586

Lt. J. Schafer

Det. Charles E Ahern #159

Wayne P.D.

FUNDAMENTALS OF
CRIMINAL INVESTIGATION

270

ABOUT THE AUTHORS

Charles E. O'Hara (1912–1984) received his bachelor's and master's degrees from St. Peter's College, Jersey City, N.J. where he was an instructor of physics from 1934 to 1938. As a detective in the New York City Police Department (1940–1952 and 1957–1965), Mr. O'Hara spent many years dedicated to crime scene investigation and police laboratory work. During the Korean War he enlisted in the U.S. Air Force and was assigned to the Office of Special Investigations in Washington, D.C. From 1955 to 1956, Mr. O'Hara taught at the Suburban Officer's Training School of Western Reserve University (now Case Western Reserve) located in Cleveland, Ohio. His many publications include *An Introduction to Criminalistics* (with James W. Osterburg, 1949); *Photography in Law Enforcement* (Eastmann Kodak, 1959); and "Criminal Investigation" for *The Encyclopedia Britannica* (1970).

Gregory L. O'Hara attended Catholic University of America (B.A., 1966) and Ohio State University (M.A., 1971). He taught philosophy at Ohio State before turning his attention to the emerging field of criminal justice. In 1975, he was recruited by his father, Charles E. O'Hara, to help with the writing of the Fourth and subsequent editions of *Fundamentals of Criminal Investigation.*

Sixth Edition

Fundamentals of Criminal Investigation

By

CHARLES E. O'HARA

and

GREGORY L. O'HARA

CHARLES C THOMAS • PUBLISHER
Springfield • Illinois • U.S.A.

Published and Distributed Throughout the World by

CHARLES C THOMAS • PUBLISHER
2600 South First Street
Springfield, Illinois 62794-9265

© *1994 by* CHARLES C THOMAS • PUBLISHER

ISBN 0-398-05889-X

Library of Congress Catalog Card Number: 93-26172

First Edition, 1956
Second Edition, 1970
Third Edition, 1973
Fourth Edition, 1976
Fifth Edition, 1980
Revised Fifth Edition, 1988
Sixth Edition, 1994

With THOMAS BOOKS *careful attention is given to all details of manufacturing
and design. It is the Publisher's desire to present books that are satisfactory as to their
physical qualities and artistic possibilities and appropriate for their particular use.*
THOMAS BOOKS *will be true to those laws of quality that assure a good name
and good will.*

Printed in the United States of America
SC-HP-3

Library of Congress Cataloging-in-Publication Data

O'Hara, Charles E.
    Fundamentals of criminal investigation / by Charles E.
O'Hara and Gregory L. O'Hara. — 6th ed.
      p.   cm.
    Includes bibliographical references and index.
    ISBN 0-398-05889-X
    1. Criminal investigation.   I. O'Hara, Gregory L.
    II. Title.
HV8073.039   1994
363.2'5—dc20   93-26172
                                     CIP

To
Louis Sattler

PREFACE TO THE SIXTH EDITION

THE SIXTH EDITION has been extensively revised, incorporating the latest technical and scientific methods while maintaining the structure and the spirit of the original text. Among the most recent investigative developments appearing in this edition are DNA analysis, automated fingerprint identification system (AFIS), cognitive interviewing, and expert systems. Many traditional investigative topics that were either overlooked or not adequately treated in previous editions have now been included such as neighborhood canvassing, glass fracture analysis, laser and cyanoacrylate fingerprint techniques, sexual asphyxia, bitemarks, earprints, chemical etching, and gunshot primer residue analysis. Many subjects have been rewritten including evidence collection, crime scene photography, lineups, and safe-breaking techniques. Two new chapters, "Assault" and "Broken Glass," have been introduced and the references for each chapter have been improved, updated, and expanded.

The purpose of the "Additional Reading" sections at the end of each chapter is to direct the student to more specialized reading material when he has found a subject of interest to him. With hundreds of articles and books written each year on subjects associated with criminal investigation, it is impossible to keep track of most of the material published. Out of necessity many worthwhile publications are overlooked. Articles appearing in this section are selected not only for their quality and usefulness but also for their accessibility. For this reason, an effort is made to select articles from the more readily available periodicals, such as the *FBI Law Enforcement Bulletin, Law and Order, Police Chief,* and the *Journal of Forensic Sciences.* If a reference has helped a student to further his interest, then it has fulfilled its purpose. It is hoped that some students will continue their research in the field of criminal investigation and someday make their own contribution in the form of an article or a book.

I would like to thank Professor Paschal Ungarino, Head of the Department of Criminal Justice at Suffolk Community College (NY), for his inspiration and guidance in the preparation of the Sixth Edition. In the Fourth Edition, the corrections and suggestions of Mr. Harrison C. Allison of the Marion Institute have greatly improved the text.

G.L.O.

INTRODUCTION

T HE PURPOSE of this book is to bring the reader to an intermediate level of attainment in the main branches of investigation. From this point he may be able to proceed, with the help of other literature and his experience, to specialized fields of crime detection or non-criminal inquiry. It is not presumed that from mastery of the contents of this book the reader will become an accomplished investigator. The detection of crime is, after all, not a science but an art, whose secrets are not likely to be captured in any great part between the covers of a book. Techniques such as interrogation and surveillance are acquired mainly through patient practice and self-criticism. The student can, however, bypass months of aimless apprenticeship if he learns at the outset of his career the significance and application of the basic tools of investigation, which have been described in Chapter I as the three "I's"— Information, Interrogation, and Instrumentation.

It is the object, then, of the present book to introduce the student to investigative work in such a way that he shall, on the one hand, learn what is meant by a complete investigation and acquaint himself with the proofs of the most important crimes, and, on the other, become familiar with the employment of technical methods and services available to him. The book, as its title indicates, is intended as a presentation of the foundations of investigation. An attempt has been made throughout to lay a sufficiently broad groundwork to enable the reader to pursue his further studies intelligently, rather than to carry any single topic to exhaustive completeness. Since a selection was necessary, those offenses have been chosen for treatment which are serious in nature or relatively frequent in occurrence. The extension to other crimes of the principles elucidated here should be well within the powers of the attentive reader.

The presentation is directed to the beginning student of the art of investigation. The experienced investigator and the supervisor may, of course, find some material that is instructive or interesting. Little has been said of the administrative practices and problems of a detective division or an investigative agency, and such administrative information as is given is necessarily of a fragmentary and accidental character. The text throughout is addressed to the "investigator," a term chosen in preference to such titles as "detective" and "agent" because of its more general nature. Thus the ideas and precepts have been arranged for practical application by a city detective or plainclothesman, a private investigator, or a federal agent. Military personnel may find the work particularly useful in view of the fact that many of the paragraphs devoted to legal matters reflect the principles of the Uniform Code of Military Justice.

The many recommendations to be found in these chapters are often put in the form of rules and are sometimes permitted to stand unqualified. This manner of presentation does not imply that the recommended method is the only effective procedure for the investigation. The student will understand that, although these precepts are based on accepted practice, they have been interpreted with discretion and a reasonable elasticity. The learner, however, must be guided by rules until he knows enough about investigation to be superior to the rules. He must submit himself temporarily to this discipline, knowing well that there is a freedom beyond the rules and that this freedom is the result of discipline. The rules are the discipline of learning.

One of the problems facing a contemporary textbook writer concerns the proper use of personal pronouns. The use of the word "he" when referring in general to a person engaged in an occupation or holding a position is thought by some readers and writers to be unnecessarily exclusive, and hence, offensive. Because of this, many writers of criminal investigation textbooks have chosen to replace the pronoun "he" with "gender neutral" terms such as "he or she," "he/she," or "s/he." Others have eliminated the grammatical situations in which "he" refers back to the investigator, requiring the author to repeat the noun continually and to restrict his use of subordinate clauses. Adjusting the language of the text may solve one problem, but at the same time it creates others. While it may achieve the goal of reassuring the reader that aspiring to the role of investigator is open to everyone, it also results in a text that is difficult to read and that limits the writer's ability to express himself. The purpose of writing, after all, is communication. A solution to this problem, and the one adopted in this text, is to maintain the traditional use of the pronoun "he" to mean both "he and she" when not referring to a specific individual. In the same manner, the words "man" and "mankind" are traditionally used to refer to all members of the human species. Furthermore, it should not be necessary to state that the personality traits that make up a good investigator, namely, character, judgment, intelligence, objectivity, intuition, patience, and perseverance, are found in both men and women in equal measure.

CONTENTS

PART V

THE INVESTIGATOR IN COURT

PART VI

IDENTIFICATION AND REPRODUCTION

PART VII

SPECIALIZED SCIENTIFIC METHODS

FUNDAMENTALS OF
CRIMINAL INVESTIGATION

PART I
GENERAL

Chapter 1

METHODS OF INVESTIGATION

1. Nature of Investigation

A CRIMINAL investigator is a person who collects facts to accomplish a threefold aim: to identify and locate the guilty party and to provide evidence of his guilt. Investigation is an art and not a science; hence it must be discussed in terms of precepts and advice rather than laws and rigid theories. The element of intuition or felicity of inspiration in the choice of methods has its effect on the outcome despite the most methodical and exhausting treatment of a case. Then, too, there is the matter of chance which cannot be omitted from consideration.

In order, however, to provide a basis for a logical discussion of investigation as an applied art, it is necessary to create for ourselves the fiction that it is a science, complete with general principles and special theorems; that, if the investigator operates in harmony with the rules, the case will be inexorably solved; that a failure to solve a particular case is attributable to the employment of unorthodox methods or the neglect of prescribed procedures. With these assumptions, we can proceed to build our structure.

The tools of the investigator are, for the sake of simplicity, referred to as the three "I's," namely, Information, Interrogation, and Instrumentation. By the application of the three "I's" in varying proportions the investigator gathers the facts which are necessary to establish the guilt or innocence of the accused in a criminal trial. The remaining chapters of this book are an exposition of the nature and use of the three "I's."

It should be noted at this point that there are no normative criteria for judging the success or failure of an investigation. The fact that the crime remains unsolved does not indicate a deficiency

5

in the investigation; nor does a conviction of the accused necessarily mean that the investigation was conducted in an intelligent manner. An investigation may be considered a success if all the available information relevant and material to the issues or allegations of the case is uncovered. There is, however, no way of knowing, ordinarily, whether the information was available.

It is a common misconception that every crime is intrinsically soluble; that there is always sufficient evidence available to reveal the identity of the criminal; that the perpetrator always leaves traces at the crime scene which, in the hands of a discerning investigator or technician, will lead inevitably to his door. It is for this reason that a citizen who cannot determine which of his three children opened a forbidden jar of cookies may become indignant at the inability of his police force to locate unerringly the perpetrator of a mysterious robbery among the several million inhabitants of his city.

Many crimes are not susceptible of solution by reason of the fact that the evidence is insufficient. The absence of eyewitnesses, discernible motives, and physical clues will obviously prohibit a solution unless the malefactor confesses. Often, the *corpus delicti* or the fact that a crime was committed cannot be established, and even a confession is of little value.

The concept of "solving the crime" does not satisfy the requirements of a completed investigation. To the general public, this term describes merely the process of discovering the identity of the suspect and apprehending him. These achievements, however, are but two of the objectives of an investigation and leave the investigator far from his ultimate goal of presenting sufficient evidence in a court of law to warrant a conviction. Finding the perpetrator is frequently the simplest phase of the investigation; obtaining the evidence to support the charge in court is often an exceedingly complex task, the difficulties of which are greatly increased by the requirements placed by the court on the character, sufficiency, and mode of introduction of the evidence.

To simplify the presentation of the ideas in these chapters it will be assumed that most crimes can be solved and that the methods described are usually effective in accomplishing the solution. The investigation will be considered successful if the available physical evidence was competently handled, the witnesses intelligently interviewed, the suspect, if willing, effectively interrogated, all logical leads properly developed, and the case comprehensively, clearly, and accurately reported. The verdict of the court in regard to the guilt of the accused will not be considered a necessarily valid criterion of the success or failure of the investigation.

2. Information

The word "information" is used here to describe the knowledge which the investigator gathers from other persons. There are basically two kinds. The first type of information is acquired from regular sources such as conscientious and public-spirited citizens, company records, and the files of other agencies. The second type, which is of particular interest to the criminal investigator and which will receive special attention here, is the knowledge gathered by the experienced investigator from cultivated sources such as paid informants, bartenders, cab drivers, licensed owners and employees in general, former criminals, or acquaintances. The extent to which informants are employed varies widely with law enforcement agencies. The French police, for example, rely heavily on an elaborate network of paid informants. In the English system, however, there is little provision for paid informants. The United States in recent years has drawn away from the English model and is rapidly approaching that of the French with increasingly liberal provisions for paid informants. Many agencies, federal, state, and municipal provide routinely for informant expenditures in any case of more than ordinary importance.

Of the three "I's," information is by far the most important, since it answers the question, "Who did it?" By the marvelous expedient of simply questioning a knowledgeable and often anonymous individual, the identity of the perpetrator, and usually his motive, are revealed. The investigation at once acquires direction, and subsequent steps are meaningful and heuristic rather than merely experimental. The investigator finds himself in a position of working a mathematical problem backwards with the known solution always before him, not in the difficult sense of proving a theorem in geometry but with the mechanical ease of establishing an algebraic identity from a knowledge of the original and the derived forms.

It is commonly held that most cases involving offenses committed by professional criminals are solved in this manner; that a homicide case in which the killer has a previous record is usually broken by a tip from a paroled convict, a hint from a narcotics addict, or a few snatches of conversation gleaned by a curious bartender. The crime of the professional is ordinarily motivated by a desire for economic gain. Larceny, robbery, and burglary share this motive. Assault and homicide are often incidental to crimes of greed or are the by-product of disputes over divisions of spoils or areal rights. The crime of greed, then, when perpetrated by the professional is most frequently solved by information.

When the amateur puts his hand to criminal activity, where the crime is one of passion, sparked by love, hate, or a desire for revenge, or when the offense is "motiveless" by reason of the deranged mind of the perpetrator, information in the usual sense is seldom available. The criminal, as far as the underworld is concerned, is socially trackless; he exists without reference to the milieu of the detective. There are informative sources which may prove helpful but "information" in the second sense is not forthcoming.

The present discussion has been limited to a relatively narrow interpretation of the concept of information. The potential role of modern information technology is far too broad a subject to treat in the limited space available. The systematic storage and rapid retrieval of information by electronic data processing methods have been in operation in some of the larger police departments for a number of years. Their effectiveness has already been demonstrated in the apprehension process. Plans for an integrated information system for criminal justice have already taken concrete form. Many local police agencies have already availed themselves of computer communication with federal and state systems. The combination of modern technology with information theory has begun to mark a new era in law enforcement.

3. Interrogation

Interrogation, the second "I," includes the skillful questioning of witnesses as well as suspects. The success of "information" depends on the intelligent selection of informative sources; the effectiveness of interrogation varies with the craft, logic, and psychological insight with which the investigator questions a person who is in possession of information relevant to the case. The term *interview* will be used throughout the text to mean the simple questioning of a person who has no personal reason to withhold information and therefore may be expected to cooperate with the investigator; while the term *interrogation* will be used to describe the questioning of a suspect or other person who may normally be expected to be reluctant to divulge information concerning the offense under investigation. The ability to obtain information by questioning is the most prized talent of the investigator.

The novice investigator often overlooks the most obvious approach to the solution of a crime, namely, asking the suspect if he committed the offense. The lesson is so elementary that it is frequently neglected by the beginner in his eagerness to use the more refined techniques of modern crime detection. The guilty person is in possession of most of the information necessary for a successful prosecution, and if he is questioned intelligently, he can usually be induced to talk. A confession, moreover, which includes details that could not be known by an innocent party is a convincing form of proof.

A study of typical homicide cases will reveal the importance of obtaining confessions and admissions. It will be found that if the accused can be induced to "talk" the prospects of a successful prosecution are usually bright. If he remains silent, his chances of being acquitted are inestimably improved. Indeed, the most egregious error committed by clever criminals is that of answering, truthfully or otherwise, the questions of the police. The reason for this state of affairs is not difficult to find. In the absence of eyewitnesses and of admissions by the accused, it is only rarely that the available circumstantial evidence is strong enough to support a conviction. The physical evidence may serve to place the suspect at the scene or associate him with the weapon but will contribute little to proving malice, motive, intent, the criminality of the act or, in general, matters relating to the state of mind of the perpetrator. The accused must be asked to supply, directly or indirectly, details from which his actions and intentions can be deduced. He contributes indirectly when by evasive or untruthful statements he gives indications of actions which were not innocently motivated.

It is logical at this point to ask why, if silence so greatly favors the criminal in this system of justice, he is led so frequently to talk to the police even after being properly given the *Miranda* warnings. The reply lies in experience and observation. The normal person is possessed by an irresistible desire to talk. A great deal of his everyday conversation is devoted to justifying his actions or his opinions. He cannot, then, at a time when his reputation and record are being seriously questioned, resist the temptation to come volubly to their defense by stating the truth, if his character and training are so directed, or by resorting to even the most extravagant falsehoods. It must be remembered, too, that a guilty person under questioning by the police is often a very frightened human being who is driven by apprehension to seek comfort, however indirectly, in communication with his fellow man. Only an exceptionally strong personality or a criminal indurated by bitter experience can withstand prolonged, skillful interrogation in silence.

The investigator should look upon a suspect or a reluctant witness as a person who will yield the desired information if he is questioned with sufficient skill and patience. To acquire the necessary proficiency in interrogation is the work of several years. If he is endowed with a fair share of common sense and a capacity for perseverance, he will eventually become reasonably effective in his work. If, however, he possesses insight into personalities and acquires a knowledge of practical psychology by study and observation, he will excel in the art of interrogation by reason of his ability to establish rapport quickly with a wide variety of criminal types. Finally, he must be nimblewitted. Interrogation is an intellectual game that is often won by the player who is mentally faster afoot and who can rapidly take advantage of an opening or an indicated weakness. As in any other game or skill, the art of interrogation must be practiced constantly in order to develop and maintain expertness. It is a common observation of experienced investigators that a period of inactivity of even a few months will result in a marked falling off in their effectiveness as interrogators.

4. Instrumentation

The third "I" is meant to include the application of the instruments and methods of the physical sciences to the detection of crime. Physics, for example, offers such aids as microscopy, photography, and the optical methods of analysis. The role of chemistry is too well known for elaboration here. Biology and pathology are particularly important in crimes of physical violence.

The sum of these sciences insofar as they are applied to crime detection is called criminalistics. Their utility is associated mainly with physical evidence. By their means a part of the *corpus delicti* may be established in certain crimes — the cause of death in a homicide or the nature of the drug in a narcotics violation. They may be used to link the suspect to the scene of the crime by showing that clue materials found at the scene possess the same constituents as materials associated with the suspect. The same procedure is employed in identifying the criminal by tracing a substance found at the scene to a source that can be immediately associated with the suspect.

Instrumentation, however, is taken here to mean rather more than criminalistics. It includes also all the technical methods by which the fugitive is traced and examined and, in general, the investigation is advanced. Thus, fingerprint systems, *modus operandi* files, the lie detector, communication systems, surveillance equipment such as a telephoto lens and detective dyes, searching apparatus such as the x-ray unit and the metal detector, and other investigative tools are contained within the scope of the term.

There has been a tendency in recent years to place too great a relative value on the contribution of instrumentation to the detection of crime. The inexperienced are especially prone to place their faith in technical methods to the neglect of the more basic and generally more effective procedures of information and interrogation. Several reasons may be given to account for this frame of mind. Greater publicity is given the instruments and techniques of criminalistics because they are frequently quite picturesque and attract the attention of the newspapers, feature writers, and popular dramatists. Moreover, many of those assigned to technical duties are scientists accustomed to addressing large groups, reporting new developments in journals, and otherwise publicizing their findings. A small articulate group of persons, such as the medical examiners, by making known their work in correct fashion, will at the same time convey a highly favorable impression of their contribution to investigative work. For example, although the precinct detective may perform 95 per cent of the work in a homicide investigation, it is the remaining 5 per cent contributed by the medical examiner and other technical experts which often receives the publicity and which impresses the uninitiated. The future detective should, then, assign in his perspective of the investigative picture the correct proportions to the contributions of the three "I's" so that proper attention and effort will be given to each.

The most common use of instrumentation is in connection with the physical evidence in the case and the limitations of this tool of investigation are set by the clue materials and other traces found at the scene. In a good percentage of the cases it will be found that there is no physical evidence and that instrumentation is relatively unimportant. Larceny and robbery, for example, are usually committed without leaving physical evidence in the form of traces. In a homicide, however, clue materials and other forms of physical evidence are of paramount importance. The use of information and interrogation is applicable to nearly all cases, but instrumentation is found most effective in cases where physical evidence is abundant.

A thorough training in the resources of instrumentation is of great importance to an investigator. The technical aids are available to him, but unless he understands their applicability to his problems their utility cannot be adequately realized. He should recognize investigative situations in which the physical evidence may be fruitful or where the pattern of the crime suggests a study of the *modus operandi* file. He should be able to anticipate from the character of a surveillance the types of cameras or other optical devices which will be most useful to him. The limitations of technical methods should also be a part of his knowledge, since excessive reliance on instruments may in certain situations result in a neglect of other and more suitable investigative procedures. He may, for example, fall into the error of relying on a lie detector examination to the exclusion of the routine investigative methods.

5. Phases of the Investigation

The objectives of the investigator stated at the beginning of this chapter provide a convenient division of the investigation into three phases: (1) the criminal is identified; (2) he is traced and located; and (3) the facts proving his guilt are gathered for court presentation. This division is made for convenience of discussion, since the three phases are not necessarily separated in time but are usually fused throughout the investigation. The same evidence, moreover, can often be used for all three objectives. Throughout all phases of the investigation, the three "I's" are constantly employed. Although explicit reference to these tools will not be made, their application at each step can be readily seen.

6. Identifying the Criminal

In the first stage the criminal is identified, i.e., some person is identified as the perpetrator of the criminal acts. Ordinarily the identity of the criminal is discovered in one or more of the following ways: confession, eyewitness testimony, or circumstantial evidence.

   a. **Confession.** Admission or confession by a suspect is a major objective of every investigation. The confession is, of course, an excellent means of identifying the criminal. From the point of view of proving guilt at the trial, a consideration that will overlap this discussion, it must be supported by other corroborative evidence. The *corpus delicti* must be separately established in order to support a conviction. A confession may be denied in court and unless an affirmative show of voluntariness (*Miranda* warnings and so forth) can be presented by the prosecution, the objections of defense counsel based on charges of duress and coercion may prevail regardless of their falsehood.

b. **Eyewitness.** The ideal identification is made by several objective persons who are familiar with the appearances of the accused and who personally witnessed the commission of the crime. Where the witness and the accused are strangers and the period of observation was limited to only a few seconds, the validity of the identification depends upon the ability of the witness to observe and remember the relative "distinctiveness" of the accused's appearance, the prevailing conditions of visibility and observation, and the lapse of time between the criminal event and the identification.

c. **Circumstantial Evidence.** The identification may be established indirectly by proving other facts or circumstances from which, either alone or in connection with additional facts, the identity of the perpetrator can be inferred. Evidence of this nature usually falls into one of the following classes:

1) *Motive.* It may be inferred from circumstances and from the statements of witnesses that the suspect could have been motivated by a desire for revenge or personal gain. In offenses such as larceny, robbery, and burglary the obvious motive is monetary gain and persons in straitened financial condition may become suspects. In crimes of personal violence such as assault and murder, the existence of a strong personal hatred would be significant, and evidence of quarrels and angry statements would be relevant. Closely related to motive is a desire for criminal action formed by a pathologically disordered mind. Certain types of arson, for example, suggest the work of a deranged incendiary. Some forms of rape and other sexual offenses indicate the work of a deviate. Evidence relating to motive or state of mind is usually obtained by interviewing witnesses. A study of the crime scene and a reconstruction of the occurrence, including the suspect's prior and subsequent acts, may often be helpful.

2) *Opportunity.* It must have been physically possible for the suspect to commit the crime. He must have had access to the area, have been in the vicinity, and have had the means available. It must be shown that the suspect could have been in the vicinity of

the crime scene in the sense that it was not improbable for him to have been there. Thus the search is further limited to those who had the opportunity to commit the crime by reason of probable physical presence, knowledge of the criminal objective, and the absence of alibis. In a crime such as embezzlement the element of opportunity to commit the crime can readily lead to an identification if it is coupled with the desire and need for money. Only a few persons can participate in the financial procedures of a company. A suspect's credit ratings, gambling or investment losses, and style of living can be carefully studied to determine the existence of critical need.

3) *Associative Evidence.* The physical evidence may serve to identify the criminal by means of the clue materials, personal property, or the characteristic pattern of procedure deduced from the arrangement of objects at the crime scene. The perpetrator may leave some clue at the scene such as a weapon, tool, garment, fingerprint, or foot impression; he may unwittingly carry from the scene a trace in the form of glass, paint, rouge, hair, or blood. In offenses of personal gain, the fruits of the crime may be in his possession. Crimes of violence will leave evidence of physical struggle. Where the offense involved the application of force against property, contact with certain materials may be discernible.

7. Tracing and Locating the Criminal

The second phase of the investigation is concerned with locating the offender. Obviously many of the steps previously suggested for identifying the suspect will also lead to his location. Most commonly the answer to the question of the criminal's whereabouts falls easily out of the solution to the problem of his identity. Usually the criminal is not hiding; he is simply unknown. The professional criminal does not operate near his residence, and hence his flight from the scene is merely a return home unless, of course, he has been recognized during the commission of the offense. The amateur usually commits a crime because of the exceptional opportunity. It is to his advantage to remain in his normal haunts, since flight might betray guilt. In those cases, then, the problem is primarily one of identification. In many cases, however, it is necessary to trace a fugitive who is hiding. Tips, interviews, and in general, information as described earlier will be the most useful means. The techniques of tracing the fugitive are described in Chapters 13 and 14.

8. Proving the Guilt

It is assumed that the criminal has been identified and is now in custody. The investigation, however, is far from complete; it has entered the third and often the most difficult phase, namely, gathering the facts necessary in the trial to prove the guilt of the accused beyond a reasonable doubt. The fact that the accused has confessed to the offense and that the investigator has convincing arguments of his complicity, derived from common sense and information, is not sufficient. The court requires that guilt be proved beyond a reasonable doubt and that the evidence be presented in a certain form and in accordance with a prescribed procedure and that it satisfy certain requirements of quality, trustworthiness, and logical sufficiency.

The final test of a criminal investigation is in the presentation of evidence in court. The fact of the existence of the crime must be established; the defendant must be identified and associated with the crime scene; competent and credible witnesses must be available; the physical evidence must be appropriately identified, the chain of its custody established, and its connection with the case shown; and the whole must be presented in an orderly and logical fashion. The complete process of proof is described in the phrase "establishing the elements of the offense."

In order to instruct the investigator in the methods of gathering proof, the treatment of specific crimes has been centered around the key idea of the elements of proof. By reason and tradition a convention has been established as to the essential general facts relating to an offense which must be demonstrated to prove the guilt of the offender and which are contained in the related concepts of *corpus delicti* and elements of the offense.

9. Corpus Delicti

Early in a criminal trial the prosecution must prove the *corpus delicti* or fact that a crime was committed. Unless an offense can in fact be shown to exist, there is little basis for testing the guilt or innocence of the accused and the court may dismiss the case if a *corpus delicti* is not known. The *corpus delicti* is proved by showing (1) there exists a certain state of fact which forms the basis of the criminal act charged, and (2) the existence of a criminal agency which caused the state of fact to exist. In an arson, for example, it must be shown that there was a burning by a criminal agency; in a homicide the death of a person by a wrongful act of another must be shown. Preferably this state of fact should be established by direct and positive proof, but circumstantial evidence will suffice if it is particularly clear and cogent. The importance of proving the *corpus delicti* is illustrated in the following case. A detective, after stopping an automobile on suspicion of another crime, questioned the driver concerning a mink coat lying on the back seat. The driver confessed to stealing the coat from a restaurant and was duly arrested. Further investigation, however, failed to discover the true owner of the coat, and the case was dismissed for the reason that a larceny had not been established. In general it may be said that a confession in itself is worthless unless proof of the existence of the *corpus delicti* is available.

10. Elements of the Offense

By adding to the *corpus delicti* certain facts concerning the accused, such as his identity as the malefactor, we have the elements of the offense, the necessary and sufficient conditions which must be fulfilled by the evidence before it can be said that the guilt of the accused has been proved. For example, the elements of burglary are: (1) the accused broke into (2) a dwelling (3) in the nighttime (4) in order to commit a crime therein. A charge of burglary can be supported if, and only if, proof of these four elements of burglary is presented.

Normally the organization of the evidence in this form is the responsibility of the prosecuting attorney, but it will be found that the outline presented by the elements provides a convenient frame-work for the investigator in the development of the case. In addition it offers him the only sound criteria for testing the adequacy of his investigative efforts. Naturally, the investigative procedure does not follow the lines of the elements in its chrono-logical progress. The elements should, however, be kept constantly in mind, even at the outset, so that no evidence essential to the establishment of an element is irrevocably lost and no necessary lead is neglected.

a. **Form.** To acquire a knowledge of the elements of criminal offenses, the investigator must study the penal law of the juris-diction under which he is operating. It is not to be expected that he will have at ready recall the essentials of all the crimes which he will be required to investigate, but he should possess sufficient powers of analysis to be able to deduce the essential elements from a reading of the penal law. In their most general form the elements of an offense will consist of the following: (1) that the accused did or omitted to do the acts as alleged, and (2) the circumstances as specified. A further study of this form will demonstrate its usefulness despite its generality.

b. **Accused and the Acts Alleged.** In the first general element the identity of the accused must be established and his connection with the acts clearly shown. The methods for establishing the identity of the accused as the perpetrator of the criminal act have been discussed above in connection with the first objective of an investigation. To satisfy this element, however, a close causal connection must be established between the accused and the offense. It is not necessary to show that he willed the particular effect in its final form; it is sufficient to show that his objective in acting was one which could not have been accomplished without violating the law. The accused must be shown as responsible agent, either by physical or moral causation or by omission to perform a legal duty.

c. **Intent.** The investigation must be designed to develop facts which give evidence of the frame of mind of the accused. It must be shown that the accused knew what he was doing. Consciousness of the unlawfulness of the act is not essential, since ignorance of the law is no defense. In some crimes intent is an essential element;

in others it is merely necessary to show that the accused was aware of the consequences of his acts. Some crimes include the additional element of malice, the intent to do injury to another. Legal malice does not necessarily imply hate or ill will; it is a mental state in which an act is done, without excuse, from which another person suffers injury. Since malice is not a presumption of law, it must be inferred from the facts developed by the investigation. Motive, or that which induces the criminal to act, must be distinguished from intent. The motive may be the desire to obtain revenge or personal gain; the intent is the accomplishment of the act. Motive need not be shown in order to obtain a conviction, but intent must always be proved where it is an element to the offense. Although proof of motive does not show guilt, the absence of a motive bears on the fact of whether the accused committed the crime. In cases which depend upon circumstantial evidence, proof of motive is especially important. The relative significance of the proof of motive varies widely with the nature of the crime. In homicide, arson, and sabotage, motive is particularly important. In crimes such as robbery, burglary, and larceny, motive is of little or no value since the desire for money is almost universal and need for it quite common. The motives of revenge and hate, however, are only infrequently possessed to such a degree as to be given expression in criminal activity. To establish the motives of revenge, hate, or jealousy the investigator should look into the history of the victim. If the victim is alive he can be requested to give a simple account of his relations with people over the preceding months. If he is an employer, the matter of the promotions and frustrations of employees should be examined. In the victim's social life, the relative stability of his domestic life, his affairs with women, and his drinking habits should be examined. If the victim is dead, this information can be developed through witnesses. The witness should be encouraged to gossip during the interview since a motive is a nebulous matter difficult to detect in a prosaic recital of facts.

11. Role of Reason

Although the investigator is basically a collector of facts, he must also construct hypotheses and draw conclusions relating to the problem of who committed the crime and how it was accomplished. It is expected that his reasoning processes will be logical and that, even when he engages in speculation, good judgment and common sense will be in control. The investigator, faced with a complex crime, may be compared to a research scientist, employing the same resources of reason and resorting, where necessary, to imagination, ingenuity, and even intuition.

Both inductive and deductive reasoning are applicable to investigation. By inductive reasoning, the passage from the particular to the general, the investigator develops from observed data a generalization explaining the relationships between the events under examination. For example, from the observation of a broken window, a door left open, and overturned desk drawers, an investigator might conclude by inductive reasoning that a burglary had taken place. Again, from clues left at the scene, such as a large-sized man's jacket or glove, a footprint made by a man's shoe, or evidence of a heavy object having been moved or carried out, the investigator might infer that a large male of considerable height and weight was involved. From a comparison of the details of this burglary with those of another recent burglary, the investigator could theorize that both crimes were probably committed by the same person. This type of thinking, that is, forming a general theory from an examination of particular details, is inductive reasoning.

In deductive reasoning, proceeding from the general to the particular, the investigator begins with a general theory, applies it to the particular instance represented by the criminal occurrence, and determines whether the instance can be explained by the theory. For example, an investigator might hold to the general theory that one can tell when a burglary has been committed by an experienced burglar if the crime scene evidence reflects planning and execution. The investigator would analyze the crime scene to determine if this theory was applicable in this particular instance. If he found that the occupants were not at home at the time of the burglary and that they kept valuables on the premises, it might indicate that the job was well-"cased" and well-planned. If the burglar displayed ease in entrance and exit, left few clues, searched methodically and removed valuables selectively, it would indicate that the burglary was well-executed. From these observations, the investigator could determine that this crime scene was an instance covered by his general theory; thus, he would conclude that this particular burglary was probably committed by an experienced burglar. The application of a general theory to a particular instance to see if it is, in fact, an instance of that theory is what is meant by deductive reasoning.

In practice, the investigator shifts continually between inductive and deductive thinking. At one moment, he may be theorizing that a burglary has taken place from examining the details of the crime scene (induction). At the next moment, he may be thinking in the opposite direction, applying the general definition of what constitutes a burglary to see if in this particular crime scene the necessary elements are present (deduction). In both inductive and deductive reasoning, the passage from point to point must be managed by logical steps, a requirement that is not easily satisfied. The use of correct reasoning processes must be learned by conscious application, and constant vigilance against the pitfalls of false premises, logical fallacies, unjustifiable inferences, ignorance of conceivable alternatives, and failure to distinguish between the factual and the probable.

12. Representative Approach

In considering a crime problem no single method of reasoning may be said to be the only correct procedure for arriving at a solution to the exclusion of alternative procedures. Described below is a suggested approach to the investigation of the more complicated crimes. The steps are related to the problem of determining who committed the crime and how it was done.

　　a. The criminal occurrence or complaint is critically reviewed to determine its nature.

　　b. A painstaking and comprehensive collection is made of the data obtained from the crime scene, the witnesses, and observational inquiry.

c. The available information is arranged and correlated.

d. The issues and problems are formulated in terms of the elements of proof required to support the charge.

e. The most likely hypotheses are selected to resolve the problems along lines consistent with the available data.

f. The hypotheses are subjected to the tests of probability considerations, additional interrogation of suspects, and the development of additional witnesses. Various possibilities are eliminated systematically by considerations such as opportunity, motive, past record, observed reactions, and corroboration of alibis.

g. On the basis of consistency with known facts and a high degree of probability, the best hypothesis is selected and given final support.

h. The best hypothesis must be objectively tested and modified or rejected when contrary evidence is uncovered. The investigator must not permit his observations and interpretations to be biased in favor of the hypothesis.

This suggested approach to the systematic use of reason in an investigation may appear to be an unnecessarily abstract and complicated procedure for solving the typical crime. It is, however, given mainly for the more difficult and elaborate crimes. Frequently, it is not possible to determine at first glance whether a particular crime will present a difficult problem. Often an apparently simple crime will go unsolved by virtue of its very simplicity, while a seemingly complex crime may lend itself readily to solution, since its complexity involves parts and organization. The parts naturally supply clues. The organization, or disposition of the parts, presents a pattern to the intelligent observer from which useful conclusions can be drawn.

13. Chance

In many investigative situations reasoning alone will not yield a solution and qualities other than a facility for logic will determine the success of the inquiry. Enterprise, initiative, perseverance, ingenuity, and an insatiable curiosity are among the characteristics which are needed in addition to a rational method of procedure. Consideration must also be given to the fact that chance often plays an important part in the solution of crimes. The element of chance should not be ignored as something strange which may detract from the credit owed to a competent investigation. By training the powers of observation and maintaining a constant vigilance for the unexpected, the investigator will be prepared to take advantage of those slight clues encountered accidentally which sometimes resolve the problem. Chance merely provides an opportunity. An open and observing mind is required to grasp the opportunity and a prepared mind is needed to interpret it.

14. Intuition

Since investigation is essentially an art, consideration must be given in its study to the concept of intuition, the sudden and unexpected insight that clarifies the problem where progress by logic and experiment has been end-stopped. The phenomenon of the detective whose success in many cases appears to be attributable to "hunches" is quite familiar in police work. Some investigators possess a sensitivity to persons and crimes of a violent nature that provides inspiration or illumination when method alone will not yield a solution. The key idea may come suddenly when he is not consciously thinking of the case, or it may arrive dramatically when his mind is weighing the available information or following a routine chain of investigative thought. It may spring involuntarily to the conscious mind from a subconscious that is saturated with the data of a case and is occupied with the many facets of the problem. Intuition, in any event, is not to be despised, particularly in difficult cases where little progress is evident. The conditions of relaxation and even distraction which often encourage this phenomenon should be sought in those situations. Since there is no evidence that crimes are intrinsically soluble, the investigator can expect in many cases to reach a point where sheer plodding work and deductive reasoning are no longer fruitful and where hope would appear to lie in intuition or chance.

15. Summary

This chapter has been devoted to describing the nature of a criminal investigation and the processes by which it is accomplished. For purposes of simplification the tools and methods of investigation were grouped under the three "I's"—Information, Interrogation, and Instrumentation. An investigation was considered as consisting of three phases: (1) identifying the perpetrator; (2) locating the perpetrator, and (3) proving his guilt. To achieve the major objective of successfully presenting the case in court, it was found necessary to gather the evidence in accordance with the pattern which will fulfill the necessary and sufficient conditions for obtaining proof beyond a reasonable doubt. The concept of the *corpus delicti* was introduced as a basic necessary condition to be fulfilled, since it established the fact that a crime has been committed. By considering the *corpus delicti* together with the factor of criminal agency, the final concept of the elements of the offense was reached. The evidence gathered by the investigator must establish the elements. It was found that although many investigators manage to collect the facts to prove the elements, their procedures too often appear to be the result of habit, supervised experience, and even intuition. It was felt that more could be accomplished by a more fully trained investigator, whose conscious knowledge of the nature of the offense would enable him to advert constantly to a schema of the elements, thus providing him with an overall plan of procedure, giving direction and significance to each step, and insuring that the investigation is not concluded without proving each essential act and showing the causal connection between the acts and the accused as their conscious criminal author.

It has been seen, finally, that the terms "solving" and "investigating" a crime are used here in a sense somewhat different from that employed by mystery writers. In the tidy murders of make-believe the crime is considered solved and the investigation completed when the villain has been placed by the author in a plausible framework of guilt and has thrown up his hands in despair before the ingenious exposé by the author's detective. The tedious work of the crime scene, the interviews, tracing, identification, interrogation, assembling of proof, and presentation of testimony are passed over lightly in the world of fiction.

It is not merely a play on words to say that the succeeding chapters attempt to tell the student not "how to solve a crime" but "how crimes are solved." The process is complex and many persons aid in the solution. Notably there is the criminal, who may leave in his path the set of data which will constitute the evidence. Indications betrayed in the planning of the crime, carelessness and bad luck in its execution, admissions or confidences in the *post factum* period—these are the raw materials from which the solution is shaped.

The completed investigation is the end product of teamwork. The patrolman who discovers the crime and protects the scene, the detective who is assigned to the case, the investigators who assist him in running leads, the supervisors who aid administratively, the technical services that preserve, examine, and record the evidence, and the state's attorney who provides overall guidance of the completion of the case and its presentation in court—all of these are members of the team to whom the solution of the case may be accredited.

Finally, it is desirable to avoid the terms *success, failure,* and *accredited* in these matters because of the unfavorable connotation they give to the motive of the investigator. We have described the investigator as a collector of facts relevant to an offense and, by implication, we have described him as gathering these facts impartially. We have not, however, sufficiently stressed this point of the investigator's objectivity, namely, that he has no special interest in establishing the guilt of a particular suspect, that he regards with equal interest facts which may exonerate the accused as well as to those which are inculpating, and that a biased collecting of facts with an exclusive view to the guilt of a designated suspect is destructive of the basic purpose of an investigation, namely, the discovery of the truth concerning the criminal event.

Indeed, a prejudiced investigator is a contradiction in terms, since a biased inquiry cannot remain a comprehensive consideration of all relevant facts but becomes a polarized view of selected, pre-analyzed data. It is no longer an objective search for the truth but a testing of a preferred hypothesis by adducing the most favorable facts and by admitting for examination only the data and materials contributory to its support.

16. The Criminal Justice System

Because of the great variety of criminal investigation units at municipal, state, and federal levels, no attempt has been made to place the investigator in an administrative frame of reference or to give specific treatment to the administrative aspect of his work. As we have seen from the preceding section, he participates in a joint effort of the prosecution team, which includes members of the patrol force as well as the prosecutor and which may include other agencies. The place of the investigator in the total picture, however, can only be understood from a consideration of the criminal justice system as a whole. The reader is referred to the extensive literature that has already grown up around the general subject of law enforcement and the criminal justice system.

ADDITIONAL READING*

Criminal Investigation

Anderson, W.B.: *Notable Crime Investigations.* Springfield, Ill.: Thomas, 1987.

Bennett, W.W. and Hess, K.M.: *Criminal Investigation,* 3rd ed. St. Paul, West Publishing, 1991.

Bozza, C.M.: *Criminal Investigation.* Chicago, Nelson-Hall, 1977.

Cook, C.W.: *A Practical Guide to the Basics of Physical Evidence.* Springfield, Ill.: Thomas, 1984.

Fisher, B.A.J., Svensson, A. and Wendel, O.: *Techniques of Crime Scene Investigation,* 4th ed. New York, Elsevier, 1986.

Gilbert, J.N.: *Criminal Investigation,* 3rd ed. New York, Macmillan, 1993.

Horgan, J.J.: *Criminal Investigation,* 2nd ed. New York, McGraw-Hill, 1979.

Ingraham, B.L. and Mauriello, T.P.: *Police Investigation Handbook.* Albany, N.Y.: Matthew-Bender, 1990.

Kenney, J.P. and More, H.W., Jr.: *Principles of Investigation.* St. Paul, West Publishing, 1979.

*A number of the books in this list may be helpful for further research on many of the topics treated in this text. For the most part, they will not be subsequently listed.

Kirk, P.L.: *Crime Investigation,* 2nd ed. Edited by J.I. Thornton. New York, Wiley, 1974.

Krishnan, S.S.: *An Introduction to Modern Criminal Investigation: With Basic Laboratory Techniques.* Springfield, Ill.: Thomas, 1978.

Lyman, M.D.: *Criminal Investigation: The Art and the Science.* Englewood Cliffs, N.J.: Prentice-Hall, 1993.

Macdonald, J.M. and Haney, T.P.: *Criminal Investigation.* Denver, Col.: Apache Press, 1990.

Morgan, J.B.: *The Police Function and the Investigation of Crime.* Brookfield, Vt.: Gower, 1990.

Myren, R.A. and Garcia, C.H.: *Investigation for Determination of Fact: A Primer on Proof.* Pacific Grove, Calif.: Brooks/Cole, 1989.

Osterburg, J.W. and Ward, R.H.: *Criminal Investigation: A Method for Reconstructing the Past.* Cincinnati, Anderson, 1992.

Palmiotto, M.J.: *Critical Issues in Criminal Investigation,* 2nd ed. Cincinnati, Anderson, 1988.

Pena, M.S.: *Practical Criminal Investigation,* 2nd ed. Costa Mesa, Calif.: Custom Publishing, 1990.

Sanders, W.B.: *Detective Work: A Study of Criminal Investigations.* New York, Free Press, 1977.

Schultz, D.O.: *Criminal Investigation Techniques.* Houston, Gulf Publishing, 1978.

Swanson, C.R., Jr., Chamelin, N.C., and Territo, L.: *Criminal Investigation,* 4th ed. New York, Random House, 1988.

Vandiver, J.V.: *Criminal Investigation: A Guide to Techniques and Solutions.* Metuchen, N.J.: Scarecrow Press, 1983.

Ward, R.H.: *Introduction to Criminal Investigation.* Reading, Mass.: Addison-Wesley, 1975.

Weston, P.B. and Wells, K.M.: *Criminal Investigation: Basic Perspectives,* 5th ed. Englewood Cliffs, N.J.: Prentice-Hall, 1990.

Criminal Justice

Bennett, G.: *CRIMEWARPS: The Future of Crime in America.* New York, Doubleday, 1987.

Braswell, M.C., McCarthy, B.R. and McCarthy, B.J.: *Justice, Crime and Ethics.* Cincinnati, Anderson, 1991.

Brown, S.E. and Curtain, J.H.: *Fundamentals of Criminal Justice Research.* Cincinnati, Anderson, 1987.

Brown, S.E., Esbensen, F.A. and Geis, G.: *Criminology: Explaining Crime and Its Context.* Cincinnati, Anderson, 1991.

Cole, G.F.: *The American System of Criminal Justice,* 5th ed. Pacific Grove, Calif.: Brooks/Cole, 1989.

DeLucia, R.C. and Doyle, T.J.: *Career Planning in Criminal Justice.* Cincinnati, Anderson, 1990.

Fay, J.J.: *The Police Dictionary and Encyclopedia.* Springfield, Ill.: Thomas, 1988.

Futrell, M. and Roberson, C.: *Introduction to Criminal Justice Research.* Springfield, Ill.: Thomas, 1988.

Germann, A.C., Day, F.D. and Gallati, R.R.J.: *Introduction to Law Enforcement and Criminal Justice,* rev. ed. Springfield, Ill.: Thomas, 1988.

Gottfredson, M.R. and Hirschi, T.: *A General Theory of Crime.* Stanford, Calif.: Stanford University Press, 1990.

Inciardi, J.A.: *Criminal Justice,* 3rd ed. New York, Harcourt Brace, 1990.

Jenkins, J.P.: *Crime and Justice: Issues and Ideas.* Pacific Grove, Calif.: Brooks/Cole, 1984.

Kadish, S.H. (Ed.): *Encyclopedia of Crime and Justice.* 4 vols. New York, Macmillan, 1983.

Karem, A.: *Crime Victims: An Introduction to Victimology,* 2nd ed. Pacific Grove, Calif.: Brooks/Cole, 1990.

Pepinsky, H.E. and Jesilow, P.: *Myths That Cause Crime,* 2nd ed. Cabin John, Md.: Seven Locks Press, 1985.

Reiman, J.H.: *The Rich Get Richer and the Poor Get Prison: Ideology, Class, and Criminal Justice.* New York, Wiley, 1979.

Saney, P.: *Crime and Culture in America: A Comparative Perspective.* Chicago, University of Chicago Press, 1986.

Talarico, S.M.: *Courts and Criminal Justice: Emerging Issues.* Beverly Hills, Calif.: Sage, 1985.

Terrill, R.J.: *World Criminal Justice Systems: A Survey.* Cincinnati, Anderson, 1984.

Walker, S.: *Sense and Nonsense About Crime: A Policy Guide,* 2nd ed. Pacific Grove, Calif.: Brooks/Cole, 1989.

Westermann, T.D. and Burfeind, J.W.: *Crime and Justice in Two Societies: Japan and the United States.* Pacific Grove, Calif.: Brooks/Cole, 1991.

Wilbanks, W.: *The Myth of a Racist Criminal Justice System.* Pacific Grove, Calif.: Brooks/Cole, 1987.

Wilson, J.Q.: *Thinking About Crime,* 2nd ed. New York, Random House, 1983.

Chapter 2

THE INVESTIGATOR'S NOTEBOOK

1. Purpose

THE INVESTIGATOR who is assigned to a case is charged with the general responsibility of piecing the various parts of an investigation into a coherent whole. He must interview the complainant, search the crime scene, collect and transmit the evidence, interview witnesses, interrogate suspects, and perform the innumerable minor chores attached to an investigation. Although he submits a report of the investigation, many of the details associated with the inquiry which are not essential to the report may well become points of interest to the court when the case comes to trial. The mass of detail is so overwhelming in a major case that very few investigators can successfully rely on their memories.

a. **Repository for Details.** Experienced investigators employ a notebook to record the relevant details of a case. Adequate notes are considered a prerequisite to the future recording, evaluation, and presentation of the information developed in the course of an investigation. The intervention of time affects the quantity and accuracy of the data remembered by the investigator. A few notes taken during or immediately after an interview or a search will serve later to recall the entire interview or the circumstances surrounding a search. Many seemingly inconsequential details become important in the light of later developments. The press of duties at the time of the occurrence of a major case prevents an objective evaluation of the significance of details. The notebook serves as a repository of data until more leisurely moments permit the assay and placement of such facts or observations.

b. **Basis for the Report.** The notebook contains also the raw material from which the report of investigation is ultimately

29

fashioned. At the outset of the investigation it is not a simple matter to determine what investigative steps will be significant and should consequently be incorporated in the report. The investigator must frequently record data indiscriminately and without adverting to its relevance. Often the identity of the guilty person is completely unknown, and information must be gathered concerning a number of persons who might possibly develop into suspects.

c. **Supplement to Sketches and Photographs.** A complete description of the crime scene must rely on the notebook as much as it does on photographs or crime scene sketches. In a photograph, distances between objects are not accurately or even proportionately represented. The crime scene sketch does not purport to be other than merely schematic. The notebook must be employed to describe the true location and condition of objects, the nature and appearance of hidden objects, the texture and inscriptions of various articles, the odor and general atmosphere of the area, and, finally, the inventory of articles of value.

d. **Documentary Evidence.** The investigator's notebook may be used in court by the investigator to refresh his memory while testifying. Defense counsel may under these circumstances subsequently examine the notebook. The possibility of court examination of his notebook should act as a control for the investigator in regard to the care and accuracy which are to be employed in recording notes. Under examination by defense counsel the investigator must be able to account for all entries in the notebook. Cryptic, vague, or illegible inscriptions tend to undermine the validity of the notes and hence militate against the credibility of the witness. One of the conditions sometimes placed on the use of notes in court is that they be original notes which were taken contemporaneously with the phase of the investigation to which they pertain. For example, notes describing the crime scene should have been taken on the scene itself. Of course, exceptions may be made in regard to matters such as moving surveillances or interrogations which by their very nature require that the notes should be made at a later time.

2. Materials

There are ordinarily no official requirements regarding the maintenance of a notebook. Several precautions logically suggest themselves in regard to the manner in which a notebook should be kept. Obviously, ink is preferred to pencil for permanence. A bound notebook creates a more favorable impression in the court-room than the looseleaf type, since its form does not suggest the possible removal of pages. Ideally, the notebook should contain the notes of only one investigation so that its examination may not involve the unauthorized disclosure of information relating to a separate investigation. This procedure obviates, also, any over-lapping or confusion of notes relating to several investigations.

3. Recording Notes

Notes are gathered in chronological order corresponding to the investigative steps or receipt of the information. The sequence is not necessarily in logical order; the notes are first taken and then related to the logic of the investigation in the report. The data of the investigation should be recorded in a complete, accurate, and legible fashion so that, in the event another investigator is required to assume the responsibility for the investigation, he can make intelligent use of the notebook. Improper abbreviations and highly personal, unintelligible locutions should be avoided. In record-ing an interview of a witness the investigator should preface the notes with the case identification, hour, date and place of interview, and a complete identification of the person interviewed and of any others present. This should be followed by a summary of the interview. Important statements should be recorded verbatim, if possible. The extent of the notes will depend upon the impor-tance of the interview and the ability of the investigator to recon-struct an interview from significant data. The manner in which the notebook is used during an interview will vary. If the matter under investigation is sensitive, the obvious use of the notebook may tend to create a reluctance on the part of the interviewee to be forthright and candid in revealing information. In an interrogation it is poor technique to draw out a notebook as soon as the subject begins to make admissions. The source of information frequently dries up at the sight of a notebook with its connotation of formal procedure. In certain types of interviews, such as those incident to a routine personnel background check, there is usually no objection to the open use of the notebook. As a matter of courtesy, however, it is well to request permission of the subject before taking notes.

4. Recording Aids

In a major case the abundance of physical materials to be described, the wealth of potentially relevant data for consideration, and the number of crime-scene interviews that must be conducted suggest the need for ancillary methods of note taking. In the past, some supervisors have solved this problem by dictating to a stenographer as they examined the scene. The use of a portable tape recorder appears to be a simpler solution to the problem. By taping his observations and findings, the investigator can be more comprehensive in his acquisition of information. Subsequently, the relevant taped information can be transcribed to a more permanent form. The tape itself can be retained for a period of time as part of the case record and as a means of refreshing the investigator's memory. In a large office, investigators frequently submit their reports of investigation in taped form to the typing pool.

ADDITIONAL READING

Investigator's Notebook

Fox, R.H. and Cunningham, C.L.: *Crime Scene Search and Physical Evidence Handbook.* Boulder Col.: Paladin Press, 1988.

Chapter 3

REPORT WRITING

1. Importance

THE EFFECTIVENESS of an investigator is judged in large measure by his reports of investigations. If an otherwise satisfactory investigation is poorly reported the reputation of the investigator suffers. The investigator is part of a working team. Unless his information is available to the other members of the organization, proper action cannot be taken in the case. The information is of little use when confined to the investigator's notebook or memory; if it is not communicated to others it fails of its purpose. The report of the finished case provides the necessary basis for action at higher levels; the progress report enables co-workers to take the next logical steps; the initial report establishes the validity of a complaint and indicates the general nature and magnitude of the case. In treating of the subject of report writing the point of view will be that of an investigator who is part of a widespread organization such as a governmental law enforcement agency. In this way the most meaningful type of report can be treated. An agency covering an extensive territory relies heavily on the submission of effective reports by its agents. Often the investigation is nationwide in scope, and as many as ten of the agency's officers will assist the office of origin in covering leads. The only way in which the case can be intelligently managed is through the medium of competent reporting. To a lesser degree the report will be significant in the work of a municipal police department. Here the problem of geography does not interfere with personal communication and extended conferences. Although the report for these organizations is not used as a control mechanism, it is of equal importance as an objective summary

33

of the case findings and as such is an invaluable aid to the district attorney.

2. Purpose of an Investigative Report

In order to understand the basis for the report writing requirements that are described below, the investigator must have a clear view of the purpose of an investigative report. The investigator writes his report in order to achieve the following objectives:

a. **Record.** The report provides a permanent official record of the relevant information obtained in the course of the investigation.

b. **Leads.** The report provides other investigators with information necessary to further advance the investigation.

c. **Prosecutive Action.** The report is a statement of the facts on which designated authorities may base a criminal, corrective, or disciplinary action.

3. Nature of the Report

A report of investigation is an objective statement of the investigator's findings. It is an official record of the information relevant to the investigation which the investigator submits to his superior. Since a case may not go to trial until months after the completion of the investigation, it is important that there be available a complete statement of the investigative results. Loss of memory in regard to details, missing notebooks, and possible absence of the investigator are some of the dangers which the report anticipates.

4. Qualities

To be effective the writer of the report should strive toward the basic qualities of expository style: clarity and brevity. Since the investigator is an instrument of justice, his point of view should be objective and impartial. His purpose is not to convict but merely to describe or narrate. Since he is a reporter in the best sense of the word, he must endeavor to achieve accuracy and completeness. The report of investigation is not the place for the investigator's opinions. It should contain only the facts which he has developed. The information given in the report should be relevant. Everything relevant to the proof or disproof of the crime must be included.

a. **Accuracy.** The report should be a true representation of the facts to the best of the investigator's ability. Information both favorable and unfavorable to the suspect should be included. Statements and opinions of the subjects and witnesses should be clearly presented as such. Persons should be completely identified. Information should be verified by statements of other witnesses and by reference to official records or other reliable sources.

b. **Completeness.** The age-old questions of When? Who? What? Where? and How? should be answered. Since the case concerns a crime, the elements of the offense should be established and the additional facts developed should tend to prove these elements. Every lead should be treated, and negative results from leads should be so indicated. Where a lead is not developed, reasons for this lack of action should be given. The report should be documented by appending important statements, letters, findings of other agencies, and laboratory reports.

c. **Clarity.** The report should develop logically. The order of presentation is not fixed but is dictated by the nature of the case. It will be found that the chronological order is best suited to certain parts of the investigation, while others should be associated with the place where the facts were developed.

5. Sequence of Reports

In general all investigative effort should be reported. Obviously, trivial or irrelevant findings should not be included. The report, however, should include negative as well as positive findings in order to remove unwarranted and misleading suspicion. A single report is desirable, but usually this is not possible because of the leads which are involved in a typical case. In a major case a report should be submitted within a matter of a few days. The seriousness of the matter will warrant maximum investigative effort. Headquarters will require assurance that all possible progress is being made and will desire to initiate leads by other offices. The element of publicity attaching to major crimes will require that headquarters be kept in a position to control news releases and protect itself from charges of inactivity or negligence. Routine cases do not require any rapid dispatch of information. There should, of course, be no unjustifiable delay in investigative action. Ordinarily a lapse of ten days may be permitted before the report is submitted. Supplementary reports will be sent out as the information is developed or the leads discovered. In major cases, however, a status report should be made even when no new significant information has been uncovered. The information contained in previous reports should not be repeated. The closing report will be submitted when all leads are developed and the case does not warrant further investigation.

6. Parts of a Report

Many investigative agencies have fixed rules concerning the divisions that will be made in a report. Others provide a form with blocks for administrative data and permit the investigator to arrange the report in logical divisions. In general the report will contain the following parts:

a. **Administrative Data.** In order to properly control cases and file them in an efficient manner, the report must have identifying data on the face sheet. The following information is considered useful:

1) *Date.* The date on which the investigator's dictation or draft of the report was given to the typist will be the date of the report.

2) *File Number.* This is a matter of local custom. Standard decimal classification file numbers can be used.

3) *Subject.* If the Subject is known, his full name and address. He may subsequently be referred to in the same report as the *Subject* or by his last name in capital letters. If the Subject is unidentified a short description of crime should be given. For example: "JOHN DOE, 741 E. 97 St., assaulted with knife in front of 942 14th Ave., 3 December 1993."

4) *Classification.* The specific nature of the case should be given. This may be done by citing the name of the crime and the section of the penal code under which it is punished. If two

offenses were committed the more serious offense will determine the classification.

5) **Complaint.** The name of the complainant and the manner in which the complaint was received will be given. The complaint may have been received directly or from another office. Personal interview, telephone, or mail may have been used. The complaint will form the initial basis for the investigation. The basis and association with the original case will be explained in the first paragraph of the details.

6) **Reporting Investigator.** The name of the investigator assigned to the case will be given. Assisting investigators will be listed in the details of the report. Care should be exercised in identifying each investigative step with the person by whom it was accomplished. This is of particular importance to the prosecutor in preparing for trial.

7) **Office of Origin.** The office, squad, or precinct in which the complaint was received or which has jurisdiction over the area where the offense requiring investigation took place is considered the Office of Origin. This designation may be changed if it is found that all the investigation is to be performed at another office. Headquarters may specify the Office of Origin in some cases. Other offices which assist the case by "running leads" in their territory are termed "Auxiliary Offices."

8) **Status.** This entry should reflect the status of the case within the office or squad submitting the report. The status is either "Pending" or "Closed."

a) PENDING. This term, when used by the Office of Origin, indicates that the investigation is continuing. In effect it often means that the case is not closed. In submitting a pending report an Auxiliary Office implies either that it has developed significant information before completing leads, that it desires to set out additional leads, or that the completion of the leads is delayed.

b) CLOSED. A case can be closed only by the Office of Origin. Ordinarily it is closed for one of the following reasons: the subject has died, the investigation is completed, or further investigation is considered to be unwarranted for some reason such as the failure to establish a *corpus delicti.*

c) AUXILIARY COMPLETION. This designation of status is used

by an auxiliary office or squad on completing its assigned portion of the investigation.

9) *Distribution.* The disposition of the original and all copies of the report should be clearly stated. In some organizations, for example, the original will be directed to the Chief of Detectives, a copy to the District Attorney, where he is interested, another copy to an interested agency, and the final copy retained for file. A nationwide agency would have an entirely different distribution, transmitting, for example, two action copies to the office with primary interest in the case.

b. **Synopsis.** Each report should bear on its cover sheet a synopsis or brief description of the actions of the perpetrator as established by the body of the report and a summary of the major investigative steps thus far accomplished. This is done in a single paragraph using narrative style. An estimate of the value of property stolen or damaged should be included. If the perpetrator is known, his name should be used and his present status described. The victim's name and address should be given. The following is an example of a synopsis in a burglary case.

"Investigation revealed that on April 15, 1993, JOHN JONES entered the home of THOMAS BROWN at 6854 Dento Rd. and stole a camera and watch. On 24 April JONES was apprehended at Greyhound bus terminal in Newark.

Value of property reported stolen: $410.

Value of property recovered: $410.

JONES presently is in George County Jail."

The purpose of the synopsis is to provide a brief, informative summary of the nature and important events of the case. This procedure is of immense value to reviewing authorities and is of assistance in filing the case and facilitating subsequent reference.

c. **Details of the Report.** The "Details" section of the report has for its objective a narrative account of the investigation. It should be arranged logically with an eye to reader comprehension. Each paragraph should normally contain a separate investigative step. Paragraphs and pages should be numbered. All pertinent details uncovered by the phase of the investigation being reported should be related. The investigator should refer parenthetically to all exhibits which support details.

d. **Conclusions and Recommendations.** (Some investigative agencies do not, as a matter of policy, permit the reporting investigator to submit his conclusions or recommendations. Others require such a statement, and to these the subsequent remarks are applicable.) The investigator's opinions, conclusions, and recommendations as to the status of the case and the disposition of physical evidence should be expressed under this heading. Because of his proximity to the sources of information the investigator is in a better position than the reviewing authorities to judge the credibility of statements in his report. Great weight, therefore, is usually given to his conclusions. It is, of course, incumbent upon the investigator to justify or account for any conclusions which are not consistent with his report or not clearly supported by the facts contained there.

e. **Undeveloped Leads.** An undeveloped lead is an "uncontacted" possible source of pertinent information which appears necessary in bringing the investigation to a logical conclusion. Each undeveloped lead known to the preparer of the investigative report will be listed by him under the above heading at the end of the initial and progress reports. The investigator should try to make each lead specific, stating exactly what information is to be expected from the lead.

1) Requests for the development of a lead at a headquarters different from that of the reporting investigator are addressed under "undeveloped leads" to the commanding officer of the office or squad known to be the closest to the source of information. The report describes the character of the lead, the type of information desired, and if possible, the name and address of the source of information.

2) Undeveloped leads at the headquarters of the reporting investigator also are described, together with a recommended course of investigation.

3) If no undeveloped leads exist, the investigator enters "None" opposite this heading.

f. **Inclosures.** Photographs and sketches of crime scenes, identification photographs, and photocopies of checks are among the exhibits or inclosures that can aid an assisting office.

1) Each inclosure is assigned a letter of the alphabet and

listed. The entry of an inclosure in the report consists of the assignment of a designated letter for the inclosure followed by a brief description.

2) If the exhibit is suitable for reproduction and inclosure with each copy of the report, the fact of its inclosure is indicated by a parenthetical reference after its description in the Exhibits Section and by its additional listing in the report under the heading. "Inclosures."

3) The value and relation of the exhibit to the case are discussed under an appropriate section in the body of the report.

g. **Style.** Clear, simple language should be employed. The use of confusing pronouns should be avoided. Since many of the items are interviews of a similar nature, care should be taken to avoid stereotyped phrases that are repeated to the point of monotony. There must of necessity, however, be a good deal of repetitious use in a long report, since there are certain common terms which are part of the language of investigation. The past tense should be used. The investigator may refer to himself in the third person. Surnames should be in upper-case letters throughout for purposes of filing as well as for expediting a review of the case.

7. Initial Report

Ordinarily, an initial report should be made after the first few days of the investigation. This should set forth the basis of the investigation, i.e., how the case arose, whether by complaint or observation, and on what authority the investigation was begun. The complainant should be interviewed and the fact of the crime established by noting the presence of the elements. For example, if a larceny is reported the element of true ownership should be established. The evidence found at the scene of the crime and the actions of the investigators in searching and processing should be described. Certain details necessary for an understanding of the physical layout of the scene should be included; other details the importance of which may be later realized should be recorded in a notebook. The interviews which were accomplished on the first day should be described, and finally the proposed leads should be set out at the end of the report.

8. Progress Report

In simple cases the initial report can be the final report. In most cases, however, the investigation will require an extended period of time, from a week to a year. The investigator's headquarters should be kept apprised of the progress of the case by periodic reports describing its status. These reports should be submitted at fixed intervals of time unless developments indicate earlier submission. Another purpose served by the progress report is that of setting out new lines of inquiry. Leads may be uncovered in other areas and the appropriate offices must be furnished the necessary information.

9. Closing Report

When an investigation is terminated a closing report should be submitted. This is done under the following circumstances:

a. On successful conclusion of the case.

b. When all leads are exhausted and there appear to be no further steps to be taken.

c. On orders from higher authority. The submission of the closing report does not preclude the reopening of the case on receiving new information. The closing report should include the results of the entire investigation in summary and should present a picture of the status of the case.

10. Miscellaneous

The information given above for the composition of a report falls far short of covering the many difficulties that may arise in an individual case. The following suggestions are given to assist in reporting certain commonly occurring details.

a. **Informants.** The preservation in secrecy of the identity of the informant is of paramount importance. The informant should be referred to by a symbol such as I-2. The accompanying information should not provide a clue to the informant's identity by revealing occupation, location, habits, or other clues.

b. **Minors.** In interviewing a minor the consent of the parents should be indicated in the report and a remark should be made as to the competency of the witness.

c. **Statements.** A statement of a subject should be set forth verbatim, if practicable. Data should be given concerning the place where the statement was taken and the location of the original statement. Statements of witnesses can be given in substance and a remark made, where applicable, that a written statement was taken.

d. **Records.** Where a record of importance is referred to, the following data should be given: title; location; revealed by whom; date, and content. If the record is to become evidence in the case the name of custodian should be given and a statement should be made concerning the need for a subpoena to obtain the record if necessary.

e. **Events Witnessed by Investigator.** The details of time, place, and identification should be given for significant events witnessed by the investigator.

f. **Description of Persons and Property.** The principles outlined in Chapter 29 should be followed in describing persons or objects such as vehicles, jewelry, or other articles of significance to the report.

11. Conclusion

A report of investigation should not be weighted down by a mass of information that is hardly material or only remotely relevant. Discretion should be exercised, also, in the inclusion of negative material which merely states that certain investigative measures were fruitless and does not prove a point, clarify an issue, or aid the inquiry even by indirection. The report should be consistently functional, designed to prove or disprove the allegations. Some investigative agencies often value the report for its own sake, considering it primarily as a justification of the investigative activity described therein. Every step, whether fruitful or not, is listed to show that no logical measure has been overlooked and to demonstrate as a corollary that the reporting agent is beyond criticism. The system may be commended on a number of counts. It serves to provide reviewing authorities with a ready means of checking subordinates and provides order, method, and routine to investigative activity. In addition it offers supervisors and investigators a sense of security; the investigator knows within fairly exact limits what is expected of him and the supervisor is comforted by the knowledge that his organization may not be reasonably criticized in a particular case on the grounds of obvious omissions or inertia. To the state's attorney and others, however, who must take administrative action on the basis of the report, the irrelevant and immaterial information contravenes the purpose of the investigation by dimming the issues and obscuring the facts that are truly contributory of the proof.

ADDITIONAL READING

Report Writing

Agnos, T.J. and Schatt, S.: *The Practical Law Enforcement Guide to Writing Field Reports, Grant Proposals, Memos, and Resumes.* Springfield, Ill.: Thomas, 1980.

Clede, B.: Lakeland's Near-Paperless Reporting. 35 *Law and Order,* 10, 1987.

Cox, C.R. and Brown, J.G.: *Report Writing for Criminal Justice Professionals.* Cincinnati, Anderson, 1991.

Dienstein, W.: *How to Write a Narrative Investigation Report.* Springfield, Ill.: Thomas, 1964.

Gammage, A.Z.: *Basic Police Reporting,* 2nd ed. Springfield, Ill.: Thomas, 1974.

George, D.: Computer-Assisted Report Entry: Toward a Paperless Police Department. 57 *Police Chief,* 3, 1990.

Hess, K.M. and Wrobleski, H.M.: *For the Record: Report Writing in Law Enforcement.* New York, Wiley, 1978.

Kakonis, T.E. and Hanzek, D.: *A Practical Guide to Police Report Writing.* New York, McGraw-Hill, 1978.

Kelly, P.T.: Increasing Productivity by Taping Reports. 57 *Police Chief,* 3, 1990.

Lesce, T.: Lap Computers Aid Report Writing. 35 *Law and Order,* 2, 1987.

Levie, R.C. and Ballard, L.E.: *Writing Effective Reports on Police Investigations: Concepts, Procedures, Samples.* Boston, Allyn and Bacon, 1978.

Nelson, J.G.: *Preliminary Investigation and Police Reporting.* Beverly Hills, Calif.: Glencoe Press, 1970.

Robinson, C.C.: *Criminal Justice: Improving Police Report Writing.* Danville, Ill.: Interstate Printers and Publishers, 1977.

Romig, C.H.A.: The Improvement of Investigative Reports. 26 *Law and Order,* 3, 1978.

Ross, A. and Plant, D.: *Writing Police Reports: A Practical Guide.* Deerfield, Ill.: MTI Teleprograms, 1977.

Seay, W.T.: Report Writing: Do It Right the First Time! 57 *FBI Law Enforcement Bulletin,* 12, 1988.

PART II
INITIAL STEPS

Chapter 4

CRIME SCENE SEARCH

1. General

THE SEARCH of the scene of the crime is, in certain types of offenses, the most important part of the investigation. Obviously, many kinds of crime do not have a "scene" in the sense of an area where traces are usually found. Offenses such as forgery and embezzlement require no vigorous or exceptional physical activity in their commission. There is no impact of the criminal on his surroundings. Crimes of violence, however, involve a struggle, a break, the use of weapons, and the element of unpredictability. In homicide, assaults, and burglary, the criminal is in contact with the physical surroundings in a forceful manner. Traces may be left in the form of clothing, shoe impressions, fingerprints, bloodstains, overthrown furniture, disturbed articles in general, and jimmy marks. The scene of the crime must, moreover, be viewed in an active as well as a passive sense. There is not only the effect of the criminal on the scene to be considered, but also the manner in which the scene may have imparted traces to the criminal. The investigator must be able to visualize the way in which the perpetrator may have carried with him the available evidentiary material that may link him to the scene. Flour and coal dust, paint, seeds, soil, and many other traces, depending on the character of the locale, may later be discovered on the clothing or effects of a suspect. Samples of the trace material must also be gathered at the time of the search in anticipation of the finding of these traces on a suspect.

2. Preliminary

Before treating the search itself, it is profitable to consider the actions and duties of the investigator on first arriving at the scene of the crime. The following measures or steps will ordinarily be found necessary:

   a. Identify and, if possible, retain for questioning the person who first notified the police.

   b. Determine the perpetrator by direct inquiry or observation if his identity is immediately apparent.

   c. Detain all persons present at the scene.

   d. Summon assistance if necessary.

   e. Safeguard the area by issuing appropriate orders and by physically isolating it. All unauthorized persons must be excluded from the crime scene. Spectators, newspaper photographers, reporters, and others who are not officially connected with the investigation should be kept at a distance. Uniformed police stationed at appropriate distances will serve to perform this function. The police should be requested to refer potential witnesses to one of the investigators.

   f. Subsequently permit only authorized persons to enter the area.

   g. Separate the witnesses so as to obtain independent statements.

   h. Do not touch or move any object.

   i. Assign definite duties of the search if assistants are present.

3. Assignment of Duties

For a full discussion of the crime scene search optimum personnel conditions must be assumed. As a matter of common experience, however, the investigator will frequently find that he must perform all of the crime scene duties without assistance. It is understood, moreover, that the thoroughness of the search must often be dependent on the relative importance of the case. Where the offense is minor and the work load great, the search cannot justifiably be performed as meticulously as it would in the ideal or isolated situation. For maximum effectiveness, then, a group such as the following should be assigned to the task of the search:

a. **Officer in Charge.** Directs search, assigns duties, and assumes responsibility for the effectiveness of the search.

b. **Assistant.** Implements the directions of the officer in charge.

c. **Photographer.** Photographs the scene and individual pieces of evidence as they are discovered.

d. **Sketcher.** Makes a rough sketch at the scene and later a finished sketch.

e. **Master Note Taker.** Writes down in shorthand the observations and descriptions given by the others. Notes the time of discovery, the identity of the finder and maintains an orderly log of the proceedings.

f. **Evidence Collector.** Collects, preserves and tags articles of evidence.

g. **Measurer.** Makes overall measurements of the scene and locates by a coordinate system or otherwise each article of evidence and each significant object present.

h. **Section Leader.** In the search of a large crime scene area, such as the scene of an airplane crash, the size of the searching group will suggest a division of labor into sections consisting of a group of six persons headed by a section leader. If a searcher discovers an artifact or object of possible evidentiary significance, he should, before touching the object, call it to the attention of the section leader, who will note the discovery or finding and make the necessary arrangements for its collection, preservation, or transportation. In this way the search of the whole section can be supervised and alternative witnesses to the discovery of evidence obtained.

4. The Survey

At this stage in the investigation, prohibitions and negative advice are most useful. The investigator must initially restrain himself from taking physical action. The natural inclination is to form a quick opinion of what happened and endeavor to verify it by physically examining various articles. The most advisable measure at this point is to stand aside and make an estimate of the situation. Determine what areas bear no foot impressions so that they may be traversed without damage. A place should then be selected for a "headquarters." Notebooks, equipment, and receptacles for evidence can be placed in this designated area. Having formed the estimate, the investigator now determines the number, kind, and views of the photographs he wishes taken. With the photography accomplished, he may proceed with the search. In case of homicide, he should, of course, await the arrival and services of the medical examiner before disturbing the body.

5. The Search

Method rather than intuition should guide the basic search. The examination must, of course, be thorough. It is impossible to predict the vagaries of the criminal mind or to safely imagine all the physical effects of violent action. A plan of search should be formed which will cover all the ground. The scheme must then be doggedly followed. The spirit of the investigation at this point is caught, if the investigator assumes that the physical traces he now uncovers will be the only evidence in the crime. Since every step of an investigation must be undertaken with the thought of ulti-mate presentation in court, a notebook will be an invaluable aid. Copious methodical notes of appearances and measurements will supplement the crime scene sketches and photographs. In gather-ing the evidence some principle of selection must be employed since the indiscriminate collection of clue materials is an unscien-tific procedure which may lead to serious omissions. As a basic guide the investigator should look upon the evidence as serving to establish one or more of the following:

    a. The *corpus delicti* or the fact that the crime was committed.

    b. The method of operation of the perpetrator.

    c. The identity of the guilty person.

6. The Mechanics of the Search

If the crime scene is indoors, the search plan will naturally be dictated by the size of the room and its contents. The unlimited variety of indoor situations precludes systematic discussion. Where the scene is outdoors one of several methods described below can be selected to suit the terrain. The choice of method is not too important since the essential elements of success in implementing any of the suggested schemes are the alertness, knowledge, and experience of the participating investigators. One or more persons can cooperate in an orderly search as long as there is a clearly apparent organization and well-defined leadership. One person must undertake the responsibility of command and he must in consequence dominate the scene. We shall, for convenience, assume in this discussion that three persons are performing the actual search.

a. **Strip Method.** In this method, the area is blocked out in the form of a rectangle. The three searchers, A, B, and C, proceed slowly at the same pace along paths parallel to one side of the rectangle. When a piece of evidence is found, the finder announces his discovery and all halt until the evidence is cared for. A photographer is called for if necessary. The evidence is collected and tagged and the search proceeds at a given signal. At the end of the rectangle, the searchers turn and proceed back along new lanes as shown in Figure 1.

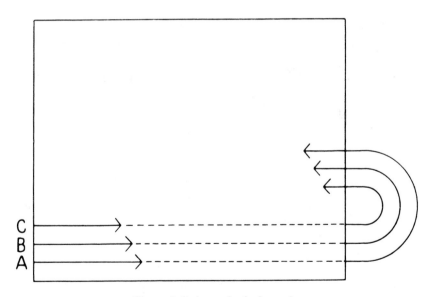

Figure 1. Strip method of search.

A modification of this plan is the *double strip* or *grid* method. Here, the rectangle is traversed first parallel to the base and then parallel to a side (see Fig. 2).

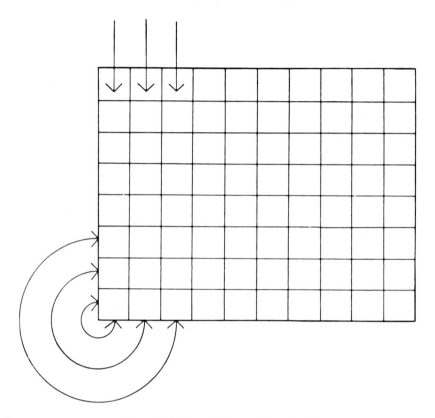

Figure 2. Double strip or grid method.

b. **Spiral Method.** The three searchers follow each other in the path of a spiral, beginning on the outside and spiraling in toward the center (see Fig. 3).

c. **Zone Method.** One searcher is assigned to each subdivision of a quadrant. Depending on the size of the area, it is divided into quadrants and then each quadrant is cut into another set of quadrants (see Fig. 4).

d. **Wheel Method.** In this method, the area is considered as being approximately circular. The searchers gather at the center and proceed outward along radii or spokes. The procedure should be repeated several times depending on the size of the circle and the number of searchers. One shortcoming of this method is the

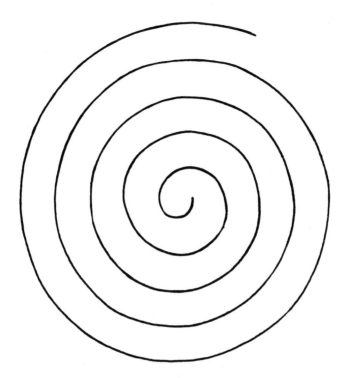

Figure 3. Spiral method.

great increase of relative area to be observed as the searcher departs from the center (see Fig. 5).

7. Precautions

The investigator should employ imagination as well as thoroughness in his search. For example, in searches of indoor crime scenes the following are typical of the points that should not be overlooked: cracks in the floor, new paint or plaster, light fixtures, closets, clothing, shades, draperies, door locks, casings, sills, stairs, banisters, garbage pails, toilets, fuse boxes, asbestos lining of pipes, washing machines, vacuum cleaners, and so forth.

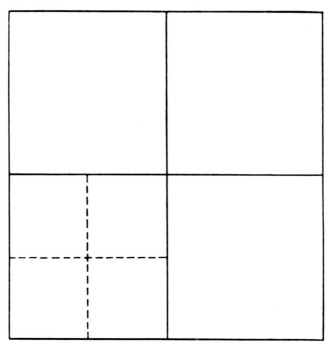

Figure 4. Zone method.

8. Evaluation

During the crime scene search the discovery of physical evidence will be guided merely by the order of path and time. Clues and evidentiary traces will have been collected and preserved without specific regard for their relation to the crime. With the completion of the main search the investigator should devote some time to developing a directive principle to determine the significance of the evidence. Thus far the clue or trace material has been viewed by the discoverer as an abnormality, a thing which is foreign to the scene or simply out of its accustomed place. Its logical position in the investigative pattern may not as yet be clear. It serves to identify or it belongs to the relation of cause and effect. Blood stains or scuffmarks are examples. The investigator

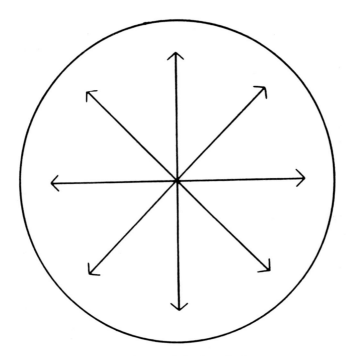

Figure 5. Wheel method.

recognizes that these traces are not part of the normal scene. He is aware that their existence is attributable to the human agency in the crime of violence that has taken place. What exactly does the evidence prove or partly prove? What additional evidence must be looked for to supplement the proof—to definitely establish an element or an identity? What norm must be employed to give coherence and pattern to the collected evidence? To answer these questions the investigator must carefully study the materials to determine their significance and probative use. Basically he is searching for two kinds of evidence. In the first category are those facts and materials which establish the elements of proof. These may show that a crime has been committed; that a certain person committed the crime; or that it was committed in a certain manner which indicates the degree of the crime or the specific offense and also reveals the *modus operandi* of the criminal. Other evidence or the same evidence looked at in a different light may serve to trace the criminal. In the latter category we have as examples the fingerprint or the dry cleaner's mark on a garment. The fingerprint establishes the fact that the criminal was at the scene and assists in tracing the criminal by means of files and comparisons.

9. Reconstructing the Crime

Subsequent to the search of the scene of a crime an effort should be made to determine from the appearance of the place and its objects what actually occurred and, particularly, what were the movements and methods of the criminal, since this latter constitutes part of the *modus operandi*. The process of ascertaining the circumstances of a crime is known as *reconstructing* the crime. It may include a physical reproduction of the positions of articles and persons during the occurrence. From a study of the evidence in this manner it is often possible to make useful inferences which may be synthesized into a reasonable theory.

a. **Physical Reconstruction.** If possible the investigator should reconstruct the physical appearance of the scene from the description of witnesses and the indications of the physical evidence. If the lighting and weather conditions are relevant, the reconstruction should be accomplished at the same time of day and under comparable weather conditions. The witnesses should be requested to reenact their movements while other persons assume the positions of the participants.

b. **Mental Reconstruction.** From the reenacting of the occurrence and the reconstruction of the arrangement of the physical objects some conclusion can now be made concerning the consistency of the accounts of the various witnesses. In reconstructing the actions of the criminal, the investigator should test his theory for logic and consistency. A theory should not be rejected merely because the investigator might not under the circumstances behave in a similar manner. The study should be conducted from the point of view of the mentality of the criminal. No assumptions should be made concerning actions which are not supported by evidence. The theory finally developed by the investigator should provide a line of investigative action but should not be stubbornly pursued in the face of newly discovered facts which are not consistent with it.

10. Equipment

To search and sketch the crime scene and to care for the evidence, a small kit containing a number of the items described below will be found useful for each of the designated activities.

a. **Searching.** Equipment for searching the crime scene consists simply of a flashlight and a magnifier.

b. **Sketching.** This equipment consists of (1) measuring devices such as a compass, steel tape, and ruler, and (2) recording implements such as pencils, pens, chalk, graph paper, a sketching pad, clip board, and a paper pad for notetaking. The scene will, of course, be also recorded photographically; cameras, however, will ordinarily be contained in a separate kit.

c. **Collection of Evidence.** This will include tools such as a cutting pliers, a knife, a screwdriver, and shears as well as tweezers, a scalpel, forceps, cotton swabs, a medicine dropper and disposable latex gloves. Fingerprint equipment, such as brushes, powders, and lifting tape, should be included.

d. **Preservation of Evidence.** The equipment for this purpose consists of various kinds and sizes of containers such as glass jars, plastic vials, paper and plastic bags, filter paper, envelopes, pillboxes, and cardboard boxes. Pins, thumbtacks, rubber bands, tape and a stapler are also useful. To mark, label and seal the evidence there should be pens, grease pencils, a metal scribe, evidence tags, gummed labels, and evidence sealing tape.

ADDITIONAL READING

Crime Scene Search

Berry, G.N.: The Uniformed Crime Investigator: A Unique Strategy to Protect and Serve. 53 *FBI Law Enforcement Bulletin*, 3, 1984.

Bevel, T.: Crime Scene Reconstruction. 41 *Journal of Forensic Identification*, 248, 1991.

Buckwalter, A.: *Search for Evidence.* Stoneham, Mass.: Butterworth, 1984.

Clede, B.: Forensic Determinations Depend on Training. 36 *Law and Order,* 3, 1988.

Fisher, B.A.J., Svensson, A. and Wendel, O.: *Techniques of Crime Scene Investigation,* 4th ed. New York, Elsevier, 1987.

Fox, R.H. and Cunningham, C.L.: *Crime Scene Search and Physical Evidence Handbook.* Boulder, Col.: Paladin Press, 1988.

Glidden, R.C.: Establishing a Crime Scene Unit. 38 *Law and Order,* 6, 1990.

Hoving, G.L.: *Crime Scene Investigation: A Manual for Patrol Officers.* San Luis Obispo, Calif.: Concepts in Criminal Justice, 1985.

Scene of the Crime: U.S. Government Forensic Handbook. Boulder, Col.: Paladin Press, 1992.

Schultz, D.O. and Scheer, S.: *Crime Scene Investigation.* Englewood Cliffs, N.J.: Prentice-Hall, 1977.

Tackett, E.: *Underwater Crime Scene Investigation.* Fountain Valley, Calif.: Lasertech, 1987.

Urlacher, G.F. and Duffy, R.J.: The Preliminary Investigation Process. 59 *FBI Law Enforcement Bulletin,* 3, 1990.

Will, J.W.: Sonar: Underwater Search and Recovery. 56 *FBI Law Enforcement Bulletin,* 5, 1987.

Chapter 5

PHOTOGRAPHING THE CRIME SCENE

1. Use of Photography

THE ESSENCE of photography is visual communication. When photographing the crime scene, the investigator will attempt to convey the maximum amount of useful information that will enable the viewer to fully understand the what, where, and how of the events depicted. The photographs will include not only the immediate area where the act itself took place but also the adjacent areas where the events leading up to and following the crime occurred. The number and kinds of photographs needed depend a great deal on the type of crime involved, its seriousness, and other circumstances. In an arson case where the physical evidence is important in establishing the elements of proof and where the crime scene may cover a large area, extensive photography will be necessary. On the other hand, an armed robbery on a city street will leave so few if any traces of the event that it will usually be unproductive to extensively photograph the crime scene. The seriousness of the crime is another important factor in determining the number of photographs: A murder may require many photographs, while a minor burglary only a few. Other circumstances, such as the complexity of the crime, the size of the premises, and the amount of physical evidence involved, are other considerations affecting the number of photographs that should be taken.

As a general rule, it is better to take too many photographs rather than too few. In most cases, the investigator has only one opportunity to photograph the crime scene in its original condition before the physical evidence is collected and removed. An object at a homicide scene may not seem important at the time. However, during the subsequent investigation, the investigator may develop information that the object was in fact the murder weapon. Its appearance and position in the crime scene photograph would then have great significance, a significance he was unaware of when he took the pictures.

Crime scene photographs are used in the investigation and prosecution of criminal cases to serve a number of purposes:

a. **To Provide a Permanent Record.** The crime scene photographs provide a permanent record of how the crime scene appeared shortly after the crime was committed, before the objects of evidence were moved or otherwise disturbed. Along with the report and the crime scene sketch, it is part of the official record of the investigation. The crime scene photographs will be used throughout the investigation, prosecution, and presentation of the case in court. They will remain on file for a long time after the case is tried. In the event that a conviction is appealed, the pictures must be available to reconstruct the crime years after it has taken place.

b. **To Understand the Crime.** A verbal description of the crime scene is always more understandable when illustrated with photographs. Many of the people involved in investigating and prosecuting a case are required to have an intimate knowledge of the details of the case. Because of time and work constraints, they usually do not have the opportunity to view the crime scene directly. For example, laboratory personnel sometimes need to see the position of a piece of physical evidence at the crime scene in order to determine its significance. The district attorney must be familiar with all aspects of the investigation in order to determine whether it is worthwhile prosecuting the case. Photographs help these people, who do not attend to the crime scene, to understand the crime.

c. **For Investigative Purposes.** Crime scene photographs are useful to the investigator for a number of purposes:

1) To establish the *corpus delicti.* Every crime has certain elements that must be shown to exist before a case can be developed. When photographing the crime scene, the investigator will be guided by the state of affairs that needs to be demonstrated to support a criminal charge. Depending on the crime in question, certain aspects of the crime scene will receive special attention: For example, in a burglary case, pictures of the area of the break-in

or the entry; in arson, the origin of the fire; in homicide, the manner and cause of death. Illustrations of this type can serve to establish the *corpus delicti* of the offense, that is, the fact that a certain crime has been committed.

2) To verify the story of a witness or a suspect. A witness's or suspect's account of what happened at the crime scene can be checked to see if it corresponds to the condition and arrangement of objects, furniture, doors, and windows as depicted in the crime scene photographs. During interrogation a suspect may confess when confronted by the investigator with a picture of the crime scene and a description of how the crime was committed.

3) To refresh the investigator's memory. A photograph makes it easy for the investigator to mentally reconstruct the crime. Doing this periodically may lead him to associate this crime with another similar offense or suggest to him a different line of inquiry.

4) To avoid excessive handling of the physical evidence. When interviewing witnesses, it is often necessary to ask them whether they recognize a particular object, such as the murder weapon. By using a photograph instead of the object, the physical evidence can be preserved from unnecessary handling and possible alteration.

d. **For Court Presentation.** The crime scene photograph is the primary means of conveying to the judge and jury an objective representation of the scene, enabling them to understand the evidence and to evaluate the actions of the accused. The purpose of the photograph is to provide a reproduction of the scene as it would appear to the average eyewitness. For photographs to be admissible in court, the photographer, or someone familiar with the crime scene, must testify that the pictures faithfully represent the subject matter. The photograph must not mislead the viewer in any significant aspect. The size and distances of the objects should appear normal to the eye and the important subject matter should be in sharp focus.

2. Evidence Rules Relating to Photographs

A few basic precautions must be observed by the investigator to insure the admissibility of his photographs in court. The following are minimal requirements:

a. The object which is represented should be material and relevant. (That is, the physical evidence should tend to establish a fact that is both significant and related to an issue in the case.)

b. The photograph should not unduly incite prejudice or sympathy. Pictures of severe injuries may arouse emotions of fear, anger, and indignation in the mind of the juror. As long as the intent of the photograph is to document the relevant facts of the case and not to prejudice the jurors against the defendant, it will be admissible as evidence. The trial judge makes the decision on admissibility.

c. The photograph should be free from distortion; it should not misrepresent the scene or object it purports to depict. Distortions ordinarily assume one of the following forms:

1) *Incorrect Point of View.* By selecting a peculiar direction from which to point the lens, the photographer is able to obscure essential objects and emphasize others.

2) *Improper Perspective.* Tilting the camera upward or downward will distort the sizes and distances of objects. Photographs have the proper perspective when the sizes and distances of objects appear normal to the average viewer. This can be accomplished by keeping the camera at eye level with the lens pointed so that it is at a 90-degree angle with an opposing wall.

Another source of distortion is the result of an improper relationship of the focal length of the lens to the print-viewing distance. For a technically correct perspective, the focal length of the lens must be equal to the viewing distance of the photograph. Practically, it is difficult, if not impossible, to control at what distance from their eyes a person views a photograph and accuracy in this regard is unnecessary as long as the photograph contains no misleading distortions.

3) *Deceptive Tones.* Tones are the representation of colors in black-and-white photography. Misrepresentation of tones, even to the point of complete obscurity, can result from the manipulation of the development or the exposure of the film, or from an inappropriate choice of film or printing paper.

3. Photographing the Crime Scene

In photographing the crime scene the investigator should endeavor to provide a series of "shots" which supply a maximum of useful information and which will enable the viewer to understand how the crime was committed. The photographer should show the relationships of the various objects to one another. Locations of articles should be clearly seen with reference to recognizable backgrounds. Since at the time the photograph is taken, the investigator cannot be expected to know the significance of all articles of evidence present, he must take a large number of photographs to insure complete coverage.

The 4 × 5 press and the 35mm are the two most widely used cameras for crime scene photography. The press camera is so called because at one time it was used extensively by newspaper reporters. It has long been favored by crime scene photographers because it's 4 × 5 inch negative can be enlarged and still retain most of the fine details of the original. The main drawback of this camera is its relatively large size and cumbersome accessories. On the other hand, the 35mm camera is easier to learn and more convenient to operate. However, enlargements from the much smaller 35mm negative will lack some of the definition and clarity of those from the larger 4 × 5 press camera.

Traditionally, the crime scene has been photographed using black-and-white film. Today, color film is being used more frequently and in some police agencies exclusively. Color pictures have the advantage of giving a more "natural" look to the crime scene. When asking a witness to identify an article of clothing or some other object from a crime scene photograph, the item will be more recognizable in a color picture. Color film is superior for photographing bodily injuries, especially bruises which change color over a period of time. But the courts will, on occasion, object to the use of a color photograph of the victim's injuries as inflammatory and prejudicing the jury against the defendant. Ideally, then, the photographer will take both black-and-white and color pictures of the crime scene

In the suggestions given below for photographing the crime scene, the homicide situation has been taken as an example because it encompasses many of the techniques which are applicable to other crimes.

a. **Overall Photographs.** Several photographs should be taken employing a general view. The camera should be carried clockwise until at least four general view photographs have been taken.

b. **Photographs of the Deceased.** A set of views should be selected to show significant aspects of the body of the deceased. The relationship of the body to surrounding furniture, for example, may be suggestive of action immediately preceding the death.

c. **Photographs of Articles of Evidence.** As the scene is examined, various objects will appear to have a direct relation to the homicide. Weapons, bloodstains, hair, fibers, papers, and similar articles should be photographed before they are moved. Two photographs are needed for a significant object which is less than 6 inches in length. The first should be at close range to obtain a fairly large image of the article. The second photograph should be taken with the camera approximately 6 feet from the object in order to bring the background in view and show the object in perspective.

d. **Markings in the Field of View.** Markers are devices placed in the field of view which aid in the interpretation of a photograph. In court exhibits markers draw attention to points of evidence and help jurors, who are ordinarily unfamiliar with the subject matter, to understand their significance and their relationship to the crime. Because placing markers in the field of view will leave the investigator open to the charge of tampering with evidence, many courts require that, if markers are to be used, two sets of photographs be taken. The first set will record the crime scene in its original state; the second set will include the markers. Markers must not misrepresent the evidence or conceal any significant part of it. There are three types of markers that are generally used:

1) *Rulers.* By including a ruler, a yardstick, or a tape measure in the photograph, the size of objects and the distance between objects can be effectively conveyed. Placing a small ruler in the field of view can also guide the photographic laboratory personnel in determining the degree of enlargement required.

2) *Location Markers.* White arrows or numbered signs are placed in the picture to draw attention to significant points of evidence.

They are quite helpful when the size of the evidence is small and it could easily be overlooked. Alternatively, a transparent overlay with the markers attached may be placed over the photograph. This technique has the advantage of not requiring a second set of photographs.

3) *Identifying Data.* A small sign placed in the field of view can be used to identify a photograph. The information will usually include the date, time, and location of the crime scene as well as the photographer's name. The data should not indicate the type of offense being investigated or any opinion concerning the crime. This precaution is taken to avoid any objection to the use of the photograph in court on the grounds that it will prejudice the jury.

e. **Special Techniques.** A wide-angle lens may be used with indoor photographs in order to include more of the contents of the room in the field of view than can ordinarily be achieved with a normal lens. Evidence such as a developed fingerprint or a tool mark should be photographed by employing special techniques. Fingerprints should, of course, be photographed with the fingerprint camera. Photomacrography, i.e., the use of an image greater than life size, should be employed for tool marks if the bellows extension of the camera permits.

f. **Photographing the Environs.** The crime scene should not be considered as a physically limited area immediately surrounding the body of the victim or the immediate objective of the criminal. If the homicide took place in a house, for example, the investigator should not consider the single room in which the deceased is found to be the whole crime scene. Any contiguous areas which may have been used in approach, pursuit, flight, or struggle should be considered part of the scene of the crime and should, therefore, be accorded appropriate attention. The nature of the crime will determine the extent to which the environs need be photographed for a fuller understanding of the events that led to the fatal occurrence. For example, the investigator may find that some of the following are significant and therefore suitable photographic subjects: the arrangement of rooms; a passageway; the location of a window; shattered glass; broken furniture; scattered clothes of the victim or his assailant; bullet holes in floors, ceilings, or walls; a trail of bloodstains; the relation of the house to the street; and the location of street lights. Many other evidence photographs will be suggested by a particular crime scene.

g. **Photographing the Body After Removal.** Additional photographs of the body may be required after the body has been carried from the scene and the clothing has been removed.

1) *Identification.* If the identity of the deceased is unknown, photographs of the face and of identifying scars or deformities will be important. The face should be photographed from both sides and from the front. The viewpoint should be the same as that used in ordinary identification photographs.

2) *Wounds.* The character of the wounds received by the victim may be of importance in the prosecution of the case. Significant wounds should be photographed with both black-and-white and color film to give a true impression of their size, shape, and appearance. These photographs can be considered as a supplement to the autopsy report.

h. **Photographic Data.** A complete record of each photograph should be made in a notebook so that the following minimum essential information is available if requested in court:

1) Data to identify the photographs with the offense.

2) Data to identify the photographer.

3) Data to orient the camera position with the scene.

4) The date and hour when each photograph was taken.

5) Data reflecting light and weather conditions when each photograph was made, *f/* number and exposure.

6) Data reflecting the type and make of camera, film, and details regarding any special photographic equipment which was used.

7) Focal length of the lens.

8) Data regarding developing, printing, and any special laboratory techniques. This is usually furnished by the laboratory technician, but the investigator should be in a position to present the data and arrange for the appearance of the laboratory technician in court.

9) Data to reflect a complete chain of custody of the photographic film used.

PHOTO LOG

Report Number   **063-85-4807**

SA   **Tim C. Winkler**   Date   **25 November 1993**

TIME   **0904**   Began taking crime scene photographs and drawing rough sketch to depict camera positions and distances. All photographs taken at eye level height (**5' 6"**) unless otherwise indicated. All interior and exterior photographs are taken with the following equipment:

TYPE CAMERA   **Canon AE-1**   BODY NUMBER   **603113**

LENS FOCAL LENGTH AND
LENS SERIAL NUMBER   **50 mm 1:1.4   10492**

TYPE OF FILM   Ektachrome   NUMBER OF EXPOSURES   **36**

ASA   **400**   FILTRATION   **Canon Haze**

F/STOP   **See Remarks**   SHUTTER SPEED   **See Remarks**

FLASH ATTACHMENT   **NA**   FLASH SERIAL NUMBER   **NA**

EXPLANATION OF TERMS USED IN REMARKS COLUMN: Camera held in horizontal format, unless otherwise noted. DA—Photograph taken from directly above the object; V—Camera held in vertical format; N—Normal lens; M—Macro lens; WA—Wide-angle lens.

TIME	PHOTO	TYPE	PHOTO DEPICTING	DISTANCE	REMARKS
0910	# 1	Outside Establishment	Distance To Building # 3262-A From Walkway	14' 7"	N, 1/500 Sec, f/11
0913	# 2	Outside Entrance	Open DoorTo Apartment 126-A	6' 9"	V, N, 1/500 Sec, f/8
0918	# 3	Evidence	Pistol On The Floor In The Doorway	2' 6"	DA, N, 1/250 Sec, f/5.6

Figure 6. A sample photo log. (Source: U.S. Army. *Field Manual, 19-20.*)

4. Selection of Point of View

The camera should be carefully placed to provide a perspective which is both normal and informative. The incorrect selection of photographic angle (formed by the camera axis and the horizontal) often results in a distorted and false impression of the scene. The height of the camera is normally taken at eye level. This is particularly important if the photograph purports to show what a witness could have seen in a certain position. The location of the camera should be recorded and indicated in the crime scene sketch.

5. Videotape

When faced with an extensive crime scene such as arson in a factory or burglary of an office building, the videotape camera or camcorder can be an invaluable aid to the investigator. A videotape of the crime scene can provide background and continuity to a collection of photographs by capturing the atmosphere of the crime scene and showing the relationship of what appears to be unrelated pictures. By "panning" across a room, the investigator can record articles of evidence that have been overlooked or whose significance has not yet been recognized. At an arson or a homicide crime scene, a videotape of a crowd of spectators, on later analysis, may yield the likenesses of important witnesses or even a suspect.

Shooting the crime scene with a camcorder is similar to the procedure followed with still photographs. First, general views are taken by "panning" across the crime scene. Then with the zoom lens, the operator will take close-ups of the physical evidence. For extreme close-ups such as for tool marks and fingerprints, the camcorder can be equipped with a macro lens. Ordinarily, the use of the camcorder requires one investigator to act as a cameraman and another to narrate the audio segment. When narrating, care must be taken to avoid the unintended remark because an erased or edited tape is not admissible as evidence in court. For this reason and because there is often noise and confusion at the crime scene, some investigators prefer to press the "mute" button on the camcorder which will eliminate the sound portion. An added feature of the camcorder is its playback capability which permits the investigator to review all the footage at the crime scene to make sure he has properly recorded all of the important evidence.

The videotape can be played on a television set. While viewing the tape the investigator can press the "pause," "slow motion," or "rewind" buttons on the remote control which gives him the opportunity to study a particular scene as long as he wants. However, it must be kept in mind that a videotape does not record the fine details of a photograph and, hence, is not a substitute for photographs. If a videotape of the crime scene is made, it should be made in addition to the photographs. The videotape should cover the same range of material as well as the same photographic angles and distances as the crime scene photographs, plus any additional footage the investigator believes will contribute to understanding the case.

The videotape is also an ideal form of evidence in other types of investigative situations. Insurance frauds, for example, are sometimes proven by this means. Where a person feigns an incapacitating injury and wishes to collect heavy damages, a videotape showing him in active use of the supposedly injured limbs is sufficient to convince the jury of the fraudulence of his claim. Stores and banks routinely monitor their customers with hidden cameras as part of a larceny and robbery prevention program. In police work there are many opportunities for the use of the video camera. Certain criminal activities take place in the street and can be readily photographed in the daytime—for example, the completion of a "buy" in narcotics, breaking into an automobile, or the offer of a bribe. Interrogations are frequently videotaped in order to obtain an accurate record of the suspect's statements and also to protect the investigator from charges of coercion. Perhaps the most important routine use of this technology is in cases involving drunken drivers. In some communities videotape cameras are mounted on the dashboards of patrol cars and record every traffic stop the officer makes. An activated wireless microphone tapes the patrol officer's verbal description of what he sees as well as his conversation with the driver. Videotaping traffic stops serves several functions. A person who is pulled over for driving while intoxicated will have a difficult time denying the charges when confronted in a more sober moment with a visual and aural record of his behavior. If the arresting officer is accused of falsifying charges or of mistreating the driver, a videotape of the defendant's driving pattern and the officer's conduct during the arrest will either verify or discredit the allegation. If the driver is able to elude the police, a picture of the car and its license plate will have been recorded.

6. "Posed" Photographs and Markers

It is sometimes desirable to illustrate the statement of a witness by means of a "posed" photograph. In this way the inadequacies of verbal testimony can be graphically remedied. To accomplish a posed photograph a person with the same general physical appearance and dress should be employed. Naturally he should be placed in the same spot and positions as directed by the witness, and the camera should be located so as to represent the point of view of the witness. If there is a plurality of witnesses, several photographs should be made to represent the version of each witness. Markers or pointers should be used to clarify important aspects of the photograph. Tire tracks and bullet holes, for example, can be more clearly indicated by delineating chalk marks. Prior to such a procedure, however, photographs should be made of the untouched scene to obviate any objection to the photograph in court on the grounds that it does not purport to show the original scene.

ADDITIONAL READING

Photography

Auten, J.: Traffic Collision Investigation: Photographing the Crime Scene. 36 *Law and Order*, 1, 1988.

Chernoff, G. and Herschel, S.: *Photography and the Law.* New York, Amphoto, 1978.

Dey, L.M.: Night Crime-Scene Photography. 21 *Law and Order*, 4, 1973.

Duckworth, J.E.: *Forensic Photography.* Springfield, Ill.: Thomas, 1983.

Giacoppo, M.: The Expanding Role of Video in Court. 60 *FBI Law Enforcement Bulletin*, 11, 1991.

Harman, A.: Videotaping by Police. 36 *Law and Order*, 9, 1988.

Kilpack, L.: Use of Video Camera for DUI Investigation. 56 *FBI Law Enforcement Bulletin*, 5, 1987.

MacFarlane, B.A.: Photographic Evidence: Its Probative Value at Trial and the Judicial Discretion to Exclude it from Evidence. 16 *Criminal Law Quarterly*, 149, 1974.

Mayer, R.E.: Minilabs in Law Enforcement. 38 *Law and Order*, 7, 1990.

—— : Versatile Compact 35mm Cameras. 38 *Law and Order*, 5, 1990.

McEvoy, R.T., Jr.: Surveillance Photography: What You Need to Know. *Law Enforcement Technology,* February/March, 1986.

Mestel, G.S.: Video Camcorders Offer a New Edge in Crime Scene Documentation. 54 *Police Chief,* 12, 1987.

O'Brien, K.P. and Sullivan, R.C.: *Criminalistics: Theory and Practice,* 3rd ed. Boston, Allyn and Bacon, 1980.

O'Hara, C.E.: *Photography in Law Enforcement.* Rochester, Eastman Kodak, 1963.

Poutney, H.: *Police Photography.* New York, Elsevier, 1971.

Redsicker, D.R.: *The Practical Methodology of Forensic Photography.* New York, Elsevier, 1991.

Samen, C.C.: Major Crime Scene Investigation—Basic Photography, Part II. 19 *Law and Order,* 9, 1971.

Sansome, S.J.: *Police Photography: Law Enforcement Handbook.* Cincinnati, Anderson, 1977.

Schmidt, J.: A Changing Picture: Instant Photography in Policing. 58 *Police Chief,* 12, 1991.

Scott, C.C.: *Photographic Evidence,* 2nd ed. 3 vols. St. Paul, West Publishing, 1969.

Siljander, R.P.: *Applied Police and Fire Photography.* Springfield, Ill.: Thomas, 1976.

Unsworth, S.H. and Forte, R.M.: Waltham Police Benefit from Focus on Instant Photography. 39 *Law and Order,* 9, 1991.

Young, P.A.: Night Photography. 28 *Police Research Bulletin,* 21, 1976.

Chapter 6

CRIME SCENE SKETCH

1. General

I N A PHOTOGRAPH of the crime scene, the distances between the various objects are not accurately or even proportionately represented. The relationship existing between objects present in the scene cannot be clearly understood unless the measured distances are known. Certain objects, moreover, are not visible in a photograph or cannot be clearly identified. A drawing or crime scene sketch is the simplest and most effective way of showing actual measurements and of identifying significant items of evidence in their locations at the scene. Sketches are divided generally into rough sketches and finished drawings.

a. **Rough Sketch.** The rough sketch is made by the investigator on the scene. It need not be drawn to scale, but the proportions should be approximated and the appropriate measurements or dimensions shown. The rough sketch may be used as a basis for the finished drawing. No changes should be made on the original sketch after the investigator has left the scene.

b. **Finished Drawing.** The finished drawing is made primarily for courtroom presentation. It is generally based on the rough sketch and drawn to scale by a person skilled in either mechanical or architectural drawing.

c. **Materials.** A sketch of a crime scene may be accomplished with little more than a pencil, a sheet of paper, and a straight edge. On the other hand, a finished drawing will require more advanced equipment. If the investigator wishes to draw an outdoor crime scene together with the surrounding terrain and achieve a reasonable degree of accuracy, he must possess an elementary knowledge of geometry. The following materials will be found useful although they should not be considered an absolute necessity.

1) *For Rough Sketching.* For a rough sketch it is generally desirable to use a soft pencil. Graph paper is excellent for sketching as it provides a guide for lines and proportions. A clipboard, or a piece of plywood or masonite, of a size which will fit in the investigator's briefcase will serve as a sketching surface. The investigator should have a compass so that he may accurately indicate directions and also a steel tape to insure correct measurements.

2) *For Finished Drawing.* When the finished drawing is to be made in the office, based on the rough sketch, the draftsman will require a drawing set, a drafting board with accessories, India ink, and a good grade of drawing paper. Since the drawing is made to scale, these materials are necessary to insure accuracy. If the finished drawing is to be made at the scene, the equipment of the draftsman should include a compass, steel tape, and alidade.

2. Elements of Sketching

The following considerations apply generally to all sketches:

a. **Measurements.** Measurements must be accurate. In portraying a large area, a sufficient degree of accuracy is obtained by measurements of yards or tenths of a mile; for small areas measurements accurate to the sixteenth of an inch may be required. Measurements should be accomplished by the sketcher himself making the actual measurement while his assistant verifies all readings. Measurements establishing the location of a movable object must be based on an immovable object. While measurements may be indicated between movable objects to establish a correlation, at least one set of dimensions must reach an immovable object.

b. **Compass Direction.** Compass direction must always be indicated to facilitate proper orientation of the sketch. The compass is used to determine "North." A standard arrow of orientation will indicate this direction on the sketch.

c. **Essential Items.** The sketch should portray those items which have a bearing on the investigation being conducted. The inclusion of unnecessary detail will result in a cluttered or crowded sketch and tends to hide or obscure the essential items. Simplicity is essential and sketches should be limited to the inclusion of only relevant material. For example, the sketch will include an outline of the room together with the doors, windows, chimney, and other large fixed objects. The furniture will then be indicated. Templates are helpful for drawing household furniture and fixtures. Templates are patterns which are placed over the crime scene sketch paper which guide the pencil in outlining the various objects. Outlines of furniture, plumbing fixtures, weapons, and human figures, both male and female, are available in different sizes to fit the scale of the drawing. The dead body or other significant object will be shown in relation to the furniture and other objects. Measurements will be made of the room, fireplace, sink, doorways, etc. The distances of the various parts of, for example, the body from these objects will be measured and recorded.

d. **Scale or Proportion.** The scale of a drawing will normally be dependent upon the area to be portrayed, the amount of detail to be shown, and the size of drawing paper available. It is normally advisable to use the smallest scale practicable. The actual or approximate scale of a sketch should always be shown by words and figures, graphically. If a rough sketch is made, the size of an object may be approximated as correlated to other objects. For example, if one dimension of a room is 30 feet and the other 10 feet, the first line would be approximately three times the length of the second.

e. **Legend.** The legend is an explanation of symbols used to identify objects in the sketch. In sketches portraying a large area, conventional signs or symbols may be used. These should be explained in the legend. If it is necessary to show considerable detail in a sketch covering a small area, the various objects may be lettered and an explanation included in the legend. Excessive lettering in the sketch generally will result in a crowded sketch and obscure essential items.

f. **Title.** The title of a sketch should contain the case identification (case file number and offense); identification of victim or scene portrayed; location; date and hour made; and the sketcher. These data authenticate the sketch.

3. Projection

The normal sketch will show the scene in two dimensions of one plane. When it becomes desirable to portray three dimensions to allow better correlation of the evidential facts of the scene, a projection sketch must be used. This projection sketch of the scene of a room is like a drawing of a cardboard box whose edges have been cut and the sides flattened.

4. Surveying Methods

When portraying large areas, some of the basic surveying methods may be used to facilitate the work of the sketcher and to help insure the accuracy and clarity of the sketch. If the investigator does not have a knowledge of surveying, he should enlist the services of a competent surveyor. The coordinate method, of which there are many simple variations, can be used to meet most of the problems in field sketching.

a. **Rectangular Coordinates.** The simplest way to locate points on a sketch is to give the distances from two mutually perpendicular lines. If the crime scene is a room, the objects can be mapped by using two mutually perpendicular walls as the reference lines. A chair, for example, can then be located by measuring its distance from each wall, e.g., 82 inches from the west wall and 43 inches from the south wall. If a graph paper is used for sketching and each unit of the graph paper represents 5 inches (for example) in the room, the chair is located on the graph paper by a point located 16.4 units from the vertical axis and 8.6 units from the horizontal axis, where the two axes are the left hand margin and the lower margin.

b. **Polar Coordinates.** A point can also be mapped by giving its distance from some chosen origin and the direction angle which the distance line makes with a chosen axis of reference. The system is particularly useful for outdoor scenes, being commonly used in daily life. Using a door of a house as the origin, a tree can be located by saying that it is 324 yards away in a direction 42°

west of south. The angle is determined by compass using the side of the house as a reference line, and the distance is measured from the door to the tree.

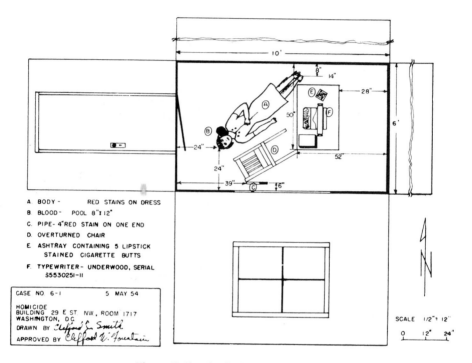

A. BODY –   RED STAINS ON DRESS
B. BLOOD – POOL 8"ı 12"
C. PIPE- 4"RED STAIN ON ONE END
D. OVERTURNED CHAIR
E. ASHTRAY CONTAINING 5 LIPSTICK
     STAINED CIGARETTE BUTTS
F. TYPEWRITER – UNDERWOOD, SERIAL
     3553025ı-ıı

CASE NO. 6-ı   5 MAY 54
HOMICIDE
BUILDING 29 E ST NW, ROOM ı7ı7
WASHINGTON, D.C.
DRAWN BY *Clifford J. Smith*
APPROVED BY *Clifford U. Fountain*

SCALE ı/2"ː ı2"

0   ı2"   24'

Figure 7. Sketch of a homicide scene.

5. Computer Method

An accurate and detailed crime scene sketch can also be generated by computer. "Compuscene" is the trade name of a software package designed to run on an Apple Macintosh computer. It consists of predrawn detailed images of objects called "templates" which are selected and moved to various positions on a computer screen. The "templates" include the common elements of both indoor and outdoor scenes, such as furniture, fixtures, vehicles, weapons and the human form in a variety of positions. When the crime scene is accurately displayed on the computer screen, the result is then printed out.

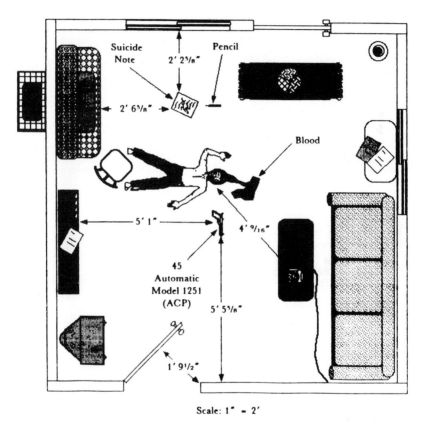

COMPUSCENE™
EXAMPLE OF A CRIME SCENE

Scale: 1″ = 2′

Figure 8. A computer-generated crime scene sketch. (Courtesy of Visatex Corp.)

The advantages of this system are:

a. It increases the number of people who can create a crime scene sketch since artistic ability is not a prerequisite.

b. All the lines of the sketch will be straight and there will be no smudges or erasures.

c. Multiple copies of different sizes can be readily printed.

d. Rescaling drawings can be accomplished easily.

ADDITIONAL READING

Crime Scene Sketch

Computer-aided Drafting for Law Enforcement. 60 *FBI Law Enforcement Bulletin*, 2, 1991.

Fox, R.H. and Cunningham, C.L.: *Crime Scene Search and Physical Evidence Handbook.* Boulder, Col.: Paladin Press, 1988.

Kehl, E.: Sketching the Crime Scene. 4 *Forensic Photography*, 11, 1976.

Samen, C.C.: Major Crime Scene Investigation, Part III. 19 *Law and Order*, 10, 1971.

Scott, J.D.: *Investigative Methods.* Reston, Va.: Reston Publishing, 1978.

Chapter 7

CARE OF EVIDENCE

1. Introduction

PHYSICAL EVIDENCE may be defined as articles and material which are found in connection with an investigation and which aid in establishing the identity of the perpetrator or the circumstances under which the crime was committed or which, in general, assist in the discovery of the facts. In order to realize the full probative value of physical evidence it must be intelligently cared for from the point of view of science and the law. A few simple rules can guide the investigator in the protection of evidence from its initial discovery at the scene of the crime until its final appearance in the court. A violation of these rules may lead to a partial loss of the value of the evidence and, in some instances, to the loss of the case.

Physical evidence discovered at the scene of the crime or during the later course of investigation may serve a number of purposes: it may be part of the body or *corpus delicti* of the crime; it may place the suspect at the scene of the crime; it may establish the identity of the offender; or it may enable the investigator to track down the suspect. These categories are obviously not mutually exclusive. In a larceny where part of the stolen money is found, the recovered property is part of the *corpus delicti* and may, through careless spending, leave a trail to the suspect. A fingerprint, by reason of location and through the process of exclusion, may identify the suspect, as well as place him at the crime scene. Finally, careless use of a credit card may describe a pattern of flight, partially identify the suspect, and help guide the investigator to the suspect's ultimate lighting place. Thus, physical evidence can serve several investigative purposes and can be divided roughly into the following categories:

79

a. **Corpus Delicti Evidence.** This consists of objects or substances that are an essential part of the body of the crime, i.e., tend to establish that a crime has been committed. For example, in a homicide the corpse or body of the decedent is part of the *corpus delicti* of the offense. The narcotic found in the addict's unlawful possession is part of the *corpus delicti* of a narcotics violation.

b. **Associative Evidence.** This kind of evidence links the suspect to the crime scene or to the offense. For example, safe lining found in a suspect's shoe may associate the owner with the scene of a safe burglary where an identical type of lining was found on the floor. The headlight glass found at the scene of a hit-and-run motor vehicle homicide can associate the scene with a car having matching glass fragments in a broken lens. Fingerprints and shoe impressions are other common examples.

c. **Identifying Evidence.** This is associative evidence that tends directly to establish the identity of the perpetrator. This can be exemplified by fingerprints, foot impressions, and quantities of blood found at the place of occurrence.

d. **Tracing Evidence.** These are articles that assist the investigator in locating the suspect. A laundry mark, for example, found among his effects may assist in tracing a fugitive. Similarly, the credit card mentioned above would provide another tracing clue.

At the risk of repetition, then, these categories are not mutually exclusive; they are simply aspects under which physical evidence may be viewed to serve four main investigative purposes.

2. Evaluation of Physical Evidence

Before an object can become evidence it must be recognized by the investigator as having significance with relation to the offense. He should endeavor to develop an ability to recognize valuable physical evidence through on-the-job experience and by broadening his informational background. The following forms of information and skill will assist his development in this direction:

a. A knowledge of the law of evidence and its application in court procedure.

b. **Ability** to recreate imaginatively the events preceding, during, and after the commission of a crime.

c. An ability to recognize indications of a *modus operandi.*

d. A knowledge of the substantive law relating to the offense under investigation.

e. A knowledge of scientific laboratory techniques and the conclusions which may be derived from their use.

3. Procedure

The ability to recognize and gather valuable physical evidence must be supplemented by a knowledge of the correct procedure in caring for evidence from the time of its initial discovery until its ultimate appearance at the trial. In order to introduce physical evidence in a trial three important factors must be considered:

a. The article must be properly identified.

b. Continuity or chain of custody must be proved.

c. Competency must be proved, i.e., that the evidence is material and relevant.

The proof of identity implies that the investigator who first found the object can testify that the exhibit offered in evidence is the same as the object he discovered at the crime scene. He should, further, under cross-examination be able to say that another similar article could not have been substituted. Both of these objectives can be achieved by a systematic procedure which would ordinarily consist of the following steps:

a. Protection	d. Preservation
b. Collection	e. Transmission
c. Identification	f. Disposition

4. Chain of Custody

The number of persons who handle evidence between the time of commission of the alleged offense and the ultimate disposition of the case should be kept to a minimum. Each transfer of the evidence should be receipted. It is the responsibility of each transferee to insure that the evidence is accounted for during the time that it is in his possession, that it is properly protected, and that there is a record of the names of the persons from whom he received it and to whom he delivered it, together with the time and date of such receipt and delivery.

5. Protection

The protection of physical evidence serves two major purposes. First, certain types of evidence, such as latent fingerprints, are so fragile in nature that a slight act of carelessness in handling can destroy their value as clues and remove the possibility of obtaining from them any information which would further the investigation. Second, it is necessary that the evidence presented in court be in a condition similar to that in which it was left at the time of the offense. In order that a physical object connected with the commission of the offense be admitted into evidence, it is necessary to show that such object is in practically the same condition, without substantial change, as at the time the offense was committed. Hence evidence should be protected from accidental or intentional change during the period extending from its first discovery after the commission of the offense to its ultimate disposition at the conclusion of the investigation.

a. **Alterations.** The exercise of a reasonable degree of care and the use of common sense will usually minimize the possibility of alteration of the evidentiary object. Special precautions must be employed with certain types of evidence such as articles bearing latent fingerprints. Alterations in the evidence such as contamination, chemical change, alterations of shape, removal of a part, or addition of extraneous characteristics are attributable to the following causes:

1) *Natural Causes.* The initial failure to safeguard evidence from exposure to the elements may result in a deterioration of the evidentiary value of an object. During the period of custody, damage from rain or deterioration from high temperatures may affect certain types of evidence unless special precautions are taken. For example, a vehicle which may bear latent fingerprints should be protected from rain. A blood sample which is not

maintained under refrigeration may lose some of its grouping properties on standing in hot weather.

2) *Negligence and Accident.* Failure to observe the ordinary precautions for the protection of property may result in breakage, loss, or the acquisition of new characteristics. Examples of this are the careless dropping of a fragile article, pointing to and accidentally marking a document to be used in a handwriting comparison, or opening a box containing fibers in an area exposed to strong drafts of air.

3) *Intentional Damage or Theft.* The investigator must keep in mind that in criminal cases there are usually several persons who would prefer that certain items of evidence did not exist. Thus measures should be taken to maintain the evidence secure from destruction, theft, and, in general, access by unauthorized persons.

b. **At the Crime Scene.** Physical evidence which is associated with a crime scene may be exposed to damaging influences prior to the discovery of its significance. Consequently all unauthorized persons should be excluded from the scene to prevent their handling or stepping on objects of evidence. The number of persons who are subsequently permitted to enter the scene should be kept to a minimum. Immediate action should be taken to prevent exposure of the evidence to the elements where there appears to be a likelihood of damage from rain, snow, wind, or sun.

c. **Receiving Evidence.** Where physical evidence is obtained not at the scene of the offense but from some other source such as an informant or from the possessions of a suspect, the investigator should take the necessary measures to protect it from any extraneous contact. For example, if the investigator, away from his office, comes into possession of a narcotics specimen such as a deck of heroin, he should place it in an envelope rather than put it unprotected in his pocket. Often he will acquire evidence when he has no equipment or containers for its protection. In situations such as this he should improvise with envelopes, boxes, or paper. Naturally, the degree of immediate protection required depends upon the physical nature of the evidence. As soon as possible after its receipt, the evidence should be transferred to a suitable container which can be sealed and labeled in the correct manner.

d. **Transporting.** Some risk of damage to evidence is incurred in the process of transporting the evidence. For example, in removing bottles bearing fingerprints from the scene of the offense to the office there is a danger of blurring the prints by contact with the interior surfaces of the vehicle or the sides of an improper container. Similarly if a jar of liquid or a plaster cast is mailed to a laboratory without being properly packaged for protection in transit, the likelihood of breakage is present.

e. **Evidence Not at the Scene.** Much of the physical evidence which is collected in connection with a typical criminal case is not found at the scene of occurrence. Evidence is often delivered to the investigator by a complainant or is found in the course of a search of a suspect's possessions. Moreover, many offenses, particularly those not involving personal violence, are not associated with a definite scene of occurrence. The investigator, therefore, will often receive evidence in circumstances where he does not have the papers, envelope, boxes, labels, and other equipment which he brings to the scene of a crime. In these situations the investigator should improvise methods of collecting the evidence until he has the proper equipment. A little ingenuity will enable him to find containers or envelopes which can serve to hold the evidence safely until he reaches his office. In receiving evidence at places other than the crime scene the investigator should make special note of the circumstances since he may later forget exactly where, when, or from whom he received evidence which was not at the crime scene.

f. **Standards of Comparison.** Known specimens to be used as standards of comparison with the questioned evidence are sometimes needed to aid in establishing a suspect's relationship to the crime under investigation. The character of the articles or materials to be collected for these comparisons is determined by the type of investigation being conducted.

g. **Containers and Packaging.** Articles which can be removed and conveniently packaged should be placed in clean containers such as envelopes, pill boxes, large cardboard boxes, and glass containers. The choice of container will depend upon the size of the specimen; its fragility; its physical state, whether solid or liquid; and whether it is to be transmitted by mail, express, or by hand carrying. Ordinarily there are two phases of the packing of evidence. The first is the transportation of the evidence from the crime scene or place of receiving it to the office. Secondly, if the evidence is to be submitted to a laboratory examination, it must be appropriately prepared for shipping.

h. **Storage.** Adequate facilities for storage of evidence should be maintained by an investigative agency. The evidence room should be so constructed and equipped that physical protection is assured against alteration or destruction from natural causes or unauthorized contacts. Changes of status as to custody of items maintained in the evidence room should be covered by hand receipts. Notations of such changes should be made in the case file. Each instance of deposit and removal of evidence should be recorded by inked entries indicating:

1) *Date* the evidence was received.

2) *File number* of case.

3) *Title* of case.

4) *Person* or *place* from whom or at which received.

5) *Person who received* the evidence.

6) *Complete description* of evidential items including size, color, serial number, and other identifying data.

7) *Disposition.* The name of the person to whom the evidence was delivered or an indication of any disposition other than delivery to a person. If at the time of receipt of real evidence any information is available as to its intended future disposition, this may be noted; care should be taken to avoid ambiguity in the notation indicating future disposition.

8) *Identify by signature* of the officer in control of the evidence room.

6. Preservation

Evidence in the form of organic matter, such as food, blood, or tissue, may present special problems relating to preservation. Most organic matter changes in character through natural decomposition, and, unless preventive measures are taken, its value for laboratory examination with a view to subsequent use as evidence may be destroyed. In taking measures against such deterioration, the factors of time and temperature should be given special consideration.

a. **Time.** In warm weather there should be a minimum of delay in placing the evidence in appropriate storage.

b. **Temperature.** High temperatures such as 95°F. greatly accelerate the decomposition of organic matter. Similarly, extreme cold may affect the evidentiary value of a specimen. Blood, for example, will lose some of its value as evidence if it is exposed to high temperatures for a long period of time or if it is permitted to freeze solidly. Ideally, the preserving temperature for blood or other perishable specimens should be between 40° and 50°F.

7. Preservatives

Certain types of perishable evidence require special preservatives to maintain their evidential value. For example, when a specimen of blood is taken for purposes of determining intoxication from alcohol, sodium fluoride may be added to the blood to preserve it for a week at room temperature or indefinitely in a refrigerator. As a general rule, however, no preservative should be used without expert advice. If it appears that the evidence specimen must be retained for a number of days and if refrigeration is not available, the investigator should seek the advice of a chemist or toxicologist concerning the need for any preservative.

8. Collection

Most of the errors committed in connection with evidence take place in the collection of the samples. Insufficiency of sample and failure to supply standards of comparison and controls are the most common errors. These investigative deficiencies are a consequence of a lack of understanding of the principles that should guide the collection from the point of view of the analyst. The employment of improper collection techniques results also in a failure to realize the full probative value of the evidence.

a. **Adequate Sampling.** A generous sample of the evidence should be collected. The analysis of evidence usually requires the consumption of part of the evidence. The laboratory expert can make his determinations with small samples, but the difficulties increase rapidly as the quantity becomes smaller. In analyzing evidence the chemist always endeavors to retain a quantity of the evidence untouched, so that the court may actually see and thus understand the nature of the evidence as well as acquire some knowledge of its original appearance. With a restricted sample the analyst may find it necessary to use almost all of the evidence. Another advantage of the generous sample is that it permits him to perform desirable confirmatory tests. Finally, an adequate sample will more nearly approach the ideal of the "representative sample," i.e., it will provide a sufficient quantity to enable the expert to determine the true nature of the substance, whereas the extremely limited specimen may be an anomalous sample containing extraneous matter not indicative of the true nature of the material.

b. **Standard or Known Samples.** Clue materials such as stains and other traces, particularly those available in only small quantities, are usually found in the presence of a foreign substance which can affect the analysis. In cases of this nature the foreign substance or background material should also be collected in the form of two samples, one bearing the stain or trace and the other free from the stain. For example, if the stain is found imbedded in wood or on linoleum, it should be collected by cutting off part of the wood or linoleum. In this way the analyst can approach his problem with an understanding of the difficulties he may encounter. A sample of the unstained wood or linoleum should also be removed and submitted for the purpose of providing a control that will enable the analyst to determine what impurities are contributed to the stain by the background material. He can, moreover, by means of the control determine what difficulties the background substances will add to the analysis. The control sample should be taken from an area near the stain. For example, if the investigation is concerned with a motor vehicle collision involving a hit-and-run car and a paint smear from the missing vehicle is found on the fender of the victim's car, the collector would proceed by first removing the smear and then taking a sample of the paint of the victim's car from an area approximately 6 inches from the smear. Another control sample would be taken from an area about a foot away. In removing the smear the collector ordinarily cannot avoid scraping some of the paint of the victim's car at the same time.

c. **Integrity of Sample.** An evidence sample should not come into contact with another sample or with any contaminating matter. This error most commonly occurs by initial, superficial comparison of the unknown and known samples. For example, if a tool impression is found on the door of the house during an investigation of a burglary and if a jimmy is found in association with a suspect, there is a temptation for the investigator to experimentally determine whether the blade of the tool fits the impression by placing the tool against the door. The result is a contamination of any paint traces that may have lain on the blade of the tool and which would have served as stronger evidence of its use in the commission of the crime than would the impression alone. A less conscionable error is the placing of the two poorly wrapped samples of known and unknown in the same envelope. To maintain individuality each piece of evidence should be separately wrapped and should not share the same container unless all danger of mingling is removed by the employment of strong protective coverings or partitions.

d. **Types of Evidence.** The simplest division of evidence into categories is that of portable and fixed evidence. If the evidence is readily portable no difficulty exists. The investigator simply removes the whole object. For example, if a fingerprint is found on a cash box, it should be developed and photographed and then the box itself should be brought back to the office or the laboratory. No attempt should be made to lift the print. If the evidence cannot be collected separately because of its size, the removal will often depend on the importance of the case. In a case involving a serious crime the investigator should not, for example, hesitate to remove a bedroom door that bears a good tool impression. Sometimes fixed evidence can also be placed in the same category as evidence not readily portable, since tools can be employed to remove that part of the installation which bears the evidence. A piece of wooden floor should be removed with the appropriate tools, if the importance of the evidence and the gravity of the case indicate the advisability of such a procedure. The decision concerning the removal of evidence will depend upon the individual case. Where it is not possible or practicable to remove the evidence, methods of reproduction such as photography and casting should be employed to accurately represent the condition of the evidence.

1) *Fingerprints.* Articles bearing fingerprints are the most common forms of physical evidence. Their handling will vary with the nature of the article on which they are found.

a) ON PAPER. A paper such as a document should be handled with tongs or forceps and placed, where the size permits, into a cellophane envelope. It should not be folded unless it is very large and then only along existing fold lines.

b) ON GLASSES AND BOTTLES. These can be placed over pegs imbedded in a board. Small crates can be built for additional protection.

2) *Firearms, Knives, and Tools.* Articles such as these can be tied to a board by means of strings passing through perforations and then packed securely in a cardboard or wooden box.

3) *Hairs and Fibers.* The hair or fiber should be picked up with a forceps and placed in a filter paper which is creased in a "druggist fold." The druggist fold is formed by folding the paper in thirds. Fold one side of the paper and then fold the opposite side over it. Folding the remaining two sides in a similar manner will form an interior square compartment in which evidence can be placed. It will also form two ends, one of which is tucked into the other to secure the contents. Cellophane tape may be used to seal the edges and the ends. The folded paper is then placed in a pillbox or a plastic vial.

4) *Dirt, Soil, Particles, Filings, and Fragments.* Minute quantities of this kind of material should be placed in a filter paper, which is folded, sealed with tape, and then put in a pillbox or plastic vial. Larger quantities should be transferred directly into an appropriately sized box or plastic vial.

5) *Bullets and Fired Cases.* These should be put in separate small boxes and surrounded with cotton.

6) *Clothing.* Unnecessary folding or folding across areas of evidentiary interest should be avoided. Each article of clothing is packed separately in a paper bag or cardboard box. Plastic bags should not be used. Wet cloths should be air-dried before packing.

7) *Blood.* When handling blood or any other biological evidence, the investigator should take the precaution of wearing

latex gloves to protect against infection by the hepatitis and the AIDS virus. Wearing gloves will also prevent the accidental contamination of the evidence from traces of perspiration, body oils, or other biological residue that may be present on the hands.

a) WET BLOOD. If there is a large pool of blood present at the crime scene, approximately 5cc should be collected with an eyedropper or a syringe and placed in a sterile test tube. No preservatives or anticoagulants should be added. To prevent deterioration, the sample should be transported immediately to the laboratory for analysis or placed under refrigeration. Liquid blood should never be frozen. If there is a possibility that a DNA analysis may be performed, an additional 5cc should be collected in another test tube containing EDTA, which will preserve the blood without interfering with the procedure. If there is a small quantity of blood, it should be collected with a cotton swab or gauze pad. The swab or gauze is then air-dried at room temperature and placed in an envelope, a test tube, or some other sterile container.

b) DRY BLOOD. When dried bloodstains are found on small objects or articles of clothing, the entire item should be collected. If the garment is dry, it is folded carefully and packaged separately in a paper bag or cardboard container. Dried stains can be scraped off walls and floors with a razor or a scalpel onto filter paper creased in a druggist fold. The paper is folded, sealed with cellophane tape, and placed in a pillbox or similar container. Bloodstains on carpet or mattress covers can be removed by cutting out the portion containing the stain, making sure to include some unstained area as a control sample. A swab or gauze pad moistened with distilled water can be used on stains which can't be scraped or otherwise removed.

Where there is more than one bloodstain, one may be the blood of the victim and the other may be that of the suspect. Therefore, instruments used to collect blood, such as an eyedropper, scalpel, or swab, should be used on only one stain to avoid contaminating the evidence.

8) *Semen.* This evidence is found primarily in those crimes in which sexual assault is involved. It is important to remember that all evidence of this kind must be air-dried before being packaged and sent to the laboratory.

a) WET STAIN. If the stain is moist, it can be collected with an eyedropper and placed in a sterile test tube to dry. A swab or gauze pad can be used to absorb smaller stains. If the semen is found on an article of clothing or bedding, the entire item is collected. After being air-dried in a well-ventilated room, it is folded carefully in order to avoid creasing the stained area. It is sent to the laboratory, in a "breathable" container—that is, a paper bag or a cardboard box.

b) DRY STAIN. When a dried semen stain is found on items that are not readily movable, it can be scraped onto filter paper, which is folded, sealed with tape, and placed in a pillbox or plastic vial. Dried stains on porous surfaces that can neither be moved nor scraped can be moistened with distilled water and absorbed with a swab. After being air-dried, swabs are usually placed in an envelope or a sterile test tube.

9) *Saliva.* Evidence of this kind is found infrequently at a crime scene. Unlike blood or semen, it is extremely difficult to see once it has dried. Saliva should be treated similarly to semen, that is, it should be collected in a test tube or with a swab and air-dried before being packaged and sent to the laboratory.

10) *Paint on Vehicles.* Paint chips on or near the vehicle are collected with a tweezers, preferably intact, and placed on a filter paper. The paper is folded, sealed with tape, and put into a pillbox or plastic vial. When a paint smear adheres to the surface of a vehicle as a result of a collision with another vehicle, it is necessary to use a metal scalpel to recover the evidence. The scalpel is used to cut through the paint layers and undercoat until bare metal is reached. A paint chip bearing the smear, approximately one-half inch square, should be removed. A comparison standard of the same size should be collected in an undamaged area adjacent to where the evidence sample was taken. The control sample and the evidence sample should be packaged separately.

11) *Glass.* See Chapter 37, Section 7.

9. Identification

Evidence should be properly marked or labeled for identification as it is collected or as soon as practicable thereafter. The

Table I
RECOMMENDED METHODS FOR
HANDLING SPECIFIC ITEMS OF EVIDENCE

Item	Method
Handguns	Use your fingers on knurled grips. Do not touch smooth grips or smooth metal parts. Use the tip of the grips. Do not touch the magazine base of pistols. Place in a box, bracing the weapon at the front and rear.
Paper money, documents, paper	Use tweezers. Do not place tweezers over any obvious smudge. Place each item in a clean envelope or bag.
Broken glass	Use your fingers on the edges of larger pieces. Do not touch flat surfaces. Use tweezers on pieces too small for your fingers. Do not grasp at point of any obvious smudges. Wrap pieces individually in clean tissue, place in a box, and stabilize to prevent rubbing, shifting, or breakage.
Dried stains on smooth surfaces of furniture	Collect portion of furniture bearing surfaces of furniture stain in original pattern, if possible; otherwise scrape with pocket knife or putty knife, removing as little of the finished surface as possible.
Bottles, jars, drinking glasses	Insert two or more fingers into large mouth vessels. Place the index fingers on the top and bottom of small mouth vessels. Do not contaminate or spill any substances in the vessel that may have evidence value.
Bullets	Use your fingers or use tweezers with taped ends. Avoid damage to rifling marks on the circumference. Place in a pillbox.
Cartridge cases	Pick up at the open end with tweezers. Avoid scratching. Place in a pillbox.
Dried stains on a floor	Collect portion of floor bearing stain in original pattern, if possible; otherwise, remove by gouging deeper than the stain with putty knife, wood chisel, or other tool. Place in pillbox or larger similar container.

Source: U.S. Army. *Field Manual 19–20.*

importance of this procedure becomes apparent when consideration is given to the fact that the investigator may be called to the witness stand many months after the commission of the offense to identify an object in evidence which he collected at the time of offense. Indeed, defense counsel may require that the complete chain of custody be established, in which case each person who handled the evidence may be called to identify the object. Obviously such an identification is most easily managed by means of marks or labels which have been placed on the evidence. An additional aid to identification is the investigator's notebook in which should be recorded a description of the evidentiary object, the position where it was found, the place where it was collected or the person from whom it was received, the names of any witnesses, and any serial number which the object may bear, together with the case reference data.

a. **Marking.** Solid objects which have a volume of approximately 1 cubic inch or greater should be marked for identification with the initials of the investigator receiving or finding the evidence. The mark of identification should not be placed in an area where evidentiary traces exist. A sharp-pointed instrument such as a metal scribe should be used for marking hard objects. Pen and ink can be used for absorbent articles. Special care should be employed in marking articles of great intrinsic value. Objects which are smaller than 1 cubic inch in approximate volume need not be marked. These may be placed in a container such as a pillbox and the container then sealed and labeled. Liquids and pastes should be retained in their original containers and appropriately sealed and labeled. If the evidence consists of a large number of similar items, the district attorney should be consulted to determine how many of the items need be brought into court and how many should be marked for identification.

b. **Sealing.** Wherever practicable, articles of evidence should be inclosed in separate containers. Pillboxes, envelopes, test tubes, and bottles containing evidentiary materials should be sealed in such a manner that they cannot be opened without breaking the seal. The investigator's initials (or name) and the date of sealing (in abbreviated form) should be placed on the seal with ink so that the marking extends over to the container from the seal.

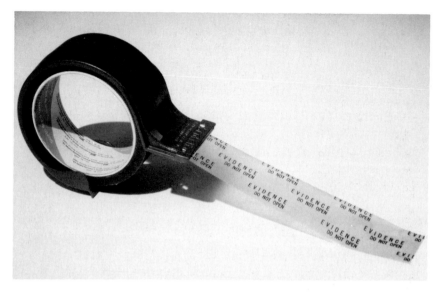

Figure 9. Evidence tape for sealing physical evidence properly and easily. The tape's frangible backing can reveal tampering. (Courtesy of the 3M Company.)

c. **Labeling.** After the article of evidence is marked and placed in a sealed container, a label should be affixed bearing identifying case information. This may take the form of paper pasted (gum label) on the container or a tag tied to the object. Thus, a bullet would be marked with the investigator's initials, placed in a pillbox which is then sealed and initialed and finally labeled by affixing a paper sticker to the box. An alleged heroin specimen would be placed in protective paper and inserted in an envelope, which would then be sealed. A paper seal would then be placed across the flap of the envelope and labeled by inscribing thereon the case information. A rifle would be marked and then tagged. The following information should appear on the label or tag:

1) Case number.
2) Date and time of finding the article.
3) Name and description of the article.
4) Location at time of discovery.
5) Signature of investigator who made the discovery.
6) Name of witnesses to the discovery.

Figure 10. A demonstration of how evidence tape resists tampering. (Courtesy of the 3M Company.)

d. **Examples.** In the following typical examples of evidence which may be received or obtained, suggestions are made for marking and labeling.

1) *Documents.* A document, like other physical evidence, should be identified by some type of marking. The best method of marking is to initial and place the date where the marking will not affect the examination. The initials and date should be inscribed with a fine-pointed pen. After initialing and dating, the document should be placed in a cellophane envelope and properly sealed. The envelope can be sealed with gummed paper tape, and the date and initials of the investigator placed thereon. Information concerning the identity of the document should be placed on the outside of the cellophane jacket. A piece of paper bearing the typed information can be stapled to the edge of the envelope for this purpose.

2) *Firearms Evidence.*

a) FIREARMS. A firearm should be unloaded prior to submission to the laboratory. It should be marked with a metal scribe on some inconspicuous area of the frame to avoid unnecessarily defacing the weapon. Ordinarily, on the bottom of the frame inside the trigger guard is a good place to mark a firearm. If the firearm is rigidly assembled so that the firing pin or barrel cannot be removed without tools this marking will be sufficient. On the other hand, if the parts which may leave an imprint on the bullet or cartridge case are removable without the aid of tools each part should be marked. Thus, in a .45 caliber semiautomatic pistol the barrel, slide, and receiver should be individually marked. Similarly in a hinge-frame type of revolver the barrel, cylinder, and frame should each be marked. In bolt-action rifles, the bolt and frame should be marked. If the barrel of a shoulder firearm is removable without tools, it should be marked.

b) LOADED WEAPONS. If the evidence weapon is a revolver containing loaded cartridges or fired cases, the investigator should make a diagram of the rear face of the cylinder to show the position of each cartridge with respect to the firing pin. The cartridges should be numbered to correspond to the numbering of the chambers. To further assist the expert, a mark should be placed on the rear face of the cylinder on both sides of the chamber which lay under the firing pin on original discovery of the weapon.

c) BULLETS. A bullet should be marked only on its base. The sides are never marked to avoid scarring any area that may bear a rifling imprint. The nose of the bullet should not be marked because it may retain evidentiary material. If the bullet has passed through clothing, the nose of the bullet might bear the impression of the fabric. It may also have minute particles of blood, tissue, fibers, paint or other materials adhering to it. Fragmented or deformed bullets should be wrapped in cotton and placed in a pillbox which is then sealed and labeled.

d) CARTRIDGE CASES. A fired cartridge case should be marked inside of the mouth or, if the caliber is too small, on the cylindrical outer surface at a point near the mouth. The case should never be marked on the head, since this area may bear breech-face markings or firing-pin indentations.

e) SHOTGUN SHELLS. If the shell is made of paper, it should be marked with ink; a plastic shell can be marked with a metal scribe. Brass shells should be treated as cartridge cases.

f) SHOTGUN WADS. The wad should be placed in a pillbox, sealed and labeled.

g) SMALL SHOT. Buckshot, birdshot and similar ammunition are too small to be marked. Hence specimens should be placed in a pillbox, sealed and labeled.

h) COMPARISON STANDARDS. In submitting a firearm for examination, an effort should be made to supply ammunition of the same type. For example, if the weapon is owned by a resident of the area, a search of his property should be made to discover similar ammunition. Approximately ten cartridges will suffice as standards of comparison.

3) *Clothing*. Articles of wearing apparel are best marked by an inked inscription on the lining of each garment. A string tag attached to a button or a button hole will serve as a label.

4) *Plaster Casts*. These should be marked on the back before the plaster has dried. When the cast has hardened the marks will be permanent. Subsequently the cast should be placed in a wooden box of suitable size and appropriately labeled.

5) *Photographs*. Each print may be marked for identification on the reverse side in a manner that will reflect appropriate data, including the date on which the photograph was taken, the name of the photographer, and the place where taken; the marking should be carefully made in order not to damage the photograph. Other data of an explanatory nature, generally restricted to technical information regarding the mechanics of making and processing the photograph, may properly be inscribed on the reverse side if the inclusion of such data augments the evidential value of the photograph. If it is found necessary to place supplementary marks (such as measurements, arrows to indicate direction, or lines leading to characteristics of a fingerprint pattern) on the emulsion side of a print, it should be understood that any marking on the front or back of a photograph must be susceptible of explanation by a qualified witness, must not detract from the merits of the

Table II
FBI RECOMMENDATIONS FOR EVIDENCE COLLECTION

COLLECTION OF PHYSICAL EVIDENCE
(five things to keep in mind)

---

1. **Obtain it legally:**
   a. Warrant.
   b. Consent.
   c. Incidental to arrest.

---

2. **Describe it in notes:**
   a. Location, circumstances, how obtained.
   b. Date, chain of custody.
   c. How identified.

---

3. **Identify it properly:**
   a. Use initials, date, case number.
   b. Preferably on evidence itself. Liquids, soils,
      tiny fragments must be placed in suitable containers,
      sealed and marked on the outside.

---

4. **Package it properly.** One case to a box:
   a. Use suitable containers such as round pillboxes,
      plastic vials, glass or plastic containers,
      strong cardboard cartons.
   b. Seal securely against leakage.
   c. Package each item separately. Avoid any
      appearance of leakage or contamination.
   d. If wet or bearing blood, **air-dry** before packaging
      (except arson cases where hydrocarbons are present).

---

5. **Maintain chain of custody.** Keep it short:
   a. Same person or persons that recovered
      the evidence should initial, seal and send
      evidence, if possible.
   b. Maintain in a locked vault, cabinet or room
      until shipped.
   c. Send by air express, registered mail, registered
      air mail or personal delivery to the laboratory
      or identification division (there is no way to trace
      parcel post, certified mail or regular mail).

Source: FBI. *Handbook of Forensic Science,* Rev. ed. Washington, D.C.: U.S. Government Printing Office, 1990.

picture, and should contribute to expressing a pertinent fact that is devoid of evidential value when considered apart from the photograph. Any abuse of discretion in this regard may render a photograph objectionable as an exhibit; hence it is generally advisable to have duplicate unmarked prints available for use if needed. Transparent overlays may be utilized when desired.

10. Transmission

If the transmission to a laboratory is desired, the evidence must be carefully packed to prevent loss or damage. In the absence of any local or state laboratory facilities, law enforcement agencies may seek the services of the FBI Laboratory. In communications to the FBI requesting examinations, a letter of transmittal should accompany the evidence, setting forth the essential facts in the case and any information which can be of assistance to the examiner. The communication should indicate that the evidence has not been and will not be examined by an expert other than one of the FBI Laboratory. In transmitting certain types of evidence by mail, cognizance should be taken of current postal regulations. For example, the postal service should not be used in transmitting live ammunition or flammable liquids (see Appendix 3).

ADDITIONAL READING

Care of Evidence

Cook, C.W.: *A Practical Guide to the Basics of Physical Evidence.* Springfield, Ill.: Thomas, 1984.

Federal Bureau of Investigation. *Handbook of Forensic Science,* rev. ed. Washington, D.C.: U.S. Government Printing Office, 1990.

Fox, R.H. and Cunningham, C.L.: *Crime Scene Search and Physical Evidence Handbook.* Boulder, Col.: Paladin Press, 1988.

Genova, J.: Automating Crime Labs and Evidence Control. 56 *Police Chief,* 4, 1989.

Goddard, K.W.: *Crime Scene Investigation.* Reston, Va.: Reston Publishing, 1977.

Hamilton, T.S.: Developing an Automated Evidence Tracking System. 58 *Police Chief,* 4, 1991.

Kennedy, D.B., Homant, R.J., and Emery, G.L.: AIDS and the Crime Scene Investigator. 56 *Police Chief,* 12, 1989.

O'Brien, K.P. and Sullivan, R.C.: *Criminalistics: Theory and Practice,* 3rd ed. Boston, 1980.
Samen, C.C.: The Evidence Collection Unit. 19 *Law and Order,* 7, 1971.
Scene of the Crime: U.S. Government Forensic Handbook. Boulder, Col.: Paladin Press, 1992.

PART III
OBTAINING INFORMATION

Chapter 8

INTERVIEWS

1. Introduction

THE EFFECTIVENESS of an investigator is largely dependent upon his ability to obtain information from complainants, witnesses, informants, and suspects. Included in these sources of information are those persons who may not be called as witnesses but who can provide useful data such as official company records or non-official information that is a matter of observation. The progress of an investigation is often a function of the knowledge gained from these sources, since most crimes are solved by "information." It is rarely that circumstantial evidence alone is sufficient to obtain a conviction. In some crimes, of course, such as robbery or assault, the eyewitness testimony may provide all of the elements. More complicated crimes such as forgery, burglary, fraud, and embezzlement ordinarily require more evidence than that of eyewitnesses. An effective interrogator may elicit much of the information necessary to the success of a case; whereas, the inexperienced or inept person will obtain little or no data on which a prosecution can be based. At the outset of an inquiry into a crime the investigator possesses only a few facts concerning the occurrence. A crime may have been committed; the true fact of its commission must be established. There is a complainant or a victim; some physical evidence of the crime; and perhaps, a suspect. Often the gap between these simple facts and a finished case that can be successfully presented in court can be bridged only by patient and intelligent questioning.

a. **Building the Case.** The elements of the offense must be established. Identifications must be obtained. Can the victim identify his assailant? Can the stolen property be recognized by definite markings, serial numbers, or a bill of sale? Can the person who cashed the worthless check recognize the passer? Is the accused the person he claims he is? What personal records are available to identify the accused or to place him in a certain area at a given time? What persons can provide information concerning the activities of the accused on the day of the crime?

b. **Tracing.** If the suspect is missing, the investigator is faced with the problem of tracing. He must know the available sources of information, official and unofficial. Custodians of records and persons dealing in services must be questioned. Police department files, hotel registers, bureaus of vital statistics, employers, associates, and many other sources will yield valuable information if approached in the correct manner. In all of these steps toward building up his case, the investigator must rely mainly upon strangers. Depending upon the technique he employs while interviewing these people, he may come away with all the desired data available or he may obtain only a few scattered facts of doubtful value. He must, moreover, develop in these persons a willingness to testify or make formal written statements if necessary.

c. **Canvassing.** If there is an absence of information about the crime itself, the investigator will have to interview people in the vicinity of the crime scene to locate a witness. The "neighborhood canvass" is the name given to the technique of systematically interviewing the people living near or frequenting the vicinity of the crime scene in order to locate someone who can provide information about the crime. The information developed may include the identity of: a witness to the crime; a witness to the flight of a suspect who may be able to identify or describe him; and/or someone who knows the victim and can provide facts concerning the identity of the victim, his friends, his reputation, his habits, his haunts, and a motive for the crime.

1) *Time.* Ideally, the canvass should take place at approximately the same time of day as when the crime occurred. This will provide the opportunity for those persons who normally conduct their business in the area at that hour to be interviewed. Shopkeepers, deliverymen, commuters, dog-walkers, and shoppers, for example, often follow a daily routine.

2) *Technique.* The neighborhood canvass is usually carried out by a team of investigators. Each investigator should be familiar with all the details of the case so that they will be able to ask the appropriate questions and recognize a valuable lead. The circumstances of the crime will determine the extent of the area to be covered. The premises to be visited will normally include the houses and stores in view of the crime scene as well as those lining the probable route of the suspect's flight. People walking on the street, parking their car, or waiting for a bus may be interviewed. The investigator will record in his notebook each address visited and the name and address of each person spoken to, whether or not they provide information. If no one is at home, that should also be recorded. This information will be important if for some reason the canvass needs to be repeated. When a possible witness or source of information is located, a more extensive interview is scheduled.

2. Definitions

An interview is the questioning of a person who is believed to possess knowledge that is of official interest to the investigator. In an interview the person questioned usually gives his account of an incident under investigation or offers information concerning a person being investigated in his own manner and words.

3. Importance

The greater part of an investigation is usually devoted to interviews. In most cases interviews constitute the major source of information. Because of the apparent simplicity of the typical interview, the novice is inclined to neglect the development of a technique. In his first year in the profession, the investigator should devote his greatest efforts to developing effective methods of interviewing. He should constantly remind himself that the next interview on his schedule may be the only way of acquiring information on a certain aspect of the case under investigation. After each interview he should subject his performance to a critical review by checking the quantity and quality of the information obtained and the extent to which he established rapport with the subject.

4. Qualifications of the Interviewer

The investigator as an interviewer should have the qualities of a salesman, an actor, and a psychologist. He is called upon to subject strangers to extensive questioning on topics of varying sensitivity. He must be measured by the discretion which he employs, and at the same time he may be criticized for a want of perseverance. He must possess insight, intelligence, and persuasiveness. His speech should be suited to the situation, compelling for the educated subject and calculated to strike a responsive note in the subject of little letters. The demands made of the ideal interviewer are too great to be fully met by any individual investigator; nevertheless, the challenge is one that will add interest to the years in which the investigator endeavors to increase his proficiency and ward off the stalemate with routine which often hinders his development.

a. **Rapport.** The relationship existing between the interviewer and the subject usually determines the success of the investigation. By establishing rapport with the subject the investigator may be able to unloose a flood of useful information. On the other hand, if the relationship is strained or marked by mistrust or a feeling of strangeness, the subject may be reluctant to give any of the desired information. The interrogator must endeavor to win the confidence of the subject wherever this is possible, since a completely voluntary offer of information is the ideal result of an interview. Where this is not possible the interrogator may have to rely on the force of his personality, persistence, or other qualities or resources which he may possess. Obviously, the interviewer cannot be a one-sided personality. He must possess a variety of character traits.

b. **Personality.** The primary trait which the interviewer should possess is that of forcefulness of personality. He should instinctively induce confidence by the strength of his character so that the subject trusts him on the first meeting and tends to seek his assistance by confiding in him. There should be no air of superiority in his manner. His demeanor should be sympathetic and understanding. Absence of exaggerated regional traits is desirable to avoid any clash with the subject's prejudices. Tolerance should mark his temperament. He is a person who is aware that prejudice frequently is the name we give to the other fellow's set of convictions.

c. **Breadth of Interests.** To establish rapport with a witness or a complainant, it may be necessary to create a meeting ground of interests. A person tends to regard a fellowman who shares common interests as a sympathetic personality. This is the first step toward placing trust in the interviewer. Obviously, the range of the investigator's interests must necessarily be broad if it is to cover those of many of the witnesses and subjects with whom he will come in contact. It is well known that a good investigator does possess a breadth of practical knowledge. He is acquainted with the habits of working men, the behavior and social life of gamblers, the temperament of storekeepers and the simple business principles by which they operate. On other levels, he knows the habits, prejudices, and modes of thinking of the more prosperous members of the community.

5. The Place and Time

In planning an interview, the investigator should, as a general rule, select a place which will provide him with a psychological advantage and conduct the questioning as soon as possible after the occurrence. Naturally this rule must be modified to suit the exigencies and nature of the case.

a. **Background Interviews.** If the interview is concerned with the background of a person being considered for a position of trust, no great difficulty arises in selecting the time and place. References such as individual businessmen and representatives of large companies can be interviewed during normal business hours. Professional men and women should be interviewed after arranging a suitable time by telephone.

b. **Routine Criminal Cases.** In criminal cases, the interview should be more carefully arranged. In order to obtain a maximum of information, a time should be selected at which the subject can have the leisure to devote his full attention to the matter. If it appears that the subject is under the press of business, the interview should be postponed until the evening. Privacy is another consideration in cases of this nature. An open office with a number of fellow workers present is not conducive to a candid expression of opinion or an accurate recollection of facts.

c. **Important Criminal Cases.** The investigator should arrange to interview witnesses in important cases at places other than their homes or office. Unfamiliar surroundings will prevent the witness from feeling confident and from controlling, through his composure, the amount and kind of information which he gives. The investigator should control the situation. He needs every psychological advantage which can serve to induce candor. The interviewee must respect him to the point where he is extremely hesitant to withhold or color information. Obviously, the investigator's own office is the ideal place.

d. **Time.** As a general principle, an interview should take place as soon as possible after the event. The information is then fresh in the mind of the witness. Moreover, he has had little time to contemplate any untoward consequences of his giving the information. It is seldom possible, however, to conduct the interview at the time set by the investigator. The witness may not be immediately available. Other developments of the case may intervene. Moreover, as a matter of strategy, it may be desirable to place certain interviews subsequent to others.

6. The Approach

On first meeting the subject the investigator should show his credentials and inform the subject of his identity. The point of identity must be stressed, since often the subject misunderstands the investigator with the result that a vague but unpleasant charge of misrepresentation may develop later. If a male investigator interviews a woman in her home, he should remain at a few paces from the door until the subject is convinced of his identification and invites him in. If at all possible, the investigator should avoid interviews at the threshold. Where necessary, he should return at a later time when the woman is reassured by the presence of a friend.

7. Background Interviews

The simplest type of interview is the one designed to develop information concerning a person who is being considered for a position of trust. The nature of the information desired should be so familiar to the investigator that he can ask the questions without reference to a checklist.

a. **Background Data.** Information on the following points is ordinarily required for a background report:

1) Date and time of the interview.
2) Name, vocation, and address of the interviewee. A request for a business card or a letterhead will supply the most accurate information.
3) Subject's full name.
4) Length of acquaintance in years.
5) Type of contact, whether business or social.
6) Degree of association, whether daily, occasional, or rarely.
7) When last seen.
8) Names—parents, brothers, and sisters.
9) Marital status and children.
10) Residence, past and present.
11) Educational background.
12) Personal and financial habits.
13) Personality traits.
14) Membership in organizations.
15) Relatives in foreign lands.
16) Honesty, loyalty, and discretion.
17) Recommendation for a position of trust.
18) Evaluation.
19) References.

b. **Credit Check.** The following additional information is important in a credit check report:

1) Recent changes in address.
2) Place of employment.
3) Name of spouse or parent.
4) Number of account.
5) Date opened.

6) Type of account.
7) Manner of payment.
8) Date closed.
9) Credit rating.
10) Eligibility for further credit.
11) Other pertinent information.
12) Evaluation.
13) Cross reference.

8. Criminal Cases

The manner in which the interview is conducted will vary with the relationship of the subject to the matter in question. The demeanor of the investigator must be suited to the requirements of the case. The following are the usual stages of this type of interview:

a. **Preparation.** Before interviewing a witness, the investigator should mentally review the case and consider what information the witness can contrib te. If the importance of the case warrants it, he should acquaint himself with the background of the witness. In this manner he may more easily strike a responsive chord. He should plan his interview, if necessary providing himself with a checklist so that no important point is overlooked.

b. **Warm-Up.** The first few minutes will determine the tenor of the interview. If the investigator permits a clash of personalities or creates a tense atmosphere, the witness may tighten up and be reluctant to divulge all of his information. After showing his credentials, the investigator should open with a few friendly remarks. Conversation on the weather, the difficulties of his profession, and matters of mutual interest will serve to warm up the atmosphere. Although friendly in his approach he should maintain a business-like manner. When he feels that the witness is in a communicative mood, he should turn the conversation toward the witness's knowledge of the case under investigation. The witness should be given every opportunity to give a complete account without interruptions. A mental note should be made of inconsistencies, and other matters requiring clarification. During the witness's recital the investigator should "size him up." Prejudices, educational attainments, moral traits, and intelligence should be assessed.

c. **Questioning.** After the witness has told his story, the investigator should review it with him and request him to amplify certain points. Matters which have not been touched upon by the witness should be treated. The elements of the offense and other points in the case should guide the investigator in his questioning.

1) *Guiding the Conversation.* Many witnesses have a tendency to ramble in giving information. Often their answers are lengthy and not responsive. The investigator must control the interview so that complete and accurate information is obtained.

2) *Corroborating.* Information obtained from one witness should be correlated with that obtained from others. Corroboration of important facts is desirable. The information on such points should be obtained in detailed and specific form.

3) *Inaccuracies.* Discrepancies, falsehoods, and inaccuracies may become apparent during the interview. Questionable points should be treated repeatedly by rewording queries and by additional questions. Honest mistakes should be distinguished from misrepresentations.

4) *Technique of Questioning.* Questions should not be asked until the person appears prepared to give the desired information in an accurate fashion. Direct questions have a restraining effect and will not be suitable until the witness has given his own story and is ready to cooperate in giving additional information.

a) One Question at a Time. A multiplicity of questions tends to confuse the person being interviewed and detracts from the orderly conduct of the interview. The answers can be more easily segregated if a leisurely, logical procedure is used.

b) Avoid the Implied Answer. The interview becomes futile if the answers are suggested in the questions. The objective is to find out what the person knows. Suggesting the answer defeats the purpose of the interrogation.

c) Simplicity of Questions. Long, complicated, legalistic questions only serve to confuse and irritate. The witness may answer that he doesn't know, when in reality he simply doesn't understand the question. In addition, such questions may embarrass him and cause resentment.

d) SAVING FACE. If his answers tend to give rise to an embarrassing situation by reason of his exaggerations or errors in matters of time, distance, and description, the investigator should cooperate with him and permit him to save face. The investigator should not ridicule his stupidity, poor judgment, or other deficiency. He should assist the subject in order to separate misrepresentation from unintentional mistakes.

e) "YES" AND "NO" QUESTIONS. Any person being questioned should have an opportunity to present relevant knowledge in its entirety. Insisting on "yes" and "no" answers is not only unfair but results in inaccurate answers and prevents a flow of information. Where such responses are concerned, qualification of the answers should be encouraged.

f) POSITIVE ATTITUDE. A common error of interviewers is the use of the negative approach in dealing with witnesses both in questioning and in arranging for the interview. An interviewer who questions a witness by saying, "You couldn't arrange to meet me this afternoon, could you?" is inviting a negative answer. He is unconsciously suggesting that a negative reply will be acceptable and that the interview can be evaded. Similarly, if the investigator puts his question by saying "You didn't see anyone near the house when you arrived, did you?" or "Would you care to sign this statement?" he is encouraging a noncommittal answer. The positive approach should always be employed. The investigator should convey by his tone of voice and phrasing that he does not contemplate the possibility of negative or non-informative answers. "I have the interview set for ten o'clock," and "How many persons were at the scene, when you arrived?" are questions that guide the mind of the witness positively. Timidity and lack of confidence are easily detected by the average man. Leadership and firmness are respected and command acquiescence.

g) CONTROLLING THE INTERVIEW. The investigator's confidence and authority communicate themselves to the witness. Hesitancy and doubt encourage evasion; weakness fosters resistance. If the witness appears to be one who will be difficult to control, small psychological gestures will bring him under control. He may be instructed to cease smoking or directed to a chair other than the one he has selected. The difficult witness must learn quickly that the investigator intends to dominate the situation.

9. Techniques for Controlling Digression

After rapport has been established and the subject has been permitted to tell his story in his own words, the most difficult task facing the interviewer is the control of digression. If the interviewer has not mastered the technique of avoiding rambling discourses, his interviewing will tend to be markedly inefficient and he may fail to obtain the desired information. Two principles should guide the interrogator in maintaining control, namely, keeping the subject on the point and preventing him from going into excessive detail in non-essential matters. The following techniques will be found useful in achieving the objective represented by these principles:

a. **Precise Questioning.** Digressions and rambling interviews are often attributable to the ineptitude of the investigator in failing to master his most effective device, namely, precision of question formulation. The question should be constructed as precisely as possible in order to restrict the range of information which the subject can give in answer. For example, to employ the question: "Can you tell me something about the habits of this man?" is encouraging a general discourse in which the subject explains his own principles. On the other hand, "Have you ever seen him intoxicated?" may in its bluntness and precision provide the interviewer with the exact information he is seeking in using the former question.

b. **Shunting.** This technique consists in asking a question which relates the digression to the original line of questioning. This maneuver is preferable to interrupting the subject since the "shunt" appears to rise out of an interest in what the subject is saying. For example, if the subject is relating his occupational history, he may dwell too much on the difficulties of one particular position he held. The interviewer can then ask quickly, "How much did they pay you for all this work?" When the subject answers, "29,000 a year," the interviewer can ask, "And how much did your next job pay?" and the interviewer has now progressed to another phase of his career.

c. **Skipping by Guessing.** Frequently the interviewer is confronted with a subject whose narration progresses in detailed and obvious steps. To speed up the recital he may ask a question such as "Was he hurt?" which anticipates a conclusion and skips intermediary details. Other such questions are: "How did he finally get home?", "Was he arrested?" A shrewd guess at the probable outcome of the various stages of the subject's recital will encourage the skipping of intervening details. For example, "You met Jones at the bar the next morning, didn't you?" " . . . and that was how you came to meet Brown?" and similar questions will greatly reduce the amount of digression.

10. Types of Interviews

The investigator must suit his techniques of interviewing to the varied personalities that are encountered in life. Some typical classes are discussed here with appropriate recommendations. Within each class one should expect to find wide variations.

a. **Children.** (Wherever possible permission should be obtained before interviewing children. Attempts to use children secretly as informants can cause serious embarrassment through the complaints of the parents.) Young children are given to flights of imagination. The inexperienced investigator will find himself quite bewildered at the turns of thought taken by children in response to questioning. The child may indulge his fancy in an imaginary journey to strange places and relate a series of unreal events. The distinction between truth and unreality may be lost on the child without any intentional desire to deceive. A child under six may invent a story in reply to a question. An older child, from six to ten, may tend to distort the story. The chief advantage of the older child as a witness, however, is the ability to observe, remember, and express himself and the absence of motives and prejudices. Such a child is an intimate of the truth although somewhat at a distance from reality. He is at least a stranger to falsehoods inspired by hate, ambition, or jealousy.

1) ***Boys.*** Most boys are alert young beings employing their minds in the direct apprehension of reality and instinctively shunning falsehood. The boy will usually describe events and objects as they appear to him. In fact, the intelligent boy can be the best of all witnesses. His perceptions are not dulled by age or preoccupation with cares, and he has a desire to communicate truth.

2) ***Girls.*** The female when young is intensely interested in the world as it reacts to her. She can be an excellent source of information because she observes with interest events intrinsically boring. She can relate facts concerning the behavior of neighbors, particularly young neighbors. She notices moral traits and psychological dispositions. Unfortunately, a girl improperly motivated can be a dangerous witness. If, in the world which in her mind centers about her person, there are individuals who do not reflect her glory or who have incurred her displeasure, she may permit herself to place fantastic interpretations on their actions. Another fault to be found in the girl witness is the tendency to exaggerate.

b. **Young Persons.** Persons in the prime of their youth are usually living too intensely to pay great heed to others, particularly to those younger or older than they. The intense preoccupation of young people with themselves prevents them from being ideal witnesses. They have not yet begun to reflect on life and to view objectively the behavior of their neighbors. They are inclined to be truthful, but their testimony is not strengthened by any great powers of observation.

c. **Middle-aged Persons.** The person who has reached the middle of his life is keenly aware of his fellow beings at other age levels. Coupled with this perception is the possession of unimpaired faculties and mature judgment. A middle-aged person is often the ideal witness.

d. **Older Persons.** Physical impairment and a tendency to regress into self-preoccupation seriously affect the value of older persons as witnesses. The intelligent older person, however, may be classed as a very effective witness, particularly since he adds maturity of judgment to a leisure for observation.

11. Types and Attitudes of Subjects

The investigator must endeavor to classify the subject as soon as possible after beginning the interview. He must then adjust his method of interviewing to the personality and attitude which he is encountering. Experience with various personality types will suggest to the investigator the best technique to be employed in a particular case. The following is a list of some of the personalities and attitudes which the interviewer will meet:

a. **Know-Nothing Type.** Some persons are reluctant to act as witnesses. This is particularly true of uneducated persons who imagine that any contact with the law means "trouble." An extensive warm-up, followed by persistent questioning, may yield results. Another technique is that of presenting the subject with a great many questions to which he cannot reply that he knows nothing, and then leading into the relevant questions. If the subject persists in his attitude, the investigator should determine whether he is stupid or unobservant before continuing. A few innocuous test questions can reveal the level of intelligence and capacity for observation attained by the subject.

b. **Disinterested Type.** The uncooperative, indifferent person must be aroused. He should be flattered at first to develop a pride in his ability to supply information. His interest should be stimulated by stressing the importance of the information he possesses.

c. **Inebriated Type.** Flattery will encourage the inebriate to respond to questions and develop an interest. Naturally, it is not advisable to take written statements from a person in this condition. At times an intoxicated person can be the best of all witnesses since he is inspired by his own potent truth serum.

d. **Suspicious Type.** His fears must be allayed. An effort should be made to win him over on the grounds of good citizenship. Failing this, the investigator should employ psychological influence. By implying that he (the investigator) already knows a good deal about the case, the investigator leaves the suspicious witness to infer that this knowledge is sufficient to work against him in the event that he does not cooperate.

e. **Talkative Type.** The garrulous witness merely requires management. The flow of information is there but it requires channeling.

The investigator should subtly lead this type back to relevant matters, by interspersing remarks that switch the subject's mind back on the desired track.

f. **Honest Witness.** If the witness possesses useful information and demonstrates honesty and cooperativeness in his attitude, the investigator has found a precious stone that is well worth polishing. Such a person, if he is normally intelligent, can be developed into an ideal witness with a little care and guidance. He should first be convinced of the investigator's mission, namely, the discovery of truth, and disabused of any notion that the investigator is determined to punish or persecute the subject. Secondly, the witness should be given a five-minute talk, with illustrative examples, of the difference between direct evidence and hearsay and the importance of accurate, relevant information.

g. **The Deceitful Witness.** The witness who is obviously lying can often be brought into the investigator's camp by careful maneuvering. He should be permitted to lie until he is well enmeshed in falsehoods and inconsistencies. The investigator can then halt the interview and dramatically announce that he recognizes the witness's statements as falsehoods. He can sustain his point by one or two examples of which he is sure and imply that he knows wherein lies the falsity of the others. A recording of the lies is extremely effective in the playback. Finally, the investigator should refer in vague terms to perjury and false statements and the probability that he may now have to investigate a case of "obstructing justice" with the witness as defendant. The case under investigation should be forgotten for the moment. About five minutes should be spent by the investigator in discoursing with great gravity on the seriousness of the witness's offense, namely false representations to an officer of the law during an official investigation. The average person is unaware that there exists no such offense. He will feel vaguely that he is punishable under the law. Now he has an excellent motive for telling the truth, namely, self-preservation.

h. **The Timid Witness.** Housewives, uneducated, foreign-born people and others may often be unusually timid and stand in awe of law enforcement procedures. The investigator must employ a friendly approach and should spend some time in explaining that the information obtained will be treated as a confidential matter.

i. **The Boasting, Egotistic, or Egocentric Witness.** Patience and flattery are necessary in dealing with the vain or self-centered person. He is potentially an excellent witness because of his drive toward self-expression. Unfortunately, he is prone to color his story and put unwarranted emphasis on his own part.

j. **Refusal to Talk.** The witness who will say nothing is the most difficult of all types. If he is a shrewd criminal with a record, he will probably remain silent. With other types the investigator must persevere. Neutral topics should be chosen to induce the atmosphere of conversation. Motivation should be exhausted before admitting defeat. The witness should be made to feel that he "owes it" to himself, his family, the victim, or even the subject to give whatever information he may possess.

12. Approaches

A direct approach is the most effective with willing witnesses. The investigator should begin in a friendly conversational tone and develop the information naturally. With difficult witnesses such as those who dislike law enforcement officers or who fear retaliation, a direct questioning may be necessary.

a. **Complainant.** The investigator should appear to be sympathetic with the complainant by expressing his interest in the case and assuring the complainant of his gratification by the report of the offense. He should convince him that full cooperation will be given and then proceed to elicit all the facts of the complaint. Privately the investigator should form an opinion of the reliability of the complainant and his complaint. He should determine whether the elements of an offense are present. The records should be checked to discover whether the person is a chronic complainant or has a criminal history. The motivation of the complainant must be considered. The existence of jealousy or grudges may have affected the complainant's point of view.

b. **Persons "Complained of."** Before questioning a person complained of (there being insufficient evidence to consider him a suspect), the investigator should refresh his knowledge of the law, acquaint himself with the facts concerning the elements present, and know the record or reputation of the person. This preliminary questioning should be impartial and probing.

c. **Informants.** The informant should be flattered. Praiseworthy motives should be attributed to his action, such as "duty to society" and "assisting law and order." The informant should be permitted to talk freely and fully. He should then be questioned for details. In concluding, a favorable estimate should be made of the importance of his information.

d. **Victims.** The victim must be treated with some care since his reactions to fancied indifference can be violent and accusations of neglect of duty may be made. The investigator should be sympathetic and listen to the complete story, permitting the victim to offer opinions. The investigator need not support or discourage the suggestions of the victim or offer any of his own at the moment. He should devote himself simply to gathering facts.

13. Evaluation

During the interview, the investigator will be forming a judgment of the credibility of his witness. Physical mannerisms, frankness, emotional state, and content of the statements will form the basis of his evaluation of the worth of the information.

a. **Physical Mannerisms.** Nervousness, evasive facial expression, embarrassment at certain questions, perspiration, and similar signs will give some indication of the trustworthiness of the person.

b. **Frankness.** The person should be tested with questions, the answers to which the investigator already knows. The investigator should compare the subject's account of certain events with the facts that he probably should have knowledge of. Significant omissions should be noted.

c. **Emotional State.** The investigator should observe carefully any unusual reaction to questions. Partial guilt can be detected by unwarranted indignation or excessive protests. Spite, jealousy, and prejudice can be easily detected.

d. **Content of Statements.** The information given by the witness can be compared with statements of other witnesses and with known facts. Discrepancies and misrepresentations can be detected by comparing the information with the known facts.

14. Notebook

The proper use of the notebook is a matter of judgment which will depend on the nature of the interview and the character of the person to be questioned. If the interview is concerned with sensitive matters, the appearance of the notebook at an early stage may instill excessive caution in the subject. After introducing himself and informing the subject of the general nature of the case, the investigator should listen to the subject's story without taking notes. At the conclusion he may request permission to put the pertinent information in writing. If necessary, he should prepare it in the form of a statement, later obtaining the subject's signature. The investigator should carry a sample statement with him to insure covering the important points. Where, however, the interview is concerned with routine matters, such as a background investigation or an interview of a custodian of official records, the notebook should be used at the outset to record the information without loss of time.

15. Hypnosis

The placing of consenting witnesses under hypnosis is increasingly becoming an investigative tool. Hypnosis may be defined simply as a sleep-like state of heightened awareness and concentration. Under hypnosis, the subconscious level of thought takes precedence over the conscious level. At the subconscious level, the mind continuously records images even while the subject is sleeping, intoxicated, or his mind is otherwise inattentive. The subconscious serves as a storehouse of sensory impressions that, when accessed, will supply the hidden details of a crime. In some cases, when the crime has been a traumatic experience, the victim will not remember it because the mind, in protecting itself, will repress the memory. In other cases, the witness has forgotten, or was not paying sufficient attention to, details of investigative significance. While under hypnosis, the subject becomes aware of those experiences, stored in his subconscious memory, that were repressed, that were forgotten, or that he was not fully conscious of at the time of their occurrence.

Many law enforcement agencies have established special units to employ hypnosis in interviewing witnesses. The training of police officers in these techniques must be conducted by a qualified psychologist or a physician skilled in medical hypnosis. The method most often used may be described as "the television technique." The subject is told to relax and imagine he is sitting in a chair in his home watching a videotape of the crime on his television set. Because reliving the actual crime may be a frightening experience, the subject is asked, rather, to watch it on television, a medium by which he can feel a sense of detachment from the event. While under hypnosis, the subject becomes very receptive to the suggestions of the hypnotist. Through hypnotic suggestion, the subject is led to believe that he can replay the imaginary videotape and stop it on important images. Under the guidance of the hypnotist, the subject can stop the tape at will and recall details of the crime. This method has enabled witnesses to provide a more complete account of the crime scene including descriptions of people, places, and vehicles. They have also remembered statements, names, and, on occasion, even license plate numbers.

However, placing the witness under hypnosis has a serious drawback. While hypnosis may enhance the witness's recollection of the details of the crime, many state courts will not permit or will severely restrict the testimony of a witness who has been hypnotized. The courts believe that the witness in a hypnotic state may become overly receptive to the suggestions of the hypnotist. Along with recalling the details of the crime, the witness may acquire misleading or false information which will make his subsequent court testimony unreliable. To avoid this problem, the use of hypnosis will generally be restricted to witnesses who are a likely source of information but who are not expected to testify. In many circumstances, the use of the "cognitive interview" described below may be a more practical approach to the problem of memory recall.

16. The Cognitive Interview

When conducting an interview, the investigator will often encounter a witness who fails to recall sufficiently all the details of the crime. It is not that the witness wasn't paying attention or is withholding information. Rather, it is the simple fact that he just doesn't remember. To deal with this problem of a witness's inability to recollect the details of a crime, Edward Geiselman of UCLA and Ronald Fisher of Florida International University developed a method called "the cognitive interview." It consists of a series of interviewing techniques designed to enhance memory recall. These techniques are meant to be used together in the order in which they appear below:

a. **Avoiding Interruption.** The witness is encouraged to speak freely about the crime while the interviewer refrains from interrupting the narrative or hurrying the witness in any way. The goal is to have the witness feel confident that he will have all the time he needs to think, speak, and reflect about the event that has occurred.

b. **Reliving the Event.** The witness is then asked to mentally recreate the period before, during, and after the crime. He is encouraged to vividly recall the setting and circumstances of the crime. The typical daily pattern of routine tasks, errands, and problems of the time leading up to the crime are reviewed. He experiences again his thoughts, his actions, his emotions, and his attitudes as they unfold in his mind. By reliving the event and placing it in the context of his normal day, the witness is led to concentrate more intensely on the details of the crime.

c. **Recalling Details.** Normally, when a witness is recounting his story, he will skip over what he considers the unimportant details to avoid boring the listener. In this technique, the witness is now instructed not to edit his impressions of the event. He is encouraged to provide every detail, no matter how insignificant it seems to him or how unsure he is that he has accurately remembered it.

d. **Changing the Order.** At the beginning of the interview, the witness narrated his story in chronological order. Now the investigator, by a series of questions, leads the witness to consider the events in a different sequence. If a reverse order is chosen, the investigator, at pauses in the interview, might ask the witness: "What did you do before that?" Step-by-step, the investigator will lead the witness backwards through each stage of the event. In the normal course of a narrative, the mind tends to truncate experiences and skip over details anticipating reaching the end. When the order of events is changed, the mind naturally pauses at each stage until instructed to continue. This technique compels the witness to consider each stage of an event as a separate incident and may result in the recall of forgotten details.

e. **Changing Perspective.** In this exercise, the witness is encouraged to view the event from a different perspective than his own. He may adopt the point of view of the victim, the suspect, another witness, or an imaginary video camera on the wall. By experiencing the crime through "someone else's eyes," the witness may recall details that had not previously occurred to him.

f. **Recollecting by Association.** The cognitive interview is concluded with a series of questions designed to elicit specific information. The witness is asked to associate his sense perceptions of the event to people, places, and things that are familiar to him. A typical question might be: "Does the suspect remind you of anyone you know? In what way? Did you ever see a hat like that one before?"

The cognitive method of interviewing will increase the amount of information obtained. It not only addresses the problem of the witness who can't remember but also lends support to the interviewer who may run out of questions and have difficulty continuing with the interview.

ADDITIONAL READING

Interview

Bennett, M. and Hess, J.E.: Cognitive Interviewing. 60 *FBI Law Enforcement Bulletin*, 3, 1991.
Copinger, R.B., Jr.: Planning the Investigative Interview. 9 *Security World*, 7, 1972.

Dexter, L.A.: *Elite and Specialized Interviewing.* Evanston, Ill.: Northwestern University Press, 1970.

Evans, D.D.: 10 Ways to Sharpen Your Interviewing Skills. 38 *Law and Order,* 8, 1990.

Geiselman, R.E. and Nielsen, M.: Cognitive Memory Retrieval Techniques. 53 *Police Chief,* 3, 1986.

Geiselman, R.E., et al.: Enhancing Eyewitness Memory: Refining the Cognitive Interview. 15 *Journal of Police Science and Administration,* 292, 1987.

MacHovec, F.J.: *Interview and Interrogation: A Scientific Approach.* Springfield, Ill.: Thomas, 1989.

Olsen, L. and Wells, R.: Cognitive Interviewing and the Victim/Witness in Crisis. 58 *Police Chief,* 2, 1991.

Royal, R.F. and Schutt, S.R.: *The Gentle Art of Interviewing and Interrogation: A Professional Manual and Guide.* Englewood Cliffs, N.J.: Prentice-Hall, 1976.

Ryals, J.R.: Successful Interviewing. 60 *FBI Law Enforcement Bulletin,* 3, 1991.

Wicks, R.J. and Josephs, E.H., Jr.: *Techniques in Interviewing for Law Enforcement and Corrections Personnel.* Springfield, Ill.: Thomas, 1972.

Yeschke, C.L.: *Interviewing: An Introduction to Interrogation.* Springfield, Ill.: Thomas, 1987.

Zulawski, D.E. and Wicklander, D.E.: *Practical Aspects of Interview and Interrogation.* New York, Elsevier, 1991.

Hypnosis

Arons, H.: *Hypnosis in Criminal Investigation.* South Orange, N.J.: Power Publishers, 1977.

Ault, R.L., Jr.: Hypnosis: The FBI's Team Approach. 49 *FBI Law Enforcement Bulletin,* 1, 1980.

Hibbard, W.S. and Worring, R.W.: *Forensic Hypnosis: The Practical Application of Hypnosis in Criminal Investigations.* Springfield, Ill.: Thomas, 1981.

Howell, M.: Profile of an Investigative Hypnosis Interview. 37 *Law and Order,* 3, 1989.

Kingston, K.A.: Admissibility of Post-Hypnotic Testimony. 55 *FBI Law Enforcement Bulletin,* 4, 1986.

Kline, M.V.: *Forensic Hypnosis: Clinical Tactics in the Courtroom.* Springfield, Ill.: Thomas, 1983.

Orne, M.T., Tonry, M.H., et al.: *Hypnotically Refreshed Testimony: Enhanced Memory or Tampering with Evidence?* Washington, D.C.: U.S. Government Printing Office, 1985.

Reiser, M.: *Handbook of Investigative Hypnosis.* Los Angeles, Lehi Publishing, 1980.

Timm, H.W.: The Factors Theoretically Affecting the Impact of Forensic Hypnosis Techniques on Eyewitness Recall. 11 *Journal of Police Science and Administration,* 442, 1983.

Wagstaff, G.F. and Maguire, C.: An Experimental Study of Hypnosis, Guided Memory and Witness Memory. 23 *Journal of the Forensic Science Society,* 73, 1983.

Chapter 9

INTERROGATIONS

1. A Fundamental Rule

THE SUPREME COURT *Miranda v. Arizona* decision has radically changed the procedural requirements for a lawful interrogation of a suspect or of a person in custody by specifying certain minimal prerequisites to insure the voluntariness of the suspect's responses. Because of its importance the Court's rule is stated at the beginning of the chapter; it will be repeated later in other, and more formal, terms to explain and develop the ideas from which it arose.

Before interrogating a suspect or a person in police custody the investigator should

a. Identify himself to the suspect as a law enforcement officer — this is done orally, together with a show of credentials.

b. Explain to the suspect in general terms the nature of the offense under investigation.

c. Inform the suspect of his wish to question him on matters relating to this offense.

d. Advise the suspect of his rights in substantially the following terms:

(1) You have the right to remain silent; you do not have to answer any questions.

(2) If you answer any questions, your answers may be used in evidence against you.

(3) You have the right to have legal counsel; that is, you may have the services of a lawyer of your own choosing.

(4) If you believe you cannot afford a lawyer, the state will appoint one for you at your request without any expense on your part.

(5) Do you understand your rights as I have explained them to you—namely, your right to remain silent and your right to be represented by a lawyer?

Miranda Rights

You must read the suspect the following information before subjecting him to custodial interrogation:

- You have a right to remain silent.
- If you choose to speak, anything you say can be used against you in court.
- You have the right to consult with an attorney and have the attorney present during questioning. If you cannot afford an attorney and wish to have one, an attorney will be provided for you before any questions are asked.
- If you choose to waive your rights and answer questions now, you have the right to cut off the questioning at any time.

Figure 11. *Miranda* warning card.

2. Options and Procedure

The fourfold warning of rights, as stated above or its equivalent, must be given by the investigator as a necessary preliminary to the interrogation of a suspect or of a person in custody. The responses of the suspect will determine the investigator's subsequent action.

a. The suspect may choose to remain silent. If before or during questioning the suspect invokes his right to remain silent, interrogation must be forgone or cease. The investigator must respect the suspect's right to remain silent. Threats, tricks, or cajolings designed to persuade the suspect to waive this right are forbidden.

b. The suspect may request counsel. No interrogation must then be attempted until the lawyer of his choosing or a state-appointed lawyer is present. If before or during questioning (assuming that he has waived his right to remain silent) the suspect invokes his right to request and have counsel, the interrogation must cease until a lawyer is procured.

c. The suspect may waive his rights. To forgo these rights an affirmative statement of rejection is evidently required. The burden of proof of waiver is on the State. Withdrawal of a waiver is always permitted. If the interrogation continues without the presence of an attorney and a statement is taken, a heavy burden rests on the Government to demonstrate that the defendant knowingly and intelligently waived his privilege against self-incrimination and his right to retained or appointed counsel. The following points should be noted:

1) Proof of waiver of constitutional rights may take the form of an "express statement that the individual is willing to make a statement and does not want an attorney, followed closely by a statement."*

2) A valid waiver will not be presumed simply from the silence of the accused after warnings are given or simply from the fact that a confession was in fact eventually obtained.

3) "Presuming waiver from a silent record is impermissible. The record must show, or there must be an allegation and evidence which show that an accused was offered counsel but intelligently and understandingly rejected the offer. Anything less is not a waiver" (*Carnley v. Cochran,* 369 U.S. 506, 516 [1962]).

4) The right to remain silent is not considered waived if the individual answers some questions or gives some information on his own prior to invoking the right.

5) "Whatever the testimony of the authorities as to waiver of rights by an accused, the fact of a lengthy interrogation or incommunicado incarceration before a statement is made is strong evidence that the accused did not validly waive his rights.... Any evidence that the accused was threatened, tricked, or cajoled into a waiver will show that the accused did not voluntarily waive his privilege."

---

*Unless otherwise noted, all of the quotations and much of the formal language used in this chapter are taken from the Supreme Court's decision in *Miranda v. Arizona,* 384 U.S. 436 (1966).

WAIVER OF RIGHTS FORM

My *Miranda* rights as they are set forth below have been read and explained to me, and I fully understand them.

Because I wish to respond to questions now and do not wish to have an attorney present, I hereby knowingly and voluntarily waive these rights.

- I have the right to remain silent.

- I have the right to consult with an attorney and have the attorney present during questioning. If I cannot afford an attorney, one will be provided for me before any questions are asked.

- I understand that anything I say in response to question may be used against me in court.

_____	_____
signature	date
_____	_____
officer's signature	date
_____	_____
witness' signature	date

Figure 12. Waiver of rights form.

3. Matters Unaffected by the Ruling

The warnings must be given when the individual is first subjected to police interrogation while in custody at the police station or while otherwise deprived of his freedom in any way. Thus, the Court's ruling does not affect other modes by which information may be acquired from persons whose freedom has been in no wise restricted by the police.

a. **Confessions without Warnings.** The Court did not purport to find all confessions obtained without warnings and counsel inadmissible. For example,

1) Any statement given freely and voluntarily is, of course, admissible in evidence.

2) There is no requirement that police stop a person who

enters a police station and states that he wishes to confess a crime.

3) Similarly, there is no requirement to stop a person who calls the police to offer a confession (or any other statement he desires to make).

4) Volunteered statements of any kind are not barred by the Fifth Amendment and their admissibility is not affected by the *Miranda* decision.

In summary, the fundamental import of the privilege while an individual is in custody is not whether he is allowed to talk to the police without benefit of warnings and counsel but whether he can be interrogated.

b. **Field Investigation.** When an individual is in custody on probable cause, the police may, of course, seek out evidence in the field to be used against him. Such investigation may include:

1) Inquiry of persons not under restraint;

2) General on-the-scene questioning as to facts surrounding a crime;

3) Other general questioning of citizens in the fact-finding process.

Questioning of this nature is not affected by *Miranda*, since in these situations the compelling atmosphere thought to be inherent in the process of in-custody interrogation is not ordinarily present.

c. **Public Safety Exception.** When there is an immediate threat to public safety such as the presence of a loaded weapon or a bomb, an arresting officer may question a suspect in custody about it without first giving *Miranda* warnings. In *New York v. Quarles* (467 U.S. 649 1984) the Supreme Court created an exception to the *Miranda* rule in those situations where the safety of the public is at stake. In this case the danger involved was a loaded handgun. The existence of a threat to the public safety is determined by an objective standard, namely, whether a reasonable officer in this situation would conclude that a threat exists.

4. Right to Counsel

After June 12, 1972, no poor person could be sentenced to a term in jail unless he had been offered free legal counsel. This Supreme Court ruling is an interesting development in view of the fact that forty years before this a person could have been legally tried and sentenced to death in a state court without a lawyer. The following are the major historical steps in this evolution and their effect on the criminal justice system:

a. **1932.** The Supreme Court first declared, in the famous "Scottsboro Boys" rape case from Alabama, that the Constitution guarantees the right to counsel in state court trials whenever the defendant's life is at stake (*Powell v. Alabama*, 287 U.S. 45 [1932]).

b. **1963.** The Court extended the rule to all felony cases (in general, those offenses carrying more than a year's imprisonment) by holding that the Sixth Amendment's guarantee of counsel in "all criminal prosecutions" required the states to furnish free lawyers to poor defendants (*Gideon v. Wainwright*, 372 U.S. 335 [1963]).

c. **1966.** In *Miranda v. Arizona* the Court ruled that a person in police custody had a right to legal counsel during interrogation; that is, a suspect must be advised of his right to counsel before interrogation. If the suspect requests counsel, no interrogation must be attempted until the lawyer of his choosing or a state-appointed lawyer is present (*Miranda v. Arizona*, 384 U.S. 436 [1966]).

d. **1972.** The Court saw no reason to limit the Sixth Amendment's right to counsel to felony cases and declared that the defendant is entitled to the "guiding hand of counsel" whenever "the actual deprivation of a person's liberty" is at stake. Thus, judges must now decide in advance of the trial of an indigent defendant if imprisonment is to be considered. Where a jail sentence is possible, the court must offer the defendant free legal counsel. Otherwise, the defendant can be given only a money fine as punishment (*Argersinger v. Hamlin*, 407 U.S. 25 [1972]). In a related development the Supreme Court decided in 1971 that a person could not be put in jail for the inability to pay a fine.

e. **The 1970s—Misdemeanor Representation.** Since fewer than a dozen states had provided counsel in all cases involving jail, the 1972 decision had affected most communities in the United States. The magnitude of the problem may be grasped by considering the fact that over five million misdemeanor cases (offenses ordinarily punishable by sentences of less than a year or a fine) had been handled by the courts as compared with 350,000 felony cases. Since the Supreme Court ruling there had been fewer guilty pleas and more trials and appeals contributing to the swollen backlog and the near breakdown in the criminal courts of some cities. The cumulative impact on the criminal justice system was a matter of conjecture. Some observers believed that this new and massive use of defense lawyers would prove too great a weight for the survival of the treadmill system of urban misdemeanor justice that must turn out a defendant every few minutes or be crushed under its growing backlog. By 1975, however, the courts had managed to contain the problem within reasonable proportions. In a five-volume report ("Counsel for Misdemeanants") on this subject by Boston University's Center for Criminal Justice we find the conclusion: "Compliance has generally been token in nature," reform "has been chaotic and uneven at best," and the assurance of legal representation remains "an empty right for many defendants." Judges have availed themselves of the key words of the *Argersinger v. Hamlin* decision permitting "a knowing and intelligent waiver" of the right to counsel. That phrase, says the Center "has resulted in a 95% waiver rate in some lower courts." In Houston and Belle Glade, Fla., according to the report, "it is assumed that a defendant has waived counsel unless he aggressively asserts (the) right." In other jurisdictions "defendants perceive, correctly or not, a tacit rule of court that those who ask for counsel are treated more harshly."

f. **The 1980s—Felony Representation.** An enormous increase in drug-related crime during the 1980s placed a tremendous strain on all branches of the criminal justice system. Resources for providing legal counsel for indigent defendants were stretched thin. In many cities, representation for even the more serious crimes was at best inadequate. For example, in Atlanta, the Fulton County Superior Court indicted 6,604 people on felony charges in

1985. That figure grew to 13,325 in 1989. Approximately three-quarters of the defendants were indigent and required counsel appointed by the public defender's office. The Georgia Indigent Defense Council, a group that helps to set the standards for the legal representation of those who cannot afford a lawyer, commissioned a study of the problem. Their research found that lawyers in Fulton County routinely handle enormous caseloads of more than 500 defendants a year, while the National Advisory Commission of Criminal Justice Standards recommends a maximum of 150 cases a year.

The arraignment is the initial step in the criminal trial process where the defendant is brought before the judge in court to be formally charged with the offense and to enter a plea of guilty or not guilty. In Fulton County, for many defendants who cannot "make bail," it is not unusual to wait three or four months in jail after the arrest for the arraignment. Because of the heavy caseloads, the court-appointed lawyer will rarely meet the defendant he is representing until the day of arraignment. At this time, the lawyer will interview the defendant for approximately 10 minutes to decide upon a plea. In the words of one defendant: "Your lawyer is not here to try to win your case but to let you know what is happening to you." Major cities, like Atlanta, make a serious effort to safeguard the constitutional rights of defendants. However, because of the extent of the problem and budgetary restraints, legal representation of the indigent is, at best, minimal.

5. Terms

To proceed now from the warning phase to the practical aspect of interrogation, the assumption must be made that the suspect has waived his right to counsel as well as his right to remain silent. As Justice Harlan has remarked (*Miranda v. Arizona*) in his dissenting opinion: "The Court's vision of a lawyer 'mitigating the dangers of untrustworthiness' by witnessing coercion and assisting accuracy in the confession is largely a fancy; for if counsel arrives, there is rarely going to be a police station confession. *Watts v. Indiana*, 338 U.S. 49, 59 (separate opinion of Jackson, J.): 'Any lawyer worth his salt will tell the suspect in no uncertain terms to make no statement to police under any circumstances.'" Nevertheless, the assumption must be made, since the professional investigator accepts with equanimity either decision of the suspect, whether he invokes or rejects his rights.

For the purpose of simplifying the practical aspect of interrogations, special meanings will be attached to some of the terms used. It should be understood that these conventions are not universally accepted.

a. **Interrogations.** An interrogation is a questioning of a person suspected of having committed an offense or of a person who is reluctant to make a full disclosure of information in his possession which is pertinent to the investigation.

b. **Witness.** A witness is a person, other than a suspect, who is requested to give information concerning an incident or person. He may be a victim, a complainant, an accuser, a source of information, an observer of an occurrence, a scientific specialist who has examined physical evidence, or a custodian of official documents. A witness is usually interviewed, but he may be interrogated when he is suspected of lying or of withholding pertinent information.

c. **Suspect.** A suspect in an offense is a person whose guilt is considered on reasonable grounds to be a practical possibility.

d. **Subject.** The term *subject* will be used here most commonly to represent the person, whether witness or suspect, who is being interviewed or interrogated. The subject in this sense is not necessarily the subject of the case under investigation. Where the term is used to refer to the subject of the case, the distinction will be apparent from the phrasing and context.

6. Purpose

The primary purpose of interrogation is to obtain information which will further the investigation. Interrogation is not simply a means of inducing an admission of guilt. It is an investigative tool of far wider application to the effective day-to-day administration of justice. It is a major means of discovering other evidence. It permits the person who appears to be implicated in a crime to present information which can establish his innocence. One of the most important functions of police questioning is that of screening cases where an arrest has been made on probable cause but where a decision to charge cannot or should not be properly made without some further investigation by the police and some evaluation by the prosecutor of the circumstances of the arrest and the availability of admissible evidence. In large metropolitan areas, each day a great number of people will be lawfully arrested for a wide variety of reasons. Routine preliminary questioning may well result in their release prior to the filing of any charge or may result in the filing of a less serious charge.

Some of the other functions served may be found in the following list of the purposes of interrogation:

a. To obtain information concerning the innocence or guilt of a suspect.

b. To obtain a confession to the crime from a guilty subject.

c. To induce the subject to make admissions.

d. To learn the facts and circumstances surrounding a crime.

e. To learn of the existence and locations of physical evidence such as documents or weapons.

f. To learn the identity of accomplices.

g. To develop information which will lead to the fruits of the crime.

h. To develop additional leads for the investigation.

i. To discover the details of any other crimes in which the suspect participated.

7. The Interrogator

The interrogator must be able to impress his subject, not through use of his formal authority but because his personality commands respect. He must be professional in attitude and performance. If he reveals any waivering tendencies the suspect may discover the means of resisting the interrogation. To inspire full confidence, the force of the investigator's personality should be tempered by an understanding and sympathetic attitude. The subject must feel instinctively that he is talking man-to-man with a person who is interested in his viewpoint and problems. The suspect who has been forced to cooperate with hostile organizations may tell his story more readily if he feels that the investigator understands his helplessness and is inclined to take his plight into consideration. The following qualifications and traits are desirable in an interrogator:

a. **General Knowledge and Interests.** To some degree, the efficiency of an investigator is commensurate with his general knowledge. To acquire this breadth of knowledge, the investigator must develop intellectual curiosity and a keen sense of observation. He must cultivate a genuine interest in people and their problems, for such knowledge will help him in determining motives as he deals with many types of personalities in a variety of circumstances. It is highly desirable that he have a wide range of general knowledge concerning professional and technical matters, since his subjects represent nearly every phase of human activity. The background and personality of these individuals, together with the information they provide, can be assessed adequately only if the interrogator is prepared to discuss their major interests intelligently and to analyze their motives in light of environmental factors.

b. **Alertness.** The variety of problems confronting him requires the interrogator to be constantly alert so he can analyze his subject accurately, adapt his technique to the requirements of the case, uncover and explore leads, and alter his tactics when necessary. A sense of logic will not in itself quickly reveal contradictions in a subject's story; it must be accompanied by a ready awareness of the contradictory information. Discovery of gaps in the subject's story after the interrogation is less satisfactory than on-the-spot recognition, because the time interval gives the subject opportunity to reflect upon the matter before questioning is renewed.

c. **Perseverance.** Every interrogation requires a great deal of patience if complete and accurate information is to be obtained. The need for patience is obvious when lack of cooperation is encountered; but perseverance frequently is required even when the suspect is willing to help but is unable to recall precisely the complex ramifications of his story or to explain discrepancies.

d. **Integrity.** If the person being questioned has reason to doubt the integrity of the interrogator, it is practically impossible for the latter to inspire confidence or trust. The interrogator must never make a promise he cannot keep; he should keep all promises he makes.

e. **Logical Mind.** The interrogator must develop the questioning along a logical line. The objectives of the questioning should be clearly defined in his own mind. A plan of questioning should be built around the requirements of establishing the elements of the offense.

f. **Ability in Observation and Interpretations.** He must not only develop the ability to "size up" an individual, but also must learn to observe and interpret his reaction to questions.

g. **Power of Self-control.** He must maintain control of himself at all times. Loss of temper results in a neglect of important details.

h. **Playing the Part.** If it will accomplish the desired results, the investigator may act as though he were angry or sympathetic as the circumstances suggest. Anger, however, should never be simulated to the degree where it might become a coercive factor.

8. Conduct of the Interrogator

The behavior of the interrogator at the outset of the questioning usually creates the atmosphere and sets the tone of the subsequent interrogation. It is of great importance for the investigator to develop an effective personality that will induce in the subject a desire to respond. Personal mannerisms must be controlled wherever they distract or antagonize. The following are some of the more useful reminders concerning attitude and demeanor:

a. **Control of the Interview.** The interrogator must always be in command of the situation. The strength of his personality must constantly be felt by the subject. He must never lose control through indignation, ill temper, hesitancy in the face of violent reactions, or obvious fumbling for questions through lack of resourcefulness.

b. **Distracting Mannerisms.** The subject must be impressed with the seriousness of the interrogator's purpose. Pacing the room, smoking, "doodling," and similar forms of behavior should be avoided, since they tend to convey a sense of inattentiveness or a lack of concentration. The investigator should seat himself close to the subject with no intervening furniture and focus his attention on the subject. The full weight of his personality must be brought to bear on the emotional situation. Distance or obstructions tend to mitigate the effect.

c. **Language.** The speech of the interrogator should be adapted to the subject's cultural level. Profanity and vulgarity should, of course, be avoided, since they diminish the effectiveness of the interrogator by compromising his dignity or antagonizing the subject. The uneducated subject must be approached in his own language. Simple, forthright diction should be employed. It is especially important in sex cases to avoid ambiguities. Slang may be used if it promotes ease of speech or fluency in the subject. The choice of words should be made with a view to encouraging a free flow of speech in the subject. Where the subject may shy away from words such as "assault" and "steal," he may not hesitate to admit that he "hit" or "took." It is a natural tendency for a person to describe his conduct in terms of euphemisms.

d. **Dress.** Civilian dress is more likely to inspire confidence and friendship in a criminal than a uniform. The accoutrements of the police profession should be removed from view. The sight of a protruding gun or billy may arouse an enmity or a defensive attitude on the part of the criminal.

e. **Attitude.** The interrogator is not seeking to convict or punish. He is endeavoring to establish the facts of the case; to discover the truth, to clarify a misunderstanding; to help the suspect to straighten himself out; to clear up this mess, to simplify matters; to rectify an unfortunate situation; to see what he can do to help the subject to help himself; to get rid of a distasteful task as painlessly as possible; to see that the subject's accomplices are not doing him an injury; and so forth. There is an extensive set of locutions available to the investigator in describing his role in the administration of justice.

f. **Preliminary Conduct.** As stated in the beginning of this chapter, the interrogator should identify himself at the outset and show his credentials to the subject. He should then state, in general terms, the purpose of the investigation. He must advise the suspect of his rights against self-incrimination and inform him that he does not need to answer questions and that, if he does answer, his answers can be used in evidence against him. He must inform the suspect of his right to counsel and of the fact that state-appointed counsel will be made available without cost to him if he so desires. If the suspect requests counsel, the interrogation may not begin until counsel is present. In any event, the interrogator may not question the suspect unless the suspect had definitely waived his right to be silent.

g. **Presence of Other Persons.** Ordinarily, the investigator should be alone with the suspect—and, of course, his lawyer, if he has requested counsel. It is desirable, for several reasons, to restrict the number of persons present at an interrogation. If a confession is obtained the defense may claim the existence of duress because of the presence of five or ten police officers. Moreover, some courts require the prosecution to produce all the witnesses of a confession. A parade of ten detectives to the witness stand creates an unfavorable impression and opens up the likelihood of inconsistencies in the testimony. Ordinarily the interrogator should be alone with the subject. Other parties may be brought in for a specific purpose, such as witnessing the signing of a confession.

9. The Interrogation Room

The room chosen for the interrogation should provide freedom from distractions. It should be designed for simplicity with a view to enhancing the concentration of both the interrogator and the subject on the matter under questioning.

a. **Privacy.** Interruptions dispel an atmosphere of concentration that may have been carefully cultivated by the investigator; hence, the following are desirable:

1) *Restricted Entrance.* A room with a single door is preferable. Several doors suggest possible interruption and destroy the sense of focused attention.

2) Absence of windows or view.

3) Sound-proofing.

4) Telephone without bell.

b. **Simplicity.** Distracting influences should be kept to a minimum. The suspect may strive to avoid the investigator's concentration by focusing his attention on some object in the room which suggests a different train of thought.

1) Medium-sized room.
2) Bare walls. Pictures and charts are distracting.
3) No glaring lights.
4) Minimum furniture.

c. **Seating Arrangement.** The subject and the investigator should be seated with no large furniture between them.

1) *Chair.* Armless, straight-back chair for the suspect.

2) *Table or Desk.* The investigator requires a flat surface on which to place papers and articles of evidence.

3) *Suspect.* Seating the suspect with his back to the door further deprives him of any hope of interruptions or distraction.

d. **Technical Aids.** Although the investigator should be alone with the subject and his lawyer, it is desirable to have facilities for others to observe and hear the suspect during the interrogation. Other investigators may suspect the subject of participation in other crimes. Thus the interrogation room can also serve as a line-up or show-up room. In an important case the investigator will require the assistance of his associates. By their listening unobserved to the interrogation they may be able to make useful suggestions and draw more objective conclusions. Persons such as the prosecuting attorney will find this opportunity to observe the prospective defendant invaluable in preparing his case. Victims and complainants are enabled to make identifications.

1) *Recording Installation.* Important interrogations and confessions should be recorded.

2) *Listening Device.* A hidden microphone such as a "live" telephone should be installed.

3) *Two-Way Mirror.* This device appears to be a plain mirror on one side but permits a person on the other side to see through without being observed. Unfortunately the typical two-way mirror installation is obvious and is familiar to the experienced criminal. A more deceptive arrangement can be devised with a little ingenuity. A framed picture with a mirror strip border is less familiar. A medicine chest with a mirror door will pass unnoticed if a small sink is installed beneath it.

e. **Interrogation Log.** In addition to his regular facilities for taking notes, it is well for the investigator to have available an Interrogation Log. This is essentially a form on which the investigator maintains in chronological order a record of the time periods of interrogation together with a time record of necessities and privileges requested by the accused and granted to him by the law enforcement agents. The interrogation log is a useful addition to the investigator's notes for special reference in answering allegations of duress.

10. Information Sought

The interrogator's primary purpose is to obtain facts or information concerning the offense under investigation for the purpose of determining the identity of the perpetrator and of substantiating a court prosecution. Initially his questions will be designed to learn whether the subject is innocent or whether there is reasonable cause to suspect his implication in the crime. If the responses indicate implication, the questioning will then seek to place the subject at the scene or to develop other associative or corroborative evidence. The identity of accomplices and the location or disposition of any fruits of the crime are, of course, matters of great interest.

To pursue a logical line of questioning, the interrogator should be acquainted with every significant detail of the case so that he is aware of what evidence is available and what evidence is needed, as well as the contributory force of each item of evidence. Thus, he should have a thorough knowledge of the nature of the offense under investigation and a mental outline of the elements of the offense together with the mode of proof required to substantiate each element.

11. Selection of Technique and Approach

In the work of an interrogation, the principle of economy of means should guide the investigator. The simplest approach is best if it achieves the desired result. The interrogator should not be unnecessarily devious. He may outwit himself with his own cleverness or antagonize the subject by creating an unwanted confusion. Ingenuity is desirable when it is required, but it should not be considered as a satisfactory substitute for intelligence. The interrogator must first classify or analyze his subject with the aid of information or criminal records. A preliminary interview will often assist in determining the character and personality of the suspect and in planning the techniques to be used.

Often, the primary purpose of an interrogation will be to obtain an admission of guilt from a suspect. When selecting an interrogation technique it is important to keep in mind the legal principles concerning the admissibility of confessions in a court of law:

    a. To be admissible in court a confession must be *voluntary* and *trustworthy* and it must have been obtained by *civilized police practices.*

    b. To be *voluntary* a statement must be essentially the product of a free and unconstrained choice of its maker rather than the result of undue pressure. In determining whether undue pressure has been exerted, the courts make use of the *totality of circumstances* test. This test consists of a review of the interrogation techniques employed in conjunction with other relevant circumstances in order to determine their effect on the defendant's decision to confess.

    c. One of the factors considered in the totality of circumstances test for voluntariness is the use of trickery and deception.

    d. The use of trickery and deception to elicit a confession is not by itself enough to render that confession involuntary and hence inadmissible. It is only one of the factors taken into consideration under the totality of circumstances test. Other coercive factors must also be present to render a confession involuntary.

    e. The Supreme Court in *Frazier v. Cupp* (394 U.S. 731 [1969]) gave tacit approval to the use of deception in obtaining a confession. In this case the defendant had been told falsely that an accomplice (Rawls) had confessed. "The fact that the police misrepresented the statements that Rawls had made is, while relevant, insufficient in our view to make this otherwise voluntary confession inadmissible. These cases must be decided by viewing the 'totality of circumstances'. . . . "

    f. Trickery and deception may be used if it is not of such a nature as to be likely to lead the subject into a false confession. In the words of Professor Fred E. Inbau, the authority on interrogation (Legally Permissible Criminal Interrogation Tactics and

Techniques. 4 *Journal of Police Science and Administration*, 249, 1976):

> A "rule of thumb" that criminal interrogators may use in determining whether or not their contemplated tactics and techniques are legally permissible is to present this question to themselves, either after a waiver of *Miranda* warnings, or where no such warnings are required:
>
> > "Is what I am about to do, or say, apt to make an innocent person confess?"
>
> If a reasonable answer to the question is "no," the interrogator should go ahead and do or say what was contemplated. On the other hand, if the answer is "yes," the interrogator should refrain from doing or saying what he had in mind. This is the only understandable test of any practical value for investigators to follow.

g. Trickery and deception should be avoided in those cases where a straightforward approach can achieve the same results. Even though the use of trickery and deception will not by itself invalidate a confession, it can still do so in conjunction with other factors as part of the totality of circumstances.

12. Interrogation Techniques

There are many techniques of interrogation which the investigator can employ. His choice should depend on the nature of the crime under investigation, the character of the subject and on his own personality and limitations. The following are some of the techniques practiced by experienced investigators.

a. **The Helpful Advisor.** The simplest of techniques is to assume that the subject is willing to confess if he is treated in a friendly spirit. The investigator is the subject's friend. Between the two of them they are going to straighten things out. The subject is bewildered by the recent happenings. If he explains the whole thing from the beginning, his friend, the investigator, will try to advise him. The investigator understands the law, the district attorney, and police procedures. Who is in a better position to help the subject?

b. **The Sympathetic Brother.** The subject needs to square things with his own conscience. For the sake of his family and himself, he should make a clean breast of the affair. His friend the investigator has seen other persons in similar circumstances. He knows the suspect is seeking, above all, to achieve peace of mind. He has his whole life ahead of him. With the help of the investigator, he can take the first long step toward rehabilitation—recite the present story from the beginning and reason out the future steps with this as a basis. The investigator wants to give the suspect a chance to help himself.

c. **Greater and Lesser Guilt.** In most crimes, there are several offenses involved. Although the investigator is only concerned with the major offense, he can represent himself as being interested mainly in a minor offense. The subject, who is afraid only of the consequences of the major offense, may resort to cleverness and in an attempt to throw the interrogator off the track or at least to placate him by throwing him a bone, may confess to a minor offense. Once he has committed himself to this, the ice has been broken and persistence should bring forth a confession of the major guilt. It must be stressed to the suspect that since he has lied about the lesser offense, it is obvious that he has lied about the greater.

d. **Knowledge Bluff.** The interrogator reveals a number of pertinent items of evidence which are definitely known. He is thus able to convince the subject that it is futile to resist since the interrogator obviously has sources of knowledge. The interrogator should prepare himself for this approach by learning a great number of facts about the crime in question and about the subject's background. He must create the impression that he possesses an unlimited store of knowledge. This is not too difficult if the subject is confused and is normally not too bright.

e. **Bluff on a Split Pair.** This is applicable where there are accomplices. The two suspects are separated and one is informed that the other has talked. Another variation, one which is less likely to run aground as a bluff, is to obtain individual, detailed stories from each suspect, no matter how fanciful or erroneous they may be, and to play the discrepancies against each suspect's story. A stronger form of this technique is to pretend to the suspect that his accomplice is placing all the blame on him. It is then suggested that the suspect would be foolish if he did not protect himself by telling the truth.

f. **Questioning as a Formality.** In this technique, the interrogator asks a series of questions as though it were a necessary formality in his routine duty. He gives the impression that he knows the answer, but that he is required to ask the question in consideration of the rights of the accused. The procedure is business-like, but the interrogator pauses meaningfully as if to give the suspect *one more* chance to tell the truth. Such phrases as the following can be used; "You were in the apartment at seven o'clock, weren't you?" "You're sure about this fact?" "Do you want me to write your answer exactly the way you said it?" "I'm going to give you a fair chance to answer this question truthfully. Think it over for a while; then, give me your answer." When the answer is not that which the interrogator expects, he puts down his pencil skeptically, looks at the suspect, stares at his note pad and shakes his head ruefully. He may make some remark such as, "I don't know what you're trying to do to yourself," or "You think you'd give yourself a break." A prolonged silence will work with equal effectiveness.

g. **Pretense of Physical Evidence.** The interrogator states that he does not need any confession and isn't particularly interested in the suspect's reasons. There are, however, a few formalities he must go through. He is required to inform the suspect of certain findings and give him an opportunity to explain certain evidence. The interrogator then pretends that certain physical evidence, appropriate to the case, has been found by laboratory experts. The average person has mystical notions of the power of scientific crime detection and will accept practically any claims that science may make. Thus the detective can mix pseudoscience in his statements. In a homicide, the interrogator can refer to hair found at the scene of the crime, which can be shown, under the microscope to be the suspect's hair. For added realism, the suspect can be invited to look into the microscope. In a document case, such as a forgery or a threatening letters case, a comparison of handwriting can be represented as being conclusive. Fingerprints are the most effective form of evidence. The layman believes that they can be left on any object. The investigator should select some object which was known to have been touched and should face the suspect with the object. It does bear fingerprints and the fingerprints have been photographed. The interrogator can show at a discreet distance a small photograph of a latent fingerprint. The imaginative investigator can create his own dramatic effects such as having the interrogation interrupted by the delivery of a message to the effect that the fingerprints on the weapon have been identified, or that the handwriting has been positively compared.

13. Control

One of the first lessons to be learned by the inexperienced investigator is the unfortunate ease with which he can lose control of the interrogation. As he questions the suspect, unexpected answers are received and his strategy is pushed off its course. Startling emotional reactions on the part of the suspect may upset him. He may become impatient in the face of obstinacy or angry with the appearance of impertinence. With the tone of the interrogation changed and the sequence of his presentation altered, he may find himself caught in a discouraging stalemate. Although experience will remedy these defects, initial training according to sound principles will enable him to avoid the pitfalls at the outset.

a. **Initial Phase.** In the beginning of the typical interrogation the investigator has little need for control. The subject should be permitted to tell his story in his own way without interruption. A few general questions will lay the groundwork. Often the suspect, after he is once launched in his narrative, will work himself into a confession. At this stage the investigator should restrict himself to assisting the subject when there is an obvious need for a word or phrase.

b. **Questioning.** After the narrative phase of the interrogation, planned questions should be put to the subject. The tone of the interrogation will now be set by the responses of the subject. Spontaneous answers which appear to be given without much reflection are particularly valuable and trustworthy. If the subject appears to be cooperating, the investigator should endeavor to develop in him a pride in his cooperation.

c. **Emotional Control.** If the subject seems reluctant to cooperate, the investigator should make every effort to remain calm. A loss of temper will cut off the small trickle of information. Anger may swiftly lead to duress. The suspect, moreover, will sense his own superiority in remaining calm. Harassing the suspect should be avoided since it can result in false statements. It is always possible that the suspect does not have the information. The indifferent type may give the desired answer regardless of its truth merely to be rid of the oppression of the interrogator. Instead of yielding to feelings of contempt, impatience, sarcasm, or anger, the interrogator can find relief in putting his efforts into the expression of emotions or sentiments such as patriotism, motherhood, childhood, religion, or fidelity to ideals.

d. **Strategic Interruptions.** When the interrogator senses that he is losing control or that his tactics are availing nothing, it may be time to pause and do additional planning or introduce a new technique. The interrogation room should be equipped with a button and buzzer under the top of the desk, which the investigator can push with his knee or foot. In this way, he can sound the buzzer, pretend it is a signal for him and leave the room.

14. Detection of Deception

Since the interrogator's main objective is to obtain true information — true, that is, in the sense that it accurately reflects what is in the subject's mind — he is necessarily concerned with the methods of distinguishing truth from falsehood. He relies, ordinarily, on his common sense, experience, and knowledge of human behavior to determine whether the subject is giving him true information, is misleading him with evasions and false statements, or is actually ignorant of the facts as he claims. Some conclusion can be drawn from inconsistencies and improbabilities evident in the subject's statements. Often, however, the interrogator must rely on the emotional reactions of the subject discernible in his features and mannerisms or in his unconscious physical behavior.

a. **Physiological Symptoms.** Careful observation of the physical state of the subject as influenced by his emotional reaction to questions has traditionally been considered a source of insight in determining guilty knowledge or deception. Primitive tribes are said to have relied on such methods as sniffing out the guilty person from a group of suspects by detecting an odor arising from an unusually nervous state; or selecting the guilty person on the basis of dryness of mouth as evinced by the relative difficulty experienced in chewing and attempting to swallow a handful of dry rice. The various symptoms observable in a subject are usually consistent with a state of nervousness as well as guilt. The following observations are generalities which can sometimes be useful if they are considered in relation to the known temperament of the subject and other relevant data:

1) *Sweating.* Perspiration on the brow may indicate excitement, nervousness, or simply the fact that the room is rather warm for the subject. Sweating palms, however, are indicative of tension and nervousness rather than warm surroundings.

2) **Color Changes.** A flushed face indicates anger or embarrassment but not necessarily guilt. An unusual pallor, considered by some a more likely sign of guilt, is often associated with fear or shock.

3) *Dry Mouth.* Frequent swallowing, wetting of the lips, and thirst are indications of dryness of the mouth, a common symptom of nervous tension that is sometimes associated with guilty knowledge and deception.

4) *Pulse.* An increase in the rate of the heart beat can be caused by the consciousness of deception.

5) *Breathing.* Deception is sometimes accompanied by an observable change in the rate of breathing or by an effort to control breathing during critical questions.

b. **The Lie Detector.** In drawing inferences from physiological symptoms, the interrogator is unconsciously serving roughly the purpose of a lie detector, since he is relying on the same principle: the bodily functions of a person are influenced by his mental state. The brain reacts to emotional disturbances by transmitting through the nervous system signals which appropriately affect and regulate the body's vital functions. A suspect's emotions will thus effect certain physiological changes such as a quickened heartbeat; a difference in the rate and volume of breathing; blushing; increased perspiring; and dryness of the mouth. These are autonomic changes, accordingly self-regulating and difficult to control consciously. A number of these changes, moreover, are measurable and can be recorded and interpreted with reasonable accuracy. A mechanical aid for measuring such changes is called a lie detector; if it serves the additional function of recording the changes, it is commonly called a polygraph.

1) ***The Lie Detection Process.*** The lie detector or polygraph does not record lies as such but simply measures changes in blood pressure, pulse rate, breathing, and in the resistance of the skin to a small electrical current. By far the most important element in the process of detecting deception is the qualified examiner, whose education, training, and experience enable him to determine whether the graphs produced with the instrument present a meaningful pattern. The interpretation of the charts is of critical importance. Without a suitable background in psychology, physiology, and scientific method, the operator of the lie detector may be little more than a shrewd mechanic, using the instrument to support conclusions already half-drawn on the basis of experience and intuition.

In practice the examiner uses both neutral questions (irrelevant to the issues of the case) as well as relevant questions. Neutral questions enable the examiner to establish a norm for the subject's reactions to questions relatively free of emotional content. The relevant questions provide the examiner with some insight into the cause of a subject's fears—the guilty person's fears usually tend to increase during a test, his reactions usually become stronger; the fear and nervousness of the innocent person, on the other hand, usually tend to decrease during the test.

In 1923, the Circuit Court of the District of Columbia ruled against the admissibility of polygraph results as evidence in a court of law. More significantly, this decision, *Frye v. U.S.* (293 F. 1013 [D.C. Cir. 1923]), set forth the criteria for the judicial acceptance of a scientific advancement. In order for expert testimony based on a scientific principle or procedure to be admissible as evidence, that principle or procedure must have already received general acceptance from scientists in the particular field to which it belongs. This came to be known as the "general acceptance" or the "*Frye* test" and is recognized as one of the two standards by which the courts evaluate the admissibility of scientific developments. The other is called the "relevancy standard" (see Chap. 25, Sec. 26d).

2) *Objectives.* Although information obtained by means of the lie detector test is not generally accepted as direct evidence in United States courts of law, the test itself is considered a valuable investigative aid in the achievement of the following objectives:

a) Ascertaining if the subject is telling the truth.

b) Testing and comparing inconsistent statements.

c) Verifying statements made by the suspect before the test.

d) Developing leads to important facts of the crime, such as the whereabouts of a wanted person or the location of stolen goods.

c. **Suitability of Test Subject.** Not all persons are fit subjects for a lie detector test, since certain physical and mental conditions may affect the subject's reactions during the test. The following factors are considered:

1) *Physical Ills.* Permanent conditions such as certain heart conditions and breathing disorders can make a person unfit to take the test. A highly nervous or excitable person may be unfit. Temporary conditions such as drunkenness, sickness, injury, pain, extreme fatigue, and certain respiratory ailments may affect a person's suitability as a test subject.

2) *Mental Ills.* Permanent mental illnesses such as mental deficiency or insanity render persons unsuitable. It may be difficult, or impossible, for them to distinguish the truth from a lie, or even to understand the purpose and procedure of the test. Persons of very low intelligence may display little moral sense or fear of being caught in an offense or a lie. Temporary conditions such as severe emotional upset or the influence of a sedative may also disqualify a person as a subject.

d. **Treatment of Subject.** The success of a test depends in part on how the person was treated before he was asked to take the test, the manner in which he was asked to take the test, and how he was treated while awaiting the test.

1) *Routine Questioning.* A proper interview seldom affects the test results, provided it is not unduly long or rigorous. The investigator should not reveal details of the offense to a person who may be asked to take the test. The interview should be straightforward, without resort to tricks or bluffs or other ruses which upset the subject or make him suspicious, thereby defeating the purpose of the test at the outset.

2) *Asking a Person to Take the Test.* The investigator should inform the subject of his right to take the test and of the fact that he may have counsel present during the test if he so wishes. He should then explain and discuss the test along the following lines:

a) Describe the test to the person in simple language, removing any misconceptions.

b) Suggest the test as a means for the suspect to indicate his innocence. Do not suggest that a refusal to take the test will indicate guilt.

c) Discuss the capability of the test for indicating, through recorded responses, whether a person is telling the truth. Do not make any false or exaggerated claims for the lie detection process.

3) *Treatment During Detention.* The subject should be treated normally, with food and exercise available at appropriate times. The test, however, should be scheduled promptly to avoid unnecessary delays. Suspects in the same case should not be allowed to communicate with each other.

e. **Planning Test Questions.** The investigator can be of great assistance to the examiner in the preparation of the test questions by giving him detailed and verified factual information about the offense. From a study of representative test questions he can become familiar with the kind of information most useful to the examiner.

1) Whenever possible, the investigator should inform the examiner of the unpublicized facts of the offense, particularly those known only to the victim, the offender, and the investigator. He should inform the examiner of the following:

a) Specific articles or exact amounts of money stolen.
b) Peculiar aspects of the offense, such as a strange or obscene act committed at the scene.
c) The exact time at which the offense occurred.
d) Known facts about a suspect's actions or movements.
e) Facts indicating a connection between suspects, victims, and witnesses, especially when they deny any connection.
f) Exact type of firearm, weapon, or tool used.
g) Results of laboratory tests.

2) The questions to be used are constructed by the examiner to be short, simple, and easily understood by the subject. They are

formulated so that only a yes or no answer is required. The examiner is interested in the subject's reaction to the immediate sense of the question and not in the subject's difficulties in understanding the question because of its form or wording.

f. **Test Procedures.** The procedure used will vary somewhat with the person tested and the facts of the case. Polygraph experts will vary, too, in their procedures, some having developed more sophisticated techniques which they have found reliable and sometimes more informative. The following are two basic techniques — the *general question test* and the *peak of tension test* — as described by the Office of The Provost Marshal, U.S. Army, in its technical bulletin (TB PMG 22):

1) *General Question Test.* This test consists of a series of relevant (concerning the offense) and irrelevant (not concerning the offense) questions asked in a planned order. The relevant questions are asked in order to obtain a specific response. The irrelevant questions are asked to give the subject relief after pertinent questions and to establish a normal tracing on the test chart. The questions are so arranged that a specific reaction to a relevant question can be compared with a normal tracing made during the answering of an irrelevant question. The reaction may be strong enough to indicate that the subject either did not tell the truth or that he was unduly disturbed by the question. In the general question test, the subject usually does not know beforehand what questions are to be asked. Repeat tests are used.

2) *Peak of Tension Test.* The second type of test depends on the building up of a peak of tension (emotional disturbance). The subject is usually told beforehand the questions that are to be asked. The series contains one question about a specific detail of the offense. The test chart of a subject who is not telling the truth or who is unduly disturbed usually shows a rise in the tracing up to the relevant question (peak of tension) and a decline thereafter. The rise is due to the fact that the subject dreads the question to which he knows he is going to lie. The decline is caused by the relief of knowing that the dreaded question is past. The peak of tension works best if the examiner knows some unpublicized details of the offense. It is also used when the examiner is probing for a weakness in the subject's testimony. Variations of this test are used as preliminary tests to ascertain if a person is capable of giving a reliable response.

g. **Examples of Prepared Questions.** The questions below are based on a sample case. Allen Rowe was found dead in the day room, killed by a bullet from a .45 caliber weapon. Rowe's wallet, which his friends say contained about five hundred dollars, was found beside his body, empty. Investigation reveals John Simpson as a suspect in the murder and robbery of Rowe. Simpson is promptly brought in for a lie detector test, after being informed of his rights and after giving the necessary waivers. The examiner decides to test him first by the *general question test* and then by the *peak of tension test.*

1) *General Question Test.* The following questions might be used: (Note that questions *c, d, f, g,* and *i* are relevant to the case.)

 a) Is your last name Simpson?
 b) Are you over 21?
 c) Do you know who shot Rowe?
 d) Did you shoot Rowe?
 e) Were you born in Indiana?
 f) Did you take Rowe's money?
 g) Did you shoot a .45 caliber pistol last night?
 h) Is your hair brown?
 i) Have you answered my questions truthfully?

2) *Peak of Tension Test.* If the details of the murder and robbery have not been made public and the investigators have not mentioned specific facts to Simpson, the following peak of tension tests might be used:

 a) FIRST TEST.
  (a) Did you stab a man?
  (2) Did you poison a man?
  (3) Did you drown a man?
  (4) Did you shoot a man?
  (5) Did you hang a man?
  (6) Did you strangle a man?
 b) SECOND TEST. [The subject is a member of the military.]
  (1) Did you shoot a submachine gun last night?
  (2) Did you shoot a carbine last night?
  (3) Did you shoot an M1 rifle last night?
  (4) Did you shoot a .45 caliber pistol last night?
  (5) Did you shoot a cannon last night?
  (6) Did you shoot a shotgun last night?
  (7) Did you shoot a .22 caliber rifle last night?

h. **Sources of Error.** It should not be expected that a positive conclusion can be reached in every lie detector test even when properly administered; nevertheless, the investigator should not contribute, through any deficiency of his own, to the inadequacy of a test. Most unsatisfactory lie detector examinations are attributable to two main factors: unsuitable subjects and unprepared examiners. The lack of preparation of the examiner may be the result of a lack of intelligent cooperation on the part of the investigator. The following precautions will assist the investigator in his contribution to the success of the examination:

1) Do not wait until the last minute to ask a person to take the test. The test should not be used as a last resort after all other methods have failed.

2) Do not tell a suspect everything you know about the offense or about him.

3) Do not fail to investigate the case before you ask a person to take the test. Faulty or incomplete investigation is a pitfall. The background information on each subject should be as complete as possible.

4) Do not depend on mass screening of possible suspects to produce a real suspect or the guilty party. The number of subjects should be narrowed as much as possible.

i. **Post-test Questioning.** A period of skillful questioning by the examiner usually follows every lie detector test. The examiner should select an approach based on the information supplied by the investigator, on the subject's background, and on the results of the test and the effects it seems to be having on the person being tested. The investigator should be available to provide any additional information that might assist the examiner.

15. Psychological Stress Evaluator

This instrument is a form of lie detector that depends on a different principle to detect emotional elements in speech production and to deduce therefrom the relative content of truth or falsity. The objective of the inventors of the Psychological Stress Evaluator (PSE) was to achieve a simpler way of detecting lies, one that would eliminate the use of restraining tapes and cords and the consequent emotional strain that might lead to incorrect readings. The subject merely speaks into the microphone or his voice is recorded by other means on magnetic tape that is fed into a machine as small as a portable typewriter which accomplishes an analysis on the voice pattern.

The key to the successful use of the PSE is the preparation of simple selected questions keyed to the individual and structured to reveal normal or truthful answers and responses that are false. Once the personal pattern has been established, any evasive or false answers reveal stress, that is, if a person is not telling the truth, the analysis of his voice pattern will show it.

The principles underlying PSE and its equipment are best described by their inventors: When one speaks, the voice has two modulations—audible modulation and inaudible. The audible portion is what we hear. The inaudible comes from the involuntary areas (those not directly controlled by the brain or thought processes). Internal stress is reflected in the inaudible variations of the voice. These differences cannot be heard, but they can be detected and recorded by the PSE. Superimposed on the audible are inaudible frequency modulations. The FM quality of the voice is susceptible to the amount of stress that one may be under in speaking. To the human ear, a person may sound perfectly normal, free of tremors or 'guilt-revealing' sound variations. The PSE senses the differences and records the changes in inaudible FM qualities of the voice on the chart. When the chart is interpreted by an experienced examiner, it reveals the key stress areas of the person being questioned.

The advantages of PSE, as suggested by their manufacturers, include simplicity, fewer moving parts, ease of operation, and the provision of a permanent record of the interview which can be reexamined at a later date. One should mention, too, the possibility of surreptitious use, since the PSE can be used to analyze tapes recorded from telephone lines or hidden microphones. Indeed, a voice-stress analyzer has been designed to work directly over the telephone and without the need for a tape recording. The ethical and legal questions raised by such an apparatus are formidable. Some indication of official reaction was given by Governor Carey of New York in 1978 when he signed into law a bill that prohibits an employer from requiring, requesting, suggesting, or knowingly permitting a worker or job applicant to be subject to a test on a psychological stress evaluator.

In evaluating the relative merits of this mode of lie detection, it should be noted that polygraph manufacturers consider voice analyzers inferior because they monitor only one supposed indicator of stress where polygraphs typically monitor three (blood pressure, respiration, and the electrical conductivity of skin surfaces).

ADDITIONAL READING

Interrogation

Aubry, A.S. and Caputo, R.R.: *Criminal Interrogation,* 3rd ed. Springfield, Ill.: Thomas, 1980.

Bruce, T.A.: *Miranda* — 20 Years Later: An Overview of Recent Restrictions on its Application. 35 *Law and Order,* 8, 1987.

Higginbotham, J.: Interrogation: Post-*Miranda* Refinements. Parts I and II. 55 *FBI Law Enforcement Bulletin,* 2 and 3, 1986.

———: Waiver of Rights in Custodial Interrogations. 56 *FBI Law Enforcement Bulletin,* 11, 1987.

Inbau, F.E.: Legally Permissible Criminal Interrogation Tactics and Techniques. 4 *Journal of Police Science and Administration,* 249, 1976.

———: Over-reaction — The Mischief of *Miranda vs. Arizona.* 73 *The Journal of Criminal Law and Criminology,* 797, 1982.

Inbau, F.E., Reid, J.E. and Buckley, J.P.: *Criminal Interrogation and Confessions,* 3rd ed. Baltimore, Williams and Wilkins, 1986.

Kamisar, Y.: *Police Interrogation and Confessions.* Ann Arbor, University of Michigan Press, 1980.

Klotter, J.C. and Kanovitz, J.R.: *Constitutional Law,* 6th ed. Cincinnati, Anderson, 1991.

MacHovec, F.J.: *Interview and Interrogation: A Scientific Approach.* Springfield, Thomas, 1989.

Riley, C.E. III: Fine Tuning *Miranda* Policies. 54 *FBI Law Enforcement Bulletin,* 1, 1985.

———: Confessions and Interrogation: The Use of Artifice, Strategem, and Deception. 51 *FBI Law Enforcement Bulletin,* 4, 1982.

———: Interrogation after Assertion of Rights. Parts I and II. 53 *FBI Law Enforcement Bulletin,* 5 and 6, 1984.

Robin, G.D.: Juvenile Interrogation and Confessions. 10 *Journal of Police Science and Administration,* 224, 1982.

Van Meter, C.H.: *Principles of Police Interrogation.* Springfield, Ill.: Thomas, 1973.

Witt, J.W.: Non-Coercive Interrogation and the Administration of Criminal Justice. 64 *Journal of Criminal Law, Criminology, and Police Science,* 320, 1973.

Yeschke, C.L.: *Interviewing: An Introduction to Interrogation.* Springfield, Ill.: Thomas, 1987.

Zulawski, D.E. and Wicklander, D.E.: *Practical Aspects of Interview and Interrogation.* New York, Elsevier, 1991.

Detection of Deception

Ansley, N. (Ed.): *Legal Admissibility of the Polygraph.* Springfield, Ill.: Thomas, 1975.

Desroches, F.J. and Thomas, A.S.: The Police Use of the Polygraph in Criminal Investigations. 27 *Canadian Journal of Criminology,* 43, 1985.

Ferguson, R.J., Jr. and Miller, A.L.: *The Polygraph in Court.* Springfield, Ill.: Thomas, 1973.

Furgerson, R.M.: Evaluating Investigative Polygraph Results. 58 *FBI Law Enforcement Bulletin,* 10, 1989.

———: Polygraph Policy Model for Law Enforcement. 56 *FBI Law Enforcement Bulletin,* 6, 1987.

Hunter, F.L. and Ash, P.: The Accuracy and Consistency of Polygraph Examiners' Diagnosis. 1 *Journal of Police Science and Administration,* 370, 1973.

Inbau, F.E. and Reid, J.E.: *Truth and Deception: The Polygraph (Lie Detector) Technique,* 2nd ed. Baltimore, Williams and Wilkins, 1978.

Lesce, T.: SCAN: Deception Detection by Scientific Content Analysis. 38 *Law and Order,* 8, 1990.

Matte, J.A.: *The Art and Science of the Polygraph Technique.* Springfield, Ill.: Thomas, 1980.

Murphy, J.K.: The Polygraph Technique: Past and Present. 49 *FBI Law Enforcement Bulletin,* 6, 1980.

Nachshon, I., Elaad, E. and Amsel, T.: Validity of the Psychological Stress Evaluator: A Field Study. 13 *Journal of Police Science and Administration,* 275, 1985.

Polygraph: A Critical Appraisal. 8 *Journal of the Beverly Hills Bar Association,* 35, 1974.

Scientific V. Judicial Acceptance. 27 *University of Miami Law Review,* 254, 1972.

Timm, H.W.: The Efficacy of the Psychological Stress Evaluator in Detecting Deception. 11 *Journal of Police Science and Administration,* 62, 1983.

Chapter 10

ADMISSIONS, CONFESSIONS, AND WRITTEN STATEMENTS

1. General

THE ART of interviewing and interrogating is properly supplemented by a knowledge of the procedures for reducing the information acquired to a formal written statement. It is, of course, required that the statement be made knowingly and voluntarily—under the same conditions, in brief, as those which should obtain before a subject is interrogated. If the subject, after intelligently waiving his rights, has brought himself to confess, it may require but a simple additional request by the investigator for him to provide a written version of his statement or to sign a typed version that accurately reflects the information he has given orally. When the spirit of confession has been invoked, the investigator should try to obtain the information in several different forms, of which the written form is considered by many to be the most desirable. It is not sufficient that he, the investigator, knows that the subject has acknowledged guilt. The persons who will prosecute the case find special encouragement in a written confession. Such a statement, freely made and correctly accomplished to include reference to each of the elements of the offense and to indicate that the confession is knowingly and voluntarily given, is a source of reassurance also to law enforcement supervisors, who somehow find such a statement more convincing in a report of investigation than a simple recounting by the investigator of the accused's acknowledgment of guilt and description of the circumstances.

By way of expectancy, the investigator should remember that almost half of all felony defendants make a confession. Defendants accused of property crimes are much more likely to confess to the police than those accused of crimes against the person— presumably because of the persuasiveness of the evidence that can be used to convince the suspect that a denial is hopeless.

2. Relative Importance

There is a tendency on the part of even professional investigators to exaggerate the value of such a confession and to misinterpret its significance. The written confession does not, for example, prove the matters to which it pertains. Often the written statement is not considered admissible and does not become part of the evidence in the case. Moreover, if the written confession is admitted in evidence it will be subjected to the closest scrutiny by defense counsel. Above all, the question of voluntariness is commonly raised by defense counsel and accusations of duress and coercion are brought against the prosecution witnesses. Finally, proof of the elements of the offense should be developed by the investigator independently of the written confession for presentation to the court. He should continue with his investigation and bring it to its completion as though the written confession existed mainly for the purpose of providing guidelines and additional leads for the inquiry as well as a number of details which must be separately proved to supply additional evidence or to serve as a check on the information already acquired.

Confessions have been called "the prime source of other evidence." Often it provides the investigator with information that would be otherwise unavailable—for example, the scope of a conspiracy, the existence and identity of accomplices, additional past offenses attributable to the same person or group, and so forth. Physical evidence that will be later analyzed through a confession or admission: the existence and location of a firearm used in the commission of a crime; the location of an automobile used in an assault; and the location of stolen property are a few examples.

3. Purpose

In addition to providing some of the general investigative advantages described above, the obtaining of written statements can serve the following specific purposes:

a. To provide a written record for the case file.

b. For use by the prosecution at the trial to refresh recollection, impeach witnesses, and, in general, monitor to some extent the testimony.

c. To discourage a witness from wrongfully changing his testimony at the trial.

d. To assist the prosecution in planning its presentation by reducing the element of surprise that unforeseen testimony would introduce.

4. Admissions

An admission is a self-incriminatory statement by the subject falling short of an acknowledgment of guilt. It is an acknowledgment of a fact or circumstance from which guilt may be inferred. It implicates but does not directly incriminate. A simple statement to the effect that the subject was present at the scene of the crime may be an admission. Coupled with such circumstances as the existence of a motive, the admission may provide an inference of guilt. Traditionally, in all courts the prosecution has been permitted to introduce an admission as evidence without first showing that it was made freely and voluntarily. The *Miranda* decision, however, would suggest that admissions and exculpatory statements are to be treated just like confessions:

> The warnings required and the waiver necessary in accordance with our opinion today are, in the absence of a fully effective equivalent, prerequisites to the admissibility of any statement made by a defendant. No distinction can be drawn between statements which amount to "admissions" of part or all of the offense. The privilege against self-incrimination protects the individual from being compelled to incriminate himself in any manner; it does not distinguish degrees of incrimination. Similarly, for precisely the same reason, no distinction may be drawn between inculpatory statements and statements alleged to be merely "exculpatory." [A statement is said to be exculpatory if it is designed to vindicate, to excuse or to free from blame or

guilt.] If a statement made were in fact truly exculpatory it would, of course, never be used by the prosecution. In fact, statements merely intended to be exculpatory by the defendant are often used to impeach his testimony at trial or to demonstrate untruths in the statement given under interrogation and thus to prove guilt by implications. These statements are incriminating in any meaningful sense of the word and may not be used without the full warnings and effective waiver required for any other statement. In *Escobedo* itself, the defendant fully intended his accusation of another to be exculpatory as to himself.

5. Confessions

A confession is a direct acknowledgment of the truth of the guilty fact as charged or of some essential part of the commission of the criminal act itself. To be admissible, a confession must be *voluntary* and *trustworthy*. In addition, the Supreme Court has stated that if a confession is to be used in a federal or state prosecution it must have been obtained by *civilized police practices*. The giving of the fourfold warning of rights is a necessary but not a sufficient condition for the voluntariness and trustworthiness of a subsequent confession. The use of coercion, unlawful influence, or unlawful inducement is obviously outside the limits of civilized police practice. Some examples of circumstances which would render a confession inadmissible are threats of bodily harm or of imposition of confinement; illegal detainment; deprivation of necessities or necessary privileges; physical oppression; promises of immunity, clemency, or of substantial reward or benefit likely to induce a confession or admission from the particular accused.

6. Demonstrating Voluntariness

The prosecution may not use statements, whether exculpatory or inculpatory, stemming from custodial interrogation of the accused unless it demonstrates the use of procedural safeguards effective to secure the privilege against self-incrimination. The investigator, then, must be able to prove, through his own testimony and that of witnesses, for example, that he informed the accused of his right to remain silent and of his right to counsel either of his own choice or appointed by the state if he is indigent. Further, the investigator should be able to make an affirmative showing to the effect that a confession was voluntarily given by evidence of one of the following:

a. The statement was not obtained by urging or by request but was a spontaneous or self-induced utterance of the accused.

b. The statement was obtained without coercion and not during an official investigation nor while the accused was in custody.

c. The statement was obtained during an official investigation after the accused had been informed of the nature of the offense, of his right to remain silent, of the fact that the evidence he might give could be used against him at a trial, and of the fact that counsel would be made available to him if he so requested.

d. The accused knowingly waived his right to remain silent and his right to have counsel before making the statement. (A written and witnessed waiver is preferable.)

7. Illustrative Case

In stressing the need for care in demonstrating voluntariness, it may appear that undue emphasis is being placed on fairly obvious points. It should be remembered, however, that the investigator presenting a written confession of the accused for admission into evidence is often looked upon with skepticism and even distrust. He has, in recent years, been given a bad press. Defense counsel, for example, may for the benefit of the jury suggest that a detective may be described as a person who collects signatures on typed confessions. The magistrate, especially, will have a keen sense of the "heavy burden resting on the Government to demonstrate that the defendant knowingly and intelligently waived his privilege against self-incrimination and the right to retained or appointed counsel." The *Miranda* case will serve to illustrate the fact that ordinary care in obtaining a statement may not suffice. The two police officers in this case, after a two-hour interrogation, "emerged from the interrogation room with a written confession signed by Miranda. At the top of the statement was a typed paragraph stating that the confession was made voluntarily, without threats or promises of immunity and with 'full knowledge of my legal rights, understanding any statement I make may be used against me.' ... The mere fact that he signed a statement which contained a typed-in clause stating that he had 'full knowledge' of his 'legal rights' does not approach the knowing and intelligent waiver required to relinquish constitutional rights."

8. Depositions

A deposition is the testimony of a witness reduced to writing under oath or affirmation, before a person empowered to administer oaths, in answer to interrogatories (questions) and crossinterrogations submitted by the party desiring the deposition and the opposite party. A deposition is used ordinarily to take the testimony of a witness who will be at a prohibitive distance from the scene of the trial at the time of the trial, or who for some reason would be unable to testify in person at the trial. Ordinarily a deposition should be taken by an attorney and not an investigator.

9. Reducing Statements to Writing

Whenever possible, important statements of witnesses and suspects should be reduced to writing. Specifically, written statements should be taken from:
    a. Subjects and suspects.
    b. Recalcitrant or reluctant witnesses.
    c. Key witnesses.
    d. Any witness who gives an indication of a tendency to change his mind.
    e. Witnesses who will not be available at legal proceedings.

10. Content of the Statement

A lengthy interrogation will develop much information that is unnecessary in the sense of being irrelevant or immaterial. When the subject finally consents to make a written statement, the investigator must then decide what information he wishes to be included in the statement. The exercise of good judgment at this point is important since the subject may subsequently refuse to make an additional statement to remedy any deficiencies in the first.

a. **Witnesses.** In taking a statement from a witness, the investigator should consider first what information he may possess and could normally be expected to give in testimony and second what information is needed for support of the case. The common ground of these two considerations should form the substance of the statement.

b. **Suspects.** The statement of a suspect should substantiate the elements of the charge or contain any information pertinent to the issues of the case. In addition, the statement should include any details of extenuating circumstances or explanations offered by the suspect. Finally, the investigator should apply to the statement the criteria applicable to judging a report of investigation. The purposes of such a report are:

1) Provision of a permanent record of the information.

2) Presentation of clear, direct, complete, and accurate communication.

3) Presentation of information that can form the basis of charges and specifications.

4) Provision of information that can form the basis of additional investigation.

11. Methods of Taking Statements

Although there should be no delay in reducing a confession to writing, the investigator should not interrupt the suspect once he has launched himself into a freely flowing recital. At this point the suspect, although quite willing to speak of his participation in the crime, may be psychologically unprepared to commit his words to the formality of writing. At no time should the investigator weaken his position by appearing excessively eager to put the confession in writing. He should expedite the procedure by having the date line and introductory matter of the statement prepared in advance. The methods which he will employ in reducing the statement to writing will depend on the intelligence and temperament of the suspect; the amount and nature of the information to be recorded; and the availability of stenographic services. The following are some of the methods that may be employed: (The methods are applicable to statements in general.)

a. The subject may write his own statement without guidance. A statement of this nature, which is sufficiently comprehensive, is the most desirable form.

b. The subject may dictate to a stenographer without guidance.

c. The investigator may give the subject a list of the essential points to be covered in the statement and suggest that he include these matters and add whatever other pertinent information he may wish.

d. The subject may deliver his statement orally in his own way to the investigator, who writes the statement.

e. The subject may deliver his statement orally to the investigator or a stenographer in response to questions put to him by the investigator. The responses are recorded verbatim.

f. The investigator may assist the subject in dictating his statement by suggesting words and locutions which will express the subject's intended meaning. Naturally, great caution must be exercised by the investigator to protect himself from a charge of influencing the subject. A taped recording is useful.

g. The investigator may prepare the statement by writing his version of the information given by the subject. He should try to use expressions employed by the subject and submit the statement to him for corrections and changes.

12. Form for Statements

Although different law enforcement agencies will employ varying formats, the following outline of a statement will be found common to many of them and generally satisfactory.

a. **Identifying Data.** The first paragraph of a statement should contain the date, place, identification of the maker, the name of the person to whom the statement is made, and a declaration by the maker that the statement is being made voluntarily, with any necessary waivers.

b. **The Body.** The body of the statement can be given in expository or narrative form. It is of great importance, particularly in a confession, that the statement include all the elements of the crime and the facts associating the subject to these elements. The words of the subject should be used, but the scope of the confession should be guided by the investigator. The investigator may write the statement himself to insure the inclusion of all the necessary details. The subject should afterwards be requested to read the statement and sign each page at the bottom. In order to establish more firmly the fact that that subject read the statement, it is well to include several errors—typographic or otherwise—and request the subject to correct any errors in reading and to initial the corrections in ink. If the subject fails to recognize the errors, they should be called to his attention. Each page should be numbered by writing in the lower right corner: "Page __ of __ Pages."

c. **Conclusion.** The concluding paragraph should state that the subject has read the document of so many pages and that he has signed it. The subject should then be requested to sign the statement on each page and initial corrections as described above.

13. Witnesses to a Confession

The presence of witnesses will provide a defense in rebutting claims that duress in the form of threats or promises was employed by the investigator. After the investigator has prepared the statement for signature, witnesses may be introduced so that they can later testify to the following:

a. That the subject read and revised the entire statement with the investigator.

b. That the subject objected to certain words, phrases, or statements.

c. That he corrected certain words and phrases and initialed the corrections.

d. That he evidently understood the contents of the confession.

e. That he was in his right senses, knew what he was doing, and acted voluntarily.

f. That he acknowledged the statement to be true and correct. Each person witnessing the signature should sign as a witness. The signatures should show their names and addresses. If the witness is a member of the law enforcement agency, his signature should be accompanied by his grade, title, and assignment.

a.   STATEMENT OF SUSPECT
Personally appeared before me, the undersigned authority for administering
oaths, _____, _____ who has been advised that he need not
make any statement and, that any statement he makes may be used against him
in any proceeding, civil or criminal and that he may, at his request, have the
benefit of free legal counsel before making any statement; and who declares that
the following statement is given freely and voluntarily, and without promise of benefit, or threat or use of force or duress; does proceed, under oath, to state as follows:
    I, _____, _____, have been advised that I
need not make any statement and that any statement I make may be used against
me in any proceeding, civil or criminal. I . . .
                      (BODY OF STATEMENT)
    I have read the foregoing statement consisting of _____ pages which I have
initialed and signed and I state that it is true and correct to the best of my knowledge and belief. (DECLARANT HANDWRITING)

                    _____
                              (Signature)
Sworn and subscribed to before me this _____ day of _____, _____.
                    /s/ _____
                    ....
    OFFICIAL TITLE /t/ _____
WITNESSED: _____   _____
                    (Signature)   (Address)

           _____   _____
                    (Signature)   Address)

b.   STATEMENT OF A WITNESS
                                        Dated _____
    I, _____, having been duly advised
that I need not make this statement and that it may be used against me in any
proceeding, civil or criminal, declare that the following statement is given freely
and voluntarily, without promise of benefit, or threat or use of force or duress, do
proceed to state as follows:
                      (BODY OF STATEMENT)
    I have read the foregoing statement consisting of _____ pages which I have
initialed and signed, and I state that it is true and correct to the best of my
knowledge and belief. (DECLARANT HANDWRITING)

                    _____
                              (Signature)
WITNESSED: _____   _____
                    (Signature)   (Address)

           _____   _____
                    (Signature)   (Address)

Figure 13. Representative forms for taking a statement: (a) from a suspect; (b) from
a witness.

14. Swearing to the Statement

If it is desired to have the subject sworn to the statement, all persons should stand. The investigator should instruct the subject to raise his right hand. The investigator should also raise his right hand and proceed to recite the oath. Although there is no fixed form for the oath, the following will be found generally applicable:

"Do you (state name of subject) solemnly swear that the statement which you have made and to which you are about to affix your signature is the truth, the whole truth, and nothing but the truth? So help you, God."

After the subject is sworn, the statement is signed by the subject, the investigator administering the oath, and the witnesses.

15. Investigation Subsequent to the Confession

At the conclusion of a successful interrogation, the investigator, although he is in possession of a written confession, should not yield to a feeling of complacency. The investigation should not be considered complete until the confession has been critically reviewed in relation to the charge. The following points should be considered:

a. On the information available, can it be said that the elements of proof have been established?

b. What substantiating evidence is needed to sustain the facts which are contained in the statement or which have been developed in the interrogation?

c. Is there sufficient evidence, independent of the confession, which can be presented in court to show that the offense charged has probably been committed by someone? The significance of the question lies in the fact that, normally, an accused cannot be convicted upon his confession or admission unless his statement is substantiated by other evidence. Moreover, the court may not consider the confession as evidence against the defendant unless there is in the record of trial other evidence, either direct or circumstantial, that the crime charged has probably been committed. Additional confessions by the accused cannot be used to corroborate information found in any one of the confessions.

16. Admissibility of Confessions

A confession which is obtained under duress or by compulsion or without the continuous presence of the prescribed constitutional safeguards is inadmissible in court. The investigator who obtains a confession through the employment of illegal practices renders inadmissible not only the suspect's statement but very likely the evidence which might subsequently be developed from the leads contained in the statement. Hence great care and sound judgment must be exercised in obtaining a confession to avoid casting a shadow on its legality. The investigator must have a thorough knowledge of the court requirements for admissibility and of the procedural safeguards and standards of conduct by which it is insured.

a. **Tests for Admissibility.** The test employed by state and federal courts for the admissibility of a confession is the following: *A confession must be voluntary and trustworthy, and it must have been obtained by civilized police practices.* The Supreme Court requires more than the voluntary-trustworthy test in demanding that the police methods should not be "inherently coercive" and should be attended continuously by the prescribed protective devices. Regardless of the actual effect of the police behavior on the accused in giving the confession, the Supreme Court requires that this behavior should not even have a *tendency* to compel a confession. Further, the Court considers the susceptibilities of the individual defendant in these cases rather than the police methods in general.

b. **Meeting the Tests.** In the present and the preceding chapter a number of the procedural safeguards for meeting the test of admissibility have been treated. They are summarized below:

1) *Fourfold Warning.* The foremost requirement, upon which later admissibility of a confession depends, is that a fourfold warning be given to a person before he is questioned.

2) *Proof of Waiver.* To forgo these rights an affirmative statement of rejection is required. No conclusion can be drawn from a suspect's silence after the warnings have been given. An express statement, preferably written and witnessed, that the suspect is willing to make a statement and does not wish an attorney may constitute a satisfactory waiver. In any event, a positive showing

should be made to meet "the high standards of proof of waiver of constitutional rights required by the Court."

3) *Proof of Voluntariness.* "The voluntariness doctrine . . . encompasses all interrogation practices which are likely to exert such pressure on an individual as to disable him from making a free and rational choice." Again, the investigator should be prepared to make a positive showing to the effect that the statement or confession was voluntarily given.

4) *Record of Conduct.* The record of the interrogation, including the investigator's notes and the interrogation log, should reflect the continuous availability of protective devices for the suspect's rights, the absence of any threats, tricks, or cajolings to obtain a waiver of rights, and the absence of all forms of duress and coercion in the conduct of the interrogation as described below. The testimony of witnesses is part of the record.

17. Forms of Duress and Coercion

Police behavior which would adversely affect the admissibility of a confession may be classified into three types of restraint: *Coercion, Duress,* and *Psychological Constraint.*

a. **Coercion.** The term *coercion* connotes the idea of physical force; it is the direct application of illegal physical methods. This obviously refers to beatings or forms of assault such as hitting with a rubber hose or newspaper, punching, using glaring lights, administering cathartics, placing a man in a brace, forms of torture, and so forth. The threat of such abuse is also included in this category.

b. **Duress.** Duress is taken here in the legal sense to mean the imposition of restrictions on physical behavior. This includes prolonged (six hours, for example) detention in a dark cell; privation of food or sleep; imposing conditions of excessive physical discomfort; and continuous interrogation over extraordinarily long periods such as twenty-four hours. If arrangements are made for appropriate intervals of rest, the investigator may interrogate over reasonable (reasonable, that is, in relation to the amount of information that is required in the case) periods of time, several days or weeks, for example, without violating this prohibition against duress provided, of course, the protective devices are continuously available to the accused—that is, the accused should at all times be able to invoke his right to remain silent and his right to have counsel present. In considering the probable effects of indirect physical abuse in the form of duress, the age, sex, temperament, and physical condition of the subject must be considered.

c. **Psychological Constraint.** The free action of the will may be unlawfully restrained by threats or other methods of instilling fear. Moral restraint by means of threats can destroy the voluntariness of a confession. Obliquely suggesting the prospect of harm to the suspect, his relatives, or his property can be interpreted as psychological abuse even though these suggestions do not assume the form of explicit threats. A susceptible person could, under these circumstances, be induced to give a false confession. It is sufficient that the subject reasonably thought he was placed in sufficient danger. To tell the subject that he will be hanged or given over to a mob unless he confesses or to state that he will be sent to jail for more serious crimes is sufficient to affect admissibility. Some courts have gone so far as to hold that the use of the following statements constitutes a threat: "You had better confess"; or "It would be better for you to confess"; or even, "You had better tell the *truth.*" However, it is permitted to employ the following techniques: to tell the subject that the police will discover the truth anyway; that the subject may tell what he wishes and run the risk of imprisonment; to display impatience with the subject's story; and to give the underlying impression that the investigator considers the subject guilty.

18. Deception and Promises

No deception, promises, threats, tricks, or cajolings may be used to obtain from the suspect a waiver of his rights. If we assume, now, that waivers have been properly obtained and the suspect has submitted to interrogation, to what extent may the investigator use deception and promises in his questioning without jeopardizing the legality of a confession or statement?

a. **Employment of Trickery and Deception.** Trickery and deception may be used if it is not of such a nature as to make an innocent person confess. The following are examples of deceptions that have been considered permissible in both state and federal courts:

1) Informing the subject that his accomplice just confessed.

2) Informing the subject that he has failed a polygraph test.

3) Pretending that his fingerprint has been found on the weapon.

4) Pretending that cogent evidence such as additional witnesses or documents exist.

b. **Employment of Promises.** The use of promises may render a confession inadmissible. The following test should be applied: Is the promise of such a nature that it is likely to cause the subject to make a confession?

Examples of the substance of promises which can render a confession inadmissible are:

1) Release from custody.

2) Cessation of prosecution.

3) Pardon.

4) Lighter sentence.

5) Grant of immunity or remission of sentence.

6) Prosecution for only one of several crimes.

19. Other Uses of Confessions

a. **Confessions of Several Crimes.** It is not desirable to permit a number of crimes to be included in the confession. In a trial for one crime it is ordinarily not permissible to bring in evidence which shows that the defendant committed another crime except where the additional crimes tend to establish:

1) Intent.

2) Guilty knowledge.

3) Identity of the defendant.

4) The scheme used in the commission of the crime being tried.

Actually, if the additional crime is part of the same transaction, the confession is admissible. A written confession, however, should be drawn up with one offense in view.

b. **Use of One Defendant's Confession Against Another.** A confession of a defendant may be used against his accomplice if the latter, when first knowing of the confession, fails to deny it. The confession cannot be used unless the confessor himself so testifies in court or unless the confession had previously been made in the presence of the accomplice and he failed to deny it. Thus, the investigator, on receiving such a confession, should have the confessor confront the accomplice with the accusation. In many states, the silence of the accomplice may be used as evidence of his guilt.

c. **Use of an Illegally Obtained Confession to Impeach the Defendant's Testimony.** Ordinarily, a confession in violation of the *Miranda* rules is not admissible in court. However, in *Harris v. New York* (401 U.S. 222 1971) the Supreme Court decided that if the defendant takes the stand to testify in his own defense, statements obtained in violation of *Miranda* rules may be used to impeach that testimony. Although an illegally obtained confession cannot be introduced as substantive evidence against the defendant, it can be used to challenge his testimony.

20. Summary

It should be apparent that the matter of a confession must be approached by the investigator with great caution. The subject must be advised of his constitutional rights. Threats or other forms of duress should be avoided. Oral confessions are valid, but written ones are obviously preferable. Witnesses should be present to the confession and its circumstances. An accused should be taken before a committing magistrate within the time limit provided by statute. Finally, if wrong police methods have been used in interrogation, it is possible to later obtain a valid confession by showing that the threats or other abusive influences had been removed and that their effect could no longer be reasonably said to exist.

ADDITIONAL READING

Confessions

Burke, J.J.: Confessions to Private Persons. 42 *FBI Law Enforcement Bulletin,* 8, 1973.

Inbau, F.E.: Legally Permissible Criminal Interrogation Tactics and Techniques. 4 *Journal of Police Science and Administration,* 249, 1976.

Inbau, F.E., Reid, J.E. and Buckley, J.P.: *Criminal Interrogation and Confessions,* 3rd ed. Baltimore, Williams and Wilkins, 1986.

Invergo, M.: Questioning Techniques and Written Statements. 5 *Police Law Quarterly,* 3, 1976.

Kamisar, Y.: *Police Interrogation and Confessions.* Ann Arbor, University of Michigan Press, 1980.

Klotter, J.C. and Kanovitz, J.R.: *Constitutional Law,* 6th ed. Cincinnati, Anderson, 1991.

Macdonald, J.M. and Michaud, D.L.: *The Confession: Interrogation and Criminal Profiles for Police Officers.* Denver, Col.: Apache Press, 1987.

Nissman, D.M., Hagen, E. and Brooks, P.R.: *Law of Confessions.* Rochester, Lawyers Co-operative, 1985.

Riley, C.E. III: Confessions and Interrogation: The Use of Artifice, Strategem, and Deception. 51 *FBI Law Enforcement Bulletin,* 4, 1982.

——: Confessions and the Sixth Amendment Right to Counsel. Parts I and II. 52 *FBI Law Enforcement Bulletin,* 8 and 9, 1983.

Robin, G.D.: Juvenile Interrogation and Confessions. 10 *Journal of Police Science and Administration,* 224, 1982.

Schafer, W.J.: *Confessions and Statements.* Springfield, Ill.: Thomas, 1968.

Tousignant, D.D.: Why Suspects Confess. 60 *FBI Law Enforcement Bulletin,* 3, 1991.

Chapter 11

RECORDING INTERVIEWS AND INTERROGATIONS

1. Methods of Reproduction

AN INTERVIEW or an interrogation may not be considered a success unless it is faithfully reproduced in its significant parts. The retention of information received in a sensitive interview is a recurring problem of investigation which may be solved in a number of ways.

a. **Mental Notes.** Relying on simple memory has the advantage of permitting an uninterrupted flow of information without inspiring caution by the appearance of pencil and paper. The disadvantages are obvious. The untrained memory may come away from an interview with little more than a general impression and a few phrases.

b. **Written Notes.** Although a great improvement over mere memory, written notes must necessarily be sketchy. They suffice to record significant data. As a tool of the routine interview, they are satisfactory. An interrogation, which may be accompanied by an oral confession, requires more exact reproduction. A flood of information may overwhelm the interrogator when dealing with a subject who suddenly becomes willing to speak freely.

c. **Stenographic Notes.** The presence of a stenographer may deter a hesitant subject. Moreover, the investigator seldom has stenographic facilities at his disposal.

d. **Tape Recording.** Tape recording has been found to be the simplest and most practical means of reproducing the interview or the interrogation. It requires, of course, physical preparation and a moderate degree of technical facility.

e. **Videotape.** The ideal solution is the videotape, that combination of sound and sight which most nearly represents to the senses the event itself. In an important case where the subject confesses, a videotape of his statement will provide the most convincing evidence for presentation to the jury.

2. Recording

One of the characteristics of modern criminal investigation is the extensive use of recording devices for the production of a transcript of interviews and interrogations. Obviously, the best evidence of an interview is the recorded voice. The words themselves are there; the tones and inflection provide the true meaning; the author of the statement is identifiable. For these and other reasons, wherever it is possible and practicable, an effort is made to record an important interview. Although the recording of a conversation appears at first glance to be a fairly simple process, the investigator who attempts a transcript without training and preparation usually must learn by the embarrassing deficiencies of his initial efforts that there is both an art and a science associated with this branch of investigative work. Because of the wide variety, both in size and quality, of the recording systems on the market, no attempt at a treatment of the technical aspects of these instruments would be feasible in this compass.

3. Types of Recording

There are two general types of recording: the overt and the surreptitious, the use of each being suggested by the nature of the case.

a. **Overt Transcripts.** Often there is no need to conceal the fact that a recording is being made of an interview. The suggestion to record the conversation may be made by the investigator or the interviewee. Some men occupying important positions make a practice of recording such interviews for their own protection. The nature of the interview will determine whether the investigator should suggest that a recording be made. If the witness is "friendly to the prosecution" and the information which he has to offer is somewhat complicated in nature, the most practical procedure is to request permission to record. A courtesy copy of the record may be given to the interviewee if he so requests. The advantage of this solution to the reproduction problem is the relative ease with which the recording can be made with the cooperation of both parties. Recordings of telephone conversations can also be more simply made with permission of the subject. Arrangements can be made with the telephone company for the necessary apparatus. A fifteen-second signal is imposed on the line to inform the subject that a recording is being made.

b. **Surreptitious Transcripts.** More commonly, the recording of an interview or an interrogation will be made without the knowledge of the subject. Sensitive interviews and interrogations should always be recorded in important cases. The following embrace most of the situations which will be encountered by the investigator:

1) *Interrogation Room.* The room set apart for interrogations or for interviews in the offices of the law enforcement agency should be equipped with a permanent recording installation. The live telephone (the mouthpiece is rewired to bypass the hook switch and transmit sound) is the preferred instrument. A leading manufacturer of security equipment produces a cassette recorder disguised as a book. It can record up to four hours while nestled inconspicuously in a bookcase.

2) *Rooms Prepared on Short Notice.* If the subject must be interviewed at some place other than the investigator's office, it will be necessary to make an installation in a relatively short time. The telephone can be made into a live microphone or one can be installed in a desk. Whatever arrangements are made, they should be carefully tested beforehand. Failures are quite common as a result of the work of inexperienced technicians.

3) *Unprepared Meeting Places.* If the interview must take place in a room, automobile, or restaurant without previous technical preparation, a pocket recorder can be used or one which is concealed in a briefcase. The investigator can be *wired* for the occasion, i.e., a microphone and small recorder can be attached to his person and concealed beneath his clothes.

4) *Telephone Conversations.* In recording interviews which take place over the telephone, special equipment must be used. In some communities, the legality of the procedure must be considered.

4. Purpose of Recording

The techniques and care exercised in making a recording will vary with the purpose of the interview or the interrogation.

a. **Interview.** If the purpose of the interview is merely to obtain information, no special technique is required. Where the information is to be used as evidence, as in the case of a witness who may later refuse to testify, the precautions described below must be observed.

b. **Interrogation.** The purpose in recording an interrogation may be one of the following:

1) *Evidence for Court Presentation.* Admissions and confessions should be reproduced. If the subject later refuses to make a formal confession or changes his "story," the recording can serve as evidence.

2) *Contradictions.* During the interrogation the subject may deny guilt or knowledge of the crime and may offer elaborate alibis and excuses. If he is persistently interrogated, he may contradict himself or fall into inconsistencies. By recording the interrogation and playing it back to the subject, he may be brought to appreciate the futility of deception.

3) *Implication of Associates.* The information supplied by the subject may tend to show the guilt of associates or accomplices. The record can later be played for the associates for the purpose of inducing them to confess.

4) *Assisting Later Interrogations.* In the first interrogation of the subject, a long and relatively complicated story or recital of facts will often be given. At the moment it may be difficult for the interrogator to detect the weak points or the inconsistencies in the subject's statement. To further question by wild guessing or improving with the data at hand may weaken the position of the interrogator and give confidence to the subject. If the interrogation is interrupted after the first recital of the story, the investigator can leisurely listen to the statement, analyze it for consistency and credibility, and check certain points for trustworthiness. After determining the weak points, he can then plan the strategy and tactics to be employed in the next interrogation session.

5. Techniques

The mechanics and physical principles of recording are described in textbooks and manuals. Additional instructions can be obtained from the manufacturer's directions for the equipment used. The present section deals with the tactics that must be employed by the investigator in order to obtain an effective recording of an interview for the purpose of evidence.

a. **Radio Techniques.** The methods of recording are those of radio broadcasting and not television. The investigator must put himself in the position of the future listener. A recording made by an untrained investigator may result in a meaningless jumble of voices and unintelligible references. The investigator must imagine himself as a radio director. The performance must be managed so that the listener can understand *what* is being said; by *whom* it is being spoken; and *what object* is being referred to at any given moment. In a surreptitious recording, the investigator is at the disadvantage of being restrained from giving explicit directions; he must avoid by obvious mannerisms divulging the fact of the recording.

b. **Identifying Persons.** The interview may involve two or three persons. Since many persons have voices which are not readily distinguishable, for the recording to serve as evidence the voices must be identified as being those of specific individuals. To achieve an identification of voices, the investigator should refer to the interviewees as often as possible by name. This can be conveniently accomplished under the guise of excessive courtesy. A statement may be associated with a definite person by tagging the conclusion with a remark addressed to the author such as, "Was that on Tuesday, Mr. Smith?" or "Was that the same check, Mr. Jones?" The statement can also be associated by a leading question such as "What did Brown say to you, Mr. Smith?"

c. **Identifying Objects.** If the recording is made by an inexperienced investigator, sentences such as the following may be heard: "I gave him this other check"; or "He made this entry in the book." Such statements are not effective for evidence purposes because the object to which reference is made cannot be identified by the listener from the recording alone. The investigator should follow such a statement by an identifying question of his own, such as "You mean check number four, Mr. Smith?" or "That is, he wrote these words 'No Sales' on line 14 of page 24. Is that correct, Mr. Jones?" Although these statements may appear stilted on paper, to the interviewee they will seem to be the normal plodding methods of the mediocre investigator. The investigator may not impress the interviewee with these tedious, repetitious questions, but he will rescue the recording from becoming a meaningless recital of untagged pronouns.

d. **Describing Physical Action.** If the interviewee's statements involve the simulation of some physical act, the investigator must manage to include a description of the action in the recording. For example, the victim of an assault may, as part of his narrative, imitate the motions of his assailant in delivering a blow and accompany the action with some non-descriptive sentence such as "He hit me here like this. . . . " The investigator can then follow such a statement with a few clarifying sentences. "Let me get this straight, Mr. Brown. You were standing sideways, 2 feet from Black when Black swung his right fist and hit you on the back of the neck just below the left ear. Have I got it right?"

e. **Overt Transcripts.** If the recording is being made with the knowledge and consent of the interviewee, more elaborate precautions can be made to clarify the identity of the speakers and the objects to which reference is made. If there are a number of persons present, the speaker may be identified before he begins. If several speakers overlap, a request can be made to repeat the statements separately. At various points in the interview, it may be necessary to make statements which are not properly part of the recording. Agreements can then be made to "go off the record." The investigator should then make specific oral statements such as "Going off the record." and "Back on the record."

f. **Surreptitious Recordings by the Interviewee.** It has been previously stated that persons occupying positions of importance often protect themselves from possible future complications such as misquotations by secretly making their own recordings. Whenever an investigator conducts an interview in the office of such a person, he should assume that such a recording is being made and guide his own conversation accordingly. He should make the supposition that the interviewee has thrown a switch and that a concealed microphone is recording his conversation. In this way he can avoid statements or remarks that are susceptible to later misinterpretation to the detriment of the investigation or the investigator's reputation.

6. Videotaping Confessions

In all important felony cases, confessions should be video-taped. In the standard hearing that takes place before a trial to decide whether the confession was voluntarily made and, hence, admissible, a videotape of the confession provides the strongest possible evidence. It is difficult for the defense attorney to claim that his client was coerced when confronted with the sight and sound of his client freely recounting his deed. By recording the conduct of the police, it protects them from false allegations. Another advantage of a videotaped confession is that it leads to a great increase in guilty pleas, saving an enormous sum in court costs. Few suspects will retract their confession and insist on their innocence knowing that the jury will be viewing the entire video record of their statement.

a. **Equipment.** The subject will be seated in a quiet room. There should not be any police equipment visible, nor should police sounds such as radios or sirens be heard. A clock is placed in view to assure that no erasures have been made. The investigator should never attempt to videotape the session himself. A trained technician should be available who can testify about the quality of the equipment, the techniques employed, as well as the identification, the sealing, and the chain of custody of the videotape evidence.

b. **Procedure.** It is important to remember that the videotape is additional documentation of the confession and is not a substitute for a written confession. For this reason a written confession should be obtained before the videotaping begins. If for some reason the videotape is found not to be admissible, the investigator may still use the written confession.

1) *Preliminary.* Normally, permission is requested from the suspect to videotape the proceedings. The investigator begins

with a statement of the date, time, and location of the interview. He identifies the people present and appears briefly on camera with the suspect. The suspect is requested to waive his rights on tape or at least make reference to the fact that he had previously understood and signed such a statement.

2) *Taping.* The tape should be kept running with the suspect and the clock continually in view. Any interruptions in the taping are to be accounted for in the interrogation log. Normal refreshments and courtesies are extended and videotaped to demonstrate that the suspect is not under duress. An object of evidence can be properly documented by having the suspect identify it and read the serial number of the object on camera. When the taping is concluded a typewritten transcript should be made so that in preparing for a trial the tape won't have to be continually played.

ADDITIONAL READING

Recording Interrogation

Gebhardt, R.H.: Video Tape in Criminal Cases. 44 *FBI Law Enforcement Bulletin,* 5, 1975.

Hollien, H.: *The Acoustics of Crime: The New Science of Forensic Phonetics.* New York, Plenum Press, 1990.

Koenig, B.E.: Making Effective Forensic Audio Tape Recordings. 56 *FBI Law Enforcement Bulletin,* 5, 1987.

McDonald, W.H.: The Use of Videotaping in Documenting Confessions. 50 *Police Chief,* 2, 1983.

Rifas, R.A.: *Legal Aspects of Video Tape and Motion Pictures in Law Enforcement.* Evanston, Ill.: Traffic Institute, Northwestern University, 1972.

Chapter 12

INFORMANTS

1. General

THE TRADITIONAL shortcut to the solution of a crime or to the location of a wanted person is the informant. The practical investigator who is pressed by a heavy case load must perforce rely heavily upon this source of information. A good proportion of important cases are solved by means of informants. The social level of the informant will vary with the nature of the offense or inquiry. The investigator must know his way about the taverns, bowling alleys, pool halls, and other hangouts of his area. He must fraternize with people at all levels of society: bartenders, cab drivers, doormen, bootblacks, waiters, maids, janitors, window cleaners, security personnel, night watchmen, milkmen, and, in general, all those who see their fellow citizens from a special point of vantage. These are the persons who will constitute the cadre of informants that may aid the investigator's work immeasurably. Often information will be voluntarily offered by those whose motives spring from good citizenship. In general, however, the motives of the informant should not prohibit the enjoyment of his confidence. At times it will be necessary to repay the informant by favors or by cash. In any case, the payment should take a form in accordance with professional ethics. For convenience we may make the following distinction between informants:

a. In general an *informant* is a person who gives information to the investigator. He may do this openly and even offer to be a witness, or he may inform surreptitiously and request to remain anonymous.

b. A *confidential informant* is a person who provides an investigator with confidential information concerning a past or projected crime and does not wish to be known as the source of the information. The investigator must take special precautions to protect the identity of such an informant since his value as a source is lost on disclosure.

2. Motives

The motives for revealing information are numerous and it becomes the investigator's responsibility to evaluate the informant and the information given in order to arrive at the truth. Some of the more common motives are:

a. **Vanity.** The self-aggrandizing person who delights in giving information to gain favorable attention from the police authorities.

b. **Civic-mindedness.** The public-spirited person of good standing in the community who is interested in seeing that justice is done.

c. **Fear.** The person under an illusion of oppression by enemies or of other impending danger.

d. **Repentance.** The person, usually an accomplice, who has a change of heart and wishes to report a crime that is preying on his conscience.

e. **Avoidance of Punishment.** The person who is apprehended in the commission of a minor offense and seeks to avoid prosecution by revealing information concerning a major crime.

f. **Gratitude or Gain.** The person who gives information to express appreciation or obtain a privilege, such as one who is arrested and desires cigarettes or other items or a former prisoner who wishes to repay the police officer's interest in the welfare of his family during his detention.

g. **Competition.** The person (usually one earning a living by questionable means) who wishes to eliminate his competitor.

h. **Revenge.** The person who wishes to settle a grudge because someone else informed against him, took advantage of him, or otherwise injured him.

i. **Jealousy.** A person who is envious of the accomplishments or possessions of another and wishes to humiliate him.

j. **Remuneration.** The person who informs solely for the pecuniary or other material gain he is to receive.

3. Obtaining Confidential Informants

An effective investigator of criminal offenses in a localized area usually has a number of confidential informants drawn from various classes and occupations. He has developed their friendship and cooperation over the course of years. In the investigation of a suspect he can sometimes find in his group of informants one or two who are in a position to observe the subject. When operating in other than his usual area the assistance of another investigator can be sought in obtaining informants.

4. Protecting the Informant

The investigator should compromise neither himself nor the informant in his pursuit of information. He should make no unethical promises or "deals," and should not undertake commitments which he cannot fulfill. He should safeguard the identity of his informant, first as a matter of ethical practice and second because of the danger of undermining the confidence of his sources. Wherever possible he should accept the information on the terms of the informant. The identity of informants should not be disclosed unless absolutely necessary and then only to the proper authorities. To preserve this secrecy, each confidential informant may be assigned a number, symbol, or fictitious name, and should be referred to by such designation in reports. To avoid discovery of identity of the confidential informant, great care must be exercised when a meeting or communication is contemplated. Confidential informants should not be called to testify in court. Such action would reveal their relationship and would terminate the informant's sources of information or invite vengeance upon him. Nevertheless, in extraordinary circumstances it may be practicable and desirable to summon a confidential informant as a witness in court. The general rule governing the safeguarding of the identity of confidential informants by law enforcement officers on the witness stand in trials has been announced in *Wilson v. United States* (59 F2d 390, 392) as follows: "It is the right and the duty of every citizen of the United States to communicate to the executive officer of the government charged with the duty of enforcing the law all the information which he has of the commission of an offense against the laws of the United States, and such information is privileged as a confidential communication which the courts will not compel or permit to be disclosed without the consent of the government. Such evidence is excluded, not for the protection of the witness, but because of the policy of the laws; . . . however, . . . a trial court must dispose of the case before it. If what is asked is essential evidence to vindicate the innocence of the accused or lessen the risk of false testimony, or is essential to the proper disposition of the case, disclosure will be compelled."

5. Treatment of Informants

After the investigator has been stationed in an area for a period of time, he has developed numerous sources of information, including persons from all walks of life. The treatment of the informant in the investigator-informant relationship is an individual problem based upon personality, education, and occupation. The investigator's sources of information are only valuable if they are able to obtain desired information or if they are willing to volunteer known information. To aid the investigator some general rules regarding this relationship with informants are listed:

a. **Fair Treatment.** The informant should be treated considerately, regardless of his character, education, or occupation.

b. **Reliability.** The investigator should be scrupulous in the fulfillment of all ethical promises which he has made. Any other policy results in distrust and a loss of the informant.

c. **Control.** The informant should not be permitted to take charge of any phase of the investigation.

6. Communicating with the Informant

In order to avoid revealing the status of the informant, careful judgment must be used in communication. The following points should be observed:

a. Meetings should be held at a place other than the investigator's office.

b. The circumstances surrounding the meetings should not be repeated to the extent that a recognizable pattern is created.

c. The proper name of the informant should not be used in telephoning. Designation by code is advisable for obvious reasons.

d. The investigator's organization should not be identified in any correspondence with the informant.

7. Dismissal of Informants

If after a period of time an informant becomes undesirable, the investigator should advise his supervisor of the situation and arrange for a debriefing of the informant. In accomplishing the debriefing, the investigator should avoid antagonizing the informant or otherwise creating a reaction unfavorable to the organization. If a record of the informant is maintained, the reasons for or the circumstances surrounding his dismissal should be also placed in writing, since the question of his usefulness may arise in the future. Among the more common reasons are ineptitude, compromise of identity, security risk, criminal record or act, and submitting false information. Often an informant will be dismissed without prejudice when he requests such action or when his services are no longer required.

8. Evaluating Informants

The investigator should continually evaluate his informants and form an estimate of their reliability. The information received should be tested for consistency by checking against information obtained from other persons. The motives and interests of the informer should be considered in the evaluation. The reports or leads from either known or unknown informers should be considered potentially valuable and should be developed by the investigation according to their significance until their true value is determined. Often these "tips" will prove to be groundless. The investigator should not, however, become excessively skeptical in the face of disappointments and should be receptive to future information. Finally, in dealing with anonymous persons who voluntarily offer information by telephone, he should remember that such persons ordinarily do not call back once they have delivered their message. Hence he should endeavor to draw out all relevant information before the anonymous caller ends the conversation.

9. Potential Informants

The following is a partial list of persons who because of their occupations may be in a position to supply useful information, depending upon the nature of the investigation:

Barbers
Bartenders
Beauty shop operators
Club and association secretaries
Deliverymen
Dry cleaners
Employment agency clerks
Gas station attendants
Grocers
Gunsmiths
Hotel managers, bellboys, telephone operators
Household servants
Insurance investigators
Janitors, maids, window cleaners
Locksmiths

Money lenders
Neighbors
Newspaper reporters, editors
Parking lot operators
Postal workers
Prostitutes
Public utility employees
Race track employees and bookmakers
Rental agency clerks and agents
Restaurant employees and entertainers
Tailors
Waiters and waitresses

10. Informant's Status

The informant belongs to the organization and not to the individual investigator. Hence, the information concerning the identity of the informant should be maintained in a central file. The following points are important:
   a. The supervisor should *personally* maintain the file.
   b. The classification of the file should be at least confidential.

c. The informant should be assigned a code designation consisting of the local office number and his number. Thus an informant in squad office 31 might have the designation 31-9.

d. The informant's name should never be used in reports. It should be referred to by symbol only.

e. Copies of the informant's file should be prepared on index cards for filing at the local office and at headquarters.

11. Methods of Private Investigators

It is appropriate at this point to discuss briefly the operations of the private investigator, who has in recent years developed to an art the work of obtaining information. Naturally the methods of the private investigator are not greatly restricted. Unembarrassed by public scrutiny, his activities can exceed the bounds that delimit the acceptable scope of the operations of the law enforcement agent. Much of the work of private investigators is devoted to credit and background reports designed to uncover insurance, security, and general personnel risks. About one-fourth of the private agency cases are concerned with domestic problems such as divorces and missing persons. Only 5 percent are criminal defense cases. It may be said that private investigative work requires two major talents: the ability to conduct surveillances and ingenuity in developing information. Some of the methods used are listed here but it is not suggested that they may be conscionably used in law enforcement work.

a. **Contacts.** Deprived of the authority that permits law enforcement agents to have access to official records and other sources of information, the private detective must rely for his intelligence on "contacts" and "cooperation." In some situations the desired information can be bought; in others it can be obtained in exchange. Thus, some private investigators by enlisting the clandestine aid of an employee can obtain unlisted telephone numbers, telephone toll calls data, telegram messages, address records of utility companies, and hotel registrations. Through a "connection," such as an unscrupulous clerk, he can obtain from federal, state and municipal agencies many types of records: civil service histories, military and social security records, automobile registrations, income tax payments, and mail covers. Even members of law-enforcement agencies are sometimes willing to become sources of information, expecting in turn to be assisted by the private detective in the same manner.

b. **Other Methods.** The ingenuity of the private detective enables him to develop temporary sources in a short time to suit the needs of a case. Trades people, such as utility service men, milk delivery men, and mailmen, owners of grocery stores, pharmacies and newsstands, disgruntled employees, unfriendly neighbors, business competitors, and many others respond to the knowing tactics of the experienced investigator. He may pose as a federal investigator or an insurance representative depending on the layman's credulity for the acceptance of his "credentials." He may manage to obtain the office trash of a company or subject by an arrangement with the collector, by renting his own trash removal truck, or by renting an office in the same building and substituting his own trash container for that of the subject. The list of ruses employed by the private investigator would, perhaps, require several chapters for adequate treatment. The following may serve as an example: One detective pursuing matrimonial cases obtains hotel registration records by requesting permission of the manager under the guise of investigating a bad check. The pretense is supported by a check, made out by the detective, bearing the subject's signature which is to be compared with the registration.

ADDITIONAL READING

Informants

Brown, M.F.: Criminal Informants: Some Observations on Use, Abuse, and Control. 13 *Journal of Police Science and Administration* 3, 1985.

Crawford, K.K.: Cellmate Informants: A Constitutional Guide to Their Use. 59 *FBI Law Enforcement Bulletin,* 12, 1990.

Earhart, R.S.: *A Critical Analysis of Investigator—Criminal Informant Relationship in Law Enforcement.* Washington, D.C.: International Association of Chiefs of Police, 1964.

Gutterman, M.: The Informer Privilege. 58 *Journal of Criminal Law, Criminology and Police Science,* 32, 1967.

Harney, M.L. and Cross, J.C.: *The Informer in Law Enforcement,* 2nd ed. Springfield, Ill.: Thomas, 1968.

The Informer Privilege: What's in a Name? 64 *Journal of Criminal Law and Criminology,* 56, 1973.

Luger, J.: *Snitch: A Handbook for Informers.* Port Townsend, Wash.: Loompanics, 1991.

McCann, M.G.: *Police and the Confidential Informant.* Bloomington, Indiana University Press, 1957.

McClean, J.D.: Informers and Agents Provocateurs. *Criminal Law Review,* 527, 1969.

McGuiness, R.L.: Probable Cause: Informant Information. Parts I and II. 51 *FBI Law Enforcement Bulletin,* 11 and 12, 1982.

Morris, J.: *Police Informant Management.* Orangeville, Calif.: Palmer Enterprises, 1983.

Mount, H.A., Jr.: Criminal Informants: An Administrator's Dream or Nightmare. 59 *FBI Law Enforcement Bulletin,* 12, 1990.

Reese, J.T.: Motivations of Criminal Informants. 49 *FBI Law Enforcement Bulletin,* 5, 1980.

Rissler, L.E.: The Informer-Witness. 46 *FBI Law Enforcement Bulletin,* 5, 1977.

Chapter 13

TRACING AND SOURCES
OF INFORMATION

1. Introduction

A GREAT PART of investigative work is devoted to "finding" missing or wanted persons. The solving of a case frequently depends upon locating the perpetrator. The proper presentation of a case in court involves the discovery and identification of witnesses. The search for a person is frequently a simple matter of a few telephone calls or a visit to a house. At other times, however, the hunt can become a lengthy and complicated ordeal.

The search for persons commonly requires a concomitant search of records and an application to various sources of information. The term *tracing* is used here to describe all of these procedures. A patient study of records and the acquisition of information from official sources and private agencies are frequently required in order to obtain additional evidence as well as to locate or to identify a person.

One of the most hackneyed aphorisms of investigative work is the maxim, "An investigator is no better than his information." Ordinarily this principle is used in reference to unofficial sources of information such as confidential informants. In a very true sense, however, it is applicable to *all* the sources of information, official as well as unofficial, which are available to the investigator. The detective who depends exclusively on tips and personal interviews to the exclusion of the official sources hinders himself in his work. He is inefficient and is, in fact, operating at only a fraction of his true capacity. Often a vital point of information can be readily obtained by a reference to so obvious a source as the telephone book or by a simple visit to the public library, but instead many investigators will spend weeks clarifying this point by personal interviewing of witnesses. This neglect of informative sources is usually attributable to the tradition in which many detectives are nurtured. Newspaper reporters and private investigators are trained to habits of research. The police, however, because of their ready access to the confidence of private persons, have a tendency to deal with these exclusively and, since they are usually pressed for time, to remain in ignorance of the methods of the research type of investigation. In the following discussion many of the available official sources are listed.

2. Tracing a Missing Person (Witness, Victim, or Other)

In searching for a person, the aim of the investigator is first to obtain the information necessary to identify him beyond question. His pedigree, social, business, and criminal history will form the basis of the identification. The facts uncovered through informants should be verified by an examination of informative records. The investigator, in locating a missing or wanted person, should use the simplest facilities first. An example of this direct procedure is given below.

a. **The Telephone.** The investigator should telephone the home of the missing person (unless, of course, the request for a search has come from the home). Ask simple direct questions. Is he home? Where has he gone? What is his present address? Naturally, for the latter questions the investigator will be required to identify himself. Telephone the employer of the missing person and ask a series of similar questions. Telephone friends and relatives and make inquiries. Obviously the investigator should follow up any leads he obtains from these sources.

b. **Visit the Home.** If telephone inquiries are fruitless, the investigator should visit the house. He can question the family; or, if the family has moved, he can make inquiries of the neighbors and discover the habits and haunts of the missing person. He should endeavor to learn as much as possible concerning the habits, haunts, and social life of the missing person. Since the average person is strongly ruled by habits, we should expect him in his new surroundings to do the things that he likes to do and to which he is accustomed. The state of mind of the missing person is important. Some conclusions can be reached concerning this by questioning the family. Was he worried or nervous? What were his plans or ambitions? Were his home and vocational conditions satisfactory? Did he draw any pay or any money from the bank? What was the condition of his room? Who saw him last? What was the conversation? How did he behave when last seen? The superintendent, landlord, or realty agent can be interviewed to find the name of the mover or to examine the lease for references. The local tavern, drug store, filling station, and stationery store should be visited.

c. **Record of Change of Address.** The following sources may have a record of the change of address:

Post Office
Board of Education
Board of Elections
Motor Vehicle Bureau
Tax Assessment Lists
Bank
Census
Haulers and Movers

(The other sources listed below should then be consulted for possible leads.)

d. **Mail Covers.** The post office can be particularly helpful in many cases. A request can be made of the post office inspector to have a mail cover placed on the homes of relatives. A copy will then be made, including the mailing place and date stamp, return address if any, and all other markings present on the front and back of each piece of mail sent to the address being covered. A cover is usually placed on mail for two weeks or a month. The post office does not open the subject's mail. It simply maintains a list of postmarks and names of return addresses on mail cover. Consideration should be given to the work involved. A request should be made only when useful results can be reasonably expected. The request should state the specific period of time for which the mail cover is needed. It should not run in excess of sixty days. If the desired information is obtained before that, the cover should be canceled. An investigation office should maintain an index of all current mail covers. Even though no obvious lead is obtained, attention should be paid to typewritten letters, especially if several are sent from a particular mailing point and no return address is given, for they undoubtedly are not business letters. If specimen handwriting of the missing person is obtained it can be compared with the copies made while the mail cover is in operation. If the writing on any piece of mail appears similar, it merits further investigation.

e. **Mail Ruse.** A useful ruse employed in tracing by mail is that of sending a special delivery or registered letter bearing the subject's name to the address of a friend or relative who may know the subject's hideout. The mail supervisor is instructed not to deliver the letter, but to say that it must be sent or called for at the post office by the addressee. Since the relative will imagine that the letter contains an important message or document, he will get in touch with the fugitive. The mail of the fugitive and the friend should, of course, be covered in this situation.

f. **Criss-Cross Directory.** When interviewing neighbors of the missing person, a lot of time and energy can be conserved with the use of the "criss-cross" or "reverse directory." This book lists the telephone subscribers of a city or a region according to their street address rather than their name. The directory is arranged with the streets listed alphabetically and the houses or apartments on that street in numerical order. The criss-cross directories are compiled from phone company records by private publishers who sell the information to business firms and private investigative agencies. Copies of the local directories can often be found in the public library or at the chamber of commerce. By looking up the address of the missing person in the directory, the investigator can quickly compile a list of the names, addresses, and telephone numbers of all of his neighbors. Another section of the criss-cross directory is indexed according to telephone numbers. It consists of a listing of all the numbers of a city or a region in numerical order along with the subscriber's name and address. Sometimes the missing person has left notes about the house with phone numbers identified only by a nickname, initials, or with a cryptic message. By looking up the numbers in the directory, the investigator can easily learn the names and addresses of the people referred to in the notes. The telephone index of the criss-cross directory is especially useful when used in conjunction with the "pen register" described below.

g. **Phone Log.** The "pen register" is a device that is attached to the telephone line which records every number dialed from a particular phone, as well as the date, the time, and the duration of the call. If the missing person is suspected of using the telephone of a friend or relative to contact his associates, a pen register can be helpful. The pen register monitors telephone use in a similar manner as the mail cover does for postal service. That is, it records the data concerning the fact that the communication was made, not the contents of the communication. However, unlike the mail cover which records the *incoming* mail, from those contacting the address, the pen register lists only the *outgoing* calls, to those contacted from the phone. The pen register is equipped to automatically print on a sheet of paper the list of telephone numbers dialed, along with the date, time, and duration of the calls. With this list and the telephone number index of the criss-cross directory, the investigator can readily determine the names and addresses of everyone receiving calls from this phone. Presumably, among those contacted will be the friends and acquaintances of the missing person.

Ordinarily, the pen register, a device the size of a briefcase, is installed and maintained for a period of thirty days by the telephone company in their office. Federal law requires that a court order be obtained before a pen register can be used. If the calls of interest are long distance ones, a pen register may not be necessary. The telephone company maintains its own record of all long distance calls for billing purposes. In an effort to insure the privacy of their customers, the phone company will usually require a court order before divulging this information to an investigative agency. As the telephone company converts to a computerized electronic switching system, it will eventually have the capability of maintaining records on all phone numbers dialed, both long distance and local. When that day arrives, the pen register will no longer be needed for this purpose.

3. Tracing the Fugitive

The technique employed in tracing a fugitive will vary with the character of the subject. In the case of an astute fugitive, discreet methods must be employed. With the inexperienced criminal a more direct approach is permissible. The methods described in the preceeding sections will be found useful. The following checklist is given as an example of a typical, routine trace. Naturally the order of these steps is not fixed and in some cases various steps can be omitted.

a. **Routine Information.**

1) Full name and alias.

2) Physical description.

3) *Modus operandi.*

4) Motive.

5) Associates past and present including girlfriends.

6) Habits, hangouts, and resorts he is known to frequent.

7) Criminal record, photograph, and fingerprints.

8) Residence, last known and previous locations.

9) Employment, last known and previous employers.

10) Relatives, names and addresses of all available.

11) Close friends, names and addresses.

12) Physical condition.

13) Motor Vehicle Bureau, check for operator's, chauffeur's, or owner's license.

14) Social Security number.

15) Selective Service history, records from local boards.

16) Handwriting for comparison with mail cover, hotel registrations, etc.

b. **Immediate Action.** The following steps can be taken with reference to law enforcement agencies, when prompt action is required:

1) Teletype.

2) Police circulars.

3) Police journals; FBI bulletins.

4) Wanted card at local and state Bureau of Criminal Information.

5) Wanted Persons File at FBI (Washington, D.C.).

6) Local Bureau of Information for information on summons and arrest cards, aid and accident cases.

7) Bureau of Motor Vehicles for accident reports or reports of lost plates.

8) Chief Magistrates Court or equivalent for fingerprint file with regard to arrests on minor charges.

9) If a parolee, the Parole Board concerned should be notified.

10) If the fugitive is known to frequent the racetracks, notify the Pinkerton Detective Agency.

11) Notify former arresting officers.

12) Place a notice or consult the monthly bulletin of the American Hotel Association, published by Wm. J. Burns International Detective Agency.

4. Agencies Possessing Informative Records and Other Sources

It should not be assumed that all of the agencies listed here will readily reveal their records to the investigator. A number of them will supply only limited information. Often the nature of the case and the authority of the investigator will determine the extent to which these agencies are permitted to cooperate.

    a. **Federal Sources of Information.**

1) Alcohol, Tobacco, and Firearms—Treasury Department.

2) Bureau of Customs—Treasury Department.

3) Civil Service Commission.

4) Coast Guard.

5) Drug Enforcement Administration—Department of Justice.

6) Federal Communications Commission.

7) Federal Compensation Offices.

8) Federal Unemployment Offices.

9) Immigration and Naturalization Service—Justice Department.

10) Intelligence Division—Treasury Department.

11) Internal Revenue Bureau—Treasury Department.

12) Federal Bureau of Investigation—Department of Justice.

13) Maritime Commission—Commerce Department.

14) Navy Department.

15) Post Office Department.

16) Post Offices—generally.

17) Probation Bureaus.
18) Provost Marshal's Offices.
19) Secret Service—Treasury Department.
20) Selective Service—administration.
21) Veterans Administration. (usually the most fruitful source)
22) Voting Registers—District of Columbia.
23) Defense Department.
  b. **State Sources of Information.**
  1) Assessor's Office.
  2) Attorney General's Office.
  3) Clerk's Office.
  4) Department of State Records.
  5) Fish and Game Warden's Office.
  6) Judges—Justices of Peace.
  7) Old Age Pension Offices.
  8) Penal agencies.
  9) Personal Property records.
  10) Probation and Parole Bureaus.
  11) Public Welfare and Social Service Offices.
  12) Relief Agency records.
  13) Secretaries of Agriculture.
  14) Tax Collectors' Offices.
  15) Treasurers' Offices.
  16) State Compensation Offices.
  17) State Unemployment Office.
  18) Voting registers.
  19) Workmens' Compensation Boards.
  c. **County Sources of Information.**
  1) Assessors' Offices.
  2) Boards of Supervisors.
  3) Clerks' Offices.
  4) Agents' Offices.
  5) Judges—Justices of Peace.
  6) Probation and Parole Bureaus.
  7) Prosecuting officials.
  8) Tax Collectors' Offices.
  9) Treasurers' Offices.
  10) Voting registers.

d. **City Sources of Information.**
1) Records of applications for Licenses: marriage, car, etc.
2) Assessor's Office.
3) Boards of Commissioners.
4) Boards of Health.
5) Clerks' Offices.
6) Coroners' or Medical Examiners' Offices.
7) Court Records, Civil and Criminal.
8) Election Boards.
9) Fire Marshals.
10) Health, Sanitation, Building, and License Inspectors' Offices.
11) Judges—Justices of the Peace.
12) Personal Property records.
13) Police Departments.
14) Probate records.
15) Prosecuting officials.
16) Public Schools.
17) Sheriffs' Offices.
18) Tax Collectors' Offices.
19) Title Records Offices.
20) Treasurers' Offices.
21) Truant offices.
22) Voting registers.
e. **Private Sources of Information.**
1) Airlines.
2) American Red Cross.
3) Banks.
4) Bonding companies.
5) Brokerage offices.
6) Commercial investigative agencies.
7) Contractors.
8) Credit bureaus.
9) Fraternal organizations.
10) Hotels.
11) Income records.
12) Industrial organizations.
13) Insurance companies.
14) Loan and Finance companies.

15) Mortgage, Debt, and Lien records.

16) Public Utility offices.

17) Railroad companies.

18) Real estate agencies.

19) Rental agencies—real estate, cars, trucks, etc.

20) Steamship companies.

21) Storage companies.

22) Telephone companies.

23) Trade union records.

24) Transportation companies, particularly bus lines, etc.

25) Water, electric, and gas companies.

f. **Directories.** The following are among the publications which will be found to contain useful information:

1) Telephone Directory—Local and out-of-town directories are available at central branch libraries. Geographical telephone lists are available to the police.

2) Criss-cross or reverse directory—A listing of telephone subscribers according to their address and their phone number.

3) Who's Who in America.

4) Who's Who in Finance and Industry.

5) Who Knows What—A listing of experts in various fields.

6) American Medical Directory.

7) Directory of Medical Specialists.

8) Who's Who in Engineering.

9) American Men and Women of Science.

10) Martindale-Hubbell Law Directory.

11) Who's Who in Education.

12) Polk's Bank Directory—A listing of bank officials, brokers and bank examiners.

13) National Change of Address System—A listing of eighty-six million postal customers who have recently relocated.

14) Postal Directory.

15) Insurance Directory.

16) Dun and Bradstreet.

5. Federal Bureau of Investigation

a. **National Crime Information Center.** The NCIC is the FBI's computerized index containing information on wanted persons, criminal histories, and stolen and/or missing property. Information concerning individuals for whom warrants have been issued is retained in the Wanted Persons File, which contains records of warrants and descriptive data on the persons wanted. The file is completely computerized with extensive communications networks among local, state, and federal law enforcement agencies, who may enter records directly into the index from computer terminals in their respective departments. Such records are immediately available in response to query by other agencies participating in the system.

Information in the Wanted Persons File relates to individuals for whom federal warrants are outstanding or for individuals who have been identified with an offense classified as a felony or serious misdemeanor for whom the jurisdiction originating the entry has been issued a warrant. Probation or parole violators with outstanding warrants are also entered in the NCIC. Law enforcement agencies in the federal government, the fifty states, the District of Columbia, Puerto Rico, and Canada have direct on-line access to the computer records; the system is used to identify suspects and apprehend fugitives.

Descriptive data recorded includes name, sex, race, nationality, date of birth, height, weight, hair color, FBI number, NCIC fingerprint classification, miscellaneous identification numbers, Social Security number, driver's license data, offense for which warrant was issued and date of warrant, and data identifying license plates and automobiles associated with the wanted person.

b. **Fingerprint and Criminal Identification Files.** A national clearinghouse for such records, the files contain over 200 million fingerprint cards divided into criminal and civil sections. The civil file is comprised of cards on federal employees and applicants, Armed Forces personnel, civilian employees in national defense industries, aliens, and persons wishing to have their fingerprints on file for identification purposes.

Fingerprint cards contain the name, signature, and physical

description of the person fingerprinted; information concerning the reason for fingerprinting; identity of contributing agency; date printed; and, where applicable, the charge and disposition or sentence. Some cards contain the residential address, occupation, and employment of the person fingerprinted.

Identification records, compiled from fingerprint cards, contain the identity of the contributors of the cards; names and aliases of the subject of the record; agency identifying numbers; dates of arrest and/or incarcerations; charges; and dispositions. No other information concerning an individual's background, personal life, personality, or habits is included in these records.

Fingerprint cards are submitted by over 14,000 contributors representing local, state, and federal law enforcement agencies, including penal institutions, the federal government, and organizations authorized by state laws to contribute fingerprints for official purposes.

The FBI's records are furnished to authorized officials of the federal government, the states, cities, and penal or other institutions for their official use only. Written record is maintained of each dissemination of an identification record, including the date disseminated and the identity of the receiving agency.

c. **Known Professional Check Passers File.** The FBI's PROCHECK is a tape storage of records containing information on prolific bad check passers. Information includes a description of the person (age and appearance), his method of operation, and the check format (how his checks are customarily filled out). Information is collected from existing FBI investigative records and is accessible only to FBI personnel involved in official investigations concerning bad checks.

6. Scope of Federal Information Gathering

Records maintained by elements of the federal government will reflect the particular function of the agency involved as well as its responsibilities and security requirements. The scope and volume of the information contained will depend on the purpose of the record and will vary also with the agency. In general, the records can be placed in one of the following categories:

a. **Civilian Personnel Records.** This is a basic class of records for a government that is the employer of millions of persons. The typical employee dossier will contain the following information: name, date of birth, social security number, educational background, professional qualifications, job assignments, and so forth. Ordinarily the dossier will include employment applications, proficiency reports, and information relating to the person's security clearance status.

b. **Military Records.** Information similar to the above is included in the personnel folders of present and former members of the Armed Forces. Data pertinent to service personnel having current duty or standby status is maintained in the active files of the Department of Defense or other appropriate agency. Records of former military personnel are maintained in several records repositories in various parts of the country and, in limited form, in the files of the Veterans Administration.

c. **Information on Private Individuals.** The federal government maintains millions of records on private persons. Some are related directly to criminal activity; some are concerned with security matters, identifying persons and specifying the reasons why a certain level of security clearance was granted or withheld; still others — a far larger class of records — contain highly detailed information on individual citizens without any specific relation to crime or security. Examples of this last category are the records of the Census Bureau, the Bureau of Internal Revenue, and the Social Security Administration.

7. Data Banks and the Threat to Privacy

a. **A New Industry.** The acquisition of data on individuals has become a major activity of a number of Federal agencies. In recent years a new era of gathering and distributing information was entered with the development of high-speed data retrieval systems, many based on computer technology. Some public officials have been led to predict the ultimate establishment of a national computerized data bank incorporating dossiers of *cradle-to-grave* information on every United States citizen. Advances in the field of communications have led to the development in some

Federal agencies of so-called *data banks* — mechanized or computerized files of instantly available information which can be rapidly transmitted, upon request, to authorized agencies and individuals throughout the country.

b. **The New Technology.** The governmental process of gathering, storing, retrieving, and disseminating data on individuals has always existed and has been recognized as a significant threat to the functioning of a free society. In the last ten years, however, incredible advances in technology have enabled government agencies to achieve surveillance capability undreamed of only a short time before. Where once methodical persistence could maintain a surveillance on a number of persons, we are now entering an era where surveillance capability is achieving the quality of inevitability. Electronic and photographic developments now permit the collection of vast amounts of data on day-to-day activities of all citizens, without so much as an inkling that the data collection is taking place. Innovations in computer technology have made possible the storage, retrieval, and dissemination of personal dossiers on millions of persons.

c. **The Threat to Privacy.** The marriage of sophisticated information-gathering techniques with computer information storage and dissemination systems has created for the first time a very real danger that the sense of privacy which has traditionally insulated Americans against the fear of state encroachment will be destroyed and be replaced, instead, by a pervasive sense of being watched. Since the protection of the sense of privacy is essential to the preservation of individuality which characterizes a democracy, legislators and a government advisory committee have proposed a number of safeguards against this new encroachment:

1) *Statute of Limitations.* We can no longer start life anew by moving to another town. A shrinking world has destroyed that procedure. An informational statute of limitations should be an integral part of any surveillance system, automatically expunging stale information after a given period.

2) *Individual Access.* The surveillance process must be hedged with rigorous safeguards. Every person about whom data is being stored by the government should be permitted access to his dos-

sier to check its accuracy and propriety. Upon receipt he should be permitted challenge.

3) **Dissemination Notice.** Prior to its dissemination, notice should be given an individual of a request for information.

4) **Transmission.** There must be a way for an individual to prevent information about him that was obtained for one purpose from being used or made available for other purposes without his consent.

5) **Reliability.** Any organization creating, maintaining, using, or disseminating records of identifiable personal data must insure the reliability of these data for their intended use and must take precautions to prevent misuse.

6) **Secrecy.** There must be no personal data record-keeping systems whose very existence is secret.

8. Rapid Transmission of Information

There are, of course, a great number of practical applications of the computer to law enforcement. By shortening the time lapse between the request for information and the transmission of data, computer technology permits the investigator to avail himself of ongoing opportunities by rapidly providing a legal basis for apprehension. Thus, the computer can facilitate on-the-street investigations by quick delivery of information about targets of opportunity. At headquarters, computer information can greatly assist in the control and direction of an extensive surveillance, a moving search, or a wide-area pursuit by giving the supervisor current information on the exact location of police vehicles. The effectiveness of many police operations relies heavily on shortening the time span between information request and appropriate police action.

ADDITIONAL READING

Information

Claggett, S.F.: REJIS: A Computer Information Network. 52 *FBI Law Enforcement Bulletin,* 3, 1983.

Criminal Justice "Hot" Files. Washington D.C.: U.S. Department of Justice, 1986.

Harris, D.R., Maxfield, M., and Holladay, G.: *Basic Elements of Intelligence: A Manual for Police Intelligence Units.* Washington, D.C.: U.S. Government Printing Office, 1976.

Harry, B.: A Diagnostic Study of the Criminal Alias. 31 *Journal of Forensic Sciences,* 1023, 1986.

Lyford, G. and Wood, U., Jr.: National Crime Information Center—Your Silent Partner. 52 *FBI Law Enforcement Bulletin,* 3, 1983.

Murphy, H.J.: *Where's What; Sources of Information for Federal Investigators.* New York, Warner, 1976.

O'Brien, K., Boston, G., and Marvin, M.: *Directory of Criminal Justice Information Sources.* Washington, D.C.: U.S. Government Printing Office, 1976.

Rapp, B.: *Deep Cover: Police Intelligence Operations.* Port Townsend, Wash.: Loompanics, 1989.

SEARCH Group, Inc.: *1986 Directory of Automated Criminal Justice Information Systems.* Washington, D.C.: National Institute of Justice, 1986.

Sparrow, M.K.: Information Systems: A Help or Hindrance in the Evolution of Policing? 58 *Police Chief,* 4, 1991.

Privacy

Albanese, J.S.: *Justice, Privacy and Crime Control.* Lanham, Md.: University Press of America, 1984.

Carroll, J.M.: *Confidential Information Sources: Public and Private,* 2nd ed. Stoneham, Mass.: Butterworth-Heinemann, 1991.

Dintino, J.J. and Martens, F.T.: *Police Intelligence Systems in Crime Control: Maintaining a Delicate Balance in a Liberal Democracy.* Springfield, Ill.: Thomas, 1983.

Eaton, J.W.: *Card Carrying Americans: Privacy, Security and the National ID Card Debate.* Totowa, N.J.: Rowman, 1986.

Federal Government Information Technology: Electronic Surveillance and Civil Liberties. Washington, D.C.: U.S. Government Printing Office, 1985.

Halperin, M.H. and Hoffman, D.: *Freedom vs. National Security: Secrecy and Surveillance.* Port Townsend, Wash.: Loompanics, 1977.

How to Use the Federal F.O.I. Act and the Privacy Act of 1974: A Citizen's Guide to Using the Freedom of Information Act and the Privacy Act of 1974 to Request Government Records. Port Townsend, Wash.: Loompanics, 1987.

Miller, A.R.: *The Assault on Privacy: Computers, Data Banks and Dossiers.* Ann Arbor, University of Michigan Press, 1971.

Petrocelli, W.: *Low Profile: How to Avoid the Privacy Invaders.* New York, McGraw-Hill, 1982.

Riggin, S.P.: U.S. Information Access Laws: Are They a Threat to Law Enforcement? 53 *FBI Law Enforcement Bulletin,* 7, 1984.

Chapter 14

MISSING PERSONS

1. General

ALTHOUGH the problem of finding and identifying missing persons is hardly the most exciting branch of detective work, it is a routine task of the first magnitude in importance. In a large city, a considerable fraction of the cases of the detective division is concerned with Missing Persons. The Missing Persons unit is ordinarily concerned with three classes of persons: (a) missing persons under about nineteen years of age; (b) unidentified dead, and (c) unidentified persons. Missing persons over eighteen years of age who are in full possession of their faculties are not ordinarily the concern of the police. Private investigators, however, are usually hired for cases of this nature.

2. Definitions

The following definitions, although not in widespread use, will serve to simplify the treatment of this subject.

a. The term *missing person* is often confused with "wanted person." The latter is a person who is sought by the police in connection with a crime. We may use for our definition the following: a missing person is anyone reported missing who is under eighteen or who, being eighteen or over, is: (1) seriously affected either mentally or physically, or (2) absent under circumstances which would indicate involuntary disappearance.

b. *Unidentified dead* will include those whose true identity is unknown and those whose relatives or friends cannot be immediately located.

c. An *unidentified person* is one who has been physically or mentally affected to a degree or in a manner requiring the attention of the police and who cannot be readily identified, or whose friends or relatives cannot be immediately located.

3. Crimes and Conditions Associated with Missing Persons

a. **Homicide.** In the disappearance of many thousands of people annually in this country, it is to be expected that personal violence should play a significant part in some of the cases. Murder, the unspoken fear of the relatives and the police, must always lie in the back of the investigator's mind as a possible explanation. The suspicions of a shrewd investigator have not infrequently uncovered an unsuspected homicide. The two most popular motives for this type of homicide are money and love. As an example of the love motive, the Feldt case is fairly representative. George Feldt walked into a police station one morning and reported his wife, Selma, age 47, missing for two days. Detective John Brandt of the Missing Persons Bureau was assigned to the investigation. In the first interview, Detective Brandt permitted Feldt to talk at considerable length. Feldt attributed various motives to his wife's disappearance. Before many minutes had passed he was accusing his wife of adultery with some unknown man. Subsequent interviews convinced the detective that Feldt was much more interested in the gratuitous vilification of his spouse than in her prompt return. In the course of these diatribes, it dawned upon Brandt that Feldt was speaking as though his wife's death were an accomplished fact. Brandt pursued the inquiry to Feldt's home. There he questioned Feldt's stepdaughter, age 18, and well-endowed by nature. The girl obviously was shaken by some fear. She confessed to an intimacy with Feldt and revealed her own suspicion of foul play. The cellar of Feldt's home was then searched for evidentiary traces. A newly cemented area attracted immediate attention. Digging in this spot, the detectives uncovered the body of Mrs. Feldt. She had been almost decapitated by a blow from a sharp instrument. The discovery of a blood-stained ax in a corner completed this part of the inquiry. Confronted with this evidence, Feldt confessed to the homicide. His infatuation with the stepdaughter had led him to conceive this violent plan to dispose of his wife. The methods employed were quite crude; nevertheless, carelessness on the part of the police might have insured Feldt's success. An intelligent investigation and a routine search had uncovered the crime.

b. **Suicide.** To the layman the suicide theory is one of the first to suggest itself in a disappearance case. Statistically, however, it can be shown that the odds are greatly against the suicide solution. Approximately one out of 2,000 missing persons cases develops into a suicide case. Suicides are ordinarily motivated by financial difficulties such as business failures, domestic troubles, or incurable disease. In the investigation of a case the detective should endeavor to discover the motive for the disappearance. A voluntary disappearance is motivated by a desire to escape from some personal, domestic, or business conflict. If the motive is founded merely in boredom or the desire for a change, suicide can be readily eliminated. A disappointment in love seldom results in self-inflicted death.

c. **Simulated Suicide.** These are usually planned by persons wishing to defraud insurance companies or to arrange for a change of spouse. The scene of this prefabricated demise is most commonly a watery one, such as a boat, bridge, or beach. This selection is obvious, since the perpetrator must leave clothing as a means of identification under circumstances which would make plausible the absence of the body. In general, no conclusion should be made concerning suicide unless the body is recovered. A drowned person will ordinarily be washed ashore within five to ten days. After twenty days, it may be concluded that the body has been carried out to sea (or that the person is still alive). A search for motives should include an inquiry into insurance policies. Naturally, the insurance company will promptly bring this matter to the attention of the police. The following are representative cases:

1) A bath house cleaner pursuing his Monday morning duties found a set of men's clothing in one of the lockers. A few hours later, detectives called at the home of Mrs. Sol Stern to inform her that her husband's clothes had been left unclaimed at a bath house on a local beach. Mrs. Stern became hysterical and was of little assistance to the detectives. A $50,000 insurance policy on the life

of Sol Stern was of more interest to them. Two months later, a report from the Montreal police informed the detectives that a man answering Stern's description had been knocked unconscious in an auto accident. The only identification was a newspaper clipping describing the disappearance of Stern at the beach. Stern later confessed to the fraud.

2) The technique of feigning suicide can be more highly developed if the perpetrator is an exceptional swimmer, as was Alfred Jones, another frequenter of beaches. Jones disappeared into the water during a heavy storm and before the eyes of several witnesses. Mrs. Jones, however, had greater faith in her husband's aquatic prowess. She insisted that he was still alive and had merely swum into some other woman's arms. This theory was vindicated two years later, when Jones was discovered living with another woman in a town fifty miles away.

d. **Extortion.** The extensive publicity which accompanies the disappearance of a person of some means usually stimulates the more unbalanced element among newspaper readers. The police department and the relatives of the missing person are besieged by crank letters suggesting false clues and absurd motives. Sometimes, however, the relatives become the target of an extortionist who pretends that he is holding the missing person in custody. The ransom note usually suggests that a large sum of money be forwarded to the writer by some means which may involve an innocent messenger or even the employment of homing pigeons. Needless to say, the writers of these letters in some cases know nothing of the location of the missing person. They are merely exploiting the disturbed emotions of the relatives. Naturally, an effort should be made to trace the extortion letter. A dummy package or some other ruse should be employed to trap the extortionist.

e. **Amnesia.** Loss of memory and with it knowledge of identity is a rare occurrence even among missing persons cases. Amnesia has its highest incidence in the confections of scenario writers. Of the authentic cases, the most frequent cause is battle shock.

f. **Psychoses.** The insane person of unknown identity is a more common type of missing person. A person of this sort is brought to the city or county hospital for examination. If he is adjudged insane, he is committed to a state hospital. The unidentified insane should form a separate file in a missing persons bureau. Psychoses which frequently result in a missing persons case are dementias caused by organic changes in the cortical brain cell. With Alzheimer's disease, the most common of these psychoses, the onset is ordinarily gradual. There is an uninterrupted deterioration of mental powers accompanied by defective memory, disorientation, and confusion. Members of the family are well aware of the condition and will readily describe the symptoms to the investigator.

g. **Abandonment.** Unhappy marriages account for a large percentage of disappearances. The voluntary disappearance of a married adult can in itself become a crime when it assumes the form of abandonment, e.g., the abandoning of a pregnant wife in destitute circumstances. Abandonment is a criminal offense and, as such, is a matter for police action.

4. Investigative Steps

The following procedure is suitable to a large city. The steps can be readily telescoped to fit the exigencies of a more limited personnel.

a. **Unidentified Dead.** The following steps are ordinarily followed in cases where the dead person is unidentified:

1) The report is received at the local detective squad.

2) The squad detective visits the scene, fills out a form with a full description of the deceased.

3) The squad detective notifies the Missing Persons Unit by telephone, giving a description of deceased. At the same time, he forwards the official form.

4) The Missing Persons Unit consults its records.

5) The Missing Persons Unit sends a detective to the morgue to see the victim.

6) Three sets of fingerprints are made to be transmitted to the local department's identification bureau, to the state's identification bureau, and to the Federal Bureau of Investigation.

7) Photographs are made as a permanent record. Particular attention is given to scars, tattoos, deformities, and other outstanding characteristics.

At the morgue, the following procedure is customary:

1) The body is immediately examined.

2) The clothing is searched for dry cleaner's and laundry marks and clothing labels.

3) The property is recorded. Documents are examined for identification.

4) An examination is made for scars caused by accidents or operations; tattoos; birth marks; moles; and other superficial characteristics.

5) Appliances, such as a truss, elastic stockings, artificial limbs, etc., can be traced through a manufacturer of prosthetic apparatus.

6) A complete description of the body is made.

7) Fingerprints of the deceased are recorded.

8) X-rays can be made to provide a more accurate description of bone structure anomalies.

9) The teeth should be described by a dentist.

b. **Missing Persons.** The steps which are to be followed in locating a missing person are quite similar to those given in the preceding chapter for tracing a wanted person. Ordinarily, however, there is one important difference between the two types of cases, namely, the motive. If the wanted person is the perpetrator of a crime, his motive for escape is quite clear; it is simply the evasion of justice. The typical missing person, on the other hand, is endeavoring to escape his present circumstances; he wishes to re-establish himself in new surroundings rather than simply to lie in hiding. The investigator should first complete the routine steps in official procedure:

1) *Notification.* A full description which places emphasis on peculiarities of the body or dress should be transmitted to other law enforcement agencies. A teletype alarm should be sent to the neighboring states. Later a general alarm should be transmitted. Circulars with a complete description and a photograph should be distributed for placement in public places such as hotels, railroad stations, and post offices. Inquiries are made at hospitals and morgues.

2) *Background Investigation.* The investigator should interview the relatives and friends of the missing person in order to

establish a motive. Information concerning the following should be developed.

a) Domestic background.
b) Personal habits.
c) Business history.
d) Associates—social and business.
e) Medical history.
f) Educational background.
g) Family history.

The methods described in the preceding chapter for tracing wanted persons will guide the investigator subsequently.

5. Illustrative Cases

Two 1952 Chicago cases will illustrate the effectiveness of these techniques in a typical large city.

a. One case involved the body of a man recovered from Lake Michigan. The fingerprints were not adequate since there was no general file. The only other clues were a pair of red swimming trunks and a red stone ring bearing the initials "T.B." and a manufacturer's marking. A visit to the manufacturer revealed that this latter was a class ring, specifically made for Wendell Phillip's High School. The school register listed a Timothy Bradley as a graduate of that class. Bradley's father denied this identity of the body. On questioning, it was found that the young Bradley had maintained a post office savings account. The prints were compared with those of the postal record and proved to be those of Timothy Bradley.

b. In another case, a man identified as Lawrence White was found dead in the street. The identification had been made by White's brother. When it was discovered that the family had no funds for burial, a further police investigation followed to save the body from a potter's field burial. Since White had been a World War II veteran, the prints were sent to Washington for verification with the hope that a burial could be achieved through the Veterans Administration. Washington reported that the prints belonged to a man named Stanley Michael Hochrek, another war veteran.

Hochrek's sister visited the morgue and identified the body as that of her brother. It was learned that Lawrence White had left town the day of Hochrek's death to take a railroad job.

6. Misconceptions Associated with Missing Persons

A great deal of the statistical and conceptual information about missing persons is unreliable and inaccurate. There are no reliable nationwide statistics on missing persons. Among the more common myths popularized by magazines and other media are the following:

a. **Number of Missing Persons.** A number of journalistic sources have maintained that one million persons voluntarily absent themselves each year. The fact of the matter is that there is no way of demonstrating how many people disappear. There is no central clearing house for such information. Even if there were a source for a reliable statistic, this would still remain a "dark figure," since it would be unduly raised by the premature alarms of parents and spouses and would be lowered by the large number of people too proud, too poor, too depressed, or too indifferent to report.

b. **Clearance Rate.** It is widely believed that the police solve 95 percent or more of missing person cases. In practice the police do not have jurisdiction to look for everyone reported missing. The great majority of the cases that are handled by the police are solved by the voluntary return of the missing person.

c. **Difficulty of Disappearance.** "It is practically impossible to disappear in today's society." This is held to be true by reason of the efficiency of the police, the claims of private investigators, and the mass of documentation that accumulates in the average person's life. The notion of the difficulty of disappearing probably has its origins in the movies and television dramas which for the past fifty years have exploited the theme of the inevitable discovery of the fugitive, the lost, and the strayed. On any television night there is some film illustrating the futility of hiding from the Mafia. In reality it is quite simple for a person to disappear in a large city without a trace. In New York he would move five miles away or take a subway to Newark. To begin his new life he would acquire a new name and would "repaper" accordingly, e.g., a new Social Security card and driver's license. His behavior must, of course, be guarded and his activities moderately restricted, since changes of identity are most commonly discovered in the course of a routine ID check in connection with some trivial offense.

7. Sources of Information

There are no sources of information about missing persons who have changed their name. If the person has retained his own name then the Motor Vehicle Bureaus of the area and the credit bureaus are the most likely sources. The following comments suggest the usefulness of these and some other sources:

a. **Motor Vehicle Bureau.** Since a license is issued to any requesting adult who can pass the test, this source is useful only if the name is unchanged.

b. **Credit Bureaus.** This is the largest private source of alphabetized information on American citizens. The Associated Credit Bureaus of America number over 2,000 interconnected bureaus which exchange information among themselves and their 400,000 clients based on the 130-million customer reports on file.

c. **Federal Bureau of Investigation.** The FBI does not conduct searches for missing persons. It does, however, maintain a Missing Person File in the National Crime Information Center and will post a notice in the file when a request is made by an authorized law enforcement agency or by an immediate relative of the individual whose location is sought. On receipt of pertinent information regarding the whereabouts of the missing person the interested party is notified immediately.

d. **Social Security Administration.** This agency annually receives thousands of requests for information concerning the whereabouts of its clients. Most of the inquiries come from state and federal officials and relate to tax investigations, immigration problems, national security, and the Aid to Families with Dependent Children program. The Social Security Administration does not accept private requests. It should be noted that a Social Security card can be obtained simply by applying. The card is designed for social security and tax purposes, not for identification.

e. **Insurance Companies.** Although these companies conduct investigations of death claims related to missing persons, they do not reveal their information to the police or to private persons. That is, even after they have discovered a missing person these companies will not inform the relative. They consider the policy holder as a client whose confidence and wish for privacy they must respect. A company such as the Prudential receives annually close to 2,000 death claims based on legal declarations of presumed death, i.e., the court has decided there is reason to concede the demise of an individual even though no corpse has been found.

f. **Private Investigators.** The resources of the private investigator are limited since he must proceed on the assumption that the missing person will not change his name from Reginald Smith to Alonzo Jones. The investigator writes letters to the state motor vehicle bureaus in the area, requesting information about the issuing of a license to anyone named Reginald Smith. If the results are negative he then writes to credit bureaus, enclosing the appropriate fee and requesting a file check by name and date of disappearance. If the missing person has not changed his name, the investigator has a good chance of finding him.

ADDITIONAL READING

Missing Persons

Bishop, D.R. and Scheussler, T.J.: The National Crime Information Center's Missing Person File. 51 *FBI Law Enforcement Bulletin*, 8, 1982.

Crnkovic, G.: I SEARCH for Missing Children. 35 *Law and Order*, 7, 1987.

Erickson, R.G. II: *How to Find Missing Persons: A Handbook for Investigators*, rev. ed. Port Townsend, Wash.: Loompanics, 1984.

Fallis, G. and Greenberg, R.: *Be Your Own Detective.* New York, M. Evans and Co., 1989.

Ferguson, A. and Mascaro, D.G.: I–SEARCH for Missing and Exploited Children. 55 *FBI Law Enforcement Bulletin*, 4, 1986.

Ferraro, E.: *You Can Find Anyone: A Complete Guide on How to Locate Missing Persons*, rev. ed. Santa Ana, Calif.: Marathon Press, 1989.

Forst, M.L.: Law Enforcement Policies on Missing Children. 38 *Law and Order*, 6, 1990.

——: *Missing Children: The Law Enforcement Response.* Springfield, Ill.: Thomas, 1990.

Gallagher, R.S.: *"If I Only Had It To Do Over Again. . . . "* New York, Dutton, 1969.

Goldfader, E.: *Tracer: The Search for Missing Persons.* Los Angeles, Nash, 1970.

Hirschel, J.D. and Lab, S.P.: Who Is Missing? The Realities of the Missing Persons Problem. 16 *Journal of Criminal Justice,* 35, 1988.

Hotaling, G.T. and Finkelhor, D.: Estimating the Number of Stranger-Abduction Homicides of Children: A Review of Available Evidence. 18 *Journal of Criminal Justice,* 385, 1990.

Hyde, M. and Hyde, L.: *Missing Children.* Danbury, Conn.: Watts, 1985.

Identifying the Unidentified. 59 *FBI Law Enforcement Bulletin,* 8, 1990.

Investigator's Guide to Missing Child Cases: For Law Enforcement Officers Locating Missing Children. Washington, D.C.: National Center for Missing and Exploited Children, 1985.

Johnson, R.S., Lt.Col.: *How to Locate Anyone Who Is or Has Been in the Military.* Port Townsend, Wash.: Loompanics, 1990.

Krauss, T.C.: Forensic Odontology in Missing Persons Cases. 21 *Journal of Forensic Sciences,* 959, 1976.

Naumann, R.: *How to Locate (Almost) Anyone.* Hayward, Calif.: PI Publications, 1985.

Parker, S.: Missing People: How to Find Them. 36 *Law and Order,* 5, 1988.

Thomas, R.D.: *How to Find Anyone Anywhere,* 2nd rev. ed. Austin, Texas, Thomas Publications, 1986.

Zoglio, M.: *Tracing Missing Persons: A Professional's Guide to Techniques and Resources.* Doylestown, Penn.: Tower Hill Press, 1982.

Chapter 15

SURVEILLANCE

1. General

I N MANY investigations a point is soon reached where little or no advantage can be obtained by further questioning of the complainant or the friendly witnesses. It is time, then, for the detective to go into the field to locate the criminal or, if he is known, to study his habits. At this juncture, the investigator must resign himself to the tedious but essential task of observing the activities of witnesses or principals in the case. The nature of the observation may be such that it is necessary to "put a tail" on certain persons or to maintain a fixed surveillance of a particular place. To the amateur these matters may appear relatively simple and readily accomplished by the use of ordinary common sense. The experienced investigator, however, is well aware of the value of a systematic procedure and the methodical employment of certain precautions. There is, in other words, a *technique* of observation. There are certain principles underlying this technique, which have been established by experiment and experience. There are pitfalls and errors which lead readily to a predictable failure. A surveillance which has failed may carry a double misfortune: the investment of time has been dissipated in the space of a few minutes, and the situation is often immeasurably worse than before because the subject of the surveillance is now alerted and will increase his precautions tenfold.

2. Definitions

Surveillance is the covert observation of places, persons, and vehicles for the purpose of obtaining information concerning the identities or activities of subjects. The surveillant is the person who maintains the surveillance or performs the observation. The subject is the person or place being watched. Surveillance may be divided into three kinds: surveillance of places; tailing or shadowing; and roping or undercover investigation. The objectives and methods will vary with each type of observation.

3. Surveillance of Places

In criminal investigations the crimes which usually require this kind of surveillance are gambling, prostitution, acting as a fence, and the illegal sale of drugs or alcohol. Private investigators will ordinarily watch a place to uncover evidence of dishonesty among the employees or of infidelity in a divorce case. In general, the objectives of place surveillance are:

To detect criminal activities.

To discover the identity of persons who frequent the establishment and to determine their relationship.

To discern the habits of a person who lives in or frequents the place.

To obtain evidence of a crime or to prevent the commission of a crime.

To provide a basis for obtaining a search warrant.

a. **Preliminary Survey.** A careful survey of the surrounding area should precede any surveillance of a place. The character of the neighborhood, the residents and the transients should be noted. The observation point should be selected after careful study. Two types of place surveillance will suggest themselves:

1) Using a room in a nearby house or business establishment and remaining undercover.

2) Remaining outdoors and posing as a person who would normally conduct his business in such an area, i.e., a laborer, carpenter, street vendor, or an employee of the building under observation.

b. **Equipment.** Whenever possible, a photographic record of visitors to the place should be obtained. A videotape camera and a 35mm camera, both equipped with telephoto lenses, can be used. A small telescope or a pair of binoculars is especially useful. If permission has been obtained, wire taps and recording apparatus can be employed. A night-viewer can be used in dark, unlit areas.

c. **Report.** A complete "log" of the activities taking place in the establishment under surveillance will form the basis of the report. The time of arrival and departure of each person should be carefully noted. Photographs and motion picture film footage should be numbered with reference to time. In addition to, or in lieu of, photographs, descriptive notes of visitors should be taken.

d. **Movements.** A certain degree of activity will be necessary to set up the observation post, move in equipment, relieve surveillants, and terminate surveillance. This should be accomplished as unobtrusively as possible. Surveillants should enter and leave separately. If it is necessary to take into confidence the residents of the observation point, the number of confidants should be held to a minimum and the purpose of the installation should not be revealed.

4. Requirements and Appearance of Surveillant

The following are the conventional requirements for an investigator selected to shadow a person:

a. Average size, build, and general appearance.

b. No noticeable peculiarities in appearance or mannerism.

c. No conspicuous jewelry or clothing.

d. Perseverance and capacity to wait for hours at a time without showing any signs of impatience or irritation, since these attract attention.

e. The appearance of attending strictly to his own business and of not being interested in what others may be doing.

f. Resourceful, versatile, and quick witted, so that he can readily conceive reasons or excuses for being in any given place.

g. A fluent speaker, able to talk his way out of embarrassing situations without arousing suspicion.

h. Trained in one or two good standard *covers*, such as canvassing for the city directory or a trade publication or selling hosiery, brushes, or other common articles. In this connection he should carry with him the necessary forms, data, or identification to give his pretense an appearance of authenticity.

5. Shadowing

Shadowing or *tailing* is simply the act of following a person. The purpose of shadowing will depend upon the nature of the investigation. In criminal work the objective may be:

    a. To detect evidence of criminal activities.

    b. To establish the associations of a suspect.

    c. To find a wanted person.

    d. To protect a witness.

In the work of the private detective we may have an objective of the following nature:

    a. To discover the associates, amusements, and habits of an employee who has been proposed for a position of responsibility.

    b. To check the loyalty of employees in an establishment where thefts have occurred.

The objective of the surveillance will determine the character of the tail:

    a. A "loose tail" will be employed where a general impression of the subject's habits and associates is required.

    b. "Rough shadowing" or shadowing without special precautions may be used when the criminal *must* be shadowed and is aware of this fact; or where the subject is a material witness and must be protected from harm or other undesirable influences.

    c. A "close tail" or surveillance in which extreme precautions are taken against losing the subject is employed where constant surveillance is necessary. For example, such a procedure would be recommended where the subject is suspected of impending criminal activities; or where the subject is suspected of past criminal activities and it is expected that these subsequent movements will yield the desired evidence; or where it is thought that the subject will lead the investigator to the hideout of the criminal.

6. Preparation

The investigator should, as always, make a preliminary survey of his task to prepare himself for contingencies that may suddenly arise:

a. Before undertaking a surveillance mission, the surveillant, assuming that he does not know the subject to be shadowed, should obtain a complete description of him and, if possible, arrange to have someone who does know the subject point him out to the surveillant. This description should particularly emphasize those details which are visible from *behind* the suspect, since that is the angle from which the surveillant will generally be watching him. It should include the type of headgear, overcoat, suit, and shoes that he ordinarily wears, the general carriage of his head and shoulders, whether his walk is fast or slow, his step short or long, and whether he acts as though he knows where he is going and goes there, or is hesitant and erratic in his pace and direction.

b. The investigator should learn as much as possible about his subject—his habits, haunts, and social life. In what areas will he be active? Are his tastes expensive? Will he dine at an expensive restaurant?

c. In the light of this information the investigator should accordingly prepare himself. He should endeavor to dress and act as though he belonged to the milieu in which he expects to find the subject. In preparation for a possible confrontation by the subject, he should have a plausible "story" which he can support with documents and knowledge.

d. He should comport himself as one belonging to the neighborhood. His manner should be casual and his interest apparently centered on matters other than the subject. Nervousness and haste should be studiously avoided. His dress should conform to his surroundings. In a commercial area he would wear a business suit; in a factory neighborhood, rough clothing would be in order; in suburban sections an informal costume would be found suitable.

e. He should study the neighborhood carefully in order to become familiar with the transportation lines and the likely pedestrian routes between certain points. In the event he loses his subject, the investigator will thus be better prepared to pick up the trail again.

f. The subject should be identified at the outset of the surveillance. Mental notes should be taken of the physical description, clothing, and the behavior of the subject.

7. Shadowing by Foot

The technique of shadowing by foot will vary with the number of men available. From one to six men can be usefully employed on a foot tail. The private investigator with a limited budget may be forced to do the shadowing by himself. A police agency should assign at least three persons to a foot tail. The purpose of using two or more persons is to minimize the risk of detection by falling into the subject's line of view too often or by being forced to make abrupt changes of direction.

a. A three-man tail is described here as typical of shadowing technique. The three men will be referred to as *A, B,* and *C. A* is closest to the subject *S.* He follows *S* at a distance which depends upon the conditions of pedestrian traffic. *B* follows *A,* at about the same distance from *A* as *A* is from *S. C* may precede *S* or, if vehicular traffic is moderate, may be approximately opposite him on the other side of the street. *B* and *C* take turns in occupying the position, thus preventing *A*'s becoming a familiar and noticeable figure to *S.*

b. A number of advantages recommend this ABC method of shadowing. If the subject becomes suspicious of any of the operators, that person can quickly drop out of the tail. If *S* suddenly turns a corner, *A* may continue straight ahead, instead of hurrying to the corner and anxiously looking for the subject. *C* may then cross the street and follow *B,* thus taking up the *B* position. *C,* moreover, has been in a position to view any sudden disappearance into a building.

c. Prearranged signals should be employed. For example, if *A* feels that he has been "made," he can signal that he is dropping out of the tail by adjusting his hat.

8. Tactics

In general, the subject should be kept unaware of the shadowing operation. The investigator should be inconspicuous. He should not be detected looking directly at the subject. He should shift from left to right, never remaining for long directly behind the subject. Both sides of the street should be used. If he suspects that

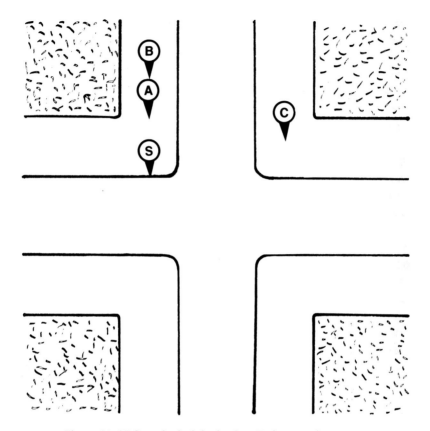

Figure 14. ABC method of shadowing: Before turning a corner.
S –Subject   **B** –Surveillant in position B
A –Surveillant in position A   **C** –Surveillant in position C

the subject has become alerted to the tail, he should request immediate removal from the assignment. A number of situations will arise that will test the resourcefulness of the investigator. A few of these are described below.

a. **Turning Corners.** If the subject turns a corner, the surveillant should not hurry. If the subject is lost, the nature of the neighborhood will determine the subsequent procedure. In most cases it is preferable to lose the subject than to alert him to the tail.

b. **Entering a Building.** If the building is a store, the operator should wait until the subject comes out. Naturally, in cases

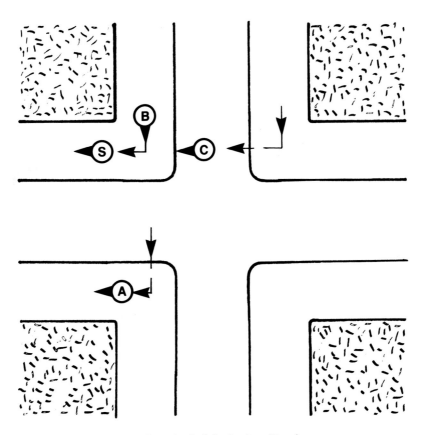

Figure 15. ABC method of shadowing: Turning a corner.
S — Subject   B — Surveillant in position A.
A — Surveillant in position C   C — Surveillant in position B.

of a department store or an establishment with a number of exits it will be necessary to follow into the store. If the subject enters the elevator of a building, the surveillant should board the same elevator. If the elevator man requests a floor number, he should give him the same one that the subject gave or else the top floor with the intention of alighting at the subject's floor. When two investigators are present, one should alight at the subject's floor but proceed in a different direction. The other investigator can then return to the first floor and wait for the subject.

c. **Taking a Bus.** The surveillant should board the same bus; sit behind the subject and on the same side. If he misses the bus, he should, of course, hire a taxi and board the bus at a point ahead.

d. **Taking a Taxi.** When the subject takes a cab, the surveillant should record the time, place, name of the taxi company, and license. He should endeavor to follow in another taxi. If this results in failure, he should trace the taxi by means of his recorded information and ascertain the destination from the taxi driver.

e. **Taking a Train.** If the subject shows his intention of buying a train ticket, the surveillant should endeavor to get in line behind him with one person intervening. If he hears the destination requested by the subject, he may buy a similar ticket. In the event he is unable to hear the destination, he should ask the agent the destination requested by the subject. If the surveillant does not intend to purchase a ticket, he should merely request a time table.

f. **In a Restaurant.** The surveillant should allow a few minutes to elapse before following the subject into a restaurant. He should then take an obscure seat and arrange to finish his meal at the same time as the subject.

g. **In a Hotel.** An inquiry can be made concerning the room of the subject. If he is registered, the surveillant can take an adjoining room.

h. **In a Telephone Booth.** The surveillant should either go into the next booth or stand near enough to hear. He should note the telephone book used and the page at which it is left open.

i. **In the Theater.** The surveillant should sit behind the subject and take note of the various exits which are available.

9. Recognition of Surveillant

There are two risks constantly incurred by a shadower—the risk of being "made," or recognized as a shadow by the subject, and the risk of being "lost," or eluded by the subject. Not even the most experienced shadow man can avoid these contingencies. He should, however, be prepared to take intelligent counter-measures.

There is a tendency among inexperienced surveillants to become easily convinced that they have been uncovered or "made" by the suspect—that the latter has found out that he is being shadowed and knows the identity of his follower. Rarely is there a real basis for the belief; it arises merely from the self-consciousness of the inexperienced shadow man. If the suspect does "make" the shadower, the latter will be left in no doubt about the matter from the actions of the suspect, who will often take a malicious pleasure in demonstrating that he is aware of the shadow. When the surveillant knows he has been recognized as such, he should drop the surveillance at once, but must exercise care in his subsequent actions. Although the suspect may have had several good views of the surveillant and has been convinced that the latter is following him, he will still be unaware of the identity of the shadow and will wish to satisfy his curiosity. Hence he is quite likely to turn shadower himself and follow the surveillant. Should the surveillant return to his home or office, followed by the suspect, the latter would then know who had been shadowing him and would be aware that the authorities had knowledge of his illegal activities. Thereafter, the suspect would either desist entirely from the pursuit of his objective or render the surveillance difficult if not impossible. The surveillant, therefore, must be quite certain that he has thrown off a shadow, either by the suspect or by someone else, before he goes to any place where the association might tend to identify him.

10. Testing a Tail

A favorite trick of suspects "testing for a tail"—ascertaining whether or not they are being shadowed—consists of boarding a public conveyance, such as a bus, streetcar, or subway train, waiting until the last possible second before the door closes and then jumping off the vehicle. The subject then looks about quickly to determine if any other person jumped off. If the shadower alights too, the suspect will study him closely to facilitate future recognition. On finding himself in this predicament, the surveillant's best tactic is to remain on the vehicle until the next stop, alight, and board the next car or train. Often he will find his subject and can continue the surveillance. To avoid being caught in this manner, the experienced surveillant will arrange to be the last passenger to board the vehicle, and will remain just inside the door until it is closed. Under these conditions if the suspect starts toward the door, the surveillant can immediately step off and appear to be waiting for another car or train.

11. The "Convoy"

When engaged upon a surveillance mission, the investigator must keep in mind that a shrewd subject is often guarding against a shadow by having one of his men follow him at a reasonable distance to observe whether or not the same person is constantly in the rear. Therefore, the shadower must keep a lookout *behind* himself to guard against this. If it is determined that the subject does have a follower or "convoy," the shadower must get behind the "convoy" and follow him instead of the subject.

12. Tailing by Automobile

The suggestions which have been offered for tailing by foot are applicable in large part to surveillance by means of the automobile. The number of persons and cars assigned to the task will be a function of the importance and difficulty of the assignment. Two cars can be used more effectively than one. By steadily interchanging positions, the risk of detection can be greatly lessened. At least two persons should follow the subject at a distance of about 100 yards. The distance of operation will become greater on highways and less in crowded traffic. If a second car is used, it should follow at an equal distance behind the first. The chief difficulty in tailing a vehicle will be encountered at night, since a great many cars will look quite similar at a distance from the rear. The subject car can be easily lost against a background of city traffic with its puzzling patterns of neon signs, traffic signals, and the taillights of other autos. The simplest solution to this problem is to mark the subject car beforehand so that it is identifiable at night. A pellet gun or even a .22 caliber revolver wrapped in a cloth can be used in an emergency to put a hole in one of the rear lights. A quick spray of a small area on the rear fender with an aerosol can of liquid glass will provide a less obtrusive means of identifying the car, since the reflective material is clearly seen from a position on a line perpendicular to the fender but is practically invisible from any other angle.

In an important case, where two or more surveillance cars are used, the movements of the cars should be closely coordinated through radio intercommunication. Depending on the radio facilities available, control can be maintained by one of the surveillance cars or by the communications center.

13. Disguising the Car

A car of popular type and color should be used. If possible, a change in vehicles should be made each day. The following precautions are sometimes useful:

a. **License Plates.** If the suspect uses a car, the surveillant, naturally, must also use a vehicle. He must be careful that the license plates cannot be identified as those of an investigator or his organization. He cannot, in general, use his own personal plates, since a check by the suspect would lead directly to the surveillant. There are three solutions to the problem:

1) Use tags borrowed from someone who is trustworthy, but who has no official associations.

2) Use rented cars.

3) Use special unregistered (dead) plates issued through the cooperation of motor vehicle authorities.

b. **Use of Rented Cars.** For an extensive surveillance job the use of rented cars is perhaps most satisfactory, since the surveillant can often change not only the license plates, but the cars themselves as the circumstances indictate.

c. **Appearance.** It is possible to alter the appearance of the car by various devices such as the use of removable stickers or other windshield adornments; changing license plates; shifting the headlights from dim to bright; using a multiple contact switch to eliminate one of the headlights; rearranging the seating of the occupants; changing the occupant's clothes, e.g., changing or removing hats; changing the number of the occupants.

14. Techniques

The manner of driving should be changed often. The driver should, for example, alternate between right and left lanes of his side of the road. A suspicious subject will suddenly stop his car to observe whether the surveillance car passes by. Obviously, to avoid detection, the surveillance car must proceed at the same speed until an opportunity is afforded to halt unobtrusively and permit the subject car to pass. Where two tail cars are employed, the stopping of the subject's car can be signalled from the first tail car to the second by flashing the brake lights in rapid succession an agreed number of times. A good part of tailing by vehicle consists in parking and awaiting the emergence of the subject from a home or business establishment. It is well to park as far away as is compatible with satisfactory observation. A car parked in the same block as that on which the subject resides will usually cause suspicion. The surveillant car should be parked in the next block, if at all possible. The building exits and the subject's car can be kept under close observation by means of binoculars. The occupants of the surveillant's car should sit in the back seat and remain inconspicuous. If they must wait a considerable time, it is advisable to leave the car and walk up and down the street casually.

15. Precautions

Among the most common errors made by inexperienced surveillants are the following: staying parked in the same spot too long; using a conspicuous car; having both surveillants in the front seat for an extended period of time; approaching the parking position furtively; parking in a prohibited zone, thereby attracting attention; operating a shortwave radio with excessive volume; failing to manage the changeover to a relieving team unobtrusively; telephoning repeatedly from the same store or filling station.

16. Notes

Since the activities observed during a surveillance may later become part of the evidence in a trial or perhaps become the basis of a subsequent interrogation, it is highly important that a record of the day's observations should be made. This should take the form of a log—a chronological record of the activities of both the surveillant and the subject. The reason for recording the movements of the surveillant lies in the importance of definitely establishing his movements for the purposes of cross-examination in a trial. An accurate knowledge of the subject's activities will prove of great value in an interrogation of the subject. By making shrewd guesses as to the purpose of the subject's movements, the interrogator can often lead the subject into the belief that his knowledge is quite detailed and intimate. The subject may more easily be persuaded into a confession. Moreover, a written record can be objectively studied in retrospect for the purpose of evaluating the results of the surveillance. By integrating the separate reports of each surveillant, the investigator may be able to construct a logical pattern of the subject's behavior which can serve as a criterion for the validity of the hypothesis that led to the surveillance. The following is a suggested log form:

Notes on a Surveillance
Case No. ....

Investigator's Name
Date: ....

1. Operator's arrival—time and place ....
2. Exact time of all items...
3. Description of premises—exits and entrances ....
4. Data on auto ....
5. First observation..
6. Telephone calls ....
7. Conversations...
8. Persons contacted by subject ....
9. Places visited by subject...
10. Period covered...
11. Time of relief...

17. Conclusion

It is not assumed that the treatment of this subject which has been given above will provide the investigator with an unfailing method of dealing with every surveillance situation. A surveillance is a minor form of conflict. No fixed pattern can be prescribed.

General principles should be studied with the prevailing reservation that the strategy will depend for its success upon an intelligent implementation of tactics. Thus, procedures must be frequently improvised to suit the requirements of the situation; the nature of these will, of course, depend upon the resourcefulness of the surveillant. When should he run the risk of being "made?" Is the time element sufficiently liberal that he may safely drop the suspect at this point to obviate the danger of recognition? When should the obviously fruitless surveillance be terminated? It should be apparent that the successful surveillant is the end product of training, experience, and native intelligence. Rigid adherence to rules and dogged perseverance alone will not suffice.

18. Methods of Private Investigators

The very nature of private investigative work requires intense concentration on the art of surveillance. As a result of extended study, exceptional ingenuity, and impressive expense authorizations, private agencies have developed a number of excellent instrumental techniques for surveillance.

a. **Automobile Surveillance.** One agency simplifies the problem of tailing a vehicle by attaching to the understructure of the vehicle a miniature transmitter with a mercury battery as the power supply. The investigator's car, equipped with a receiver and a direction-finding antenna, can then follow at a distance which precludes detection.

b. **Wiretaps and Bugs.** A *wiretap* is an electronic device that picks up both ends of a telephone conversation. A *bug* detects voices in a defined space. Protection from wiretapping is based on the Federal Communications Act of 1934, while protection from bugging relies on the Fourth and Fourteenth Amendments. Federal law authorizing both is based on Title III of the Omnibus Crime Control and Safe Streets Act of 1968. The short description of some of these eavesdropping devices given below overlooks the technical difficulties associated with their use:

1) *Wiretaps.* The telephone can be tapped at a number of places along the line, either in the building, along the street lines, or even at the telephone exchange. The tapped line is monitored

by earphones or run into a recorder. Instruments are available that record only when the line is in use. The more common forms of tapping are the following:

a) DIRECT TAP. This is the most common form. A direct tap is placed right on the phone pair in the phone company's bridge box, usually located in the basement. A set of wires is attached to the specified pair in the box and run into a tape recorder or a headset concealed nearby.

b) PARASITE TAP. This is a miniature transmitter wired into and drawing power from the telephone line. A variant of this device is the so-called *parallel tap,* which includes a small microphone as well as a transmitter. It has a self-contained battery but can draw auxiliary power from the telephone itself.

c) INDUCTION COIL. Various types of coils and pick-up loops can be used in coupling to an active telephone line for the purpose of monitoring the conversations.

2) *Bugs.* The bug is a sophisticated radiating device in the form of a self-contained receiver and transmitter. In size some of these instruments are no larger than a fingernail and thus can be readily concealed in some part of a room. The listener can be in an adjoining room or even outside the building, depending on the nature of the instrument. Another device in this category is the body-worn transmitter. The capacities and limitations of concealed microphones in general can be studied in the references at the end of this chapter.

c. **Recorder.** The problem of surreptitiously recording conversations has been greatly simplified by the development of small instruments such as the pocket-sized recorder. These instruments are tape recorders of the approximate size of the 35mm camera. They may be readily concealed in a pocket and will record for two hours. Other recorders, with longer running time, are concealed in suitcases and briefcases.

d. **Television.** The television camera and receiver have been added to the resources of the private investigators. By means of a closed circuit television system the activities of the subject can be observed by the surveillant at a distance. A number of private companies have installed these circuits to watch the activities and general behavior of their employees. In one factory four concealed cameras were installed to visually monitor the production line. A receiving set, connected to the cameras by a coaxial cable, was installed in the office of the plant manager. The employees of any section of the production line could then be observed by the manager surreptitiously and leisurely.

19. Eavesdropping and the Law

The increased use of wiretapping and the rapid development of microphones and transmitting devices in miniature form have aroused concern in the courts and among lawmakers for the protection of individual privacy. Responding to this need Congress passed Title III of the Omnibus Crime Control and Safe Streets Act of 1968, 18 U.S.C. 2510–2520 prohibiting the interception of wire and oral communications by federal law enforcement officers except in one of the following circumstances:

1) Where one party consents;
2) Where a court order authorizing the interception is granted;
3) Where an officer determines that an emergency situation exists involving national security or organized crime, under the condition that he later obtains judicial authorization.

Except in cases of consent of one party, state officers do not have the right to intercept communications unless a state law authorizes it. To be admissible in court, all evidence must be obtained according to the provisions of this federal law.

20. Surveillance and Society

The scientific revolution of the past few decades has provided a technology that vastly increases the potential scope and effectiveness of technical surveillance. The threat to individual privacy has grown in proportion, while the problem of imposing protective controls on the use of technical surveillance has become equally formidable in size and complexity. Since the investigator is closer to the base of the problem, he should acquire an appreciation of its true scope and a sense of his personal responsibility to contribute to an ethical solution consistent with his claim to professional status. After all, the essential element in the definition of a professional man is this—he is a person who answers to himself for his own conduct.

a. **Categories of Surveillance.** Three broad categories of surveillance have been suggested to correspond respectively to what a person is doing, what he is thinking, and what he has done and thought in the past:

1) *Physical Surveillance* is concerned with what a person is doing or saying; hence it embraces those activities which can be apprehended by the senses, mainly sight and hearing. The methods described in this chapter belong in this category. Included, also, are eavesdropping, wiretapping, picture-taking, and spying. The technological facilities for accomplishing these forms of surveillance are impressive in variety and sophistication.

2) *Psychological Surveillance* is concerned with what a person is thinking and feeling. It is concerned with man's mind—his thinking, beliefs, opinions, feelings, and reactions. The tools of this form of surveillance include lie detectors, employment forms, personality tests, and the use of mind drugs. The areas of interest may include sex, religion, ethics, politics, and the normative references of behavior in general.

3) *Data Surveillance* is concerned with what a person *has* done or *has* thought. It consists, therefore, of the innumerable records man leaves behind in his journey through life—birth certificates, church records, school records, records of offenses, of credit and debt, of employment and of employers' estimates of character, of military service, and so forth. The major tool is, of course, the giant computer, centralized, comprehensive, infinite in appetite, instant in response, and forever faultless in memory.

Business has now supplanted the government as the chief data collector in our country. The corporate computer has become a repository of both the mundane and the intimate details of our lives. The kind and the extent of this personal information is dismaying. Telephone companies have a record of every long distance call we make. Banks have a copy of every check we write and a record of every credit card purchase. Insurance companies know our complete medical history while the pharmacies have a computerized list of all the medicines we take. Airline and car rental companies know where we have been and where we plan to go. Video stores have a list of every movie we have rented and the cable television company has a record of every pay-per-view show that we have ordered from the "privacy" of our own homes.

   b. **Applications.** The uses of these forms of surveillance are too many and too familiar to enumerate. Many of these applications are well intended, but most of them can be adapted to questionable purposes and worse. The businessman, for example, may in good faith conceive the notion of researching customer reaction by means of hidden microphones, but subsequently he will find it difficult to resist the temptation of taping a sample of his employees' conversations, especially if his industrial psychologist supports his inspiration with a suitable label, such as "Employee-Attitude Sampling," or if his security chief seconds the recommendation on the grounds that it may provide a clue to the perpetrators of a series of inside merchandise thefts. Thus, the steps leading from legitimate inquiry into unjustified snooping are insensibly graduated to suit the spiritual gait of all but the most scrupulously honorable.

   Together these three categories of surveillance with their highly sophisticated supporting apparatus represent a massive threat to the individual as such. They menace that aspect of the person which makes him, in his own mind, an individual—namely his privacy. The acknowledgment of human dignity takes the primary form of conceding the individual the privacy of his thoughts and converse.

   c. **Supervision and Control.** Ordinarily we should look to the Supreme Court for protective rules against the invasion of privacy. In recent years the Court has tended to lay down objective standards for law enforcement conduct designed to permit close judicial supervision, despite the cost of such control in terms of convictions. The problems presented by the immensely broadened field of surveillance, however, cannot be solved by federal controls or restrictive rules similar to those prescribed for testing the legality of wiretapping. The Supreme Court cannot police the policeman by means of exclusionary rules issued and enforced by Washington. It must inevitably bow to the reality that the people of each community must shoulder much of the responsibility for enforcing the Constitution in their own area. The local law enforcement agencies, as the key representatives of the community in these matters, must assume major responsibility for the proper conduct of surveillances and the lawful use of the resources of the various categories of surveillance. The ultimate determinant in this area, however, must be the ethical judgment of the individual investigator, guided by the spirit of the law as interpreted through court decisions and by the policy statements of his organization.

In this connection, we should recall that the investigator is selected for three major qualities—character, judgment, and the ability to deal with people—and that the most important of these is character, the habit of acting on principle. The efficacy of any policy or set of rules will depend on the character of the investigator to whom they are issued. In this sense the law enforcement agencies constitute the propylon of the temple of justice. And in this spirit, too, we can understand Justice Oliver Wendell Holmes's observation that the law of the land may be the United States Constitution but to most of us it's whatever the policeman on the beat says it is.

ADDITIONAL READING

Physical Surveillance

Buckwalter, A.: *Surveillance and Undercover Investigation.* Stoneham, Mass.: Butterworth, 1984.

Degarmo, J.W., Jr.: The Nature of Physical Surveillances. 42 *Police Chief,* 2, 1975.

DiPietro, A.L.: Aerial Surveillance: Fourth Amendment Considerations. 58 *FBI Law Enforcement Bulletin,* 12, 1989.

Hough, H.: *A Practical Guide to Photographic Intelligence.* Port Townsend, Wash.: Loompanics, 1990.

Lapin, L.: *How to Get Anything on Anybody—Book II: The Encyclopedia of Personal Surveillance.* Port Townsend, Wash.: Loompanics, 1991.

Kingston, K.A.: Reasonable Expectation of Privacy Cases Revive Traditional Investigative Techniques. 57 *FBI Law Enforcement Bulletin,* 11, 1988.

McEvoy, R.T., Jr.: Surveillance Photography: What You Need to Know. *Law Enforcement Technology,* February/March, 1986.

McGuiness, R.L.: In the *Katz* Eye: Use of Binoculars and Telescopes. Parts I and II. 50 *FBI Law Enforcement Bulletin,* 6 and 7, 1981.

Rapp, B.: *Shadowing and Surveillance: A Complete Guide Book.* Port Townsend, Wash.: Loompanics, 1985.

Sighting in the Dark. 34 *Law and Order,* 6, 1986.

Siljander, R.P.: *Applied Surveillance Photography.* Springfield, Ill.: Thomas, 1975.

————: *Fundamentals of Physical Surveillance.* Springfield, Ill.: Thomas, 1978.

Siuru, W.D., Jr.: Turning Night into Day. 37 *Law and Order,* 7, 1989.

Vandiver, J.V.: Electronic Visual Surveillance. 36 *Law and Order,* 10, 1988.

Electronic Surveillance

Bourniquel, P.M.: Visiophone: French High-Tech Security. 60 *FBI Law Enforcement Bulletin,* 7, 1991.

Church, G.J.: The Art of High-Tech Snooping. 129 *Time,* 16, April 20, 1987.

French, S. and Lapin, L.: *Spy Game: Winning Through Super Technology.* Port Townsend, Wash.: Loompanics, 1985.

Hollien, H.: *The Acoustics of Crime: The New Science of Forensic Phonetics.* New York, Plenum Press, 1990.

Jones, R.N.: *Electronic Eavesdropping Techniques and Equipment.* Washington, D.C.: National Institute of Law Enforcement and Criminal Justice, 1975.

Moran, W.B.(Ed.): *Covert Surveillance and Electronic Penetration.* Port Townsend, Wash.: Loompanics, 1983.

Neville, H.C.: Foiling the Electronic Eavesdroppers: A Survey of Available Countermeasures. 12 *Security World,* 4, 1975.

Pollock, D.A.: *Methods of Electronic Audio Surveillance.* Springfield, Ill.: Thomas, 1984.

Surette, R.: Video Street Patrol: Media Technology and Street Crime. 13 *Journal of Police Science and Administration,* 78, 1985.

Vandiver, J.V.: Surveillance: Eavesdropping and Wiretapping: Equipment and Techniques. 36 *Law and Order,* 9, 1988.

Electronic Surveillance and the Law

Carr, J.C.: *The Law of Electronic Surveillance,* 2nd ed. New York, Boardman, 1986.

Courtney, J.: Electronic Eavesdropping—Wiretapping and Your Right to Privacy. 26 *Federal Communications Bar Journal,* 1, 1973.

Federal Government Information Technology: Electronic Surveillance and Civil Liberties. Washington, D.C.: U.S. Government Printing Office, 1985.

Fiatal, R.A.: The Electronic Communications Privacy Act: Addressing Today's Technology. Parts I, II and III. 57 *FBI Law Enforcement Bulletin,* 2, 3 and 4, 1988.

————: Lights, Camera, Action: Video Surveillance and the Fourth Amendment. Parts I and II. 58 *FBI Law Enforcement Bulletin,* 1 and 2, 1989.

————: Minimization Requirements in Electronic Surveillance. Parts I and II. 56 *FBI Law Enforcement Bulletin,* 5 and 6, 1987.

Hall, J.C.: Electronic Tracking Devices: Following the Fourth Amendment. Parts I and II. 54 *FBI Law Enforcement Bulletin,* 2 and 3, 1985.

Paulsen, M.G.: *The Problems of Electronic Eavesdropping.* Philadelphia, American Law Institute, 1977.

Saunders, E.F.: Electronic Eavesdropping and the Right to Privacy. 52 *Boston University Law Review,* 831, 1972.

Sharp, A.G.: The Rights and Wrongs of Taping Phone Calls. 38 *Law and Order,* 2, 1990.

U.S. Attorney's Manual on Electronic Surveillance. Port Townsend, Wash.: Loompanics, 1988.

Chapter 16

UNDERCOVER ASSIGNMENTS

1. Information

U NDERCOVER work or "roping," as it is sometimes called, is a form of investigation in which the investigator assumes a different and unofficial identity in order to obtain information. It may be classed as a method of surveillance. In its most effective form the investigator wins the confidence of the subject and induces him to reveal the desired information. The investigator, by adopting an identity compatible with the surroundings in which he will work, places himself in a position where he will be able to observe and gain the confidence of the subject.

Undercover work is a useful technique in crimes which require organization. "Selling crimes" involving drugs, alcohol, pornographic literature, stolen goods, frauds, contraband, or black market operations will constitute a large part of undercover work. In the investigation of subversive activities and systematic thefts undercover operations are almost indispensable. Undercover work is most successfully used when there is knowledge that certain persons are engaged in criminal activity but proof that may be used in court is lacking. It is especially effective in the investigation of ongoing offenses, such as blackmail or extortion. In such cases the undercover agent must gain the confidence of a criminal whose identity is known but against whom more evidence must be gathered. Verbal admissions may be obtained if the acquaintance is sufficiently developed, or better, a microphone can be placed surreptitiously in the rooms occupied by the suspect so that a recording can be made of any conversations concerning the blackmailing operations.

An investigator of the same ethnic background is sometimes

placed in the cell of a criminal. The undercover agent is selected, among other reasons, because he speaks the foreign language used by his "cell mate." The common national background and language compatibility, sympathy, reticence, or other assumed attitude needed to gain the confidence of the criminal has frequently been the means of gathering information about a particular crime or the activities of an organized mob which could not be obtained in any other way. The undercover agent who has infiltrated into a criminal gang is in a position to learn the operations, feelings, past activities, and future plans of his "confederates." This information coupled with that obtained by intercepting telephone conversations among gang members can lead ultimately to the building of a successful case against the gang or any individual in it.

2. Objectives

The general objective of an undercover investigation is the obtaining of information. Usually the information is desired for the purpose of evidence. There are situations, however, where the information is sought simply to lay the groundwork for a separate and major investigative step. The following objectives comprehend most of the investigative situations in which undercover work is employed:

a. **Obtaining Evidence.** The undercover worker places himself in an excellent position for obtaining evidence, either direct or physical. He can observe criminal activities, listen to conversations, photograph documents, and perform many other useful services.

b. **Obtaining Information.** The undercover worker is close to the most reliable source of information—the criminals themselves. He may find himself in the position of having the criminal explain to him the very details of the crime.

c. **Checking Informants.** If it is suspected that an informant's reports are prejudiced, misleading, or inaccurate, an undercover check can be made.

d. **Fixed Surveillance.** The most effective position for a surveillance is in the bosom of the criminal family. The undercover worker can even become a friend of the subject so that he is aware of every move made by him. He can also assist in the installation and maintenance of investigative equipment.

e. **Preliminary to Search.** The investigator can lay part of the legal basis of the search by determining the presence of contraband, for example, or by observing criminal activities. In addition he can assist the surreptitious approach of the searchers.

3. Selection of the Undercover Worker

Since the undercover assignment is the most sensitive type of investigative work, the selection of the operator must be made with great care. The ideal undercover agent is a combination of an actor and a good investigator. The selection should be made with consideration of the following elements:

a. **Background.** If the assignment places the agent in a special milieu, he must fit into the environment. His physical and other racial characteristics should not stand out. He must be able to suit his speech and line of thinking to that of his associates. His educational and technical background must rise to the required level. His conversation, knowledge of hobbies, and sports, as well as general information should suit the particular social stratum in which he will find himself.

b. **Temperament.** A calm, affable, enduring personality is required. He should have the necessary self-confidence to carry him through the more trying moments and the resourcefulness to adjust to a change of plans or situation.

c. **Intellect.** The undercover agent must above all be intelligent. He should have a clear view of the objective of the mission and the overall strategy that must be employed in its accomplishment. A retentive memory and keen imagination will serve him in good stead. Finally he should be an excellent observer and a person of sound judgments. Major decisions may be required during the course of the assignment. A mere tactical adjustment may be insufficient in a crisis. A critical situation will require the judgment of a good mind to avoid jeopardizing the whole investigation.

4. Assignment

The nature of undercover work can vary widely. A given assignment may require the investigator to place himself in several different social settings, testing to the fullest his resourcefulness, adaptability, and endurance. As a general rule the more complex assignment is more demanding in the completeness and flawlessness of the cover story which is employed. An assignment, for example, to perform undercover work with a group of competent racketeers entails serious hazards and requires the utmost attention to details. Among the more common types of assignment are the following:

a. **Neighborhood Assignment.** Here the investigator must move into the neighborhood of the subjects. In some situations it may be necessary to move into the rooming house of a subject. The assimilation of the undercover agent into the neighborhood background must be gradual and natural. A long period of time is required before the agent is accepted and his comparatively recent accession to the neighborhood is forgotten.

b. **Social Assignment.** In this type of work the investigator must frequent clubs, taverns, or other social meeting places visited by the subject or known to be centers of illegal activity.

c. **Work Assignment.** In the investigation of systematic thefts in a place of business it is usually necessary for the investigator to assume the role of a fellow employee. The work assignment can also be employed in place of the neighborhood type. The part of the employee is one of the simplest of undercover roles. The agent is not required to explain or justify his presence. If the job which the agent fills is a sales or clerical position, the assignment is relatively simple. Professions and trades require some experience or training prior to engagement in the assignment.

5. Preparation for the Assignment

If an investigator is working under the control of a superior, he should not undertake an undercover assignment without the express authorization of his superior officer. The type of character which the investigator should assume will be determined by the subject of the investigation. The following preparations for undercover work are recommended:

a. **Study of the Subject.** Unless the investigator has a thorough knowledge of his subject, he will find himself frequently at a disadvantage. The investigator should, as a first step in the preparation, draw up a checklist of the details of the subject's character and history.

1) *Name.* Full name, aliases, and nicknames. If he holds public office, then the title and the name of the department.

2) *Addresses.* Past and present, residential and business.

3) *Description.* A portrait parlé as given in Chapter 29.

4) *Family and Relatives.* An acquaintance with members of the family may suggest another source of information.

5) *Associates.* This knowledge is essential to an understanding of the subject's activities.

6) *Character and Temperament.* The strengths and weaknesses of the adversary should be known. Likes, dislikes, and prejudices are particularly helpful.

7) *Vices.* Drug addiction, alcohol, gambling, etc.

8) *Hobbies.* Suggest a simple way of developing acquaintance. A common interest of this nature creates a strong bond of sympathy.

9) *Education.* This knowledge suggests the limitations of the subject and will indicate the desired level of education in the investigator.

10) *Occupation and Speciality.* These suggest, again, a possible meeting ground and are also indicative of the character of the subject.

b. **Knowledge of the Area.** The investigator should make a thorough study of the area in which he is to operate. If he is to pretend previous residence there, he should possess an intimate knowledge of neighborhood details. The following checklist can be used.

1) *Maps.* The general layout and features of the area can be learned from a street map. Bordering areas should be included in the study.

2) *National and Religious Background.* The predominant racial characteristics of the inhabitants can be learned from a resident or from police officers assigned to posts in the area.

3) **Transportation.** The routes of surface lines and subways should be known together with their service schedules.

4) **Public Services.** The investigator should have a general familiarity with the schedule of mail delivery, trash pickup, utility meter reading, and other public services.

5) **Restaurants, Bars, and Stores.** It is important to know the location of the most popular neighborhood restaurants, fast-food outlets, bars, nightclubs, supermarkets, and convenience stores.

c. **Cover Story.** A fictitious background and history for the new character of the investigator should be prepared, including the names, addresses, and descriptions of the assumed places of education, employment, associates, neighborhoods, trades, and travels. The investigator's background story should seldom, if ever, be wholly fictitious. It is usually advisable for the investigator to maintain that he is from a city in which he has lived and with which he is well acquainted. If it can be avoided, the home town of one of the subjects should not be selected as the origin of the investigator. Arrangements should be made to have principals in the fictitious history ready to corroborate the assertions of the undercover investigator, as the criminals may investigate his claims. It is good practice to select corroborating principals who are engaged in occupations which will not cause suspicion or arouse too much interest on the part of the subjects. It is imperative for the successful undercover investigator to possess all of the requisites for the assignment, such as appropriate personality, ability, background story, and attention to details.

Provisions should be made in the cover story for some of the following:

1) Frequent contact with the subject.

2) Freedom of movement and justification for actions.

3) Background that will permit the investigator to maintain a financial and social status equivalent to that of the subject.

4) Mutual points of interest between agent and subject.

5) Means of communication with agent's superiors.

6) Alternate cover story in the event that the original cover story is compromised, i.e., "Plan B."

7) A method of leaving the area quietly at the conclusion of the mission.

d. **Physical Details.** Personal possessions should be obtained for the undercover investigator which are appropriate to the character assumed in quality, price, age, fit, degree of cleanliness, laundry marks, and manufacturer's design; and ostensibly obtained from the place which the undercover man will claim as his origin. Personal possessions may include clothes, a wallet, a watch, a ring, a token, a suitcase, stubs of tickets from movie theaters and transportation agencies, cigarettes, matches, photographs, letters, certificates, or amounts of money. The undercover investigator must not possess any articles which will suggest his true identity. Badge or credentials must never be found on the person of an undercover agent; and a firearm or other weapon may be carried only where compatible with the investigator's background story.

e. **Testing.** The investigator should memorize all details in connection with his assumed role and the fictitious portions of his biography. He should be tested by prolonged questioning and surprise inquiries.

f. **Disclosure of Identity.** The investigator should be instructed whether to disclose his identity or remain undercover if arrested by other authorities. A plan or act should also be laid out against the contingency of accidental disclosure of identity.

6. Conduct of the Assignment

a. **Demeanor.** The undercover man must in every respect live the part which he plays. His appearance, language, attitude, opinions, interests, and recreations must support the assumed role. He should speak little, but let his actions carry conviction. When required, he must speak and act with assurance regarding his assumed past and trade, as he may be called upon to demonstrate his knowledge of the assumed trade. An undercover man should not ask questions except as part of the assumed identity, because inquiries usually attract attention. Bragging or showing too much knowledge may also invite unwanted attention.

b. **Approach.** Making contact with the subject or subjects is normally the first hurdle for the undercover investigator. As a general rule, the undercover man should create a situation where the subject or subjects become interested in and approach him, thinking he is what he purports to be. Many a subject has become interested in an undercover man who lived in the same rooming house, one whom he encountered frequently in the neighborhood or at a club or business house, or one who supposedly was vacationing, hunting a job, or a reputed expert in a matter which was a hobby of the subject.

c. **Entrapment.** It is against public policy for an officer of the law to incite or participate in the commission of a crime; the undercover man must, therefore, take care not to get involved as an accessory to a crime. He may pretend to fall in with their plans, but should never make any suggestions or promises, or render any real assistance with regard to the perpetration of crime. He should not be guilty of planting the criminal idea into the mind of the subject. At the trial the subject may plead entrapment and fix the responsibility for his actions on the agent.

Narcotics undercover work is particularly susceptible to entrapment charges. The accused may assert that the police provided the money, motivation, and connections to make the deal or that the police forced him to supply heroin. The undercover agent can protect himself from these charges by making several buys from the same dealer and also by obtaining testimony relating to the character and reputation of the accused. As a general rule the undercover worker can avoid such a charge if he maintains a restrained and passive role and does not engage in "creative activity" with respect to the commission of the offense.

7. Taking Notes

Written notes should be made by an investigator only when they are of unusual importance and when they cannot otherwise be remembered: They should be written in such a manner as to be unintelligible to anyone else. Numbers may be written as parts of a mathematical problem or as a telephone number. They may be written on inconspicuous materials such as chewing gum or cigarette wrappers, toilet paper, paper napkins, match boxes and covers, magazines, or on the wall paper in certain types of dwellings. Exposed film should not be kept in the agent's possession. It should be sent in immediately even though there is only one exposure on the roll.

8. Communication with Headquarters

a. **Telephone.** Communication between headquarters and the undercover investigator must be accomplished by secret methods. When contacting headquarters, it is best to call from a public telephone. To lessen the possibility of wiretapping, the investigator should use a different telephone for each call.

b. **Written reports** may be addressed to a fictitious girlfriend at a prearranged general delivery address which is under the control of officials from headquarters. It is best not to put the undercover investigator's return address on the envelope as the post office department might return it to the investigator's dwelling for insufficient postage or other reason, in which case it might fall into improper hands. Since criminals usually have little correspondence, the investigator should not become conspicuous by the posting of numerous letters. To preclude the possibility of the reports falling into improper hands before mailing, they may be written in the post office and mailed there.

c. **Meetings** at secret, prearranged rendezvous may be held with representatives from headquarters, but this method of communication is dangerous, as the investigator may be tailed to the rendezvous. If the investigator, en route to the rendezvous, discovers he is being followed he may "lose" his follower in such a manner as not to show a deliberate attempt, or he may forgo the rendezvous and pursue a course which would appear natural to the "shadow."

d. **Emergency.** The possibility of making telephone reports to one's superiors while in the presence of the subjects should not be overlooked when it is imperative that headquarters be notified immediately of the latest developments. This communication may be accomplished by calling an unlisted number at headquarters or at the home of an associate investigator, under the pretext of calling a friend or business person on some routine matter. In such cases, the investigator should be sure that the person telephoned knows the alias with which he is addressed, understands the situation, and will cooperate.

9. Arrest of the Undercover Investigator

If the investigator is arrested by the police he will act in accordance with his orders. If he has not received orders regarding the disclosure of his identity in case of arrest by other law enforcement officers, he must act according to his judgment. In such a case, if retaining his assumed character does not serve a useful purpose, the investigator should refuse to make a statement except to a member of his own organization.

10. Departure

The undercover investigator should not "vanish." A plausible reason for departure should be invented. Discharge from employment, family illness, and fear of local police are among the many reasons that can be offered. The agent should leave open the avenue of return; otherwise a resumption of the assignment becomes too difficult.

11. Large-Scale Operations

Undercover work varies widely in the period of time consumed and the extent of the cover. The simplest activity is the buy and bust operation in which the undercover agent, on finding an unwary narcotics seller, tries to make a deal and thereafter arrest the dealer. More sustained and elaborate operations have been set up by a number of police agencies in the form of illegal "fences"—a rented warehouse and several plainclothesmen posing as criminals, one of whom, of course, is "Mr. Big." The purpose of the operation is to recover stolen property and to identify and arrest the thieves and fences responsible. Most charges relate to the stolen goods unwittingly sold to the police before hidden cameras and microphones, but these operations have led also to arrests for murder, rape, bank robbery, arson and other offenses. The buying and selling of stolen property permits the development of close relationships with suspects who think they are dealing with fellow criminals.

ADDITIONAL READING

Undercover Assignments

Anderson, K.P.: *Undercover Operations: A Manual for the Private Investigator.* Boulder, Col.: Paladin Press, 1988.

Barefoot, J.K.: *Undercover Investigation,* 2nd ed. Stoneham, Mass.: Butterworth, 1983.

Buckwalter, A.: *Surveillance and Undercover Investigation.* Stoneham, Mass.: Butterworth, 1984.

Hicks, R.D. II: *Undercover Operations and Persuasion.* Springfield, Ill.: Thomas, 1973.

MacInaugh, E.A.: *Disguise Techniques.* Port Townsend, Wash.: Loompanics, 1984.

Pistone, J.D. and Woodley, R.: *Donnie Brasco: My Undercover Life in the Mafia.* New York, NAL–Dutton, 1989.

Rapp, B.: *Undercover Work: A Complete Handbook.* Port Townsend, Wash.: Loompanics, 1985.

Sample, J.: *Methods of Disguise.* Port Townsend, Wash.: Loompanics, 1984.

Schiano, A. and Burton, A.: *Self-Portrait of an Undercover Cop.* New York, Dodd Mead, 1973.

Vasquez, I.J. and Kelley, S.A.: Management's Commitment to the Undercover Operative: A Contemporary View. 58 *FBI Law Enforcement Bulletin,* 2, 1989.

Wade, G.E.: Undercover Violence. 59 *FBI Law Enforcement Bulletin,* 4, 1990.

Sting Operation

See Chapter 20, Additional Reading, **Criminal Receiving.**

PART IV
SPECIFIC OFFENSES

Chapter 17

ARSON

E VERY FIRE IS assumed to be from natural causes unless proven otherwise. A fire does not become arson until it has been inspected and declared to be so by a fire marshall, a member of the fire department who is trained in arson investigation. During the course of a year, there may be hundreds of suspicious fires in a major city that, for lack of manpower, will not be investigated. In a recession, the arson statistics are expected to rise because many owners will burn their unprofitable businesses or their homes that have decreased in value in order to collect insurance money. At the same time, if the city is conserving money by laying off fire marshalls, the number of arson cases reported will decline. Paradoxically, there will be an increase in arson activity while the statistics reflect a decline in the number of arson incidents.

Besides a lack of trained fire investigators, there are other difficulties in determining the number of arson fires. There is usually a lack of witnesses because arson is a crime of stealth, often taking place at night under the cover of darkness. Moreover, the physical evidence that would connect the offender with the offense is often consumed in the blaze. Because of the difficulty of determining how many of the fires of "unknown causes" are in fact deliberately set fires, there are no accurate figures for the number of arson incidents in a given year. The National Fire Protection Association, a private organization that publishes annual statistics for arson, estimates for the year 1990 that there were 97,000 structural fires that were "deliberately set or suspicious" causing approximately $1.394 billion in property damages. In its *Uniform Crime Reports* for 1991, the FBI records a rate of arrest of about 1 suspect for every 6 arson incidents reported to them. Arson is a crime committed primarily by young men. Of the arson offenders arrested,

255

87 percent were male, 47 percent were below the age of 18, and 66 percent below the age of 25.

Arson is not always a solo activity. It will sometimes involve a conspiracy, that is, a group of persons organized to accomplish the offense in a professional manner. In a case in Suffolk County, Massachusetts, an organized arson ring took on the character of a commercial enterprise, complete with entrepreneurs, brokers, middlemen, and agents. In one morning, as part of a state police raid, twenty-two persons were arrested, among them six attorneys, eleven real estate operators, four public insurance adjustors, one police officer, and a retired fire chief. A total of twenty-six men were ultimately arraigned on charges as varied as fraud, bribery, and murder—and all were alleged to have committed arson. In general, they were accused of contracting with landlords, financially troubled shopkeepers, warehouse owners, and others to burn down their buildings for insurance with a provision for sharing in the claim.

Smaller-scale operations are, of course, more common. For some landlords arson is seen as a means of profitably liquidating otherwise unprofitable assets. The following pattern has been discerned in areas such as the South Bronx: the tenants are driven out by cutting off the heat or water; the fire insurance is paid up or even increased with a promise of improvements; finally the firesetter is hired. From one point of view the landlord is selling his building to the insurance company because no one else will buy it.

The traditional problem in the investigation of arson is that of proof—the fire too often consumes the evidence and the clues. The traces of the arsonist's activity are burned with the property. In the choice of method the arsonist can still rely on the simple approach of matches, fuses, and gasoline. There are, however, expert firesetters whose ingenuity is impressive. In one case the arsonist deactivated the sprinkler system by building a wooden collar around the main pipe, filling it with dry ice, and thereby freezing the water in the pipe. In the subsequent blaze this clever contrivance disappeared and it was only through other investigative bypaths that its use was discovered.

Because the arsonist may be part of a conspiracy, investigators have to reach out farther than the fire scene for means of proof. For example, federal prosecutors have used the federal mail fraud statutes (the mails are used for false insurance claims) because it is often easier to prove mail fraud than to establish the perpetrator at the scene or to prove interstate travel to plan arson. The formidable difficulties encountered in proving arson are best shown by insurance company records. Although the companies bring only 10 percent of questionable fire cases to civil court, they still lose eight out of ten such suits.

I. BURNING OF BUILDINGS

1. Arson Defined

Arson is the malicious burning of another's house. The gravity of the offense lies in the danger to the lives of persons who may be dwelling in the house at the time of the fire. The spirit of the common law implies that arson is a crime against the security of a dwelling house as such and not against property. Various state statutes, however, provide for the punishment of burning property as such under the law of arson. The elements of proof required in the aggravated form of arson are concerned with the "burning," "malice" and "dwelling" aspects of the offense:

a. **Burning.** A structure is not burned within the meaning of an accusation of arson until some part of it is heated to the point of ignition. Any appreciable burning is sufficient. It is not necessary that there be a flame or that the structure be consumed or materially injured. The ignition satisfies the requirement of burning.

b. **Inhabited Dwelling.** If the structure is used exclusively or in part specifically for dwelling purposes it is classed as an *inhabited dwelling*. The essential consideration is the use which is made of the building; it is not essential that a human being be actually present in an "inhabited dwelling." Thus a trailer, tent, church, or theater can be the subject of an aggravated arson. The value and ownership should be proved even in aggravated arson, since they provide an additional method of identifying the dwelling or structure. Facts related to the identity of the actual occupants should be obtained.

c. **Malice.** Unless there is a malicious intent to burn, no crime of arson exists. Malice is the intent to do injury to another. Fires caused by negligence or accident do not constitute arson. The intent is to be inferred from the facts. The conditions surrounding the act such as threats, quarrels, expressions of dislike, applications of fire insurance, and so forth, may supply a basis for inferring intent. The prosecution must show that a burning was accomplished with criminal design. The law presumes that a fire is accidental in origin; hence the criminal design must be shown beyond a reasonable doubt.

2. Attempted Arson

Attempted arson is an act done with specific intent to commit arson which, except for the intervention of some preventing cause, apparently would result in the actual commission of the offense. The attempt, consequently, must be accompanied by some overt act designed to carry out the intent. The mere gathering of incendiary materials with malicious intent to burn a structure is not an attempt to commit arson. If, however, a lighted match is applied to the structure or other property, the act is an attempt to commit arson even though the match may be immediately extinguished by the elements or otherwise.

3. Methods of Proof

The investigation of arson often presents a complex problem because the methods employed by incendiaries and the manner in which they operate are far greater in number and more varied in aspect than those employed by most other types of criminal. Proof of the commission of the offense is rendered more difficult because the physical evidence, normally providing material assistance in an investigation, is often destroyed by the criminal act itself. The same basic elements of all criminal investigations, however, are required of arson inquiries, namely, the establishment of the *corpus delicti* and the identification of the perpetrator.

a. **Corpus Delicti.** Since in law every fire is presumed to be of accidental origin until proved otherwise, this presumption must be overcome before an arson charge can be established. Evidence must be adduced to show the *corpus delicti* of the offense, that is, the existence of the essential facts demonstrating that the offense had been committed. It must be emphasized that the unsupported confession of a person with respect to the burning is insufficient and inadmissible in the absence of a substantial and independent showing of the *corpus delicti.* To establish the *corpus delicti* the following two facts must be established:

1) *Burning.* It must be shown that there was a fire, i.e., a burning or charring as distinguished from a mere scorching. The burning of the property and its location can be established by the direct testimony of the complainant, fire department personnel, or other eyewitnesses. Physical evidence in the form of burned parts of the building may also be offered as proof.

2) *Criminal Design.* It must be shown that the fire was willfully set by a person criminally responsible. This may be established directly by the discovery of an incendiary device or plant such as a candle or mechanical arrangement, by the unexplained presence of accelerants such as kerosene or gasoline, or by eyewitness testimony. Negatively, the incendiary nature of the fire can be shown by the elimination of accidental and natural causes. The testimony of technical experts, expressing the opinion that the fire was not of an accidental or natural origin, can be used. Electrical, heating, or structural engineers, for example, can, if properly qualified, testify to the absence of wiring deficiencies, structural defects, or other conditions which could cause fire. The evidence should be sufficient to exclude every reasonable hypothesis other than that the property was feloniously burned.

b. **Other Evidence.** Once the *corpus delicti* is established, any legal and sufficient evidence, direct or circumstantial, may be introduced to show that the act was committed by the accused and that it was done with criminal intent. In arson cases direct evidence is ordinarily lacking with respect to the connection of the offender with the crime and great reliance must be placed on circumstantial evidence. The following general types of evidence will usually be encountered in addition to those discussed in the preceding paragraphs.

1) *Evidence Associating the Suspect with the Scene.* Clue materials such as tools, matches, and articles of clothing may be found at the scene and sometimes traced to the suspect. Similarly, the suspect may have carried on his person or clothing traces which link him to the scene.

2) *Evidence Showing Intent.* The actions of the suspect can frequently offer evidence of criminal intent. For example, anticipation of a fire may be shown by such circumstances as the removal of valuable articles or the substitution of inferior articles. Ill feeling or unfriendly relations between the accused and occupants of the burned building may be shown. The absence of any effort to extinguish the fire or to turn in the alarm in the presence of an opportunity is significant. The flight of the suspect may be incriminating.

4. Motives

Although it is not absolutely necessary to establish a positive motive, the fact that the element of intent is essential in proving arson suggests the importance of showing a motive. In cases where great dependence is placed on circumstantial evidence it is especially important to prove a motive. Experience has shown that five motives predominate in arson cases, namely, economic gain, concealment of a crime, revenge, intimidation, and pyromania. Since government property is not insured the importance of economic gain as a motive in fires on government-owned property is greatly diminished. In a significant number of arson cases there is no apparent motive or the motive isn't clearly defined. For example, a riot will usually be accompanied by random incendiary acts. A juvenile will often set a fire out of a pure sense of mischief.

a. **Economic Gain.** The burning of property can profit the assured directly or can provide a means of gain for the perpetrator indirectly without regard to the insurance.

1) *Insurance Fraud with Assured Directly Benefiting.* The business motives which underlie the defrauding of an insurance company are often complex and not readily apparent to the investi-

gator. Although reference is made here to business establishments, the motives described are applicable to such simple cases as the housewife who burns a sofa or some clothes for the purpose of replacing the property with new articles. The following are among the more common motives attributed in the past to businessmen:

a) Desire to Move. The premises may no longer be desirable because of the condition of the building, the fact that the quarters are outgrown, or because of the locality.

b) Disposing of Merchandise. The stocks on hand may have lost value by reason of the seasonal nature of the business, obsolescence, scarcity of materials necessary to complete contracts, overstock in the absence of expected orders, or a changing market.

c) Property Transaction. The business itself may no longer be desirable because of impending liquidation, settlement of an estate of which it is part, the need for cash, prospective failure, the comparatively greater value of the land, or the comparatively greater value of the insurance benefits.

2) *Profit by a Perpetrator Other Than the Assured.* Although the beneficiary of the insurance on the business or the premises may be innocent, the perpetrator may achieve economic gain. Offenders of this type can usually be placed in one of the following categories:

a) Insurance agents wishing more business.

b) Insurance adjusters desiring to adjust a loss by securing a contract.

c) Business competitors.

d) Persons seeking jobs as security personnel.

e) Salvagers or "strippers" who set fires in order to steal the copper pipes, the boiler, or the plumbing fixtures after the building is abandoned.

f) Contractors wishing to increase business by obtaining a repair contract.

g) Apartment residents who are dissatisfied with their housing may arrange for a fire to be set. Fire victims often can collect special cash benefits from the city as well as priority in new public housing.

b. **Concealment of a Crime.** The arsonist may set fire to a building in order to conceal a projected or past crime. He may, for example, wish to divert attention in order to loot the burning premises or burglarize others. Another motive is the desire to break out of confinement in the confusion caused by the fire. The most common of these motives, however, is the desire to destroy evidence. For example, a person whose office records would not pass inspection may conceal mismanagement by burning the documents. Supply personnel can conceal a stock shortage by arranging a fire in the supply room. Finally, it is not uncommon for a criminal to attempt to conceal crimes such as larceny or murder by burning the building in which the crime was perpetrated.

c. **Punitive Measure.** An arsonist may use fire as a means of punishing another person for reasons of jealousy, hatred, or revenge. For example, a military person suffering a real or imaginary grievance may set fire to a barracks or a chapel.

d. **Intimidation and Economic Disabling.** Fire is a favorite means of warfare, both private and international. It can be used as a weapon of the saboteur, the unscrupulous striker, or the racketeer to intimidate or to disable economically as a step toward forcing submission to certain demands.

e. **Pyromania.** Strictly speaking, pyromania, an uncontrollable impulse toward incendiarism, is a mental affliction and not a motive. Indeed, pyromania is a term used to describe a condition of mind leading to an act of arson that is not rationally motivated. This type of person has a passion for fire that can be satisfied only by watching flames. Ordinarily the pyromaniac works alone. He may not run from the scene, turn in an alarm, or do anything observable which could associate him with the fire. Among the various types of pyromaniacs are the following:

1) *The Abnormal Youth.* Included in this group are mentally deficient persons of both sexes who set fire without any realization of the seriousness of the act. Their enthusiasm and rapture at the sight of the blaze, together with their general conduct, which is easily recognized as that of a mentally disturbed person, can make them noticeable even in the throng that gathers at the scene of a fire.

2) *The "Hero" Type.* Occasionally cases occur in which the person sets a fire, subsequently pretends to discover it, and turns in the alarm. Persons of this type wish to appear as "heroes" to the public. A person who desires to be a fireman, for example, or a

watchman, may set fire to a building and endeavor to achieve spectacular rescues in order to attract the attention of spectators.

3) *Alcoholics and Drug Addicts.* Persons who subject themselves to intense artificial stimulants such as alcohol or narcotics sometimes develop a strong urge toward incendiarism. In their normal condition these persons do not evince any sign of pyromania. Under the influence of the stimulant, however, they become victims of an uncontrollable desire to see a fire.

4) *Sexual Deviates.* This type of pyromaniac, usually a male, is said to derive sexual stimulation from setting a fire and watching the flames. He is thought to be a person given to chronic self-abuse, whose sexual gratification is enhanced by acts of arson.

5. Factors Influencing Burning

Most ordinary combustible substances are compounds of carbon and hydrogen, often containing mineral matter and oxygen. When they burn freely and completely in the air, the carbon reacts with the oxygen to form carbon dioxide; the hydrogen combines with the oxygen to form water; and the mineral matter remains behind as ash. In the first stages of a fire the building structure and the materials, such as wood and cloth contained in building, are merely heated and give off gases and vapors. With increased heat and exposure to flames these materials finally reach the ignition point and burst into flame. The rate and extent of the spread of fire depend on a number of factors, chief among which are the following:

a. Wind velocity and direction.

b. Relative humidity, dryness of the materials, and the absence of rain.

c. Air temperature.

d. Nature and condition of any vegetation surrounding the building.

e. Nature of the building construction; in particular the presence of wood and the arrangements for drafts. Partitions, laths, eaves, roofs, and shingles which are constructed of wood will aid the spread. Drafts created by stairwells, elevator shafts, and open doors and windows will obviously hasten the conflagration.

6. Causes of Fire

A fire originates intentionally or accidentally. One method of proving that a fire was intentionally set is to eliminate systematically the possibility of accident. An accidental fire may arise from the working of certain forces of nature or from negligence in the use of equipment or materials. The following are the most common accidental causes:

a. Carelessly discarded cigarettes and matches.

b. Careless disposition of readily combustible materials such as oily waste and painting equipment.

c. Poorly managed or defective heating systems. This includes overheated and overturned stoves; clothes dried too close to a fireplace; lint from fabrics coming in contact with open fires or radiant heaters; faulty chimneys and flues; explosions resulting from kerosene stoves; and leaks in pipes of gas stoves.

d. Spontaneous combustion arising from the storage of oily or chemically saturated materials such as cloth, paper, or cotton waste deposited in poorly ventilated places.

e. Sun rays focused by bubbles in window panes, shaving mirrors, or by some other peculiarly shaped glass article which may serve as a convex lens.

g. Lightning. If a thunderstorm took place in the vicinity of the fire at the time of occurrence, an examination should be made for traces of lightning. Metal parts of the building may exhibit melting. Paint will be streaked with burned areas. Cracks in the walls, broken bricks, and soot driven into the rooms from the chimney are among the other signs. Lightning usually strikes a high point of the building and may be traced in its path to the ground.

h. Electrical mishaps. As a subdivision of accidental causes of fire, electrical sources deserve more extended treatment because of the frequency with which such accidents arise. Modern buildings are heavily equipped with electrical wiring to operate fixtures, appliances, air-conditioning units, and heating apparatus. Defects in any part of the system may result in fire. Specifically, the cause is either an arc or sparking or excessive heat. A combination of these may also be found as the cause.

1) Arc or sparking. These will be discussed together since an arc may be considered as a sustained sparking. When an inductive circuit is suddenly broken, the electromotive force induced in the inductive coil may rise to a very large value causing a current to jump across the opening contact points in the form of a spark. The breaking of the circuit may be caused by the opening of a switch or the loosening of a contact. If an electric circuit is carrying a current larger than that for which the switch was designed, the spark, when the switch is opened, may vaporize sufficient metal to cause an arc across the mains and so open the circuit breaker or destroy the switch. On high potential circuits, switches are immersed in oil to prevent this danger. The presence of combustible material in the area surrounding the arc may readily provide fuel for a fire.

2) Overheating. One effect of current flowing through a wire is the production of heat, which is proportional in quantity to the resistance multiplied by the square of the current. The smaller the diameter of the wire, the greater the heat produced. A short circuit may lead to a greater current through the circuit than the wire can maintain. The result is a melting of the insulation and the ignition of nearby combustible materials. The National Electric Code prescribes maximum current loads for various sizes and kinds of wire. Among the other causes of overheating are faulty wiring, improper voltage, low line capacity, neglected electric motors, soldering, curling, and flat irons. Other appliances such as vacuum cleaners and refrigerators can overheat if they are neglected.

7. Methods of the Arsonist

The techniques, devices, and materials employed by the arsonist vary with his mentality and with his emotional condition immediately prior to the commission of the offense. A person who plans an incendiary fire for an insurance fraud or to conceal a series of embezzlements will ordinarily plan his crime carefully and employ ingenuity in its execution. A pyromaniac of the mentally deficient type or a person concealing an unplanned crime of violence usually acts in haste and is indifferent

to the need for cleverness. It may be noted that excessive ingenuity frequently betrays the arsonist, since the fire is often
under control before the incendiary device is destroyed by the
flames.

a. **Incendiary Materials.** Obviously to create a fire there must
be present combustible material. The burning material or fuel
may be already present or later introduced. It may be a solid,
liquid, or gas. Strictly speaking, only gases burn. The solids
and liquids must be heated to liberate flammable gases. The gases
in turn must be raised to the proper temperature before ignition
occurs. Hence there must be present the material to burn and a
source of heat to raise the temperature of the fuel to the kindling
point. Finally there must be a supply of oxygen, since burning is
an oxidation process. If the supply of oxygen is only 17 percent of
the atmosphere present, the flame is extinguished and the fire
cannot be supported. Oxygen may be supplied from the air or
from oxidizing agents.

1) *Liquids.* Liquids such as gasoline or ether with low flash
points do not require open flame for ignition. In the presence of a
spark, rapid and explosive fires may result from the mixture of
these vapors with air. The following liquids possess excellent
incendiary properties and as a consequence are often used by the
arsonist as accelerants:

Liquid	Flash Point (Fahrenheit)
Alcohol (grain)	61°
Benzol	40°
Petroleum ether	24°
Gasoline	45°
Kerosene	100°
Naphtha (safety)	100°
Turpentine	95°

2) *Gases.* Certain gases when mixed with air possess excellent
ignition properties and when present in an enclosed area can lead
to an explosion. In an arson investigation, however, it should be
remembered that a slow fire, poorly ventilated, will often provide
its own explosive gases. The following are the more common gases
resulting in fires from explosions.

Gas	Explosive Limits
Acetylene	2.6%–55.0%
Butane	1.6%–6.5%
Carbon Monoxide	12.5%–74.0%
Ethylene	3.0%–35.0%
Hydrogen	4.1%–75.0%
Natural Gas	4.8%–13.5%
Propane	2.3%–7.3%

3) *Solids.* When solids exist in finely ground or powdered condition they form an excellent combustible substance. Coal dust, grain, metals, and other materials will burn rapidly when combined with air and ignited. Some substances generate intense heat on contact with water. Notable among these are sodium, sodium peroxide, potassium, and calcium carbide. Certain solids, called oxidizing agents, give off oxygen on decomposition thus aiding combustion. Incendiary pencils, for example, can be made with potassium chlorate, an oxidizing agent, and sugar separated from a fragile capsule of concentrated sulfuric acid. When the capsule is broken, the acid extracts water from the sugar, leaving charcoal and giving a sufficient heat reaction to liberate the oxygen from the chlorate and ignite the charcoal. The following are typical families of oxidizing agents:

Chlorates
Perchlorates, including Perchloric Acid
Chromates, including Chromic Acid
Bichromates
Nitrates, including Nitric Acid
Permanganates

b. **"Plants" and Other Contrivances.** The "plant" is a device which is designed to ignite combustible material sometime after the initiating action. During this period of time the arsonist has an opportunity to escape from the premises or leave the neighborhood. With a sufficient time delay the criminal may establish an alibi by being present at another place at the time of the fire. Exceptionally clever arsonists employ remote control devices to accomplish ignition thus obviating the necessity of being at the premises to start the fire. The following methods are used in conjunction with the combustible materials described previously:

1) *Heating Appliances.* Gas and electrical appliances can be employed to supply the heat necessary to ignite a combustible material. The following have been used by arsonists:

a) *Heaters* such as flat irons, toasters, soldering irons, hot plates, and lamps. The heater is placed in contact with a combustible material, switched on, and abandoned. The arsonist thus has sufficient time to leave the scene.

b) *Sparkers* such as electrical switches, door bells, short circuits, and telephone boxes. If the vapor of a volatile fluid such as gasoline is present in high concentration, the spark may be sufficient to set off an explosive flash. It can be seen that a plant of this nature permits the criminal to be at another place when some other person innocently performs the initiating action.

2) *Mechanical Devices.* These are usually time delay arrangements such as the following:

a) *Clock mechanisms* which can be arranged so that the alarm movement starts the action.

b) *Altered equipment* such as broken pipes on oil burners or sprinkler systems in which combustible fluids have been placed.

c) *Magnifying glasses* focusing sunlight on a combustible material.

d) *Animals* tied to ignition devices.

3) *Trailers.* A favorite device of the criminal is a slow burning initiating arrangement constructed in one of the following ways:

a) *Streamers* may be made out of candlewick, rope, or cloth saturated with an inflammable liquid such as kerosene. They are strung from room to room to provide a path for the fire.

b) *Cigarettes* can be employed for this purpose by lighting and placing them on a book or box of matches.

c) *Candles* can be placed in straw, excelsior, or paper. Often a piece of the candle may be recovered from the neck of the supporting bottle.

4) *Inflammable Gases.* The combination of a plant and an inflammable gas is a particularly dangerous arson technique. The result is usually an explosion followed by a fire. The more common gases employed for this purpose are the following:

a) *Natural gas* may be made to fill the interior of a building by sawing off a low-lying pipe or by simply turning on a jet. A spark or pilot light will ignite the gas.

b) *Sewer gas* may be caused to seep into a structure in certain city areas by removing the water from a toilet, sink drain, or trap.

5) **Chemical Devices.** These became well known as offensive weapons in World War II.

a) *Thermite bombs* are found exceedingly difficult to control. The main body of the bomb consisted of powdered aluminum and titanium oxide.

b) *Phosphorous* can be used to impregnate cards, so that, on drying, the cards burst into flame.

c) *Molotov Cocktails* in the crude form of a soda bottle filled with gasoline and a streamer of cloth or paper are the favorite incendiary device of rioters.

6) **Explosives.** Bombs are ordinarily used to cause physical damage to machinery or personnel. Any ensuing fire is usually not intended. However, since fire is one of the common consequences of such an act, the use of explosives can become an act of arson. Nitroglycerin, TNT, mercury fulminate, gunpowder, and gun cotton are the common explosives employed for this purpose.

8. Investigation During the Fire

Since there is much valuable evidence and information to be gathered during the fire, the investigator should respond to any serious or suspicious fire affecting property within his assigned area of responsibility. By maintaining appropriate liaison with the fire department servicing the area, it is possible to arrange for prompt notification in the event of such a fire. It will be assumed throughout the following discussion that the burning property includes a building.

a. **Observations During the Fire.** The extent to which the investigator can conduct a preliminary investigation during the actual burning will vary with the nature and severity of the fire. General observations can, of course, be made from an appropriate distance and certain examinations of the peripheral area can sometimes be made at this stage. Much of the information suggested below can also be obtained later from eyewitnesses.

1) *Smoke and Vapors.* The characteristics of the smoke, steam, or other vapors which emanate from the fire are useful indications in determining the nature of the burning substances, including the accelerants used. In the following list the color of the smoke is related to the most common incendiary agent which may emit it.

a) STEAM AND SMOKE. The presence of steam indicates that humid substances have come in contact with the hot combustible substances. The water present in the humid substance is evaporated before the substance begins to burn.

White smoke is given out by the burning of phosphorus, a substance that is sometimes used as an incendiary agent.

Grayish smoke is caused by the emission of flying ash and soot in loosely packed substances such as straw and hay.

Black smoke is produced by either incomplete combustion or the preponderance in the burning material of a product with a petroleum base such as rubber, tar, coal, turpentine, or petroleum.

Reddish-brown or yellow smoke indicates the presence of nitrates or substances with a nitrocellulose base. Thus, smoke of this color can be emitted from the burning of nitric acid, nitrated plastics, film, or smokeless gun powder. A number of these substances are suitable as accelerants.

2) *Color of Flame.* The color of the flame is indicative of the intensity of the fire and sometimes of the nature of the combustible substances present. The temperature of the fire may vary from 500 to 1500 degrees Centigrade with the color of the flame ranging from red, through yellow, and finally becoming a blinding white. Some accelerants may give a characteristically colored flame. For example, burning alcohol is characterized by a blue flame. Red flames may indicate the presence of petroleum products.

3) *Size of Fire.* The size of the fire should be noted at the time of arrival and at subsequent intervals thereafter. This information may be significant in relation to the time at which the alarm was received. An unusually rapid extension of the fire is indicative of the use of accelerants or some other method of physical preparation. Naturally the opinion of the experienced firemen present at the scene is of value in this matter. A knowledge of the type of

construction, the ventilation facilities, and the normal contents of the building will enable a professional observer to form an opinion as to whether the fire has traveled abnormally fast.

4) *Direction of Travel.* Since hot gases rise and fire normally sweeps upward, the direction of travel of a fire is predictable from a knowledge of the construction of the building. It will be expected that the flames will tend to rise until, on meeting obstacles, they project horizontally to seek other vertical outlets. The extent and rate of travel in the horizontal direction will depend primarily on the direction of the wind and on ventilating conditions such as open doors and windows. The spread of fire in an unusual direction or at an exceptional rate should arouse suspicion as to the presence of accelerants or a prepared arrangement of doors and windows.

5) *Location of Flames.* The investigator should note carefully whether there is more than one apparent point of origin and should try to estimate the approximate location of each. Unrelated fires in different places are indicative of arson. The incendiary may, for example, arrange timing devices in different places with the result that the separate outbreaks of flames will be apparent.

6) *Odors.* Many substances which may be used as accelerants emit a characteristic smell. Naturally the odors detectable at the scene of a fire are determined mainly by the substances which are stored, manufactured, or used on the premises. The smell of a highly inflammable substance in an area where it is not normally used should arouse suspicion. Turpentine, alcohol, kerosene, and gasoline are among the accelerants which emit characteristic odors.

b. **Examinations During the Fire.** In addition to his observations of the flame and smoke, the investigator can at this time make many important examinations of the building and the scene.

1) *Exterior Openings.* The investigator should note the condition of the windows, doors, or other openings. Locked outside doors and obstructed entrances may indicate an intent to impede the firemen in their efforts to extinguish the fire. Open windows and interior passageway doors may suggest an arrangement for ventilating the fire and promoting its rapid progress. Drawn shades or windows covered with blankets where such arrangements are unusual indicate an effort on the part of the arsonist to conceal his preparations and work.

2) **Preliminary Examination of the Scene.** A limited search of the area surrounding the fire may be made at this time. The attention of the investigator should be directed to two types of evidence: first, equipment that may have been used by the arsonist such as containers, matchbooks, and tools; and secondly, traces which may lead to the perpetrator, such as shoe and tire impressions.

3) **Photography.** The progressive stages of the burning should be photographed from various angles. Photographs of the spectators are sometimes made in the hope that the incendiary may be present in the crowd and that in the event of a series of criminal fires the face of the arsonist may be revealed by his repeated presence in the photographs of the spectators. Such a procedure is advisable if it is thought that a pyromaniac is operating in the area. A camcorder is especially useful at the scene of a suspected arson not only for recording the faces in the crowd but also for documenting the development of the fire.

4) **Observation of the Spectators.** Some types of arsonist, such as the pyromaniac, remain at the scene to watch the fire. By observing the spectators the experienced arson investigator is occasionally able to identify the incendiary. An exceptional appearance of personal satisfaction or excitement is sometimes indicative of the pyromaniac. If the fire takes place during normal sleeping hours, the arsonist may be sometimes distinguishable by being one of the few fully clothed persons among the spectators.

9. Investigation of Scene After the Fire

The difficulties that may be encountered in the search of the suspected arson scene depend primarily on the extent to which the building or other property has been consumed. If the fire has been promptly reported and quickly extinguished, the discovery of incriminating evidence may be a relatively simple matter. On the other hand, where the fire has gone beyond control and has reduced a considerable portion of the property to ashes, it may be exceedingly difficult to uncover traces of value. Whatever the condition of the scene, however, it will be found that a patient, methodical study of the area will often reveal indications of criminal design and sometimes will permit a logical reconstruction of the arsonist's method of operation. It is of paramount importance in arson cases to know what type of evidence is significant.

a. **Safeguarding the Scene.** In order to preserve and safeguard the evidence prior to a search the investigator must prevent unnecessary disturbance of the debris and the intrusions of unauthorized persons. This may be achieved by liaison with the fire department and uniformed police. An agreement should be made with the firemen in the case of suspected incendiarism to postpone clean-up operations until the investigator has completed his examination of the premises. It will, of course, be necessary for the firemen to perform a certain amount of washing down and overhauling, but it may be requested of their commander that extreme care be exercised in this activity to prevent excessive disturbance of potential evidence. The senior police officer may be requested to issue orders excluding from the scene all persons not officially concerned with the extinguishment of the fire or the investigation of its origin.

b. **Order of Searching.** The area immediately surrounding the burned property should now be more thoroughly examined for evidentiary traces and clues. The doors and windows of the building should be studied for evidences of a break, particularly if the premises are normally locked during the period in which the fire took place. Tool impressions, broken window panes, and forced locks are the obvious marks of such a break. The investigator should now progress to the interior, directing his observations to the charred remains of the fire primarily for evidence of the use of accelerants or other incendiary devices. Assuming that the burning has been extensive, the following order will normally be followed: the outer shell of the remains, the first open area of floor from the point of entry, the first inner shell or wall of an inside room, and the general area suspected of being the point where the fire first broke out.

c. **Locating the Point of Origin.** One of the major objectives of the search is the location of the point of origin, since it is in this area that the physical evidence of criminal design is most likely to be discovered. Multiple points of origin are usually an indication of arson. The region in which the fire originated may be determined by information obtained from witnesses and by an examination of the debris.

1) ***Depth of Charring.*** In searching for the exact point of origin, the investigator should follow the path of the burning to its source by observing the intensity of the destruction. Because heat builds up under the ceiling and enters an adjacent room through the space underneath the door jamb, heavy charring on the ceilings and walls will be apparent directly above the doorway through which the fire entered the room. An examination of the charred uprights will indicate the direction of the flames. Fire that envelops a wooden beam tends to round the edges on the side away from the source of the flames. As the investigator draws closer to the point of origin he will find the charring becoming deeper. By using a metal probe and a ruler or a depth gauge such as the kind used to measure tire treads, the investigator can compare the relative depths of charring. The charring will be the deepest at the point of origin, the place where the fire usually has its greatest intensity and duration.

2) ***The "V" Pattern.*** Fire characteristically burns upward and outward in a "V"-shaped pattern from the point of origin. As the fire climbs vertically it will spread out slightly horizontally. The flames in a room will rise in a "V" pattern until blocked by the ceiling. The fire will then travel across the ceiling and if unable to burn upward will begin burning in a downward direction on the walls. Once the room of origin has been determined by the extent of the destruction of the ceilings and walls or by the depth of charring, locating the bottom of the "V" pattern will indicate the point of origin.

3) ***Other Indicators.*** Because the point of origin of the fire is usually characterized by intense heat, recognizing the effects of high temperatures on household materials may be helpful in locating it.

a) *Alligatoring.* The surface of charred wood will bear a pattern of crevices that is similar in appearance to the skin of an alligator.

b) *Spalling* is the chipping, flaking, and discoloration of concrete or brick due to intense heat. Brown stains may indicate the use of an accelerant.

c) *Craze lines* are a pattern of thin irregular lines found in glass that has been exposed to high temperatures. Crazing suggests the possible use of an accelerant.

d) When light bulbs are subjected to high temperatures the glass will expand and become deformed. A bulge will sometimes form on the side of the bulb closest to the source of the heat and the point of origin.

e) Furniture springs will sag when subjected to intense heat indicating either that the fire originated in the cushions or that an accelerant was used to cause the high temperatures.

d. **Examining the Point of Origin.** The debris at the point of origin should be studied carefully for the purpose of determining the cause of the fire, whether accidental or incendiary. A search should be made for traces of combustible materials. Substances such as peculiarly colored ashes, soot, unusual formations of clinkers, and impregnated materials should be collected for laboratory examination. In conducting his search the investigator should recall the nature of the materials ordinarily stored in the area so that he will be able to detect extraneous or misplaced objects such as fuel and oil cans. Peculiar odors should be noted. The remains of streamers or other plants should be observed and protected. The degree of burning, general appearance, carbonization, and oil content of burned objects should be noted.

e. **Traces of Accelerants.** The investigator should give special attention to any evidence of the use of a liquid accelerant such as gasoline, kerosene, or turpentine. Often the point of origin may be located by tracing such substances to the place of spillage. Since a fluid will flow downward to lower levels, the search for traces of an accelerant should be extended to the floors or cellar below the level of the fire, in the hope that some of the substance may still remain there in an unburned state. A study of the manner in which wood is charred sometimes reveals indications of an accelerant. If wood is soaked with a petroleum product, such as gasoline or kerosene, prior to burning it, it will acquire a distinctive appearance in charring. The "alligator effect" will be more easily observed. The char marks will be deeper where the liquid has seeped into the wood. Thus, the charring will follow the pattern of the spilled liquid. If a soaked trailer was used, the charring will follow the outline since the burning will be deeper in the area occupied by the impregnating substance. Sometimes the burning pattern will indicate the removal of certain objects after the fire had begun.

f. **Detection of Hydrocarbons.** A portable hydrocarbon vapor detector, called a "sniffer", is often used to determine the presence of hydrocarbons at fires of suspicious origin. This device draws in the surrounding air and passes it over a heated filament. The heated filament will oxidize any flammable vapor causing a rise in temperature which will be recorded on the instrument's meter. It is very useful in screening burnt material at a fire scene to detect articles and areas containing unconsumed hydrocarbons which may have been used as an accelerant.

g. **Arson Dogs.** Impressive results have been achieved with the use of dogs specially trained to detect accelerants. A dog's nose is a more sensitive instrument than the hydrocarbon vapor detector. The vapor detector cannot differentiate between the hydrocarbons from burned plastics and those from unburned accelerants. This results in a number of samples which are not accelerants being sent to the laboratory for costly analysis. On the other hand, an "arson dog" has no trouble identifying accelerants. Furthermore, because he does not labor under preconceived notions of where accelerants should be, he will often find them in a places a trained investigator might overlook.

h. **Altered Protective Devices.** To insure destruction the arsonist sometimes tampers with the sprinkler system or the alarm devices, rendering them ineffectual. For example, he may pour paraffin into the main sprinkler line or mute the water flow alarm. The investigator should arrange to have the fire protection system of the building inspected. The condition of the supply valves should be carefully checked. The water flow should be examined for signs of tampering. Abnormal conditions of fire doors, transoms, and windows should be observed.

10. The Physical Evidence and Its Collection

The task of collecting physical evidence in an arson case is complicated by the delicate condition of the materials. Any piece of evidence that appears to have unusual significance should be photographed and located on a sketch before it is moved since the act of collecting the evidence sometimes results in an alteration.

The following are typical of the significant articles of evidence that may be present in a fire of incendiary origin.

a. **Containers:** The arsonist uses bottles, cans, barrels, pails, or boxes to hold the combustible liquid. Any residual gasoline or similar fluid should be poured into a glass container, such as a mason jar, covered, and sealed with paraffin. This may be the most important piece of evidence; it should not be permitted to evaporate by placing it in a container with a loose cover. The original container should be collected and preserved in a similar way if possible. Wrapping paper, cardboard boxes, string or cord, or similar articles which may have been used to cover the substances in transporting it, should also be collected. These articles may sometimes be traced to the perpetrator of the offense.

b. **Ashes and Debris.** If it is found that the ashes or debris contain traces of accelerant or some other significant clue, these materials should be collected for transmission to a laboratory. Where straw or excelsior has been used in a "plant," the ashes will retain their characteristic shape. The burned remains of clothing are sometimes significant. The degree to which cloth will burn is normally limited. Wool, for example, is ordinarily not completely consumed unless it is soaked with an inflammable liquid. In the collection of debris the investigator should not overlook materials which have fallen to lower floors or to the cellar since these sometimes contain valuable evidence such as the remaining parts of a "plant."

c. **Fingerprints and Impressions.** A search for fingerprints should be made in the usual manner, giving special attention to such objects as containers for accelerants. A fingerprint should be developed, if necessary, and photographed. The object bearing the print should, if its size permits, be transported to the office for preservation. Impressions made by tools, shoes, or tires should be photographed and cast.

d. **Incendiary Devices.** The investigator should be alert during the search for suspicious articles such as wires, fuses, straw, or candles which could have formed part of an incendiary device. Since the arsonist may arrange for several points of origin, the search for such devices should be extensive. Closets and obscure corners should be searched for heating appliances.

e. **Stoves and Fireplaces.** The arsonist sometimes insures the destruction of clothing, records, and papers by first burning them in one of the ordinary heating devices. The ashes remaining in stoves and fireplaces should be observed to determine if they are hot and should then be examined for evidence of burned materials that may be significant in the case.

f. **Tools.** A careful study should be made of all tools present in the building. They may have been brought there and abandoned by the arsonist, thus providing a tracing clue, or they may have been employed by a resident arsonist in his preparations. Wax on knife blades; sawdust and chips on saws, augers, and bits; and metal particles on axes are important, depending on the materials used to set the fire. If tool marks are present on door jambs or window sills as a result of forcible entry, the blades of the screwdrivers and crowbars should be examined for a comparison of size and for paint particles.

g. **Documents.** In certain types of incendiary fires such as those designed to conceal evidence of embezzlement or other irregularities of records, the arsonist will attempt to arrange the incriminating documents so that they will be exposed to the flames. For example, he may arrange ledgers in tented fashion on a table to aid the burning. Since, however, masses of paper, such as books, do not burn as well as the novice arsonist imagines, often incriminating documents which were intended for destruction are left by the fire in salvageable condition. In the examination of such documents, the absence of certain papers, such as insurance policies, which are normally kept in the area, should be investigated.

11. Interior Arrangement

The condition and contents of various areas in the building should be noted. An occupant planning a fire will be tempted to remove certain items such as articles of value or sentimental significance. Fur coats and jewelry, for example, may have been removed before setting fire to a dwelling house. The insurance policy and the inventory may be removed from a commercial building. A movement of a large part of the more valuable contents may be accomplished. Sometimes certain articles may be placed in a more exposed position in order to accomplish their destruction before the fire is placed under control. The closet door in a dwelling will often be purposely left open to insure the burning of other clothing ordinarily placed with the fur coat. An account book may be arranged in tented fashion on a desk to accomplish the destruction of evidence of financial irregularities.

12. Witnesses

The gathering of physical evidence is merely the first phase of the investigation, and is primarily concerned with establishing the *corpus delicti* and, secondarily, with the discovery of traces leading to the identity of the perpetrator. Additional evidence can be obtained by carefully questioning the various persons associated with the discovery and control of the fire, the security personnel, the occupants of the building, and the owner. Suggested checklists of important points of information are given in Section 16.

a. **Persons First Arriving at the Fire.** Every effort should be made to locate and question the person who first saw the fire. Passersby, security personnel, and police officers are among those who may have made important observations. The identity of the person who turned in the alarm should be learned. These persons should be questioned concerning the exact place where the fire began, the number of places where they have seen flames, and the manner in which the fire spread. Their opinions should be sought on the probable origin of the fire, the color of the smoke, and the general appearance of the conflagration. An inquiry should be made about suspicious actions on the part of anyone near the premises, such as hastily leaving the scene on foot or in an automobile.

b. **Firemen.** The most reliable information concerning the fire can be obtained from the firemen, who are professional observers of these occurrences. They should be questioned concerning the nature of the fire, the color of the flames and smoke, and the perceptible odors. Information can also be obtained concerning the condition of doors, windows, and shades. The firemen may also have observed the arrangements of stock, packing cases, and furniture.

c. **Security.** If a security person is employed in the building, he should be able to provide detailed information concerning the condition of the building prior to the fire. He should be questioned at great length concerning the building and the fire. In addition, inquiries should be made concerning the occupants of the building in regard to their recent behavior and movements of stock or furniture. He should be asked about his suspicions and his theory concerning the origin of the fire. Finally, he should be asked to identify the last person to leave the building.

d. **Occupants.** The occupants and employees of the building should be interviewed separately. They should be encouraged to give their own accounts, theories, and suspicions of the fire. The identity of the last person to leave the building should be determined. Was it customary for him to be last? Who ordinarily locked the premises?

e. **Owner.** The owner of the damaged property should be questioned concerning his activities at the time of the fire. Any aliases which he may have employed should be determined. He should be questioned also regarding prior arrests, apprehensions, convictions, previous fires, financial standing, businesses, domestic conditions, and hobbies or amusements that could have caused reverses in his financial situation.

13. Photography and Sketching

A photographic record should be made of the destruction accomplished by the fire and of physical evidence uncovered by the search. The photographer should follow the order of the search, photographing each area of significance to the investigation prior to the search. When the point of origin is located it should be thoroughly photographed to show such points as the type and extent of "alligatoring" and charring and the remains of any incendiary device. As each important piece of evidence is discovered it should be photographed in its original condition and in its position when it is completely uncovered. In addition to the photographs a sketch of important areas should be made showing the location of the various articles of evidence. As an aid in the construction of his sketch the investigator will find that the blueprints of buildings maintained in the files of housing and building departments are particularly useful in giving the dimensions and other details of the structure.

14. Packaging and Forwarding of Evidence

Articles of physical evidence which have been collected to determine the possible presence of an accelerant or which, in general, may contain traces of an inflammable substance should be placed in airtight containers, such as mason jars, in order to prevent the evaporation of volatile components. The containers should be packaged to provide adequate protection and forwarded or hand-carried to the laboratory as soon as possible. Postal regulations should be carefully observed in forwarding through the mails. The post office facilities should not be used to ship flammable evidence. Couriers or other means of delivery should be employed in such instances. In the examination of debris samples the laboratory expert can be greatly assisted by the provision of certain information relating to the fire. The following data are usually found of assistance and should be included in the letter of transmittal in addition to the regularly required information:

a. An itemized list of the evidence being submitted with information concerning the means by which it is being forwarded.

b. The date and time of burning.

c. A brief description of the type and construction of the burned building or object and the extent of damage or destruction caused by the fire.

d. A list of the chemical agents used in extinguishing the fire. Water, carbon tetrachloride, and carbon dioxide are the most common agents employed.

e. Photographs and scaled sketches on which are indicated the points where the various articles of evidence were collected.

15. Sources of Information

The identification files should be searched for the names of any persons associated with the building or with the fire. The local fire department may be consulted for records of previous fires.

Depending on the nature of the fire the following may be consulted: local police records of known incendiaries; records of recent repairs or alterations in the building; records such as inventories, financial statements, and bills of sale where it is suspected that the fire was designed to conceal embezzlement or theft; personnel rosters of persons employed and of persons recently discharged where the fire is thought to be inspired by hatred. In addition to these records the investigator can, where appropriate, avail himself of the following central indices:

a. **Material Files.** Reference collections of incendiary materials such as match folders, rope, and celluloid are useful. A discarded match found near the scene of a fire can offer a valuable tracing clue in an arson case. In some cases the type of matchbook from which the match was taken can be identified and the match itself associated with a matchbook found on the person of a suspect. Some match folders contain advertising of places such as taverns and restaurants. Since the places of distribution for such folders are limited in number, these establishments can often provide an identifying eyewitness. Similar tracing can be accomplished with cord and string that have been used to wrap incendiary materials.

b. **Property Insurance Loss Reporting System.** One of the more helpful insurance company efforts is the establishment of the Property Insurance Loss Reporting System (PILR) by the American Insurance Association located in New York City. The PILR is a computerized record of all fire losses designed to detect patterns of arson fraud and to trace firesetters who change insurance companies or geographic locations. It is organized under categories such as fires at the same address, fires with the same insurer, and fires in which one adjustor is associated with a number of similar fires. The PILR contains over 100,000 case histories and is on-line 24 hours every day.

c. **Insurance Companies' Files.** Because of the tremendous financial loss that results from arson, insurance companies are prepared to offer active cooperation to law enforcement agencies in their investigation of this crime. It should be noted that these sources of information are most useful where a peculiar *modus operandi* has been repeatedly observed. For example, cases involving pyromaniacs can usually be investigated with the characteristic pattern of the outbreak of the fires a starting point.

16. Checklist

The list found below is given as an aid to the investigator in an arson case. The list does not purport to be comprehensive, nor are the points covered applicable to every case. It will be found, however, that in the investigation of an arson involving a building many of these points are relevant and their coverage by means of interviews, observation, or search of records will make for a more complete report.

    a. **Official Data.**

1) Address, location, and description of the building.

2) Date and time of burning.

3) Time of receipt of alarm by the fire station.

4) Fire station receiving the alarm.

5) Fire units responding.

6) Time of arrival and departure of fire units.

7) Designation of the building in terms of construction, material, size, age, and materials stored there.

8) Designation of type of fire by the fire department records.

    b. **Date of Ownership, Occupancy, and Property Value.**

1) Owner of the building.

2) Tenants of the building.

3) Occupants.

4) Value of the property.

5) Insurance coverage.

6) Name of insured.

7) Name of insurer.

8) Loss of property through fire.

    c. **Discovery of the Fire.**

1) Who reported the fire?

2) When was the fire reported?

3) How was the fire reported? Verbally, telephone?

4) Did the person who reported the fire have any motive for doing so?

5) Who discovered the fire?

6) When was the fire first discovered?

7) Under what circumstances was the fire first discovered?

8) What was the time interval between discovery and report? How was the time interval accounted for?

d. **Conditions Surrounding the Fire.**

1) Initial observations of the fire.

2) Point of origin of fire. In what building? In what room?

3) Direction of winds; weather conditions such as temperature and humidity; electrical storms.

4) Type of fire—flash or otherwise.

5) Explosion.

6) Speed of travel.

7) Odors—gasoline, kerosene, etc.

8) Appearance of smoke—shape and color.

9) Appearance of flames—size, intensity, color, and area of spread.

10) Hissing or crackling noises.

11) Direction of spread.

12) Were any windows or doors, normally closed and locked, left open?

13) Evidence of forced entry.

14) Chemical agents used to extinguish fire—water, foam, CO_2.

e. **Condition of the Building.**

1) How was the room or building furnished? Was there a stove of any kind? Was there a fire in the stove? What fuel was used? Was the stove well insulated? When were ashes last removed? Where were they placed?

2) Check for changes in building while occupied by present tenant, such as partitions, electric wiring, stoves, etc.

3) Was any electric wiring exposed? What was its condition? Were they ever repaired? When? By whom? What was the load carried by these wires? Was there ever any heat observed in the wires or terminals?

4) Number and kind of electric motors in the room or building. Provisions for safeguarding against dust.

5) Were there any machines in the room or building? What type? When were they last used? What power did they consume? When were they last tested and lubricated?

6) Location and condition of pipes, particularly gas pipes.

7) Location and condition of all electric lights, appliances, and wiring, including the condition of fuses.

8) Existence of devices for focusing sun's rays.

9) Degree of care exercised in storing inflammable materials.

10) Condition of fire-fighting equipment.

f. **Persons Associated with the Building.**

1) Persons present in building at time of fire. Last person in the building. Persons in and around in the last 24 hours. Loiterers in the area.

2) Possessors of keys to the building.

3) Persons responsible for the security of the building.

4) Names and addresses of all occupants, tenants, employees, and all persons frequently around premises.

5) Last person to leave the building—were his actions customary?

g. **Motive.**

1) Description of all property on premises; when it arrived, value, and amount of insurance.

2) Recent movements of property.

3) Possible substitutions of less valuable property.

4) Financial condition of owners of the property.

5) Impending inspections, investigations, inventories, and audits.

6) Relations between property owners—friendly or inimical. Recent defections from partnerships or severance of employment.

7) Possibility of concealment of a crime.

8) Existence of previous criminal record on the part of any of the occupants.

9) Existence of a record of confinement to a mental institution.

10) Possible association of any persons with other mysterious fires.

h. **Evidence of Intent.**

1) Failure to summon the fire unit within a reasonable time.

2) Tampering with warning devices or communications systems.

3) Doors, windows, transoms, and ventilating systems left in an other than normal position.

4) Placement of incendiary materials, such as gasoline, oil,

Table III
EXAMINATION OF THE FIRE SCENE

Point of Origin

a. Exterior of structure—note fire-damaged areas.
1) Charring and/or smoke deposits over doorways, windows, attic vents, eaves or soffits.
2) Determine whether doors and windows were open or closed during fire.
3) Check for forced entry.
4) Determine if fire originated at the building's exterior.

b. Interior of structure.
1) Locate the area or room of most severe damage.
2) Check the ceiling to find the worst area of damage.
3) Find the lowest point of burning within the area of origin or "V" patterns.
4) Look for directions of heat flow. Observe effects on light bulbs, window glass, metal objects, interior doors and other furnishings.
5) Look for multiple or non-communicating fires.
6) Observe alligatoring/depth of char, to determine speed and duration of fire.
7) Spalling—indicates intensity of fire on masonry material.

Cause of Fire

a. Elimination of all accidental and natural causes.
1) Electrical malfunctions.
2) Heating or cooking equipment.
3) Smoking materials.
4) Accidental explosions.
5) Spontaneous combustion.
6) Lightning.

b. Identify and document evidence of incendiarism.
1) Trailers.
2) Devices.
3) Chemicals or flammables.
4) Special burn patterns.
5) Altered or misused electrical equipment or appliances.
6) Multiple fire sets.
7) Preparations of premises for fire.
   a) Blocked windows/obscured view.
   b) Ventilation holes in interior.
   c) Missing furnishings, equipment or stock.
8) Evidence of fire to conceal other crime.

Source: Bureau of Alcohol, Tobacco and Firearms. *ATF Arson Investigative Guide.*

candles, matches, timing devices, and cans containing residual inflammable material, in the building.

5) Tampering with fire-fighting equipment or fire-control systems.

6) Removal of property of value prior to the fire.

7) Bringing personal property into the building.

II. AUTOMOBILE FIRES

17. Motive

When a car is stolen, it is often driven to a remote place where it is stripped of its parts and then set on fire either by the thief or someone else who happens to find it. An automobile burning may be an act of revenge, rioting, or vandalism. Sometimes a car is set on fire to conceal a crime. In many instances, deliberately setting fire to a vehicle is done to defraud the insurance company. A policy-holder will hire a "torch" to burn his car to obtain ready cash. Among the more common motives for this offense are the following:

a. **Financial Difficulties.** These are similar to those encountered in other arson cases with the following additions:

1) Inability to meet the payments on the car or to return it to the dealer.

2) Demands by the finance company that payments be made or the vehicle surrendered.

3) Inability to sell the equity in the car.

b. **Domestic Problems.** A divorce may be pending or one of the spouses may object to the ownership or improper use of the car.

c. **Dissatisfaction with the Automobile.** The car may have a long history of mechanical trouble. Excessive depreciation and unsuit-ability for the owner's needs are additional reasons.

18. The Burning of Automobiles

It is extremely difficult to accomplish the total loss of a vehicle, since an automobile is mainly composed of noninflammable materials. With the exception of the upholstery, wires, and tires, there is very little that can be burned. Experiments have shown that a short in the wiring will almost always burn itself out without setting fire to the other parts of the automobile. When the upholstery is set on fire it will smolder for hours without breaking into open flame.

19. Examination of the Burned Car

The burned automobile should be examined before the owner is interviewed. The point of origin should be located and the manner in which the fire spread should be determined. The following areas should receive special attention:

a. **The Electrical System.** The owner may claim that the fire started because of a short. A total fire loss from this cause is extremely rare.

1) Locate the wiring area where the short was first suspected.

2) Look for melted strands of wire with beaded ends at the broken points.

3) Burned out head lamps indicate a battery short.

4) Check the battery charge. A short will usually lead to a run-down battery.

5) Examine the distributor points for fusing due to a short while the motor was running.

b. **Gas Tank and Gas Line.** Gasoline may have been obtained from the tanks, gas line, or the fuel pump.

1) Examine the *gas line* for breaks or other tampering such as disconnection.

2) Examine the *gas cap* for signs of fire. If there are no signs it may have been placed on after the fire. If an explosion took place the cap will bear signs of this occurrence.

3) The *fuel pump* should be examined for missing parts or tampering. Determine whether the line from the fuel pump was disconnected to obtain gasoline.

c. **Under the Hood.** The possible points of origin under the hood are the fuel pump, carburetor, and wiring. The use of incendiary substances is indicated by lead melted from the lower or outside seams of the motor, burned fan belt, and burned rubber cushions in the front of the motor. Another indication is the presence of burned spots on the paint. When the perpetrator pours gasoline over the motor he sometimes spills a few drops on the front fender. These areas will burn even though they are not in the direct line of the fire.

d. **Body.** Often an excess of inflammable fluid is used to burn a car with the result that the fluid seeps through the floor of the car and the fire produces oil or gasoline soot on the underside of the car. Similarly, soot deposits on the underside of the frame and springs indicate the use of inflammables.

e. **Other Indications.** Often the criminal commits the error of making small economies. The investigator should check the accessories to determine whether any of the extra equipment has been recently removed. The radio, tape deck, emergency repair kit, jack, spare tires, and similar equipment may have been first removed from the car. In fact, the complete set of tires has been removed in some cases. Where total burning has taken place the tires may be completely consumed but wires will remain on the metal rims. An inspection should also be made for the substitution of inferior equipment prior to burning.

20. Interviewing the Assured

After the car has been examined the investigator should obtain a statement from the assured, permitting him to give his account of the burning without interrupting. Subsequently the assured should be questioned in detail along the following lines:

a. **Purchase.** All data concerning the sale of the car and its financing should be obtained, including such details as the name of the salesman.

b. **Conditions.** Amount of extra equipment on the car at the time of fire; mileage; defects; name of service station to which the car was customarily brought.

c. **Movements.** The assured should be questioned in detail concerning his movements during the hours preceding the loss. Information may be developed in this way to establish motive or deception.

d. **Observations.** The assured's recital of the discovery and progress of the fire are often revealing. Most persons have never observed the accidental burning of a car. If the assured has no experience in these matters, he will describe details that are peculiar to a fire contrived with an inflammable material.

e. **Assured's Theory.** The investigator should display a great interest in the owner's explanation of the cause of the fire and his opinion on the point of origin. These statements should be compared with the results of the physical examination.

f. **Subsequent Movements.** The manner in which the owner left the scene is significant. If the fire is arranged to take place in an isolated place, the perpetrator makes prior arrangements for transportation.

g. **Other Witnesses.** Other persons who observed the fire should be interviewed separately. The lines followed in interviewing will be dictated by the nature of the fire and the statement of the owner.

h. **Subsequent Checks.** The complete investigation should include a check of the following items:

1) Dealer's records; reconditioning records before sale; prior owner's reason for sale.

2) Assured's title to determine if he has an insurable interest.

21. Law

In common law and in most jurisdictions the malicious and willfull burning of an automobile is not considered arson but is prohibited under statutes relating to the malicious destruction of property. In some jurisdictions, however, the term *simple arson* is used to describe the criminal burning of property other than a dwelling and the term *aggravated arson* is used for the burning of an inhabited structure.

ADDITIONAL READING

Arson

Arson Trends and Patterns – 1989. Quincy, Mass.: National Fire Protection Association, 1991.

ATF Arson Investigative Guide. Washington, D.C.: U.S. Government Printing Office, 1986.

Bennett, W.W. and Hess, K.M.: *Investigating Arson.* Springfield, Ill.: Thomas, 1984.

Bouquard, T.J.: *Arson Investigation: The Step-by-Step Procedure.* Springfield, Ill.: Thomas, 1983.

Carroll, J.R.: *Physical and Technical Aspects of Fire and Arson Investigations.* Springfield, Ill.: Thomas, 1983.

Clede, B.: Arson Dog. 36 *Law and Order* 7, 1988

DeArmond, H.T.: Automobile Arson Investigation. 25 *Fire and Arson Investigator,* 3, 1975.

DeHaan, J.D.: *Kirk's Fire Investigation,* 3rd ed. Englewood Cliffs, N.J.: Prentice-Hall, 1990.

Ferrall, R.T.: Arson Information: Who – What – Where? 50 *FBI Law Enforcement Bulletin,* 5, 1981.

Goodnight, K.M.: Arson for Profit: The Insurance Investigation. 57 *Police Chief,* 12, 1990.

Hart, F.: The Arson Equation: Arson + Circumstantial Evidence = Conviction. 57 *Police Chief,* 12, 1990.

Hartnett, D.M.: Bombing and Arson Investigations Enhanced by Advances in ATF Labs. 57 *Police Chief,* 4, 1990.

Hobson, C.B.: *Fire Investigation: A New Concept.* Springfield, Ill.: Thomas, 1992.

Icove, D.J.: Serial Arsonists: An Introduction. 57 *Police Chief,* 12, 1990.

Icove, D.J. and Estepp, M.H.: Motive-Based Offender Profiles of Arson and Fire-Related Crimes. 56 *FBI Law Enforcement Bulletin,* 4, 1987.

Inciardi, J.A.: The Adult Firesetter: A Typology. 8 *Criminology,* 145, 1970.

Kennedy, J. and Kennedy, P.: *Fires and Explosions: Determining Cause and Origin.* Chicago, Investigations Institute, 1985.

Levin, B.: Psychological Characteristics of Firesetters. 27 *Fire and Arson Investigator* 3, 1977.

Molnar, G., Keitner, L. and Harwood, B.T.: A Comparison of Partner and Solo Arsonists. 29 *Journal of Forensic Sciences,* 574, 1984.

O'Connor, J.J.: *Practical Fire and Arson Investigation.* New York, Elsevier, 1986.

Phillips, C.C. and McFadden, D.A.: *Investigating the Fireground.* Englewood Cliffs, N.J.: Prentice-Hall, 1982.

Rider, A.O.: The Firesetter: A Psychological Profile. Parts I and II. 49 *FBI Law Enforcement Journal,* 6 and 7, 1980.

Roblee, C.L., McKechnie, A.J. and Lundy, W.: *The Investigation of Fires,* 2nd ed. Englewood Cliffs, N.J.: Prentice-Hall, 1988.

Swab, S.E.: *Incendiary Fires: A Reference Manual for Fire Investigators.* Bowie, Md.: Robert J. Brady, 1983.

Thomas, R.B., Jr.: The Use of Canines in Arson Detection. 58 *FBI Law Enforcement Bulletin,* 4, 1989.

Tower, K. and Matson, D. (Eds.): *Arson Guide.* 5 vols. New York, National Fire Protection Association, 1982.

Yereance, R.A.: *Electrical Fire Analysis.* Springfield, Ill.: Thomas, 1987.

Chapter 18

NARCOTICS VIOLATIONS

1. Introduction

THE PROBLEMS ASSOCIATED with narcotics and other dangerous drugs are too well publicized to require elaboration here. It is the common belief that the illicit trade in narcotics is centrally controlled by a few powerful criminals who exercise an extraordinary influence over large sections of the country. This chapter does not pretend to establish the truth or falsity of this belief. The extent to which propositions of this nature are true and the reliability of the associated statistics will not be treated here. The subject of narcotics is a land of dark figures, myths, and unprovable propositions. We shall content ourselves in this chapter with activities within the ken and scope of the operations of the individual investigator. He should understand the nature of the drugs he is dealing with, the probable nature of the addict, the typology of sellers at various levels, and the action he can take to circumvent criminal activities connected with narcotics and other dangerous drugs.

2. Drug Addiction

The state of addiction may be described as a condition in which a person through repeated use of a drug has become dependent on it for his sense of well-being and, if deprived of the drug, suffers a psychic craving usually manifested by characteristic withdrawal symptoms due to an alteration of certain physiological processes.

a. **Causes.** Most commonly it is found that drug addiction is attributable to the availability of an addicting drug coupled with the existence of a personality disorder such as a psychoneurosis or a constitutional psychopathic inferiority. Initially the future addict makes his acquaintance with the drug through another addict or a criminal seller. It is only rarely that his introduction to the drug will be in the form of a prescribed medical treatment or self-medication. The psychoneurotic individual will take drugs to relieve an emotional or physical distress, while the psychopathic person resorts to them for their intoxicating effect. The first experiment, however, will usually be prompted by curiosity or a desire for adventure. The beginner feels confident that he will avoid addiction but continues to experiment until he is a victim of the habit. Although an initial venture into the use of drugs may have been prompted by a pleasure-seeking curiosity, a quest for euphoria or excitement, the narcotics addict, after he has fully acquired the habit, is definitely pursuing neither pleasure nor dreams—he is simply easing the pain. The condition is summed up in the words of a heroin addict to a reporter: "You don't even know what I'm talking about; *you* feel okay all the time. *Me,* it costs me $100 a day just to stop hurting so much."

b. **Addict.** The Controlled Substances Act defines an addict as follows: "The term 'addict' means any individual who habitually uses any narcotic drug so as to endanger the public morals, health, safety, or welfare, or who is so far addicted to the use of narcotic drugs as to have lost the power of self-control with reference to his addiction."

c. **Physical Dependence.** Through continued use the addict gradually reaches a state where he finds the drug necessary to maintain his normal sense of physical well-being. The need is an actual physical one, which is attributable to physiological changes, particularly in his nervous system. It is more than the mere psychological craving that attends a habit. If deprived of the narcotic, the addict becomes physically ill to such an extent that he will resort even to criminal methods to obtain the source of his relief.

d. **Tolerance.** The body adjusts itself to repeated use of narcotics so that the addict soon finds his customary dosage failing to give the expected reaction. Increased quantities of the drug are required to give the needed stimulation or even to maintain a feeling of physical normality. The increase in dosage is inevitably followed by correspondingly increased tolerance as the body seeks to develop relative immunity to the toxic effects of the drug. In a short time the addict finds himself able to absorb quantities of the narcotic which formerly would have been fatal.

e. **Moral Degeneration.** Social disapproval of drug addiction demands that the use of narcotics be surrounded by secrecy. Deceit, subterfuge, and evasion must be employed by the addict to disguise his condition. The source of drug supply, moreover, is associated with the criminal element of society and the addict finds himself dealing and even associating with the underworld. The great cost of the drug may create a serious problem. The addict of limited means finds himself in financial straits and is driven to petty larceny and worse in his efforts to support the habit.

f. **Drug Dependence.** In addition to developing a physical dependence the addict also acquires a psychic dependence on the drug. From repeated usage he begins to associate a sense of satisfaction and mental well-being with the periodic administration of the drug. The two concepts—physical and psychic dependence— are closely related and their various aspects are not readily distinguishable. For this reason the World Health Organization introduced the broader concept of *drug dependence,* a state which may include either or both the physical and psychic dependence. In this connection WHO recommended that the nature of the dependence be identified by specifying the nature of the drug, such as drug dependence of the morphine type, of the barbiturate type, of the amphetamine type, and so forth.

3. Definitions

The following definitions are used in the Controlled Substances Act:

a. **Narcotic.** The term "narcotic" drug means "opium, coca leaves, and opiates" or "any compound, manufacture, salt, derivative, or preparation" of them, or any substance chemically identical with any of these substances.

b. **Opiate.** The term "opiate" means any drug or other substance having an addiction-forming or addiction-sustaining liability similar to morphine or being capable of conversion into a drug having such an addiction-forming or addiction-sustaining liability.

c. **General.** Several points should be noted in the definitions given above. The term "opiate" is not used here in the customary sense of an "opium derivative" but rather as a catch-all designed to include synthetic drugs which have a similar addicting effect as morphine. Modern chemistry periodically synthesizes drugs which may be used medically as a substitute for morphine and hence should be placed under legal control. The Attorney General may declare these new drugs to be within the meaning of the term "narcotic" and thus subject to the same regulations. Other drugs with abuse potential are similarly placed in the appropriate schedules of the Controlled Substances Act.

4. Legal Provisions

In general, federal and state laws forbid the unauthorized manufacture, sale, use, or possession of narcotics. Since the laws are quite lengthy and technical, they may be described only briefly here.

a. **Federal Law.** The following are some of the important federal laws in effect prior to the Controlled Substances Act which initially regulated the sale and use of drugs:

1) *Harrison Act (1914).* Taxed the importation, manufacture, distribution, and sale of narcotics and gave them a legal definition.

2) *Narcotic Drug Import and Export Act (1922).* Limited the importation of opium and coca leaves to that required for medical and scientific needs. The importation and manufacture of heroin and smoking opium were prohibited.

3) *Marihuana Tax Act (1937).* Controlled the distribution of marihuana by a system of registration and taxation, making it difficult to obtain legally.

4) *Drug Abuse Control Amendments (1965).* Placed amphetamines, barbiturates, and hallucinogens under repressive controls.

b. **Controlled Substances Act (1970).** Laws relating to narcotics and dangerous non-narcotic drugs were incorporated in the Comprehensive Drug Abuse Prevention and Control Act. This act is divided into four titles. Title II, which is concerned with control and enforcement, is called the Controlled Substances Act. This act is the controlling federal statute, superseding all other federal narcotics laws. It divides narcotics and other dangerous drugs into five schedules according to medical usage and abuse potential. Responsibility for enforcement is shared by the Drug Enforcement Agency and the Food and Drug Administration who monitor production, procurement, and sale of the controlled substances. Criminal penalties for violations are based on the classification of the drug, the nature of the offense (possession, sales, or manufacture) and whether it is a first or subsequent offense.

c. **State Laws.** Because state laws are not always consistent with federal law, a violation in one state may not be a violation in another. The federal government encourages each state to adopt similar drug laws not only to facilitate enforcement but also to benefit manufacturers, pharmacists, doctors, and their patients. To assist states in making their drug-control laws consistent with federal legislation, the Uniform Controlled Substances Act was developed, which many states have adopted with only minor revisions.

5. Opium

Opium is derived from the oriental poppy plant (*papaver somniferum*) which is grown chiefly in Asia but is found in other areas such as Mexico and the Balkans. The plant is usually 3 or 4 feet high with smooth, dull foliage and flowers approximately 4 inches wide. The opium itself is a latex or milky substance obtained by slitting open the capsules of the plant and scraping the sides. The small cakes thus obtained are pressed into a larger mass, the shape of which will depend on local custom. Raw opium is dark brown or black in color and is bitter to the taste. A number of alkaloids are derived from this substance, the most important of which are morphine, heroin, and codeine.

a. **Prepared Opium.** By a process of boiling, fermentation, and roasting, a dark brown extract of the raw opium is obtained which may be smoked, chewed, or eaten. This is the opium which is offered to the market for consumption. Opium for medicinal purposes is obtained in powder or granulated form or in solution. In powder form medicinal opium is light brown or dark yellow in color. Solutions of opium such as laudanum were popular analgesics in Europe during the eighteenth and early nineteenth centuries when they could be readily purchased without prescription.

b. **Smoking Opium.** The use of the opium pipe is largely confined to Asians and persons of Asian origin in this country. The pipe consists of a long stem and a detachable bowl with an extremely narrow opening. It is usually smoked in a prone position because of the requirements of the operations. The opium is heated by means of a small lamp employing peanut oil as a fuel to avoid smoking and unpleasant fumes. The lamp is covered by a cone-shaped device to direct the heat. The opium is heated until it is viscous fluid. A long metal needle (yen hock) is dipped in the opium and a small pellet is gathered with a twirling motion. The pellet is cooked over the flame, kneaded against the lamp to express moisture, and placed over the opening of the pipe. The addict draws in the smoke with slow, deep inhalations. After the opium has been smoked, a usable residue remains in the pipe in the form of a charcoal-colored mass. This is called opium dross or yen shee and contains carbon, unburned opium, and morphine. After soaking in water, draining and evaporating, the yen shee can be smoked again. It may also be mixed with tea or wine and is even injected into the body by some addicts. Because of the narcotic potential of yen shee the possession of the opium pipe itself is considered illegal.

c. **Effects.** The use of opium produces a feeling of well-being and relieves bodily pains. The drug is absorbed slowly into the body, gradually renders the smoker drowsy, and finally induces a deep sleep accompanied by fantastic dreams of a pleasant character. Continued use of opium results in addiction. The user acquires a physical dependency on the narcotic and suffers severely if it is withdrawn.

6. Opium Derivatives

The consumption of opium by smoking or other means is relatively uncommon in the United States. The use of opium derivatives constitutes the major narcotics problem. These are far more powerful in their stimulating effect and in the addiction which they produce. The opium derivatives are a group of some twenty alkaloids which possess complex organic structures. Their general appearance is that of a white powder. The alkaloids most commonly used illegally are morphine, heroin, and codeine.

a. **Morphine.** Morphine in the form of morphine sulphate, morphine hydrochloride, and morphine tartrate is widely used by the medical profession as an analgesic. It is the most important of the alkaloids and constitutes about 12 percent of the use of raw opium. For legitimate use it is found in the form of a small white cube or tablet approximately one gram in weight. Illegally it is usually sold as a white powder, a small quantity of which is wrapped in a glassine paper. In this form the quantity is referred to as a "deck." Almost invariably the morphine is "cut" or diluted by the sellers to obtain greater profits. The actual amount of morphine present in a deck may be as low as 3 percent; the remainder is a harmless white substance such as milk sugar.

1) *Method of Use.* Although morphine may be taken orally, the method is considered wasteful. Ordinarily the addict injects it into his body by means of a hypodermic needle or its improvised equivalent. For medical purposes the drug would be injected under the skin or into the muscles. To achieve a more rapid and stimulating effect, however, the addict usually injects it directly into the blood stream. A user employing this method is called a "mainliner." The investigator should become familiar with the apparatus characteristically employed by the addict. A bent spoon, medicine dropper, needle, and rubber band constitute the user's "kit." The drug is dissolved in water placed in a bent spoon. A match is applied to the bottom of the spoon to accelerate the dissolving by heat. The medicine dropper is used in place of the conventional hypodermic syringe. The needle, attached to the dropper by the rubber band, is used to penetrate the skin. Still cruder methods may be employed by the addict. In place of the

needle, the end of the dropper may be broken to present a jagged edge to the skin. Again, the user may simply incise the skin with a sharp blade and insert the end of the dropper.

2) *Effects.* With the injection of the drug the addict experiences an extraordinary stimulation. A sense of euphoria pervades his being. His spirit is invigorated, his mind becoming keener and his self-confidence increasing greatly. The effect lasts for several hours, after which he gradually subsides into his former state. With prolonged use of the drug the addict will develop great tolerance and require a daily dosage many times more than that which originally supplied a stimulus.

3) *Identifying the Addict.* When in possession of his normal supply of the drug, it is difficult to distinguish an addict on the basis of his appearance. Experienced narcotics investigators are unable to detect the addict by merely looking at his face. His conduct will appear quite normal since he ordinarily has adjusted himself to the use of the drug. There will be no irrational or otherwise exceptional behavior beyond a possible excess of enthusiasm. When the effects of the drug have worn off, however, the addict may be betrayed by an unusual drowsiness; prolonged abstinence may also result in identifiable symptoms. With the lapse of twenty-four hours after withdrawal, the addict will begin to experience severe pains in his back and legs. He may be overcome by nausea and suffer pains in his stomach. His eyes and nose begin to run in continuous lachrymation.

4) *Physical Marks.* Under the influence of morphine the eyes of the user will be characterized by a contracted pupil which does not react normally to changes of intensity of illumination. Since the addict must inject the drug quite frequently, his arms will be marked by punctures and scabs. The recent application of the needle will be shown by a small red spot on which a small drop of blood has coagulated. The scab formed over this mark will remain for approximately ten days. Dark blue scar tissue may be seen where the vein walls have broken down through repeated punctures. Some addicts, especially women, will inject in the area in back of the thighs.

5) *Sources of Supply.* The use of morphine as a sedative or an analgesic is quite common in the medical profession; hence the

drug can be legally manufactured. The illegal trade is supplied by smuggling, clandestine manufacture, or theft from legitimate users such as hospitals or pharmacies. Morphine has for the most part been supplanted by heroin as the drug of choice in the illicit trade.

b. **Codeine.** Methylmorphine or codeine is similar in many respects to morphine, but its effects are very much weaker in intensity. It is a natural alkaloid of opium and is in common medical use as a sedative in cough mixtures and an analgesic in tablet form. Its physical state in its pure form is that of a crystalline powder or of long, slender, white crystals. Although codeine, like all psychoactive drugs, represents a certain hazard for dependence-prone individuals, the problem of drug abuse with codeine does not remotely approach that of morphine or heroin. Primary codeine dependence can occur, but because of its rarity is considered to be a medical curiosity, and vast clinical experience supports the view that the danger of inducing drug dependence with the usual therapeutic dose is slight. Instances of abuse of codeine cough syrups, particularly by juveniles, have at times been publicized by the news media, leaving the impression that the problem is widespread. There are no adequate statistical data on the true incidence of this type of abuse, but the opinion of authorities in the field of drug abuse, after reviewing what data are available, has been that abuse of codeine-containing cough syrups is minimal and sporadic, and of little significance with respect to the general drug abuse problem.

c. **Heroin.** Heroin is a synthetic drug made from morphine as a diacetyl derivative. It is by far the most common drug occurring in cases of narcotic addiction. In appearance it is usually a white, crystalline powder; occasionally it is found in cubes or tablets. The method of use is similar to that of morphine. Rarely the user absorbs it by sniffing or rubbing into the gums. The effects of heroin are the same as those of morphine but greatly magnified in intensity. "Four times more powerful" is a phrase commonly used in comparing these two drugs. The withdrawal symptoms are qualitatively identical. Heroin differs from morphine and codeine in that it may not be legally manufactured in the United States. It is not recognized as an authorized drug by the U.S. Pharmacopoeia.

Thus, the licenses granted to possess other narcotics do not extend to heroin, and its possession by persons other than law enforcement officers acting in performance of duty may ordinarily be considered illegal. The drug is, however, used legitimately by members of the medical profession in certain foreign countries. It is considered a particularly effective analgesic for use in the terminal stages of such diseases as tuberculosis and cancer. Large quantities of heroin are manufactured abroad for illicit traffic in this country. Perhaps one reason for its popularity in the illegal market has been the desire of narcotic dealers to increase their sales through the medium of a drug which can easily obtain a grip on the victim and produce an addiction most difficult to conquer.

7. The Heroin Problem

a. **The Magnitude of the Problem.** The worldwide American war on opium growing and heroin smuggling promises to be at least as protracted, and perhaps as inconclusive, as the conflict in Vietnam. As awareness of the dimension of the effort spreads, officials are beginning to scale down their expectations. There is less talk of burning the world's poppy fields. The emphasis is now on disrupting supply routes by pinching off the flow of heroin into this country and by reducing availability on the street. Fifty-seven nations have been selected for diplomatic attention — either as producing or transshipment areas. The combination of furious diplomatic activity abroad and the continuing ravages of addiction at home often gives the impression that American addicts have a corner on the world opium market. Yet, in fact, they are the marginal consumer. The annual illicit world production of opium is estimated at 1,000 to 1,500 tons and the illicit American consumption is 60 to 100 tons — that is, 6 to 10 tons of heroin. And the American market, it is reckoned, can be supplied through the cultivation of little more than 5 square miles of arable up-country land. The task of stopping the flow of heroin into this country is overwhelming. In a typical year approximately 250 million people enter the United States in 65 million vehicles, 306,000 planes and 157,000 ships. Obviously, the most scrupulous search could discover only a minute fraction of the innumerable sites where illicit narcotics might be secreted.

b. **The Problem of Addiction.** Although there is no doubt that using certain psychoactive drugs predisposes a person to repeat the experience, opinion is divided on whether this results from a biochemical change or from a purely psychological or behavioral response. Whether addiction results from a biochemical change or from an unconsciously learned behavior pattern, or both, there is no doubt among researchers that certain chemicals have a molecular structure capable of inducing varying degrees of pleasure in the user. Psychological dependence is a response in behavior patterns that leads a person to want to take the drug again and again, often simply because it feels so good. Depending on the individual's personality, almost any drug can produce a psychological dependence. One indication of its strength is the difficulty tobacco smokers have in quitting the habit. Physical dependence, on the other hand, involves actual biochemical changes in the body so that the brain cells appear to function normally only in the presence of the drug. A phenomenon often confused with physical dependence is tolerance. This is an adaptation of the brain cells in which they become able to function normally in the presence of the drug but do not require the drug. Increasing tolerance makes it necessary to increase the dose to achieve the same effects.

c. **The Problem of Contagion.** One of the hardest-dying myths is that the dope pusher is the person most responsible for spreading addiction among the young. By now we know that the biggest culprit is not the pusher, who plays an indispensable backup role, but the youthful, enthusiastic addict who thinks he's onto a good thing and wishes to share it with his friends. This applies to many different drug addictions, but when it comes to heroin, initiation in the use of the needle is an important ritual that requires one addict to teach another. Hence, heroin maintenance is no solution as long as there are young, enthusiastic users constantly enlarging the addict population.

A number of studies have been made of this phenomenon of contagion, of which the Nils Bejerot experiment is particularly informative. Bejerot plotted the explosion of amphetamine mainlining from a tiny group of Stockholm poets and Bohemians in 1949 to a runaway epidemic claiming 12,000 addicts twenty years later. Drug epidemics, Bejerot finds, are spread by "personal initiation from established addicts"; they begin within certain defined class or ethnic boundaries, and then spread outward into a larger society. The debut age is low; there are usually 3 to 6 male addicts for every female addict and, most alarmingly, epidemics spread "by geometric progression if other conditions remain unchanged." The one factor that correlates most highly with the epidemic spread of addiction is the availability of the drug in question. Heroin may be fairly available today; as it is made more available there will be more junkies—many more.

d. **Institutional Response.** Those who look for a cure, e.g., for heroin, through methadone or heroin antagonists (or through law enforcement) must constantly be reminded that for every drug eliminated ten can be found to take its place that will produce nearly equivalent euphoria, addiction, and trouble. The problems of addiction are not the problems of an isolated drug, whether alcohol or methaqualone, but rather are symptomatic of sociological and economic conditions.

8. Synthetic Analgesics

Modern medical research has developed a series of drugs designed to be used as substitutes for the opium derivatives. These chemically synthesized drugs produce the same effects as the narcotics previously discussed. They are prescribed as analgesics, that is, substances which relieve pain. Since their effects are similar to those of morphine they have been declared opiates and their manufacture, sale, and use are strictly regulated by the Controlled Substances Act. Among the more important of these synthetic analgesics are the following: meperidine, methadone, Dilaudid®, and Percodan®.

a. **Meperidine.** Meperidine hydrochloride is also known by the following names: Demerol®, Dolantin®, Dolantol®, Endolat®, and the international generic name, pethidine. For relief of pain this drug lies somewhere between morphine and codeine in its effects. Opinions vary in regard to its capacity to develop physiologic dependence. The drug does have a moderate degree of addiction liability. Mild withdrawal symptoms are observable. These are qualitatively similar to morphine but considerably milder.

b. **Methadone.** Methadone hydrochloride is also known by the following trade names: Methadon®, Amidone®, Amidon®, Dolophine®, and Adanon®. Its pharmacologic action is like that of morphine, except for its failure to produce a "high." Methadone can definitely produce an addiction. The withdrawal symptoms are more gradual in their appearance and are less severe than those of morphine. In treating addiction to heroin, physicians commonly substitute methadone to alleviate withdrawal pains. A number of cities have instituted programs of methadone maintenance to care for their heroin addicts.

c. **Dilaudid (Dihydromorphinone Hydrochloride).** This substance is closely allied to morphine in its chemical nature and in its physiological effects. It is effective in doses considerably smaller than are necessary with morphine. The withdrawal symptoms are qualitatively identical with and just as severe as those attending abstinence from morphine.

d. **Percodan (Oxycodone Hydrochloride** and other analgesic ingredients). An effective and widely used pain reliever, Percodan has achieved great popularity in the illegal market among youths. It is a semisynthetic opium derivative sold in yellow or pink pills. Percodan is similar to codeine in its effects and is somewhat greater in its addictive potential. Under the trade name of Percobarb® this substance is offered in combination with a barbiturate in the form of a blue-and-white or blue-and-yellow capsule.

9. Cocaine

This drug is a sparkling white crystalline powder which is obtained from the leaves of the coca shrub, *Erythroxylon coca*, a plant cultivated by Andean Indians before the Spanish occupation. The raw coca leaves are either chewed or brewed as a tea by the Indians to deaden pain, allay fatigue, diminish hunger, and relieve altitude sickness. Cocaine is derived from the coca leaves either as an alkaloid powder or a more water-soluble hydrochloride. It has a legitimate medical use as a surface anesthetic. Illegally, the drug is taken through the nose by sniffing or is injected in the vein. The initial effect is stimulating, pleasurable, and productive of self-confidence.

a. **Source.** The legitimate medical needs of the world are met by 200 to 500 tons. The annual yield of Bolivia and Peru alone, however, is estimated to be about 15,000 tons, most of which is consumed by the native Indians. Importation of coca leaves and the manufacture of cocaine are under the strict control of federal narcotics laws. Only a single chemical company is licensed by the Justice Department to import leaves and produce pure cocaine.

b. **Illegal Traffic.** During the last ten years there has been a marked increase in the flow of illegal cocaine into the United States. The Drug Enforcement Administration has reported an enormous increase in the official seizure of cocaine being smuggled into this country. "Body carriers," who a few years ago brought only 5 to 10 lb. of cocaine concealed on their persons or in their baggage, are now found to carry from 80 to 100 lb. The mountains of western South America are the leading source of cocaine smuggled into this country.

The first step in processing coca leaves into cocaine is performed by the highland Andean Indians who pluck the leaves from the small bushes. To a gasoline drum filled with the leaves they add kerosene and one or more solvents, leaving the mixture to soak. After the fluid is drawn off and the soggy leaves removed, the residual thick, coffee-colored paste is ladled into small containers and sold to laboratory agents. These clandestine laboratories then refine the paste into white cocaine, sometimes pressing it into small pills. There are many such clandestine laboratories presently in operation. Some of these are mobile units, thus presenting an additional police problem.

c. **Ingestion.** The typical price to the cocaine dealer is several hundred dollars an ounce. Ordinarily, the pure cocaine will be diluted with lactose, dextrose, or quinine and sold at an exorbitant price to the customer. The user takes the substance either by sniffing or by injection. Oral ingestion is ordinarily confined to the coca leaf chewing or brewing by Indians.

1) *Sniffing.* It is still a common practice to administer the drug by sniffing. A small amount is placed on the back of the hand and

snuffed up. This direct application, however, can result in the destruction of body cells and the consequent erosion of the septum or middle part of the nose. Excessive use is accompanied by a characteristic deformity—the so-called "rat's nose."

2) *Injecting.* Injecting is done as with heroin: a water solution of cocaine is drawn into a hypodermic (or its equivalent) and injected into the vein. "Mainlining" is preferred because of the intense, quick-acting, and longer-lasting effect.

d. **Physical Effects.** Cocaine is an intense central nervous system stimulant, affecting the higher brain centers to render the user alert, restless, and apparently more energetic. The sense of fatigue is diminished and the appetite suppressed. In extreme cases, paranoia and psychosis may appear with nausea and hallucination. Although relatively rare, cardiac failure and subsequent death can result from an overdose of cocaine in the bloodstream.

e. **Mental Effects.** Following an injection, the cocaine user experiences great exhilaration and even a sense of ecstasy. He becomes restless and garrulous. With heavy use hallucinations and illusions of a paranoid nature may develop; the user may become an irresponsible victim of his imagination. The chief evil in the immoderate use of cocaine is thought to be an excessive freedom from inhibitions and a consequent predisposition to reckless action, aggressive behavior, and confusion.

f. **Dependence and Withdrawal.** Neither tolerance nor physical dependence develops with the continued use of cocaine. It is not addicting in the sense in which the opiates are addicting; that is, there is no characteristic abstinence syndrome. Although withdrawal is normally uneventful, the heavy user may experience severe depression, great fatigue, and a confused state of mind. The continued use of cocaine can develop a strong psychic dependence, leading to a profound and dangerous type of abuse. It should be kept in mind that there is a dearth of scientific knowledge about the abuse of cocaine and very little experimentation on its effects is being performed.

g. **Law.** Cocaine is classed as a narcotic under federal law and its unauthorized sale, use and possession are prohibited by the same laws that proscribe the opiates. The state laws controlling cocaine are also characterized by harsh penalties—heavy fines and sentences up to life imprisonment. The classification of this drug under the same laws as the addicting opiates is a historical fact of a less sophisticated age, since medically and pharmacologically cocaine, a stimulant, has been found to be the opposite of heroin and morphine, which act on the sense as depressants. In the absence of any clear knowledge of the dangers of cocaine, the prospect of placing it under new and separate legislation is not bright.

h. **The User.** There is no typical cocaine user, and the range of personalities covered by the term is quite broad. The user may be a young adult in search of a new experience or a depressed person seeking to recapture his interest in life. As a hallucinatory drug, cocaine has an attraction for the rock-drug culture, in which mind-expansion and the atmosphere of illusion have a special value. As a stimulant, cocaine appeals to the imaginative but unsure person looking to acquire a feeling of self-confidence. Among the regular users of cocaine are said to be a sizable number of well-known public personalities who wish to project an enthusiastic and energetic image. In brief the cocaine user can be described as a person who wishes to change an impression—either his impression of the world about him or the impression he gives to the world.

10. Crack

In 1983, "crack," a new form of cocaine, appeared on the streets of New York City. Within three years, more than half of all cocaine arrests involved crack. Crack filled the drug dealer's need: an easily prepared, low-cost form of cocaine that produced a euphoric effect while being highly addictive. Because of its relatively low cost, dealers could offer free samples to attract new customers. Its highly addictive nature would eventually lead users to spend their money impulsively for long crack-smoking sessions. Eventually, when their finances are depleted, the user will turn to drug dealing, robbery, burglary, prostitution and other crimes to support his habit. By 1986, there had been significant growth in crime in New York City attributed to the spread of crack. Murder and assault also increased dramatically as drug dealers would fight amongst themselves for control of this lucrative trade.

Cocaine in its usual form is cocaine hydrochloride. As we have seen in the previous section, cocaine hydrochloride is a refinement of coca paste which in turn is derived from the cocoa leaves cultivated in the Andes Mountains. Cocaine hydrochloride can be further refined by a method called "freebasing," where the active cocaine alkaloid is "freed" from its "base," the hydrochloride salt. The extraction technique involves dissolving the cocaine hydrochloride in water, adding a catalyst of either ammonia or baking soda, and then heating the mixture. This blend is then filtered and the precipitate is permitted to dry. The result takes the form of small yellow crystals which can be placed in a pipe and smoked. One gram of cocaine hydrochloride yields approximately one-half gram of crack.

a. **Characteristics.** The drug dealer now has a product with the following characteristics:

1) It is 70 to 90 percent pure which leads to a more intense euphoria.

2) It can be smoked. The lungs are designed for inhaled oxygen to pass quickly into the bloodstream. Inhaled crack enters the bloodstream and is carried to the brain in a matter of seconds.

3) It is economical. Because smaller amounts of cocaine are required, $1,000 worth of cocaine can be converted to over $2,000 worth of crack.

4) It is highly addictive. While crack produces an intense euphoria, the depression that follows is equally severe. Smoking crack can lead a susceptible individual to compulsive use in six to ten weeks.

b. **Distribution.** In a typical urban setting, crack dealing evolved into a highly efficient organization, usually involving:

1) *Supplier.* He hires the dealer to sell his drugs. In a large operation the supplier may have as many as five dealers working for him.

2) *Dealer.* He does the actual selling of the crack and hires the doorman, the steerer, and the lookout.

3) *Doorman.* He guards the dealer from being robbed by other drug dealers or by customers.

4) *Steerer.* The function of the steerer is to conduct customers met on the street to the dealer.

5) *Lookout.* Usually a young boy on a bicycle will tip off the doorman in the event of trouble.

6) *Courier.* Frequent deliveries of drugs by a courier is essential. In the event the crack dealer is apprehended by the police, he will usually be carrying no more than a dozen crack vials, a supply well below the amount necessary to support a felony charge of selling drugs.

c. **Marketing.** Crack is most commonly sold in plastic vials or in self-sealing plastic bags. The smallest size, containing 100 milligrams, will sell for $10; the largest, containing 500 milligrams, will sell for $40 or $50. Crack vials are sometimes heat-sealed in plastic to prevent adulteration of its contents. To give the impression of quality control, they are often sold under brand names. This is important to insure customer satisfaction and thus repeat business. The vials are small enough so that they can be transferred from seller to buyer with a handshake.

d. **Location.** Different types of premises are often used for the manufacturing, buying, and consuming of crack.

1) *Crack Factory.* This is a house or apartment where the crack is manufactured for distribution to dealers.

2) *Crack House.* Crack cannot be smoked openly in the streets. A crack house is a facility where the drug can be purchased and consumed on the premises. Pipes for smoking crack are rented or sold here.

3) *Crack Spot.* This is a house or apartment where money is exchanged for drugs through a small opening in a door, a wall, or a window.

4) *Street.* In large cities some drug dealers conduct business openly in the streets.

e. **User.** The typical crack smoker is a young lower-income urban male.

11. Marihuana

Marihuana or *Cannabis sativa* is the most widely used of the illicit drugs. The smoking of marihuana cigarettes is especially popular among adolescents, who experience a mild intoxication in this manner. The hemp plant from which the drug is obtained

Table IV
COMPARISON OF COCAINE HYDROCHLORIDE AND CRACK

	Cocaine Hydrochloride	*Crack*
Street Price	$5 and up.	$5 and up.
Average Buy	$10 and up.	$10 or $20.
Speed of Drug Reaction	Snort: 1–3 minutes.	Smoked: 4–6 seconds.
Purity	15–25 percent. Always adulterated and/or diluted.	70–90+ percent. Sometimes adulterated and/or diluted.
Average Amount Used per One Hour Session	Two or three $10 bags.	Five or more $10 vials often used continuously.
Packaging Methods	Folded pyramid paper or aluminum foil; more difficult to hide; packets must be unfolded to examine contents.	Small vials, very easy to transport and conceal; see-through vials need to be opened to examine contents.
Convenience of Use	Snorting can be accomplished relatively quickly and unobtrusively.	Smoking with marijuana or freebasing in a pipe is likely to be observed if done in public.
Average Length of High per $10 Buy	20–30 minutes.	5–7 minutes.
Euphoric Reaction	Injection produces a more intense euphoria than snorting.	More intense than snorting or injecting cocaine hydrochloride.

Source: U.S. Customs Service. *Narcotics Identification Manual.*

is a hardy weed which can be grown in a variety of climates. In warm regions the plant develops a resinous substance which has a strong narcotic effect. The hemp plant grows wild or is cultivated in Turkey, Greece, Syria, India, Africa, Brazil, Mexico, and the United States. The appearance of the plant varies widely with the region in which it is found. Most commonly it is approximately five feet in height; green in color with stalks fluted lengthwise; compound palmate leaves usually containing seven leaflets; flower (in the male plant) like greenish yellow sprays about 6 inches in length; fruit or seed (in the female plant) in the form of a brown or greenish yellow moss enclosed in a green, sticky hull.

a. **Preparation and Use.** Marihuana is made from the female hemp plant. As the plants ripen, their flower and seed heads exude a resin that contains the highest natural concentration of active cannabis chemicals. The pure resin is hashish, a combination of powerful chemicals that rarely reaches the United States. The typical seizure of marihuana is a variable combination of female cannabis seed heads with leaves, chopped-up stalks, flowers, and hulls. Marihuana is illegally imported into this country, mainly from Mexico, either loose or in the form of a pressed brick, called a "key" because of its one kilo (2.2 lb.) weight. Marihuana is usually consumed by smoking it in cigarette form (*joint*). The potency of the cigarette will depend on the region in which the plant is grown and the amount of resin used. At best, it is only one-tenth as strong as hashish. Marihuana may also be eaten when mixed with foods such as sweetmeats and it may be consumed as a beverage by steeping it in the same manner as tea.

b. **Identification.** The hemp plant itself may be readily recognized by the serrations and vein structure of the leaf. Familiarity with the appearance of the plant is essential. Prepared marihuana has the general appearance of catnip. In this form it may be recognized by an experienced microscopist. Several chemical tests are available. One of these, the Duquenois test, can be applied by the investigator as a corroborative measure prior to a seizure. Although not conclusive it is a fairly reliable indication of the presence of marihuana. A small amount of the suspected material is placed in a test tube. Two cubic centimeters of the Duquenois reagent are added to the substance and shaken for thirty seconds. One cubic centimeter of concentrated hydrochloric acid is added. If marihuana is present, the solution will turn pink, change to violet and finally become a deep blue. A supply of the Duquenois reagent can be obtained from a chemist or pharmacist.

c. **Effects.** The pattern of behavior induced by smoking marihuana will vary widely with the individual and the quality of the cigarette ingredients. Most physicians agree that the only physical effect of marihuana smoking is a temporary impairment of visual and muscular coordination. As for mental effects, the Medical Society of the County of New York has classified marihuana as a mild hallucinogen, although hallucinations are only one of many effects the drug can produce. It can impair judgment and memory and can cause anxiety, confusion, or disorientation. It does not appear to cause any severe mental illness (psychosis)—in contrast with the frequency of such breakdowns among persons taking LSD. However, when pre-psychotic people take marihuana, there can be a serious psychotic reaction, with marihuana serving as a catalytic rather than a causative agent.

Figure 16. Marihuana leaf.

There is a substantial difference of opinion on the relationship of marihuana use to criminal behavior and violence. One view is that marihuana is a major cause of crime and violence. Another is that marihuana has no association with crime and only a marginal relation to violence. The 1972 report of the National Commission on Marihuana and Drug Abuse found no evidence to substantiate the reputation of marihuana for inciting people to antisocial acts. Marihuana does have a tendency to release inhibitions, but the effect of the drug appears to depend on the individual and the circumstances. Thus, with regard to sexual acts, marihuana might predispose the user to friendlier relations but could hardly be considered an aphrodisiac. Similarly, with regard to acts of violence, the response will depend more on the individual than on the drug.

Some members of the medical profession take a more severe view of the effects of marihuana. To present this point of view it should suffice to quote Doctor Nicholas A. Pace, President, New York Affiliate, National Council on Alcoholism: "Scientific studies worldwide have shown that chronic marihuana use causes inhibition of cellular growth, reduction in sperm production, development of abnormal sperm cells, interference with the synthesis of important genetic material in the cell, interference with the immune system, destruction of chromosomes, abnormal embryonic developments and birth defects in experimental animals, and, above all, brain damage." (*New York Times,* Letters, May 16, 1977)

d. **Tolerance and Withdrawal.** Marihuana is not an addicting drug. No tolerance is developed with continued use; that is, no increase in quantity is required to produce the desired effect. The use of marihuana does not develop a physical dependence, nor does sudden abstinence from the drug result in anything resembling the severe withdrawal syndrome with its intense physical suffering and uncontrollable craving that characterizes the opiates or narcotics. At worst withdrawal may leave the habitué depressed and irritable, since marihuana can lead to a psychic dependence as can many other substances, especially those which alter the state of consciousness.

e. **The Marihuana User and the Law.** Although the smoking of marihuana is a habit and not an addiction, its use and possession are prohibited by most state laws. Under the Uniform Narcotic

Drug Act, in force in most states, marihuana is defined and controlled as a narcotic drug. The controlling federal statute, although ostensibly a tax law, in practice is simply a criminal law imposing sanctions on persons who sell, purchase, or possess marihuana. These legal prohibitions with respect to marihuana are based on the drug's supposed liability to lead to petty offenses and even serious crime through underworld associations and, in particular, on the supposed tendency of the habitué to experiment with heroin in search of more intense excitement.

Responding to a considerable increase in the number of marihuana users and an even greater increase in the number of those who consider the laws controlling this drug excessively severe, some states have passed laws to "decriminalize" the possession of small quantities of marihuana or to institute non-criminal treatment for those who use marihuana. This view looks upon marihuana as a substance similar to alcohol—not especially harmful when used in moderation and, even when in excess, attended by evil effects attributable to the individual rather than the drug.

The opposite view is held by many reputable physicians and public officials, who consider the alcohol analogy a weak argument since it seeks to justify the adoption of a new vice by trying to show that it is no worse than a presently existing one. This group indicts marihuana on three counts: 1) it builds up an addictive need for continued use; 2) it impairs mental functioning at least temporarily and may damage the mind permanently; 3) it leads often and almost inevitably to the use of "hard" narcotics such as heroin.

Those who seek relaxation of the rigor of present marihuana laws deny the truth of all three charges. With respect to the first charge they point out that marihuana use leads to a habituation and not an addiction—that marihuana is not a narcotic in the medical sense, since it is not physiologically addicting as evidenced by the absence of withdrawal pains and by the absence of any buildup of tolerance that would lead to increasing doses. The second charge, too, is rejected on the grounds of insufficient supporting evidence and because of the existence of a significant body of evidence to the contrary, namely, that no physical damage and no permanent mental impairment have been linked to the use of marihuana.

Greater difficulty, however, is encountered in dealing with the third charge, namely, that marihuana habituation "leads" to the use of heroin. It is denied in the sense that marihuana has any intrinsic quality that results in a heroin liability. There is evidence that a majority of the heroin users who come to the attention of public authorities have in fact had some prior experience with marihuana. Nevertheless, there are too many marihuana users who do not graduate to heroin, and too many heroin addicts with no known prior marihuana use to support the theory that there is any special quality in the drug that leads to heroin use. There is sufficient evidence, however, to permit the conclusion that some people who are predisposed to marihuana are also predisposed to heroin use, and the further conclusion that through the use of marihuana a person forms personal associations that later expose him to heroin.

In summary, it would appear that the third charge is rejected here by requiring rigorous scientific proof, a much higher order of proof than is ordinarily available in sociological areas. The practical investigator would readily and instinctively concede that there is no pharmacological causal connection between the continued use of marihuana and an ultimate heroin addiction. He would, nevertheless, point to the need for a closer examination of the economics of the illegal drug trade—the likelihood, in view of the equivalent sanctions, that the marihuana seller is also a seller of the far less bulky and considerably more profitable heroin and that ordinary business sense would encourage the sale of heroin, particularly in the presence of a predisposed market. Finally, since the third charge presents a problem that is not academically soluble within at least the next decade, he would suggest that a meeting ground of the two groups be found in a consideration of the desirability of separating the marihuana dealer from the heroin dealer by a modification of the marihuana laws which would establish a penalty for selling this substance markedly less than the sanctions imposed on the sale of heroin.

f. **Identifying the User.** It is not possible for the investigator to identify definitely the marihuana user in his normal state, but certain indications will be found helpful. The confirmed user may develop a yellowish skin particularly about the eyes. In addition the eyes may appear exophthalmic, i.e., "pop-eyed." During a period of use a characteristic odor, resembling that of cubeb cigarettes, is detectible on the breath. The general behavior of a suspect may be compared with the typical pattern previously described.

12. Dangerous Non-narcotic Drugs

Certain drugs, although not prohibited under federal narcotics laws, deserve extended treatment because of their popularity and the deleterious effects attending their misuse. Some of these drugs — the tranquilizers and stimulants — are obtainable only on prescription; others, such as the hallucinogens, cannot be obtained even in this manner. For the illegal sale of both classes of drugs a considerable market exists and an illicit traffic has developed accordingly.

a. **Laws.** A series of federal enactments that had been found inadequate to deal with the traffic in dangerous non-narcotic drugs was replaced by the Controlled Substances Act of 1970. This, the principal federal law in the field, limits manufacture, sale, and distribution of any controlled drug to designated classes of persons, such as registered wholesale druggists and licensed physicians. It requires that inventories be taken and records of receipts and dispositions be maintained. It also places restrictions on the refilling of prescriptions. Criminal penalties are provided for violations, including manufacture, sale, or distribution by unauthorized persons. The first offense is a misdemeanor; the second, a felony. Possession of drugs for personal use is not an offense under this statute.

All of the amphetamines and the barbiturates are controlled by specific language in the statute. In addition, any other drug with potential for abuse because of its depressant, stimulant, or hallucinogenic effect may be placed under control by designation. The statute is enforced by the Bureau of Drug Abuse Control, an agency within the Food and Drug Administration.

b. **Addictions, Tolerance, and Withdrawal.** Opinions vary with respect to the addicting properties of the dangerous non-narcotic drugs. The medical profession generally considers the confirmed use of these drugs to be a habit and not an addiction. Except perhaps in the case of the barbiturates no physical suffering follows withdrawal. Very little tolerance to these drugs is developed even by prolonged use. While these drugs may not be considered addicting in the strict sense, it must be noted that a great psychic dependence can be developed and hence that users may in some cases require medical care in their efforts to break the habit.

13. Barbiturates

By far the most commonly abused of this class of drugs are the barbiturates or derivatives of barbituric acid, which are prescribed by physicians as soporifics or sedatives. In correct dosage the barbiturates are a harmless and invaluable aid to the treatment of insomnia, nervousness, and related conditions. They are readily obtainable, and their use is common at institutions such as hospitals. An excessive dose is toxic and may result in death. In fact an overdose of barbiturates is the most fashionable and one of the most common methods of suicide. The drug was once prescribed by many physicians without the exercise of any exceptional forethought. With some doctors it had replaced the old-fashioned placebo. Drugstores are the ordinary source of supply. A few unscrupulous pharmacists sell them under the counter. Operators on the criminal fringe peddle barbiturates in lodging houses, poolrooms, and bars.

a. **Identification.** Barbiturates are usually found in the form of white powder. Occasionally, they are dispensed in solution. For the most part, however, they are sold as tablets or capsules. The names of the various barbiturates would form a long list which could, according to frequency of usage, be headed by phenobarbital, sodium Amytal®, Seconal®, Nembutal®, and Tuinal®. The nomenclature is variable, different terms being used in England and Japan, for example. The various barbiturates are distinguishable by the color series employed by the manufacturers in their gelatin capsules: sodium Amytal is usually found in a blue capsule, Seconal in red, Nembutal in yellow, and Tuinal in a capsule with a blue body and an orange cap. Phenobarbital is usually manufactured in the form of a white tablet.

b. **Effects.** The barbiturates vary widely in the duration and the speed of action. Phenobarbital acts slowly but is effective for a long period of time. Seconal is felt within fifteen minutes but its effect is short-lived. Tuinal is rapid in the onset of its effects and is relatively long lasting. All of the barbiturates affect the higher cortical centers, partially removing control over learned behavior and inhibitions governing instinctive behavior. The user loses consciousness as the intermediate centers are reached, and in the final stages the respiratory and circulatory systems may be affected by the action of the drug. Death may ensue if the depression of the central nervous system is sufficiently severe. Because of the wide latitude of dosage, the margin of error is sufficiently great to preclude accidental death except under circumstances of unusual ignorance. The fatal dose is considered to be fifteen times greater than the sleeping dose. This estimate must be drastically modified, however, if an alcoholic drink is taken in connection with the drug. As with many other poisons, the effect of barbiturates becomes more toxic with alcohol. The synergistic action of alcohol and the barbiturates is well known to habitués and it is a common practice among them to drink whiskey together with two or three capsules of Seconal.

c. **Identifying the User.** According to the President's Commission on Violence there is no reliable evidence to the effect that tranquilizers (including barbiturates) are associated with antisocial behavior. "Behavior may change and some observers may disapprove of the changes, but crime itself has not been shown to occur." Although the use of barbiturates is not illegal, the identification of the user is sometimes helpful in the investigation of an illegal sale. The habitué is usually a maladjusted person who seeks escape from reality through the medium of the drug. Occasionally, he is a narcotic addict who is deprived of his opiate supply and seeks relief from the withdrawal symptoms. The barbiturate user enjoys a mild sense of well-being on taking the drug. He appears intoxicated and lapses into mental confusion. His speech is slurred, reflexes are diminished, and muscular control is seriously affected. Sleep supervenes after a period of time which depends on the type of the barbiturate and the extent to which alcohol has been taken. Even after awaking the effects are still felt and the user may still be recognized by his "out-of-focus" eyes, imprecise movements, and difficulty of articulation particularly with respect to distinguishing the dentals. Tests are available for the detection of barbiturates in the urine. The confirmed addict sometimes suffers from amnesia and may incur serious injuries from falls. Tranquilizers can result in an impairment of driving ability.

d. **Withdrawal Symptoms.** Usually there are no physical symptoms following the abstinence from barbiturates. Some medical authorities, however, have observed that, if a person has been taking as much as one gram of a powerful barbiturate daily for a period of two months, the abrupt withdrawal of the drug may be followed by epileptiform seizures within two to seven days.

e. **Illegal Use.** Although a serious attempt to control the use of barbiturates was made by the Controlled Substance Act of 1970, great quantities of these substances are apparently diverted from the enormous supply used legally by the medical profession. Some barbiturate supplies are illegally manufactured in laboratories in Mexico and California. Some quantities are acquired by forged prescriptions and drugstore burglaries. The main sources, however, would appear to be those supplies which are manufactured for legal use but which somehow are diverted to illegal sales by an organized black market or by unscrupulous retailers. Among illegal users the most popular of the barbiturates is Seconal.

14. Amphetamine (Benzedrine)

The use of amphetamines has become prevalent in the United States and is one of the more common complications of opiate addiction. This drug is representative of a broad class of stimulants known as "pep pills." Ephedrine and epinephrine may also be placed in this category. The drugs in this group (sympathomimetic agents) are aromatic compounds, all of similar chemical structure, which affect the sympathetic nervous system, stimulating certain nerve impulses and inducing a primary action on the cortex of the brain. They uplift the spirit, dispel fatigue, and impart a sense of great work capacity. Their use without medical supervision is disapproved because of the danger of overwork attending the removal of the normal signals of fatigue. During World War II they were used to instill energy and confidence in the troops and to assist pilots in long bomber missions.

a. **Appearance.** Amphetamine may be found as a colorless liquid with a burning taste and a strong odor or in the form of white, crystalline powder. At one time amphetamine was readily available in the form of an inhalant. The paper strips containing the amphetamine could be removed by addicts and swallowed. The drug is now found in the form of orange-colored, heart-shaped tablets. Other tablet colors such as the green, heartshaped Dexamyl®, are found as well as other shapes. Benzedrine® and Dexedrine® are the common trade names.

b. **Effects.** Amphetamine has been called the modern cocaine, since the effects are similar although milder in degree; it is used widely by narcotic addicts, prisoners, and maladjusted adolescents. Users experience increased muscular efficiency, exhilaration, sleeplessness, and a loss of appetite. Persons with unstable personalities may experience untoward reactions. Habituation and excessive use can result in overexertion and collapse. Little tolerance is developed. It has been observed by the President's Commission on Violence that research done to date contradicts the claims linking amphetamine use either to crimes of violence, sexual crimes, or to accidents.

c. **Sources.** The most common illegal sources of amphetamine are the unlicensed and unscrupulous manufacturers who supply the drug to unauthorized distributors. The retail outlets are too many and too varied to permit any useful description.

15. Sedatives and Hypnotics

There are other drugs besides barbiturates that act as behavioral depressants reducing the level of alertness and activity, and these may be conveniently grouped under the heading of sedatives and hypnotics. Sedatives are drugs used to decrease anxiety and motor activity by depressing the central nervous system. Hypnotics tend to depress the system even further, thus inducing a state resembling a normal sleep. Usually both kinds of drugs can be used for either sleep or sedation by increasing or decreasing the dosage. Included in this group are the minor tranquilizers, glutethimide, methaqualone, and chloral hydrate.

a. **Minor Tranquilizer.** This is a pharmacological classification for those drugs which are used to relieve the less severe psychological disorders. They are commonly prescribed for relief of anxiety, sedation, and as a muscle-relaxant. Included in this group are meprobamate (Miltown®, Equanil®), chlordiazepoxide (Librium®, Librax®), and diazepam (Valium®). Although these drugs are less powerful than barbiturates, abrupt withdrawal after an extended period of overuse may cause comparable ill effects.

b. **Glutethimide.** Sold under the trade name Doriden®, this drug is used as a sedative and as a hypnotic with effects similar to barbiturates, useful in treating various types of insomnia.

c. **Methaqualone.** This is a powerful sedative-hypnotic sold under various trade names, the most familiar of which are Sopor® and Quaalude®. This drug is used medically in the treatment of insomnia or for daytime sedation. Recommended dosages for sleep are between 150 and 300 milligrams. Large overdoses of the drug may lead to delirium and coma, progressing to convulsions. The effect of the drug is heightened when used with other sedatives or with alcohol. Thus, the danger of overdose is greater for students, who tend to use the drug while drinking alcohol.

d. **Chloral Hydrate.** This drug deserves special mention because it is sometimes put to criminal use. In planning a larceny the criminal may administer a heavy dose of the drug to his victim in the form of "knockout drops." Chloral hydrate is found in the form of colorless, transparent crystals, strong in odor and sharp in taste. Since it is highly soluble in water and alcohol, it may be readily mixed in the victim's drink. On ingestion the central nervous system is depressed, and pulse and respiration slowed, and the victim quickly sinks into a deep sleep. When combined with alcohol the effect of the drug is considerably enhanced; hence the name "knockout drops." An overdose may paralyze the respiratory center or the heart and result in death. Chloral hydrate has a legitimate use in the field of medication, where it is prescribed as a sedative or soporific. It is dispensed in the form of tablets or capsules.

16. Hallucinogens

This group of drugs named for their capacity to cause hallucinatory effects includes several natural chemicals, mescaline and psilocybin, and a number of synthetics, LSD, STP, and DMT. Although marihuana can also be placed in the class of hallucinogens, it has been treated separately because of its long established use and the special legislation which it has attracted.

a. **Natural Hallucinogens.** These are considered relatively mild in comparison with the synthetics. Their use was discovered from observation of the practice of Indians.

1) *Mescaline or Peyote.* This drug has religious and cult associations in northern Mexico and the southwestern United States. Studies of the effects of mescaline gave rise to the present research into the use of synthetics for *mind-expanding* purposes. Mescaline is taken from the spineless peyote cactus in the form of a flower or *button* which resembles a dried brown mushroom, about the size of a half dollar and a quarter-inch thick. The button is eaten or brewed in a concoction for drinking. Narcotics agents in the 1970s reported that the use of peyote, alternately sipped with orange juice, had grown in popularity among the young. The drug produces hallucinations, described by some as an appearance of geometric figures against a kaleidoscopic background of colors. Although bitter in taste and tending to produce nausea, the drug does not appear to have any serious after effects. The user experiences a sense of well-being but is not incited to violent action. The chemical name is 3,4,5-trimethoxyphenethylamine.

2) *Psilocybin.* This substance is extracted from Mexican mushrooms. It is considered far more powerful than mescaline. This drug may be obtained in capsules containing either spores or dried, ground mushrooms.

Table V
CONTROLLED SUBSTANCES: MEDICAL USES

	Drugs	Schedule	Trade or Other Names	Medical Uses
NARCOTICS	Opium	II, III, V	Dover's Powder, Paregoric, Parepectolin	Analgesic, antidiarrheal
	Morphine	II, III	Morphine, Pectoral Syrup	Analgesic, antitussive
	Codeine	II, III, V	Codeine, Empirin Compound with Codeine, Robitussin A, C	Analgesic, antitussive
	Heroin	I	Diacetylmorphine, Horse, Smack	Under investigation
	Hydromorphone		Dilaudid	Analgesic
	Meperidine (Pethidine)	II	Demerol, Pethadol	Analgesic
	Methadone		Dolophine, Methadone, Methadose	Analgesic, heroin substitute
	Other Narcotics	I, II, III, IV, V	LAAM, Leritine, Levo-Dromoran, Percodan, Tussionex, Fentanyl, Darvon, Talwin, Lomotil	Analgesic, antidiarrheal, antitussive
DEPRESSANTS	Chloral Hydrate	IV	Noctec, Somnos	Hypnotic
	Barbiturates	II, III, IV	Amobarbital, Phenobarbital, Butisol, Phenoxbarbital, Secobarbital, Tuinal	Anesthetic, anti-convulsant, sedative, hypnotic
	Glutethimide	III	Doriden	hypnotic

Table V
CONTROLLED SUBSTANCES: MEDICAL USES

	Drugs	Schedule	Trade or Other Names	Medical Uses
DEPRESSANTS (continued)	Methaqualone	II	Optimil, Parest, Quaalude, Somnafac, Sopor	Sedative, hypnotic
	Benzodiaze-pines	IV	Ativan, Azene, Clonopin, Dalmane, Diazepam, Librium, Serax, Tranxene, Valium, Verstran	Anti-anxiety, anti-convulsant, sedative, hypnotic
	Other Depressants	III, IV	Equanil, Miltown, Noludar, Placidyl, Valmid	Anti-anxiety, sedative, hypnotic
STIMULANTS	Cocaine	II	Coke, Flake, Snow	Local anesthetic
	Amphetamines	II, III	Biphetamine, Delcobese, Desoxyn, Dexedrine, Mediatric	Hyperkinesis
	Phenmetrazine	II	Preludin	narcolepsy
	Methylphenidate	II	Ritalin	weight control
	Other Stimulants	III, IV	Adipex, Bacarate, Cyclert, Didrex, Ionamin, Plegine, Pre-Sate, Sanorex, Tenuate, Tepanil, Voranil	

b. **Synthetic Hallucinogens.** This group of drugs is presently the subject of considerable controversy, with its proponents extolling its "mind-expanding" capability and its potential for research while its opponents decry the use of such dangerous substances in our present state of knowledge.

Table V
CONTROLLED SUBSTANCES: MEDICAL USES

	Drugs	Schedule	Trade or Other Names	Medical Uses
HALLUCIN-OGENS	LSD	I	Acid, Microdot	
	Mescaline and Peyote	I	Mesc, Buttons, Cactus	None
	Amphetamine Variants	I	2.5 DMA, PMA, STP, MDA, MMDA, TMA, DOM, DOB	
	Phencyclidine	II	PCP, Angel Dust, Hog	Veterinary anesthetic
	Phencyclidine Analogs	I	PCE, PCP, TCP	
	Other Hallucinogens	I	Bufotenine, Ibogaine, DMT, DET, Psilocybin, Psilocyn	None
CANNABIS	Marijuana	I	Pot, Acapulco Gold, Grass, Reefer Sinsemilla, Thai Sticks	Under Investigation
	Tetrahydro-cannabinol	I	THC	Under investigation
	Hashish	I	Hash	None
	Hashish Oil	I	Hash Oil	None

1) *LSD, STP, and DMT.* Of these three well-known synthetic hallucinogens, LSD (d-lysergic acid diethylamide) is considered the most important in several respects—first, LSD appears to be the most widely used (and abused) and second, it is by far the most powerful hallucinogen yet developed. The ingestion of as little as one quarter-millionth of an ounce can cause hallucinations that last for four hours. In addition to causing hallucinations and distortions of perception, LSD may also give rise to psychological reactions, such as, feelings of panic, violent impulses, suicidal tendencies, and even what might be termed acts of insanity. Long-term physical damage is also suspected by

biochemists. Abnormal chromosomal patterns have been observed in persons who have taken LSD. Although not as powerful as LSD, STP (also known as DOM [dimethoxymethylamphetamine] and DMT (dimethyltriptamine) have equally dangerous psychological sequelae.

2) *Use and Abuse.* The hallucinogens have no recognized medicinal use, although LSD is being used experimentally in the treatment of alcoholism and certain forms of mental illness. Against the questionable promises of inconclusive research and the dubious claims of enhanced creativity and widened scope of spiritual sensitivity must be set the known dangers associated with the use of these drugs and the dangers of the unknown. In the rapidly expanding world of psychopharmacological knowledge the "dangers of the unknown" cover a sizeable area of formidable contingencies. In addition to the hazards of brainwashing or mind control, there is the possibility of "mind dulling" and a picture of a society of people "manipulating their central nervous system by the use of psychoactive agents. . . . Different individuals, using different drugs to achieve different conditions of heightened stimulation or tranquilization, may be unable or immotivated to question existing social thought and standards of behavior and thus become a conforming mass. . . . Because such frightening conditions as mind controlling or conforming may be possible, it is imperative that we recognize (that) the threat of our exploding knowledge in biochemistry and behavior lies precisely in the abuse of this knowledge to coerce, to control and to conform." (Dr. Eiduson, *Science Journal,* May, 1967)

3) *The Drug Culture.* The use of LSD and other hallucinogenic drugs, such as marihuana, hashish oil, and cocaine, is fostered in drug-oriented religious cults, particularly in the California area. In 1972 a task force of federal, state, and local narcotics agents conducted a raid on a ranch of the Brotherhood of Eternal Love, an offshoot of O'Leary's League of Spiritual Discovery (LSD). The raid, said to be one of the largest coordinated police efforts against illegal narcotics traffic, revealed an operation that smuggled 1,000 pounds of hashish into the U.S. every month. A seizure was made of more than one million pink LSD tablets. As fronts for the sale

and distribution of drugs the Brotherhood used popular counter-culture businesses such as health food stores, juice bars, psychadelic shops, record stores, surf equipment stores, used car lots, a rug company, and a beach club.

4) *PCP or "Angel Dust."* Phencyclidine (PCP) is the most dangerous drug to appear on the streets since LSD became widely available a decade ago. There are few specific controls over PCP. At present it is synthesized in home factories—an investment of $100 can produce a quantity of PCP worth $100,000 in retail value. The drug, a white, crystalline substance, is a hallucinogen that can be snorted, swallowed, injected, spread over comestibles or taken with marihuana. PCP or angel dust has proved to be a very potent psychoactive drug capable of causing convulsions and violent behavior and occasionally producing death. During 1976 PCP was responsible for 214 deaths in the Detroit area alone. Unpredictable and irrational behavior is typical of chronic users. The rapid proliferation of PCP is attributable to the difficulties of control. Specific legislation is still under study. The manufacture of PCP is a simple, relatively odorless process that can be managed in the average home. The possible control of PCP suggests another, more formidable and more general problem in legislation, namely, the possibility of home manufacture from easily obtainable materials of an indefinite number of hallucinogenic drugs. The investigation of drugs like PCP depends on information from disgruntled users, fires from unexplained causes, and mysterious explosions.

17. Investigative Methods

The proof of a narcotics violation usually consists in establishing the following elements: (a) that the accused did or failed to do the acts as alleged and (b) the circumstances as specified. The act to which reference is made is the possession or use of a habit-forming narcotic drug or marihuana. In establishing these elements the investigator will usually be required to place emphasis on the points which are developed in the succeeding paragraphs.

a. **The Nature of the Substance.** A basic but essential step in the investigation is the establishment of the fact that the substance in question is a narcotic or other controlled drug. A *corpus delicti* must be proved independently of any confession. Occasionally the trial of a user is permitted to take place before the receipt of the laboratory report because the accused agrees to plead guilty to the charge of possession, and subsequently the laboratory analysis fails to reveal the presence of a narcotic. The accused is deceived in this matter by the unscrupulous "pusher" who sells a harmless white powder instead of a narcotic. The accused's admission should not be accepted as proof. The laboratory analyst must testify to the chemical contents of the substance. Some courts will accept a written affidavit from the chemist; others require the court appearance of the expert since his written report, being only hearsay evidence and not an official record or business entry, may not be admitted into evidence on the grounds that its admission would be prejudicial to the rights of the accused. If the chemist occupies an official position, however, his affidavit is usually accepted in the absence of any objection by defense counsel.

b. **The Unlawful Act.** The investigator must prove that the accused's relation to the narcotic was without legal authorization, i.e., that he illegally possessed, sold, or used the drug. Since the three acts are never completely separable, the following discussion will overlap in some areas.

1) *Possession.* The most common act is that of possession since it is assumed at some phase of the use or sale of the narcotic. It is necessary to prove that the narcotic was in the possession of the accused. Possession of a narcotic is presumed to be wrongful unless the possessor can prove otherwise. The possession is innocent if the drug has been duly prescribed by a physician or when it is possessed in performance of duty or when it is in his possession through accident or mistake. The subject should be searched in the presence of witnesses if any are available. If the narcotic is found on the person of the subject he should be confronted with it in order to induce an admission. Often the investigators will discover the drug in a cache. The

confirmed user or experienced seller will usually have several places where he may hide his narcotics. The problem of the investigator is to associate the subject directly with the hidden drug. He should not under ordinary conditions remove the substance from the cache; a surveillance should be maintained for the purpose of observing the subject's return to the hiding place to recover the narcotic. Naturally the surveillance should be terminated after a reasonable period of time, but every effort should be made to prove that the subject had personal, conscious, and exclusive possession of the substance. To show merely that the accused had access to it is not sufficient to establish possession.

2) *Use.* Proving use of the drug is important chiefly in cases conducted for organizations which have requested an investigation of an employee as a possible drug user. In addition, proof that the accused is a user may corroborate a charge of possession. The subject may claim that his possession is attributable to accident or mistake or that the drug was prescribed by a physician and was obtained with a legitimate prescription. A number of steps can be taken by the investigator to test these claims. Incident to apprehension he may obtain a statement from the subject concerning his intent to use the narcotic. The accused should be interrogated extensively concerning all the details of any explanations he offers. If the name of the prescribing doctor or a dispensing druggist is given, verification of these facts should be obtained. If the subject admits the use of drugs he should be questioned concerning such details as the frequency of injections, methods of administration, amount of dosage, cost of the drugs, circumstances under which the drug was first used, growth of the habit, sources of supply, and identities of sellers.

a) APPARATUS. The subject's person and dwelling should be searched for hypodermic needles, medicine droppers, bent spoons, and other instruments that are used in administering narcotics. These should be submitted for laboratory analysis to determine the presence of any residual narcotics. It should be noted that possession of the apparatus cannot by itself support a charge of use of an opiate unless some residue of a narcotic is present in the instrument.

b) WITNESSES. Information concerning the habits of the accused may be helpful. It is possible that there may be an eyewitness to the actual administration of the drug. Again, witnesses may be developed to whom the accused has confided his addiction.

c) MEDICAL TESTIMONY. The accused should be examined by a physician for physical marks, conditions, and symptoms which indicate addiction. Analysis of the urine and blood will reveal the presence of narcotic if the specimens are taken soon after administration. The withdrawal syndrome is the most reliable indication of addiction.

3) *Selling.* The illegal sale of narcotics is a more serious offense than possession or use; hence the chief objective of a narcotics investigation should ordinarily be the location of the source of supply or at least the immediate seller of the drug. The proof of a drug sale is established by testimony of the investigator or other eyewitness who has observed the exchange of money or other thing of value for a narcotic substance. In some states the proof of a selling charge is less demanding. Several states have enacted legislation under which the illegal possession of drugs in excess of specified amounts creates a presumption of intent to sell. The law also permits the prosecutor to establish a presumption of possession by all persons present in a motor vehicle wherein drugs are found. Although both presumptions are rebuttable, the shifting of the burden of proof considerably lightens the task of the prosecution. Moreover, the necessity of employing informants to make purchases of drugs for the purpose of establishing the fact of a sale no longer exists, since the mere possession of certain amounts is *prima facie* evidence of intent to sell.

a) LOCATING THE SELLER. Intensive questioning of a user will usually lead to the identity of the seller. In most cases the user knows the seller only by nickname and is able to give only the addresses of places frequented by the seller. The user should be taken to the identification division and requested to study the photographs of convicted narcotic sellers.

b) UNDERCOVER ASSIGNMENTS. An investigator can be assigned to work undercover, posing as an addict. After locating the seller he should arrange to make a "buy." This operation, of course, is not a simple matter and the assistance of informants and others may be required. The investigator may make the purchase himself but it is preferable to have a confederate make the purchase with the investigator as a witness to the sale. It may be possible for the investigator to witness a sale to a user who is not a confederate. This latter arrangement has the advantage of avoiding the complication of a charge of entrapment.

c) SURVEILLANCE. Fixed and moving surveillances are sometimes needed to witness the sale and to gather other evidence. Binoculars should be used in fixed surveillances in order to observe the details of the purchase. Photographic methods provide excellent corroborative evidence. In order to obtain identifiable images, while working at a discreet distance, a telephoto lens should be used. A Camcorder and a 35mm camera will provide a satisfactory film record.

d) OTHER TECHNICAL AIDS. The investigation will often be greatly assisted by the use of imagination. Certain scientific techniques will aid in connection with proving the sale. For example, marked money should be given to the seller in making the purchase. If the serial numbers of the bills are recorded, they can be later identified when recovered incident to a search of the seller. Another valuable technique is the employment of tracing powders. A fluorescent powder may be lightly dusted on the bills or on the envelope in which the bills are passed. Particles and smears of the powder will be transferred to the hand and clothing of the seller. Although the powder is relatively invisible, it will fluoresce brilliantly under the ultraviolet light. Thus it will be possible to identify the seller even after he has disposed of the money and detect also any confederates who have subsequently handled the money. Tracing powders of this type are especially useful in a surveillance conducted to trail the seller to his employers and, perhaps, to the ring leaders of the local narcotics trade. In one case, for example, it was possible to locate the headquarters of a narcotics ring by following a seller until he disappeared into a multiple dwelling house. A portable ultraviolet light was then directed on the door knob of the entrance of each apartment until the characteristic fluorescence of the tracing powder was observed (see Chap. 41).

e) SEARCHING. A thorough search of the suspect's person and clothing should be made incident to an apprehension in order to discover any narcotic substance or apparatus for the administration of drugs. Since the narcotic is usually small in quantity and the apparatus readily hidden, exceptional care and considerable ingenuity must be employed in the search. The following suggested places of concealment have been gleaned from case histories: The shipment and possession of narcotic drugs are hidden in every conceivable and bizarre manner. Grooved plants, hollow bedposts, false-bottomed stoves, hollow heeled and soled shoes, false-backed water closets, hidden compartments in various articles of furniture, the inside of stereo speakers, the backs of cuckoo clocks, sealed tubes or pockets in automobile tanks, whiskey, fish and pickle barrels, coffee, gypsum, and flour sacks, hollowed-out tombstones and grindstones, tins in blocks of wax, hollowed-out candles, specially constructed corsets and other underclothing, belts tied to various parts of the body beneath clothing, rolled-up magazines and newspapers, falsely manifested packages, and hollowed-out staves in shipped barrels, are some of the methods which have been used. Heroin has been stuffed inside a live boa constrictor and in a toy llama. Prisoners have obtained narcotics tied to cats' bellies, and in Egypt drugs have been transported by camel under an excised flap of hide. The various body orifices, the toes, underarms and fingernails are places where drugs may be hidden. As a mode of concealment the inconspicuousness of the obvious should not be forgotten; carrying drugs openly in the guise of familiar and legitimate objects is perhaps the most subtle means of avoiding detection in some circumstances.

18. Laboratory Examination

In order to conclusively identify a substance as being a narcotic, it should be submitted for analysis by a qualified chemist. The admission of an accused as to the nature of the substance bears no weight in proving that a narcotic is present in the substance. Several tests have been developed for the identification of certain narcotics in the field; since, however, the tests are not conclusive or entirely reliable, they should not be attempted by the investigator. In addition to diminishing the quantity of available narcotic, the employment of these tests incurs the additional risk of misinterpreting the results in cases involving synthetic narcotics. If the charge brought against the suspect is a violation of the federal law, the evidentiary substance should be forwarded directly to the nearest District Supervisor of the Drug Enforcement Administration, Department of Justice. State, county, and municipal laboratories may be used for violations of laws committed within the corresponding jurisdictions. In connection with some laws, it may be desirable to obtain quantitative analysis. Often, however, the quantity of substance available is insufficient for this purpose.

a. **Letter of Transmittal.** The evidence forwarded to the laboratory should be accompanied by a letter of transmittal containing, in addition to the usual data, a statement concerning the circumstances under which the evidence was seized, any statement of the suspect regarding the nature of the substance, and any other information which the investigator may possess as to the type of drug suspected. Such information is particularly valuable when the evidence sample is small. It is customary for peddlers to adulterate the narcotic by the addition of an innocuous substance such as milk sugar or aspirin. This adulteration adds to the difficulty of analysis. If the chemist is provided with a hint concerning the nature of the narcotic, he can eliminate from consideration a number of drug groups and concentrate on one or two indicated groups, thus conserving that part of the evidence which would necessarily have been consumed in more exhaustive tests.

b. **Disposition.** Since narcotic drugs are placed in the category of contraband, they must be disposed of in accordance with the laws and regulations of the Drug Enforcement Administration. When retention of the evidence is no longer required it may be transferred to the Drug Enforcement Administration or disposed of in accordance with local laws.

19. Care of Evidence

The handling of narcotics evidence requires exceptional care because it is usually limited in quantity and an accounting must be made for weight and the number of items of evidence. All of the available evidence should be forwarded to the laboratory in a manner that insures freedom from contamination.

a. **Original Container.** Ordinarily the evidentiary material should not be removed from its original container. It may be removed for purposes of inventory, but subsequently it should be returned to the container. It is important to preserve any boxes, cans, bottles, envelopes, or wrappers connected with the evidence, since these may serve as additional clues to a removed source. These containers should be marked for identification. In addition, in the case of a purchase the wrapper may identify the establishment of the seller. In one case, where a narcotic user confessed to obtaining the substance from a drugstore, it was possible in the face of the druggist's denials to show by means of glue spots and paper cutter marks that the glassine envelope had been removed from the top of a pile of such envelopes found in the store.

b. **Inventory.** All suspected narcotics should be accurately weighed or counted by the investigator in the presence of a witness. When the evidence is in the form of tablets or capsules it should be both counted and weighed since it is possible to remove some of the drug without altering the number of items present. A record of the inventory should be made in a notebook.

c. **Packaging.** When the inventory is completed the evidence should be placed in a suitable container. Tablets, pills, capsules, and powders can ordinarily be placed in a small envelope or a pillbox; liquids should, of course, be placed in a bottle. Seals should be placed across the flap of the envelopes and the edge of the bottle cap. The seal should bear the investigator's name. If the evidence is to be shipped to the laboratory, it should be placed in an appropriate box, with precautions taken to prevent breakage or loss.

d. **Labeling.** A label should be affixed to the container of the evidence before packaging. This label should bear the following information:

1) Case number.
2) Name, rank, and title of the investigator.
3) Weight and substance or number of items.
4) Time and date when seized.
5) Place of seizure.

20. Medical Examinations

A medical examination of a suspect often provides corroborative evidence of the use of a narcotic. Such a procedure should be accomplished in accordance with the laws of the jurisdiction and with due consideration of the rights of the accused. A physician experienced in narcotics cases should be employed.

a. **Use and Addiction.** By observing such signs as contracted pupils and especially the abstinence syndrome, the physician can give an opinion as to the use of drugs. Needle scars and ulcerations on the arms and legs may indicate addiction.

b. **Body Fluids.** A urine analysis or blood examination will provide the best evidence of recent use of a narcotic. The physician or a qualified medical technician should draw the samples of the suspect's blood and urine, which should then be transmitted to a toxicological or pathological chemist. Approximately thirty milliliters of blood should be taken. The test tube containing the sample should be corked and sealed with a piece of white tab tape, covering part of the cork and tube. The accused's name, the time and date of taking the sample and the name of the physician or technician should be written on the top. Although 30 cubic centimeters of urine are adequate for a test, a more generous sample should be taken. A witness of appropriate sex should be present when it is voided. A screw-top jar may be used and labeled in the manner previously described.

c. **Nalorphine.** One of the methods used to detect a narcotics user is the administration of nalorphine, followed by observation of the subject's eyes. If the pupils dilate, the person has been using narcotics. Nalorphine (Nalline) is a substance which affects the same part of the central nervous system as the narcotic analgesics but which does not achieve any marked degree of euphoria or pain killing. That is, nalorphine, although it affects the same receptors and has even a greater receptor affinity than heroin, morphine, or methadone, does have enough intrinsic activity to be considered useful as an analgesic. Because of this very high receptor affinity, nalorphine will displace previously administered heroin, morphine, or methadone molecules from the receptors and will precipitate a classic morphine abstinence syndrome. This explains why in cases of narcotics overdose with opiates the administration of nalorphine is a potentially lifesaving diagnostic therapeutic measure. It also explains why nalorphine testing is used in the State of California for testing narcotics abuse in parolees. The administration of nalorphine to a *clean* subject usually results in pupillary constriction. However, as predicted from the theory, the administration of nalorphine to someone whose CNS morphine receptors are occupied will result in pupillary dilatation as part of the precipitated abstinence syndrome.

The nalorphine test is not foolproof and the results of the test should be considered as circumstantial medical evidence. In general, nalorphine testing is correct in about 85 per cent of the cases.

21. Narcotics and Crime

The exact relationship between drug addiction and crime is not known. The fact that drug addicts are crime prone is well accepted. Certainly the drug addict is associated with drug offenses, that is, violations of the various narcotics laws, especially those relating to possession and use. The extent of the drug addict's responsibility for non-drug offenses cannot be estimated with any great degree of accuracy. In any discussion of the subject, however, a clear distinction must be made between drug offenses (violations of narcotics laws) and non-drug offenses.

a. **Drug Offenses.** Although addiction in itself is not a crime under either federal or state law, it is a condition which easily, if not inevitably, leads to violations of the narcotics laws. To maintain his habit, the addict must necessarily buy and possess the drugs before he can use them. Unauthorized purchase and possession are violations of both federal and state laws. Moreover, to finance his expensive habit the addict frequently becomes a seller, thus greatly increasing his liability to arrest. Finally, in many states the non-medical use of narcotics is an offense, as well as the mere possession of a hypodermic needle or the equivalent paraphernalia such as a needle and syringe. Since a habit must be ministered to daily, the addict must violate each day a number of narcotics laws and run to some degree the concomitant risk of arrest.

b. **Non-Drug Offenses.** "Criminals become addicts, but opiate addicts do not become criminals through the maddening or deteriorating effects of drugs." This finding of the 1962 addiction study of Lawrence Kolb is increasingly confirmed by the proliferating literature on addicts—most addicts are definably deviant, delinquent, or criminal before becoming addicted. Most addicts have a greater tendency than their socioeconomic peers to be delinquent.

Addicts as a group do not specialize in violent crime. There is a clear and highly significant tendency for heroin users to be charged with property crimes as opposed to crimes against the person. Non-users appeared, on the basis of the charges against them, to be more violent in their criminal behavior. James M. Markham, in an article appearing in the *New York Times Magazine,* March 18, 1973, summed up the current expert opinion on the relation of heroin to crime in the following words:

> Given the current state of ignorance, it is impossible to answer with any pretense of precision the question—"If I am mugged, what are the chances that my mugger is an addict?" But, as we have seen, we do know this much: The image of the decent young fellow suddenly plunged into a desperate economic struggle to "feed his habit" is far too simplistic. Typically, an addict was deviant or criminal before addiction; the onset of addiction tends to continue, not create, a pattern of antisocial behavior. Getting hooked and "taking care of business" may in fact increase the new addict's level of criminality. But available evidence suggests strongly that addiction thrusts our hypothetical addict into property crimes, not muggings or other crimes of violence. Some addicts may have been violent criminals before they were addicts—and may continue to be violent. But there are some indications that the over-all rate of violence in the junkie population decreases slightly after the onset of addiction.

c. **The Cost.** The average heroin addict requires 5 grams a day at a cost of about sixty dollars. Obviously, the typical addict cannot afford the expense of his drug supply and, because of the

Table VI
CONTROLLED SUBSTANCES: METHODS OF ADMINISTRATION AND EFFECTS

	Drugs	Methods of Administration	Possible Effects	Effects of Overdose	Withdrawal Syndrome	Physical Dependence	Psychological Dependence	Tolerance	Duration of effect in hrs.
NARCOTICS	Opium	Oral, smoked	Euphoria drowsiness, respiratory depression constricted pupils, nausea	Slow & shallow breathing, clammy skin, convulsions, coma, possible death	Watery eyes, runny nose, yawning, loss of appetite, irritability, tremors panic, chills & sweating, cramps nausea	High	High	Yes	3–6
	Morphine	Oral, smoked, injected				High	High	Yes	3–6
	Codeine	Oral, injected				Moderate	Moderate	Yes	3–6
	Heroine	Injected, sniffed, smoked				High	High	Yes	3–6
	Hydromorphone	Oral, injected				High	High	Yes	3–6
	Meperidine (Pethidine)	Oral, injected				High	High	Yes	3–6
	Methadone	Oral, injected				High	High	Yes	12–24
	Other narcotics	Oral, injected				High–Low	High–Low	Yes	Variable
DEPRESSANTS	Chloral Hydrate	Oral	Slurred speech, disorientation, drunken behavior without the odor of alcohol	Shallow respiration, cold & clammy skin, dilated pupils, weak & rapid pulse, coma, possible death	Anxiety, insomnia, tremors, delirium, convulsions, possible death	Moderate	Moderate	Possible	5–8
	Barbiturates	Oral, injected				High–Mod.	High–Mod.	Yes	1–16
	Glutethimide	Oral, injected				High	High	Yes	4–8
	Methqualone	Oral, injected				High	High	Yes	4–8
	Benzodiazepines	Oral, injected				Low	Low	Yes	4–8
	Other depressants	Oral, injected				Moderate	Moderate	Yes	4–8

Table VI (Continued)

Drugs	Methods of Administration	Possible Effects	Effects of Overdose	Withdrawal Syndrome	Physical Dependence	Psychological Dependence	Tolerance	Duration of effect in hrs.
STIMULANTS								
Cocaine	Sniffed, injected	Increased alertness, excitation, euphoria, increased pulse rate and blood pressure, insomnia, loss of appetite	Agitation, increase in body temperature, hallucinations, convulsions, possible death	Apathy, long periods of sleep, irritability, depression, disorientation	Possible	High	Yes	2–4
Crack (Free-Base Cocaine)	Smoked				Possible	High	Yes	2–4
Amphetamines	Oral, injected				Possible	High	Yes	2–4
Phenmetrazine	Oral, injected				Possible	High	Yes	2–4
Methylphenidate	Oral, injected				Possible	High	Yes	2–4
Other stimulants	Oral				Possible	High	Yes	2–4
HALLUCINOGENS								
LSD	Oral	Illusions and hallucinations, poor perception of time and distance	Longer, more intense "trip" episodes psychosis, possible death	Withdrawal syndrome not reported	None	Deg. unknown	Yes	8–12
Mescaline and Peyote	Oral, injected				Unknown	Deg. unknown	Yes	8–12
Amphetamine variants	Oral, injected				Unknown	Deg. unknown	Yes	up to days
Phencyclidine	Smoked, oral, injected				Deg. unknown	High	Yes	Variable
Phencyclidine Analogs	Smoked, oral, injected				Deg. unknown	Deg. unknown	Possible	Variable
Other hallucinogens	Oral, injected, smoked				None	Deg. unknown	Possible	Variable
CANNABIS								
Marijuana	Smoked, oral	Euphoria, relaxed inhibitions, increased appetite, disoriented behavior reported	Fatigue, paranoia, possible psychosis	Insomnia, hyperactivity, & decreased appetite occasionally	Deg. unknown	Moderate	Yes	2–4
Tetrahydrocannabinol	Smoked, oral				Deg. unknown	Moderate	Yes	2–4
Hashish	Smoked, oral				Deg. unknown	Moderate	Yes	2–4
Hashish Oil	Smoked, oral				Deg. unknown			2–4

nature of drug addiction, he must supplement his income by any available means. Thus he finds himself drifting into a career of small-scale crime — larceny, burglary, selling narcotics, procuring, prostitution, and other offenses which will yield the increment necessary to support his habit. For the most part he concentrates on theft of cash or of property which can be converted to cash.

No doubt, if we were to total the number of addicts and the cost of the crimes attributable to them in their efforts to obtain the price of each day's drug supply, we should obtain an impressive set of figures. With the value of the property loss running into many millions of dollars, we should be drawn to the conclusion that the drug addict is responsible for a great part of the country's crime burden. We must, however, set against this array of statistics the overriding consideration that the heroin addict is a special kind of offender — his criminal acts are directed toward the support of an addiction of which he is usually the unwilling captive. There is also the consideration that the nature of his crime is not assaultive or violent; the offenses rarely betray a personal malevolence or capricious cruelty. The element of malice seems to be missing from his criminal conduct, so that his behavior, and even his life, is better described as extrasocial rather than antisocial. Indeed, the great loss to the nation is not in the stolen property or cash but in the usufruct of citizens whose lives have lost all major direction and purpose other than the acquisition of the day's drug ration.

ADDITIONAL READING

Controlled Substances

Andrews, G. and Solomon, D. (Eds.): *The Coca Leaf and Cocaine Papers.* London, Harcourt Brace, 1977.

Brown, F.C.: *Hallucinogenic Drugs.* Springfield, Ill.: Thomas, 1972.

Cohen, S., et al.: *Frequently Prescribed and Abused Drugs.* New York, Haworth, 1982.

Drug Enforcement Administration. *Controlled Substances Analogs.* Washington, D.C.: U.S. Government Printing Office, 1985.

Emboden, W.: *Narcotic Plants.* New York, Macmillan, 1979.

Fay, J.J.: *The Alcohol/Drug Abuse Dictionary and Encyclopedia.* Springfield, Ill.: Thomas, 1988.

Griffith, H.W.: *Prescription and Non-Prescription Drugs.* Tucson, Ariz.: HP Books, 1983.

Henderson, G.L.: Designer Drugs: Past History and Future Prospects. 33 *Journal of Forensic Sciences,* 569, 1988.

Inciardi, J.A. (Ed.): *Handbook of Drug Control in the United States.* Westport, Conn.: Greenwood Press, 1990.

Julien, R.M.: *A Primer of Drug Action,* 5th ed. New York, W.H. Freeman, 1988.

Kirsch, M.M.: *Designer Drugs.* Minneapolis, CompCare Publication, 1986.

Lee, D.: *Cocaine Handbook: An Essential Reference.* Berkeley, Calif.: And/Or Press, 1981.

Lowry, W.T. and Garriott, J.C.: *Forensic Toxicology: Controlled Substances and Dangerous Drugs.* New York, Plenum, 1979.

Maurer, D. and Vogel, V.H.: *Narcotics and Narcotic Addiction,* 4th ed. Springfield, Ill.: Thomas, 1973.

McLaughlin, G.T.: Cocaine: The History and Regulation of a Dangerous Drug. 58 *Cornell Law Review,* 537, 1973.

Peoples, J.T. and Hahn, L.M.: Indoor Cannabis Cultivation: Marijuana in the '90s. 58 *Police Chief,* 10, 1991.

Shafer, J.: Designer Drugs. *Science,* March, 1985.

Stafford, P.: *Psychedelics Encyclopedia.* Berkeley, Calif.: And/Or Press, 1977.

Narcotics Investigation

Benson, C.C.: K-9 Sniffers. 39 *Law and Order,* 8, 1991.

Brown, L.P.: Strategies for Dealing with Crack Houses. 57 *FBI Law Enforcement Bulletin,* 6, 1988.

Cameron, J.: Pressure Point: One City's Solution to Crack Cocaine. 36 *Law and Order,* 6, 1988.

Carroll, P.J.: Operation Pressure Point: An Urban Drug Enforcement Strategy. 58 *FBI Law Enforcement Bulletin,* 4, 1989.

Entrapment Defense in Narcotics Cases: Guidelines for Law Enforcement. Washington, D.C.: Institute for Law and Justice, 1991.

Florez, C.P. and Boyce, B.: Laundering Drug Money. 59 *FBI Law Enforcement Bulletin,* 4, 1990.

Harney, M.L. and Cross, J.C.: *The Narcotics Officer's Notebook,* 2nd ed. Springfield, Ill.: Thomas, 1973.

Hermann, S.: Clandestine Drug Lab Raid. 38 *Law and Order,* 9, 1990.

James, R.D.: Hazards of Clandestine Drug Laboratories. 58 *FBI Law Enforcement Bulletin,* 4, 1989.

Kingston, K.A.: Hounding Drug Traffickers: The Use of Drug Detection Dogs. 58 *FBI Law Enforcement Bulletin,* 8, 1989.

Lyman, M.D.: Minimizing Danger in Drug Enforcement. 38 *Law and Order,* 9, 1990.

——: *Practical Drug Enforcement: Procedures and Administration.* New York, Elsevier. 1989.

Macdonald, J.M. and Kennedy, J.: *Criminal Investigation of Drug Offenses: The Narcs' Manual.* Springfield, Ill.: Thomas, 1983.

Mangan, R.J.: Exploiting the Financial Aspects of Major Drug Investigations. 53 *FBI Law Enforcement Bulletin,* 11, 1984.

McCormack, W.U.: Detaining Suspected Drug Couriers: Recent Court Decisions. 60 *FBI Law Enforcement Bulletin,* 6, 1991.

Moore, M.H.: *Buy and Bust.* Lexington, Mass.: Lexington Books, 1977.

Moriarty, M.D.: Undercover Negotiating: Dealing for Your Life. 57 *Police Chief,* 11, 1990.

Narcotic's Investigator's Manual. Washington, D.C.: Drug Enforcement Administration, 1978.

Ross, C. and Block, J.M.: K-9 Narcotics Detection Training. 55 *Police Chief,* 5, 1988.

Snow, R.L.: Street Level Narcotics Enforcement. 38 *Law and Order,* 7, 1990.

Wade, G.E.: Undercover Negotiating: Flashrole Management. 57 *Police Chief,* 11, 1990.

——: Undercover Violence. 59 *FBI Law Enforcement Bulletin,* 4, 1990.

Ware, M.: *Operational Handbook for Narcotic Law Enforcement Officers.* Springfield, Ill.: Thomas, 1975.

Drug Identification

Angelos, S.A., Raney, J.K., Skowronski, G.T. and Wagenhofer, R.J.: The Identification of Unreacted Precursors, Impurities, and By-Products in Clandestinely Produced Phencyclidine Preparations. 35 *Journal of Forensic Sciences,* 1297, 1990.

Baumgartner, W.S., Hill, V.A. and Blahd, W.H.: Hair Analysis for Drugs of Abuse. 34 *Journal of Forensic Sciences,* 6, 1989.

De Faubert Maunder, M.J.: The Rapid Detection of Drugs of Addiction. 14 *Medicine, Science and the Law,* 243, 1974.

Field Testing for Controlled Substances. Washington, D.C.: Drug Enforcement Administration, 1973.

Heroin Paraphernalia: Breakdown of a Fix. 10 *Criminal Law Bulletin,* 493, 1974.

Hider, C.I.: The Rapid Identification of Frequently Abused Drugs. 11 *Journal of the Forensic Science Society,* 257, 1971.

Hutton, G.W.: Marijuana Problems: A Legal Problem. 42 *Police Chief,* 5, 1975.

Klein, M., Krugel, A.V. and Sobol, S.P. (Eds.): *Instrumental Applications in Forensic Drug Chemistry.* Washington, D.C.: U.S. Government Printing Office, 1979.

Manura, J.J., Chao, J.-M. and Saferstein, R.: The Forensic Identification of Heroin. 23 *Journal of Forensic Sciences,* 44, 1978.

Moffat, A.E., et al. (Eds.): *Clarke's Isolation and Identification of Drugs,* 2nd ed. London, Pharmaceutical Press, 1986.

Nakamura, G.R. and Thorton, J.I.: The Forensic Identification of Marijuana: Some Questions and Answers. 1 *Journal of Police Science and Administration*, 102, 1973.

Oteri, J.S., Weinberg, M.G., and Pinales, M.S.: Cross-Examination of Chemists in Narcotics and Marijuana Cases. 2 *Contemporary Drug Problems*, 225, 1973.

Rajananda, V., Nair, N.K. and Navaratnam, V.: An Evaluation of TLC Systems for Opiate Analysis. 37 *Bulletin of Narcotics*, 35, 1985.

Rangel, C.B.: Heroin Paraphernalia: Accessories of Death. 2 *Journal of Drug Issues*, 42, 1972.

Rasmussen, K.E. and Knutsen, P.: Techniques for the Detection and Identification of Amphetamines and Amphetamine-like Substances. 37 *Bulletin of Narcotics*, 95, 1985.

Shellow, J.M.: The Expert Witness in Narcotic Cases. 2 *Contemporary Drug Problems*, 81, 1973.

Sidle, A.B. and Widdop, B.: Nitrate Test for Methaqualone. 6 *Forensic Science*, 135, 1975.

Thornton, J.I. and Nakamura, G.R.: The Identification of Marijuana. 12 *Journal of the Forensic Science Society*, 461, 1972.

Troop, W.M. and Lovitt, J.: The Kentucky State Police Drug Testing Policy. 60 *FBI Law Enforcement Bulletin*, 9, 1991.

Watling, R.: Hallucinogenic Mushrooms. 23 *Journal of the Forensic Science Society*, 53, 1983.

Wyatt, D. and Grady, L.: Analytical Profiles of Drug Substances: Heroin. 10 *Analytical Profiles of Drug Substances*, 357, 1981.

Zeese, K.B.: *Drug Testing Legal Manual.* New York, Clark Boardman, 1988.

Drugs and Crime

America's Habit: Drug Abuse, Drug Trafficking, and Organized Crime: Report to the President and the Attorney General. Washington, D.C.: U.S. Government Printing Office, 1986.

Anglin, M.D. and Speckart, G.: Narcotics Use and Crime: A Multisample, Multimethod Approach. 26 *Criminology*, 197, 1988.

Ball, J.C., Shaffer, J.W. and Nurco, D.N.: Day to Day Criminality of Heroin Addicts in Baltimore—A Study in the Continuity of Offense Rates. 12 *Drug and Alcohol Dependence*, 119, 1983.

Chaiken, J. and Chaiken, M.: Drugs and Predatory Crime. In Torry, M. and Wilson, J.Q. (Eds.): *Crime and Justice*, vol. 13, 239. Chicago, University of Chicago Press, 1990.

Constantine, T.A.: Why Legalization Won't Work. 57 *Police Chief*, 5, 1990.

Cushman, P., Jr.: Relationship between Narcotic Addiction and Crime. 38 *Federal Probation*, 38, 1974.

Deschner, E.P., Anglin, M.D. and Speckart, G.: Narcotics Addiction: Related

Criminal Careers, Social and Economic Costs. 21 *Journal of Drug Issues,* 383, 1991.

Gandossy, R.P., et al.: *Drugs and Crime: A Survey and Analysis of the Literature.* Washington, D.C.: U.S. Government Printing Office, 1980.

Greenberg, S.W. and Adler, F.: Crime and Addiction: An Empirical Analysis of the Literature, 1920–1973. 3 *Contemporary Drug Problems,* 221, 1974.

Inciardi, J.A. (Ed.): *The Drugs—Crime Connection.* Beverly Hills, Calif.: Sage, 1981.

Johnson, B.D., et al.: *Taking Care of Business: The Economics of Crime by Heroin Abusers.* Lexington, Mass.: Lexington Books, 1985.

Lyman, M.D.: *Gangland: Drug Trafficking by Organized Criminals.* Springfield, Ill.: Thomas, 1989.

——: *Narcotics and Crime Control.* Springfield, Ill.: Thomas, 1987.

McGlothlin, W.H., Anglin, M.D. and Wilson, D.B.: Narcotic Addiction and Crime. 16 *Criminology,* 293, 1978.

Miller, R.L.: *The Case for Legalizing Drugs.* Westport, Conn.: Greenwood Press, 1991.

Rice, B.: *Trafficking: The Boom and Bust of the Air America Cocaine Ring.* New York, Macmillan, 1989.

Speckart, G. and Anglin, M.D.: Narcotics and Crime: An Analysis of Existing Evidence for a Causal Relationship. 3 *Behavioral Sciences and the Law,* 259, 1985.

Stephens, R.C. and Ellis, R.D.: Narcotics Addicts and Crime: Analysis of Recent Trends. 12 *Criminology,* 474, 1975.

Watters, J.K., Reinarum, C. and Fagan, J.: Causality, Context and Contingency: Relationships between Drug Abuse and Delinquency. 12 *Contemporary Drug Problems,* 3, 1985.

Weisheit, R. (Ed.): *Drugs, Crime and the Criminal Justice System.* Cincinnati, Anderson, 1990.

Wisotsky, S.: *Breaking the Impasse in the War on Drugs.* Westport, Conn.: Greenwood Press, 1986.

Drug Abuse

Abadinsky, H.: *Drug Abuse: An Introduction.* Chicago, Nelson-Hall, 1989.

Babicke, T.C.: Pharmaceutical Diversion and Abuse. 60 *FBI Law Enforcement Bulletin,* 6 1991.

Cohen, S.: *The Substance Abuse Problems.* New York, Haworth, 1981.

Cull, J.G. and Hardy, R.E.: *Types of Drug Abusers and Their Abuses.* Springfield, Ill.: Thomas, 1974.

DuPont, R.L., Goldstein, A. and O'Donnell, J. (Eds.): *Handbook on Drug Abuse.* Rockville, Md.: National Institute on Drug Abuses, 1979.

Harvey, A.J.: Drug Abuse and Testing in Law Enforcement. 60 *FBI Law Enforcement Bulletin,* 6, 1991.

Harvey, J.G.: Drug Related Mortality in an Inner City Area. 7 *Drug and Alcohol Dependence,* 239, 1981.

Hofmann, F.G.: *A Handbook on Drug and Alcohol Abuse,* 2nd ed. New York, Oxford University Press, 1983.

Keiman, M.A.R.: *Marijuana: Costs of Abuse, Costs of Control.* Westport, Conn.: Greenwood Press, 1989.

Kozel, N. and Adams, E.: *Cocaine Use in America: Epidemiologic and Clinical Perspectives.* Monograph 61. Washington, D.C.: National Institute on Drug Abuse, 1985.

Lane, J.D.: The Respectable Pusher. 60 *FBI Law Enforcement Bulletin,* 10, 1991.

Lyman, M.D. and Potter, G.W.: *Drugs in Society: Causes, Concepts and Control.* Cincinnati, Anderson, 1991.

Newcomb, M.D. and Bentler, P.M.: *Consequences of Adolescent Drug Abuse: Impact on the Lives of Young Adults.* Newbury Park, Calif.: Sage, 1988.

Pascarelli, E.F.: Methaqualone Abuse, the Quiet Epidemic. 224 *Journal of the American Medical Association,* 1512, 1973.

Petersen, R.C. and Stillman, R.C.: *Phencyclidine (PCP) Abuse.* Monograph 21. Washington, D.C.: National Institute on Drug Abuse, 1978.

Riley, T.L.: Toward a Drug Free Military. 5 *Criminal Justice,* 4, 1991.

Schinke, S.P., Botvin, G.J. and Orlandi, M.A.: *Substance Abuse in Children and Adolescents: Evaluation and Intervention.* Newbury Park, Calif.: Sage, 1991.

Sessions, W.S.: Working Toward a Drug-free America. 59 *FBI Law Enforcement Bulletin,* 4, 1990.

Spotts, J.V. and Spotts, C.A.: *Use and Abuse of Amphetamine and Its Substitutes.* Washington, D.C.: National Institute on Drug Abuse, 1980.

Stead, A.H., et al.: Drug Misuse—The Barbiturate Problem. 21 *Journal of the Forensic Science Society,* 41, 1981.

Swanson, C., Gaines, L. and Gore, B.: Abuse of Anabolic Steroids. 60 *FBI Law Enforcement Bulletin,* 8, 1991.

Chapter 19

SEX OFFENSES

1. Introduction

T HE TERM *sex offenses* is used here to include rape, carnal knowledge, sodomy, and deviant sexual practices related to the condition of homosexuality. An investigation of these offenses is particularly demanding of the investigator because of the discretion and tact which must be employed. Moreover, since the accusation of a sex offense, although easily made, is often difficult to substantiate or disprove, the investigator has a special responsibility to protect the reputations of innocent subjects of such charges.

Sex offenses may be divided into two groups. The first, and generally more serious, involves physical aggression against unwilling victims, as in forcible rape, violent homosexual attack, or indecent assault. The second involves such acts as illicit intercourse or voluntary homosexual relations, acceptable only to the immediate participants but offensive to relatives, neighbors, or a substantial part of the community. This latter group presents distinctive problems in law enforcement. Fortunately, the authorities receive few complaints from voluntary participants in prohibited sexual behavior, and since the offenses are ordinarily committed in private, only a relatively small proportion of this activity is brought to the attention of law enforcement agencies.

One important result of employing the penal law to suppress behavior that is condemned primarily because it affronts the moral sense of non-participants is the great variety of laws and enforcement policies that ensue. Nations and states, as well as groups within states, differ widely in the gravity with which they view violations of sexual mores and in their estimates of the seriousness of the associated police problem. The discussion given in this chapter has been restricted to those offenses on which the law is fairly uniform and basically uncontroversial. Included, too, are certain sexual deviations (such as practices related to homosexuality and sadism) whose expression may carry implications (such as security considerations) having a far-reaching social effect.

I. RAPE

2. Nature of Rape

The act of having sexual intercourse with a female without her conscious and voluntary permission is traditionally forbidden by law. If the act is committed without the consent of the female, regardless of age, it is considered rape. Special provision is made for the protection of those females who are considered incapable of giving consent. Thus, if a woman is of unsound mind, unconscious, or in an advanced state of intoxication and the accused is aware of this condition, the act is rape. Similarly, if the victim is a female child who is not old enough to understand the nature of the act, the accused may be charged with rape. The act of sexual intercourse with females below a certain age under circumstances not tantamount to rape is called carnal knowledge or statutory rape. The elements of proof required to support a conviction on a charge of rape are discussed below.

a. **The Accused Had Sexual Intercourse with a Certain Female.** Penetration, however slight, is sufficient to complete the offense. It must be shown beyond a reasonable doubt that the private parts of the male entered at least to some extent those of the female. It is not necessary to prove emission. Corroboration of the victim's testimony with respect to penetration is not required. Finally, penetration can be established in the absence of the victim's testimony by circumstantial evidence such as expert medicolegal opinion.

b. **The Act Was Done by Force and without Her Consent.** The force required is simply that used to effect the act of penetration. If the woman is in normal condition the act must be committed against the utmost reluctance and resistance which she is capable of making at the time. Since the degree of resistance is a relative matter, it must be judged in the light of all of the circumstances of the occasion such as the degree of force employed by the assailant and the apparent uselessness of the resistance. In the case of girls too young to understand the nature of the act or women of unsound mind or relatively unconscious (to the offender's knowledge), the absence of consent is considered to exist regardless of the actions or statements of the victim.

c. **Legal Changes.** Recent changes in state laws reflect a growing national trend to view rape not as a deviant sexual offense but as a violent crime of assault. Rape is considered the major crime least reported to the police—the FBI says only one offense in five is reported. Reluctance to report the crime was due in part to the fear of having one's prior sexual conduct explored in court. Furthermore, the law seemed to express and support the view that claims of rape were to be treated with scepticism and that the behavior of the victim was to be given greater emphasis than that of the assailant. To remedy these and other inequities in the law, a number of legal changes were enacted.

1) *"Rape Shield" Laws.* Most states have changed the rules of evidence in a rape case to limit the introduction of material about a victim's personal sex life. "Rape shield" laws prohibit courtroom inquiry into the prior sexual conduct of the victim. However, these laws afford only limited protection to the victim because an exception is often made to admit into testimony the description of a past relationship if it was with the accused. Furthermore, a skillful defense lawyer can circumvent the intent of these laws by impuning the victim's moral character with questions about lifestyle, living arrangements and marital status. Juries tend to approve of traditional married life and look askance at any deviation from it. They are most likely to take seriously the accusation of a victim who is married and assaulted at night by a stranger in her own home. The jury is often reluctant to believe the victim when she lives alone and knows the assailant. For this reason, and the victim's desire to spare herself the embarrassment that a court trial entails, "date rape" and "acquaintance rape" go largely unreported and unpunished.

2) *"Rape Trauma Syndrome."* Some jurisdictions have admitted into court the expert testimony of a psychiatrist that a victim's behavior was consistent with "rape trauma syndrome." This term describes characteristic behavior patterns frequently exhibited by rape victims, such as fear of men, fear of the offender, fear of being alone, shame and repression of the incident. Evidence of this condition is ordinarily used in court to establish the victim's lack of consent. Repression, the mind's attempt to exclude from consciousness the details of a traumatic event, is an aspect of rape trauma syndrome. It is offered in court as an explanation for the difficulty the victim sometimes experiences in making a positive identification of the assailant.

3) **Rape Crisis Counselor Privilege.** In a few jurisdictions, the confidentiality of the relationship between the rape victim and the professional rape crisis counselor is protected. It is considered a privileged communication similar to that between a psychiatrist and a patient and prohibits the disclosure of the counselor's notes and records in court. This permits the victim to use crisis services without running the risk of her private statements appearing in court.

4) **Eased Evidence Requirements.** Many states have enacted changes in their law to ease the evidence requirements necessary to support a conviction for rape. For example, New York no longer requires a witness to the act itself. Connecticut and Iowa repealed their laws requiring corroborative evidence. In Massachusetts law, proof that the victim was physically forced to submit is no longer required; the threat of physical force is sufficient.

5) **Videotaped Testimony.** Some jurisdictions permit the courtroom use of videotaped testimony of children who are victims of sexual offenses. This eliminates the requirement of confronting the assailant, sparing the children further psychological trauma and making the parents more inclined to have their children testify.

6) *"Marital Exemption."* Traditionally, a husband could not be charged with raping his wife. Since 1975, when South Dakota became the first state to make spousal rape a crime, twenty-five states have enacted similar legislation. In 1984, New York's highest court, the Court of Appeals, unanimously struck down the "marital exemption" in the state's rape law because it denied a wife the

Constitutional guarantee of equal protection under the law. According to the Clearinghouse on Marital Rape, from 1978 to 1985, 118 husbands were prosecuted for this offense and 104 were convicted.

3. Characteristics of the Offense

One source of information on the offense of rape is a study by the Israeli sociologist Menachem Amir (*Patterns in Forcible Rape*) based on the investigation of 646 cases in Philadelphia. The study shatters, again, several popular myths, e.g., that black men assault white women. In 77 percent of the cases victim and offender were both black; in 18 percent both were white. In this urban study, rape was found to be an overwhelmingly intraracial event in which the victims were mostly black. Other findings from this study are given below.

    a. **Characteristics**

    1) *Alcohol* was a factor in only one-third of the cases.

    2) *Acquaintanceship.* In two-thirds of the cases the offender and victim were hitherto unknown to each other.

    3) *Place.* Most rapes are committed indoors; one-third take place in the victim's homes. The dark-alley event is rare.

    4) *Time.* Most rapes are committed on weekends; the peak time is Friday evening.

    5) *Age.* Offenders tended to be under 25; victims tended to be under 20. Both offenders and victims tended to be unmarried.

    6) *Occupation.* Only 10 percent of the offenders were in occupations above the level of skilled worker.

    7) *Resistance.* More than 50 percent of the victims failed to resist.

    b. **The Offender.** The rapist is usually described as an emotionally immature person, with deep feelings of inferiority and a sense of inadequacy with respect to social relations. Some psychologists distinguish two general classes of offenders—criminal and psychiatric. The distinction has been found useful, medically and legally, in the treatment of sex offenders. In a few states a sex offender must be examined by a board of psychiatrists. In New Jersey, for example, if he is diagnosed as a "repetitive/compulsive offender," an indeterminate sentence (with an upper limit of 30 years) is prescribed at a specialized treatment center. If he is otherwise diagnosed, he is sentenced as a criminal. The following are some of the characteristics of the two groups:

1) *Psychiatric Offenders.* Compared with the criminal offenders, the psychiatric offenders have a higher average IQ, have a broad range of educational and achievement levels, and vary widely in social position. The typical psychiatric offender is said to be gentle and even naive about sex, living on fantasy and retreating from normal life out of a sense of inadequacy. Many are latent homosexuals who overcompensate by the overt, aggressive heterosexual act of rape. The psychiatric rapist knows that he is sick and typically feels tremendous guilt and shame, and even concern for his victim.

2) *Criminal Offenders.* In contrast, the criminal rapist feels no guilt, has no concern, and does not accept the idea that anything is wrong with him. He is a sociopath, of course, but he is not *sick* in the psychiatric sense. His action is frequently motivated by a contempt and hostility toward females.

4. Medical Examination of the Victim

It is important that a complete medical examination take place soon after the occurrence not only for the health and welfare of the victim but also for the preservation of the fragile biological evidence involved. Hospital emergency rooms are now staffed with physicians trained in these medicolegal matters and have established a high priority for treatment of these cases.

a. **Consent.** If the victim is an adult, permission for the examination must be obtained. With regard to persons under the age of sixteen, permission should be obtained from a parent or guardian, since those under that age may not be considered sufficiently adult to give permission. The object of the examination should be explained to the victim and the examinee informed that the findings will be embodied in a medical report. Another woman should be present during the examination.

b. **Significance of Signs of Physical Resistance.** Physical signs of rape will vary in different cases and may even be absent although the offense was in fact committed. Hence the medical examiner may not affirm in the absence of physical evidence that rape was not accomplished. Where evidence does exist, the range of physical signs will usually vary according to the capacity for physical resistance. In the case of young children or unconscious women, the evidential results of resistance will probably be absent, while the local signs of accomplishment of the act may be well marked, this latter condition varying with the previous experience of the victim. Where a vigorous woman is involved, it is to be expected that signs of violence such as wounds, bruises, and scratches will be present and in their absence an explanation should be sought. Fear and threats can sometimes render the victim incapable of physical resistance. The acts and demeanor of the victim immediately after the assault should be subject to critical investigation in these cases.

c. **Examination.** In his report the physician will include the following information:

1) The recent medical history of the victim.

2) The details of the assault.

3) The general physical appearance and demeanor of the victim.

4) The presence or absence of marks of violence on the body; their character and position, when present.

5) The presence or absence of marks upon the clothing.

6) The condition of the affected parts with respect to bleeding, bruising, and previous experience.

d. **Evidence Collection.** Physicians in almost every hospital are supplied with a sexual assault evidence kit. It includes detailed instructions for collecting, preserving, securing, and transporting the physical evidence to the forensic laboratory. The evidence is collected in order to establish the *corpus delicti* and to identify the assailant. The types of evidence will include the following:

1) Any debris acquired during the assault.

2) Dried secretions such as semen, blood, and saliva which are collected with a moistened swab.

3) Fingernail scrapings which are collected to obtain traces of such evidence as blood, hair, skin, and fibers, acquired while resisting the assailant.

4) Pubic hair combing to obtain hairs or fibers left by the assailant.

5) Pulled pubic hairs and pulled head hairs for comparison with those found at the scene of the crime and on the assailant.

6) Vaginal swabs and smear if vaginal assault occurred. The swab is used to collect semen evidence. A smear involves the placing of this evidence on a glass slide for microscopic examination.

7) Rectal swabs and smear if rectal assault occurred.

8) Oral swabs and smear if oral-genital contact occurred.

9) Blood samples for blood typing and DNA analysis which will be compared with any biological evidence found at the crime scene or on the assailant.

10) Saliva samples to determine if the victim is a secretor. A secretor is one whose ABO blood group can be determined from any of their body fluids. Eighty percent of the population are secretors. This sample can be compared with respect to secretor status with any biological fluid or stain found at the crime scene, on the victim, or on the suspect.

5. Medical Examination of Suspect

An examination of the suspect by a physician, if conducted soon after the occurrence, may provide valuable evidence. In addition to medical evidence of recent sexual activity, the physician may discover traces which may link the suspect to the crime. A pubic hair combing may reveal foreign hair or fibers. Pulled pubic and head hairs are collected for comparison with any that may be discovered on the victim or at the crime scene. Similarly, blood and saliva samples are obtained to compare with any fluids or stains associated with the crime. Fingernail scrapings should be taken as in the case of the victim. In addition the hands should be carefully examined for traces of cosmetics which may have been acquired by contact with the victim.

6. Examination of Clothing

Since in a sexual assault intimate contact takes place between the clothing of the assailant and that of the victim and, in some cases between the garments of both and the ground, a careful examination of the clothing of the suspect and the victim should be made for traces of grass, weeds, seed, and soil. If traces are found which correspond to similar materials found at the crime scene, this evidence may serve in the case of the suspect's clothing to associate him with the scene or, in the case of the victim, to partially corroborate her story. Clothing is collected during the physician's examination by having the subject, whether it is the victim or the suspect, disrobe on a white sheet of paper. As each article of clothing is removed it is packed in separate paper bags. The paper sheet is refolded to retain any trace evidence present and placed in a bag. The bags are then sent to a forensic laboratory for examination.

7. Identification of Semen

When there is a question of identifying the assailant, the locating of semen on the victim, the victim's clothing, or at the crime scene is of paramount importance. Semen is the grayish-white fluid produced by the male reproductive organs. It is a viscous adhesive fluid usually discovered in the form of stains on clothing or bedding, imparting a starchy stiffness to the portion of the fabric on which it is contained. If the semen stains are not apparent, inspection of the evidence with an ultraviolet light can help locate them. Semen stains will display a bright luminesence under ultraviolet radiation.

a. **Acid Phosphatase Color Test.** If the semen stain cannot be discovered by sight or touch, the acid phosphatase color test can be used. Acid phosphatase is an enzyme found in all body fluids but found in semen in great concentration. A detection of high levels of acid phosphatase is a good indication that the stain is semen.

1) A few drops of alpha-napthylphosphate is allowed to soak into the stain.

2) One drop of fast blue B dye is added.

3) If the stain is semen, a blue-violet color will appear in approximately 30 seconds.

Other substances, such as vegetables and vaginal secretions, will also react, but not with the same speed that semen will. It is usually considered a screening test; that is, if the stain does not react, it is definitely not semen. A positive reaction, however, requires a further confirmatory test.

b. **Microscopic Test.** A portion of the stain is dissolved in a saline solution and placed on a slide. The finding of *spermatazoa* through a microscope is considered conclusive evidence that the stain is semen. *Spermatazoa* or *sperm* are the male reproductive organisms in semen which fertilize the female egg. They are tadpole-like creatures with long tails and in humans have a characteristic appearance. Though there are hundreds of millions of sperm in a small quantity of semen, it is often difficult to locate one because of their fragile nature. Moreover, some individuals have low sperm counts (*oligospermia*) or lack sperm altogether (*aspermia*). The latter condition is becoming more common with the increase in vasectomies.

8. Interview of the Victim

The victim should be interviewed as soon as possible after the medical examination. Another woman should be present during the interview. The victim should be questioned thoroughly concerning the occurrence, the circumstances surrounding it, and her movements before and after the commission of the offense. Questions should be asked concerning her acquaintance with the suspect. Since charges of rape are easily made, the necessity of close scrutiny of the victim's complaint is evident. Logical inconsistencies in the victim's story may indicate the falsity of a charge. Sometimes when the girl is a consenting party, she becomes frightened after the act and, to save her reputation, brings a charge against her escort. Young girls may bring a false charge through fear of their parents' knowledge of their consent to the act. The following special points should guide the investigator in his questioning.

a. **Fresh Complaint.** The victim should be questioned concerning the manner and time in which she complained about the attack. In prosecutions for sexual offenses, such as rape and sodomy, evidence that the victim made complaint a short time thereafter is admissible. Under this rule evidence that the complaint was made, the offender identified, or other details may be given. The sole purpose of receiving the fresh complaint in testimony is the corroboration of the victim's story. The investigator should verify this information through witnesses such as the person who first heard or received the complaint.

b. **Consent.** To establish lack of consent, it must appear that the victim resisted to the extent of her ability at the time and under the circumstances. Useless or perilous resistance is not required. In regard to the acquiescence of a female child, the question of her ability to understand the nature of the act arises as a question of fact to be determined by the court. It has been held by some courts that a child under the age of ten years is presumed incapable of consenting to the act.

c. **Relations with the Accused.** In many jurisdictions specific prior sexual acts with the accused are admissible. The defense may raise the possibility of the victim having consented to the act charged and thus bringing into question her credibility.

9. Examination of the Crime Scene

If there are no eyewitnesses and little direct evidence, the investigator must rely on circumstantial evidence. The scene of the crime should be carefully examined as soon as practicable after the reporting of the offense. Described below are some suggested investigative steps and types of evidence found at outdoor scenes. For indoor scenes and automobiles the same general principles are applicable with appropriate modifications.

a. **Photography.** Photographs of the crime scene are sometimes useful in verifying or disproving statements of the victim or suspect concerning their activities at the scene. These should include an overall photograph of the area, a close-up of the immediate locale of the activity, and photographs of special points of interest to the case such as approaches, broken branches, and so forth.

b. **Tire Impressions.** The approaches and surrounding area should be examined for tire impressions. These should be photographed and cast if they appear helpful.

c. **Shoe Impressions.** The shoe impressions of the suspect at the crime scene can constitute valuable evidence, particularly if he later denies having been at the place. Photographs and casts of male shoe impressions should be made. Shoe impressions of the female victim may also be of importance under certain circumstances.

d. **Clothing and Other Personal Belongings.** Personal articles such as clothing, handkerchiefs, papers, or jewelry should be carefully collected and preserved.

e. **Matches.** Used matches and match booklets discarded at the scene sometimes provide valuable clues. The match, for example, may fit a match booklet later found on a suspect. The match booklet may bear the advertisement of an establishment patronized by the suspect.

f. **Fingerprints.** Surfaces capable of bearing latent fingerprints should be appropriately processed.

g. **Soil, Seeds, and Pollen.** Particles of soil and excrescences of the flora sometimes adhere to the person or clothing of the perpetrator. The investigator in his search of the crime scene should be alert for any characteristic material which might be used to identify the suspect. Samples of soil, seeds, and pollen should be collected from the immediate scene and preserved for possible comparison with similar material that may be later found on the person of a suspect.

10. Neighborhood Inquiry

Persons living in the neighborhood of the crime scene should be interviewed to ascertain whether there are any witnesses who heard outcries or who saw the suspect or the victim during the broad period of time including the occurrence. Particular attention should be given to any spontaneous exclamations which may have been heard. A notable exception to the hearsay rule of evidence is the admissibility of utterances concerning the circumstances of a criminal act made by a person without deliberation or design while he also is in a state of excitement caused by participation in or observation of the event. The utterance may be an exclamation, statement, or oral manifestation of pain and suffering.

11. Abettor as a Principal

An accused may be found guilty as a principal in rape, attempt to commit rape, and assault with intent to commit rape, even though he had no intercourse with the alleged victim, if he shared the criminal intent or purpose of the active perpetrator of the crime, and, by his presence, aided, encouraged, or incited the major actor to commit it. There must be an intent to aid or encourage the person who actually commits the crime; the aider or abettor must be shown to have associated himself in some manner with the venture, and it must be shown that he participated in it as something that he wished to bring about, and that he sought by his action to make it successful. For example, one who stands guard while his companions commit a rape is guilty as a principal even though he did not have intercourse with the victim.

12. Carnal Knowledge or Statutory Rape

The absence of consent is an essential element of rape, whereas in carnal knowledge the victim assents to the act. If the consenting victim is of unsound mind or so young as to be unable to understand the nature of sexual intercourse, the act is one of rape since such a female is considered legally incapable of consent. Carnal knowledge can, however, be made a lesser included offense of a charge of rape when there is evidence pointing to consent by a victim under sixteen years of age (or other age given in the statute) rather than the application of force by the accused. The techniques employed in the investigation of carnal knowledge are similar to those of rape with the added requirement of proof of age. Documentary proof of the child's age is desirable. In view of the youth of the victim, the investigator should obtain the consent of the parents prior to such investigative steps as the arranging for a medical examination.

13. Attempt to Commit Rape

Charges of attempts to commit rape and assaults with such intent are common occurrences in criminal investigative work.

They deserve special study on the part of the investigator both for their frequency and their relative complexity. An attempt to commit rape is a lesser included offense of the crime of rape. To constitute an attempt to commit rape, there must be a specific intent to commit rape accompanied by an overt act which directly tends to accomplish the unlawful purpose.

a. **Elements of Proof.** The following matters must be proved in order to establish the offense of attempted rape:

1) That the accused did a certain act.

2) That the act was done with specific intent to commit rape.

3) That the act amounted to more than mere preparation and apparently tended to effect the commission of the intended offense.

b. **Specific Intent.** The specific intent required is the accomplishment of unlawful sexual intercourse with a woman by force and against her will. This may be established, either by direct evidence, such as statements proved to have been made by the accused at the time of the alleged offense, or by circumstantial evidence, such as an inference as to intent drawn from the nature of the act committed. A statement of intent may be proved by the testimony of anyone who heard it being made, or by other competent evidence.

c. **Overt Act.** An overt act is one that amounts to more than mere preparation to commit an offense, and must be one which in the ordinary course of events would result in the commission of the offense. To constitute an attempt to commit rape, the overt act must have proceeded far enough so that the crime would have been completed but for extraneous intervention.

d. **Consummation of Offense.** An accused may be convicted of an attempt to commit an offense although at the trial it may appear that the offense was consummated.

14. Assault with Intent to Commit Rape

In some cases specific provision is made in the criminal statutes for the punishment of assaults with intent to commit rape. The offense is discussed here in order to distinguish it from an attempt to commit rape. An assault with intent to commit rape is not necessarily the equivalent of an attempt to commit rape, for an assault can be committed in furtherance of the intended act without thereby achieving that degree of proximity to the consummation of the act which is essential to constitute an attempt to commit the act. An "assault with intent" differs from an "attempt" in that it lacks the element of the overt act which would have led to the accomplishment of the crime except for some unlooked for interference. The procedure followed in the investigation of an assault with intent to commit rape is similar in many respects to that employed with respect to rape itself. Additional points requiring special attention are the following:

1) *The Assault.* The victim should be interviewed to obtain a complete and detailed description of the assault. Where physical force was not actually applied, the nature of the threats or menacing gestures becomes of critical importance and must be thoroughly explored. If a weapon was employed, the investigator should obtain a detailed description of it from the victim. In the event that he is successful in finding the weapon, he should endeavor to establish its ownership. Where the weapon is a gun, it should be submitted for laboratory examination.

2) *The Intent.* The purpose of the assailant to have sexual intercourse can be established by statements made at the time, by indecent expressions suggestive of sexual preoccupation, by gestures or by the intimate nature of the application of hands, and by the obvious, demonstrable absence of any other rational motive. A thorough interrogation of the accused can often establish the absence of any rational motive other than rape even though the questioning may not succeed in obtaining an explicit admission of the intent.

3) *Use of Force.* The accused must have had a purpose to carry out the plan with force and against the will of the female. This purpose cannot be proved by direct evidence unless the accused had been overheard to make a statement to this effect. However, it will suffice to establish the intent by circumstantial evidence, that is, by facts and circumstances from which, alone or in connection with other facts, the existence of the intent can be inferred on the basis of the common experience of mankind.

15. Indecent Assault

Provision has been made under criminal statutes for the punishment of men who satisfy their desire for erotic pleasure by touching females in a sexually intimate manner. Indecent assault is the term used to describe the action of a male in taking indecent, lewd, or lascivious liberties with the person of a female without her consent and against her will with the intent of gratifying his lust or sexual desires. More simply stated, the offense consists of an intimate caressing or fondling of a female against her will. The investigation of a complaint of this nature should include a complete and detailed description of the occurrence by the female, an interview of witnesses, and an interrogation of the suspect. In questioning the suspect particular stress should be placed on the activities and location of the suspect before, during, and after the time of the occurrence of the alleged offense. The details of any alibi which the accused offers should be thoroughly explored. An effort should be made to find witnesses who can offer information concerning the accused's actions during the broad period of time that includes the occurrence. A search should be made for any past record of a similar offense on the part of the accused. The background and history of the female should also be investigated to detect any record of involvement in sex crimes or a propensity for placing similar complaints.

16. Indecent Acts with a Child Under the Age of Sixteen Years

More vigorous provisions are usually found in the criminal code for the protection of girls under sixteen years of age from the dangers of indecent assault. In addition, the law is equally applicable to cases involving youthful male victims. The offense comprises the taking of any immoral, improper, or indecent liberties with the body of a child of either sex under the age of sixteen years. It differs basically from indecent assault in that consent by the victim is not an element and does not constitute a defense. The investigation of this crime is similar to that of indecent assault. An interview of the parents should, however, be conducted with a view to determining the child's credibility. Ordinarily the major difficulties encountered in the investigation of this offense lie in the unreliability of the child's account. If the child is quite young, it is not a simple matter to obtain an accurate relation of the events in specific detail. In addition, the identification of the offender is sometimes a problem. The investigator should permit the child to give an account of the occurrence without interference or suggestion and should then explore ways of eliciting other necessary information without stimulating any latent tendency towards fantasy.

17. Checklist for Rape and Lesser Included Offenses

In addition to the usual who, when, what, how, why, and where questions the following points should be covered where they are relevant:

a. Employment, marital status, and family relationships of the victim.

b. Previous history of similar occurrences or related offenses in which the present complainant was the victim.

c. Exact location of the commission of the offense.

d. Locations where preparations may have been made.

e. Places visited prior to the occurrence.

f. Persons seen prior to the occurrence.

g. Road followed in arriving at the place of occurrence.

h. Location of rooms, houses, or other establishments from which the occupants could have heard or seen the events. Names and addresses of occupants.

i. What physical force did the accused employ?

j. Detailed description of any weapon used by the accused.

l. Statements or utterances of the accused at the crime scene.

m. Nature and degree of resistance offered by the victim.

n. Duration of efforts at resistance.

o. Utterances of the victim at the time of the offense.

p. Screams or outcries of the victim.

q. Movements of the accused and the victim subsequent to the offense. Paths followed, roads used, places passed, and persons seen.

r. To whom did the victim make the first report of the offense?

s. Was the victim's report made voluntarily or was it the result of persuasion?

t. Exact time of the victim's report.

u. Was the report made as soon as possible after the act took place? What reasons are given for any delay?

v. Results of the medical examination: Do they offer proof of the use of violence? Resistance? Penetration? Was the victim pregnant at the time of the offense? How long had she been in this condition?

w. Reputation of the victim: Chastity? Had she engaged previously in sexual acts? If so, with whom and when? Has she previously made similar complaints? Does she have any motive for false accusation?

x. Victim's relation to the accused: Were they previously acquainted? How long were they acquainted? How often did they see each other? What were the typical circumstances of their meetings? When did the accused make the first advance? How often did he make advances? What were the victim's overt reactions to these advances?

y. Statement of the Accused: Accused's responses to those inquiries listed above which are applicable to his actions, viz., movements at the scene, utterances, relationship with the victim, and so forth. Details of any alibi of the accused. Detailed log of accused's movements during the broad period of time including the occurrence. Verification of details concerning his alibi and movements.

z. Reputation of the accused: Criminal record; military record; social history; marital status; previous involvement in similar or related offenses; associates.

II. SODOMY

18. Elements

Sodomy has traditionally been known as the "crime against nature." The term *sodomy* as it is used here includes sodomy proper, which is the carnal copulation of human beings in other than the natural manner, and bestiality or carnal copulation by a human being with an animal. Although sodomy is usually practiced by homosexuals, it may take place between male and female, as well as between two males or two females. Both parties are guilty of sodomy if they participate willingly. Proof in the offense of sodomy consists in showing that the deviant act took place as alleged. The sexual connection in a deviant manner is the essence of the offense. Penetration of the body must be shown, but it need not be any particular distance, since any sexual penetration, however slight, is sufficient to complete the offense. The fact of penetration may be proved by circumstantial evidence. It should be noted that emission is not a necessary element and need not be proved to make out a consummated offense.

19. Investigative Procedures

The proof of sodomy is by no means a simple matter, since the act is usually performed in circumstances designed to insure great privacy. Ordinarily a sodomy case develops as an outgrowth of an investigation into homosexuality. A number of the investigative methods employed in rape and homosexuality cases are applicable to the investigation of sodomy.

a. **Eyewitnesses.** The investigative problems are greatly simplified if an eyewitness, other than the participants, can be found. The witness should be questioned in detail concerning the action he observed. The specific anatomical detail of the act is of great importance and the witness should be encouraged to describe the occurrence fully. He should also be asked to describe the participants and to state the significant points by which he would be able to identify them. Finally, he should be requested to account for his presence in the vicinity of the place of occurrence at that time or, where this is not applicable, the reason why his attention was drawn to the activity.

b. **Participants.** In the absence of eyewitnesses the interrogation of the other witnesses is of vital importance to the success of the case. Although both participants are guilty of the offense of sodomy, a different approach is usually employed in the interrogation of the active party as distinguished from the passive. In difficult situations the one should be played against the other in order to induce a confession. The passive participant or pathic is usually the weaker of the two and should be interrogated accordingly. It should be noted that in certain cases no clear distinction can be made between active and passive parties since the nature of the occurrence may have been such as to involve reciprocation or mutual and equally active participation. Naturally, where the crime is one of bestiality the distinction is of no value. It is understood here that the rights of a suspect are scrupulously protected during any interrogation (see Chap. 9).

1) *Active Participant.* The investigator should, as far as practicable, acquaint himself with the background of the accused prior to the interrogation. Some knowledge of the reputation, record, and associates of the accused should be required to enable the investigator to form an estimate of the suspect's character. Since in the interrogation the first approach is usually one designed to induce admissions, the investigator should employ euphemisms in referring to the offense. Terms such as "sodomy," "bestiality," "unnatural act," or "crime against nature" should be avoided. In the preliminary phases words such as "contact," "caress," and "connection" will serve to create an atmosphere conducive to frank discussion. After admissions have been obtained the interrogator can shift gradually to a restatement of the nature of the occurrence in terms of explicit, anatomical detail. In the preliminary stages it is often useful to follow the lines of the suspect's history. The interrogator can ask a series of questions relating to the following data:

a) Participation in similar offenses prior to present occurrence.

b) Arrest record for similar offenses.

c) Marital status: single; married (no children); married (children); divorced (no children); divorced (children).

d) First act in which subject participated: Active oral, passive oral, active anal, passive anal, bestial, mutual masturbation, or other.

e) Principal cause of first act: experimentation; compelling inner urge; intoxication; submission to force; or other.

f) Usual case of subsequent acts, particularly recent ones: continuing experimentation; compelling inner urge; intoxication; or other.

g) Frequency of acts.

h) Partners in such acts, viz., whether the acts are performed promiscuously or are confined to one or several partners.

2) *Passive Participant.* The pathic or passive party in a sodomy case is usually the more vulnerable of the suspects. In many cases, particularly if he is not confirmed in the sex habit, he will be under the impression that he is relatively innocent by comparison with his partner. As in dealing with the active party, the investigator should not impart by his reactions any sense of the gravity of the offense. Expressions of shock or abhorrence in the initial stage of the interrogation may strengthen the suspect's resolve to remain silent. Restraint on the interrogator's part leads the passive suspect to believe that he will be receptive to any admissions which would indicate that he, the passive partner, was practically an unwitting victim. From the opening wedge of an admission of this type the interrogator should endeavor to work toward a full confession. An inquiry into the subject's personal history along the lines described in the previous paragraph may develop the spirit of clinical candor. It should be noted, however, that the suggestions given here represent the simplest line of approach to the problem of interrogation. Different types of subjects with varying degrees of experience will require different treatment. The interrogator should be sufficiently resourceful to try several different approaches where one has failed. Corroboration of admissions by the pathic must be shown in those cases where he consented to the act, since, being a willing participant, he must be regarded as an accomplice.

c. **Physical Evidence.** The scene of occurrence should be examined for evidence of the criminal act, such as stained handkerchiefs, and if necessary, for traces or clues which will associate the suspects with the place. In addition, arrangements should be made for a physical examination of the suspects by a medical examiner. When the offense is based on penetration of the anus, a medical examination can also provide corroboration founded on the abnormal condition of the anal region. On young persons the examination may disclose great tenderness around the anal sphincter, accompanied by signs of bruising, and laceration. In the older subject or in habitual offenders the anus becomes dilated, loses its natural, puckered orifice and develops a thickened, hardened skin. If the examination takes place soon after the act, the physician may discover seminal stains on the person of the passive offender or victim and fecal soiling on the active participant. Bestiality or sodomy committed with an animal is usually difficult to prove because of the lack of direct evidence. Medical examination is ordinarily successful only in demonstrating the presence of animal hair on the accused. Occasionally, semen may be found on the coat of the animal.

III. HOMOSEXUALITY

20. The Nature of Homosexuality

Homosexuality is the sexual propensity for persons of one's own sex. Normal behavior, the sexual attraction to a person of opposite sex, is termed *heterosexuality.* In homosexuality the person is subject, with varying degrees of compulsion, to sexual fixations or erotic attachments to persons of the same sex. The condition may be latent or may be overtly manifested. It is with the latter type that the investigator must be concerned. Male homosexuals often commit sodomy, particularly in the form of fellatio, and sometimes practice mutual masturbation. Female homosexuals, also called *lesbians,* may engage in cunnilingus and tribadism. Both types may engage in fondling, embracing, and kissing as a means of achieving sexual satisfaction.

21. Recognizing the Homosexual

It is a popular belief that the male homosexual can be identified by his feminine mannerisms and physical characteristics. This theory, however, is by no means generally true, not even in regard to the great majority of homosexuals. Many male homosexuals are virile in appearance and athletic in physical demeanor.

Similarly the lesbian, while disliking men, may attract them strongly by her feminine beauty. On the other hand, there are many males possessing a feminine appearance and females with a mannish face and manner who are not in the least homosexual. Finally, to add to these difficulties of recognition, there is the phenomenon of bisexuality. Many homosexuals are married and conduct normal sexual relations with their spouses while practicing their preferred mode of deriving erotic stimulation in secrecy with another of their own sex. As a general rule, then, the investigator cannot trust his unaided observation of a person to deduce that a condition of homosexuality exists, but rather must rely on eyewitness testimony and other evidence to support such a judgment. The investigator should, in fact, as in other types of investigations, make no conclusions but simply describe the facts and amass evidence.

22. The Homosexual Problem

The condition of homosexuality is not a crime. Although overt manifestations of the condition, such as sodomy with a person, are otherwise punishable under criminal statutes, these considerations are, in the strict sense, irrelevant to the question of homosexuality itself. Although there is no specific penal provision for homosexuality in view of the fact that it is only a condition or tendency, the homosexual frequently creates a security or a morale problem which is of investigative interest. Homosexuality among members of large organizations is looked upon as highly undesirable in that it serves to impair efficiency and *esprit*. Further, such individuals are considered security risks because of the influence that may be exerted upon them through a homosexual relationship with a person desiring "sensitive" information. Moreover, homosexuality tends to be epidemic: the hard-core homosexual, frequently unable to control his inclinations or desires, will usually look for a sexual partner, and, unless he can find another homosexual, he will tend to recruit some other person for his purpose. It will be found that the discovery of one homosexual in the course of an investigation often leads to the uncovering of a number of others.

23. Lesbianism

Homosexuality among women is tolerated more readily by society, attracting far less attention than its male counterpart and arousing less antipathy. Indeed, lesbianism is heeded so little that it is difficult to find anywhere in the United States a record of conviction or prosecution of a female under state sodomy laws. This is partially explained by the fact that the character of the female homosexual is less aggressive, her activities less overt, and her efforts at recruitment less obvious. Further explanation is offered by the statistics of the Kinsey research, which indicated that only one-third to one-half as many females as males were primarily or exclusively homosexual at any age.

While lesbianism poses no general police problem, it does, however, represent a danger to morale in organizations such as the armed services in which large numbers of women are employed. The nature of military life, with its necessary sharing of accommodations and close association during and after working hours, provides a satisfactory arrangement for the unscrupulous female homosexual who wishes to recruit from the innocent or the ignorant.

24. Initiating and Controlling Homosexual Cases

An investigation of an allegation of homosexuality should not, ordinarily, be initiated except on specific information. The informational basis of the case should not consist of non-specific facts such as mere acquaintance, neutral correspondence, past residence, or the presence of the subject's name in a homosexual's address book or letter. Moreover, an investigation founded on specific information should be carefully controlled to prevent unnecessary extension. Leads should be carefully evaluated for relevancy and materiality. If it is necessary to interview supervisors or associates of the subject the questions should be limited to reputation and character. The element of homosexuality should not be introduced unless information of this nature is first proferred by the interviewee. Minor children who are victims in sex offenses will present special interviewing problems. It is essential that a tactful approach be employed to preclude any subsequent serious psychological disturbance in the child. The interview should be conducted in the presence of a parent, guardian, or juvenile authority. A slow, friendly, manner should be used to avoid exciting the child. Allegations and statements made by a child should be evaluated on the merits of the child's maturity and tendency to indulge in fantasy.

25. Investigative Steps

Witnesses such as associates and supervisors, both past and present, should be interviewed if the information available to the investigator indicates that these persons are logical sources of additional evidence. Valuable clues may sometimes be obtained by means of a trash cover and a discreet search of quarters in which special attention is given to diaries, letters, and other written material. Because of the tendency of some homosexuals to commit their thoughts and feelings to writing and to employ certain characteristic terms of endearment and other locutions, their communications are often fruitful sources of information. Other articles which should be noted in a search are items ordinarily associated with females such as cosmetics and feminine garments.

26. Interviewing the Homosexual

In suggesting techniques of interviewing persons suspected of homosexual tendencies or practices it is not possible to prescribe fixed rules or even widely applicable principles, because of the variety of personality types which is encountered in these cases. The recidivist homosexual whose sex habits are confirmed by years of indulgence will by dint of experience be able to resist the moral pressure of prolonged and vigorous questioning. On the other hand, the immature person who has under the influence of alcohol and without full volition committed an isolated homosexual act may be impelled by remorse to a ready confession of his lapse. Since the majority of unknown homosexuals are relatively young and inexperienced, the simplest assumption that can be made for the purposes of discussion is that they will more readily yield to an initial display of interest on the part of the investigator that is free from manifestations of animosity or hostility. The suggested techniques described in some of the subsequent paragraphs can be abandoned without difficulty in favor of more effective tactics when the course of the questioning indicates the necessity of such a shift.

a. **Qualifications of the Interviewer.** The investigator who is assigned to interview a homosexual should be carefully selected on the basis of maturity, experience, and criminological knowledge. He should understand the various aspects of sex and marital relations and should be able to maintain rapport with the various types of offenders in discussing these matters. Finally, he should be well versed in the terminology of sex discussions so that he can word his questions in a manner calculated to elicit candid and accurate responses.

b. **Establishing Rapport.** To win the confidence of the subject the interrogator should convey the impression that his mission is not one of prosecution and that he is sincerely desirous of discovering the origin and causes of his sex problem.

c. **Diction.** The choice of words and phrases will directly affect the investigator's success. Initially the interrogator should form his questions so that they carry an assumption that the subject has participated in abnormal sex acts. For example, the question "When did you first do this?" should be used rather than "Did you ever do this?"

d. **Order of Question.** If the suspect is shy or guilt-ridden, the order in which the questions are arranged will be important. Embarrassing questions about sex habits should not be asked too early in the interrogation. Preparation should be made for critical questions by a series of neutral inquiries concerning schooling, physical health, and relations with parents.

e. **Introduction.** Initially the interview should not suggest too strongly a criminal investigation. The investigator should appear to be conducting a personnel background inquiry. At first the conversation should be casual and related to everyday affairs, common acquaintances, or recreational interests. The experienced investigator will be able to establish rapport without conveying to the subject the impression that he is making an exceptional effort to put him at ease. After devoting an appropriate length of time to the introduction, the investigator should shift smoothly to more pertinent questioning. He may state that a situation has arisen that requires him to obtain information concerning the background of certain persons. He should further state that the inquiry may make it necessary for him to ask a number of questions of a personal nature. The following information should then be obtained as a means of "warming up" to the sexual topics:

1) *Background history* including the subject's birthplace, the family income during his boyhood, parents' educational background and compatibility, number of children, class of neighborhoods, type of dwellings, and other factors relating to his boyhood.

2) *Educational history* including the types of schools attended, the courses pursued, relative academic success, relationships with instructors, and extracurricular activities.

3) *Social life* including general background of friends, extent and nature of social activities, and club memberships.

4) *Recreational interests* including types of sports, names of athletic clubs, extent of athletic interests, and summer camp activities.

5) *Military history* including circumstances of separation from the service.

6) *Medical history* including any consultations with a psychiatrist or psychologist.

f. **Body.** Naturally the most important part of the interrogation will deal with the subject's homosexual activities and the commission of substantive sex offenses. Little practical guidance can be given in regard to inquiries concerning sex offenses since the techniques to be employed will vary widely with the character of the subject. The questioning should, however, develop the following information, which, in addition to furthering the inquiry, will serve to supply useful data for use by reviewing authorities:

1) Arrest record for sexual offenses.

2) History of homosexual activity (if he divulges this readily many of the subsequent topics will be covered at this point).

3) Circumstances surrounding the first act of homosexuality — age, cause, initial desires, degree of urges and desires, submission to force, inducement, exact physical nature of the act.

4) Exact physical nature of subsequent acts.

5) Nature of present sexual life; include any tendencies toward bisexuality.

6) Associates in homosexual activities—character of persons and manner of developing acquaintanceship.

7) Efforts to cure the condition, such as psychiatric treatment or change of social habits.

8) Identity of associates in homosexual activities.

9) Identity of places frequented for the purpose of associating with homosexuals.

10) Marital history including number of children, compatibility, and desires for normal domestic life.

IV. OTHER FORMS OF SEXUAL DEVIANCE

27. Significance

In the interests of public decency, law enforcement must take cognizance also of those forms of sexual deviance, other than sodomy, which directly affect persons other than the deviant himself and his partner. This effect is usually an affront of sensibilities or an outrage of personal dignity, but occasionally it may be bad example and constitute a deleterious influence on the conduct of others. No attempt will be made here to treat the subject of sexual deviance comprehensively, since a complete listing of the various forms would require a book in itself and would be, in large part, a treatise of chiefly academic interest. It is not possible to give a strict definition of the term *sexual deviance.* The generalized psychiatric acceptance of this term has in recent years been broadened to include any sexual act which constitutes a deviance from the heterosexual act of coitus. A convenient division of deviant acts may be made into those which constitute a misuse of the parts of the body designated by nature for normal sexual union and those which indicate a deviance from a normal sexual aim. In the first class would lie fellatio, cunnilingus, and anilingus; while the second class would embrace those acts which use a substitute object in place of the normal one, such as fetishism, voyeurism, and sadism.

28. Indecent Exposure

Indecent exposure is the exposure of the genitalia to one of the opposite sex under other than the conventionally lawful circumstances. Usually this offense is committed by a male in the presence of one or more females. In psychiatry this compulsive neurosis is termed *exhibitionism*. The personality of individuals given to this practice is characterized by timidity and lack of aggressiveness and there is in them little desire and often no psychological capability for the normal sexual act. In exposing himself the exhibitionist irrationally hopes that the woman will be attracted to him and will likewise expose her own person. The manner in which the exhibitionist operates will vary considerably. Some expose themselves at windows to female passersby. Others frequent parks and reveal themselves to individual females by rapidly drawing aside their overcoats or a covering newspaper. Still others accomplish their objectives while seated in automobiles and even in public conveyances.

29. Voyeurism

A voyeur (from the French word meaning a "looker" or "viewer" is a "Peeping Tom." Voyeurism is the derivation of sexual excitement and satisfaction from viewing the genitalia or naked body of another. Ordinarily the voyeur prefers to remain unseen and finds particular pleasure in watching the disrobing of women. His activities are frequently followed by masturbation. In general the voyeur does not constitute a danger to society. Indeed his viewing activities do not even constitute an offense other than in some cases the incidental trespass of property. If the Peeping Tom remains in his own quarters and views the undressing of a woman in another building he commits no substantive offense although his conduct, if it is commonly observable by his associates, is reprehensible as having a deleterious effect on the morale of others and he may be classed as a public nuisance.

30. Sadism and Masochism

The sadist achieves sexual excitement by inflicting physical punishment on another. The masochist, on the other hand, derives his pleasure from submitting to physical ill treatment at the hands of a sadist or another. In some persons both of these deviances are mingled. The most common forms of punishment employed are those of whipping and biting. Although these deviances are practiced by both male or female, it is found that the female is seldom a sadist, her nature being more inherently passive. While the masochist will derive sexual pleasure only from submitting to punishment by one of the opposite sex, the sadist may derive lascivious excitement from inflicting torture on a member of either sex.

31. Fetishism

This deviance involves the use of an object, usually intimate wearing apparel, of a person of the opposite sex to derive sexual satisfaction. The fetishist's mind is such that he can conduct most of the acts of lovemaking with this over-evaluated object with the exception of the sexual act itself. Pure fetishism is not uncommon among men but is a rarity in women. Fetishists sometimes break into houses to remove a certain type of article, such as shoes, lingerie, stockings, or other feminine wearing apparel.

32. Transvestitism

The practice of wearing the clothes of the opposite sex with the erotic desire of simulating attributes thereof is termed *transvestitism*. Male homosexuals occasionally dress up in feminine garments and solicit attention openly. At homosexual parties some of the members may array themselves in female costumes. Transvestitism is considered offensive in males and is explicitly forbidden by the laws of many states. The same offense among females, although more common, is considered socially acceptable, since this action does not appear in females to possess the deviant interest which it provides for males.

33. Frottage

This is a sexual deviance in which excitement is aroused and satisfaction achieved by rubbing against the clothing or anatomical parts, usually the buttocks, of a person of the opposite sex. The frotteur is almost invariably a male, the deviance being practically unknown in females. *Toucherism* is closely allied to frottage. The toucheur is subject to an irresistible impulse to touch the body of another person. He is encountered most commonly in large crowds, deriving sexual excitement from intimately touching women, apparently inadvertently. Such acts as pinching or caressing are made to appear like a casual contact.

34. Tribadism

Tribadism, the mutual vis-à-vis friction between women, is a common and effective method of achieving sexual excitement between female homosexuals. The tribadist is often bisexual; that is, she practices intercourse regularly with a person of opposite sex and yet derives intense pleasure in physical contact with members of her own sex.

35. The Social Problem

A change in public attitude toward the homosexual has taken place during the last two decades in the direction of a broader understanding of his problem and his need for protection in certain areas of social life. The homosexual represents a problem that will not disappear by the public's looking the other way. The experts do not understand the causes of homosexuality. Family background, cultural environment, and even genetics are looked upon as key factors influencing the development of this condition. It is generally agreed that an adult homosexual will probably always be a homosexual. Since the number of hard-core homosexuals is estimated at more than 4 per cent of the male population, society cannot ignore their existence and should permit them to achieve a *modus vivendi.* At present a great many homosexuals live in fear—fear for their jobs or fear of blackmail, knowing that their vulnerability increases as they rise in their fields. The following case vividly illustrates the dangers that beset the career and peace of mind of the sexual deviate.

In early 1967 the New York City police and FBI agents broke up an extortion ring of 70 persons that had blackmailed over 700 homosexuals for a profit running into hundreds of thousands of dollars. According to the *New York Times:*

> The victims included men from the heights of eminence: two deans of Eastern universities, several professors, business executives, a motion picture actor, a television personality, a California physician, a general and an admiral, a member of Congress, a British theatrical producer and two well-known singers. Another victim, a high-ranking military officer, committed suicide the night before he was to testify to a New York County grand jury investigating the racket.
>
> All were shaken down by crooks posing as police officers after decoys from the ring got the victims into hotel rooms. In every case the extortionists made the same threat, to expose the homosexuals unless they paid up.

As a remedy for the plight of the homosexual, a number of organizations are endeavoring to make sexual acts between consenting adults an issue of morality not law. They point to the example of Great Britain, where, as a result of the Wolfenden Report, the sex law regards that which consenting adults do in private as a matter of private conscience rather than public law. Public solicitation, however, and sexual acts between minors still carry severe penalties. The American Law Institute has urged reform of the United States law along these lines, stating in its 1955 report that "no harm to the secular interests of the community is involved in atypical sexual practice in private between consenting partners." In 1967 The American Civil Liberties Union took a similar position, stating that "the right of privacy should extend to all private sexual conduct and should not be a matter for invoking the penal statutes." The policy statement added, however, that "the state has a legitimate interest in controlling, by criminal sanctions, public solicitation for sexual acts and, particularly, sexual practice where a minor is concerned."

The homosexual, too, argues that the abolition of sodomy laws would change his status from "that of covert criminal to open deviate, thereby putting the blackmailers out of business." Further, he believes that a change in policy regarding public employment of homosexuals would remove the major threat of the blackmailer and that as a result he would no longer be a security risk. "He would be different but trustworthy," they argue.

The argument, however, is unsound. A change of laws or regulations would have little effect on the point of view of society, and it is the attitude of society and not the law that determines the vulnerability of men in high position to extortion and blackmail. The homosexual's susceptibility as a security risk would be negligibly affected by a change of legislation. Moreover, in the absence of sodomy laws the police would still invoke nuisance and loitering statutes to control homosexuals as public attitude indicated.

Finally, it should be noted that the laws penalizing homosexual conduct are honored more in the breach than in practice. Although twenty-four states have sodomy statutes, the application of these laws is an unusual occurrence. Police attention is ordinarily directed toward the suppression of public solicitation and the molestation of minors. The homosexual's plight can hardly be attributed to police harassment or excessive zeal in specialized application of the law. It may more accurately be considered a reflection of public attitude, the ultimate determinant of public policy.

Those who hold the view that homosexual conduct is a matter of private conscience rather than of public law suffered a major setback with the 1986 Supreme Court decision, *Bowers v. Hardwick*. In upholding Georgia's sodomy statute by a 5-to-4 majority, the Supreme Court ruled that private homosexual conduct between consenting adults is not protected by the Constitution. The Court did not consider the issue of heterosexual sodomy in this decision. Up until 1961, all fifty states outlawed sodomy. By 1993, only twenty-four states, mostly in the more conservative southern and western regions, still had sodomy laws.

ADDITIONAL READING

Rape and Sexual Assault

Ageton, S.S.: *Sexual Assault among Adolescents.* Lexington, Mass.: Lexington Books, 1983.

Amir, M.: *Patterns in Forcible Rape.* Chicago, University of Chicago Press, 1971.

Bart, P.B. and O'Brien, P.H.: *Stopping Rape.* Elmsford, N.Y.: Pergamon Press, 1985.

Bessmer, S.: *The Laws of Rape.* Westport, Conn.: Praeger, 1984.

Blair, I.: *Investigating Rape: A New Approach for Police.* Wolfboro, N.H.: Longwood Publishing, 1985.

Bradway, W.C.: Stages of a Sexual Assault. 38 *Law and Order,* 9, 1990.

Burgess, A.W.(Ed.): *Rape and Sexual Assault: A Research Handbook.* New York, Garland, 1985.

Burgess, A.W., et al.: *Sexual Assault of Children and Adolescents.* Lexington, Mass.: Lexington Books, 1978.

Estrich, S.: *Real Rape.* Cambridge, Harvard University Press, 1987.

Eyman, J.S.: *How to Convict a Rapist.* Briarcliff Manor, N.Y.: Stein and Day, 1980.

Field, H.S. and Bienen, L.B.: *Jurors and Rape: A Study in Psychology and Law.* Lexington, Mass.: Lexington Books, 1980.

Finkelhor, D. and Yllo, K.: *License to Rape: Sexual Abuse of Wives.* New York, Free Press, 1987.

Green, W.M., M.D.: *Rape: The Evidential Examination and Management of the Adult Female Victim.* Lexington, Mass.: D.C. Heath, 1988.

Griffiths, G.L.: Psychological Factors: The Overlooked Factors in Rape Investigations. 54 *FBI Law Enforcement Bulletin,* 4, 1985.

Grispino, R.R.J.: Serological Evidence in Sexual Assault Investigations. 59 *FBI Law Enforcement Bulletin,* 10, 1990.

Groth, A.N.: *Men Who Rape: The Psychology of the Offender.* New York, Plenum, 1979.

Hazelwood, R.R.: The Behavior-Oriented Interview of Rape Victims: The Key to Profiling. 52 *FBI Law Enforcement Bulletin,* 9, 1983.

—— : The Criminal Sexual Sadist. 61 *FBI Law Enforcement Bulletin,* 2, 1992.

Hazelwood, R.R. and Burgess, A.W.: An Introduction to the Serial Rapist: Research by the FBI. 56 *FBI Law Enforcement Bulletin,* 9, 1987.

Hazelwood, R. and Burgess, A.W.(Eds.): *Practical Aspects of Rape Investigation: A Multidisciplinary Approach.* New York, Elsevier, 1987.

Hazelwood, R.R. and Warren, J.: The Criminal Behavior of the Serial Rapist. 59 *FBI Law Enforcement Bulletin,* 2, 1990.

Hazelwood, R.R. and Warren, J.: The Serial Rapist: His Characteristics and Victims. Parts I and II. 58 *FBI Law Enforcement Bulletin,* 1 and 2, 1989.

Hertica, M.A.: Interviewing Sex Offenders. 58 *Police Chief,* 2, 1991.

Lanning, K.V. and Hazelwood, R.R.: The Maligned Investigator of Criminal Sexuality. 57 *FBI Law Enforcement Bulletin,* 9, 1988.

Mills, J.K.: The Initial Interview of Sexual Assault Victims. 56 *Police Chief,* 4, 1989.

Morneau, R.H., Jr.: *Sex Crimes Investigation: A Major Case Approach.* Springfield, Ill.: Thomas, 1983.

Olson, D.T.: Rape: Understanding Motivations an Aid in Investigations. 37 *Law and Order,* 4, 1989.

Parrot, A. and Bechhofer, L. (Eds.): *Acquaintance Rape: The Hidden Crime.* Somerset, N.J.: John Wiley, 1991.

Stewart, G.D.: Sexual Assault Evidence Collection Procedures. 40 *Journal of Forensic Identification,* 69, 1990.

Other Sex Offenses

Alicea-Diaz, A.: Child Sexual Abuse: Investigative Problems. 57 *Police Chief,* 10, 1990.

Bierker, S.B.: *About Sexual Abuse.* Springfield, Ill.: Thomas, 1989.

Davidson, H.A.: Sexual Exploitation of Children: An Overview of Its Scope, Impact and Legal Ramifications. 53 *FBI Law Enforcement Bulletin,* 2, 1984.

Goldstein, S.L.: Investigating Child Sexual Exploitation: Law Enforcement's Role. 53 *FBI Law Enforcement Bulletin,* 1, 1984.

——: *Sexual Exploitation of Children: A Practical Guide to Assessment, Investigation and Intervention.* New York, Elsevier, 1986.

Goodwin, J.M.: *Sexual Abuse: Incest Victims and Their Families.* Littleton, Mass.: PSG Publishing, 1982.

Hertica, M.A.: Police Interviews of Sexually Abused Children. 56 *FBI Law Enforcement Bulletin,* 4, 1987.

Ingersoll, S.L. and Patton, S.O.: *Treating Perpetrators of Sexual Abuse.* Lexington, Mass.: D.C. Heath, 1990.

Holmes, R.M.: *The Sex Offender and the Criminal Justice System.* Springfield, Ill.: Thomas, 1983.

Lanning, K.V. and Burgess, A.W.: Child Pornography and Sex Rings. 53 *FBI Law Enforcement Bulletin,* 1, 1984.

Lanning, K.V.: *Child Molesters — A Behavioral Analysis — For Law Enforcement Officers Investigating Cases of Child Sexual Exploitation.* Washington, D.C.: National Center for Missing and Exploited Children, 1986.

Lester, D.: *Unusual Sexual Behavior: The Standard Deviations.* Springfield, Ill.: Thomas, 1976.

Macdonald, J.M.: *Indecent Exposure.* Springfield, Ill.: Thomas, 1973.

Parker, T.: *The Hidden World of Sex Offenders.* Indianapolis, Bobbs-Merrill, 1969.

Rosen, D.H.: *Lesbianism.* Springfield, Ill.: Thomas, 1974.

Schur, E.M.: *Crimes Without Victims: Deviant Behavior and Public Policy.* Englewood Cliffs, N.J.: Prentice-Hall, 1966.

Underwager, R. and Wakefield, H.C.: *The Real World of Child Interrogations.* Springfield, Ill.: Thomas, 1990.

Wakefield, H.C., Underwager, R., et al.: *Accusations of Child Sexual Abuse.* Springfield, Ill.: Thomas, 1988.

Chapter 20

LARCENY

I. LARCENY IN GENERAL

1. Definition

A PERSON who wrongfully takes, obtains, or withholds, by any means whatsoever, from the possession of the true owner or any other person, any money, personal property, or article of value of any kind is guilty of larceny if he intends to permanently deprive or defraud another person of the use and benefit of the property or to appropriate the same to his own use or the use of any person other than the true owner. If the intent is simply to temporarily deprive another person of the use or benefit (and so forth) the offense is sometimes called *wrongful appropriation.*

2. Elements

The elements of larceny and the points of proof which must be established by the investigator are the following:

a. That the accused wrongfully *took, obtained,* or *withheld* the property described in the specification.

b. The *ownership* of the property, i.e., that such property belonged to a certain person named or described.

c. The *value* of the property.

d. The *intent* to deprive.

3. Taking, Obtaining, or Withholding

Generally the taking is accomplished by the thief so that he can acquire actual possession of the property, but this specific action is not necessary. A person may take constructive possession by employing an agent or by other means. For example, a person may steal electrical energy by fraudulently adjusting the electric company's wiring so as to bypass the meter. He may steal an animal by enticing it through food to leave the owner's premises. He may have funds of another transferred to his own bank account. Examples of *withholding* are a failure to return, account for, or deliver property to its owner when a return, account, or delivery is due. Again, a person may devote property to a use not authorized by its owner. It should be noted, however, that a debtor is not guilty of larceny because he refuses to make payment to a creditor, since he is not withholding specific property.

4. Ownership

The taking must be from the possession of the true owner or any other person. Care, custody, management, or control are forms of possession. Unless an owner of the property can be found the charge of larceny cannot be supported. Ownership is commonly shown by a bill of sale or a record of continued possession. The following points should be noted in connection with ownership.

a. A *true owner* is a person who at the time of the taking had the superior right of possession, i.e., the organization as against the custodian of the funds or as against a member; the estate as against a trustee.

b. The term *"any other person"* refers to an owner of the property by virtue of his possession or right to possession, who is other than the one who takes the property.

c. A *general owner* is a person who has title of the property.

d. A *special owner* is a person who has not title but who has the care, control, custody, management or use of the property.

e. The word *person* includes a government, corporation, estate, and so forth.

5. False Pretense

Property can be larcenously obtained by a false representation of a fact. For example, a person can collect money by representing himself as an agent of some creditor. A person may misrepresent the extent of his funds in a bank and utter a check without intending to meet payment.

6. Intent

The intent to steal must be present to constitute larceny. This intent may exist at the time of the taking or may be formed afterward. For example, a person may drive off in a car with the intent to ride a short distance and return. After driving a while he may conceive the intent to keep the car. The intent must in most cases be inferred from the circumstances:

a. If a person takes property, hides it, and denies that he knows about the property, the intent to steal can be inferred.

b. Conversely, if he takes the property openly and returns it, his actions would tend to disprove intent.

c. A proof of subsequent sale of the property is strong evidence of intent to steal and can be introduced to support a charge of larceny.

d. A person may be guilty of larceny even though he intends to return the property ultimately, if his intent to return it is made to depend on some future condition or happening, such as an offered reward.

e. A person who pawns the property of another, intending to redeem it at a future date and return it to its owner, may be guilty of larceny.

f. Once a larceny is committed, a return of the property or a payment is no defense.

7. Value

The investigator must not only show that a thing of value was taken but he must be able to establish the approximate value of the item. This element is important also in establishing the degree of larceny and in fixing punishment. The general rule is that value in larceny is the local, legitimate market value on the date of the theft. The following points should be noted:

a. In thefts of government property serviceable items are

deemed to have values equivalent to the prices listed in official publications such as catalogues of the military services.

b. Market value may be established by proof of the recent purchase price paid for the article on the legitimate market. The testimony of a person who has ascertained the price of similar articles by adequate inquiry in the market will be accepted.

c. With certain kinds of property the value is clearly apparent and can be inferred by the court from its own experience. An automobile in fairly new condition or a collection of precious stones is known to the court to have a value in excess of five thousand dollars.

d. An owner may testify to market value if he is familiar with the quality and condition of the object.

8. Miscellaneous

Since the circumstances that surround a larceny can be infinitely varied, it is not possible to treat this offense comprehensively. The following are some of the more common questions that may arise:

a. **Finding Property.** A person finding property and taking it away with an intent to keep it is guilty of larceny, if there is a clue to the identity of the owner or if the owner may be traced by the character, location, or marking of the property.

b. **Theft of Several Articles.** If a number of articles are stolen at substantially the same time and place, a single larceny is charged even though the articles may belong to different persons. When several articles are stolen at the time and the accused is found in possession of some of the articles, this fact tends to show that he stole them all.

c. **Total Value of Separate Larcenies.** If several larcenies are committed at different times from different owners, the value of the stolen items cannot be summed up for the purpose of presenting a charge of grand larceny.

d. **Unexplained Possession.** The facts that the accused cannot explain possession of stolen property; that it has been in his possession since it was stolen; and that he had an opportunity to steal it are sufficient to support a larceny conviction. Possession of stolen property normally raises a presumption that the accused stole it.

e. **Flight.** The fact that the accused absconded at the time of the larceny is a circumstance tending to establish his guilt, but it is, by itself, not sufficient to support a conviction.

9. Motives

Obviously, the most common motive of larceny is economic gain. Kleptomania, an obsessive impulse to steal, is not uncommon. A person suffering from this mental peculiarity will usually have a long history of similar thefts and will not have any definite plan for converting the property to his own use. Revenge and malicious mischief are other motives of larceny. A person will sometimes steal solely for the purpose of exposing another to a serious inconvenience.

10. Investigative Procedure

The techniques to be employed in a particular case will be determined by the type of thief involved. The remainder of this chapter is devoted to a discussion of the different kinds of thieves and the *modus operandi* employed by each. As a general basis of procedure, however, the investigator will find it worthwhile to record the following data in the initial states of the inquiry. Many of the suggestions can be disregarded in minor or uncomplicated cases.

a. Date and hour of the theft. If this is unknown the period between the time when the stolen object was last seen and the discovery of the theft should be established.

b. A complete list and description of the missing property. If there are several witnesses who can offer this information, it should be obtained independently from each as a means of checking.

c. The location of the property immediately prior to the larceny; other places in which the property had been previously located; places searched for the property.

d. Reasons for placing the property in the location described above. The investigator should reflect on the logic of placing the property in this location. Safeguards employed or the absence of safeguards where logically indicated.

e. Identity of person who first discovered the loss. How did it come to his attention? Was he the logical person to make the discovery? Who should have ordinarily made the discovery? Other witnesses to the discovery.

f. A list of persons who knew the location of the property.

g. A list of persons who knew of the existence of the property.

h. A list of persons who had access to the property.

i. Movements of persons having access prior and subsequent to the loss in cases where the time interval is reasonably short.

j. List of absentees in commercial establishments.

k. Ownership of the property: true owner, person having possession at the time of theft, person responsible for the property.

l. Proof of ownership, custody, or responsibility.

m. Estimated value of the property. Bills of sale. Where documentary evidence is absent, the approximate date of purchase and the identity of the vendor.

n. Suspects named by the owner or others. Reasons for their suspicions. Employees exhibiting unusual behavior within the last month.

o. Suspects in financial straits, faced with future money problems, or maintaining a standard of living inconsistent with their incomes.

p. Reconstruction of the larceny; *modus operandi* of the thief; means of access; selection of time; method of concealing the larceny; in larceny by false pretenses, the conversations and transactions which took place between the perpetrator and the victim or other parties.

q. Character of property; saleability; uses; convertibility.

r. List of possible markets for the property.

s. Interrogation of each suspect: activities prior and subsequent to the larceny; time at which he last saw the property; time at which he was last near the location of the property; persons who can verify his alibi; financial circumstances; present indebtedness; contemplated investments or purchases; relations with the owner.

t. Records: previous larceny complaints made by the victim; history of periodic or systematic thefts; employees with police records; background of suspects.

u. Interviews of building employees, and others who may have observed persons approaching the area containing the property at unusual times or in a peculiar manner. Complete physical descriptions of any suspects developed in this manner.

v. Physical evidence such as latent fingerprints, shoe prints, articles of clothing, or similar traces left at the scene.

II. AUTOMOBILE LARCENY

11. Automobile Thefts

Approximately one million automobiles are stolen in the United States each year. Many of these stolen cars are recovered because a high percentage of auto thefts are perpetrated for temporary use rather than for resale. However, in urban areas where professional car thieves operate, less than half are recovered. To combat auto theft activity special measures have been adopted for its prevention and trained groups of investigators are assigned to the problem. The annual monetary loss from the larceny of cars is so great that insurance companies have established the National Auto Theft Bureau to assist local law enforcement agencies in the recovery of cars and the apprehension of the criminals. Another agency set up for the same general purpose is the recently established Federal Interagency Committee on Auto Theft Prevention. Large municipal police departments have organized Auto Squads or Auto Theft Details to counteract this criminal trend. These squads consist of detectives who have received special training in the methods of operation of automobile thieves and who have an intimate knowledge of the identity of known auto thieves and the organization of their gangs. Every state has a special law relating to larceny of automobiles. These laws are not uniform; at present, there appears to be no immediate possibility of the enactment of a uniform law. Section 408 of Title 18, U. S. Code, provides for the punishment of persons who transport in interstate or foreign commerce a stolen motor vehicle, knowing it to have been stolen. In addition, this law relates to the receiving, storing, selling, or disposing of such a motor vehicle, knowing it to have been stolen. These offenses are investigated by the FBI. In considering the larceny of automobiles, a distinction should be made between wrongful appropriation and true larceny. A large number of thefts of automobiles are temporary appropriations. Vehicles in this category are frequently recovered. Obviously there are two distinct classes of auto theft.

a. **Temporary Appropriation.** Many cases of automobile larceny fall in this category. The motive is temporary use. The car is stolen, remains missing for a few days, and is abandoned. Later, it is observed for a period of days unattended in the street. A resident of the neighborhood or the patrolman assigned to the post makes the report. The license is checked against the registrations of vehicles reported stolen and the auto is returned to its owner. The following are the more common types of this offense.

1) *Juveniles and Joy Riders.* The most serious aspect of auto theft is represented by the statistics relating to the age of the typical offender. Many auto thefts are committed by juveniles—in 1991, 44 percent of the persons arrested for auto theft were under eighteen years of age and 62 percent were under twenty-one. In addition, auto theft is a common statistical starting point of a criminal career—in an FBI sample of juvenile auto theft offenders 41 per cent had no previous arrest record. A substantial contribution to crime prevention can be made by adults by removing the ignition key and otherwise securing their unattended automobiles.

2) *Professional Criminals.* In perpetrating a "big job" (usually robbery) the professional criminal is faced with the problem of obtaining transportation and at the same time avoiding the danger of exposing a license plate as a clue. The obvious solution to this problem is to steal a car, use it in the commission of the crime, and abandon it in an unpopulated neighborhood. The larceny is committed as near as practicable to the time of perpetration of the major crime in order to avoid the danger of a pickup by local police through teletype or radio transmission of the license plate. In planning a robbery, the criminals arrange to use the stolen car at the scene of the crime, drive to a secluded spot,

and then switch to their own car. Since the stolen car is readily recovered, the investigator is concerned with the major crime rather than the car theft.

3) *False Report by Owner.* Occasionally the owner will falsely report the theft of his vehicle in order to cover up a serious accident. While driving he may have injured a pedestrian and left the scene without stopping. On reflection he becomes aware of the seriousness of a hit-and-run charge and of the probability that a witness may be able to recognize the car. He then forms the plan of simulating a car theft. He may damage the car door or side window in order to give the appearance of a forced entry. He then abandons the car and proceeds to report the "theft" to the police. Naturally the investigator should be suspicious of any "theft" where the recovered car shows signs of an accident. An inquiry should be made into all hit-and-run cases which took place during the pertinent period in order to determine whether the vehicle reported stolen is implicated.

b. **Professional Automobile Thieves.** The true automobile thief steals a car so that he can profit by its sale. Subsequently the car may be resold as a unit or stripped for the sale of its parts. Frequently the thief belongs to a well-organized group that is set up to steal cars, disguise them, obtain fraudulent registration, and sell them in a prepared market.

1) *Stealing the Car.* The actual work of stealing a vehicle is carried out by a professional within the space of a few minutes. The following are representative steps in the operation:

a) TARGETING. The thief selects a car on a street where he thinks he can work for a short time without drawing attention.

b) OPENING THE DOOR. In the absence of a key the problem of the locked door is attacked through the window by means of a *snake*, a sharp-bladed tool that is passed between the top of the window and the rubber insulation to catch the lock button and raise it.

c) THE IGNITION CYLINDER. With the door open the thief may jump the ignition behind the dash or under the hood by means of a set of alligator clips. The more professional approach uses one of the following methods:

i. Master Keys. Although it is time-consuming, the thief may use a set of keys, one of which is sure to work for any given line of cars.

ii. Code Cutter. This is a punch device for cutting blank keys according to a car's ignition code number.

iii. "Slapper." This is a tool (also known as the "slam hammer") originally designed to pull dents out of auto bodies. It can be adapted to pulling out the ignition cylinder in three or four good whacks. The thief then slips in a standard replacement cylinder (a "deadlock"), which is equipped with keys.

d) Steering Column. With the advent of locking devices on steering columns, the simple breaking into a car and jumping the wires to drive it off has become rare. Auto thieves now use long, thin saws that can be inserted into the steering column to break the lock. After this operation the ignition lock is managed by one of the methods previously described.

e) Towing Away. Some thieves employ the simple method of using a tow truck to take the car away. Still others employ vans and cranes to lift the auto from the ground, place it into a truck, and drive off.

f) Copying the Key. Another common procedure of auto thieves is to establish a connection at a car wash, parking garage, or restaurant with a parking service and then make copies of the keys of selected cars, noting down their tag numbers. Later, after locating the car on the street, the thief uses his stolen copy of the key to drive off.

g) Neutralizing Alarms. Although the professional thief would rather steal a car without an alarm system, he is prepared to neutralize the standard systems if necessary with a special key to turn them off or by cutting the right wire or bypassing them with a pair of alligator clips. Most alarm systems and locks can be neutralized by so innocent-appearing a mechanism as a tow truck.

2) *Disguising the Car.* Automobiles can be identified by means of the Vehicle Identification Number (VIN). A visible VIN will be found on a plate on top of the dash for police inspection. A hidden VIN is stamped on a part of the car which varies from model to model and which is changed each year. The auto industry has entrusted the looseleaf binder filled with VIN location diagrams from each manufacturer only to the FBI and the private National Auto Theft Bureau, rather than to local or state police

departments. The NATB owes its privileged status to the International Association of Chiefs of Police, which has designated NATB as the national clearing house for stolen cars and as a source of expert witnesses to answer auto-identification questions. The professional car thieves will locate VIN stampings on new cars by buying a Cadillac, for example, and removing the body to examine the chassis. Car theft rings in the United States buy or steal the latest models as soon as they appear and make a microscopic examination of the auto frames to find the hidden VINs. Knowing the locations, the car thieves can quickly have the true numbers abraded and new ones inscribed. Often the dies which are used to punch in the new numbers are defective and a recovered car can be linked to a set of tools. About a third of the cars stolen are renumbered and usually repainted for resale.

3) *Fraudulent Registration.* The car-theft organization must provide apparently legitimate papers for the stolen vehicle, if they wish to sell it. To accomplish this a study is made of the various state laws and regulations controlling registration and transfer of ownership. For example, the thieves are aware that most states have a "certificate-of-title" law and that it is less difficult to transfer stolen cars in the others. A certificate of title is a history of the car's ownership. A New York registration stub, however, may be used to transfer a car with no more information about the owner than his name. The thief can alter the information on a faded and tattered but bona fide stub to fit a car he wishes to sell.

4) *Market.* The outlet chosen by the car thief for his merchandise will depend on the thief's specialty and his *modus operandi.* The following are some of the usual outlets:

a) "CAR CLOUTS" and "BOOSTERS" are persons who steal parts and property out of cars. Articles such as hub caps, CB units, or tape decks will be brought to second-hand dealers.

b) SALEABLE PARTS. A car can be cut up into parts for sale within a few hours after it is stolen. The operation is highly professional. A short time after the vehicle is stolen it disappears into a well-equipped junkyard where a team of specialists or "cutters" proceeds to cut off the saleable parts and destroy the remainder.

c) SELLING "TO ORDER". Professionals who steal and sell to order are the most skillful and systematic of all. In one scheme they recruit car wreckers who will sell them the identification plates and registration papers of late-model wrecks. They then repaint stolen cars to match the wrecks in all but color.

d) EXPORT. In recent years an export market for stolen cars has been developed in places such as Mexico, Puerto Rico, Brazil, and the Dominican Republic.

12. Automobile Fraud

A variety of frauds, many of them connected with insurance, are practiced by car thieves. It will be noted that a number of these schemes require for their success an elaborate organization, sometimes extending over several states. The following are representative of frauds that have come to the attention of law enforcement agencies:

1) *Insuring a Wreck.* This is sometimes called the phantom car fraud. The perpetrator first buys a late model, completely wrecked car from a salvage yard. At the same time he will obtain a title and the vehicle identification number. With this identification he will register and insure the car without even taking possession of the vehicle. Several months later he will report his "car" as stolen. By that time what was once a car will have disappeared as scrap. Under state law, however, the insurance policyholder must receive the market replacement value of the car. Thus the policyholder makes a profit on the insurance and the salvage dealer receives payment for a car that did not exist.

2) *Duplicating from Salvage.* In this operation the thieves buy a wrecked car to obtain the identification papers that go with it. Subsequently they steal an identical car in good condition. The stolen car is then taken apart and the parts put back together again on the frame of the wrecked car. They have now duplicated the car for which they have legal papers and can sell it.

3) *Stripping the Car.* The perpetrator of this fraud strips his car to the frame, stores the parts, and dumps the skeleton in a lot. After reporting the car to the police as stolen, he subsequently informs them anonymously of the location of the frame. The insurance company pays for the loss of the car.

4) *The "Erector Set" Fraud.* As a continuation of the previous fraud, the owner will buy the frame from the insurance company for a few hundred dollars and take it to the garage for reassembly with the dismantled parts.

5) *Changing the VIN.* After the theft of a car, the VIN is abraded and a new number is impressed with a set of steel stamps. The numbers are changed also on other parts, such as air-conditioners, which manufacturers have lately been stamping with identification numbers. Ostensibly, the vehicle is now a new car. Papers are obtained for it, often from another state. After a series of fabricated transactions, the car is put up for sale with an apparently genuine pedigree.

6) *Odometer Rollback Scheme.* The object of this fraud is to disguise a heavily used automobile so that it can be sold at the higher price of an almost-new vehicle. An automobile dealer buys a one- or two-year-old rental vehicle with a polished appearance but with a high-mileage reading. He replaces the mats, the brake pedals, the tires and any other parts that show wear. The dealer then hires a mechanic called a "clocker" to turn back the odometer gauge. Using tools such as a pick, a screwdriver, and wires, a professional "clocker" can adjust the mileage indicator in a matter of minutes. Either the title to the car is altered by an artist or calligrapher to reflect the new mileage, or a new title with the changed mileage is obtained through a series of out-of-state transactions. The car is then sold by the dealer directly from his lot or, more commonly, through one of the many automobile auction houses. There are laws that prohibit tampering with odometers. In 1972, Congress passed the Motor Vehicle Information and Cost Saving Act which made it a federal violation to disconnect, reset or replace an odometer for the purpose of disguising a vehicle's true mileage.

13. Indications of a Stolen Automobile

The investigator sometimes encounters an automobile which is not listed in the alarms or notifications as stolen but which arouses his suspicions in connection with its ownership. Certain indications are helpful in confirming or dispelling these suspicions:

a. **Tags.** Automobile license plates are changed every five or ten years depending upon the state. New tags found on a used car in the middle of tag period are suspicious. The auto thief sometimes buys new tags for a stolen vehicle for the purpose of registering the car in the name under which it is to be sold. The tag bolts should be examined for rust and other signs of age. New bolts with an old tag suggest that the tag was stolen. In estimating the time when the bolts were placed on, it should be remembered that bolts will usually show signs of rust after a month's exposure.

b. **Registration.** Recent registration of a used car indicates the possibility of preparation for the sale of a stolen car, since lawful owners do not ordinarily re-register a car prior to selling.

c. **Bill of Sale.** A notarization on a bill of sale for a used car is suspicious since, in most cases of used cars, the bill of sale is not notarized.

d. **Keys.** Are the keys original factory keys or are they duplicates? A duplicate key will ordinarily be imprinted with some identifying data such as a small number or the name of the locksmith.

e. **Vent Glass.** In stealing a car the thief frequently forces open the vent window or breaks it. The vent area should be examined for tool marks and the vent glass should be studied to determine whether it is a replacement. Vent glass which is original equipment will ordinarily have a trademark in the lower corner. On the replacement glass the open edge will be found rough as compared with the corresponding surface of factory glass.

f. **Ignition.** Is there evidence of tampering with the ignition switch? Among the signs of such tampering are the following: Coil wire stripped of insulation near the points where it enters the coil; a new switch with wire taped in the area of previous stripping; and the presence of extraneous wires.

14. Prevention

It is difficult to defeat a determined professional car thief. If his heart is set on a particular car, the experienced thief will find some way of entering it or, as a last resort, he may tow the car away or remove it bodily into a van. The car owner can, however, improve his chances for continued possession by adopting sound security habits with respect to ignition keys, safeguarding of registration, and strategic parking. In addition, a growing industry of car-theft prevention has made available a wide range of devices for further security, e.g., burglar-alarm systems, some of which lock the hood and cut off the ignition; horn and light flashers; mercury switches; gas-line cutoffs; four-digit ignition switches; and locks that join the gas pedal and steering wheel. The list is endless; the devices actually delay or discourage the thief but in the end the owner is left with the sobering reflection that what man can devise the thief can bypass.

In the past decade auto manufacturers have assisted greatly in this problem by developing and installing devices that significantly increase the difficulty of car theft. These include less accessible ignition system locations, increasing the number of ignition key combinations, and making the ignition system connector cable more difficult to remove from the ignition lock. Recently the auto industry introduced a combination ignition, transmission, and steering column lock on all new cars. It far surpassed the security of the old locks which could be easily defeated by *hotwiring,* i.e., crossing ignition wires in back of the dash or under the hood.

15. Bicycle Theft

a. **The Problem.** The nationwide rise in the popularity of bicycle riding has been accompanied by an equal rise in the incidence of bicycle stealing. The increase is attributed to two factors: 1) The popularity of bicycling in many parts of the country has produced both a market and a supply for the thieves.

2) The value of bicycles has increased greatly. The problem has changed from a situation of "a few kids stealing bikes" to one where organized groups sweep through the city, fill a truck with stolen bikes and take them to a factory where they are sandblasted to remove the paint and serial numbers and then repainted and sent out to be sold as new bikes. Some 10-speed models cost as much as $500 and can be sold by thieves for as much as $200.

b. **Prevention.** The need for special enforcement efforts has become apparent during the last ten years. Pittsburgh, New Orleans, Chicago, and Dade County, for example, have instituted mandatory bicycle registration programs. There is, however, a growing demand in some states for a computerized master registration system for all bicycles sold in the state to permit a rapid check of the ownership of a questionable bicycle.

c. **Investigation.** The method of investigating bicycle thefts will vary with the nature of the case. A single, casual theft is best handled by the patrol force. Where it appears that a ring of bicycle thieves is involved, a full-scale investigation is required.

1) *Description.* The investigator should obtain the necessary information on the make, model, year of purchase, cost of the bicycle, and most important of all, the serial numbers. The color of the paint, the nature of the accessories, any marks of personal identification, defects, and marks of damage are additional data to be recorded.

2) *The Factory.* In the investigation of an organized group of bicycle thieves the investigator should endeavor to locate the factory where the processing takes place. Since this can become a fairly big operation—one group, operating in central California was processing 100 bicycles a week—floor space, equipment, and materials are required. Precinct business files should be examined and the assistance of members of the patrol force should be enlisted to determine the character of any suspected business operations which could lend themselves to this work. Automobile body shops are an example of a business which can be diverted to bicycle conversion work. Sources of materials such as quality enamel paints should be explored. Consultation with bicycle manufacturers may prove useful in ascertaining the nature of the equipment and the types of paint that would be used on the bicycles.

3) *Field Investigation.* The patrol force is best suited to the field investigation of smaller operations. Bicycle riders should be questioned concerning ownership. This procedure is, of course, much simpler in cities which require registration of bicycles or encourage property registration with the police. Places where bicycles are sold should receive police attention. Sometimes stolen bicycles show up in bicycle stores. More commonly they are sold to bargain hunters on the street, in parks, or in flea markets.

III. PICKPOCKETS

16. Pickpockets

The pickpocket is a species of criminal indigenous to large cities. An urban population with its many places of congregation and its crowded transportation systems provides unending opportunity for the pickpocket. This type of criminal is, however, restricted in number because of the great skill that is required for successful operation. Moreover, his skill in itself is a handicap because it endows him with a reputation and thereby makes him known to the police. In the criminal argot, he is known as a "cannon." There are numerous other slang terms employed in this branch of crime which will not be used here since, despite their picturesqueness, they belong to a dying dialect. In the age of the checkbook and the credit card the pickpocket is becoming less common. Few of the younger generation have either the patience or the professional pride to devote years to an apprenticeship in this demanding art.

a. **Operational Techniques.** The equipment and preparation of the pickpocket are of extreme simplicity. Given a crowd of moderate dimensions, he can ply his trade with his bare hands. He may work alone or with one or more confederates. The purpose served by the confederates is that of distracting the attention of the victim. The element of *modus operandi* is of great importance in detecting pickpockets. Most pickpockets employ the same technique throughout their criminal careers. In studying the methods described below, the investigator should make the assumption that the pickpocket is a person of great skill. Some of these techniques may be seen on the stage. The performer, while talking to his voluntary victim, can remove his suspenders, belt, or watch without the victim's knowledge. The techniques of the professional magician are employed by the pickpocket. Distraction of the victim's attention and swiftness of operation are the most important elements of the pickpocket's success. A pickpocket is known by his style. His designation is derived from the clothing area in which he operates.

1) ***Fob Worker.*** Although the pickpocket who takes money

from the fob pocket is fast disappearing along with the type of garment from which his name was derived, he is worth discussing because his equivalent, the operator who works in the front of the victim, is still current. This operator is held in low esteem by his professional colleagues. His method consists in abstracting money from the most accessible place—the fob pocket. Usually he gathers only small change. The fob worker is usually also a tailpit worker, i.e., he steals from the side pocket of a man or woman's jacket. The fob worker is ordinarily an old man who, through hebetude or age, has lost his nerve or his touch. He employs a handkerchief or "wipe" to cover his operations. The "wipe" serves also to hide the coins. On observing an approaching detective, the fob worker will raise the handkerchief to his mouth and, if necessary, swallow the coins. Since many of these criminals have five or six felonies in their records, they fear an additional conviction for grand larceny, which would, in some states, be constituted by the taking of so little as twenty-five cents from the person of another.

2) *Inside Worker.* This is a more advanced operator. Considerable skill is required to remove a wallet from the inside pocket of a man's coat. To cover his operations, an inside worker usually employs a "stiff," i.e., a newspaper which he places against the victim. Very few pickpockets resort to inside work.

3) *Pants Pocket Workers.* The pickpocket who operates in the trousers is considered the cleverest of this class of thief. A highly developed skill is necessary to abstract a wallet from a man's side pocket without his knowledge. The pants pocket worker uses only two fingers—the index and middle finger—to perform this operation. Sometimes this type of worker employs as many as two assistants. One of the assistants—the "stall"—distracts the victim by jostling him and excusing himself. A newspaper may be employed in these motions. The other assistant receives the wallet in a quick pass from the operator. The "mechanic" or "tool" performs the actual picking of the pocket. The whole operation is accomplished with the dispatch and precision of a football play. As the victim boards a subway train or other vehicle, the "stall" will fall or push against him from the front and mutter regrets or muffled curses. Simultaneously, the "mechanic" will have lifted the "poke" or wallet from the victim and passed it to his assistant.

If the victim feels the operation and turns suspiciously, the pickpocket will run away. Since he no longer has possession of the "poke," his apprehension is of little avail for police purposes, for there can be no case unless the money is found in his possession. The person who receives the "poke" remains in the same position to avoid arousing suspicion. This person is usually a man without a previous conviction. Thus, he will at most receive a suspended sentence under the current court customs.

4) *The Lush Worker.* Probably the lowest form of pickpocket is the criminal who steals from a drunk or a sleeping passenger in a train. Lush workers operate in trains, buses, street cars, waiting rooms, and parks. They observe a prospective victim who is apparently sleeping or unconscious. Sometimes they test their victim by gently kicking his foot as they pass by. If the victim does not react, the lush worker proceeds to take his money and other valuables.

5) *Bag Stealers.* A woman's handbag suspended from her arm is an inviting target for the petty thief. In crowded areas such as department stores or trains, the thief may remove the bag or its contents without attracting attention. There are several forms of this theft. The *bag opener* surreptitiously opens the bag suspended from the woman's arm and then removes the change purse or wallet. The *bag clipper* cuts the strap by which the bag is suspended, removes the wallet, and throws the bag away. The *bag snatcher* jerks the bag away from the woman's grasp.

b. **Apprehending the Pickpocket.** If the pickpocket is a professional, he will undoubtedly have a record. The crime can then be solved by means of the *modus operandi.* The techniques of pickpockets are well known. The detective can restrict the number of suspects by paying close attention to the victim's story. By consulting the known pickpocket file and showing photographs to the victim, he may be able to obtain a preliminary identification. The difficulties of finding a lush worker are much greater. Where the lush worker confines his activities to a certain neighborhood or a particular transportation line, the outlook is somewhat brighter. The great weakness of the lush worker is his tendency to take such valuables as fountain pens and watches. Strong proof of his guilt is provided if he is apprehended with these in his possession. The apprehension of pickpockets is considered specialized work in large cities. Some police departments have pickpocket squads or details consisting of a few detectives who are well acquainted with the appearance and habits of known pickpockets. These detectives are assigned to subways, railroad and bus terminals, and racetracks. In a city such as New York, the transit police are assigned to the task of apprehending lush workers.

IV. MISCELLANEOUS THIEVES

17. Miscellaneous Thieves

a. **Automobile Baggage Thieves.** This form of theft, though little publicized, accounts for larceny losses amounting to hundreds of thousands of dollars each year in a large city. The thieves usually operate in pairs and work in the hotel section of the city. Visitors to the city, frequenting the hotels, theaters, and restaurants in the area, often park their cars with clothing and suitcases in the rear seat part of the vehicle. One of the pair of thieves acts as a lookout and also serves as a shield. This part is sometimes played by a woman to lend a natural air to the proceedings. The other member opens the car or breaks into it by means of the vent glass. The clothing and baggage, usually valued at several hundred dollars, are removed and the thieves walk away with the loot. If the thieves wish to perform their work rapidly, they break the glass and push the handle down. To prevent any noise of the shattering, they may first fix a sheet of flypaper over the windows. The apprehension of this type of thief is best accomplished by means of a plainsclothesman plant. A casual patrol of an area may reveal suspicious activity on the part of two persons. Discreet surveillance from a distance will enable the plainclothesman to observe the actual theft. A panel truck equipped for viewing from within is useful.

b. **Package Thieves.** There are a number of forms of package thievery. All of them can be classed as minor operations. The success of these thieves depends upon the carelessness of the agent in guarding or delivering the property. Since the theft is a minor one, it does not warrant extensive investigation. It will suffice to periodically caution merchants and their associations of the prevalence of this form of crime and to instruct them in precautionary measures. The following are some of the techniques employed by the package thief:

1) *Fraudulent Receiving.* The thief acquires knowledge of the identity of the consigned. He places himself at the entrance of the consignee's residence or place of business. When the delivery boy approaches, he advances to meet him and chides him on his tardiness thereby convincing the delivery boy that he is the consignee. He takes the package, signs the receipt, and sends the boy on his way. Some thieves employ a confederate to learn the address of the consignee by striking up a conversation with the delivery boy. In a variation of this type of offense, the thief telephones an order to the company in the name of an old customer and waits outside of the address.

2) *Packages from Vehicles.* Deliverymen tend to be careless in the protection of their vehicle while they bring the package from the vehicle into the building occupied by the consignee. Often they leave the ignition key in the vehicle. A pair of thieves will study the habits of the driver along his route. Waiting until the driver enters a building, they hop into the vehicle and drive away. Another type of thief simply steals a package from the unattended vehicle. The thieves may drive up in their own vehicle and transfer the merchandise.

3) *Sidewalk Thieves.* Parcel post packages left on top of a full mailbox; packages left by express deliverers in front of the building; garments hanging on small trucks in front of factories; and similar unattended property may be observed in the business streets of a larger city. Opportunities such as these are quickly noted and exploited by the "small-time" package thief.

4) *Senders.* The delivery boy is accosted and requested to carry a message to a fictitious person while the thief guards his package. The boy is rewarded with two dollars for his service. This type of thief is rapidly becoming extinct, partially because the old-fashioned delivery is also rapidly disappearing. Occasionally, this petty trick is perpetrated on a boy carrying a musical instrument.

c. **Dishonest Employees.** The systematic larceny of merchandise by collusion of dishonest employees can result in serious losses. Prevention of this type of theft is accomplished by careful background investigations of applicants prior to employment. Detection of the thieves usually is the result of intelligent surveillance. Undercover work or roping by an investigator posing as an employee will ordinarily yield results in the space of a few weeks. The following techniques may be used by the criminal:

1) *Checkers and Order Clerks.* By arranging for the shipment of merchandise in excess of the actual order these thieves can transfer a considerable amount of property before the loss is discovered.

2) *Drivers.* The truckman leaves the unattended vehicle in the street with the ignition key in the lock. His confederates steal the truck while he is making a telephone call or eating in a restaurant.

3) *Express Loaders.* Express companies frequently report losses of merchandise apparently delivered in a regular manner. In one form of this type of larceny the loader changes the address on the carton and the driver delivers the package to the loader's confederate unwittingly. The investigation should center around the fact that a knowledge of the truck routes is necessary for the success of the operation. Spot checking the loaded merchandise may reveal the existence of an altered or obliterated address on a package.

4) *Waterfront Pilferage.* In the past the losses through thefts attributable to dock workers, longshoremen, and other waterfront workers have been estimated in the millions. The unloading of a ship involves the transfer of property of enormous value. A conspiracy to systematically divert such property into the hands of thieves can result in overwhelming losses. This form of larceny can be so great in magnitude and so intricate in the details of its accomplishment that the subject cannot be treated in this limited space. Waterfront pilferage, moreover, is usually a racket centrally managed by criminals who also directly control the hiring of waterfront personnel. The investigation of this offense must be undertaken by a fairly large squad of detectives. In the New York area a Waterfront Commission was established for this purpose.

Surveillance and undercover work are required. It is not suffi
cient to apprehend one or two workers in the act of diverting
merchandise. The investigation should lead to the discovery of
the drops, fences, and bosses.

d) **Sneak Thieves.** The term *sneak theft* is used to include a
number of forms of petty larceny involving unattended property.

1) *Baggage Thieves.* Travelers in railroad and bus terminals frequently have occasion to place their baggage down while
they attend to some business such as purchasing a ticket. The
baggage thief takes advantage of the unguarded moment, swiftly
picks up the bags and walks calmly away. The detection or apprehension of this type of thief is ordinarily the responsibility of the
railroad police.

2) *Shoplifters.* Department stores annually suffer considerable losses from the operation of store thieves. Female shoplifters
are in the majority since their presence in a store is more likely to
pass unnoticed. The techniques employed by shoplifters are many
and varied. The department stores usually have their own methods
and even their own detective personnel for dealing with this
problem. Larger department stores have a definite policy in dealing with the apprehended store thief. The possibility of a suit for
false arrest is often present and, therefore, special measures are
taken to obviate such a danger. The kleptomaniac, or person who
suffers from a psychological disturbance impelling him to steal,
sometimes finds a convenient area of activity in shoplifting. The
shoplifter working in collusion with a dishonest employee presents
another obstacle to retail security. The emergence of well-organized
rings composed of trained full-time shoplifters has added an
element of dedicated professionalism to this offense. The major
problems with respect to shoplifting, however, are its rapidly
increasing incidence and the fact that the majority of offenders are
teenagers.

e. **Pennyweighting.** One or two thieves engage a jeweler in a
discussion of a prospective sale. The jeweler's goods are displayed.
In the course of the discussion, the attention of the jeweler is
drawn away from the goods, and false, imitation jewelry is substituted for it. The operation must be "cased" and planned so that a
reasonably similar substitute can be acquired.

f. **Hotel Thieves.** This type of thief steals jewelry, furs, or money from hotel rooms. He sometimes works in collusion with bellboys or hotel clerks who advise him concerning the guests' property and habits. Entrance to the room may be achieved without the cooperation of the hotel employees in the following ways: stealing the key from the desk; obtaining a duplicate key by previous rental of the room; skeleton keys; picking the lock; forcing the lock with a piece of celluloid or similar material. Hotel thievery in the past decade has grown to great proportions. The owners of hotels are often reluctant to install effective locks or lock systems. Recently, however, a number of hotels in New York, where the problem is most severe, have begun to take advantage of modern technology to protect their residents. At a cost of more than $1 million the Americana installed a computerized system designed to protect guests against burglars. After the guest unlocks his door with his regular key, he has about thirty seconds to insert a special card into a box on his television set; otherwise a light flashes on a console summoning a security man. The Algonquin Hotel spent about $200 a room to replace its keys with a computerized system that uses individually programmed cards to unlock doors. When a guest checks out, the electronic combination is changed. Other hotels are expected to follow the Algonquin lead.

g. **Credit Card Thieves.** For a number of years the fraudulent use of stolen or lost credit cards was a source of worry to credit men and financial officers throughout the nation. The thief, after acquiring the credit card by taking one from an unguarded counter or by stealing a wallet or pocketbook, would apply it to making a great number of small purchases from stores or in a series of larger purchases at widely separated places. Unless checked in time, the thief could acquire a sizeable amount of goods, services, and money.

Remedial measures have been devised to discourage the use of stolen or lost credit cards by rapidly transmitting the appropriate information to those authorized to grant credit. Countertop data processing units have been introduced into the retailing industry and in service stations and airline reservation desks to link up with computers storing the required information. A clerk can now punch the numbers of a credit card into the unit and receive a rapid response regarding the current status of an account, charge plate, or credit card.

The larceny involved in credit-card loss does not represent a serious law enforcement problem, since the corrective measures of stricter controls of distribution and use lie well within the resources and administrative capabilities of the businesses concerned. Clearly the profits resulting from this freedom of distribution of credit cards and permissiveness in their use more than compensate for any losses, and the expense of introducing stricter controls would not be offset by the amounts of the larcenies prevented. Moreover, as the credit-card system becomes permanently embedded among our purchasing habits, businesses will not be reluctant to consider losses incident to their misuse a part of their overhead, warranting an appropriate adjustment of prices. There are, however, those who would look upon this degree of permissiveness and resilience in business policy as an implicit subsidy of larcenous conduct.

V. CONFIDENCE GAMES

18. Confidence Games—Swindles

The obvious reader interest in the subject of "con" men or swindlers is an open invitation to an author to dwell extensively on this aspect of criminal activity. It is difficult to touch even lightly on this topic without allotting to it a space in the crime world far out of proportion to the small number of people who practice professionally the art of swindling. We must, of course, omit from our discussion a number of aspects of this crime, since swindling is defined in general as the art of obtaining money or property from another by fraud or deceit. Such a definition would readily lead us into embezzlement, stock manipulation, and other high level commercial operations that depend for their effectiveness on a background of a stable and substantial business structure. Our concern is chiefly with confidence games, and this type of fraud is a short-term operation that is equivalent to a one-night stand in business. The distinguishing characteristic of most confidence games is the fact that the victim is knowingly engaging in a dishonest act. It is in the very act of perpetrating a larger fraud upon another that the victim is himself defrauded.

a. **The Spanish Prisoner.** The Spanish (or Mexican) prisoner is a mail fraud which depends for its success on the victim's romantic view of life in the Latin countries. The victim receives a letter requesting money to obtain the freedom of the sender, who claims to be falsely imprisoned. In return, the sender promises on his release to share a hidden treasure with the victim. After sending the money the victim hears no more from the prisoner.

b. **The Sir Francis Drake Swindle.** The victim receives a letter or a visitor informing him of the pleasant discovery that he is one of the descendants of Sir Francis Drake and as such is entitled to a share in the fortune left by that famous adventurer. Since the estate is not completely settled, a certain sum will be required for litigation. The victim agrees to put up the money. A few months later, he is informed that the court proceedings will be more protracted than first estimated. An additional sum is requested. The mulcting continues until the victim is exhausted in either finances or credulity. In the 1910s this swindle was practiced throughout the midwest with extraordinary success. In common faith, the victims banded together to form a Sir Francis Drake Club to advance their interests in the estate and even to support the defense of the swindler against the government's prosecution. Needless to say the swindle is still practiced today with success.

c. **The Money-Making Machine.** The victim is shown a machine which will literally make money for him. The con man demonstrates its efficiency by showing the production of several bills. The machine is then sold to the victim at an appropriate price. The money-making machine may appear in different forms, either as small as a cigar box or as large as a peanut roaster. As recently as 1966, money-making machines were being sold in this country.

d. **Stock Swindles.** The sale of worthless stocks in Canada oil wells, for example, is still a staple of the swindler. According to the Better Business Bureau, approximately one million dollars is lost each week through frauds of this kind.

e. **Wallet Dropper (Dropping the Leather).** This is another "short con" played by two men, A and B. The victim, V, is walking peacefully along the street when A walks past him rapidly and drops a wallet. Before V can reach down to pick it up, B comes from behind and seizes it. Since the wallet contains no means of identification, B pretends to recognize V's claim to a share and agrees to divide the contents. A is now well out of calling distance. The wallet contains a few small bills and a counterfeit one-hundred dollar bill. If V can change the bill, B will walk away with the fifty dollars leaving the wallet to V. When V cannot produce the change, B consents to settle for security in the form of money or jewelry. He leaves the wallet in V's possession and agrees to meet him tomorrow to arrange a proper division.

f. **The Smack Game.** This is a small con game which is worked by two men, the roper and the insideman. The roper develops a chance acquaintance with the victim at a railroad station or a bar. The insideman accidentally encounters the two men and joins their company on some pretext. The roper suggests that they match coins for drinks or for cigars. Money bets are finally suggested. The game is played by tossing coins in the air. The odd coin is the winner. While the insideman is absent for a few moments, the roper, feigning a dislike for the insideman, suggests to the victim that they arrange to fleece the third player. The scheme is described in which the roper will always call opposite to the victim. Thus, if the victim calls "heads" the roper will call "tails." In this way they continue to always have one or the other winning the play. They agree to divide the spoils later. The scheme, of course, is highly successful. The bets mount until a substantial sum has changed hands. The insideman manages to lose all the large bets to the roper, who thus acquires a considerable amount of the victim's money. When the insideman finally concedes defeat, the roper and the victim walk off together. At this the insideman expresses vehemently the suspicion that he has been fleeced by professional sharpers. He threatens to call the police unless they show evidence of the absence of conspiracy by departing in different directions. The roper suggests to the victim that he will meet him later at a designated point to divide the money. Naturally, there is no later meeting and the victim is left to meditate upon his experience.

VI. EMBEZZLEMENT

19. Embezzlement

A study of the penal law of a state will reveal the fact that the crimes of larceny and fraud occupy many more pages than the serious offenses of murder and robbery. The obvious reason for this is the ingenuity of the criminal in devising new schemes of illegally obtaining money. In the present treatment these forms of theft, frauds, and cheats have been placed under the general heading of "larceny," since they are all methods of depriving an owner of his property against his will. The difference between the various forms of larceny lies ordinarily in the title or type of ownership or custody which the criminal enjoys at the time of the offense. Since only the most important of these "white-collar crimes" can be touched upon in this text, an effort is made to stress the general principles which govern investigations of this type so that the reader can extend the application of appropriate techniques to other forms of larceny. Certainly one of the most lucrative and popular of the "white-collar crimes" is embezzlement, the fraudulent appropriation of money or goods by a person to whom they are intrusted. It is an obvious crime in the sense that it is committed by a person confronted with a combination of opportunity and temptation. The motivation is simple — profit. Beyond the immediate prompting of a desire for profit are the proximate motives of financial straits and a desire for power. It is the crime of the unfaithful steward, a larceny possible only in an office of trust.

a. **Statistics.** Since the offense of embezzlement involves no violence, does not affect the person of another, and is committed at the expense of a fairly wealthy organization, no great odium attaches to the criminal. The embezzler is simply dishonest in the least disreputable sense of the word. The terms "clever" and "master mind" are applied to his "defalcations" by newspaper reports. The embezzler's deeds are sometimes recounted with ill-concealed admiration as though he were a Robin Hood of the land of file cabinets and computing machines. It is little known that several thousand embezzlers are arrested each year and that the loss from this crime amounts to millions of dollars annually.

To a considerable degree the financial damage is absorbed by surety companies and is reflected in the adjustments of fidelity bond insurance. In 1975, an estimated 189 million dollars was lost by banks alone through embezzlement, more than five times the amount lost through bank robbery during that same period. The tolerance of society toward the embezzler is reflected in the comparison of sentencing patterns for both crimes—91 percent of those convicted of bank robbery serve time in jail, compared with only 17 percent of those convicted of embezzlement of bank funds.

b. *Modus Operandi.* The methods employed by the embezzler depend upon the nature of the transactions over which he has control in the performance of his duties. In the banking business the employee may have control of the recording of accounts and may manipulate several accounts so that the loss cannot be detected except by a complete audit. The criminal has a thorough understanding of the financial operations of the organization. In some instances, where the criminal is the firm's accountant or bookkeeper, he may be the only person in the organization with a comprehensive knowledge of the working of the company's finances. His criminal operations may take place over a period of months or years. In a typical case a bank cashier was found to have been embezzling over a period of eighteen years.

c. **Investigation.** An inquiry into a charge of embezzlement often requires the services of an accountant. The investigator who does not possess such a knowledge should avail himself of the services of an experienced accountant who is not an employee of the company. Before proceeding with the case it is well for the investigator to ascertain the company's policy in these matters. Many companies do not choose to prefer charges against the dishonest employee. Their policy is to avoid unfavorable publicity by simply discharging the guilty person. If it is the intention of the company to press charges, the investigator should carefully note the documentary evidence which will be needed to substantiate the charges. Photographs of the documents can be made as the case progresses. These photographs will aid in the preparation of the case until the records are formally offered in evidence.

d. **Discovery of the Loss.** The first notice of the defalcation may be in one of many ways:

1) *Disappearance.* The embezzler may suddenly flee his surroundings. He will leave town and take up residence in another city. The disappearance of an employee entrusted with large sums of money gives rise to natural suspicions. In a famous New York case a bank official left the city with over $400,000. The discovery of the loss was made after his departure. After spending a few days in Florida he voluntarily surrendered.

2) *Inspection.* The annual audit of the company's records may reveal the loss. In some cases the embezzler devises covering methods which will withstand the scrutiny of the auditors.

3) *Information.* If the criminal is not clever and particularly if he is quite young, a sudden display of prosperity will arouse the suspicions of neighbors or friends. Jealousy may motivate them to notify the company or bank of their suspicions. Rival employees, an abandoned wife, a trusted consort, or disgruntled accomplices are other likely sources of information.

4) *Accident.* Some unusual circumstance of business operations may require a review of certain accounts. In such a situation another employee may stumble over the irregularity.

e. **Establishing the Loss.** Before taking any serious action with respect to any suspect, the investigator should first satisfy himself that a crime has in fact been committed. To this end he should have an accountant examine the "books" and make a record of the financial irregularities.

f. **Suspects.** The number of suspects is usually quite small. The guilty person must first have access to the funds and the accounts. Often there is only one logical suspect. In more complicated cases the investigator may have to conduct background investigations. The following points should be noted.

1) *Office Behavior.* Was there anything unusual in the behavior of the suspect during office hours? Did he appear nervous or worried? Did he take his annual vacation at the regular time? In some forms of embezzlement the criminal may not risk a day's absence for fear of detection.

2) *Living Habits.* Does the suspect live within his means? Who are his associates? Does he drink? Frequent night clubs? Are his social aspirations inconsistent with his income? A discreet neighborhood check will reveal this information.

3) *Financial Status and Credit.* Is the suspect solvent? What is the extent of his debts? What is the state of his bank account? Does he keep a number of accounts? Do these accounts show great activity even though the total value is not large? Does he have accounts in other states? Does he have a safe deposit box? Credit investigating agencies can assist in this phase of the investigation.

g. **Checklist.** The following points should receive special attention.

1) The relation of trust and confidence should be proved.

2) It must be shown that property was entrusted to the accused as agent, bailee, or trustee to keep for the owner or to treat in accordance with the owner's instructions.

3) The property was received by the accused.

4) The property is accurately described.

5) A fraudulent intent was formed.

6) The property was appropriated by the accused for some use other than that intended by the owner. The fraudulent intent and appropriation are often established by one or more of the following facts:

7) The disposition made of the property or money such as deposits in a bank.

8) Failure to perform the assigned duty relating to the property.

9) Failing to return the property after a demand for the return was made subsequent to the dereliction of duty.

10) Denial of having received the property.

11) False entries in documents or ledgers recording the transaction.

VII. THE CRIMINAL RECEIVER

20. Receiving Stolen Property

A larceny investigation will often branch out into a case of receiving stolen property. On locating stolen property the investigator should exercise great care in conducting the search and exhaustively interviewing the criminal receiver, the thieves, and other persons. The elements of receiving stolen property are described below together with the usual methods of proof. It should be noted that this crime is difficult to prove and consequently all the suggested avenues of approach should be explored. The evidence in cases of this nature is largely circumstantial. The accused usually hides behind a legitimate business front and the testimony of the thieves is looked upon with skepticism by the jury. The activities of the receiver should be investigated in minute detail. His responses under extensive questioning should be checked carefully for discrepancies as to detail.

a. **The property was stolen.** The testimony of the thieves will prove this element. Since the thieves are not considered accomplices to this offense, they may be induced to give a statement as to the stolen character of the property.

b. **The property was received by the accused.** Again, the thieves can offer testimony to this fact. Proof is also offered by the fact that the property was found in the possession of the accused. If the room wherein the property is found is occupied only by the criminal receiver, no difficulty exists. If there is more than one occupant, each must be interviewed to eliminate all but the guilty. The investigator should endeavor to develop additional evidence such as the fact that the stolen goods were located in immediate association with other property of the accused or the accused was observed in physical possession of the property.

c. **The receiver knew that the property was stolen.** Testimony that the thieves informed the receiver of the theft would prove this fact indirectly. Other evidence includes the absurdly low purchase price; the fact that the person from whom it was received could not have been the legitimate owner; and the fact that it was not bought from a responsible person or from an established business concern.

d. **The accused had the intent to convert the property to his own use.** Evidence should be obtained of any effort to dispose of the property. During the search particular attention should be given to any arrangements for concealment of the stolen goods.

21. "Operation Sting"

A new approach to the apprehension of burglars and their associates was initiated with the establishment of "Operation Sting," a method whereby the police, posing as fences, would buy the stolen property from the burglars. In conjunction with and financed in part by the Justice Department's Law Enforcement Assistance Administration, forty-seven such operations were set up in thirty-five cities during the last three years.

Typically the strategy called for undercover detectives to rent stores and warehouses in neighborhoods where burglaries and street thefts were common and pass themselves off as prospective buyers of stolen goods. The building would be refitted to meet the requirements for surveillance, communications, and safety. An appropriate "front" would be devised in the form of a small cleaning business or trucking operation. About six officers were required to man the operation. One officer dealt with the sellers of stolen property. Another, hidden from view, operated surveillance equipment. Other surveillance officers were stationed in a building across the street from the store to record license plates, make other observations, and provide additional protection.

The site of the fencing operation was selected with a view to accessible parking and inconvenience with respect to public transportation to induce the sellers to use their cars. Transactions were videotaped and clean-surfaced objects were available for accidental fingerprints from handling. Negotiations were managed so that the seller would find it convenient to leave the phone number of a location where he could be reached. In the course of casual conversation the client would sometimes be led to reveal the identity of other fences or the general nature and approximate date of the burglary offense.

The effectiveness of "Operation Sting" is difficult to evaluate. As a strictly business enterprise the venture in New York City ("Operation Fence") cost about $800,000 in police salaries (at eight sites) and another $345,000 for equipment and "buy money." It is estimated, however, that a "gross" of $8.3 million in recovered property was achieved, ranging from stolen government checks (purchased for 10 cents on the dollar) to brand new automobiles

($250 apiece). Also recovered were two original bronze statues by
Frederic Remington, valued at $100,000.

Some of the police aspects of the operation were favorable.
About 480 persons were arrested for illegal possession of stolen
goods, including a man reputed to be the biggest underworld
fence in Queens. Most of them pleaded guilty on being shown the
videotapes of their selling stolen goods to the undercover officers.
The arrests were made after the operation had been closed down.

VIII. LOAN SHARKING

22. Introduction

Loan sharking is the lending of money at exorbitant rates of
interest. A fuller definition would include the threat of violence
that is later brought to bear on the debtor in the event he defaults.
The victim, of course, is a person in serious financial straits. The
loan shark himself is usually an underworld character. The importance of loan sharking lies in the fact that it is considered one
of the largest sources of revenue in organized crime. (Gambling is
the largest.)

Although loan sharking is ordinarily a violation of the laws
relating to usury and extortion, it is placed in this chapter partly
for convenience, partly because a loss of money is involved, and
partly because of its kinship with confidence games in that the
victim of the offense is also a victim of his own self-deception in
money matters. The typical victim, short of credit and collateral
and attempting to discharge a heavy, short-term money obligation,
undertakes another and more formidable financial burden.

23. The Offenders

As a highly lucrative branch of organized crime, loan sharking
is controlled by well-organized units, each divided into about four
levels of operating personnel and headed by a chief or boss.

a. **The Boss Loan Shark.** At the top of a unit is the "boss loan
shark," a high-ranking man in a well-organized crime group.

Although he may also be the head of a legitimate business (such as the underworld-owned First National Service and Discount Corporation in New York) as an avocation, his loan sharking operation is conducted without any established headquarters and without the bookmaker's corps of runners or banks of telephones. Since he seldom carries less than $5,000 on his person, he is not susceptible to a vagrancy charge. An Assistant District Attorney of New York has testified: "We have known a loan shark who lent a million dollars in the morning and another million in the afternoon." One boss loan shark is known to have turned a half-million dollars into 7.5 million dollars in about five years. In Manhattan alone there are at least ten men comparable to him.

b. **Organization.** There are about four levels of operation in the organization of a big loan shark.

1) *At the top level* is the boss loan shark himself, providing the financing and the overall supervision. For example, at the beginning of the year he will distribute a million dollars among his ten lieutenants with the simple instruction: "I don't care what *you* get for it, but *I* want one percent per week."

2) *Second Level.* Each of the ten lieutenants must now farm out $100,000 among his subordinates with similar instructions, requiring however, 1.5 to 2 percent interest per week.

3) *Third Level.* Each of the lieutenants may have about thirty subordinates who may themselves do the lending, if the loan is large enough, or may farm out the money in turn to their own subordinates for lending. Again the interest requirement will be raised.

4) *Fourth Level.* Most of the actual operations are conducted at this level, which may consist of working bookmakers and street-corner hoodlums. The interest rate at this level is usually 5 percent of the principal per week and may be higher. This interest is known in the business as "vigorish."

c. **Operation.** The basic operation of loan sharking has already been outlined: a pyramid of distributors or lenders, at each (descending) level of which a higher interest rate is used so that ultimately the customer is being charged 260 cents per dollar per year, and ultimately, at the top, the million dollars outlay by the boss loan shark should show a half-million dollars in profit at the end of the year. The two objectives of the operation are the acquisition of money and the acquiring of legitimate businesses. The means by which they are achieved may be summed up by the word "enforcement," a term covering the truly criminal aspect of loan sharking, namely, extortion.

24. "Enforcement"

Since a successful business must be based on a sound policy, calculated to yield predictable results, loan sharking has developed a reliable procedure for dealing with the critical matter of default.

a. **"Lender Makes the Rules."** The arbitrary manner in which the loan shark determines the rules is illustrated by a case which began with a $6,000 loan to a businessman. The borrower made three payments and then missed two. As a penalty, the loan shark declared that the debt was now $12,000, with the 5 percent interest per week now on this larger sum. Again, the businessman failed to pay and the declared principal was increased to $17,000. Finally, the debt had grown to $25,000 and the debtor was called to account. The loan shark declared himself a half-partner in the victim's business. Now he was to collect half of the business profits *and* the weekly payments on the old loan. Eventually the situation became hopeless and the loan shark issued his final declaration: "You forget about the business and we'll forget about the loan. It is now all mine."

b. **"The Sit Down."** When it appears that the victim is in serious trouble and can no longer meet the payments, a "sit down" is called. This is a meeting presided over by a recognized underworld chief and called to decide what lump sum the loan and the accumulated vigorish can be settled for. It is a court from which there is no appeal. As an example, we may consider the case of an optical company whose chief executive received a loan of $22,000 with interest payable at $1,100 per week. Later another $6,500 was lent, and the total interest payments became $1,425 per week, without diminishing the amount owed. Soon the executive was convinced that he couldn't maintain the payments. Although he had already paid $25,000 in interest, he still owed the entire principal of the loan, $28,500 and was still faced with the prospect of continuing the interest payment of $1,425 per week. A "sit down" was called, with Chief Frank Eboli presiding. It was ruled that Don Ferraro should take over the optical company and operate its plant. In a few months the company had been looted of its assets and driven into bankruptcy.

c. **Sanctions.** Failure to meet payments is met with grave disapproval and followed usually by the imposition of severe sanctions. Depending on the nature of the case and especially on the victim's assets, a decision is made,—unilaterally, as we have seen—and a penalty imposed which may take the form of assault, murder, or expropriation of the customer's property.

1) *Assault and Murder.* Depending on the amount of his indebtedness, the defaulter may be punished by a beating or by killing. The underworld-owned First National Service and Discount Corporation employed two "enforcers" for this purpose, Anthony Scala, "The Leg Breaker," and Anthony (Junior) Franco. A victim who had borrowed $11,600 unable to meet his payments for a number of weeks found that he now owed $16,898, with diminishing prospects of meeting future payments. He was subsequently found murdered.

2) *Appropriation of Property.* If the victim still possesses business assets, the presiding chief at the "sit down" frequently rules that the loan shark should take over the property in discharge of the indebtedness. In this way the loan shark can become an invisible partner, if not the outright owner, of a legitimate business. Using this procedure, members of the underworld have acquired a controlling interest in nightclubs, optical stores, brick companies, and even Wall Street brokerage houses and banks.

3) *Exploitation of Services.* It may be decided that the services of the victim can be made to compensate for his debt. Thus, in the case of a well-known sports announcer who could no longer meet his payments it was decided that, because of his reputation and wide range of acquaintances, he would prove valuable as a "steerer." When the sports announcer would come in contact with persons in financial difficulty, he would recommend the services of a friend who liked to lend money. The friend, of course, would be the loan shark.

25. The Victim

An interesting aspect of loan sharking is the character of the victim. One would suspect that a person agreeing to take on a hard obligation to pay 5 percent interest per week for an unpredictable term must be short of business acumen and bereft of any vestige of prudence. Actually, the victim is typically a man of common sense and experience, and not infrequently he is intelligent and well educated. In fact, substantial business and professional men appear to be the preferred victims of the loan shark. The Marcus Case of 1968 was not atypical. James Marcus, New York City's Commissioner of Water Supply, Gas and Electricity, was an intelligent, experienced person who, finding himself in financial difficulties, had resorted to the loan shark and found himself a few months later in deeper financial trouble. He also discovered that when he was in trouble with the loan shark he was in trouble with the underworld. Subsequently, he was accused of accepting an alleged bribe of $40,000 on a city contract worth $840,000 for the cleaning and repair of a reservoir. Like other victims, swept up by the pressures of the moment and the optimism of the sudden, solitary hope afforded by the loan shark, he had committed himself irrevocably to a spiraling financial obligation.

26. Investigation

Loan sharking is a difficult crime to investigate because it is a personal transaction to which there may be no witnesses other than the principals. Some loans are negotiated under circumstances which the victim is reluctant to reveal. For example, gambling losses are a common source of the financial difficulties we have spoken of. There is usually a loan shark at a floating crap game. In fact, the people who run the game may be more interested in the loan sharking than in the gambling. One of the gamblers in the dice game may run short of money. He feels that another $500 would enable him to recoup and accordingly applies to the loan shark in the corner of the room. Since the loan shark knows his customer—indeed, he may have already checked his credit ratings—he lends him the $500. If the gambler wins, he returns $600 for the $500 he has just borrowed. If he loses the money, he will have to come up with $600 within twenty-four hours. In the victim's mind the circumstances of such a loan preclude the confidence of the police.

a. *Evidence.* Even though the victim does talk to the police, there is little evidence beyond his uncorroborated statements. Occasionally (as in the case described in the next section) the enforcers make the mistake of telephoning their threats and intentions, and the investigators may obtain more convincing evidence. A search of the loan shark or of the place where he is thought to keep his records is ordinarily not fruitful. Even when the records are seized, they are usually found to be too meager or too cryptic to serve as evidence. In one case, a search yielded a typical record sheet bearing a list of sums ranging from $13,000 to $43,000, after which were placed a set of initials to represent the client. Sometimes mnemonic devices or substitute names are used, but even if the real names are used, the records do not constitute adequate supporting evidence.

b. *Undercover Men.* The use of an undercover man is probably the best, if not the only, solution to the problem of proof in loan shark cases as it is in many other criminal activities of organized crime. The harvest reaped from the activities of Herbert Itkin, a Manhattan labor lawyer who for six years served as an undercover agent for the FBI, is impressive proof of the effectiveness of a well-placed informer. From his testimony in the 1968 federal bribery conspiracy trial known as the Marcus Case it appeared that Itkin infiltrated the world of organized crime in 1962 and faithfully mapped it for the FBI until "his cover was blown" with the arrest of his friend Marcus. By the time Itkin left the witness box, his disclosures as the Government's star witness had implicated a number of people in corrupt and criminal schemes including persons reputed to be well-known members of the underworld.

27. Remedial Measures

Because of the formidable difficulties encountered in obtaining evidence against loan sharks as compared with the obvious effectiveness of employing undercover agents such as Itkin, the latter appears to be the logical course for law enforcement. There is, however, a peculiar reluctance on the part of law enforcement officials to approach the problems of loan sharking and other aspects of organized crime in this manner. In part this reluctance can be attributed to the unfavorable reaction of the public to the use of undercover men and informers, with its European connotation of police spies prepared to extend their surveillance over other citizens. Part of it, too, is caused by the difficulty involved in recruiting satisfactory agents, since the unfavorable reception given by the public to their work and the patent dangers of such employment are not offset by any great personal reward. Another remedy proposed for the control of loan sharks is the passage of special legislation. In most states, however, the legislation would appear to be adequate. In New York, as in many other states, there are laws to control usury. All states have statutes covering extortion and conspiracy. At present, then, it would appear that the best remedy would be a program of education of the prospective victims (through the general public) in the methods of the loan shark and the dangers inherent in such borrowing. In particular, potential victims should be encouraged to enlist the cooperation of the police if they find themselves the subjects of threats and extortion. The importance of this step was seen in the recent case of a defaulter who, after receiving a number of threatening telephone calls, went to the local detective squad. While he was explaining his situation to the detectives, the "enforcers" called his wife to tell her that they would be there that night to break her husband's arms and legs. This, of course, was a poor tactic on the part of the criminals, since the investigators and the state police arranged to be present when the enforcers appeared at the door, repeating their threats and demanding payment. They were arrested for assault and extortion. The victim was not molested further — again, a matter of good business policy: why bother with a victim under police surveillance when the city is filled with customers ready to pay 5 percent per week?

ADDITIONAL READING

Larceny

Albrecht, W.S., et al.: *How to Detect and Prevent Business Fraud.* Englewood Cliffs, N.J.: Prentice-Hall, 1982.

Aylesworth, G.N. and Swan, M.: Telecommunications Fraud Devices. 56 *FBI Law Enforcement Bulletin,* 9, 1987.

Bailey, L.L.: Medicaid Fraud. 60 *FBI Law Enforcement Bulletin.* 7, 1991.

Chadd, G.L.: Retail Theft Investigation: Embezzlement, Falsely Reported as an Armed Robbery. 39 *Law and Order,* 4, 1991.

Dubé, D.M.: Bank Employee Embezzlement. 60 *FBI Law Enforcement Bulletin,* 4, 1991.

Fennelly, L.J.: *Museum, Archive, and Library Security.* Stoneham, Mass.: Butterworth, 1983.

Gates, D.F. and Martin, W.E.: Art Theft—A Need for Specialization. 57 *Police Chief,* 3, 1990.

Glick, R.G. and Newsom, R.S.: *Fraud Investigation.* Springfield, Ill.: Thomas, 1974.

Hollinger, R.C. and Clark, J.P.: *Theft by Employees.* Lexington, Mass.: Lexington Books, 1983.

Keeley, M.P. and Gannon, J.J.: Sneak Thefts. 58 *FBI Law Enforcement Bulletin,* 12, 1989.

Keogh, J.E.: *The Small Business Security Handbook.* Englewood Cliffs, N.J.: Prentice-Hall, 1981.

Nemeth, C.P.: *Private Security and the Law.* Cincinnati, Anderson, 1989.

Pratt, L.: *Bank Frauds,* 2nd ed. New York, Free Press, 1975.

Rudnitsky, C.P. and Wolff, L.M.: *How to Fight Industrial Larceny and Pilferage.* Babylon, N.Y.: Pilot Books, 1975.

Seger, K.A. and Icove, D.J.: Power Theft: The Silent Crime. 57 *FBI Law Enforcement Bulletin,* 3, 1988.

Siljander, R.P.: *Introduction to Business and Industrial Security and Loss Control.* Springfield, Ill.: Thomas, 1991.

Smith, J.C.: *The Law of Theft,* 6th ed. Stoneham, Mass.: Butterworth, 1989.

Timm, H.W. and Christian, K.E.: *Introduction to Private Security.* Pacific Grove, Calif.: Brooks/Cole, 1991.

Weber, T.L.: *Alarm Systems and Theft Prevention.* Stoneham, Mass.: Butterworth, 1985.

Yeager, W.B.: *Techniques of the Professional Pickpocket.* Port Townsend, Wash.: Loompanics, 1990.

Automobile Theft

Beekman, M.E. and Daly, M.R.: Motor Vehicle Theft Investigations: Emerging International Trends. 59 *FBI Law Enforcement Bulletin,* 9, 1990.

Beekman, M.E.: Automobile Insurance Fraud Pays . . . and Pays Well. 55 *FBI Law Enforcement Bulletin,* 3, 1986.

Brickell, D. and Cole, L.S.: *Vehicle Theft Investigation.* Santa Cruz, Calif.: Davis Pub., 1975.

Chilimedos, R.S.: *Auto Theft Investigation.* Los Angeles, Legal Book Corp., 1971.

Clede, B.: Lo-Jack. 36 *Law and Order,* 10, 1988.

Colombell, W.E.: Examination of Vehicle Identification Numbers. 46 *FBI Law Enforcement Bulletin,* 6, 1977.

Cook, C.W.: *The Automobile Theft Investigator.* Springfield, Ill.: Thomas, 1986.

Frazier, S.F.: A Comprehensive Approach to Auto Theft. 35 *Law and Order,* 2, 1987.

Gifford, J.D.: *The Automotive Security System Design Handbook.* Blue Ridge Summit, Pa.: TAB Books, 1985.

National Automobile Theft Bureau Passenger Vehicle Identification Manual, 64th annual ed. Palos Hills, Ill.: NATB, 1993.

Nilson, D.W.: Vehicle Recovery: New Technology Captures Chicago's Attention. 38 *Law and Order,* 2, 1990.

Poplinger, C.A.: VINSLEUTH: Outsmarting the VIN Changers. 53 *Police Chief,* 5, 1986.

Rapp, B.: *Vehicle Theft Investigation: A Complete Handbook.* Port Townsend, Wash.: Loompanics, 1989.

Ratledge, M.W.: *Hot Cars! An Inside Look at the Auto Theft Industry.* Boulder, Col.: Paladin Press, 1982.

Scripture, J.E., JR.: Odometer Rollback Schemes. 59 *FBI Law Enforcement Bulletin,* 8, 1990.

Stern, G.M.: Effective Strategies to Minimize Auto Thefts and Break-Ins. 38 *Law and Order,* 7, 1990.

Shoplifting

Baumer, T.L. and Rosenbaum, D.P.: *Combating Retail Theft: Programs and Strategies.* Stoneham, Mass.: Butterworth, 1984.

Brindy, J.: *Shoplifting: A Manual for Store Detectives,* rev. ed. Matteson, Ill.: Cavalier, 1975.

Curtis, B.: *Retail Security: Controlling Loss for Profit.* Stoneham, Mass.: Butterworth, 1983.

Farrell, K.L. and Ferrara, J.A.: *Shoplifting: The Antishoplifting Guidebook.* Westport, Conn.: Praeger, 1985.

Murphy, D.J.I.: *Customers and Thieves.* Brookfield, Vt.: Gower, 1986.

Rapp, B.: *Shoplifting and Employee Theft Investigation.* Port Townsend, Wash.: Loompanics, 1989.

Sklar, S.L.: *Shoplifting: What You Need to Know about the Law.* New York, Fairchild, 1981.

Credit Card Theft

Credit Cards: Distributing Fraud Loss. 77 *Yale Law Journal,* 1418, 1968.

Dodge, R.L.: Credit Card Fraud Investigation. 8 *Security World,* 24, 1971.

Lipson, M.: Crime and the Credit Card. Parts I and II. 39 *FBI Law Enforcement Bulletin,* 6 and 7, 1970.

Paul, P.: Credit Cards. 32 *International Criminal Police Review,* 307, 1977.

Rapp, B.: *Credit Card Fraud.* Port Townsend, Wash.: Loompanics, 1991.

Confidence Games

Bell, J.B. and Barton, W.: *Cheating and Deception.* New Brunswick, N.J.: Transaction Publishers, 1991.

Blum, R.H.: *Deceivers and Deceived.* Springfield, Ill.: Thomas, 1972.

Hancock, R. with Chetz, H.: *The Compleat Swindler.* New York, Macmillan, 1968.

Heintzman, R.J.: Confidence Schemes and Con Games: Old Games with New Players. 55 *FBI Law Enforcement Bulletin,* 6, 1986.

Henderson, M.A.: *How Con Games Work.* Secaucus, N.J.: Citadel Press, 1986.

Maurer, D.W.: *The American Confidence Man.* Springfield, Ill.: Thomas, 1974.

Rosefsky, R.S.: *Frauds, Swindles and Rackets.* Chicago, Follett, 1973.

Santoro, V.: *Frauds, Rip-Offs and Con Games.* Port Townsend, Wash.: Loompanics, 1988.

——: *The Rip-Off Book: The Complete Guide to Frauds, Con Games, Swindles, and Rackets.* Port Townsend, Wash.: Loompanics, 1984.

Smith, L.E. and Walstad, B.A.: *STING SHIFT: The Street-Smart Cop's Handbook of Cons and Swindles.* Littleton, Col.: Street-Smart Communications, 1989.

Criminal Receiving

Cappell, D. and Walsh, M.: "No Questions Asked": A Consideration of the Crime of Criminal Receiving. 20 *Crime and Delinquency,* 157, 1974.

French, M.P.: Is a Sting Feasible for Your Agency? 57 *Police Chief,* 4, 1990.

Klockers, C.B.: *The Professional Fence.* New York, Free Press, 1975.

Klose, K., Lewis, A.B. and Shaffer, R.: *Surprise! Surprise! How the Lawmen Conned the Thieves.* New York, Viking, 1978.

Langworthy, R.H. and LeBeau, J.L.: Spatial Evolution of a Sting Clientele. 20 *Journal of Criminal Justice,* 2, 1992.

Law Enforcement Assistance Administration. *Strategies for Combatting the Criminal Receiver.* Washington, D.C.: U.S. Government Printing Office, 1976.

McGuire, M.V. and Walsh, M.E.: *The Identification and Recovery of Stolen Property Using Automated Information Systems: An Investigator's Handbook.* Washington, D.C.: U.S. Government Printing Office, 1981.

Nielsen, S.C.: The Small Agency and Sting Operations. 35 *Law and Order,* 6, 1987.

Raub, R.A.: Effects of Antifencing Operations on Encouraging Crime. 9 *Criminal Justice Review* 78, 1984.

Sharp, A.G.: Stings are not Just for Large Departments. 38 *Law and Order,* 5, 1990.

Steffensmeier, D.J.: *The Fence: In the Shadow of Two Worlds.* Totowa, N.J.: Rowman and Littlefield, 1986.

Trainum, J., Brown, N., and Smith, R., Jr.: ROP-ing in Fences. 60 *FBI Law Enforcement Bulletin,* 6, 1991.

Walsh, M.E.: *The Fence: A New Look at the World of Property Theft.* Westport, Conn.: Greenwood Press, 1976.

Weiner, K.A., Stephens, C.K. and Besachuk, D.L.: Making Inroads Into Property Crime: An Analysis of the Detroit Anti-Fencing Program. 11 *Journal of Police Science and Administration,* 311, 1983.

Computer Crime

Arkin, S.S., et al.: *Prevention and Prosecution of Computer and High Technology Crime.* Albany, N.Y.: Mathew Bender, 1989.

Bequai, A.: *How to Prevent Computer Crime.* New York, Wiley, 1983.

——: Technocrimes—The Computerization of Crime and Terrorism. Lexington, Mass.: Heath, 1987.

Burger, R.: *Computer Viruses and Data Protection.* Port Townsend, Wash.: Loompanics, 1991.

Conly, C.H.: *Organizing for Computer Crime Investigation and Prosecution.* Washington, D.C.: National Institute of Justice, 1989.

Cook, W.J.: Thefts of Computer Software. 58 *FBI Law Enforcement Bulletin,* 12, 1989.

Coutourie, L.: The Computer Criminal: An Investigative Assessment. 58 *FBI Law Enforcement Bulletin,* 9, 1989.

Harry, M.: *The Computer Underground: Hacking, Piracy, Phreaking, and Computer Crime.* Port Townsend, Wash.: Loompanics, 1985.

Lobel, J.: *Foiling the System Breakers: Computer Security and Access Control.* New York, McGraw-Hill, 1986.

McAfee, J. and Hayes, C.: *Computer Viruses, Worms, Data Diddlers, Killer Programs, and Other Threats To Your System: What They Are, How They Work, and How to Defend Your PC, Mac or Mainframe.* Port Townsend, Wash.: Loompanics, 1989.

McEwen, J.T.: *Dedicated Computer Crime Units.* Washington, D.C.: National Institute of Justice, 1989.

Mehnert, G.: *Computer Searches and Seizures: A Primer for Law Enforcement.* 36 *Law and Order,* 11, 1988.

Moulton, R.T.: *Computer Security Handbook: Strategies and Techniques for Preventing Data Loss or Theft.* Englewood Cliffs, N.J.: Prentice-Hall, 1986.

Schweitzer, J.A.: *Computer Crime and Business Information.* New York, Elsevier, 1986.

Sessions, W.S.: Computer Crimes: An Escalating Crime Trend. 60 *FBI Law Enforcement Bulletin,* 2, 1991.

Tien, J.M., Rich, T.F. and Cahn, M.F.: *Electronic Transfer System Fraud: Computer Crime.* Washington, D.C.: U.S. Department of Justice, 1986.

Organized Crime

Abadinsky, H.: *Organized Crime,* 3rd ed. Chicago, Nelson-Hall, 1990.

Albanese, J.: *Organized Crime in America,* 2nd ed. Cincinnati, Anderson, 1989.

Herbert, D.L. and Tritt, H.: *Corporations of Corruption: A Systematic Study of Organized Crime.* Springfield, Ill.: Thomas, 1984.

Keene, L.L.: Asian Organized Crime. 58 *FBI Law Enforcement Bulletin,* 10, 1989.

North, D.V.: RICO: A Theory of Investigations. 55 *Police Chief,* 1, 1988.

Pace, D.F. and Styles, J.C.: *Organized Crime: Concepts and Control,* 2nd ed. Englewood Cliffs, N.J.: Prentice-Hall, 1983.

Chapter 21

BURGLARY

1. Importance of Burglary

BURGLARY IS CONSIDERED by many to be the most important form of theft. The frequency, expense, and difficulty of controlling this crime place great demands on law enforcement personnel. Moreover, a burglary is usually the average citizen's only contact with crime, and hence, as a taxpayer, he demands attention. The importance of the burglary problem is recognized, too, by detective commanders at every level, since their efficiency records and their career progress frequently—and often unfairly—depend on the fluctuations of the burglary statistics for their areas of operation. It is not expected, of course, that the incidence of burglary can be made to approach zero in any large urban district, and the failure of a detective command to achieve this millennial objective is of little significance. What can, however, be reasonably expected in the way of efficiency is the apprehension of criminal groups employing definite crime patterns which are indicative of organization and method. For example, the operations of a safe mob using a torch should be curtailed after the first five jobs. Similarly, it should not be too difficult to apprehend a mob that specializes in jewelry stores or liquor shops. The use of plants, information, tails, *modus operandi* files, and physical evidence can be effectively focused, if a meaningful pattern of target selection and technique is apparent.

2. Definitions

a. **Burglary.** The definition of burglary varies in different states. In some jurisdictions degrees of burglary are defined in the law to take care of the distinction between burglary of a dwelling house at night, which is considered a serious crime, and house-breaking. For present purposes, a definition taken from the common law will suffice. Burglary is the breaking and entering in the nighttime the dwelling house of another, with intent to commit a crime therein. The "crime therein" is usually taken to mean larceny or an offense which is a felony against the person such as rape or assault.

b. **Housebreaking.** This offense is simply the unlawful entering of the building of another with intent to commit a crime therein. The elements of "dwelling house," "nighttime," and a specification of the crimes are absent. All of these elements must be present in order to constitute the crime of burglary. It is apparent that a discussion of burglary will necessarily include the lesser crime of housebreaking; the present treatment will be restricted to the major offense, since its investigation includes the techniques and procedures applicable to housebreaking.

3. Proof

The following elements must be established in proving the offense of burglary:

    a. Breaking and entering.
    b. Dwelling house of another.
    c. Nighttime.
    d. Intent to commit a crime therein.

4. Elements of the Offense

a. **Breaking and Entering.** There must be a breaking either actual (physical force) or constructive (trick or ruse). Entering a hole in the wall, an open skylight, door, or window will not constitute breaking. The essence of the break is the removal or putting aside of some material part of the house on which the dweller relies for security against intrusion.

1) *Actual Breaking.* This term describes the application of physical force to effect entry. Opening a closed door or window; unlocking or unlatching a door; lifting a fastening hook; pushing

open a closed transom or trapdoor; removing a fastened screen; cutting a pane of glass or the netting of a screen are examples of physical force. If a guest, lodger, or servant, already lawfully in the building, forces an inner door, he has committed a break.

2) **Constructive Breaking.** The use of collusion, trick, ruse, intimidation, or impersonation to gain entry constitutes a break. Thus, a person who gains entry by impersonating a repairman has accomplished a break.

3). **Entry.** The insertion of any part of the body into the building constitutes entry. The insertion of a long pole or hook into the building is considered sufficient entry.

4) **One of Two Accomplices.** To support a conviction of two persons for burglary it is not necessary that both enter. If one enters, the other also commits burglary by being present and aiding in the entry.

b. **Dwelling House of Another.** The term *building* as used in defining housebreaking refers to a structure having four sides and a roof which is used by man to shelter himself or his property. Thus, a *building* includes freight cars, booths, tents, warehouses, a watchman's shanty, and a tool house. The term *dwelling house* means a building used as a residence. Thus, a store is not a subject of burglary unless part of it is used as a dwelling house. Temporary absence of the occupant does not deprive a dwelling house of its character as such. The house must be in the status of being occupied at the time of the breaking and entering. This does not mean that someone must be actually present in the structure. If the occupant leaves it temporarily with the intention of returning, though he may remain away for some time, the house remains a dwelling house. Hence, a dwelling used only during vacation periods and over weekends can be the subject of a burglary. The test lies in the occupant's or owner's intention to return.

c. **Nighttime.** Both the breaking and the entering must be in the nighttime, which is the period between sunset and sunrise, when there is not sufficient daylight to discern a man's face. It is not necessary that both the breaking and the entering occur on the same night.

d. **Intent.** To constitute burglary, there must be an intent to commit a specific offense within the dwelling house. The fact that the actual commission of the felony was impossible is immaterial. The breaking and entering are, ordinarily, presumptive evidence of an intent to commit a crime therein. The crime intended by the burglar is in most cases larceny.

e. **Proof on a "Plant."** The detective who is assigned to a tail or a plant detail should keep constantly in mind the requirements of proof. On observing the criminal, the first impulse is to make an arrest. Often, this is done while the burglars are occupied with the preliminaries of forcing entrance. An arrest at this time permits the criminals to escape the onus of the full crime, since they can be charged only with attempted burglary or illegal entry by reason of the overt act. A patient investigator will permit the burglars to enter and apprehend them *in flagrante delicto* or while making their exit.

5. Criminal Type

Traditionally the burglar, and in particular the safecracker, has been portrayed as a masked, bewhiskered, burly individual whose daring was matched only by his ruthlessness in disposing of interference. This legend undoubtedly had its origin in the facility with which the safecracker could be caricatured by cartoonists. His safe, mask, blackjack, and flashlight have come to be the picturesque symbols of the professional criminal. By this intimate association, the safe burglar has acquired in fiction the attributes of character corresponding to the physical properties of the safe itself—steely toughness of fiber and impregnability to moral suasion. Historically, this picture may, indeed, have been true, but modern criminal society is far more democratic. The safecracker category, for example, includes all races, colors, and creeds: the skilled craftsman and the bungler; the timid and the bold; the lone wolf and the pack member; the professional criminal and the young amateur trying his wings; the local thug and the strong boy from a distant city. The occupation of safecracker has proved so remunerative to some practitioners that its membership has swollen beyond the limits imposed by any of the restrictions of qualifications in the form of skill.

6. Safe-Breaking

The work of the safeman is one of the more demanding of criminal pursuits. Knowledge of safe construction, experience with power tools, physical conditioning, and the character traits of patience and tenacity are all prerequisites for a successful career in safecracking. The most proficient are the ones who possess both a detailed knowledge of safe construction and a mastery of the techniques of the locksmith trade. The professional safeman is aware that if he knew the locksmith's "secrets," he would be able to open almost any safe. He recognizes that there is an innate contradiction in the safe manufacturer's business. On the one hand, the company must design a safe to prevent entry by a burglar. On the other hand, in the case of a mechanism malfunction or if a customer loses the combination, a locksmith must be able to gain entry without destroying the safe or its contents. For this reason, the locksmith will rely on "drilling," "combination deduction," and "manipulation" as the preferred methods of opening a customer's safe.

a. **Safe-Breaking Methods.** A thoughtful examination of the crime scene will reveal the extent of the safeman's expertise. Choice of method, ease of entry, quality of equipment, and precision of toolmarks are all indicative of the safeman's level of proficiency. The following procedures are currently in practice:

1) *Punch.* The "punch job" is a common method of opening safes. When performed by an expert, this operation is clean, rapid, and not unduly noisy. For its successful execution there are four requisites: a moderate degree of skill and experience; a reasonable portion of luck; the correct selection of a safe; and the simple tools, viz., a sledge hammer and a drift pin or center punch. The technique is relatively simple. The dial is first knocked off the safe with a hammer, exposing the end of the spindle. The spindle is an axle on which the tumblers or locking wheels rotate. The punch is then held against the spindle and hit sharply with the hammer. The spindle is driven back into the safe, knocking the locking mechanism out of position, releasing the lock, and allowing the handle to turn. Unfortunately for the safeman, most of the newer safes are "punch-proof." Some are equipped with a

relocking device which is activated by a punch attempt. Others will have a drive-proof spindle made out of a malleable metal which will flatten on impact and can't be driven back against the lock. The investigator should look for toolmarks on the dial and the spindle. The typical burglar is successful in only a small percentage of punch jobs and usually must resort to additional techniques.

2) *Peel.* While the punch takes only a few minutes when performed by a professional, the "peel" is physically demanding and may require several hours of strenuous work. It is a common practice to resort to this method after an unsuccessful punch. The objective of the peel is to separate the metal layers on the door, which have been riveted or spot-welded, and to curl back the top layer to expose the lock or bolt. To start the peel, a corner of the door is attacked, penetrating the top metal layer so that a pry bar or jimmy can be inserted. The initial opening can be accomplished in a number of ways: hammering the corner of the safe door to buckle the metal and then cutting it with a hacksaw; using a hammer and chisel to pop the spot welds or rivets; or using a drill or an acetylene torch to open a small hole. A pry bar is then inserted into the opening and the top layer is curled back. A sectional pry bar is often carried in a suitcase and assembled at the job; the added length gives greater leverage, making the effort that much easier. This technique will not work on the newer, seam-welded, burglar-resistant safes.

3) *Ripping.* A "rip" involves cutting through the metal layers either to expose the locking mechanism or to make a hole in the safe large enough to remove the contents by hand. The tools of choice are a hammer and chisel or an ax. The rip can be directed to any surface of the safe, though many safemen prefer attacking the underneath. Cutting a whole through the bottom of the safe is sometimes called "chopping" or a "chop job." On older safes, the insulation in liquid form was poured in through a hole in the bottom and then covered with a twelve-inch-square metal plate. This plate is the weakest section of the safe and can be punctured with a reasonable amount of force. The application of a jimmy further simplifies the process. With a hole in the bottom of the safe, the burglar has access to its contents. One of the drawbacks of

this method is that safes are often quite heavy and can be difficult to overturn. Ripping or chopping will not be effective on the reinforced steel of a modern burglar-resistant safe.

Figure 17. A "chop job." After overturning the safe, the burglar "ripped" through the bottom and bent the metal back. The dial on the right indicates the attack was preceded by an unsuccessful "punch." (Courtesy of Paschal Ungarino.)

4) *Carry out.* In this operation, the safe is simply physically removed from the house and brought to a location where the burglar can work on it, at his leisure and without detection. Most commonly, this method is used in private dwelling houses, in which the safe is usually quite small and movable. A passenger car is used to transport the safe from the house. Stores and other establishments which are located near the street level are also likely places for this type of job. A dolly cart and a truck must be used for a larger safe.

5) ***Blasting.*** Blowing the safe with nitroglycerine is one of the traditional as well as picturesque methods in the safeman's repertoire. However, its use has been firmly discouraged by the federal government which provides harsh penalties for the sale, possession, and use of explosives for illegal activities. The noise and the danger involved are other serious drawbacks. Measuring the correct amount of explosive requires both knowledge and experience. Too little and the safe won't open; too much and the contents of the safe will be destroyed, or even worse, the burglar could be severely injured. In "the jamb shot," the nitroglycerine is permitted to drip slowly into the space between the safe door and the door jamb. If done correctly, when the charge is detonated, the door will be blown open. In the "spindle" or "gut" shot, the dial of the safe is knocked off, the spindle is punched, and the nitroglycerine is poured through the spindle into the lock. The explosion will destroy the locking mechanism allowing the door to be opened. Other explosives, such as, dynamite or military explosives, are also used.

6) ***Burning.*** The "burn" or the "torch" technique is one of the more effective methods of penetrating the burglar-resistant safe. The safeman will use either the oxyacetylene torch, that can operate at temperatures over 4000 degrees, or the "thermal lance" or "burning bar," that can produce heat in excess of 7000 degrees. Such temperatures will burn a hole through almost any metal.

a) OXYACETYLENE TORCH. Because of its widespread industrial application, it is not surprising to find the oxyacetylene torch employed in the service of the safeman. Training in its use can be acquired in schools, garages, factories, shipyards, and other places where welding is performed. Unfortunately, an acetylene tank can be quite dangerous in the hands of the amateur. It is necessary, moreover, to intelligently control the relative amounts of oxygen and acetylene in order to obtain the proper temperature. Hence, the operator of the torch must be a reasonably skilled workman. The size of the tank which is carried to the job is variable. Small tanks are available which are suitable for inconspicuous conveyance. Although any point on the safe can be attacked, a common method is to burn a circular hole around the dial to permit access to the lock. The investigator should bear in mind that clean, even cuts in appropriate areas are the hallmarks of an experienced torchman. An excess of black soot around the burn indicates an incorrect proportion of oxygen to acetylene. Any tanks, torches, and gauges left at the scene may have serial numbers that are often traceable.

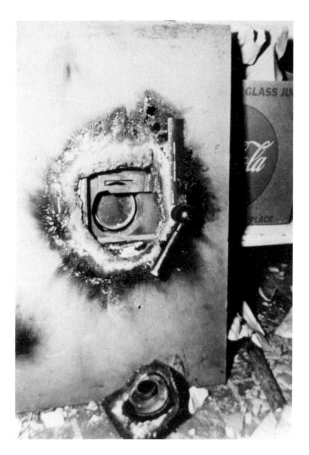

Figure 18. The use of an oxyacetylene torch around the dial. The rough cuts and black soot are indicative of a lack of skill. (Courtesy of Paschal Ungarino.)

b) THERMAL LANCE. The "thermal lance" or "burning bar" is a tool used for cutting steel and other metals for construction, demolition, shipbuilding, and other industrial purposes. It consists of a 10-foot section of a 3/8-inch-diameter pipe filled with a dozen wires or rods of which eleven are made of steel and one of an alluminum-magnesium alloy. On one end is a coupling which connects the pipe to an oxygen tank via a hose and regulator. Oxygen flows through the pipe and is ignited on the other end usually with an acetylene torch. Capable of reaching temperatures in excess of 7000 degrees, the thermal lance can penetrate any metal surface. At first sight, it would seem to be the ideal instrument by which the safeman could gain an insurmountable advantage over the safe manufacturer. However, the thermal lance has had only limited use in safe burglaries because of the extensive equipment required and other difficulties associated with it. A 10-foot section of pipe burns for only 5 minutes, so that several sections will be needed to burn a sizeable hole in a safe wall. Moreover, the thermal lance consumes oxygen at a rapid rate so that extra tanks will be required. Another disadvantage is the great amount of smoke, gases, and slag produced which make it difficult just to see and breathe, let alone operate a torch in a confined area. Moreover, some safe manufacturers have taken a defensive measure by inserting into the wall of the safe a layer of metal that conducts heat, such as copper. This layer disperses the heat over a wider area protecting temporarily the steel underneath and slowing the progress of the torchman. Another development is the portable thermal lance equipped with a flexible cable instead of the long rigid pipes which makes it easier to handle and less conspicuous to transport.

7) **Drilling.** In skilled hands, the drill is perhaps the most effective as well as the most practical tool in overcoming the defenses of a burglar-resistant safe. Two kinds are generally used:

a) HIGH–TORQUE DRILL. Equipped with carbide or diamond-tipped bits and held in place by a "jig" bolted to the safe, the high-torque drill can be used to pierce drill-resistant metal. Success with this method requires a degree of skill because the drill bits have a tendency to bind and break with any movement of the drill or when the drill passes through metals of different temper and thickness. Knowledge of safe construction is necessary in order to pinpoint the drill hole over an appropriate objective. Locksmiths who specialize in safes have access to "drilling instructions" provided by the manufacturer for the simplest and least destructive method of opening any safe model. Templates that are placed against the side of the safe provide the locksmith with the precise point at which to drill. Another helpful instrument for both locksmith and the safeman is the "borescope." This is a lighted fiber-optic instrument designed to be inserted into small holes to look into and around darkened cavities. It is used extensively in medical and industrial applications. After a hole has been drilled in the safe, a "borescope" can be used to peer inside in order to examine its contents or to align the wheels so that the combination can be deduced.

b) CORE DRILL. Instead of using a solid drill bit, a safeman sometimes employs the core drill with a hollow cylindrical bit. The core drill will create a circular hole in the safe large enough to reach in and remove its contents. It is bolt-mounted onto the safe because any movement will result in a binding and breaking of the bit. For the investigator, the broken drill bits and the marks of the drill mounts should be photographed and preserved for a possible comparison with tools found in the possession of a suspect.

8) *Combination Deduction.* This is a general phrase used to describe those safe burglaries in which the safeman determines either the combination of the safe or how to open it from circumstances in the office.

a) DAY–LOCK. Manipulation may be defined as the art of opening a safe without prior knowledge of the combination using only the senses of sight, hearing, and touch. The few who are adept at this skill are usually in the employ of a locksmith or a safe manufacturer and not among the criminal class. The fiction of the safecracker listening to the tumblers is maintained by careless office employees who neglect to close the safe properly or who leave the combination hidden in some fairly obvious place. The experienced safeman is well acquainted with the habits of the office-worker species in his native haunt. He is aware, for example, of the evening custom of careless employees giving the dial only a half turn to lighten the burden of their morning labors. The safe is not actually locked. The burglar has merely to reverse the half turn to make his night's work profitable. The practice of closing the safe door and turning the combination dial slightly is called putting the safe on "day-lock." It derives its name from the habit

Figure 19. A core drill was used to expose the locking mechanism. The stains on the front of the safe are from a lubricant for the drill. (Courtesy of Paschal Ungarino.)

of businessmen leaving the safe in this condition during the day so that they would not have to redial the entire combination every time they need to open it.

b) HIDDEN COMBINATION. The safecracker is also aware of the tendency of some office employees of leaving the combination "hidden" in some fairly obvious place to make sure they won't forget it. It may be written on the inside cover of a record book, on the side of a desk drawer, or on a door or window frame. It will be somewhere near the safe "where they won't lose it."

c) SIGNIFICANT NUMBERS. Safe owners will often use their birthday, their wedding day, their social security number, or some other significant number in their lives to supply the digits for their combination number.

d) TRIAL COMBINATIONS. When you buy a safe, it will already be equipped with a combination set by the manufacturer. This is called a "trial" or "try-out" combination. Each manufacturer has a set of trial combinations so that they will be able to open any safe coming from their factory. It is up to the purchaser of the safe to install a new combination. Some owners are too lazy or forgetful to do this and thus become vulnerable to a safecracker who has access to these numbers.

e) SURVEILLANCE. Surveillance methods may include: a "bug" placed near the safe door to hear any conversation concerning the combination, a hidden video camera timed to photograph the opening of the safe each day, or just observing the dial regularly. If the dial is observed to rest on the same number after each opening, one may assume it is the last number of the combination. With a three-digit lock, it is feasible over the course of several nights to try out all of the possible combinations in order to determine the other two numbers.

9) *Manipulation.* Determining the combination of a safe by perceiving the sight, sound, and feel of the dial as it turns the wheels of the lock is called "manipulation." Each wheel has a notch on it. When the notches of all three wheels of the lock are aligned, a lever will drop into the notched area releasing the bolt. When the wheels are not aligned, the lever will make a noise as it drops slightly as it passes over the notch. The points at which the lever enters and leaves the notched area are called the "contact points." Recording the numbers that are on the dial as the lever passes over the contact points on each wheel will provide the information needed to determine the combination. Manipulation is a challenging but by no means impossible skill to acquire. The stethoscope and electronic equipment such as earphones, audio amplifiers, and noise filters are very helpful. However, safe manufacturers make the task more difficult with the use of quieter wheels, false wheel notches, and the addition of extraneous sounds, all introduced to foil the would-be manipulator.

b. **How Safe Is a Safe?** It is an almost daily experience of detectives in some sections of large cities to be summoned to the scene of a safe burglary. The proprietor will usually be striding about the office, a dazed look in his eyes, exclaiming, "Look what they did to my safe! Is it possible?" The scene before the detective's eyes will indeed be depressing. The safe will be lying on its back, the door pried open, and the carefully maintained records scattered about the room. A thin coat of white powder covers the documents.

Tools and miscellaneous debris are strewn about the safe. "Is it possible?" the proprietor asks. The detective knows that not only is it possible, but it is a fact discouragingly repeated in his daily experience. The proprietor of the safe has spent his years of ownership in a pleasant but unfounded sense of security. A safe (i.e., a metal container with a combination lock) means to the proprietor a burglarproof iron box. He fancies it an impregnable fortress resisting valiantly the night-long ministrations of six masked men with acetylene torches and nitroglycerin. The possibility of a theft of the combination always exists, but mere physical assault will, he feels, avail nothing against these steel barriers.

Safe manufacturers, however, take a different view of this matter. They do not think (nor do they intend that the proprietor should so consider) the average safe to be burglarproof. To them, it is a strongbox, a deterrent to casual larceny and a protection in the event of fire. That it will not resist the determined efforts of a moderately skilled cracksman is a fact of which they are keenly aware. The heavy doors, which appear to the layman as an eight-inch wall of steel, are in reality relatively thin metal layers containing an insulation of fireproofing material. The safe manufacturers (and the insurance companies) have endeavored to make safe owners aware of the nature and limitations of their safes. Naturally, no safe is completely "burglarproof," since time and equipment will eventually prevail over the strongest construction. However, safe companies do produce burglar-resistant safes which they consider "proof" against the average burglar. The construction of such a safe is entirely different from that of the fireproof strongbox.

c. **Safe Construction.** The ordinary safe is simply fire resistant. It is constructed of sheet-steel boxes separated by several inches of insulation. It serves also as a deterrent to the thief, since it is equipped with relocking devices and burglar-resistant locks. The burglar-resistant safe, on the other hand, is built to withstand the efforts of an experienced burglar for a number of hours. It will be seam-welded with laminated steel and is designed to repel any attempt at "peeling" or "ripping" the safe walls. The walls will be layered with drill-resistant and torch-resistant metals. The more advanced models may have features to guard the safe against explosion or manipulation. As a protection from fire, the safe will be imbedded in concrete or placed within a larger fire-resistant safe.

7. Breaking into Commercial Establishments

Most burglars are unskilled; a few, such as the loft burglar, described in the following section specialize and develop suitable skills for their selected work. For the most part, then, the selection of the point of entry and the method of breaking in can be considered choices made after a quick survey of the opportunities and weaknesses of the building and its condition. The findings of the President's Commission on Crime in the District of Columbia shed some light on the representative methods used in breaking into commercial establishments: In 21 (7 percent) of the 313 commercial burglaries surveyed, burglars entered through unlocked doors and in 70 cases (22 percent) through unlocked windows. In 111 cases the burglars broke windows to gain entry, and in 95 cases locks were forced. A total of 105 of the commercial establishments burglarized were reported to have burglar-resistant locks; 65 of these establishments, however, were entered by means other than by tampering with the lock. Sixty-four percent of the burglarized commercial establishments were located on the first floor.

8. Loft Burglars

This type of burglar specializes in stealing merchandise from lofts. He may, as part of his loft work, open a safe if one is available. Indeed, loft burglars carry practically the same tools as a safe burglar. A loft burglar, however, is something more than a crude mechanic. He must possess some knowledge of the worth of merchandise; he must be a judge of different kinds of material. For example, if the loft mob is stealing bolts of cloth, one of them should be able to select the most expensive goods. In addition, the loft burglar must be acquainted with a receiver who will dispose of the goods.

a. **Planning.** A loft job is usually elaborately "cased." The leader has accurate knowledge of the plant layout, the protection system, the amount of merchandise on hand, and the habits of the personnel. This information may sometimes be obtained through a dishonest employee. More often, it is acquired by ruse, observation, and personal inspection.

b. **Gaining Entry.** The entry into the chosen premises usually takes place at night, preferably over the weekend when the area is relatively quiet. A common point of entrance is the skylight. The burglars have knowledge of ready access to a nearby building. From the roof of this building, they may reach the roof of their objective. They may then kick in the glass of the skylight and let themselves down by means of a rope. If the windows are not wired or barred, they may descend the fire escape ladder and break a window. In deserted streets, the burglars are emboldened to make a more direct entry by forcing open the main door or by pulling down the swinging ladder of the fire escape. Another means of entry is an open delivery chute. Still another kind of loft burglary is represented by the "lay-in-mob." Members of a "lay-in-mob" will acquire the confidence of a legitimate businessman, visit him in the late afternoon on an apparently honest mission, and subsequently secrete themselves in another part of the building until the personnel has departed at the close of business.

c. **Removing the Goods.** The loft mob usually employs a truck to remove the merchandise; since the burglary takes place in a business section of the city, the presence of a truck passes unnoticed. The goods are then brought to a "drop-off" to be later inspected by the receiver.

9. Apartment House Burglars

Large multiple dwelling buildings offer many advantages to the burglar who operates in a large city. Ordinarily, the majority of the tenants are unknown to each other, and consequently the appearance of a new face on the premises will not arouse suspicion. Similarly, when the burglar has once gained entrance, his activities within the apartment will seldom attract the attention of the neighbors. The following are among the techniques commonly employed:

a. **Gaining Entry.** This type of burglar usually selects the target by observing the lights from the street and noting apartments with darkened windows. Entry may be gained to the buildings by ringing the doorbell of a resident who is home at the time, opening the front door, and jamming the locking mechanism with a thin piece of wood such as a toothpick. A period of time is permitted to lapse while the tenant is convinced that his bell was sounded by mistake. The burglar then enters the building and frees the lock. Entry into the apartment is accomplished by means of a strip of celluloid applied to the lock or by jimmying a window accessible from a fire escape. If the building is guarded by a doorman, the burglar may enter an unguarded entrance, proceed to the roof, and select the apartment of choice. By using the roof he may "hit" four or five apartments in one night. Finally, it should be noted that many apartment dwellers are careless about locking their doors—a fact which is well known to the "door shaker," a burglar with minimal technique who simply goes through a big apartment building or a hotel, usually between 9:30 A.M. and noon, trying doors until he finds one unlocked or ajar. In a New York Police Department survey of apartment houses in the borough of Queens, 25 out of 150 apartment doors were found unlocked.

b. **Procedure.** The burglar searches the closets and dressers for valuables such as jewelry and furs. Sometimes he empties the drawers of the dresser on the bed or floor to facilitate the search.

c. **Leaving the Building.** On departing, the burglar may leave the loot in the hallway and emerge empty-handed to see if a tail is waiting to pick him up. If the road appears clear, he returns, picks up the loot, and departs.

10. The Suburban Burglar

Dwelling houses in middle-class suburbs are considered simple and staple targets for the burglar. The houses are sufficiently detached to enable him to operate unnoticed, and the target can be selected without difficulty by driving about and observing the familiar signs—the absence of any lights in the early evening and the doors flung open to reveal an empty garage. For reassurance the burglar will approach from the rear to try the bell.

Failing any response or other signs of activity, he will break a pane on the door or window to let himself in. In a few minutes he will have made the evening rewarding. Should he decide not to break and enter, he can still turn a tidy profit by picking up the bicycle, the lawn mower, and a few power tools from the garage. A moderately industrious burglar can, in this way, average over $500 a week. His success as a burglar is attributable to the carelessness of the householders rather than to any specially developed skills. Although he may eventually be picked up through a neighbor's phone call or as an incident of patrol, the long series of depredations could be easily prevented by a few common-sense precautions.

11. The Hit-and-Run Burglar

The suburbs have proved such an inviting target that a number of variations in daytime burglary technique have been introduced, which in turn have led to the adoption of new protective measures.

a. **The Commuter Burglar.** Where the suburban burglar tends to work alone and operates not far from where he lives, the *commuter* burglar is definitely a city dweller, will travel as far as 30 miles for his target, and spends very little time in its selection. These burglars present an even more difficult problem to the police, since they operate in a much greater area and are rarely seen twice in the same locality. Working in pairs, the commuter burglars drive out from New York City or Newark, for example, drop off the Garden State Parkway into a residential development and cruise about until they find a house that appears to be unoccupied. While one drives around the block, the other rings the doorbell. If the homeowner answers, the thief asks directions to a fictitious address. If no one answers, he smashes in the glass of a rear window or door and quickly goes through the house, picking up small appliances, cameras, money, and jewelry, leaving when his confederate returns in the car.

b. **Delivery Trucks.** Some of these burglars drive up in a delivery van to cart away items such as television sets, VCRs, stereo equipment, and similar appurtenances of an affluent community. Delivery trucks are too common in these areas to attract special attention. Another ruse is to pose as a television repairman and pull up at the selected house in an appropriately marked truck. In one case, the burglar was a genuine repairman, half of whose calls were legitimate. In other calls he would choose a likely house and, if the occupant was away, enter by the rear, quickly remove any money and jewelry and leave in his van.

c. **Dinner-time Burglars.** The wealthy suburbs of New York, such as the North Shore communities and Westchester County, have recently become the targets of "dinner-time burglars." While the family and guests are collected in one area of a large house preoccupied with dinner, the burglar busies himself in the relatively remote bedroom area, searching the rooms for jewelry and cash. The early evening hours are propitious for this sort of activity, since it is too early for the burglar alarms to be switched on. Obviously, a sensible protection against this type of intruder is the possession of an intelligent dog.

12. Summer Home Burglary

The breaking and entering of vacation homes in the off-season is becoming a relatively common offense in rural and resort areas. Thousands of vacation homeowners throughout the country are discovering that their rural havens have become targets for off-season burglars and vandals. The sharp increase in these offenses has followed the growing resort population. Each year more vacation homes are built and each year they become more elaborate in their furnishings and equipment. With the burgeoning population these homes are scattered over a much wider area, presenting a serious problem to a police force that is geared to the local population. Many of these houses are located on the farther side of a lake or are hidden away in the mountains at the end of a road that is little used in the summer and is impassable in the winter. The normal patrol of the sheriff's department or of the state troopers is not suited to burglary protection in these areas.

13. Physical Evidence

On arriving at the scene of a reported burglary, the investigator should first search the building for the burglar. This may appear to be an odd piece of advice, but experience has shown that the burglar is sometimes interrupted in his work and finds his path of escape blocked. This is particularly true of loft buildings where the area is so large that the burglar deems it safer to conceal himself than to risk dashing out of the building. It is assumed that police officers responding to the call will search the neighborhood for the burglar. The next investigative step is the search for physical evidence.

a. **Heelprints.** The most common clue left at the scene of a safe burglary is a heelprint on paper. The burglar, after opening the safe, throws the papers on the floor and carelessly steps on them. In wet weather, the prints may be exceptionally good. If a sufficient number of defects are observable in the heels, an excellent identification can be made.

b. **Fingerprints.** The complainant in a burglary case always relies heavily on the discovery of a fingerprint for the solution of the crime. Experienced investigators, although they do not neglect this investigative technique, understand that relatively few burglaries are solved each year through the medium of fingerprints. If the importance of the case warrants a photographic record, pictures should be taken of the affected room and the point of break and entry before processing for fingerprints. In the development of latent fingerprints, the following area and objects will receive attention:

1) *Area of Break.* If this is on the outside, weather effects usually prevent the deposit of good prints. Immediately inside of the area of the break, however, prints may be found. This is especially true if it has been necessary for the burglar to climb through a window. The inside of the window and the sill are good surfaces for prints.

2) *Closets.* Prints are often found on door and jamb of a closet. Naturally, most of the prints will be those of the occupants.

3) *Door Knobs.* Fingerprints are practically never found on door knobs. The manner in which the knob is handled ordinarily prevents the retention of fingerprints.

4) *Dressers.* In a house burglary, the dresser is searched by the burglar. The color of the wood and the presence of furniture polish usually prevent developing prints. Polished boxes and glass covers may bear prints.

5) *Furniture.* The chairs, bed, and tables are not likely sources.

6) *Bottles and Glasses.* Burglars often drink the owner's liquor. The glasses and bottles are ideal surfaces for receiving prints. It may be safely said that bottles and glasses are the most likely of all sources of prints in a burglary investigation.

7) *Cartons and Crates.* Objects found in a loft, such as wooden containers, seldom bear prints.

8) *Safe.* If the safe is "crinkled" or if the paint is old and quite worn, the search for prints will usually be unsuccessful. A new, smooth, enamel surface will yield prints. A particularly good source is the cash box. The bottom of the change shelf of the cash box should receive special attention.

9) *Walls.* Success depends primarily on the nature of the paint. The areas near light switches and in back of the safe should be processed.

10) *Tools.* Although it is possible to find a print on a tool, such a discovery is quite rare.

11) *Papers.* Again, there is a possibility, but small probability. Sized paper and heavy smooth stock can be powdered at the scene. Other papers should be removed to the laboratory for silver nitrate treatment.

12) *Desks.* It is seldom that a print is found on a plain wooden desk, either on the top or on the fronts of the drawers.

c. **Clothing.** In a house burglary, the criminal sometimes exchanges his own jacket or suit for that of the owner of the house. Dry cleaner's marks present on the clothing will offer an invaluable clue.

d. **Glass.** If a window was broken in effecting entry, glass particles may be present in the pockets of the suspect. Samples of the broken glass should be collected for possible future comparison in the event that a suspect is picked up.

e. **Paint.** If a jimmy has been used to force the door or window, paint may adhere to the tool. Paint samples should be taken for future comparison.

f. **Tool Marks.** In jimmying a door or window, tool impressions are left by the criminal. These should be photographed from a distance of a few feet and also in a one-to-one shot. Impressions in wood serve only to indicate the size of the jimmy. Marks in metal may sometimes be positively identified as having been made with a particular tool. In safe burglaries, excellent tool marks are left on the dial in "knocking" it off with a cold chisel and hammer or with the hammer alone (see Chap. 36).

g. **Tools.** The preceeding two paragraphs have assumed that the burglar departed with his tools. In most instances, however, the criminal leaves his tools behind him. The reason for this is his fear of being picked up with the tools in his possession. In some states, it is a crime for a person to be found at night with burglar tools in his possession. Consequently, the experienced burglar purchases his equipment before the job and leaves it at the scene. In the case of an "inside job" in a factory, the burglar may use the tools present on the premises. An effort should be made to trace the tools to the store in which they were purchased. If the subject of the burglary is a factory or garage, the burglar may depend on finding the instruments in the building. This is particularly true if the burglary is an inside job or if it has been "fingered" by a former employee. Certain types of tools, such as sectional jimmies or very fine drills, suggest a special *modus operandi* and may limit the suspects to a small number.

h. **Peculiar Habits.** Some burglars are given to odd behavior such as defecation on the floor, stealing desk ornaments, eating candy, or drinking excessively from bottles found on the premises. Peculiarities of behavior should be noted and checked against the *modus operandi* index.

i. **Safe Insulation.** Samples of safe insulation should be taken for possible future comparison. Since the typical safe is of the fire-resistant kind, it contains insulating material. The burglar, in breaking into such a safe, scatters the insulation on the floor. In some burglaries, so much of this material is strewn about the room that the layman is under the impression that an explosion has taken place. The insulation material falls on the clothing of the burglars and is picked up by their shoes. Sometimes, the insulation material can be found in the nail holes of the heels weeks after the commission of the burglary.

1) *A Clue Material.* Safe insulation material can serve as excellent clue material. Some safe manufacturers make their own insulation material; others order it from outside firms according to

certain specifications. It has been found that the materials differ sufficiently to constitute a medium of identification. Thus, if a suspect is found with safe insulation material on his clothing which on spectrographic comparison is found to be chemically the same as the sample of material from the broken safe, there is a strong indication of guilt.

2) *FBI File.* The FBI Laboratory maintains a Petrographic File, one section of which consists of safe insulations and data concerning such substances. Specimens have been obtained from the products of the major safe companies of the United States. This file has assisted often in the solution of safe burglaries. As an example of the usefulness of the file, a case of the Kentucky State Police may be cited. A drug store in Albany, Kentucky, was "burglarized" and the safe containing money and narcotics was removed to an isolated area where it was broken into. The Kentucky State Police picked up a suspect near Albany and on searching him found light grey material in his trouser cuffs. The trousers, evidence material, and samples of insulation from the safe were sent to the FBI Laboratory for comparison. Under the microscope, the material from the trousers appeared to be the same as that from the safe. It was found, by reference to the Petrographic File, that the insulation material was relatively rare. Thus, it could be concluded with a high degree of probability that the sample in the cuff was acquired at the scene of the burglary.

ADDITIONAL READING

Burglary

Barnard, R.L.: *Intrusion Detection Systems: Principles of Operation and Applications.* Stoneham, Mass.: Butterworth, 1981.

Bennet, T. and Wright, R.: *Burglars on Burglary: Prevention and the Offender.* Brookfield, Vt.: Gower, 1984.

Bopp, W.J.: A Profile of Household Burglary in America. 59 *Police Journal,* 168, 1986.

Conklin, J.E. and Bittner, E.: Burglary in a Suburb. 11 *Criminology,* 206, 1973.

Cromwell, P.F., Olsen, J.N. and Avary, D.W.: *Breaking and Entering: An Ethnographic Analysis of Burglary.* Newbury Park, Calif.: Sage, 1991.

Davis, M.: *Prevent Burglary: An Aggressive Approach to Total Home Security.* Englewood Cliffs, N.J.: Prentice-Hall, 1986.

Dunckel, K.: Unsafe Safes. 36 *Law and Order,* 9, 1988.

Dussia, J.: Safe Burglary Investigation. 36 *FBI Law Enforcement Bulletin,* 11, 1967.

Green, E.J. and Booth, C.E.: Cluster Analyses of Burglary M/Os. 4 *Journal of Police Science and Administration,* 382, 1976.

Macdonald, J.M.: *Burglary and Theft.* Springfield, Ill.: Thomas, 1980.

Maguire, M. and Bennet, T.: *Burglary in a Dwelling: The Offense, the Offender and the Victim.* Brookfield, Vt.: Gower, 1982.

Meiners, R.P.: Store Diversion Burglaries. 59 *FBI Law Enforcement Bulletin,* 3, 1990.

Murphy, R.B. and Horton, S.: Focus on Burglary: A Management Approach to Prevention of Crime. 42 *Police Chief,* 11, 1975.

Pope, C.E.: *Crime Specific Analysis: An Empirical Examination of Burglary Offender Characteristics.* Washington, D.C.: U.S. Government Printing Office, 1977.

—— : *Crime Specific Analysis: The Characteristics of Burglary Incidents.* Washington, D.C.: U.S. Government Printing Office, 1977.

Rapp, B.: *The B & E Book: Burglary Techniques and Investigation.* Port Townsend, Wash.: Loompanics, 1989.

Rengert, G. and Wasilchick, J.: *Suburban Burglary: A Time and a Place for Everything.* Springfield, Ill.: Thomas, 1985.

Safe Insulation and Its Value in Crime Detection. 43 *FBI Law Enforcement Bulletin,* 11, 1974.

Scarr, H.A.: *Patterns of Burglary,* 2nd ed. Washington, D.C.: U.S. Government Printing Office, 1973.

Seamon, T.M.: The Philadelphia Scene Team Experiment. 57 *Police Chief,* 1, 1990.

Shover, N.: Structures and Careers in Burglary. 63 *Journal of Criminal Law, Criminology and Police Science,* 540, 1972.

Waegel, W.B.: Patterns of Police Investigation of Urban Crimes. 10 *Journal of Police Science and Administration,* 452, 1982.

Walsh, D.: *Heavy Business: Commercial Burglary and Robbery.* New York, Methuen, 1986.

Webb, D.B.: *Investigation of Safe and Money Chest Burglary.* Springfield, Ill.: Thomas, 1975.

Weber, T.L.: *Alarm Systems and Theft Prevention.* Stoneham, Mass.: Butterworth, 1985.

Weiss, J.: Residential Burglaries: Nuts, Bolts and Demographics. 36 *Law and Order,* 11, 1988.

Yeager, W.B.: *Techniques of Safecracking.* Port Townsend, Wash.: Loompanics, 1990.

Chapter 22

ROBBERY

1. Introduction

Robbery is perhaps the most glamorous of the major crimes. We speak of "robber knights" and "robber barons," of "bold robbers" and "daylight robbery." The element of reckless courage is usually associated with robbery, since the criminal often declares himself in the most forthright manner imaginable. He stands with his weapon bared and demands from his victim the property on which he has set his heart. There is present in this situation the imminent possibility of resistance, of a chase and a vigorous pursuit by the police. The daring character of the typical robbery does not imply that the planning of the crime is without ingenuity or that the executants are devoid of finesse. On the contrary, a truly first-rate robbery is as much an achievement of timing and precision as a skillfully executed play of a professional football team. At the other end of the scale we have the truly low class robber—the common "mugger" who employs all the subtlety and delicacy of a pile driver.

There is considerable confusion in the mind of the layman concerning the meaning of the term *robbery*. The average citizen uses it as a synonym for burglary and for larceny. There is a fundamental difference; indeed, from the point of view of the criminal it is a vital difference, since the offense of robbery may mean a few additional years in jail. Robbery is considered a very serious crime because it involves immediate personal danger to the victim. Robbery is the taking of property from another in his presence and against his will. Larceny is simply the taking of someone else's property. (Thus robbery implies the additional but lesser crime of larceny.) Burglary is the breaking into a building with the intention to commit a crime—any crime, be it larceny, murder, or simple mischief.

Table VII
ROBBERY, TYPE OF OFFENSE, 1991

Street/Highway	56.2%
Commercial House	11.7%
Gas or Service Station	2.6%
Convenience Store	5.7%
Residence	9.8%
Bank	1.6%
Miscellaneous	12.3%

Source: FBI. *Uniform Crime Reports—1991.*

Table VIII
ROBBERY, TYPE OF WEAPONS USED, 1991

Firearms	39.9%
Knives or Cutting Instruments	11.0%
Other Weapons	9.3%
Strong-Armed	39.8%

Source: FBI. *Uniform Crime Reports—1991.*

2. Law

Robbery is the unlawful taking of personal property from the person or in the presence of another against his will, by means of force, violence, or fear of injury, immediate or future, to his person or property, or the person or property of a relative or member of his family, or of anyone in his company at the time of the robbery. Robbery is similar to larceny with the element of violence, actual or threatened, added. It includes some of the elements of larceny plus the taking of the property from the person by force or fear.

a. **Proof.** The following elements must be established:

1) The taking of the property.

2) That the taking was from the person or in the presence of the person.

3) That the taking was against his will, by force, violence, or putting in fear.

b. **Taking of the Property.** The reader is referred to Chapter 20 for those elements relating to the property involved.

c. **From the Person.** The words "from the person" are not to be taken in a literal or strict sense. If the property is taken in the presence of the owner it is, in the contemplation of the law, taken from his person. For the condition "in the presence" to be satisfied, it is not necessary that the owner be within a certain distance of his property. If the victim is left tied up in one room, while the robber takes his money in another room, the taking is considered to have been done in his presence.

d. **Force or Violence.** The force must be actual violence, but the amount is immaterial. The violence is sufficient if it overcomes the actual resistance of the person robbed, or puts him in such a position that he can make no resistance. If resistance is overcome in snatching the article, there is sufficient violence. If, however, an article is merely snatched from the hand of another or if a pocket is picked by stealth, the offense is not robbery.

e. **Fear or Threats.** Putting the victim in fear of bodily injury is sufficient intimidation to sustain a charge of robbery. Actual fear need not be proved, since a legal presumption of fear will arise from facts clearly indicating the cause. The fear may be aroused by word or gesture where the victim is threatened with a gun or knife.

3. Bank Robbery

For an adequate understanding of the crime of robbery, we shall focus our attention on the robber *par excellence,* the bank robber. The most highly skilled professional criminals concentrate on bank robbery. The reason for this is fairly simple. At one time, the rewards of safe burglary tempted the professional criminal. Before the development of the time lock, an expert burglar could steal a half-million dollars by opening a bank safe. In modern times, the bank has become almost invulnerable because of the time lock, which can be set to jam the bolt mechanism for a period of time during which the vault cannot be opened even by an employee possessing the combination.

The safes of business firms yield little to the burglar in the way of cash since business is carried on by means of checks and securities which are ordinarily not negotiable. Stolen jewelry will realize less than 20 percent of its true value. Hence, the modern criminal who is in search of the big "score" must resort to bank robbery.

4. The Bank Robber

Persons who rob banks cannot be placed in simple categories. They range in background from all walks of life; they may be of any age from eight to sixty; color, creed, and sex do not prescribe boundaries. The most practical division of bank robbers would yield two general classes: individuals and groups.

a. **Individuals.** These are persons who operate singly. He (or she) may be motivated by greed, want, the desire for a thrill, or the need for extreme self-testing. Most commonly he is a person who enters a bank, passes a note to the teller demanding a large amount of cash and informing the teller that he is armed with a pistol or an explosive device. He may be armed or unarmed; since the weapon is concealed, the teller is instructed to make the safe assumption and to surrender conveniently available cash without further questions. Wishing to avoid injury to clients or employees, banks ordinarily issue standing instructions for the teller to concede to the robber's wishes. This policy, in turn, has encouraged robbers in the commission of twenty or more offenses before they have been caught. The robber's confidence is such that he may periodically revisit the same bank and successfully use the same technique for many months.

b. **Groups.** This class consists of criminals whose records include several serious offenses. They operate in small groups of three or four persons. They are serious-minded, fairly competent, and often dangerous. The methods of procedure described in the succeeding paragraphs will give additional insight into the character of the professional bank robber.

5. Patterns

The method of operation of the bank robber varies widely with the individual criminal. The target he selects, for example, may be located in the center of a populous area and protected by all the approved safety devices and measures; or it may be an isolated bank far from the nearest policeman. The bank may never have been previously robbed or it may have been robbed several times within recent years. The preparation given to the robbery may be a matter of months or even years, or the perpetrator may have conceived the plan on the spur of the moment. Despite these wide variations, however, a number of trends are apparent. The following generalizations will provide a rough picture of the typical robber.

a. **Selection of Target.** The small branch bank or savings and loan association is preferred. Larger institutions involve a greater hazard because of the number of employees and customers.

b. **Time.** Wednesday and Friday are favored slightly over the other days. If the job is closely cased, the day selected may be one on which large payroll deliveries are expected. The time of day is selected so that the least number of people will be present. Opening time, lunch hour, and closing hour are preferred. As an example of time selection one should consider the Bank of Manhattan Company Robbery in Queens, New York City, in which $305,243 was lost. Three men escorted a young bank clerk as he left his home in Queens, ushered him at gunpoint into his Ford and drove with him fourteen blocks to his office, one of the thirty-five branch banks of the Bank of Manhattan Company in Queens. They waited on the sidewalk until the manager arrived and showed him their submachine gun. At 8:52 A.M., with all the bank employees accounted for, the bandits entered, herded eleven people into a vault, locking the inner gate with a chain and padlock which they had brought for that purpose. Within eight minutes they had gathered the money. At 9:00 A.M., they quietly drove away with the most money ever taken in a U.S. bank robbery. During the holdup one of the bandits said: "We've been casing this joint for six months." They knew the bank employees' names and faces. They also knew that the vaults contained an extra $200,000 that day to meet local payrolls.

c. **Disguises.** Hoods and masks are increasingly worn. Sunglasses are the most common disguise. Most robbers wear hats or caps, frequently for the purpose of concealing the color of their hair.

d. **Weapons.** In the majority of cases guns are carried; in others they are simulated. Toy guns are used in about 10 percent of the cases. The weapons are frequently disposed of by throwing from the window of the getaway car, by burying, or by hurling into a body of water. The weapons are not often discharged, the trend being away from unnecessary brutality and murder. Each year, however, the records show a sufficient number of fatalities to discourage foolhardy resistance.

e. **Escape Methods.** The typical bank robber uses a rented or stolen car to make his getaway from the bank and later transfers to his own car. A popular make such as a Ford or Chevrolet is chosen to avoid attracting attention. The robbers may use their own car for a getaway and equip it with stolen license plates, which will be discarded later. It is found that the vehicle and articles left in the vehicle provide the most useful clues in tracing the criminal.

f. **Criminal Group.** The typical robbery is perpetrated by a pair of criminals. Approximately 75 percent of the robbers have records of previous arrests for crimes such as robbery, burglary, and larceny. In an FBI study of 100 robberies it was found that in the large majority of cases persons from the local area were involved. In seventy-eight of the cases the robbers lived within a radius of approximately 100 miles from the scene of the robbery. In thirty-three of the seventy-eight cases at least one of the robbers resided in the city or town where the crime took place.

6. Modus Operandi of the Professional

Since the criminal type in robbery varies so widely, a narrow selection must be made in treating *modus operandi.* In the description found below the techniques of skilled professional robbers are given. These methods represent "best practice"; they are the product of experience and mature planning. Although this discussion of the methods of operation of robbers is concerned mainly with bank robbery, it will be found that the same techniques are applicable to other forms of this crime.

a. **Fingering the Job.** Professional thieves do not leave the selection of the target to chance or a good guess. Some of their marks (targets) are "dug up," that is, discovered by the criminals themselves. Experience coupled with shrewd observation and surveillance will suggest profitable and practicable targets to the thief. Often, the robbers are tipped off to a target by "small-time" criminals. Pickpockets, gamblers, and ordinary "grifters" will tip off the robber with an agreement for a 10 percent share in the proceeds. Legitimate business people will also tip off "heist" men. A truck driver or parking lot attendant may finger a truck as a hijack target for a share in the proceeds. A bank manager will tip off a criminal, supplying all the necessary information for the safe and profitable accomplishment of the robbery in order to cover up embezzlements which he has perpetrated. An unscrupulous jeweler will encourage a robbery of his own shop in order to put in an excessive claim with the insurance company.

b. **Casing the Job.** The professional robbers do not attack the bank at random and improvise their tactics to suit the needs of the situation. The mob must equip itself with a plan. The initial step, then, is reconnaissance or "casing." Experience has shown that there are no limits to the extent of the mob's preparation. The mob obtains information on the layout of the bank building; the surrounding terrain; avenues of approach; location and movements of bank personnel; fixed police posts; location of bank guards. One famous bank robber would spend weeks in casing a bank, extending his study even to an examination of the "Bankers' Directory" for information concerning the bank, its officers, and other personnel. Often, the bank robber will employ ruses to gather information concerning the interior of the bank, its operations, and its personnel. The following are a few of the ruses employed:

1) *Loitering.* A member of a mob may simply loiter about a bank in order to obtain information. He may appear to be waiting for someone inside the bank or may stand outside and observe at a distance. This form of casing is, however, likely to draw suspicion.

2) *Feigned Business.* The caser may enter the bank on the pretext of cashing a check, changing large bills, opening an account, or making a small deposit.

3) *Salesman Pretext.* One ingenious bank robber obtained considerable information about a bank in one of the southern states by posing as a salesman for an aluminum screen firm. The vice president of the bank escorted him on a tour of the bank ostensibly for the purpose of surveying the bank's need for screens. The spurious salesman obtained a signed contract for the screens after closing time. He followed the bank official into a vault, pulled out a gun, and obtained $17,000. He was apprehended within five hours after the robbery. It should be noted that this example illustrates an operational technique as well as a method of casing.

c. **The Group.** The "heist mob" is usually a group of three or four experienced criminals. Ordinarily there is no leader or "mastermind." The members of the group act as equals with an authority to which their knowledge and experience entitle them.

d. **Assignments.** Each member of the mob may have his own special activity in which he has acquired experience through previous "jobs." The following are some of the specifically designated functions:

1) *The Wheelman.* The wheelman or driver undertakes to solve all the problems relating to the transportation of the mob from the scene of the stickup. He must undertake, first, to obtain a car for transportation at the scene. He usually steals this car and provides it with another set of license plates. The car selected is fairly new, inconspicuous, and capable of rapid acceleration. It is not the only car employed in the job. At a distance from the scene, the criminals will shift from the stolen or getaway car to the "front" car, which is owned by one of the mob.

2) *The Rodman.* One person is assigned to the task of gathering and transporting the guns which are to be used. He is usually a good marksman and is expected to specialize in gunplay if the situation demands. Submachine guns are avoided.

3) *Insidemen.* These persons must perform the actual work of the robbery. The rodman is also an inside man, and occasionally the wheelman may be called upon to go inside a building.

e. **Planning.** The details of the robbery are planned with scrupulous attention even to seemingly trivial matters. The wheel-man studies the geography of the area, together with its streets and traffic conditions. The getaway route is carefully laid out. The mob assembles at a "meet" shortly before the appointed time for the job. The plan or layout is once again studied in a general briefing. The mob changes clothes if necessary. For example, in a factory district, they would don overalls. The members leave the "meet" separately and go to the mark by separate routes. They gather within a few blocks of the mark and "rod up." They proceed on foot to the bank, the wheelman driving up and parking near the entrance. If it is practicable, the inside men occasionally work with masks on their faces. (Rubber masks were used in the Brink's case.) One of the mob is assigned to do the talking. He speaks evenly and avoids dramatics, since he is the center of attention and most likely to be identified. After obtaining the money, the robbers depart in the getaway car and drive to the "front" car. If they are not being pursued, they shift to the front car. During the journey, they change their clothes and transfer the money to paper bags. Some of the mob take the money and guns in the front car to the place selected for the "meet." The wheelman goes to another part of the city with the getaway car. Sometimes, the front car is changed for a third car.

7. Reactions at the Scene

There are many points of view from which the bank is regarded during a holdup.

a. **Executives.** A decreasing number of executives choose to look upon their bank as a beleagured fortress whose flag, the greenback, must be preserved at whatever cost and whose vaulted heart of gold must be contested by bitter inches. The robber, of course, brings a different philosophy of the situation. He views the banker as an intransigent misanthrope suffering from an overvaluation of his responsibility to the insurance company. He considers himself a just aggressor whom society has grieviously wronged in denying him an access to a reasonable share of its riches.

b. **The Bank Employee** is guided by mixed motives. In his loyalty he is keenly aware of the traditional heroism of fictional and factual bank cashiers. The cinematic *coup de main* may endear him to his superiors and win him the lavish attention of the television cameras. On the other hand, his instinct for clerical order rebels against any procedure as untidy as resistance by physical violence.

c. **Bank Guard.** The special case of the bank guard is difficult to analyze. After years of incredulous expectancy that poor unfortunate may be left helpless in trauma or given over to a panicky self-sacrifice. However, if he is a trained professional or a retired police officer, he may be the only one present whose behavior is intelligent and effective.

d. **Customers.** The state of mind of the customers is ordinarily the least involved. Their concern is usually simple and primal—the preservation of their own invaluable persons. There are, of course, the unpredictable few; but the courageous and the panic-stricken alike can aggravate the danger.

e. **Police.** Apart from all these groups and occupying a middle ground of motives are the police. They are sensible of their responsibilities for the protection of life and property and the apprehension of the criminals, but they prefer the event to be uncomplicated by homicide.

8. Instructions for Employees

a. **During the Robbery.** The behavior of the employees and customers during the robbery should have safety as its objective.

1) The persons present should follow the instructions of the robber. Since the criminals are extremely nervous, an unexpected action on the part of an employee may precipitate gunfire.

2) Employees instructed to hand over money should endeavor to keep the loss of money at a minimum. In other words, while obeying an order to hand over money, they should not volunteer to reach for money not visible to the robbers.

3) The employees should observe the robbers carefully. Physical descriptions, peculiarities of behavior, method of operation, voice, and exact words are invaluable aids to the investigators. If

an employee has a view of the street he should note any accomplices standing outside and also try to remember details of the getaway car.

4) When the robbers are leaving, the employees should remain until the danger is removed.

5) Employees should be conscious of the presence of physical evidence and should avoid obliterating evidence such as fingerprints.

b. **After the Robbery.** As soon as the robbers have gone, an employee should put into action the "robbery plan." He should first telephone the police and keep the telephone line open. The following information should be given:

1) The fact that the robbery has occurred.

2) The exact time of the departure of the robbers.

3) The number of robbers.

4) An accurate description of each robber, referring to them as "Robber No. 1," "Robber No. 2," etc.

5) The make, year, color, style and license plate of the getaway car and direction in which it departed.

After giving this information, the employee should keep the line open and monitor the telephone. Another employee should request the customers to remain until the police arrive. If the customers are sufficiently composed, he should take down their names and addresses. Cooperative customers should be requested to write down descriptions of the robbers and their behavior. The customers should be discouraged from comparing notes and endeavoring to arrive at a common denominator in their descriptions. An effort should be made to find witnesses in the street.

9. Investigation

a. **General.** There are several major obstacles to the solution of the crime of robbery. First, there are usually very few traces left behind by the criminals. The actual physical work of robbery as compared with burglary is of such a minor nature that the criminal scarcely leaves any impress on his surroundings. Secondly, the time allotted to the work is of such short duration that the victim is not sufficiently composed to note the exact appearance of the robbers. In addition, the probability of interruption becomes quite small in an operation that occupies the space of only a few minutes. Finally, the violent manner of the robber dismays the victims and prevents civilian cooperation.

Robbery belongs to that category of crimes in which the criminals are perfect strangers. There is ordinarily no one remaining at the scene of the crime who would be suspected. It is seldom that an inside accomplice is employed to provide information concerning the physical layout or the habits of the personnel. The motive of robbery is simple and uncomplicated and hence can yield no clues.

The physical clues, although they should by no means be overlooked, are ordinarily of little value in the original detection of the perpetrators. Their true worth is later realized in the additional proof which they may offer. The solution of a robbery will most often be reached through "information." Intelligent use of stool pigeons and a friendly association with known criminals constitute the most valuable key to the crime. In subsequent arrests for other serious crimes, the detective should closely interrogate the criminal concerning his activities at the time of the robbery in question. The list of daily arrests should be scrutinized for persons who have a robbery conviction in their records. These persons should then be checked against the recorded descriptions of the wanted robbers. If the physical descriptions and the interrogation justify such a measure, the detective should personally check the criminal's story concerning his location, occupation, working hours, friends, and residence during the time of the robbery.

b. **Interrogation.** If the suspect waives his right to be silent, he should be interrogated by a person thoroughly familiar with bank robbery operations. Since the suspect may be a professional bank robber, special techniques of questioning may be required. For example, in questioning such a suspect it may be found useful for the interrogator to refrain from showing his special interest in the robbery actually under investigation. Without in any way violating his rights, the suspect may be permitted to assume that he is being interrogated concerning a different crime. A burglary, or better a homicide (fictitious or factual), which took place at a distant town will serve the purpose. The crime selected should have taken place at the same time as the robbery. The suspect will then feel quite free in establishing his alibi and may even risk an alibi in which he is placed near the scene of the robbery. If he is guilty and somewhat naïve, he may even suggest the names of his confederates as a substantiation of his alibi. The investigator should not reveal his true intent until he has exhausted the possibilities of this line of inquiry. Later, the direct accusation of the true crime should be brought in with the full impact of the existing evidence—eyewitnesses, knowledge of subsequent activities, and other identifying elements. A sudden psychological onset of this sort frequently results in utterly confusing the suspect. He has been picked up for one crime, has presented an alibi for a second, and finds himself maneuvered into a third. The prospect of a confession is now at its brightest.

c. **Interviewing Witnesses.** On receiving a telephoned report of a robbery, the proprietors of the establishment should be immediately instructed to detain all witnesses. When the police arrive, the witnesses should be quietly separated and instructed not to discuss the crime with anyone until they have been interviewed. Each witness should then be individually interviewed concerning the event and the appearance of the participants. This procedure is of great importance since, if the witnesses are permitted to congregate and engage in random conversation, the value of their subsequent descriptions of the criminals will depreciate. Listening to other opinions will dissuade the witness from his original impression. He will be tempted to follow the "party line." His description will then share the consensus and will not have the value of an independent observation. Witnesses should subsequently be taken to the local bureau of identification to look at the photographs of known robbers. If possible, they should also be shown the FBI bank robbery album.

10. Clues and Investigative Techniques

a. **Vehicle.** One of the best tracing clues in the crime of robbery is the getaway vehicle. The amateur may sometimes use his own car. The professional will usually employ a stolen car and switch later to his own car. At other times, the robber may use his own car with a stolen license plate or with no license plates. Quite often, the car has been rented from an agency. As a starting point, the investigator should obtain detailed descriptions of the car from as many witnesses as possible. Naturally, if one of the witnesses noted the license plate number, the investigator is at a marked advantage. The alarm should be sent out immediately with this information. The registration should be obtained as soon as possible from the state bureau of motor vehicles. The list of alarms for stolen cars should be checked both for the license plate and the type of car. Local car rental agencies should be canvassed to determine whether a car answering to the description of the robbery vehicle has been recently rented. The combination of a rented car and a stolen license plate has a strong appeal for the ingenious robber. In checking the car rental agency, the investigator may further assume that the witnesses have erred in their descriptions of the vehicle and should obtain a list of cars rented since the day preceding the robbery together with the exact times of checking out and returning. The manager of the agency may be able to give a good description of the person renting a car resembling the getaway car.

A robbery which took place in Carlisle, Iowa, offers a good illustration of this latter technique. After holding up the bank and obtaining $4,500, the two robbers were seen departing in a dark green Plymouth with no license plates. The car was going in the direction of Des Moines. The police of that city canvassed car rental agencies. At one agency, it was found that a dark green Plymouth had been checked out at 9:42 A.M. on the day of the robbery and had been returned at 12:15 P.M. The man who rented the car was described by the owner of the agency. Working with this description, the police succeeded in apprehending the criminals.

b. **Latent Prints.** The counters and other furniture touched by the robbers should be processed for latent prints. Occasionally, the robber may handle papers, checks, or currency. These should be processed with silver nitrate. In one sample case, the robber, observing that a bank employee was watching him with great care, picked up some advertising circulars, threw them to the employee, and ordered him to write his name on one of them. The robber placed the signed paper in his pocket. Subsequently, the circulars were processed for latent prints. On one of the circulars a print of value was developed. A search of the FBI Identification Division files yielded a successful comparison. The witnesses were requested to study photographs in the FBI bank robbery album. A positive identification was made with one of the photographs. The criminal in the identified photograph was found to be the possessor of the fingerprint developed on the circular. He was subsequently apprehended and convicted. The getaway car, which is usually recovered shortly after the crime, is an excellent source of fingerprints. The rearview mirror, front doors, and side windows are the most fruitful areas for processing. Each year, one or more robberies are solved by means of a print deposited on the rearview mirror by a robber adjusting it to his sitting height.

c. **Restraining Devices.** In order to restrain the victim or his employees, the robbers frequently tie them up with rope, towels, sheeting, or adhesive tape. The robbers may bring the tying materials or ligatures with them in anticipation of the need or will use the materials at hand when the emergency arises. For example, in a robbery involving the theft of narcotics from a hospital, the criminals, on encountering resistance, may resort to the use of adhesive tape. The persons finding the victim tied up should endeavor to release him without disturbing the knots. A characteristic type of knot may offer a clue to the identity of one of the criminals. Similarly, in removing adhesive, care should be taken to avoid obliterating fingerprints on either side of the tape. In addition to the significance of the knots and the fingerprints, the restraining material may sometimes be traced to its source, if it has been brought to the scene by the criminals. The cord, for example, may have been removed from a Venetian blind. The edge of the adhesive tape may match the end of a roll of tape found on the suspect.

d. **Stolen Property.** The robbers are not always careful in the selection of loot. Money bags, paper bags, and small traveling bags are used to hold the loot. In addition to cash, they may take securities and traveler's checks. The latter are excellent tracing clues. In one robbery, the stolen traveler's checks were traced for several months as they were passed by the criminals. The trail led through a number of eastern cities. The investigators were able to construct a pattern from these peregrinations and finally made a shrewd forecast of the next stop in the criminals' itinerary. Plants were staked out in the city and the criminals were apprehended as they were about to cash another traveler's check.

e. **Other Physical Evidence.** Footprints may be left on the bank floor by the robbers if the streets are wet or snowy. A discarded newspaper may provide a clue to the area which they have passed through. The newspaper should, of course, be processed for latent prints. Discarded garments such as gloves, hats, or jackets may bear dry cleaners' marks or tags. A gun or other abandoned weapon may provide a tracing clue after it has been processed for prints.

f. **Voice.** An important part of the *modus operandi* of the crime of robbery is the manner of speech of the criminals. The opening and closing speeches of the robber are highly characteristic. The criminal in his planning has usually determined a set of orders which he will give the victims, e.g., "This is a stick-up, keep your hands down and walk to the back." Some criminals will repeat this without modification at each job. While intimidating his victim, the robber may employ the language of violence and vulgarity that is closest to his fancy and hence is part of his character. It is important, then, for the detective to obtain an exact statement of the language used by the robber.

12. *Modus Operandi*

In the investigation of the crime of robbery, the *modus operandi* file is of great importance. In the absence of physical clues, the techniques and mannerisms of the robbers are often the most valuable clues to the identity of the robber.

a. **The *Modus Operandi* File.** The robbery index can be arranged profitably along the following lines:

1) *Type of Robbery*

Bank	Gasoline Station
Bank Messenger	Warehouse
Payroll at Premises	Hotels

Payroll Messenger	Dentists and Doctors
Armored Car	Gambling Games
Cab Driver	Residences
Store (with subdivisions	Mugging
according to type of store)	Private Cars
Theater	

2) *Method of Attack*

Threatening	Binding
Assault	Drugging

3) *Weapon*

Mugging	Revolver or Automatic
Blackjack	(Specify size and type)
Brass Knuckles	

4) *Object*

Money	Jewelry
Clothing	Goods

5) *Vehicle*

6) *Voice and Speech*
(Characteristic orders, threats, or phrases)

7) *Peculiarities*

Takes clothes of victim	Slashes tires
Cuts telephone wires	

13. Loan Companies and Savings Associations

These organizations are similar to banks except for the fact that the building is relatively weak in structure and permits a forced entry. Thus, the robbers can enter at night, await the arrival of employees in the morning, and force them to open the safes. In a sample robbery of this type the robbers approached the savings association building from an empty lot in the rear. Using a spread jack they forced apart the bars protecting a window. One robber jimmied open the window, entered, and hid in the toilet. At 8:45 A.M., the manager "opened up" the building, preparatory for business. As he entered the back room, the robber met him with his gun in hand. He ordered the manager to crawl out, below eye level, to the small burglarproof safe in the front room. The manager opened the safe and handed $2,500 to the robber, who escaped through the rear.

14. Jewelry Stores

The robbery of jewelry stores is usually practiced in large metropolitan shops where the value of the stock may run into the hundreds of thousands of dollars. In the typical jewelry job the robbers dress exceptionally well in order to appear as customers during the first few minutes of the operation. Various ruses are employed. The "gentleman robber" has become popular in recent years. This type of criminal has all the appearances of a wealthy customer. He is fastidious in his tastes and requests the jeweler to show him the best of his stock in a certain line, preferably diamonds. At the opportune moment, when a big "take" is on the trays before him and the road appears relatively clear, the robber displays his gun and takes the jewels.

Other types of bandits use a more direct approach, but still rely on initially gaining the confidence of the salesman. In stores which are not visible from the street, the robbers will avoid all formalities and conduct the operation in the manner of a bank robbery. Methods of detecting jewelry store robbers rely heavily on locating the fence. A market is needed in order for even 20 percent of the value of the jewelry to be realized. Tips are obtained from jewelers and pawn brokers who recognize the exceptional value of the merchandise and question its origin.

15. Closing-Time Shop Robberies

Chain stores, haberdasheries, druggists, restaurants, and many other kinds of business establishments usually have a fairly large sum of money at hand in the evening, especially on Saturday night. A gang of three robbers may attack a series of these shops in an evening. One of the criminals will remain in the getaway car while the other two proceed to hold up the store. The employees are herded into the back room, the money taken from the cash register, and the bandits disappear. Since the employees have an excellent opportunity to observe the robbers closely and listen to their voices, effective clues can be derived from physical descriptions and the *modus operandi.*

16. Liquor Stores, Gasoline Stations, and Delicatessen Stores

These are three very popular targets for the modern robber. The liquor store usually has several hundred dollars in cash on hand and is attended by only one or two persons. The delicatessen store is a likely objective because of the late hours kept by the employees on Saturday and Sunday nights. This is particularly true in New York City (Manhattan) where periodically there is a wave of robberies of delicatessen stores. Gasoline stations, because of their isolation and all night service, are also obvious targets.

These three targets have been grouped together because they form part of the *modus operandi* of the robber. A criminal will "specialize" in liquor stores alone, for example, on one evening robbing two or three. The apprehension of this type of robber depends upon the likelihood that he will pull the same kind of job in the near future. Thus, the "plant" or "stake-out" is the technique sometimes used by the police.

17. Robbery of Individuals

The term "individual" is used here to mean a person not at the time representing a business. The form of robbery is a "small time" operation practiced by a criminal wanting the imagination or daring required for the robbery of an establishment. Although the perpetrator may lack the courage for larger endeavors and may be armed with only a blackjack or a knife, he may possess a viciousness and savagery that make him exceedingly dangerous.

a. **Mugging.** The term *mugging* is derived from the assailant's technique of seizing the victim from behind with one arm locked around his neck or head and the other being used to frisk his valuables from him. Muggers may act alone or in concert. They attack men and women. A person, preferably one intoxicated, returning home at night from a social engagement is the ideal victim. The mugger may operate with a female accomplice whose function it is to entice the victim into a building.

1) ***The Offense.*** Mugging may be described as the robbery of
an individual accompanied by an assault. The offense usually
takes place indoors—in hallways, elevators, stairways, and apartments. Thus, more than half of the muggings occur outside of the
purview of the patrol force. Many of the victims are chronic
drunks or men seeking the company of prostitutes or homosexuals.
The habits of these persons obviously render them especially
vulnerable to the mugger. On the average, the mugger strikes
many times before he is arrested, and even when arrested and
convicted, he will usually be on the streets again in a relatively
short time. Because of an overloaded judiciary system, the desire
to avoid a costly and time-consuming trial or deficiencies in the
evidence, the defendant is permitted to plead guilty to a lesser
offense (plea-bargaining) than the armed robbery and assault
charge for which he was originally arrested. Parole further reduces
the time served in prison for an offense. Many offenders are
juveniles and are often treated leniently with suspended sentences.
Hence, the time served is minimal and there are many repeat
offenders.

2) ***Plea-Bargaining.*** The judiciary and the prosecuting attorney have often been criticized, perhaps unfairly, for the number
of repeat offenders preying on the public. A study conducted by
the Vera Institute of Justice explains in good part the apparent
indulgence shown by judges and prosecuting attorneys in plea-
bargaining. An arrest-to-disposition examination of fifty-three
randomly selected robbery cases showed that fifty-two were plea-
bargained or dismissed outright and only twenty-seven went to
jail. Of the twenty-seven jailed only eleven were imprisoned for
more than a year.

A closer study of the cases, however, indicated that simple logic
rather than misplaced magnanimity directed these court decisions.
In nineteen of the fifty-three robbery cases the defendant and
victim were known to each other, i.e. they were "non-strangers."
Robberies by non-strangers have a high clearance rate, since the
offender is identified and located by the victim. Convictions,
however, are not necessarily forthcoming because of the later
reluctance of the victim to press charges. Thus, fifteen out of the

nineteen non-stranger arrests resulted in no jail sentence and the few jail sentences were for periods of less than a year.

Of the thirty-four robbery cases not involving a relationship between defendant and victim, i.e. "stranger" robberies, twenty-three resulted in jail sentences of five years or more. The arrests that did not result in jail terms were cases in which the victim failed to testify or proved to have questionable reliability. In some cases the defendant's lack of criminal record suggested judicial clemency.

3) *Investigation.* The investigation of a "stranger" mugging requires prompt action. Ordinarily, the patrol force is more effective in this kind of case. The local police officer has some knowledge of the neighborhood, its inhabitants, and the sources of information. Personal inquiry of possible witnesses and the owners of taverns and restaurants is the most helpful beginning. In the absence of a struggle, few traces may be found at the scene or on the victim. Since in the mugging of a female the criminal usually puts his hand over the mouth to prevent an outcry, the investigator should examine the palms of suspects for lipstick stains. Sometimes a mugging case can be solved by spectrophotometric comparison of a female victim's lipstick with a red stain removed from the hand of a suspect.

4) *Decoy Units.* The use of a disguised police officer to pose as a potential victim of a mugger has proved a successful technique in an increasing number of cities. The project requires a person experienced in amateur theatricals, including make-up procedures. In larger cities like New York and San Francisco, decoy street crime units are broken down into full-time day and night decoy teams. One male or female officer in each team is designated as the decoy with two to five other members acting as backup. Through the police department's property clerk an impressive array of disguises was made available to the unit. Dressed as clergyman, little old ladies, cabbies, tennis players, bums, and sometimes Santa Claus, these policemen pretend to be innocent bystanders and likely victims in areas of high street crime. In a typical case, a policewoman arrested two men who had tried to rob her as she sat on a park bench, wearing a shabby dress and a gray wig. She was a

seemingly helpless decoy, but hidden nearby were several "backup men" — plainclothesmen who were ready to come to her aid.

b. **Lovers' Lane.** A particularly vicious type of robber is the criminal who selects as his victims couples sitting in parked cars in secluded spots. Quite frequently, after taking the man's money, the robbers will force him to witness the rape of his female companion. These robberies are difficult to solve because of the victim's desire to withhold information and avoid publicity.

c. **Hitchhikers.** Probably the most fruitful of all robbery fields is that of hitchhiking banditry. Indeed, if he is disguised by a military uniform, the robber cannot fail to be successful in soliciting a ride on the highway. The masquerading soldier thumbs a ride, seats himself alongside of the driver, and pulls out a gun. He alights and is picked up by a confederate who is driving nearby on a different road. Alternatively, he may order the driver out of the car and drive to a place near his own vehicle.

d. **Doctors and Dentists.** Professional men such as dentists and doctors are likely subjects for robbery since their offices are open to prospective patients. Selecting a time which will permit him to be the last patient, the robber "sticks up" the dentist and takes whatever money is available. The victim is usually too intelligent to offer resistance but can often give an excellent description of the criminal.

Twenty such robberies were attributed to Martin Nicholosi, a former convict who allegedly gained entry by deceiving dentists into believing he needed root-canal work. In 1975 he was arrested and charged with the armed robbery of more than twenty dentists and physicians in Brooklyn. In the words of Sgt. Emidio Ponzi of the Brooklyn Robbery Squad: "He pulled off a couple of jobs in the offices of physicians where he complained of chest pains. When the coast was clear, he whipped out his revolver and said, 'This is a stickup.' " The robberies had netted the suspect thousands of dollars in money and jewelry over a period of six months.

e. **Residence.** The homes of certain types of wealthy businessmen are targets for the robber. The typical victim lives in an area which is on the outskirts of the city without being isolated. Thus, the robber is afforded to some degree the "cover" of a populated neighborhood, and his presence does not attract unusual attention.

Often, the owner of the house is professionally engaged in a business which falls somewhat short of the respectable. Income tax evaders who must conceal large sums of money in their houses are representative of this class of victim. The job is usually fingered. The most important lead in a case of this type is frequently the servant. Obviously, former employees should also be investigated. The victim is usually the housewife or the maid, who is tied up with rope or sheeting. Adhesive tape is sometimes used to prevent an outcry. Since the robbers must handle the furniture and other objects in their search for the loot, an examination for latent prints may be profitable.

In house robberies which also involve rape, the crime is usually committed haphazardly without any previously conceived plan. In one of the author's investigations, a single fingerprint developed on the middle of a closet door led to a conviction. The robber forced his way into the apartment by threatening the housewife with a knife. After raping her, he stole some jewelry and money. The robber was described as a small, young man in rough clothes. The area was canvassed within a radius of a mile for errand boys until one answering the description was discovered. Although the victim was doubtful of his identity, having fainted during the assault, the fingerprint on the closet door served to substantiate the suspicion.

f. **Elderly.** One development in the rising crime pattern of New York is the marked increase in the number of assaults and robberies of elderly people. Young men, teen-age boys, and even young women are known to be preying on the elderly. The favorite method of operation is to induce the elderly people to open the apartment door and then, rushing in, to threaten and rob them. Various ruses are used. One team of two men and a young woman employ the following procedure: the young woman informs the elderly person that she has mistakenly received her (or his) mail. When the door is opened, her two male companions rush into the apartment, overpower the elderly person, and remove the valuables.

g. **The Hooker's Knockout Scam.** With the popularity of travel for business, conventions and major sporting events, the success-ful businessman, away from home with time on his hands, is often the target of a type of enterprising, sophisticated, well-dressed prostitute. She poses as a business representative, a health technician or a school teacher and strikes up a conversation with a man in a hotel bar or lobby. The man is selected for his professional dress and demeanor. An expensive wristwatch, such as a Rolex, is often the mark of a worthwhile prospect. After casually engaging the man in conversation, she will eventually arrange to have herself invited to his room. At the first opportunity she will "spike" his drink with a sedative such as diazepam (Valium) in sufficient quantity to insure that the victim will pass out for a period of at least eight hours. After removing his wallet, watch and other valuables, the perpetrator, with ample getaway time, moves on to another resort or convention center in a different state. When the victim recovers he is often too disoriented to remember what happened to him or, as a married man, too embarrassed to bring it to the attention of the police. For these reasons, the crime, more often than not, is never reported.

ADDITIONAL READING

Robbery

Banton, M.P.: *Investigating Robbery.* Brookfield, Vt.: Gower, 1985.

Baumer, T.L. and Carrington, M.D.: *Robbery of Financial Institutions: Executive Summary.* Washington, D.C.: U.S. Department of Justice, 1986.

Bellemin-Noel, J.: Combatting Armed Attacks on Financial Establishments. 31 *International Criminal Police Review,* 296, 1976.

Conklin, J.E.: *Robbery and the Criminal Justice System.* Philadelphia, Lippincott, 1972.

Dunn, C.S.: *The Patterns of Robbery Characteristics and their Occurrence among Social Areas.* Washington, D.C.: U.S. Government Printing Office, 1976.

Einstadter, W.J.: The Social Organization of Armed Robbery. 17 *Social Problems,* 64, 1969.

Feeney, F. (Ed.): *Prevention and Control of Robbery,* 5 vols. Davis, University of California Center on Administration of Criminal Justice, 1973.

Gabor, T., et al.: *Armed Robbery: Cops, Robbers, and Victims.* Springfield, Ill.: Thomas, 1987.

Gates, D.F. and Roberge, N.N.: Updated Solutions for Armored Car Robberies. 58 *Police Chief,* 10, 1991.

Harry, B.: A Diagnostic Study of Robbers. 30 *Journal of Forensic Sciences,* 50, 1985.

Lamson, P.A.: A Concentrated Robbery Reduction Program. 40 *FBI Law Enforcement Bulletin,* 12, 1971.

Macdonald, J.M. and Brannan, C.D.: The Investigation of Robbery. 4 *Police Chief,* 1, 1974.

Macdonald, J.M.: *Armed Robbery: Offenders and Their Victims.* Springfield, Ill.: Thomas, 1975.

McCormick, M.: *Robbery Prevention: What the Literature Reveals.* La Jolla, Calif.: Western Behavioral Science Institute, 1974.

McDonald, W.F.: *Plea Bargaining: Critical Issues and Common Practices.* Washington, D.C.: U.S. Government Printing Office, 1985.

Ozenne, T.: The Economics of Bank Robbery. 3 *Journal of Legal Studies,* 19, 1974.

Rapp, B.: *The 211 Book: Armed Robbery Investigation.* Port Townsend, Wash.: Loompanics, 1989.

Sagalyn, A.: *The Crime of Robbery in the United States.* Washington, D.C.: U.S. Government Printing Office, 1971.

Waegel, W.B.: Patterns of Police Investigation of Urban Crimes. 10 *Journal of Police Science and Administration,* 452, 1982.

Walsh, D.: *Heavy Business: Commercial Burglary and Robbery.* New York, Methuen, 1986.

Ward, R.H. and Ward, T.J.: *Police Robbery Control Manual.* Washington, D.C.: Law Enforcement Assistance Administration, 1975.

Hostage Situations

Carlson, E.R.: Hostage Negotiation Situations. 25 *Law and Order,* 7, 1977.

Marlow, J.R.: The Sacramento Situation: A Case History of Managing a Hostage-Terrorist Situation. 39 *Law and Order,* 9, 1991.

Maher, G.F.: *Hostage: A Police Approach to a Contemporary Crisis.* Springfield, Ill.: Thomas, 1977.

Strentz, T.: 13 Indicators of Volatile Negotiations. 39 *Law and Order* 9, 1991.

Chapter 23

FORGERY

1. Introduction

"IT WAS wonderful what could be done with a piece of paper."
These words are attributed to Ivar Kreuger, a remarkably
clever manipulator of securities, whose forgeries at one time
threatened the stability of international finance. The words are
unfortunately true today as they have been for hundreds of years.
Forgery, as we know it today, the alteration of documents that
impose a financial obligation, dates from the days of the merchants who first instituted the procedure of transferring money by
means of a piece of paper. This measure, taken to thwart the
robbers who harried the highway shipments of gold and silver,
introduced a new and even greater evil than that which it was
intended to cure. In place of the armed thug, forthright, brutal,
and direct, there arose the penman, a person of education,
talent, and imagination, whose crime affected only property and
hence did not incur popular odium.

Since forgery attacked the landed and the moneyed classes it
was not viewed with equanimity by the law. Financial transactions
in business depend on credit and in turn on the paper which
represents credit. Negotiable instruments, bills of lading, bills of
hand, checks, and similar documents are the tools of commerce.
Destroy their trustworthiness and the transactions of finance suffer accordingly. So serious did the threat of forgery become that
the English instituted the death penalty for this offense. In 1819
an issue of one-pound notes consisting of simple pen and ink
inscriptions on ordinary white paper proved irresistible to a great
mass of the populace. During the succeeding seven years, 94,000
persons were arrested for the crime of forgery. Of this number
7,700 were sentenced to death.

2. The Forger

Forgery in the early twentieth century was a much more complicated procedure in which a variety of false instruments such as
bank notes, drafts, bills of exchange, letters of credit, registered
bonds, and post office money orders as well as checks were manufactured or altered and foisted off. A knowledge of chemicals,
papers, inks, engraving, etching, lithography, and penmanship as
well as detailed knowledge of bank operations were prime requisites for success. The amounts of money sought were relatively
large and often they had to be obtained through complex monetary transactions. The technological characteristics of this kind of
forgery made planning, timing, specialization, differentiation of
roles, morale, and organization imperative. Capital was necessary
for living expenses during the period when preparations for
the forgeries were being made. Intermediates between the skilled
forger and the passers were necessary so that the latter could swear
that the handwriting on the false negotiable instruments was not
theirs and so that the forger himself was not exposed to arrest. In
short, professional forgery was based on the technology of the
period. The forger of extensive knowledge and highly developed
skills is rapidly becoming a figure of history. The universal prevalence of checking accounts and credit cards has greatly simplified
the forger's task. He is now a "loner" following one of the types
described below:

a. **General Type.** Forgery is practiced by a wide variety of
types, male and female, young and old. Elderly women have
plied the forger's trade successfully. Prisoners have produced
forgeries during their confinement. It is of little use to enumerate
the endless number of types except to illustrate the element of
variety, the range of social levels, and the differing backgrounds.
The most useful conclusion to be drawn from such a study is
the existence of two prerequisite qualifications: a degree of clerical skill and elementary business knowledge and an exceptional
amount of that type of courage which is best described as "nerve."
A high-school education would seem to be indicated by the former qualification. In the nineteenth century, when such academic
training was far less common, this degree of knowledge and skill

would have served to screen out a great number of adults from the domain of suspects. The compulsory education of modern times has equipped most of the population with the technical facility and basic knowledge of the forger. At present the most practical way of studying the forger is to classify him by his *modus operandi.*

b. **The Habitual Check Passer.** This type has spent many years in passing checks. Often he spends a year or two in jail between short periods of freedom. One well-known check passer has spent a good part of fifty years in prison. His profits have been meager, barely sufficient to offer a comfortable living. He is typical of the mediocre check passer who has not had any great degree of success in passing even small checks. He has become familiar to the police and his chances of future success naturally diminish with each arrest.

c. **The Successful Check Passer.** A small group of forgers manage to make a distinguished success of their criminal careers. They are the "gentlemen" of the profession, the aristocrats who manage to evade the law for many years. They are characterized by an unusually "honest" appearance, which borders on distinguished prosperity. Their apparent good character and honesty quickly hurdle the first barrier, the suspicions of the person cashing the check. This type of forger is professional in his operations. His manner, story, dress, face, and his check are calculated to avoid raising the slightest suspicion. It is as simple for him to cash a fraudulent check as it is for the honest person to change a fifty-dollar bill.

d. **The Roving Check Passer.** This type of forger passes several checks in one community and moves on to another. He goes from one jurisdiction to another often leaving the state before his checks have been found to be fraudulent. He presents a great problem to the police, since he is an exceptionally clever criminal and his true identity is difficult to determine.

e. **The Disguised Check Passer.** By changing his appearance this check passer is able to escape arrest for long periods of time. He may employ such simple tricks as horn-rimmed glasses, mustache, or dyed hair. Recently one check artist enjoyed great success by disguising himself as a clergyman. He would pass five or six checks for a total of $200 in one evening in the same community and then would pass on to another area. Finally he came to a city were police had been expecting him and had alerted the merchants. His error lay in working the same disguise too often.

3. Techniques of the Forger

To pass a forged check, the criminal must first obtain blank forms on which to write the forgery, or he may obtain checks meant for another person and merely add the endorsement. He may use equipment to make the check look more genuine. Finally, he must have identification papers to support the story.

a. **Obtaining Blank Forms.** The following are the two most common methods:

1) *Theft.* The forger may steal blank checks from an office. Posing as a salesman, telephone repair worker, or window cleaner, he will await an opportunity to steal a number of checks from the back of a book. Another method is to pilfer mail and thus obtain cashed or uncashed checks.

2) *Printing.* Using a stolen check as a model, the forger can have facsimiles printed. Alternatively, he may print a check bearing the name of a fictitious company.

b. **Equipment.** The professional check passer will equip himself with mechanical devices for practicing his trade: Checkwriters, protectographs, typewriters, rubber stamps, date stamps, and even printing equipment. With these he can produce the perforations in a check that convince the bank cashier of its authenticity. He can stamp *certified* on the check to remove any residual doubts of the passer. Finally, he can print the names of reputable companies such as General Electric or Exxon.

c. **Identification Papers.** Supporting papers are necessary for a successful forgery operation. Documents such as Social Security cards, automobile registration, driver's license, ID card, and service discharge papers can be used by the forger to identify himself to the check casher.

d. **Official Papers.** The business of selling a variety of official identification documents has broadened out to include a much wider market than that of supplying supporting identification papers for forgers. The largest market now accommodates persons with no criminal connections. Driver's licenses, for example, are bought by non–English-speaking persons who are not able to pass the written parts of license examinations. Persons without qualifying high school or college education buy blank diplomas and degree certificates on which their own names will be filled in. Professional criminals are able to obtain birth certificates, licenses, car registrations, diplomas, armed forces discharges, Social Security cards, and even passports. Some of these documents are counterfeit, but most are genuine document blanks stolen from government offices and printing houses. Gangsters concentrate primarily on the wholesale end of this business. They arrange to buy blocks of documents from inside contacts and then sell them to retailers. In turn, the retailer sells them to individual customers at a great markup. Normally, he will assist the customer in filling out the document or form to insure its correct appearance. A diploma, for example, may require calligraphy or special lettering in affixing the customer's name.

4. Examples of Forgery Techniques

The techniques and methods which have been described above are shown below in the actual operations of successful forgers.

a. **Using Checks in Excess of Purchases.** One passer of fraudulent checks successfully pursued his career of forgery for a half century by limiting his gain from each illegal transaction to a small sum such as ten or twenty dollars. His method consisted of purchasing several hundred dollars worth of merchandise and giving a forged check slightly in excess of the bill. He would receive in change the small excess and would avoid receiving the goods by stating that he would pick them up at a later time or by having them delivered to a fictitious address.

b. **Use of Elaborate Credentials.** Another accomplished forger, Courtney Taylor, selected as victims jewelry and department stores. Posing as a representative of one of the well-known firms whose names were printed on his checks, he successfully passed the bogus instruments in twenty-eight states. In eighteen months he obtained $55,000 in this manner. Entering a store and leisurely selecting an item for purchase he would offer in payment a "salary" check or "bonus" check from the concern whose name was printed on the face. For identification he would display company credentials, selective service cards, Social Security cards, operator's licenses, and similar papers, all fraudulent. While waiting for the check to be approved he would discuss the product of his concern and even produce samples. The preparation which Taylor made for his career of forgery is of particular interest. While serving a prison term, he devoted his reading time to a study of the literature relating to printing. Eventually he became the possessor of such printing equipment as a hand printing press, trays of type, printer's ink, and a trimmer. A search of Taylor's apartment at the time of his arrest revealed 172 completed checks for amounts totaling in excess of $16,000, fifty-seven Selective Service cards, assorted fraudulent identification cards, railroad and airline ticket stubs, a stampmaking kit, assorted stamps, a checkwriter, and a typewriter. Apparently Taylor had extensively applied his knowledge of printing. In one particular month he printed up check forms of thirty-two widely known business establishments and divisions of state and city governments. Typical of Taylor's operations was the use of the "voucher system." He would first obtain a photograph of a widely known trademark such as that of Smith Brothers Cough Drops® and have a cut prepared. At a legitimate printing concern he would pose as the District Sales Manager for Smith Brothers, present the cut and order the printing of a number of new sales contracts. He would lay the basis for the order by explaining that he had encountered a shortage of promotional-type sales agreements. The form which the printer was requested to prepare consisted of a sheet of paper, the upper portion of which bore the same design and printing that would be found on a legitimate check. The lower part contained an agreement for the signature of the merchant whereby for a sum of money he contracted for a 25 percent increase in his purchases of Smith Brothers products. By detaching the upper part, Taylor would have a typical check form. Naturally, precautions were taken before calling for the completed printing order to determine whether the printer's suspicions had been aroused. Using the check portion, Taylor would prepare an apparently genuine check by using a numbering machine, a date stamp, a typewriter for the payee's name, a checkwriter for the amount, and the signature of a fictitious officer of the company. With the support of appropriate credentials, Taylor successfully passed a great number of such checks drawn on a number of companies.

c. **The Dual Signature Scheme.** Probably the most accomplished forger of this century was Alexander Thiel who was active from 1930 to 1943, cashing four-figured checks at New York banks several times a year. Thiel is noteworthy also because of his association with the Campbell case. Bertram Campbell, an innocent stockbroker, was arrested and convicted for forgeries committed by Thiel on the testimony of eyewitnesses, the chief point of identification being his small mustache. After serving three years in prison, Campbell was released after Thiel's confession. In his statement Thiel confessed to forgeries amounting to $250,000 and described in detail the schemes he used so successfully.

Blank checks were obtained by committing a burglary in the offices of a businessman. After removing the checks from the book Thiel would write on the check stubs "void, imperfect" or "checks removed, defective printing." If a checkwriter was used in the office, he would stamp the blank checks. Next, Thiel would break into the office of a second individual—the person whose name he intended to use in forging the checks—and appropriate necessary papers for identification such as letters and office letterheads and canceled checks with model signatures. Equipped with these papers he would open a bank account in the name of the latter person and deposit a forged check for several thousand dollars, drawn on the account of the first individual. Thiel would now test both persons to determine whether either had become suspicious. He would telephone the first man, stating that he was a person of the same name and was inquiring about another person of that name. If the victim had discovered the loss of the blank checks, he would at this time indicate this knowledge. In addition Thiel would learn in this way whether the bank had communicated with the impersonated man to verify the fact that he had opened an account. With these assurances the stage was satisfactorily set. Allowing time for the clearance of the deposited checks through the bank on which they were drawn, Thiel would then cash checks on the account which he had opened under the assumed name. The whole operation would be completed within a given month, before the victim received his monthly bank statement.

Thiel's success was attributable mainly to his "dual signature" scheme and his remarkable facility for simulating signatures. The key to his method lay in the authenticity of his references. On opening an account he would use an assumed name and give as a reference the bank in which the true owner of the name had an actual account. In addition he would write the signature of the impersonated man in the presence of the bank official. This signature would be forwarded to the reference bank where invariably it would be declared genuine.

5. Law

Forgery laws are quite lengthy and vary with states. Only the basic parts of these laws are discussed below.

a. **Definition.** Forgery is committed by a person who, with intent to defraud, knowingly makes or utters (passes, offers, or puts in circulation) a false writing that apparently imposes a legal liability on another or affects his legal right or liability to his prejudice. The term *false* as used here refers to the making of the writing and not to the content of, or the facts contained in, the writing. For example, a check which bears the signature of the maker and which is drawn with intent to defraud on a bank wherein the maker has no credit is not a forgery but is simply a bad check. Signing the name of another to an instrument without authority and with intent to defraud is forgery since the signature is falsely made. The distinction here is that the falsely made signature purports to be the act of another. Although forged checks are the most common, other instruments such as railroad tickets, wills, pari-mutuel tickets, and receipts are also subject to fraudulent alteration and making.

b. **Elements of Proof.** To support a charge of forgery the following elements must be established.

1) *False Making.* It must be shown that a writing was falsely made or altered. The writing concerned is usually a signature

or a number on a check. An alteration may be shown by the document examiner using physical methods. A false signature can be established by a comparison with the true signature which it purports to be. A statement should be obtained from the person whose signature was forged showing that he had not signed the document himself and that he had not authorized the accused to do so for him. If the name of a fictitious person was used as the purported drawer of the check, proof of falsity may include evidence that the purported drawer of the check had no account in the bank on which the check was drawn. An interview with a bank officer should provide this information. The forged instrument itself should be produced, if it is available.

2) *Legal Liability.* The signature or writing must be of a nature which would, if genuine, impose a legal liability on another or change his legal right or liability to his prejudice. The writing must on its face appear to impose a legal liability on another as, for example, a check or note. It is not forgery to alter or falsely make with intent to defraud a writing which does not operate to impose a legal liability. For example, a falsely made letter of introduction would not be a forgery in the legal sense. For an alteration to constitute forgery, it must effect a material change in the legal tenor of the writing; for example, an alteration whereby an obligation is apparently increased, diminished, or discharged would be material. The date, amount, or place of payment would be material alterations in the case of a note. The change in legal liability or prejudice may be quite obvious, as in the case of a check. In other situations it may be necessary to obtain the testimony of a bank officer or a company officer as to the effect of the writing or alteration.

3) *Identity of the Forger.* It must be shown that it was the accused who falsely made or altered the writing or who knowingly uttered, offered, or issued the false instrument. This may be established by the confession of the accused, statements of witnesses, or by the testimony of a document examiner.

4) *Intent to Defraud.* The intent to defraud must be shown; it need not be directed toward a particular person nor be for the advantage of the offender. It is immaterial whether anyone was actually defrauded. The carrying out of the intent need not go

beyond the false making or altering of the writing. The intent can often be inferred from the act. Evidence of other forgeries is admissible to prove intent to defraud; hence, other business establishments and towns which the suspect has passed through should be visited for the purpose of discovering similar, additional forgeries or attempts at uttering. It must also be shown that the suspect knew that the instrument he was uttering was a forgery. This is not difficult if the forgery is the handiwork of the suspect, but may become a problem when the utterer and the forger are different persons. In fact the most common defense to a charge of uttering a forgery is that the accused had honestly received the forged instrument and believed it to be genuine. Another claim is that the accused was cashing the check for an acquaintance. To meet such claims the investigation should develop all possible evidence to show the existence of guilty knowledge. Evidence of the existence of other similar checks or other attempts to utter forgeries is admissible.

6. Tracing and Apprehending the Forger

Ordinarily the nature of the forged check is not discovered until long after the forger has departed. Hence, the investigator is usually at a disadvantage of a time lapse of several days. The tracing of the forger is not a simple problem. The actual arrest, however, presents no difficulties since this type of criminal is not given to violent action.

a. **Detection by Cashier.** Naturally the most effective method of catching the forger is to detect him in the act. Alert bank cashiers, storekeepers, and hotel clerks can sometimes spot the forger as he attempts to pass the check. Employees who keep abreast of circularized information on forgers can aid greatly in this work.

b. **Plants.** Persons who steal checks from mailboxes can be caught by means of plants or stakeouts. If the police are aware of the general area of his operations, they can send out investigators to cover certain spots on days on which government checks are delivered.

c. *Modus Operandi.* The check passer will usually have his own peculiar way of operating. His "story" or disguise will become well known. Employees can be alerted to the danger and instructed to call the police on the arrival of the suspect.

7. Interviewing the Victim

Three victims are to be considered: the person who cashed the check; the person whose signature has been forged; and the bank on which it was drawn.

a. **Person Who Cashes the Check.** This is usually a bank cashier or a storekeeper. Bank cashiers are often careless in their habits of accepting checks. In a bank in a large Eastern city, the management subjected one of its cashiers to a test. One of the other employees stepped to the window and submitted a rubber check (the check was actually made of rubber). The cashier took the check, stamped it, made the deposit, and placed the check in its proper place. Although this is an extreme case, lesser degrees of carelessness are common among bank employees. Store personnel are similarly careless. Large chain stores make a rule of cashing the checks of government employees. Chain grocery stores may suffer losses running into the hundreds of thousands of dollars annually. The added business resulting from the check cashing service, however, more than compensates for the losses. The interview with the person who cashed the check should develop the following information:

1) *Physical Description.* A detailed physical description of the check passer should be obtained (see Chap. 29). Descriptions should also be obtained from other persons who may have seen the check passer.

2) *Circumstances.* The manner in which the check was cashed, the story given by the passer; the exact words used; credentials offered; conversation and behavior after the check was passed.

3) *Date and Time.* Date and time of the occurrence.

4) *Number of Persons Present.* Was the store or bank crowded at the time?

5) *Record.* A record of the cashier in regard to cashing checks. History of the establishment with regard to forged checks.

6) *Handwriting.* Did the check passer sign or write the check in the presence of the person cashing?

b. **The Person Whose Signature Appears on the Check.** It is important to interview this person early in the investigation. In military services where fraudulent checks are quite common because of the relative ease with which they may be passed at Officers' Clubs and post exchanges, it is found that in approximately one-third of the cases an error has been made: The person who first alleged that his name had been forged subsequently remembers or is convinced that the signature is his own. The interview should include the following points:

1) The subject should examine and identify the document. The check may be marked for identification by inscribing small initials on a corner of the reverse side.

2) *Authenticity.* He admits or denies that the signature is his.

3) *A Statement* to the effect that he has not given authority to another person to use his signature.

4) *Handwriting Specimens,* signatures, and other writings similar to those forged, should be obtained.

5) *Check Writing Habits.* Does he write many checks? For what purpose? In what amounts? Manner in which he writes his checks, viz., writing of amounts, assigning check number, manner of writing date.

6) *Access to Check Forms.* Where kept? Who has access to the area?

7) *Records of Employees and Associates.* Inquiries should also be made about acquaintances.

8) *Suspects.* He should be encouraged to name any persons whom he may suspect and to give his reasons for his suspicions.

9) *Financial Status.* What is the condition of his credit? Does he have an account at the bank on which the check was drawn? In what bank does he have accounts. Has he had any bad checks, i.e., complaints of insufficient funds? Has he been connected in any way with a previous forged check case?

c. **Bank.** The bank on which the check was drawn should be visited to ascertain certain facts. Information relating to the proof of the crime must be obtained as well as any clues which they may offer.

1) Is the check invalid?

2) Does the person whose name appears on the check have an account there? Has he ever had an account there?

3) Have they had any forged checks similar to the evidence check?

8. False Identity Papers

Advances in printing and photocopying techniques have made it increasingly difficult to detect bogus or altered birth certificates, resident alien or "green cards," driver's licenses, and Social Security cards. What is more disturbing is the ease with which dealers and aliens themselves are able to obtain authenticated copies of genuine documents such as birth certificates from lax state and local agencies. With a birth certificate, an impressive array of other genuine ID cards can easily be acquired. Birth certificates are the most common means of establishing identity, and birth certificate frauds are among the easiest to perpetrate, according to the Federal Advisory Committee on False Identification. Approximately 10 million certified copies of birth certificates are issued yearly on 1,000 different forms by more than 7,000 local and state offices. More than 80 percent of them are requested and sent out by mail, sometimes to foreign countries. Even unsigned requests are generally honored, as are requests from supposed relatives or other interested parties. State vital records offices also allow thousands of applicants each year to "create" birth records. (A person born in the United States can claim U.S. citizenship.) The applicant simply states that he was born at a certain location but that his parents did not register his birth. "Evidence" such as an affidavit signed by a friend, relative or minister, a notation in a family Bible, a church census, and other easily forged papers will be acceptable. Because so many different forms are used and because they are generally made by photostat, birth certificates are among the easiest documents to counterfeit or alter.

9. Physical Evidence in Forgery

The questioned check is part of the *corpus delicti* and should, accordingly, be safeguarded as a valuable piece of evidence. When not under examination the check should be protected by a transparent envelope. For identification, the investigator's initials and the date should be placed on the back of the check.

The examination of the check for physical evidence should be performed by a competent document expert. If an expert is unavailable, a properly trained investigator can perform some of the preliminary work of the examination. The handwriting comparison of signatures of a suspect with signatures on the check should be performed only by a person qualified to testify as an expert witness. Law enforcement agencies should submit the evidence to the laboratory without tampering with it in any way.

a. **Photographs.** One-to-one photographs of the front and back of the check should first be made.

b. **Latent Fingerprints.** If the forgery is detected early and the check has not been handled to any great extent, the possibility of latent fingerprints exists. The check can be dipped in a 5 percent solution of silver nitrate, dried, and then exposed to bright light (see Chap. 32). The check can be later cleared of the nitrate and restored to its previous condition by immersing in a bath of mercuric chloride and drying. If it is found (by spot testing) that the ink is water soluble, iodine fuming can be used. Checks consisting of heavily sized paper can be processed with black powder.

c. **Forging Methods.** The techniques employed by the forger will depend upon his skill. Some of the most common methods of reproducing a signature are given below:

1) *Free hand.* If the forger is an experienced and skilled penman, he may simulate the signature from the model which he has obtained. This is the most difficult of all methods. If the forger's work is slow and painstaking, an examination under a low-power microscope will reveal the hesitation and the interruptions at points where the pen was lifted.

2) *Tracing.* The signature can be traced from a model. Proof of forgery in this case lies in the fact that the questioned signature

is an exact duplicate of an authentic signature. It is practically impossible to write the same signature twice in exactly the same way. The forged signature can be superimposed over the model in front of a strong light. There are two common methods of tracing:

a) CARBON PAPER TRACE. A piece of carbon paper is placed over the check. The genuine signature is placed over the carbon. With a pencil, the genuine signature is traced and a light carbon outline is produced on the check. The forger then inks in the outline with his pen. This type of trace may be detected by examining under a low-power microscope. Traces of the carbon will be visible in the forged signature.

b) TRANSMITTED LIGHT. The check is placed over the genuine signature and the two are placed over a piece of glass the under side of which is illuminated from below by a strong light. The forger now traces the signature which is visible over the light. This type of trace can sometimes be detected by the abnormal shading and the signs of slow, painstaking movement. Nervousness, retraced lines, varying density, interruptions caused by pen lifts, and tremor may be apparent.

d. **Alterations.** The check may be altered to change the amount, the name, or some other element. The existence of any changes can be discovered by holding the check under an ultraviolet lamp.

1) *Additions.* If the check has been "raised," additional writing is present. The difference in the inks may be apparent to the unaided eye or under the ultraviolet lamp. The use of filter photography or of infrared film will often visibly emphasize the difference in the inks.

2) *Erasures.* When an eraser is used on the paper, the sizing and the fibers are disturbed. The new ink writing placed on the erased area will have a tendency to spread or "feather." If chemical eradicators are used, a bleaching stain usually is apparent. Ultraviolet examination or merely holding the check in front of a light will usually reveal the erasure.

e. **Watermark.** The watermark can be used to trace the source of the check paper. To reproduce the watermarks a photograph can be taken of the check illuminated from the back so as to emphasize the mark. Sometimes, the watermark can be printed directly on photographic paper. When the design cannot be clearly

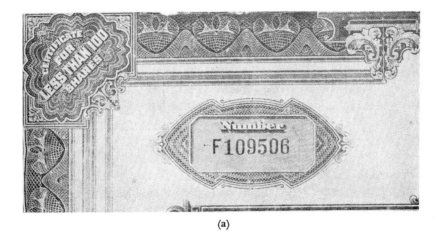

(a)

(b)

Figure 20. The stock certificate, of which the upper left corner is shown in (a), appears to bear the number F 109506. Microscopic examination, however, revealed that the second "0" has been changed from a "9." The photomicrograph (b) shows the disturbance of the fibers. (Courtesy of Edward Palmer.)

photographed because there is writing or printing in the water-mark area, a radiograph can be made using soft x-rays. In this way the writing or printing is eliminated and a picture of the water-mark alone is obtained.

f. **Rubber Stamps.** A rubber stamp found in the possession of the suspect often can be related to the stamp impressions on forged checks. In order to give an appearance of genuineness to their work, some forgers stamp the check with the word "CERTI-FIED." The stamp may have individual characteristics which are reproduced in each impression. The stamp will, of course, have class characteristics that establish a similarity, but not an identity. The stamp itself should be submitted to the laboratory for comparison with the impressions. Some of the characteristics which may be present are the following:

1) *Mold Defects.* In making a "one-piece" mold, the defects existing in the type of the mold are reproduced in the series of stamps made from the mold.

2) *Accidental Nicks.* Careless use of the mold results in individual nicks in the rubber. These can be distinguished from mold defects.

3) *Mounting Defects.* When a "one-piece" stamp is cut out and mounted on its sponge rubber cushion, characteristics may be observed along the border of the stamp.

4) *Alignment.* Stamps which are made by the forger from individual letters will have a poor alignment because of the limitations of the hand-setting process with rubber letters. The investigator should carefully protect the stamp so that the alignment is not disturbed.

5) *Foreign Matter.* Dirt and other foreign material may become imbedded in the letters of the stamp. The result in use is a defective impression which is highly characteristic. Again, the investigator on coming into possession of such a stamp should protect its original condition and should not disturb any foreign matter by mishandling or haphazard testing.

g. **Checkbook.** If a checkbook is found among the effects of the suspect, it should be examined as a possible source of the forged check.

1) *Perforations.* Particular attention should be paid to the perforated line of the checkbook stub and the check. Sometimes, it can be shown that these match and thus it is established that the check was extracted from the suspect's checkbook.

2) *Watermark.* Sometimes the watermark of the check paper overlaps the stub and the check. A matching of the two parts of the watermark is convincing proof of the source of the check.

10. Obtaining Exemplars

Exemplars should be obtained from each person whose name appears on a questioned check as well as from the accused. The methods for obtaining exemplars are described in Chapter 44. There are several reasons for this procedure:

a. To establish the fact of forgery where it exists.

b. To determine whether an attempt has been made in the questioned endorsement to simulate the genuine signature.

c. To verify the genuineness of the endorsement in cases where the complainant actually endorsed and cashed the check but denies the facts in order to obtain a second payment.

d. To verify the genuineness of the check in cases where the complainant suffers from a faulty memory.

11. Sources of Information

a. **General.** Since the nature of the forger's occupation requires that he change his scene frequently, moving about a great deal, patronizing a variety of stores, banks, hotels, and other businesses, and sometimes leaving a trail of bad checks in his wake, the proprietors of these establishments and their security personnel should be consulted where appropriate. Additional clues to the identity and location of the forger may be obtained in this manner. Further help may be sought from retail credit, protective, hotel, and bankers associations.

b. **FBI Resources.** Because of the travel aspects of the offense, the Federal Bureau of Investigation is in a position to offer considerable help in the investigation of a forgery. This assistance relates both to the materials used by the forger and the identification of the offender.

1) **Standards Files.** The FBI document section maintains the following:

   a) Checkwriter Standards File
   b) Ink Standards Collection
   c) Rubber Stamp and Printing Standards File
   d) Typewriter Standards File
   e) Watermark File

2) **PROCHEK.** A computerized file of professional check passers, containing information on their description, habits, and methods of operation.

3) **National Fraudulent Check File.** This is a large (about 100,000 specimens) collection of fraudulent checks gathered by encouraging local police agencies to submit copies of fraudulent checks written in excess of a specified amount. The file is said to aid in the identification of forgers and writers of bad checks.

ADDITIONAL READING

Forgery

Brocklehurst, E.R.: Computer Methods of Signature Verification. 25 *Journal of the Forensic Society,* 445, 1985.

Cain, S. and Winand, J.E.: Striation Evidence in Counterfeiting Cases. 28 *Journal of Forensic Sciences,* 360, 1983.

False Identification: The Problem and Technological Options. Port Townsend, Wash.: Loompanics, 1988.

Federal Advisory Committee on False Identification. *The Criminal Use of False Identification.* Washington, D.C.: U.S. Government Printing Office, 1976.

Flynn, W.J.: Forgery by Phone. 4 *Journal of Police Science and Administration,* 326, 1976.

Fraudulent Credentials. Port Townsend, Wash.: Loompanics, 1985.

Gilliam, V.J.: Taking the Bounce Out of Bad Checks. 60 *FBI Law Enforcement Bulletin,* 10, 1991.

Hargett, J.W. and Dusch, R.A.: Classification and Identification of Checkwriters. 4 *Journal of Police Science and Administration,* 404, 1976.

Herkt, A.: Signature Disguise or Signature Forgery? 26 *Journal of Forensic Science Society,* 257, 1986.

Hogan, B.: The Rise and Fall of Forgery. *Criminal Law Review,* 81, 1974.

I.D. Checking Guide. Redwood City, Calif.: Drivers License Guide Co., 1986.

Lemert, E.M.: The Behavior of the Systematic Check Forger. 6 *Social Problems,* 141, 1958.

Levinson, J.: Passport Examination. 29 *Journal of Forensic Sciences,* 628, 1984.

Rapp, B.: *Check Fraud Investigation.* Port Townsend, Wash.: Loompanics, 1991.

Seleno, J.: Check Print. 58 *FBI Law Enforcement Bulletin,* 2, 1989.

They Write Their Own Sentences: The FBI Handwriting Analysis Manual. Boulder, Col.: Paladin Press, 1987.

Throckmorton, G.J.: Disappearing Ink: Its Use, Abuse, and Detection. 35 *Journal of Forensic Sciences,* 199, 1990.

Traini, R.: Beating the Forger. 15 *Security Gazette,* 10, 1973.

Vastrick, T.W. and Smith, E.J.: Checkwriter Identification—Individuality. 27 *Journal of Forensic Sciences,* 161, 1982.

Williams, G.: Forgery and Falsity. *Criminal Law Review,* 71, 1974.

Williamson, D.M. and Meenach, A.E.: *Cross-Check System for Forgery and Questioned Document Examination.* Chicago, Nelson-Hall, 1981.

Chapter 24

HOMICIDE

I. LAW

1. Introduction

T HE UNLAWFUL killing of a human being is still looked upon as
the classic crime. The detection of the murderer is considered the most severe test of the abilities of the investigator. With
the proliferation of handguns in a more violent society, murder
has become a serious problem. In the 1950s there were approximately five thousand non-negligent homicides a year. Today there
are about twenty-five thousand annually. As a cause of death,
however, murder still lags considerably behind suicide (about
thirty-three thousand a year) and traffic fatalities (about forty-six
thousand annually). Hit-and-run homicides are especially disturbing because the deceased in a motor vehicle death is ordinarily an innocent, law-abiding citizen, frequently a child. It is for
this reason that great stress has been placed in the present treatment on the investigation of motor vehicle homicides, with particular reference to the hit-and-run driver. Of course the problems
of murder and manslaughter in general have been given the
customary emphasis. The crime of murder permits a discussion of
the full resources of the science of investigation. The varieties of
physical evidence, the motives of the culprit, and the efforts which
he will make to evade detection combine to give this crime an
interest, both academic and dramatic, that can be found nowhere
else in the whole catalogue of the penal law.

2. Definitions

Homicide is the killing of a human being. Depending on the circumstances, it may be criminal or innocent.

a. **Criminal Homicide.** A homicide which is not excusable or justifiable is considered a criminal homicide. The crime is considered to have been committed at the place of the act or omission although the victim may have died elsewhere. The death must have occurred within a year and a day of the act or omission and must have been the result of an injury caused by the act or omission. There are two major categories which will be later discussed in detail:

1) *Murder.* Killing with malice aforethought (premeditation) is considered murder. The law presumes all homicides to be committed with malice aforethought and thus to be murder. The burden is on the defendant to show otherwise, i.e., that there was an excuse, justification, or alleviation.

2) *Manslaughter.* This term is used to describe an unlawful and felonious killing without malice aforethought (premeditation).

b. **Innocent Homicide.** There are two kinds of homicide which do not involve criminal guilt, namely, excusable and justifiable homicide:

1) *Excusable Homicide.* For practical purposes we need only consider two kinds of excusable homicide: first, a homicide which is the outcome of an accident or misadventure while doing a lawful act in a lawful manner and without negligence. For example, a hunter accidentally shoots a concealed man; or a lawful operation, performed with due care and skill, results in the death of the patient. Second, a homicide which is committed in self defense. In order to excuse a person for killing on the ground of self-defense, it is required that he must have believed on reasonable grounds that the killing was necessary to preserve his own life or the lives of those whom he might lawfully protect. If the grounds actually exist, the homicide is justifiable; if the grounds, although believed for good cause to be present, do not actually exist, the homicide is excusable. For example, if a person threatened by an assailant who is armed with an imitation pistol reasonably believes the

weapon to be lethal and so kills, the killing, although not authorized by law, is excusable because of the reasonable mistake of fact.

2) *Justifiable Homicide.* A killing is justifiable if it is authorized or commanded by the law. A killing to prevent the commission of a violent felony such as rape, robbery, or other felony against the person is authorized by the law. Other examples are: killing an enemy on the field of battle in time of war, within the rules of war, and executing a death sentence pronounced by a competent tribunal. The acts of a subordinate performed in good faith in compliance with supposed duty or orders, within the scope of authority and without negligence, are justifiable.

3. Murder

A criminal homicide is murder if one of the following four conditions exist:

a. There is a premeditated design to kill.

b. The accused intended to kill or commit great bodily harm.

c. The accused is engaged in an act inherently dangerous to others and shows a wanton disregard of human life.

d. The accused is engaged in the perpetration (or attempt) of a felony against the person such as robbery, burglary, sodomy, rape, or aggravated arson.

4. Premeditated Design to Kill

The term "malice aforethought" is sometimes used in place of "premeditated design to kill." The taking of the human life must be consciously intended. A well-laid plan is not essential; the slaying may be conceived and executed in a short interval of time.

5. Intent to Kill or Inflict Great Bodily Harm

Since a person is presumed to have intended the natural and probable consequences of an act purposely performed by him, where such an intentional act is likely to result in death or great bodily injury, it may be presumed that the accused intended death or great bodily harm. Premeditation is not required. For example, A accidentally meets B, a person who has previously wronged him, and, on the impulse of the moment, shoots and kills him. Great bodily harm refers to serious injuries such as shooting to break a person's leg.

6. Act Inherently Dangerous

To kill while engaged in an act inherently dangerous and evidencing a wanton disregard of human life can constitute murder. Examples of this behavior are: shooting into a room or train in which persons are known to be present; throwing a live grenade to another person as a practical joke.

7. Felonies Against the Person

Certain felonies have been attended so frequently by death or great bodily harm, even when not intended by the wrongdoer, that they must be classified as dangerous. Hence a homicide committed during the perpetration (or attempt) of burglary, sodomy, rape, maiming, robbery, and aggravated arson is considered to constitute murder, even though the killing was unintentional or even accidental. For example: A robbery victim in attempting to disarm his assailant is killed by the accidental discharge of the assailant's firearm. Another example: A robber orders his victim at gunpoint to throw up his hands. The victim staggers back, fall, dies of a fractured skull. In both examples the robber is guilty of murder.

8. Proof of Murder

In order to prove the crime of murder the following elements must be established:
   a. The person named or described is dead.
   b. The death was the result of an act of the accused.
   c. The circumstances show that the accused had a premeditated design to kill; or intended to kill or inflict great bodily harm; or was engaged in an act inherently dangerous to others and evidencing a wanton disregard of human life; or was engaged

in the perpetration or attempted perpetration of burglary, sodomy, rape, robbery, maiming, or aggravated arson.

9. Manslaughter

Any homicide which is neither murder nor innocent homicide is called *manslaughter*. It is the unlawful killing of another without malice aforethought. Manslaughter may be voluntary or involuntary depending upon whether there existed an intention to kill.

10. Voluntary Manslaughter

An unlawful killing, although committed in the heat of sudden passion caused by adequate provocation, is not murder but voluntary manslaughter even though there was an intent to kill or commit great bodily harm. It is recognized that a man may be so overcome by sudden passion that he may strike a fatal blow before he can bring himself under control. The law recognizes that in the light of the provocation such homicide does not amount to murder. The provocation, however, must be such that the law considers adequate to arouse uncontrollable passion in a *reasonable* man. In judging provocation the following requirements are considered: *Adequate* provocation, *sudden* heat of passion, and causal connection between the provocation, the transport of passion, and the fatal act.

a. **Adequate Provocation.** Adequacy is determined by an objective test: What effect would the provocation have on the *average, reasonable* man? If the nature of the provocation is such that it is calculated to inflame the passions of the ordinary reasonable man, it is considered adequate. The following are forms of provocation which commonly occur:

1) *Battery*. An unlawful, hard blow inflicting great pain or injury may be sufficient.

2) *Assault*. The attempt to commit serious personal injury, although not accompanied by a battery, may be calculated to excite sudden and uncontrollable passion and, hence, may constitute adequate provocation. For example, A fires a gun at B, misses, and runs away. B shoots A in the back as he flees. This is not

considered self-defense, but sufficient provocation may exist to reduce the grade of homicide to manslaughter.

3) *Mutual Combat.* All the circumstances of the combat must be considered. Who was the original assailant? Was the fight truly mutual or was one person clearly the attacker? Did the original assailant have an intent to kill? Did the counter-attack exceed the requirements of self-defense? If both parties engage in an altercation with unlawful intent to kill, there is no mitigation on either side.

4) *Words.* Insulting words alone are not adequate provocation.

5) *Trespass.* A trespass may be sufficient if it is upon a dwelling house and involves personal danger to the slayer. The consideration here is of a trespass of a nature insufficient to authorize the use of deadly force. If the force used is permitted by law under the circumstances, no question of provocation arises because no crime is committed in the slaying. A purely technical trespass, even in a dwelling house, is not recognized as sufficient for this purpose.

6) *Outrageous Acts.* It is generally recognized by law that certain outrageous acts constitute provocations. For example: Adultery, seduction of the slayer's infant daughter, rape of a close female relative of the slayer, or felonious injury inflicted upon a close relative of the slayer is considered adequate provocation.

b. **Heat of Passion.** The accused must have killed in the heat of passion. It is not necessary that the passion be so great that the killer does not know what he is doing at the time. It is sufficient if the passion is so extreme that the slayer's action is directed by passion rather than by reason. A subjective test must be applied: Did the slayer kill in the actual heat of passion? This is different from the objective test used in determining adequate provocation where the reaction of the ordinary reasonable man was considered. It should be noted here that *both* adequate provocation and heat of passion must be present to reduce the homicide to manslaughter. Either alone is insufficient.

c. **Suddenness.** The heat of passion must be sudden. The time lapse between the provocation and the fatal act should not have presented a reasonable opportunity for the slayer's passion to cool. An objective test is applied: Would the mind of the ordinary reasonable man have cooled sufficiently so that the act could be considered to have been directed by reason rather than passion? The length of the cooling time will vary with the circumstances. The severity of the provocation and the occurrence of intervening acts are factors to be considered.

d. **Causal Relation Between Provocation, Passion, and the Fatal Act.** It is not sufficient that the provocation, passion, and the fatal act occurred in rapid sequence. It must be shown that the adequate provocation aroused the passion and that heat of passion immediately led to the fatal act. If, for example, the intent to kill existed before the provocation, the fatal act would be a murder since the provocation would not have been the cause of the fatal act.

11. Involuntary Manslaughter

Involuntary manslaughter is defined as an unlawful homicide committed without intent to kill. Negatively, it is an unintentional killing which is neither justifiable nor excusable. Involuntary manslaughter is an unlawful homicide committed without an intent to kill or inflict great bodily harm; it is an unlawful killing by culpable negligence, or while perpetrating or attempting to perpetrate an offense other than burglary, sodomy, rape, robbery, or aggravated arson, directly affecting the person.

a. **Culpable Negligence.** Culpable negligence is a degree of carelessness greater than simple negligence. It is a negligent act or omission accompanied by a culpable disregard for the foreseeable consequences to others of such act or omission. Thus, the basis of a charge of involuntary manslaughter may be a negligent act or omission which, viewed in the light of human experience, might forseeably result in the death of another, even though death would not, necessarily, be a natural and probable consequence of such act or omission. Examples of culpable negligence are: Negligently conducting target practice so that the bullets go in the direction of an inhabited house within range; pointing a pistol in fun at another and pulling the trigger, believing, but without taking reasonable precautions to ascertain, that it would not be dangerous; carelessly leaving poisons or dangerous drugs where they may endanger life.

b. **Legal Duty.** When there is no legal duty to act, there can, of course, be no neglect. Thus, when a stranger makes no effort to save a drowning man, or a person allows a mendicant to freeze or starve to death, no crime is committed.

c. **Offense Directly Affecting the Person.** By an offense directly affecting the person is meant one affecting some particular person as distinguished from an offense affecting society in general. Among offenses directly affecting the person are the various types of assault, battery, false imprisonment, voluntary engagement in an affray, maiming, and the use of more force than is reasonably necessary in the suppression of a mutiny or riot.

d. **Proof of Manslaughter.** The following elements must be proved to establish the offense of manslaughter: That the victim named or described is dead; that his death resulted from the act or omission of the accused, as alleged; and facts and circumstances showing that the homicide amounted in law to the degree of manslaughter alleged.

II. THE IDENTITY OF THE DECEASED

12. Introduction

In the proof of criminal homicide the first element is the establishment of the fact that the victim named or described is dead. To support a criminal charge, it must be shown that someone is dead. Every effort should be made to identify the victim. It is not, however, considered absolutely essential that an identification be made. Convictions have been obtained for causing the death of an unknown person.

13. The Fact of Death

Obviously, one of the first actions of the investigator on arriving at the scene of an allegedly fatal occurrence is the verification of the death. He may not consider a person dead until the fact has been established by a competent person. All deaths will be verified by a licensed physician. In the event that the investigator is the first to arrive at the scene of an apparent homicide, he should summon a physician to examine the victim and determine whether he is dead.

a. **Definition of Death.** An individual is said to be dead in a medical sense when one of the three vital functions is no longer performed by the body, namely, respiration, cardiac activity, and central nervous system activity. In a legal sense, death is considered to have occurred when all three of these vital functions have irrevocably ceased.

b. **Presumptive Signs and Tests for Death.** The following are a few of the signs indicative of death:

1) Cessation of breathing and respiratory movements.

2) Absence of heart sound.

3) Loss of flushing of nail beds when pressure on nail is released.

c. **Suspended Animation.** Death may be superficially simulated. Cardiac activity, breathing, and the functioning of the nervous system may reach such a low level of activity that an observer is deceived into an assumption of death. Although such advice is irrelevant to the topic, the investigator is naturally encouraged to devote his full energies to resuscitation in the absence of obvious signs of death. Intelligently applied first aid may obviate the need of a homicide investigation. Among the conditions which will produce the simulated appearance of death are the following:

1) Electrical shock.

2) Prolonged immersion.

3) Poisoning from narcotic drugs.

4) Barbiturate poisoning.

5) Prolonged exhausting diseases such as typhoid fever.

6) Certain rare mental diseases.

d. **Brain Death.** With the advent of heart transplantation medical experts have stressed the importance of brain death, or the cessation of brain activity, as an acceptable criterion. In ordinary cases brain death usually coincides with the stoppage of heart and breathing and the old criteria are adequate. Beginning in the early 1950s, however, the need arose for better ways of determining brain death independently because respirators were developed which allowed a patient's breathing to be maintained artificially even though the brain was dead. Under these circumstances the heart would often continue beating too because the artificial breathing was giving the blood the oxygen it needed to nourish the heart. For the purpose of a heart transplant, the respirator would be used to maintain the heart's breathing capability (and the heart's condition) even though the donor's body, because of brain death, was no longer capable of spontaneous respiration. In 1972 a court in Richmond, Virginia, accepted the concept of brain death as an adequate definition of death.

14. Identification Procedure

Identifying the victim is obviously a critically important investigative step. First, the identity of the deceased may arouse suspicion in a mysterious death, since the victim may be a person whose life has been threatened or whose death was desired for criminal purposes. Second, the identity of the dead person provides a focal point for the inquiry, since the investigators can then center their attention on the associates and haunts of the deceased. Moreover, police agencies maintain files of missing and wanted persons and the identification of the deceased can sometimes be related to previous convictions, property claims, insurance claims, desertion claims, and similar matters. Several cases must be distinguished, depending upon the condition in which the body was found. The whole body discovered soon after death does not present any serious problems. Drowned, mutilated, and cremated bodies, however, require expert attention. In any case, the clothes and other possessions of the victims, where they are present, provide the simplest clues.

a. **Clothes and Other Articles.** In the absence of the next of kin of a deceased person, a representative of the law enforcement agency having jurisdiction takes possession of all property of value found on the person of the deceased, making an exact inventory and delivering the property to the agency. Subsequently, the property is surrendered to the person entitled to its custody or possession. The medical examiner or his equivalent may take possession of any portable objects useful in establishing the cause of death and deliver them to the agency. The circumstances under which the body is found usually determine the number of identifying clues that are present in the form of possessions. In the deceased's hotel room, an abundance of clues may be found. In other circumstances, there will usually be simply the clothes and a few personal articles. Licenses, Social Security cards, draft cards, ID cards, letters, and similar articles are obviously most helpful. In the absence of such items, the investigator may sometimes establish an identification by means of the clothes alone. If a name or set of initials is in the jacket or hat, the problem is greatly simplified. The clothes may sometimes be traced by one of the following methods:

1) *Tracing by Purchase.* The clothing (and also some other manufactured articles found on the person) will bear some of the following identifying data: brand name; type; model; retail price; size; code number; color; outlet; date; and characteristic marks. It is the aim of the investigator to trace the clothing to the retail store, where an employee may know of the identity of the purchaser.

2) *Laundry and Dry Cleaner's Marks.* One of the best means of tracing the owner of a garment is through the laundry mark on shirts and underwear and the dry cleaner's marks on jackets, trousers, and hats. The law enforcement agencies of large cities and states usually maintain a file of these marks through which the mark can be traced to the launderer or dry cleaner. In some laundries and dry cleaning establishments, a record is maintained of the customer' name and address and the associated clothing marks. Many cases of unknown identity are solved each year by means of such files (see Chap. 34).

b. **Identifying a Whole Body.** The procedure to be followed in identifying a whole body is similar to that for identifying living persons.

1) *Physical Description.* Procedures for describing living persons are given in Chapter 29. In composing a description of a deceased person, the investigator should not be misled by characteristics that are acquired after death. For example, the color of the deceased undergoes certain postmortem changes. The skin tends, with time, to take on a negroid appearance, assuming such

colors as blue, blue-black, and brown. The hair is similarly subject to change; brown and red hair becomes lighter and gray and blonde hair darker. Since the color of the hair can be altered, the hair on the head should be compared with that on the other parts of the body. If the color of the head hair is patchy or if it varies close to the scalp, a dye should be suspected. Samples of the head hair should be requested from the medical examiner for microscopic and chemical examination to determine the presence of coloring matter. A sample of head hair should be preserved in any case in anticipation of the discovery of hairs as a clue. In cases of sexual assault, samples of torso hair should also be taken. Postmortem changes affect even the contours of the body. The features broaden and run together. The body is subjected to swelling. Thus, the weight of the deceased may be grossly overestimated. The fit of the clothing, however, will give an indication of the degree of swelling.

2) *Fingerprints.* This is the best means of identification. Special techniques must be employed if the fingers have been deteriorated from putrefaction, drowning, mutilation, or burning (see Chap. 31). A set of fingerprints may be forwarded to the FBI with a request for a search. The assistance of other agencies, such as police departments which maintain fingerprint files, should be sought.

3) *Photographs.* Photographs should be taken of the whole body and of the head alone, full face and profile. Significant features such as scars, deformities, and amputations should be photographed. These photographs can be shown to persons who may have known the deceased. They can also be checked against the files of photographs in the identification bureaus of law enforcement agencies.

4) *Age.* The apparent age of the deceased can be estimated only roughly from the teeth and the joining of the bones. The medical examiner, by means of an x-ray examination, can estimate the age from a study of the epiphyses of the bones (the stage of uniting of bones, a condition varying with age). This procedure is helpful only in persons below the age of about twenty-five years. Histological examinations are informative.

5) *Teeth.* Dental structure and dental work provide an excellent means of identification. With the invention of the high-

powered drill four decades ago, permitting more sophisticated dental restoration such as tooth capping and root canal work, dentists have been making extensive x-rays and plaster molds, both of which are accurate records of oral anatomy not dependent on the recordkeeping ability of the dentist. The forensic dentist is especially helpful in the identification cases where the corpse is burnt or dismembered. He can determine the approximate age of a person by wear on the teeth, or in the case of preadolescence, by the amount of tooth blood left in the jawbone. The degree of abrasive wear gives a clue to the socioeconomic status of the corpse because it tells something about the diet. Jawbone construction provides anatomical landmarks that never change, no matter how much dental work is performed. Fillings and caps are helpful, since they are highly individual. Probably the most celebrated recent case in which dental evidence played a significant role was the identification of Diane Oughton, as one of the three bodies in the remains of a Greenwich Village town house explosion. A fragment of a little finger and of a jaw with three and one-half teeth were sifted out of the debris. The FBI found a childhood orthodontist of Miss Oughton's and, by comparing the shape of the roots and the bone structure with x-rays taken fifteen years before, was able to confirm the identification they had already made with the fingerprint.

6) *Fractures.* The existence of old fractures may serve as a point of identification.

7) *Blood Group.* Samples of the deceased's blood should be taken for grouping purposes as well as for autoptical reasons. The group and Rh factor provide an additional means of identification. It is the custom of military services to include this information on identification cards.

c. **Mutilated Remains.** To make identification difficult, the criminal sometimes removes or disfigures the head, hands, and feet. Identification then becomes a difficult matter in which the investigator must rely heavily on the medical examiner. Frequently, the assistance of anatomists, dentists, and radiologists is required. The following significant information may be established by the examinations:

1) ***Human or Animal.*** If a reasonable amount of material is present, this determination is not difficult.

2) ***Time Elapsed Since Burial or Death.*** A considerable number of years are required for the disappearance of tissue in a buried body. If only bones are discovered, it may be said that they have been buried for a long time. If the organic matter is present, some conclusion can be drawn from the state of decomposition. Again, the ease of the determination will depend on the amount of material available.

3) ***Means Used to Cut Up the Body.*** It can readily be determined from a study of the body whether skill was used in its dissection or whether it was cut up without regard for anatomical considerations.

4) ***One or Several Bodies.*** The examiner can determine usually whether the parts belong to one body or several bodies.

5) ***The Sex.*** Differences in the weight and structure of the skeleton will indicate the sex.

6) ***The Structure.*** To form an accurate estimate of the height, it is usually necessary to have the greater part of half the skeleton. A rough estimate can be made from a single bone.

III. THE INVESTIGATION AT THE SCENE

15. Introduction

The proper investigation of a homicide is one of the most exacting tasks with which the investigator can be confronted. He is faced, first of all, with an occurrence of the utmost gravity; hence, the responsibility of competent inquiry is exceptionally great. Secondly, a criminal homicide is a complex crime, since the motives are devious and varied and the methods that can be employed by the criminal are great in number. The variety of physical evidence that may be discovered in connection with a homicide can tax the full resources of the laboratory experts. The investigator arriving on the scene of his first homicide case soon becomes aware of the complexity of the work ahead of him. He is the key man in the investigation; yet he must rely greatly upon the assistance of others. He is, in a way, the coordinator for the various forces that will be brought to bear on the inquiry—the medical examiner, the laboratory technicians, the detective force, the district attorney, and other civilian investigating agencies. To properly utilize these aids the investigator must be aware of the potentialities of the services that are available to him and he must know the appropriate assisting action to be taken. The medical examiner is able to inform him as to the probable cause of death if the body has not been moved or tampered with prior to his examination. The physical evidence may be eloquent in proving important points if it has been discovered by a competent search, collected and preserved according to best practice, and transmitted to the laboratory experts with accurate information. Most important of all, the investigator brings to the investigation, in addition to training, knowledge, fidelity to directions, and adherence to regulations, the invaluable ingredients of good judgment and imagination. Common sense will enable him to establish causal relations between the various elements that are discovered in the course of the inquiry. Imagination will aid him in reconstructing the crime—the process whereby the scene of the crime, the physical evidence, and the information obtained from witnesses are woven together to produce a logical pattern of the course of events that culminated in the fatal act.

16. Preliminary Procedure

On receiving notification or information concerning a possible homicide, the investigator should at once resort to methodical procedure. He should resist impulses arising out of curiosity, a false sense of urgency, or a desire for immediate action. The investigator's initial activities may determine the success or failure of the subsequent investigation. The first step should be the recording of the receipt information. The following data should be recorded:

    a. Date and exact time of receiving the information.

    b. Method of transmission of the information.

    c. Name and other data identifying the person giving the information.

    d. Complete details of the information.

17. Action on Arrival

The procedures to be followed with respect to the control, recording, and collecting of evidence at the crime scene have been described fully in Part I. It will be found that the usefulness of the suggestions given there is most fully realized in a homicide case.

IV. BLOOD AND OTHER BODY FLUIDS

18. Introduction

One of the most common clues to be found in connection with homicides is the bloodstain. Homicidal assaults can be especially productive of the victim's blood, traces of which may be carried from the scene on the perpetrator to later connect him with the crime. As an identifying medium, blood is of the highest value. Through a series of increasingly complex tests, it is possible to progress from the general finding that a stain is blood to the specific identification of its origin. Thus, blood is a medium of unique identification which can establish with certainty the suspect's association with the crime scene.

19. The Victim's Blood

In Paragraph 14 it is recommended that samples of the deceased's blood should be taken and the blood group determined in all cases of homicide and suicide. The purpose of this procedure is to provide a standard with which suspicious bloodstains on possible weapons or on the suspect's clothing or other possessions can be compared. This precaution is repeated here since experience has shown that in the absence of insistent attention to this point at the time of the autopsy there is a possibility of overlooking this obvious procedure.

20. Bloodstains

From an examination of bloodstains found in connection with homicides, a number of valuable conclusions may be drawn. Blood can be positively identified with an individual using DNA analysis. DNA analysis can be performed on old and dried bloodstains, so that deterioration is not the enormous problem it is with other tests. Before the introduction of DNA analysis, often no more could be done with a deteriorated bloodstain than to show that it was of human origin or that it belonged to one of the ABO groups. Among the questions that can be answered by an examination of bloodstains are the following:

    a. *Could* this minute stain be blood?

    b. *Is* this stain blood?

    c. Is it animal or *human* blood?

    d. Does this blood have the same distinctive properties as the suspect's blood (ABO group, "genetic markers")?

    e. Is this the suspect's blood (DNA analysis)?

21. Tests—Preliminary Field Test—Could the Stain be Blood?

In the investigation of a homicide, numerous stains may be brought to the attention of the investigator. The discoverer of the stains may be quite positive that they are blood. On testing it will be found that some are blood and others are lipstick, rust, or one of many substances which appear similar. The investigator should make no conclusions as to the nature of the stain from its appearance. Of course, if the substance is fresh, liquid, and appears to be blood, it can be concluded that it is blood and collected without hesitation. If the stain is questionable, it should be tested by a preliminary chemical test such as the following:

    a. **Tetramethylbenzidine.** The "benzidine test" was for many years a frequently used test to determine the presence of blood at the crime scene. Because benzidine has been found to be carcinogenic, its manufacture and use has been banned in the United States. Tetramethylbenzidine has proved to be an effective and apparently safe substitute. This is an extremely sensitive test that can be applied to minute stains. If the stain reacts positively, the investigator can conclude that it may be blood. Unfortunately, a number of other substances give the same reaction. If the stain reacts negatively, it is not blood. In all cases, the reagent should first be tested with known blood.

1) A minute part of the stain is scraped or tweezed onto a filter paper.

2) A medicine dropper is used to place a few drops of tetramethylbenzidine reagent on the stain fragment now in the filter paper.

3) A few drops of 3% hydrogen peroxide are added.

4) If the stain is blood, a blue-green color appears in a short time.

b. **Other Color Reaction Tests.** The following is a list of frequently used tests for blood and their color reaction:

1) Phenolphthalein (pink).

2) Leucomalachite (green).

3) Orthotolidine (blue).

c. **Luminol.** This test is especially useful for detecting minute traces of blood while searching large areas such as walls or carpeting. It is sensitive enough to locate blood even after the crime scene has been cleaned up. Luminol is applied as an aerosal spray and reacts with blood by producing a blue-white luminescence. One drawback of this method is that the room must be dark or an article with the suspected trace must be carried into a dark room in order for the luminesence to be visible. Sometimes outlines of shoe impressions or cleaning marks can be observed and photographed.

22. Confirmatory Tests—Is It Blood?

The preliminary field tests described above are called screening tests. If the appropriate color does not appear, then you know the specimen *is not* blood. A positive result means that the specimen *could be* blood. Because there are other substances that could cause positive reactions such as many kinds of fruits and vegetables, a confirmatory test that is specific for blood will be necessary. To determine definitely that the stain is blood, a small portion of the stain is dissolved in a saline solution and subjected to one of the following tests.

a. **Teichmann or Hemin Crystal Test.** This is the most common test. It is not effective on blood that has been heated. Identification depends on the formation of hemin crystals upon the application of an appropriate reagent.

b. **Microspectroscopic Test.** A drop of the dissolved stain is placed on the stage of a microscope to which a spectroscope is attached. The appearance of certain lines or bands in the absorption spectrum establishes the fact that the stain is blood.

23. Precipitin Test—Is the Blood of Human or Animal?

With a larger stain, additional tests can be made. The precipitin reaction distinguishes between the blood of a human being and that of an animal. The test is based on the fact that when an animal is injected with the protein of an animal of a different species, an antibody is developed in its serum which causes the latter to react specifically with the protein of any other species. A test animal such as a guinea pig is injected with human blood serum and with whole blood over a period of time. The blood of the test animal provides an antihuman serum. To perform the test, a few drops of the bloodstain dissolved in salt solution are placed in a test tube. A few drops of the anti-human serum are added to the test tube. The formation of a gray precipitation ring at the interface of the two layers within twenty minutes indicates that the stain is human blood.

24. Blood Grouping

A further classification of blood can be achieved by the recognition of certain clumping reactions caused by the presence in human blood of two factors known as *antigens* and *antibodies.* By means of clumping properties, it is possible to divide blood into four major groups, namely, A, B, AB, and O. In the ABO blood grouping system, there are two antigens A and B and two antibodies anti-A and anti-B. If a person is in blood group A, he has the A antigen in his blood. If he is in group B, he has the B antigen. If he is in group AB, he has both A and B antigens. The O blood group has neither A nor B antigens. When group A blood is exposed to anti-A antibodies, it will clump or *agglutinate*. B blood will clump in the presence of anti-B antibodies. AB will clump with either anti-A or anti-B, and O blood, which has neither A nor B antigens, can have both anti-A and anti-B antibodies present without agglutination. By testing blood with known serums containing anti-A and anti-B antibodies to see if clumping occurs, the ABO grouping of that blood can be determined. Each person's blood can be placed in one of these groups. The blood group of a human does not change throughout life. The grouping of fresh human blood is a straightforward laboratory procedure, while old bloodstains may present difficult problems in blood grouping. There are a number of other antigen grouping systems besides ABO, the most famous of which are the Rh and the MN systems. However, blood found at the crime scene has usually deteriorated too much to identify these systems.

25. Enzymes and Proteins ("Genetic Markers")

There are other elements in blood besides antigens which can be grouped for identification purposes, namely, enzymes and proteins. Each of the enzymes and proteins grouped are "polymorphic," that is, having several forms, and are inherited independently of each other, making them ideal for identification. Because these enzymes and proteins are components of a body fluid that exhibit inheritable variations, they are often referred to as "genetic markers." For each form of an enzyme and protein, statistics are kept to determine their relative frequency in human blood. If several forms are identified in an evidence sample, it can greatly restrict the number of possible sources of the blood. More than a dozen enzyme and protein grouping systems have been discovered. Several of the more common ones are:

PGM	Phosphoglucomutase
ADA	Adenosine deaminase
AK	Adenylate kinase
EsD	Esterase D
EAP	Erythrocyte acidphosphatase

When blood is subjected to heat, sunlight, or moisture, it deteriorates rapidly so that it is often not possible to detect many of these grouping systems. Where the blood is adequately preserved, many of these genetic markers can be identified and can be used to eliminate up to 99.9% of the population as possible donors.

Enzymes and proteins are located and separated by a technique called *electrophoresis.* Blood cells are placed in a gel that is situated on a glass sheet. The gel is subjected to an electric current that causes the enzymes and proteins to separate from the blood and migrate across the gel. A chemical dye is used to stain these genetic markers. The resulting patterns are photographed and then analyzed to identify the specific forms of enzymes and proteins present.

26. DNA Analysis

In 1985, Doctor Alec Jeffreys with a research team from the University of Leicester produced one of the most remarkable discoveries in the history of forensic science, a technique for the positive identification of genetic material. Biological evidence left at the scene of the crime can be analyzed and compared with a specimen obtained from the suspect. Using this technique of DNA analysis, it can be stated with certainty that the evidence did or did not originate from the suspect. DNA or *deoxyribonucleic acid* is the complex genetic material found in the cells of an organism that provides the "blueprint" for its development. The DNA in each cell, whether it is blood, bone, or tissue, is identical to the DNA in all of the cells throughout the human body. Although the DNA is identical with the DNA in the other cells of the same human body, it is unique to that individual. As far as science has determined through speculation and observation, no two individuals that are alive or who have ever lived have the same DNA. The only exception is identical twins who share the same genetic material having originated from the division of a single fertilized egg.

DNA is comprised of *nucleotides.* A nucleotide is a molecule consisting of sugar, phosphates, and a nitrogenous base. There are only four different kinds of nucleotides: adenine (A), guanine

(G), cytosine (C), and thymine (T). Nucleotides combine with each other in a specific manner called complimentary base pairing. Adenine (A) pairs with thymine (T) and guanine (G) pairs with cytosine (C). These pairs form long chains that contain millions of nucleotides. The almost infinite number of combinations of pairs possible in these long chains of nucleotides account for the diversity in the genetic code that insures no two individuals will be alike.

a. **Procedure.** DNA analysis is also commonly called "DNA typing," "DNA profiling," and "DNA fingerprinting." The goal of DNA analysis is to obtain a visual image that will characterize each DNA sample. The resulting image will take the form of a pattern of bands, that resemble the "bar codes" on store products, which can then be examined visually or by computer-assisted image analysis. DNA analysis consists of the following steps:

1) *Collection.* DNA is found in the chromosomes of every cell in the human body that has a nucleus. This will include blood, semen, hair roots, skin cells, tissue, bone, teeth, saliva, and urine. In blood only the white cells have a nucleus. Red blood cells cannot be used because they have no nucleus and hence no DNA. Only semen with sperm cells present have DNA. The condition of "aspermia," the absence of sperm cells in the semen, would make it unacceptable for DNA analysis. Only hair with root cells can be used for DNA testing.

2) *Extraction.* DNA is chemically extracted from the cells and purified.

3) *Cutting. Restriction enzymes* are added to the DNA to cut the long chain of nucleotides into short fragments of varying lengths. These enzymes recognize the different sequences of nucleotides and by means of a chemical reaction cut these chains at specific points.

4) *Sorting.* The DNA fragments are then sorted according to length by a process called *electrophoresis.* The fragments are placed on a gel-covered flat plate and charged with an electrical current. The negatively charged fragments will migrate across the gel to the positive end. The smaller DNA fragments will travel farther than the larger segments. The result will be that, after several

hours, the fragments will be arranged in parallel lines according to length.

5) *Splitting*. Chemicals are introduced that will split the DNA fragments into two strands, dividing the complementary pairs of nucleotides.

6) *Transfer*. A nylon membrane is placed over the gel absorbing the fragments and fixing their position. This procedure is called *Southern blotting*, named after its innovator, Edward Southern.

7) *Probes*. "Probes" are synthetic DNA fragments which are designed to combine with the split fragments on the nylon membrane. They are a known sequence of nucleotides which will naturally pair with a complementary fragment. The probes are made radioactive so that they can be detected by X-ray film. The radioactive probes are added to the split fragments on the nylon membrane. The probes will target specific sequences and will combine with the fragments making them radioactive and hence detectable. This process is called *hybridization*.

8) *X-ray Film*. After the excess probe is washed away, x-ray film is placed near the membrane and is exposed for several days. When the x-ray film is developed, the radioactive fragments will appear as black bands on a white background. The developed film is called an *autoradiograph* or *autorad*.

9) *Comparison*. A visual comparison of the autoradiographs is performed. If a *single-locus* probe has been used, only two black bands will be observed on the autoradiograph. A *multi-locus* probe will have multiple band patterns. The autoradiograph of the evidence sample from the crime scene is compared with the autoradiographs of the samples submitted by the suspect and the victim to determine if there is a match. A single-locus probe will have to be performed more than once to establish identity. The whole DNA analysis procedure takes approximately two weeks to complete.

c. **Advantages.** There are many advantages to using DNA analysis for identifying biological evidence:

1) DNA analysis yields positive identification. It can identify the evidence donor to the exclusion of all other individuals.

2) Only small amounts of body fluid or tissue are needed.

3) DNA analysis can differentiate sources of mixed stains, which are fairly common in sexual assault cases. When semen is combined with vaginal secretions or blood, the DNA from each individual can be identified.

4) Dried or old stains can be analyzed.

5) DNA band patterns can be computerized.

d. **Judicial Acceptance.** On January 9, 1992, the U.S. Court of Appeals ruled that DNA evidence was admissible in criminal trials. In the *U.S. v. Jakobetz,* the court accepted as valid the general theory and procedures of DNA analysis. It instructed the lower courts to take "judicial notice" of DNA analysis, that is, the courts could accept as fact the general theory and specific techniques of DNA testing. Lower courts would no longer be required to conduct lengthy hearings to determine the admissibility of DNA results.

The courts generally use either of two standards to determine the admissibility of new scientific evidence.

1) *The Frye Standard.* In 1923, the U.S. Court of Appeals rejected the admissibility of the polygraph technique in the landmark *U.S. v. Frye* (293 F 1013 D.C. Cir. 1923) decision. In so doing, it set forth a standard by which new scientific evidence could be judged. The court ruled that for expert testimony to be admissible, the scientific theories and techniques must have general acceptance in the particular field in which it belongs.

2) *The Relevancy Standard.* Many courts have adopted the "relevancy standard" as an alternative to the *Frye* standard in determining the admissibility of new scientific evidence. The relevancy standard, based on the Federal Rules of Evidence, directs the courts to consider other factors in judging admissibility besides the general acceptance in a particular scientific discipline. These factors include: a) the relevancy of the expert's opinion; b) the expert's qualifications; c) the existence of a specialized literature on the topic; d) the reliability of the testimony; e) the potential for error; and f) the potential for unfair prejudice against the defendant. Although general scientific acceptance is considered an important factor in the relevancy standard, it is not the only or overriding factor taken into consideration. The relevancy standard is considered less stringent than the *Frye* standard. In *U.S. v. Jacobetz,* the

Appellate Court used the relevancy standard in judging the admissibility of DNA evidence.

27. Other Group-Specific Substances

A number of other serological fluids which the body contains also have the property of possessing a characteristic group.

a. **Secretors.** It has been estimated that approximately 80 percent of the population carry in the bloodstream a group-specific substance which makes it possible to determine the blood group of other body fluids such as saliva, semen, tears, urine, perspiration, and nasal secretion. Individuals in this category are known as *secretors.* Studies of innumerable cases have established the following biological conclusions concerning body fluids:

1) The body fluid group of a secretor will always be identical with his blood group.

2) A secretor will never change to a non-secretor (or vice versa) during his life.

b. **Application.** The practical application of the secretor phenomenon lies in the fact that garments and non-blood stains may also provide evidence. The perspiration present in an abandoned shirt or the semen stain on the victim's garment may be sufficient to determine the blood group of the perpetrator. Saliva and urine stains provide similar opportunities. Success in these procedures, however, is infrequent.

28. Location of Stains

a. **Perishable Nature of Blood.** Blood is a type of evidence which undergoes a rapid change in its character with the passage of time, as the process of clotting and drying commences almost immediately on exposure to air. Furthermore, blood offers little resistance to decomposition, especially when exposed to certain conditions and influences which, if prolonged, will cause the specimen to lose its identity. It is, therefore, extremely important that blood samples be sent to the laboratory as soon as possible after their discovery. Prior to a general search of the crime scene, the floor should be examined carefully in order to minimize the danger of loss or destruction caused by being walked upon by persons otherwise engaged in the investigation.

b. **Clothing.** All articles of wearing apparel of the victim and the suspect should be collected for further scrutiny. The shoes, in particular, should be given special attention. No article of clothing should be discarded simply because a superficial examination fails to reveal suspicious stains. Garments which have been washed may still retain sufficient blood to produce a positive reaction.

c. **Fingernails.** It is not unusual to find traces of the blood of the victim under the fingernails of the suspect or under the cuticle at the base of the nail. Similar traces, torn from the suspect, may be found in the same locations on the fingers of the victim. In the latter instance, lacerations of the face and hands of the perpetrator of the crime may have been produced by the victim's instinctive attempts to protect himself. Moreover, the victim would be less likely, and sometimes unable, to wash his hands after the offense in order to remove incriminating traces.

d. **Furniture.** No search for bloodstains on furniture is complete until the *under* sides, as well as the tops, of tables, chairs, desks, radios, and other articles have been examined. This will also apply to the bottoms of all drawers in dressers, vanities, desks, and similar items. It frequently happens that fingerprints in blood are left in these places, and a reconstruction of the movements of the suspect may indicate that such articles have been lifted or otherwise moved during the commission of the crime. Special effort should be directed toward all pieces of furniture which do not appear to be in their accustomed locations.

e. **Motor Vehicles.** The location and amount of blood on the exterior, interior, or in the vicinity of a motor vehicle may often have an important bearing on an investigation. A serious crime such as murder, rape, or assault may have been committed in the vehicle; a body may have been transported from the scene of an offense to another spot for disposition; the automobile itself may have been the instrument of aggression; or the crime may have been of the hit-and-run variety in which the operator of a vehicle has failed to stop after knowingly causing death or personal injuries to another. The search for incriminating bloodstains should be conducted on the exterior as well as the interior of the automobile, with special attention directed to the undercarriage and the front assembly.

f. **Weapons.** Any instrument suspected of having been used to cut, stab, or strike a victim should be forwarded to a laboratory for blood examination. In many cases, it will be found that no attempt has been made to remove telltale stains, particularly when the weapon has been discarded in the immediate area of the offense. It frequently happens, however, that the guilty person will retain possession of the weapon, and at the earliest opportunity, will try to destroy traces of incriminating residue by washing in water or other solvent. In spite of the time and effort expended in this manner, it is sometimes possible to detect bloodstains on certain parts of the instrument, if it has come in contact at any time with the blood of the victim. In his examination, the laboratory technician will devote particular attention to cracks in wooden clubs or handles, to the junction of the blade with the handle of a knife, to the space between the grip and the frame of a pistol or revolver, or in any place where the blood may have seeped while still in a liquid state. It sometimes happens that the stains on exposed surfaces may present an aspect that will deceive the average person. Blood on rusty metal, for example, may appear as a slightly glazed area which blends into the background, or the same reddish, shining, and cracked appearance may be noted in rusty iron when there is no blood present. The possibilities in this phase of investigation are so vast that searches for blood traces cannot be conducted too carefully. It is emphasized that a liberal supply of bloodstained or suspected objects be collected, regardless of the subsequent work entailed in their examination.

g. **Plumbing.** The bathroom and kitchen offer to the criminal a means of disposing of blood, either through the washing of stains from articles of clothing and cleaning rags, or through the use of the bathtub for the dissection of the body of the victim. The mere washing of blood from the hands may leave identifiable traces in a sink or washbowl. When this action is suspected, the towels and washcloths should be collected and submitted for examination, especially if it appears that there has been an attempt to conceal the articles in the laundry or in discarded rubbish.

Drain pipes and joints in the plumbing fixtures may be dismantled and examined, sometimes with positive results.

h. **Rugs and Similar Material.** Any dark stain, wet or dry, on rugs, upholstery, tapestry, overdrapes, or similar fabrics, should be examined carefully and considered with suspicion, pending a decision concerning its potential value in the investigation.

29. Other Conditions Observed at the Scene

a. **Amount of Blood Near Body.** The average male body of 154 pounds contains approximately 12¾ pints of blood. As soon as a considerable amount of bleeding takes place, a defense mechanism lowers the blood pressure, which has been forcing the blood from a wound, thus decelerating the flow. Some bleeding will occur, therefore, if death is not instantaneous. After death, the blood pressure drops to zero and bleeding ceases. Consequently, it may be said that dead bodies do not bleed; they drain. When a body is found with wounds which indicate that much blood has been lost, but the amount of blood near the body appears to be less than what one would normally expect to find, the logical assumption is that the crime was committed elsewhere. Every effort must be directed to the establishment of the other location. The distance between the two points may provide a clue to the method employed in moving the body, such as by dragging or carrying from a location nearby or by automobile transportation from a more distant spot. The nature of the terrain will indicate the type of search for such evidence as tire tracks, bent or broken bushes, or a trail caused by a heavy object being dragged through grass or some type of soil. A similar search should be conducted if it appears that the body has been moved in an urban area, as, for example, from an automobile to a building or vice versa, from one building to another, from a building to an outside area, from floor to floor, or from room to room. Blood traces may be deposited in the passage of the body between the indicated points.

b. **Clotting of Bloodstains.** The mechanism of blood-clotting is due in part to the existence in the blood of very small, fine-grained particles which are without nuclei and whose origin is unknown. These are known as platelets. On exposure to air, a fibrous coating forms on a bloodstain, generally in three to five minutes, and under normal conditions the entire process of clotting will be completed in ten to twenty minutes, accompanied by a change in the color from red to dark brown. Physically, the blood changes from its liquid state to a mass resembling jelly, surrounded by a wet area produced by the serum, which has separated from the other components. Prolonged clotting and drying of blood in a wound cause the formation of a scab, which acts as a protective seal in the process of natural healing.

c. **Drying of Bloodstains.** A bloodstain begins to dry at the edges and the process continues toward the center of the stain. The length of time required after the complete drying of the stain is governed by many conditions, specifically as follows:

1) *Temperature.* The higher the temperature the greater will be the increase in the speed of drying.

2) *Humidity.* An increased percentage of humidity will slow down the drying speed.

3) *Material.* Bloodstains dry faster on smooth and non-absorbent surfaces.

4) *Exposure to Elements.* Drying is speeded when the stains are exposed to wind and sunlight. Contact with moisture in the form of rain, snow, etc., has a tendency to prolong the process of drying.

5) *Size of Stain.* The larger the stain or pool, the longer it will take to dry.

d. **Direction and Distance of Fall.** A study of the shape and size of a splash or stain of blood, and a comparison with other stains created by a fall at a known angle and from a known height can lead to an approximation of the angle and distance from which the questioned drop of blood has fallen. In this type of experiment, animal blood may be used to prepare standards of comparison.

1) The vertical fall of drops is characterized by a round stain, with or without a surrounding pattern of droplets, depending on the distance of the fall.

2) Drops falling at an angle other than 90 degrees from the horizontal will form a blot, roughly oval or tear-shaped, with the point extended in the direction of fall. Frequently, droplets will be found in prolongation of or extending from the pointed

end, and small splashes from the parent blot will be seen in the area beyond the original point of impact.

30. Collection and Transmission of Blood Specimens

All activities and observations of the investigator pertaining to the evidential use of blood and body fluids must be conducted in a methodical and meticulous manner. Instructions pertaining to the handling of evidence in general are particularly applicable to blood specimens. It frequently happens that blood is overlooked at the crime scene because its familiar characteristics are missing, and it is not recognizable in the form and condition ordinarily associated with blood. It putrefies rapidly at high temperatures and excessive humidity. Specimens submitted for examination are often insufficient for laboratory use. Dried stains are easily cracked, chipped away, and lost through improper handling and packing. The following procedures are suggested as being conducive to the effective preservation of specimens between the time of finding and the ultimate disposition:

a. **Notes.** These should be copious and should be made concurrently with the events described rather than as a result of later recollection. Specific information should relate to the following:

1) Whether the suspect stain is liquid, moist, or solid.
2) The color of the specimen.
3) What photographs were taken and when.
4) When sketches were made.
5) The method of removal.
6) How specimen was marked for identification.
7) The methods used for the protection of the evidence.
8) Facts relating to the transmission to the laboratory, such as the laboratory to which sent and the date of transmission.

b. **Sketches.** A rough sketch should be made of the scene and the immediate area, with measurements and complete information regarding indicated features. In the detailed sketch, small stains may be traced for size and shape, while large stains may be plotted on graph paper. If a sketch of the crime scene has already been accomplished, the detailed sketch will suffice.

c. **Removal of Stains.** If the article on which the stain is found can be sent to the laboratory, it should be submitted intact. In cases where the bulk or weight of the article prohibits its shipment, the stains may be removed using the methods described in Chapter 7.

V. OTHER PHYSICAL EVIDENCE

31. Hairs and Fibers

Hairs from the assailant are sometimes found on the deceased. Fibers from the clothing of the criminal may be found on the clothing of the deceased. Similarly, hairs or fibers from the deceased may be found on the clothing of a suspect. Since these items of evidence are light in weight and difficult to see, great care must be exercised in handling and packaging. The following recommendations will be found useful in collecting hair and fiber evidence and transmitting it for expert examination.

a. Hairs and fibers from different locations at the scene should be placed in separate containers.

b. Hairs and fibers should be placed in round pillboxes or wrapped in druggists' powder paper. The box or paper should then be sealed with transparent tape, marked for identification, and placed in an envelope which is also sealed and marked for identification.

c. Where hairs are found attached to an object, particularly one which has been used as a weapon, such as a hammer or wrench, the object itself should be forwarded to the laboratory for examination without detaching the hairs. In such instances, the area bearing the evidence should be protected by a cellophane or paper wrapping secured with tape before the object itself is packaged for transmittal. Where the object itself is too large to forward to the laboratory, the hairs should be removed and submitted as previously described.

d. **Clothing.** Since the clothing is to be submitted to a laboratory examination by an expert, as described below, there is no need to remove such evidence for separate transmission.

e. **Standard Specimens.** In collecting hair specimens from a suspect and a victim for comparison purposes, obtain several hairs from different sections of each region of the body as may be pertinent to the individual case. For example, in selecting known samples of scalp hair for comparison purposes, at least twelve to fifteen hairs from various areas of the head and preferably full length should be obtained. This precaution is necessary in view of the known fact that the characteristics of hair from one area of the scalp may vary from those of hair taken from other portions of the same head. Where it becomes material to examine the hair of a victim who has sustained a scalp injury, several of the specimens should be taken from the vicinity of the wound. Chapter 42 describes more fully hair and fiber evidence.

32. Shoe and Tire Impressions

Restrictions must be placed on the movements of even authorized personnel until the area has been thoroughly searched for shoe and tire impressions. The approaches to the scene should first be examined. The impressions in earth should be photographed and plaster casts made following the procedures described in Chapter 35.

33. Shoe and Footprints

The violence associated with indoor homicides is often attended by a disturbance of furniture and a scattering of paper. The floor should be searched for the presence of papers which bear shoe prints. In wet weather, particularly, such prints may contain a wealth of detail far exceeding that of an impression in the earth. On tiled surfaces such as bathroom floors, consideration should be given to the possibility of latent footprints which may be developed in the same manner as fingerprints. Foot and shoe prints should be first photographed with the 4×5 camera, with the axis of camera perpendicular to the ground.

34. Clothing of the Deceased

a. **Importance.** The clothing of the deceased is an important article of evidence in the investigation of a homicide since it may be part of the *corpus delicti* and can yield valuable information concerning the manner of death. The garments should be described and marked for identification by the medical examiner. The marks and locations of weapons in relation to the body should be studied. Stains, cuts, and holes may be encircled with chalk in patterns which will facilitate repeated location and study without interfering with the examination. It will be found that the deceased's clothing is of great importance in shooting cases. For example, the medical examiner can determine whether the firearm was discharged from a distance or close to the body. Where the bullet has passed through the body, the holes in the clothing aid in establishing the direction of fire under circumstances in which the entrance and exit holes are not readily differentiable.

b. **Disposition of Clothing.** The clothing of a person who is the victim of a homicide should not be given to the family after it has been examined. Ordinarily, it is delivered by the identifying officer to the prosecuting attorney. If the deceased dies in a hospital, the authorities of that institution should be requested to retain the clothes for examination by the medical examiner.

c. **Care of Clothing.** The clothing should be obtained from the morgue or hospital as soon as possible. If moist stains are present on the garments, they should be placed on hangers to dry. After the clothing is thoroughly dry, it should be placed in a large box with as little folding as possible. Each piece should be separated by a layer of paper.

d. **Example of Evidence.** As an example of the importance of an examination of clothing in homicide investigation, a recent case may be cited where the defendant, while admitting the fatal shooting, claimed that it was done in self-defense. The fatal bullet passed completely through the body. In the course of an operation performed on the victim before death, a bullet wound in the front of the abdomen was obliterated. The physician performing the autopsy erroneously interpreted a bullet perforation on the back as an entrance wound and, as a consequence, the plea of self-defense was held in great suspicion despite the presence of strong corroborative evidence. During the trial, it was discovered that the deceased's clothing had not been examined. On studying the garments, it was found that the bullet had perforated all the articles of clothing in front, but not in the back. This fact supported the claim of self-defense.

35. Ligatures and Gags

A careful study should be made of all ligatures, gags, or wads which may be found in the area of the neck and head, or in the mouth and throat in cases of strangulation by ligature or choking. In other cases, ropes, wires, and improvised ligatures and restraining devices may be found on the limbs or body. These articles can sometimes be traced to their source, and their probable ownership can thus be established.

36. Fingernail Scrapings

The fingernails of the deceased sometimes contain indications of an assault. In a struggle with his assailant the victim may scratch him or scrape his clothing. Minute fragments of skin, strands of hair, cloth fibers, and other materials which can serve as useful clues may sometimes be found, particularly in cases of strangulations, smothering, choking, and homicidal assaults with clubs or knives. The medical examiner will ordinarily take fingernail scrapings in these cases. Fingerprinting of the deceased should be postponed until the scraping procedure has been accomplished. The scrapings from each fingernail should be placed in a separate filter paper and appropriately labeled.

VI. POSTMORTEM EXAMINATION

37. General

The term *postmortem* examination is used here to include the procedures followed by the medical examiner, coroner, or other qualified person in the investigation surrounding certain types of death. The procedure includes the examination at the scene of the crime, the identification of the body, the external examination of the body, the autopsy, and subsequent technical examinations, such as toxicological analysis, which the case may require. The postmortem examination may all be accomplished by one physician or it may be performed by a physician in association with a pathologist, toxicologist, serologist, or histologist. The primary purpose of the examination is to determine the cause of death. It is considered the function of the investigator to determine who committed the offense.

38. Qualifications of the Examining Physician

The postmortem examination, especially the autopsy, should be performed preferably by a forensic pathologist. The branch of medicine called pathology is the study of abnormal changes in bodily tissues or functions caused by diseases, poisons, or other bodily affections. By certain techniques, such as the microscopic examination of samples of tissues from vital organs, the pathologist can draw reliable conclusions concerning the causes of bodily conditions. The forensic pathologist employs special techniques to gather evidence concerning how, when, and where the victim came to his death. His special study is the problem of sudden, unexpected, and violent death. He endeavors to determine whether the nature of the violence employed was suicidal, accidental, homicidal, or other.

39. Availability of Expert Assistance

Since local laws and customs are the determining factors, no definite requirements can be given concerning the qualifications of the physician who will perform the postmortem examination in investigations of homicide. Obviously, an effort should be made to obtain the most qualified persons available. The investigator will, however, be usually restricted to personnel locally available, and to the laws and customs of the community serving such agency. If qualified personnel is not available, the investigator should seek a physician with some experience in postmortem work. Failing this he should obtain the services simply of a person with a degree of doctor of medicine. Where the investigator does not have authority and responsibility in the case, he must abide by local laws and customs. He should, however, remember that the services of the Armed Forces Pathological Institute, FBI Laboratory, and other law enforcement laboratories are available to him for toxicological, pathological, and serological work. Organs and other specimens can be properly collected, preserved, and transmitted over great distances for ultimate examination by qualified persons.

40. When Should an Autopsy be Performed?

As a general rule a postmortem examination including an autopsy should be performed in every death where there is a suspicion of homicide (including suicide). Specifically the following types of death should be the subject of a preliminary examination by a physician: deaths from criminal violence, accidental deaths, suicides, sudden deaths where the person had been in apparent good health, deaths unattended by a physician, deaths occurring in prison, and deaths occurring in any suspicious or unusual manner. The physician should go to the scene of the death and take charge of the dead body. He should then fully investigate essential facts concerning the circumstances surrounding the death. If the cause of the death is established beyond a reasonable doubt, the physician should so report. If, however, in his opinion an autopsy is necessary, this should be performed by a qualified physician. An autopsy is performed when the cause of death is doubtful or when it appears that criminal violence has been employed.

The term *qualified physician* has been used here in referring to the person making the initial examination. Ideally, this person should be a medical examiner, i.e., a doctor of medicine who is a skilled pathologist. Lay persons, whether private citizens, police officers, prosecuting attorneys, or physicians not trained to carry out medicolegal investigations often cannot decide the nature of sudden death, or of death where there has not been any medical attention, and accordingly should not be burdened with that responsibility. Their opinion of any such death should not preclude an investigation by a medical examiner with the authority to decide upon the advisability and necessity of an autopsy and to perform such autopsy. The investigator should not be satisfied with the procedure in practice in some communities of referring only the obviously violent, suspicious cases to the medicolegal department. Laxity in this regard is responsible for the exhumation of bodies which are embalmed and buried too hastily because the violence was not apparent or suspected at the time of death. The later development of new evidence necessitates an exhumation. Often a careful routine postmortem examination in cases first reported as non-suspicious leads to the detection of a number of violent deaths each year in those communities where rigorous medical examiner's laws are in effect.

41. Coroners and Medical Examiners

It should be remembered that the term *medical examiner* is not in universal use even in the United States, nor is the *medical examiner system* (substantially the investigative practice recommended in the preceding paragraph) in widespread use. The term *medical examiner* will be used throughout here on the assumption that the investigator is endeavoring to conform to the best practice in homicide investigation. It is understood that he will frequently find himself in communities and jurisdictions where he must be satisfied perforce with something less than the best practice. The term *pathologist* is used in some communities with the same connotations as *medical examiner.* The title *coroner* is neutral in regard to the degree of education and skill possessed by its owner. This will vary widely with the community; in some states it will be the equivalent of a medical examiner, while in others the coroner may be an undertaker or a barber. In dealing with the latter type of coroner, the investigator may suggest the advisability of further examination by a professional medical man.

42. Removal of the Body

After completing his preliminary examination, the medical examiner orders the removal of the body to the mortuary. An identification tag should first be attached to the body. The transportation of the body must be carefully supervised in order to avoid mutilation and interference with anatomical lesions which may be present on the surface. If the body is handled roughly, new injuries may be produced which are not easily distinguishable from the antemortem injuries. In moving the body it is important to avoid soiling the clothing with foreign dirt or body discharges. Powder marks, hair, dust, and other fragile evidence should not be disturbed.

43. Identifying the Body

The identification of the body to the medical examiner is an obvious and simple procedure which although important may be readily overlooked by the inexperienced. The body of the deceased is identified to the medical examiner by the first representative of the law enforcement agency having jurisdiction who saw it. This identification is a vital link in the chain of evidence. Without it the body autopsied by the medical examiner is not connected to the particular crime of which a suspect will be later accused. The identification may be made at the scene or later at the mortuary. In those cases where the victim survives for a period of time and later dies in a hospital, the identification is of particular importance, since the medical examiner will have first seen the body only at the mortuary. The time and place of identification should be recorded in the investigator's notes and should later become a part of his report of investigation. The manner of identification and the persons to whom it is made should also be made a part of the report.

44. Responsibilities of the Investigator

Obviously, the investigator does not engage in any autopsy work himself. He may, however, be expected to assist in making the necessary arrangements where responsibility has been assumed by another agency. The investigator should be capable of determining whether the medicolegal purposes of the autopsy are being adequately served. He should, moreover, place himself in a position where he can report whether the circumstances under which the autopsy was conducted were proper. For example, he should know whether the body was properly identified to the persons performing the autopsy. He should also make sure that evidence requiring further examination is properly preserved, packed, and transmitted.

45. Procedures in Autopsies

At the time of the autopsy, it is impossible to determine initially all the lines along which the case may develop. Hence, it is desirable that a complete examination be carried out in a systematic manner. The examination is not limited to the region in which the cause of death is supposed to exist and ordinarily does not even begin in this area. The requirements of the case dictate the order of procedure but in all cases a fixed routine governs the operation. This routine is established on anatomical considerations, mechanical convenience, and the general principle that a structure should be examined before it is disturbed. The customary order is as follows: external examination, head and brain, incision of the body, thorax, abdomen, pelvis, extremities, and an examination of the various regions. Microscopic studies of selected portions supplement the unaided visual examinations.

46. Reporting the Autopsy

A record of the findings of an autopsy is called an autopsy *protocol.* The preferred protocol is one which is dictated by the operator as the examination progresses. Negative as well as positive findings are recorded. Many physicians employ a prepared autopsy blank which guides the procedure and assures completeness as well as order.

47. Legal Considerations

An autopsy must be conducted in accordance with the laws of the state or territory governing the conditions under which an autopsy is performed. The investigator should scrupulously avoid any violation of these laws in his efforts to cooperate with the authorities. The following general information will serve as a guide in many situations.

a. **Authorization.** Generally speaking, an unauthorized autopsy is a tort (the offending party is subject to civil suit for damages). Authorization for an autopsy may be made by consent of the person entitled to custody of the body, by the coroner or medical examiner, or by the will of the deceased. Since the dead have no right to privacy, the liability for an unauthorized autopsy is based on the outraged sensibilities of the person entitled to custody. The coroner, or medical examiner, can authorize autopsy only for statutory purposes. It should be noted that unauthorized spectators or unauthorized use of photographs may constitute grounds for damage claims.

b. **Privileged Communications.** Ordinarily the information which is obtained by an autopsy is not privileged.

c. **Property Rights.** A dead body is not property and a person cannot own a dead body or acquire title thereto. Since, however, the duty of burial falls on the next of kin, the custody of the body is given to this person. Interference with rights of custody and interment of the dead may result in recovery of damages for mental pain and suffering.

d. **Disposition of the Body.** The regulations of the state department of health control the embalming, transportation, and interment of a dead body.

e. **Exhumation.** The principle of the sanctity of the tomb controls disinterment. The coroner or medical examiner may request the sheriff in writing to disinter a body for examination.

48. Results of the Autopsy

In a homicide investigation, the findings of the autopsy will be useful in providing new information to the investigator as well as confirming or negating his suspicions concerning the event. The following is a list of some of the essential facts that an autopsy may establish:

    a. The probable cause of death.

    b. An estimate of the time of death.

    c. The number and nature of the wounds on the body.

    d. The identity of the fatal wound.

    e. Whether the wound was self-inflicted.

    f. The kind of weapon used.

    g. An estimate of the time elapsed between receiving the wound and death. *probably amount of blood lost*

    h. An assessment of the victim's ability to move after receiving the wound.

    i. The probable manner of death.

    j. The blood type.

    k. Evidence of alcohol or drug use.

    l. Evidence of sexual assault.

VII. TIME OF DEATH

49. Determining the Time of Death

One of the first steps in an investigation of a homicide is to determine the time of death. Although it may not be possible to set the time precisely, good estimates within certain limits can be established by observation of the following changes that take place in the body after death:

    a. Temperature and rate of cooling.

    b. Postmortem lividity.

    c. Rigor mortis.

    d. Putrefaction.

These changes can provide information on the following points:

    a. Time of death.

    b. Alterations in the position of the body after death.

    c. Whether the death was suicide or a murder.

Other circumstances and conditions which help to establish the time of death include:

    a. Indicative acts.
    b. An autopsy examination of the stomach contents.
    c. Insect activity.
    d. Chemical changes.

50. Temperature

Normally the temperature of the body is 98.6°F. The rate of cooling depends on the following factors:

    a. Temperature of the air and the manner in which the body is clothed. On cold days the rate of cooling is greater. Heavy clothing will retard the cooling.

    b. The age, size of a person, and the amount of fat on the body. A fat person of 250 pounds will tend to cool slowly. Aged persons with less subcutaneous fat will cool more rapidly.

51. Postmortem Lividity

This is the dark blue discoloration that is observable on the parts of the body which are nearest the ground. The blood settles under its own weight into the lowest parts of the body. This coloring appears about two hours subsequent to death. After the blood has settled, it tends to clot in the tissues. Hence, although the body is moved after death, the lividity remains. If a body is found with postmortem lividity on the upper surface, it can be concluded that the body was moved after death. It is important to differentiate between discoloration due to lividity and that due to bruises. Close observation will reveal distinct differences.

    a. The bruise may have a swelling or an abrasion; lividity does not have these indications.

    b. The color of the bruise is variable; that of lividity is uniform.

    c. Lividity appears only on the low-lying parts of the body; bruises may appear on any part.

    d. In the case of lividity, an incision will reveal the fact that the blood is still in the vessels; in bruises an incision shows that the blood has broken out of the vessels.

52. Rigor Mortis

The muscles of the body stiffen after death, because of the chemical changes that take place within the muscle tissue (the accumulation of waste products causes the coagulation of the myocin in the muscles). Immediately after death the body is limp and relaxed. A relaxing of the sphincters leads to incontinence. With the onset of rigor mortis the body becomes exceptionally stiff. The stiffening process begins at the neck and lower jaw and spreads downward. All the muscles, voluntary and involuntary, including the heart muscle, contract.

a. **Time Required.** Rigor mortis may begin to set in fifteen minutes after death or fifteen hours after. On the average, it commences in about five to six hours after. The upper part of the body is affected within about twelve hours and the whole body within about eighteen hours.

b. **Duration.** Rigor mortis usually disappears within thirty-six hours. The head and neck once more become relaxed and the limpness gradually extends to the lower parts of the body. The process may take from eight to ten hours.

c. **Estimating Time of Death.** Many variables enter into the speed with which rigor mortis sets in and disappears. Great heat will accelerate the process by coagulating the proteins in the muscles. Individual differences such as relative muscular development affect the time. In general, however, the investigator may employ the following rough rule:

1) Rigor mortis should begin within ten hours after death.

2) The whole body should be stiff within twelve to eighteen hours after death.

3) Stiffening disappears within thirty-six hours after death.

d. **Cadaveric Spasm.** Sometimes, stiffening occurs immediately after death. This happens when there is a severe injury to the central nervous system or when there was great tension at the moment of death. The body becomes stiff rapidly and the hand may be found clutching the weapon. In such cases it is strong presumptive evidence of suicide. Ordinarily, the hand relaxes after death and the weapon falls away. If a weapon is subsequently placed in the hand of a dead person, it will lie there loosely. It is not possible to force the hand to grasp the weapon tightly. The tenacious grasp is characteristic of cadaveric spasm; hence, its importance in questions of suicide.

53. Putrefaction

In cases where the elapsed time interval is a matter of days, the changes of the body attributable to putrefaction become important. The onset and rate of development of putrefaction are influenced mainly by the temperature of the environment. Thus putrefaction may be well developed within a day in tropical surroundings or may be scarcely observable after months of exposure to a freezing atmosphere. The principal perceptible changes are:

a. *Bloating* of the body by gas. With the passage of time the gas escapes and the bloated tissues collapse. Disintegration or desiccation sets in depending on the humidity of the body.

b. *Darkening* of the skin in suspended parts of the body.

c. Green *discoloration* of the skin of the abdomen.

d. Formation of *blisters* filled with fluid or gas.

54. Indicative Acts

Logical deductions concerning the true time of death can often be made by careful study of the crime scene and the reports or evidence of the activities of the deceased prior to death.

a. **Acts Performed by the Deceased While Alive.** Certain evidence present at the scene may indicate activities of the deceased and establish the fact that he was alive at a certain time.

1) *Lights.* The fact that the lights in a house are on or off will suggest whether the crime occurred during the day or night.

2) *Collections.* Milk, mail, and newspapers are ordinarily collected within a definite span of time. The presence or absence of these objects from their place of delivery is significant.

3) *Preparations.* Meals prepared or eaten indicate the lapse of time intervals. The shining of shoes, brushing of teeth, bathing, and other actions may be related to a definite time by one familiar with the personal habits of the deceased.

b. **Acts Not Performed.** The failure to perform certain customary acts indicates that death had already occurred. Thus, negative conclusions can be associated with the actions listed in the preceding paragraph.

c. **Correlation of Other Events with Death.** Independent events which affect the crime scene can be used to set certain time limits to the time lapse since death. For example, in an outdoor crime scene the area beneath the body may be found to be unaffected by a rainfall or snowfall. Obviously the body must have been situated on the spot prior to the time set by weather bureau statistics for the beginning of the precipitation.

55. Stomach Contents

From an examination of the stomach contents of the body during the autopsy, the medical examiner can sometimes make an estimate of the time of death based on information about the eating habits of the deceased. It is necessary to know the time of his last meal and the size of the meal. It is helpful to know the specific food eaten and the interval between his last two meals.

a. **Position in the Stomach.** Food travels through the stomach into the intestines. The stomach begins to empty approximately ten minutes after eating a meal. It may take up to two hours for a light meal to travel through the stomach and enter the intestines. A large meal may require up to six hours to pass completely out of the stomach. At death, the stomach activity ceases. By knowing the size of the last meal and observing its position in the stomach, the medical examiner can approximate the number of hours that have elapsed between the deceased's last meal and his death.

b. **Degree of Digestion.** Digestion is the physical and chemical breakdown of food into an absorbable form. There are a number of factors that will affect digestion, such as the kind of food eaten, the particle size, the amount of liquid consumed and the strength of the stomach acids. However, the rate of digestion depends primarily on the length of time the food is in the stomach and intestines. By noting the progress of digestion, the medical examiner can make a rough estimate of the time elapsed between the deceased's last meal and his death.

57. Insects

An entomologist can sometimes estimate the time elapsed since death by an examination of the insects present on the remains.

a. **Age of Maggots.** Flies may lay eggs between the lips and the eyelids within a few minutes after death. Maggots, the fly larvae, may be present within twenty-four hours. An entomologist who can determine the approximate age of a maggot can then make an estimate of the minimum time that could have elapsed since death. If the weather conditions during the entire period in question were conducive to insect activity (e.g., temperatures exceeding 40 degrees), the entomologist can assume the minimum time elapsed is the probable time of death.

b. **Species of Insects Present.** The types of insects that are attracted to the body change as decomposition progresses. An entomologist who can identify the different species of insects presently on the corpse can often approximate how long ago the death occurred. Furthermore, the presence of species not native to the area may indicate that the body was moved as well as provide a clue to the actual place of death.

58. Chemical Changes

Chemical analysis of unputrefied bodies may provide valuable information concerning the time of death. The numerous chemical changes which take place in orderly sequence enable the pathologist to draw some useful conclusions.

VIII. ASPHYXIA

59. Asphyxia

Asphyxia or suffocation is a suspension of breathing due to a deficiency of oxygen in the red blood cells. Among the forms which asphyxia may take are drowning, hanging, strangulation, choking, and smothering. Death results if the oxygen supply to the blood and tissues falls below a certain level. If breathing stops for a period of three to four minutes, movement ceases. The heart, however, will continue to beat for another five minutes.

a. **Forms.** Asphyxia can occur in a number of ways. In all of these forms of death, postmortem examination can yield only the information that death resulted from asphyxia. The following may cause death from asphyxia:

1) Disease such as pneumonia.
2) Cutting off air externally as in drowning or smothering.
3) Cutting off air in the throat by choking or hanging.
4) Breathing certain gases.
5) Poisoning or wounds.

b. **Postmortem Appearance.** Lividity of the mucous membranes is apparent; lips are pale blue to black; blue fingers and toenails can be seen; face is usually calm, but may be distorted; sometimes froth appears at the mouth; postmortem lividity is well marked because the blood is dark venous in color. The postmortem appearance of asphyxia is not an indication that death did not come from natural causes. Death of this kind is due to lack of oxygen in the tissue. It is, then, of extreme importance to discover the cause of asphyxiation.

60. Hanging

Usually, hanging is suicidal; sometimes it is accidental. Rarely is it used as a means of murder. It is not necessary that the body be suspended clear from the ground for death to take place. The body may be half-prone or in a sitting position.

a. **Causes of Death.** There are several causes of this type of death:

1) Asphyxia attributable to the tongue pressing upward and backward. This is the most common cause.

2) Occlusion or tightening of the great vessels of the neck. With the supply of blood to the brain cut off, unconsciousness intervenes. This may take place in a few seconds or in the space of several minutes. This rapidity of occurrence is an explanation of those cases of accidental hanging in which it appears that a minor effort would have freed the person.

3) Inhibition of the heart due to pressure on the vagus.

4) In legal hangings, the fracture-dislocation of the spine is the most common cause of death.

b. **Postmortem Appearance.** The knot is usually on the left side. If a small rope is used a deep groove will be made in the neck, under the jaw bone. Black and blue marks are visible along the edges of the groove. After several hours, the tongue protrudes slightly from the mouth.

c. **Accident, Suicide, or Murder.** The following indications are helpful in distinguishing accident from purpose:

1) *Accident.* Accidental hanging of adults is extremely rare. If a young boy is found dead from hanging or a child is found hung by the cords of the venetian blinds, the occurrence can usually be attributed to accident. Unconsciousness takes place so rapidly that death intervenes before discovery.

2) *Suicide.* Hanging is a common form of suicide. The person may bind his hands or feet. If the body is not completely suspended, it is usually a case of suicide, since a murderer will strive to achieve complete suspension.

3) *Murder.* Hanging, as remarked above, is a very infrequent form of murder. Ordinarily, it would be necessary for the victim to be unconscious from drugs, alcohol, or a blow before succumbing to the hanging procedure.

4) *Hanging After Death.* Hanging may be employed after a murder has been committed by other means in order to give the appearance of suicide. Other signs of violence may be visible about the neck to indicate prior strangulation.

5) *Sexual Asphyxia.* This is an unusual kind of hanging involving bizarre sexual practices. Incidents of sexual asphyxia will present the appearance of suicide but will be, in fact, an accident. In the typical case, a male body, often dressed in female undergarments, will be found suspended in a closet, a basement, or some other private area. The body may be bound with rope, usually in an elaborate interconnected fashion. There may be evidence of self-inflicted pain and ritualistic behavior. Pornography, literature and equipment for bondage, and paraphernalia for sexual self-stimulation are often present at the scene. Hence, the term *autoerotic death* is frequently used in describing cases of this nature. The victim enhances his sexual gratification by diminish-

ing the oxygen supply to the brain. He achieves this by suspending himself by a rope around his neck which will constrict the blood vessels. In the experience of light-headedness and euphoria that follows, he neglects to unloosen the rope in time. Unconsciousness occurs and death follows shortly after. A death of this type is an accident and not a suicide because there is no conscious intent to take one's life.

61. Drowning

In drowning, death is the result of asphyxia. The lungs ordinarily are not filled with water. In the process of drowning the person takes some water in the mouth and begins to choke. Irritation of the mucous membranes result in the formation of a great deal of mucus in the throat and windpipe. Efforts to breathe produce a sticky foam which may be mixed with vomit. The foam prevents the passage of air into the lungs.

a. **Appearance.** Drowning presents a characteristic appearance if the body has not been in the water too long. In addition to the fine foam about the mouth and nose, the body is usually pale, although some areas may redden because of the sudden lowering of temperature in cold water.

b. **Diagnosis.** Was the death of the deceased due to drowning or was the person dead before being thrown into the water? This question can sometimes be answered by the medical examiner from an examination of the body. The following indications are looked for in determining true drowning:

1) Articles grasped in the hand, such as seaweed.
2) Swelling of the lungs.
3) Signs of asphyxia.
4) The nature of the water in the stomach.
5) The mouth is usually found open.
6) Comparison of the chloride content and the magnesium content in the right and left ventricles of the heart.

c. **Emergence of the Drowned Body.** Invariably a submerged body will rise again. The bacteria in the body cause the formation of gases which distend the body until it is again buoyant. The time required for emergence depends on the fat content of the body and upon the temperature of the water. Weights attached to the body will, of course, increase the required time. Eventually, the gas escapes from the tissues and the body sinks once again.

IX. BURNING, LIGHTNING, AND ELECTRIC SHOCK

62. General

The finding of a body in a burned building or vehicle presents a number of special problems in homicide investigation. The fire may be incendiary or accidental in origin; the death may be accidental or intended; finally, the cause of death may be other than the fire itself. Combining these possibilities will present the following possible situations.

a. **Accidental Fire and Accidental Death.** The investigation in this situation is centered around the question of negligence. The improper storage of fuel, amateur electrical work, or other careless act or omission may point to negligence. The techniques of arson investigation are applicable.

b. **Accidental Fire and Intended Death.** It is possible that after the commission of a homicide, a fire accidentally broke out. The investigator is faced here with the problem of investigating a homicide in which much of the evidence has been destroyed.

c. **Arson and Accidental Death.** Although the arsonist may not have been aware of the presence of a human being in the building, he can be charged with murder if a death is caused by the fire.

d. **Arson and Intended Death.** A criminal may use fire as the lethal agent or, more commonly, he may employ the fire for the purpose of concealing a homicide. An attempt may be made to conceal a suicide by fire.

e. **Arson and Death from Natural Causes.** It may be desired by the criminal to make death by natural causes appear to be the result of accidental fire in order to collect additional insurance.

63. Cause of Death

From the preceding outline of the problems resulting from the combination of fire and death it is apparent that the establishment of the cause of death is the most significant step in the investigation. Among the more common causative factors in the death of a person in a burning building are the following:

a. **Exposure to Gases.** During the course of a fire noxious gases are generated. The gases can cause death either because they are so searingly hot that they burn the skin and air passages or because they are toxic.

b. **Direct Exposure to Flame.** A vital organ exposed to flames can be completely incapacitated or destroyed to the point where life can no longer be supported.

c. **Falls While Attempting Escape.** In an effort to escape from the flames, the victims of a fire will take extraordinary risks in climbing, often falling to their deaths. Theater and hall fires may result in death from trampling or crushing as a consequence of panic.

d. **Falling Beams and Masonry.** The burning of a building naturally loosens the elements of its structure with considerable hazard to persons trapped within.

64. Mechanisms of Death

The precaution that should underlie the investigator's point of view in the investigation of conflagration deaths is the avoidance of the assumption that death occurring in a fire is necessarily attributable to exposure to the flames. A list of the actual mechanisms of deaths in fires must include the following:

a. **Carbon Monoxide Poisoning.** Obviously, there is a great amount of incomplete combustion in a building fire. The result, which is a source of comfort to relatives, is that the victim dies by asphyxiation or by the incapacitation due to the carbon monoxide in the blood. Persons sitting too close to an ordinary fire in a brazier are sometimes overcome by carbon monoxide and fall face forward into the fire.

b. **Pulmonary Irritants.** Fires in factories or other commercial establishments where certain chemicals are stored are characterized by the generation of great amounts of unusual gases such as pulmonary irritants, the inhalation of which can rapidly cause death. Among the gases sometimes found in fires are oxides of nitrogen; acrolein; refrigerant gases such as ammonia, freon, and methyl chloride; and phosgene, which is generated on burning carbon tetrachloride.

65. Antemortem and Postmortem Changes

The critical question in many investigations of deaths in fires is concerned with whether the deceased was alive at the time of the fire. Often a person desiring to conceal a homicide will look on arson as the only practical solution to his problem. The body, however, does not burn as readily as the arsonist imagines. It resists the destructive forces of fire with astonishing durability, and frequently there is sufficient evidence remaining for the medical examiner to draw some useful conclusions.

a. **Life Probably Present During Fire.** The following signs suggest that the victim may have been alive during the conflagration although unconscious or dying from other causes:

1) Smoke stains about the nostrils, in the nose and the air passages.

2) Carbon monoxide in the blood.

3) Blistering and marginal reddening of the skin.

b. **Life Not Necessarily Present During Fire.** A conclusion of this nature can be made only by an experienced pathologist who is aware of the origin of the anatomical changes that can result from exposure of a dead body to fire. The so-called *pugilistic posture,* in which the arms and wrists are flexed in a boxer's pose, is of no value in this determination, since a body exposed to heat can acquire this attitude as a consequence of heat rigor regardless of the cause or time of death. Similarly, skin splits, fractures, and other signs suggestive of injury will have no significance for the investigator until they are interpreted by the pathologist in terms of their cause and probable time of occurrence in reference to the fire.

66. Lightning

Death from lightning is due either to fibrillation of the heart (marked change in strength and rhythm of the heartbeat) or paralysis of the respiratory center. There is no characteristic appearance. When a person is struck by lightning, he may be thrown into the air for a considerable distance, with consequent fractures and lacerations. Burns may be observed particularly in the areas covered by metal objects worn near the skin, such as religious medals or garter clips. At times, highly typical superficial burns may be observed in the shape of arborescent (treelike) markings caused by variations in skin conductivity. To decide whether lightning is the cause of death, the following steps are useful:

a. Eliminate all other common causes.

b. Determine, by interview, the storm and lightning activity in the immediate neighborhood.

c. Look for signs of lightning strikes on trees and other tall objects near the scene.

d. Look for skin burns under metal objects and for treelike markings.

67. Electrocution

Deaths from electric shock are similar to those from lightning. A combination of small voltage and high current or high voltage and small current may cause death. Potentials as low as 50 volts have been known to be fatal. The electric chair is ordinarily charged with 1700 volts. Most important in determining the danger of electricity is the question of good contact with good ground. Wet hands on plumbing fixtures combined with standing in water cause many deaths in bathrooms; wires falling into pools of water present another hazard. A high voltage will send the heart into a spasm with death rapidly following. Low voltage such as 110 volts can cause death if the person is well grounded, but death does not occur with the same rapidity. Fibrillation of the heart takes place (the strength and rhythm of the heartbeat are altered). As a consequence, there is a failure of blood supply to the brain and the person lapses into unconsciousness. If this continues, the heart ceases to beat and death follows.

a. **Skin Appearance.** Although the resistance of the skin causes the electrical energy to be transformed into heat, an electrical injury is not necessarily a burn. Often no mark is apparent where contact was made. The true electrical injury is an elevated, round, grayish-white or yellow, wrinkled area. The dried skin may peel. The surrounding area may be black or may be burned.

b. **Postmortem Appearance.** Ordinarily the appearance is not sufficiently characteristic to exclude all other causes. Pulmonary edema (swelling) and the appearance of asphyxia are usually present. Entrance and exit lesions together with the physical surroundings are helpful in forming a diagnosis.

X. WOUNDS IN GENERAL

68. Classification

For the purposes of investigation, wounds may be classified according to the nature of the instrument used in their production as follows: Wounds due to cutting or stabbing; wounds caused by an instrument having no blade; gunshot wounds. In making the postmortem examination the doctor attempts to answer questions relating to the following points:

a. The nature and extend of the wound and the extent of damage to the organs. From this examination it may be possible to determine the nature of the weapon used.

b. **The Cause of Death.** It should not be assumed that the victim died as a direct result of the wounds. Although the body may bear severe wounds, it is possible that death was caused by a fall or by heart failure.

c. The time elapsing between the infliction of the wounds and death.

d. **The Nature of the Occurrence.** Is it accident, suicide, or murder?

e. The condition of the victim with regard to speech and the use of his limbs after receiving the wound.

69. Stabbing and Cutting Wounds

A common form of homicide is that resulting from the use of a knife, or other instrument possessing a blade.

a. **Nature and Extent of the Wound.** It should not be concluded from a simple visual examination that a wound was caused by a knife. Sometimes gunshot wounds striking the body surface at an angle may have the appearance of a slash. A person falling and striking his head on a curb, radiator, or on ice may suffer a laceration resembling a knife wound. The nature of the wound made by a knife will in general depend on the following:

1) The type of knife used, and the area, shape, and length of the blade, whether single or double-edged, sharpness.

2) The manner in which the knife was used. The action of stabbing, i.e., plunging the knife into the body, is usually accompanied by a cutting motion before it is withdrawn. One result of this motion is that the length of the entry slit or hole is larger than the blade of the knife.

3) *Part of the Body.* The elasticity and thickness of the skin vary in different parts of the body, thus determining in part the size and shape of the wound.

4) *Depth of Stab.* An indication of the length of the knife can be obtained from the depth of the stab. The dissecting surgeon can usually determine the depth of the wound during the autopsy.

b. **Cause of Death.** In determining the cause of death in cases where the deceased bears stab wounds, the doctor does not assume that death resulted from the wounds. The actual cause is determined by means of an autopsy. The following causes are considered:

1) *Primary Causes.*

a) HEMORRHAGE. Where the large artery is cut, the death can be attributed to bleeding. The quantity of blood visible is also an indication.

b) VITAL ORGAN. Injury to a vital organ is readily determined by the autopsy.

c) SHOCK. The victim may have been subjected to a number of small injuries, no one of which is sufficient to cause death. In these cases the death may be attributed to shock. Fear, inhibitions, total affected area, trauma, and other considerations assist in the diagnosis of shock.

2) **Secondary Causes.** The victim may not die from the original wounding but rather from an ensuing complication such as pneumonia or tetanus.

c. **Time Elapsed.** By observing the condition of the wound the doctor can estimate within twelve hours the time elapsed between receiving the injury and death. It is possible also to determine whether a wound was received before or after death. Such information is of value when an effort has been made to conceal true causes of death by inflicting stab wounds. If the wound is received before death, it gapes and usually bleeds profusely; if received after death, the wound does not gape and bleeds but slightly.

d. **Accident, Suicide, or Murder.** Usually a death by stabbing or cutting presents a murder or a suicide case. Rarely is it an accident.

1) *Accidental.* Accidental deaths due to cutting or stabbing are ordinarily the result of a fall. For example, if a person falls on a pitchfork, picket fence, or against a long needle the projection may puncture a vital organ.

2) *Suicide.* The throat, left wrist, left chest, and femoral artery are the parts of the body most commonly attacked in suicides by stabbing or cutting. Of these, the most frequently occurring form of suicide is that of cutting the throat with a razor or knife. The razor is usually held in the right hand; the cut is begun below the left ear and drawn under the chin to the right side. One common indication of suicide is the existence of superficial cuts, approximately one inch long, at the point of origin of the wound. These cuts are referred to as *hesitation marks.* They ordinarily indicate that the person tested the razor on his skin before summoning sufficient courage to make the fatal slash. The presence of the razor or knife tightly clenched in the hand of the dead person is also considered strong evidence of suicide. Another indication of suicide is the finding of the body at the point where the cutting or stabbing was done. In cases of homicide the victim in an effort to escape or pursue his assailant runs away from the point of occurrence leaving blood drops and other traces as he goes.

3) *Homicide.* If the victim is awake at the time of the attack, it is difficult to kill him by cutting alone. Stabbing strokes of the

knife must ordinarily be employed. In defending himself the victim may receive wounds on the palms of the hands and outer surfaces of the forearms. If the victim grasps the knife, deep gashes may be observed in the palm or under surface of the fingers. The fatal wounds are usually in the neck or the upper chest. Wounds in the back are obviously indicative of homicide.

e. **The Crime Scene.** In addition to the usual matters connected with the crime scene there are certain points of special interest in stabbing and cutting crimes. The investigator should note the condition of the clothing; the photographs should show the position of the hands. If a hand is gripping a knife, attention should be directed to the firmness of the grip, the direction in which the blade is pointing with relation to the hand, and the direction in which the cutting edge is pointing. The presence or absence of defense wounds should be observed. The extent of the bleeding and the condition of the blood should also be noted.

f. **Information Obtained from the Autopsy.** Ordinarily in cases where death appears to be attributable to a knife wound, an autopsy is performed. The investigator may then obtain from the surgeon information such as the following:

1) *The Cause of Death.* It is not to be assumed that the victim died of the knife wounds. The true cause must be ascertained from the surgeon.

2) *The Type of Weapon.* An estimate of the size, shape, and sharpness of the knife or other weapon can be made from an examination of the wounds. The depth of penetration and the dimensions of the wounds are indications of these characteristics of the weapon.

3) *Circumstances Surrounding the Attack.* The character and location of the attack suggest the vigor of the resistance offered by the victim to the assault.

70. Blunt Force or Direct Violence

Under this heading will be placed deaths caused by the application of direct violence, a category including by far the largest proportion of the homicides with which the investigator must deal. Clubbing over the head, kicking in the stomach, and hurling the victim to the ground or into some other stationary object are examples of the work of blunt force. In general, assaults, motor vehicle homicides, and negligent homicides frequently involve the use of blunt force. Although death by direct violence is accomplished in a crude manner, the cause of death may be difficult to establish. The external appearance of bruises is not a reliable indication of the seriousness of the internal damage. The part of the body directly affected, the nature of the instrument used, and the degree of force exercised in the application of the instrument are determining factors.

a. **Head Injuries.** In approximately 45 percent of the fatal motor vehicle accidents, the cause of death is an injury to the head. Similarly, in death from assaults and falls, damage to the head is the most important factor. The scalp lying over the hard skull is easily lacerated by blunt force with a resulting appearance suggestive of the use of a sharp instrument. Injury to the scalp and a state of unconsciousness are not reliable indications of the extent of serious damage to the brain. The medical examiner by examining the injuries to the skull and brain can make certain deductions as to the nature, extent, and direction of the force and the type of instrument used. His description of the damage to the head employs the introductory term *fracture of the skull.*

b. **Spine.** Fracture of the spine occurs most commonly in falls and motor vehicle accidents. Sometimes spine fractures are due to indirect violence such as a punch on the chin, diving into shallow water, and a fall of a weight on the head.

c. **Neck.** A broken neck in itself is not the cause of death. Death will follow a broken neck if there has been sufficient damage to the spinal cord. A diagnosis of an injury of this type can only be made by an autopsy.

d. **Chest.** Blows or crushing wounds on the chest may fracture the ribs, causing them to pierce the lung or heart and thus resulting in death. In motor vehicle accidents in which the driver is thrown against the steering wheel, the heart becomes squeezed between the sternum and the vertebral column and death may follow from heart failure. If the violence is exceptionally severe, the heart may be crushed, ruptured, or torn out of place.

e. **Abdomen.** An injury to the abdomen may result from a fall, kick, or motor vehicle accident. Although only slight abrasions may be visible externally, the damage to the organs may be fatal. The liver, spleen, and kidneys may be ruptured, resulting in death from hemorrhage. A rupture of the stomach and intestines can follow as a result of crushing against the spine. For example, in a street fight an assailant may drive his knee into the abdomen of the victim, with fatal consequences.

XI. GUNSHOT WOUNDS

71. General

In the investigation of a death caused by firearms the wound is examined for the purpose of determining the nature and type of the weapon employed; the distance and direction of fire; and the relative positions of the victim and the assailant at the time of occurrence. If the bullet is still remaining in the body, the surgeon will recover it. From the fatal bullet additional information can be obtained concerning the character of the weapon. If a gun is discovered which is thought to be the murder weapon, it may be possible to identify or exclude it by means of a comparison between fatal and test bullets. In the investigations of unexpected death all weapons, bullets, and shells should be submitted for expert examination as described in Chapter 7.

72. Nature and Extent of the Wound

The two types of wounds, entrance and exit, are studied with regard to certain characteristics which vary with the kind of ammunition used; the firing distance; ricocheting (striking another object before hitting the body); passage through clothing; and path through the body.

a. **Entrance Wounds.** The shape, size, and appearance of the entrance wound are affected by the distance of discharge, the type of weapon, the nature of the gunpowder, and the affected part of the body. The terms near and far discharge are used below in a relative sense. At one time when black powder was in common use, a gun fired from a distance of a few feet would leave distinct evidence of the closeness of discharge. With modern ammunition this effect is not apparent when the distance of discharge exceeds a few inches. Wounds, however, vary with the discharge distance and some useful conclusions can be drawn from a consideration of certain characteristics of the wound.

1) *Near Discharge.* When a bullet strikes the skin, it pushes against a tough, elastic surface which it stretches and indents. A part of the skin removes the grime from the sides of the bullet and forms a gray ring around the entrance wound. The wound itself is larger than the bullet, since at close distance it is affected by undispersed explosive gases. Powder, clothing, and, in cases of shotguns, a wad may be discovered in the wound. The powder is not completely burned, and small particles of the unburnt powder are driven into the skin by the explosive gases, resulting in a "tattooing ring." Powder marks and scorching are more prominent on the side from which the bullet came.

2) *Far Discharge.* The entrance wound reveals no discharge products such as tattooing or scorching. Because of the absence of explosive gases the wound is smaller than the bullet. The edges of the skin are usually inverted.

3) *Shotguns.* This type of discharge is recognized by the presence of shot in the wound. The most common type of shotgun found at the scene of a murder is the 12-gauge shotgun. This weapon, when fired from a distance of 1 to 3 feet, will make a hole in the body of 1½ to 2 inches in diameter. When fired from greater distance the gun produces no central hole but rather a number of small wounds. The size of the pattern will depend on whether or not the shotgun is chokebored, i.e., narrowed slightly in the muzzle to concentrate the pattern. A search should always be made for the wadding since it gives an indication of the gauge of the gun. If the discharge distance is less than 10 feet, the wad will usually be found in the body. Outdoors the wadding can usually be found within a radius of 50 feet from the gun.

b. **Exit Wounds.** If the bullet passes through the body unobstructed by bone, the typical exit wound is small and everted (skin edge turned out). Where the bullet strikes bone, it may turn over on its axis, push fragmented matter ahead in its path, and produce a large exit wound. It is difficult to draw useful conclusions from the relative sizes of the entrance and exit wounds. If the gun is fired from a distance, both entrance and exit wounds may be of the same size. At a close distance the relative size will depend on whether the bullet struck bone in its path.

73. Accident, Suicide, or Murder

In the absence of eyewitnesses it is not always a simple matter to determine whether a death from gunshot wounds is an accident, suicide, or murder. The circumstantial evidence is helpful in some cases. Often, however, no conclusion can be drawn.

a. **Accident.** Gunshot deaths attributable to accident are quite common. Pulling a gun through a hedge; carelessly cleaning rifles; pointing guns at other people in jest; untutored handling of guns; and similar misuse of a firearm can result in a fatal accident. Questions of motive and opportunity must be investigated before a judgment of accident can be made. One of the most important factors to be considered in drawing any conclusion is the distance from which the shot was fired.

b. **Suicide.** The determination as to whether a death due to a gunshot wound is suicidal in nature can often be a difficult problem. A suicidal death can be contrived to appear accidental for the purpose of defrauding an insurance company. For the same purpose the suicide may arrange the circumstances surrounding his death so that the conclusion of murder will be drawn.

1) *Location of Wound.* The position of the wound in the body is of great importance. In murder the wound may be found in any part of the body. Certain areas, however, are relatively inaccessible to the suicide. Typically, suicides select an area such as the right temple, the mouth, the center of the forehead, beneath the chin, the left chest, behind the right ear, and in the center of the back of the head. The majority of suicide wounds are inflicted in the head, at the right temple. The gun is usually held against the skin so that the imprint of the muzzle and the front sight may be seen. The next most popular area for suicides is the mouth. The muzzle of the gun is placed in the mouth.

2) *Distance of Discharge.* Without the aid of some ingenious mechanical device a person cannot commit suicide unless the gun is within a few feet of his body. If the gun is fired close to the victim (a distance less than 18 inches), a discoloration is visible on the exposed skin about the entrance wound. Two types of discoloration can be found, namely, smudging and tattooing. These are not visible if the bullet has gone through clothing. Ordinarily, however, the suicide is reluctant to shoot through clothing and bares the skin covering the area in which he intends to shoot.

a) Smudging. Burnt powder produces a smoke and powder which is deposited on the skin when the gun has been held at a distance of from 2 to about 18 inches. The result is a dirty, grimy appearance at the entrance. The size of the smudge is a function of the caliber of the bullet, the type of powder used, and the firing distance.

b) Tattooing. When the gun is fired, unburnt powder and particles of molten metal are also discharged in the blast. On striking the body surface the powder and particles imbed themselves in the lower layers of skin. The effect is known as "tattooing." The size of the tatooed area is a function of the caliber, powder charge, and the discharge distance from the victim. In estimating the distance of discharge the expert fires test shots from varying distances with the fatal gun and similar cartridges.

3) *Position of the Body.* Useful conclusions can often be made from the position in which the body is found with relation to other objects. In some cases it is obvious that the "stage has been set." Before shooting himself the person may have removed a garment to bare his chest and may have so placed himself that he would fall on a bed. Preparations such as these eliminate the probability of accident and point to suicide.

4) *Actions After Receiving Wounds.* Although a person has shot himself fatally, he may still be capable of rational acts. Even a person who has shot himself through the temple may still be able to move and alter the scene of death. The investigator cannot conclude, therefore, that the scene has not been changed since the shots were fired.

5) *Clenching the Weapon.* A strong indication of suicide is the presence of the weapon clenched in the hand. It is said to be

impossible to reproduce this tension in the grip by placing the gun in the hand after rigor mortis has set in. If the weapon lies loosely in the hand or if it apparently has fallen away from the hand, no conclusion can be drawn (see Sec. 52d).

c. **Murder.** The conclusion that a particular homicide is a murder is often made by the exclusion of accident and suicide. In murder the wound can be found on any part of the body; wounds in the back are particularly indicative of murder. The position from which the shot was fired can usually be determined from a study of the body wounds. If the shooting took place indoors and the bullet passed completely through the body, the location of the bullet in the wall, floor, or furniture will assist in determining the direction of fire. In making this determination the lodging place of the bullet is aligned with the entrance and exit holes of the body.

1) *The Body.* The body should be photographed from various angles to show its relationship to doors, windows, and furniture in the room. The distance of the body from these objects should be measured. The exact position of the body should be noted.

2) *The Bullet.* The floors, ceiling, walls, and furniture should be examined for bullet holes, shells, fired bullets, and shotgun wadding. A recovered bullet or shell should be marked for identification as described in Chapter 7.

3) *The Weapon.* The investigator should note the exact position of the gun; the type (automatic, revolver, shotgun, rifle) and caliber or gauge should be recorded together with the make, lot number, and serial number. Chapter 7 describes the procedures to be used in connection with this evidence.

74. Chemical Tests for Powder Residue

The discharge of a firearm may deposit certain gunpowder residues from which useful conclusions can be drawn. Several tests are available for the detection of powder residue. The gunshot primer residue test may be applied to the hand of the deceased to determine whether he was recently in close proximity to a discharged firearm. It is more often used on the hands of a suspect to associate him with the use of a firearm. This test will determine the levels of trace elements which are present in the gunpowder blown back on discharge. The Walker test is used to determine the presence of nitrites on the skin or clothing as an indication of powder residue and of the proximity of discharge. Both of these tests are discussed at length in Chapter 39.

XII. POISONING

75. Definition

A poison is a substance which when introduced into the body in small quantities causes a harmful or deadly effect. The emphasis in this definition should be placed on the term "small quantities." The word "small" is used relatively. Many substances such as alcohol become poisons when they are used in excessive amounts. Alcohol, however, is not a substance which would be employed by a murderer. The essence of the poisoner's technique is the administration of the fatal dose surreptitiously. The substance has been consumed before the victim is aware of the noxious presence, and the problem becomes one of detecting traces. Substances which become poisonous when taken in excessive quantities or after being contaminated do not ordinarily present difficult investigative problems. Poisonous materials fatally effective in small quantities are adaptable to the purpose of the murderer. Substances producing lethal effect in large quantities may be found in cases of manslaughter and negligent homicide.

76. Classification

Poisons may be classified in a simple manner according to the following scheme:

a. **Irritants.** This class of poisons produces vomiting and acute pains in the abdomen. The autopsy effects are recognizable by the redness or ulceration of the gastrointestinal tract. An extremely active irritant is termed a *corrosive.* The following are some of the more common irritants.

1) Mineral Acids and Alkalis. Among the most common are the following:

a) *Sulphuric Acid* (Vitriol). Deaths from this acid are usually accidental and occasionally suicidal. In assaults motivated by jealousy and revenge, a bottle of this acid may be thrown at the victim.

b) *Hydrochloric Acid* (Muriatic Acid) is the most commonly used poison among the inorganic acids. It is a strong corrosive acid similar to, but less destructive in its effects, than sulphuric acid.

c) *Nitric Acid* (Aqua Fortis) is similar to hydrochloric acid.

d) *Ammonia* is a common cause of death in industrial accidents attributable to the bursting of refrigerators.

2) *Organic Acids.* This group includes three of the quickest and most powerful of all poisons.

a) *Carbolic Acid* (Phenol, Cresote, Lysol®) in its pure state is colorless. For industrial use as a disinfectant, it is mixed with impurities and assumes a darker color. Carbolic acid, sold under the manufacturer's name of Lysol, is one of the more common means of suicidal poisoning. The characteristic smell and the staining about the mouth are indicative of poisoning by carbolic acid.

b) *Hydrocyanic Acid* (Prussic Acid). A colorless liquid, hydrocyanic acid is commonly employed in trades such as photography and engraving. Its use as a gaseous disinfecting agent on ships occasionally results in accidental death. The extreme rapidity of the onset of symptoms discourages its use in murders.

c) *Oxalic Acid* is used extensively in industry as an analytic reagent and as a bleach. Printing, dyeing, cleaning, paper, photography, and rubber are some of the industries in which it is employed. As a poison it is one of the most sure and rapid means of killing. Since it is inexpensive and easily obtained, it is often used by suicides. A burning of the throat and stomach, vomiting of bloody matter, an imperceptible pulse, and a quiet spell followed by death in about twenty minutes are indications. The drinking vessels and vomitus should be examined for characteristic white crystals.

b. **Metallic Poisons.** Two of the most commonly used poisons in murder are arsenic and antimony. In suicides and in deaths from industrial diseases mercury and lead are common. Traces of metallic poisons remain in the body long after death. Occasionally, a body is exhumed long after burial for the purpose of verifying a belated charge of murder.

1) *Arsenic.* This is the most commonly occurring poison in cases of murder. It is also one of the most readily available. Compounds of this metal are used as insecticides for spraying trees, as rat poison, and for medicinal preparations. Arsenic is extremely effective in minute doses. Quantities as small as a one and one-half grains have been known to cause death. For the purpose of murder, the poisoner sometimes avoids administering the large fatal dose and induces chronic progressive poisoning.

2) *Antimony.* This is a less commonly used poison and is ordinarily available in two forms: tartar emetic and butter of antimony, a substance used in veterinary practice. It differs from arsenic in that the onset of symptoms is immediate. The postmortem appearances of death by antimony are similar to those of poisoning by hydrochloric acid. The body remains in an excellent state of preservation for a period of years after burial.

3) *Mercury and Lead.* These are in common use for industrial purposes. Accidental deaths may occur through the use of certain preparations designed to prevent contraception or to induce abortion. These poisons are not used by murderers and only occasionally are they the means of suicide.

c. **Organic or Vegetable Poisons.** A large and effective group of poisons is extracted from various plants. They may be classified as *alkaloids* and *non-alkaloids.* These are sometimes called *neurotics* because they act mainly on the nervous system. The chief symptoms are drowsiness, delirium, coma, and sometimes convulsion and paralysis. Postmortem examination usually does not reveal any obvious physical effects on the organs as in the case of irritants.

1) *Alkaloids.* These are organic compounds which are alkaline in their chemical characteristics. They are poisonous in small quantities, affecting mainly the nervous system.

a) Opium Derivatives. At one time, opium and its derivative alkaloids were extensively used as a poison. Suicidal poisonings were accomplished in the great majority of these cases by drinking laudanum. Although their popularity as poisons has diminished considerably in modern times, opium derivatives are still widely used. Opium itself is a dried juice of the opium poppy. Among the alkaloids which it contains are morphine, codeine, and papaverine. Heroin, a synthetic derivative of morphine, although the most commonly used narcotic in the world of illegal consumption, is rarely used as a poison. Morphine is the most common of these poisons. On absorbing a small amount of an opium derivative, such as morphine, the victim passes through a short period of mental excitement into a phase of nausea and finally into a coma. Convulsions may precede death. The skin becomes blue and clammy, bathed in sweat. Death follows from asphyxia, since the respiratory function ceases. The pin-point pupils, blue skin, gasping breath and the odor of opium on the breath are the chief points in diagnosis.

b) BELLADONNA GROUP. This class includes atropine and scopolamine or hyoscine. Symptoms develop in one-half to three hours. Respiratory failure is the cause of death. The pupils become dilated, the throat husky, and the face flushed. A mild delirium precedes death. Since these drugs are extensively used in medicine and rarely employed in homicides, a strong possibility of accidental death always exists.

c) STRYCHNINE. Poisoning from strychnine is also likely to be accidental, since salts of this substance are used in medicines such as cathartics. Taken in quantities such as a grain, strychnine is a deadly poison which acts rapidly to affect the spinal cord and ultimately results in a cessation of breathing. Characteristic of this form of poisoning is a series of extremely violent convulsions. Within approximately fifteen minutes, muscular twitchings begin, followed by a sensation of suffocation and constriction of the chest. The sudden onset of a convulsion is attended by stiffening of the body and an apparent cessation of breathing. The head and feet are bent backward in a tetanic spasm, the face becomes blue and the mouth is contracted in a fixed grin—the *risus sardonicus.* Within a few minutes, the spasm passes and is succeeded by a relaxed exhaustion, while the victim awaits in terror and dread the onset of another convulsion. After three or four increasingly severe convulsions, the victim dies of exhaustion, the respiratory function becoming completely inactive.

2) **Non-Alkaloids.** Certain soporifics (sleeping potions) are commonly used as poisons. Since their purpose is the inducement of sleep, obviously an overdose may lead to permanent unconsciousness.

a) BARBITURATES. The most common sleeping pills in use today are barbiturates or derivatives of barbituric acid. Since most pharmaceutical concerns produce these drugs with their own trade names, the nomenclature of these substances varies. The most popular of these sleeping pills or sedatives are phenobarbital, Seconal, and Nembutal (see Chap. 18). They may appear as tablets or as white powders in colored capsules. In ordinary dose, a natural sleep is induced. Excessive doses (eight or ten grams) result in profound coma and subsequent death. As a method of suicide, the barbiturates in recent years have achieved an impressive popularity. The barbiturate is an ideal poison; moreover, it is simple to obtain since physicians are not reluctant to prescribe it. Digestion is no problem, for the substance is practically tasteless. The first sensations are pleasant, amounting to an uneventful relaxation in inhibitions. Sleep overcomes the victim and death follows easily. The required dose for poisoning by barbiturates can be considerably lessened by drinking whiskey or strong wine before and after the poison. The coma resulting from an overdose of barbiturates may last several days. (Consequently, prolonged efforts to recall life by stomach lavage and stimulants are justified in the light of the experience.)

b) CHLORAL HYDRATE. Another widely used soporific is chloral hydrate, the active ingredient of the so-called "Mickey Finn." This is a white crystalline substance that is prescribed by physicians for sedation of the nervous system. Again, through overdose the victim becomes comatose and respiration is shallow.

d. **Gases.** 1) *Hydrogen Sulphide.* Sulphuretted hydrogen is the toxic agent in sewer gas. It is found in sewers, cesspools, privies, and other places where decayed animal or vegetable matter is present. In heavy concentrations, it produces immediate unconsciousness. Poisoning from this source is almost always accidental.

2) **Phosgene.** This gas is formed through the decomposition of chloroform or carbon tetrachloride by heat. The use of certain fire extinguishers in confined spaces can result in the decomposition of the carbon tetrachloride and the formation of phosgene.

3) **Carbon Monoxide.** The most common cause of death from chemical asphyxiation is carbon monoxide, a colorless, odorless, and tasteless gas. Deaths are almost always accidental or suicidal. Often a person attempting suicide will use the exhaust from an automobile as the source, closing the garage doors and starting the motor. Obvious suicides are those in which the person lies on the floor with his head near the exhaust pipe. If the person is sitting in the car and the weather is cold, it is difficult to draw definite conclusions. Accidental deaths are sometimes associated with defective gas refrigerators. Since the symptoms of carbon monoxide poisoning are those of asphyxiation, the problem of distinguishing accident from murder can arise.

a) CHARACTERISTICS. Carbon monoxide is the product of the incomplete combustion of carbinaceous materials such as wood, coal, and gasoline. The toxicity of carbon monoxide depends upon the fact that it has a greater affinity for the haemoglobin of blood than oxygen. In effect, by combining with the haemoglobin, carbon monoxide prevents the ordinary diffusion of oxygen to the cell tissues. Thus, the body processes are no longer supported and as a result the victim is suffocated rather than poisoned. The factors on which the effects of carbon monoxide depend are:

(1) *Concentration* of the gas.

(2) *Length* of time exposed.

(3) *Temperature* and *humidity* insofar as they affect blood circulation.

(4) *Individual characteristics,* some persons having greater resistance than others.

(b) INVESTIGATIVE TECHNIQUES. Death from carbon monoxide should be suspected if the skin has a cherry red color. The source of the gas is usually an apparatus such as an automobile or a gas refrigerator in which combustion is incomplete. On arriving at the scene of a refrigerator death, the investigator should inquire about the state of the windows, doors, and transoms. In the excitement of the initial discovery of the body, the windows are usually thrown open and the premises aired. Thus, it is impossible to determine accurately the original concentration of carbon monoxide which was present at the time of death. If tests are to be run with the assistance of a chemist, the original conditions should as far as possible be reproduced. The machine should be turned on and permitted to operate for some time. Tests can be conducted with special apparatus for determining the concentration of carbon monoxide. In lieu of this, air samples can be collected by the chemist and later analyzed. A concentration of forty parts of carbon monoxide to 10,000 parts of air is usually fatal if the exposure takes place in an inclosed room for a period of an hour or more.

4) *Carbon Dioxide.* Another common cause of death from asphyxiation is carbon dioxide. Deaths from this gas may appear to be of a suspicious nature until the cause is determined. In rooms where heating and cooking appliances are being used without proper ventilation, the oxygen is depleted and the carbon dioxide content is built up to a level at which the air of the room can no longer support life. The condition of the windows and other openings to the room at the time of discovery should be ascertained. Usually, the room is well ventilated by the time the investigator arrives at the scene. In certain situations, however, the gas may still be present in lethal concentrations. In a manhole, for example, the hold of a ship, or a silo, the original concentration will still be present. A sample of the gas can be obtained by filling a gas collector with water and subsequently permitting the water to run out and be replaced by the atmosphere. The sample can be analyzed with little difficulty by a competent chemist.

e. **Food Poisoning.** In civilian jurisdictions, cases of accidental food poisoning are investigated by the local Department of Health or its equivalent. The interest of the police in a case of accidental food poisoning is concerned with the question of negligence. It is possible that acts or omissions amounting to ordinary negligence have led to death from poisoning. The investigation is directed toward the discovery of the origin of the poisoning, the violation of sanitary regulations in food service, and the failure to report existing disease. Naturally, if the poisoning is non-accidental, the case is treated in the same manner as other poison cases. Where a number of persons are afflicted by the poisoning, the possibility of sabotage must be entertained by the investigator.

1) **Physical Effects.** The word *ptomaine* poisoning is a misnomer. Food poisoning is usually a synonym for bacterial food poisoning. The bacilli belong to the salmonella group. The affected food does not yield any abnormal appearance or smell. The diagnosis is not difficult. Proof is established by isolating bacteria from the excreta. In dead persons, the spleen, liver, and intestines are examined for bacteria.

a) ELAPSED TIME. The time of onset is usually between six and twelve hours after ingestion. It can take place as early as half an hour or even twenty-four hours after ingestion, depending on whether the poison was already formed in the food or was formed after eating or drinking.

b) SYMPTOMS. Headache, abdominal pain, vomiting, and diarrhea mark the onset.

c) POSTMORTEM APPEARANCE. The appearance is similar to that resulting from gastrointestinal irritation and toxemia.

2) **Botulism.** Bacterial food poisoning may also be due to eating sausages or canned foods. The bacillus is *B. botulinus.* This anerobic organism produces symptoms slightly different from those of ordinary food poisoning. There is no fever or pain. Partial paralysis takes place. The respiratory muscles and heart become affected, and the patient finally dies. Loss of consciousness and vomiting do not occur.

3) **Non-bacterial Food Poisoning.** This type of affliction is caused by eating certain plants and animals containing a naturally occurring poison. The following substances are the most common causes: certain kinds of mushrooms such as *Amanita muscaria* and *Amanita phalloides;* immature or sprouting potatoes; mussels at certain undetermined times of the year; grain, especially rye which has become contaminated with the ergot fungus; fruits containing metallic contaminants such as substances sprayed with salts of arsenic or lead and food stored in cadmium-lined containers.

4) **Physical Evidence.** The advice of the attending physician or a forensic chemist should be sought in the collection of physical evidence. Food, vomit, and feces are of basic importance. These should be collected in separate, stoppered jars. Utensils used in

the preparation of the food should also be preserved. In some instances, kitchen fixtures such as faucets may be of importance to the case.

77. Investigative Techniques in Poisoning Cases

Ordinarily, the investigator does not enter a poisoning case until the death is an accomplished fact. He is thus presented with an investigation in which there are no witnesses to the crucial events. Often, there will be no "crime scene"; i.e., the exact place where the poison was consumed may be unknown. Further, any immediate association of the victim with the perpetrator may be absent, since the poison may have been planted in an accessible place at some indefinite time prior to its consumption. In cases of poisoning, the link between the criminal and the victim is most commonly established by motivation. Revenge, profit, jealousy, and hate are the seeds of poison cases. The following general procedure is applicable to these investigations:

a. The crime scene should be visited as soon as possible.

b. A detailed history of events immediately preceding the death should be compiled. This chronology will serve two purposes:

1) The physical circumstances surrounding the death and the nature of the antecedent illness may supply useful information to the medical examiner in determining whether a poisoning case exists and, if it does, the type of poison employed. The diagnosis of poisoning is often difficult without this information.

2) A knowledge of the victim's activities may enable the investigator to discover witnesses and suspects.

c. A brief history of the victim's life during the preceding year should be obtained as far as practical from his friends, relatives, and associates in employment. In this way the motive may be established.

d. The report of the physician who first attended the victim should be obtained.

e. The medical examiner performing the autopsy should be interviewed and a complete report obtained.

f. The report of the toxicologist should be obtained and the toxicologist should be interviewed for a more detailed discussion of the poison found, its common forms, its availability, the commercial sources, the techniques of administration, and the probability of accidental absorption. The report is a simple, factual statement of findings. The interview will supply a number of leads and provide the investigator with the necessary background knowledge for the investigation of the poisoning.

g. The investigator should next establish whether the poisoning is a case of accident, suicide, or homicide. He has now assembled a considerable body of data. His interviews with the attending physician, medical examiner, and toxicologist will have explored the possibility of suicide from the point of view of physical evidence and practical experience. The crime scene, if any exists, may have revealed significant clues. The strongest evidence for or against a suicide theory will be available in the information obtained from friends and relatives.

78. Physical Evidence

If there is a reasonable suspicion of poisoning, an investigation should be initiated immediately. Several days or even months may confirms the suspicion. In that time, some or all of the evidentiary traces at the scene will have disappeared. In addition to the regular crime scene search that has been recommended in cases of homicide, the following matters should receive attention:

a. **Excretions.** The victim may have vomited or defecated at the scene. The material should be gathered up and placed in separate containers. Since some poisons are volatile, the containers should be carefully sealed to avoid evaporation.

b. **Refuse.** The remains of meals should be similarly collected and preserved. Garbage and remnants in cooking vessels are important. The pail or vessel should be taken together with its contents.

c. **Medicine Closet.** The entire content of the medicine closet should be collected for examination. It is not advisable to choose from among the medicines present, since the containers may be incorrectly labeled.

d. **Food.** The kitchen should be searched for food that may contain poison. Certain foods need receive little attention if they are found intact. It is difficult to place poisons in food that is large in unit size or which has a readily identifiable surface. For example, vegetables and fruits which appear intact are not likely carriers of poison. Prepared cereals such as corn flakes can usually be rejected after brief inspection. Powdered or granulated foods, however, should be collected without questioning. Flour, baking powder, sugar, salt, and spices, for example can be readily diluted with a poison which is not detectable by visual inspection.

e. **Alcoholic Beverages.** Probably the most common method of administering a poison is to first mix it in an alcoholic drink. The alcohol serves as an excellent solvent and, in addition, the beverage dulls the senses of taste and smell. Thus, whiskey, wine, and beer bottles should be collected as well as any dry soiled glasses that are present.

f. **Insecticides.** Insecticides and vermicides should be collected. Plant sprays, roach powders, and rat exterminators are often employed by the poisoner.

79. Suspect's Residence

If a suspect has been "developed" and it is possible to obtain a search warrant, his premises should be examined for the presence of poisons. The preceding paragraph will suggest the substances to be looked for. If the medical examiner has already given his opinion on the type of poison employed, the search can be greatly simplified.

80. Special Points of Proof

In poisoning cases, the following points of proof should receive special attention:

a. **Access to the Poison.** It must be shown that the accused had access to the poison. This fact may be demonstrated by showing one of the following:

1) *Common Substance.* The poison may be a common substance, readily available to any person.

2) *Purchase.* The investigator should canvass the places where the poison could have been purchased in that area or in an area

which the accused had recently visited. Pharmacies, exterminator companies, garden supply companies, and chemical houses are the likely sources. It should be ascertained whether the seller is required by law or company rules to make a record of the purchase.

3) *Occupation.* In various industrial operations it is necessary to employ poisons. A plater, for example, will use cyanide. The investigator should inquire concerning the industrial uses of the poison and draw up a list of acquaintances employed in such occupations.

b. **Access to the Victim.** It must be shown that the accused had access to the victim. The testimony of friends or neighbors can be used to show that the accused was with the victim prior to death. If the substance was sent through the mails, as, for example, nuts salted with cyanide, it may be possible to associate the package with the sender by various traces. Fingerprints on the package, of course, are excellent proof. Wrapping paper, twine, and boxes can be traced to the suspect's house. The handwriting on the package is of great importance.

c. **Intent.** Aside from the usual questions of motive and the relation of the accused to the deceased, there must also be established as part of the element of intent the fact of the accused's knowledge of the poison. It is necessary to show that this chemical substance, which has caused the death and which was presumably administered by the accused, was known by the accused to be a poisonous substance. This fact may be proved by showing that the education or occupation of the accused presumed such knowledge or by showing that the accused made inquiries or conducted library research concerning poisons.

d. **Clothes.** Garments, sheets, and similar articles should be thoroughly dried before they are packed. In packing, the clothing should not be unnecessarily folded. On folding, stains that may still be moist will produce similarly stained areas in other parts of the clothing. Tissue paper should be used to separate layers of clothing in placing it in a box.

81. Diagnosis of Poisoning

To determine whether or not a poisoning has taken place, an extensive investigation must be made. The events preceding the death must be studied. The manner of death and the nature of the illness that preceded it are important. The symptoms of poisoning can be presented by many other medical conditions. Epilepsy, heart disease, uremia, gastric ulcer, gastritis, intestinal obstructions, diseases of the central nervous system, and other conditions present symptoms similar to those of poisoning. The following conditions should give rise to a suspicion of poisoning:

a. **Acute Poisoning.** The following signs suggest acute poisoning:

1) Shortly after taking food, drink, or medicine.

2) A person in apparent good health.

3) Suffers a sudden attack, accompanied by

4) Vomiting, together with convulsions or coma.

5) More than one person is affected in a similar manner.

b. **Chronic Poisoning.** The perpetrator sometimes conducts the poisoning operation over a long period of time. The victim appears to suffer from malaise and chronic ill health. The following history should arouse suspicion:

1) The medical diagnosis was difficult and inconclusive.

2) The patient's condition improved when he was away from home, but not otherwise.

3) The doctor's instructions were not properly followed in caring for the patient.

82. Toxicology

Toxicology is the science which deals with poisons, their effects and antidotes, and recognition. The method of obtaining conclusive proof of the presence of poison is that of chemical analysis, accomplished by separation, purification, and identification.

a. **Autopsy.** A complete autopsy is always desirable and usually necessary in a case of suspected poison. In the event that the autopsy reveals evidence of poisoning, the organs of the deceased, food, and other substances suspected of containing poison must be subjected to a toxicological analysis. Since poisoning is a crime of stealth and the substance is usually administered surreptitiously, only small quantities of the poison are taken into the body. As a result, only microscopic quantities of the absorbed poison are found in the tissues and fluids of the body. The toxicological analysis requires an examination of the vital organs, viz., the liver, kidneys, heart, and brain. In addition, all the urine in the bladder is collected and a pint of blood is taken. In certain instances, sections of the intestines and lungs are used.

b. **Expert Services.** The medical examiner handling the case in question may possess an adequate knowledge of toxicology. More often, he does not, and the investigator will be required to seek the services of another agency for a toxicological examination. Ordinarily a local agency will provide such services. The FBI Laboratory offers the services of trained toxicologists in the analysis of substances and material sent to them for a determination of the presence of poisons. Organs and substances to be examined for poisons should be packed and shipped with dry ice as described below.

c. **Autopsy Report.** A copy of the autopsy report should accompany the specimens. The observations of the autopsy surgeon or the medical examiner are often useful to the toxicologist. Postmortem appearances such as discoloration of the skin, nails, and blood; unusual odors emanating from the body cavity; charring, corrosion, and staining of tissues are indicative of certain poisons.

83. Postmortem Evidence of Poisons

The pathologist performing the autopsy should be experienced in recognizing the effects of poisons on the body. Naturally, the investigator can contribute little to this phase of the inquiry. He should, however, for purposes of background information, possess some familiarity with the general nature of the evidence which the pathologist and toxicologist look for.

a. **Visual Observation.** Some of the effects of poison are visible to the unaided eye. Corrosion of tissues, perforation of the stomach, gastrointestinal irritation, and marked congestion are some of the more obvious effects. Sometimes, the poisonous substance itself may be found in the stomach. Grains of arsenic and belladonna leaves, for example, may sometimes be discovered. Ordinarily, alkaloidal poisons and the barbiturates do not leave visible signs. The diagnosis in this case rests on before-death symptoms and analysis of the organs.

b. **Chemical Analysis.** It is the pathologist's duty to examine the organs and perform some of the more simple qualitative tests in which he is experienced. Familiarity with the basic tests for oxalic acid, hydrocyanic acid, carbon monoxide, and arsenic are desirable; in rural districts, the pathologist may find it more convenient to perform these tests himself. In urban areas, however, a toxicologist or analyst will be available for the examination of the organs to detect poisons. In the analysis, it will usually be possible to place the poison in one of four groups:

1) *Volatile.* Volatile poisons such as carbolic acid, chloroform, and hydrocyanic acid. These are suspected by smell and are isolated by distilling the suspected fluid in a flask and collecting the distillate. Appropriate tests are then applied.

2) *Non-volatile.* Non-volatile inorganic poisons such as arsenic, mercury, and lead. In this type of analysis the organic matter is broken down and the metal is obtained as a chloride.

3) *Alkaloidal Poisons.* Morphine and other opium derivatives are the most commonly used alkaloidal poisons. The principle used in analyzing is based on the fact that alkaloids unite with acids to form salts which are soluble in water but not in ether.

4) *Miscellaneous Poisons.* This group contains poisons which are not contained in any of the preceding three classifications. Food poisons are an example of this group.

84. Submission of Evidence

Toxicological evidence such as body organs and fluids to be submitted for examination should be treated in accordance with the instructions of the controlling jurisdiction. The following additional recommendations will be found useful:

a. **Containers.** Only glass containers should be used since metals may react with the substances present. Pint and quart jars with clean glass caps and new rubber seals are satisfactory.

b. **Sealing.** Each container should contain but one substance, fluid, or organ. It should be sealed by the investigator or the physician performing the autopsy, and the seal should bear the name of the investigator or the autopsy surgeon. An identifying tag or label should be affixed to each container providing the following information: the name of the investigator, the autopsy surgeon, and the victim; the type of organ or fluid submitted; the date and place of the autopsy; and the case number.

c. **Preservatives and Packing.** No preservatives should be added. The containers should be placed in separate bins in one carton. This should be sealed and initialed on the seal. If practicable, the investigator himself should transport the carton to the toxicologist, obtaining a receipt for the package. If the evidence is to shipped a great distance, a wooden box should be used and a lining of insulating material such as rock wool should be provided. The evidence should then be packed with dry ice.

d. **Letter of Transmittal.** A letter of transmittal should accompany the evidence if it is hand-carried or should be forwarded by airmail if the evidence is sent by registered mail. A carbon copy of the letter should be inclosed with the evidence for purposes of proper identification on arrival. The letter should contain all pertinent facts, including an autopsy report concerning the history of the case. This information should include the following:

1) *Duration of the Illness.* The length of time during which the victim suffered from the ill effects may indicate the type of poison or may suggest chronic poisoning.

2) *Treatment by a Physician.* If the deceased was treated by a physician or if he received any other medical treatment, a statement from the physician should be obtained if possible. A note should be made of drugs administered during the treatment.

3) *Background Information.* Pertinent case information should be made available to the toxicologist. The signs and symptoms observed by witnesses may offer useful information to the toxicologist. Reactions such as dilation or contraction of the pupils, vomiting, convulsions, respiratory rate, and other physiological disturbances suggest the possibility of certain poisons. The toxicologist is also interested in the various clues that may be suggested by the physical circumstances surrounding the victim. Thus, the

occupation of the victim, the poisons available to him at work and at home, any suspected medicines or unlabeled materials available to the victim, health habits and peculiarities of the deceased, and similar information should be obtained.

e. **Substances to be Submitted.** The most important tissues and fluids to be obtained at an autopsy will vary with the case. Usually, the following are desirable:

1) The stomach and stomach content.
2) The intestines and their contents.
3) The liver.
4) The gall bladder.
5) Both kidneys.
6) Urinary bladder and its contents.
7) Blood in a quart jar.
8) Brain.
9) Heart.
10) Lungs
11) Bone—Parts of the rib or portions of exposed sections of the spinal column.
12) Hair—This should be taken in generous quantities from the back of the head and near a head wound if one is present. It should be pulled out.

XIII. SUICIDE

85. Definition and Law

Suicide is the killing of one's self. It is a voluntary and intentional destruction. At one time suicide was considered a felony by common law and was punished by ignominious burial and forfeiture of goods. An attempt at suicide was considered a misdemeanor by common law. Under many of the state laws no specific provision has been made for the punishment of suicide or attempted suicide, but it is considered that the attempt is punishable.

86. The Problem of Suicide

The investigator is often called upon to provide factual information which will assist in deciding whether the death in question is murder, suicide, or accident. Since most injuries can be found in one of these three occurrences, the successful solution of the problem must depend to a great extent on the investigator's experience and fund of information. The problem of distinguishing suicide from accident and murder has been touched upon at various places in discussing the causes of death. In the absence of eyewitnesses, a conclusion of suicide is drawn only after a careful study of the type of injury, the presence of the weapon or instrument of death, the existence of a motive, and elimination of a theory of murder, accident, or natural causes.

87. Type of Injury

The cause of death is one of the best indicators in determining whether the case is one of suicide. The type or nature of the injury is not a conclusive indicator but can establish to a degree the improbability of self-infliction.

a. **Position and Awkwardness.** As a general principle, it may be stated that any part of the body accessible to the suicide is also accessible to the murderer; i.e., a wound produced by a suicide could also have been produced by a murderer. Certain types of wounds, however, are readily excluded from suicide; for example, knife wounds in the back indicate murder; cuts on the palms of the hands indicate a struggle against an assailant. Suicides are prone to select the front of the body for attack. With a knife, they will select the throat, wrist, and heart region. With a gun the choice is usually among the temple, forehead, center of the back of the head, mouth, and heart. The position of the wound or the difficulty of self-infliction does not exclude suicide as an explanation. An example of this is a case in which a person shot himself in the top of the head at a range of twelve inches. In another case a man tied a stone to his legs and then bound his arms to his legs to insure death by drowning.

b. **Combination of Methods.** A combination of methods or a choice of several sites is indicative of suicide. For example, a person who is found with a hanging noose or a revolver, while he is actually dead from poisoning, is probably a suicide. Indecision or insurance of one method by another method is characteristic. Cutting of the wrist as well as the throat, for example, is another indication of suicide.

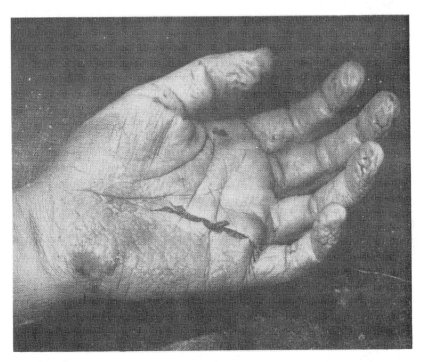

Figure 21. Defense wound, indicating murder rather than suicide.

c. **Extent of the Wound.** It is difficult to draw a conclusion from the extent or number of wounds. Often a deranged suicide will inflict very severe wounds in great numbers. Experimental wounds and hesitation marks may be observed in suicides performed with a knife.

d. **Direction of Wound.** In cases of firearms, the investigator can determine whether the person could have fired the fatal shot from a consideration of the direction involved and the limitations of the human body in "positioning" the weapon. In stab wounds, the presence of purposeless incisions is indicative of an assailant trying to discover a vital spot. A series of parallel slashes on the left side of the head and neck would suggest suicide.

e. **Painfulness.** It is logical to expect that a suicide will select the least painful way of dying. The popularity of carbon monoxide and the barbiturates as suicidal agents is attributable to the desire to avoid excessive pain. It must not be concluded, however, because the form of death is too horrible to contemplate from the point of view of self-infliction, that the death must be a murder. The following examples, although obviously illustrating the work of deranged minds, are indicative of the extremes of pain to which suicides may subject themselves:

1) A woman cut off her feet and her left hand before cutting her throat.

2) A woman poured kerosene over her clothes and set fire to herself.

3) A girl enucleated both of her eyes. This is an example of psychopathic self-mutilation.

4) A sexual psychopath killed himself with an axe.

f. **Disfigurement Considerations.** A female suicide will tend to avoid purposely disfiguring her face. Her natural anxiety concerning her appearance extends even to the impression she will make on viewers in her death. Another characteristic of the suicide is the care taken to push aside clothing so that the weapon may be in direct contact with the body. It is difficult to determine whether this action is prompted by a natural reluctance to mark a useful garment or whether it is part of the measures taken to insure the effectiveness of the gun or knife.

g. **Incapacitating Sequence.** Certain combinations of wounds suggest a physical impossibility. To draw a conclusion of suicide, the wounds should be physically not improbable. The existence of two fatal shots at some distance apart does not suggest suicide. For example, shots through the heart and temple are unlikely as the work of self-infliction.

88. Presence of Weapon

The means by which death was accomplished should be apparent. As an obvious example: If the cause of death was a gunshot wound, the firearm should be present. A search for the weapon should be made. If the weapon is not found near the body, a search of adjoining areas must be made since a person, even though mortally wounded, is capable of considerable activity. Persons fatally shot through the head or heart have been known to travel as much as a hundred yards before succumbing.

a. **Concealment.** The weapon is sometimes deliberately concealed by the victim or by others. For example, in one case, a banker arranged for the disappearance of the weapon in order that his suicide should appear to be a murder committed during robbery. In another case, a conclusion of suicide rather than murder was reached after the discovery of a few fragments of broken brick at the fireplace. The victim, by means of strong elastic attached to the gun, had arranged for the firearm to disappear into the chimney after he had shot himself. The possibility of the relatives' concealing the weapon must also be entertained. Among the motives of relatives in concealing the weapon are the collection of insurance and the avoidance of unfavorable publicity.

b. **Accidental Disappearance.** The weapon is sometimes stolen. For example, on finding a man in a deserted house, dead from a bullet wound, a conclusion of murder was first made until it was discovered that the gun had been stolen by neighborhood boys. Sometimes the weapon or instrument may not be apparent. In one case the victim had committed suicide by hanging himself from the cord of a venetian blind. The hanging and death took place quickly and the body slipped away from the unknotted cord. On finding the body on the floor with no obvious means of hanging, it was at first thought that strangulation by garroting was the cause of death.

89. Motive and Intent

The intent to commit suicide may have been evinced by the victim through his oral statements during the period preceding his death or by a statement contained in a death note.

a. **Motive.** Motive is deduced from a study of the victim's behavior during and just prior to the fatal act. It has been found that mental uneasiness or worry is the chief cause of suicide. In fact, there is a general tendency to officially regard suicides as persons temporarily insane. Worry and alcohol, considered together, account for a large percentage of the total number of suicides. Certain occupations which tend to produce anxiety and tension, notably the medical and legal professions, are characterized by a higher incidence of suicides. The investigator should make an inquiry into the state of mind of the deceased by interviewing members of the family, business associates, intimate friends, and social acquaintances. The line of inquiry should be pointed toward discovering the existence of any domestic, business, or financial troubles. It should be noted in this connection that marital harmony, pregnancy, and love are negligible factors when considered as possible motives for suicide. Hence, the deceased's anxiety over his position or work and his financial condition should receive the greater emphasis in this phase of the investigation. The interviews should stress factual information rather than opinions concerning the deceased's state of mind. For example, a history of failures in regard to promotion in rank and the financial statistics in regard to debts should be learned if a witness proffers the observation that the deceased was depressed over professional failure or money.

b. **Intent.** The stated intention of the deceased to commit suicide is of obvious importance. In the course of the interviews, the investigator should endeavor to learn of any statements made by the deceased which would indicate a purpose of self-destruction. A search should be made for a diary, unmailed letters, or other personal writings containing sentiments from which a desire for suicide can be inferred or bearing an explicit statement of the intention. The most typical communication of this nature is the "suicide note." In its classical form, the suicide note contains a clear expression of both the motive and the intent. On finding such a note, the investigator should not accept it at its face value. It must be regarded, at first, with an investigator's skepticism. Is the document what it purports to be? Was it written by the deceased? Was it written voluntarily? To answer these questions the suicide note must be submitted to a qualified document examiner. The note should be picked up with a pair of tongs and placed in a transparent envelope. As a matter of regular procedure the note should be photographed and transmitted to the laboratory or other qualified agency together with adequate samples of the deceased's handwriting. At the same time a request for a comparison of the known writing of the deceased with the writing of the suicide note should be forwarded. Precautions should be taken throughout the handling of the document to avoid contact with the fingers. In the event that the handwriting on the note is found to have been made by someone other than the deceased, it will become necessary to process the note for fingerprints. This conditional request should be included in the original letter.

c. **Young Persons.** It is estimated that between 70,000 and 80,000 young people, between the ages of 15 and 24, will attempt suicide in a typical year. About 5,000 will succeed. Fewer than 30 percent of these young suicides will leave notes. More girls will attempt suicide but more boys will succeed. One explanation offered for this is that the girls will generally use methods (razor and pills) which are less certain than those chosen by the boys (guns and hanging). The increase in young suicides has been attributed to an inability to communicate and a feeling of isolation and loneliness.

90. Accidents

A fatal accident which is not witnessed may involve injuries suggestive of suicide. If the injuries are compatible with self infliction and if eyewitness accounts are absent or unreliable, there is a danger that a conclusion of suicide will be made where the subject is in ill health or beset by financial or familial problems. Often the circumstances surrounding a death do not permit any conclusion to be drawn. Cases where persons fall from windows, fall in front of oncoming trains, drown, or are overcome by carbon monoxide often remain mysteries because of the absence of eyewitnesses or of any oral or written statement of intentions. Physical evidence may sometimes be helpful in these cases. For example, in a case involving a fall from a window in a high building, the wall areas at the sides of the windows and the sill area should be processed for latent fingerprints and palm prints which may indicate preparations for a leap. If a carbon monoxide death is intentional, certain precautionary arrangements, such as locked garage doors or a position near the exhaust, may be observed.

91. Natural Causes

A death from natural causes may appear to be suicide in the preliminary stages of any investigation. A person suffering from an unsuspected disease may suffer an attack, fall into an unexpected collapse, and die. Again, deaths from falls or drowning will serve as examples. A man is seen to fall from a ladder which had begun to slip. He is dead when examined and the question arises: Is the death an accident or did he suffer a dizzy spell and lose his coordination? The question is not trivial since on that determination may depend the awarding of the industrial accident insurance indemnity to the estate of the deceased. In suicides these questions sometimes arise when the motive is the escape from a painful disease. For example, in one case, the dead body of a man was found with a revolver nearby. It was apparent that the deceased had killed himself by firing the gun with the muzzle in his mouth. A full hot water bottle was found on the bed. In the autopsy it was discovered that the deceased had suffered a ruptured aorta. To relieve the excruciating pain of this condition he apparently prepared the hot water bottle and, on applying it, had failed to find alleviation. In despair he finally shot himself. The perforating wound in his head, however, was not the cause of his death. The ruptured aorta had supervened and the death was natural rather than suicidal. We may divide "death from natural causes" into two categories: first, a person dies from natural causes, but there is an appearance of violence; and, second, a person dies of violence but the apparent explanation is one of natural causes.

a. **Appearance of Violence.** The possibility of death from natural causes should never be excluded in the initial phase of the investigation because of presence of obvious marks of violence. The appearance of a struggle can be created by the abnormal activity of a person suffering from an acutely painful attack.

There are over seventy diseases the onset of which can produce sudden death. A person experiencing such an attack may disarrange his clothing and injure himself severely by falling. Prominent among these diseases are those associated with heart failure. Coronary involvement is precipitated in a large number of cases by a sudden stress resulting from an emotional crisis or undue physical exertion. Where signs of violence and severe injury are present and a fatally diseased condition also exists, a number of questions arise concerning the relationship of the injury and the disease to the death. The autopsy surgeon can provide the investigator with information bearing on the following questions:

1) Has the natural disease any unusual relation to the injury or is it a distinct process?

2) Could the natural disease by itself have caused the death?

3) Had the disease progressed to such a state that death could have been expected?

4) Is the injury sufficiently severe to cause death by itself?

5) Is the disease merely a contributory factor in the death, which is due to the injury?

6) Is the injury merely a contributory factor to the death, which is due to natural causes?

b. **Appearance of Natural Causes.** A death may be a suicide even though it has the appearance of being the result of natural causes. For purposes of defrauding the insurance company or to protect the family reputation, the person may contrive the circumstances surrounding his death to give the impression of natural causes. For example, a person may kill himself by injecting an adequate quantity of absolute alcohol into his veins. If he has also taken a few drinks to give his breath the odor, the conclusion may be reached that he died from drinking excessively. A more common example is that of a death attributable to an overdose of sleeping pills. The increased and more lenient use of barbiturates helped to make these the drugs of choice among suicides. In a case of this nature or in a similar poisoning case, the investigator should ascertain whether the deceased obtained the drugs legally and whether he was aware of their lethal effect.

XIV. INTERVIEWING WITNESSES

92. Classification

After completing his work at the scene of the crime, the investigator must direct his attention to the witnesses. This phase of the investigation is equal in importance to the examination of the physical evidence. Often the scene of the crime offers only evidence bearing on the *corpus delicti.* The vital question of the identity of the perpetrator will be answered ordinarily by the intelligent interviewing of witnesses. Most witnesses should be questioned as soon as possible since the lapse of time permits a deterioration of the memory and opens the door to the entry of motives for discreet silence. The order in which the witnesses are interviewed will initially depend on their availability. A more logical order will suggest itself as the development of information gives form to the case and meaning to the events. Witnesses may be classified according to the type of testimony they are expected to give. Thus, we may place them in the following categories:

a. **Eyewitnesses.** Persons who saw the fatal act.

b. **Circumstances.** Persons who can give information concerning the circumstances surrounding the crime, as for example, the druggist who sold the poison or the dry cleaner who can identify the jacket left at the scene.

c. **Motive.** Persons who can give information concerning the motive for the fatal act.

d. **Flight.** The persons who can testify to acts of the accused subsequent to the slaying and indicative of flight. The landlady of the suspect's rooming house, for example, may testify to the fact that the suspect failed to return home after the fatal act.

e. **Expert Witnesses.** Persons qualified to give expert opinions on the significance of the physical evidence.

f. **Suspects.** Logical suspects should be interrogated in appropriate order.

93. Witnesses to Circumstances

Interviewing witnesses of circumstances surrounding the crime should consist of a comprehensive examination of details concerning the physical evidence:

a. **Categories of Physical Evidence.** For convenience of discussion, physical evidence will again be placed in the following useful but arbitrary categories:

1) *Corpus Delicti Evidence.* This evidence tends to show that a crime has been committed. In a murder, for example, it must be proved that a person is dead through the criminal agency of another. This kind of physical evidence is ordinarily given by the medical examiner.

2) *Associative Evidence.* This evidence can be used to show that the accused was linked to the crime scene or with the act in general. It includes such diverse matters as the accused's previous possession of the objects left at the scene and the identity of the automobile used in flight. Since lay witnesses are usually the ones who offer such information, it will be the investigator's responsibility to conduct interviews to obtain the evidence.

3) *Identifying Evidence.* This evidence tends directly, from the clues at the scene, to establish the identity of the person who brought about the death. Fingerprints, foot impressions, and quantities of blood are examples of this kind of evidence.

4) *Tracing Evidence.* These are articles and materials that help to locate the suspect. A laundry mark found on his clothing in a furnished room may assist in tracing the fugitive. His use of a credit card during flight may establish a pattern leading the investigator to his place of incidence. Of course, it may also serve as a means of identifying the suspect.

Since our categories of evidence are simply aspects under which the evidence may be considered for investigative purposes, the student should not be disturbed by an apparent overlapping, i.e., an object of evidence can sometimes be placed in two or more of these classes. The latter three classes are of special interest to the investigator since his concern is to establish the identity and whereabouts of the perpetrator and to link him logically to the scene. For example, botanical material clinging to the suspect's clothing and peculiar to the flora of the crime scene may provide a critical link. In homicide involving a firearm or a poison, the investigator's procedures may include the following.

a) TRACING THE GUN. (1) *Ownership.* In cases where the lethal weapon is found at the scene, the investigator must try to trace the history of the weapon. Who is the owner? The records of state and municipal law enforcement agencies should be consulted to determine the owner of the gun. Available data concerning the distribution of the weapon must be obtained from the manufacturer. The weapon must then be traced to the wholesaler, and finally to the retailer. If the sale of the weapon has been legal, the retailer's books should yield the name and address of the purchaser. To facilitate this search, the Bureau of Alcohol, Tobacco and Firearms has set up the National Firearms Tracing Center for the use of all federal, state and local law enforcement agencies. This federal agency routinely traces all firearms associated with crimes from the manufacturer to the last retail purchase. If the trace is successful, the investigator will be provided with the name, address, physical description and age of the purchaser. Not all firearms are traceable because of their age (before accurate records were kept) or because they were stolen at some point between the time of the manufacture and the time of the criminal act.

(2) *Stolen Gun.* If the gun has been stolen, an inquiry into the larceny must be made. Local police records or the National Crime Information Center's stolen gun file might provide the identity of the owner if the theft of the gun had previously been reported. If the larceny has been solved, information must be obtained concerning the disposition of the gun. To whom was the gun sold? Was the thief involved in the killing?

b) TRACING THE SOURCE OF POISON. The investigator in this case must canvass drugstores, garden supply houses, hardware stores, chemical companies, and other places where the particular type of poison could be sold. The poison may have been purchased by the accused or by a friend offering the pretext of destroying rodents or a sick animal. The friend is usually innocent and when interviewed will relate the details concerning the poison: from whom it was bought; how he came to buy it; when and where he gave it to the killer; and any conversation relating to poisons that took place. The killer himself may have knowledge of poisons and may have obtained it from available sources at his place of employment. The inquiry must then follow the line of the killer's education in poisons, his opportunities to obtain them, and his possession of them.

(1) The accused's familiarity with the locus of the crime.

(2) The accused's knowledge of the victim, his location, and his habits; or, if the victim is unknown to the accused, the latter's acquaintance with someone who could supply information concerning the victim.

(3) Information concerning the accused's normal style of living; his wealth or lack of it; and his legitimate income.

(4) The accused's financial condition before and after the killing; his activities, lawful and criminal, during this period.

(5) Actions of the accused which indicate an effort to establish an alibi on the day of the crime or to provide an excuse for any change in his financial condition after the crime.

94. Witnesses to Establish Motive

Although it is not necessary for the prosecution to prove a motive in a homicide, such a failure is considered a serious strategic weakness in the presentation of the case. The progress of the investigation will also suffer in the absence of a reasonable motive to give form and logic to the line of inquiry. The investigator, drawing from his ingenuity, experience, and available data, must base his investigation on a theory that rationally explains the fatal act. Among the common motives are revenge, love, degeneracy, financial gain, and robbery. In addition to the many possible motives, the investigator must also consider the fact that the crime may be relatively free from motive.

A brutal, sadistic assault or a reckless expression of drunken rage may provide a seemingly inexplicable problem to the investigator, whose first encounter with the suspect finds him a calm and relatively pleasant person bearing little resemblance to the psychopathic killer. The investigator must be a particularly astute interviewer in questioning witnesses for the purpose of establishing a motive. For example, he must be courteous, sympathetic, and discreet in questioning members of the killer's family who may allege that they were outraged by the victim. In killings resulting from a group conspiracy, he can obtain a great deal of information if he can convey to individual members the impression that he is in possession of the inside facts or create discussion by implying that one of the members has talked. In cases involving an illicit love affair, the third party should be questioned closely and persistently about his or her relations with the accused. Usually, the character of such a person is weak and he will supply the desired information for the purpose of protecting himself.

95. Witnesses to Flight

Flight is a sign of guilt. The absence of the suspect from his home and haunts can be interpreted as flight. A search should be made for the suspect in these places. Someone should be in a position to testify that the accused did not return to his home or visit his usual haunts. If the suspect lived in a lodging house or in a hotel, the cooperation of the landlady or manager can be enlisted to testify to the lodger's absence after the occurrence of the homicide.

96. Eyewitnesses

The investigator must be patient and exhaustive in his interviewing of the eyewitnesses. A background history of the witness should be developed. He should be asked to give a brief history of himself which will include any criminal record or involvement. He should be asked to account for his presence at the scene of the crime and the fact of his acquaintanceship with either the victim or the accused. The witness should then be requested to tell his story in his own way. He should be subjected to detailed questioning concerning the identification of the accused. The following is a list of representative questions which will suggest many others to the investigator in an actual case:

    a. Do you know the accused?

    b. Was this the first time you have ever seen the accused?

    c. How long a time did you observe him?

    d. From what position?

  e. What attracted your attention to the accused?
  f. What attracted your attention to the victim?
  g. Have you identified the accused since his apprehension?
  h. What were the circumstances surrounding that identification?

97. Classifying the Witness

The investigator should observe the witness closely and classify him from a moral, intellectual, and physical point of view. Is he of weak character, one who would be subject to such influences as corruption, intimidation, or the solicitation of a mutual friend? Is he aware of the seriousness of his position as a witness and of the grave responsibility of adhering to the truth in his statements? Is he honest but not of strong character, one who could be easily led into confusion and vacillation? All these mental notes will aid in estimating the strength of the case from the standpoint of the quality of the available witnesses.

98. Physical Competency of the Witness

During the interview the investigator should observe the physical condition of the subject who is a prospective witness. Direct questioning can also be used to acquire information on an aspect of physical condition which may affect his credibility as a witness. If the witness is to testify to what he saw under difficult conditions of visibility, the possession of normal vision, natural or corrected, becomes an important point. Impairment of hearing would affect the reliability of his testimony in regard to things heard. The investigator should be able to make some estimate of the witness's powers of observation and his ability to relate facts briefly, correctly, and clearly without becoming emotionally disturbed. Finally, the physical condition of the witness should be noted with a view to his availability at the time of trial.

XV. TRENDS AND PATTERNS IN HOMICIDE

99. Application

It is decidely advantageous in the investigation of homicide to possess a general understanding of the patterns and trends of this offense. Cases of murder and manslaughter frequently fit into conventional patterns. The investigator who can readily recognize types of homicide can also mentally classify the offender and shorten the process of locating a logical suspect. Some of the information given below will serve to provide a background in homicide trends in large urban communities of heterogeneous population. The figures given should be considered as rough estimates.

100. Circumstances

a. **Time.** More than half of all homicides are committed over the weekend. Most homicides are committed during leisure hours, particularly between the hours of 8:00 P.M. and 2:00 A.M.

b. **Place.** Usually the highest rates of homicide exist in areas which have the highest delinquency rates, such as low-income residential areas surrounding industrial business areas. A significant number of homicides occur in the home.

c. **Weapon.** There is a growing tendency toward the use of firearms in homicide. More than 65 percent of all murders are committed with firearms while less than 20 percent are accomplished with cutting instruments. Knives are often used (as well as guns) in those murders arising spontaneously, while the gun figures prominently in premeditated murder where the perpetrator has time to arm himself. Women are more inclined than men to select a knife or icepick rather than a firearm.

d. **Alcohol.** The majority of the homicide cases involve alcohol as a factor, with the assailant or the victim, or both, drinking heavily.

Table IX
MURDER, TYPE OF WEAPONS USED, 1991

Total[1]	21,505	100%
Total Firearms	14,265	66.3%
Handguns	11,411	53.0%
Rifles	741	4.5%
Shotguns	1,113	5.2%
Other Guns	30	0.1%
Firearms Not Stated	970	4.5%
Knives or Cutting Instruments	3,405	15.8%
Blunt Objects (Clubs, Hammers, Etc.)	1,082	5.0%
Personal Weapons (Hands, Fists, Feet, Etc.)	1,193	5.5%
Poison	12	
Explosives	16	
Fire	194	
Narcotics	22	
Drowning	39	
Strangulation	326	
Asphyxiation	113	
Other Weapons or Weapons Not Stated	838	

1. Total murder victims for which supplemental homicide data were received. The total number of murders reported to the FBI for 1991 was 24,703. Supplemental information was available for 21,505 of these cases. Nonnegligent manslaughter is included under the category of murder. Murder and nonnegligent manslaughter, as defined in the Uniform Crime Reporting Program, is the willful (nonnegligent) killing of one human being by another. Source: FBI *Uniform Crime Reports—1991.*

101. Victim—Offender Relationships

a. **Sex.** Males commit more than three-fourths of the homicides and comprise more than three-fourths of the victims.

b. **Race.** Generally, whites murder whites and blacks murder blacks. Blacks are more likely both to commit murder and to be the murder victim.

c. **Acquaintance.** In about three-fourths of the cases, the victim knows his assailant. In about one-fourth of the cases, the victim is a member of the family.

d. **Quarrels.** 1) *Sexual.* A significant number of murders are attributable to quarrels over a woman. A sexual reason ordinarily lies behind a slaying of a woman by a man. Among the middle-income groups, the slaying is usually of the ordinary sex-triangle type, the man killing his wife or her lover. Where a male kills a female, the victim is usually his wife or his girlfriend. In the lower-income groups, the slaying of a woman by a man may arise out of a sex triangle or out of a orgiastic drinking-sex party.

Occasionally, the cause is trivial and unrelated to sex. The conflict over sexual rights to a woman is much more likely to give rise to murder among the lower-income groups. The unstable marital arrangements and the primacy of physical strength among the very poor are a combination from which murder can easily spring. Slayings by middle-class females are quite rare. The lower-class female is more inclined to defend her sexual rights to a man by slaying him or her rival. In some cases, the woman will slay her husband or lover to protect herself from a beating.

2) *Property.* Quarrels arising out of gambling or from a disputed claim to property are an important source of homicide among the lower-income classes. In fact, the quarrel over property is a more common cause than the sexual factor.

3) *Quarrels of Trivial Origin.* Oddly enough, the most common causes of homicide are trivial in nature. A fancied insult, a jostle, or a choice bit of profanity when properly mixed with alcohol can readily lead to a fatal struggle. This is particularly true of the lower-income groups, where minor affronts are often greatly magnified and then subjected to the arbitrament of the knife.

XVI. INFANTICIDE AND OTHER INFANT DEATHS

102. Definition

Infanticide is the slaying of a newborn infant. This form of homicide is concerned only with the period from the time of birth until the time when the birth is reported to the authorities as required by law. The general term *homicide* is applied to the killing of an infant after the time of reporting. The destruction of a fetus during labor for the purpose of saving the mother's life is not considered infanticide. An infanticide must be treated as any other homicide. The slaying can be murder, manslaughter, or negligent homicide depending upon the circumstances.

103. Motive

If the death is not accidental, the motive of infanticide is obviously the desire to be rid of an unwanted child. The child can be unwanted for any of a number of reasons. Usually, infanticide is preceded by a secret birth. The mother is unwed and fears the stigma of giving birth to an illegitimate child. Among other reasons for not wanting the child are economic family straits and deformities of the body.

104. Autopsy Determinations

The discovery of a dead infant under circumstances giving rise to suspicion does not justify a hasty conclusion of homicide. Higher probability of accidents is associated with secret births. The many misadventures that are easily avoided or readily corrected under the care of a physician in a hospital can quickly result in the death of an infant born to an inexperienced woman under rigorous physical conditions. A careful pathological examination must form the basis of any conclusion that the death resulted from criminal violence rather than accidental injury. Among the specific questions which the autopsy surgeon can answer in regard to infanticide are the following:

a. **Viability.** Was the infant able or likely to live? It is necessary to show that the infant could have lived under normal care. The accepted criterion is normal formation and a gestation period of at least seven months in the uterus. An infant fulfilling these conditions is considered viable, i.e., capable of survival.

b. **Live Birth.** It must be shown that the baby was born alive. Pathological examination of the lungs will determine whether the infant actually breathed.

c. **Cause of Death.** The autopsy is the only reliable means of determining whether the baby was stillborn or died of natural causes, accidental birth injuries, or criminal violence.

d. **Infanticide.** Is the death due to infanticide? This determination is accomplished in the same manner as in ordinary homicides. The likely methods employed in the criminal act are known from experience: Drowning in tubs, dropping in privies, smothering, and the other simple methods of accomplishing asphyxia that are invited by the helplessness of the infant.

105. Innocent Deaths of Infants

The causes of deaths in children under two years of age are frequently mysterious at the outset of an investigation and often result in erroneous conclusions on the part of the investigators. A knowledge of some of these causes can serve to obviate unnecessary suspicions of homicide.

a. **Common Causes.** The following four classes include most of the common causes of infant deaths requiring autopsies:

1) *Sudden Infant Death Syndrome.* This is a medical term given to the sudden and unexpected crib deaths of seemingly healthy infants. It is the leading cause of death for infants from one week to one year of age with 2 out of every 1000 succumbing to this condition. Sudden Infant Death Syndrome occurs with the highest frequency between the ages of two and four months. Though the mechanism of death is described as spontaneous cessation of breathing, the cause of this condition is mysterious. It is often accompanied by a minor viral infection and some congestion of the lungs. Neither of these conditions are considered sufficient to cause death. The infant, apparently in good health or at worst suffering from a slight cold, is put to bed and later fed at some period during the night. In the morning, the parents find the child dead with little evidence of disturbance other than a spot of blood on the bed clothing or a slight discharge from the nose.

2) *Disease.* Bacterial and viral infection can fatally overwhelm a child in a short time because of its size and the absence of defenses possessed by adults.

3) *Birth Defects.* The child may be afflicted at birth with some defect unknown to the parents. The absence of a vital structure, a defective heart, or a poorly functioning kidney or liver may be the cause.

4) *Birth Injuries.* The child may have been injured at birth by the forces of labor and delivery. Most commonly the skull is affected by compression and subsequent release of pressure, and the brain is damaged.

b. **Accidents.** A suspicious injury is sometimes the result of a fall from a bed. Asphyxia may result from food caught in the respiratory passages.

c. **Smothering.** It is a common error of investigators and even physicians to jump to an erroneous conclusion of death from accidental smothering, where the cause is not obvious. As a matter of practical experience, accidental suffocation is rarely the cause of death. It has been stated by competent authority that it is "almost impossible for an unrestrained normal infant, three weeks of age or older, to be accidentally smothered by a pillow or bed clothing. . . . Most deaths attributed to smothering are interstitial pneumonias although they may also be terminal conditions following other serious illness." The self-accusing parent can be relieved of remorse only through the information offered by an autopsy.

d. **Non-bacterial Food Poisoning.** This type of affliction is due to eating certain plants and animals containing a naturally occurring poison. The following substances are the most common causes: certain kinds of mushrooms such as *Amanita muscaria* and *Amanita phalloides;* immature or sprouting potatoes; mussels at certain undetermined times of the year; grain, especially rye which has become contaminated with the ergot fungus; fruits containing metallic contaminants, such as substances sprayed with salts of arsenic or lead, and food stored in cadmium-lined containers.

XVII. MOTOR VEHICLE HOMICIDES

106. General

In the investigation of traffic accidents as in the investigation of all criminal offenses, the objective is to determine all of the facts relating to the incident under examination. However, in motor vehicle accidents, particularly hit-and-run cases, the reconstruction of the occurrence is more dependent upon proper evaluation of physical evidence than upon the statements or testimony of witnesses. Scientific methods of examination and evaluation of physical evidence have become accepted and approved procedure of modern accident investigation. The proper examination and correct evaluation of physical evidence is a responsibility of the technician or expert, who by reason of his training and experience is qualified in the particular field involved. It is not practical to train the investigator in all of the techniques necessary to scientifically examine physical evidence which may come to his attention. He should know, however, what scientific aids are available, and he should be sufficiently familiar with the basic principles of the techniques common to scientific examination that he can perform the following functions in connection with a motor vehicle accident investigation:

    a. Isolate and safeguard the scene of the accident.

    b. Interview witnesses and obtain statements.

    c. Photograph the initial appearance of the accident and significant evidence found at the scene.

    d. Evaluate evidence of potential value and transmit it for expert examination.

107. Hit-and-Run Accidents

The classical problem of motor vehicle accident investigation is the establishment of the identity of the hit-and-run vehicle. This is the most difficult problem and consequently the investigative procedures described below will be based on the assumption that the identity of the hit-and-run vehicle is unknown. The solution of lesser problems will follow readily from a study of the techniques employed in this type of an investigation. It should be remembered that a driver who leaves the scene of a motor vehicle accident without properly identifying himself is guilty of an offense under state laws. If a driver remains at the scene he may be found guilty under the state laws of reckless driving or drunken driving, depending, of course, upon the circumstances and his culpability.

108. Scientific Aids

Experience has shown that materials found at the scene of an accident are of great importance in the case, and evaluation of these materials will sometimes involve complicated analyses. It is a safe rule to consider that all materials, traces, or conditions found at the scene which cannot for the moment be satisfactorily explained as having no bearing whatsoever upon the investigation at hand are physical evidence until their relative importance can be definitely determined. Ordinarily the immediate objectives of scientific aids in the investigation of a motor vehicle accident are:

a. To identify a car as having been on the scene of the accident.

b. To establish conclusively that a suspected car has been in an accident.

c. To reconstruct the circumstances surrounding the accident in order to determine the causative factors.

d. To corroborate or to disprove statements of the persons involved.

109. Scientific Techniques

The most common techniques employed in the scientific evaluation of physical evidence may be roughly divided into five general divisions:

a. **Preservation.** Photography is the most important means of preserving the initial appearance of the scene and the evidentiary materials. Casting is used to preserve such traces as tire and foot impressions.

b. **Physical Comparisons.** The most common of these are visual comparisons of missing parts. These may be conducted with magnifiers or low-power microscopes.

c. **Analytical Examinations.** Chemical analysis and spectrographic examinations of paint and soil are the most common analytical procedures.

d. **Physiological Examinations.** These include the facts developed by the autopsy; the examination of the body of the victim with a view to determining facts of the accident; and the analysis of body fluids to determine alcoholic content and blood group.

e. **Psychological Examinations.** These are related to the examination of persons involved in the accident to determine mental condition and superficial evidence of drunkeness. Also included are the techniques of deception detecting by mechanical means or by purely psychological means such as the word association test.

110. Examination of the Scene

The chief responsibility of the investigator at the scene is the discovery and preservation of the evidence. In regard to the other techniques it is expected that he will be aware of their potential value and will avail himself of their use. He must also provide the evidentiary materials to which the investigator can most effectively operate with regard to the physical evidence. The investigation of the hit-and-run accident will be divided into three phases:

1) The scene of the accident.
2) The superficial examination of the injured persons.
3) The examination of the suspected vehicle.

In hit-and-run accidents the scene of the occurrence frequently provides the only clues to the identity of the missing car. The scene moreover may contain sufficient evidence to enable the investigator to prove certain facts concerning the manner in which the accident took place. Traces, conditions, and material objects left at the scene are often more conclusive evidence of what happened than the oral testimony of eyewitnesses. All the factors of faulty perception, varying degree of memory, different levels of intelligence, and emotional stability enter into the testimony of witnesses but the physical facts provide objective evidence for the investigator.

a. **Principles of Searching.** As in the search of crime scene areas, the site of a motor vehicle accident must be subjected to a complete search. Every part of the scene must be examined, attention being given not only to the center of activity but to all the surrounding area as well and particularly to the approaches to the scene. This can be accomplished only if the search is planned and systematized. The particular pattern of search will vary with the individual case. Some of the most important factors to be considered in a plan of search are:

1) The scene should be isolated so that perishable traces are not destroyed.

2) Perishable traces such as tire tracks, foot impressions, and stains should be preserved before attention is given to the less destructible items.

3) No significant area should be overlooked.

4) Notes should be taken as the search progresses.

5) Physical evidence should be scrupulously marked for identification as it is picked up.

b. **Pattern of Search.** In the typical scene of a motor vehicle accident the search can be organized according to the following plan:

1) The point of impact should serve as the center of the search. The area immediately surrounding the center should be searched, and the perishable evidence cared for as the search progresses.

2) The path of the escaping car should be examined for glass particles, metal fragments, and paint flakes that may have fallen from the vehicle.

3) The approach to the point of impact should be examined for skid marks and tire impressions.

4) The path of the wrecked car, i.e., the car of the victim, should be studied. The car itself should be examined for transfer traces which were acquired from the other car at impact. Metal parts, impressions of bumpers, and paint are typical examples of this type of evidence.

c. **Collecting and Marking Evidence.** Evidence should be properly marked for identification as it is collected. The data concerning the evidence should be recorded in the investigator's notebook at the same time. Typical data for recording evidence are the following:

1) The exact position of the article of evidence with reference to fixed objects in the roadway and with reference to the vehicle.

2) Condition of the article, i.e., whether it was broken, dirty, and so forth.

3) Identifying description and information as to its probable source.

4) The names of the investigators who witnessed the finding.

The articles which can be removed should be placed in clean containers, envelopes, or cardboard boxes and properly marked. Large objects should be marked with an identifying mark. A tag should then be attached. They should then be removed to a safeguarded place for later, more detailed examination. Envelopes, containers, and boxes should be sealed and labeled as described in Chapter 7.

111. Photography of Motor Vehicle Accidents

Photographs of motor vehicle accidents are the most common type of court exhibit. Since the photograph is taken outdoors, it appears to be a relatively simple matter to make such a picture. Yet, a great number of traffic accident photographs are unacceptable because of distortion, misrepresentation, or some other inadequacy. The principles for producing accurate traffic accident scenes are complicated. It will be understood in the present discussion that a tripod should be used with the 4 × 5 camera.

a. **Completeness.** A photograph intended as evidence in a motor vehicle homicide should include all significant elements of the scene. Several photos should be taken to insure that all the facts are pictorially present. Contributing factors such as foliage obstructing vision should be shown clearly. Since different impressions of a scene are received from different points of view, the camera should be shifted so as to photograph the scene from several significant angles. Particularly important are the points of view which were available to the drivers of the vehicles and of any pedestrian involved in the accident.

b. **Distance from the Subject.** The camera should be located at a distance from the subject matter that will give a normal perspective for the lens employed. If the viewpoint of the camera is too close, perspective will seem distorted. If the camera is at too distant a point the scene will be lacking in depth and the objects will appear to be too near to each other.

c. **Height of Camera.** As a general rule in photographing traffic accidents, the camera should be at eye level. This is particularly important if it is desired to show the view available to a pedestrian at a given point. There are, of course, situations where other points of view are desirable. For example, if the investigator wishes to photograph an intersection to be used as a chart of the scene on which the approximate course of the colliding cars can be shown, a view from a very high camera position will be better than a photograph taken at eye level.

d. **Focusing.** Since the field of view in an accident photograph is so extensive, it is sometimes difficult to achieve proper focusing of all the significant objects in the scene. The simplest procedure to follow is to focus on the principal object and stop the diaphragm down to the next to the last opening. In this way considerable depth of field can be achieved. Modifications of this procedure must be made when lighting conditions are poor and background movement is present.

e. **Subject Matter.** The scene of the accident should be first photographed to show general conditions, approaches to the point of impact, and the views of the different drivers. These photographs should be taken after the vehicles are moved to show the nature and course of tire tracks and skid marks. Skid marks should next be photographed. The length of the skid mark is an indication of the speed at which the vehicle was traveling. Knowing the coefficient of friction of the roadway and the length of the skid marks, an expert can determine with fair accuracy the minimum speed at which the vehicle was traveling before the brakes were applied. A camera is placed at eye level to photograph the marks. Tire impressions on dirt roads and tire imprints on wet pavements are useful in identifying the unknown car. Photographs should be made of the tire tracks with the camera lens at a distance of approximately 5 feet and with the plate parallel to the surface of the road. A ruler should be included in the field to provide a reference scale for later measurements on the photograph. A plaster cast of tire impressions of the unknown vehicle should then be made. Evidentiary materials, such as glass pieces and metal fragments, lying on the surface of the roadway should be photographed before they are collected. Close-up photographs should be taken to insure a recognizable image. One of the views should include sufficient background to enable the viewer to locate the articles with reference to the scene in general.

112. Evidence at the Scene

The following types of evidence are among the most common clues which the investigator will find at the scene of a hit-and-run accident:

a. **Skid Marks.** These are the black marks left by a deposit of rubber from the tires. They are visible only when the wheels are almost locked by the forceful application of brakes. Skid marks help to locate the point at which the brakes were first applied. The length of the marks is an indication of the speed at which the vehicle was traveling prior to the application of the brakes. On finding skid marks at the scene of a motor vehicle accident, the investigator should photograph them and carefully measure their length. For an interpretation of the skid marks in terms of the original speed of the car, the investigator should request the services of an expert in this type of investigation.

b. **Tire Marks.** Tire impressions in mud, dirt, snow, and tar often contribute useful evidence. If the impression is clear, it may be possible to determine the manufacturer of the tire and the size of the wheel. If a sufficient number of characteristic defects are present it is sometimes possible to identify the tire itself. Tire prints on hard surfaces should be photographed with the plate parallel to the ground and a ruler in the field of view. An overall photograph of the tire print should be made in the same manner. In addition, the tire mark should be cast by means of plaster of paris.

c. **Dirt from Impact.** It is possible to obtain useful evidence from the mud and dirt which become caked on the undersurface of the fenders of an automobile. On collision with another vehicle or, in some cases, with a pedestrian, part of this mud or dirt is loosened and falls on the road. Dirt of this nature is easily recognized in the roadway. Samples should be collected and preserved for a possible later comparison with dirt obtained from the undersurfaces of the fenders of the suspected vehicle. Spectrographic analysis is used by laboratory experts in order to compare samples of this material chemically. In many cases this comparison will yield no evidence of value because the dirt or soil is common in nature and is found over a wide area. If, however, there are some elements or substances in the dirt which are highly characteristic, it is possible through this means to establish the fact that the vehicle passed over the area of the accident scene. Evidence of this nature is seldom conclusive because of the wide variety of soil which a vehicle may travel over in collecting fender dirt. Sometimes the shape of a piece of dirt may be significant. If the impact caused a large piece of dirt to fall intact it may be possible to find a corresponding cavity in the dirt remaining on the fenders.

d. **Cloth.** It is sometimes possible to find small fragments of cloth, usually in the path of the skid marks. When the injured person is run over by the wheels of the vehicle, these small fragments of cloth are removed and left in the roadway. Consequently, in subsequent examinations of suspected vehicles, attention should be given to the tires for the purpose of finding similar pieces of cloth or fibers.

e. **Blood, Tissue, and Hair.** When these substances are found on the roadway at the accident scene the investigator may make certain conclusions concerning the evidence which he may expect to find on a suspected car. It is unnecessary, ordinarily, to collect blood, tissue, or hair that is found at the scene of the accident since samples of these can be obtained from the autopsy surgeon. Sometimes, however, particularly when this type of evidence is found at a distance from the body, it is helpful to preserve the samples since their presence in a particular location is useful in reconstructing the accident. The collection of blood and tissue has been described in a preceding section.

f. **Chipped Flakes of Paint.** When two cars collide it is to be expected that there will be an exchange of paint smears and even that small flakes of paint will shaken loose and fall to the ground. This is particularly true of collisions involving an old car on which the paint has already begun to flake. It is possible from the examination of a flake of paint to determine the make and year of a car. The FBI Laboratory maintains a national automotive paint file which is used to provide such information. In addition, it is possible to state that a certain sample of paint came from a certain car. This is especially true where the car has been repainted several times and has thus acquired a number of individual and characteristic layers of paint. All samples of paint found at the scene of an accident should be collected in order to enable a future spectrographic analysis to be made by a comparison with the paint from the suspected car. If the paint is found in flake form it should be preserved intact so that it will be possible later to establish that the flake fit into the outline of a certain area of the metal surface of the suspected vehicle.

g. **Broken Equipment.** One of the best types of evidence for the purpose of showing that a suspected vehicle was at the scene of the accident is a broken piece of equipment such as the side mirror, headlights, or radiator emblem. These ornaments or accessories are sometimes detached from the vehicle by the shock of the collision. If on locating a suspected car it is found that a corresponding piece of equipment is missing, a photograph should be made which will show the part found at the scene in juxtaposition with the area of the vehicle from which it was detached. By the use of appropriate photographic techniques it is possible to show an exact correspondence between the part and its source.

h. **Headlights.** One of the most common clues found at the scene of a hit-and-run accident is broken headlight glass. From an examination of this glass it is sometimes possible to establish the exact type of lens and from this to discover the year and type of the car which was involved in the accident. The tendency to equip cars with a standard type of headlight, namely the "sealed beam" headlight unit, is a limiting factor. In nighttime accidents the condition of the headlights can be an important element. One of the first steps of the investigator is to check the position of the light switch. The headlights themselves should be examined with special reference to the filaments. If the lamp was on at the moment of impact, the coils may have suffered a deformation. The effects of impact on a headlight will be different for lighted and unlighted lamps.

1) *Identifying Make and Model.* When glass fragaments are discovered at a hit-and-run accident scene the investigator should first photograph them as they lie on the ground and should then collect them in an envelope. The pieces may be placed together in

the manner of a jigsaw puzzle. Transparent tape will facilitate the procedure by holding together pieces that are found to match. If a sufficient number of pieces of glass are present, it will be possible to determine the trade name of the lens, the name of the manufacturer, and sometimes the make and model of the car.

2) *Matching.* If pieces of headlight glass are later found in an automobile, it may be possible to match them with pieces found at the scene.

113. Examination of the Injured

The deceased may bear marks from the car on either his body or his clothing. Both should be examined carefully for traces.

a. **Clothing.** The clothing should be removed and studied for the following:

1) *Grease* from the understructure of the vehicle.

2) *Tire marks.* These may be irregular because of the yielding action of the clothing.

3) *Paint.* The buttons and sometimes the cloth may retain paint from the car.

b. **The Body.** The chest or back of the deceased sometimes bears a distinct tire mark.

114. Examination of the Suspected Vehicle

The determination of whether a suspected vehicle has been in an accident is by no means simple. Often the body of the deceased is cast aside on impact and leaves no trace on the car. If the car collides squarely with the body, traces may be left.

a. **Dents and Scratches.** These provide a special problem to the investigator. It is not a simple matter to determine the recency of the damage or the exact cause of it. The owner should be questioned concerning the origin of the damage and the story checked at a later date.

b. **Broken Parts.** Pieces of glass may remain in the headlight or may fall into the grillwork. A broken emblem or side mirror should also attract attention. Questions should be raised concerning the cause of this damage.

c. **Fibers.** Contact with the victim's clothing may leave fibers or even cloth on the vehicle.

d. **Cloth Marks.** If the victim is struck with sufficient force, an outline of clothing pattern may be seen on the paint.

e. **Blood and Tissue.** In a particularly violent accident, blood stains and tissue may be found on the radiator, the door handles, and other parts.

f. **Characteristic Soil.** When the accident has taken place on a dirt road, particles of soil may be found adhering to the fenders and the tires. If the chemical composition of the soil is highly characteristic, it may be possible to associate the vehicle with the scene of the accident.

g. **Understructure of the Vehicle.** The car should be placed on a service station jack for the purpose of studying the understructure for various traces such as impressions in the grease or fibers.

ADDITIONAL READING

Death Investigation

Abel, E.: *Homicide.* Westport, Conn.: Greenwood Press, 1987.

Adelson, L.: *The Pathology of Homicide.* Springfield, Ill.: Thomas, 1974.

Baden, M.M. with Hennessee, J.A.: *Unnatural Death: Confessions of a Medical Examiner.* New York, Random House, 1989.

Browne, A.: *When Battered Women Kill.* New York, Free Press, 1987.

Catts, P.E. and Haskell, N.H. (Eds.): *Entomology and Death: A Procedural Guide.* Clemson, S. Car.: Forensic Entomology Associates, 1990.

Copeland, A.R.: Accidental Death by Gunshot Wound. Fact or Fiction. 26 *Forensic Science International,* 25, 1984.

——: Homicidal Drowning. 31 *Forensic Science International,* 247, 1986.

DiMaio, D.J. and DiMaio, V.J.M.: *Forensic Pathology.* New York, Elsevier, 1989.

Erzinclioglu, Y.Z.: Forensic Entomology and Criminal Investigation. 64 *The Police Journal,* 1, 1991.

Falk, G.: *Murder: An Analysis of Its Forms, Conditions and Causes.* Jefferson, N. Car.: McFarland, 1990.

Fisher, B.A.J., Svensson, A. and Wendel, O.: *Techniques of Crime Scene Investigation,* 4th ed. New York, Elsevier, 1987.

Geberth, V.J.: Investigation of Drug-Related Homicides. 38 *Law and Order,* 11, 1990.

———: *Practical Homicide Investigation: Tactics, Procedures, and Forensic Techniques,* 2nd ed. New York, Elsevier, 1990.

Gormsen, H., Jeppesen, N. and Lund, A.: The Causes of Death in Fire Victims. 24 *Forensic Science International,* 107, 1984.

Harries, K.D.: *Serious Violence: Patterns of Homicide and Assault in America.* Springfield, Ill.: Thomas, 1990.

Harris, R.I.: *Outline of Death Investigation.* Springfield, Ill.: Thomas, 1973.

Hazelwood, R.R., Dietz, P.E. and Burgess, A.W.: *Autoerotic Fatalities.* Lexington, Mass.: Lexington Books, 1983.

Hazelwood, R.R. and Douglas, J.E.: The Lust Murderer. 49 *FBI Law Enforcement Bulletin,* 4, 1980.

Hughes, D.J.: *Homicide: Investigative Techniques.* Springfield, Ill.: Thomas, 1974.

Lipskin, B.A. and Field, K.S. (Eds.): *Death Investigation and Examination: Medicolegal Guidelines and Checklists.* Colorado Springs, Col.: Forensic Sciences Foundation Press, 1984.

Johann, S.L. and Osanka, F.: *Representing . . . Battered Women Who Kill.* Springfield, Ill.: Thomas, 1989.

Macdonald, J.M.: *The Murderer and His Victim,* 2nd ed. Springfield, Ill.: Thomas, 1986.

Morse, D. and Dailey, R.C.: The Degree of Deterioration of Associated Death Scene Material. 30 *Journal of Forensic Sciences,* 119, 1985.

Ressler, R.K., Burgess, A.W., and Douglas, J.E.: *Sexual Homicide: Patterns and Motives.* Lexington, Mass.: D.C. Heath, 1988.

Revitch, E. and Schlesinger, L.B.: *Sex Murder and Sex Aggression: Phenomenology, Psychopathology, Psychodynamics and Prognosis.* Springfield, Ill.: Thomas, 1989.

Riedel, M. and Zahn, M.A.: *The Nature and Patterns of American Homicide.* Washington, D.C.: U.S. Government Printing Office, 1985.

Rodriguez, W.C. III and Bass, W.M.: Decomposition of Buried Bodies and Methods that May Aid in their Location. 30 *Journal of Forensic Sciences,* 836, 1985.

Snyder, L.: *Homicide Investigation: Practical Information for Coroners, Police Officers, and Other Investigators,* 3rd ed. Springfield, Ill.: Thomas, 1977.

Spitz, W.V. and Fisher, R.S. (Eds.): *Medicolegal Investigation of Death,* 2nd ed. Springfield, Ill.: Thomas, 1980.

Stickevers, J.: The Investigation of Fatal Fires: Views of the Fire Investigator. 55 *FBI Law Enforcement Bulletin,* 8, 1986.

Wilson, M. and Daly, M.: *Homicide.* Hawthorne, N.Y.: Aldine de Gruyter, 1988.

Wilson, W.: *Good Murders and Bad Murders: A Consumer's Guide in the Age of Information.* Lanham, Md.: University Press of America, 1991.

Multiple Murder

Brooks, P.R., et al.: Serial Murder: A Criminal Justice Response. 54 *Police Chief,* 6, 1987.

Egger, S.A.: *Serial Murder: An Elusive Phenomenon.* Westport, Conn.: Greenwood Press, 1990.

——: A Working Definition of Serial Murder and the Reduction of Linkage Blindness. 12 *Journal of Police Science and Administration,* 348, 1984.

Fox, J.A. and Levin, J.: *Mass Murder: America's Growing Menace.* New York, Plenum, 1985.

Geberth, V.J.: The Serial Killer and the Revelations of Ted Bundy. 38 *Law and Order,* 5, 1990.

Goodroe, C.: Tracking the Serial Offender: The NCAVC Connection. 35 *Law and Order,* 7, 1987.

Hickey, E.W.: *Serial Murderers and Their Victims.* Pacific Grove, Calif.: Brooks/Cole, 1991.

Holmes, R.M. and DeBurger, J.: *Serial Murder.* Newbury Park, Calif.: Sage, 1988.

Jenkins, P.: Serial Murders in England 1940–1985. 16 *Journal of Criminal Justice,* 1, 1988.

——: Serial Murders in the United States 1900–1940: A Historical Perspective. 17 *Journal of Criminal Justice,* 5, 1989.

Keppel, R.D.: *Serial Murder: Future Implications for Police Investigations.* Cincinnati, Anderson, 1988.

Kozenczak, J.R. and Henrikson, K.M.: In Pursuit of a Serial Murderer. 35 *Law and Order,* 8, 1987.

Leyton, E.: *Compulsive Killers: The Story of Modern Multiple Murder.* New York, Columbia University Press, 1986.

Terry, G. and Malone, M.P.: The "Bobby Joe" Long Serial Murder Case: A Study in Cooperation. Parts I and II. 56 *FBI Law Enforcement Bulletin,* 11 and 12, 1987.

Suicide

Cimbolic, P. and Jobes, D.A.: *Youth Suicide: Issues, Assessment, and Intervention.* Springfield, Ill.: Thomas, 1990.

Fisher, D.: High School Suicide Crisis Intervention. 59 *FBI Law Enforcement Bulletin,* 5, 1990.

Geberth, V.J.: Investigating a Suicide. 36 *Law and Order,* 12, 1988.

Johnson, A.P.: Hammer Spur Impressions: Physical Evidence in Suicides. 57 *FBI Law Enforcement Bulletin,* 9, 1988.

Lester, D.: *Suicide as Learned Behavior.* Springfield, Ill.: Thomas, 1987.

——: *Why People Kill Themselves: A 1990's Summary of Research Findings on Suicidal Behavior,* 3rd ed. Springfield, Ill.: Thomas, 1992.

——: *Why Women Kill Themselves.* Springfield, Ill.: Thomas, 1988.

Massello, W. III: The Proof in Law of Suicide. 31 *Journal of Forensic Sciences,* 1000, 1986.

Stone, I.C.: Observations and Statistics Relating to Suicide Weapons: An Update. 35 *Journal of Forensic Sciences,* 10, 1990.

Bloodstain Evidence

Cox, M.: A Study of the Sensitivity and Specificity of Four Presumptive Tests for Blood. 36 *Journal of Forensic Sciences,* 1503, 1991.
——: Effect of Fabric Washing on the Presumptive Identification of Bloodstains. 35 *Journal of Forensic Sciences,* 1335, 1990.

Eckert, W.G. and James, S.H.: *Interpretation of Bloodstain Evidence at Crime Scenes.* New York, Elsevier, 1989.

Gaensslen, R.E. and Lee, H.C.: *Procedures and Evaluation of Antisera for the Typing of Antigens in Bloodstains.* Washington, D.C.: U.S. Government Printing Office, 1984.

Gaensslen, R.E.: *Sourcebook in Forensic Serology, Immunology, and Biochemistry.* Washington, D.C.: U.S. Government Printing Office, 1983.

Grispino, R.R.J.: Serological Evidence in Sexual Assault Investigations. 59 *FBI Law Enforcement Bulletin,* 10, 1990.

Hunt, S.M.: *Investigation of Serological Evidence: A Manual for Field Investigators.* Springfield, Ill.: Thomas, 1984.

Laux, D.L.: Effects of Luminol on the Subsequent Analysis of Bloodstains. 36 *Journal of Forensic Sciences,* 1512, 1991.

Lytle, L.T. and Hedgecock, D.G.: Chemiluminescence in the Visualization of Forensic Bloodstains. 23 *Journal of Forensic Sciences,* 550, 1978.

MacDonell, H.L.: *Flight Characteristics and Stain Patterns of Human Blood.* Washington, D.C.: U.S. Government Printing Office, 1971.

Miller, L.S. and Brown, A.M.: *Criminal Evidence Laboratory Manual,* 2nd ed. Cincinnati, Anderson, 1990.

Murch, R.S.: The FBI Serology Unit: Services, Policies, and Procedures. 54 *FBI Law Enforcement Bulletin,* 3, 1985.

Pizzola, P.A., Roth, S. and De Forest, P.R.: Blood Droplet Dynamics—Parts I and II. 31 *Journal of Forensic Sciences,* 36 and 50, 1986.

Walton, G.: *A Laboratory Manual for Introductory Forensic Science.* Encino, Calif.: Glencoe Publishing, 1979.

Wilber, C.G.: *Forensic Biology for the Law Enforcement Officer.* Springfield, Ill.: Thomas, 1974.

DNA Analysis

Bigbee, D., Tanton, R.L. and Ferrara, P.B.: Implementation of DNA Analysis in American Crime Laboratories. 56 *Police Chief,* 10, 1989.

Burke, T.W. and Rowe, W.F.: DNA Analysis: The Challenge for Police. 56 *Police Chief,* 10, 1989.

Fiatal, R.A.: DNA Testing and the *Frye* Standard. 59 *FBI Law Enforcement Bulletin,* 6, 1990.

Geberth, V.J.: Application of DNA Technology in Criminal Investigations. 38 *Law and Order,* 3, 1990.

——: DNA Print Identification Test Provides Crucial Evidence in Lust Murder Case. 36 *Law and Order,* 7, 1988.

Hicks, J.W.: DNA Profiling: A Tool for Law Enforcement. 57 *FBI Law Enforcement Bulletin,* 8, 1988.

Ingraham, B.L. and Mauriello, T.P.: *Police Investigation Handbook.* Albany, N.Y.: Mathew Bender, 1990.

Kelly, K.F., Rankin, J.J. and Wink, R.C.: Method and Application of DNA Fingerprinting: A Guide for the Non-Scientist. *Criminal Law Review,* 105, February 1987.

Miller, J.V.: The FBI's Forensic DNA Analysis Program. 60 *FBI Law Enforcement Bulletin,* 7, 1991.

Saferstein, R.: *Criminalistics: An Introduction to Forensic Science,* 4th ed. Englewood Cliffs, N.J.: Prentice-Hall, 1990.

Sylvester, J.T. and Stafford, J.H.: Judicial Acceptance of DNA Profiling. 60 *FBI Law Enforcement Bulletin,* 7, 1991.

Poisoning

Arena, J.M. and Drew, R.H. (Eds.): *Poisoning: Toxicology, Symptoms, Treatments,* 5th ed. Springfield, Ill.: 1986.

Cravey, R.H. and Basett, R.C. (Eds.): *Introduction to Forensic Toxicology.* Davis, Calif.: Biomedical Publications, 1981.

Curry, A.: *Poison Detection in Human Organs,* 4th ed. Springfield, Ill.: Thomas, 1988.

Kaye, S.: *Handbook of Emergency Toxicology: A Guide for the Identification, Diagnosis, and Treatment of Poisoning,* 5th ed. Springfield, Ill.: Thomas, 1988.

Lance, D.: Product Tampering. 57 *FBI Law Enforcement Bulletin,* 4, 1988.

Wilber, C.G.: *Forensic Toxicology for the Law Enforcement Officer,* Springfield, Ill.: Thomas, 1980.

Motor Vehicle Homicide

Badger, J.E.: Investigating Vehicular Homicide. 36 *Law and Order,* 3, 1988.

Baker, J.S. and Lindquist, T.: *Lamp Examinations for On or Off in Traffic Accidents.* Evanston, Ill.: The Traffic Institute, Northwestern University, 1977.

Barrette, R.: Accident Scene Evidence: Placing the Driver behind the Wheel. 13 *Police: The Law Officer's Magazine,* 12, 1989.

Basham, D.J.: *Traffic Accident Management.* Springfield, Ill.: Thomas, 1979.

Brown, J.F. and Obenski, K.S.: *Forensic Engineering Reconstruction of Accidents.* Springfield, Ill.: Thomas, 1990.

Collins, J.C.: *Accident Reconstruction.* Springfield, Ill.: Thomas, 1979.

Daily, J.: *Fundamentals of Accident Reconstruction.* Jacksonville, Fla.: Institute of Police Technology and Management, 1989.

McGrew, D.R.: *Traffic Accident Investigation and Physical Evidence.* Springfield, Ill.: Thomas, 1976.

Rivers, R.W.: *On-Scene Traffic Accident Investigators' Manual.* Springfield, Ill.: Thomas, 1981.

——: *Traffic Accident Investigators' Handbook.* Springfield, Ill.: Thomas, 1980.

von Breman, A.: The Comparison of Brake and Accelerator Pedals with Marks on Shoe Soles. 35 *Journal of Forensic Sciences,* 14, 1990.

Woods, J.: Headlights are Tools in Traffic Accident Investigation. 25 *Law and Order,* 6, 1977.

Zeldes, I.: Speedometer Examination: An Aid in Accident Investigation. 49 *FBI Law Enforcement Bulletin,* 3, 1980.

Dental and Skeletal Identification

Barry, R.J.: Forensic Odontology: Identification through Dental Evidence. 55 *Police Chief,* 8, 1988.

Barsley, R.E., Carr, R.F., Cottone, J.A.: Identification Via Dental Remains: Pan American Flight 759. 30 *Journal of Forensic Sciences,* 128, 1985.

Bastiaan, R.J., Dalitz, G.D. and Woodward, C.: Video Superimposition of Skulls and Photographic Portraits: A New Aid to Identification. 31 *Journal of Forensic Sciences,* 1373, 1986.

Iten, P.X.: Identification of Skulls by Video Superimposition. 32 *Journal of Forensic Sciences,* 173, 1987.

Johnson, D.E.: Forensic Anthropology. 38 *Law and Order,* 10, 1990.

Katz, J.O. and Cattone, J.A.: The Present Direction of Research in Forensic Odontology. 33 *Journal of Forensic Sciences,* 1319, 1988.

Killiam, E.W.: *The Detection of Human Remains.* Springfield, Ill.: Thomas, 1990.

Krauss, T.C.: Forensic Odontology in Missing Persons Cases. 21 *Journal of Forensic Sciences,* 959, 1976.

Krogman, W.M. and Iscan, M.Y.: *The Human Skeleton in Forensic Medicine,* 2nd ed. Springfield, Ill.: Thomas, 1986.

Mann, R.W. and Ubelaker, D.H.: The Forensic Anthropologist. 59 *FBI Law Enforcement Bulletin,* 7, 1990.

Micozzi, M.S.: *Postmortem Change in Human and Animal Remains: A Systematic Approach.* Springfield, Ill.: Thomas, 1991.

Morse, D., Duncan, J. and Stoutamire, J.: *Handbook of Forensic Archaeology and Anthropology.* Tallahassee, Fla.: Rose Printing, 1983.

Pane, P.: Dental Identification Program: An Overview. 51 *FBI Law Enforcement Bulletin,* 8, 1982.

Rathbun, T.A. and Buikstra, J.E.: *Human Identification: Case Studies in Forensic Anthropology.* Springfield, Ill.: Thomas, 1984.

Reichs, K.J. (Ed.): *Forensic Osteology: Advances in the Identification of Human Remains.* Springfield, Ill.: Thomas, 1986.

Rodgers, S.L.: *Personal Identification from Human Remains.* Springfield, Ill.: Thomas, 1987.

———: *The Testimony of Teeth: Forensic Aspects of Human Dentition.* Springfield, Ill.: Thomas, 1988.

Sopher, I.M.: *Forensic Dentistry.* Springfield, Ill.: Thomas, 1976.

Sperber, N.: Identification of Children and Adults through Federal and State Dental Identification Systems. 30 *Forensic Science International,* 187, 1986.

Stewart, T.D.: *Essentials of Forensic Anthropology.* Springfield, Ill.: Thomas, 1979.

Xiaohu, X., et al.: Age Estimation from the Structure of Human Teeth: Review of the Literature. 54 *Forensic Science International,* 23, 1992.

Chapter 25

ASSAULT

1. Introduction

SOME OF THE more frustrating moments of police work are spent responding repeatedly to scenes of domestic violence, to intervene in family disputes. Most frequently, the wife has been hit by the husband and she or a neighbor has telephoned the police. The husband demands to know why the police have been called; after all, "it is a family argument." Occasionally, the wife will decide to press charges against her spouse. But after several days of reflection on the incident and of cajoling by her husband, the wife will usually decide it is more conducive to family harmony and less embarrassing to overlook the incident. In the absence of a complainant, the charges against the husband are dropped.

The traditional police response to a violent family quarrel of this type has been initially to placate both parties and to follow this with a stern warning to the husband about the illegality of his actions. The underlying problem, namely, the husband's need to resort to violence and intimidation, is never addressed, understood, or properly dealt with. This approach, while well intentioned, does little to prevent or even slow the gradual escalation of violence. Typically, the husband's behavior follows a predictable pattern of more frequent and hostile outbursts leading eventually to a violent confrontation in which the husband or wife is seriously injured.

In some of the more enlightened jurisdictions, an effort is being made to break this cycle of domestic violence. In Sussex County, New Jersey, for example, the police are instructed to follow what is called a "pro-arrest" policy. When called to a domestic dispute, if an assault is committed in their presence, they are required to make an arrest. Once the police have witnessed the assault and made the arrest, the prosecution will pursue the case even if this course of action goes against the wishes of the victim. Ordinarily, if a wife presses charges, she feels responsible for punishing her husband. If the decision to proceed is taken out of her hands, it removes this burden to some extent. The wife can no longer be intimidated into dropping charges by the threat of a future beating, or by the fear of the social or economic consequences she would share in if her husband were convicted.

The husband may be permitted to plead guilty to a lesser charge if he is a first-time offender and he agrees to enroll in a program of counseling. Even then he is still required to spend a weekend or two in jail so that he fully understands the seriousness of the offense. This new policy clearly establishes the principle that it is never acceptable for husbands and wives to hit each other. Preliminary evidence suggests that this policy of intervening in the early stages of domestic disputes is instrumental in reducing the number of repeat offenses.

2. Assault and Battery Defined

The words "assault and battery" are commonly used together in the same expression as if one of necessity followed from the other. In order to understand the nature of assault, it is important to distinguish clearly between these terms.

a. **Assault.** An assault is a willful attempt or immediate threat to do physical harm to another with unlawful force or violence. The meaning of "immediate threat," in this context, is the placing of another in the fear of imminent physical harm. In a strictly legal sense, an assault is limited to the immediate threat or the attempt. The actual commission of the injury is a battery. In ordinary conversation, however, the term "assault" generally includes the battery. For example, the sentence, "He was the victim of an assault," conveys the meaning that the person referred to has suffered physical harm from an attack.

b. **Battery.** Battery is the unlawful application of force to another. The crime of battery includes not only intentional bodily injury but also offensive touching. The injury must be done intentionally or be occasioned by culpable negligence. The act must also be unlawful. It is not a battery to lay hands on another to attract his attention or to seize another to prevent him from falling. Likewise, there is no battery, if the act was done in lawful self-defense.

c. **Differences.** Assault involves the attempt or immediate threat of force; battery is the physical application of that force. While assault is committed without physical contact, battery requires the bodily injury or the offensive touching of another. Not every assault involves a battery, because not every threat is carried out and not every attempt is successful. However, every battery involves an assault, that is, it is the result of a willful attempt or of culpable negligence. Battery may be looked upon as the completion of an assault. Consequently, in many jurisdictions, the crime of battery is often referred to as "assault and battery."

3. Kinds of Assault

Assaults can be classified into two groups, simple assault and aggravated assault, depending on the severity of the attendant circumstances.

a. **Simple Assault.** An assault unaccompanied by aggravating factors is a simple assault. A simple assault is a misdemeanor, while an aggravated assault is a felony. A felony is a crime of a more serious nature than a misdemeanor that is usually punishable by a prison term of more than a year. In order to make an arrest for a misdemeanor, such as simple assault, it is generally required that a law enforcement officer witness the infraction or have an arrest warrant.

b. **Aggravated Assault.** An aggravated assault can be defined as an assault with serious attendant circumstances. These aggravating factors include the causing of severe bodily harm, the use of a dangerous weapon, or the intent to commit a serious crime. The status of the victim may also be an aggravating factor. For example, assaulting a police officer or a prison guard while they are acting in the line of duty is an aggravated assault in some jurisdictions. An aggravated assault is a felony. To make an arrest for a felony, a police officer is not required to have witnessed the offense. For a felony not happening in his presence, a police officer must have "probable cause" to believe that the offense has occurred before making the arrest. "Probable cause" exists when the facts and circumstances of an event would lead a reasonable person to conclude that the person to be arrested has committed a felony. A felony arrest, as with a misdemeanor arrest, may also be made with a warrant obtained from the court.

In some jurisdictions, the categories of simple and aggravated assault have been replaced by degrees of assault. An offense is classified as a first, second, or third degree assault according to the severity of the accompanying circumstances. The three most important kinds of aggravated assault are:

1) *Assault with a Dangerous Weapon;*

2) *Assault in Which Grievous Bodily Harm is Intentionally Inflicted;* and

3) *Assault with Intent to Commit Certain Other Offenses.*

4. Simple Assault

a. **Elements of Proof.** In order to prove the offense of simple assault, it is necessary to show:

That the accused attempted or made an immediate threat to do bodily harm to a certain person with unlawful force or violence.

b. **Immediate Threat and Attempt.** There is a distinction made between an immediate threat and an attempt. An immediate threat to do bodily harm to another is the placing of the other in reasonable fear that force will be at once applied to his person. An attempt, on the other hand, may be made without the victim being aware of it and, consequently, he would have no fear of bodily injury. This distinction is best illustrated by the following examples:

1) If *A* points an unloaded pistol at *B* who is unaware of the act, no assault has been committed. *B* has not been placed in fear of bodily injury and *A* is fully cognizant of his inability to shoot *B* because he knows the gun is unloaded.

2) If, in the preceding example, *B* was aware of the attack and was thereby placed in reasonable fear of bodily injury, *A* may be guilty of an assault. *A*'s act constitutes an immediate threat but not an attempt under these circumstances, since, knowing the gun to be unloaded, he is unable to shoot *B*.

3) If, on the other hand, *A*, with intent to shoot, points a loaded gun at *B* who has his back turned and is unaware of the impending danger, *A* has committed an assault in the form of an attempt to do bodily harm even though *B* was not put in fear.

Preparation not amounting to an overt act, such as picking up a stone without any attempt or threat to throw it, does not constitute an assault nor does the mere use of threatening words. If an apparent attempt to assault is accompanied by an announcement clearly indicating an intention not to consummate the assault, no assault is committed. This principle was applied in a case in which the accused raised his whip and shook it at another within striking distance, saying, "If you weren't an old man, I would knock you down." However, a threat to inflict bodily injury upon another instantly, if the other does not comply with a demand which the assailant has no lawful right to make, is an assault.

c. **Negligent Acts.** An assault may consist of a culpably negligent act or omission which forseeably might and does cause another reasonably to fear that force will at once be applied. A person who places another in fear by failing to restrain his attack dog may be charged with an assault.

d. **Apparent Ability to Injure.** In order to constitute an assault, there must be an apparent present ability to inflict the injury. Threats of physical violence over a telephone, for example, do not constitute an assault. It is no defense to a charge of assault that for some reason, unknown to the assailant, his attempt was bound to fail. Thus, if a person loads his gun with what he believes to be a good cartridge and, pointing it at another, pulls the trigger, he may be guilty of assault although the cartridge was, in fact, so defective it would not fire.

5. Assault with a Dangerous Weapon

A weapon, to be considered dangerous, need not be inherently dangerous. The test is whether it is used in the particular case in such a manner that it is likely to produce death or serious bodily injury. Thus, a bottle, glass, rock, bowl, piece of pipe or wood, boiling water, or a number of other substances may be considered a dangerous weapon, depending upon the manner in which it is used in committing the assault. To constitute an offense of aggravated assault with a dangerous weapon or other means or force likely to produce death or grievous bodily harm, it is not necessary that death or grievous bodily harm actually be inflicted. In order to prove this offense, it is necessary to show:

a. That the accused assaulted a certain person with a certain weapon, means, or force; and,

b. That such weapon, means, or force was used in a manner likely to produce death or grievous bodily harm.

Table X
AGGRAVATED ASSAULT[1], TYPE OF WEAPON USED, 1991

Firearms	23.6%
Knives or Cutting Instruments	18.4%
Other Weapons (Clubs, Blunt Objects, Etc.)	30.8%
Personal Weapons (Hands, Fists, Feet, Etc.)	27.1%

1. In the Uniform Crime Reporting Program, aggravated assault is defined as an unlawful attack by one person upon another for the purpose of inflicting severe or aggravated bodily injury. Source: FBI. *Uniform Crime Reports—1991.*

6. Assault in Which Grievous Bodily Harm Is Intentionally Inflicted

Grievous bodily harm includes fractured or dislocated bones, deep cuts, torn members of the body, serious damage to internal organs and other serious bodily injuries. It does not include minor injuries such as a black eye or a bloody nose. When grievous bodily harm has been inflicted by means of intentionally using force in a manner likely to achieve that result, it may be inferred that grievous bodily harm was intended. For example, intentionally knocking a person from a height such as a grandstand, so that the resulting fall breaks his leg, is an aggravated assault. In order to prove an offense of this kind it is necessary to show:

a. That the accused assaulted a certain person;

b. That grievous bodily harm was thereby inflicted upon such person; and,

c. That such bodily harm was intentionally inflicted.

7. Assaults with Intent to Commit Certain Other Offenses

This type of aggravated assault includes assaults with intent to commit murder, voluntary manslaughter, rape, robbery, sodomy, arson, burglary or housebreaking. An assault to commit an offense is not necessarily the equivalent of an attempt to commit the offense. An assault may be committed in furtherance of an intended act without thereby achieving the degree of proximity to consummation of the act essential to an attempt to commit that act. For example, if *A* assaults *B* with the intention of robbing *B* but is interrupted before he can take or demand *B*'s property, the offense committed lacks an essential element of an attempted robbery charge. In order to prove an offense of this kind, it is necessary to show:

　　a. That the accused assaulted a certain person; and

　　b. That the assault was committed with intent to murder, or to commit voluntary manslaughter, rape, robbery, sodomy, arson, burglary or housebreaking. (For assault with intent to commit rape and for indecent assault, see pp. 360–363.)

8. Investigative Procedure

Many of the techniques followed in the investigation of homicide are applicable in those cases of aggravated assault in which the victim has been badly injured. In a case of this kind the investigator's notes should be as extensive and complete as in a homicide investigation.

　　a. **Crime Scene.** The crime scene and any evidence located there should be photographed in the same manner as in a homicide case. A sketch of the scene should be made if the circumstances warrant it. Weapons and any other evidence which will serve to identify the assailant or associate him with the crime scene should be collected in the approved manner. Steps should be taken to trace any weapons or other physical evidence bearing on the case when the necessity of such action is indicated.

　　b. **Victim.** The victim should be interviewed as early as practicable. If he knows the identity of his assailant, the task of the investigator is greatly simplified. A complete account of the incident should be obtained from the victim including the circumstances immediately preceding, information relative to motives, the names of corroborating witnesses and any other details which will serve to further the investigation. With the victim's permission, color photographs of the wounds should be taken. In order to show the full extent of the injuries, another set of photographs may be recorded approximately three days later. The clothes of the victim should be obtained and forwarded to the laboratory for evidentiary traces. This should be done in cases involving violent physical contact between the victim and his assailant where the identity of the assailant is unknown. This should also be done in cases where the identity of the assailant is known but corroboration as to his participation is needed. If there is any suspicion that the victim had been drinking to excess or had taken narcotics, appropriate tests should be requested.

c. **Witnesses.** The investigator should interview all eyewitnesses to the incident and any other persons who can furnish material information relative to the circumstances preceding the crime, the motive for the assault and the identity of the assailant. A medical report on the victim should be obtained from the attending physician. The investigator should also discuss the case with the doctor if there is a possibility that his findings with respect to the nature and location of the wound will be of assistance in the investigation. If the injured person was the victim of a gunshot wound and the bullet became lodged in the body, it should be obtained from the attending physician for transmittal to the laboratory.

d. **Suspect.** The procedures to be followed with regard to the suspect will depend on the circumstances of the case. If the suspect is taken into custody at the scene or shortly thereafter, he should be questioned in detail about the alleged offense and his motive. If there are any indications that he had been drinking or was under the influence of narcotics at the time of the offense, appropriate tests should be conducted. The location of any physical objects known to have been connected with the case, such as the weapon employed, should be determined during the investigation. The necessity for an examination of the suspect's clothing will depend upon the possibility of finding incriminating evidence on them and the amount of corroborating evidence needed in the particular case. Any justification, excuse, or alibi offered by the suspect should be fully explored.

ADDITIONAL READING

Assault

Besharov, D.J.: *Child Abuse: A Police Guide.* Washington, D.C.: American Bar Association, 1987.

Bopp, W.J. and Vardalis, J.J.: *Crimes Against Women.* Springfield, Ill.: Thomas, 1987.

Cameron, J.M. and Rae, L.J.: *Atlas of the Battered Child Syndrome.* New York, Longman, 1975.

Chamelin, N.C. and Evans, K.R.: *Criminal Law for Police Officers,* 4th ed. Englewood Cliffs, N.J.: Prentice-Hall, 1987.

Clark, R.S.: *Deadly Force: The Lure of Violence.* Springfield, Ill.: Thomas, 1988.

DiMaio, V.J.M.: *Gunshot Wounds: Practical Aspects of Firearms, Ballistics, and Forensic Techniques.* New York, Elsevier, 1985.

Gil, D.: *Violence Against Children.* Cambridge, Mass.: Harvard University Press, 1970.

Harries, K.D.: *Serious Violence: Patterns of Homicide and Assault in America.* Springfield, Ill.: Thomas, 1990.

Horgan, J.J.: *Criminal Investigation,* 2nd ed. New York, McGraw-Hill, 1979.

Johann, S.L. and Osanka, F.: *Representing . . . Battered Women Who Kill.* Springfield, Ill.: Thomas, 1989.

Meier, J.H. (Ed.): *Assault Against Children.* San Diego, Calif.: College Hill Press, 1985.

Pagelow, M.D.: *Family Violence.* New York, Praeger, 1984.

Shepherd, J.R.: The Law Enforcement Role in the Investigation of Family Violence. In Helfer, R.E. and Kempe, R.S. (Eds.): *The Battered Child,* 4th ed. Chicago, University of Chicago Press, 1987.

Wolfgang, M.E. and Weiner, N.A. (Eds.): *Criminal Violence.* Beverly Hills, Calif.: Sage, 1982.

Chapter 26

CRIMINAL EXPLOSIONS

1. Introduction

I T IS NOT the purpose of the present treatment to provide detailed descriptions of explosive devices such as bombs, *suspicious packages,* infernal machines, or incendiary devices. Information of that nature should not be made easily available to the general public. The problems associated with bomb threats, unexploded bombs, and bomb scene procedures are basically the problems of the patrol force. The student who wishes to learn about explosives, protective response, and preventive measures against bombs is referred to the series of excellent publications of The National Bomb Data Center of the International Association of Chiefs of Police. It is assumed in this chapter that an explosion has already taken place and an investigative problem exists. The investigator, then, is faced with a scene of wreckage; the physical clues appear either non-existent, irrevocably scattered, or mutilated beyond recognition; even the eyewitnesses may have been killed in the blast.

2. Initial Action

Appropriate attention to routine police tasks is also assumed throughout so that space can be devoted to the special features of an explosion investigation. For example, the injured will have been cared for, measures will have been taken to extinguish fires or prevent their subsequent outbreak, and the possibility of further accidents or explosions from utility hazards or other dangers will have been eliminated. The investigator must determine the nature and cause of the explosion. Initially, he must distinguish

623

between an accidental explosion and one produced intentionally or by criminal negligence.

All persons who witnessed the explosion or observed any significant attendant circumstances should be detained, identified, and interviewed. Observations concerning the number and nature of the explosions, the color of smoke, the presence of peculiar odors and other observations of the senses will be important. Recollections concerning the movements of persons before and after the occurrence should be recorded while they are fresh in the witnesses' memories.

The scene of the explosion should be placed under safeguard as soon as possible by assigning an adequate number of officers to the duty of rigorously excluding unauthorized persons. To preserve the crime scene as far as possible, rescue workers should be cautioned against unnecessary disturbance of the wreckage and the fire chief requested to restrict overhauling to a minimum.

3. Types of Explosions

The investigator should be able to distinguish between the two basic types of explosions. A low explosive results in a *push* effect, leaving a diffuse pattern with no marked progression of effect from a point source. The high explosive incident is marked by a definite *seat* of origin. Movable objects are blown outward from this point, the force of the blast diminishing in intensity with distance.

a. **Low Explosives** are characterized by the relatively low velocity with which the energy wave is transmitted—a few thousand feet per second. Gunpowder, gasoline, and carbon monoxide are examples of low-explosive substances. The explosion is identifiable by two characteristics: a low-frequency sound, which has been variously described as a *puff, boom,* or *pop,* and the absence of relatively severe damage in the area of the explosion.

b. **High Explosives**, on the other hand, such as dynamite and nitroglycerine, have velocities as high as 25,000 feet per second, are accompanied by a shattering high-frequency sound, and reveal a definite crater of explosion. On the basis of these differences it is often possible to identify the character of the explosion even though no traces of the explosives remain.

4. Crime Scene Action

Crimes involving explosions present many of the difficulties usually associated with arson, paramount among which is the partial or total destruction of evidence tending to establish a *corpus delicti.* Hence, although the usual investigative steps are followed at the crime scene, great care must be taken in handling the articles of evidence and interpreting the pattern suggested by their location.

a. **Defining the Scene.** Depending on the severity and location of the explosion, the crime scene area may be restricted to a room or may extend over an area of several acres. Determine the outer limits of the area to be searched and post a guard to prevent the entrance of any unauthorized persons and the removal of any object from the area. The posting of placards marking the limits of the crime scene area is helpful in these situations. Of course, special problems will be presented by certain kinds of explosion. For example, a time bomb exploding on a plane in flight may result in the distribution of wreckage over more than a mile of territory.

The Colorado aircraft disaster of November 1, 1955 provides an example of an exceptionally difficult "crime scene," since the mid-air explosion resulted in the distribution of fragments over a wide area. In this case a twenty-three-year-old youth had plotted to kill his mother for the sake of the insurance money and the prospect of a major share of a $150,000 estate. The perpetrator had tied together twenty-five sticks of dynamite and attached the timing device connected with a dry cell battery and two blasting caps. The ensemble was concealed in a suitcase which his mother took aboard the plane. In the mid-air explosion forty-four persons were killed. It was found later that the perpetrator had bought $37,500 in vending machine insurance policies on his mother's life before planting the bomb on the DC-6B. Further investigation revealed a previous forgery charge against the bomber. The

Colorado explosion was the first known case of successful bomb sabotage in the history of this country's airline operations.

b. **Documenting the Scene.** Because of the significance of the pattern of strewn objects created by the explosion and the importance of tracing the point of origin through this pattern, documentation should be unusually painstaking.

1) *Photography.* Overall photographs of the scene and sectional views of important areas should be taken before anything is disturbed. During the search close-ups of articles of evidence should be taken as they are discovered. If it is helpful to include markers or signs in the field of view, it is advisable to make two sets of such photographs, one with and one without the markers. The use of transparent overlays with unmarked photographs should also be considered. Significant objects and places can be marked on the transparent overlay to correspond to the exact location of such items on the corresponding photograph. The report of investigation should include photographs as a supplement with text references to evidence objects and areas at the scene keyed to the symbolism used in the photographs and sketches.

2) *Sketches.* A representation of the scene should be made by means of sketches—an overall sketch for the whole scene and individual sketches for separated areas such as rooms. Significant items of evidence should be located by symbol and accurate measurements from fixed points. Rectangular coordinates are preferable for indoor scenes, while polar coordinates are more suited to outdoor explosions extending over broad areas. Compass directions, legends, and other essentials should be given in each sketch.

3) *Investigator's Notes.* Although photographs and sketches can be invaluable supplements to the investigative report, they should not be expected to take the place of the investigator's notes. These should contain detailed descriptions of the scene and each important object in it. Identifying data for each evidentiary article should be inscribed in the notebook.

c. **Searching the Scene.** The investigator should enlist the aid of any available technical assistance in his search of the crime scene. Accompanied by a member of the Bomb Squad or Explosives Unit, a police laboratory expert, an explosives specialist, or an arson investigator, he should search the scene for physical evidence. If a point of origin can be located, a spiral method of search can be used effectively. The searchers should begin at the point of origin and progress outward using increasingly larger circles. Limitations on this procedure are naturally set by the extent of the area.

The searchers should look for evidence which will establish a *corpus delicti,* viz., the fact that an explosive device was used and that there was an intent to injure some object or person. They should, of course, be constantly alert for clues which may lead to the identity of the perpetrator or link him to the scene. Pieces of metal such as pipe fragments, wire, or parts of a timing device; string, paper, leather, wood, and other fragments which may have been used to package the bomb; unexploded materials, pieces of paper that may have been part of the explosives wrapping; and any other trace evidence which may have been part of an explosive device or its container should be carefully collected after its location and initial appearance have been documented as described. This procedure was used in the case of the New York World's Fair bomb with the result that a sufficient quantity of clue materials was recovered to enable the experts to identify the clock, explosive materials, and suitcase, to reconstruct the bomb, and to trace some of its components.

The value of trace evidence in the investigation of an explosion was dramatically shown in a California case in which a dynamite bomb found near the home of a prominent citizen was submitted to a microanalyst, the late Doctor Albert Schneider, dean of the Berkeley School for Police Officers. Doctor Schneider examined every part of the package minutely—burlap, paper wrappings, the dynamite sticks, caps, fuses, and a piece of string. Particles clinging to this latter item provided considerable information under the microscope. Doctor Schneider drew the following conclusions from his examination: "This twine came from a farm upon which will be found a fast-running stream of water, pine trees, black and white rabbits, a bay horse, a light cream colored cow, and Rhode Island red chickens."

On reading this report there was considerable head shaking and exchanging of glances among the more cynical officials; nevertheless, they filed the data for future reference. The dynamite was traced to an explosives dealer in Novato, California, who gave the police details concerning three recent sales of dynamite in the neighboring communities. On investigating the three purchasers, the police officers found that one of them lived adjacent to a farm which matched that of Doctor Schneider's description in every detail. The farmer was innocent of the crime. The dynamite, however, had been stolen from his premises by two farm hands, comparative strangers in his employ, who later proved to be the guilty parties.

d. **Examination of Victims.** Deceased persons should not be disturbed until the medical examiner (or other person serving in a medicolegal capacity) has made his examination to determine such matters as the cause and manner of death, the time of death, and whether death took place before or after the explosion. Where the victims have been mutilated or burned to a degree that prevents recognition by relatives or associates, identification may be made by means of fingerprints, teeth, and bones. The medical examiner can provide information as to age, height, and weight, even though only part of the body is available. He can also provide data on operations, including the length of time since the operation, and pathological findings as to physical ailments which can lead to identification. Further information can be obtained through the laboratory examination of clothing, documents, and personal items, particularly metal articles, such as watches, rings, or cigarette lighters. Since the position of all such articles with relation to the body is important for identification purposes, the exact location of each item should be recorded before it is collected.

e. **Utilities.** A bomb which is set off unknowingly by the action of an occupant of the premises may present a problem in regard to the source of electrical energy required for detonation. Electrical or telephone equipment can be used to supply the necessary power. Check such devices as telephones, electric clocks, heaters, coffee pots, and lamps for breaks or additions in the wiring. The wiring systems of the engines of powered devices, such as lawn mowers, compressors, and pumps, should also be examined. The presence in any of these motors of extraneous wires or fragments of fuses, caps, or detonators should provide a lead. In certain cases, as for example those of suspected sabotage, the entire electrical system including motors, appliances, and other apparatus should be examined for defects such as exposed wires, incorrectly installed wiring or fuses that could result in overheating or sparking. The investigator should enlist the aid of a safety expert or an electrician in this phase of the search for evidence. Experienced assistance of this character is required not only because of the complexity of the investigative problem but also because of the need for expert testimony on the matters in the event of a trial.

In a New York case to which the newspapers gave the garish title "The Case of the Golden Bomber," a pipe bomb was wired to the utility lines so that when the intended victim switched on the cellar light an explosion would take place. The victim survived, however, and assisted in the solution of the case by indicating the motive: $985 concealed in a metal container in the cellar was missing. The perpetrator proved to be an electrician who had access to the cellar for storage facilities. Part of the evidence that linked him to the pipe bomb was a gilt (gold) paint which through some whim he had chosen to decorate the bomb. The search of the cellar in this case required extreme care, since the defendant had stored away 220 pounds of powder, 259 flares, and 115 bombs.

5. Nature of the Criminal

A number of elements in crimes involving explosions render the investigation of these crimes unusually difficult. Particularly significant is the fact that quite often the bomber is not a criminal by record or inclination. Thus we are faced with a disturbing paradox: the perpetrator of one of the most heinous of crimes may not at heart be a professional criminal. In all likelihood he may be a man with a grievance nurtured out of all proportion by psychopathic brooding and hence requiring some abnormal emotional outlet. Another *non-professional* type is the political agitator or self-styled patriot whose twisted mind urges him to this dramatic gesture.

The jealous suitor and the deceived husband are other examples of normally law-abiding citizens who, through protracted anguish and prolonged contemplation of an unpleasant social situation, resort to drastic measures to resolve their difficulty.

In many cases involving bombers of this type, the investigator will find it difficult to obtain logical leads. Established sources of information are effective mainly in cases involving professional criminals or at least adult delinquents. The common bond of greed or dedication to a degraded mode of existence throws these persons together socially, constraining them to mutual associations and meeting places. The non-criminal type of bomber, however, provides no ordinary source of information through his contacts or haunts. The investigator must rely on the special circumstances surrounding the case, particularly the existence of personal grievances.

Some of the more useful factors which will serve to guide the investigator are the following:

a. **Target.** What person, property, or activity was the objective of the bombing?

b. **Opportunity.** Who had the capability, means, knowledge, and access necessary for the destructive act?

c. **Means.** What explosive materials, mechanism, and camouflage were used in the bomb?

d. *Modus Operandi.* What technique, tactic, or method of operation did the perpetrator use?

e. **Motive.** Why was the crime committed?

The answers to these questions will ordinarily form the basis of a successful investigation. In the absence of an on-the-spot apprehension, these answers must be sought for in the statements of eyewitnesses, in conclusions drawn from the physical evidence gathered at the crime scene, and from the suspect's possessions.

f. **Bomb Threats.** Any communication by the perpetrator of an explosion can provide useful clues. Telephone calls should be carefully monitored. The operator should be instructed to recall the exact words of the caller in answer to the following five questions:

1) When is the bomb to explode?
2) Where is the bomb right now?
3) What kind of a bomb is it?
4) What does it look like?
5) Why did you place the bomb?

The operator should also be asked to describe the caller's voice by sex, accent, age, and tone and to say whether or not it is familiar. Any background noise should be noted.

6. Determining the Target

The nature of the offense committed should be determined by a study of the circumstances surrounding the explosion, the nature of the explosive device, the type of target, and the evidence tending to show design or intent. An offense has been committed if it can be established that an explosion took place through criminal intent or through criminal negligence. Usually, the most helpful factor is the determination of the target.

If the explosion was directed against a person, the device will often be such that an act of the intended victim is required to detonate the explosive. Examples of this are: a bomb placed in an automobile and wired to the ignition; a package sent through the mails with the victim's address; a bomb connected to the house wiring so that, when the light is turned on in the victim's room, the explosion occurs. Bombs placed in airplanes and in buildings can be timed to insure the victim's presence when the explosion occurs.

Ordinarily, the laws pertaining to homicide will cover an act in which an explosive was used to take a man's life. Some states, however, have special statutes for the specific crime of using an explosive to injure or kill a person. Suicide by means of explosives presents no special problems unless the perpetrator was unsuccessful in his attempt and seriously endangered the lives of others by his act.

Deaths as a result of simple or criminal negligence present special problems. They relate ordinarily to the statutes dealing with explosives and with death caused by negligence. In bombings designed to effect the death of a person, if there appears to be no apparent motive, consideration should be given to the possibility of mistaken identity or an error in locating the vehicle or place in which to plant the bomb.

Two persons were killed in this manner when a bomb was planted in the automobile of Doctor E. H. Rebhorn, the Director of Public Health in Scranton, Pennsylvania. Rebhorn's son and daughter were killed a moment after they attempted to step into the family car. Apparently a bomb had been connected to the door handle so that the act of opening the door would trigger the device. The deaths seem to have been a tragic mistake. Rebhorn had no enemies and was engaged in no controversies. The best police theory held that the bomb had been intended for a resident of a house further down the block, a superintendent of a coal company whose home had been dynamited during a labor dispute a few years earlier.

7. Evidence Connecting a Suspect

Since the construction of an explosive device requires preparation, labor, and considerable handling of materials, trace evidence may be found on the suspect's person, in his lodgings, place of work, or vehicle. Guided by a knowledge of the evidence found at the crime scene, the investigator should conduct a thorough search of the suspect and his possessions.

a. **Suspect's Person.** Examine the suspect's hands and clothing for trace materials from the bomb. Burns or discolorations may be present if acids were used. If the suspect was near the explosion, traces of debris may be found on his person. Fingernail scrapings and even ear wax have been found to contain significant microscopic traces.

b. **Place of Dwelling or Work.** If a search is made of the suspect's lodging or place of employment, the investigator should look for evidence to link the suspect to the crime scene. The nature of the materials on which the search should particularly concentrate will, of course, depend on the physical evidence gathered at the scene. In general, the following clue materials may prove helpful:

1) *Explosive Substances* — If professional explosives were used, look for dynamite, nitroglycerine, gun cotton, black powder, smokeless powder, and similar substances. In addition to professional materials such as blasting caps, fuses, and primacord, search for improvised devices such as filaments, handmade squibs, and fuses. In cases involving low-explosive homemade bombs, chemicals such as the following should be collected:

Ammonium nitrate	Potassium nitrate
Ammonium dichromate	Potassium permanganate
Chromic acid, chromates	Powdered aluminum
Metallic peroxides	Powdered iron
Metallic potassium	Powdered magnesium
Metallic sodium	Powdered zinc
Nitric acid	Sulphur
Potassium chlorate	Sulphuric acid

Military explosives are occasionally encountered, though they are more common in countries where terrorists have access to military supplies. They are found in two basic forms: sheet explosives and plastic explosives or composition. Sheet explosives are manufactured in thin rubbery sheets that can be cut with a knife. They contain a high explosive, either RDX or PETN, and are used both militarily and commercially. Plastic explosives, also known as composition, are so called because of the plasticizers included in their ingredients which make them pliable at warm temperatures and give them a doughy appearance. RDX, the most powerful of the military explosives as well as the most common, is the explosive element in this mixture.

2) *Construction Materials.* A disguised bomb involves considerable work in the construction of the basic bomb and in camouflaging the container. The suspect's dwelling place or workshop should be searched for tools and construction materials. The type of tools to look for will be indicated by the nature of the bomb. A pipe bomb, for example, with a special thread suggests access to a lathe. All tools of possible evidential value should be collected and placed in separate containers. Paint, wood fibers, metal pieces, and other traces clinging to the faces of the tools can sometimes be linked to the materials used in constructing the bomb.

c. **Vehicle.** A search of the suspect's car may disclose evidence relating to explosives or associating the vehicle with the scene of the explosion. Tools should be examined for indications of use in assembling the bomb or forcing entry. Traces of materials used to construct the bomb, blasting caps, special matches, unnecessary batteries, and wires are among the articles that may be uncovered.

The car should be examined for soil or other traces that may link it to the explosion scene.

d. **Sources of Explosives.** In determining the source of the explosives, consideration should be given to the possibility of a local theft. Although it is possible to obtain the explosive materials directly under the guise of intending to use them to clear land or perform some other minor blasting operation, it is more common for the perpetrator to acquire the dynamite and blasting caps by theft or other illegal means. Carelessness in the safeguarding of explosives results in frequent thefts from local contractors and persons engaged in large-scale construction work. In one city, four thefts were reported within a period of several months with the following respective losses: (1) 103 sticks of dynamite, (2) 150 blasting caps, (3) 50 blasting caps, (4) 86 sticks of dynamite. In the near future, it is expected that taggants or chemically coded additives will be mixed with explosives to provide a clue to their origin (p. 861).

8. Motive

In some explosion cases the motive may be obvious. For example, the throwing of a lighted dynamite bomb into the house of a union official recently involved in an election dispute suggested the obvious motive of revenge. Similarly, in a case of an automobile bombing, investigation disclosed that the victim had been conducting an affair with a married woman. Interrogation of the aggrieved husband led to a confession. Often, however, the motive for a bombing is difficult to discern, and the investigator must explore every lead in an effort to locate a person who might have cause for criminal designs against the victim. In determining the motive the following matters should be given consideration:

a. **Profit.** Who stood to gain or lose by the explosion? If the victim was a person, did someone stand to gain by the explosion? If property was destroyed, what was the financial condition of the owner? Were there any recent movements of property, such as substitutions of less valuable property?

b. **Sabotage.** Was the target some special machinery, materials, or activity that could logically be the subject of enemy, industrial, or labor sabotage?

c. **Concealment of a Crime.** An explosion can be used to disguise the existence of another crime, such as a homicide or larceny, or, in a business establishment, the existence of financial irregularities.

d. **Hatred and Revenge.** Jealousy, family quarrels, and other personal reasons may result in a desire for inflicting injury. Labor disputes, racial enmities, and religious hatreds lead to the malicious destruction of property.

In order to determine the motive the investigator should gather all pertinent information about the victims and other persons who are normally in the area, scheduled to be in the area, or suspected of being in the area before and after the time of the explosion. The relationship of such persons to the victim should be explored by interviewing witnesses.

The form of the bomb will often provide a clue to the criminal's purpose. The terrorist, for example, whose intent is to intimidate a religious or racial group may attempt no disguise, since he wishes to publicize the existence of the terrorist group. The saboteur and the bomber with a more personal motive, on the other hand, will usually employ camouflage. Sabotage seeks to diminish the war potential of a nation or an industry; hence, the saboteur, to remain effective, must play the role of a concealed agent. Where the bombing is motivated by fraudulent insurance gain, the desire to conceal a crime, or the achievement of some psychological satisfaction, disguise is usually in accord with the criminal's purpose. The crank, crackpot, and psychopath, in general, despite the existence of mental disturbance, will ordinarily possess sufficient acumen to disguise his infernal machine in a suitcase or a parcel.

9. Access

If it was necessary to gain entry by force in order to plant the bomb, the investigators should be alert for typical evidence of a burglary, e.g., signs of a break, direction in which window panes were broken, or tool marks. Trace evidence relating to the perpetrator's movements, in general, should be collected or photographed.

a. **Doors and Windows.** Note the condition of all doors and windows, particularly with reference to the locks.

b. **Entry and Exit.** Paths of access and points at which the premises could have been entered should be examined for tire marks, foot impressions, fingerprints, and similar clues.

c. **Security Conditions.** Through interviews, observation, and study of available directives, ascertain the exact nature of entry and exit. Check on controls and deliveries: personnel receiving and handling incoming shipments; receipt systems; protection in transit and during storage. Check on the nature of materials recently delivered. In some cases it may be found that the materials for the construction of the bomb were sent into the plant separately and the bomb assembled within the plant. During the last war a worker in an important defense plant endeavored to show the inadequacy of the installation's security system by smuggling in the components of a bomb and then constructing the infernal machine on the premises. The assembled explosive device was a lunch-box bomb containing four sticks of dynamite, an electric detonator, a dry cell battery, and the timing mechanism from an alarm clock. On observing the finished product, a police captain who was also the explosives expert of a nearby city described the bomb thus: "As perfect a bomb as I have ever seen." The maker of the lunch-box bomb claimed that he had "sneaked" the parts into the plant, piece by piece. The detonators and dynamite were stolen from a nearby quarry. The other components were readily obtainable at local stores. At the time of the young man's arraignment the court conceded that the defendant had most dramatically pointed up certain deficiencies in the plant security system.

d. **Shipping Materials.** If the bomb was shipped in the disguise of a package, fragments of the packing, wrapping, and binding materials are of particular importance in tracing the perpetrator and in linking him to the explosion. Special attention should be given to pieces of paper bearing writings. In addition to the tracing value of the materials themselves, the edges of such items as stamps, paper, and cardboard may prove valuable in establishing a common origin with similar materials found in the lodgings or working place of a suspect.

e. **Files.** A check of all pertinent files should be made. In particular, records pertaining to bombers and arsonists and *modus operandi* files will be of special interest.

10. Determining the Crime

The nature of the offense under investigation is, of course, a matter of immediate importance. Where there is obviously no intent to injure a person or to damage property, the gravamen of the charge will usually lie in the misuse or mishandling of explosives, that is, the essence of the matter will be a violation of the laws relating to the transportation, manufacture, sale, storage, and handling of explosives. The statutes of nearly every state will be found to contain laws controlling explosives and their use. The extent and rigor of the legislation vary considerably among the states. In most, however, legislation along the following lines will be found in some form:

a. **Manufacture.** The place of manufacture will be licensed with respect to location, construction, qualifications of specialized personnel, and the manner in which the products are labeled for shipment.

b. **Transportation.** Restrictions are placed on the type of carrier. Shipment on common carriers with passengers is forbidden. In some states the controls extend even to the type of motor used in the carrier.

c. **Storage.** The magazines used for storing explosives are subject to laws, that describe their size, construction and location.

d. **Sale and Use.** Safety regulations are usually established to restrict the sale of explosives to legitimate users such as owners of construction works, mines, quarries, and even farm lands on which it is necessary to blast stumps or perform other clearance operations. Ordinarily it is required that the record of sales be maintained.

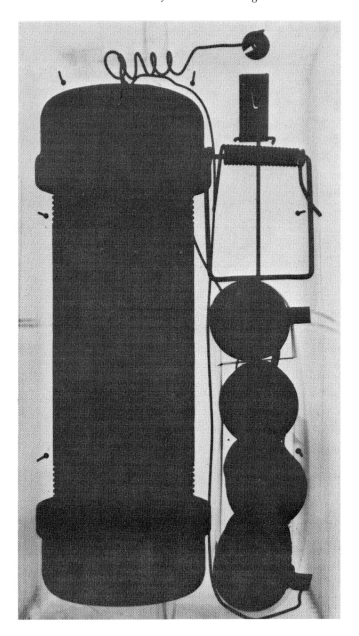

Figure 22. Radiograph of a suspected package, revealing a pipe bomb and trigger mechanism.

11. Dog-Handler Teams

In 1972 a Trans World Airlines jet bound for Los Angeles was turned back to Kennedy Airport on receiving an anonymous phone call warning that a bomb was aboard. After the passengers were evacuated, a German shepherd went to work, sniffing out the bomb within twelve minutes before it was set to detonate. This success has been repeated a number of times in the intervening years. It is estimated that the trained dogs have saved more than 100 lives and prevented millions of dollars in property damage. More than twenty-seven city airports are presently protected by bomb squad dog teams, which spend 40 percent of their time at airports and the remainder in patrol work and bomb detection work in the city. In non-airport searches the dogs have found sixty-eight explosive devices, including a letter bomb addressed to the former mayor of Los Angeles. In 2,000 airport and aircraft searches, most of them false alarms, the dogs and their handlers have found explosives twenty-one times, seven of them on aircraft. The handlers are local police officers, trained at Lackland Air Force Base, Texas, who use male German shepherds because of their stamina, adaptability, intelligence, and size.

ADDITIONAL READING

Criminal Explosion

Berluti, A.F.: Connecticut's Explosive-Detecting Canines. 58 *Police Chief*, 10, 1991.

Brodie, T.G.: *Bombs and Bombing.* Springfield, Ill.: Thomas, 1973.

Chisholm, J.J. and Icove, D.J.: Targeting Bombers. 58 *Police Chief*, 10, 1991.

Hartnett, D.M.: Bombing and Arson Investigation Enhanced by Advances in ATF Labs. 57 *Police Chief*, 4, 1990.

Hoffman, C.M. and Byall, E.B.: ATF Field Kit for Identifying Explosive Residues in Bomb Scene Investigations. 4 *Journal of Police Science and Administration*, 106, 1976.

Kennedy, J. and Kennedy, P.: *Fires and Explosions: Determining Cause and Origin.* Chicago, Investigations Institute, 1985.

Kennedy, J.: *Fire, Arson and Explosion Investigation.* Chicago, Investigations Institute, 1977.

Laposata, E.A.: Collection of Trace Evidence from Bombing Victims at Autopsy. 30 *Journal of Forensic Sciences*, 789, 1985.

Macdonald, J.M.: *Bombers and Firesetters.* Springfield, Ill.: Thomas, 1977.

McLuckey, S.A., Glish, G.L. and Carter, J.A.: The Analysis of Explosives by Tandem Mass Spectrometry. 30 *Journal of Forensic Sciences,* 773, 1985.

Stoffel, J.: *Explosives and Homemade Bombs,* 2nd ed. Springfield, Ill.: Thomas, 1972.

Styles, S.G.: The Car Bomb. 15 *Journal of the Forensic Science Society,* 93, 1975.

Thurman, J.V.: Interpol Computers Keep Track of Firearms, Explosives. 58 *Police Chief,* 10, 1991.

Twibell, J.D., et al.: The Persistence of Military Explosives on Hands. 29 *Journal of Forensic Sciences,* 284, 1984.

——: Transfer of Nitroglycerine to Hands During Contact with Commercial Explosives. 27 *Journal of Forensic Sciences,* 783, 1982.

Yallop, H.J.: *Explosion Investigation.* Harrogate, Eng.: Forensic Science Society Press, 1980.

Yinon, J. and Zitrin, S.: *The Analysis of Explosives.* Oxford, Eng.: Pergamon Press, 1981.

PART V
THE INVESTIGATOR IN COURT

Chapter 27

RULES OF EVIDENCE

1. General

THE SUCCESS or failure of a criminal prosecution usually depends upon the evidence presented to the court. It is in the court that the investigator must present the evidence which he has so laboriously collected over a period of months. Will his evidence be admitted? Has he taken precautions to obtain evidence that is admissible? Has he observed the rules which govern admissibility? A failure through ignorance on the part of the investigator may lead to the rejection of a vital piece of evidence by the court with the result that a conviction cannot be sustained. Since the investigator is occupied constantly with the business of evidence, it is an indispensable part of his training to understand the purpose of evidence and the rules that control its admissibility. It is only in this way that he can serve the cause of justice efficiently. The rules of evidence lie at the heart of modern judicial systems, and their understanding is necessary for an intelligent participation in prosecutive procedures.

2. Purpose

The term *evidence* includes all the means by which an alleged fact, the truth of which is submitted to scrutiny, is established or disproved. The purpose of evidence is the discovery of the truth of the charge. The laws of evidence are the rules governing its admissibility. This system of rules does not constitute a science of logical proof. From long experience with witnesses, jurors, and litigant parties, it has been found that certain types or forms of information tend to possess risks of irrelevancy and to confuse the issues rather than assist in determining truth. The rules of evidence have as their primary aim the screening out of all evidence having these risks and tendencies from consideration by the jury and court members. There is no universal law of evidence. The rulings of the different states vary. For example, common law exists in some states, while in others, a different law exists or the common law prevails side by side with statutes. In federal courts, the common law has been superseded by procedural rules.

3. Classifications and Definitions

Evidence may be divided into three major classifications:

a. **Direct Evidence.** Evidence which directly establishes the main fact of issue (elements of the crime) is called *direct evidence.* For example, an eyewitness account of a criminal act is direct evidence; the witness is here describing an event which he actually saw.

b. **Circumstantial Evidence.** Evidence which establishes a factor or circumstance from which the court may infer another fact at issue is called *circumstantial evidence.* Where direct evidence is the immediate experience on the part of a witness, the essence of circumstantial evidence is inference. As an elementary example we may consider the following:

> *Example:* X and Y go into a closet together and close the door. A shot is heard and Y rushes out with a smoking gun in his hand. X is found lying on the floor. An eyewitness relating this event would be offering circumstantial evidence since he did not see Y fire the shot. The facts, however, are so closely associated that it may reasonably be inferred that Y shot X.

c. **Real Evidence.** This comprises tangible objects introduced at a trial to prove or disprove a fact in issue. The evidence speaks for itself. It requires no explanation, merely identification. Examples of real evidence are guns, fingerprints, and blood stains. Real evidence may be direct or circumstantial.

4. Admissibility of Evidence

Evidence to be admissible must be material and relevant. The rules of evidence are concerned with the admissibility of facts and pertinent materials and not with their weight. With respect to given evidence, the weight is a question of fact for the judge or jury to determine.

a. **Materiality.** If the fact which the evidence tends to prove is part of an issue of the case, the evidence is material. Evidence which proves something that is not part of an issue is immaterial. To be material the evidence must affect an issue of the case significantly. Example: X is being tried for larceny of a crate of oranges. His attorney discourses at length on the fact that the oranges were yellow in color. Such evidence is unimportant to the trial and is, therefore, immaterial.

b. **Relevancy.** Evidence which tends to prove the truth of a fact at issue is relevant. Example: A murder has been committed with a bow and arrow. It is relevant to show that the defendant did know how to use a bow and arrow. It would be irrelevant to show that he was well acquainted with firearms.

5. Competency of Witnesses

A competent witness is one who is eligible to testify. The competency, both mental and moral, of a witness over thirteen years of age is presumed. Mental competency refers to the ability to see, recall, and relate. Moral competency implies an understanding of the truth and the consequences of a falsehood. The competency of children is not dependent on age and may be shown by apparent understanding and a recognition of the moral importance of telling the truth. A record of conviction of crime is unrelated to competency but may affect credibility.

6. Impeachment of a Witness

Impeachment is the discrediting of a witness. A witness may be disqualified by showing, for example, a lack of mental ability, insufficient maturity, previous conviction of a crime, or a reputation for lack of veracity.

7. Judicial Notice

Certain kinds of facts need not be proved by formal presentation of evidence, since the court is authorized to recognize their existence without such proof. This recognition is called *judicial notice.* The general rule prescribes that the court will not require proof of matters of general or common knowledge. Examples: historical and geographical facts; a state's own laws; weights and measures; and so forth.

8. Burden of Proof

No person is required to prove his innocence. The burden of proof for a conviction rests solely with the prosecution. In criminal cases, the prosecution has the burden of proving the accused guilty *beyond a reasonable doubt.* The accused, however, must prove his own allegations such as alibis, claims of self-defense, and insanity.

9. Presumption

A presumption is a justifiable inference. It is an inference as to the existence of one fact from the existence of some other fact founded upon a previous experience of their connection. Presumptions generally serve the purpose of shifting the burden to the other party to establish the contradictory facts.

a. **Conclusive Presumption.** This presumption is considered final, unanswerable, and not to be overcome by contradictory evidence. The following are examples:

1) Everyone is presumed to know the law.

2) Children under seven years are presumed to be incapable of committing a crime.

3) A boy under fourteen years cannot commit the crime of rape.

b. **Rebuttable Presumptions.** These can be overcome by proof of their falsity:

1) Every man is presumed to be innocent.

2) Presumption of sanity.

3) One intends the natural consequence of his acts.

4) Presumption of good character, chastity, or sobriety.

5) That an officer properly performs his tasks.

6) Legitimacy of children and validity of marriage.

7) Presumption of death after an unaccounted absence of seven years.

10. Rules of Exclusion

Much of the body of the rules of evidence concerns itself with the *rules of exclusion*. These latter deal with the conditions under which evidence will *not* be received. They are often extremely technical in nature with the consequence that their purpose is obscured.

a. **Purpose.** The rules of exclusion were primarily evolved to control the presentation of evidence in a trial before a jury. It was supposed that the juror who decided the facts in controversy was inexperienced in legal matters and would be unable to separate the immaterial and unimportant from matters truly germane to the issue. It was feared that the layman would not discriminate properly between gossip and fact, or between allegation and truth.

b. **Function.** The function of the rules is to limit the evidence which a witness may present to those things of which he has a direct, sensory knowledge. The witness may relate what *he* saw, felt, and smelled. The jury endeavors to put itself in the place of the witness and to judge the reliability of the witness.

c. **General Rule.** All direct and circumstantial evidence, if material and relevant, is admissible except:

1) Opinion evidence.

2) Evidence concerning character and reputation.

3) Hearsay evidence.

4) Privileged communications.

5) Secondary evidence.

There are exceptions as regards admissibility to all of the categories of evidence listed above.

11. Opinion Evidence

a. **The Opinion Rule.** The general rule is that opinion evidence is not admissible in a trial. A witness may testify only to facts, not to their effect or result, or to his conclusions or opinions based on the facts. He can bring before the court only those facts which he has observed, directly through the medium of his senses — sight, hearing, touch, taste, or smell. The reasons for this restriction lie in the fact that it is a function of the jury to weigh the evidence and to draw conclusions. Moreover, where a witness adds opinion to observation, a confusion may arise in the minds of the jurors as to what is the observed fact and what is the witness's derived interpretation of the fact originally apprehended by his senses.

b. **Exceptions to the Opinion Rule.** Several exceptions are attached to the opinion rule. These exceptions recognize first the fact that certain simple judgments based immediately on sensory observation are so much a matter of common practice in the mind of the average man that they may be given with much greater reliability than the word "opinion" ordinarily connotes. Second, the court recognizes that the opinions of certain specialists in regard to their specialty should be treated with greater consideration than mere opinion.

1) *The Lay Witness.* The layman may express an opinion on matters of common observation. This exception arises in cases where an opinion is the only logical way to receive the information concerning the fact, since a recounting of all the facts which caused the formation of the opinion would tend to confuse the jury. Necessity and expediency dictate the exception. These opinions, of course, are permitted only concerning subjects in which the average man has considerable experience and knowledge.

The following are examples of matters of common observation in which an opinion may be expressed:

a) Physical properties such as color, weights, size, and visibility.
b) Gross estimates of a person's age.
c) Implications of race, nationality, and language.
d) Emotional states.
e) The apparent physical condition of a person.

f) Intoxication.

g) Speed of vehicles.

2) *Expert Testimony.* An expert is a person skilled in some art, trade, or science to the extent that he possesses information not within the common knowledge of men. Medical doctors, fingerprint specialists, and collectors may be considered experts. The testimony of an expert can be admitted to matters of a technical nature that require interpretation for the purpose of assisting the judge and jury in arriving at a correct conclusion. Expert testimony is not proof, but evidence that can be accorded its own credibility and weight by each member of the court.

a) TESTS OF ADMISSIBILITY. An expert may not testify as such until he has satisfied the court that he has the proper skill, knowledge, and background of experience or education. In other words, he must possess qualifications. He must, moreover, testify concerning a subject on which expert testimony should be received. The facts concerning which he gives an opinion are of such a technical nature that the judge and jury may not be expected to have sufficient knowledge, skill, and understanding of such matters.

b) EXAMPLES OF EXPERT TESTIMONY. Among the innumerable examples of subjects on which expert opinion may be received are the following:

1) Medical matters.

2) The direct movement of a car before a collision based on a study of tracks left by the vehicle.

3) Minimum distance required to bring a vehicle to a stop from certain speeds.

4) Extent of damage to a vehicle.

5) The field of police science, viz., fingerprints, photography, casting, etc.

6) Chemical analysis, e.g., drugs, paint, etc.

7) Serology, i.e., the study of body fluids such as blood and semen.

12. Character and Reputation

As a general rule, testimony concerning a person's character and reputation cannot be introduced for the purpose of raising an inference of guilt. This exclusion is based on the difficulty that the jury may experience in separating the fact that a defendant has a previous record of crime from the question of his guilt in the crime under consideration. The following are among the usual exceptions to this rule:

a. **Character.** The defendant may introduce evidence of his own good character and reputation to show the probability of innocence. Such testimony may either be given by himself or by character references. It should deal with specific character traits such as sobriety and chastity. When such testimony has been introduced, the "door is open" for the prosecutor to introduce evidence concerning those specific areas of character treated in the defendant's testimony. For example, if the defendant introduces testimony concerning his sobriety, the prosecution may produce evidence relating to instances of drunkenness.

b. **Exceptions.** Previous acts of crimes of the accused may be introduced in evidence if they tend to show that the defendant actually committed the crime for which he is being tried. Some examples of this type of testimony are the following:

1) *Modus Operandi.* The prosecution may show that the pattern of previous crime is similar to that of the present crime, i.e., they may show that "this is the way the defendant operates."

2) *Previous acts.* These may be brought in to rebut a defense of *mistake* or *ignorance.* Example: A wife claims that the arsenic in the meal which her husband ate and which caused his death was the result of a mistake. The fact that three previous husbands died of a mixture of arsenic in their meals would be admissible.

3) *Identifying Evidence.* The evidence is admissible if it serves to identify the defendant as the perpetrator of the crime. Example: In a case of burglary, it may be shown that the pistol found at the scene was stolen previously by the defendant. This evidence is specifically designed to show that the pistol was in the possession of the defendant before the crime and not to show guilt of a theft.

4) *Guilty Knowledge or Intent.* An example of this would be a case in which it is shown that the defendant had previously been a fence for stolen goods and hence was aware that the goods in the present case were stolen.

13. Hearsay Evidence Rule

a. **Definition.** Hearsay evidence proceeds not from the personal knowledge of the witness but from mere repetition of what the witness has heard others say. It does not derive its value from the credit of the witness but rests mainly on the veracity or competency of other persons. Example: A witness states, "I know X hit Y because Z told me." Hearsay applies not only to oral statements, but also to written matter. Wherever the matter is quoted or is not within the personal knowledge of the witness, it may be adjudged hearsay.

b. **Exclusion.** Hearsay evidence is excluded for the following reasons:

1) The author of the statement is not present and under oath.

2) No opportunity for cross-examination is afforded the defense.

3) There is no opportunity for the court to observe the author's demeanor.

4) No consideration is given to the defendant's right to confront witnesses against him.

5) There is a possibility of error in the passage of information from one person to another.

c. **Exceptions to the Hearsay Rule.** There are numerous exceptions to the exclusion of hearsay evidence. These exceptions are of sufficient importance and of such common occurrence that they should be treated in detail. It will be noted that the circumstances surrounding the exception tend to greatly minimize the possibility of error or fraud.

1) *Confessions.* (See Chapter 10 for an extended treatment of confessions.) Since a confession is a direct acknowledgment of guilt, it is not likely that a person would voluntarily so commit himself.

2) *Conversations in the Defendant's Presence.* If the defendant is confronted with an accusation of guilt before apprehension and fails to deny it, the circumstances can be offered in evidence.

3) *Dying Declaration.* In a trial for criminal homicide, the dying declaration of the alleged victim concerning the circumstances of the act which induced his dying condition, including the identity of the person who caused his injury, is admissible in evidence to prove such circumstances. The following specific con-

ditions must be fulfilled in order for a dying declaration to be admissible:

a) The evidence must be given in a trial for homicide.

b) The statement must be that of the victim.

c) The statement must concern the circumstances of the act causing his condition, including the identity of the person who caused the injury.

d) The victim must believe he is dying.

e) The victim must in fact have died.

f) The victim must have been competent at the time the statement was made.

4) *Spontaneous Exclamations.* Ordinarily, if a person speaks before he has time to reflect or to fabricate a lie, he will speak the truth. The element of surprise tends to minimize the possibility of design or deliberation.

a) DEFINITION. A *spontaneous exclamation* is an utterance concerning the circumstances of the startling event by an individual in a condition of excitement, shock, or surprise, which warrants the inference that it was spontaneous and not the product of deliberation or design. Such a statement is admissible when made by anyone who heard it. The spontaneous exclamation can be made either in favor of or against the person making it. It can be made by anyone present at the event and not simply by the victim. The term *res gestae* literally means: "things which happened." Thus, testimony concerning spontaneous actions is included in this broader term, but exclamations relate specifically to the hearsay rule.

b) TESTS OF VALIDITY. A spontaneous exclamation must be carefully examined before it is admitted into evidence. The following points should be considered:

1) The statement or action should be close in time to the main act, i.e., it should precede, follow, or be concurrent with the main act very closely in time.

2) The spontaneous character of the statement should be clear so as to preclude the possibility of fabrication or deliberation.

3) The declaration should not have been made in response to a question.

4) The statement should tend to elucidate or explain the character of the act.

5) In general, only a person who committed, participated in, or witnessed the act may be the declarant.

c) FRESH COMPLAINT. In prosecutions for sexual offenses such as rape, carnal knowledge, or sodomy, evidence that the victim made complaint within a short time thereafter is admissible in certain jurisdictions. In fresh complaint only the victim's statement is considered; the statement may relate only to *who* and *what* caused the conditions; the complaint may be made within any reasonable time after the event. These three points differentiate fresh complaint from spontaneous exclamation.

5) *Documentary Evidence.*

a) BEST EVIDENCE. Documents may be introduced in evidence as an exception to the hearsay rule. Their submission is controlled by several rules, the most important of which is the "best evidence" rule. Basically, this rule requires that a person bring into court the best evidence available to him. Thus, whenever possible, the original of a written document should be produced.

b) SECONDARY EVIDENCE. This evidence, which includes copies, carbons, and other duplicates of the original, is not ordinarily admissible. Under the following exceptional circumstances, secondary evidence may be admissible:

1) When the original is lost or destroyed.

2) When it is in the hands of the defendant, who refuses to surrender it.

3) When it is of such official nature that its production in court is not deemed advisable.

4) When there is some other valid reason for which it cannot be produced.

c) OFFICIAL RECORDS. These can be introduced by duly authenticated copies because their maintenance is required by law, regulation, and custom, and they can be attested to by the custodians. It is reasoned that it would disrupt the machinery of government to require the appearance of the recording official at each time the records are required. Moreover, it would be difficult to have the official testify to every record because of distance, death, and changes in office.

d) INVESTIGATOR'S NOTES AND MEMORANDA. Notes covering the period of time when the events in question occurred may be used by the investigator to refresh his memory in testifying. They may be entered into evidence under the conditions described in Chapter 2.

e) FORMER RECORDED TESTIMONY. Under certain conditions former recorded testimony may be introduced. The requirements are as follows: The witness who gave the testimony is not now available and the former trial involved the same or similar defendants in substantially the same issues.

f) DEPOSITION. The testimony of a witness who will be beyond the processing of the court at the time of trial may be formally reduced to writing and is ordinarily admissible. Written interrogatories are submitted by both prosecution and defense and the answers of the witness by both parties may be reduced to writing. The right of cross-interrogation is protected, since both parties may use the deposition. Special requirements are placed on the qualifications of the persons taking the depositions.

g) REGULAR ENTRIES IN THE COURSE OF BUSINESS. It is reasoned that an entry made in the conduct of a regular business is sufficiently credible to make it admissible as evidence. Tests of admissibility must be applied:

1) The entry must have been made at a time close to the occurrence of the fact in issue.

2) The entry must have been made with personal knowledge of the person making the entry or the regularity of the bookkeeping system.

3) The entry must have been made within the usual course of business.

4) The original entry in the book must be offered.

6) *Matters of Pedigree.* Formerly, much of our knowledge relating to matters of death, birth, marriage, and family relationships was based on the knowledge of members of the family. Statements relating to pedigree made by a member of the family circle (including old friends and servants) before the beginning of a controversy in which pedigree arises as a question can be received in evidence when the person making the statement has died.

14. Privileged Communications

Information obtained in certain confidential relationships will ordinarily not be received in evidence. The court considers such information to be privileged communication and in the interest of public policy will refuse to receive evidence by the person whom it benefits. The court may, however, receive this evidence from a person not bound by the privilege. The following are examples of privileged communications:

a. **State Secrets and Police Secrets.**

1) Informants to public officers in the discovery of a crime are privileged.

2) Deliberations of petit and grand juries.

3) Diplomatic correspondence.

4) Official communications, the disclosure of which would be detrimental to public interest.

b. **Personal Privileged Communications.**

1) *Husband and Wife.* Neither can divulge in the trial of either confidential information imparted to each other, unless the consent of both is obtained. The person entitled to the benefit is the spouse who made the communication.

2) *Attorney and Client.* The communication is privileged if it was made while the attorney-client relation existed and in connection with the matter for which the attorney was engaged.

3) *Penitent and Clergyman.* The communication is privileged if made as a formal act of religion or while seeking spiritual advice on a matter of conscience.

4) *Doctor and Patient.* Confidential information given by the defendant to a doctor while he is a patient of the doctor is privileged in a few jurisdictions.

15. Real Evidence and Admissibility

The question of self-incrimination arises in connection with certain types of real evidence. The privilege against self-incrimination is based primarily on the Fifth Amendment to the Constitution: No one shall be compelled to be a witness against himself in a criminal case. This privilege is not limited to the person on trial but extends to any person who may be called as a witness. Ordinarily, the prohibition against compelling a person to give evidence against himself relates only to the use of compulsion in obtaining from him a verbal or other communication in which he expresses his knowledge of a matter. In other words, if the fact involved is a *testimonial utterance,* a compulsory answer involves self-incrimination. If the presentation of the fact does not demand the *intervention of the mind,* it will ordinarily be admissible. The privilege usually does not apply to such physical circumstances as may exist on the defendant's body or about his clothing.

a. **Personal Evidence.** A person may be required to give certain personal evidence. In some jurisdictions, for example, he may be required to try on clothing or shoes, place his feet in impressions; produce a sample of handwriting; and utter words for voice identification. The taking of fingerprints or photographs does not violate the prohibition.

b. **Scientific Tests.** A person may be required to give a sample of blood for group-comparison purposes. He may also be subjected to blood, urine, saliva, and breath tests for the purpose of determining alcoholic content in connection with tests for intoxication. These practices, however, vary with jurisdictions, and reference must be made to local court rulings for guidance.

16. Entrapment

In obtaining evidence of a crime, the investigator must not permit his zeal to involve him in a situation where he becomes the inciting cause of the criminal's commission of a crime. The term *entrapment* is given to an act of a peace officer or agent of the government in inducing a person to commit a crime *not contemplated* by him, for the purpose of instituting a criminal prosecution against him. Entrapping a subject into committing a crime is illegal. The mere act of an officer, however, in furnishing an accused an opportunity to commit a crime where criminal intent was already present in the accused's mind is not entrapment. In entrapment, the officer plants the seed or "puts the idea" into the other's mind. Normally, the danger of entrapment will arise for an investigator only in an undercover assignment. It is against public policy for an officer of the law to incite or participate in the commission of a crime. The undercover investigator must be careful to avoid involvement as an accessory to a crime. He may pretend to fall in with the criminal's plans, but he should never render active assistance in the preparation or commission of the offense. A defense of entrapment may be used where the crime was actually planned and instigated by officers of the law and the accused was lured into its commission by persuasion or fraud. An investigator may, however, employ decoys and supply opportunities to commit crime, as a matter of detective technique. "If the defendant's criminal design originated with him or if he intentionally committed or carried out his own criminal purpose, whether it originated with him or not, at the suggestion of another person, the fact that someone other than the accused facilitated the execution of the scheme or that an officer appeared to cooperate with him will not be a defense."

17. *Corpus Delicti*

It is a general rule that a criminal charge should not be supported unless the *corpus delicti* is established. In its simplest terms this rule states that one must have the essence of the crime before one can have a conviction. The *corpus delicti* or body of the crime consists of all the facts relating to the commission of a particular crime and of the fact that the crime was committed by some human agent. In a charge of criminal homicide, for example, it is necessary to first establish the *corpus delicti,* or actual elements of the offense committed. This will consist of the following facts: That the person alleged to be dead is in fact dead; that he came to his death by violence and under circumstances which preclude the supposition of death by accident or suicide and warranting the conclusion that such death was inflicted by a human agent and leaving the question of who the guilty agent is to after consideration. The following rules relate to the *corpus delicti:*

    a. A confession cannot be used to establish the *corpus delicti.*

    b. Proof of *corpus delicti* must be sustained before there can be a conviction.

c. The *corpus delicti* does not have to be proved beyond a reasonable doubt. It suffices to show substantial corroborative evidence of the existence of an offense.

d. Confessions of co-accuseds may be used to establish *corpus delicti.*

e. Proof of *corpus delicti* can be direct, real, or circumstantial evidence.

f. Negative proof of *corpus delicti* has in some recent cases been permitted. Thus in the offense of arson, it can be shown negatively that the fire was initiated by criminal agency by logically eliminating all natural or accidental causes.

ADDITIONAL READING

Rules of Evidence

Chamelin, N.C. and Evans, K.R.: *Criminal Law for Policemen,* 4th ed., 1987.

Donigan, R.L., et al.: *The Evidence Handbook,* 4th ed. Evanston, Ill.: Traffic Institute, Northwestern University, 1980.

Hanley, J.R. and Schmidt, W.W.: *Legal Aspects of Criminal Evidence.* Berkeley, Calif.: McCutchan, 1977.

Inbau, F.E., Aspen, M.E. and Carrington, F.: *Evidence Law for the Police.* Philadelphia, Chilton Book, 1972.

Kaplan, E.J.: *Evidence: A Law Enforcement Officer's Guide.* Springfield, Ill.: Thomas, 1979.

Klein, T.J.: *Law of Evidence for Police,* 2nd ed. St. Paul, West Publishing, 1978.

Klotter, J.C. and Meier, C.L.: *Criminal Evidence for Police,* 4th ed. Cincinnati, Anderson, 1986.

Klotter, J.C.: *Criminal Evidence,* 5th ed. Cincinnati, Anderson, 1992.

Murphy, D.: Hearsay: The Least Understood Exclusionary Rule. 17 *Journal of Criminal Justice,* 265, 1989.

Pellicciotti, J.M.: *Handbook of Basic Trial Evidence.* Lanham, Md.: University Press of America, 1985.

Schloss, J.D.: *Evidence and Its Legal Aspects.* Columbus, Ohio, Merrill, 1976.

Entrapment

Callahan, M.: Predisposition and the Entrapment Defense. Parts I and II. 53 *FBI Law Enforcement Bulletin,* 8 and 9, 1984.

Entrapment Defense in Narcotics Cases: Guidelines for Law Enforcement. Washington, D.C.: Institute for Law and Justice, 1991.

Hardy, B.A.: The Traps of Entrapment. 3 *American Journal of Criminal Law*, 165, 1975.

Heydon, J.D.: The Problems of Entrapment. 32 *Cambridge Law Journal*, 268, 1973.

Miller, J.D.: The Entrapment Defense. Parts I and II. 42 *FBI Law Enforcement Bulletin*, 2 and 3, 1973.

———: Entrapment. 42 *FBI Law Enforcement Bulletin*, 10, 1973.

Park, R.: The Entrapment Controversy. 60 *Minnesota Law Review*, 163, 1976.

Mathematics and Proof

Fairley, W.B.: Probabilistic Analysis of Identification Evidence. 2 *Journal of Legal Studies*, 493, 1973.

Finklestein, M.O. and Fairley, W.B.: The Continuing Debate over Mathematics in the Law of Evidence. 84 *Harvard Law Review*, 1801, 1971.

Kingston, C.: A Perspective on Probability and Physical Evidence. 34 *Journal of Forensic Sciences*, 6, 1989.

Kingston, C.R.: Application of Probability Theory in Criminalistics. 60 *Journal of the American Statistical Association*, 70, 1965.

Lenth, R.V.: On Identification by Probability. 26 *Journal of the Forensic Science Society*, 197, 1986.

Mode, E.B.: Probability and Criminalistics. 58 *Journal of the American Statistical Association*, 629, 1963.

Van Gelder, D.: An Examination of the Application of Bayes' Theorem to Trace Evidence Evaluation—The Criminalist's Perspective. 11 *Journal of Police Science and Administration*, 377, 1983.

Chapter 28

TESTIMONY IN COURT

1. General

T HE APPEARANCE of the investigator as a witness before a court
of law is the final and most severe test of his efficiency. The
preparation of the case is made with the goal of ultimate presentation before the jury constantly in view. The precautions taken
at the crime scene, the meticulous preservation of the evidence,
the patient gleaning of information from scattered witnesses, the
dogged search for the fugitive, the painstaking interrogation of
the suspects, the preparation of exhibits, the detailed report of
investigation—all of these exhausting and time-consuming stages
of the inquiry culminate in the trial. The probative value of the
accumulated evidence depends in no small degree upon the manner of its presentation to the jury. Finally, the effectiveness of the
evidence is a function of the impression which the investigator
makes as a witness.

Since the reputation of the investigator rests in great part on his
courtroom performance, he should give some heed to the art and
science of behavior on the witness stand. In external demeanor he
should possess dignity and should behave with a decorum conso-
nant with his surroundings. On the witness stand the investigator
represents the agency which employs him. Deficiencies or irregularities in his behavior will reflect upon his organization. Errors of
judgment and misrepresentations, moreover, may unjustly affect
the fate of the defendant and thus defeat the aims of justice.

When the investigator takes the witness stand he is subject to
the most critical censure he will encounter in his career. He is no
longer dealing with the admonitions of a friendly supervisor. He
must contend now with the objective and critical eye of the court

and at times with the outright animosity of defense counsel. Regardless of the proficiency with which the investigation was conducted prior to the trial, a failure in the vital task of testifying on the witness stand may render worthless much of the commendable work he has performed in the case. The court trial is the test which is weighed most heavily by the public and by his organizational supervisors. Although the substance of the investigator's testimony is of paramount importance, an almost equally great significance is attached to his conduct on the stand and to his manner of informing the court of the facts discovered during the course of the case. It is not to be expected that the investigator become a proficient witness in his first appearance in court. He can, however, assist his rapid development in this aspect of his profession by complying with the elementary principles of "witnessmanship."

2. Training in Laws of Evidence and Court Procedure

To become trained and skilled in the work of testifying on the witness stand the investigator should first become thoroughly conversant with the laws of evidence. In this way he can guide his investigation so that evidence relevant to the issues receives primary consideration. Through an understanding of the rules of evidence the investigator will acquire a general knowledge of what is taking place in the courtroom at any given time. He will understand what the prosecution or defense counsel is attempting to achieve by means of a particular tactic. Finally, he will be able to avoid the pitfalls and traps of the unscrupulous cross-examiner.

a. **Rules of Evidence.** A knowledge of the rules of evidence is indispensable to the investigator on the witness stand. He must be able to recognize relevant and material evidence. He should know the rules governing the admissibility of evidence, particularly those relating to hearsay, confessions, and documents. He may testify only to facts whose knowledge he has acquired through his own senses, i.e., he may not give opinions but may testify only to facts that are part of his personal knowledge. If he is asked a question by counsel, the answer to which would in his mind be inadmissible, he should pause for a short space to give opposing counsel an opportunity to object. A knowledge of the laws of evidence will suggest many of these small but important points in the technique of testifying.

b. **Knowledge of Court Procedure.** In addition to knowing the jurisdiction of the various courts, the investigator should have an understanding of the court procedure. The positions occupied by the judge and the other members of the bar should be clear to him. He should understand the functions of the court clerk and the court attendants. A familiarity with the terms and operations of the courts will enable him to understand each step in the trial.

3. Preparation

On the stand the investigator should give the impression of being prepared while at the same time avoiding any parrot-like recital which would imply that he has been rehearsed. In preparation, the investigator should review his notes and endeavor to fix in his mind the highlights of the case. He should refresh his recollection on all important happenings in the events which he intends to relate.

Prior to testifying in a case, the investigator should prepare his testimony in anticipation of logical questions. He should be cognizant of the rules of admissibility and of the evaluation factors that govern the probative value of his evidence. The full history of his association with the evidence should be at his fingertips. A careful study of his notes will refresh his memory and enable him to select the significant parts of the accumulated data of the investigation. He should be so familiar with his case that at all times he is prepared to use his wits to his best advantage, expressing his information upon the issues in a fair, convincing, and forceful manner. He must avoid errors, confusion, and inconsistencies which may lead to a loss of poise and composure and thus undermine the confidence of the jury in his credibility.

Although the investigator is permitted to use his notes in court, he will convey a better impression if he is able to narrate the facts without reference to a memorandum book. If a witness must look up each point in his notebook, his testimony loses force and he becomes ineffective. He must know his case well enough to report all facts without reference to notes except data such as numbers, dates, addresses, and the spelling of names. Thus, his appearance on the stand must be preceded by a conscientious, thoughtful review of the facts and the points with which they are involved. A failure to conduct a review of a case will result in misstatements, omissions of material facts, and even contradictions. This is particularly true of those cases which involve events that occurred some months in the past.

4. On the Witness Stand

On being called as a witness the investigator should step up to the stand and permit himself to be sworn in. In sitting he should assume a comfortable but alert posture. He should identify himself and his membership in his organization. His testimony should then be given *slowly, audibly,* and *distinctly.* The court stenographer should be given an opportunity to hear and record every word. The investigator should address his testimony to the jury and not to counsel or judges.

Ordinarily the investigator is asked to relate a series of incidents that he observed. This recital can be accomplished in simple chronological fashion. Using straightforward language, the witness should describe the observed events in the order in which they took place. The narrative should enable the jury to understand clearly the incidents that occurred.

Since the prosecuting attorney is prevented from asking leading questions, the testimony in which he is particularly interested should be anticipated by the investigator. He should endeavor to place appropriate emphasis on the highlights. The narration of events should be designed to present certain elements of proof.

In giving his testimony, the investigator should present a modest demeanor and should display a sincere interest in accuracy and truth of statement. Bias, prejudice, and antipathy should not color the testimony, since they will affect the court adversely. The investigator must give the appearance of an officer whose interest lies not in the conviction of the accused but in the presentation of the facts of a case.

On assuming his position on the witness stand, the investigator should picture accurately his position in the court. Although he may view himself as an objective collector and retailer of the facts, unbiased and unprejudiced because of his official position and professional experience, others in the court will look upon him as an interested party, ready to accuse a person of a crime on slight suspicion or out of excessive zeal for prosecution. The defense counsel will endeavor to portray him as a police officer who is trying to solve a case by seizing the nearest suspect at hand regardless of the dearth of evidence. Thus, the investigator must not display any extraordinary interest in presenting his testimony. He must play the part of the impartial, conscientious public servant endeavoring in his modest way to achieve the aims of justice. His calm and forthright presentation must be designed to win over the judge and jury to a belief in his honesty and integrity. This effect can be accomplished by following a few simple rules:

a. **Personal Knowledge.** The investigator must tell only what he knows from personal knowledge to be the truth. This is the sole function of the witness. It is in this way that he will assist the court in arriving at a just decision in the case, whether the verdict be a conviction or acquittal. The truth is told not only by an accurate choice of words but also by a careful control of emphasis and tone to avoid exaggeration or underestimation.

b. **The Appearance of Candor.** The professional investigator should train himself to give the impression of telling the truth. (No suggestion of duplicity is intended by this statement.) It is the misfortune of some scrupulously honest souls that their appearance does not convey to their hearers an impression of unquestionable honesty. Nervousness and timidity give them an almost evasive manner. Such a deficiency is almost fatal to the investigator whose professional duties include testimony in court. He must school himself carefully so that poise, lack of timidity, and forthrightness are evidenced in his demeanor.

c. **Courtesy.** An attitude of respect must be maintained at all times. The investigator must not engage in sarcasm, witticisms, or ridicule. Even obviously absurd questions should be answered seriously and temperately.

d. **Direct Answers.** The witness must answer the question asked, i.e., his answers must be responsive. He should listen to the question and gather its exact meaning. If he does not understand it, he should request clarification. If he knows the answer, he should offer it without hesitation. The answer should do no more than reply to the question. It should not express a view of the case, draw a conclusion, or present an argument. Further, it should not gratuitously provide "ammunition" for opposing counsel.

e. **Control.** A witness who becomes angry or otherwise loses control of his emotions is an easy prey to astute counsel. Emotional composure is a paramount virtue in a witness. He must ignore insults, badgering, and innuendoes. He should, in other words, take a professional view of the proceedings. Every effort should be made to avoid the impression of being contentious.

f. **Appearance and Manner.** The witness should speak in natural, unaffected tones. His speech should be clear and sufficiently loud to be heard by all concerned parties. It should be directed to the jury or to the judges as the nature of the court may be. The posture of the witness should be erect and comfortable, since slouching or other appearance of carelessness suggests an indifference to the issues.

5. Expert Testimony

Although the investigator does not hold himself to be an expert witness in the sense of a professional laboratory expert, he will occasionally find himself in a position where he is an expert to a limited degree. There are a number of techniques such as photography and casting which are required in the investigator's profession. In testifying concerning these technical procedures, the investigator should know something of expert testimony.

a. **Expert Testimony.** The expert witness deals in opinion testimony. Ordinarily a witness must state facts and may not express his opinions or conclusions. He may testify to impressions of common experience such as the speed of a vehicle, whether a voice was that of a man, woman, or child, or to a person's state of intoxication. Beyond that he is closely limited. An expert witness is one who possesses a special skill, be it an art, trade, or science, or one who has special knowledge in matters not generally known to men of ordinary education and experience. Possessing this knowledge the expert may express an opinion on a state of facts within his specialty and related to the inquiry. Before he expresses such an opinion, however, it must be established that he is an expert in the specialty.

The testimony of the expert is given in a number of ways. He may, for example, be requested to state his relevant opinion based on his personal observation or from an examination which he has conducted without specifying hypothetically in the question the data upon which his opinion is based. On the other hand he may be asked to express an opinion upon a hypothetical question if the question is based on facts in evidence at the time the question is asked or, at the discretion of the court, on facts later to be received in evidence.

b. **Common Experience.** Treated more simply, expert testimony is a valuable means of arriving at the truth; it consists most commonly of experiments conducted to prove or disprove a fact or statement of the defendant or one of the witnesses. The following are some examples which investigators will frequently encounter:

1) Visibility—the possibility of seeing one place from another.
2) The length of time required to go from one place to another.
3) The distance traveled in going from one place to another.
4) The nature and audibility of a sound.
5) The length of time required for a candle to burn.
6) The results of firing with a given weapon.
7) Whether a particular firearm will give a visible flash with certain ammunition.

c. **Evidence of Experiment.** Facts such as those listed above can be proved by experiments conducted by the investigator. These experiments must be made under substantially the same conditions as those existing at the time of the incident in question.

d. **Professional Experts.** In matters requiring a depth and breadth of technical knowledge, the investigator should have recourse to the professional expert. The success of the case is jeopardized if a person of limited knowledge or experience endeavors to give an opinion that is within the realm of the scientific criminologist or other expert. For example, questions relating to microscopy, biology, handwriting, or fingerprint identification should be resolved only by experts. The investigator can assist the expert by acquiring an understanding of the scope and limitations of the expert's scientific knowledge. He should know what can be fairly expected of science and what lies out of the realm of possibility in the expert's field. Thus he will understand the methods of collecting and preserving evidence and of properly transmitting them to the expert so that their full probative value can be realized.

e. **Expert Investigative Techniques.** In relation to the professional techniques in which the investigator, himself, can be considered an expert, he should be able to show on the witness stand that he possesses the necessary training, experience, and knowledge of the literature. Photography, casting, and the development of latent fingerprints are the subjects most commonly mastered by investigators. Before testifying concerning these matters the investigator should review some standard work on the particular technique which was employed in acquiring the evidence. He should inform the prosecutor of his qualifications and, in particular, of instances where he has previously testified in similar matters.

ADDITIONAL READING

Courtroom Testimony

Anderson, P.R. and Winfree, L.T., Jr. (Eds.): *Expert Witnesses: Criminologists in the Courtroom.* Albany, State University of New York Press, 1987.

Bratton, W.J. and Esserman, D.M.: Post-Arrest Training. 60 *FBI Law Enforcement Bulletin,* 11, 1991.

Burke, J.J.: Testifying in Court. 44 *FBI Law Enforcement Bulletin,* 9, 1975.

McDonald, W.F. (Ed.): *The Defense Counsel.* Beverly Hills, Calif.: Sage, 1983.

Mogil, B.M.: Maximizing Your Courtroom Testimony. 58 *FBI Law Enforcement Bulletin,* 5, 1989.

Petersen, R.D.: *The Police Officer in Court.* Springfield, Ill.: Thomas, 1974.

Reynolds, D.W.: *The Truth, the Whole Truth, and Nothing But . . . A Police Officer's Guide to Testifying in Court.* Springfield, Ill.: Thomas, 1990.

Rutledge, D.: *Courtroom Survival: The Officer's Guide to Better Testimony.* Costa Mesa, Calif.: Custom Publishing, 1984.

Tierney, K.: *Courtroom Testimony: A Policeman's Guide.* New York, Funk & Wagnalls, 1970.
Whitaker, M.W.: *The Police Witness: Effectiveness in the Courtroom.* Springfield, Ill.: Thomas, 1985.

PART VI
IDENTIFICATION
AND REPRODUCTION

Chapter 29

OBSERVATION AND DESCRIPTION

I. OBSERVATION

1. Gathering Information

IN THE ACQUISITION of information the investigator relies mainly on indirect sources, such as the accounts of witnesses, the reports of investigation prepared by associates, photographs, sketches, and the reports of laboratory experts. There are occasions, however, when he must rely on the reports of his own senses. In a surveillance, for example, the appearance of the subject and the persons whom he contacts must be recorded in the investigator's mind. At the scene of a crime, although the assistance of the camera and the sketcher is available, the investigator must ultimately rely on his own observations for a comprehensive and truly significant representation. The accuracy of his observations will depend chiefly upon his training and experience. Their usefulness, however, will often depend on his ability to communicate their purport to others, either orally or in a report. In other words, he must be trained to describe as well as to observe.

2. The Senses in Observation

In recording the data of a scene or occurrence the investigator must employ his senses, primarily that of sight and secondarily hearing, smell, touch, and taste. The eye is the most fruitful source of information, but in the absence of training it is also one of the most unreliable because of the tendency of the observer to fill in the gaps that inadequate observation may leave. Hearing is the most objective sense; nevertheless the observation of a sound is subject to such errors as mistaken estimates of distance and illogical comparisons. The sense of touch is usually unreliable because of the inexperience of most persons in the accurate use of this sense. Smell, the olfactory sense, is considered relatively unreliable because of its susceptibility to suggestion. The sense of taste suffers from the same defect. It has been estimated by psychologists that approximately 85 percent of our sensual knowledge is gained through the medium of sight; 13 percent through hearing; and the remaining 2 percent through smell, touch, and taste. The reliability of the information obtained through the senses may be considered to be in the same relation.

3. Psychological Elements

For the purposes of the investigator the process of observation can be divided into three stages—attention, perception, and report.

a. **Attention.** The psychological process of being brought into the presence of a fact is called *attention.* The observer cannot observe a phenomenon until he is aware of it. A convenient division of attention consists of three phases, namely, involuntary, voluntary, and habitual. Each of these phases is influenced by such factors as size, change, interest, physical condition, suggestion, and repetition.

b. **Perception.** Recognition of the significance of a phenomenon is termed *perception.* In this stage the observer not only *apprehends* a phenomenon but also *understands* it. In understanding the fact to which attention has been drawn the following factors are contributory:

1) *Intelligence.* The mental capacity of the observer is an obvious factor.

2) *Educational Background.* Observation depends upon reference. The educated person is at an obvious advantage in being able to refer observed phenomena to matters which he has learned.

3) *Experience and Occupation.* These elements constitute a frame of reference for the observer.

c. **Report.** The third element of observation is the identification of a fact, i.e., the subject identifies, names, or otherwise subconsciously becomes aware of the significance of a fact.

II. PHYSICAL DESCRIPTIONS

4. Description of Persons

The ability to describe persons accurately has traditionally been highly prized in the investigative profession. Before the advent of fingerprint classification physical descriptions were considered to be the basis of identification files. Alphonse Bertillon (1853–1914), an employee of the Paris police department, recognized the importance of standardizing physical identification. He developed a system of classification based on body measurements. As the director of the newly founded Bureau of Identification (1882), he refined the art of describing a person in custody to a procedure consisting of a series of measurements of various physical features. This system was accorded the impressive title of anthropometry or *bertillonage.*

During this period, great stress was placed on the ability to describe persons after a short period of visual observation. Again, Bertillon introduced method and precision into this endeavor. He called his systematic procedure for such a verbal description the *portrait parlé,* a term that is still in general use at the present time. Although the talent for verbal description has lost much of its former emphasis among modern investigators, the logic that underlay this nineteenth century development remains undiminished in its validity for purposes of criminal inquiries.

5. General Information

To fully identify a person, the following background data should be obtained:

a. **Name, Aliases, and Nicknames.** The full name should be obtained and not merely the initials. The varied spellings of the different aliases should be included.

b. **Social Security Number.**

c. **Military Serial Number.**

d. **Fingerprint Classification.**

e. **Present and Former Addresses.**

f. **National Origins.** An exceptionally useful item in a description is the national origin of the person. Thus, Irish-American or Italian-American are more descriptive terms than those used to list the facial characteristics.

g. **Scars and Marks.** Cicatrices, birthmarks, and tattoos are valuable identification points. Both visible (normally dressed) and invisible scars and marks should be reported where known.

h. **Physical Traits.** Significant physical habits are important.

1) *Walk.* The manner of walk is highly individual. Such terms as the following are commonly used: athletic, limping, shuffling, bowlegged, flatfooted, and pigeon-toed.

2) *Voice.* The voice may be high- or low-pitched; loud or soft; or, more typically, it may lie between these extremes.

3) *Speech.* The most obvious trait of speech is the local characteristic of enunciation, viz., southern, midwestern, New York, Boston, etc. Foreign speech should be associated with the country of origin. "Educated" and "uneducated" speech can sometimes be discriminated.

i. **Personal Habits.** Despite any efforts at disguise, the personal habits that characterize an individual are seldom changed.

1) *Dress.* The standard of dress is usually maintained by a well-dressed fugitive as a matter of personal pride, whereas the person used to slovenly attire will remain in that condition out of ignorance or inertia. Tendencies toward sport clothes or loud dress will be retained. Slovenly, neat, expensive, cheap, or conservative are a few of the adjectives that may be employed.

2) *Other Habits.* A number of other personal habits are found useful in identification. A propensity for frequenting bars, theaters, bowling alleys, and other forms of entertainment; a "weakness" for women or other forms of sex diversion; an addiction to narcotics; a desire to engage actively in sports such as fishing or bowling— any of these habits can serve to provide a line of inquiry or search for a wanted person.

j. **Relatives and Associates.** The names, addresses, and occupations of relatives, friends, associates, and acquaintances should be listed.

k. **History.** This should include his education, military history, criminal record, and professional or occupational background.

6. Physical Description

The verbal description or *portrait parlé* is still considered a reliable aid in the field of identification. The degree to which the investigator can place detail in such a description will depend on his training and natural gifts in this direction. The following items are basic in a verbal description.

a. **General Impression.** Type; personality; apparent social status; comparison by name with an actor, political figure, or other well-known person.

b. **Age and Sex.**

c. **Race or Color.**

d. **Height**, estimated within 2 inches.

e. **Weight**, estimated within 5 pounds.

f. **Build.** Thin, slender, medium, and stout.

g. **Posture.** Erect, slouching, round-shouldered.

h. **Head.** Size, whether small, medium, or large; and shape, whether round, long, dome-shaped, flat on top, or bulging in the back.

i. **Hair.** Color; sheen; part; straight or curly; and area of baldness.

j. **Face.** General impression, followed by a description of the features.

1) *Forehead.* High, low, bulging, or receding.

2) *Eyebrows.* Bushy or thin; shape.

3) *Mustache.* Length; color; shape.

4) *Eyes.* Small, medium, or large; color; clear, dull, bloodshot; separation; glasses.

5) *Ears.* Size; shape; size of lobe; angle of set.

6) *Cheeks.* High, low, or prominent cheekbones; fat, sunken or medium.

7) *Nose.* Short, medium, big, or long; straight, aquiline, or flat; hooked or pug.

8) *Mouth.* Wide, small, or medium; general expression.

9) *Lips.* Shape; thickness; color.

10) *Teeth.* Shade; condition; defects; missing elements.

11) *Chin.* Size; shape; general impression.

12) *Jaw.* Length; shape; lean, heavy, or medium.

k. **Neck.** Shape; thickness; length; Adam's apple.

l. **Shoulder.** Width and shape.

m. **Waist.** Size; shape of stomach.

n. **Hands.** Length; size; hair; condition of palms.

o. **Fingers.** Length; thickness; stains; shape of nails; condition of nails.

p. **Arms.** Long, medium, or short; muscular, normal or thin; thickness of wrist.

q. **Feet.** Size; deformities.

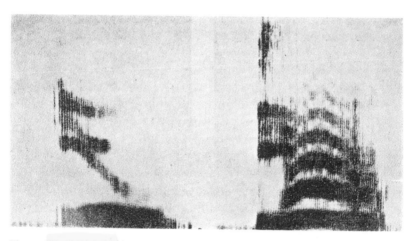

Figure 23. *Voiceprints* are visual representations of characteristics of the human voice that permit identification by comparison. The spoken word "you," for example, can be recorded to provide "spectrograms" such as these, in which an expert can find an adequate base of similarities and differences for a definite opinion as to the identity of the speaker.

7. Voice Identification

The recognition of a human voice is a common experience. Picking up a telephone we may recognize immediately, from the sound of a few words, the voice of a person whom we have not seen for months or even years. Although we may attribute this ability to recognize an individual voice to some special capacity of perception and memory, there is an implicit acknowledgment of the fact that voices are distinctive—that each individual can be uniquely associated with his voice and that the sounds emitted in human speech possess characteristics, such as pitch, intensity, and "quality," which impose a unique pattern upon the human ear.

The investigator, however, is interested not so much in recognizing a human voice as in the problem of proving for court purposes the identity of the voice with relation to its owner. The need for this form of proof can arise in a variety of ways. For example, the identity of the speakers in a taped recording of a conversation during which no names are mentioned can be essential to the prosecution of a conspiracy case. Similarly, the identity of a person accused of telephoning bomb threats can be established from a study of recordings of the voice in question. Voice identification would prove valuable also in kidnapping and extortion cases.

A solution to the problem of objective proof of voice identification has been offered in the form of an electronic recording of the energy output of the subject's voice in producing a specified word (specified for purposes of comparison). The result is a sound "spectrogram" that can be used for comparison purposes. Whenever the person says the word—"you," for example—regardless of pitch, volume, or attempt to disguise his voice, the "spectrogram" or "voiceprint" will be substantially the same.

The consistency is said to arise out of the fact that voice quality is determined by the physical characteristics of the vocal cavities (in the throat, the nasal system, and the mouth) and by the structure and use of more than half a dozen "vocal muscles" such as the lips, the jaw, and the tongue. Since speaking is a randomly learned process, in which the infant tries thousands of vocal combinations before coming up with his own, the end product is a unique voice. The factors used in voiceprint identification are those which are not under speaker's conscious control. Thus, the identification ignores loudness, rapidity of speech, and pitch, since these can be controlled consciously. Even the use of a different language does not affect the identification.

The usefulness of voiceprints can be seen in the following 1970 case of the St. Paul Police Department. Shortly after midnight an anonymous telephone call was received at headquarters, requesting aid for a woman about to give birth. A two-man patrol car arrived at the given address to find only a darkened house. While one patrolman went around to the back door, a sniper opened fire from across the street, fatally wounding the other patrolman. The shooting appeared to be a senseless attack on police in general. The only clue was a taped recording of the telephone call. The investigation sought to identify the voice by interviewing thirteen neighborhood women and recording their voices. As a result of voiceprint analyses, Caroline Trimble, 18, was arrested and later indicted for murder.

Two earlier cases involving voiceprints came before courts in New Jersey (1967) and California (1968), and both times the appeals courts rejected the method as unreliable. In another 1967 case, a voiceprint identification in a grand jury investigation of police corruption was later admitted to be an error. The subject of the voice comparison, a deputy inspector of police, was identified as the owner of a voice recorded in a telephone conversation with a known gambler. The identification, made in 1967, was acknowledged to be an error in 1971 only after the police official, through his own investigative efforts, had found and produced the true owner of the recorded voice.

At this stage in the development of voice identification great care must be exercised in view of the technical uncertainties and the substantial lack of agreement among speech scientists. The method is ill served by excessive claims with respect to specificity and infallibility. Even though a method falls short of 100 percent reliability, it can still be quite useful to the courts and the police provided the users are aware of present limitations. The actual physical mechanism of voice production is still a dark area of science. The investigator should not be misled by nomenclature such as "voiceprints" and "voice spectrograms" with their implied analogies of fingerprints and spectrography into attributing a comparable degree of scientific reliability to voice identification. He should be aware of the inherent limitations in the method and in the performance of the examiners.

8. Lost or Stolen Property

One of the most effective methods of recovering lost or stolen property is the employment of a central index of articles which have been reported lost, stolen, pawned, or sold at second hand. Many thieves lack the imagination or underworld associations which would enable them to dispose of the property with a reasonable gain and relative safety. Ordinarily they resort to a haphazard sale of the stolen goods and run the risk of detection. The usual modes of disposal of the property are sales to pawnbrokers, secondhand dealers, innocent friends, strangers, or fences.

9. Lost Property Files

Whichever of these channels of disposal is employed, there exists the likelihood that the stolen object will eventually find its way to a pawn shop or a secondhand dealer. In most cities it is required that pawn shops and secondhand dealers daily report the pawning or purchase of certain types of property on official police department forms. These forms are then filed at the central office. A detective investigating a larceny can readily check on property by merely communicating with the lost property office. The following files are usually maintained: lost property; stolen property; property pledged at pawn shops; and property sold in secondhand stores. In one scheme of reporting, these four types of reports are filed together. This system theoretically eliminates the possibility of an object being reported in groups 3 and 4 without the knowledge of the staff. If these are maintained separately, it is possible through carelessness that an object may be reported pawned and not be checked in the stolen property file. The mingling of reports 1 and 2 is logical, since an object which is thought to have been lost may have actually been stolen through a clever larceny.

10. Description of Property

Property is primarily filed according to classification of article, e.g., watches, automobiles, fur. Thus, one set of file cases will be devoted to watches alone, another to automobiles, and so forth.

Certain types of property can be readily subclassified according to serial number. Watches, automobiles, typewriters, and cameras, for example, usually bear a stamped serial number. Unfortunately, many owners (and even dealers) keep no record of these numbers. Where they exist, however, they should determine the system of filing. In describing property the following basic data should be included:

    a. *Kind* of article (e.g., watch or camera).

    b. *Physical appearance* (model, size, shape and condition).

    c. *Material* of which it's composed (the more expensive substance, such as gold or silver, should be mentioned where it is applicable).

    d. *Brand name.*

    e. *Number* of articles or weight.

    f. *Identifying marks* such as serial numbers or personal inscriptions.

11. Examples

Listed below are examples of some of the more common types of stolen property, together with the more important identifying characteristic:

    a. **Automobiles.** License, "VIN" number, make, model, color.

    b. **Watches.** Case number, movement number, make, model, metal, inscriptions, setting.

    c. **Jewelry.** Kind; style; metal; setting; kind and number of stones. Rings should be classified according to type: engagement, wedding, cocktail, etc. If no initials or inscriptions are present, the number and kind of stones is the determining factor in filing at the Lost Property Unit. Matching with pawned or purchased property is possible only if the accurate number and size of stones are given. The shape and cut of the stones should also be given.

    d. **Fur.** Kind of fur; style; manufacture. (Fur coats can be filed according to manufacturer.)

    e. **Cameras.** Kind, manufacturer, model, number; kind of lens including lens focal length, f/number, and serial number.

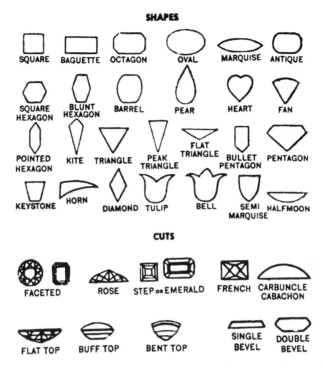

Figure 24. The identification of jewelry is one of the most effective clues in a burglary investigation. Shown above are the various shapes and cuts of stones, together with the terms used in their description.

12. Personal Marking

To facilitate property recovery in the event of theft, a number of police departments are encouraging citizens to engrave their Social Security numbers on their valuables and register them with the police. By means of an electric needle-tipped device the citizen *tattoos* his number on his bicycle, television set, silverware, camera, and jewelry. A record of the numbered article is then registered with the police department's Lost Property Unit. If an item is subsequently stolen and later recovered in a pawnshop or with a secondhand dealer, the department's computer can match the article with the owner in a matter of minutes. Ordinarily the police must check their lists of stolen property or go through a manufacturer's list of serial numbers in a time-consuming procedure that may require several weeks to trace the owner of recovered property. The scheme is especially useful in discouraging bicycle thefts, since a policeman can check a numbered bike with the cyclist's Social Security card in the space of a minute.

III. MODUS OPERANDI

13. Basis of Method of Operation

The criminal aspires to the status of a professional man, trained by experience and instruction in the most effective techniques of his occupation. He is, of course, limited or enhanced by his mental and physical capabilities and influenced by such factors as his fugitive status or the availability of a "fence." Ordinarily he judges the value of his methods solely on the basis of successful accomplishment. Having achieved a few minor successes he is loath to alter his operational procedure, his reluctance stemming from superstition, lack of imagination, and inertia. A summary of the habits, techniques, and peculiarities of behavior is often referred to as the *modus operandi* or MO, a term which means no more than *method of operation.*

14. Purpose

Large law enforcement agencies maintain MO Files to enable their investigators to recognize a pattern of criminal behavior, to associate a group of crimes with a single perpetrator, to enable them to predict, approximately, the next target of the criminal, and to assist complainants, eyewitnesses, and investigators to recognize the perpetrator by means of the recorded information concerning the characteristics of his criminal activity. It has been found that the MO File is most effective in crimes involving personal contact, such as felonies against the person, confidence games, and forgery. Apparently the physical description, mannerisms, and speech of the criminal are important elements in the effectiveness of such a file.

15. Organization

The traditional MO arrangement devised by Atcherley has been found to be still effective eighty years after its inception. In the Atcherley system the following were considered the significant elements in the detection of offenders:

a. **Property.** The nature of the stolen property provides an excellent clue in crimes which involve a larceny.

b. **Description.** If the criminal was observed, a verbal description is usually the most important clue to the identity of the perpetrator.

c. **Observations at the Scene.** The data of the senses are important since they may result in a useful pattern. Thus the objects and substances seen, heard, smelled, tasted, or felt will contribute to the complete picture.

d. **Motive.** In addition to the acquisition of property there are many other criminal motives. Thus, in murder, rape, or assault, in general, a pattern of behavior may be discerned in the course of a series of crimes. This observation is particularly true with regard to the crimes accomplished by the psychopath.

e. **Time.** The time at which the crime was committed is an important element in the pattern. Naturally, since the exact moment of occurrence cannot be readily established in many cases, the investigator must endeavor to establish the time of occurrence between determinable limits.

f. **Peculiarities.** From evidence, weaknesses of character will ordinarily reveal themselves in the uninhibited surroundings of the crime. Peculiarities such as partaking of the victim's liquor, psychopathic defecation, and theft of inconsequential items such as ties or cuff links are particularly significant.

g. **Observed Peculiarities.** An observer of the offense may be able to supply valuable clues in the form of personal idiosyncracies. Speech is one of the most important clues. Enunciation, dialect, and diction can be closely described.

IV. PERSONALITY PROFILE

16. Criminal Profiling

a. **Method.** The manner in which an activity is performed expresses the psychological make-up of the person performing it. Criminal activity is no exception. Thus a knowledge of the habits and personality traits of people who have committed crimes can be used to develop personality and behavioral descriptions of the typical offender.

If, in examining the circumstances of a crime, the investigator can determine that the criminal's behavior is consistent with a typical pattern, he will be able to screen possible suspects. Those who do not fit the description of the type of person who commits a crime in this manner can be safely eliminated for consideration as suspects.

From a study of the behavioral traits of people who have committed the same offense, a knowledge of the typical offender emerges. When this knowledge is combined with a study of the details of the crime under consideration, a description of the personality and behavioral traits of the perpetrator can be developed. This technique is called criminal profiling.

b. **Factors Considered.** The details of the crime that are considered include:

1) The activities of the criminal as evidenced by the arrangement and disposition of materials at the crime scene.

2) The description of the criminal act by witnesses.

3) The background and activities of the victim.

4) Any other detail of the crime that could express the personality of the perpetrator, such as the type and condition of the getaway car.

c. **Types of Crimes.** Most crimes do not lend themselves to personality profiling. Crimes in which there is minimal contact with the crime scene and the victim are usually not conducive to profiling. Robberies and thefts usually fit into this category. Crimes in which the act itself does not indicate a psychological disorder, such as burglary, are ordinarily not suitable for this technique. In these cases, little of the personality of the offender can be determined from the crime scene and the motivation, greed, is too common to be of much help to the investigator.

Crimes that are suitable for criminal profiling are those in which there is much evidence at the crime scene or considerable interaction with the victim wherein the offender displays severe mental disturbance. Sexual homicide, pyromania, and mutilation fit this description. Ritualistic crimes, torture, and murders involving post-mortem disfigurement are especially conducive to this kind of analysis because they are committed by criminals with pronounced psychological disorders. People exhibiting the behavioral characteristics associated with these crimes are extremely rare. Thus a personality profile of the typical offender would be useful in eliminating potential suspects.

d. **FBI Criminal Profiling Program.** The FBI's Behavioral Science Unit offers assistance in profiling to all official law enforcement agencies. Each of the FBI's fifty-nine field offices have criminal profile coordinators to review the cases presented to them to determine if they are suitable for profiling and to provide preliminary investigative advice. If the case warrants it, the coordinator will draw up a preliminary profile and submit it to the Behavioral Science Unit at the FBI Academy. After the profile is reviewed, it is then supplied to the requesting agency.

e. **Psycholinguistic Analysis.** Anonymous letter writers and telephone callers who threaten violence can be profiled by a psycholinguistic analysis of the contents of their messages. Psycholinguistic refers to the characteristic of all communication that it expresses not only its primary message but also the personality, background and frame of mind of the communicator. Word usage is catalogued by computer and then compared with ordinary speech or writing to determine any linguistic patterns. Investigators can use this analysis to determine whether the messages are originating from the same person. It also provides information about the author's personality and educational background.

f. **Example.** The FBI interviewed thirty-six convicted sexual murderers and studied their crime scenes and their behavior during the crime. From this information, they were able to classify sexual murder into two types, "organized" and "disorganized", and to develop the following charts:

**Crime Scene Differences Between Organized
and Disorganized Murderers**

Organized	*Disorganized*
Planned offense	Spontaneous offense
Victim a targeted stranger	Victim/location known
Personalizes victim	Depersonalizes victim
Controlled conversation	Minimal conversation
Crime scene reflects overall control	Crime scene random and sloppy
Demands submissive victim	Sudden violence to victim
Restraints used	Minimal use of restraints
Aggressive acts prior to death	Sexual acts after death
Body hidden	Body left in view
Weapon/evidence absent	Evidence/weapon often present
Transports victim or body	Body left at death scene

Profile Characteristics of Organized and Disorganized Murderers

Organized	*Disorganized*
Average to above-average intelligence	Below-average intelligence
Socially competent	Socially inadequate
Skilled work preferred	Unskilled work
Sexually competent	Sexually incompetent
High birth order status	Low birth order status
Father's work stable	Father's work unstable
Inconsistent childhood discipline	Harsh discipline as child
Controlled mood during crime	Anxious mood during crime
Use of alcohol with crime	Minimal use of alcohol
Precipitating situational stress	Minimal situational stress
Living with partner	Living alone
Mobility with car in good condition	Lives/works near crime scene
Follows crime in news media	Minimal interest in news media
May change jobs or leave town	Significant behavior change (drug/ alcohol abuse, religiosity, etc.)

Source: 54 *FBI Law Enforcement Bulletin,* 8, 1985.

An "organized" sexual homicide crime scene indicates that a possible suspect should display some of the profile characteristics of the organized murderer. If an investigator can determine that the crime scene is either "organized" or "disorganized", he will have some indication of the character traits of the assailant.

V. EXPERT SYSTEMS

17. Artificial Intelligence

When an investigator retires, his organization loses some invaluable assets, namely, his knowledge and experience. However, through the means of an "expert system" or "artificial intelligence," as it is often called, this knowledge and experience can be preserved and put to use. An expert system is a computer program that is designed to solve problems by simulating human intelligence. A detective who is considered to be an expert in a particular type of crime, such as burglary or robbery, is asked to contribute the most useful information he has acquired over the course of his career. This information is formulated into rules that simulate the process of deductive reasoning. The rules take the form of "if . . . then" statements. For example, if the medicine chest at a burglary was rifled through, then the suspect probably has a history of drug abuse. If no fingerprints have been found at the crime scene of a burglary, then there is a possibility that the burglar wore gloves. The knowledge of other detectives can be added to the expert system and the system itself can be constantly revised as new information or techniques emerge. The study of an expert system is an excellent training method for future detectives.

The Baltimore County Police Department has a fully operational expert system to combat burglary. The Residential Burglary Reporting System (REBES) is designed to identify possible burglary suspects from clues left at the crime scene using a system of rules developed from the expertise of their detectives. This expert system combines three elements:

a. The details of the criminal histories of more than 600 burglary offenders that are recorded on data-coded forms and stored in the computer. This information will include physical and psychological characteristics as well as all the information found in a traditional *modus operandi* file.

b. The clues found at the crime scene which are entered on data-coded forms.

c. A collection of approximately 110 "if . . . then" rules that are applied to the clues left at the crime scene.

By applying the "if ... then" rules to the crime scene data an indication of the *modus operandi* is developed. This information is then matched with the criminal histories of the past offenders and a list of possible suspects will be produced. They will be listed in the order in which the suspect's record matches both the crime scene data and the rule-based inferences from this data. The purpose of the REBES program is to inform investigators of possible suspects. Similar systems have been developed for robbery, sex offenses, and other violent crimes.

ADDITIONAL READING

Observation and Description

Basinger, L.F.: *The Techniques of Observation and Learning Retention: A Handbook for Policeman and Lawyer.* Springfield, Ill.: Thomas, 1988.

Davies, H.M., Ellis, H.D. and Shepherd, J.W. (Eds.): *Perceiving and Remembering Faces.* London, Academic Press, 1981.

McGuire, M.V. and Walsh, M.E.: *The Identification and Recovery of Stolen Property Using Automated Information Systems: An Investigator's Handbook.* Washington, D.C.: U.S. Government Printing Office, 1981.

Nash, D.J.: *Individual Identification and the Law Enforcement Officer.* Springfield, Ill.: Thomas, 1978.

Penry, J.: *Looking at Faces and Remembering Them. A Guide to Facial Identification.* London, Elek Books, 1971.

Rogers, S.L.: *The Personal Identification of Living Individuals.* Springfield, Ill.: Thomas, 1986.

Starrett, P. and Keegan, J.M.: *Police Identification Guide.* Palo Alto, Calif.: Starrett Publishing, 1983.

Zavala, A. and Paley, J.J. (Eds.): *Personal Appearance Identification.* Springfield, Ill.: Thomas, 1972.

Criminal Profiling

Bradway, W.C.: Crime Scene Behavioral Analysis. 38 *Law and Order,* 9, 1990.

Crime Scene and Profile Characteristics of Organized and Disorganized Murderers. 54 *FBI Law Enforcement Bulletin,* 8, 1985.

Douglas, J.E. and Burgess, A.E.: Criminal Profiling: A Viable Investigative Tool Against Violent Crime. 55 *FBI Law Enforcement Bulletin,* 12, 1986.

Douglas, J.E. and Munn, C.: Violent Crime Scene Analysis: *Modus Operandi, Signature, and Staging.* 61 *FBI Law Enforcement Bulletin,* 2, 1992.

Holmes, R.M.: *Profiling Violent Crimes: An Investigative Tool.* Newbury Park, Calif.: Sage, 1989.

Lesce, T.: Computer-Assisted Profiling: Help for Small Departments. 37 *Law and Order,* 7, 1989.

Pinizotto, A.J.: Forensic Psychology: Criminal Personality Profiling. 12 *Journal of Police Science and Administration,* 32, 1984.

Voice Identification

Albrecht, S.: *Catching Crooks with Voiceprints.* 35 *Law and Order,* 7, 1987.

Bloch, E.: *Voiceprinting.* New York, David McKay, 1975.

The Evidentiary Value of Spectrographic Voice Identification. 63 *Journal of Criminal Law, Criminology and Police Science,* 349, 1972.

Greene, H.F.: Voiceprint Identification: The Case in Favor of Admissibility. 13 *American Criminal Law Review,* 171, 1975.

Hollien, H.: *The Acoustics of Crime: The New Science of Forensic Phonetics.* New York, Plenum Press, 1990.

Jones, W.R.: Evidence Vel Non: The Non Sense of Voiceprint Identification. 62 *Kentucky Law Journal,* 301, 1973–1974.

Kersta, L.G.: Voiceprint Identification. 3 *Police Law Quarterly,* 3, 1974.

Koenig, B.E.: Speaker Identification (Part 1) Three Methods—Listening, Machine, and Aural-Visual. (Part 2) Results of the National Academy of Sciences' Study. 49 *FBI Law Enforcement Bulletin,* 1 and 2, 1980.

On the Theory and Practice of Voice Identification. Washington, D.C.: National Academy of Sciences, 1979.

Tosi, O. and Nash, E.: Voiceprint Identification Rules for Evidence. 9 *Trial,* 1, 1973.

Tosi, O.: *Voice Identification: Theory and Legal Applications.* Baltimore, University Park Press, 1979.

Voice Identification Research. Washington, D.C.: U.S. Government Printing Office, 1972.

Voiceprint Identification: The Trend Towards Admissibility. 9 *New England Law Review,* 419, 1974.

Voiceprint Technique: How Reliable is Reliable? 63 *Illinois Bar Journal,* 260, 1975.

Artificial Intelligence and Expert Systems

Bayse, W.A. and Morris, C.G.: Automated Systems' Reasoning Capabilities: A Boon to Law Enforcement. 57 *Police Chief,* 6, 1990.

Cameron, J.: Artificial Intelligence: Expert Systems, Microcomputers and Law Enforcement. 36 *Law and Order,* 3, 1988.

Kingston, C.: Expert Systems in Forensic Science. 35 *Journal of Forensic Sciences,* 1404, 1990.

Ratledge, E.C. and Jacoby, J.E.: *Handbook on Artificial Intelligence and Expert Systems in Law Enforcement.* Westport, Conn.: Greenwood Press, 1989.
Reboussin, R. and Cameron, J.: Expert Systems for Law Enforcement. 58 *FBI Law Enforcement Bulletin,* 8, 1989.

Chapter 30

IDENTIFICATION BY WITNESSES

1. Difficulties

THE TYPICAL witness is a layman unskilled in the techniques of investigation and unaware of the special terminology that is used in the *portrait parlé*. In addition, he is not a trained observer. As a consequence, when he is asked to describe a wanted criminal he offers a confusing set of generalities from which it is difficult for the investigator to form a definite picture or even to establish one useful peculiarity. The investigator obviously must assist the witness in describing the criminal, but he must avoid the introduction of errors that may result from suggesting characteristics to an impressionable witness.

2. Identifying Wanted Criminals

The aim of the investigator in questioning a witness concerning the appearance of a fugitive from justice is to obtain a complete verbal description and, with the aid of an artist, a pictorial representation. Two cases are distinguished: the known fugitive and the unknown criminal who was observed by the witness.

a. **Known Fugitives.** The known fugitive belongs to a definite neighborhood. Police records and even photographs may exist. A limited background investigation including a local agency check will develop the desired information. Relatives and other friends can offer a description. Emphasis should be placed on peculiarities and defects. Social acquaintances and barroom companions are more likely to stress odd characteristics and peculiarities of dress. By obtaining copies of all available photographs and by gathering a number of verbal descriptions, it is quite possible to

691

acquire an excellent pictorial and verbal representation of the fugitive.

b. **Unknown Criminal Observed by Witness.** The problem of identifying the unknown criminal by means of an eyewitness must be approached with special caution by the investigator. The fallibility of eyewitness identification was made clear in 1932 with the publication of E. M. Borchard's book, *Convicting the Innocent.* Documenting sixty-five cases of innocent persons who had been convicted of crimes, Borchard showed that twenty-nine were victims of mistaken identity. In one case identification had been made by seventeen witnesses, and later the real offender was found to bear little resemblance to the falsely accused. Convictions are still being obtained on erroneous identifications. One of the more famous cases involved Campbell, a respectable stockbroker, who was identified as a wanted forger by several eyewitnesses. The main point in the identification was his mustache; a minor point was the fact that he used green ink. After Campbell had served a good part of his jail term, the true forger was apprehended and confessed to a series of crimes which included the Campbell offense. The real forger also wore a mustache and used green ink.

3. Identifying Methods

Three methods may be recommended for identifying an unknown criminal by a witness.

a. **The Verbal Description.** The *portrait parlé* may be used. Its inadequacies have been described, and the investigator should judge its worth by the capacity of the witness to describe persons known to the investigator. The description of the known person can serve as a control in judging the reliability of the description of the unknown criminal.

b. **Photographic Files (Rogues' Gallery).** The witness may be taken to the headquarters of the law enforcement agency and requested to examine the photographs in the Known Criminals' File. The *modus operandi* of the crime under investigation should suggest a group of photographs for viewing by the witness. It should be brought explicitly to the attention of the witness that the wanted criminal's photograph may not be contained in the file. The witness should also be instructed to call the investigator's attention to any strong similarity in the photograph of a single feature such as the nose or mouth.

c. **General Photographs.** An additional photographic identification technique employs a variety of facial types which do not necessarily represent criminals. The investigator should make up his own file of photographs representing different features in each photo. The image should be of the same size in all the pictures. The selection of photos should include the varieties of various features such as degree of baldness, length and shape of nose, shape of ear, and so forth.

d. **Artist's Assistance.** Law enforcement agencies have had considerable success in identification by employing an artist to depict a composite of the features as described by the eyewitness. The witness is shown a chart which contains representations of the various types of human features such as noses, eyes, and ears and is requested to select the individual features that most nearly represent those of the unknown criminal. From this selection the artist draws a composite face which may be a close approximation to the criminal. The following steps may be used:

1) *Separation of Witnesses.* If there are a number of witnesses to the appearance of the unknown criminal, they should be separated or advised not to exchange opinions on this matter. A witness who is susceptible to suggestion may readily acquiesce in the opinion of a more forceful person. To retain the value of the witness's initial impression it is necessary to obtain a description before he has spoken at length with others.

2) *Written Description.* After listening to the witness's oral account of the occurrence and his description of the criminal, the investigator should request the witness to reduce his description to writing. The form given in the preceding chapter will be found satisfactory.

3) *The Composite Description.* After studying the written descriptions given by each of the witnesses, the investigator will be able to establish a common denominator for each of the features of the unknown criminal. He should, of course, weigh the description according to his personal observation of the witness's reliability.

4) *Preliminary Sketches.* An artist should be called in at this point to assist the investigator. On the basis of the composite written description, he should make up several sketches which are variants of the common impression. The witnesses are separately requested to examine the sketches, select the closest approximation, and write their suggestions for improvement.

5) *Final Sketch.* On the basis of these suggestions the artist can now draw a second sketch. The witnesses are now called in as a group and may discuss the second and the preliminary sketches with the artist. Suggestions are offered, studied, and incorporated into a final sketch which can be printed on a wanted notice and distributed. It may be noted that a final sketch of this type was employed in the Lindbergh kidnapping and in a number of other prominent cases. In many instances it was found that the sketch was a close resemblance to the suspect.

e. **Identification Kits.** There are presently on the market a number of mechanical and optical systems to aid the investigator or the artist in assembling an image of the suspect corresponding to the witness's description and recollection. The kit consists of a variety of facial features that can be systematically composed into a single face in response to the direction of the witness.

f. **Electronic Aids.** The Supreme Court itself has recently suggested the use of modern technology in identification practice. The following are a few of the technical aids available:

1) *Videotape in Identification.* Videotaping is mechanically simple and requires no expertise or special training for its operation. The actual pre-trial confrontation would consist of having the eyewitness view a series of videotaped "bits," each bit consisting of a sequence of actions, profiles, and spoken words by a single line-up participant. One of the bits, the sequence of which would be identical to the others, would involve the suspect. The identification, if any, would take place during the viewing. A library of available bits with identical sequences can be established by routinely videotaping persons at booking when fingerprints and other information are present. Videotaping for identification purposes offers significant practical advantages over present corporeal identifications. It would eliminate the present difficulty of procuring on short notice a group of line-up participants similar in age, height,

race and other characteristics to the suspect. The risk of an unfairly composed line-up would be minimized. Videotaping would also preserve the confrontation itself for reproduction at trial. This could be accomplished by merely showing the bits used at the identification in court.

2) *Miracode.* This is a computer-like information retrieval system that facilitates the identification of criminal suspects by a witness. Instead of requesting the witness to thumb through mug books, he is seated in front of a screen similar to the kind used to read microfilm copies of a newspaper. Miracode uses cassette cartridges of microfilm onto which have been coded twenty-five characteristics of recently arrested criminals. The viewer is first asked to provide a verbal description of the suspect, which a systems operator translates into numerical symbois that determine what the scanner is to look for once it receives the microfilm cartridge. Each cassette can hold information on 600 suspects.

3) *Computer Sketch.* The enormous data storage and graphics display capability of the computer make it ideally suited to the task of the composite sketch. A computer system can store up to 100,000 different facial features which can then be combined to form billions of different faces. In a matter of seconds, with a touch of the keyboard, a new feature can be added or taken away from the computer display. One such system, "Compusketch", is a composite sketching software designed to operate with an Apple or an I.B.M. computer. In this system, the sketch on the computer display is formulated according to the responses obtained by a standardized witness interview. The questions are designed to help the witness remember important facial features, to provide unbiased answers and to eliminate guessing. The uniform interpretation of descriptions which this system provides can be important if there are several witnesses describing the suspect or if there are several police departments exchanging information on a suspect (see Fig. 25).

The advantages of the computer-generated composite sketch are:

a) It increases the number of people who can produce a composite sketch since artistic ability is not required.

b) Redrawing or making changes in a sketch can be done easily, in seconds rather than minutes.

c) The drawing will have precise lines with no smudges or erasures.

d) Multiple copies for circulation can be readily printed.

Figure 25. Compusketch, a computerized composite sketch system. Facial features are selected and arranged on the computer display according to responses obtained by a standardized witness interview. The printer on the right provides multiple copies for circulation. (Courtesy of Visatex Corp.)

4. Identification of a Suspect

a. **Lineup.** When there is an absence of other evidence, an eyewitness identification will often be of critical importance to a criminal investigation. To insure that the identification is an independent and honest recollection by the witness, the investigator must be familiar with the techniques and precautions involved. The three important methods of eyewitness identification are the "lineup," the "showup," and the photographic identification. The lineup is the customary means of identification of a suspect. When conducted properly, it is considered more accurate than the other methods. The showup, or single suspect confrontation, is used in emergency situations, such as when the victim is dying, or in other circumstances when a lineup is impractical. Photographic identification is often employed when a lineup cannot be held because the suspect is not in custody.

1) *Purpose.* "Is this the man whom you saw at the scene of the crime?" This is the critical question that is asked of the eyewitness after he is permitted to view a suspect in custody. Years of unfortunate experience have instilled in the investigator a deep-seated suspicion of the reliability of eyewitness testimony. Mistaken identifications are still common occurrences. The investigator can, however, greatly increase the reliability of identifications by eyewitnesses through the medium of an intelligently conducted "lineup." A lineup is a police identification procedure in which the suspect of a crime is exhibited with a number of other participants so that a witness can identify him. It is used as a means of selecting a suspect from a group of similar-looking persons. The purpose of the lineup is the elimination of the power of suggestion as a factor in identification.

2) *Necessity.* A lineup should only be used when the identification by a witness is an important factor in the case. The lineup may be dispensed with in the following situations:

a) When there is a significant amount of other incriminating evidence and the eyewitness recollection is weak.

b) When the witness knows the suspect and recognized him during the offense.

c) When the suspect's appearance is so unusual that suitable lineup participants cannot be located.

d) When the suspect is being held in custody at a great distance from the witness. Identification from photographs may be used instead.

3) *Procedure.* To conduct a lineup, a group of at least six persons, including the suspect, should be assembled. The procedure is designed to provide for an accurate and reliable identification. Nothing is to be said or done by the investigator or the lineup participants that unfairly distinguishes the suspect from

the other participants in the lineup. For this reason, the following precautions should be observed:

a) APPEARANCE. The persons participating in the lineup should have the same general appearance as the suspect with respect to race, sex, height, hair and clothing. Persons known to the witness should not be used in the lineup.

b) LOCATION. The lineup should be held in a room away from the public view so that there is little opportunity for disturbance. The room must at least be large enough to accommodate six lineup participants side-by-side while still leaving room for their freedom of movement. Though not required, consideration should be given to installing a screen or a two-way mirror, so that the witnesses can view the lineup unobserved.

c) POSITION. The suspect should be permitted to select his own position in the lineup. This can be done after the investigator has left the room to bring in the witness.

d) WITNESS's CONDUCT. The witness should be instructed before entering the lineup room that the suspect may or not be among the persons in the group and that he should simply enter the room and study the group without pointing, shaking his head, or otherwise indicating a decision. The witness is given a form on which he can indicate his selection. The form consists of numbered boxes to represent the positions of each member of the lineup and an additional box to indicate no selection. While the lineup participants are in view, the witness marks the appropriate box. He should not state whether he has recognized the suspect until he has left the room. The suspect should not be made aware of any decision on the part of the witness, since this knowledge may interfere with techniques that the investigator is using. Where, however, the witness has positively identified the suspect, the investigator may wish to confront the suspect with the witness in order to induce a confession.

e) CONDUCT OF MEMBERS OF LINEUP. The lineup members should not talk while in the room unless voice identification is required. Before bringing in the witness, the investigator should determine whether it will be necessary to have the lineup members wear hats, walk, show certain physical areas, sit down, or otherwise demonstrate any characteristics. If during the lineup the witness desires the lineup members to perform certain actions, he should communicate this information in a quiet aside to the investigator.

f) NUMBER OF WITNESSES. If there is more than one witness, they should make their identification separately and should not be permitted to confer with each other until they have indicated their individual decisions to the investigator. It is recommended, also, that the written description of the suspect be obtained prior to the lineup.

g) CONDUCT OF THE SUSPECT. A suspect does not have the right to refuse either to participate in a lineup or to perform the acts or utterances requested by the investigator. A court order may be obtained to compel his participation and evidence of his refusal may be used against him in court. When a suspect has been detained for a lineup identification, ordinarily he does not have a legal right to representation by lawyer. (However, it is important to note that some states, such as California, Michigan, and Alaska, have stricter safeguards for the rights of the accused than the federal standard and attach the right of legal counsel to all lineup identifications.) Only after the suspect has been formally charged with a crime does the right to counsel at a lineup commence and only for that offense. The suspect may be compelled to appear in a lineup for other unrelated offenses without the benefit of legal representation. The suspect may waive his right to counsel by filling out a waiver form which is signed by the suspect and two witnesses. As with a confession, a valid waiver must be voluntary and the product of a suspect's free choice.

h) CONDUCT OF THE DEFENSE ATTORNEY. A suspect's request for legal counsel at a lineup should be honored, even if by law it is not necessarily required. The defense attorney's presence at a lineup is that of an observer. He is not permitted to participate in any way in the conduct of the lineup or converse with any of the witnesses or the participants. However, he is permitted to make suggestions to the investigator about the procedure of the lineup to insure fairness for his client. If the requests are reasonable, they should be adopted.

i) RECORDING THE LINEUP. Color photographs of the front and profile of the lineup participants should be taken. The witness lineup identification forms should be retained. The investigator in charge of the lineup should prepare a report describing where and how the lineup was held and the names and addresses of all the participants. Statements by the witnesses and objections and suggestions from the defense attorney should be noted.

4) **Supreme Court Ruling.** After the *Miranda* decision of 1966 the Supreme Court addressed itself in the following year to the related problem of the right of a suspect to have a lawyer present at the lineup. In *U.S. v. Wade*, 388 U.S. 218 (1967) the Court ruled that, since lineups are critical stages of prosecutions, the right of counsel guaranteed by the Sixth Amendment must be observed. The requirement for the presence of a lawyer at the lineup led to new problems. The most serious of these difficulties concerned suspects who, while protesting their innocence, were compelled to wait about four hours until their lawyer appeared. The lineup was then arranged only to have them quickly cleared. Consequently, the Supreme Court in *Kirby v. Illinois,* 406 U.S. 682 (1972) ruled that only suspects who had been indicted, that is, formally charged with a criminal offense, are entitled to have lawyers at lineups. Most suspects, however, are identified long before they are indicted. The Court retained the rule that identifications would be barred from evidence whenever a defendant could show that a lineup was unfair.

b. **Showup.** A showup is the confrontation of a single suspect by a witness for the purpose of identification. If a suspect is seized shortly after the commission of an offense in the vicinity of the crime scene, he may be returned to the crime scene or detained in place for identification by a witness. One hour after the commission of the crime is usually considered a reasonable time period, but the special circumstances of the case may justify an extension.

1) *Purpose.* Because a single suspect confrontation is inherently suggestive, it is, in most cases, preferable to use a lineup for identification. However, forming a lineup is not always practical. It can cause a substantial delay and the time elapsed may affect the witness's ability to recollect and, hence, diminish the reliability of the identification. There are several other circumstances where the single suspect identification may be necessary: (1) When there are a number of suspects and the crime was committed by a single

individual. Conducting a lineup for each of the suspects would take a long time and require the detention of innocent parties unnecessarily. (2) When the victim has been seriously injured and may die before lineup preparations have been completed.

2) *Procedure.* If a suspect has been arrested, he may be brought back to the crime scene for identification. If the suspect has not been arrested and he does not voluntarily return to the crime scene, the witness should be brought to where he is being temporarily detained. Unless there is a state law to the contrary, a suspect does not have the right of legal representation at a showup.

The investigator should make every effort to make sure that the confrontation between suspect and witness is accomplished in a fair and reasonable manner. If possible, the suspect should not appear in handcuffs. The investigator should not relate to the witness details of the apprehension of the suspect. The witness should merely be informed that a person fitting the description of the suspect has been detained for questioning. The witness, when confronting the suspect, should be asked "Is this the person?" The investigator should not comment on the identification in the presence of the suspect or the witness. A written report of the procedure should be made and retained in the case file.

c. *Photographic Identification.* An identification in which a witness selects the photograph of a suspect from a series of other photographs is called a photographic identification. The same consideration of fairness applies to the photographic identification as to an ordinary lineup. The photographs must be of people who have a similar general appearance and they must be displayed in a manner that is not suggestive.

1) Purpose. Photographic identification is most often used where there is a suspect but he is not in custody. The suspect may have eluded capture or the police may have a picture of him from a surveillance photo but not know who he is or where he can be located. A photographic identification may also be used at those times when a lineup is impractical. There may not be enough people available who resemble the general appearance of the suspect or the witness may live at too great a distance from where the suspect is being held.

2) PROCEDURE. At least six photographs, including that of the subject, should be used. Each photograph should resemble the general appearance of the suspect and should be of someone whose identity is known. As the investigator displays the photographs, he will explain to the witness that the person who committed the crime may or may not be among those presented. If the witness recognizes a photograph of that person, he should select it. The investigator will ask the witness to initial the back of the photograph he has chosen. The investigator will also initial it and will request the witness to furnish details of the identification in a signed statement. The investigator should not comment on the selection or the lack of a selection. If there are other witnesses, they should not be permitted to know whether or not any of the previous witnesses made an identification or not.

3) RECORDING. If an identification is made, all the photographs used in the display should be retained along with the identifying information of the persons represented. The investigator will draw up a written report containing the details of the investigation. This report will include: the date, time, location, and procedure of the identification; the identities of the investigators, witnesses, and the persons depicted in the photographs; any statements made by the witnesses pertaining to the identification; and the presence or absence of any marks, scratches, writing, or other physical characteristics on the photographs.

4) LEGAL REQUIREMENTS. The suspect does not have the right to have a lawyer present at a photographic identification whether or not he has been formally charged with a criminal offense. Nor does the suspect need to be informed that a photographic lineup has taken or will take place.

5. Self-Incrimination

The Fifth Amendment guarantees that "No person . . . shall be compelled in any criminal case to be a witness against himself." This right against self-incrimination is violated when a person is required to give testimonial evidence against himself, i.e., when he is required to make a conscious communication in testimony.

Questions relating to self-incrimination often arise in the pre-trial stage in matters concerning identification.

a. **Blood Samples.** In *Schmerber v. California,* 384 U.S. 757 (1966) a blood sample was taken from the defendant after he had been arrested at a hospital where he was being treated for injuries sustained in an automobile accident. Subsequently, the chemical analysis of the blood sample was used to show that the defendant was intoxicated. The court held that the taking of the blood sample did not violate the defendant's rights against self-incrimination, since the withdrawal of the blood sample and its use in evidence was neither the defendant's testimony nor relating to some act by the defendant. Thus, the defendant had not been compelled to testify against himself.

b. **Handwriting.** The U.S. Supreme Court has held that the taking of handwriting exemplars from a defendant after his arrest and their subsequent use against him, over his objection, does not violate the privilege against self-incrimination. The mere handwriting sample is an identifying characteristic like the voice and the body itself and as such is outside the protection afforded by the Fifth Amendment against self-incrimination. This is to be distinguished from the matter contained in the writing, which may be incriminating (*Gilbert v. California,* 388 U.S. 263 [1967]).

c. **Fingerprinting.** The privilege against self-incrimination is not violated by taking the fingerprints of a defendant despite his objections (*U.S. v. Laub Baking Co.,* 283 F. Supp. 217 [1968]).

d. **Voice.** Requiring a suspect in a line-up of six persons to repeat the words used by the robber in a bank holdup was held not to violate his privilege against self-incrimination. The defendant was being required to use his voice as an identifying physical characteristic. He was not being compelled to disclose knowledge or make a testimonial utterance (*U.S. v. Wade,* 388 U.S. 218 [1967]).

e. **Line-up.** Since in a line-up the defendant is not compelled to make a testimonial utterance but is simply required to exhibit his person, his privilege against self-incrimination is not violated. Matters relating to the conduct and fairness of a line-up are treated in the preceding section.

f. Summary. The attitude of the courts has been summed up in the following words:

> ... both federal and state courts have usually held that it (the privilege against self-incrimination) offers no protection against compulsion to submit to fingerprinting, photographing, or measurements, to write or speak for identification, to appear in court, to stand, to assume a stance, to walk, or to make a particular gesture. The distinction which has emerged, often expressed in different ways, is that the privilege is a bar against compelling communications or testimony, but that compulsion which makes a suspect or accused the source of real or physical evidence does not violate it (*Schmerber v. California,* 384 U.S. 757 [1966]).

6. Compelling Non-Testimonial Evidence.

Non-testimonial evidence may be defined generally as any evidence taken from the person of the suspect which does not involve his comment on his own guilt. (Examples: fingerprints, blood samples, hair, identification photographs, items of clothing, and handwriting samples.) In general, the suspect or accused under lawful arrest for an offense has no constitutional right to refuse to provide non-testimonial evidence and no right to warnings such as those given under *Miranda.* Non-testimonial evidence may be forced from him against his will and used to convict him. The preferred method of compulsion is the use of a court order directing the suspect to surrender the type of non-testimonial evidence desired.

ADDITIONAL READING

Identification by Witness

Bocklet, R.: Suspect Sketches Computerized for Faster Identification. 35 *Law and Order,* 8, 1987.

Brown, E., Deffenbacher, K. and Sturgill, W.: Memory for Faces and the Circumstances of Encounter. 62 *Journal of Applied Social Psychology,* 311, 1977.

Buchanan, D.R.: Enhancing Eyewitness Identification: Applied Psychology for Law Enforcement Officers. 13 *Journal of Police Science and Administration,* 303, 1985.

Clede, B.: Computerized ID Systems. 36 *Law and Order,* 1, 1988.

——: The Psychology of a Composite ID. 34 *Law and Order,* 11, 1986.

Clifford, B.R. and Bull, R.: *The Psychology of Person Identification.* Boston, Routledge and Kegan Paul, 1978.

Cohen, A.A.: Number of Features and Alternatives Per Feature in Reconstructing Faces with the Identi-Kit. 1 *Journal of Police Science and Administration,* 349, 1973.

Ellis, H.D.: Recognizing Faces. 66 *British Journal of Psychology,* 409, 1975.

Geiselman, R.E., et al.: Enhancement of Eyewitness Memory: An Empirical Evaluation of the Cognitive Interview. 12 *Journal of Police Science and Administration,* 74, 1984.

Hinkle, D.P.: *Faces of Crime* (True crime stories from the files of a police artist). Atlanta, Peachtree Publishers, 1989.

——: *Mug Shots: A Police Artist's Guide to Remembering Faces.* Port Townsend, Wash.: Loompanics, 1990.

Hopper, W.R.: Photo-Fit—The Penry Facial Identification Technique. 13 *Journal of the Forensic Science Society,* 77, 1973.

Laughery, K.R., et al.: Time Delay and Similarity Effects in Facial Recognition. 59 *Journal of Applied Social Psychology,* 490, 1974.

Loftus, E.F., Altman, D. and Geballe, R.: Effects of Questioning upon a Witness' Later Recollections. 3 *Journal of Police Science and Administration,* 162, 1975.

Morton, D.W.: Composite Drawings as Evidence and Investigative Tools. 35 *Law and Order,* 5, 1987.

Owens, C.: Identi-Kit Continues to Score. 55 *Fingerprint and Identification Magazine,* 1, 1973.

Lineup

Adams, T.F.: *Police Field Operations,* 2nd ed. Englewood Cliffs, N.J.: Prentice-Hall, 1990.

Compelling Nontestimonial Evidence by Court Order. 40 *FBI Law Enforcement Bulletin,* 2, 1971.

Doob, A.N. and Kirshenbaum, H.M.: Bias in Police Lineup—Partial Remembering. 1 *Journal of Police Science and Administration,* 287, 1973.

Klotter, J.C. and Kanovitz, J.R.: *Constitutional Law,* 6th ed. Cincinnati, Anderson, 1991.

Levine, F.J. and Tapp, J.L.: The Psychology of Criminal Identification: The Gap From *Wade* to *Kirby.* 121 *University of Pennsylvania Law Review,* 1079, 1973.

Pitts, M.E.: How Sound is Your Lineup? 40 *FBI Law Enforcement Bulletin,* 12, 1971.

Rifas, R.A.: *Legal Aspects of Video Tape and Motion Pictures in Law Enforcement.* Evanston, Ill.: Traffic Institute, Northwestern University, 1972.

Ringel, W.E.: *Identification and Police Line-ups.* Jamaica, N.Y.: Gould Pub., 1968.

Tobias, M.W. and Petersen, R.D.: *Pre-Trial Criminal Procedure.* Springfield, Ill.: Thomas, 1972.

Trapp, W.H., Jr., Pretrial Identification Confrontations. 45 *Mississippi Law Journal,* 489, 1974.

Eyewitness Testimony

Borchard, E.M.: *Convicting the Innocent: Errors of Criminal Justice.* New Haven, Conn.: Yale University Press, 1932.

Buckhout, R.: Eyewitness Testimony. 231 *Scientific American,* 6, 1974.

Ceci, S.J., Toglia, M.P. and Ross, D.F. (Eds.): *Children's Eyewitness Memory.* New York, Springer-Verlag, 1987.

Hinkle, D.P. and Malawista, D.: Sudden Fear and Witness Reliability. 35 *Law and Order,* 7, 1987.

Lipton, J.P.: On the Psychology of Eyewitness Testimony. 62 *Journal of Applied Social Psychology,* 1, 1977.

Lloyd-Bostock, S. and Clifford, B.R. (Eds.): *Evaluating Eyewitness Evidence.* Chichester, Eng.: Wiley, 1983.

Loftus, E.F.: *Eyewitness Testimony.* Cambridge, Mass.: Harvard University Press, 1979.

Sagatun, I.J. and Edwards, L.P.: The Child as Witness in the Criminal Courts. 56 *Police Chief,* 4, 1989.

Sobel, N.R.: *Eyewitness Identification: Legal and Practical Problems.* New York, Clark Boardman, 1972.

Wall, P.M.: *Eyewitness Identification in Criminal Cases.* Springfield, Ill.: Thomas, 1966.

Wells, G.L. and Loftus, E.F. (Eds.): *Eyewitness Testimony.* Cambridge, Eng.: Cambridge University Press, 1984.

Woocher, F.D.: Did Your Eyes Deceive You? Expert Psychological Testimony on the Unreliability of Eyewitness Identification. 29 *Stanford Law Review,* 969, 1977.

Chapter 31

FINGERPRINTS AND THE MECHANICS OF RECORDING

1. Importance

THE SEARCH for a valid identification medium has been a constantly recurring quest in the history of investigation. Tattooing, branding, physical description, measuring, and photographing have had their successive vogues. The latter three methods are still in current use. More imaginative procedures have been suggested in recent years. For example, identification by retinal patterns has been put forward as a useful method. Nose prints (nasal pore patterns) are used to identify horses and dogs. Apes and men alike have an intricate set of ridges on the palmar surfaces of their hands and on the soles of their feet, which appear to be non-skid adaptations like the tread of a tire. Along these ridges are irregularly scattered ends of tiny ducts that discharge perspiration from the sweat glands a millimeter or so down in the dermal layer. Formed in the third or fourth fetal month, these ridges persist from birth to death. They change only in size with growth. The slight distortions caused by pressing the fingers against a surface are relieved as soon as the pressure is withdrawn. The topology—the whorls, loops, deltas, arches, and other characteristics—remains unchanged throughout life.

The one-to-one identification of fingertips is made by direct comparison of details of ridge endings, bifurcations, and other small features of the print on a submillimeter scale. A number of such points must be found to agree in topology and direction, although not in measurement, before an identity is firm. Traditionally, there was thought to be a minimum number of corresponding characteristics ("the twelve-point rule") necessary to establish an identification. In 1973, the International Association for Identification, after examining this issue for three years, decided there was no scientific basis for this requirement. There is no minimum number of points of agreement between the ridge characteristics of two fingerprints necessary to establish a positive identification. Other factors, such as the frequency of occurrence of a particular pattern type and the absence of dissimilar characteristics, enter into the fingerprint examiner's evaluation.

At present the most successful means of identifying a person is that of fingerprint classification, which dates from the beginning of this century. This method possesses the major qualities of an effective identification medium, namely, permanence, universality, unicity, ease of recording, and simplicity of classification.

a. **Permanence.** The medium should be fixed and relatively unalterable by deformation or replacement. Fingerprints are present at birth and last throughout a person's life. Although cuts, burns, and skin diseases may produce temporary disfigurement of the ridge pattern, the ridges will ordinarily resume their original appearance on healing. Permanent destruction of the ridges is possible but unusual. Disease and injury of the glands in the lower skin level can destroy the ridge pattern. Criminals have occasionally accomplished this destruction by mutilation or illegal operations. The grafting of a new ridge pattern on to a finger is considered surgically impossible.

b. **Universality.** The medium must be found on each person. This is obviously true of fingerprints. Where fingers have been amputated or mutilated, the scars of such destruction serve equally well the purposes of identification.

c. **Uniqueness.** The medium must possess a unique form for each person; the uniqueness can be established in two ways. First, the employment of the empirical method has not revealed the existence of two persons sharing a common fingerprint pattern (for even one print). Secondly, theoretical considerations exclude the probability of such an occurrence. Putting the case at its weakest and simplest, if we consider a print to be made up of approximately twenty characteristics and if we assume that the probability of finding one of these characteristics in a fingerprint to be one chance out of ten, then the probability of finding a fingerprint with a particular set of twenty characteristics is $1/10^{20}$ or one divided by one followed by twenty zeroes. This is a negligible probability if we place the population of the world at six billion.

d. **Simplicity of Recording.** An effective identification medium should be susceptible of being recorded in a simple manner. The fingerprint satisfies this condition, since the record can be accomplished by merely inking a finger and pressing it against paper. So marvelously simple is the recording process that soiled or perspiring fingers leave their own record without the knowledge of their owner. Thus, fingerprints are potentially extremely valuable clues.

e. **Simplicity of Classification.** This quality must be considered from two points of view. First, the classifying process must not be so complex as to require hours for its accomplishment. Obviously, such a system defeats its purpose when a large number of prints must be dealt with. Second, each person should have an almost unique position in the files; that is, there should be a unique correspondence between persons filed and classification formulas. This position should be simple to find by means of the system. The fingerprint classification systems in common use adequately fulfill this requirement.

2. The Nature of a Fingerprint

If we consider the nature of a fingerprint, the remarks previously made concerning the uniqueness of the fingerprint pattern for each person will appear quite obvious. One of the basic principles of criminal identification, whether of prints or handwriting, is that no two objects are alike. Fingerprints, paper clips, sheets of paper, blades of grass, or peas cannot be found in identical pairs, and sufficiently close examination will always reveal differences. If the differences are sufficiently great, the scientific detective can draw useful conclusions. Objects are essentially collections of molecules, which are the bricks with which nature builds its structures. The number and position of all of these elements in an object can never be exactly reproduced. We should as soon expect a builder to construct two identical houses. The fingerprint pattern is a configuration of ridges and intervening depressions or valleys. The ridges are dotted irregularly with pores, the orifices from which perspiration is emitted. These pores can in themselves provide a valid, though perhaps impractical, means of identification, since their position is unchanged throughout life. When the finger is inked and rolled against a white card, the ink from the ridges is transferred to the paper, leaving a picture of the ridge lines separated by white (inkless) lines corresponding to the depressions between the ridges.

3. Recording Fingerprints

In order to provide a permanent record of fingerprints for comparison, identification, and filing in an indexed series, the ridge patterns are covered with a black ink and rolled on a stiff paper form. The procedure appears in description to be relatively simple. Unfortunately, many investigators fail through carelessness to master this elementary technique. As a consequence, many fingerprint cards are submitted daily to identification bureaus with defectively recorded prints that are partially illegible and relatively worthless in a reliable fingerprint file. An hour's practice in the inking and rolling of fingerprints will reward the investigator with a lasting mastery of the basic technique.

a. **Equipment.** The essential equipment for rolling fingerprints consists of a tube of ink, a rubber roller, and a slab of glass. More complete equipment will include the following:

1) *Ink.* Fingerprint ink is similar to printer's ink, containing an admixture of oil which permits the ink to dry rapidly.

2) *Rubber Roller.* A hard rubber roller, 4 inches in length and 1 inch in diameter, is used to distribute the ink evenly on a glass plate.

3) *Slab.* A piece of plate glass, 4 by 10 inches, is used as a bearing surface for the ink. Aluminum, stainless steel, porcelain, and other non-porous substances will serve the purpose.

4) *Card Holder.* A piece of wood with metal strips serves to hold the conventional 8-inch square fingerprint card.

5) *Fingerprint Card-Form.* The standard fingerprint form of the FBI or other law enforcement agency is used. The front is marked with allotted spaces for single fingers and for the grouped

fingers. The back of the card provides for descriptive data of the subject.

6) *Table.* A shelf or table 40 inches in height will provide a comfortable surface for fingerprinting.

b. **Inking the Slab.** One of the main causes of illegible prints is an excess of ink on the pad. The exercise of care in two simple operations will eliminate this difficulty.

1) Squeeze four small (⅓-inch diameter) blobs of ink on the slab.

2) Spread the ink evenly over the slab by applying the roller in a back-and-forth motion.

c. **Cleaning the Fingers.** The subject's hands should be cleaned of perspiration, grease, and dirt by wiping with a small cotton ball dipped in carbon tetrachloride.

d. **Rolling the Prints.** The operator must control the rolling process completely. Smooth rolling, even pressure, and relaxed fingers are the key to successful rolling. The following steps are recommended:

1) Place the fingerprint card in the holder and request the subject to sign his name in full in the signature block of the card.

2) Instruct the subject to relax his fingers, look away from the card, and permit the operator to do the work without assistance.

3) Roll each finger of the right hand separately on the glass, placing the finger so that it is inked from below the first joint to a point as close as possible to the tip and from nail edge to nail edge. The thumb should be rolled first.

4) Beginning with the thumb, the finger is rolled in the appropriate space in the card. The right hand of the operator should be used to grip the subject's finger between the first and second joint. The left hand should control the pressure and guide the movement of the finger in rolling. The finger is first rolled on the inked plate through an arc of 180°. The finger is then rolled through the same 180° arc in the appropriate card space. The pressure should be light and the direction of roll away from the operator. The card is moved up to the correct space after each print.

5) At the bottom of the card, a space is provided for inking all four fingers simultaneously without rolling. This serves as a check

on the sequence in which the rolled prints were taken. Again, without rolling, each thumb is printed in the proper space. A notation of scars and deformities is made. The subject should then be requested to sign the card. Naturally, each print should be checked carefully for clarity and legibility.

6) A paper towel and detergent should be given the subject to clean his hands. The operator should now fill out the front of the card with the data relating to the subject and should sign the card. The descriptive data on the reverse of the card should be completed. The card should not be folded.

e. **Reasons for Rejection.** The following are the more common reasons given for the rejection of prints when they are submitted for identification:

1) The ink was unevenly distributed.

2) The entire first joint of each finger has not been entirely inked and rolled.

3) Too much ink was used.

4) Insufficient ink was used and the ridge characteristics are indistinct.

5) Some of the impressions are blurred or smudged as though the fingers slipped while being rolled.

6) Moisture or some other foreign substance may have been present on the fingers, as the impressions are blurred and indistinct.

7) The ridge characteristics are not distinct, possibly because they may have been partially effaced due to the nature of the subject's employment, to some skin disease, or to some other temporary cause. In many instances, legible prints can be obtained in cases of this type by retaking the prints after a lapse of several days.

8) The hands have been reversed, i.e., the left hand fingers placed in the spaces provided for the right hand.

9) The impressions of the fingers of one of the hands were taken twice, and the impressions of the fingers of the other hand not at all.

10) One or more of the rolled or plain impressions is missing or partially missing. It is necessary to have the complete impressions of all ten fingers, unless amputations appear. In cases of bent or paralyzed fingers a spoon or similar instrument should be used

and the fingers printed individually and then mounted on the card in the appropriate block.

11) The impressions have not been recorded in correct sequence.

12) Printer's ink was not used in recording the impressions. Fingerprints taken with ordinary writing fluid, stamp pad ink, or chemicals are not usually legible or permanent.

f. **Judging Acceptability.** The experienced investigator should judge the recorded prints critically before he forwards them to the identification bureau. If, upon examination, it appears that any of the impressions cannot be classified, new prints should be made. If not more than three impressions are unclassifiable, new prints of these fingers may be taken and pasted over the defective ones. If more than three prints are unclassifiable, a new chart should be made. The following points are to be observed in judging the quality of the rolled impressions:

1) A delta, the point at which the lines forming the loop or whorl pattern spread and begin going in different directions, should be clearly defined. All loops have one delta. Whorl prints have two.

2) Loop prints cannot be classified unless the center of the loop and the delta and the lines between them are clear.

3) Whorl prints cannot be classified unless the two deltas and the lines connecting the deltas are clear.

4) Arch fingerprints can be classified only if a sufficiently clear impression is obtained to permit identification of the pattern as being an arch.

4. Sole Prints

Certain purposes of identification can be served by areas of the body surface (other than fingers) bearing a permanent and relatively complex set of ridges or lines. The palm of the hand and sole of the foot are especially suitable, since their latent prints are sometimes found on crime scene surfaces and evidentiary objects and hence can be used to place a suspect at the scene. Although there is no generally accepted system of classification of these prints, they can nevertheless be identified with comparable prints of a suspect. Identifications of this nature have been accepted in court.

Another important purpose of identification is served by infant footprints. Sole prints of the baby recorded soon after birth can later be used to identify the child in the event of a baby "switch," accidental or otherwise. In both civil and criminal cases the importance of infant footprints has been demonstrated. In two cases of kidnapping a positive comparison of the child's footprint with a hospital record was accepted by the court as conclusive proof of the child's identity.

a. **Infant Footprints.** Both the ridge areas and flexure lines can be used to identify an infant. When ridge areas are present there is a tendency to structure the identification about the ridges. However, no inference should be drawn from this concerning the validity of the flexure lines of the child's foot as a means of identification. Indeed, sometimes the child's foot does not present any legible ridge areas, but the flexure lines of the sole are sufficient in number, complexity, and variance in distribution to permit an identification.

Two kinds of flexure lines are observable on the foot of the newborn child. One group of lines tends to disappear after about seven months. The other group is more permanent; the same set of lines in the same relative location is observable over a period of years. These latter lines form the basis of foot identification in infants, since, like fingerprints, they will remain unchanged during the period in question and the number and distribution of the lines provide a complex sufficiently distinctive for purposes of comparison and differentiation. Naturally, the case can be further strengthened by the existence of a ridge area.

b. **Hospital Records.** The maintenance of adequate footprint records at the hospital is basic in any attempt at infant identification. In some jurisdictions private as well as public hospitals are required to record the footprints of newborn infants. The records of many hospitals, however, have been found inadequate because of unsatisfactory printing technique.

c. **Recording Footprints.** A group of hospital employees should be instructed in the elements of inking and recording footprints. The first lesson for the group should be devoted to the purpose of footprinting, the nature of the footprint, and the recognition of a correctly recorded footprint. Instruction in footprint recording procedure should stress the importance of using a limited quantity of ink and of applying the correct pressure. Finally, to maintain footprint recording technique at a satisfactory level, the records should be inspected regularly by an experienced hospital supervisor.

Police departments can aid greatly in a hospital's identification program by instructing personnel in printing technique, periodically reviewing the hospital's file, and conducting an informal critique of recent records by pointing out examples of good and bad footprinting procedures.

d. **Latent Sole Prints.** By this term is meant a print made with the bare foot, ordinarily at the crime scene. If the sole print is already clearly visible, it should be photographed before further treatment. Occasionally a relatively invisible, or truly latent, sole print can be developed by the methods used for latent fingerprints on comparable surfaces. Large, tile bathroom floors, paper on floors, polished wood, and similar surfaces are receptive to such prints. The friction ridges on the sole of the foot sometimes leave a deposit of perspiration (or, perhaps, moisture) and dirt which will respond to the appropriate methods of development used for fingerprints. The investigator will first become aware of the presence of such prints through the faintly observable outlines of the foot. After development the print should be photographed on a one-to-one scale, using a $3\frac{1}{4} \times 4\frac{1}{4}''$ fingerprint camera, which ordinarily will cover the relevant friction ridge area. A camera of larger film size—such as the $4 \times 5''$ or preferably a view camera—should be used for larger footprint areas (e.g., where flexure lines may be present in addition to a ridge area) and for the usual overall picture, which will include the background in the field of view. Comparison prints of a suspect should be made using the procedures described above for infant footprinting.

5. Deceased Persons

The investigator in the field occasionally is confronted with situations in which it is necessary to establish by fingerprinting the identity of a deceased person. The technique employed in this type of fingerprinting will depend upon the condition of the corpse. In extreme cases it may be necessary to amputate the hands of the person and forward them to the criminal investigation laboratory. A surgeon or other medically qualified person may perform the operation. Legal authority is frequently necessary before cutting a corpse in order to fulfill the requirements of federal or state law. As a general principle, the action taken by the investigator in printing a deceased person should be guided by the fragility of the skin of the fingers. Non-destructive methods such as photography should precede any removal or printing action that might damage the friction ridges. In severe cases, every effort should be made to preserve the fingers intact until the body can be transported to a place where the services of a physician or laboratory technician are available.

a. **Recently Dead.** If death has taken place within the last ten hours and rigor mortis has not set in, the following techniques may be used: (It should be noted that the presence of an assistant greatly simplifies the operation.)

1) Cut a fingerprint card in such a manner that the five spaces for the fingers of each hand are on two separate strips.

2) Insert the strip for the right hand in a curved holder or "spoon," the strip fitting into the curve of the spoon. With this piece of equipment it is possible to achieve the effect of rolling the finger by pressing against the spoon. The entire pattern can be obtained in this manner.

3) Extend the arms of the deceased forward and ink the fingers by means of a plate or a spatula.

4) If the fingers are clenched, they can be extended by standing behind the deceased's shoulders and lifting his arms as though extending them above the head. Another method is that of massaging the hands or soaking them in warm water until relaxation is felt.

5) If the fingerprinting of the deceased is not accomplished at the crime scene, paper bags should be placed over the victim's hands to protect evidential material during transportation. Traces such as blood, fibers, hair, and debris should be removed from the victim's hands before fingerprinting. Since it is necessary to clean

the deceased's hands prior to printing, valuable evidence can be lost if this precaution is not taken.

6) If the fingers are wrinkled from immersion in water, it is frequently necessary to fill out the finger before a satisfactory impression can be made. This can be done by means of a hypodermic needle and a suitable filling fluid such as warm water or glycerin. The fluid is injected in the finger in sufficient quantity to restore its normal contour. A piece of string may be tied around the finger at a point immediately above the hole to prevent the fluid from leaking out.

b. **Advanced Decomposition.** In cases involving bodies that are in a more advanced state of decomposition, the techniques of the laboratory and the medical examiner should be employed. Since these are highly specialized procedures, a full explanation will not be attempted here. The investigator under these circumstances should exercise great care to avoid damaging the remaining evidence. His initial step should be to photograph the fingerprint using careful lighting to emphasize the ridge outlines. In the subsequent steps the state of putrefaction of the fingers will dictate the procedures. The investigator should seek the advice of a qualified technician or a physician, if he himself has not had the training.

With extreme care the fingers should be cleaned with water or with xylene and then gently inked and printed in the usual manner. In some cases the epidermis or outer skin may be destroyed. Since the second layer of skin has the same ridge outline in a less pronounced form, it can sometimes be used in the same manner to obtain fingerprints. Remaining fragments of the outer layer should first be removed. The second layer is then cleaned, inked, and rolled as previously described. If the resulting prints are not satisfactory, it is often because the ridge detail is too fine to record. In this situation, photography should be again employed.

c. **Desiccation and Charring.** Desiccated and shriveled skin presents the problem of smoothing out the print surface. This may be done by first softening the skin and then attempting to fill it out by the previously described methods. Charred skin is quite brittle, depending on the degree of charring, and is best approached by preliminary photography. Inking and rolling should not be attempted if there is any indication that the charring is sufficiently severe to result in crumbling on manipulation.

d. **Drowned Persons.** The prints of "floaters" or persons subjected to prolonged immersion can sometimes be taken by actual removal of the skin. The operator places the removed skin over his own finger (which is first protected by a rubber glove) and proceeds to print as though it were his own finger.

e. **Dusting-Tape Method.** For extremely fine or worn ridge detail the dusting-tape method has been found by some experts to be superior to the inked method of friction ridge impression. Ordinary black fingerprint dusting powder is applied to the cleaned (alcohol or xylene) fingers of the deceased using a fingerprint brush or cotton ball. A piece of white-backed, opaque pressure-sensitive tape is then applied to the dusted ridges of each finger, peeled off and pressed against a piece of glass or transparent vinyl.

ADDITIONAL READING

Fingerprint Recording

Collins, C.G.: *Fingerprint Science: How to Roll, File and Use Fingerprints,* 2nd ed. Costa Mesa, Calif.: Custom Publishing, 1989.
Federal Bureau of Investigation. *The Science of Fingerprints: Classification and Uses,* rev. ed. Washington D.C.: U.S. Government Printing Office, 1984.
Olsen, R.D., Sr.: Scott's Fingerprint Mechanics. Springfield, Ill.: Thomas, 1978.

Palm Prints and Sole Prints

See Chapter 36, Additional Reading, **Palm Prints and Sole Prints.**

Chapter 32

LATENT FINGERPRINTS

1. General

T HE SEARCH for fingerprints should be conducted before any of the objects present at the scene are moved. The fingerprints found may be placed in three classes:

a. **Latent Fingerprints.** These, the majority, are "hidden" or relatively invisible and must be developed by one of the special methods described below.

b. **Plastic Fingerprints.** These may be found on such objects as soap, butter, putty, melted wax, etc. Impressions are depressed below the original surface.

c. **Visible Fingerprints.** These are left by fingers covered with a colored material, such as paint, blood, grease, ink, or dirt.

2. Searching for Fingerprints

If the scene is outdoors there will be few articles which are suitable for bearing fingerprints and the order in which the objects are processed will not present any problem. For indoor scenes the search for fingerprints is conducted in accordance with rules which are extremely flexible. Some system must be followed, however, in order to insure complete search and positive results under varying conditions produced by the type of crime, the *modus operandi* of the culprit, and the existence of surfaces capable of retaining fingerprint impressions. A clockwise order can be followed in processing a room filled with articles. In addition, observation should be made of points of entrance and departure, and such objects as doorknobs, window sills, door panels, window-panes, and porch railings.

a. **Searching for Latent Fingerprints.** Latent fingerprints of value for comparison are not frequently found at the scene of a crime. This is attributable to the delicate nature of the print. To deposit a thin layer of perspiration or grease in the complicated pattern of the friction ridges optimum conditions must be present. The surface must be such that it can retain the print without absorbing and spreading it. Thus hard, glossy objects such as glass and enamel painted walls and doors present ideal surfaces. Dirty surfaces and absorbent materials do not readily bear prints. The fingerprint, moreover, must be deposited with the right amount of pressure. The object must not be touched with an excess of pressure, since this tends to spread the print. A movement of translation of the finger will result in a smear. The fingers of the person depositing the prints must have a certain degree of moisture or should have some body grease on the ridges. When all these requirements are fulfilled a good latent fingerprint is deposited. Despite the infrequency with which a latent fingerprint examination meets with success, the unsurpassed value of a print as evidence warrants the expenditure of effort that this search entails. No general rules can be given concerning the finding of fingerprints. Although it is known that prints are seldom found on certain types of surfaces, the fact that such impressions under unusual circumstances are sometimes discovered should suggest to the investigator the necessity of exhausting all possibilities before abandoning the search for latent fingerprints. Some useful comments can be made on the likelihood of finding prints on certain typical surfaces encountered at the scene of a crime. The following are representative of articles to be examined in serious crimes:

1) Suspected poisoning—glasses, bottles, cups, saucers, spoons, medicine cabinets, bathroom, kitchen, etc.

2) Shooting—firearms, unfired cartridges, ammunition boxes, desk or cupboard where ammunition or firearm was habitually kept, etc. For fingerprints on guns (see Chap. 39, Sec. 12).

3) Cutting or stabbing—all sharp pointed or edged instruments, broken glass, or crockery.

4) Automobile used in the commission of a crime and abandoned—rearview mirror, rear deck, edges of doors, radio, all

glass, glove compartment, hood, and other accessible, smooth areas.

5) Burglary and larceny—areas necessary for access and containers, closets and objects probably handled in searching for valuables.

b. **Pertinent Techniques.**

1) The beam from a flashlight held at an acute angle with a surface may reveal impressions that are not otherwise visible.

2) The examination of a surface from different angles may produce a like effect.

3) Breathing on a surface may cause fingerprints to be visible on certain types of materials.

3. Developing the Impression

To serve the purposes of investigation the latent fingerprint must be converted into a visible image—a few hundred micrograms of residue left behind by evaporating sweat on a glass or handle must be changed to reveal a legible ridge pattern. Some method of developing latent fingerprints must be used to provide a contrast between the ridge lines and the background. The term *developing,* used in this sense, should not be confused with the developing of photographic negatives in the darkroom. The nature of the surface, the degree of visibility before development, and the type of camera available should be the deciding factors in the determination of the proper technique in each case. Experiments should be conducted in order to study the effects of the different mediums, but any latent fingerprint which is a part of the evidence should never be used in an experiment. A latent impression should be placed on the same or a similar surface for this purpose. The following methods of development have stood the test of time and are highly recommended: powder, vapor, liquid, and laser light.

a. **Powder.** This method is recommended for the development of latent impressions on a hard, dry, and smooth surface. Effective fingerprint powders may be obtained commercially, although there are many acceptable substitutes which lend themselves to this type of investigation.

1) **Qualities.** The powder selected should possess the following qualities:

a) It should be adhesive to the extent that it clings readily to the ridges of the fingerprint.

b) It should not absorb water.

c) It should "photograph" well, i.e., provide good contrast.

2) **Colors.** Powders of many colors are obtainable, but it is believed that the following will take care of every condition that may be encountered.

a) White or grey powder will provide sufficient contrast when used on a dark surface.

b) Black powder is used to provide a contrast against a light-colored surface.

c) Fluorescent powder, such as anthracene, is recommended for the development of latent fingerprints found on a multicolored background. Illumination by means of ultraviolet light causes the powder to fluoresce vividly while the colors in the background remain only faintly visible.

3) **Application.** Of the available methods for developing fingerprints with powder the use of the brush is the simplest and most effective. The others, however, have their special uses.

a) BRUSH. If haste and haphazard techniques are avoided, the following steps will successfully develop latent prints on suitable surfaces.

1) A good brush is needed. One with soft hairs approximately 1½ inches long with a 3-inch handle is recommended. It is advisable to paint the handle in a color to match that of the powder with which it is to be used. One brush should not be used with powders of different colors.

2) Powder should be used sparingly. A small quantity is placed on a piece of paper and is picked up with the brush as required. It is poor practice to push the brush into the bottles, as this tends to lump the powder and damage the brush.

3) The brush is used to distribute the powder lightly across the fingerprint until the characteristic outlines of the ridge become visible.

4) More powder is added, if necessary, and the desired density built up gradually. As soon as the maximum development is

completed, the surplus powder is tapped from the brush, which is now used to "clean" the impression by a continuation of the brushing motion. It is sometimes of advantage to follow the contour of the ridges in removing the surplus powder.

Figure 26. The Zephyra II fingerprint brush features a soft fiberglass bundle composition on a balanced aluminum handle. (Courtesy of ACE Fingerprint Equipment Laboratories, Inc.)

b) ROLLING OR SIFTING. An excellent procedure for latent prints on a surface such as well-sized paper is to sift or place a quantum of powder on the sheet and then, by tilting the paper, roll the powder back and forth over the areas of response. When the print is fully developed, the excess powder is removed by a few sharp taps of the fingers. Black powder is especially effective with this method.

c) FERROMAGNETIC MIXTURES. The Magna-Brush® method achieves the same effect as rolling by using a ferromagnetic powder and moving it across the paper by means of a magnet passed beneath the paper. The excess powder is removed by the magnet when the print is developed.

d) SPRAYING. To process large areas, some identification men prefer the use of a spraying apparatus such as an atomizer. By squeezing the bulb a fine stream of powder is made to pass over the surface under examination. Sprays have a tendency to clog if the powder is not of the proper consistency or if it is affected by moisture.

e) Aerosol Spraying. Thirty years ago the aerosol can was brought into use as a means of spraying fingerprint powder. Efforts have been made to overcome the problems of clogging and unevenness of distribution. The manufacturers recommend the supplementary use of the brush, at least for the removal of excess powder. In the opinion of a leading expert in the field: Fingerprint spray is mainly useful on large areas. Since the broad and indiscriminate application of fingerprint powder is often demanded by suspicious complainants and nervous supervisors, the spray will do much to improve public and departmental relations for the identification man. However, for the effective development of latents he will rely mainly on the brush to apply powder with discrimination, skill, and purpose.

b. **Chemical Development.** Different methods must be used on absorbent surfaces such as paper, cardboard, and wood. Of the many methods that have been suggested for this purpose, fuming and immersion enjoy the widest use. Although the processes are described here, the investigator is encouraged to submit the evidence to a law enforcement laboratory whenever possible.

1) *Fuming.* Developing a fingerprint by exposing it to a chemical vapor is called fuming. The two most frequently used fuming techniques are the iodine method, which is excellent on porous surfaces such as paper and cardboard, and the cyanoacrylate method, which works well on nonporous surfaces such as glass, metal, plastic, and leather.

a) Iodine. If a sheet of paper is exposed to a flow of iodine vapor, latent fingerprints can be made visible. They can be suspended in a glass case over a crucible containing iodine crystals, which, since they sublime at room temperature, will emit a flow of vapor upward toward the paper surface. The crystals may be heated to hasten the process. A portable iodine fuming apparatus — consisting of an open-ended glass tube containing the iodine crystals separated by means of glass wool from a quantity of calcium chloride, a drying agent — is available for treating objects at the crime scene such as papers and greasy surfaces. The warmth of the operator's breath serves to enhance sublimation and provide a stream of vapor that can be directed as desired. (Since iodine fumes can be poisonous, the use of this vapor should always be managed with care.) The fingerprints should be photographed as soon as it appears that maximum contrast has been reached, since the iodine-vapor image is not permanent.

b) CYANOACRYLATE (SUPER GLUE). The cyanoacrylate method is a fuming technique, invented by the Japanese National Police in 1978, that is effective in developing fingerprints on nonporous materials such as glass, metal, tin foil, wax paper, and leather. It is especially useful on plastic bags and other pliable plastics. It is often referred to as the Super Glue method because this product is composed of approximately 98 percent cyanoacrylate ester and was the original source of this chemical when this fingerprint method was first introduced.

The article to be processed is placed in an airtight glass or plastic container in such a way as to insure that all of its sides are exposed to the vapor. If the item is light enough, it can be suspended from the top of the container. The fuming process is accelerated by heating a few drops of glue to approximately 180 degrees or by adding the glue to cotton dipped in a sodium hydroxide solution. In the latter method, a two-inch square of cotton is saturated in a solution of twenty grams of sodium hydroxide and one liter of distilled water. The cotton is allowed to dry and then placed in the container. Several drops of cyanoacrylate are added to the cotton. In about one-half hour to an hour, a gray or white image will appear as the glue vapor adheres to the friction ridges of the print. When it is fully visible, the fingerprint is photographed and then developed by the powder method. The resulting print can be lifted several times because the glue has hardened the impression.

2) *Immersion.* A variety of substances has been proposed for the chemical development of latent fingerprints on paper and wood. Of these, silver nitrate and ninhydrin appear to be the most widely used.

a) SILVER NITRATE. A reagent such as silver nitrate can be used to convert the sodium chloride content of the latent print into silver chloride, a photosensitive substance which darkens on exposure to a strong light. The envelope or sheet of paper to be processed is dipped in a 3 percent solution of this reagent (4 ounces of silver nitrate dissolved in a gallon of water) and hung to dry in a darkened room. On drying, the paper is exposed to sunlight or suitable artificial light until the print areas have darkened sufficiently. The prints are then photographed. If it is desired to preserve the prints, the document should be placed in a light-tight container, such as an empty film box. The paper can be restored to its original color by immersion in a mercuric chloride solution followed by rinsing in water.

b) Ninhydrin. For the development of old fingerprints, particularly on paper, some identification experts favor the use of ninhydrin, a substance known to react with amino acids. A solution of ninhydrin with ethyl alcohol or acetone (0.2 to 0.4%) is sprayed over the document or other surface by means of an atomizer. Care should be exercised to guard against over-spraying, since the excess may dissolve the prints. After optimal spraying, the document is heated in an oven at a temperature between 80° and 140° C until pink areas are observed. With the passage of time the fingerprints will acquire a deeper shade of pink, improving in contrast for photographic purposes even after several days. Ninhydrin can also be applied by immersing the document in a tray of the solution. Aerosol containers of ninhydrin are marketed for convenience in spraying.

c. **Laser Detection.** The use of laser light to illuminate fingerprints is a recent and valuable addition to the investigator's arsenal of techniques. Laser detection was pioneered in 1976 in a joint venture of the Ontario Provincial Police and the Xerox Research Center. In this method, a concentrated beam of blue laser light produced by an argon ion laser is directed on the area to be examined. Fingerprint residues, which consist primarily of perspiration and body oils, contain chemical compounds which will become luminescent in the presence of laser light. These fingerprint residues will absorb the light and re-emit it at different wavelength. With the use of specially filtered goggles, the latent print becomes visible as a yellow-orange luminescence. Using a similarly filtered lens, the print can then be photographed.

The laser method requires no pretreatment of the specimen. It is non-destructive, that is, it will not alter the evidence. Thus, it can be used prior to the application of powder and chemical methods. Laser detection is especially useful on difficult surfaces, such as styrofoam, cloth, skin, and, in general, places where conventional methods will not work. This method is also helpful with old prints; using the laser technique, the FBI was able to detect a fingerprint of a Nazi war criminal on a postcard dating from the 1940s. Chemicals, such as zinc chloride and rhodamine 6G, are often applied in conjunction with the laser technique to enhance the image.

d. **Photography.**

1) *Fingerprint Camera.* A specially designed camera with a fixed focus is used to copy fingerprints that are developed on a flat or nearly flat surface. The fingerprint camera produces a copy of the latent print at its natural size, that is, a 1:1 replication. Because it is fixed-focus, the focal point will be flush with the open end of the camera. Consequently, the fingerprint must be on a nearly flat surface or otherwise it will be out of focus and the resulting picture will be blurred. If the print extends beyond the camera opening, only a partial picture will be obtained. The fingerprint camera has a self-contained light source powered by batteries or household current. The film for the various models ranges in size from $2^{1}/4''$ × $3^{1}/4''$ to $4''$ × $5''$. The larger sizes can accommodate multiple fingerprints or partial palm prints in one exposure. The basic fingerprint camera is easy to use, requiring only a minimum of photographic training and experience.

2) *Polaroid Photography.* A Polaroid camera or Polaroid attachment that provides for "instant viewing" of the results is especially helpful in fingerprint photography. The photographer, experimenting with different types of film, illumination, or composition, will be able to tell at once whether the pictures have captured the important details. Polaroid also manufactures positive-negative film. In addition to providing an instant photograph, it also produces a negative that can be used for obtaining more prints

and enlargements. This eliminates the need to take duplicate pictures with another camera.

3) *Use of Other Cameras.* The investigator who has a more advanced knowledge of photography may prefer to use a camera other than the fixed-focus fingerprint camera, such as a 35mm or a Speed Graphic which will provide for filters, variable shutter speeds, and "ƒ stops" in addition to permitting greater latitude in angles of illumination.

e. **Identification.** A small tab of paper on which is inscribed appropriate identifying data should be placed in the field of view in a manner that will insure its inclusion in the photograph. This suggestion is particularly advisable in order to avoid confusions in overlapping investigations.

f. **Chain of Custody.** If the person who made the photographs permits another person to complete the darkroom processing, the taker should be sufficiently familiar with the operation to enable him to state that the work was performed under his supervision. Courts will generally allow the photographs to be admitted as exhibits if the photographer identifies them properly, even though the darkroom processing was accomplished by a second party.

g. **Curved Surfaces.** Photographs of latent impressions on a curved surface may be made with the fingerprint camera, provided that the arc of the curve is not too pronounced. Persons who use this camera should familiarize themselves with the restriction in depth of focus imposed by the absence of the iris diaphragm. If it appears that the subject is beyond the capabilities of the fingerprint camera, another type should be used.

4. Handling and Transmission

The removal and transportation of objects bearing fingerprints must be accomplished with great caution. The following procedures will be adaptable in most cases:

a. Gloves may be worn.

b. Articles should be touched only in those places where there is the least likelihood of disturbing a latent fingerprint.

c. Objects should *never* be wrapped in a handkerchief or a towel.

d. Small objects should never be placed in a paper bag.

e. Cellophane sheets or envelopes may be used for protecting papers.

f. Fired bullets and cases should be packed separately in absorbant cotton and placed in a small box.

g. Prior to removal from the scene, the latent print should be photographed one-to-one, or actual size, and also in a way to show relationship with the surrounding area.

h. Articles bearing fingerprints should be marked for identification and packed according to instructions.

i. If it is inconvenient to move an object because of its excessive size or weight, it may be necessary to detach the part bearing the fingerprint. For example:

1) Doors may be removed from hinges.

2) Windows may be removed from frames or panes of glass taken from sashes.

3) Legs and arms may be removed from chairs and tables.

4) Drawers and desks and dressers may be handled separately.

5) Boards may be lifted from floors or paneling from walls.

6) Any part of an automobile may be detached.

j. Under ordinary circumstances, it is advisable to leave the fingerprint impression on the surface where it was found. Its subsequent introduction in court in its original location serves to enhance its evidential value.

5. Elimination of Persons Legitimately at the Scene

When fingerprints are found at the scene of the crime, immediately consideration should be given to the possibility that the impressions may belong to persons whose presence has been legitimate.

a. Rolled impressions should be made of members of the household, the servants, and police officers who may have touched anything carelessly, or in the ordinary course of their activities prior to the commission of the crime.

b. In many cases where there are obvious discrepancies between the patterns being compared, the fingerprints of innocent persons may be eliminated by means of a visual examination of the fingers, thus obviating the necessity of making fingerprint records.

6. Lifting

Lifting is the process which involves the physical removal of a latent fingerprint from its original surface. Under ideal conditions, using the proper equipment, a skilled operator may expect to produce the desired results by employing this method. There are, however, attendant dangers involved, among which the following should be mentioned.

a. **Disadvantages.**

1) Accidental air bubbles under the lifting material, which may be unnoticed by the operator, will leave a blank spot in the lifted impression.

2) If the attempt is not successful, it is generally useless to repeat the lifting process on the same latent impression.

3) The admissibility of lifted impressions in court may be subject to objection on the ground that the evidence has been altered through tampering.

4) Many authorities on the subject of fingerprint identification state that the lifting process should be employed only when it is impossible to secure good photographs.

b. **Techniques.** If a decision has been made to lift a latent fingerprint, there are two types of material which may be used effectively. The choice of one in preference to another will generally be based on personal reasons.

1) *Transparent Tape.* When transparent tape is used as a means of lifting fingerprints, it is necessary that the width be at least 1 inch in order to cover the area to be treated. All subsequent examinations and photographs should be made from the dry or non-adhesive side so that the details of the impression will not be reversed. Direct projections may be made in the enlarging camera by using the transparency as a negative. The adhesive side of the tape should be protected by covering it with a small section of fairly stiff cellophane.

2) *Rubber Lifter.* This material resembles an ordinary inner tube patch. Being opaque, the lifted impression must be exam-

ined and photographed on the reverse side only. Under these conditions, it is necessary to print or enlarge photographs with the negative reversed; otherwise, a true picture of the fingerprint will not be obtained.

3) *Application.* The technique of lifting fingerprints is the same for transparent tape and rubber lifter.

a) Press the sticky side of the tape or rubber against the powdered fingerprints, carefully avoiding the production of air bubbles.

b) Insure complete adhesion by rubbing the entire surface with a smooth round object.

c) Beginning at one edge or corner, peel the lifter gently from the surface and cover the sticky surface with cellophane.

d) A small tab or paper, inscribed with pertinent identifying data, may be attached to the lifter by placing it between the lifter and the cellophane cover at one corner.

Table XI
LATENT FINGERPRINT DEVELOPMENT

Property of Print	Method	Operation	Effect	Color	Surfaces
Stickiness	Powder	Brush or Spray	Adhere to Ridges	Color of Powder	Smooth, Glazed or Sized
Fatty Material	Iodine Reagent	Fuming	Darkens Ridges	Brown	Paper and Wood
Chloride Ion	Silver Nitrate	Immersion and Exposure to Light	Sensitive to Sunlight and U.V. Lamp	Dark Brown	Paper and Wood
Amino Acids	Ninhydrin	Spray or Immersion	Organic Reagent	Pink	Old prints on a variety of surfaces

ADDITIONAL READING

Latent Fingerprints

Allison, H.C.: *Personal Identification.* Boston, Holbrook Press, 1973.

Bridges, B.C.: *Practical Fingerprinting.* Rev. by C.E. O'Hara. New York, Funk & Wagnalls, 1963.

Brooks, A.J., Jr.: Frequency of Distribution of Crime Scene Latent Prints. 3 *Journal of Police Science and Administration,* 292, 1975.

——. Techniques for Finding Latent Prints. 54 *Fingerprint and Identification Magazine,* 5, 1972.

Clements, W.W.: *The Study of Latent Fingerprints.* Springfield, Ill.: Thomas, 1987.

Cowger, J.F.: *Friction Ridge Skin: Comparison and Identification of Fingerprints.* New York, Elsevier, 1983.

Crown, D.A.: The Development of Latent Fingerprints with Ninhydrin. 60 *Journal of Criminal Law, Criminology and Police Science,* 258, 1969.

Federal Bureau of Investigation. *The Science of Fingerprints: Classification and Uses,* rev. ed. Washington, D.C.: U.S. Government Printing Office, 1984.

Gidion, H.M. and Epstein, G.: Latent Impressions on Questioned Documents. 39 *Police Chief,* 8, 1972.

Lambourne, G.: Glove Print Identification: A New Technique. 48 *Police Journal,* 219, 1975.

Lee, H.C. and Gaensslen, R.F. (Eds.): *Advances in Fingerprint Technology.* New York, Elsevier, 1991.

Micik, W.: Latent Print Techniques. 56 *Fingerprint and Identification Magazine,* 4, 1974.

Moenssens, A.A.: *Fingerprint Techniques.* Philadelphia, Chilton Book, 1971.

Nutt, J.: Chemically Enhanced Bloody Fingerprints. 54 *FBI Law Enforcement Bulletin,* 2, 1985.

Olsen, R.D., Sr.: *Scott's Fingerprint Mechanics.* Springfield, Ill.: Thomas, 1978.

Petersilia, J.: *Processing Latent Fingerprints — What are the Payoffs?* Santa Monica, Calif.: Rand Corp., 1976.

Trowell, F.: A Method for Fixing Latent Fingerprints Developed with Iodine. 15 *Journal of the Forensic Science Society,* 189, 1975.

Wilson, J.C.: Developing Latent Prints on Plastic Bags. 56 *Fingerprint and Identification Magazine,* 6, 1974.

Laser Detection of Latent Prints

Burt, J.A. and Menzel, E.R.: Laser Detection of Latent Fingerprints: Difficult Surfaces. 30 *Journal of Forensic Sciences,* 364, 1985.

Creer, K.E.: Operational Experience in the Detection and Photography of Latent Fingerprints by Argon Ion Laser. 23 *Forensic Science,* 149, 1983.

Goodroe, C.: Laser Based Evidence Collection and Analysis. 35 *Law and Order,* 9, 1989.

Herod, D.W. and Menzel, E.R.: Laser Detection of Latent Fingerprints: Ninhydrin Followed by Zinc Chloride. 27 *Journal of Forensic Sciences,* 513, 1982.

Menzel, E.R.: Comparison of Argon-Ion, Copper-Vapor and Frequency-Doubled Neodymium: Yttrium Aluminum Garnet (ND:YAG) Laser for Latent Fingerprint Development. 30 *Journal of Forensic Sciences,* 383, 1985.

Menzel, E.R., et al.: Laser Detection of Latent Fingerprints: Treatment of Glue Containing Cyanoacrylate Ester. 28 *Journal of Forensic Sciences,* 307, 1983.

Ridgely, J.E.: Latent Print Detection by Laser. 54 *FBI Law Enforcement Bulletin,* 6, 1985.

Chapter 33

CLASSIFICATION OF FINGERPRINTS

1. Introduction

To the layman's eye, the rolled print is a meaningless array of curved and relatively straight lines which are obviously highly individual but which do not appear to lend themselves to any system of ordered filing or indexing. The problem of classification — to convert a fingerprint into a significant label — has challenged many ingenious minds and has been successfully solved by several practical "systems." The most commonly used method of fingerprint classification is the Henry System. The present discussion is directed toward an exposition of this system. The investigator should bear in mind that fingerprint classification is a comparatively simple branch of knowledge. By approaching the study as a practical problem, the various steps of development will suggest themselves as straightforward and logical. Basically, the problem of fingerprint classification is that of representing an array of lines by a formula, consisting of numbers and letters, which can be easily indexed. Three considerations present themselves: The elements or types of ridges; the location of the ridges; and a method of counting the lines. The matter of counting ridges implies a point of reference, that is, a point from which one can by convention begin to count.

2. Ridge Characteristics

The ridges are the basic elements in the system of classification. From a study of the ridge lines, it is found that these lines can be satisfactorily classified by eight types which form the bases for comparing prints. The accompanying illustrations are self-explanatory.

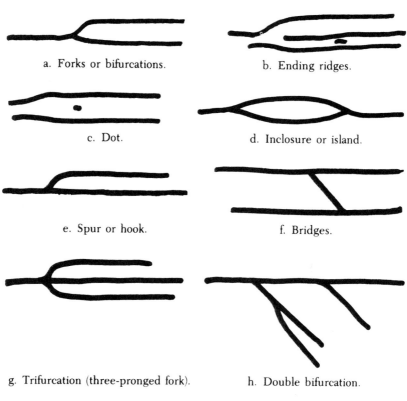

a. Forks or bifurcations.

b. Ending ridges.

c. Dot.

d. Inclosure or island.

e. Spur or hook.

f. Bridges.

g. Trifurcation (three-pronged fork).

h. Double bifurcation.

Figure 27. a. Forks or bifurcation.
        b. Ending ridges.
        c. Dot.
        d. Inclosure or island.
        e. Spur or hook.
        f. Bridges.
        g. Trifurcation (three-pronged fork).
        h. Double bifurcation.

Figure 28. Pattern area or working area of classification.

3. Basic Features

Certain ridges are basic to the fingerprint patterns in the sense that they either form or locate the pattern frame of reference.

a. **Pattern Area.** This is simply that part of the fingerprint which contains the ridges necessary to determine classification. It is the working area of classification.

b. **Type Lines.** These lines are the innermost ridges which start as parallel lines, diverge, and bound the pattern area. They define the working area of classification. Type lines may not be continuous and may even be absent.

c. **Delta.** Referring to the figure immediately above, it will be noted that an imaginary point has been indicated where the type lines began to diverge. This is called the center of divergence. The delta is defined as the first fork or bifurcation nearest the center of divergence. The delta need not be a fork but may be any type of ridge formation.

Where a choice appears between two formations, either of which seems to fulfill the definition of a delta, the following rules may be applied:

1) The delta may not be located at a bifurcation which does not open toward the core.

2) If there is a choice between a bifurcation or some other type of delta, the bifurcation is selected.

3) The delta may not be placed in the middle of a ridge running between the type lines, but only at the nearest end of the ridge.

d. **Core.** The core is the approximate center of the pattern area. It is located according to the following rules:

1) The core is located on or within the innermost looping ridge.

2) The shoulders of a loop are the points where the ridges begin.

3) If the innermost loop has no ending ridge or rod rising as high as the shoulders, the core is placed on the end of the center rod (whether or not it touches the looping ridge).

4) If the innermost loop has an even number of rods rising as high as the shoulders, the core is located on the end of that one of the two center rods farther from the delta.

Figure 29. Type lines.

Figure 30. Typical delta.

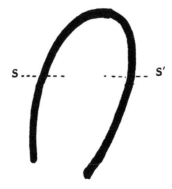

Figure 31. Loop shoulders.

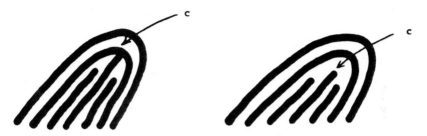

Figure 32. Locating the core for an odd number of rods.

Figure 33. Locating the core for an even number of rods.

4. Pattern Types

The basic fingerprint patterns can be conveniently divided into the following eight types under three pattern groups:

- a. Arches.
    1) Plain arch.
    2) Tented arch.
- b. Loops.
    1) Radial loop.
    2) Ulnar loop.
- c. Whorls.
    1) Plain whorl.
    2) Central pocket loop.

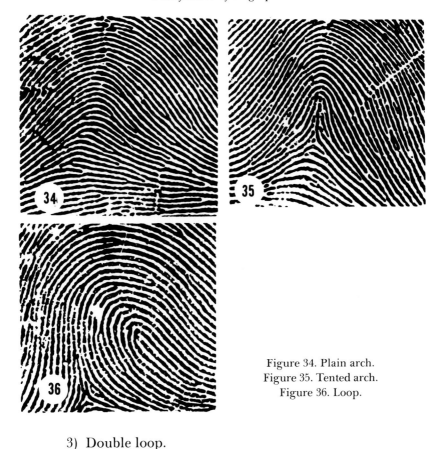

Figure 34. Plain arch.
Figure 35. Tented arch.
Figure 36. Loop.

3) Double loop.
4) Accidental whorl.

5. Arches

a. **Plain Arch.** This is made up of a series of ridges that enter from one side of the pattern and flow without interruption across the finger, terminating at the other side after a slight rise in the center. There are no recurring ridges in the true arch.

b. **Tented Arch.** This is similar to the plain arch except that there is a sharp rise in the center of the pattern. A very sharp peak is noted in most tented arches and a definite angle is formed by the upward thrust of the ridges.

6. Loops

A loop is formed by one or more ridges entering at one side of the pattern, continuing up to the center of the pattern, and recurving around a core to form a loop, then flowing in the opposite direction and terminating on the same side from which they entered. One essential requirement is that the recurving ridge pass freely between the core and the delta. A series of such ridges permits a ridge count between the delta and core, following an imaginary straight line between these two points. If no ridges are found between the core and the delta, the pattern is a tented arch. As loops are the most common of all the patterns, an additional breakdown of the loop is made by classifying it according to the side of the finger from which it starts and terminates, as described below.

Figure 37. Downward slope of radial loop, recurving toward the thumb.

Figure 38. Radial and ulnar loops (the directions will vary depending on whether it is the left or right hand).

a. **Radial Loops.** Radial loops are those that have a flow of ridges starting and terminating in the direction of the thumb of the same hand on which they are found. The term *radial* is given this type of loop because of the fact that the thumbs are nearest to the point where the radius, or large bone of the forearm, joins the hand.

b. **Ulnar Loops.** The term *ulnar* denotes a trend of the flow of ridges in the direction of the little finger of the hand. On this side of the forearm is a small or ulnar bone, which joins the hand in line with the little finger. It should be noted that loops are divided into radial and ulnar according to the way they flow on the hands and not according to the arrangement on the fingerprint card. It is impossible to know whether a loop is ulnar or radial unless it is known from which hand the impression was obtained.

7. Whorls

a. **Plain Whorl.** A *whorl* is a pattern in which one or more ridges appear to revolve around a center point, called the *core,* often making a complete circuit. All whorls have two or more deltas, located below and to the right and left of the center of the pattern. In the whorl pattern an imaginary straight line drawn between deltas will cut one or more of the recurving ridges that completely encircle the core. The name of the pattern was derived from the whirling formation of the ridges. All whorls are not circular in shape, but may be elliptical or oval. Deltas in whorls may be found very close to the core or at any point extending out to the extreme edge of the impression, but never above an imaginary horizontal line running through the center of the pattern.

b. **Central Pocket Loop.** The central pocket loop, which closely resembles an ordinary loop, has a recurving ridge or ridges in the center of the pattern, which forms a pocket within the loop. The recurve of the ridge inside the loop must be at right angles to the axis of the pattern. In order for the pattern to be a pocket loop, the recurving ridge or ridges forming the inner pocket must be of a circular formation. Any convergence or sharp angle of the ridge or ridges in the direction of the axis of the pattern makes the pattern a plain loop.

c. **Double Loop.** This pattern consists of two separate but not necessarily unconnected loop formations. There are two distinct sets of shoulders and two deltas. Two forms of the double loop were described by Henry and at one time they were commonly recognized: 1) the *twinned loop* and 2) the *lateral pocket loop.* Because of confusion between the two forms caused by difficulties in locating and tracing the loops, the FBI no longer makes this distinction. Both forms are now considered part of a single classification, the double loop.

d. **Accidental.** The accidental derives its name from the unusual formation of the ridge pattern which appears to have been formed by accident and does not conform to any of the rules that would apply to the other patterns. This accidental formation is a natural condition and is not caused by any injury to the finger. As most accidentals have two or more deltas, this pattern is classed as a composite.

8. Classification of fingerprints

The goal of a classification system is to assign a formula to a set of fingerprints impressions so that the set can be readily located in a file. This formula consists of letters and numbers written above and below a horizontal line. All ten fingers are used. The formula will include a key and major division and the primary, secondary, subsecondary, and final. The following is an illustration of a typical classification:

Key	Major	Primary	Secondary	Sub-Secondary	Final
17	L	1	U	III	4
	S	1	U	IIO	3

a. **Blocking Out.** After examining the rolled impressions to determine by comparison with the simultaneous impressions whether they are in their correct square, the operator "blocks out" or marks the pattern symbol below each pattern. The following symbols are used:

1) *Symbol.*
a) Arch — A, a.
b) Tented Arch — T, t.
c) Radial Loop — R, r.
d) Ulnar Loop — / (in left hand); \ (in right hand).
e) Whorl — W, w.

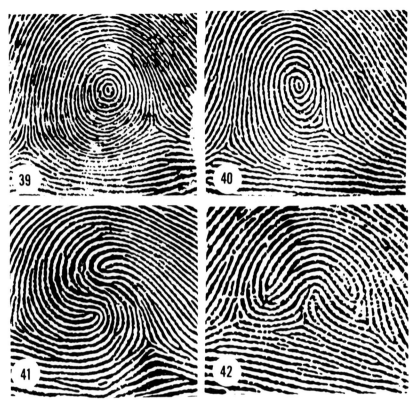

Figure 39. Plain whorl.
Figure 40. Central Pocket Loop.
Figure 41. Double loop.
Figure 42. Accidental.

2) *Block Out Rules.*

a) INDEX FINGERS. The appropriate *capital* letter is placed under the index fingers for all patterns except the ulnar loop.

b) ALL OTHER FINGERS. The appropriate *small* letter is placed under all other fingers for every pattern except the ulnar loop.

c) ULNAR LOOP. Slanting lines are used for all fingers. The slant should be in the direction of the loop.

b. **Ridge Counting.** The classification of fingerprints depends largely on ridge counting. The method of counting ridges differs in loops and whorls.

1) **Loops.** The following rules apply to loops and whorls.

a) The *ridge count* is the number of ridges counted on an imaginary straight line drawn from the point of the delta to the point of the core.

a) The *ridge count* is the number of ridges counted on an imaginary straight line drawn from the point of the delta to the point of the core.

b) The core and delta are not counted.

c) A white space must come between the first ridge and the delta. This condition defines the first ridge.

d) If there is a bifurcation on the line of count, two ridges are counted.

e) If the line crosses an island, two ridges are counted.

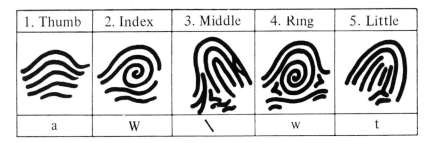

1. Thumb	2. Index	3. Middle	4. Ring	5. Little
a	W	\	w	t

Figure 43. Right hand block out.

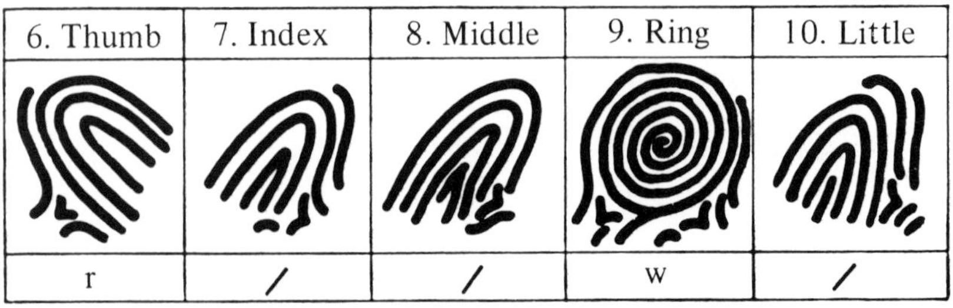

6. Thumb	7. Index	8. Middle	9. Ring	10. Little
r	/	/	W	/

Figure 44. Left hand block out.

f) Dots and short ridges are counted if they are cut by the line and are heavy and thick.

2) **Whorls.** To distinguish the various types of whorls the symbols I, M, and O are used for *Inner, Meeting,* and *Outer* whorls. The appropriate letter is placed in the upper right hand corner of a whorl print after being selected by means of the following steps:

a) The deltas are located.

b) A tracing line is established by starting with a ridge at the lower side or point of the extreme left delta and continuing to the point nearest or opposite the extreme right delta.

c) The number of ridges between the tracing line and the right delta is counted.

d) If the traced ridge passes inside or above the right delta with three or more ridges intervening between the traced line and the delta, the whorl is called *inner* and is indicated by the letter I.

Figure 45. Ridge counting.

e) If the traced ridge passes outside (below) the right delta and there are three or more intervening ridges between the traced line and the delta, the whorl is termed *outer* and is indicated by the letter O.

f) If the traced ridge meets the right delta or not more than two ridges intervene when passing inside or outside of the delta, the whorl is called a *meeting whorl* and is represented by the letter M.

g) If the traced ridge forks, the lower branch of the fork is used to continue the trace.

Figure 46. Inner whorl.

Figure 47. Outer whorl.

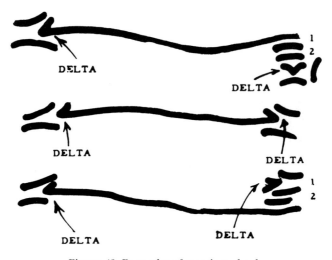

Figure 48. Examples of meeting whorls.

h) If the traced ridge ends abruptly, the trace is resumed on the next lower ridge.

9. Primary Classification

In making the primary classification, certain conventions are assigned in the form of designated numerical values to the fingers in the following manner:

Right Hand	Thumb	Index	Middle	Ring	Little
	16	16	8	8	4
Left Hand	Thumb	Index	Middle	Ring	Little
	4	2	2	1	1

a. It is seen that fixed values are assigned to pairs of fingers.

b. These values are counted only for whorls; when arches, tented arches, or loops appear, they are given no value.

c. Beginning with the right thumb and using every *odd* numbered finger of both hands, each time a whorl appears, the numbers in the corresponding boxes are added. The sum, plus one, is the denominator of the primary classification symbol, i.e., the number is the lower part of a symbol which will be in the form of a fraction.

d. Beginning with the right index finger and using every even numbered finger of both hands each time a whorl appears, the numbers in the corresponding boxes are added. The sum plus one is the numerator (upper number of a fraction) of the primary classification symbol.

> *Example:* Let us assume that whorls have been found on the right index, right ring, left index, and left little finger. These are fingers no. 2, 4, 7, and 10 respectively. To find the denominator, we must first add from the illustrated box the value of 2.

e. The lowest primary classification is 1/1.

f. The highest primary classification is 32/32.

Sum for odd numbered fingers = 2
Adding 1
Denominator = 3

To find the numerator, we add values for the even numbered fingers (2, 4, and 10), thus,

Sum for even numbered fingers	= 16 + 8 + 1 = 25
Adding	1
Numerator	26
	26
Hence, the primary classification is:	3

10. Secondary Classification

Secondary classification is the assignment of letters to the fingers. The symbols are in the form of a fraction. Symbols representing the right hand are placed in the numerator; left hand symbols are placed in the denominator.

a. **Index Fingers.** The capital letters are used for the index fingers, viz., A, T, R, U and W for Arch, Tented Arch, Radial Loop, Ulnar Loop, and Whorl, respectively.

> *Examples:* A radial loop on the right index and an ulnar loop on the left index would give the secondary classification: R/U. (This is actually only part of the secondary classification.)
>
> If the right index is an arch and the left index a whorl, we have: A/W.

b. **Other Fingers.** Small letters are used when arches, tented arches, and radial loops are found on fingers other than index fingers.

c. Ulnar loops and whorls appearing on thumbs are ignored. If they appear on the middle or ring finger and there is an arch, tented arch, or radial loop to their right, they are represented by a dash.

d. If successive fingers have the same small letter, they are represented by a numerical coefficient and the letter. Thus, r would be 2r.

t	W	a	a	r
u	W	r	t	r

The secondary classification is:

tW2ar
———
Wrtr

11. Sub-secondary Classification

The thumb and little fingers are not considered in the subsecondary classification. Again, right hand fingers appear in the numerator and left hand in the denominator.

a. **Whorls.** The symbols I, M, and O are used for Inner, Meeting, and Outer whorls, which are determined by the procedure described in paragraph 2 above.

b. **Arches** are not considered or represented.

c. **Loops** are represented by letters I and O.

1) *Index Fingers.* A ridge count of 1 to 9 inclusive is represented by I; a ridge count greater than 9 is represented by O.

2) *Middle Fingers.* A ridge count of 1 to 10 inclusive is represented by I. Greater than 10 is represented by O.

3) *Ring Fingers.* A ridge count of 1 to 13 inclusive is represented by I; more than 13 is O.

Example: A sub-secondary classification would be

$$\frac{IOI}{OMM}$$

12. Final Classification

For the identification bureau of a small police department the primary, secondary, and sub-secondary classifications are sufficient. In larger identification bureaus where there are a great number of cards with the same primary, secondary, and sub-secondary classifications, a final classification is used. A number indicating a ridge count on the little finger is the final classification and is obtained as follows:

a. **Loop on Right Little Finger.** The ridge count of this finger is placed in the numerator at the right of the subsecondary classification. The complete final classification is this number.

b. **Loop on Left Little Finger.** If there is no loop on the right little finger, but there is a loop on the left little finger, the ridge count of the latter is the final classification and is written in the denominator.

c. **No Loop on Little Finger.** In this case there is no final classification. Some identification bureaus in treating this case consider the whorl as an ulnar loop and use the ridge count of the whorl. The count is taken from the left delta to the core in the right hand and from the right delta to the core in the left hand.

13. Extension of the Henry System

At times there is a need for further sub-classification of finger-prints and a key and major division are used for this purpose. Their use is recommended by necessity.

a. **The Key.** The key is always placed to the left of the numerator regardless of the finger on which it is found. The key consists of the ridge count of the first loop found in a set of prints beginning with the right thumb but omitting the little finger.

b. **Major Division.** Only the thumbs are considered. The major subdivision is written immediately to the right of the key in the numerator and on the extreme left in the denominator. The right thumb is recorded in the numerator and the left thumb in the denominator.

1) *Both Thumbs Whorls.* The major division consists of one of the symbols I, M, and O, representing the tracing as Inner, Meeting, or Outer.

2) *Both Thumbs Loops.* The ridge count of the left thumb is represented in the denominator by the symbols S, M, and L, representing respectively the words Small, Medium, and Large. Ridge counts 1 to 11 inclusive are represented by S; counts 12 to 16 inclusive by M; and above 17 by L. For the right thumb the ridge counts are represented in the numerator by the symbols S, M, and L, arrived at by the same designation of ridge counts as described for the left thumb. A ridge count of 14 on the right thumb and 9 and on the left would give a major division of $\frac{M}{S}$.

3) *Combinations of Loops and Whorls.* The same system as described in the preceding two paragraphs is employed. Ridge

counting is used for the loop, and ridge tracing for the whorls with the appropriate symbols.

14. Identification Records

The function of the identification bureau of a police department is twofold: it must maintain conveniently and efficiently the various files of identification records of criminals, and it must provide for the rapid and reliable searching and filing of these records.

a. **Identification Files.** Typically, the records of the identification bureau can be placed in four or more major classifications such as the following:

1) *The Master Criminal File.* This contains the criminal records and fingerprints in serial-number sequence.

2) *The Fingerprint File.* This contains card-size (8″ × 8″) fingerprint records, together with criminal record sheets.

3) *The Index File.* This consists of 3 × 3-inch cards filed alphabetically and by fingerprint classification.

4) *The "Mug" Shot File.* Identification photos are placed on file, together with the prisoner's record and other useful data, such as his height, weight, age, and a description of his significant characteristics. "Mug" pairs (side and front views) are usually printed on 3 × 4¾-inch paper to be filed in a standard 3 × 5-inch card file.

15. NCIC Fingerprint Classification System

One of the files in the National Crime Information Center (NCIC) is the computerized Wanted Persons File on individuals for whom federal warrants are outstanding or who have committed or been identified with an offense which is classified as a felony or serious misdemeanor under the existing penal statutes of the jurisdiction originating the entry and a felony or misdemeanor warrant has been issued for the individual with respect to the offense. This includes probation and parole violators.

When a wanted person's fingerprint classification is available, the National Crime Information Center fingerprint classification (NCIC FPC) should always be included in the wanted person's record. While not a positive identifier, the NCIC FPC can be of assistance in establishing the identity of a suspected wanted person. The following information and instructions, which include a modification of the Henry System, have been issued by the FBI to aid police officers in the submission of criminal data and fingerprint records.

In November, 1971, a file known as Computerized Criminal History (CCH) was added to the NCIC data base. The file contains data concerning personal descriptions of those individuals arrested for violations of serious crimes, the nature of the charge, and the disposition of the arrest. This file is meant to service all agencies in the criminal justice system. Developed in conjunction with local, state, and federal NCIC participants, this file was designed to meet the needs of police, as well as those of prosecutors, courts, and correctional institutions for prompt up-to-date information concerning an individual's past criminal history. One field of data which has been provided for and which should be used in the CCH record is the subject's NCIC FPC. The NCIC FPC is not a positive identifier, but it can aid in establishing the identity of an individual, particularly when a subject possesses a common name and the search for his CCH record is being made against a vast repository of computerized data based records.

To alleviate problems existent due to the various methods of fingerprint classification, the following method was devised and should be utilized in classifying fingerprints for entry into the fingerprint classification (FPC) field of the wanted person record format, as well as the FPC of the CCH record. This is a twenty character field.

The fingers are numbered beginning with the right thumb as number 1, and continuing through number 10 with the left thumb being number 6. Two characters are to be used for each finger as shown below:

Pattern Type	Pattern Subgroup	NCIC FPC Code
ARCH....................	Plain ARCH....................	AA
	Tented ARCH.................	TT
LOOP	Radial LOOP.................	2 numeric characters. Determine actual ridge count and add fifty (50). E.g., if the ridge count of a radial loop is 16, add 50 to 16 for a sum of 66. Enter this sum (66) in the appropriate finger position of the FPC field.
	Ulnar LOOP	2 numeric characters indicating actual ridge count (less than 50). If the ridge count is less than 10, precede actual count with a zero. E.g., ridge count of 14, enter as 14; ridge count of 9, enter as 09.
WHORL	Plain WHORL	Enter "P" followed by tracing of whorl.
	Inner tracing	PI
	Meeting tracing	PM
	Outer tracing	PO
	Central Pocket Loop WHORL	Enter "C" followed by tracing of whorl.
	Inner tracing	CI
	Meeting tracing	CM
	Outer tracing	CO
	Double[1] Loop WHORL .	Enter "d" followed by tracing of whorl. In double loop whorl pattern the small letter "d" is utilized when classifying prints in lieu of the capital "D" in order to make the handwritten character more distinguishable from the handwritten letter O. When entered in a computer data base or when the NCIC FPC is otherwise typed or printed out

the capital "D" will be
used instead of the small
letter "d" to avoid the
complications involved in
having to provide both
upper (capital letter) and
lower (small letter) case
character sets.

Inner tracing	dI
Meeting tracing	dM
Outer tracing	dO
Accidental WHORL	Enter "X" followed by tracing of whorl.
Inner tracing	XI
Meeting tracing	XM
Outer tracing	XO
MISSING/AMPU-TATED FINGER[2]	XX
COMPLETELY	SR
SCARRED OR MUTILATED PATTERN[3]	

---

[1]In double loop whorl patterns the small letter d is utilized in lieu of the capital D in order to make it more distinguishable from the handwritten letter O.

[2]Used only in instances of missing and totally/partly amputated fingers making it impossible to accurately classify an impression according to the above instructions for NCIC FPC. It is recognized that under the Henry System of classifying fingerprints, if a finger is missing or amputated, it is given a classification identical with the opposite finger; however, this should not be done in the NCIC FPC, since the precise identity of the finger or fingers missing/amputated is not preserved.

[3]Used only in instances in which the fingerprint cannot be accurately classified due to complete scarring or mutilation and a classifiable print cannot be obtained. As in the case of missing and amputated fingers, the procedure for assigning the classification of the opposite finger, as is done under the Henry System of classifying fingerprints, *should not be used* for the NCIC FPC.

It shall no longer be necessary to place a diagonal line through the number zero. The computer program now distinguishes the difference between the number 0 in a loop classification and the outer tracing whorl designation capital O.

An example of the NCIC FPC for a set of fingerprints made up of all ulnar loops might thus read: 12101116141109111713. The same fingerprints with #2 and #7 fingers being radial loops would appear as follows: 12601116141159111713.

Suppose then for an example, a set of fingerprints is classified under the Henry System and contains the following: #1 finger is an ulnar loop with 12 ridge counts, #2 finger has been amputated, #3 finger is a plain arch, #4 finger is a Central Pocket loop with outer tracing, #5 finger is an ulnar loop with 4 counts, #6 finger is completely scarred, #7 finger is a radial loop with 9 ridge counts, #8 finger is a tented arch, #9 finger is a double loop with a meeting tracing, and #10 finger is an ulnar loop with 10 ridge counts. Applying the foregoing rules, the correct NCIC FPC would be: 12XXAACO04SR59TTdM10. (If typed or machine printed, the small letter "d" would be a capital letter "D" in this classification.)

16. Automated Fingerprint Identification System (AFIS)

In 1985, California unveiled its new automated fingerprint identification system. Its first assignment was the identification of a latent print found on an orange Toyota in Los Angeles two days before. The print was believed to have been left by the "Night Stalker," a brutal serial killer believed to be responsible for the deaths of fifteen women, who had been terrorizing Los Angeles for seven months. A few minutes after the fingerprint was entered into the system and compared with the 380,000 prints stored in its memory, it printed out a list of suspects with a similar fingerprint. At the head of the list was the name of Richard Ramirez, a 25-year-old drifter who had previous convictions for drug offenses and auto thefts. When the computer assigned him a probability rating of four times the next person on the list, the Los Angeles Police knew that they had their man.

The identification of single fingerprints found at crime scenes has always been a laborious and time-consuming job for identification experts. In what is called a "cold search," where there is little information to go on except the latent fingerprint, the examiner would search through reams of fingerprint cards by hand, comparing the latent print with those on file using a magnifying glass. In a typical case, they would first examine the prints of those suspects living in the area of the crime scene and expand in a widening circle to adjacent neighborhoods. In a large city with a mobile criminal population, this system was only rarely successful. Because "cold searching" was so time consuming and unproductive, latent fingerprints found at the crime scene were used primarily to confirm the identification of a suspect. That is, if the victim, after examining a collection of mug shots, identifies a suspect, the latent print would be compared to the suspect's fingerprints on file in order to confirm the identification. Now, with an automated fingerprint identification system (AFIS), when the investigator finds a print, he simply enters it into the computer to find out who it belongs to. The Los Angeles Police can compare a latent print with the approximately two million sets of fingerprints presently on file in about one hour.

An AFIS consists primarily of two technological instruments, a scanning machine, which translates the images of the fingerprint into a numerical code, and a computer, which compares the numerical code of the print with those on file. The computer compares the codes, not the images of the fingerprints. Ultimately, the goal is to maintain all fingerprints only in digital form rather than in images. What is needed is a computer that can classify fingerprints automatically into the Henry System subgroups. Computer experts are currently at work on this project.

a. **Recording.** A scanning machine uses a beam of light to record what are referred to as "minutiae." (Minutia is a word of Latin origin meaning a small detail; minutiae is its plural form.) The minutiae are the points at which ridge lines end or split. The following information on each minutia is recorded in digital form:

1) *Type.* Whether the minutia is on a ridge line that either splits or ends.

2) *Location.* The position of the minutia with respect to landmarks such as the "core," the center of the fingerprint pattern.

3) *Direction.* The angle of the ridge line on which the minutia is located with respect to the "axis." The "axis" is the fingerprint pattern direction.

4) *Ridge Count.* The number of ridge lines that are counted between the minutia and each of the four closest minutiae.

This information is recorded for each minutia. The scanner has the capability to process up to 100 minutiae for each finger-

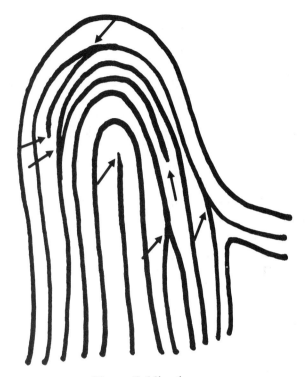

Figure 49. Minutiae.

print, although the computer can make an identification using as little as 8 minutiae. Blurred areas of a fingerprint are ignored.

b. **Comparing.** The computer will compare the numerical code of the "questioned" print with the numerical code of the "known" prints on file. It will then list and rank, in probable order, the names of the people whose fingerprints most closely resemble the "questioned" print. A technician will make a decision on a possible match. An AFIS is claimed to have a 97 percent accuracy rate.

ADDITIONAL READING

Classification of Fingerprints

Allison, H.C.: *Personal Identification.* Boston, Holbrook Press, 1973.

Bridges, B.C.: *Practical Fingerprinting.* Rev. by C.E. O'Hara. New York, Funk & Wagnalls, 1963.

Clements, W.W.: *The Study of Latent Fingerprints.* Springfield, Ill.: Thomas, 1987.

Collins, C.G.: *Fingerprint Science: How to Roll, Classify, File and Use Fingerprints,* 2nd ed. Costa Mesa, Calif.: Custom Publishing, 1989.

Cowger, J.F.: *Friction Ridge Skin: Comparison and Identification of Fingerprints.* New York, Elsevier, 1983.

Federal Bureau of Investigation. *The Science of Fingerprints: Classification and Uses,* rev. ed. Washington D.C.: U.S. Government Printing Office, 1984.

Olsen, R.D., Sr.: *Scott's Fingerprint Mechanics.* Springfield, Ill.: Thomas, 1978.

The Fingerprint Identification System. Boulder, Col.: Paladin Press, 1988.

Automated Fingerprint Systems

Brotman, B.J. and Pavel, R.K.: Identification: A Move Toward the Future. 60 *FBI Law Enforcement Bulletin,* 7, 1991.

Fjetland, R. and Robbins, C.: The AFIS Advantage: A Milestone in Fingerprint Identification Technology. 56 *Police Chief,* 6, 1989.

Hildreth, R.: The Tenprinter. 37 *Law and Order,* 7, 1989.

Neudorfer, C.D.: Fingerprint Automation: Progress in the FBI's Identification Division. 55 *FBI Law Enforcement Bulletin,* 3, 1986.

Rundell, P.: AFIS Today: An Overview. 35 *Law and Order,* 7, 1987.

SEARCH Group, Inc.: *Automated Fingerprint Identification Systems: Technology and Policy Issues.* Washington, D.C.: U.S. Department of Justice, 1987.

Shonberger, M.F.: Miami Police and A.F.I.S. Complete First Decade. 38 *Law and Order,* 11, 1990.

Slahor, S.: Leading the Way. 38 *Law and Order,* 7, 1990.

What is an AFIS? 56 *Police Chief,* 6, 1989.

Chapter 34

LAUNDRY AND DRY CLEANER MARKS

1. Introduction

I T WAS a routine house burglary. At two o'clock in the morning the detectives received a call from a couple who had returned from a theater party to find their suburban house burglarized. The detectives visited the house and examined the scene of the crime. Entrance had been made through a kitchen window, which had been unlocked by means of a "shove knife." The dresser drawers had been overturned on the bed. Jewelry and clothes had been taken. The owner remarked that the burglar must have worn one of his expensive jackets, since he had left his own jacket on the floor of the bedroom. The detectives examined the jacket and found a dry cleaner's tag on the inside of a sleeve.

The detectives brought the jacket to the identification bureau of their department. The identification man on duty examined the tag and searched through his file on dry cleaner's marks. He extracted one card which bore an inscription similar to that of the evidence tag. Printed on the card was the name of a tailor who used the mark to identify the clothing of his customers. In the morning the detectives visited the tailor, showed him the tag, and requested information concerning the customer. The tailor gave them the customer's name and address of a house just four blocks away. In a few minutes the detectives were in the room of the burglar. The criminal quickly confessed and showed them the stolen property.

2. Importance

Investigations as simple as that described above occur every month in the police departments of large cities. For every case which is "solved" by a latent fingerprint, there are probably two solved by laundry and dry cleaner's marks. These marks form a direct link between the crime and the criminal. They are attached to his clothing and associate him positively with the garment. The prosaic dry cleaner's mark has fortunately received little publicity, being ignored alike by criminals, fiction writers, and newspaper reporters.

3. Procedure in Brief

Laundries and dry cleaners are faced with a basic processing problem. The retailer receives clothing from the customer, records it, marks it, gives it to the wholesaler for processing, receives it on completion, and returns it to the customer. Obviously he must employ some reliable system of marking the clothes in order to insure the return of the proper garments to each customer. Thus, trousers, jackets, hats, dresses, shirts, handkerchiefs, towels, and similar articles which have been laundered and cleaned become, through the medium of the identifying mark, invaluable clues in a variety of cases that come to the attention of the police. The marks are not infallible clues. Some retailers do not record customers names and addresses. Moreover, there is no uniform system of marking.

4. Cases

Clothing as a clue enters into a large number of police cases, criminal and otherwise. The following list is representative of the more common types of cases:

a. **Crimes of Violence.** In murder, rape, assault, and robbery the elements of physical contact, violence, and rapid escape are present. The criminal may lose his hat, jacket, or shirt in the struggle or may simply forget them in his hurry to escape.

b. **Tracing.** The marked garment may serve as a tracing clue:

1) *Unidentified Persons.* When a dead body is found the clothing provides the most direct clue in the absence of identifying papers. Unconscious persons, lost children, and persons susceptible to mental disturbance can be identified in this manner.

2) *Wanted Persons.* Often the police are end-stopped in their pursuit of a fugitive when they arrive at his hotel or furnished room. If the fugitive has departed hurriedly, clothing may be left in the closet. By tracing the clothing marks, the detectives will obtain additional leads such as aliases and former addresses.

5. Marking Systems of Laundries and Cleaners

There are two types of numbers used to identify clothing in processing, namely, the *line number* and the *customer's receipt number.* This system has been built up by the laundries and dry cleaners themselves. As yet there is no uniform system imposed on the industry by the police as a control. Such a system would, of course, be invaluable in criminal identification work. The procedure described below is typical of the systems employed by most laundries and dry cleaners.

a. **Line Number.** This is the number used by the wholesaler to designate a particular retail store. The line number is the link between the wholesaler and the retailer. The wholesaler "picks up" clothing from a large number of retailers and lays out routes for the delivery trucks. A wholesaler with five routes will designate these as the 100 route, 200 route, and so forth. The retail stores on the 200 route, for example, will be given line numbers such as 201, 207, 205, and so forth. The system is not necessarily uniform. Some wholesalers may use letters such as MX or LY or even symbols such as triangles or squares. Some retailers may send their clothing to two or more wholesalers.

b. **Customer's Receipt Number.** The retailer must be able to associate the clothing with the customer. To do this he must add a customer's number to the line number. Receipts are issued to the customer and the number of the receipt is placed on the garment. The retailer may maintain a receipt book in which he records the customer's name and address. Some retailers can remember the owner of each garment or bundle and do not employ receipts or numbers. Where a receipt book is maintained, the retailer usually keeps his records for approximately one year before destroying them. The placing of the line number on the article of clothing is done by either the retailer or the wholesaler.

6. Marking Clothing and Other Articles

The methods of marking vary widely with wholesalers, retailers, and with communities. The common methods are described below.

a. **Marking Area.** Certain conventions are commonly observed in regard to the place where the garment is marked or tagged.

1) *Coats and Jackets.* Inside of the sleeve, usually the right sleeve.

2) *Vests.* In the lining, usually under the right arm pit.

3) *Trousers.* Waist band, fob pockets, or right rear pocket lining.

4) *Shirts.* Collar band, shirt tail, or front of shirt (invisible marks).

5) *Sheets, Pillowcases and Towels.* On the edges.

6) *Gloves.* On the inside, near the center.

7) *Hats.* On the sweat band, front or rear, or on the lining.

b. **Marking Media.** There are three common ways in which a garment is marked.

1) *Hand Marking.* Ink or indelible pencil is used.

2) *Tagging.* A small rectangular tag is clipped or affixed by a wire frame to the garment. The tag varies in size, color, material, and marking. It may be printed or hand marked.

3) *Machine, Stamp, or Stencil.* These methods are employed mainly by laundries. The type varies in size with the individual laundry.

7. Identifying the Mark

The following is typical of the procedure followed in identifying a mark:

a. **Locating.** The mark is located by turning the garment inside out and examining the lining. An ultraviolet lamp is used to search for invisible marks that fluoresce.

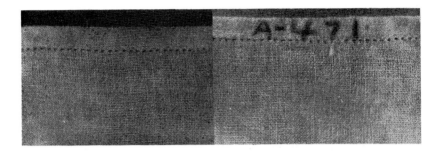

Figure 50. Obliterated laundry mark on a handkerchief.

Figure 51. Rendered visible by use of infrared film and Wratten 87 filter.

b. **Line Number.** A search of the file is made for the line number, and the cards under the given numbers are withdrawn.

c. **Comparison.** The mark is compared with the filed numbers until a matching number is located which is made with the same type of printing or with the same handwriting. In cases of tags, the color, size, and material are considered. The comparison of the type or handwriting is the most difficult part of the search. If a successful match is found, the retailer's name and address are recorded.

d. **Visiting the Retailer.** The investigator now takes the garment to the retailer and requests an identification. The retailer may at this point be able to give him the name and address of the customer by means of his records or through memory.

e. **Doubtful Cases.** Quite often the files do not yield a mark which has the same type of printing or handwriting. In these cases the numbers most closely resembling the evidence number are recorded and a visit is made to various wholesalers or retailers for further identification. Dry cleaners' associations can also be consulted.

f. **Illegible Marks.** The difficulties of marking cloth frequently result in illegible marks. In these situations the police laboratory can assist in rendering the mark legible. Photographs made with process or infrared film may provide the contrast necessary for clarifying the number. Sometimes the symbols are strongly impressed on the garment but their identity cannot be established because of the poor writing. The investigator must then visit those

Figure 52. Invisible laundry mark fluorescing under ultraviolet radiation.

establishments using symbols most nearly resembling the evidence inscription.

8. Identification Bureau Files

Separate files are maintained for laundries and dry cleaners in identification bureaus. A standard 3″ × 5″ card is ordinarily used. The cards are cross-indexed by means of various possible combinations. The name and address of the laundry or cleaner, wholesaler and retailer, are recorded on the card and a sample mark is affixed thereto. The cards are filed in numerical and alphabetical order. Finally, a file is made of all cards of the establishments according to address. The person assigned to the file must obtain samples of marks and tags by visiting each retailer and wholesaler. Annually, each establishment must be revisited for new marks or marks made by new personnel.

9. Sources of Information

The investigator will find that there are a number of agencies which maintain files of laundry and dry cleaner's marks, ranging from the local to the national level. Ordinarily the local agency, usually the municipal police department, maintains the most effective file, since efficiency in this activity requires frequent personal contact. The following are some of the available sources.

a. Crime laboratories or identification divisions of municipal, county, and state law enforcement agencies.

b. The Federal Bureau of Investigation maintains a file of invisible laundry mark systems.

c. Laundry and dry cleaning establishments in the local area.

Chapter 35

CASTING

1. Application

A NOTHER METHOD of recording the appearance of evidence at the crime scene is to reproduce its external form in three dimensions by making a cast. Ordinarily, the purpose of making casts is to enable a scientific comparison to be made with the objects suspected of having made the impression and thus to establish that the object, and by inference its owner, were at the scene of the crime. Impressions such as those produced by shoes, tires, teeth and tools can be reproduced by casting.

Both photography and casting play an important part in the accurate recording of an impression. A photograph will often provide more overall details than the cast. On the other hand, the cast, if successful, will reproduce the raised areas of the object, such as a shoe or tire, that made the impression. These are the areas that have the most wear and thus have more of the identifying characteristics. Often these areas are not represented as well on a photograph.

2. Shoe and Tire Impressions

Although a number of materials can be used to make a cast, plaster of paris is the most widely used, particularly in outdoor scenes. It is simple to prepare, provides a durable cast, and is capable of reproducing fine detail. Another casting material, class 1 dental stone, is preferred by many investigators because of its superior strength, durability and convenience. It does not require reinforcing the cast.

a. **Preparation.** Before the evidentiary indentation or impres-

766

sion is cast, it should be photographed from several points of view. First, an overall photograph should be made to show the impression in its background. Second, close-up pictures should be taken both with and without a ruler in the field of view and with the camera plate parallel to the base surface of the impression. A ruler, placed alongside the impression and depressed into the surface at the same depth as the impression, permits an accurate enlargement of the photographs reflecting the true size of the impression. Ideally, the camera will be held by a tripod placed over the impression and a fine-grained, slow speed, black and white film will be used. In order to preserve fine details, a 4″ × 5″ camera is preferable to a 35mm. camera because the negatives will not have to be enlarged as much. Finally, photographs should be taken from various angles which may reveal significant detail. An oblique light source, that is, one held at a low angle to the ground, is helpful in making the impressions more distinct. Relatively large particles of extraneous matter should be removed to prevent the obscuring of parts of the impression.

b. **Spraying.** If the receiving surface consists of a soft substance such as dust, sand, or flour, a quick-drying fixative such as plastic spray or shellac should be applied prior to casting. The spray should be directed against a piece of cardboard and permitted to settle over the impression. When the fixative is quite dry, a fine layer of machine oil should be sprayed over the surface to facilitate separation of cast from the fixative. If the impression is in snow, instead of the above sprays, several coats of a spray wax product called "snow print wax" should be used.

c. **Mixing the Plaster.** An estimate of the amount of material required for an inch-thick cast should be made and a corresponding quantity of water placed in a glass, porcelain, or rubber container. The plaster is then sprinkled evenly over the surface of the water until sufficient has been deposited to extend in a mound from the bottom of the vessel to the surface of the water. The plaster is not stirred thoroughly until the mixture has the consistency of cream. Plaster or water is added to achieve the proper consistency.

d. **Pouring.** The mixture is poured over the impression at a low level. The fall of the liquid should be broken by means of a flat piece of wood. When a depth of ½ inch is reached, the pouring should be interrupted and the cast reinforced by laying on pieces of fine mesh wire or light, flat pieces of wood. The remainder of the plaster is then poured on the first layer.

e. **Setting.** The cast should be permitted to set for approximately thirty minutes. In hardening, the plaster first becomes warm and subsequently cools on setting.

f. **Identification.** Before the plaster has completely set, it should be marked by the investigator for identification. The date, case number, and initials of the investigator can be scratched on the upper surface.

g. **Cleaning.** After hardening, the cast should be removed and permitted to further dry for several hours. It can then be washed and lightly brushed in water to remove the adhering debris.

3. Tool Marks

Casts are made of tool marks when it is impracticable to remove the impression to the laboratory for examination. There are a number of materials suitable for casting including silicone rubber, dental impression creams, moulage, modeling clay and thermosetting plastics. Silicone rubber casting compounds are an excellent medium for producing the fine details of tool marks. A retaining wall of modeling clay or a similar substance is built around the mark at a distance of one inch from the mark. The silicone compound consists of two liquids: (1) a rubber base material and (2) a small quantity of a catalyst. The two are mixed together in a container and poured into the retaining wall, hardening in about ten minutes. The result is a high quality reproduction that does not adhere to the mark and is flexible enough to be removed easily from the impression.

ADDITIONAL READING

Casting

Bodziak, W.J.: Shoe and Tire Impression Evidence. 53 *FBI Law Enforcement Bulletin*, 7, 1984.

Ojena, S.M.: A New Improved Technique for Casting Impressions in Snow. 29 *Journal of Forensic Sciences,* 322, 1984.

Vandiver, J.V. and Wolcott, J.H.: Identification of Suitable Plaster for Crime Scene Casting. 23 *Journal of Forensic Sciences,* 607, 1978.

See also Chapter 36, Additional Reading, **Foot Impressions.**

Chapter 36

VARIOUS IMPRESSIONS

1. Impressions in General

THE EVIDENTIAL value of impressions made by a shoe, hand tool, or other article is based on the theory that no two physical objects are alike and hence that impressions made by such objects often are marked by uniquely identifying characteristics which can be detected upon close scrutiny. In general there are two types of characteristics associated with an impression. First, there are the *class* characteristics which identify the kind, make, or model of the object that produced the impression. For example, the general shape of the tool mark may indicate to the observer that it was made by a screwdriver with a broad blade. The pattern of a tire impression may reflect that the imprint came from a Firestone tire. Secondly, there are *individual* characteristics which serve to identify the specific object which causes the impression. Illustrative of this type are the individual striations in the tool mark which correspond exactly with the defects of the suspect tool, or the nicks and cuts in the tire impression which match the defects in one of the tires on a suspect car. It is readily seen that individual characteristics are of much greater probative value than simple class characteristics. Unfortunately, they are more difficult to discover, and only occasionally are sufficient distinctive features found to permit a fairly conclusive identification of the impression with the object. Class characteristics do have some probative value. Although a class characteristic does not positively identify an impression as being made by a specific object, it can be used to narrow the field of objects to be considered in the preliminary stages of an investigation, often quite significantly. If one considers the thousands of makes and models

770

of shoes available, the identification of a shoe print as being of a type that is worn by less than one percent of the population is an important clue. If another class characteristic, the size of the shoe, can be determined, it would further limit the number of people who could have made the shoe print.

2. Foot Impressions

a. **Casts.** The process of making plaster casts of foot impressions is described in Chapter 35. Once the cast has been obtained it should be carefully examined for distinguishing characteristics. The fact that shoes are usually mass-produced tends to lessen the probative value of any class characteristics which may be present and, therefore, particular attention should be given to individual characteristics which would serve to identify the impression with a shoe having the same distinctive marks. Marks of wear, protruding nails, and other defects are usually helpful in effecting a comparison.

b. **Walking Patterns.** Where a number of consecutive footprints are found, it is sometimes possible to detect some distinctive characteristics which may be helpful in the course of the investigation. For example, the angle of walk, the length of step, and any infirmities which are characteristic of the person will normally be reflected in the impressions. However, such characteristics are merely indicative and should not be made the basis of positive conclusions with respect to identification.

3. Surface Footprints

The surface footprint is produced by the depositing of material on the surface by the foot or shoe. Whereas the foot impression deforms the surface, the footprint merely deposits a layer of dust, liquid, mud, or perspiration upon it. The most common prints of this type are shoe prints. These are often found in connection with office burglaries where the perpetrator has, in the course of this search, carelessly scattered papers from the drawers or safe and has stepped on the sheets. Usually a heel print can be found on the paper. If the weather is rainy, it may be possible to find excellent imprints of the heel and part of the sole. A shoe print found on any surface should first be photographed. Where it is difficult to see the print, oblique lighting should be used. Wherever possible, the camera should be placed directly over the print with the lens and plate parallel to the surface. A scale should be included in the photograph. If a suspect is found, his shoes should be examined to see if they compare favorably in size and shape with the questioned print. In many cases the investigator can eliminate shoes which do not correspond, particularly if the evidence print bears some class characteristic which is dissimilar. Where it appears that a good match has been obtained, he should endeavor to obtain the shoes of the suspect to forward to the laboratory for comparison with the evidence prints. If the shoes cannot be obtained, sample prints can be secured by coating the shoes with fingerprint ink and pressing them against plain white paper.

4. Sole Prints

Prints made with the bare feet are called *sole prints.* Occasionally such prints can be developed by the usual methods employed in connection with latent fingerprints. Large tile bathroom floors, paper on floors, polished wood, and similar surfaces are receptive to such prints. The friction ridges on the sole of the foot sometimes leave a deposit of perspiration and dirt which will respond to the appropriate methods of development used for fingerprints. The investigator will first become aware of the presence of such prints by faint outlines of the foot. The print should be photographed in one-to-one size after it has been developed. A fingerprint camera of the $3\frac{1}{4}''$ × $4\frac{1}{4}''$ type will usually include the major part of the friction ridge pattern. An overall picture should be made with the $4''$ × $5''$ camera to include the background in the field of view. Comparison prints of a suspect can be obtained by the regular inking method used for fingerprints.

5. Palm Prints

Quite frequently, palm prints are discovered at a crime scene, particularly in burglary cases. The act of climbing in and out of windows and other activities associated with a burglary often involve pressing the palms on the window sills and casements. In the absence of latent fingerprints, palm prints are particularly useful for comparison purposes in the event that suspects are found. The basis of a palm print identification is the same as that of fingerprints. The permanent, unalterable pattern of friction ridges and flexure lines on the palm varies with the individual, and thus, when two patterns are found to correspond in a sufficient number of characteristics, the expert may conclude that they were made by the same hand. Palm prints are developed and photographed in the same manner as fingerprints. Comparison prints of a suspect can be obtained by inking the palm and pressing it on a card. Best results can be realized by placing the card on an appropriate convex surface so that the pattern of the entire palm area will be reflected.

6. Poroscopy

The friction ridges of the palms and fingers of the hand contain an additional means of identification in the characteristic formation of the pores. Each ridge is dotted by pores which differ in position, shape, and size. Thus it is possible to establish a pore pattern in a small area containing only a few friction ridges and to use this pattern as a basis of identification of a suspect. Since the pores are permanent in structure throughout a person's lifetime and since they appear in an infinite variety of patterns, an identification effected in this manner has the same theoretical validity as that attached to fingerprint identification.

a. **Application.** Poroscopy can be used where a latent partial fingerprint is developed and prints of suspects are available for comparison. In order for a latent fingerprint to be of value in establishing an identification there must be a significant number corresponding characteristics in the friction ridges. If enough of these corresponding characteristics cannot be found, the techni-

Figure 53. A Fingerprint in which the pores are visible. The wide variation in the shape of the pore outline is apparent.

cian may resort to a pore pattern study. The technique is not commonly used because of the fact that outlines of the pores are so delicate, they are generally not clearly visible in latent prints.

b. **Developing Latent Pore Prints.** Since pore prints are extremely delicate and easily destroyed, special care is required in their development and subsequent protection. Iodine fuming has been recommended for development on hard polished surfaces. Powders such as lead carbonate and mercuric oxide may be used on other surfaces with satisfactory results. When using powder, the brush should be held over the print and tapped gently so that the powder will be sprinkled lightly over the impression. By delicate brushing the powder is subsequently spread and the excess removed.

c. **Pore Prints of Suspects.** Although ink has a tendency to fill the pores and spoil the outline of pore patterns when it is used carelessly, it is possible to obtain a satisfactory reproduction of pores if the ink is applied to the finger lightly and the finger is not pressed too forcefully against the recording card. Special chemical formulae exist for obtaining superior pore prints for comparison purposes; however, their use is generally confined to the laboratory.

7. Earprints

At his trial in Lusanne, Switzerland, in 1990, George Roman, a suspect in more than 30 burglaries, was convicted on the basis of earprint evidence found at the scene of the crime. Before entering an apartment, Roman would place his ear against the door to listen for activity inside. In this way, he would make sure that no one was at home at the time of his entry. As a result, his earprints were recovered and identified by the police in 11 of the cases.

a. **Latent Earprints.** While dusting for fingerprints, sometimes a barely visible outline of an ear is recognized. It is usually found on an outside door or window, or occasionally on a safe door. Latent earprints are produced by the deposit of a thin layer of perspiration and body oils when the ear is pressed against a hard glossy surface, such as glass, metal, plastic, or painted wood. They are imprints of the flesh lines that form the anatomical structure of the external ear.

Latent earprints are developed with fingerprint powders; magnetic powders work especially well. After developing the print, two kinds of photographs should be taken: an overall view illustrating the location of the developed print at the crime scene and a close-up picture reproducing the details of the earprint. After the print is photographed, it can then be lifted, in the same manner as a fingerprint, with either transparent tape or a rubber lifter. The earprint is then transferred to a white index card.

b. **Comparison Prints.** When taking comparison prints from a suspect or someone associated with the crime scene, it is necessary to try to duplicate the amount of pressure which produced the original earprint. Usually taking several prints at varying degrees of pressure and later selecting the most suitable ones is the best course. When dealing with partial prints, reproduce only that part of the ear which appears in the original.

c. **Value as Evidence.** An earprint found on a door or window is helpful to the investigator for estimating the height of a potential suspect. More importantly, it is an excellent means of positive identification because ear structure patterns are unique in each individual and remain constant throughout life. "Through 38 years of research..." writes Alfred V. Iannarelli, the author of *Ear Identification,* "... in literally thousands of ears that were examined by visual means, photographs, earprints, and latent earprint impressions, *no two ears were found to be identical* — not even the ears of any one individual. This uniqueness held true in cases of identical and fraternal twins, triplets, and quadruplets."

7. Tire Impressions

In crimes such as murder, rape, and robbery the criminal usually employs a vehicle to escape from the scene of the crime. If the area of criminal operations is unpaved the possibility of finding tire impressions exists. Often the tire tracks are the only clue left at the crime scene. Unless the car has traveled backwards only the rear tire tracks will be visible. In some cars in which the rear wheels are farther apart than the front, part of the front tire tracks may be visible.

a. **Direction of Travel.** If oil is dripping from the car the shape of the drops will be such that on hard surfaces they will taper toward the direction of travel of the car. On unpaved roads small masses of dirt may be thrown up by the side of the wheels so that they taper in the direction of travel.

b. **Measurements.** The distance between the wheels should be measured as well as the breadth of the tire track. A photograph of the track should be made with the plate and lens board parallel to the tire impression and a rule in the field of view. The impression should then be cast with plaster of paris.

c. **Tire Tread File.** The FBI maintains a collection of photographs of tire tread patterns provided by the tire manufacturers which may be helpful in determining the make and possibly the model of the tire that made the impression.

8. Tool Marks

Another form of impression that sometimes provides a valuable clue is the mark left by a tool such as a jimmy applied to a relatively hard surface. The blade or working face of a tool is

Figure 54. A tire impression photographed before casting. The careful selection of the right angle of illumination serves to emphasize the pattern.

seldom the smooth, unmarred surface which it appears to be to the eye. Low-power magnification will reveal certain imperfections. If there are a sufficient number of these and if they are sufficiently characteristic, it is possible for the expert to conclude that the mark was made by a particular tool in question. The theory that underlies the study of tool marks is similar to that applied in firearms identification. A bullet or a shell is quite frequently impressed with the characteristic markings of the gun from which it was discharged. If the evidence bullet is not mutilated on contact the expert can usually determine whether it could have been discharged from the suspect firearm. Tools, like guns, differ in size, width, thickness, and general shape. Even where the tools are alike in these characteristics, minute differences will exist which may be attributable to manufacturing, finishing, and grinding; uneven wear; unusual use or abuse; sharpening; or modifications made by the owner. These imperfections are usually visible under a low-power microscope. If the tool is applied to a soft metal surface, these individual characteristics are transferred to the metal. Occasionally the defects are sufficient in number to permit the expert to assert, on the basis of a comparison, that a certain mark was produced by a certain tool.

a. **Findings.** Although positive identifications are relatively rare, the evidence of tool marks is often found useful for one of the following purposes:

1) *Association.* The tool impression found at the scene of the crime may be matched with a tool found on a suspect or a tool found at the scene.

2) *Linking.* A series of burglaries may be linked together to show common authorship by means of similar tool impressions.

3) *Modus Operandi.* The tool marks often indicate the manner in which force was applied to a door, window, or safe. Similar applications of force in separate crimes may point to a common *modus operandi.*

4) *Searching.* The search for the tool used in perpetrating an offense may be greatly limited by determining the type of tool employed, from a study of the tool mark.

b. **Types of Tool Impressions.** Tool impressions will vary depending upon whether the tool was moved along the surface or was merely pressed in. If a tool, such as a screwdriver, is used simply as a lever, the resulting impression may not contain as many identifiable characteristic markings as the impressions from a tool such as a wrench, pliers, or saw which is usually moved along or around the surface. Of course, if an instrument such as a crowbar or jimmy is forced into a narrow space and then used as lever, both types of marks may be imparted to the surface.

c. **Handling of Tool Mark Evidence.** Tool impressions are usually found in burglary investigations. They most commonly occur at the point of the break and, in burglaries involving larceny, on the safe or strongbox which was rifled. The following is a suggested method of procedure at crime scenes of this kind.

1) *Discovery.* Openings, such as doors, windows, transoms, and skylights, should be examined for signs of forcible entry. Broken, forced, or cut locks, latches, and bolts should be studied for marks. Finally, desks, cabinets, safes, and cash boxes are examined. Tool impressions and tools should be carefully noted and included in pictures and sketches of appropriate parts of the crime scene.

2) *Protection.* Arrangements should be made for guards to protect the evidence until the examination or collection is complete. Doors and other openings which have been found to bear tool marks may, in addition, require careful processing for fingerprints and hence should not be touched unless absolutely necessary and then only with extreme care.

3) *Removal.* After appropriate photographs and sketches have been made, the investigator should, if necessary, remove the surfaces bearing tool impressions for the purpose of forwarding them to the laboratory together with any tools which are logical instruments for a comparison. Several precautions should be observed in removing such evidence.

a) MARKING. The item removed as evidence should be marked with the investigator's initials, the date, and if known, the case number. The evidence should also be marked to show the inside, outside, top and bottom surfaces, and the area bearing the tool impression. This marking should, of course, be done after the photographs have been taken.

b) PROPERTY CONSIDERATIONS. The investigator should make arrangements with the owner or custodian of the property for the return of, replacement, or compensation for items to be removed as evidence.

c) BASIS OF A DECISION TO REMOVE. The wholesale removal of property or integral parts of valuable structures and equipment is neither desirable nor necessary. The decision for removal should be based on the importance of the case, the probative significance of the tool impression in comparison with other available evidence, and the distance from the crime scene to the laboratory. Where it is impractical to remove the original evidence, the investigator can photograph and cast the evidence or, if feasible, request the presence of a technical expert at the scene of the crime to perform the comparison.

d. **Photographing Tool Marks.** Before the tool mark is disturbed or altered by casting, molding, or removal it should be carefully photographed to provide a permanent pictorial record of the evidence in its original condition. The photograph will also serve to identify original evidence with any casts or molds that may be made and thus satisfy legal requirements for records of original evidence. Two types of photographs are required: one showing the tool marks together with the background for identification purposes and a close-up photograph (at least one-to-one size) to show minute details of the tool mark. In both photographs a ruler should be placed in the field of view and to one side, in order to provide laboratory technicians with a reference scale for examination and comparison purposes.

e. **Casting and Molding Tool Marks.** A cast or mold of the tool mark should be made only when the investigator is unable to remove the original evidence. The methods described in Chapter 35 are applicable to this work. The investigator should not attempt the casting or molding until he has practiced the particular method on a similar wooden or metallic surface unassociated with the evidence. The most satisfactory method of making a cast of a tool mark is the use of modeling clay or plasticene. The casting material is kneaded between the hands and pressed against the mark until it fills the area and is conveniently shaped in the back. The method is applicable to both wooden and metallic surfaces. The resulting cast is in the shape of the blade or other portion of the tool used to make the impression. A reproduction of the tool mark itself can later be made from this cast by using plaster of paris.

9. Laboratory Findings

The investigator may submit to the laboratory for examination the original tool impression, suspect tools, casts, and photographs. In the ideal situation the investigator is seeking to conclusively identify a suspect tool with the tool mark. A number of lesser but still useful findings may result from the examination. The following are the possible conclusions that can be made in the laboratory.

a. The mark can be compared with a suspect tool to determine whether it was made by the tool.

b. A tool mark from a crime scene can be compared with similar tool marks from the scenes of other crimes. A positive finding can aid in establishing the guilt of, or in obtaining a confession of guilt from, a suspect who may be responsible for more than one crime.

c. Information can be obtained concerning the nature of an unknown tool from a study of the mark, thus narrowing the search.

d. By matching pieces of wire it may be possible to determine whether the pieces were cut from the same wire and whether a given tool or machine was used to make the cuts.

10. Number Restoration by Chemical Etching

In cases involving stolen property, the investigator will sometimes find metal objects with their serial numbers filed away, removed by grinding, or otherwise altered. Thieves will often do this in order to disguise the ownership or the origin of stolen equipment. Serial numbers that are stamped in metal are found on all types of motor vehicles and their parts, bicycles, construction equipment, firearms, appliances, cameras, watches, office machines, and many other types of products. Manufacturers place these numbers on their products in order to monitor their quantity, quality, and location as they pass through the various stages of production, distribution, and warranty coverage. The serial numbers, along with the information contained in the manufacturer's and dealer's records, are instrumental in determining the ownership of the questioned property. When these numbers are removed or altered, it is sometimes possible for the investigator to restore their visibility through the use of what is called a "chemical etching" method.

a. **Purpose.** The removal of serial numbers from automobiles, firearms, and other equipment is against the law in most states. However, for the investigator to prove the more serious crime of larceny, it is necessary to establish the ownership of the stolen object. This can often be accomplished if the serial number can be restored to visibility.

b. **Theory.** When the metal is stamped with the serial number during the manufacturing process, the force exerted on the surface compresses the molecular structure of the metal directly below the numbers. This region becomes permanently stressed to a depth of from one-half to several times that of the printed number depending on the type of metal involved. Not only will this compressed metal take on an altered structure, but it will also react differently in chemical reactions. In the presence of an acid or a base, the metal beneath the serial number will oxidate at a different rate than the surrounding metal. This may cause the imprint to become faintly visible on the metal surface. Thus, if the serial number has been filed away, the imprint of the number can still be restored by the application of a dilute acid or base called an "etching solution." This solution will dissolve the compressed metal at a faster rate than the surrounding metal, making the outline of the numbers visible.

c. **Application.** The chemical etching method can only be used if the stress pattern of the stamped metal has not been altered. Filing or grinding away the number to too great a depth, pounding it with a hammer, welding it or heating it with a torch relieves or changes the strain in the metal. The region beneath the numbers will no longer contain the original stress pattern of the stamping. Overstamping will also destroy the underlying pattern of the serial number, unless the new number has been accidentally placed off-center. In this case, the application of the etching solution might develop the original number above, below, or alongside the new number.

d. **Etching Solutions.** There are a number of effective chemical etching solutions containing either dilute acids or bases in various concentrations. Because every metal reacts at a different rate, there are formulas for each metal. A solution should be selected that is not too strong so that it will not react too quickly. Otherwise it will dissolve the metal through the compressed area too rapidly and will not allow enough time for the visibility of the numbers to develop. The time it will take for the numbers to become visible may vary from a few minutes to an hour or longer.

1) *Cast Iron or Steel.* A small magnet is helpful in identifying iron or steel. A solution of the following chemicals will produce satisfactory results:

> 120 cc of concentrated hydrochloric acid (HCL)
> 90 cc of distilled water (H_2O)
> 75 cc of ethyl alcohol (C_2H_5OH)
> 15 g of copper chloride ($CuCl_2$)

2) *Aluminum.* This metal and its alloys tend to react more rapidly than iron or steel to an etchant. The following is a suitable formula:

> 1 g of sodium hydroxide (NaOH)
> 99 cc of distilled water (H_2)

e. **Technique.**

1) Photograph the object, particularly the area where the numbers will appear.

2) Clean the surface. Any organic solvent such as alcohol, acetone, or benzene can be used.

3) Polish the surface with an emery cloth. If possible, attempt to achieve a mirror-like finish.

4) Apply the etching solution by means of a cotton swab. Alternatively, build a one-half inch retaining wall of modelling clay around the polished area, pour in the etching solution and allow it to stand.

5) When the numbers appear, photograph them immediately. Often, the numbers are visible for only a short time.

6) Add water to halt the chemical reaction.

7) Record the numbers or partial numbers with pen and paper.

11. Bite Marks.

Bite marks are occasionally found as part of the physical evidence in a wide variety of criminal investigations, including burglary, homicide, and assault cases. Each set of teeth has both natural and acquired characteristics. Teeth differ naturally in size, shape, spacing, and direction of growth. There are ridges on the edges of teeth as well as grooves on the front and back. These ridges and grooves are different in each individual; they gradually become smooth with constant wear. Besides wear, teeth acquire additional distinctive characteristics during the course of a lifetime through breakage, loss, fillings and other dental work. All of these natural differences and acquired alterations combine to make every set of teeth significantly different.

A bite mark on a receptive surface may provide enough detail so that it can be compared with a dental impression obtained from a suspect. The comparison of bite marks with dental impressions is performed by a *forensic odontologist,* a dentist trained in the recovery and analysis of dental evidence. A bite-mark comparison is often useful in excluding a suspect. One unexplained discrepancy between the bite mark and the exemplar, that is, the dental impression of the suspect, is sufficient for the forensic odontologist to conclude that they were of different origin. If several points of similarity are discovered with no unresolved differences, the bite mark will be described as consistent with the exemplar. In rare cases, a positive identification is made. When there are a significant number of similar characteristics with no disqualifying inconsistencies, the odontologist may conclude that the bite mark and the exemplar were made by the same teeth.

a. **Bite Marks on Food.** A burglar, on his way through the kitchen will occasionally sample food left on the countertop, leaving his teeth impressions on a discarded portion. Fruit, cheese, and chocolate have a consistency that is especially receptive to retaining these impressions. Bite marks are made by the upper and lower teeth as they compress and then scrape across the surface of the food. Due to the perishable nature of the evidence, it is necessary to photograph and cast the bite marks as soon as possible.

1) *Photography.* Bite marks on food are photographed in a manner similar to tool marks, requiring two different kinds of shots. One photograph locates the object bearing the bite mark, showing its position and background in the crime scene; the

other, a close-up of at least one-to-one size, records the details of the bite mark. A 4″ × 5″ press camera or a high-quality 35mm camera can be used. Oblique lighting is often helpful in highlighting the teeth indentations. In some of the photographs, a ruler should be placed in the field of view so that it would be possible to compare the size of the bite mark with the size of a dental impression obtained from a suspect. Including a ruler in the photograph is also helpful as a guide for the laboratory personnel when enlarging the picture.

2) *Casting.* A cast will sometimes record fine details missed by a photograph. Casting may be done with a silicone rubber casting compound or some other dental impression material. Care should be taken with this step because of the fragile nature of the evidence. Sometimes the cast can only be done once because the process alters the details of the impression.

b. **Bite Marks on Skin.** Bite marks occur most frequently in homicide and assault cases. They appear in a variety of forms including the characteristic doughnut and double-horseshoe patterns. When the teeth have not broken the skin, the bite mark can take on the appearance of a bruise, with the black-and-blue coloring becoming more visible with time. When the investigator suspects biting is involved, a visual inspection of the entire body should be made. Often the bite mark is hidden because the victim has been bitten through his clothing. If a suspect is in custody, the investigator must also consider the possibility that the victim has bitten his assailant. A defensive bite mark can be valuable associative evidence linking the suspect to the victim.

1) *Occurrence.* Bite marks occur frequently in the following types of criminal cases:

a) Child Abuse. In these incidents a parent or guardian becomes enraged at a child and retaliates with a single bite. This occurs out of frustration with the perceived misbehavior of the child, often during disagreeable activities, such as diaper changing or toilet training.

b) Sexual Assault or Homicide. These cases involve multiple bite wounds, often done slowly and sadistically, on or near the genital area. The biting is characteristically followed by a sucking of the skin. The sucking will leave a bruised area of tissue or, in the more severe cases, a *hematoma* in the center of the bite mark. A *hematoma* is an accumulation of blood in the tissues following a rupture of the blood vessels. These bite marks occur both in heterosexual and homosexual attacks. Because the biting is done slowly and deliberately, it will often leave fine details on the skin.

c) NON–SEXUAL ASSAULT AND HOMICIDE. While defending himself, the victim will sometimes leave a single bite mark on the hands, arms, neck, or face of the attacker.

2) *Photography.* The color and appearance of bite marks change with the passage of time; frequently they become more distinct after a day or two. For this reason, bite marks are photographed on both live and deceased victims at 24-hour intervals for a period of 5 days. In homicide cases, the morgue is instructed to refrigerate rather than embalm the victim. Embalming tends to wash out the color of the bite wound. Photographs should be taken both in black and white and in color. From the color of the bruise the approximate time that the bite was inflicted can often be determined.

Two types of photographs are required: 1) an orientation photograph, to illustrate the position of the bite mark on the body; 2) a close-up photograph, to render the details of the bite mark. A ruler is included in some of the close-up pictures to indicate accurately the size of the impression. Distortion can be a problem in the photography of curved surfaces. To avoid this, it is essential to position the camera perpendicular to the bite mark. In one of the photographs, two or more non-flexible rulers can be included to demonstrate the lack of distortion. When photographing a bite mark on a living victim, it is helpful to place him in the position he was in at the time of the bite. Because of the elasticity of the skin, the shape and appearance of the bite mark will sometimes change, depending on whether the victim is standing, sitting, or lying down.

3) *Swabbing.* Approximately 80 percent of the population are secretors, that is, they have a group-specific antigen in their body fluids which reveals their blood type. By examining the saliva from a bite wound, a laboratory technician may be able to determine the blood type of the assailant or the fact that he belongs to the non-secretor group. Saliva may also be used for DNA analysis

which can lead to the positive identification of a suspect. The collection process requires cotton swabs dipped in distilled water or a saline solution. Swabbing is done in concentric circles working toward the center of the bite mark. The swabs are replaced frequently. They are allowed to dry and are then placed in sealed, sterile test tubes to be sent to the laboratory for analysis. Control swabs of the body areas are included. Blood and saliva specimens are collected for comparison from the victim as well as from any suspect in custody.

4) *Casting*. The forensic odontologist or an experienced laboratory technician will cast the bite mark using a silicone rubber casting compound or some other dental impression material. The bite mark is placed in an upright position so that the liquid casting compound does not flow off. The liquid is then poured over the bite mark and allowed to set. After the casting material has dried, gauze or orthopedic tape warmed in hot water is placed gently over the bite mark area to give the cast support. Another thin layer of casting compound is added to secure the tape in place. When the cast has hardened completely, it is removed and then initialed and photographed. The result of the casting is a reproduction of the teeth that made the bite mark. A model of the bite mark itself can be made in the laboratory from the cast.

5) *Analysis*. When a suspect is in custody, dental impressions and photographs are obtained either by the informed consent of the suspect or by court order. If possible, the suspect's dental records are secured. The forensic odontologist compares these materials with the photographs, casts, and models of the bite mark and renders his expert opinion.

ADDITIONAL READING

Foot Impressions

Abbott, J.R.: *Footwear Evidence: The Examination, Identification, and Comparison of Footwear Impressions.* Springfield, Ill.: Thomas, 1964.
Bodziak, W.J.: *Footwear Impression Evidence.* New York, Elsevier, 1990.

——: Manufacturing Processes for Athletic Shoe Outsoles and Their Significance in the Examination of Footwear Impression Evidence. 31 *Journal of Forensic Sciences*, 153, 1986.

——: Shoe and Tire Impression Evidence. 53 *FBI Law Enforcement Bulletin*, 7, 1984.

Cassidy, M.J.: *Footwear Identification*. Ottawa, Royal Canadian Mounted Police, 1980.

Cook, C.W.: Footprint Identification. 57 *Fingerprint and Identification Magazine*, 6, 1975.

Davis, R.J.: An Intelligence Approach to Footwear Marks and Toolmarks. 21 *Journal of the Forensic Science Society*, 183, 1981.

Facey, O.E., Hannah, I.D. and Rosen, D.: Shoe Wear Patterns and Pressure Distribution under Feet and Shoes, Determined by Image Analysis. 32 *Journal of the Forensic Science Society*, 15, 1992.

Fawcett, A.S.: The Role of the Footmark Examiner. 10 *Journal of the Forensic Science Society*, 227, 1970.

Giles, E. and Vallandigham, P.H.: Height Estimation from Foot and Shoeprint Length. 36 *Journal of Forensic Sciences*, 1134, 1991.

Hueske, E.E.: A Superior Method for Obtaining Test Prints from Footwear and Tires. 41 *Journal of Forensic Identification*, 165, 1991.

Laskowski, G.E. and Kyle, V.L.: Barefoot Impressions—A Preliminary Study of Identification Characteristics and Population Frequency of their Morphological Features. 33 *Journal of Forensic Sciences*, 378, 1988.

Laskowski, G.E.: An Improved Technique for the Visualization of Footprint Impressions in the Insoles of Athletic Shoes. 32 *Journal of Forensic Sciences*, 1075, 1987.

Lorring, M.: Bloodhound Trailing Evidence, Is It Admissible? 36 *Law and Order*, 7, 1988.

McGonigle, C.: Tracking: An Ancient Skill Makes a Comeback. 36 *Law and Order*, 2, 1988.

Ojena, S.M.: New Electrostatic Process Recovers Visible and Invisible Dust Particles at Crime Scenes. 36 *Law and Order*, 7, 1988.

Petty, C.S., et al.: The Value of Shoe Sole Imprints in Automobile Crash Investigations. 1 *Journal of Police Science and Administration*, 1, 1973.

Robbins, L.M.: Estimating Height and Weight from Size of Footprints. 31 *Journal of Forensic Sciences*, 143, 1986.

——: *Footprints: Collection, Analysis and Interpretation*. Springfield, Ill.: Thomas, 1985.

Thomson, M.W.: Photographic Reproduction of Footprints. 2 *Forensic Photography*, 4, 1973.

Vandiver, J.V.: Footwear Marks. 24 *Law and Order*, 9, 1976.

Van Krunkelsven, H.: Improved Photographic Method for Making Hand and Footprints. 2 *Forensic Photography*, 5, 1973.

Tire Marks

Given, B., Nehrich, R. and Shields, J.: *Tire Tracks and Tread Marks.* Houston, Gulf Publishing, 1978.

Lloyd, J.B.F.: Luminescence of Tyre Marks and Other Rubber Contact Traces. 16 *Journal of the Forensic Science Society,* 5, 1976.

McDonald, P.: *Tire Imprint Evidence.* New York, Elsevier, 1989.

Vandiver, J.V.: Tire Marks. 25 *Law and Order,* 7, 1977.

Tool Marks

Biasotti, A.A.: The Principles of Evidence Evaluation as Applied to Firearms and Tool Mark Identification. 9 *Journal of Forensic Sciences,* 428, 1964.

Burd, D.Q. and Gilmore, A.E.: Individual and Class Characteristics of Tools. 13 *Journal of Forensic Sciences,* 390, 1968.

Davis, J.E.: *An Introduction to Tool Marks, Firearms and the Striagraph.* Springfield, Ill.: Thomas, 1958.

Ojena, S.M.: A New Silicone Rubber Casting Material Designed for Forensic Science Application. 29 *Journal of Forensic Sciences,* 317, 1984.

Peterson, J.L.: Utilizing the Laser for Comparing Tool Striations. 14 *Journal of the Forensic Science Society,* 57, 1974.

Scott, J.D.: *Investigative Methods.* Reston, Va.: Reston Publishing, 1978.

Townshend, D.G.: Photographing and Casting Toolmarks. 45 *FBI Law Enforcement Bulletin,* 4, 1976.

Vandiver, J.V.: Identification and Use of Tool Mark Evidence. 24 *Law and Order,* 7, 1976.

Bite Marks

Barry, R.J.: Forensic Odontology: Identification through Dental Evidence. 55 *Police Chief,* 8, 1988.

Dinkel, E.H., Jr.: The Use of Bite Mark Evidence as an Investigative Aid. 19 *Journal of Forensic Sciences,* 535, 1974.

MacDonald, D.G.: Bite Mark Recognition and Interpretation. 14 *Journal of the Forensic Science Society,* 229, 1974.

Mittleman, R.E., Stuver, W.C. and Souviron, R.R.: Obtaining Saliva Samples from Bitemark Evidence. 49 *FBI Law Enforcement Bulletin,* 11, 1980.

Souviron, R.R., Mittleman, R.E. and Valor, J.: Obtaining the Bitemark Impression (Mold) from Skin. 51 *FBI Law Enforcement Bulletin,* 1, 1982.

Rao, V.J. and Souviron, R.R.: Dusting and Lifting the Bite Print: A New Technique. 29 *Journal of Forensic Sciences,* 326, 1984.

Sperber, N.D.: Bite Mark Evidence in Crimes Against Persons. 50 *FBI Law Enforcement Bulletin,* 7, 1981.

——: Chewing Gum—An Unusual Clue in a Recent Homicide Investigation. 23 *Journal of Forensic Sciences*, 792, 1978.

Vale, G.L., et al.: Unusual Three-Dimensional Bite Mark Evidence in a Homicide Case. 21 *Journal of Forensic Sciences*, 642, 1976.

West, M.H. and Frair, J.: The Use of Videotape to Demonstrate the Dynamics of Bite Marks. 34 *Journal of Forensic Sciences*, 88, 1989.

See also Chapter 24, Additional Reading, **Dental and Skeletal Identification.**

Palm Prints and Sole Prints

Alexander, H.L.V.: *Classifying Palmprints: A Complete System of Coding, Filing and Searching Palmprints.* Springfield, Ill.: Thomas, 1973.

Guide to Taking Palm Prints. Washington, D.C.: U.S. Government Printing Office, n.d.

Kolb, P.A.: *H.I.T.—A Manual for the Classification, Filing, and Retrieval of Palmprints.* Springfield, Ill.: Thomas, 1979.

Myers, D.A.: *Sole Prints: A Reference Guide for Law Enforcement Personnel,* 2nd ed. Beaverton, Ore.: S.O.L.E. Publications, 1982.

Rogers, S.L.: *The Personal Identification of Living Individuals.* Springfield, Ill.: Thomas, 1986.

Shimoda, S.C. and Franck, F.E.: Writer's Palmar Impressions. 34 *Journal of Forensic Sciences*, 468, 1989.

Wentworth, B. and Wilder, H.H.: *Personal Identification,* 2nd ed. Chicago, T.G. Cooke, The Fingerprint Publishing Association, 1932.

Earprints and Lip Prints

Iannarelli, A.V.: *Ear Identification,* rev. ed. Freemont, Calif.: Paramont Publishing, 1989.

Rogers, S.L.: *The Personal Identification of Living Individuals.* Springfield, Ill.: Thomas, 1986.

Schnuth, M.L.: Lip Prints. 61 *FBI Law Enforcement Bulletin*, 11, 1992.

Williams, T.R.: Lip Prints—Another Means of Identification. 41 *Journal of Forensic Identification*, 190, 1991.

Chapter 37

BROKEN GLASS

1. Introduction

IT IS NOT unusual for an investigator to be called to the scene of a crime in which broken glass will be of critical importance. Burglary, arson, assault with a firearm, and motor vehicle homicide are among a wide variety of cases in which glass fragments are often part of the physical evidence. There are four different types of investigative problems commonly associated with broken glass:

a. **The Direction of Impact.** In burglary and arson cases, it is often important to determine whether a window was broken from the inside or the outside.

b. **An Analysis of Bullet Holes.** Assault cases involving firearms may require an examination of a bullet hole in a window in order to determine the direction and angle of the shot, and, if there were several shots, which one was fired first.

c. **A Physical Fit.** In a hit-and-run case, a fragment of glass may become embedded in the victim. Fitting the fragment into the reconstructed headlight glass of a suspect's vehicle, like a missing piece in a jigsaw puzzle, would positively identify its source.

d. **A Comparison of Particles.** In burglary cases involving broken windows, minute particles of glass may be discovered on the suspect. A comparison of these particles with the remaining glass in the window can be conducted in the laboratory. Tests comparing density and refractive index will indicate whether it was possible for the particles to have originated from the broken window.

2. Kinds of Glass

Glass is primarily a composite of the oxides of silicon, sodium and calcium. It is formed when silica sand (silicon dioxide, SiO_2), soda ash (sodium carbonate, Na_2Co_3) and limestone (calcium carbonate, $CaCo_3$) are melted at high temperature and then mixed together until they fuse. The mixture is worked while in a heated state, being stamped, molded, rolled or blown. It will retain its shape when cooled. Cooling is done rapidly without allowing time for crystallization to occur. The result is a rigid, brittle, amorphous (non-crystalline) substance. Lacking a crystalline structure, it is not a true solid; lacking viscosity, it is not a true liquid. Thus, it is sometimes described paradoxically as a "rigid liquid" or as a "solid solution" of oxides.

A major glass company may have hundreds of different glass formulas in production. These different compositions are, for the most part, formed (1) by varying the proportions of the original ingredients—the silicon, sodium and calcium oxides; (2) by substituting another metal oxide in whole or in part for one or more of the ingredients; or (3) by introducing an additional metal oxide to the original formula.

For example, to achieve the clarity and light-gathering properties of lead glass which is used in "crystal" tableware and chandeliers, a composition of approximately 80 percent lead monoxide and 20 percent silicon dioxide is used. To produce the heat and corrosion-resistant properties of borosilicate glass which is used in headlight lamps, pyrex cookware and laboratory containers, boron oxide is added to the ingredients, becoming approximately 10 percent of the total mixture. The sodium and calcium oxides are decreased and the silicon dioxide is increased. The color of glass is obtained through the addition of an appropriate metal oxide. For example, the addition of cobalt oxide into the glass formula produces blue glass. The introduction of chromium oxide accounts for the green of soda and beer bottles.

The following are the more common forms of glass that the investigator might encounter at the crime scene:

a. **Window Glass.** Clear soda-lime-silica glass is used for ordinary window panes. It is sometimes called flat glass.

b. **Plate Glass.** Because of its thickness, the plate glass used in store windows is especially resistant to breakage. It is a clear soda-lime-silica glass that is formed when molten glass is rolled into a plate and then ground and polished.

c. **Tempered Glass.** Compressing glass strengthens it. Rapidly heating and cooling the glass will compress the surface of the glass and, at the same time, place the interior of the glass under a state of tension. The compressed surface of tempered glass will resist breaking. If, however, the glass does break, the interior glass which is under tension will fragment or "dice" into thousands of tiny cubes with few sharp edges or splinters. Tempered glass is used on the rear and side windows of automobiles, shower doors, storm doors, and wherever its safety features are required.

d. **Safety Glass.** Safety glass consists of two panes of window glass separated by a thin sheet of a transparent adhesive plastic. When the glass is broken, the fragments tend to remain in place in the window. Because of this feature, safety glass, which is also called laminated glass, is used for windshields in automobiles.

e. **Headlight Glass.** Borosilicate glass is a heat- and corrosion-resistant form used in headlight lamps, laboratory vessels and pyrex cookware. It is produced by adding boron oxide to and increasing the proportion of silicon dioxide in the basic soda-lime-silica glass formula.

f. **Bottle Glass.** The glass used in soda and beer bottles consists of the soda-lime-silica formula with the inclusion of a metal oxide or some other additive to impart color.

3. Determining the Direction of Impact

An investigator at the scene of a burglary will attempt to mentally reconstruct the course of events. One of his primary considerations is to eliminate the possibility of an "inside job." An employee, who intends to burglarize the warehouse in which he works, might break a window to create the appearance that a thief entered the building from the outside. To avoid being seen by people in the neighborhood, the employee will break the window from the inside. The glass fragments found around the window frame, when assembled and examined by the investigator, will indicate on which side the glass was broken.

One of the curiosities of glass examination is that the direction of impact cannot be reliably determined by noting the position of the broken glass pieces around the window frame. A large amount of glass found on the floor or ground on one side of a broken window does not necessarily mean that the force which broke the window had to have come from the opposite side. In the breaking of a window, there are other forces at work besides that of the initial blow. These are reactionary forces working in the opposite direction which effect the distribution of glass around the window frame.

a. **Theory.** Glass will break first on the side opposite the point of impact. When a force is applied to glass, it bends on the impact side causing the opposite side to stretch. Glass will withstand more bending than it will stretching. Bending compresses the glass molecules together, while stretching separates the molecules, creating a state of tension. Eventually, the elastic limit will be reached and the glass will crack. It will break first in the area where the most stretching has occurred, on the side opposite the point of impact (Fig. 55).

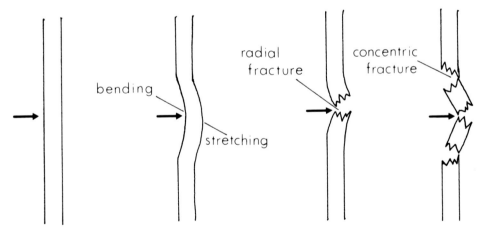

Figure 55. Side view of the breaking of a piece of glass. The arrow indicates the direction of impact.

b. **Radial Fractures.** The spoke-like cracks in glass emanating from the area of impact are called radial fractures. When the glass is stretched to its limit, it will crack first on the side opposite the impact side along lines radiating outward. In safety glass, where the pieces tend to remain in place after they are broken, the radial lines can readily be observed (Fig. 56).

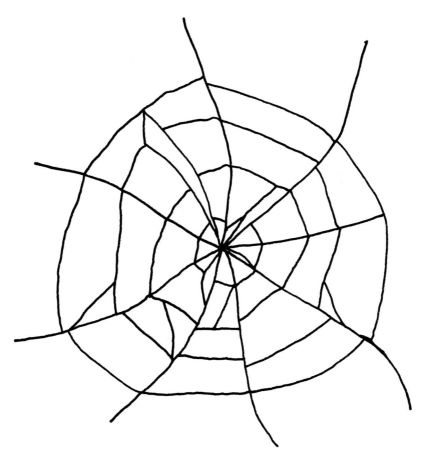

Figure 56. A broken window showing radial and concentric fractures.

c. **Concentric Fractures.** These are secondary cracks which open on the side of impact due to forces working in the opposite direction of the initial blow. The stretching of the glass in one direction will cause the bending of the glass in the opposite direction. The stretching that causes the radial fractures around the breaking point will cause other areas of the glass to bend in toward the side of impact as a reaction. This will result in a series of secondary cracks called concentric fractures. Because the glass is now bending toward the impact side, it will stretch and break on that side (Fig. 55).

Concentric fractures form a set of circular patterns around a central point. The word "concentric" means having a common center. Concentric fractures appear as a series of lines connecting the radial lines in circular patterns around the point of impact. A crack will not cross a pre-existing crack. Because the radial cracks occur prior to the concentric ones, all of the concentric lines are stopped at both ends when they meet the radial lines. Thus, concentric fractures are a series of interrupted lines in a circular pattern around the point of impact. In some textbooks, the concentric fracture is called a spiral fracture. They are not always present in every broken window. Again, this phenomenon can be best observed in safety glass where the broken pieces are held in place (Fig. 56).

d. **Rib Marks.** The curved lines of stress that are faintly visible on the edge of a piece of broken glass are called rib marks. These lines run almost parallel to one surface and then curve to become nearly perpendicular to the opposite surface. They are called rib marks because the series of curved lines together resembles a rib cage. Alternatively, the rib mark is referred to in some textbooks as a conchoidal striation because an individual curved line appears like the outline of a seashell. Rib marks are always perpendicular to the side of the glass that broke first (Fig. 57).

e. **Reassembling the Glass.** From a single isolated piece of broken glass, the investigator cannot reliably determine the direction of impact. It is necessary to establish whether the glass fragment was facing inside or outside and whether the edge being examined is a radial or a concentric fracture. This can be accomplished by collecting the pieces of glass and reassembling or partially reassembling the window. The first consideration is to have the pieces of the pane replaced with the inside and the outside sur-

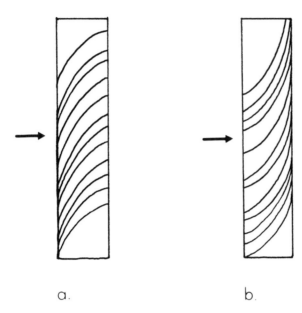

Figure 57. Rib marks: (a) on a radial fracture; (b) on a concentric fracture. The arrows indicate the direction of impact.

faces in their original position. Dirt on the window, water spots and putty marks are helpful in distinguishing the outside surface. When the window is sufficiently reconstructed, the investigator can identify the radial and concentric fractures. An examination of the rib marks on the edge of either a radial or concentric fracture will indicate the direction of the blow.

   f. **Determining the Direction of Impact.**

   1) *Radial Fractures.* Because (a) radial fractures break first on the side opposite the side of impact and (b) rib marks are perpendicular to the side that breaks first, it follows that:

   Radial fractures have rib marks that are perpendicular to the side opposite the side of impact.

To remember this principle, the investigator can employ a simple mnemonic device known as the **4R rule:**

   Rib marks on Radial cracks are at Right angles to the Reverse side.

   2) *Concentric Fractures.* Because (a) concentric fractures break

first on the side of impact and (b) rib marks are perpendicular to the side that breaks first, it follows that:

Concentric fractures have rib marks that are perpendicular to the side of impact.

g. **Glass Fracture Examination.**

1) *Summary of Procedure:*

a) Reassemble the window, identifying the inside and outside surfaces and the radial and concentric fractures.

b) Select a radial crack.

c) Examine the rib marks. They will be perpendicular to the side opposite the side of impact.

2) *Exceptions to this Procedure.* Certain types of glass do not lend themselves to this kind of examination:

a) Glass that, after breaking, falls on a hard surface and breaks again will have an additional set of cracks which will complicate the examination.

b) Glass that does not bend because the window is small or the glass is too loosely secured.

c) Tempered glass that will "dice" on impact rather than form radial and concentric cracks.

d) Windows broken by heat, wind, or an explosion that do not have a point of impact. A glass window subjected to the intense heat of a fire will crack with characteristic long wavy lines. The edge of a glass fragment will be smooth and without the rib marks indicating a point of impact. The pieces of glass tend to fall inward toward the fire sometimes creating the deceptive appearance of the window being pushed in from the outside by an intruder. In actuality, it is theorized that the fire consumes the oxygen creating a vacuum which draws the glass inwards.

e) Safety glass that is not hit with sufficient force to complete the fracture. In this case, the radial and concentric cracks will not extend all the way through to the other side of the glass. By running the back of his fingernail across the surface of the glass, the investigator can determine: (1) the impact side, that is, the side where only the concentric cracks are felt; and (2) the side opposite the impact side, that is, the side where only radial cracks are felt. An additional test for determining the direction of force depends on the tendency of safety glass to bend and remain bent when struck. The investigator places a long ruler across the surface of the glass and observes the space between the ruler and the surface. The concave side, the surface of the glass that bends inward, is the impact side.

h. **Hackle Marks.** These are the minute irregular lines found on the edge of a piece of broken glass. Hackle marks are formed when two glass surfaces scrape against each other at impact causing small particles to flake off and fly backwards. The presence of hackle marks indicates that the glass has been broken by a sudden powerful force. Hackle marks are best viewed under low magnification where they appear as short lines of varying length. They are located on the edge nearest the impact surface running in the direction of the force. On a radial edge, they are at right angles to the rib marks. Thus hackle marks provide an additional indication of the direction of impact (Fig. 58).

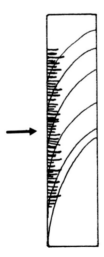

Figure 58. Hackle marks on a radial edge.

4. Bullet Holes in Glass

a. **Is It a Bullet Hole?** It is often difficult to determine whether window glass has been broken by a bullet or by some other

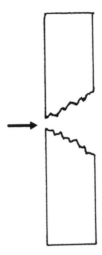

Figure 59. Bullet hole in glass.

projectile, such as a small stone or pebble. When a bullet penetrates glass, it leaves a small, clean-cut entrance hole and a much larger saucer-shaped exit hole as it pushes the glass particles ahead of it (Fig. 59). A pebble thrown from the tire of a passing car can cause a similar hole in a windshield. Finding the projectile may solve the problem. If a bullet is discovered and suspected, sometimes minute glass particles can be found embedded in the nose of the bullet. Also, the bullet, in contrast to the pebble, will generally leave a more symmetrical system of radial and concentric cracks in the immediate area surrounding the hole.

When a shot is fired from very close range, the force from the blast of the muzzle gases will shatter a window. A stone will break a window in a similar manner. If the projectile cannot be found, gunshot residue particles found on the pieces of glass are a reliable indication that the window was broken by gunfire. When a shot is fired from long range, a bullet will lose its velocity before it reaches the window. It may turn end over end and enter the glass sideways, making it difficult to determine whether the window was broken by a stone or a bullet. Again, locating the projectile is of prime importance.

b. **Determining the Direction of the Gunfire.** A bullet penetrates glass leaving a smooth entrance hole and a crater-shaped exit hole. The direction of the bullet can be determined by a visual inspection of the glass. Running the fingers across the surface of the glass provides an additional test for direction. The entrance side will feel smooth until the fingers touch the hole. On the exit side, the depression in the glass will be felt as well as the chipping around the hole.

c. **Determining the Angle of the Gunfire.** When a bullet enters a window, it pushes the glass particles ahead of it, creating the saucer-shaped depression as well as the chipping around the exit hole. When the bullet strikes the glass at right angles, the chipping will be distributed uniformly. If the bullet is fired from the right side of the glass, it will leave an elliptical hole with little chipping on the right side of the exit hole and considerable chipping on the left side. The more acute the angle of fire, the greater the chipping on the opposite side. From this observation, the investigator can approximate the angle of fire. Test firing bullets from a known angle into similar glass using the same type of weapon and ammunition may provide a more precise determination.

d. **Which Bullet Hole Was Made First?** In cases involving an exchange of gunfire coming from opposite sides of a window, it is often important to know which shot was fired first. A radial fracture caused by a bullet will travel across the glass unless it is interrupted by a previously formed fracture. The first bullet hole will have radial cracks that are complete and uninterrupted. The second bullet will cause radial cracks that will be terminated by the radial and concentric cracks formed by the first bullet. If there is a third bullet, its radial lines will be interrupted by those lines emanating from the first and second bullet holes (Fig. 60).

e. **Determining the Type of Weapon or Ammunition.** Many kinds of guns and ammunition produce characteristic bullet holes in glass. Test firing different weapons into similar glass under similar conditions may indicate the type of weapon or caliber of ammunition that was used. This may be useful in cases where the spent bullets, the cartridges, and the weapon have not been located and a particular type of weapon or caliber of ammunition is suspected.

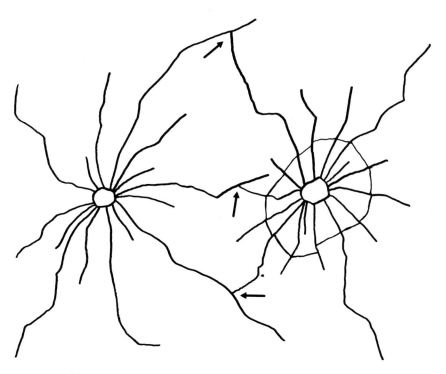

Figure 60. Bullet holes from two shots fired in sequence. The bullet hole on the left was made first. The arrows show where the fracture lines of the second bullet terminate at the lines caused by the first.

5. Physical Fit

a. **Positive Identification.** Glass evidence takes on its greatest significance when a laboratory glass examiner can render an opinion of positive identity: that this particular piece of glass was joined together with another piece of glass as part of the same window, headlight or other glass object. The phrase "physical fit" is used here to describe this precise meshing of the two glass fragments. However, there is no agreement among laboratory experts on what name to use to refer to this exact and unique relationship between the two glass fragments. "Physical match," "edge match," and "mechanical fit" are some of the terms commonly employed. A "jigsaw fit" is another phrase that is both appropriate and descriptive. In a jigsaw puzzle, only one piece will have the particular shape and surface pattern to fit in each position. However with broken glass, the fit is much tighter than even this analogy suggests. On a jigsaw puzzle piece, the edges are smooth and even; while on broken glass, the edges are slightly ridged and uneven. Because of this, a glass piece broken off from an adjacent piece will tend to lock into place and resist any movement when fitted together with its complementary piece.

When glass breaks, no two fragments will be the same. Even if two glass pieces have a similar shape, the rib marks, the lines of stress on the edge of the glass, will form a unique pattern. When the edges of two pieces are fitted together, it is the rib marks which mesh, holding the pieces in place and resisting any tendency to slip when pressure is applied. When a fragment is broken off from a glass object, no other piece of glass will fit securely into that same position.

b. **Evidence Collection.** In hit-and-run incidents where the headlight is broken, a physical fit may be of the utmost importance. If a piece of glass embedded in the victim can be proven to have originated from the headlight of the suspect's automobile, it can link the suspect to the victim. If a physical fit is to be attempted, it is important for the investigator to try to collect all of the broken glass. This will include all of the headlight glass at the accident scene, as well as the glass fragments on the victim and the remaining headlight glass on the suspect's vehicle. The glass should be marked for identification and wrapped in paper or cotton to prevent breakage. The glass from each location should then be placed in separate containers which are labeled to identify their contents. The containers are then transported to the laboratory for comparison.

c. **Laboratory Comparison.** To determine which piece is missing, it is helpful to reconstruct the headlight lens from the glass remaining on the suspect vehicle and the glass from the accident scene. It will then become apparent where the piece found on the victim fits into the "puzzle." An adjacent piece from the reconstructed headlight glass can be selected for comparison. To avoid confusion, the pieces are labeled the "known" (the piece that is part of the headlight) and the "questioned" (the piece from the victim). The two pieces of glass are placed in juxtaposition, that is, side by side. The examiner first screens the pieces to be certain that they are similar in color, thickness, curvature, texture, surface pattern, and other obvious physical characteristics. The pieces of glass are then carefully joined together and gentle pressure is applied to make sure there is "the feel" of a proper fit. Next, the edges of both pieces are examined under a low-power comparison microscope and then photographed with the rib marks and hackle marks (if present) of both pieces properly aligned. These photographs provide additional evidence of a physical fit and thus of a positive identification of the "questioned" glass.

6. Comparison of Glass Particles

When a window is broken with a heavy metal instrument, such as a tire iron or a hammer, minute glass particles will fly backwards up to a distance of ten feet. These minute particles may adhere to a burglar's shirt or be caught in his pockets. If he walks across a surface where the particles have fallen, they may become embedded in the soles or heels of his shoes. When a suspect is apprehended, particles found on his person may be compared with particles found at the crime scene.

Laboratory glass examination is often concerned with a comparison of glass particles in order to determine whether they originated from the same piece of glass. In the current state of knowledge, a glass examiner cannot "individuate" a particle of glass; that is, he cannot say with certainty that one or more glass particles came from a particular glass object. There are no physical or chemical properties that can be used to uniquely identify an individual piece of glass. In fact, there are often slight variations in both the physical properties and the chemical composition in different areas of the same pane of glass. Two of the more useful physical properties for comparing glass are those of density and refraction.

a. **Density.** Density is a measurement of the weight of a substance in relation to the volume it occupies. Lead has a greater density than glass; it has more weight per unit of volume it occupies. The density of a substance is also a measure of its buoyancy. A substance will float or sink in a liquid depending on its density in comparison with the liquid. When wood is placed in water it will float because it has a lesser density than water. Glass, on the other hand, will sink because it has a greater density than water. When a substance is placed in a liquid having the same density as itself, it will remain suspended, neither floating nor sinking. This phenomenon provides a convenient method of determining density as well as comparing the relative density of two glass particles.

A density gradient tube is filled in layers with mixtures of bromoform and bromobenzene in different concentrations. Bromoform is a liquid having a greater density than glass, in which glass will float. Bromobenzene is a liquid having a lesser density than glass, in which glass will sink. By combining these chemicals in different proportions and adding them in stages to the density gradient tube, a series of liquid layers reflecting the whole range of glass densities is formed. The mixture with the greatest density is at the bottom of the tube while the mixture with the least density is at the top. Two glass particles, the "known" whose source is certain and the "questioned" whose source is uncertain, are compared with respect to density in order to show that they originated from the same piece of glass. In a burglary case, the "known" particle would be taken from the remaining glass in the broken window, while the "questioned" particle might be one found adhering to the suspect as a result of having broken the window. The "known" glass particle is placed in the density gradient tube where it will sink until it reaches the level of the liquid mixture having the same density as itself. It will remain suspended at this level. A "questioned" glass particle of approximately the same size is added to the tube. If it becomes suspended at the same level as the "known" particle, it can be concluded that the two particles have the same density and *could* have come from the same source. If the "known" particle and the "questioned" particle remain suspended at different levels, it can be concluded that each particle has a different density and *must* have come from a different source. (A precise numerical density reading for a glass particle is obtained by placing some of the liquid from the same level at which the particle is suspended into an electrical instrument called a density meter.)

b. **Refractive Index.** If the "known" and the "questioned" particles have the same density, they should be further tested to see if they correspond with regard to refractive index. Refraction is the bending of light when it passes at an angle through substances of varying densities. When light passes from air through water, from a substance of lesser density through a substance of greater density, the velocity of the light is reduced. The light refracts or bends as it slows. To illustrate this principle, place a pencil in a glass of water and observe that the pencil will appear bent where it enters the water. This visual effect is caused by the light travelling at a slower speed and refracting when it enters the water. The refractive index of a substance is the measurement of the degree light will bend when it passes through that substance.

Light will not bend when it travels between substances having the same refractive index. When a clear glass particle is immersed in a clear liquid having the same refractive index, it will lose its visibility. The outline of the glass particle will disappear and the particle will appear to be part of the liquid. At this point, if you know the refractive index of the liquid, you will know the refractive index of the glass particle. Unlike solids, such as glass, where the refractive index remains constant, liquids will change their refractive index with a change in temperature. To determine the refractive index of a glass particle, a liquid, whose relationship with temperature and refractive index has already been calculated, is selected. A microscope with an attachment called a hot stage is used. A hot stage is a device for heating the specimen to be examined; it holds a slide containing the glass particle immersed in the liquid. As the examiner looks through the microscope, the temperature is slowly increased. When the outline of the glass particle disappears, the liquid and the glass particle will have the same refractive index. Because the index of the liquid is known, the index of the glass particle is also known. By using this method, the refractive index of both the "known" glass particle and the "questioned" glass particle can be determined and compared.

c. **Findings.** Glass may show slight variations in both density and refractive index within the same object. By comparing the "known" particle with the "questioned" particle, the glass examiner may establish:

1) *Non-Identity of Source.* Because of significant differences in either the density or the refractive index, the "known" and the "questioned" glass particles do not have the same source. They were not originally part of the same glass object.

2) *Probable Source.* If there are no significant differences in either the density or the refractive index of the two particles, then they are probably from the same source. An opinion of this nature can range from mere possibility to high probability and can sometimes be very significant. Some densities and refractive indices are quite rare in glass. If it can be shown that the two glass particles have either a density or a refractive index found only in approximately 1 percent of the glass manufactured, then it can be claimed that there is a high degree of probability that they came from the same object. To facilitate assigning such a probability, the FBI has analyzed over a thousand different glass objects to record their density and their refractive index. On the basis of the FBI's statistical data on the relative frequency of density and refractive index values, the glass examiner may approximate the probability that two specimens originated from the same source.

7. Collection of Glass Evidence

The collection of glass evidence should be guided by the investigative purpose that this evidence will serve. If there is a question concerning the direction from which a window was broken, then all of the glass from the pane should be collected. For other purposes, such as particle comparison, only a small sample of glass pieces from the window will be required.

a. **Collecting.** Before the investigator moves or even touches the glass evidence, the crime scene should be properly recorded, that is, described in the notebook, sketched, and photographed.

1) *Evidence on Glass.* When examining broken glass at the scene of a burglary, the investigator's first concern is locating evidence on the glass itself. The smooth surface of glass may yield

excellent fingerprints. After breaking a window to gain entry, the burglar will often find that much of the glass remains stuck to the frame. In order to have sufficient room to reach in and unlock the door or window, he may be forced to remove pieces of glass by hand. While picking up the pieces with his thumb and index finger, the burglar will leave his fingerprints on the glass. Blood is another kind of physical evidence commonly associated with broken glass. While handling the sharp fragments, the burglar may cut himself, depositing blood on the glass, the window frame, the sill, or the floor. The investigator should also be alert for hair, fibers, dirt, or other debris adhering to the glass.

2) **Broken Windows.** When direction of impact is at issue and the seriousness of the case warrants it, reassembling the window may be necessary. All of the glass from the broken window pane should be collected. If glass fragments remain attached to the frame, it is often easier in reconstructing the pane to remove the frame rather than pull the remaining pieces from the window. If the frame is not removed, samples of the wood, paint, and putty should be obtained.

3) **Headlight Glass.** Because it can be the most significant evidence in a hit-and-run accident investigation, all of the broken headlight glass at the scene should be collected. By piecing together the glass fragments, the laboratory examiner may determine the manufacturer and the exact type of lens used. With this information, the examiner can contact the manufacturer or consult auto parts reference books to learn the various makes, models, and years of the cars for which this headlight was manufactured. If a suspected car is located, all of the remaining broken glass from the headlight should be recovered so that the headlight can be reassembled in the laboratory. A "physical fit," between a glass fragment found on the vehicle and a glass fragment found at the crime scene, can positively link the car to the crime scene. Pieces of the headlight reflector from both the vehicle and the scene of the accident should be collected for laboratory comparison. The lamp filament may also be important if there is a question of whether the lights on the vehicle were on or off during the accident. Other hit-and-run accident debris, such as fragments of plastic lenses and metal

grillwork, will contribute to identifying a suspect vehicle and should, of course, be recovered.

4) *Particle Comparison.* In a burglary case involving a broken window, a suspect apprehended shortly after the crime should be searched for minute glass particles. These particles may adhere to his hair or clothes, be caught in his pockets or cuffs, or become embedded in the soles or heels of his shoes. All of the glass particles found on the suspect should be collected. Comparison standards should be taken preferably from the glass remaining in the window rather than from the fragments lying on the floor. This avoids the possibility of confusing the broken window glass with broken glass from another source. The samples should be removed from an area of the pane close to the point where the window was broken. This will be in close proximity to that part of the window which was the probable source of the particles found on the suspect. Several samples of about one-square inch in area will be sufficient for laboratory analysis.

b. **Handling.** Care must be taken in handling glass fragments to avoid smudging fingerprints or disturbing evidence on the glass. For this reason, glass pieces should be held with the fingers on the edges rather than on the flat surfaces. To avoid being cut, gloves made of rubber or cloth may be worn. For small pieces and particles, rubber-tipped tweezers or metal tweezers with adhesive tape placed over the tips should be used to avoid scratching the glass.

c. **Marking.** Sizeable glass pieces can be marked for identification by the investigator with a sharp-pointed instrument such as a diamond point or carborundum pencil. The investigator will inscribe his initials and the date on a flat area of the glass of no evidential value. Alternatively, adhesive tape with the investigator's inscription may be affixed to the glass. A grease pencil can also be used. On window glass, the inside and the outside should be indicated. This can be accomplished with an additional mark on the glass or by consistently placing all the markings on the inside surface of the window. When there are many glass fragments to be collected, marking each piece with a number which would indicate its location on the crime scene sketch may be helpful. Smaller glass pieces and particles are not marked but rather are placed in a small container, such as a pillbox, and then sealed and labeled.

d. **Transporting.** To avoid confusion and evidence contamination, glass from different locations should be placed in separate containers. Wrap each piece of glass separately in tissue paper or cotton and pack them tightly in a container so that the contents will not shift and break. If the evidence containers are to be shipped, the outside package will, of course, be marked "Fragile."

ADDITIONAL READING

Glass

Fong, W.: The Value of Glass as Evidence. 18 *Journal of Forensic Sciences,* 398, 1973.

McJunkins, S.P. and Thornton, J.I.: Glass Fracture Analysis: A Review. 2 *Forensic Science,* 1, 1973.

Miller, E.T.: Forensic Glass Comparison. In Saferstein, R. (Ed.): *Forensic Science Handbook.* Englewood Cliffs, N.J.: Prentice-Hall, 1982.

Pearson, E.F., May, R.W. and Dabbs, M.D.: Glass and Paint Fragments Found in Men's Outer Clothing—A Report of Survey. 16 *Journal of Forensic Sciences,* 283, 1971.

Slater, D.P. and Fong, W.: Density, Refractive Index, and Dispersion in the Examination of Glass: Their Relative Worth as Proof. 27 *Journal of Forensic Sciences,* 474, 1982.

Stahl, C.J., et al.: The Effect of Glass as an Intermediate Target on Bullets. 24 *Journal of Forensic Sciences,* 6, 1979.

Stoney, D.A. and Thornton, J.I.: The Forensic Significance of the Correlation of Density and Refractive Index in Glass Evidence. 29 *Forensic Science International,* 147, 1985.

Woods, J.: Headlights are Tools in Traffic Accident Investigation. 25 *Law and Order,* 6, 1977.

PART VII
SPECIALIZED SCIENTIFIC METHODS

THE INVESTIGATOR
AND SCIENTIFIC TECHNIQUES

I T IS NOT to be expected that the investigator also play the role of laboratory expert in relation to the physical evidence found at the scene of the crime. Obviously his opinions on many aspects of the evidence such as a chemical analysis or a physical test would in great likelihood be rejected by the court. Criminalistics, the work of the police laboratory, is a separate study associated with the main field of investigation. It suffices that the investigator investigate; it is supererogatory that he should perform refined scientific examinations. Any serious effort to accomplish such a conversion would militate against the investigator's efficiency.

Although the investigator may not aspire to the function of the laboratory expert, there does remain for him a great deal of elementary police science that he can profitably master. Photography, physical methods of reproduction, the development of latent fingerprints, and many other simple techniques should be part of the investigator's professional knowledge. In general the investigator should know the methods of discovering, "field-testing," preserving, collecting, and transporting evidence. Questions of analysis and comparison should be referred to the laboratory expert.

A certain degree of medicolegal knowledge should also be part of the investigator's background to assist him in problems of suspicious deaths. A knowledge of the medical examiner's resources will enable him to understand and implement the methods used in determining the cause of death and the lethal agents employed. The investigator can greatly aid the inquiry into a homicide if he is acquainted with the common symptoms of violent death. He should recognize the appearance of typical poisons. Most important, he should know what evidence is significant in the varied circumstances of homicides. This topic has already been treated in the chapter on homicide.

In the following chapters a selection has been made of scientific topics in accordance with the frequency of application of the techniques. Consequently, the subject of document examinations has been treated more extensively than the others. It will be found in practice that the most common use of the laboratory expert is in connection with questioned documents. Unless the investigator has a fair knowledge of the services which the document examiner is prepared to offer and of the procedures in relation to the evidence whereby he can assist the examiner, his effectiveness is seriously limited.

The scientific and technological future is typically described in terms of general benefits deriving from the application of operations research and systems analysis to the various problem areas. Multidisciplinary teamwork is expected to achieve impressive breakthroughs in police science in such areas as communications, information storage and retrieval, police management and operations, and criminalistics. Describing the future capabilities of law enforcement, however, would be to adjourn our main purpose to skirmish with difficulties of desirability and practicality. The interest of the investigator is in the present and the text has held closely to the presently available methods. The reader should, nevertheless, be conscious of the greatly increased rate of obsolescence that has been projected for the present methods of police science.

ADDITIONAL READING*

Scientific Techniques

Cunliffe, F. and Piazza, P.B.: *Criminalistics and Scientific Investigation*. Englewood Cliffs, N.J.: Prentice-Hall, 1980.

---

*A number of the books in this list should be considered references for the scientific and technical chapters in this work. For reasons of space they will not be found at the ends of the chapters.

Davies, G. (Ed.): *Forensic Science,* 2nd ed. Washington, D.C.: American Chemical Society, 1986.

DeForest, P.R., Gaensslen, R.E. and Lee, H.C.: *Forensic Science: An Introduction to Criminalistics.* New York, McGraw-Hill, 1983.

Federal Bureau of Investigation. *Handbook of Forensic Science,* rev. ed. Washington, D.C.: U.S. Government Printing Office, 1990.

Hall, J.C.: *Inside the Crime Laboratory.* Englewood Cliffs, N.J.: Prentice-Hall, 1974.

Krishnan, S.S.: *An Introduction to Modern Criminal Investigation: With Basic Laboratory Techniques.* Springfield, Ill.: Thomas, 1978.

Miller, L.S. and Brown, A.M.: *Criminal Evidence Laboratory Manual: An Introduction to the Crime Laboratory,* 2nd ed. Cincinnati, Anderson, 1990.

Moenssens, A.A., Inbau, F.E. and Starrs, J.E.: *Scientific Evidence in Criminal Cases,* 3rd ed. Mineola, N.Y.: Foundation Press, 1986.

O'Brien, K.P. and Sullivan, R.C.: *Criminalistics: Theory and Practice,* 3rd ed. Boston, Allyn and Bacon, 1980.

O'Hara, C.E. and Osterburg, J.W.: *An Introduction to Criminalistics.* Bloomington, Indiana University Press, 1972.

Osterburg, J.W.: *The Crime Laboratory: Case Studies of Scientific Criminal Investigation,* 2nd ed. New York, Clark Boardman, 1982.

Peterson, J.L., Mihajlovic, S. and Bedrosian, J.L.: The Capabilities, Uses and Effects of the Nation's Criminalistic Laboratories. 30 *Journal of Forensic Sciences,* 10, 1985.

Peterson, J.L., Mihajlovic, S. and Gilliand, M.: *Forensic Evidence and the Police: The Effects of Scientific Evidence on Criminal Investigations.* Washington, D.C.: U.S. Government Printing Office, 1984.

Saferstein, R.: *Criminalistics: An Introduction to Forensic Science,* 4th ed. Englewood Cliffs, N.J.: Prentice-Hall, 1990.

Saferstein, R. (Ed.): *Forensic Science Handbook,* vols. 1 and 2. Englewood Cliffs, N.J.: Prentice-Hall, 1982 and 1988.

Walls, H.J.: *Forensic Science,* 2nd ed. New York, Praeger, 1974.

Willard, H.H., Merritt, L.L., Dean, J.A., and Settle, F.A., Jr.: *Instrumental Methods of Analysis,* 7th ed. New York, Wadsworth, 1988.

Zonderman, J.: *Beyond the Crime Lab: The New Science of Investigation.* New York, Wiley, 1990.

Chapter 38

STAINS, TRACES, AND CHEMICAL ANALYSIS

ONE OF the most common laboratory operations is that of chemical analysis to compare two substances or to establish the constituents of a questioned substance. When large quantities are available to the chemist, the difficulties are naturally diminished. Investigative work, however, frequently leads to situations where the available traces at the scene of the crime consist of a minute sample such as a fragment of glass, a smear of lipstick, or a stained garment. In order to appreciate the potentialities of evidence of this nature and to guide him in the collection of samples, the investigator should have some knowledge of the analytical methods and instruments which are available to the laboratory technicians for this work. The techniques employed in collecting evidence in the form of stains and particles have been described in Chapter 7.

1. Spectrographic Analysis

The classical problem in the treatment of physical evidence is the analysis of minute traces. A faint smear of paint or a minute fragment of glass may constitute the vital link in the chain of evidence. To be able to establish the exact nature of the constituents of the sample and its distinctive impurities may be an essential step in the proof. Because of the minuteness of the evidence sample, ordinary methods of chemical analysis are not effective. The techniques of microanalysis can often be used in these situations, but the difficulties of these methods are sometimes discouragingly formidable. The ideal solution to such problems is the use of optical methods, of which spectrographic analysis is the most familiar and the most generally effective.

a. **Advantages.** The spectroscope has been in practical use for over a century. The spectrograph (a spectroscope with an

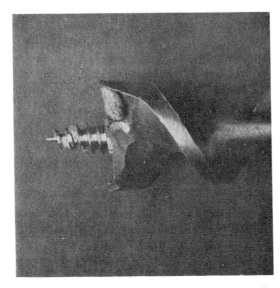

Figure 61. A small trace, such as that shown above, found on a burglar's tool can be analyzed for its constituents. By means of the trace, the tool and its possessor can be associated with the crime. (Courtesy of Dr. James J. Manning.)

Figure 62. A comparison of the spectrograms of a known and an unknown substance showing similarities of basic constituents and trace elements.

arrangement for recording on film the field of view) has been employed in chemical analysis for some fifty years. In that time its many advantages have become known to the world of chemistry. By means of this instrument it is possible to analyze minute samples in amounts of the order of a small fraction of a gram. Since only a minute part of the available physical evidence is required, subsequent tests may be made by interested parties with the remainder. The spectrograph, in addition, is an extremely rapid means of accomplishing the analysis and provides a permanent photographic record of the findings. In this latter respect, the spectrograph is, to a great extent, an objective method of analysis.

b. **Nature of the Spectrograph.** The essentials of a spectroscope are remarkably simple in view of the complex problems which it solves. If a substance is burned and the resulting light dispersed through a prism, a crude spectroscope analysis has been performed. The principle of the spectroscope may be understood by reflecting on the common observation that different substances burn with different characteristic colors. When a substance is heated its characteristic atomic arrangement is disturbed; the displaced atoms send out waves of energy which are observed as colors. If this light is passed through a slit and dispersed through a prism, a broad band of different constituent colors can be seen. When an image of this color pattern is focused on a photographic plate, a series of parallel lines is presented to the photographic plate (colored lines, if color film were to be used and black lines of varying density with the ordinary film which is almost exclusively employed.) The short black lines on the film represent different colors or, in the language of physicists, wavelengths. Different lines represent different elements. Variations in the density (heaviness) of the lines correspond to varying proportions of different substances. In summary, the analysis of a substance can be reduced to the study of an arrangement of black lines on a photographic plate. A unique arrangement of lines "fingerprints" a substance for the analyst.

c. **Illustrative Cases.** In general, the spectrographic method is useful in analyzing inorganic substances. Modifications of the instrument are employed for organic substances. Inorganic materials include many common clue materials such as paint, glass, and metals. The following examples will illustrate the application of the spectrograph to criminal investigation:

1) *Hit-and-Run.* A police officer pursuing a criminal fired to the side of him in warning. The bullet struck the fugitive and killed him. The deceased was a member of a politically active minority group, and his death was readily attributed to police brutality since the offense of which he had been suspected was not serious. The police officer claimed that the bullet had ricocheted from a nearby automobile. Laboratory technicians examined the car and found a crease in a significant area. The medical examiner, on examining the bullet recovered from the body of the deceased,

found that it bore traces of paint. Spectrographic analysis of this minute sample of paint established that it was identical with the paint on the car, thus verifying the police officer's story.

In a typical hit-and-run case, bits of paint from the missing car may be found on the buttons or belt of the victim. As soon as a car is picked up on suspicion, a sample of its paint is sent to the laboratory for comparison by spectroscope. While in most paints the main ingredients are the same, a specific batch of paint may be identified by its content of trace elements, or impurities. Here the police scientist resorts to the theory of probability. If, to take an over-simplified case, we assume that the probability of finding a specific impurity in a given batch of paint is one in ten, and if we find ten such impurities, the probability that just this combination of impurities will be found in any other batch of paint is only one chance in ten billion. Obviously such a coincidence is far beyond the leeway provided by reasonable doubt; the chances of finding two identical batches of paint of this composition may be even smaller than of finding two human fingerprints exactly alike. In practice the situation is not usually so clear-cut. Some elements are more common than others; some tend to run in groups. The probability calculation is often exceedingly complex, and part of the technician's job is to phrase the results in accurate terms that are comprehensible in the courtroom.

2. The Spectrophotometer

The spectrophotometer also has proved its worth in crime detection. It can detect tiny differences in inks, dyes, lipsticks, and other organic materials. Moreover, it provides evidence in precise, objective mathematical terms and is especially valuable in court. The spectrophotometer was used effectively in a typical mugging case. A woman walking home from the subway was gripped from behind by an assailant who clapped his hand over her mouth, grabbed her handbag, and ran. She screamed for help. A few minutes later a man was picked up by the police three blocks from the scene. The woman had not seen the thief's face, and there was no evidence to link the suspect to the crime except his proximity, his suspicious behavior, and a red smear on the palm of his left hand. But a spectrophotometric analysis showed that the substance on his hand gave the same absorption spectrum as the woman's lipstick. This, with supporting evidence, was sufficient to convict the accused.

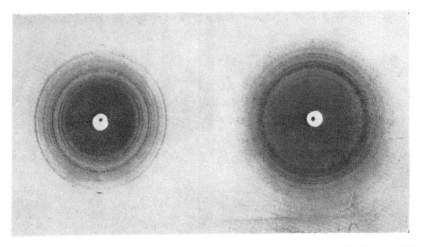

Figure 63. Analysis of x-ray diffraction patterns of (a) phenobarbitol and (b) sodium pentobarbitol.

3. X-ray Diffraction

When a stain can be made to yield crystals, or at least a substance which is not truly amorphous, it may be analyzed by x-ray diffraction. An x-ray diffraction camera can distinguish substances identical in chemical constituency but differing in atomic arrangement. Not long ago a man was found dead on the ground beneath the window of his garret room. It was supposed that he had committed suicide. But on the low, slanting ceiling near the window were some black smudges. An x-ray diffraction picture showed that the material was the same as that in the heels of the deceased's shoes. The smudges could hardly have been made on the ceiling if he had jumped; he must have been picked up and pushed out. After further investigation two casual acquaintances of the man were arrested, and they admitted they had been with him. X-ray diffraction is used to identify and compare barbiturates, which are ordinarily distinguishable only by their melting points. Grease stains can also be recognized by this device. In one case the prosecution claimed that the stain on a defendant's clothing was kitchen grease from the scene of the crime. The defense maintained that it was auto grease. X-ray diffraction analysis of the sample, less than a milligram, proved that the stain was kitchen grease.

4. The Electron Microscope

The electron microscope will often yield valuable information from such clue materials as dust, metals, fibers, inks, and other materials whose particle size and distribution cannot be differentiated by less sensitive instruments. It was used effectively in connection with the murder of a woman by a burglar. A suspect was "developed," but the police could discover no stolen property in his possession, nor could they trace his activities on the night in question. They did, however, find in his room a towel bearing a pink stain. The laboratory determined that this small stain was face powder, and under the electron microscope it was identified with powder in the woman's compact. Faced with this evidence, the suspect confessed to the crime.

5. Neutron Activation Analysis

The principle of neutron activation analysis depends on measuring the wavelength and intensity of the radiation given off by the radioactive substances that are induced in the specimen (or evidence sample) when it is subjected to a stream of neutrons. These measurements serve as qualitative and quantitative determinations of the constituents of the sample and as a means of unique identification. The method is a non-destructive, ultramicroanalytical tool of extreme sensitivity. It is anticipated that measurements of the major and minor constituents of hair, fingernails, blood, and other substances, performed by this means, can serve as a means of identification.

At least seventy elements can be readily identified and quantitatively determined in terms of measurements made on radioactive end products resulting from the interaction of their stable isotopes with a neutron source. Each of these end products (induced radionuclides) decays according to a fixed half-life period, emitting a characteristic radiation as it decays. Since many of the radionuclides emit radiation in the gamma region of varying intensities, the technique of gamma scintillation spectrometry is applied to give a graphic picture of the analysis. A plot of the intensity of radiation against wavelength results in a set of photopeaks or, perhaps, in a single photopeak that characterizes a specific radionuclide and, in turn, the stable element of which it is an end product. A measure of the intensity of radiation in the photopeak can be used as a measure of the quantity of the stable element in the sample. Thus, the location and height of the photopeaks can provide a uniquely identifying picture of the sample.

The analytical potential of this method is illustrated by its use in gunshot primer residue tests for detecting trace elements from recently discharged firearms. When a gun is fired, primer residue particles are dispersed throughout the vicinity of the discharge. If trace elements from these residues can be identified on the hands of the suspect, they can be used to associate him with the discharge of a firearm. Neutron activation analysis has proven to be an effective procedure for determining the presence of gunpowder residue on the back of the firing hand. Tests performed on such residue indicate that all revolver ammunition leaves readily measurable traces of antimony on the back of the hand; in many cases traces of barium are deposited and in some cases traces of copper can be found. Following the procedure described above, the residue, after being removed from the hand, is subjected to activation for thirty to sixty minutes in a TRIGA reactor; the induced substances (radionuclides) are separated radiochemically; their half-life periods, radiation wavelengths, and intensities are measured. The radionuclides in this examination would be Sb-122 (an isotope of antimony with a half-life of 28 days); Ba-189 (a barium isotope with an 85 minute half-life); and Cu-64 (a copper isotope with a 12.8-hour half-life). Lead is not used in this analysis since the induced activity of Pb-209 is a pure beta radiation.

ADDITIONAL READING

Electron Microscopy

Andrasko, J. and Maehly, A.C.: Detection of Gunshot Residues on Hands by Scanning Electron Microscopy. 22 *Journal of Forensic Sciences*, 279, 1977.

Basu, S. and Millette, J.R. (Eds.): *Electron Microscopy in Forensic, Occupational and Environmental Health Sciences.* New York, Plenum Press, 1986.

Brown, J.L. and Johnson, J.W.: Electron Microscopy and X–Ray Microanalysis in Forensic Science. 5 *Journal of the Association of Official Analytical Chemists*, 930, 1973.

Hearle, J.W.S., Sparrow, J.T., and Cross, P.M.: *The Use of the Scanning Electron Microscope.* Oxford, Pergamon, 1972.

Hicks, J.W.: *Microscopy of Hair: A Practical Guide and Manual.* Washington, D.C.: U.S. Government Printing Office, 1977.

Microscope and Crime. 236 *Nature*, 427, 1972.

Paplauskas, L.: The Scanning Electron Microscope: A New Way to Examine Holes in Fabric. 1 *Journal of Police Science and Administration*, 362, 1973.

Singh, R.P. and Aggarwal, H.R.: Identification of Wires and the Cutting Tool by Scanning Electron Microscope. 26 *Forensic Science International*, 115, 1984.

Taylor, M.E.: Scanning Electron Microscopy in Forensic Science. 13 *Journal of the Forensic Science Society*, 269, 1973.

Chromatography

Challinor, J.M.: Forensic Applications of Pyrolysis Capillary Gas Chromatography. 21 *Forensic Science International*, 269, 1983.

Gupta, R.N. (Ed.): *Handbook of Chromatography: Drugs*, vols. III and IV. Boca Raton, Fla.: CRC Press, 1986.

Jain, N.C., et al.: Identification of Paints by Pyrolysis-Gas Chromatography. 5 *Journal of the Forensic Science Society*, 102, 1965.

Kline, B.J. and Soine, W.H.: Gas Chromatography: Theory, Instrumentation, and Pharmaceutical Applications. 2 *Drugs and Pharmaceutical Science*, 1, 1981.

Permisohn, R.C., Hilpert, L.R. and Kazyak, L.: Determination of Methaqualone in Urine by Metabolite Detection via Gas Chromatography. 21 *Journal of Forensic Sciences*, 98, 1976.

Rajananda, V., Nair, N.K. and Navaratnam, V.: An Evaluation of TLC Systems for Opiate Analysis. 37 *Bulletin of Narcotics*, 35, 1985.

Sullivan, R.C., et al.: Evaluation and Selection of Gas Chromatography/Mass Spectrometry Systems for the Identification of Dangerous Drugs. 2 *Journal of Police Science and Administration*, 185, 1974.

Neutron Activation Analysis

Chan, R.K.H.: Identification of Single-Stranded Copper Wire by Non-destructive Neutron Activation Analysis. 17 *Journal of Forensic Sciences,* 93, 1972.

Hackleman, R.P. and Graber, F.M.: *Applications of Neutron Activation Analysis in Scientific Crime Investigation — Final Report.* Springfield, Va.: National Technical Information Service, 1970.

Lukens, H.R. and Guinn, V.P.: Neutron Activation Analysis. 16 *Journal of Forensic Sciences,* 301, 1971.

Ostroff, E.: Restoration of Photographs by Neutron Activation Analysis. 154 *Science,* Oct. 7, 1966.

Schlesinger, H.L., et al.: *Special Report on Gunshot Residues Measured by Neutron Activation Analysis.* Springfield, Va.: National Technical Information Service, 1970.

Metals

Lingane, J.I.: *Analytical Chemistry of Selected Metallic Elements.* New York, Van Nostrand Reinhold, 1966.

Wilson, M.L.: *Nondestructive Rapid Identification of Metals and Alloys by Spot Test.* Tech Brief 70-10520. Hampton, Va.: NASA Langley Research Center, 1970.

Cosmetics

Andrasko, J.: Forensic Analysis of Lipstick. 17 *Forensic Science International,* 235, 1981.

Barker, A.M.L. and Clarke, P.D.B.: Examination of Small Quantities of Lipsticks. 12 *Journal of the Forensic Science Society,* 449, 1972.

Choudhry, M.Y.: Comparison of Minute Smears of Lipstick by Microspectrophotometry and Scanning Electron Microscopy/Energy-Dispersive Spectroscopy. 36 *Journal of Forensic Sciences,* 366, 1991.

Keagy, R.L.: Examination of Cosmetic Smudges Including Transesterification and Gas Chromatography/Mass Spectrometric Analysis, 28 *Journal of Forensic Sciences,* 623, 1983.

Reuland, D.J. and Trinler, W.A.: A Comparison of Lipstick Smears by High-Performance Liquid Chromatography. 20 *Journal of the Forensic Science Society,* 111, 1980.

Russell, L.W. and Welch, A.E.: Analysis of Lipsticks. 25 *Forensic Science International,* 105, 1984.

Vegative Materials

Bock, J.H., Lane, M., and Norris, D.: *Identifying Plant Food Cells in Gastric Contents for Use in Forensic Investigations — A Laboratory Manual.* Washington, D.C.: National Institute of Justice, 1988.

Joce, C.R.B. and Curry, S.H.: *The Botany and Chemistry of Cannabis.* London, Churchill, 1970.

Stahl, E. (Ed.): *Drug Analysis by Chromatography and Microscopy.* Ann Arbor, Mich.: Ann Arbor Press, 1973.

Thornton, J.I. and Nakamura, G.R.: The Identification of Marijuana. 12 *Journal of the Forensic Science Society,* 461, 1972.

Soils

Bridges, E.W.: *World Soils.* Wolfe City, Texas, University Press, 1970.

Heinrich, E.W.: *Microscopic Identification of Minerals.* New York, McGraw-Hill, 1966.

Muckman, H. and Brady, N.C.: *The Nature and Properties of Soil,* 7th ed. New York, McGraw-Hill, 1969.

Murray, R.C., and Tedrow, J.C.: *Forensic Geology.* New Brunswick, N.J.: Rutgers University Press, 1975.

Murray, R.C.: Soil and Rocks as Evidence. 24 *Law and Order,* 7, 1976.

Robertson, J. et al.: Particle Size Analysis of Soils. A Comparison of Dry and Wet Sieving Techniques. 24 *Forensic Science International,* 209, 1984.

Wanogho, S., et al.: A Statistical Method for Assessing Soil Comparisons. 30 *Journal of Forensic Sciences,* 864, 1985.

Paint

Cardosi, P.J.: Pyrolysis-Gas Chromatographic Examination of Paints. 27 *Journal of Forensic Sciences,* 695, 1982.

Cousins, D.R., Platoni, C.R. and Russell, L.W.: The Variation in the Colour of Paint on Individual Vehicles. 24 *Forensic Science International,* 197, 1984.

Crown, D.A.: *The Forensic Examination of Paint and Pigments.* Springfield, Ill.: Thomas, 1968.

Haag, L.C.: Element Profiles of Automotive Paint Chips by X–Ray Fluorescence Spectrometry. 16 *Journal of the Forensic Science Society,* 255, 1976.

Leete, C.G. and Mills, R.M.: *Reference Collection of Automotive Paint Colors.* Washington, D.C.: National Bureau of Standards, 1975.

May, R.W. and Porter, J.: An Evaluation of Common Methods of Paint Analysis. 15 *Journal of the Forensic Science Society,* 137, 1975.

O'Neill, L.A.: Analysis of Paints by Infrared Spectroscopy. 7 *Medicine, Science and the Law,* 145, 1967.

Paint Examination Techniques Utilized in the FBI Laboratory. 42 *FBI Law Enforcement Bulletin,* 4, 1973.

Reeve, V. and Keener, T.: Programmed Energy Dispersive X–Ray Analysis of Top Coats of Automotive Paint. 21 *Journal of Forensic Sciences,* 883, 1976.

Rodgers, P.G., et al.: The Classification of Automotive Paint by Diamond Window Infrared Spectrophotometry. Part II, Automotive Topcoats and Undercoats. 9 *Canadian Society of Forensic Science Journal,* 2, 1976.

Ryland, S.G. and Kopec, R.J.: The Evidential Value of Automobile Paint Chips. 24 *Journal of Forensic Sciences,* 140, 1979.

Schlesinger, H.L. and Lukens, H.R.: *Forensic Neutron Activation Analysis of Paint.* Springfield, Va.: National Technical Information Service, 1970.

Steinberg, H.L.: *Standard Reference Collections of Forensic Science Materials.* Washington, D.C.: U.S. Government Printing Office, 1977.

Tweed, F.T., et al.: The Forensic Microanalysis of Paints, Plastics and Other Materials by an Infrared Diamond Cell Technique. 4 *Forensic Science,* 211, 1974.

Trace Elements

Bosen, S.F. and Scheuing, D.R.: A Rapid Microtechnique for the Detection of Trace Metals from Gunshot Residues. 21 *Journal of Forensic Sciences,* 163, 1976.

He, Z.-N.: Application of Trace Evidence in the Forensic Medical Examination. 34 *Journal of Forensic Sciences,* 391, 1989.

Krishnan, S.S.: Detection of Gunshot Residues on the Hands by Trace Element Analysis. 22 *Journal of Forensic Sciences,* 304, 1977.

——: Examination of Paints by Trace Element Analysis. 21 *Journal of Forensic Sciences,* 908, 1976.

Obrusnik, I., et al.: The Variation of Trace Element Concentrations in Single Human Head Hairs. 17 *Journal of Forensic Sciences,* 426, 1972.

Petraco, N.: Trace Evidence—The Invisible Witness. 31 *Journal of Forensic Sciences,* 321, 1986.

Trace Metal Detection Technique in Law Enforcement. Washington, D.C.: U.S. Government Printing Office, 1970.

Chapter 39

FIREARMS

1. Introduction

T HE WIDESPREAD use of firearms is, perhaps, the most individual characteristic of American crime. The United States,
the birthplace of the revolver, has been prolific in its production of firearms and indiscriminate in their distribution. As a
consequence, most serious crimes in this country have, as an
attending circumstance, the use or at least the possession of a
firearm. Quite frequently the crime is solved by tracing or otherwise establishing ownership of a pistol or revolver. The evidence found at the scene is usually one of the following: the
bullet, the cartridge case, the firearm, the wound, or indication
of the trajectory. A study of these five elements can sometimes
lead to the owner of the weapon and thence to the establishment
of criminal responsibility. Since a criminally owned weapon is
often used in a series of crimes, this type of evidence is of
paramount importance. Moreover, in many states the mere custody of small arms without a license is a felony, and the criminal,
in the absence of other evidence more intimately associating
him with the crime at hand, is charged with illegal possession
of a firearm. Every investigative agency should foster a firearms
specialist. This is not a difficult matter, since the study of firearms is a popular hobby to which a considerable number of
investigators are addicted. Naturally, the firearms hobbyist should
not be confused with the firearms identification expert, whose
status can be attained only by years of study and experience.
Small communities can usually refer the difficult aspects of a
firearms identification to an expert in the FBI, state police, or
in a neighboring city. There should, however, be locally available

a firearms specialist who can properly make an initial examination at the scene of the crime; collect, mark, and label the evidence; establish the possible value of the evidence; and, with reasonable accuracy, indicate the issues in question.

2. National Firearms Tracing Center.

The Bureau of Alcohol, Tobacco and Firearms (ATF) is the only Federal agency to have authorized access to the records of gun manufacturers, importers, wholesalers and retailers. In 1972, the ATF established the National Firearms Tracing Center to provide a tracing service to all federal, state and local law enforcement agencies. From 1972 to 1984, over 500,000 firearms traces were conducted. The ATF estimates that, when successful, over half of these traces played a significant part in either solving a crime or apprehending a suspect. When a firearms trace is requested, ATF personnel contact the manufacturer and provide him with a complete description of the gun. The manufacturer then gives the name and address of the importer or wholesaler who, in turn, supplies the identity and location of the retailer. If the gun is traceable, the retailer will have on record the name, address, age and physical description of the purchaser.

The effectiveness of this procedure is illustrated by the following example. In the attempted assassination of President Reagan in 1981, the ATF was called upon to run a trace of a handgun, Roehm model RG14, serial number L731332, found in the possession of the assailant. With a telephone call to RG Industries in Miami where the imported German guns are assembled, the identity of the North Carolina wholesaler was obtained. The wholesaler was then contacted and his records indicated that the gun had been shipped to Rocky's Pawn Shop on Elm Street in Dallas. A call to the store revealed that the firearm had been sold in 1980 to a 25 year old man who identified himself as John Hinkley, Jr. The ATF had traced the gun by telephone from the assembly plant in Miami to the retail sale in Dallas all within fifteen minutes.

A firearms trace will not always be successful or produce the identity of the user. Many firearms are not traceable because they were manufactured before accurate records were kept. If the gun was lost or stolen, the trace will lead only to the lawful owner. Often the theft of the firearm has not been reported to the police, or if it has, the theft has not been entered into the local or the National Crime Information Center's stolen gun file. Only if the gun was purchased legally in the United States and has not been lost, stolen or disposed of in some other way, can the trace lead to the identification of the user.

3. Problems Concerned With Firearms

The services of a firearms examiner can be used whenever a gun comes into the custody of the police under suspicious circumstances, especially in connection with cases of robbery, assault, suicide, and homicide. The classical question raised in a homicide case is: "Who fired the fatal shot?" "This inquiry raises further questions: "Who owned the gun?" "Is this the gun that fired the fatal bullet?" and so on. The subsequent investigation of the firearms problems will center about the following points:

a. **Identification.**

1) From what type of gun was the evidence bullet fired? The type of firearm may often be established through an examination of the bullet or the case.

2) Is this the gun that fired the fatal bullet? Here the questioned bullet is compared with a specific firearm.

3) Is this the gun from which the evidence case or shell was fired?

4) Were these filler wads or top-wads fired by a shotgun such as the one in question?

b. **Trajectory and Distance.** The location and point of view of the person firing the fatal shot are of importance in the investigation of homicide. A knowledge of the discharge distance assists in distinguishing suicide from murder. The approximate discharge distance can be estimated from a study and comparison of powder patterns on clothing and skin or, in the case of shotguns, from an examination of the shot pattern.

c. **Other Problems.** It should be borne in mind that in practice only a small percentage of forensic firearm examinations limit themselves to identification. The firearms examiner concerns himself with a great many other practical considerations (for example the workability or functioning condition of the weapon) too numerous to detail here.

4. Describing The Firearm

If the investigator comes into possession of a firearm in the course of official action, he must mark, label, and describe the handgun so that it can be unquestionably identified in any subsequent legal action. As a minimum the description should contain the following information in the order given: *caliber, make, model, type, serial number,* and *finish.*

a. **Caliber.** The more common are .22, .25, .32, .38 S&W, .38 S&W Spl., and .45. In doubtful cases consult an experienced firearms man.

b. **Make.** The manufacturer's name is usually stamped on the barrel of revolvers and on the slide and frame of automatics. The most common American makers of handguns are Colt, Harrington and Richardson, Iver Johnson, and Smith and Wesson.

c. **Model.** Since two revolvers of the same caliber and make can have identical serial numbers, designation of the model is essential. Some examples are Colt "Official Police"; Smith and Wesson "Military and Police"; Iver Johnson "Trailsman 66"; and Harrington and Richardson "Young America."

d. **Type.** A term describing in general the manner of operation, such as *revolver, automatic, semi-automatic,* and *single shot.* Some knowledge of firearms is required in distinguishing certain types. Several single shot target pistols, for example, resemble automatics and are best identified as to type by the absence of a magazine in the grip.

e. **Serial Number.** These are located in various areas on handguns. Even on guns of the same manufacture, the positions of such numbers may be reversed. On the very old Colt revolvers, for example, the serial number is located in the area where the parts number would be found on the modern Colt. On some handguns the serial numbers are not visible unless the weapon is disassembled. The investigator should not dismantle a gun to find hidden serial numbers, if it is planned to submit the gun later to a firearms expert for examination.

f. **Finish.** This term describes the color and surface of the firearm. The most common examples are *Blue, Nickel,* and *Parkerized* (the dull gray appearance of military handguns).

g. **Additional Data.** If the gun is difficult to describe, include such other characteristics as *barrel length, overall length,* and the number of chambers or magazine capacity. Barrel length of a revolver is measured from the muzzle to the front end of the cylinder. The barrel length of an automatic is measured from the muzzle to the face of the breech. Items such as "ducks-bill hammer," "ramped sights," or a broken trigger guard should be recorded. With foreign-made automatics give any markings stamped on the slide or frame, since these often are indications of the model and place of manufacture. Remember: Too much information rather than too little should be the rule in describing handguns. Why? For the simple reason that size, model, make and serial number do not identify firearms. The description ".32, H. & R., Serial #12345," for example, is inadequate, since the description may fit eight or more different firearms. Finally, consider the Remington .41 cal. Derringer. It has been estimated that about 250,000 were distributed; yet most of these weapons have only *three-digit* serial numbers.

5. Outline of Firearms Identification

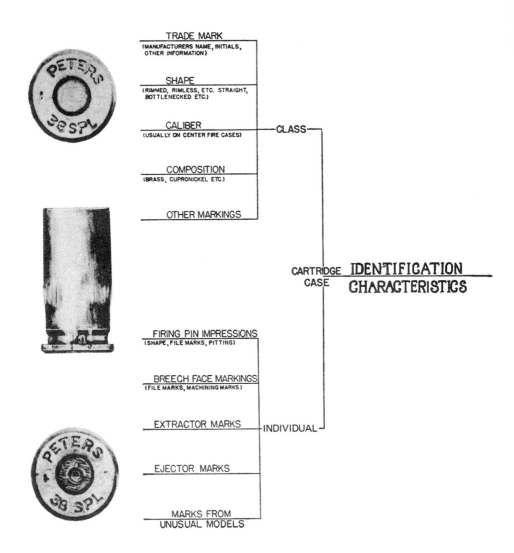

TRADE MARK
(MANUFACTURERS NAME, INITIALS, OTHER INFORMATION)

SHAPE
(RIMMED, RIMLESS, ETC. STRAIGHT, BOTTLENECKED ETC.)

CALIBER
(USUALLY ON CENTER FIRE CASES)

COMPOSITION
(BRASS, CUPRONICKEL ETC.)

OTHER MARKINGS

CLASS

CARTRIDGE CASE

IDENTIFICATION CHARACTERISTICS

FIRING PIN IMPRESSIONS
(SHAPE, FILE MARKS, PITTING)

BREECH FACE MARKINGS
(FILE MARKS, MACHINING MARKS)

EXTRACTOR MARKS

EJECTOR MARKS

MARKS FROM UNUSUAL MODELS

INDIVIDUAL

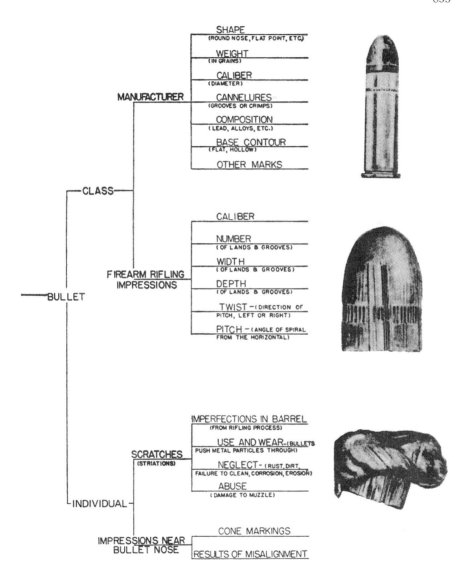

Figure 64. Outline of firearms identification.

6. Identification Procedure

The term *firearms identification* is concerned primarily with two problems: first, from a bullet or cartridge case found at the scene of the crime to determine the kind of firearm used; second, from the bullet or cartridge case to determine whether an individual, "suspected" firearm was used. The first problem is more commonly solved. The second problem is more difficult and is less likely to be treated with success. The class and individual characteristics of the bullet and case form the bases of the solutions.

a. **The Bullet.** In the manufacture of ammunition, the bullet is produced with certain gross physical properties or general characteristics. Many of these properties remain intact after firing and serve to indicate the nature of the firearm for which they were intended. After being discharged from a firearm, the bullet is stamped with an additional set of general characteristics which more closely identify the types and make of gun. In addition, the firearm may impress upon the bullet a set of individual characteristics which serve to identify the individual gun.

1) *General Characteristics (Manufacture).* Although weight, approximate diameter, and approximate length of a fired bullet are not always proof of caliber, these and other characteristics are unquestionably helpful in determining the nature of the ammunition.

a) *Weight* in grains is characteristic but variations of several grains are within the limits of tolerance and hence not significant.

b) *Material.* Soft-nosed, lead, and other designations.

c) *Diameter* is measured to determine caliber. Obviously this and other dimensions are often greatly distorted in striking hard objects.

d) *Cannelures* are knurled grooves on the curved surface.

e) *Contour* or shape, although subject to distortion from impact, is often retained after firing.

f) *Base,* whether flat or hollow, is another useful characteristic.

g) *Size and weight* serve to identify shotgun pellets.

2) **General Characteristics (Rifling Impression).**

a) *Land impressions* slant to the left or right, corresponding to the direction of twist in the bore of the firearm. These impressions are produced by the "lands" of the barrel, which are raised ribs running in a spiral (helix) lengthwise through the bore. The lands are impressed in the barrel by the cutting of grooves. The surfaces of the lands are the original surfaces of the interior of the barrel before the rifling is cut.

b) *Groove impressions* correspond to the grooves or indentations produced by the rifling cuts. They are equal in number to the lands. In different manufacturers they vary in width; depth (usually from .0035 to .005 inches deep); driven edges (whether rounded or not); and angle of spiral. The width of the lands is usually slightly less than that of the grooves except in the case of firearms using small bullets.

c) *Rifling* is the result of cutting grooves in the barrel and serves to impart a spin to the bullet, thus providing the necessary rotational inertia and permitting elongated instead of round bullets to be used. The cutting tools used in the rifling process often produce characteristic marks in a series of guns.

d) *Diameter* is measured in two ways: Bore diameter is the distance from land to land; groove diameter is the distance from bottom to bottom of opposite grooves.

e) *Number of Lands and Grooves* varies from four to sixteen.

f) *Direction of Spiral or Pitch.* The majority of firearms are made with clockwise (right) direction to the pitch. In the United States the Colt and several other firearms have a left (counterclockwise) pitch.

g) *Pitch,* the measure of the rate at which the direction of the grooves changes is calculated by the quotient of the circumference of the bullet and the tangent of the angle of twist. In practice the pitch is not really constant, is not accurately measurable, and does not in general provide a means of positive identification.

3) **Individual Characteristics.** Imperfections in the barrel are produced in the process of manufacture or may be the result of

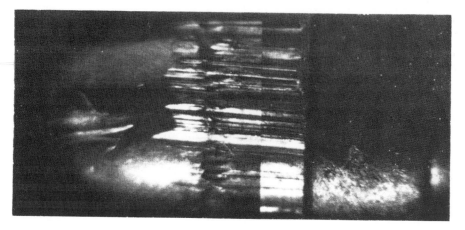

Figure 65. Photomicrograph made with the comparison microscope. The fatal bullet is seen on one side of the fine line near the center and the test bullet fired from the suspect's gun on the other. The striations of one bullet appear to run into those of the other, thus showing that they were discharged from the same weapon.

wear and rust. They are constantly changing in a small degree because of the fragments of lead which remain in the barrel after a discharge. Succeeding bullets push forward the particles and alter the scoring. Imperfections near the muzzle of the barrel produce the most marked effect on the bullet.

To answer the question "Was the fatal bullet fired from this gun?" a test bullet is compared to the evidence bullet. The test bullet is obtained by firing the gun into either a box of cotton wadding approximately five feet in length or a slightly longer water tank. The water tank is often preferred because cotton is mildly abrasive and could polish away some of the finer striations from the surface of the bullet.

Actual comparison is attempted only after it has been determined that there are no disqualifying dissimilarities in the general characteristics of the test and evidence bullets. A comparison microscope, consisting of two stages, two matched objectives, and a comparison eyepiece which permits viewing both bullets at the same time, is used to examine the evidence bullet in conjunction with the test bullet. The viewer sees corresponding parts of the two bullets in the same field. If striations are found to match, they can be aligned to appear collinear. The entire circumference of both bullets is studied under low magnification. Striations are found on the groove impressions as well as on the land impressions because of the fact that the bullet diameter is greater than the groove diameter of the barrel. Thus the bullet will be in contact with the entire inner surface of the barrel during passage. Rifling impressions nearer the nose of the bullet will sometimes be parallel to the longitudinal axis of the bullet. These are known as "skid marks" or "slippage." They are considered by some to be produced by worn rifling or by the action of a revolver in which the bullet travels a distance without a spinning motion, due to the absence of rifling in a cylinder.

b. **The Case.**

1) *General Characteristics.* The following class characteristics are common to large numbers of guns:

a) *Manufacture* is indicated by the name or initials stamped on the head for center fire cases and by initial or trademark for .22 caliber. Some makes are not marked.

b) *Shape* can be divided first into rim, rimless, and semi- or auto-rim, and second into straight, tapered, or necked.

c) *Caliber* is stamped on center fire cases generally.

d) *Composition* may be brass, nickel-plated, copper, plated steel, paper, or plastic.

2) *Individual Characteristics.* The case is ejected in automatics but remains in the cylinder of revolvers until discarded by a separate ejection action. Hence, with automatics, the case is usually found at the crime scene.

a) *Firing pin indentations* are produced when the hammer striker hits and explodes the cap of the cartridge. The tip of the pin produces its own shape and also may leave a record of its file marks and pitting.

b) *Breech face markings* are produced on the case when the pressure of the generated gas drives it against the breech face or, in rifles, the bolt head. File marks and machining marks are present on the breech face as a result of manufacturing processes or from use in firing and are impressed on the soft face of the primer.

c) *Extractor marks* are produced on the rim of a rimmed case and the flange, as well as sometimes on the groove of a rimless case. The cylindrical surface of the case just below the rim or groove is also marked. These marks are formed from the use of automatic, autoloading, bolt-, pump-, and lever-action rifles and shotguns, and automatic pistols. The extractor, under spring tension, is forced over the rim of the case at the moment of loading the cartridge into the chamber.

d) *Ejector marks* are found on the base of the case, the rim, or the flange. They are usually located on the side opposite the extractor marks. When the fired case is drawn from the chamber by the extractor, the base of the shell strikes against the fixed ejector and receives characteristic marks.

e) *Peculiarities* are apparent in certain gun models. The following are examples of peculiarities of two well-known firearms.

1) *Colt Automatics.* When the fired case is thrown from the firearm by the combined action of the extractor and ejector, the open end of the case strikes against the side of the slide with sufficient force to leave a flat area in one section of the circular opening. When the cartridge is in the chamber of this weapon, in firing position, the entire case is supported by the chamber except for a section near the base. At this point, a ramp has been cut away at the rear of the chamber in order to facilitate the loading operation. The expansion due to the interior pressure is not restricted in this area, so that a noticeable "hump" is left in the case after firing.

2) *Thompson Submachine Gun.* The bolt travels some distance behind the upper cartridge in the magazine. As it moves forward, the face of the bolt strikes a sharp blow against the head of the cartridge, leaving a mark on the head in the shape of a half-moon.

7. Powders

Three types of powder may be used in the ammunition for small firearms, namely, smokeless, black, and semi-smokeless. The use of black powder and semi-smokeless is practically negligible.

Figure 66. Comparison photomicrograph of firing-pin marks on two cartridge cases. The left side of the test shell is merged with the right side of the evidence shell. The fine scratches appear to run continuously from one shell to the other.

a. **Smokeless Powder.** This consists of cellulose nitrate with or without glycerol nitrate. In the trade these substances are called respectively nitrocellulose and nitroglycerine. To act as stabilizers, aid the firing rate, and minimize gun corrosion, substances such as nitrates, bichromates, oxalates, nitrobenzene, graphite, and petroleum jelly (Vaseline®) are added.

b. **Black Powder.** The traditional gunpowder is a mixture of saltpeter (potassium nitrate), charcoal (carbon), and sulphur in the approximate proportions of 75:15:10.

8. Gunshot Primer Residue (GSR) Test

When a gun is fired, invisible primer residues are dispersed throughout the area within 10 feet of the discharge. More importantly, these minute particles will be deposited on the hands of the shooter. If a suspect accused of a shooting is apprehended a short time after the event, invisible particles of gunshot primer, particularly the elements of antimony and barium, can be collected from his hands as evidence to associate him with the use of a firearm.

a. **Conclusions.** The following conclusions may be drawn from the Gunshot Primer Residue Test:

1) *Positive.* The chemical elements of antimony and barium are found at trace levels throughout our environment. A control group is used to determine the levels of these elements found on the hands of persons who have recently fired a gun. If there are elevated readings from the suspect's hands within the range of these levels, the test result will be positive. A positive finding will not verify that the suspect has fired a gun, but only indicates that he was in the presence of a discharged firearm. He may have been there as the shooter, as the victim who happened to place his hand near the gun as it discharged, or as a bystander who handled a firearm after it was discharged. This information is important if the suspect denies having been in the presence of a firearm.

2) *Negative.* There can be many explanations for a negative finding besides the suspect not having been in the presence of a discharged gun. Occasionally, a firearm when being discharged will not leave any significant amount of residue on the hand. Gunshot residue primer will rub off easily. If too many hours have elapsed or if the suspect has washed his hands, there may not be sufficient quantities of the elements present for identification. Also many brands of .22-caliber ammunition may be missing either antimony or barium, or both elements in their primer. Thus, a failure to find GSR on the hands of the suspect does not indicate that the suspect was not associated with a discharged firearm. A negative result means that no conclusion can be drawn.

b. **Conditions for Testing.** GSR tests should not be routinely given to victims. At a shooting from close range, it is not possible to differentiate residues deposited on the hands of the shooter and those on the hands of the victims, especially if the victim was reaching for the gun. Thus, this test is not helpful in distinguishing between a suicide and a homicide where the victim is shot from close range.

To avoid useless analysis, the GSR test should be performed on a suspect only if:

1) There are no witnesses to testify to his use of a firearm.

2) No more than a few hours have elapsed since the shooting.

3) The suspect has not washed his hands.

4) The ammunition from the suspected firearm is known to contain both antimony and barium.

c. **Collecting Evidence.** GRS evidence is collected by swabbing the hands of the suspects with a 5 percent solution of nitric acid that has been prepared with distilled or demineralized water and stored in a plastic container. Cotton-tipped applicators with plastic shafts are used as swabs. Glass containers or applicators with wooden shafts are not used because these materials may interfere with the test results. Swabbing is done wearing disposable latex gloves to avoid evidence contamination. There are four areas to be swabbed: 1) the back of the right hand on the thumb, the forefinger, and the connecting web; 2) the right palm; 3) the back of the left hand (as above); 4) the left palm. Two swabs are used for each area and are placed in four plastic bags, one for each area. In addition, two control swabs are moistened with the nitric acid solution and placed in their own plastic container. A spent cartridge case, if available, is also submitted.

d. **Testing.** The evidence samples will be tested by neutron activation analysis (NAA) (see Chap. 38) or by atomic absorption spectrophotometry (AA) to determine the concentration of antimony and barium present. Another method using scanning electron microscopy/energy dispersive x-ray analysis (SEM/EDX) requires a different evidence collection procedure. SEM/DEX has the advantage of providing a visual image of the residue particles showing size and shape as well as a chemical analysis of their composition.

9. Powder Residue

A positive and reliable test has been devised by Walker for the detection of powder residue on the skin and clothing of a victim of a shooting. The test detects the presence of nitrites and is designed to reproduce the pattern of the powder residue about the bullet hole. The pattern is useful in estimating distance of discharge, a problem often arising in suspicious suicide cases. Grains of burned and unburned powder are deposited on the skin or clothing of the victim, if the muzzle of the firearm was held within 6 feet in the case of black powder and 24 inches (or even more depending on the load and other factors) in the case of smokeless powder. Ordinary glossy photographic paper (unexposed) is desensitized by immersing in a hypo bath for twenty minutes and washing in water for fifty minutes. After the paper is dried, it is placed in an 8 percent solution of C-acid (2-naphthylamine-4, 8-disulfonic acid), for ten minutes. The paper is again hung to dry. A towel is laid on a table and the prepared paper placed on it face up. The fabric bearing the bullet hole is placed face down on the paper. Three layers of thin toweling are now placed on top of the fabric. The middle layer is slightly moistened with 20 percent acetic acid. The other layers are dry. A warm electric iron is pressed on the arrangement for about eight minutes. On removal the prepared paper will be found to have red-orange spots corresponding in position to the partially burned powder grains about the bullet hole. A one-to-one photograph is made of the pattern. The test is specific for nitrites and insensitive to other common chemicals.

As an early example of the application of the powder residue test a 1937 case may be cited in which a special patrolman, George Schuck, shot and killed an alleged burglar, James Keenan. The special patrolman stated that he had approached Keenan in the act of removing six men's caps from a showcase in front of a hat store. Keenan had wrestled with him and attempted to escape. Thereupon Schuck discharged his revolver, the bullet striking Keenan in the heart. A question arose in the minds of the investigators as to the distance that separated Schuck and Keenan at the time of fire. The decedent's overcoat and other apparel were subjected to the powder residue test. From the residue present on the overcoat and from the bullet hole in the coat, it was concluded that the bullet had traveled from 4 to 7 feet before it struck Keenan. Thus, the special patrolman's account of the occurrence was corroborated and the issue of manslaughter was not raised.

10. Other Techniques for Bullet Hole Areas

Photography and radiography should precede chemical testing of bullet hole areas to provide a pattern of the powder residue, lead fouling, or smoke residue left by a discharge of a firearm.

a. **Process Film.** A simple but effective photograph can be taken with process film. The great contrast of the film provides an outline of the residue on light clothing.

b. **Infrared.** By using infrared film and a Wratten 87 filter excellent contrast can be obtained in photographing dark clothing. A fingerprint camera can be used for this purpose.

c. **Soft X-rays.** If a soft x-ray apparatus is available, a radiograph can be made of the bullet hole to reveal the lead fouling or minute particles of metal impregnated in the cloth. The following settings are satisfactory: Distance from tube to cloth, 8 inches; 15 kilovolts; 10 milliamps; and 3 seconds exposure.

11. Trace Metal Detection Technique (TMDT)

This is a technique for determining whether a person's hand or clothing has recently been in contact with a metal object such as a tool or weapon. The surface (usually the hand) to be examined is treated with a test solution and placed under the ultraviolet light, where its fluorescence can be studied and photographed. The traces left by different metals differ in the color of their fluorescence. The pattern left by handling a metal object will be determined by its shape and the way it is used. From a study of the fluorescent pattern on a person's hand the examiner can draw some useful

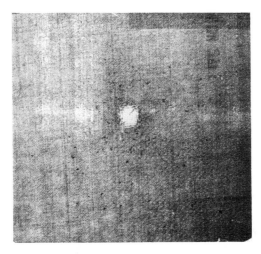

Figure 67. Powder residue about a bullet hole in dark clothing revealed by means of an infrared photograph.

conclusions as to whether or not he had been handling a weapon or tool. The test is not conclusive in the sense of permitting the conclusion to be drawn that the fluorescence could only have been caused by *this* particular weapon or tool. Nevertheless, it does provide additional useful information for the investigator, since a positive test suggests a strong probability.

a. **Equipment.** The TMDT test solution is a 0.1–0.2 percent solution of 8-Hydroxyquinoline in isopropanol (CP grade). This is applied with a plastic spray-type container, having no metal parts. In the field a battery-powered ultraviolet light source is used together with a shielding arrangement for excluding visible light.

b. **Application.** The area most commonly selected for examination is the palm and undersurface of the hand, since the investigation is usually concerned with the handling of a firearm or other metal weapon. The TMDT test solution is sprayed thoroughly over the area with the test surface held vertically to prevent puddling. After about four minutes of drying time the surface is examined under the ultraviolet lamp.

c. **Examination.** Under the ultraviolet lamp the TMDT solution produces a yellow fluorescent background. Metal trace patterns will be visible against this background in colors that are characteristic of the metal. In the case of a handgun, the examiner will look on those parts of the hand that came in contact with the gun: the index finger, which rested on the trigger; the remaining fingers and thumb which enclosed the gun; the palm; and the degree of protrusion beyond the junction of the thumb and index finger. He looks for any irregularities or distinctive marks in the pattern which may have been made by screws, protrusions, ornamentations, and other markings. A photograph is then made of the pattern produced under ultraviolet light.

d. **"Signature" Catalog.** To facilitate these examinations the police laboratory should maintain a collection of the distinctive patterns or *signatures* which are specific to types, makes, models, and calibers of these signatures. For this purpose a catalog of signatures should be prepared of as many types of specimen handguns as can reasonably be obtained. This will actually be a collection of fluorescent patterns of handguns left on the hand and photographed under the ultraviolet lamp. It should be accompanied by a record of observation of the colors and other characteristics.

e. **Conclusions.** A positive reaction will give confidence depending on the intensity and character of the color and the details of the pattern outline. It will serve as a guide to the investigator, suggesting the preferred line of inquiry.

12. Fingerprints on Guns

"Why were no fingerprints found on the gun?" This is a favorite question raised by defense counsel and an effective tactic with a jury whose criminalistics information is drawn mainly from remembered scenes of movies and television. On film it was customary for the evidence technician to develop the latent fingerprints of the perpetrator on the pistol or to draw the firm conclusion that the perpetrator wore gloves. This, of course, is mostly nonsense. Although it is not impossible to find a print on a pistol, it is highly improbable. The point is so important that we have taken the liberty of quoting from *The New York Times* (Mar. 13, 1973) a report of relevant testimony in this matter:

A police expert testifying at the trial of H. Rap Brown said yesterday that it was virtually impossible to obtain usable fingerprints from a firearm.

Sgt. William Torpey, who has been assigned to the Crime Lab for 18 of his 19 years on the force, was called to the stand in the State Supreme Court where Brown is on trial with three co-defendants in the armed robbery of a West Side bar and the attempted murder of several policemen in a subsequent gun battle on Oct. 16, 1971.

The prosecution apparently introduced yesterday's testimony in anticipation of a defense challenge that would ask why it had not introduced fingerprint evidence linking the defendants to the various weapons that are already in evidence.

Sergeant Torpey testified that during his 18 years at the Police Crime Laboratory he had examined more than 500 firearms for fingerprints and had found only one identifiable print.

"Even when fingerprints are found on a firearm," Sergeant Torpey said, "they are almost always too smudged to be useful. One reason," he said, "is that these weapons are likely to be slightly oily, especially if well kept. Another is that the person using the weapon holds it so tightly that the prints are smeared. And if the weapon is fired," he added, "the jolt smears any prints that might otherwise have been useful."

ADDITIONAL READING

Firearms

Burrard, G.: *Identification of Firearms and Forensic Ballistics.* Prescott, Ariz.: Wolfe Publishing, 1990.

Lewis, J. (Ed.): *Handguns '91.* Northbrook, Ill.: DBI Books, 1990.

Mathews, J.H.: *Firearms Identification,* 3 vols. Springfield, Ill.: Thomas, Vols. I and II, 1962, Vol. III, 1973.

Millard, J.T.: *A Handbook on the Primary Identification of Revolvers and Semiautomatic Pistols.* Springfield, Ill.: Thomas, 1974.

Scroggie, R.J.: Firearm Silencers. 46 *FBI Law Enforcement Bulletin,* 5, 1977.

Shaw, W.: The Electronic Stun Gun. 24 *Law and Order,* 8, 1976.

Wilber, C.G.: *Ballistic Science for the Law Enforcement Officer.* Springfield, Ill.: Thomas, 1977.

Williams, M.: *The 9mm and Law Enforcement Today.* Springfield, Ill.: Thomas, 1989.

——: *Practical Handgun Ballistics.* Springfield, Ill.: Thomas, 1980.

Firearms Investigation

Biasotti, A.A.: Rifling Methods—A Review and Assessment of the Individual Characteristics Produced. 13 *Association of Firearms and Tool Mark Examiners Journal,* 34, 1981.

Copeland, A.R.: Accidental Death by Gunshot Wound. Fact or Fiction. 26 *Forensic Science International,* 25, 1984.

Di Maio, V.J.M.: Accidental Deaths Due to Dropping of Handguns. 3 *Forensic Science Gazette,* 5, 1972.

Hill, T.: Firearms Tracing: A Crimefighting Weapon. 54 *FBI Law Enforcement Bulletin,* 7, 1985.

Maiti, P.C.: Powder Patterns around Bullet Holes in Bloodstained Articles. 13 *Journal of the Forensic Science Society,* 197, 1973.

Martiney, B.J.: Study of Spent Cartridge Cases. 28 *International Criminal Police Review,* 270, 1973.

Messler, H.R. and Armstrong, W.R.: Bullet Residue as Distinguished from Powder Pattern. 23 *Journal of Forensic Sciences,* 687, 1978.

Nennstiel, R.: The Determination of the Manufacturer of Ammunition. 31 *Forensic Science International,* 1, 1986.

Rathman, G.A. and Ryland, S.G.: Use of the SEM–EDXA as an Aid to the Firearms Examiner. 19 *Association of Firearms and Tool Mark Examiners Journal,* 388, 1987.

Rowe, W.F.: Firearms Identification. In Saferstein, R. (Ed.): *Forensic Science Handbook,* vol. 2. Englewood Cliffs, N.J.: Prentice-Hall, 1988.

Smith, O.C. and Harruff, R.C.: Evidentiary Value of the Contents of Hollow-Point Bullets. 33 *Journal of Forensic Sciences,* 1052, 1988.

Steinberg, M., Leist, Y. and Tassa, M.: A New Field Kit for Bullet Hole Identification. 29 *Journal of Forensic Sciences,* 169, 1984.

Stone, I.C., Di Maio, V.J.M. and Petty, C.S.: Gunshot Wounds: Visual and Analytic Procedures. 23 *Journal of Forensic Sciences,* 361, 1978.

Stone, I.C.: Observations and Statistics Relating to Suicide Weapons: An Update. 35 *Journal of Forensic Sciences,* 10, 1990.

Thurman, J.V.: Interpol Computers Keep Track of Firearms, Explosives. 58 *Police Chief,* 10, 1991.

Gunshot Residue Analysis

Aaron, R.W.: Gunshot Primer Residue: The Invisible Clue. 60 *FBI Law Enforcement Bulletin,* 6, 1991.

Andrasko, J. and Maehly, A.C.: Detection of Gunshot Residues on Hands by Scanning Electron Microscopy. 22 *Journal of Forensic Sciences,* 279, 1977.

Basu, S.: Formation of Gunshot Residues. 27 *Journal of Forensic Sciences,* 72, 1982.

Bosen, S.F. and Schewing, D.R.: A Rapid Microtechnique for the Detection of Trace Metals from Gunshot Residues. 21 *Journal of Forensic Sciences*, 163, 1976.

DeGaetano, D. and Siegel, J.A.: Survey of Gunshot Residue Analysis in Forensic Science Laboratories. 35 *Journal of Forensic Sciences*, 1087, 1990.

Goleb, J.A. and Midkiff, C.R., Jr.: Firearms Discharge Residue Sample Collection Techniques. 20 *Journal of Forensic Sciences*, 701, 1975.

Havekost, D.G., Peters, C.A. and Koons, R.D.: Barium and Antimony Distributions on the Hands of Nonshooters. 35 *Journal of Forensic Sciences*, 1096, 1990.

Krishnan, S.S.: Detection of Gunshot Residue on the Hands by Trace Element Analysis. 22 *Journal of Forensic Sciences*, 304, 1977.

Krishnan, S.S., Gillespie, K.A., and Anderson, E.J.: Rapid Detection of Firearm Discharge Residues by Atomic Absorption and Neutron Activation Analysis. 22 *Journal of Forensic Sciences*, 144, 1977.

Pillay, K. and Sagans, J.: Gunshot Residue Collection Using Film-Lift Techniques for Neutron Activation Analysis. 2 *Journal of Police Science and Administration*, 388, 1974.

Schlesinger, H.L., et al.: *Special Report on Gunshot Residues Measured by Neutron Activation Analysis.* Springfield, Va.: National Technical Information Service, 1970.

Tassa, M., et al.: A Field Kit for Sampling Gunshot Residue Particles. 27 *Journal of Forensic Sciences*, 671, 1982.

———: Characterization of Gunshot Residues by X–Ray Diffraction. 27 *Journal of Forensic Sciences*, 677, 1982.

Wolten, G.M., et al.: Particle Analysis for the Detection of Gunshot Residue. I: Scanning Electron Microscopy/Energy Dispersive X–Ray Characterization of Hand Deposits from Firing. 24 *Journal of Forensic Sciences*, 409, 1979.

Firearms Issues

Brill, S.: *Firearms Abuse: A Research and Policy Report.* Washington, D.C.: Police Foundation, 1977.

Kates, D.B., Jr. (Ed.): *Firearms and Violence: Issues of Public Policy.* Cambridge, Mass.: Ballinger, 1984.

Kleck, G.: *Point Blank: Guns and Violence in America.* Hawthorne, N.Y.: Aldine De Gruyter, 1991.

Lester, D.: *Gun Control: Issues and Answers.* Springfield, Ill.: Thomas, 1984.

Robin, G.D.: *Violent Crime and Gun Control.* Cincinnati, Anderson, 1991.

Wright, J.D. and Rossi, P.H.: *The Armed Criminal in America: A Survey of Incarcerated Felons.* Washington, D.C.: U.S. Government Printing Office, 1985.

Wright, J.D., et al.: *Under the Gun: Weapons, Crime and Violence in America.* Hawthorne, N.Y.: Aldine De Gruyter, 1986.

Chapter 40

TESTS FOR INTOXICATION

1. Alcohol and Crime

THE PRESIDENT's Commission on Drunkenness has observed that arrests for alcohol use account for more than half of all reported offenses in the United States. It has been estimated that 40 percent of all people who are victims of a homicidal assault and 50 percent of those who commit fatal assault are intoxicated. A comparable percentage of suicides takes place under the influence of alcohol. The incidence of other crimes is similarly affected. In addition, the mental instability and abnormality of alcohol intoxication predispose to a wide variety of accidental deaths. In fatal motor vehicle homicides, approximately 50 percent of the responsible drivers have been drinking heavily. Obviously, the person who is investigating a homicide will be seriously interested in the relative sobriety of the victim and his assailant. If a suspect is found soon after the fatal occurrence, it may be possible to determine whether he was intoxicated at the time of the commission of the crime. The most common method of making this determination is to observe the actions of the suspect and to smell his breath. Evidence of this nature is valuable, but is far from conclusive. Shock, disease, and personal traits may suggest a state of :toxication. The odor of alcoholic beverages is deceptive and gives little indication of the amount of the beverage consumed. To present valid evidence of intoxication to a court, the investigator must request the services of persons who are capable of performing the accepted chemical tests for this determination. The investigator should at all times request a physician to take samples of the blood of the deceased for the purpose of determining alcohol concentration. In situations where there is reason to believe that a suspect is

850

under the influence of alcohol, the investigator should endeavor to obtain the voluntary consent of the suspect for submission to a blood sampling by a physician or other qualified person.

2. Effect of Alcohol

On entering the stomach, some of the alcohol (approximately 20 percent) is absorbed through the stomach walls and passes into the blood vessels of the intestines. At the end of fifteen minutes, the absorption of the liquor is more than half accomplished and, at the end of two hours, it is almost complete. Eventually, a fraction of the alcohol reaches the brain where it upsets the delicate mechanism that guides judgment and controls skills. According to the drinker's emotional makeup, he becomes bellicose, melancholy, friendly, or joyful. Contrary to the popular conception, alcohol is not a stimulant, but a depressant. It has a drugging action on the brain cells, slowing down their activity and affecting coordination.

3. Blood-Alcohol and Intoxication

It has long been known that there is a definite relation between the amount of alcohol in a person's blood and the degree of intoxication which he manifests, i.e., the amount of alcohol in his brain. The relation appears to be fairly simple—the more alcohol in the blood, the more intoxicated the subject. It is found that when the alcohol concentration is greater than 1.5 parts per 1000, a person is definitely intoxicated. At three parts per thousand, he is in a stupor, at four parts per thousand, he becomes unconscious, after five parts per thousand he will probably die. It is possible, then, by analyzing a blood sample from the victim of a homicide to determine whether he was intoxicated at the time of his death. It may also be stated, although this aspect of the subject is not the chief concern of this section, that it is possible to determine whether a suspect in a homicide was under the influence of alcohol at the time of the fatal act if samples of his blood are taken soon after the occurrence. Although blood is the most reliable body medium for this determination, other body substances such as urine or breath can be used.

4. Sampling from Dead Bodies

In cases of homicide or suicide, the investigator should request the surgeon performing the autopsy to take a sample of blood for the purposes of a blood-alcohol analysis. The blood must, of course, be taken before an embalming fluid is used. The specimens should be taken as soon as possible. Two blood specimens should be reserved for use by the defense in the event there is a request for another analysis. A 4 or 6-ounce size bottle should be used. In order to preserve the sample, 20 to 30 grains of sodium fluoride should be added to each bottle. The specimens should be sealed and labeled in the presence of witnesses. The label should show an identification number, the date, time, and place at which the specimen was obtained and the signature of the person taking the specimen.

5. Intoxication Tests for Persons Living

The question of the sobriety of a suspect in a criminal case has an important bearing on such matters as intent and negligence. This statement is particularly applicable in motor vehicle homicides. In other types of homicide, the problem of drunkenness will also arise. A suspect who is relatively sober may later claim that he was intoxicated at the time of the fatal act. More commonly, a guilty suspect who performed the act in a moment of drunken recklessness may appear to be sober and pretend to have been dissociated from the social events preceding the homicide. In any of these situations, the value of a sobriety test is obvious.

6. Rights Against Self-Incrimination

The constitutionality of compulsory chemical tests to determine alcoholic intoxication has been the object of extensive study in legal circles. At present the taking of samples of blood and urine for intoxication tests is not, in most jurisdictions, considered to be in violation of the suspect's rights, and conclusions drawn as a result of a chemical analysis of the samples may be used as evidence of his intoxication in a trial. In some jurisdictions refusal to submit to the test subjects the driver to the penalty of revocation of his operator's license for a lengthy period of time.

7. Media for Testing

An analysis of a blood sample is the most direct and reliable way of measuring alcohol concentration in a person's blood. Urine and breath are the other body substances used for this purpose. Since intoxication tests are most commonly used in connection with motor vehicle accident investigations, law enforcement agencies have found the breath tests most convenient. The breath sample, collected by means of a balloon, is analyzed for alcohol content by means of an apparatus (such as the "Breathalyzer") designed to give direct readings in blood-alcohol percent after a few simple operations.

8. Taking Blood Specimens

Blood specimens should be taken only by a physician, medical technologist, or other person with similar qualifications. In jurisdictions requiring this condition, they should be taken only with the consent of the person, unless he is in an unconscious condition. When taking the specimen, the skin and the instruments must not be disinfected with alcohol, ether, or other volatile reducing organic fluid. A 1:1000 bichloride of mercury solution should be used as a disinfectant. Two samples of at least 10 cubic centimeters should be taken. The samples should be collected in wide-mouth bottles and closed tightly with rubber stoppers. Approximately five grains of sodium fluoride should be added as a preservative. Each specimen should be sealed with gummed paper in the presence of witnesses. The label should show an identification number, the date, time, and place at which the specimen was obtained, and the signature of the person taking the specimen. The person who supervises the taking of the specimens should deliver them personally to the chemist, technologist, or physician who is to analyze

Figure 68. The ALCO–SENSOR is a hand-held breath analyzer with a disposable mouthpiece used for the roadside screening of drivers to measure their blood-alcohol levels. The oxidation of the alcohol in the breath sample produces an electrical current in proportion to the amount of alcohol present. The blood-alcohol percentage is then indicated on a digital display. (Courtesy of Intoximeters, Inc.)

them. If they are to be sent to a distant laboratory, he should supervise the mailing. If the specimen is to be stored, it should be kept under lock and key in a cool place. The addition of the preservative will maintain the value of the specimen during any considerable lapse of time between the taking of the sample and its analysis.

ADDITIONAL READING

Tests for Intoxication

Alcohol and the Impaired Driver. A Manual on the Medicolegal Aspects of Chemical Tests for Intoxication with Supplement on BreathAlcohol Tests. Chicago, National Safety Council, 1976.

Brain, P.F. (Ed.): *Alcohol and Aggression.* Wolfeboro, N.H.: Longwood Publishing Group, 1985.

Brent, S.M. and Stiller, S.P.: *Handling Drunk Driving Cases.* Deerfield, Ill.: Clark Boardman, 1985.

Campane, J.O., Jr.: The Constitutionality of Drunk Driver Roadblocks. 53 *FBI Law Enforcement Bulletin,* 7, 1984.

Clede, B.: HGN. 38 *Law and Order,* 7, 1990.

Collins, J.J. (Ed.): *Drinking and Crime.* New York, Guilford, 1981.

Drunk Driving Laws and Enforcement: An Assessment of Effectiveness. Washington, D.C.: American Bar Association, 1986.

Emerson, V.J.: *The Measurement of Breath Alcohol.* New York, Columbia University Press, 1981.

Erwin, R.E.: There is No Danger of a Fair Trial in a Drunk Driving Case. 51 *California State Bar Journal,* 3, 1976.

Fitzgerald, E.F. and Hume, D.N.: *Intoxication Test Evidence: Criminal and Civil.* Rochester, N.Y.: Lawyer's Co-operative, 1987.

Garriott, J.C.: *Forensic Alcohol Determination,* vol. 1. Littleton, Mass.: PSG, 1987.

Garriott, J.C., et al.: Incidence of Drugs and Alcohol in Fatally Injured Motor Vehicle Drivers. 22 *Journal of Forensic Sciences,* 383, 1977.

Gullberg, R.G.: Variations in Blood-Alcohol Concentration Following the Last Drink. 10 *Journal of Police Science and Administration,* 289, 1982.

Hannigan, M.J.: California's Ongoing Battle Against DUI. 57 *Police Chief,* 7, 1990.

Hoffman, J.: DWI—Police and the Criminal Justice System. 38 *Law and Order,* 5, 1990.

Jacobs, J.B.: *Drunk Driving: An American Dilemma.* Chicago, University of Chicago Press, 1989.

Jones, A.W., Jonsson, K.-A. and Neri, A.: Peak Blood-Ethanol Concentration and the Time of Its Occurrence after Rapid Drinking on an Empty Stomach. 36 *Journal of Forensic Sciences,* 376, 1991.

Jones, I.S. and Lund, A.K.: Detection of Alcohol-Impaired Drivers Using a Passive Alcohol Sensor. 14 *Journal of Police Science and Administration,* 153, 1986.

Kilpack, L.: Use of Video Camera for DUI Investigations. 56 *FBI Law Enforcement Bulletin,* 5, 1987.

Lewis, M.J.: Blood Alcohol: The Concentration-Time Curve and Retrospective Estimation of Level. 26 *Journal of the Forensic Science Society,* 95, 1986.

Lewis, R.R. and Sherman, L.W.: *Drunk Driving Tests in Fatal Accidents.* Washington, D.C.: Crime Control Institute, 1986.

Neuteboom, W. and Jones, A.W.: Disappearance Rate of Alcohol from the Blood of Drunk Drivers Calculated from Two Consecutive Samples: What Do the Results Mean? 45 *Forensic Science International,* 107, 1990.

Norfolk Goes after Drunk Drivers. 36 *Law and Order,* 3, 1988.

Pernanen, K.: *Alcohol in Human Violence.* New York, Guilford Press, 1991.

Ross, H.L.: *Deterring the Drinking Driver.* Lexington, Mass.: Heath, 1982.

Taylor, L.: *Drunk Driving Defense,* 3rd ed. Boston, Mass.: Little Brown, 1991.

Chapter 41

TRACING MATERIALS
AND DETECTIVE DYES

1. General

A N IMPORTANT technical aid for the investigation of systematic petty larcenies and, in general, for the detection of unknown perpetrators of localized acts is the use of staining powders such as methylene blue and uranyl phosphate which will temporarily mark a culprit in a recognizable manner. To detect a thief, for example, a planted wallet may be dusted with a methylene blue, a powder. When the thief touches the wallet, the powder clings to his hands and in the presence of perspiration is turned into a deep-staining dye. A surveillance of washrooms and towels will usually reveal the culprit. A more elaborate use of tracing powder is illustrated by the following case in which the problem of trailing a narcotics seller was solved. The narcotics pusher would sell his wares to an addict in the street and disappear into a five-story tenement building where it was believed a ring of sellers had their headquarters. The police planned to conduct a surprise raid to trap the leaders of this group. An addict was employed as confederate. He was given a number of dollar bills which had been dusted with uranyl phosphate, a powder fluorescing brilliantly under ultraviolet radiation. The currency was placed in an envelope. The addict then used the money to buy a deck of heroin from the pusher in a street sale. Before completing the transaction the seller felt within the envelope to count his money. Subsequently he disappeared into the tenement house. The sale had been kept under surveillance by the investigators who now drove up to the tenement and alighted with a portable ultraviolet lamp. The lights on each landing were dimmed and the ultraviolet lamp was played on the doorknobs. Finally, one of the knobs was found to bear some bright, shining particles of the powder. A raid was quickly arranged and the local headquarters of the narcotics ring was discovered.

2. Methods

There are three basic methods of employing tracing powders:

a. **Staining.** In this method a powder is employed which on touching the skin will be converted to a dye by the moisture. The powder is selected for the permanence of its stain and for its color. If a brown wallet, for example, is to be treated, a powder of similar color is selected. The following are some of the powders which have been found useful:

Name	*Color-Dry*	*Color-Wet*
Crystal Violet	Green	Violet
Chrysoidine	Maroon	Orange
Malachite Green	Green	Green
Methylene Blue	Dark Green	Blue
Rhodamine B	Brown	Cherry

b. **Fluorescent.** One of the disadvantages of using staining powders is the necessity for maintaining surveillance, since the stain can be removed by persistent washing. To avoid this requirement a powder which fluoresces under ultraviolet radiation can be used. The powder is used in small quantities and is invisible to the culprit. Under the ultraviolet lamp each speck of the substance fluoresces brightly. The following powders can be used for this purpose:

Name	*Visible Color*	*Color in Ultraviolet*
Fluorescein	Maroon	Yellow
Rhodamine B	Brown	Orange
Uranyl Nitrate	Yellow	Yellow

c. **Chemical Detectors.** As a tracing material for liquids which are subject to theft or illicit use, a chemical indicator or a fluorescent material can be added. These techniques are discussed more fully in the following section.

3. Application

The investigator will find that tracing materials can be used in a wide variety of cases. A number of these are described below, but the investigator's imagination will readily suggest many others.

a. **Thefts.** Systematic petty larcenies in barracks, dormitories, or locker rooms provide the most obvious use of detective dyes. The object of the larceny, a wallet or pocketbook, is powdered with one of the tracing substances selected for its color in relation to that of the background. A close surveillance should be maintained to note any effort to wash off a stain. The culprit may wipe off the stain with a handkerchief or may wear gloves. These objects should be seized in such contingencies. On apprehension the subject's hands should be examined. Traces of the stain will usually be visible in the borders of the fingernails. If a fluorescent powder is used, a loose surveillance will suffice. An ultraviolet lamp should be brought to the premises where the thefts are taking place. It will be found that particles of the fluorescent powder cling to the clothes of the subject. Hence, it is possible to detect the offender many hours after the occurrence.

b. **Burglaries.** Systematic burglaries can be detected by these methods, if there is a known and limited group of suspects. Fluorescent powders can be used at the areas where a break can be logically expected. Doorknobs, locks, latches, and sills should be dusted with the powder. Care should be exercised so that other persons do not innocently touch these areas without the knowledge of the investigator. A line-up of suspects or, in general, personnel having access to the area should be conducted on the morning after a burglary. In place of powders, which may wash off in the rain, the technique described in the next paragraph is useful in solving some types of burglary.

c. **False Alarms.** An excellent means of detecting persons who have a penchant for pulling fire alarm boxes is the use of a dye which will withstand varying weather conditions. A saturated solution of crystal violet or one of the other stains in oleic acid ("red oil") is painted on a part of the handle which is not in the line of view.

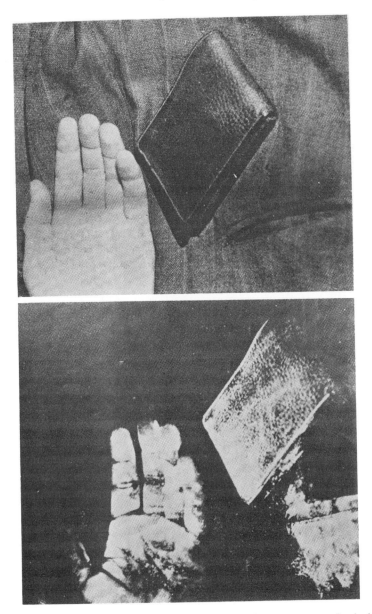

Figure 69. Fluorescent powder can be used to detect the perpetrator of a theft. At the top, objects labeled with this powder are seen under ordinary light. At the bottom the same objects are photographed under ultraviolet light.

d. **Gasoline Thefts.** By adding a chemical indicator to the gasoline supply, theft of the gas can be detected through a chemical examination of samples taken from the cars of suspects. A quantity of fifty-six milligrams of phenolphthalein is used for each gallon of gasoline. If the gas tank has a capacity of 500 gallons, one ounce of phenolphthalein is dissolved in fifteen ounces of isopropyl alcohol and added to the gas reservoir. To detect the phenolphthalein a sample is taken from the suspect's tank. One cubic centimeter of a 5 percent solution of sodium hydroxide is mixed with 10 cubic centimeters of the gasoline. If a red layer is observed at the bottom, the gasoline contains phenolphthalein. Another technique consists of adding a fluorescent substance to the gasoline. Fluorene or anthracene is satisfactory. A tablespoon of the powder added to a 500-gallon tank will cause the gasoline to fluoresce under an ultraviolet lamp.

e. **Explosives.** The lethal 1993 explosion at New York's World Trade Center revived once more the project of adding innocuous chemicals to explosives to provide trace substances that would survive detonation, leaving vital clues to the source of the explosive. These minute additives would remain after the explosion to be collected and traced to the origin of the explosives. It is anticipated that the taggants will provide immediate investigative leads and that the knowledge of their existence will prompt explosives dealers and users to employ greater security measures. The extension of this detection method to ammunition materials, in general, would greatly facilitate the investigation of crimes involving firearms.

4. Radioactive Tracers

With the widespread availability of radioactive substances it is practicable for the investigator to use these materials as tracing substances. Their presence can be detected by means of a survey meter.

ADDITIONAL READING

Hackl, F.-X.: Trap Substances. 27 *International Criminal Police Review*, 108, 1972.

Chapter 42

HAIR AND FIBERS

1. Significance

THE STRAY HAIR found at the scene of the crime, adhering to the murder weapon or even in the grasp of the victim, has long been considered one of the classic examples of physical evidence. Unfortunately there is little to recommend hair as a medium of identification. It has no unique chemical characteristics; there is little of a special nature in its shape; and its color, although highly characteristic, is not readily subjected to a color (spectrophotometrical) analysis. At best the expert can say that two specimens of hair are similar; in his present state of knowledge he may not say that they are identical in source. Nevertheless, hair specimens provide valuable exclusionary evidence. Although one may not say that the evidence specimen of hair belongs to a particular person, it can at least be asserted that the hair did not come from certain other persons. It is not often that hair is an important contributing factor to a case; such evidence, however, and its potential application to the case under investigation, must never be considered as worthless. A negative finding may serve to disprove erroneous theories. A positive finding, although merely suggesting the implication of an individual, is of importance when it is correlated with other newly discovered facts. The following are the possible findings:

a. **Non-Identity of Sources.** Establishing the fact that the evidence sample and the standard sample did not come from the same source serves the purpose of elimination.

b. **Possible Source.** Establishing that the evidence sample is similar to the standard sample may only indicate that a hypothetical event is possible or probable. In the presence of other evidence this fact may provide valuable corroboration.

2. Laboratory Examination

A number of determinations can be made in the laboratory, chiefly with the aid of a microscope.

a. **The Specimen Is Hair.** This may be established by the three parts of hair: the medulla or core, varying in thickness and continuity; the cortex or body surrounding the medulla; and the cuticle or outer covering formed by overlapping scales which vary in size, shape, and number per unit length.

b. **The Hair Is Human.** Often a suspect maintains that an incriminating hair specimen found on his person came from an animal. The difference between animal and human hair is readily apparent because of the relative diameter of the medulla and the location and distribution of pigment.

c. **Characteristics.** Hair possesses a number of useful characteristics such as the color, length, diameter, dye, or bleach.

d. **Determinations.** In addition to forming an opinion concerning the similarity of the evidence and the standard specimen, the laboratory expert is sometimes able to make some other useful deductions from a hair specimen. The sex of the owner is suggested by the thickness and length; gray hair indicates age; hair from different parts of the body varies; the race is sometimes indicated by the shape of the cross section; foreign matter may give a clue to the occupation of the owner; the nature of any dye present may be revealed by microchemical analysis; in assaults and homicides some clue to the nature of the instrument used to inflict a blow may be derived from the impression left on the hair; arsenic may be found in small traces in the hair of a person poisoned by this substance.

e. **Scanning Electron Microscope.** The Scanning Electron Microscope (SEM) far surpasses other microscopes for examining surface characteristics of hair such as scale count, hair shape, scale structure, and physical or chemical damage.

f. **Drug Testing by Hair Analysis.** Because hair will absorb any drug that is ingested, it is an excellent medium for determining long-term drug use. Hair will grow on average one-half inch a

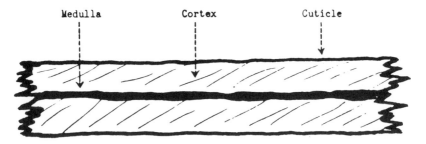

Figure 70. Longitudinal cross section of a hair.

month. Thus, two inches of hair growth will reflect drug use over a period of four months. The hair samples are first treated to extract and concentrate the drug-related material and are then analyzed using the same techniques that are used for urine analysis, namely, immunoassay and gas chromatography. Hair analysis has clear advantages over short-term testing. Because the opiates and cocaine are water soluble, they can be eliminated from the body in about two days. A subject can disguise months of drug use by abstaining a few days before a test. In this situation hair analysis will give a more accurate picture of drug use. It is also a less intrusive means of testing. Moreover, the hair from the scalp can be plucked by the person doing the testing, affording the subject no opportunity to switch the samples.

3. DNA Analysis of Hair Roots

The advent of DNA analysis will have a lasting impact on hair identification. While it is still true, as stated above, hair of itself is a poor medium for identification, it is not the case with a hair root. Although DNA typing is performed primarily on blood and semen evidence, it can be used to positively identify any biological sample which contains cells with a nucleus. The hair root cells fit this description. If there are a sufficient number of hair root cells to extract DNA from, an identification can be made. Usually ten hair roots are adequate for DNA analysis. However, it is possible to make an identification with only a single specimen. Hair roots from any part of the body can be analyzed. The following is an example of how this evidence could be used in an investigation. A victim while defending himself against a violent assault may rip out a sufficient number of hair roots from his assailant that a DNA sample could be extracted. A comparison of this DNA evidence with a DNA from a blood sample taken from a suspect would positively identify the suspect as the assailant.

3. Fibers

The clothing of persons involved in crimes of personal violence is a source of valuable clues. The fibers from the clothing may adhere to the person of the victim. In hit-and-run cases fibers from the victim's clothing may be found on the radiator, grille, or tires of the vehicle. Since fibers vary widely in composition, source, color, and shape, they possess many more identifying characteristics than hair. The following examples illustrate the value of these clues.

a. **Rope.** The victim of a homicide had been trussed with a three-strand rope. The probable manufacturer of the rope was located. It was possible to identify the rope by the marks of the machine that had been used during a certain period and by means of the characteristic chemical properties of the substance that had been used for impregnation. An examination of shipping records revealed that a wholesaler in the home town of the suspect and victim had received a shipment of the rope. A search of the garage of the suspect disclosed a length of rope similar in every respect to that used in tying the victim.

b. **Cloth and String.** Parts of the dismembered body of a woman were discovered in different locations of an Eastern city. Each part was found as a package, wrapped in the same type of cloth and tied with string made from twisted paper. It was found after diligent search that the cloth and string had been obtained at a small store devoted to the manufacture of window shades. Further investigation revealed that the suspect lived in a room on the second floor above the shop and could have obtained the cloth and string from piles of scrap in the rear of the building.

4. Types of Fibers

For the purpose of the laboratory expert, fibers may be divided into the following classes:

a. **Animal.** A number of fibers were derived from animal products, the most important being wool, silk, camel's hair, and fur.

b. **Vegetable.** This class includes most of the inexpensive clothing fibers. The familiar types are cotton, linen, jute, hemp, ramie, and sisal.

c. **Mineral.** Minerals provide such useful fibers as glass wool and asbestos. Fibers of this kind are used in safe insulation.

d. **Synthetics.** Applied chemistry has produced a number of fibers among which are rayon, nylon, orlon, and dacron.

5. Fiber Examination

The problems of fiber comparisons should be submitted to the laboratory expert. The investigator should not attempt to make such a comparison for the official record. He may, however, make preliminary examinations which are not destructive to the evidence in situations where the expert is not available. In this way he can avoid the pitfalls of false leads.

a. **Animal or Vegetable.** These fibers can be distinguished by the application of flame. After the flame is withdrawn and the fibers are permitted to continue burning, it is noted that animal fibers will burn for a short time only, emitting a characteristic odor of burned animal matter and assuming a swollen appearance at the ends. On the other hand, vegetable fibers will burn easily with a smell resembling burning wood and with the burned end appearing sharp. This type of experiment should not be considered in an actual case when the amount of evidence is limited to a few fibers.

b. **Microscopic examination** of fibers is made in comparing unknown with known specimens in order to establish similarities and variations. The complete study of woven or spun material will include data on the following characteristics: nature of the fiber; color; method of weaving; number of threads per inch, both laterally and longitudinally (lateral threads are called the filler and the longitudinal threads are called the warp); number of twists per inch in a thread; direction of the twist; position and nature of any stains and marks; nature of any dust or dirt.

c. **Examination of String and Rope.** String is identified in much the same manner as yarn from cloth or other fabrics. Rope is identified by the "lay" or angle at which the strands are twisted; the circumference; number of strands; number of yarns per strand; number of fibers per yarn; chemical processing involving sizing, lubricants, preservatives, or insect repellents.

ADDITIONAL READING

Hair

Barnett, P.D. and Ogle, R.R.: Probabilities and Human Hair Comparison. 27 *Journal of Forensic Sciences,* 272, 1982.

Baumgartner, W.S., Hill, V.A. and Blahd, W.H.: Hair Analysis for Drugs of Abuse. 34 *Journal of Forensic Sciences,* 1433, 1989.

Bisbing, R.E.: The Forensic Identification and Association of Human Hair. In Saferstein, R. (Ed.): *Forensic Science Handbook.* Englewood Cliffs, N.J.: Prentice-Hall, 1987.

DeForest, P.R. and Kirk, P.L.: Forensic Individualization of Hair. 8 *Criminologist,* 27, 1973.

Don't Miss a Hair. 45 *FBI Law Enforcement Bulletin,* 5, 1976.

Forslev, A.W.: "Nondestructive" Neutron Activation Analysis of Hair. 11 *Journal of Forensic Sciences,* 217, 1966.

Gaudette, B.D.: Strong Negative Conclusions in Hair Comparison—A Rare Event. 18 *The Canadian Society of Forensic Science Journal,* 32, 1985.

Hicks, J.W.: *Microscopy of Hair: A Practical Guide and Manual.* Washington, D.C.: U.S. Government Printing Office, 1977.

Lee, H.C. and DeForest, P.R.: Forensic Hair Examination. In Wecht, C.H. (Ed.): *Forensic Science,* vol. 3. Albany, N.Y.: Mathew-Bender, 1984.

Niyogi, S.K.: A Study of Human Hairs in Forensic Work. 2 *Proceedings of the Canadian Society of Forensic Science,* 105, 1963.

Obrusnik, I., et al.: The Variation of Trace Element Concentrations in Single Human Head Hairs. 17 *Journal of Forensic Sciences,* 426, 1972.

Petraco, N., Fras, C., Callery, F.X. and DeForest, P.R.: The Morphology and Evidential Significance of Human Hair Roots. 33 *Journal of Forensic Sciences,* 68, 1988.

Proceedings of the International Symposium on Forensic Hair Comparisons. Washington, D.C.: U.S. Government Printing Office, 1987.

Strauss, M.: Forensic Characterization of Human Hair. 31 *The Microscope,* 15, 1983.

Verhoeven, L.E.: The Advantage of the Scanning Electron Microscope in the Investigative Studies of Hair. 63 *Journal of Criminal Law, Criminology and Police Science,* 125, 1972.

Vernall, J.: A Study of the Size and Shape of Cross Sections of Hair from Familiar Races of Man. 19 *American Journal of Physical Anthropology,* 345, 1961.

Fibers

Appleyard, H.M.: Fibre Identification and Analysis of Fibre Blends. 101 *Analyst,* 595, 1976.

Bresee, R.R.: Evaluation of Textile Fiber Evidence: A Review. 32 *Journal of Forensic Sciences,* 510, 1987.

Budworth, G.: Identification of Knots. 22 *Journal of the Forensic Science Society,* 327, 1982.

Deadman, H.A.: Fiber Evidence and the Wayne Williams Trial. Parts I and II. 53 *FBI Law Enforcement Bulletin,* 3 and 5, 1984.

Dixon, K.C.: Positive Identification of Torn Burned Matches with Emphasis on Crosscut and Torn Fiber Comparisons. 28 *Journal of Forensic Sciences,* 351, 1983.

Fong, W.: Analytical Methods for Developing Fibers as Forensic Science Proof: A Review with Comments. 34 *Journal of Forensic Sciences,* 295, 1989.

——: Fiber Evidence: Laboratory Methods and Observations from Casework. 29 *Journal of Forensic Sciences,* 55, 1984.

Fong, W. and Inami, S.H.: Results of Study to Determine Chance Match Occurrences Between Fibers Known to be from Different Sources. 31 *Journal of Forensic Sciences,* 65, 1986.

Grieve, M.C.: The Role of Fibers in Forensic Science Examination. 28 *Journal of Forensic Sciences,* 877, 1983.

Grieve, M.C. and Kowtowski, T.M.: The Identification of Polyester Fibers in Forensic Science. 22 *Journal of Forensic Sciences,* 390, 1977.

Kidd, C.B.M. and Robertson, J.: The Transfer of Fibres During Simulated Contacts. 22 *Journal of the Forensic Science Society,* 301, 1982.

Martin, E.P.: Wool Fibres as Evidence: Their Probative Value in Criminal Procedure. 30 *International Criminal Police Review,* 288, 1975.

McKenna, F.J. and Sherwin, J.C.: A Simple and Effective Method for Collecting Contact Evidence. 15 *Journal of the Forensic Sciences,* 277, 1975.

Petraco, N., DeForest, P.R. and Harris, H.: A New Approach to Microscopical Examination and Comparison of Synthetic Fibers Encountered in Forensic Science Cases. 25 *Journal of the Forensic Sciences,* 571, 1980.

Pounds, C.A.: The Recovery of Fibres from the Surface of Clothing for Forensic Examinations. 15 *Journal of the Forensic Science Society,* 12, 1975.

Proceedings of the International Symposium on the Analysis and Identification of Polymers. Washington, D.C.: U.S. Government Printing Office, 1985.

Rouen, R.A. and Reeve, V.C.: A Comparison and Evaluation of Techniques for Identification of Synthetic Fibers. 15 *Journal of Forensic Sciences,* 410, 1970.

Snyder, P. and Snyder, A.: *Knots and Lines Illustrated.* Tuckahoe, N.Y.: De Graff, 1970.

Strell, I. and Kennedy, R.W.: *Identification of North American Pulpwoods and Pulp Fibers.* Toronto, University of Toronto Press, 1967.

The Textile Institute. *Identification of Textile Materials,* 7th ed. Manchester, Eng.: The Textile Institute, 1975.

Chapter 43

INVISIBLE RADIATION

I. ULTRAVIOLET RADIATION

1. Nature of Ultraviolet

ONE OF more common problems of the police laboratory scientist and the document examiner is the decipherment or discernment of the relatively invisible. Thus, a stain on a garment or an obscured writing on a document can be rendered visible by the use of certain techniques. One of these methods is the employment of rays which border the visible, i.e., radiation which is slightly longer (infrared) or slightly shorter (ultraviolet) in wavelength than visible light. The wavelength of ultraviolet light is in the region from 136 to 4000 angstrom units.

2. Effect of Ultraviolet Light

When ultraviolet radiation strikes a surface it is absorbed by some substances and its energy transformed and radiated back in light of different colors. Thus, although the original ultraviolet is invisible, its effects on an object as observed in a dark room are distinctly visible. The object is then said to *fluoresce*. This interesting phenomenon is useful to the investigator who may in this manner detect stains on a garment, alterations on a check, or secret writing in a letter.

3. Sources of Ultraviolet

To obtain ultraviolet light a special lamp must be used. Although the sun is rich in ultraviolet and may be used as a source by

9. Applications

As in the case of ultraviolet the usefulness of infrared radiation has been learned by experience. The following are some of the typical applications:

a. **Documents.** The most fruitful field to which infrared can be applied is that of documentary evidence.

1) *Inks.* Two inks which appear to the eye to be the same can sometimes be differentiated by an infrared photograph.

2) *Obliterations.* If ink has been used to obliterate writing, it may be possible to determine the nature of the writing by means of infrared photography. If the obliterating ink is transparent to the infrared and the lower writing is opaque, it is a relatively simple matter to render the writing legible. Some inks such as Chinese and india inks, iron tannate inks, and chrome logwood inks are opaque to the infrared. Others, particularly colored inks containing aniline dyes, are transparent.

3) *Erasures.* When writing is mechanically erased, small particles of the ink or pencil sometimes remain in the outline. It may be possible to increase the contrast of the residual writing by means of infrared.

4) *Secret Writing.* Infrared photography is another method of detecting secret writing.

5) *Unopened Letters.* If the paper is transparent to infrared and the ink opaque to this radiation, it is possible to read the contents of the letter without opening it. The letter is placed in contact with an infrared film in a printing frame and exposed to a light filtered through an infrared glass.

6) *Charred Documents.* Burned documents can sometimes be deciphered by an infrared photograph. Success depends upon the nature of the ink or pencil and the degree of charring.

b. **Comparison Tests.** In the course of an investigation it sometimes becomes necessary to compare a known and questioned sample of a substance in an effort to prove identity of source. Infrared provides a preliminary screening test for certain materials such as cloths and paints. If the two samples reflect infrared to distinctly varied degree, it can be said that they have different sources.

c. **Powder Marks.** Infrared photography is an excellent means of determining the presence of powder marks surrounding a bullet hole. It is particularly useful when the bullet hole is found in a dark suit.

d. **Stains.** Infrared provides an additional method of detecting and differentiating stains.

10. Infrared Photography

A special film such as Eastman Kodak® Infrared film must be used in this type of photography. Filters must be employed which exclude the visible to a great extent and transmit the infrared. The procedures are similar to those of ordinary photography. The following data will be found useful:

a. **Light Source.** A tungsten lamp such as a photoflood is a good source of infrared radiation. Varying the angle of illumination sometimes affects the results. Special flash bulbs can also be used as described below.

b. **Film.** Kodak Infrared film is available in standard sizes. In photographing a small area, such as that of an altered signature, a $2\frac{1}{4} \times 3\frac{1}{4}$-inch film size may be used conveniently with a fixed-focus fingerprint camera in which a filter has been placed.

c. **Filter.** If it is desired to exclude all the visible light a Wratten No. 87 filter should be used. The Wratten No. 25 filter, which transmits visible light also, can be used to obtain a different effect. It is possible to dispense with the filter over the lens by using flashbulbs dipped in a special lacquer and photographing in darkness. A No. 22R lamp is recommended. By using a $f/3.5$ opening a photograph can be made up to a distance of 20 feet in a dark room. This procedure is useful for surreptitious photography. A dull red glow is visible only by looking directly at the lamp.

d. **Camera.** No special camera is required.

e. **Focusing.** Since infrared rays come to focus in an image plane slightly behind the visible plane, the exposure should be made at about $f/16$ to allow for any error in focusing. Alternatively the bellows extension can be increased by 3 percent of the focal length of the lens to compensate for any error.

f. **Exposure.** A filter factor is provided for the Wratten No. 25 filter. For the Wratten No. 87, exposures must be greatly increased. A set of test exposures should be made. A test exposure for photographing a document in the infrared with two No. 1 photoflood lamps at 3 feet from the object is four seconds at $f/16$ with a Wratten No. 87 filter.

III. X-RAYS

11. Introduction

X-rays provide the investigator with another method of seeing objects invisible to the normal eye. In this respect they are similar to ultraviolet and infrared radiation. Among the situations in which the investigator would find these rays useful are the following: a "suspicious package," i.e. a package which is thought to contain a bomb; a locked suitcase thought to contain contraband; loaded dice; fraudulent paintings; the detection of lead fouling in contact bullet holes on clothing; and, in general, the presence of metallic objects in non-metallic surroundings.

12. Nature

X-rays are similar in nature to light; they are electromagnetic radiations differing from light in that they are much shorter in wavelength, a characteristic which gives them great penetrating power. In the same way as light, x-rays affect a photographic plate. A film exposed by means of x-rays is called a *radiograph.* The technique of making radiographs is relatively simple and need not present any more difficulty than ordinary photography. A few lessons in the manipulation of the x-ray apparatus suffice to provide a facility adequate for the demands of police radiography. The subtleties of medical x-ray methods are not necessary in this branch of criminalistics.

Figure 72. Examination of antiques. The photograph shows what appears to be the original face of the clock.

Figure 73. The appearance of the same clock recorded with infrared illumination. The superimposition of paints is apparent. Note that the paint used for the numbers on the overlayer is not transparent to infrared radiation.

13. The X-ray tube

The source of x-rays is a vacuum tube containing a cathode and an anode with a potential difference ranging from 20,000 to 60,000 volts or 20 to 60 kilovolts. The apparatus operates from an ordinary 110 volt AC line. A transformer supplies the needed voltage. When the cathode is hot enough, electrons fall from the cathode to the anode at high speeds and strike a target in front of the anode. The target thus bombarded gives out x-rays, which penetrate non-metallic objects. Since they are blocked by metallic objects, these latter produce a shadow on the photographic plate. This shadow picture is the radiograph. The intensity of the shadow and the penetrating power of the rays can be controlled by varying the voltage and current of the tube.

a. **Voltage.** If the voltage is increased, the wavelength of the x-rays becomes shorter and the radiation is more penetrating. X-rays in the range of 4 to 25 kilovolts are called *soft x-rays;* those from 50 to 140 kilovolts are *hard x-rays.* A different x-ray apparatus is required for each type. Hard x-rays of great penetrating power are useful in examining suspected bombs.

b. **Current.** The intensity of the shadow depends also on the tube current, which is measured in milliamperes. When the current is increased, the filament becomes hotter and gives off a greater quantity of electrons. Current does not affect the speed of the electrons and consequently the penetrating power of the x-rays. The greater the current, the shorter the exposure time.

c. **Tube-Film Distance.** To take a radiograph of a suspicious box, the photographic holder containing film is placed under the "head" of the x-ray tube. If the holder is on the level of a table, the x-ray head will be about 2 feet away from it. The box is placed on top of the holder. Since the box is between the head and the holder, metal objects will cast a shadow on the film when x-rays are emitted from the head. It is not necessary to remove the dark slide, since the x-rays penetrate this material. The exposure will depend on the distance of the head or tube from the box. The tube-to-object distance also controls definitions or sharpness of image. The object-to-film distance is also a factor. The definition or sharpness improves as the tube-to-object distance becomes greater.

If the object is placed as close as possible to the film, the sharpness is improved.

14. Film and Screens

Practically any film is satisfactory for the exploratory work of police radiography. An ordinary 8 × 10-inch wooden and plastic film holder with commercial film will yield satisfactory results. Metal film holders should not be used. The development procedures are the same as those of ordinary photography.

The above procedures have been described in order to impress the reader with the simplicity of radiography. Naturally, a more professional technique can be developed by employing equipment specifically designed for x-ray work by the manufacturers. For more exacting work special x-ray films such as Eastman Kodak type F should be used.

Another method of improving x-ray work is to employ cassettes containing x-ray screens. An x-ray cassette is a film holder equipped with intensifying screens. The purpose of the screens is to decrease exposure time. When x-rays strike a film only 1 percent of the radiation affects the screen, the remainder passing uselessly through. The screen permits more of the radiation to be utilized. The exposure time is greatly decreased, since the screen renders the film approximately thirty times faster. Polaroid backs or filmholding arrangements are available for rapid work in the field.

15. Protection

X-rays, because of their penetrating power and peculiar effect on human tissue, are dangerous if used carelessly. A lead apron and gloves should be used by the operator to absorb the rays. It should be remembered that the effect of x-rays is "summed up" or cumulative. The doses received on different days are additive, and thus a massive dosage can be accumulated by successive exposures over a period of weeks.

16. Fluoroscopy

For quick inspection of an object under x-rays, a fluoroscope is used. The fluoroscope is a small box with a viewing aperture for both eyes on one end and calcium tungstate (or similar substance) screen on the other. X-rays striking the screen fluoresce and present a shadow picture to the viewer.

17. Use of X-rays in Police Work

a. **Soft X-rays.** These rays range from 4 to 25 kilovolts. For most work a potential of 12 kilovolts and a current of 8 milliamps will suffice. The distance of the tube to the film can range from 4 inches to 3 feet. An average distance of 20 inches suffices. The exposure time may range from one second to four minutes depending on the other factors.

1) *Paintings.* Cases of fraudulent paintings and of superimposed paintings have been solved by the use of soft x-rays. The different compositions of the paints produce different effects on the film under x-rays. Where an old picture, in which paints relatively opaque to x-rays have been used, lies under a new painting with relatively transparent paints, the x-ray will reveal the presence of the older painting.

2) *Fabrics.* Two samples of cloth visually similar can be differentiated by means of x-rays.

3) *Paper.* The texture of paper can be studied with x-rays and in this way two apparently similar specimens can be distinguished. Handmade papers can be differentiated from machine-made papers because of the differing opacities of the fillers and the fiber structure.

4) *Jewelry.* Imitation diamonds such as rutile and zircon can be distinguished from the genuine. Similarly, differences in natural and synthetic pearls can be detected.

5) *Gunshot Wounds.* When a gun is discharged at a close distance from the body, lead fouling is distributed about the hole. To determine whether a hole in a garment was made by a bullet and also to acquire information about the discharge distance, x-rays can be used to produce a picture of the lead fouling.

is ordinarily (i.e., disregarding the coefficient's dependence on x-ray wavelength) a monotonically increasing function of atomic number. Neutron absorption, however, is almost independent of atomic number, because it involves a nuclear interaction determined by nuclear properties not specifically related to atomic number.

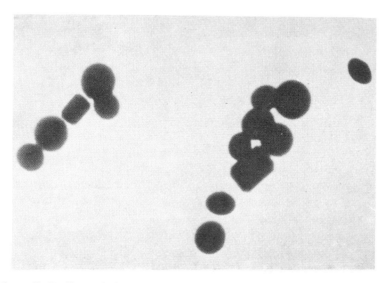

Figure 75. Radiograph that located two packets of smuggled diamonds secreted in a pillow. Lack of sharpness is the result of the separation of the diamond packets and the film by part of the pillow.

4) *Examples.* The advantages of neutron radiography can be illustrated by the ordinary cigarette lighter. An x-radiograph can show all the metal parts of a lighter and their relationship but not whether there is any cotton or wick. In a neutron radiograph most or all of the parts visible in the x-radiograph are discernible; in addition, the cotton, wick, and flint are clearly visible, since they are highly hydrogenous and thus opaque to neutrons. For the same reason, it can be established even that the lighter has been filled with fluid. Another example is given by Figure 78 in which the packing condition of the increments in an electrically initiated detonator are examined by neutron radiography and x-radiography. For example, two out of the five increments comprising the train

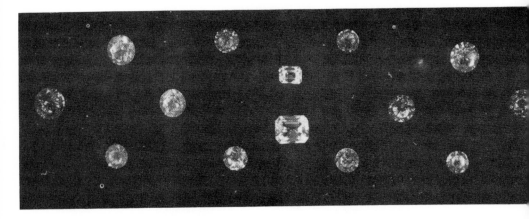

Figure 76. A one-to-one photograph of the fourteen diamonds recovered from the pillow. Notice the two emerald cut gems, which may also be identified in Figure 24 by their rectangular shape.

can be shown in the neutron radiograph to have been passed together to a higher density, since their images will be darker than those of the other three. The thin layer of case material, offering little resistance to neutrons, will be barely discernible, whereas in the x-radiograph only the case material will be visible.

5) *Applications.* The effectiveness of neutron radiography as a non-destructive inspection technique suggests its applicability to a number of investigative problems. In general, neutron radiography is applicable to the examination of assembled or sealed objects which are beyond the reach of x-radiography because their internal components are transparent to x-rays or their coverings or casings are opaque to x-rays. Some of the obvious applications are listed below.

a. **Explosive Devices.** A concealed bomb or "infernal machine" can be examined by means of neutron radiography to show the arrangement and condition of the internal components and thus provide a basis for subsequent decisions on its disarming, transportation, and disposal. Although the method is particularly applicable to bombs in metal enclosures or casings, such as pipe bombs, it is also a useful supplement to an x-ray examination, since it will detect the presence of substances such as fluids which will not be shown by an x-radiograph.

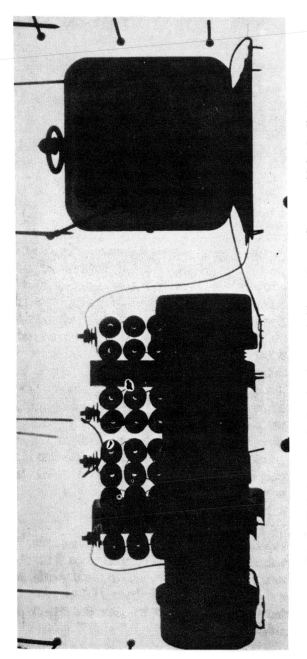

Figure 77. Radiograph of a time bomb concealed in a suitcase. (Courtesy of John Bealler.)

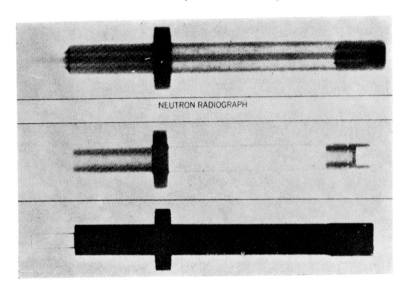

NEUTRON RADIOGRAPH

Figure 78. Neutron radiograph and light and dark positive x-radiographs of the same explosive device. The explosive train visible (down the middle of the device) is obscured in the x-radiographs but clearly visible in the neutron radiograph.

b. **Contraband.** The search for illegally possessed objects or substances can be aided by this inspection technique where the materials are visually inaccessible or undiscernible by x-rays because of their own nature or because of the nature of their protective covering.

c. **Espionage Materials.** An unusual spy case will serve as an example. Faced with the problem of transmitting a copy of highly classified security information which had been made on 8mm film, an enemy agent conceived the scheme of inserting the tightly rolled, undeveloped film segment into a small hole drilled into the edge of a half-dollar piece. Fortunately, the laboratory examiner, on detecting the plug placed over the hole to protect the film and conceal its hiding place, had the foresight to remove the plug in the darkroom, using only a green safelight to determine the condition of the film. Neutron radiography is especially suitable to an examination of this nature, particularly when the method of concealment is not easily detectable and film is readily spoiled by x-rays.

d. **Art Objects.** It has been said by Burroughs that in an x-radiograph "one studies the use of white in painting." The effect of pigments containing white lead predominates in x-radiographs of the work of early Renaissance painters, who used white lead to raise the tone of pure colors and to provide highlights and greater luminosity. X-radiographs of the fourteenth, fifteenth, and sixteenth centuries are characterized by the clarity, delineation, and almost modeling of the figures, attributable in great part to the use of white lead in the colors and of non-attenuating materials for the ground. In the latter half of the sixteenth century, however, the use of white lead as a priming coat came into general use with the result that the x-radiographs of paintings after this period tend to be thin and lacking in the clear delineation of the figures. We have seen the application of secondary radiation as a means of acquiring information concerning a painting which is not amenable to x-ray methods. Similarly, neutron radiography can be used on works of art that present special problems. The blocking effect of the support or other background material can sometimes be overcome in this manner. The author has found neutron radiography especially useful in exploring the internal structure of a figurine or other small object of art. For a small metal figure such as the famous horse of the Metropolitan Museum of Art this would appear to be the obvious method of choice.

ADDITIONAL READING

Invisible Radiation

Cantu, A.A. and Prough, R.S.: Some Special Observations of Infrared Luminescence. 33 *Journal of Forensic Sciences*, 638, 1988.

Cason, J.L.: Neutron Radiography with ^{252}Cf in Forensic Science. 17 *Journal of Forensic Sciences*, 79, 1972.

Costain, J.E. and Lewis, G.W.: A Practical Guide to Infrared Luminescence Applied to Questioned Document Problems. 1 *Journal of Police Science and Administration*, 209, 1973.

Ellen, D.M. and Creer, K.E.: Infrared Luminescence in the Examination of Documents. 10 *Journal of the Forensic Science Society*, 159, 1970.

Frair, J.A., West, M.H., and Davies, J.A.: A New Film for Ultraviolet Photography. 34 *Journal of Forensic Sciences*, 234, 1989.

Graham, D.: *The Use of X-Ray Techniques in Forensic Investigations.* Edinburgh, Churchill Livingstone, 1973.

Kraus, T.C. and Warlen, S.C.: The Forensic Science Use of Reflective Ultraviolet Photography. 30 *Journal of Forensic Sciences,* 262, 1985.

Misner, A.H.: Ultraviolet Light Sources and Their Uses. 41 *Journal of Forensic Identification,* 171, 1991.

Richards, G.B.: The Application of Electronic Video Techniques to Infrared and Ultraviolet Examinations. 22 *Journal of Forensic Sciences,* 53, 1977.

Riordan, W.M.: Detection of Nonvisible Writings by Infrared Luminescence and Ultraviolet Fluorescence. 36 *Journal of Forensic Sciences,* 466, 1991.

Schwartz, S. and Woolridge, E.D.: The Use of Panoramic Radiographs for Comparison in Cases of Identification. 22 *Journal of Forensic Sciences,* 145, 1977.

Von Bremen, U.: Invisible Ultraviolet Fluorescence. 10 *Journal of Forensic Sciences,* 368, 1965.

West, M.H., Frair, J.A. and Seal, M.D.: Ultraviolet Photography: Bite Marks on Human Skin and Techniques for the Exposure and Development of Reflective Ultraviolet Photography. 32 *Journal of Forensic Sciences,* 1204, 1987.

Chapter 44

DOCUMENTARY EVIDENCE

I. INTRODUCTION

I. Importance

T HE IMPORTANCE of documentary evidence can scarcely be overemphasized. The investigator will find that documents in one form or another will account for approximately 70 percent of the physical evidence which he will encounter. Checks, claims, marriage certificates, various types of executed forms, record cards, sworn statements, and many other forms of writing may be encountered as evidence in the course of an investigation. The investigator should understand the various types of questioned documents, the proper submission of documentary evidence, and the ways in which he can assist the document expert.

2. Document Problems

The most common document problem is that of questioned authorship. The origin, contents, and circumstances of preparation may also be questioned. The following are typical document problems:

a. The identity of the writer of a document.

b. The determination, removal, or decipherment of erasures, interlineations, deletions, additions, and other alterations.

c. The age of a document.

d. The source of the paper.

e. The source and age of typewriting.

f. Comparisons of handwriting and typewriting.

3. Investigator and the Expert

The technical information contained here is given in order that an investigator may understand the potentialities of expert document examination. The investigator may aid the examiner by properly collecting, preserving, and transmitting the evidence. The opinions or views formed by an investigator concerning a questioned document should not be included in an investigative report. When document examinations are relevant and material to the case, the documents should be submitted only to a recognized expert qualified to make such examinations. The value of a document diminishes with careless treatment. Although a certain amount of handling is necessary in any document examination, the document can be carefully preserved throughout the proceedings. The following rules are useful:

a. Preserve the document initially by handling with wooden or plastic tongs.

b. Retain the document in a transparent envelope or protected by thin tissue paper unless it is under examination by an expert.

c. Determine initially if a fingerprint processing is required.

d. Do not alter the document unnecessarily by chemical treatment.

e. Preserve the document from dampness, heat, and sunlight.

f. Do not fold the document along new lines.

g. Do not make a tracing on the document.

h. Mark each document for identification by writing the case number, investigator's name or initials, and the date in some neutral area on the back of the document. If the document must first be processed for prints, the identification should be placed on the protective envelope.

i. Record relevant data such as the circumstances surrounding the acquisition of the document, the name of the person submitting it, the date, and a brief description of the paper.

4. Document Examination

There are two phases of the document examination—the investigator's and the expert's.

a. **Examination by the Investigator.** The investigator may perform a limited examination of the evidence document in cases, such as those involving anonymous letters, where the authorship is questioned. He should study the document and compare it with any available standards. His attention should be directed to the contents of the letter, similarities in writing, typing, spelling, locutions, punctuation, and the type of paper. Immediate precautionary action or investigative leads may be indicated as a result of this study. Conclusions concerning the document should remain within the province of the expert.

b. **Laboratory Examination.** At the laboratory the expert employs scientific techniques using appropriate instruments. Microscopy, chemical analysis, micrometry, colorimetry, photomicrography, ultraviolet and infrared photography are among the available techniques.

II. HANDWRITING IDENTIFICATION

5. Importance

The majority of questioned document cases are concerned with proving authorship. Samples of a suspect's writings are obtained and compared with questioned writing. The following determinations may be involved in comparisons of handwriting.

a. Whether the document was written by the suspect.

b. Whether the document was written by the person whose signature it bears.

c. Whether the writing contains additions or deletions.

d. Whether a document such as a bill, receipt, suicide note, or check is a forgery.

6. Basis of Handwriting Comparison

The principles underlying the comparison of handwriting are similar to those on which the science of fingerprint identification is based. No two products of man or nature are identical, and differences are perceptible if a sufficiently close study is made.

Through years of practice each individual acquires permanent habits of handwriting. The group of characteristics which form his script constitutes an identifiable picture. In comparing two specimens of handwriting the expert searches for characteristics which are common to both the questioned and standard writing. If the characteristics are sufficient in kind and number and there are no significant unexplainable differences, he may conclude that the writings were made by the same person.

7. Handwriting Characteristics

Although document examiners may differ in their interpretation of the significance of various characteristics of handwriting, they usually concentrate on the same elements. The following characteristics provide the basis of the examination.

a. **Quality of Line.** The lines which form the letters will vary in appearance with pen position, pressure, shading, rhythm, tremor, continuity, skill, and speed.

b. **Form.** The formation of letters is highly characteristic. Slant, proportions, beginning and ending strokes, retracing, and separation of parts will vary with different persons. Ornamentation and flourishes at the beginning and end of the words and sentences are peculiarly individual.

c. **Spacing.** Letters, words, and lines are separated in a consistent fashion.

d. **Spelling and Punctuation.** The degree and kind of education will determine these elements.

8. Conclusions

It is a common misconception of the layman that a conclusion can be reached by the expert in the majority of handwriting cases. Unfortunately this belief is far from true since, in many cases, the available questioned writing is too limited in quantity or may contain few individual elements. The problem of the examiner is a difficult one, particularly in forgery cases; he is limited not only by the nature of the evidence but also by the degree to which the investigator can assist him in providing standards of comparison.

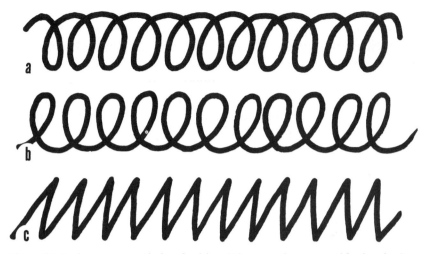

Figure 79. Basic movements in handwriting. It is convenient to consider handwriting as composed in three basic motions: (a) clockwise motion; (b) counterclockwise motion; and (c) straight line motion. These movements suggest the direction as well as the curvature of the motion. Strictly speaking, an individual's handwriting encompasses all directions and curvatures; it will be found, however, that there is a characteristic tendency toward certain shapes and slopes, which assists in identification.

9. Preliminary Examinations

It is not the purpose of this treatment to train the investigator to be a handwriting expert. A certain amount of technical knowledge, however, should be mastered so that while examining a file or record during an investigation, his suspicions may be aroused regarding the validity of certain documents. It is a great convenience for an investigator to be able to segregate the genuine documents from the suspicious ones in order that he may submit the questioned ones for technical examination and report. The following illustrations should provide him with the basic knowledge for this differentiation.

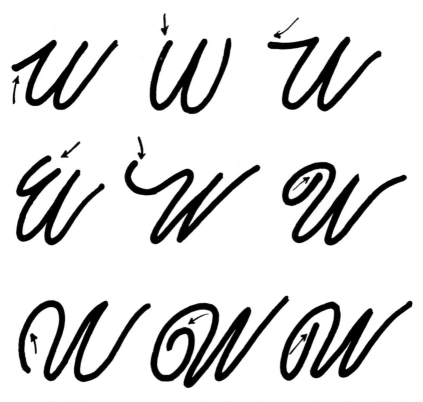

Figure 80. Initial or approach strokes. It is found that approach strokes are highly individual. The direction of the motion, the relative position of the beginning, and its height above the writing line serve to characterize an individual's handwriting. The more common variations are shown above.

III. STANDARDS OF COMPARISON

10. Definitions

One of the most important functions of the investigator in relation to a questioned document examination is the provision of suitable exemplars or standards with which the questioned writing or typing can be compared. An exemplar is a standard of writing of known authorship which can be used by the expert in a

Figure 81. Curvature. The manner in which certain letters, particularly those with loops, are curved provides an important characteristic.

comparison. The exemplar may be in the form of writing, printing, typing, a stamp or seal impression. Request standards are exemplars which have been prepared at the request of the investigator; non-request standards are usually specimens which have been prepared prior to the investigation.

11. Genuineness

In order that an exemplar be admitted in evidence, its genuineness must first be established. It must be shown that the exemplar is directly and unquestionably connected with the suspect. At the time of obtaining the exemplars the investigator must, by appropriate measures, lay the groundwork for the formal proof of authenticity which may be later required at the trial.

12. Writing Instruments

For suitability an exemplar should be prepared with the materials similar to those apparently used for the questioned document. The appearance of writing depends on the kind of pen or pencil employed; consequently, arrangements must be made to permit a suspect to use a similar writing instrument in preparing a request standard. Naturally, if it is thought that he used his own pen, he should be asked to prepare the exemplar with it.

a. **Pens.** If fountain or dip pen and ink were used, the suspect should not be permitted to use a ball-point pen. From an examina-

Figure 82. Terminal strokes. The manner in which an individual ends a word or letter is significant. Again, the direction, relative position of the terminal point, and its height above the base line are important.

tion of the questioned writing some conclusion can be drawn concerning the nib. If it appears that a fine, medium, broad, or stub point was used, a comparable nib should be provided. The ink used should be similar in color and tint to that on the questioned document.

b. **Ball-Point Pens.** Unless it is obvious that the perpetrator used such a pen, a ball-point pen should not be employed in preparing an exemplar. The ball-point pen obscures the writer's ability to exhibit his characteristic habits of quality, rhythm, shading, and skill. It fails to reveal pen position or the angle at which the instrument was held with relation to the body and the paper. Often it does not respond to normal pressure. Finally, unusual writing habits are created by the use of these pens.

c. **Pencils.** The hardness of the lead and the sharpness of the point affect the appearance of pencil writing. By testing with pencils of different numbers and varying degrees of sharpness, the investigator can choose an appropriate pencil for the production of exemplars.

d. **Crayons, Chalk, and Brushes.** Since these media vary widely in color and composition, the likely one should be selected after experiment. Naturally, the choice can be narrowed by considering the availability of specimens and also the types in the suspect's possession or area of activity. The problem of brushes will arise in oriental countries where ideographic writing is used.

Figure 83. Line quality is the term used to describe the relative smoothness of a line. The hand of a normal person accustomed to writing is shown in (a) where the lines are flowing and free from hesitation. In (b) tremor or hesitation is indicated. Certain types of forgery are detected by defective line quality.

13. Handwriting Standards

The most important phase of a typical document case is concerned with obtaining suitable handwriting standards. The subsequent examination by the expert will depend for its success upon the submission of satisfactory specimens of the suspect's writing or handprinting.

a. **Kind.** The exemplars should be suitable in word and form. Ordinarily, the suspect should be required to write the actual text of the questioned document. In some instances it may be desirable to avoid divulging the exact text of the document; it will then be necessary to use a different text which includes, however, the key words and letter combinations appearing in the questioned writing. Correspondence in form means the use of similar writing materials in preparing the exemplars. Thus, if the questioned document is an anonymous letter, paper of the same size, texture, and quality should be used together with a similar ink and pen. It is especially important that correspondingly lined paper be used where appropriate.

Figure 84. Pen pressure and shading. Some persons tend to vary the pressure of the pen in certain strokes. The degree to which variations in pressure are visible depends also on the flexibility of the nib. A similar effect can be obtained by varying other factors such as the degree of intentional shading with a broad nib, the selection of pen position, and the intensity of applied pressure.

b. **Writing Requirements.** The suspect should be required to use the same type of script as that found on the questioned document. He should write on only one side of the paper unless, of course, he is writing exemplars of a check and an endorsement on the back is desirable.

c. **Procedure.** The suspect should be first seated and provided with writing materials. The investigator should then dictate the comparison text. He should not, ordinarily, suggest the punctuation, spelling, or paragraphing. The material should be dictated several times, the speed of dictation being increased each time so that the suspect will be inclined to lapse into his normal writing habits. Each sheet should be removed as soon as it is completed. In this way the suspect will not be able to imitate the first exemplars which he has prepared and thus maintain any disguise he is attempting.

d. **Number of Exemplars.** If the questioned writing consists only of a signature or a few words, twenty specimens prepared by the suspect will suffice. Where the questioned writing consists of a few paragraphs, five exemplars will usually suffice. If the text is longer, fewer standards will be required. In addition to using the same type of writing instrument for these exemplars, in cases where a ball-point pen or a pencil was used in the questioned writing, the suspect should also be required to prepare several specimens using a fountain pen.

Figure 85. Proportion and alignment. The relative size of the various parts of the letters and the ratio of the lengths of capital and miniscule letters are significant.

e. **Identification.** The exemplar sheets should be identified by writing on the back of them the case number, date, investigator's initials, and the writing instrument used. If there are several suspects, each suspect should be designated by a letter of the alphabet and his exemplars should be numbered in order as they are prepared. Where different hands are used in different exemplars, a notation should be made to indicate whether it is the right or left.

f. **Auxiliary Request Standards.** When the text of the questioned writing is obscene or contains classified information, it should not be reproduced unless it is so limited in length that the exact wording is unavoidable. Similarly, the text should not be repeated if it is thought that the subject's awareness of the purpose of obtaining the exemplars will lead him to attempt to disguise his handwriting. In these situations auxiliary request standards, that is, specimens which do not repeat the questioned writing, should be used. A little imagination will suggest a suitable text that includes many of the words and the apparently characteristic letter combinations. As an alternative the investigator may use a paragraph in which the words include all the letters of the alphabet and most of the punctuation marks.

g. **Handprinting.** If the questioned text was handprinted, the suspect should be required to use the same style of printing. The exemplars should be written completely in capital letters when the text was thus prepared. If minuscule and capitals were used, the same arrangement should be followed. Because of the difficulties presented to the expert by handprinting, a greater number of exemplars is usually desirable.

h. **Check Exemplars.** Check standards should be prepared on a blank check similar to the one under investigation. If regular check blanks or printed forms are used, the word *void* should be marked on each in the view of the suspect. In forwarding fraudulent checks to the laboratory, the letter of transmittal should state whether any part of the evidentiary check is genuine, whether any of the signatures on the check are those of actual persons, and whether any of the suspects are presently in custody.

14. Rights of the Suspect

The Supreme Court, in *Gilbert v. California*, held that a suspect may not decline to provide a handwriting sample. Hitherto many organizations (e.g., the military investigative units), guided by the theory of handwriting being a testimonial utterance, that is, a conscious act of the mind and body, had required their agents to first obtain the assent of the suspect to the making of standards. It was considered best practice to obtain from the suspect, if possible, a statement to the effect that the specimens were prepared voluntarily.

15. Non-Request Standards

If the subject is absent or refuses to provide specimens of his handwriting, it is obviously necessary to obtain exemplars from other sources. Non-request standards are also desirable even where request specimens are given, because they are free of intentional disguise and indicate whether the request standards reflect the suspect's normal writing habits and characteristics. Good judgment will suggest in a given case the number and kind of nonrequest documents that should be submitted. Ordinarily all available specimens that can be found should be forwarded to the document examiner.

a. **Sources.** The sources of non-request standards are numerous. In addition to documents such as motor vehicle registrations and personal records which may be discovered among his possessions, a number of agencies will be found to possess files containing specimens of his writing. Most of these agencies are included in the list given in Chapter 13. In addition, school papers, letters to the suspect's family, personnel and finance records will usually provide satisfactory exemplars.

b. **Proof of Authorship.** If the non-request standards are to be admitted in evidence in court, it will be necessary to provide proof of the fact that the suspect is the author. If the suspect does not admit writing the standards, persons who witnessed their preparation may testify to the fact. Witnesses who are familiar with the suspect's writing can also offer testimony.

16. Letter of Transmittal

Suggestions for the protection of documentary evidence are given in Chapter 7. The questioned documents should be placed in a cellophane envelope which is then labeled "Questioned." The standards should be placed in a separate cellophane envelope and labeled "Known Writings" or "Standards." Both can now be placed in a third envelope and forwarded with a letter of transmittal identifying the case and the offense, describing the evidence by exhibit numbers, and specifying the type of examination desired or the nature of the information which is sought. The investigator should furnish the document examiner with any additional information which he thinks will be helpful to him. For example, he should give the reasons why the document is thought not to be genuine, or describe the circumstances under which the document was stored if the appearance of the paper shows signs of exposure or wear. The nature of such additional information will obviously depend on the case at hand.

IV. SPECIAL PROBLEMS IN HANDWRITING

17. Disguised Writing

a. **Techniques.** Writers of anonymous letters and unwilling suspects producing request writings are among those who will attempt to disguise their own handwriting. Forgers may disguise their writing in two ways: they may imitate the handwriting of another person or they may endeavor to invent an entirely new style of writing. The success achieved by a person attempting a disguise is naturally dependent on his skill and imagination. Among the physical methods used in disguising are the following:

1) *Slant.* Changing the direction of the slant is the most common disguise. The forger may employ a distinct backhand slant instead of the usual forehand slant.

2) *Speed.* By writing very rapidly or very slowly a different appearance is achieved.

3) *Irregularities.* Deliberate carelessness will disguise the writing by producing an inferior style.

4) *Size.* The letters may be written unusually large or small.

5) *Printing.* Handprinting may be substituted for script.

6) *Change of Hand.* The forger may use the left instead of the right hand.

7) *Inverted.* The writing may be made "upside down."

b. **Detecting.** Since handwriting is the result of a lifetime of practice and is actually a collection of muscular and nervous habits, it is not a simple matter to disguise all the characteristics of one's hand. The reader may be convinced of this by experimenting with the left hand or with a different slant. Although it is theoretically possible to disguise successfully, as a matter of actual practice it is found that, where the writing is abundant, a sufficient number of characteristics appear through the disguise to permit an identification. When the disguised writing is limited to a few signatures, the problem of identification becomes practically impossible. The document examiner will probably be successful in dealing with a long anonymous letter but will often fail when confronted with only one or two forged checks.

c. **Unaccustomed Hand.** The use of the unaccustomed (usually the left) hand in disguising can ordinarily be detected. Since the same mind dictates the action and since little care is given to style, design, and other qualities, the characteristics present in the normal writing can be detected. The major changes will be a difference in slant and a general deterioration of the style. If the examiner has standard specimens prepared with the left hand, his task is greatly simplified.

18. Guided Writing

A person weakened by sickness or age may require assistance in writing his signature. The result will be an unnatural appearance marked by misalignment, abnormal letter formations, abrupt changes in direction, and poor spacing of the letters. If the writing does not show these defects but appears to be fluid in style and well controlled, it can be safely concluded that the hand was not guided.

19. Illiteracy

The writing of an illiterate is marked by an absence of style and the appearance of unorthodox designs. If an attempt has been made to forge the handwriting of an illiterate person, the deception can be detected in the grammatical errors, misspellings, and peculiar phrasing. It is difficult for the forger to know the form which the illiterate's expressions will take. If other samples of

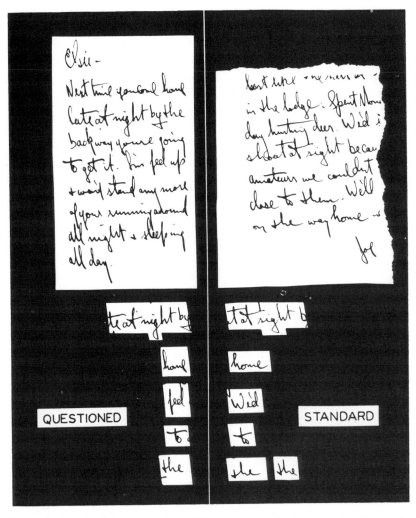

Figure 86. Handwriting comparison. This is an example of an effective choice of a non-request standard. Line quality, curvature, proportion, and other qualities are similar in each specimen, and there are no important unexplained differences. The most characteristic portions have been selected for comparison. (Courtesy of Joseph McNally and Francis Murphy.)

the illiterate's writings are available, it is possible to compare the peculiarities of the phrasing in the more common locutions of letter writing.

20. Handprinting

A very common method of disguise is the use of handprinting. In filling out a false automobile registration blank, for example, the criminal often resorts to handprinting in the belief that it is an unfailing disguise. Handprinting can, however, be successfully identified, if the questioned specimens are sufficient in quantity. The request writings must, of course, be handprinted. Since most persons do not habitually or even occasionally employ handprinting, their rare attempts at it are marked by distinct peculiarities. The design and form of the letters and the choice of small or capital letters will reveal characteristics.

21. Family Similarities

Since each person inherits part of his mental, muscular, and nervous make-up from his parents and since, further, he is exposed to environmental influences including, at times, the same form of education, it should be expected that family resemblances will appear in handwriting. The existence of such a possibility is of interest to the investigator in cases where several members of a family may be logical suspects in a case. The existence of certain similarities in the writing of members of the same family does not seriously affect the examiner's problem of detecting the individualities.

22. Foreign Handwriting

The examination of handwriting made in a European language is accomplished by means of the same principles employed for English. Certain Asiatic languages such as Chinese and Japanese which employ ideographs or picture writing present less difficult problems, since there is an absence of standardization of symbols. The writing of these Oriental languages reflects the individual mind more closely than European handwriting.

V. TYPEWRITING IDENTIFICATION

23. Applications

The typewriter also possesses characteristics which can serve to identify the source of documents. The following are the most common objectives of a comparison of typewritten materials:

a. To identify the manufacturer and model of a typewriter.

b. To identify a specific typewriter.

c. To prove that changes in a document were made with a typewriter other than the one used to type the original document.

d. To establish a limit that can be placed on the age of a document by showing that the machine was not manufactured before a certain year.

24. Obtaining Typewriter Standards

As in the case of handwriting, the success of a typewriting examination will often depend on the manner in which the standards are prepared and the number submitted to the laboratory. In obtaining standards the investigator should make an inquiry to determine whether the typewriter was repaired since the date when the questioned documents were believed to have been typed. The following problems are representative of cases involving typewritten documents.

a. **Age of Document.** To determine the maximum age of a document by establishing the make and model of the typewriter, only the questioned document itself should be submitted to the laboratory.

b. **Make and Model of an Unknown Typewriter.** This determination is usually a preliminary step in the search for the particular typewriter which was used to prepare the questioned document. The document itself should be submitted to the examiner.

c. **Identification of a Typewriter.** To determine whether a particular typewriter produced the questioned document, the latter must be compared with standards prepared with the typewriter. Samples of typing made with the machine in question should be submitted together with the evidentiary document. In cases where it is suspected that the evidentiary typing was recently made, it is sometimes possible to detect portions of the text on the ribbon of the typewriter. Hence, if the ribbon is obviously new, it should not be used to prepare the samples but should be removed and submitted for examination. Two types of standards should be prepared as follows:

1) *Regular Specimen.* The text of the questioned document should be copied exactly. A paper similar in quality and color should be used. Ten such copies should be made, if the text consists of approximately fifteen lines. If the text is lengthy only the first ten or fifteen lines need be copied. Each copy should be made on a separate sheet of paper. The ribbon used in preparing the standards should be selected to produce inked impressions of approximately the same intensity and depth as those of the questioned document. Finally, the entire keyboard, including the shift and non-shift positions, should be typed to provide a copy of each letter and character for the examiner.

2) *Carbon Specimen.* To enable the document examiner to detect dirty, defective, or scarred type, a carbon specimen of a page of the text should be typed on the machine in question. The ribbon should first be removed or the ribbon guide set in stencil position. A piece of white paper and a fresh piece of carbon paper are inserted in the machine with the carbon facing the white paper in such a manner that the keys will strike directly upon the carbon paper, leaving a carbon impression on the white paper.

25. Identifying Typewriter Standards

To identify standards prepared with a typewriter the following information should be typed on the face of each sheet:
   a. Name of the person typing the standard.
   b. Manufacturer and model of the typewriter.
   c. Serial number of the machine.
   d. Date of preparation.
   e. Case number.
   f. Exhibit number, consisting of a letter of the alphabet to identify each typewriter and a number to identify each exemplar prepared with the typewriter.

g. Additional information for the examiner, such as the date on which the typewriter was last repaired.

26. Procedure in Comparing Typewriting

Typewriting identification is based on the same principles that form the basis of the identification of handwriting. A sufficient number of characteristics may be found present in a specimen of typewriting to enable the expert to state that the typing could have been done on only one machine. The methods for identifying typewriting are similar to those of handwriting. A specimen is obtained from a known typewriter and compared with the typing specimen of unknown origin with respect to certain class and accidental characteristics. Class characteristics such as the design and size of the letters will enable the examiner to determine the make and model of the typewriter, while accidental characteristics such as alignment, slant, and other acquired defects will help in identifying the individual machine within the class. Thus, known specimens are collected as previously described and compared with the questioned typewriting with respect to the following major qualities:

a. **Design and Size.** The design and size of the letters and figures vary with different makes and different models of typewriters. Naturally, if the typewriting was made on a relatively rare model of a machine, the examiner's task is simplified. The following points of comparison will aid the examiner in determining whether the known and unknown specimens were made on the same model of typewriter.

1) Overall size of letters.

2) Lengths of serifs (small bars at the top and bottom of strokes).

3) Length and curvature of endings, in *f, g, m, t,* and *y.*

a) *f*—length of horizontal lines; curvature at top.

b) *g*—proportion of area of upper oval to that of lower; space between ovals; relative positions; shape and position of joining line; and ending at upper right.

c) *m*—relation of height to width; length of serifs and upper left and lower right.

d) *t*—curvature at lower extremity; length and location of crossbar; ratio of lengths of divided vertical line.

e) *y*—angle found in center; relative lengths of parts; length of serif; curvature.

4) Size and design of figures.

a) *8*—relative areas and shapes of ovals.

b) *5*—the design of this figure is particularly characteristic.

c) *4*—proportions of component lines.

d) *2* and *3*—characteristic shape.

e) *6, 7,* and *9*—length.

b. **Alignment.** If a typewriter is in perfect alignment, a letter will fall in the middle of an imaginary space. All letters and figures occupy the same area. The machine is designed so that a set number of characters occupy a given length. Approximately 90 percent of the older typewriters have pica type, in which ten characters occupy an inch length of the paper. Many machines have elite type, in which there are twelve characters to an inch. It should be noted also in a page of typing that the characters are aligned vertically as well as horizontally. The lines in a single space sheet of typewriting are spaced six to the inch. Thus, each character should fall in a fixed position in an area of $1/10 \times 1/6''$. With extended use or maladjustment, the character may acquire a tendency to fall in a different position. The misalignment of a letter can be detected by means of a glass plate ruled in one direction at intervals of $1/10''$ and in the perpendicular direction at intervals of $1/6''$. By placing the plate in an appropriate position, the alignment of many letters can be checked at a glance. For example, the alignment of the bottoms of all small letters should be the same except for *g, j, p, q,* and *y;* for the tops of small letters also, except for *b, d, f, h, k, l,* and *t.* A misaligned letter can be determined in this manner, and the extent of its misalignment with respect to an imaginary line can be measured.

c. **Slant.** An aberration in the slope of a letter can be considered as another form of misalignment. Loosely speaking, the letter should be perpendicular to the base line. However, even new machines will be defective in regard to the slant of some of the letters. Older machines develop these defects. The typebar becomes twisted so that the character no longer prints perpendicu-

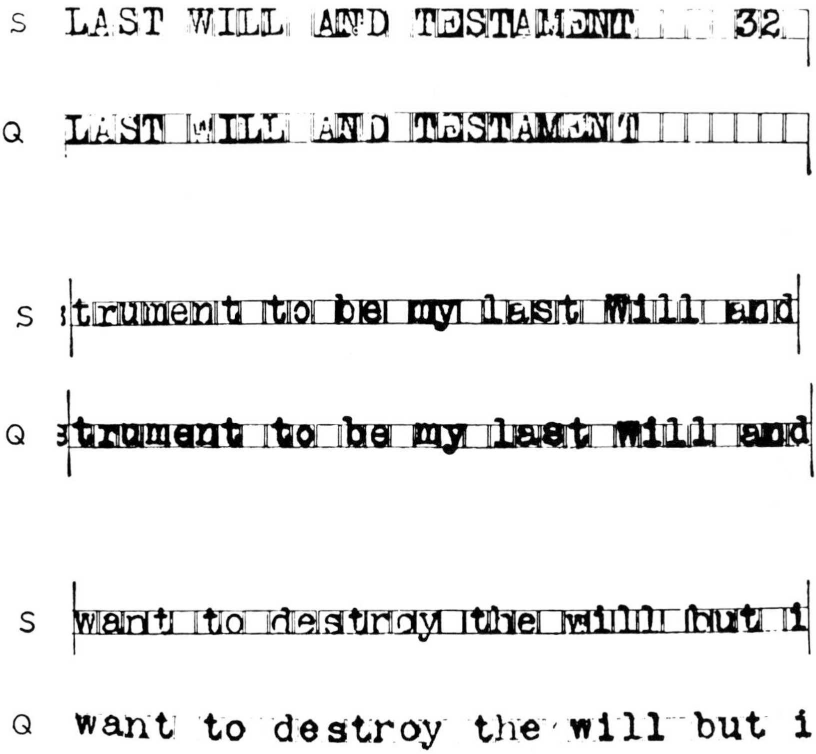

S LAST WILL AND TESTAMENT   32.

Q LAST WILL AND TESTAMENT

S trument to be my last Will and

Q trument to be my last will and

S want to destroy the mill but i

Q want to destroy the will but i

Figure 87. Typewriting comparison. Typewriting comparison between standard (S) and questioned (Q) specimens in a case of a contested will. The specimens represent the work of several typewriters. It may be seen from the characteristic defects present in each pair of specimens that the same typewriter was used in each case. The ruling of the spaces emphasizes the misalignment of the type.

lar to the line of writing. The defect is more readily detected in the tall letters such as *l, h, f, d, b, k, t,* and the capitals.

d. **"Off Its Feet."** In a new machine, the typeface should be adjusted to strike with equal pressure over the entire surface. Divergences frequently occur through maladjustment, use, or wear. The typeface no longer strikes the roller with equal pressure on all parts and variations in the density of the ink impression can be observed. The typeface is then said to be "off its feet." The fault is more readily observed in the broader small letters such as *g, m, o, s,* and *w* and in the capitals.

e. **Other Defects.** A typewriter is made of hundreds of small parts which may become loose, bent, or broken. The resulting small defects provide combinations of characteristics that definitely identify a machine as the source of a typewriting sample. Broken typefaces in which a letter prints with a part missing and worn typewriters which cause characters to print with varying density on successive strokes are among the most common defects.

f. **Electric Typewriters.** The document examiner is faced with additional problems in examining typescript made on a single-element typewriter. In regard to the class characteristics he must, in addition to the make and model of the machine, identify the type element used. Although IBM has dominated the electric typewriter market for years, there are more than a dozen single-element machines available. Different type-style single elements are interchangeable on different machines.

In identifying the individual type element the examiner must rely on acquired characteristics and imperfections in manufacture such as damage to type characters, broken detent (a stopping and releasing mechanism) teeth, and electroplating peeling from the surface of the character. This last characteristic is acquired during manufacture in the course of the molding and electroplating process. Small plastic particles may be accidentally electroplated on the type-character faces in the form of raised beads, randomly placed or distributed. Depending on its size and shape, the bead will indent or even puncture the paper on impact, in some cases leaving an embossed impression on the back of the type sheet. Since the beads are randomly produced, the spacing, size, and shape of the punctures may provide a recognizable and even individual pattern for the examiner's eye. The defects are even more apparent both on the paper and the ribbon if a one-time carbon ribbon was used in producing the questioned typescript.

27. Determining the Age of a Typed Document

It is possible to set a limit to the maximum age of a typewritten document by determining the model of the typewriter. For example, if the typing was done with a model that was first made in 1967, obviously the document must have been made since that date.

The FBI and other large law enforcement agencies maintain a reference file of typewriter specimens. If a specimen of typing is submitted to these agencies, the expert can determine the make and model of the typewriter and also can provide information concerning the year of manufacture of a particular model of a typewriter.

28. Determining the Typist

The ideal solution to a problem involving the determination of the source of a typewritten document is to specify not only the particular typewriter, but also the typist who performed the work. This latter determination is of great importance in cases of anonymous letters. Sometimes, the typewritten document contains a sufficient number of clues to permit such identification. The following points are noted by the examiner:

a. **Language Habits.** If the typist composed as well as typed the letter, certain errors of the other characteristics of language will be present. Errors of punctuation, spelling, diction, and grammar may be present in the text. If sample writings of the suspect are available, similar errors may be detected.

b. **Mechanical Habits.** The general appearance of the typing is characteristic. The pressure used in certain letters, margins, length of lines, spacing, indention of paragraphs, and many other points may reveal habits of the typist that can readily be checked by means of comparison of samples of typewriting.

c. **Electric Typewriting.** With an electric typewriter, identification of the typist rests on far fewer factors than with a manual one. The pressure on the keys is uniform because the driving force behind the typeface is a motorized mechanism rather than the manual pressure of the typist. On some machines, the tension on the keys can be adjusted to various settings. This uniformity of pressure on every key all but eliminates what is called the "touch" of a particular typist. Margins are automatically adjusted and spelling is corrected, further reducing the number of individuating characteristics.

Identification depends heavily on the arrangement of material on the paper, the characteristic grammatical constructions and the use of unusual characters or symbols. With this in mind, the need for extensive quantities of collected typing, preferably from the suspected typist's routine office work, becomes apparent. Collected standards are preferable to prepared standards as a precaution against an attempt by the typist to disguise normal typing habits.

29. Alterations to a Typewritten Document

Questions sometimes arise concerning suspected additions to a typewritten document. If an erasure and a misaligned addition are present, the problem is not difficult. If the addition has been made with great skill, a close examination by means of measuring devices and a low-power microscope is necessary. The following procedure will be found practicable:

a. **Machine.** The examiner may determine whether the addition was made by the same machine or at least by the same make and model of typewriter. The success of this examination will depend on the amount of typing in the added text.

b. **Ink Density.** If the suspected text was truly part of the original text, no difference in the density of the ink impression should be observed since a similar part of the ribbon was used. The examiner will examine the addition under a microscope and compare the inking with that of the accepted part of the text.

c. **Alignment.** It is exceedingly difficult to replace a sheet of paper in a typewriter and perfectly align added letters with those previously made. The examiner tests the suspected additions for alignment by means of a glass plate. It can readily be determined whether a given letter is falling in its proper place in the $1/10 \times 1/6''$ rectangle.

VI. EXAMINATION OF PAPER

30. Application

The origin of paper may arise as a question in the course of an investigation. Cases of anonymous letters, for example, are sometimes solved by discovering the source of the paper. One of the clues to the operations of a forger is the source of his blank checks. Papers can often be identified and distinguished by means of their composition, processing, and marking. In addition, the handling of papers subsequent to manufacture may result in identifying marks. The following are the typical objectives of a comparison with paper standards:

a. To determine whether the standard is similar to the paper bearing the questioned writing.

b. To determine whether a sheet of paper was taken from a particular pad or tablet. For example, it can be shown by matching the partially perforated edges that a questioned check was taken from a particular checkbook. Again, by matching perforated edges, it is sometimes possible to show that the stamp on a questioned envelope was removed from another stamp or a sheet of stamps found in the possession of a suspect.

c. To show that one document was in contact with another. This may be established by the shape of a blot, for example, which had seeped through the questioned document and stained some of the underlying sheets of a tablet. In a recent narcotics case it was possible to show that the glassine envelope containing the morphine found in the addict's possession had been removed from a stack of envelopes on the counter of a suspected pharmacy. The glue with which the lower end of the envelope was sealed in the process of manufacture had, in drying, caused the envelope to adhere to the next lower one in the stack. On separating, the fibers of the lower envelope had been disturbed in a recognizable outline.

31. Standards of Comparison

Standards will be required whenever the source of paper becomes a point of interest in the investigation. It is found that forgers and writers of anonymous letters often exercise great care in selecting a suitable paper, even making a special purchase to suit their needs. The investigator may discover paper standards in the suspect's quarters or place of business, or he may be required to search for the place of purchase. In the latter event the advice of a stationer or a paper manufacturer should be sought on the problem.

At least five sheets should be submitted as standards. Each sheet should be identified by writing appropriate case information on the back. In addition, there should be included any appropriate information concerning the circumstances surrounding the discovery or location of the sheets.

32. Examination by the Laboratory

The chemical and physical processes to which paper is subjected in its manufacture often provide identifying characteristics which permit the expert to distinguish one sample from another. By comparing the characteristics of two samples, the analyst can readily determine dissimilarities and eliminate the possibility of identity of source. In some cases, it is possible for him to definitely conclude that two specimens came from the same source. Some of the methods listed cause a physical change in the document and ordinarily are not used by the document examiner without obtaining specific authorization from the contributor.

a. **Physical Tests.** The following physical characteristics and measurements serve to differentiate paper: thickness, measurement of length and width; weight per unit area; color; finish, such as bond, laid, smooth, or glossy; opacity, i.e., capacity of the paper for the transmission of light; folding endurance as determined instrumentally by the number of alternate folds the paper will stand before breaking; bursting strength as determined by the measurement of the pressure necessary to burst a hole in a sheet of the paper; accelerated aging tests performed by means of high temperatures or strong artificial light.

b. **Chemical Tests.** Chemical tests may be conducted to determine the fiber composition, loading material, and the sizing used in the manufacture of the paper. Like the physical tests previously described, chemical tests are of little value unless a side-by-side comparison can be conducted between the paper in question and the known standards submitted for comparison. The use of the chemical tests causes a small change or alteration in the document; hence, extensive testing may consume a part of the evidence, and the investigator should indicate to the expert the degree to which the testing may be carried. The following tests are commonly employed:

1) *Sizing Tests.* By the use of a few drops of chemical reagent, the sizing of two different specimens of paper can be compared. A small perceptible stain results from these tests.

2) *Loading Materials.* This test is performed by burning and ashing the greater part of an ordinary sheet of paper, then analyzing the ash. Obviously, where only a limited sample of evidence is available, this test is not recommended.

3) *Fiber Composition.* Chemical reagents are applied to small sections of the paper in order to determine the nature of the constituent fibers.

4) *Absorption.* Strips of the paper are suspended in liquids to determine either the rate of absorption or the total absorption of the paper.

c. **Watermark.** The chief characteristic indicating the source or origin of paper is the watermark. It is a distinctive mark or design placed in the paper at the time of its manufacture by passing the paper under a *dandy* roll. Several designs are present on the dandy roll, similar to each other, but bearing individual characteristics, particularly if the roll has been subjected to wear or damage. By examining the watermark, the examiner is able to identify the paper as the product of a particular manufacturer.

VII. REFERENCE FILES

33. Use

An investigation involving the source of a questioned document is often quite general in nature, with no logical suspects from whom standards may be obtained for comparison. In this situation a reference file can assist in narrowing the area of investigation and drawing up a list of possible suspects. Thus, a file containing fraudulent checks may serve to identify a questioned check with the work of a known forger. A file containing samples of type from all known machines will aid in identifying the manufacturer of the machine that was used to prepare an anonymous extortion letter.

34. Files of Law Enforcement Agencies

Described below are some of the reference files maintained by law enforcement agencies. The number and extent of the files will usually vary with the size of the agency. Organizations such as the Post Office, the Treasury Department, the Bureau of Alcohol, Tobacco and Firearms, the FBI, and the New York Police Department maintain a number of these files to suit their special needs.

a. **Typewriting Standards.** This file contains impressions of all the type faces of machines of various manufacturers. Their most common application is in determining the make and model of the machine that was used to produce a questioned document submitted for examination.

b. **Watermarks.** Individual paper manufacturers use characteristic watermarks to identify the source, period, and sometimes the quality of their product. A watermark appearing on a questioned document may be compared with those in the reference file to determine its origin and approximate date of manufacture.

c. **Paper.** The paper reference file contains samples of the manufacturer's product with data relating to weight, color, composition, and quality. It is particularly useful in determining the manufacturer of papers which do not bear watermarks. A reference file for the paper used in checks is maintained by the FBI and is called the Safety Paper Standards File.

d. **Inks.** The process of thin-layer chromatography can be used to analyze the properties of inks, by separating the dye components of each ink and recording the distinctive separation patterns. The Bureau of Alcohol, Tobacco and Firearms (ATF) maintains a reference file of all commercially available pen inks catalogued according to dye patterns which can be helpful in determining the age and manufacturing source of an ink. During the 1970's, the ATF reached an agreement with major ink manufacturers to place rare-earth elements in their inks, changing them periodically. These "taggants" are used to identify the manufacturer and the age of an ink.

e. **Checkwriters.** A file of checkwriter and protectograph standards of the machines of various manufacturers is maintained to determine the make and model of the machine used on a questioned check.

f. **National Fraudulent Check File.** This file consists of photostatic and photographic copies of fraudulent checks in excess of a specified amount. Law enforcement agencies throughout the country forward such copies to the FBI, which maintains the file and provides document examination services in connection with the file. Police agencies may forward copies of fraudulent checks for a search and comparison with the files. By means of this centralized collection it is possible to identify the work of professional forgers who travel through the country passing fraudulent checks. With the information obtained from this file a police department can communicate with other communities where a particular forger has operated to obtain a physical description of the suspect and information concerning his *modus operandi.*

g. **Rubber Stamps.** This file is used to trace documents bearing stamped impressions.

h. **Anonymous Letters.** Files of anonymous letters are maintained by the FBI and municipal police departments. In this way, threatening, obscene, and annoying letters can be classified and, in some instances, the work of a habitual anonymous letter writer can be identified.

i. **Bank Robbery Notes.** The FBI retains photocopies of holdup notes used in actual or attempted bank robberies and the writings of known and suspected bank robbers.

j. **Other.** Other files maintained by the FBI that might be helpful to the investigator are:

1) Office Copier Standards File.

2) The National Motor Vehicle Certificate of Title File. This includes original state motor vehicle certificates as well as manufacturer's statements of origin and vehicle emission stickers. It also includes photographic copies of fraudulent versions of these documents.

3) The National Vehicle Identification Number Standard File and Altered Numbers File.

4) Pornographic Materials File.

35. Private Firms

Law enforcement agencies can often obtain the assistance of manufacturers of writing materials in tracing the source of paper, ink, pens, and pencils and in making comparisons with materials used in questioned documents. Many manufacturers maintain extensive reference files of their own products and employ technical experts with a broad knowledge of the industry.

VIII. AGE OF DOCUMENTS

36. Introduction

A question of the age of a document may arise in connection with papers such as wills or contracts. Documents which impose an obligation, give a title, or grant a benefit may depend for their effectiveness or validity on their date; hence, they are susceptible to the work of the forger. A document can be treated by a skilled forger so that it appears to be fifty years older than it actually is. An experienced document examiner can often detect the falsity of such a document.

37. Methods of Aging

To give the document an appearance of age, it is subjected to chemical and physical treatment. Among the techniques employed are the following:

a. **Heating.** The document may be treated in an oven or over a hot stove to give it the brittleness and discoloration of age. Baking and scorching are variations of this method.

b. **Sunlight.** Exposure to sunlight produces the yellow color of age. Carbon arc and ultraviolet lamps can be used for the same purpose.

c. **Abuse.** The paper may be crumpled, smeared, or discolored to give it the appearance of neglect that is associated with age.

d. **Chemical Treatment.** The document can be subjected to one or more of the many chemical processes that will simulate the appearance of age.

38. Determinations

It is not a simple matter to determine the age of a document. Obviously, the fixing of an exact date is an impossibility in the absence of eyewitnesses to the making of the document. Among the problems which the examiner can sometimes answer successfully are the following:

a. **Purported Age.** Is the document as old as the date or other signs would indicate?

b. **Probable Date.** What is the approximate date on which the document was made? This can be answered by setting a maximum or a minimum age to the document. For example, if the model of the typewriter used to produce the document was not made before 1921, a minimum age can be set. Similarly, if the watermark of the papers was not used by the manufacturer after 1940, a probable maximum can be fixed. The use of a ball-point pen would likewise limit the age.

c. **Several Documents.** A question may arise concerning the priority of production of several documents. Was one document produced before or after another document?

39. Age Indicators

To determine the appropriate age of a document, a study must be made of the physical and chemical properties of the paper and the writing and of the text and its meaning. Among the indicators that can assist the examiner are the following:

a. **Ink.** The age of inks is discussed in Section 69.

b. **Typewriting.** Makes and models of typewriters are associated with definite manufacturing dates. The typewritten paper *must* have been produced after the particular model of typewriter was first put on the market by the manufacturer. Another indication of date is a physical defect in the type faces, the existence of which can be associated with a date by another independently made document which bears a date. If another document bearing a date exhibits the defect in the type, then the defect is *at least* as old as the document. The date of the questioned document can now be related to the fixed date by a determination of the existence of the defect. A plurality of defects will obviously serve to narrow the date limits.

c. **Dated Mechanical Styles.** The use of certain styles of mechanical impressions is associated with the date of their first appearance. The following mechanical impressions can be used to set a date limit by their period of manufacture or by the first appearance of defects: printing; lithograph, multigraph, multilith, and mimeograph work; seals and watermarks.

d. **Stamps.** Rubber stamps can be referred to a date by their manufacture or by the appearance of defects on other dated paper. Cancellation stamps on envelopes; bank stamps; certification stamps; and date stamps are useful for this purpose.

e. **Textual Contents.** The document may contain information that suggests a date limit. The letterhead, names of officers on the letterhead, address, titles, and similar matters relate to the history of an organization and thus set a date.

f. **Writing Media.** The chemical or physical properties of the media used to produce the document can be referred to manufacturing periods. Thus, copying pencils, colored pencils, blotters, typewriter ribbons, and pens produce impressions or traces that can be associated with dates. (Ink and typewriting have, because of their importance, been placed in separate categories.)

g. **Physical Characteristics.** If the document consists of several pages, additional evidence of age may be present. Binding method; eyelets; fasteners; staples; and punch holes are among the physical characteristics that may set a date. Thus, if they were dropped from use after a certain date or have been in continuous use after a certain date, an age limit can be specified.

h. **Style.** The very term *style* suggests a date. There are fashions in the arrangement of the various elements of a letter. The disappearance of old styles and the innovations of the new place a date on a letter or other document. Among the elements and details to be noted are the following: the address, heading, form of salutation and complimentary close, abbreviations, and indentation of paragraphs.

i. **Paper.** The composition, size, and condition of the paper are important factors in age determination. The manufacturer of the paper can often be determined from the watermark. The manufacturer's technical employees can then be interviewed in regard to the date of production of certain types of paper. In this way, a maximum age can be set to the document.

40. Procedures

The methods of age determination have been suggested in the preceding section and in the section treating of inks. The details of the procedure and additional points of examination are suggested below:

a. **Storage Conditions.** How was the document kept? Was it stored in the basement or attic? What was the climate?

b. **Paper.** The paper is examined and tested for brittleness, undue soiling, and mutilation. Is the discoloration even or uneven? Is the paper yellow with age, especially near the top and the edges?

c. **Parts.** If the document is soiled, the examination should determine whether the inside or folded portion is more soiled on the inside than on the outside. Such a condition suggests a simulated aging.

d. **Books.** Where the document is in book form, the bindings and torn portions should be studied. Evidence of the removal of pages is significant.

e. **Clips and Marks.** The conditions of areas where clips, pins, fasteners, staplings, and punch markings have been used should be studied to determine if these articles or markings were recently added. For example, if a paper clip has been attached to a document for a long period of time, evidence of discoloration about the edge of the clips should be apparent. The area under certain types of clips will exhibit less discoloration than other areas.

IX. PHOTOGRAPHY OF DOCUMENTS

41. General

The document examiner is necessarily a photographer. Although the volume of his cases may prevent his personally doing the photographic work, he understands its need at each stage of an examination and gives specific directions concerning its accomplishment. He must employ photographs as a record, as a means of examination, as a method of discovery, and as a form of demonstration in court. Many phases of photography are employed. Copy and photostat work, filter photography, photomicrography, photomacrography, ultraviolet, infrared, and even x-ray techniques constitute his basic photographic knowledge.

42. Reproduction for Record

On receiving a case the investigator or document examiner photographs the front and back of the questioned documents to preserve their original appearance as part of the case. A one-to-one copy is made using a reproduction camera such as the "Identiscope." A fixed-focus camera is considered a great convenience for this work. A ruled scale is sometimes placed in the picture to show the exact size and to facilitate later enlarging procedures.

43. Photostats

The use of photostats is quite limited in document work. The photostat is at best an inferior reproduction. It cannot serve as an adequate substitute for the original in any but the crudest type of examination.

44. Substitutes for Handling in Examination

Document examiners handle the questioned documents as little as possible. Every effort is made to avoid the unnecessary touching of the evidence materials. The questioned documents are placed in transparent envelopes and subsequently referred to in this state. Since a document examination requires a great deal of handling of specimens, the expert often uses the photographs as substitutes for the originals.

45. Photomicrography and Photomacrography

To demonstrate certain minute details that are important in the evidence the examiner must make enlarged pictures of the significant areas. To demonstrate, for example, the sequence of strokes, the crossing must be greatly enlarged to show the paper fibers. To make an ordinary enlargement is an unsatisfactory procedure, since there is no great resolution in the original negative. Photomacrography, the process whereby an enlarged image is achieved on the negative, is the most commonly used technique. The use of a 32mm lens usually supplies all the magnification that is required. Sometimes, particularly where a magnification of over 10× is needed, photomicrography must be employed. In this technique the photograph is made with a microscope objective and eyepiece.

46. Transparencies

To demonstrate in forgery cases the exact superimposition of writings such as the genuine and the traced signatures, a set of transparencies is made. A film is used instead of a sheet of photographic paper.

47. Filter Photography

In obliterated writing it is often necessary to discern writing that lies beneath other writing. If the two writings were made with different colored inks, a photograph is made using a filter of the same color as the upper ink. Thus, the upper layer of writing is rendered transparent and the lower becomes visible. This is but one of the many uses of filters in document photography. The filter is often employed to provide contrast in preparing exhibits. For example, if the questioned writing is found on a green registration form, a green filter will be used to give the form an appearance of whiteness.

48. Ultraviolet

The use of radiation slightly shorter in wavelength than that of visible light is quite common in document photography. Inks and papers which appear similar in the visible light often are strikingly different under ultraviolet light. Under the ultraviolet radiations some substances transform the energy into fluorescent light. Thus, a document will take on a different appearance under the ultraviolet lamp. The following are some of the uses of this form of radiation.

   a. **Inks.** To emphasize differences in inks.

   b. **Invisible Writing.** A fluid such as lemon juice or milk can be used to produce writing invisible to the naked eye. Under the ultraviolet light the fluid fluoresces in a highly legible fashion.

   c. **Erasures.** Chemical erasures are sometimes made visible.

   d. **Identification of Papers.** The fluorescent quality of paper is highly characteristic.

   e. **Tampering.** Alterations in seals, checks, and other documents can be readily seen.

   f. **Counterfeits.** Invisible markings are used to identify pari-mutuel tickets and lottery receipts. A counterfeit can be detected by means of its fluorescent qualities.

   g. **Resealing Envelopes.** Differences in mucilage can be seen in the ultraviolet.

49. Infrared Photography

Some of the dyes used in inks are transparent to infrared radiations, others are opaque and, consequently, are recorded on infrared film. This phenomenon is useful in dealing with obliterations. A filter such as a Wratten 87 is used with infrared film and the photograph is made with incandescent light. As in other forms of filter photography, the lower layer of writing may be seen. The infrared properties of ink, pencil, and paper are used in a number of ways:

   a. **Erasures.** Residual ink or pencil in an erasure will appear in contrast to its surroundings, thus giving a more legible appearance.

b. **Burned Documents.** Charred or burned documents can sometimes be made legible.

c. **Faded Writing.** Illegible writings such as old, discolored, or soiled documents should be photographed in the infrared. Obliterated matter on embossed seals, faded stamp cancellations, or postmarks can often be restored.

d. **Sealed Envelopes.** It is sometimes possible to make a legible photograph of a document in a sealed envelope by using infrared film. If the paper is transparent to the infrared radiation and the ink opaque, ideal conditions exist. Electron radiography can also be used.

50. Soft X-rays

The texture of paper takes on a new appearance in a radiograph made with soft x-rays. Chapter 43 deals with this technique in detail. Obliterated watermarks and, in some cases, erasures can be made legible in this way.

51. Court Exhibits

In order to demonstrate his findings to the court, the document examiner must use enlarged, mounted photographs. In handwriting comparisons he must juxtapose the standard and questioned writing so that the similarities are apparent at a glance. In cases of obliterated writing or erasures he must show the document as it appeared normally as well as its appearance with the concealed elements made legible. Normal size photographs as well as enlargements should be submitted.

X. VARIOUS DOCUMENT PROBLEMS

52. General

In addition to the major problems of documentary evidence such as handwriting and typewriting comparisons and forgery determinations, there are numerous other questions that may arise in relation to documents. The present section endeavors to present the more common of these problems and to indicate in some places the methods applied by the document examiner in their solution. The purpose of this section is to acquaint the investigator with the potentialities of certain types of evidence, which might otherwise be neglected.

53. Sequence of Line Strokes and Paper Folds

In tampering with a document the criminal will often perform some operation which affects the writing or the paper and which can be determined as having been performed after the original document with its writing had been completed.

a. **Sequence of Line Strokes.** An interlineation (writing between the original lines), qualifying statement, or signature may be placed on the document after other writings have been made thereon. It is of great importance in some instances to show the order in which signatures were written on a document. If the spuriously added writing crosses the original writing, the document examiner by examination under the microscope can sometimes determine which writing was made first. If ink was used in both cases the determination is not too difficult. With ink writing and typewriting the determination of sequence is more difficult. The sequence of two rubber stamp impressions or of writing and a rubber stamp impression can also occasionally be determined.

b. **Punch Marks.** Was the writing prepared before or after the area had been perforated with a "paid" or "cancelled" punch? The edges of the punch holes should be examined for the presence of ink stains. If the punch was made after the writing, the edge will not reveal an ink stain, whereas if the writing was made later, the ink will run into the broken surface. Another indication may be present in the form of a tearing or bruising of the paper as the pen catches in the new edge formed by the punch. If it is obvious that the writer studiously avoided the holes, it can be assumed that the writing was made later.

c. **Sequence of Paper Folds.** When a paper is folded the fibers will be affected in the broken area, the extent of the breaking or changing depending on the number of times it is folded and the force employed in the action. If ink writing is added after the folding, the ink will flow or "bleed out" into the crease. Where a pencil has been used, carbon particles will adhere to the disturbed fibers. These effects are not visible when the writing existed prior to the folding. The quality of the paper as well as the extent of the folding treatment will determine the degree to which these phenomena are observable.

54. Alterations of Documents

The significance of a document can be materially altered by changing a number or a word. If the alteration is made by the author of the document, it is simply a correction and, as such, may serve as additional proof of authenticity. The problem of alterations, substitutions, interlineations, and additions is concerned with carefully executed work that would escape ordinary perusal. The alteration of a check, draft, money order, or other negotiable instrument can result in the loss of thousands of dollars. The mere addition of a zero to a number on a check can increase its value tenfold. This process is called "raising" the check. An alteration is detected by the difference in handwriting, typing, or ink or by the presence of an erasure. The document is examined under ultraviolet light for differences in the characteristics of the ink. Photographs are made with filters and process film. Differences may be discovered in the infrared region by photographing the document under incandescent lamps using a Wratten 87 filter and infrared film.

55. Indented Writings

One of the most common document problems is the so-called "indented writing." If the original writing is made on a pad of paper, indentions are produced on the bottom sheets. Thus, although the top sheet is removed, it may still be possible to decipher the writing from the sheet that lay immediately under it. If pencil was used in the original writing, the task is made simpler since a greater degree of pressure has been employed. A number of methods are recommended for the purpose of making such writing legible.

a. **Photography.** The pad is illuminated from the side so that the indentations are placed in relief. A photograph is made using commercial film. A series of photographs should be made, if necessary, varying the angle of illumination. This is the preferred method.

b. **Iodine Fuming.** The pressure applied in the writing process affects the paper fibers and makes them different from the untouched fibers. If the paper is fumed with iodine vapors, this difference is emphasized. A photograph is taken since the fumes further sublime. The fuming process should take place in a glass container with the document suspended over a crucible of iodine crystals. The process is accelerated by heat.

c. **Indented Writing Solution.** Another method of emphasizing the alterations in the fiber structure is to dab the document with a piece of cotton dipped in the following solution:

Water	8 cc
Potassium iodide	4 gm
Iodine	1 gm
Glycerin	20 cc

The document can be restored to its original condition by dabbing with a 1 per cent solution of hypo ($Na_2S_2O_3$).

d. **Electrostatic Imaging.** The document is covered with a polymer film which is charged electrically and sprayed with a toner powder. An image of the indented writing will become visible. It can then either be photographed or fixed with an adhesive transparent plastic sheet. This method has achieved excellent results and is available commercially.

56. Sealed Envelopes

Has the envelope been opened and resealed? This question may arise in connection with money or confidential documents transmitted in sealed envelopes. To detect such tampering the investigator should be familiar with the common techniques employed in the surreptitious opening of envelopes and with the effects of such tampering on the envelope.

Figure 88. Indented writing. By oblique illumination the indentations on a lower sheet of a bookmaker's pad are made legible. (Courtesy of William Stackpole.)

a. **Transmitted Light.** The envelope is held before a strong light. Alterations in the paper can be observed where the flap has been opened and resealed. To make a photographic record of the evidence, the envelope is used as a negative and printed onto photographic paper of good contrast. The variation in opacity is thus vividly reproduced.

b. **Postmarks.** If postmarks appear on the flap of the envelope, the resealing process will result in a slight misalignment.

c. **Mucilage.** In resealing, mucilage is usually added. The excess of and difference in the mucilage can be observed under a low-power microscope. A clever operator will reseal the envelope by using another envelope of the same type to provide mucilage by wetting its flap and placing it in contact for a few seconds with the flap of the old envelope.

d. **Raising the Stamp.** Another technique of surreptitiously opening mail consists of loosening and rolling back the stamp and then cutting out the area beneath the stamp. The contents can thus be removed and the stamp replaced in its original position.

e. **Rolling.** A thin rod can be inserted between the flap and the body of the envelope in the loose area near the top. The paper within can then be removed by rotating the rod until it catches the sheet and rolls it up tightly so that it can be withdrawn with the rod.

XI. ILLEGIBLE WRITINGS

57. General

Writings may become illegible through use, mishandling, or exposure to the elements. Sometimes an incriminating writing is rendered illegible by intentional obliteration or erasure. Illegible evidentiary writings submitted to a document examiner can often be rendered legible or be deciphered.

58. Alterations of Evidence

Some of the methods employed in rendering a writing legible may alter the appearance of the writing; therefore, the document examiner does not employ such techniques without the permission of the contributing agency. This permission should not be given without thought, since at trial, a valid objection may be made to the admission of evidence on the grounds that it is not in its original condition, or that it has been tampered with. Photographic copies should be made by the document examiner before the examiner in order to show the original appearance of the document at the time he received it.

59. Existence of Erasures

One of the simplest types of inquiries is that of determining whether or not an erasure was made. Visual observation of the surface of the paper will usually reveal an alteration of this type. Pencil writing on good grades of paper can escape casual observation, but ink erasures are difficult to conceal. Physical inspection under ultraviolet light and iodine fuming are additional techniques.

60. Obliterated Writing

Writing may be obliterated by mechanical action; by covering with an overlaying substance; by eradication with a chemical ink remover; or by a combination of these methods. Physical and chemical methods are used in restoring such writings to a state of legibility.

61. Used Carbon Paper

One of the traces that is sometimes overlooked by a criminal is the carbon paper which was used to make a duplicate copy of some message or record used in illegal activity. Frequently, it is possible to decipher the complete original text by a careful examination of the carbon. If a carbon which has been used often is submitted to a laboratory, a legible copy of the desired writing can sometimes be made by the use of special photographic techniques. In handling or shipping the carbon paper, care should be taken to avoid folding or wrinkling.

62. Burned or Charred Documents

Documents which have been accidentally burned in a fire or which have been purposely destroyed in this manner may sometimes be deciphered in the laboratory. If a paper has been subjected to intense heat, reducing it to ashes, it is practically impossible to develop any of the original writing. If the combustion is incomplete, some success can be realized when the pieces are large enough to form a coherent message. Great care must be exercised in packing and shipping evidence of this type. The pieces should be placed between layers of cotton and shipped in a strong, rigid box.

XII. ANONYMOUS LETTERS

63. General

In any large city the anonymous letter writer poses a peculiar problem to the detective division. He may be a harmless crank, a sexual psychopath, an extortionist, or simply a troublemaker. The last mentioned is the most insidious of this type of offender. With a few lines on paper he can disrupt the harmony of a home, create dissension in a business organization, or undermine the structure of an established career. Eminent figures in public life become accustomed to receiving letters traducing their own reputation or casting suspicion on their trusted subordinates. These persons usually follow the simple rule of ignoring the letters or referring them to an investigative agency for the purpose of discovering the identity of the author rather than with any intention of testing the truth of the contents. Persons with less confidence permit the anonymous letter to create doubts and suspicions in their own minds; thus, they grant to the writer the mean success to which he aspired.

64. Types

Anonymous letters lend themselves to classification. Four convenient categories may be used to include the person with information, the person with criminal intent, the malcontent, and the crank.

a. **Information.**

1) *Reliable Informer.* A person may write to the police department to inform them of the identity of a criminal. Sometimes the "tip" will be a reliable one. A person witnessing a crime or knowing of the existence of a conspiracy will, out of public spirit or out of personal dislike for the criminal, inform the authorities of the name and address of the perpetrator and of the circumstances surrounding the crime. There is no problem connected with such a letter. The investigator may avail himself of the information with gratitude and test its reliability by discreet preliminary inquiry. It is understandable that the informant does not wish to expose himself or his family to possible recriminations. The most common example of this type of letter writer is the informant on tax delinquencies.

2) *Crank Informants.* A crime which receives a great deal of publicity will inspire a number of slightly unbalanced minds to write letters conveying their suspicions. The writer will usually be

Figure 89. Charred documents. In order to destroy evidence the suspect threw the incriminating bonds into a fire. The charred remains were collected and photographed with infrared film and filter. In this way the printing and writing were made legible. (Courtesy of John Stevenson and Dominic Paolo.)

obsessed by some *bête noire* and will accuse it of the most heinous crimes including the one under discussion. The language of accusation is appropriately wild and can be readily recognized and profitably ignored.

b. **Criminal Intent.** This is the threatening letter of the extortionist. The writer usually demands a sum of money. Alternatively the receiver of the letter must accept the punishment which is threatened.

1) *Kidnapping.* The criminal may threaten to kill the captive unless a stipulated sum of money is delivered under stated conditions. Wealthy persons are the usual receivers of such letters. The bitter history of such cases points to the advisability of immediately referring them to the police. The Lindbergh case and the Greenlease affair of the 1950s suffice to illustrate this lesson. The captive is, in some instances, dead before the letter is sent. If he has not been killed by that time, the criminals ordinarily have no intention of carrying out their threat.

2) *Extortion and Blackmail.* Blackmail is a form of extortion. In committing the crime of extortion the criminal obtains property from another with his consent induced by the wrongful use of force of fear. In blackmail a letter is used to convey the threat. The blackmailer sends, or causes to be sent, for the purpose of extorting money, a letter or writing which threatens one of the following:

a) To accuse a person of a crime.
b) To do any injury to any person or property.
c) To publish or connive at publishing a libel.
d) To expose or impute a deformity or disgrace.

Again, it is usually unwise to accede to the blackmailer's demand. The payment of the sum does not deprive the blackmailer of his weapon. He reasons logically that, if his criminal method was successful once, he has grounds for greater faith in the outcome of the second trial. The victim by repeated acquiescence finds himself hopelessly enmeshed. He must inevitably take the stand that his conscience originally dictated.

c. **Malcontents.** This is the most common type of anonymous letter writer. In some communities his action is called "dropping a letter." Typically, he is associated with a large organization, in private industry or civil service. His merits have not received true recognition. A rival has been preferred to him and has risen to a relatively high station. He has observed improper behavior in the office or in his rival's private life. He wishes to bring this behavior to the attention of the proper authorities. In police departments the letter writer will accuse his victim of accepting graft. In other civil service work and in private industry he will usually accuse his victim of taking undue credit for work done by others, of petty thievery, or of preferring his friends for promotion.

d. **Cranks.** This term covers a wide range of letter writers. Some of them are harmlessly insane and can be ignored. Others may give violent vent to their feelings and are potentially dangerous.

1) *Attacking Public Figures.* This is the religious or political crank. He addresses anonymous letters to persons in public office or at the head of a large private organization. He recognizes the fact that the public figure is in reality at the head of a conspiracy to promote some political or religious doctrine. The writer is usually a victim of the *idée fixe,* and little can be done to disabuse him of his illusions. He is often a fanatic of a familiar stripe—anti-Semitic, anti-Christian, anti-Black, a believer in a white conspiracy, anti-Communist, or pro-Red. Sometimes he is simply an utter fool giving voice to his convictions in confused implications and vilifying. On the other hand, he may be the insidious master of the smear, with just the right touch of truth in each stroke to prevent outright denunciation. Since he is usually not associated with the public figure under attack, he is difficult to identify. However, he is not to be considered a serious problem except in those rare cases where he convinces himself of his destiny to relieve the world of an oppressor by assassination.

2) *Obscene Letters—the Sex Deviate.* Some persons derive great satisfaction, usually sexual in nature, from writing obscene or scurrilous letters to a person of the opposite sex. A neighborhood youth may select a physically well-endowed girl for his epistolary attention and send her anonymous letters informing her of his sexual ambitions. An office worker may send letters to the girl who sits three desks away. In a recent case, which is not atypical, a female school teacher was writing obscene letters to herself and complaining to authorities of the receipt of the missives. Characteristic of these letters is the description of abnormal sexual activity.

The writer describes his desire for the woman; he relates how this ardency affects him privately and causes him to seek relief; he outlines his amorous ambitions; he writes in detail of the deviations from normal sexual relations which he intends to pursue. Ostensibly he is seeking acquiescence on the part of the woman. Actually he makes no arrangement for her to communicate with him. The letter is scurrilous and only rarely imaginative. The writer may, however, be dangerous; hence the investigator should, if possible, refer the letter to a psychiatrist in order to determine whether the unknown author is potentially a menace. The writer can sometimes be identified by questioning the victim concerning her acquaintances.

65. Identifying the Writer

In cases involving a complainant, the identity of the author may sometimes be established if he is writing a series of letters and if he is within the circle of the complainant's associates, acquaintances, or neighbors. One or more of the following methods may be used:

a. **Latent Fingerprints.** The complainant should be instructed to submit each suspected letter unopened so that it may be processed for latent fingerprints.

b. **Handwriting.** Often a generous sample of the culprit's handwriting is present. Occasionally he resorts to hand printing or pasting together of words cut from newspaper headlines. If it is suspected that the letters were written by a member of a business or other organizations with which the complainant is associated, handwriting standards of selected suspects can be obtained for comparison.

c. **Typewriting.** If a typewriter is used, the make and model of the machine can be determined from the anonymous letter and the search can be limited to the offices and quarters containing similar typewriters. A little ingenuity will be required to obtain samples from these machines or to obtain standards known to have been produced on them. In this way it may be possible to identify the individual typewriter and the persons using the machine. If more than one person uses the typewriter a study of personalities, habits, education, and typing peculiarities should precede an interrogation. Alternatively a trap may be set by arrangement with the predetermined innocent users.

d. **Paper and Ink.** The writing materials in general should be examined for peculiarities which would serve to identify the source.

e. **Plants.** If one or more suspects have been identified, the investigator may obtain conclusive evidence by means of a plant. The use of marked stationery and ink is recommended. If the type of stationery used in the anonymous letters is fairly common or in general supply from a common source, the investigator can arrange to place a small invisible number in fluorescent ink on a corner of each sheet of stationery. Each suspect should be assigned a definite number. On receiving a subsequent letter it should be possible to determine the guilty party by the fluorescent number revealed under ultraviolet light. Another method applicable to a situation in which there is a limited number of suspects is the use of fluorescent ink. Using a substance such as that described in Chapter 41, the suspect's source of ink is contaminated with a tracing material. When the complainant receives a subsequent anonymous letter, the missive is placed under the ultraviolet lamp to detect any fluorescence. To hasten the procedure, where it is desired to test a number of suspects, variations can be made in the color of the fluorescence by the selection of appropriate materials. If a typewriter is used for the letters, a plant can be made by impregnating the ribbon with a fluorescent liquid which will not interfere with the normal inking properties of the ribbon.

XIII. INKS

66. Inks

In the examination of questioned documents it is sometimes necessary to investigate questions concerning the ink used in the writings. For example, if it is alleged that alterations have been made, it is advisable to compare the type of ink used in the undisputed original writing with that of the alleged alteration. If the chemical examination shows that two different types of ink were used, the inference to be drawn is obvious. Another point of interest lies in the question of the age of inks: is the writing as old as the date it bears; were the writings of chronological business entries all made at the same time or over a period of time as would be natural in the course of business? Finally, it is sometimes of great interest to learn whether a particular bottle of ink was used for the writings on two different documents, e.g., the ink bottle that may be the common source for the ink used on a series of anonymous letters.

67. Types of Ink

The determination of the specific type or age of ink is a very difficult problem for the document examiner because of the number of uncontrollable variables, namely, insufficiency of available ink sample in any writing; inadequate quality control in manufacture; and mass production by a few large manufacturers. The chief concern of the manufacturer is viscosity rather than the quantitative mix of the ink. With the widespread use of the ballpoint pen the specific identification of ink has become an even more elusive problem.

The general problem of differentiating between the inks used in two specimens of writing depends for its solution on an understanding of the physical and chemical characteristics of the major classifications of inks. The following types of ink are most frequently encountered in document work:

a. **Iron Gallotannate Ink.** This type of ink has long been used for entries in record books and for business purposes in general. Iron gallotannate or nutgall inks are true solutions and not merely suspensions of solid coloring matter in a liquid medium. Hence the ink is capable of penetration into the interstices of the fibers of the paper, thereby inscribing the writing in the body of the paper and not on the surface alone, thus rendering its removal more difficult. The general constituents of black and blue-black nutgall inks are gallic acid, tannic acid, and ferrous sulfate. These produce a colorless solution which will oxidize and darken when exposed to air. Upon contact with paper, this solution reacts to form a black iron compound in the fibers. A dye material such as Soluble Blue is added to render the writing immediately legible. Iron ink remains on the paper indefinitely if the paper is undisturbed. It is considered the best permanent ink for document purposes. Some organizations require that this ink be used in maintaining records.

b. **Logwood Inks.** From the wood of the logwood tree a natural coloring material (haemotoxylin) is obtained by extraction with water. The color of logwood inks depends upon the inorganic salt which is added; but, on drying and standing, they turn black. The addition of chromium salts will yield the deepest black. At the present time logwood inks are practically obsolete, although they are reported to be still in use in Germany.

c. **Nigrosine Ink.** This is a water solution of a synthetic black compound prepared from aniline and nitrobenzene. This synthetic type of ink is usually referred to as *Nigrosine ink* but is also known as *induline ink* and *black aniline ink*. No new compound is formed by oxidation after this ink is applied to the paper, so that lines are merely deposited organic solids that were in solution before the ink dried. It should be expected, then, that water would affect this ink by redissolving the nigrosine. Hence, inks in this class are easily smudged, affected by moisture, and washed from the paper with little difficulty, regardless of the length of time they have been on the document.

d. **Chinese, India, and Carbon Writing Inks.** Inks containing carbon are the oldest writing substances known. Chinese and india ink are the most common forms. In modern times finely divided carbon held in colloidal suspension is used to produce deep black drawing and writing ink. Since carbon is chemically inert to the usual testing reagents, it will resist all attempts at oxidation or reduction, and will remain uninfluenced by changes in acidity. This type of ink, however, does not penetrate deeply into the fibers of the paper and hence may be washed off.

e. **Ball-Point Ink.** Because of the differences in construction of the ball-point pen, a different type of ink is required. In place of the fluid type of ink, a thick, pasty substance is used which will present suitable dye to the ball-point but which will not flow readily. The permanency of these inks is not known with any accuracy. It has been noted that many ball-point inks have a tendency to fade. One approach to the analysis of ball-point ink samples is the use of the Aminco-Bowman spectrophotofluorometer to obtain a "fingerprint" of the dye components. Thin-layer chromotography (TLC) is used to separate ink components. The TLC plates are automatically scanned spectrophotometrically to determine the proportion of dyes in the ink sample.

68. Comparison of Inks

To determine whether two documents were written with the same type of ink various physical and chemical methods are available. The inks are compared visually for color. The naked eye, color filters, and infrared photography usually reveal differences in color. A 5 percent solution of hydrochloric acid is the most generally useful chemical reagent. The reagent may be applied with a sharpened wooden toothpick to a small area of the writing. When hydrochloric acid is placed on iron nutgall ink, the color disappears or turns a light blue; on logwood ink a red color developes; on nigrosine or carbon ink there is no reaction. To distinguish nigrosine from carbon ink a 10 percent solution of sodium hypochlorite (acidified) is used. Nigrosine ink turns brown with this reagent, but carbon ink is unaffected. It should be noted that these reactions sometimes take place over a period of hours. The investigator should test inks only as a screening procedure where a number of suspected documents are available.

69. Age of Inks

It may be said, in general, that under ordinary circumstances it is practically impossible to determine the age of inks. A limit can sometimes be placed to the age by color matching with standards to determine the degree of fading and by chemical reactions which depend on oxidation. The chemical methods are not applicable to nigrosine and carbon inks, which are not oxidized after being deposited on the paper. In any case, age determination will depend on the composition of the ink, its condition with respect to fluidity and impurities, the nature of the paper used in the writing, and the conditions under which the paper was preserved.

ADDITIONAL READING

Document Examination

Bartha, A. and Duxbury, N.W.: Restoration and Preservation of Charred Documents. 1 *Canadian Society of Forensic Science Journal,* 2, 1968.

Bates, B.P.: *Identification System for Questioned Documents.* Springfield, Ill.: Thomas, 1970.

Buquet, A.: New Techniques for the Detection of Alterations in Documents. 10 *Forensic Science,* 185, 1977.

Caputo, L.V.: *Questioned Document Case Studies.* Chicago, Nelson-Hall, 1982.

Casey-Owens, M.: The Anonymous Letter Writer — A Psychological Profile? 29 *Journal of Forensic Sciences,* 816, 1984.

Caywood, D.A.: Decipherment of Indented Writing — A New Technique. 1 *Journal of Police Science and Administration,* 50, 1973.

Conway, J.V.P.: *Evidential Documents.* Springfield, Ill.: Thomas, 1959.

Edwards, J.: Preliminary Document Screening. 25 *Law and Order,* 7, 1977.

Ellen, D.M., Foster, D.J. and Morantz, D.J.: The Use of Electrostatic Imaging in the Detection of Indented Impressions. 15 *Forensic Science International,* 53, 1980.

Ellen, D.: *The Scientific Examination of Documents: Methods and Techniques.* New York, Wiley, 1989.

Harrison, W.R.: *Suspect Documents: Their Scientific Examination.* London, Sweet and Maxwell, 1958.

Hilton, O.: *Detecting and Deciphering Erased Pencil Writing.* Springfield, Ill.: Thomas, 1991.

——: *Scientific Examination of Questioned Documents,* rev. ed. New York, Elsevier, 1982.

——: Special Considerations in Deciphering Erased Writing. 13 *Journal of Police Science and Administration,* 93, 1985.

——: The Evolution of Questioned Document Examination in the Last 50 Years. 33 *Journal of Forensic Sciences,* 310, 1988.

——: The Influence of Easy Correction Devices on the Security of Documents. 12 *Journal of Police Science and Administration,* 105, 1984.

Jackson, K.S.: Identification of a Checkwriter Based on Ink Deposit Pattern. 36 *Journal of Forensic Sciences,* 257, 1991.

Luisi, C., Zeins, W.R. and Brill, A.E.: Executing Search Warrants in an Office Automation Environment. 57 *FBI Law Enforcement Bulletin,* 3, 1988.

Miller, L.S.: Bias Among Forensic Document Examiners: A Need for Procedural Changes. 12 *Journal of Police Science and Administration,* 407, 1984.

Moore, D.S.: Evaluation of a Method Using Powder to Detect the Site of Rubber Erasures. 26 *Journal of Forensic Sciences*, 724, 1981.

Osborn, A.S.: *Questioned Documents*, 2nd ed. Reprint of 1926 ed. Chicago, Nelson-Hall, 1974.

Purtell, D.J.: Obtaining Questioned Document Standards for Comparison. 5 *Police Law Quarterly*, 4, 1976.

Riker, M.A. and Lewis, G.W.: Methylene Blue Revisited: The Search for a Trouble-Free Erasure Sensitive Powder. 33 *Journal of Forensic Sciences*, 773, 1988.

Rissler, L.E.: Documentary Search Warrants—A Problem of Particularity. 49 *FBI Law Enforcement Bulletin*, 7, 1980.

Sauls, J.S.: Documents and Compulsory Self-Incrimination: Fifth Amendment Considerations. 57 *FBI Law Enforcement Bulletin*, 12, 1988.

Stewart, L.F.: Artificial Aging of Documents. 27 *Journal of Forensic Sciences*, 450, 1982.

Taylor, L.R.: The Restoration and Identification of Water-Soaked Documents: A Case Study. 31 *Journal of Forensic Sciences*, 1113, 1986.

They Write Their Own Sentences: The FBI Handwriting Analysis Manual. Boulder, Col.: Paladin Press, 1987.

Whiting, F.I.: Inconclusive Opinions: Refuge of the Questioned Document Examiner. 35 *Journal of Forensic Sciences*, 938, 1990.

Williamson, D.M. and Meenach, A.E.: *Cross-Check System for Forgery and Questioned Document Examination.* Chicago, Nelson-Hall, 1981.

Handwriting Identification

Alford, E.F., Jr. and Dick, R.M.: Intentional Disguise in Court-Ordered Handwriting Specimens. 6 *Journal of Police Science and Administration*, 419, 1978.

Armistead, T.: Issues in the Identification of Handprinting: A Case Study in Anonymous Death Threats. 12 *Journal of Police Science and Administration*, 81, 1984.

Baxter, P.G.: Classification and Measurement in Forensic Handwriting Comparison. 13 *Medicine, Science and the Law*, 166, 1973.

Bradford, R.R.: Obtaining Exemplars from All Arrestees. 55 *Fingerprint and Identification Magazine*, 6, 1973.

Chodrow, M.M. and Bivona, W.A.: *Study of Handprinted Character Recognition Techniques.* Springfield, Va.: National Technical Information Service, 1966.

Franck, F.E.: Disguised Writing: Chronic or Acute. 33 *Journal of Forensic Sciences*, 727, 1988.

Hilton, O.: Effects of Writing Instruments on Handwriting Details. 29 *Journal of Forensic Sciences*, 80, 1984.

Masson, J.F.: Felt Tip Pen Writing: Problems of Identification. 30 *Journal of Forensic Sciences*, 172, 1985.

McAlexander, T.V., Beck, J. and Dick, R.M.: The Standardization of Handwriting Opinion Terminology. 36 *Journal of Forensic Sciences,* 311, 1991.

McAlexander, T.V.: The Meaning of Handwriting Opinions. 5 *Journal of Police Science and Administration,* 43, 1977.

Muehlberger, R.J., et al.: A Statistical Examination of Selected Handwriting Characteristics. 22 *Journal of Forensic Sciences,* 206, 1977.

Shimoda, S.C. and Franck, F.E.: Writer's Palmar Impressions. 34 *Journal of Forensic Sciences,* 468, 1989.

Smith, E.J.: *Principles of Forensic Handwriting Identification and Testimony.* Springfield, Ill.: Thomas, 1984.

Waggoner, L.R.: Handwriting Evidence for the Investigator. 53 *FBI Law Enforcement Bulletin,* 6, 1984.

Webb, F.E.: The Question of Disguise in Handwriting. 23 *Journal of Forensic Sciences,* 149, 1978.

Ink and Paper Examination

Browning, B.I.: *The Analysis of Paper.* New York, Dekker, 1969.

Brunelle, R.L. and Reed, R.W.: *Forensic Examination of Ink and Paper.* Springfield, Ill.: Thomas, 1984.

Brunelle, R.L., Breedlove, C.H. and Midkiff, C.R.: Determining the Relative Age of Ballpoint Inks Using a Single-Solvent Technique. 32 *Journal of Forensic Sciences,* 1511, 1987.

Cantu, A.A. and Prough, R.S.: On the Relative Aging of Inks—The Solvent Extraction Technique. 32. *Journal of Forensic Sciences,* 1151, 1987.

Cantu A.A. and Prough, R.S.: Some Special Observations of Infrared Luminescence. 33 *Journal of Forensic Sciences,* 638, 1988.

Cantu, A.A.: Comments on the Accelerated Aging of Ink. 33 *Journal of Forensic Sciences,* 744, 1988.

Crown, D.A., Brunelle, R.L. and Cantu, A.A.: The Parameters of Ballpen Ink Examinations. 21 *Journal of Forensic Sciences,* 917, 1976.

Fryd, C.F.M.: Examination of Inks on Documents. 14 *Medicine, Science and The Law,* 87, 1974.

Leukens, H.R. and Settle, D.M.: *Forensic Neutron Activation Analysis of Paper.* Springfield, Va.: National Technical Information Service, 1970.

Lyter, A.H. III: Examination of Ball Pen Ink by High Pressure Liquid Chromatography. 27 *Journal of Forensic Sciences,* 154, 1982.

Patterson, P.: The Chemistry of Inks for Writing, Printing and Copying. 4 *Journal of the Forensic Science Society,* 200, 1964.

Riordan, W.M.: Detection of Nonvisible Writings by Infrared Luminescence and Ultraviolet Fluorescence. 36 *Journal of Forensic Sciences,* 466, 1991.

Stewart, L.F.: Ballpoint Ink Age Determination by Volatile Component Comparison—A Preliminary Study. 30 *Journal of Forensic Sciences,* 405, 1985.

Tewari, S.N. and Tripathi, S.S.: Paper Chromatographic Identification of Ink

Dye-Stuffs and Its Importance in Document Examinations. 29 *International Criminal Police Review,* 278, 1974.

Throckmorton, G.J.: Disappearing Ink: Its Use, Abuse, and Detection. 35 *Journal of Forensic Sciences,* 199, 1990.

———: Erasable Ink: Its Ease of Erasability and Its Permanence. 30 *Journal of Forensic Sciences,* 526, 1985.

Witte, A.H.: The Examination and Identification of Inks. In Lundquist, F. (Ed.): *Methods of Forensic Science,* vol. 2. New York, Wiley-Interscience, 1963.

Typewriting Identification

Anthony, A.T.: Letter Quality Impact Printer Hammer Impressions. 33 *Journal of Forensic Sciences,* 779, 1988.

Attenberger, D.W. and Kanaskie, W.G.: Examination of a Typewritten Document. 50 *FBI Law Enforcement Bulletin,* 6, 1981.

Bates, B.P.: *Typewriting Identification.* Springfield, Ill.: Thomas, 1970.

Behrendt, J.E. and Muehlberger, R.J.: Printwheel Typescript Variations Caused by the Manufacturing Process. 32 *Journal of Forensic Sciences,* 629, 1987.

Behrendt, J.E.: Class Defects in Printwheel Typescript. 33 *Journal of Forensic Sciences,* 328, 1988.

Crown, D.A.: Landmarks in Typewriting Identification. 58 *Journal of Criminal Law, Criminology and Police Science,* 105, 1967.

Davis, E.A. and Lyter, A.H. III: Comparison of Typewritten Carbon Paper Impressions. 27 *Journal of Forensic Sciences,* 424, 1982.

Estabrooks, C.B.: Differentiation of Printwheel and Conventional Typescript. 16 *Canadian Society of Forensic Science Journal,* 19, 1983.

Gupta, S.A.: A Scientific Analysis of Typewriting Identification. 28 *International Criminal Police Review,* 265, 1973.

Hilton, O.: Some Practical Suggestions for Examining Writing from Electric Typewriters. 3 *Journal of Police Science and Administration,* 1, 1975.

Leslie, A.G.: Identification of the Single Element Typewriter and Type Element. Part I—Type Elements. 10 *Canadian Society of Forensic Science Journal,* 87, 1977.

Photocopy Identification

Crown, D.A.: The Differentiation of Electrostatic Photocopy Machines. 34 *Journal of Forensic Sciences,* 142, 1989.

Hilton, O.: Detecting Fraudulent Photocopies. 13 *Forensic Sciences International,* 117, 1979.

Holland, N.W.: Photocopy Classification and Identification. 24 *Journal of the Forensic Science Society,* 23, 1984.

James, E.L.: The Classification of Office Copy Machines from Physical Characteristics. 32 *Journal of Forensic Sciences,* 1293, 1987.

Kelley, J.H.: *Classification and Identification of Modern Office Copiers.* Colorado Springs, Col.: The Forensic Sciences Foundation, 1983.

Morton, S.E.: A Look at Newer Photocopiers. 34 *Journal of Forensic Sciences,* 461, 1989.

Shiver, F.C. and Nelson, L.K.: Nondestructive Differentiation of Full-Color Photocopies. 36 *Journal of Forensic Sciences,* 145, 1991.

Totty, R.N.: Analysis and Differentiation of Photocopy Toners. 2 *Forensic Science Review,* 1, 1990.

Totty, R.N. and Baxendale, D.: Defect Marks and the Identification of Photocopying Machines. 21 *Journal of the Forensic Science Society,* 23, 1981.

Appendix 1

WHITE-COLLAR CRIME

W HITE–COLLAR crime was first given substantial recognition in 1949 by the publication of Edwin H. Sutherland's book, in which he introduced the definition: "white-collar crime may be defined approximately as a crime committed by a person of respectability and high social status in the course of his occupation." The definition was considerably broadened in 1970 by Herbert Edelhertz in his paper, "The Nature, Impact and Prosecution of White-Collar Crime," published by the National Institute of Law Enforcement and Criminal Justice. Edelhertz expanded the idea of white-collar crime beyond restrictions of class and occupation by defining it as: "an illegal act or series of acts committed by nonphysical means and by concealment or guile, to obtain money or property, to avoid the payment or loss of money or property, or to obtain business or personal advantage."

Throughout this text white-collar crime has been touched upon lightly, without imparting proportionate emphasis to an area of crime that many experts consider as costly to society as street crime. Employee theft, for example, is estimated at $10 million a day by Norman Jaspan Associates, an organization that specializes in the detection and prevention of white-collar crime. Dishonesty is considered to be prevalent at all levels—from the warehouse loading dock to the executive suite. Since 1949 the problem has expanded in scope and deepened in complexity.

It is not part of the purpose of this book to treat the investigation and prosecution of white-collar crime. The student will, however, find the following outline of Edelhertz highly informative:

Categories of White-Collar Crimes

In the list given below, white-collar crimes have been classified by the general environment and motivation of the perpetrator. Comprehensive (except for the exclusion of organized crime) and distinctive, these categories are intended to provide the following benefits: (1) to assist the study of motivation as an aid in preventive programs; (2) to suggest a basis for altering environments which may give rise to criminal violations; and (3) to give insight into the psychology, susceptibility, and other exposed weaknesses of victims.

a. **Personal Crimes.** These are crimes by persons operating on an individual, *ad hoc* basis for personal gain in a non-business context.

1) Purchases on credit with no intention to pay; purchases by mail in the name of another.

2) Individual income tax violations.

3) Credit card frauds.

4) Bankruptcy frauds.

5) Title II home improvement loan frauds.

6) Frauds with respect to social security, unemployment insurance, and welfare.

7) Unorganized or occasional frauds on insurance companies (theft, casualty, health, etc.).

8) Violations of Federal Reserve regulations by pledging stock for further purchases, flouting margin requirements.

9) Unorganized "lonely hearts" appeal by mail.

b. **Abuses of Trust.** These are crimes committed in the course of their occupations by persons operating inside business, government, or other establishments in violation of their duty of loyalty and fidelity to employer or client.

1) Commercial bribery and kickbacks, i.e., by and to buyers, insurance adjusters, contracting officers, quality inspectors, government inspectors and auditors, etc.

2) Bank violations by bank officers, employees, and directors.

3) Embezzlement or self-dealing by business or union officers and employees.

4) Securities fraud by insiders trading to their advantage by

the use of special knowledge or causing their firms to take positions in the market to benefit themselves.

    5) Employee petty larceny and expense account frauds.

    6) Frauds by computer causing unauthorized payouts.

    7) "Sweetheart contracts" entered into by union officers.

    8) Embezzlement or self-dealing by attorneys, trustees, and fiduciaries.

    9) Fraud against the government
        a) Padding payrolls.
        b) Conflicts of interest.
        c) False travel, expense, or per diem claims.

    c. **Business Crimes.** These offenses are incidental to and in furtherance of business operations but not the central purpose of the business.

    1) Tax violations.

    2) Antitrust violations.

    3) Commercial bribery of another's employee, officer, or fiduciary (including union officers).

    4) Food and drug violations.

    5) False weights and measures by retailers.

    6) Violations of Truth-in-Lending Act by misrepresentation of credit terms and prices.

    7) Submission or publication of false financial statements to obtain credit.

    8) Use of fictitious or over-valued collateral.

    9) Check-kiting to obtain operating capital on short-term financing.

    10) Securities Act violations, i.e., sale of non-registered securities to obtain operating capital, false proxy statements, manipulation of market to support corporate credit or access to capital markets, etc.

    11) Collusion between physicians and pharmacists to cause the writing of unnecessary prescriptions.

    12) Dispensing by pharmacists in violation of law, excluding narcotics traffic.

    13) Immigration fraud in support of employment agency operations to provide domestics.

    14) Housing code violations by landlords.

15) Deceptive advertising.
16) Fraud against the government:
    a) False claims.
    b) False statements:
        (1) to induce contracts
        (2) AID frauds
        (3) Housing frauds
        (4) SBA frauds, such as SBIC bootstrapping, self-dealing, cross-dealing, etc., or obtaining direct loans by use of false financial statements.
    c) Moving contracts in urban renewal.
17) Labor violations (Davis-Bacon Act).
18) Commercial espionage.

d. **Confidence Games.** White-collar crime considered as a business or as the central activity of a business takes the form of the systematic frauds which are referred to as *con games*.

1) Medical or health frauds.
2) Advance fee swindles.
3) Phony contests.
4) Bankruptcy fraud, including schemes devised as salvage operation after insolvency or otherwise legitimate business.
5) Securities fraud and commodities fraud.
6) Chain referral schemes.
7) Home improvement schemes.
8) Debt consolidation schemes.
9) Mortgage milking.
10) Merchandise swindles:
    a) Gun and coin swindles
    b) General merchandise
    c) Buying or pyramid clubs.
11) Land frauds.
12) Directory advertising schemes.
13) Charity and religious frauds.
14) Personal improvement schemes:
    a) Diploma mills
    b) Correspondence schools
    c) Modeling schools.

15) Fraudulent application for, use and/or sale of credit cards, airline tickets, etc.

16) Insurance frauds:
    a) Phony accident rings.
    b) Looting of companies by purchase of over-valued assets, phony management contracts, self-dealing with agents, inter-company transfers, etc.
    c) Frauds by agents writing false policies to obtain advance commissions.
    d) Issuance of annuities or paid-up life insurance, with no consideration, so that they can be used as collateral for loans.
    e) Sales by misrepresentation to military personnel or those otherwise uninsurable.

17) Vanity press and song publishing schemes.

18) Ponzi schemes.

19) False security frauds, i.e. Billy Sol Estes or De Angelis type schemes.

20) Purchase of banks or control thereof with deliberate intention to loot them.

21) Fraudulent establishing and operation of banks or savings and loan associations.

22) Fraud against the government:
    a) Organized income tax refund swindles, sometimes operated by income tax "counselors."
    b) AID frauds, i.e. where totally worthless goods are shipped.
    c) FHA frauds through home improvement schemes or by obtaining guarantees of mortgages on multiple family housing far in excess of the value of the property with foreseeable inevitable foreclosure.

23) Executive placement and employment agency frauds.

24) Coupon redemption frauds.

25) Money order swindles.

ADDITIONAL READING

White-Collar Crime

Albrecht, W.S., et al.: *How to Detect and Prevent Business Fraud.* Englewood Cliffs, N.J.: Prentice-Hall, 1982.

Arlidge, A. and Parry, J.: *Fraud.* Elmsford, N.Y.: Pergamon, 1985.

Bailey, L.L.: Medicaid Fraud. 60 *FBI Law Enforcement Bulletin,* 7, 1991.

Edelhertz, H.: *The Nature, Impact and Prosecution of White-Collar Crime.* Washington, D.C.: U.S. Government Printing Office, 1970.

George, B.J., Jr.: *White-Collar Crime: Defense and Prosecution.* New York, Practicing Law Institute, 1971.

Green, G.: *Occupational Crime.* Chicago, Nelson-Hall, 1990.

Hutton, G.W.: *Welfare Fraud Investigation.* Springfield, Ill.: Thomas, 1985.

Investigation of White-Collar Crime. Washington, D.C.: U.S. Government Printing Office, 1977.

Kramer, W.M.: *Investigative Techniques in Complex Financial Crimes: Fraud and Corruption, Racketeering, Money Laundering.* Washington, D.C.: National Institute on Economic Crime, 1988.

Mann, K.: *Defending White-Collar Crime: A Portrait of Attorneys at Work.* New Haven, Conn.: Yale University Press, 1985.

Ogren, R.W.: The Ineffectiveness of the Criminal Sanction in Fraud and Corruption Cases. 11 *American Criminal Law Review,* 959, 1973.

Oughton, F.: *Fraud and White-Collar Crime.* London, Elek Books, 1971.

Villa, J.K.: *Banking Crimes: Fraud, Money Laundering, and Embezzlement.* New York, Clark Boardman, 1988.

Weisburd, D., Wheeler, S., Waring, E. and Bode, N.: *Crimes of the Middle Class: White-Collar Offenders in the Federal Courts.* New Haven, Conn.: Yale University Press, 1991.

Weiss, J.P.: Policing White Collar Crime. 37 *Law and Order,* 3, 1989.

Welling, S.N.: Smurfs, Money Laundering, and the Federal Criminal Law: The Crime of Structuring Transactions. 41 *Florida Law Review,* 2, 1989.

Appendix 2

ARREST, SEARCH, AND SEIZURE

1. Arrest

T HE POWER of a criminal investigator to make an arrest depends
upon the federal law and the local state laws of arrest in the
area in which he is operating. A criminal investigator possesses, of
course, the same right as the private citizen to make an arrest. He
may arrest for a felony or a breach of the peace committed in his
presence and for a felony not committed in his presence if the
felony has in fact been committed and he has reasonable cause to
believe that the person arrested committed the felony. In making
arrest under other circumstances the investigator ordinarily first
obtains a warrant. A military investigator may arrest persons
subject to military law for violation of the Uniform Code of
Military Justice or as otherwise provided by regulation.

a. **Police Arrest.** This term describes the act of taking an offender
into custody and imposing restraint upon him with formal notification that he is "under arrest." Military law employs the term
arrest to mean a moral restraint imposed on a person by oral or
written order of competent authority limiting his personal liberty
pending disposition of charges and binding upon the person
arrested, not by physical force as in the police arrest, but rather by
virtue of his moral and legal obligation to obey such an order of
arrest.

b. **Police Restraint.** In addition to the police arrest, criminal
investigators also employ the other specific types of physical
restraints which involve the deprivation of liberty by taking into
custody. These restraints are usually called "detaining for questioning," "protective custody," and "holding on a short affidavit."

957

2. Technique of Arrest

The manner in which the arrest is accomplished will naturally depend on the circumstances in which the investigator finds himself. He can in some cases exercise control over these conditions. In other situations, he must take advantage of his opportunities. The safety of bystanders and of himself should be a primary consideration. The force employed should be sufficient to overcome resistance. The use of excessive force is subject to censure and, if employed to a marked degree, renders the investigator liable to prosecution. In any event such an abuse of authority is prejudicial to the case.

a. **Behavior in Making an Arrest.** The arrest should be made in a straightforward manner whenever possible. The suspect should be notified of the fact that he is being placed under arrest. The investigator should then display his credentials or badge to establish his authority. An inconspicuous, courteous manner should be employed. The investigator must, however, convey the seriousness of his intention by his demeanor, voice, and movements. He should, at all times, control the situation. There should be no show of nervousness or indecision. A preliminary search can be accomplished in an inconspicuous manner. The subject can then be removed to a place where a more thorough search can be made without the danger of interference and without attracting a crowd.

b. **Employment of Force.** Unnecessary force or violence is to be avoided. The degree and kind of force should be calculated only to overcome the resistance offered and will depend on the nature of the case, that is, whether the case involves a misdemeanor or a felony.

1) *Misdemeanor.* In misdemeanor cases the investigator may not use force calculated to cause grave bodily harm. Although a law enforcement officer need not, under any circumstances, retreat in the face of resistance, it is preferable to permit a person accused of a misdemeanor to escape rather than inflict serious injury in effecting his apprehension. Firearms should not be used in arresting for a misdemeanor.

2) *Felony.* Deadly force may be used when required in felony cases, but only such force as is necessary to accomplish the arrest

or prevent the escape of the suspect. Since a law enforcement officer is characterized by his capacity to use judgment in extraordinary situations, it is expected that his decision to use force will not rest solely on the simplistic distinction between a misdemeanor and a felony. He will not, that is to say, decide to use deadly force simply because he is dealing with a felony case. The kind of felony should also be taken into consideration. For example, the few dollars that may distinguish a grand larceny from petty theft may not justify the use of a deadly weapon simply to prevent an escape. Similarly, a person wanted for armed robbery and a person who has forged and cashed a check for $500 may both be guilty of a felony, but the investigator, in planning an apprehension, would assign widely differing values to the potential of each offender for resistance to arrest and would be prepared to act accordingly.

A general principle of minimum violence should guide the investigator's tactics in making an apprehension so as to provide maximum safety for innocent persons in the area, suitable precautions for his own protection, and necessary, but not excessive, force in overcoming resistance.

3. Search of the Person

A search of a person is conducted to discover weapons or evidence, or to determine identity. Taking custody of property found by searching is called seizure, a term which implies a forcible dispossession of the person arrested. A preliminary search of a person ordinarily is made at the time and scene of an arrest; its primary purposes are the discovery of concealed weapons and the seizing of incriminating evidence which might otherwise be destroyed. At the place of detention (usually a station house) a more complete search is made. A suspect is stripped, and his clothing and other possessions carried on his person thoroughly examined. Female investigative personnel search women prisoners.

The Supreme Court has traditionally interpreted the Fourth Amendment's prohibition against "unreasonable searches and seizures" to mean that policemen could not search unless they had either a search warrant or enough evidence to arrest the suspect and take him into custody. In 1968 the Supreme Court announced a rule of reasonableness that authorizes the police to detain subjects for questioning and search them "when a reasonably prudent man in the circumstances would be warranted in the belief that his safety and that of others was in danger." If a legal search turns up a weapon or any other evidence, it can be used in court. With this ruling the Supreme Court clarified the "stop and frisk" situation, in which the policeman stops a person whom he suspects but could not legally arrest and whose clothing, if he looks dangerous, the officer pats down for weapons before questioning. Concerning the subjective test of "reasonableness" the Court concluded that "no judicial opinion can comprehend the protean variety of the street encounter," and that local judges would have to be trusted to judge the reasonableness of each one on a case-by-case basis (*Terry v. Ohio,* 392 U.S. 1 [1968]).

4. Search of the Area

The investigator should not, in the busy moments of taking the prisoner into custody, overlook the possibility of evidence being in the area. When the arrest has been made, and the prisoner has been subjected to a preliminary search and secured, the area surrounding the place of arrest should be searched for weapons, narcotics, or other evidence. The prisoner may have taken the advantage of the moments elapsing between his being surprised and his apprehension to throw evidence away. If the prisoner was in a vehicle, both the vehicle and the area should be searched. In a hotel room or house, the premises should be searched. In a train or bus the seat and its surrounding area should be examined.

5. Seizure of Evidence

In gathering evidence from a premises, especially from the subject's home, the investigators should be guided by the Fourth Amendment's prohibitions against unreasonable searches and seizures. In general, officials cannot seize in a search, or use as evidence, any items except illegal articles or contraband, such as narcotics, or the instrumentality of a crime, such as a weapon, or

Table XII
SUBMITTING EVIDENCE TO THE FBI LABORATORY

Specimen	Amount Desired		Send By	Identification	Wrapping and Packing	Remarks
	Standard	Evidence				
Abrasives, including carborundum, emery, sand, etc.	Not less than one ounce	All	Registered mail or Federal Express	On outside of container. Type of material. Date obtained. Name or initials	Use containers, such as ice-cream box, pillbox, or plastic vial. Seal to prevent any loss	Avoid use of envelopes
Acids	100 milliliters (ml)	All to 100 ml	Contact FBI Chemistry Unit for instructions	Same as above	Plastic or all-glass bottle. Tape stopper. Pack in sawdust, glass, or rock wool. Use bakelite or paraffin lined bottle for hydrofluoric acid	Label acids, glass, corrosive
Adhesive tape	Recoverd roll	All	Registered mail	Same as above	Place on waxed paper or cellophane	Do not cut, wad, or distort
Alkalies—caustic soda, potash, ammonia, etc.	100 ml 100 gr	All to 100 ml All to 100 gm	Contact FBI Chemistry Unit for instructions	Same as above	Plastic or glass bottle with rubber stopper held with adhesive tape	Label alkali, glass, corrosive
Ammunition (Cartridges)			UPS or Federal Express. Cannot be sent by U.S. Mail	Same as above	Follow the regulations of the U.S. Department of Transportation	Unless specific examination of cartridge is essential, do not submit

Source: FBI. *Handbook of Forensic Science,* Rev. ed. Washington, D.C.: U.S. Government Printing Office, 1990.

| Specimen | Amount Desired | | Send By | Identification | Wrapping and Packing | Remarks |
	Standard	Evidence				
Anonymous letters, extortion letters, bank robbery notes		All **original** documents	Registered mail	Initial and date each document unless legal aspects or good judgment dictates otherwise	Place in proper enclosure envelope and seal with "Evidence" tape or transparent cellophane tape. Flap side of envelope should show **(1)** wording "Enclosure(s) to FBIHQ from (name of submitting office)," **(2)** title of case, **(3)** brief description of contents, and **(4)** file number, if known. Staple to original letter of transmittal	Do not handle with bare hands. Advise if evidence should be treated for latent fingerprints
Blasting caps	(Contact FBI Explosives Unit for instructions)					
Blood:						
1. Liquid Known Samples	One tube each (sterile) 5 cc–10 cc, blood only. No preservatives	All	Registered airmail special delivery	Use adhesive tape on outside of test tube. Name of donor, date taken, doctor's name, name or initials of investigator	Wrap in cotton, soft paper. Place in mailing tube or suitable strong mailing carton	Submit immediately. Don't hold awaiting additional items for comparison. Keep under refrigeration, not freezing, until mailing. No refrigerants and/or dry ice should be added to sample during transit. Fragile label

Specimen	Amount Desired		Send By	Identification	Wrapping and Packing	Remarks
	Standard	Evidence				
2. Small quantities:						
a. Liquid Questioned Samples	All		Registered airmail special delivery	Same as above	Same as above	If unable to expeditiously furnish sample, allow to dry thoroughly on the nonporous surface, and scrape off; or collect by using eye droppers or clean spoon, transfer to nonporous surface and let dry; or absorb in sterile gauze and let dry.
b. Dry stains Not on fabrics		As much as possible	Registered mail	On outside of pillbox or plastic vial. Type of specimen, date secured, name or initials	Seal to prevent leakage	Keep dry. Avoid use of envelopes
c. For toxicological use		20 cc (blood and preservative mixture)	Registered airmail, special delivery	Same as liquid samples	Medical examiner should use a standard blood collection kit	Preservatives desired (identify preservation used). Refrigerate. **Can freeze.**
3. Stained clothing, fabric, etc.		As found	Registered mail Federal Express, United Parcel Service (UPS)	Use tag or mark directly on clothes. Type of specimens, date secured, name or initials	Each article wrapped separately and identified on outside of package. Place in strong box placed to prevent shifting of contents	If wet when found, dry by hanging. USE NO HEAT TO DRY. Avoid direct sunlight while drying. Use no preservatives

Table XII (Continued)

Specimen	Amount Desired		Send By	Identification	Wrapping and Packing	Remarks
	Standard	Evidence				
Bullets (not cartridges)		All found	Registered mail	Initials on base.	Pack tightly in cotton or soft paper in pill, match or powder box. Label outside of box as to contents	Unnecessary handling obliterates marks
Cartridges (live ammunition)		All found	UPS or Federal Express. Cannot be sent by U.S. Mail	Initials on outside of case near bullet end	Same as above	
Cartridge cases (shells)		All	Registered mail	Initials preferably on inside near open end and or on outside near open end	Same as above	
Charred or burned documents		All	Registered mail	On outside of container indicate fragile nature of evidence, date obtained, name or initials	Pack in rigid container between layers of cotton	Added moisture, with atomizer or otherwise, not recommended
Check (fraudulent)		All	Registered mail	See Anonymous Letters	See Anonymous Letters	Advise what parts questioned or known. Furnish physical description of subject
Check protector, rubber stamp and/ or date stamp known standards (Note: send actual device when possible)	Obtain several copies in full word-for-word order of each questioned check-writer impression. If unable to forward rubber stamps, prepare numerous samples with different degrees of pressure		Registered mail	Place name or initials, date, name of make and model, etc., on sample impressions	See Anonymous Letters	Do not disturb inking mechanisms on printing devices

Table XII (Continued)

| Specimen | Amount Desired | | Send By | Identification | Wrapping and Packing | Remarks |
	Standard	Evidence				
Clothing	Entire garment or other cloth item	All	Registered mail, Federal Express or UPS	Mark directly on garment or use string tag. Type of evidence, name or initials, date	Each article individually wrapped with identification written on outside of package. Place in strong container	Leave clothing whole. Do not cut out stains. If wet, hang in room to dry before packing
Codes, ciphers and foreign language material		All	Registered mail	Same as Anonymous Letters	Same as Anonymous Letters	Furnish pertinent background and technical information
Drugs:						
1. Liquids		All	Registered mail, UPS or Air Express	Affix label to bottle in which found including name or initials and date	If bottle has no stopper, transfer to glass-stoppered bottle and seal with adhesive tape	Mark "Fragile." Determine alleged normal use of drug and if prescription, check with druggist for supposed ingredients
2. Powders, pills and solids		All to 30 gm	Registered mail, UPS or Air Express	On outside of pillbox, name or initials and date	Seal to prevent any loss by use of tape	
Dynamite and other Explosives	(Contact FBI Explosives Unit for instructions)					
Fibers	Entire garment or other cloth item	All	Registered mail	On outside of sealed container or on object to which fibers are adhering	Folder paper or pill-box. Seal edges and openings with tape	Do not place loose in envelope

Table XII (Continued)

| Specimen | Amount Desired | | Send By | Identification | Wrapping and Packing | Remarks |
	Standard	Evidence				
Firearms		All	Registered mail, UPS or Federal Express	Mark inconspicuously as if it were your own. String tag gun, noting complete description on tag. Investigative notes should reflect how and where gun marked	Wrap in paper and identify contents of packages. Place in cardboard box or wooden box	Unload all weapons before shipping. Keep from rusting. See Ammunition, if applicable
Flash paper	One sheet	All to 5 sheets	Contact FBI Document Section for Instructions	Initials and date	Individual polyethylene envelopes double wrapped in manila envelopes. Inner wrapper sealed with paper tape	Fireproof, place in vented location away from any other combustible materials, and if feasible, place in water tight container immersed in water. Mark inner wrapper "Flash Paper." "Flammable"
Fuse (safety)	(Contact FBI Explosives Unit for complete instructions)					
Gasoline	500 ml	All to 500 ml	Contact FBI Chemistry Unit for instructions	On outside of all-metal container, label with type of material, name or initials, and date	Metal container packed in wooden box	Fireproof container
Gems		All	Registered mail insured	On outside of container	Use jeweler's box or place in cotton in pillbox	

Specimen	Amount Desired			Send By	Identification	Wrapping and Packing	Remarks
	Standard	Evidence					
General unknown							
1. Solids (nonhazardous)	500 gm	All to 500 gm		Registered mail	Name or initials, date on outside of sealed container	Same as Drugs	If item is suspected of being a hazardous material, treat as such and contact FBI Explosives Unit for shipping instructions
2. Liquids (nonhazardous)	500 ml	All to 500 ml		Registered mail	Same as for Liquid Drugs	Same as Drugs	Same as above
Glass fragments		All		Registered mail, UPS or Air Express	Adhesive tape on each piece. Name or initials and date on tape. Separate questioned and known	Wrap each piece separately in cotton. Pack in strong box to prevent shifting and breakage. Identify contents	Avoid chipping and mark "Fragile"
Glass particles	All of bottle or headlight. Small piece of each broken pane	All		Registered mail	Name or initials, date on outside of sealed container	Place in pillbox, plastic or glass vial; seal and protect against breakage	Do not use envelopes
Glass wool insulation	1″ mass from each suspect area	All		Registered mail	Name or initials, date on outside of sealed container	Sealed container	
Gunpowder residues							
1. Cotton applicator swabs with plastic shafts (**Do not use wood shafts**)		All		Registered mail	On outside of container, date and name or initials. Label as to name of person and which hand	Place swabs in plastic containers	Do not use glass containers
2. On cloth		All		Registered mail			

Table XII (Continued)

| Specimen | Amount Desired | | Send By | Identification | Wrapping and Packing | Remarks |
	Standard	Evidence				
Hair	Dozen or more full-length hairs from different parts of head and/or body	All	Registered mail	On outside of container. Type of material, date and name or initials	Folded paper or pill-box. Seal edges and openings with tape	Do not place loose in envelope
Insulation (see Glass wool insulation)						
Handwriting and hand printing, known standards	Obtain several samples in full word-for-word order from dictation, including some not commonly used	All	Registered mail	Name or initials, date, from whom obtained, and voluntary statement should be included in appropriate place	Same as Anonymous Letters	
Matches	One to two books of paper. One full box of wood	All	UPS or Federal Express	On outside of container. Type of material, date and name or initials	Metal container and packed in larger package to prevent shifting. Matches in box or metal container packed to prevent friction between matches	Keep away from fire, "Keep away from fire" label
Medicines	(See Drugs)					
Metal	One pound	All to one pound	Registered mail, UPS or Air Express	On outside of container. Type of material, date and name or initials	Use paper boxes or containers. Seal and use strong paper or wooden box	Melt number, heat treatment, and other specifications of foundry if available. Keep from rusting

| Specimen | Amount Desired | | Send By | Identification | Wrapping and Packing | Remarks |
	Standard	Evidence				
Oil	250 ml together with specifications	All to 250 ml	UPS	Same as above	Metal container with tight screw top. Pack in strong box using excelsior or similar material	DO NOT USE DIRT OR SAND FOR PACKING MATERIAL. Keep away from fire
Obliterated eradicated, or indented writing		All	Registered mail	Same as Anonymous Letters	Same as Anonymous Letters	Advise whether bleaching or staining methods may be used. Avoid folding
Organs of the body		200 gm of each organ	UPS, Air Express, or Register Airmail special delivery	On outside of container. Victim's name, date of death, date of autopsy, name of doctor, name or initials	Plastic or glass containers. Metal lids must have liners	"Fragile" label. Keep cool. Send autopsy report. Add no preservatives to the organs. Use dry ice on the package
Paint:						
1. Liquid	Original unopened container up to 1 gallon if possible	All to 1/4 pint	Registered mail, UPS or Air Express	On outside of container. Type of material, origin if known, date, name or initials	Friction-top paint can or large-mouth, screw-top jars. If glass, pack to prevent breakage. Use heavy corrugated paper or wooden box	
2. Solid (paint chips) or scrapings)	At least 1/2 sq. inch of solid, with all layers represented	All. If on small object send object	Registered mail, UPS or Air Express	Same as above	If small amount, round pillbox or small glass vial with screw top. Seal to prevent leakage. Envelopes not satisfactory. Do not pack in cotton	Avoid contact with adhesive materials. Wrap so as to protect smear

| Specimen | Amount Desired | | Send By | Identification | Wrapping and Packing | Remarks |
	Standard	Evidence				
Plaster casts of tire treads and shoe prints	Send in shoes and tires of suspects. Photographs and sample impressions are usually not suitable for comparison	All shoe prints; entire circumference of tires	Registered mail, UPS or Air Express	On back before plaster hardens. Location date, and name or initials	Wrap in paper and cover with suitable packing material to prevent breakage. Do not wrap bags	Use "Fragile" label. Mix approximately four pounds of plaster to quart water. Allow casts to cure (dry) before wrapping
Pornographic Materials		All	Registered mail, UPS or Air Express	Same as Anonymous Letters	Same as Anonymous Letters	Mark **inner** wrapping "OBSCENE," advise if evidence should be treated for latent fingerprints
Powder patterns	(See Gunpowder Residues)					
Rope, twine, and cordage	One yard or amount available	All	Registered mail	On tag or container. Type of material, date, name or initials	Wrap securely	
Saliva samples	1.5″ diameter stain in center of filter paper	All	Registered mail	On outside envelope and on filter paper put type of sample, name of donor, date of collection and collector's initials or name	Seal in envelope	Stain should be circled in pencil for identification. Filter paper available from hospitals and drug stores. Allow to dry
Safe insulation	Sample all damaged areas	All	Registered mail, UPS or Air Express	On outside of container. Type of material, date, name or initials	Use containers, such as pillbox, or plastic vial. Seal to prevent any loss	Avoid use of glass containers and envelopes
Shoe print lifts (impressions on hard surfaces)	Photograph before making of dust impression	All	Registered mail	On lifting tape or paper attached to tape. Name or initials and date	Prints in dust are easily damaged. Fasten print or lift to bottom of box so that nothing will rub	Always secure crime scene area until shoe prints or tire treads are located and preserved against it

Specimen	Amount Desired			Send By	Identification	Wrapping and Packing	Remarks
	Standard	Evidence					
Soils and minerals	Samples from areas near pertinent spot		All	Registered mail	On outside of container. Type of material, date, name or initials	Pillbox or plastic vial	Avoid glass containers and envelope
Tools			All	Registered mail, UPS or Air Express	On tools use string tag. Type of tool, identifying number, date, name or initials	Wrap each tool in paper. Use strong cardboard or wooden box with tools packed to prevent shifting	
Toolmarks	Send in the tool. If impractical, make several impressions on similar materials as evidence using entire marking area of tool		All	Registered mail, UPS or Air Express	On object or on tag attached to or an opposite end from where toolmarks appear. Name or initials and date	After marks have been protected with soft paper, wrap in strong wrapping paper, place in strong box, and pack to prevent shifting	
Typewriting, known standards	Obtain at least 1 copy in full word-for-word order of questioned typewriting		All	Registered mail	Place name or initials, date, serial number, name of make and model etc., on specimens	Same as Anonymous Letters	Examine ribbon for evidence of questioned message thereon
Urine	Preferably all urine voided over a period of 24 hours		All	Registered mail	On outside on container. Type of material, name of material, name of subject date taken, name or initials	Bottle surrounded with absorbent material to prevent breakage. Strong cardboard or wooden box	Use any clean bottle with leak-proof stopper

Table XII (Continued)

Specimen	Amount Desired		Send By	Identification	Wrapping and Packing	Remarks
	Standard	Evidence				
Vaginal samples						
1. Slides (microscope)		Minimum of two slides	Registered mail	On outside envelope and on filter paper put type of sample, name of donor, date of collection and collector's name or initials	Use commercial slide box	Slide box available at hospitals. Doctor should not fix slides. No cover slips. Air dry
2. Swabs	Two unstained swabs from same package as stained.	Minimum of two swabs	Registered mail	Same as above	Seal in envelope	Allow swabs to dry before packaging
Water	2 liters	2 liters	Registered mail	Same as Urine	Same as Urine	Same as Urine
Wire (See also toolmarks.)	Three feet. (Do not kink.)	All. (Do not kink.)	Registered mail	On label or tab. Type of material, date, name or initials	Wrap securely	Do not kink wire
Wood	One foot or amount available.	All	Registered mail	Same as above	Wrap securely	

INDEX

THRASONIC

Thrasonic is from Thraso, a swaggering bully and bragging soldier in Terence's play, *The Eunuch*. Hence, thrasonical means swaggering, bullying, vainglorious, and boastful.

a thrasonic air

THRINACIAN

Thrinacian refers to the sacred cattle of Hyperion, the father of Helios and the precursor of Apollo the sun-god. These flocks of oxen and sheep were tended on the island of Thrinacia (Trinacria, or Sicily) by Hyperion's daughters, Lampetia and Phaethusa, and could not be violated nor killed for food, however grievous the hunger of any voyagers to the island; if they were, destruction was sure to fall on the impious. When adverse winds detained Ulysses and his men there, famine drove the crew to slaughter some of the cattle during Ulysses' absence. Though they vainly endeavored to exculpate themselves by offering a portion to the owner in propitiation, the hides crept along the ground and the joints of meat bellowed on the roasting spits. When they left Thrinacia, their vessel was demolished by a storm and all aboard were lost except Ulysses.

as untouchable as the Thrinacian flocks

THRYM

Thrym, in Scandinavian mythology, is the giant who fell in love with Freyja and devised a theft in the hope of receiving her hand as a reward for returning the stolen object. He hid under Jotunheim the hammer of Thor, Mjoelnir, a boomerang type of mallet which, however far it was cast, never became lost, for it always returned to the hand that had thrown it. In order to retrieve it, Thor donned the goddess's attire. When Thrym handed it to him as a wedding present, Thor slew him and all the tribe of giants with it.

as light-fingered as Thrym

THUCYDIDES

Thucydides (c. 460-400 B.C.) was the Athenian writer whose *History of the Peloponnesian Wars* was called by its author "a possession for all time" and has ever since been admitted to be one of the greatest historical works of all time. In a condensed, direct and graphic style it tells of the dramatic struggle between Athens and Sparta for supremacy. Seeing a causal connection between events, the author wrote with exemplary fairness and a sound scientific method. The *History* is distinguished by the forceful inclusion of speeches between the principal historical characters of the day, who debate the political reasons for and against a particular course of action.

Thucydidean fairness of judgment

THULE

Thule, or Ultima Thule, was a vaguely defined region north of Britain, and discovered by the Greek voyager, Pytheas of Massilia (Marseilles), who so named it. To the ancients it represented the most extreme and northernmost end of the earth. Its actual location has been disputed, and various identifications link it to Iceland, Norway, the Shetland islands, and the Orkneys. In literature, and metaphorically, it signifies some far-away objective or goal, often unattainable and purely visionary.

the Ultima Thule of his imagination

THUMB, TOM

Tom Thumb is the name of a diminutive person celebrated in the legendary history of England of the time of King Arthur. He is said to have been buried at Lincoln, where a little blue flagstone was long shown as his monument. His diminutive stature (he was only an inch in height) enabled him to perform marvelous exploits, including riding in a horse's ear. The name was later used by a midget, Charles Stratton (1838-1883), exhibited by P. T. Barnum in his famous circus.

an incredibly tiny Tom Thumb

THYESTES

Thyestes, a son of Pelops and Hippodamia, was the brother of Atreus, with whose wife, Aerope, he committed adultery. To avenge this act, Atreus invited Thyestes to a feast at which he made him innocently eat the flesh of his own son, and when Thyestes learned the awful truth of his cannibal meal he consulted an oracle to learn how he might avenge himself. Having been told that offspring by his own daughter, Pelopia, should avenge him, he had incestuous relations with her, begetting Aegisthus who afterward slew Atreus and his son, Agamemnon.

vengeful as Thyestes

THYIA

Thyia, from the Greek root meaning "to rage frantically," was a daughter of Castalius and became by Apollo the mother of Delphus. Said to have been the first to have sacrificed to Dionysus, she established and celebrated orgies in his name. From her the Athenian women who went annually to Mt. Parnassus to attend the orgies in the god's honor received the name of Thyiades, which name has come to signify the violence and turbulence of drunken and roistering women.

as frenzied by drink as Thyia

THYRSIS

Thyrsis is the name of a herdsman in the Idylls of Theocritus, and of a shepherd in Vergil's seventh Eclogue, where he has a poetical contest with Corydon, another pastoral swain. Hence, in modern usage the name connotes any shepherd or rustic.

bucolic as Thyrsis

TIAMAT

Tiamat, in the Assyro-Babylonian Creation Epic and mythology, is a personification of primeval chaos in the form of marine waters. The wife of Apsu, another conception of shapeless disorder, she revolted against Marduk, the chief deity in that pantheon, and was destroyed by him. Her emblem was a dragon.

spreading confusion like Tiamat

TIBBS, BEAU

Beau Tibbs, a prominent character in Goldsmith's *Citizen of the World,* was a shabby-genteel fop and dandy, said by Hazlitt to be "the best comic sketch since the time of Addison — unrivaled in his finery, his vanity, and his poverty."

like Beau Tibbs, lavishes his little money on fine clothes

TIBERIAN

Tiberian refers to the reign and the character of Tiberius Claudius Nero Caesar, commonly known as Tiberius and emperor of Rome from 14 to 37 A.D. At first capable and beneficent, he became sullen and morose after Augustus, his step-father and predecessor on the throne, forced him to divorce his beloved wife, Vipsania Agrippina, in order to marry his own dissolute daughter, Julia (*q.v.*). After a seven year retirement on the island of Rhodes, he returned to Italy and was summoned to the throne on the death of Augustus. His character was now cruel, vicious, and tyrannical, and he was under the baleful influence of Sejanus (*q.v.*). After abolishing freedom in Rome and enslaving the senate, he withdrew to Capri, indulging his strong sensuality and practicing debauchery and astrology.

typical Tiberian despotism

TIBERINUS

Tiberinus was an ancient Italian king of Alba who was drowned in the river Albula and thereafter was revered as the god of the watercourse, the name of which was changed to Tiberis (Tiber) in his honor. In art he is represented as a reclining victor, crowned with laurel, holding a cornucopia and a rudder, and with the she-wolf and the infants Romulus and Remus by his side. He is also known under the cult-name Volturnus ("rolling"), and his festival of the Volturnalia was held on the 27th of August. After heavy rains the river frequently flooded, and it was called *flavus* by the Romans because of its muddy yellow color.

another Tiberinus, victim of a river

TIBULLAN

Tibullan refers to Albius Tibullus (60-19 B.C.), the Roman elegiac poet and friend of Horace. He wrote two books of poems addressed to his mistresses under the Greek pseudonyms of Delia and Nemesis. A gentle and melancholy genius, he dwelled on the themes of love, peace and rural simplicity. His work is marked by a quiet charm and tenderness, and absorbed in self-pity he frequently envisaged himself on the funeral pyre with his weeping and inconsolable friends forever bewailing him.

a Tibullan love for the countryside

TIDDLER, TOM

Tom Tiddler's Ground, in a child's game, is the space marked off for the chief player. He may be crowded off by any other player, who then has the right to the space. Hence, Tom Tiddler's ground means any place where the chance comer may take whatever he wishes with no one to question him.

quarreling endlessly over Tom Tiddler's ground, a futile argument

TIGLATH-PILESER

Tiglath-Pileser was the name of several kings of Assyria, of whom the first (1115-1102 B.C.) was renowned as a mighty hunter. Tiglath-Pileser III (or, according to others, IV), who reigned from 745 to 727 B.C., was the monarch who reduced Pekah, a king of Israel, to vassalage (2 *Kings*, xv, 29) and subjugated Samaria, putting it also under tribute. Defeating the Philistines, he captured the cities of Gaza and Damascus, and effectively controlled Babylon, too, by crushing a revolt there.

a Tiglath-Pileser exulting in power

TIKI

Tiki is the Polynesian and Maori god who is said to have created the first man. The name, hence, connotes an ancestor or progenitor. It also designates a wood or stone idol made in the likeness of man.

counts his forebears as far back as Tiki

TILBURINA

Tilburina, in Sheridan's play *The Critic,* is a young lady whose love-lorn ravings burlesque the sorrows of tragic heroines. The daughter of the governor of Tilbury Fort, she is "inconsolable to the minuet in *Ariadne.*"

a mawkish and lackadaisical Tilburina

TIM, TINY

Tiny Tim was the little crippled son of Bob Cratchit, in Dickens' *Christmas Carol,* whose childlike blessing, "God bless us every one!" as the preliminary to the Christmas dinner in the cheerful little home of the Cratchits, has become a part of the language.

tugging the heart-strings like Tiny Tim

TIMIAS

Timias, squire to Prince Arthur in Spenser's *Faerie Queene,* represents the spirit of chivalrous honor and generosity. Allegorically his affection for Belphoebe alludes to Sir Walter Raleigh's pretended admiration of Queen Elizabeth.

as courtly and gallant as Timias

TIMOLEON

Timoleon (died c. 337 B.C.) was the scion of a noble Corinthian family who loved liberty so passionately that he acquiesced in the murder of his own brother, Timophanes, when the latter endeavored to make himself tyrant of his native city. Exiled for his fratricide by the wrath of his family, he was sent to Sicily in command of a Greek force to repel the Carthaginians from that island. After a brilliant victory over the invaders, he proceeded to expel the tyrants from the other Greek city states of the island and to establish democracies instead.

a liberty-loving Timoleon

TIMON

Timon was a Greek misanthrope and sour cynic, notable in history for opposing and predicting ill of the schemes of Alcibiades, and in literature for his towering wrath and bitterness at mankind. In Shakespeare's *Timon* he is first the wealthy friend, lavishing gifts, generosity, and hospitality on his friends in his fortunate days, only to be incurably enraged and embittered when those same friends in his adversity were indifferent to his needs and forgetful of his generosity. He abjured the society of man, and, with only a faithful steward, lived in solitude. When he found a great hoard of gold, he gave some to Alcibiades, whom he hated, to use against the Athenians, whom he hated more, and the rest to his steward with directions to get out.

He never wished to see him again and destroyed himself in a passion of disappointment in the human race.

Timonian irony

TINTAGEL

Tintagel is the storied castle situated on the coast of Cornwall. Said to have been the work of giants, it was renowned in romance as the birthplace of King Arthur and the residence of King Mark and Queen Isolde. Its walls were washed by the sea and behind it were extensive and beautiful meadows, forests abounding with game, and rivers filled with fish. The name conjures up thoughts of romance, idyllic scenery, abundance and legendary magic.

an estate by the sea as beautiful as Tintagel
visions of Tintagel

TINTORETTO

Tintoretto (1518-1594), whose real name was Jacopi Robusti, acquired his diminutive nickname from the fact that his father was a *tintore,* or "dyer." This gifted master of the Venetian school of painting was sent to Titian (*q.v.*) for art study in his youth, but returned home after ten days in the latter's studio, either because Titian was envious of his great originality or because Tintoretto's talent was already so far developed that there was nothing for the older artist to teach him. Aiming, as expressed in a motto over the entrance to his atelier, at an ideal combination of Michelangelo's design and Titian's coloring, Tintoretto executed numerous church murals, easel pictures, and portraits, among them the *Last Judgment,* the *Crucifixion, Ecce Homo, St. George and the Dragon,* and a *Self-Portrait.* The magnificent *Paradise,* which measured 74 ft. by 30 ft., was the largest painting ever done on canvas.

sublime as Tintoretto's Paradise

TIRESIAS

Tiresias was the renowned blind sooth-sayer of Thebes who played a prominent part in the mythical history of Greece. His blindness was said to have resulted from some offense which he inadvertently gave to Juno or Minerva, or from imprudently revealing to men things which the gods did not want them to know. After a preternaturally long life he retained his clairvoyance even in the lower world.

with Tiresian foreknowledge

TIRONIAN

Tironian is from Marcus Tullius Tiro, freedman of Cicero and his stenographer in the first century B.C. A man of highly cultivated intellect and amiable disposition, he was not only the great orator's amanuensis but his assistant in literary work as well. He was the inventor of an art of shorthand writing, called *notae Tironianae,* or "Tironian signs," that lasted over 1000 years and included over 5000 abbreviations.

an abbreviated Tironian hand

TISIPHONE

Tisiphone, a daughter of Nox (Night) and Acheron, the river of woe in the lower world, was one of the three Furies and a minister of the vengeance of the gods. She punished the wicked in Tartarus and, like her sisters, Alecto and Megaera, was armed with a lighted torch. Her head was wreathed with snakes and her manner was terrifying as she lashed out retribution with her whip.

exacted Tisiphonean vengeance
vindictive as Tisiphone

TITANIA

Titania is the wife of Oberon and the queen of the fairies in Shakespeare's *Midsummer-Night's Dream.* Since in his day it was believed that the fairies were the same as the nymphs of classical times, the attendants of Diana, the fairy queen was therefore the same as Diana, whom Ovid also calls Titania in his *Metamorphoses,* III, 173. The name evokes such ideas as daintiness and elfin charm.

a dainty Titania to dream about

TITANIC

Titanic is from the Titans, a legendary race of deities of prodigious size and invincible strength who attempted to overthrow the first ruler of the earth, Saturn, but were themselves overthrown by Zeus, his son, in a struggle in which the opposing forces tore up the earth and threw mountains at each other. Hence, the word means mighty, huge, gigantic, colossal.

tumbled and jumbled as in Titanic wars

TITHONUS

Tithonus, the brother of Priam, king of Troy, was loved by Aurora, the goddess of the dawn. She entreated the gods to make him immortal, but neglected to ask them to grant eternal youth as well. In consequence of this oversight he withered into a decrepit old man, and his name became proverbial for wizened senility. Aurora then changed him into a cicada, or grasshopper.

a wrinkled Tithonus of a dotard

TITIAN

Titian (1477-1576), or Tiziano Vecelli, the chief master of the Venetian school of art, painted simply, leaving out all unessentials and centering light on whatever he wished to emphasize in his subject. Achieving notable chiaroscuro, a blended pattern of light and dark, he was a supreme colorist, creating a tremendous single impression. The reddish-gold blondness of women's hair in his paintings has made of his name a byword in the English language to describe that shade today. Among his famous pictures are *The Assumption of the Virgin, Ecce Homo,* and the *Worship of Venus.*

> *a shade of hair borrowed from one of Titian's paintings*

TITMOUSE, MR. TITTLEBAT

Mr. Tittlebat Titmouse, the hero of Warren's *Ten Thousand a Year,* is a conceited linen-draper's shopman who inherits fraudulently an estate of 10,-000 pounds sterling a year. A vulgar, ignorant coxcomb, through the instrumentality of rascally attorneys he is exalted to the third heaven of English aristocracy, because of a defect in the pedigree of a worthier claimant.

> *another Tittlebat Titmouse, raised from ignoble obscurity to nouveau riche prominence*

TITUS VESPASIANUS

Titus Flavius Sabinus Vespasianus, Roman emperor from 79 to 81 A.D., was entrusted by his father, Vespasian, with the siege of Jerusalem, during which he showed great talents as a general, capturing the beleaguered city and sacking its Temple. Though in early life he had shown a dissolute character, on his accession to the throne he displayed great concern for the welfare of his people, earning for himself by his beneficence the sobriquet "Delight of Mankind." The Arch of Titus at the one end of the Forum commemorates his taking of Jerusalem, and during the first year of his reign occurred the catastrophic eruption of Vesuvius that buried Pompeii and Herculaneum. He also completed the great Flavian amphitheater, the so-called Colosseum, in Rome. His death was rumored to have been caused by poison administered by his brother and successor, Domitian.

> *like Titus, the darling of the people*

TITYRE-TU

A Tityre-tu was one of a class of roistering streetbullies and brawling idlers who swaggered about London by night in the reign of Charles II. They broke windows, upset sedans, beat up quiet citizens, and rudely caressed pretty women. Dissolute young men and wastrels, they took their name from the first line of Vergil's first Eclogue, *Tityre, tu patulae recubans sub tegmine fagi* ("Tityrus, you take your ease in the shade of a spreading beech-tree").

> *a night-prowler as boisterous as a Tityre-tu*

TITYRUS

Tityrus is a character in Vergil's first Eclogue. Borrowed from Greek literature, the name is a common one to denote a shepherd and rustic herdsman. Vergil's Tityrus is a freedman, and is thought to represent the poet himself. Indeed, Propertius calls him by that name in one of his Elegies. In Spenser's *Shepherd's Calendar,* Chaucer is affectionately commemorated under the name Tityrus.

> *a modern Tityrus with his pipe, whistling around the animal pens at dusk*

TITYUS

Tityus was a famous giant, the son of Jupiter and Terra (Earth). At Juno's suggestion he attempted to ravish Diana (Artemis), and for this crime he was tortured in the lower world by having two vultures or snakes feeding on his liver, which continued to grow so that they never consumed it or left him. As he lay there his body was so huge that it was said to cover nine acres of ground.

> *as vast as Tityus*
> *the gigantic body of a Tityus*

TLALOC

Tlaloc was the Aztec god of rain and thunder, identical with the Mayan Chac-Mool. His cult, one of the most ancient in Mexico, centered at the great pyramid of Tenochtitlan. In the month of "diminishing waters" he was propitiated by a procession of priests with music of flutes and trumpets. His victims, usually children or maidens gayly dressed and with brightly painted faces, were carried on plumed litters to be sacrificed on the mountains or in a whirlpool in the lake.

with the thunderous crash of a Tlaloc

TOBIT

Tobit, the pious Israelite of the Assyrian captivity in the apocryphal book of the Old Testament that bears his name, was sleeping one night outside the wall of his courtyard and was blinded by sparrows "muting warm dung into his eyes." His son, Tobias, was attacked on the Tigris by a fish, which jumped out of the water to assail him. Later Tobias married Sara, seven of whose previous fiancés had been successively carried off by the evil spirit Asmodeus. But the angel Azarias protected Tobias from Asmodeus, driving the demon into the extremity of Egypt and binding him there. Old Tobit was then cured of his blindness by applying to his eyes the gall of the fish that had attempted to devour his son. Rembrandt has done a painting of the Family of Tobias and the Angel.

cursed like Tobit by blindness

TOBY, UNCLE

Uncle Toby, the real hero of Sterne's novel, *The Life and Opinions of Tristram Shandy, Gent.,* is depicted as a retired captain who had been wounded at the battle of Namur and forced to withdraw from the service. He is remarkable for his kindness and benevolence, his bravery, gallantry and simplicity. His love interest in the Widow Wadman and his military tastes, habits, and discussions are forcibly presented, and it is thought that he was intended as a portrait of Sterne's father.

a courter of widows, like Uncle Toby

TODGERS, MRS. M.

Mrs. M. Todgers, a character in Dickens' *Martin Chuzzlewit,* is the proprietress of a "Commercial Boarding-House" in London. She has a "soft spot" for Mr. Pecksniff.

found a kindly Mrs. Todgers to indulge his rent arrears

TOLBOOTH

Tolbooth, the Edinburgh city jail demolished in 1817, was popularly known as "the heart of Midlothian," whence the title of one of Sir Walter Scott's romances. The English word *tolbooth* or *tollbooth* has come from it, and means a town hall or guildhall, especially the jail or prison in it.

detained in Tolbooth

TOLSTOI, LEO

Count Leo Tolstoi (1828-1910), Russian novelist and reformer, not only advocated but practiced the doctrine that manual labor, simple living, non-resistance, and poverty were the real virtues. So ardently did he believe this that he gave up a great estate in order to be without property. He held it a sin to be wealthy, and rejected all preachings and teachings except those of Christ himself. *War and Peace* and *Anna Karenina* are his finest novels.

a Tolstoi disciple

TOM O' BEDLAM

Tom o' Bedlam was a name formerly given to wandering mendicants discharged from the hospital of St. Mary of Bethlehem (Bedlam) in London on account of incurable lunacy, or because their cure was doubtful. They were licensed to beg.

> *aimless and empty-headed as Tom o' Bedlam*

TOM, UNCLE

Uncle Tom is the negro slave, faithful, pious, devoted to his "white folks," in Harriet Beecher Stowe's *Uncle Tom's Cabin.* Sold, Uncle Tom is so cruelly treated that he dies as a result. The story was a powerful bit of propaganda against slavery in America.

> *the Uncle Toms have joined the Uncle Remuses and the Old Black Joes*

TOODLE, MR.

Mr. Toodle, in Dickens, *Dombey and Son,* is the stoker-husband of Polly Toodle, Paul Dombey's nurse, and the sire of Robin Toodle, known as "the Biler." His hair and whiskers were deepened by smoke and coal-dust, and cinders could be combed out of his beard. His canvas working suit was besmeared with oil and reeked of half-slaked ashes.

> *as grimy as Mr. Toodle*

TOOTS, MR.

Mr. Toots is an innocent, honest, and warm-hearted character, in Dickens' *Dombey and Son,* "than whom there were few better fellows in the world." His favorite saying is, "It's of no consequence," and he is a swain hopelessly in love with Florence Dombey. Her wealthy, shy, dull, and ingenuous friend, he does not succeed in winning her.

> *a suitor as dull as Mr. Toots*

TOPHET

Tophet was a place outside Jerusalem in the valley of Hinnon, where fires were kept burning continuously for the destruction of rubbish. Hence, it is sometimes used to refer to the everlasting fires of hell. In Tophet also, the idolatrous Jews worshiped the fire-gods (*Jeremiah,* vii, 31-32).

> *Tophet, hence, and black Gehenna called the type of hell*

TOPSY

Topsy, the little black girl in Harriet Beecher Stowe's *Uncle Tom's Cabin,* is the single comedy touch in the book, furnishing all the humor and some of the pathos of the story, but universally known for her comic but significant statement that she "just growed." The name is now applied to any girl-child who has come well toward her teens without special individualized care or training, by "just growin'!"

> *reform bill will take care of the Topsys*

TORQUEMADA

Tomás de Torquemada (1420-1498), Spanish Dominican monk, was the organizer of the infamous Spanish Inquisition, of which he was appointed Grand Inquisitor. This notorious "Dog of the Lord" became proverbial for his severe judgments and fiendish tortures, burning 10,220 persons and condemning 6860 others to be burned in effigy during his 18 years of office, albeit he was so austere and modest personally that he refused to accept the degree of Doctor of Theology, the highest prize in his order. Intolerant of Jews, Moors, and backsliding Christians alike, he was constantly alert with a fiery zeal for persecution, and the name of Torquemada stands for intolerance of the most narrow, despotic, and fanatical type.

> *a Torquemada, aglow with a cruel passion for exacting repentance*

TOSCA, LA

La Tosca, heroine of Sardou's brutal melodrama and of Puccini's derivative opera, is a famous singer who is passionately jealous of her lover, Mario Cavaradossi, a revolutionist in Rome during Napoleonic times. Scarpia, profligate chief of police, takes advantage of his knowledge of her character in order to force her to yield herself to him on promise of signing a safe conduct for herself and her trapped lover. The lecherous roué, dressed in formal attire of velvet knee-breeches and black silk stockings for his rendezvous with her, signs a genuine execution order for Cavaradossi, telling Tosca that it will only be a mock shooting. Tosca then stabs him to death to spare herself his odious attentions, and rushes to the Castel Sant' Angelo just as her lover falls dead under a volley of gunfire. As Scarpia's henchmen arrive to arrest her for the murder of their double-dealing chief, Tosca hurls herself from the parapet of the fortress in which her patriotic lover had been immured.

double-dealing as Tosca

TOTTLE, WATKINS

Watkins Tottle is a bachelor of some fifty years, in Dickens' *Tales*. Haunted all his life by the idea of matrimony, he combines "strong uxorious inclinations with an unparalleled degree of anti-connubial timidity." Clean, plump, and rosy, he has a formal manner and a "carriage like a kitchen poker." He lives on a small annuity, which he receives in periodical payments on alternate Mondays, running himself out after the expiration of the first week "as regularly as an eight-day clock."

as shy with girls as Watkins Tottle

TOUCHSTONE

Touchstone is a philosophical professional clown who accompanies Rosalind in the Forest of Arden, in Shakespeare's *As You Like It*. He is a facet-

ious buffoon whose mouth is filled with quips, wit, and repartee, very often delivered extempore.

as droll and humorous as Touchstone

TOULOUSE-LAUTREC

Henri Marie Raymond de Toulouse-Lautrec Monfa (1864-1901) was the grotesque and misshapen French artist who spent his interest in dissipation and in recording in art the lives and characters of dissipated people. Famous for such paintings as *Le Promenoir* and *Les Femmes Qui Dansent*, he was an outstanding designer of posters and a lithographer as well.

a deformed Toulouse-Lautrec at his easel

TOX, MISS

Miss Tox is a little, lean old maid in Dickens' *Dombey and Son*. "The very pink of general propitiation and politeness," she exhibits her "respectability" by being ever ready with an appropriate allusion to ancient mythology.

"I do not think, I will tell you candidly, that Wickham is a person of very cheerful spirit, or what one could call a —."

"A daughter of Momus," Miss Tox softly suggested. (*Dombey and Son*, ch. viii)

another Miss Tox at finding the exact word for you

TRADDLES, THOMAS

Thomas Traddles, in Dickens' *David Copperfield*, is the hero's simple and honest friend whose "porcupine hair" was brushed so extremely upright that it gave him an expression of perpetual surprise. It was so buoyant that even if he carried a half-hundredweight on his head all the way to Putney, it would be up again the minute the load was off. In school days the whipping boy of the class and caned daily, he loved to draw skeletons in order to remind himself that all punishment must ultimately cease. His talent for cultivating difficulties led him, as a poor lawyer in later life, to marry one of the ten daughters of an indigent curate.

as resilient as Thomas Traddles's hair

TRAJAN, MARCUS ULPIUS

Marcus Ulpius Trajan, Roman emperor from 98 to 117 A.D., was of Spanish birth and trained to arms, serving with distinction in the East and Germany. His great accomplishment was in extending the frontiers of the Roman empire to include Dacia (modern Rumania) and Parthia to the northwest of Persia. His victories over Decebalus of Dacia are commemorated in the triumphal column in Rome with its pictorial bas-reliefs of the war spiraling up to the top of the shaft. A strong and laborious man, simple in his mode of life, he contributed to the beauty of Rome several impressive structures, including the Basilica Ulpia, the Ulpian public library, and the Forum Trajanum.

the conquering instincts of a Trajan

TRASIMENE LAKE

The Trasimene Lake between Chiusi and Perugia in Etruria was the scene of a clever ambuscade in which Hannibal trapped the Roman army under Flaminius in B.C. 217. The Carthaginian forces had occupied the heights overlooking the narrow road that followed the shore, and as the Romans marched into the snare their visibility was impaired by fogs and early morning mists. So fierce was the fighting that as Flaminius's troops were forced into the water and slaughtered there by Hannibal's cavalry nobody heard a great earthquake that devastated northern Italy. Some 15,000 Romans were slaughtered, only a few escaping by hacking their way over the heights to the rear.

ensnared as hopelessly as those at the Trasimene Lake

TRAVIATA, LA

La Traviata ("the woman gone astray") is the heroine of Verdi's opera of the same name, based on Dumas's *Camille*. A beautiful courtesan, she abandons the gay, immoral life of Paris for a young lover, Alfred Germont, with whom she lives in idyllic content in the country until his father implores her secretly not to spoil the youth's career. She leaves for Paris in Alfred's absence, where, heart-broken and misunderstood by the young man, she is publicly insulted by him. When he learns the truth behind her noble rejection of him, he rushes to her deathbed as she expires of consumption.

the unhappy Traviata of the community

TRICOTEUSES, LES

Les Tricoteuses ("the women knitting") were female insurgents who frequented the tribunals and places of execution during the French Revolution, knitting calmly and apathetically while they watched the guillotine doing its bloody work. In *A Tale of Two Cities* Dickens has given a superb literary portrait of such a woman in the person of Mme. Thérèse Defarge. The bloodthirsty wife of a Parisian wine seller, she works into her constant knitting a secret record to be used against the aristocrats.

hard-hearted and merciless as Les Tricoteuses

TRILBY

Trilby is the heroine of George du Maurier's novel of the same name. Professionally a laundress and model of the Parisian art-studios, she becomes famous as a singer while under the hypnotic influence of the sinister Svengali, an erratic Jewish musician whose power over her is ultimately broken by her lover. She was also noted for her beautiful figure, and the name Trilby is still used to connote a dainty and tiny foot.

a dainty Trilby of a foot

TRIM, CORPORAL

Corporal Trim, in Sterne's *Tristram Shandy,* is Uncle Toby's faithful military attendant. He is noteworthy for his fidelity, affection, respectfulness, and garrulity.

a loquacious Corporal Trim to companion him

TRIMALCHIO

Trimalchio, in the *Satyricon* of Petronius Arbiter (*q.v.*), is a wealthy and tasteless *nouveau riche* who gives a fantastically sumptuous dinner party. A vulgar, though good-natured parvenu, he makes a grotesquely ostentatious display of his riches and of the art treasures he has collected without having the faintest conception of their intrinsic values. His confused notions of mythology descend into illiteracy, as he imagines Hannibal attending the siege of Troy, Cassandra (instead of Medea) gory from the infanticide of her own children, and Daedalus penning Niobe in the Trojan horse. As he advances in inebriation he becomes absurdly maudlin in discussing his will and his funeral wishes. He is a perfect type of the flashy and uncultured parvenu, fancying himself a connoisseur of elegance.

an upstart and the Trimalchio of the town's society

TRINCULO

Trinculo is a drunken sailor and jester in the train of the King of Naples, in Shakespeare's *Tempest.* Along with Stephano and Caliban, he is made the butt of Ariel's tricks. He is dishonored and discommoded by the loss of his bottle in a horse-pool.

as witty as Trinculo when inebriated

TRIPTOLEMUS

Triptolemus was the son of Celeus and Metanira of Eleusis. When Demeter came to them in her sorrowing search for her lost daughter, Proserpina, she rewarded their kind hospitality by holding their child, Triptolemus, in the fire to purge him of mortality and make him immortal. The favorite of the goddess of the earth and its fertility, he was the inventor of the plow and agriculture, and of civilization which is the result of it. The great hero of the Eleusinian Mysteries, he was given a chariot with winged dragons, and seeds of wheat. In this vehicle he rode over the earth, acquainting mankind with the blessings of agriculture. In art he is represented as a youthful hero, holding in his hand a sceptre and corn ears.

needs Triptolemus to teach him how to run his farm

TRISMEGISTUS

Trismegistus, or "thrice greatest," is an epithet of Hermes, especially as identified with the Egyptian god Thoth, regarded as the originator of hieroglyph writing, the occult and mystical sciences, art, magic, alchemy, music, astrology, and religion.

a Trismegistus, learned in mysticism

TRISSOTIN

Trissotin ("thrice-foolish" or "blockhead") is the name of a pedantic poet and coxcomb in Molière's comedy *Les Femmes Savantes* ("The Learned Ladies"). Under this character the author satirized the Abbé Cotin, a personage who affected to unite in himself the inconsistent characters of a writer of poems of gallantry and of a powerful preacher.

a fool like Trissotin

TRISTAN

Tristan was a gallant knight of King Arthur's Round Table, beloved of Isolde, the Cornish King Mark's bride. His story of a hopeless love is one of the most romantic and beautiful of the tales built around that theme, and is used by Wagner in his opera *Tristan and Isolde,* in Tennyson's *Idylls of the King,* and by A. E. Robinson in his supremely poetic version of the story, *Tristan.* The illicit love, the treachery of a malicious confidant, the discovery by Mark, the death scene of Tristan and the "Love-death" of Isolde animate the most beautiful of Wagnerian music. Tristan suggests love, renunciation, tragedy, tenderness.

another tragic Tristan situation

TRITON

Triton, the son of Neptune, is pictured usually with the head and trunk of a man and the tail of a fish, and is usually accompanied by sea deities and attendants upon the sea gods. He rises from the sea blowing on a trumpet of conch shell, with the sound of which he raises or calms the waves as he pleases.

Triton loosing the waves

TRIVIA

Trivia, in Roman mythology, is a name given to Diana-Artemis-Hecate (*qq.v.*) in her character as the three-faced goddess worshiped at places where there was a conjuncture of three roads (*trivium*), a crossroads. From this word for a meeting-place of streets is derived the meaning "common," hence "unimportant," as found in our word *trivial.*

the Trivia of the intersection

TROGLODYTAE

Troglodytae ("cave dwellers") was a name given by the Greek geographers to the savage and uncivilized peoples who lived in caverns on the west coast of the Red Sea, along the shores of Upper Egypt and Aethiopia, and on the banks of the Danube in Moesia. The name, uncapitalized, has since been given loosely to any person living in primitive, coarse, brutal, or degraded fashion. Figuratively, it connotes a hermit, anyone living in seclusion and unacquainted with the affairs of the world.

a recluse like the Troglodytae

TROILUS AND CRESSIDA

Troilus is a stock example of the faithful lover, and Cressida of the impure coquette. A Trojan prince, Troilus wins Cressida through the procurer's services of her uncle, Pandarus (hence, the word *pander,* originally spelled *pandar*), but after a passionate love affair with the young Trojan, Cressida joins her father, Calchas, a renegade, in the Greek camp, where she becomes the mistress of Diomedes. Informed by Ulysses of her unchastity and faithlessness, the disillusioned Troilus curses her uncle, Pandarus. A post-classical story, it was told by Chaucer and in Shakespeare's play of the same name.

as faithful as Troilus
as wanton as Cressida

TROJAN

The Trojans, the early defenders of Troy in the Trojan War (1184 B.C.), were marked by their strength, patriotism, courage, loyalty, energy and spirit, giving rise to the phrase, "worked like a Trojan."

Trojan horse: See Greeks bearing gifts a very Trojan for accomplishment

---

TROPHONIUS

Trophonius was the son of legendary Erginus of Boeotia, Greece. He and his brother, Agamedes, built the temple of

Apollo at Delphi and the treasury of Hyrieus there. They subsequently robbed the treasury periodically by means of a movable stone which they left in the wall (v. *Rhampsinitus*). When Agamedes was caught in a trap that had been set, Trophonius cut off his head to preserve their incognito. He then was swallowed up in the earth at Lebadia, where he was consulted as an oracle in a subterraneous chamber at night. Since his suppliants always emerged from his cave pale and dispirited, persons of a melancholic or grave aspect were proverbially said to have consulted Trophonius.

as dejected as a client of Trophonius

TROTSKY, LEON

Leon Trotsky (1877-1940) was the Russian revolutionist and Communist leader who, after an exile in Siberia, escaped to England and joined Lenin in the plot that was to hatch in the overthrow of the Czarist regime in Russia. Becoming people's commissar for foreign affairs in the newly organized Soviet government in 1917, he organized labor battalions to improve the economic life of his country. Defeated by Stalin for control of the party after the death of Lenin, he was banished, and escaped to Mexico where he was subsequently murdered. He was the author of *The Defense of Terrorism* and *A History of the Russian Revolution*.

the political machinations of a Trotsky

TROTTER, JOB

Job Trotter, in Dickens' *Pickwick Papers*, is the servant of Alfred Jingle. His tears flow so profusely that Sam Weller thinks he must have "a main in his head as is always turned on."

as lachrymose as Job Trotter

TROTWOOD, BETSY

Betsy Trotwood, the temperamental aunt of David in Dickens' *David Copperfield*, was abrupt, severe, eccentric, but kind-hearted. She had certain persons she befriended and dominated in gruff kindliness, and included young David, whom she obstinately called Trotwood, her nearest approach to the Betsy Trotwood she had determined he should be. Terse, ogreish, generous, she is a memorable portrait in the book.

a regular Betsy Trotwood of an aunt

TRULLIBER, PARSON

Parson Trulliber, in Fielding's *Adventures of Joseph Andrews*, is a fat clergyman noted for being ignorant, selfish, and slothful. A coarse, bigoted, brutal, and uncharitable curate, he is the antithesis of the same novel's Parson Adams.

a pastor as unworthy as Parson Trulliber

TRUNNION, COMMODORE

Commodore Hawser Trunnion is an eccentric retired naval veteran and seadog in Smollett's novel *The Adventures of Peregrine Pickle*. Withdrawn from the service because of injuries received in engagements, he yet retains his rigid nautical and military habits. He keeps garrison in a house which is defended by a ditch and entered through a drawbridge, forcing his servants to sleep in hammocks and to take turns on watch all the year round. Lieutenant Jack Hatchway is his attendant and boon companion.

as much a victim of habit as Hawser Trunnion

TSCHAIKOVSKY

Peter Ilitch Tschaikovsky (1840-1893) is a name that has become a popular byword for music that is tempestuously passionate, intense and broodingly melancholy. Profoundly subjective, his haunting melodies often mirror his own experiences in life. A platonic friendship with Mme. von Meck, a wealthy widow and benefactress whom he never wished formally to meet and to whom he never spoke except in correspondence, is characteristic of his sensitive psychology. *Romeo and Juliet*, a tone poem, his 4th, 5th and 6th (Pathetique) Symphonies, and his piano concerto are his most abidingly popular works, though several operas and ballet suites (the *Nutcracker* and *Swan Lake*) are still widely played. A Slavic spirit pervades his work.

a Tschaikovskian mood of despair tinged with Tschaikovskian melancholy

TUBAL-CAIN

Tubal-cain, the son of Lamech and Zillah, was a pioneer in brass and iron work, according to *Genesis,* iv, 22. "The forger of every cutting instrument," he was the teacher of artificers in those metals as well. He may have been the progenitor of an ancient people whose chief industry was the production of vessels and instruments of bronze and iron. Philo of Byblus says that he also discovered enchantment and sorcery.

the Tubal-cain of the forge

TUCK, FRIAR

Friar Tuck, one of the Merry Men of Sherwood Forest, Robin Hood's sworn friends, outlaws all, became Robin Hood's chaplain, and is ordinarily pictured as pudgy, paunchy, self-indulgent, humorous, wearing a russet Franciscan habit tucked in under his red-corded, gold-tasseled girdle, red stockings, and carrying a wallet. The tucked-in robe made Robin Hood call him Friar Tuck, and he gaily made him solemnize every occasion that called for a ceremony.

found the Friar Tuck of the village

TULKINGHORN, MR.

Mr. Tulkinghorn is a discreet, elderly bachelor lawyer, in Dickens' *Bleak House.* Numbering only noble families among his clientele, he is the personal solicitor of Sir Leicester Dedlock (*q.v.*) and is in possession of family secrets which are of no importance to anyone, and which he never divulges.

as cautious and circumspect as Mr. Tulkinghorn

TULLIA

Tullia was the name of the two daughters of Servius Tullius, sixth king of early Rome, the elder being called Tullia Major, the younger Tullia Minor. The elder, the ambition-crazed Lady Macbeth of classical legend, conspired with her sister's husband to advance their rank, and he, Tarquinius Superbus (*q.v.*), consented to her plans to do away with their respective spouses and merge their strength in their drive for power. This achieved, Tullia Major and Tarquinius conspired to oust the former's own father from the throne and to usurp it for themselves. When Servius Tullius had been murdered by his patricidal daughter and son-in-law, his body was flung into the street where Tullia drove her chariot exultantly over it, splattering herself with his blood. The street was thereafter known as *Vicus Sceleratus,* or Wicked Street.

a merciless Tullia, mad for power

TULLIANUM

The Tullianum was the dismal subterranean dungeon added by Servius Tullius (*q.v.*) to the Mamertine prison in Rome. Jugurtha, Vercingetorix, and some of the Catilinarians were cast into it, either to be strangled or starved to death, and Saints Peter and Paul were said to have been confined in its gloomy depths.

as cheerless as the Tullianum

TULLIVER, MAGGIE

Maggie Tulliver, in George Eliot's *Mill on the Floss*, is the generous, impulsive, and ardent miller's daughter whose imaginative nature led her to violate the standards of conduct of her community. Exposed to the condemnation of the unsympathetic and to that of her own beloved brother, Tom, she is drowned in a flood with him.

an unconventional Maggie Tulliver

TULLUS HOSTILIUS

Tullus Hostilius was the third legendary king of early Rome and such a constant militarist that be made an armed barracks out of the peaceful city of his predecessor, Numa Pompilius (*q.v.*). The story of the combat between the three Roman Horatii and the three Alban Curiatii (*q.v.*) occurred during the war with Alba in his reign, and at its end he cruelly tore the body of Alba's king, or dictator, Mettius Fufetius, asunder with two chariots. He also instituted wars with Veii and Fidenae, neighboring towns, in his desire to emulate Romulus, and vowed temples to Pallor and Pavor (paleness and panic) during battles. For his belligerence and pride he and his whole house were struck dead by lightning, and he is said to have disappeared during the ensuing storm.

as military-minded as Tullus Hostilius

TUPMAN, TRACY

Tracy Tupman, a character in Dickens' *Pickwick Papers*, is the amorous member of the Pickwick Club, and of so susceptible a disposition that he falls in love with every pretty girl he meets.

an ardent Tracy Tupman

TUPPERIAN

Tupperian refers to the contents, style, and spirit of a long, dreary, and moralizing didactic poem in uninspired blank verse, *Proverbial Philosophy*, by Martin Farquhar Tupper (1810-1889), a dull English poet. Hence, the word has come to mean trite, commonplace, vapid, and jejune.

a volume of Tupperian tedium

TURCARET

Turcaret, a character in a comedy of the same name by Le Sage, is a coarse and illiterate man who becomes *nouveau riche* by stock-and-bond operations. The name is proverbially applied to any one who grows suddenly rich by more or less dishonest means, and who, having nothing else in the way of intellectual accomplishments to show, makes a display of his wealth.

a flashy, Turcaret-like speculator

TURNUS

Turnus was the king of the aboriginal tribe of ancient Italians known as the Rutuli, and was betrothed to Lavinia, daughter of king Latinus of the Latin tribe, at the time of Aeneas's arrival in Italy. When Latinus declared a preference for Aeneas as his son-in-law, Turnus became the latter's fierce rival and opponent, opening up the hostilities that form the subject matter of the last six books of Vergil's *Aeneid*. A fiery warrior and the most spirited character in the poem, he is at last defeated and killed by Aeneas.

a rival as stubborn as Turnus

TURPIN, DICK

Dick Turpin was a notorious robber and highwayman, executed at York for horse-stealing in 1780. His celebrated ride to York on his good Black Bess is dramatically described in Ainsworth's *Rockwood*.

prosecuting the Dick Turpins

TURVEYDROP, MR.

Mr. Turveydrop, a character in Dickens' *Bleak House*, is a selfish and pompous elderly dandy who lives on the earnings of his son, a dancing-master. This fatuous parasite and dependent is considered a perfect "master of deportment" by his slavishly reverential son.

a Mr. Turveydrop leeching to his foppery

TUSSAUD, MME. MARIE

Mme. Marie Tussaud (1760-1850) was a Swiss woman who brought her collection of wax models of the heads of victims and leaders of the French Revolution to London in 1802, establishing it in the famous Tussaud Museum on Marylebone Road. To her original collection of curiosities she added a macabre Chamber of Horrors, containing re-enactments of famous crimes and replicas of Inquisitional tortures. The lifelike figures give the spectator the eerie effect of witnessing the infliction of death, or of experiencing the unpleasantness of a visit to a mortuary parlor.

as lifelike and yet unreal as a figure by Mme. Tussaud

TUTANKHAMEN

Tutankhamen was the Egyptian pharaoh of the fourteenth century B.C. whose tomb was found by the Earl of Carnarvon and Howard Carter in the Valley of the Kings in 1922, bringing to light fabulous riches and archaeological wealth. A popular superstition of an ancient curse on the rifler of the tomb spread with the opening of the sarcophagus and claimed to find realization in the subsequent ill-luck of the discoverers.

afraid of King Tut's curse

TUTIVILLUS

Tutivillus is the name of the celebrated medieval evil spirit and demon who is said to have collected all the fragments of words which the priests had skipped over, slurred, and otherwise mutilated in the performance of the service, and to have carried them to hell.

A very Tutivillus of an elocution-teacher

TVASHTRI

Tvashtri in Vedic mythology, is the artisan of the gods, the Hephaestus (Vulcan) of the Hindu pantheon. He is an artificer and maker of the divine weapons and of all other kinds of objects of skill.

an obsolete weapon, dug out of the arsenal of Tvashtri

TWAIN, MARK

Mark Twain, the pen name of Samuel Clemens (1835-1910) assumed for his earliest Mississippi river stories, was a phrase used by the canal boatmen in his day. So humorous are his stories and so pleasant and genial the atmosphere that his name is synonymous with natural, genial, pleasant, laughing humor. Sometimes it is whimsical and fantastic, but always of a sound, deep chuckling sort.

the inimitable Mark-Twain flavor

TWEED, WILLIAM M.

William M. Tweed (1823-1878) was the notorious American politician and sachem in the Tammany organization who organized the Tweed Ring, which seized control of New York City finances and swindled the treasury of millions of dollars, supplying the city with marble from his privately owned marble company and with printing contracts with another of his firms. Exposed and convicted of embezzlement, he fled to Spain but was returned to this country to die in jail.

a cheat and peculator of the Tweed type

TWEEDLEDUM AND TWEEDLE-DEE

Tweedledum and Tweedledee originally meant a low-pitched (dum) fiddle and a high-pitched (dee) fiddle, but they are better known as the names of two idiotic characters in Lewis Carroll's *Alice in Wonderland* who are constantly wrangling and fighting about nothing. The phrase originated from a couplet written by John Byrom (1763) about the senseless contention between Handel's adherents and the devotees of the music of his rival Buoncini:

"Strange all this difference should be 'Twixt Tweedledum and Tweedledee."

Hence, the names suggest triflers, idlers, bickering, "tweedling" — persons who differ over anything, no matter how insignificant.

a spirited Tweedledum and Tweedledee board meeting

TWELVE PEERS

The term Twelve Peers refers to the most famous warriors of Charlemagne's court, who were so called because of the equality which reigned among them. They were also known as "paladins," a term originally signifying officers of the palace. The romancers do not agree on the names of the twelve, but the most famous were Orlando, Rinaldo, Astolfo, Oliver, Ogier le Danois, Ganelon, Florismart, Namo, Otuel, Ferumbras, and Malagigi.

as co-equal in ability as the Twelve Peers

TWIST, OLIVER

Oliver Twist, the hero of Dickens' novel *Oliver Twist*, is a workhouse orphan, starved, beaten, suppressed, and always subjected to the worst of influences, yet remaining honest. His story was aimed at the existing abuses in almhouses in Dickens' time.

strange, how normal and wholesome many of the Oliver Twists grow to be

TWITCHER, JEMMY

Jemmy Twitcher is the name of a cunning robber in Gay's *Beggar's Opera*. The sobriquet was also conferred on John Montagu, fourth Earl of Sandwich (1718-1792), by his contemporaries because of his use of bribery and political jobbery.

a Jemmy Twitcher at graft

TYBALT

Tybalt, Juliet's cousin in Shakespeare's *Romeo and Juliet*, is a fiery young noble, hotheaded, impetuous and always spoiling for a fight. Welcoming feuds and wrangles, he finally kills Mercutio and is himself killed by Romeo. His name suggests hotheaded, impetuous, hasty, quarrelsome.

separated two young Tybalts

TYCHE

(see *Fortuna*)

TYDEUS

Tydeus, son of Oeneus, the king of Calydon, was compelled to leave his home because of some murder that he had committed. Fleeing to Adrastus, king of Argos, he was purified by him and married his daughter, Deipyle, who bore him a son, Diomedes (*q.v.*), often called by the patronymic Tydides. At the expedition of the *Seven against Thebes* (*q.v.*) he greatly distinguished himself in the siege, but was wounded by Melanippus, whom he slew. When Athena appeared with a remedy to make him immortal, she turned away in disgust upon seeing him eating the brain and some of the flesh of the head of Melanippus. Left to his fate, he died.

a flesh-eating Tydeus

TYLER, WAT

Wat Tyler was the leader of a peasant revolt in England in the fourteenth century in protest against a burdensome tax. In the course of the revolt the peasants killed several important persons and brought about great destruction as they marched to London, but the Mayor of London ordered Tyler executed as a rebel.

the Wat Tylers of the world nevertheless give matters a sharp shove

TYNDAREUS

Tyndareus was the king of Sparta and the husband of Leda of "swan" fame. By her he became the undisputed father of Timandra, Clytemnestra, and Philopoë. But one night his wife was embraced both by himself and by Zeus (in the guise of a swan), and the resultant issue of uncertain fatherhood comprised Castor, Pollux, and Helen of "Troy" fame. Pollux and Helen were, however, generally assigned to Zeus's parenthood.

another Tyndareus, uncertain of the paternity of his wife's child

TYNDARIS

Tyndaris, meaning "daughter of Tyndareus" (*q.v.*), the king of Sparta, can be applied to either of his female offspring, the husband-murdering Clytemnestra (*q.v.*) or the equally devastating *femme fatale*, Helen of Troy. Their mother, Leda, was erotically visited on the same evening by both her husband, Tyndareus, and Zeus, who loved her in the guise of a swan. Four children resulted from the conjuncture, Helen and Pollux being the offspring of Zeus, and Clytemnestra

and Castor those of Tyndareus. The male twins are often called Tyndarides, or "sons of Tyndareus."

as tempting as Tyndaris

TYPHON-TYPHOEUS

Typhon or Typhoeus was a monster of the primitive world, variously described as a destructive hurricane and a fire-breathing giant. Homer says that he was concealed in the earth in the land of the Arimi, which Zeus lashed with flashes of lightning. In Hesiod, Typhon, or Typhaon, is a fearful hurricane and the father of Cerberus, the Lernaean hydra, the Sphinx, and the Chimaera. Typhoeus, on the other hand, is described as a hundred-headed monster with fiery eyes and terrible voices. Wishing to acquire the sovereignty of gods and men, he was subdued by Zeus and buried under Mt. Aetna, the workshop of Hephaestus (Vulcan).

more hideous than Typhoeus

TYR

Tyr, in Scandinavian mythology, is a son of Odin, and the younger brother of Thor. The god of battle, war, and victory, he is the protector of champions and brave men, and is also noted for his sagacity. When the gods wished to bind the wolf Fenrir, Tyr put his hand into the demon's mouth as a token and promise that the bonds should be removed later. But Fenrir, finding that the gods had no intention of adhering to their word, took a measure of revenge by biting it off, making Tyr one-handed from that time on. At Ragnarok (*q.v.*), Tyr is slain by Garm, but not before he in turn despatches that bloody-breasted and ferocious monster dog.

a veritable Tyr in battle

TYRTAEUS

Tyrtaeus was the seventh century B.C. Greek poet whose martial war-songs inspired the Spartans to defeat their neighbors, the Messenians. He also wrote anapestic marching songs and elegies exhorting the people to political peace and order, to virtue and bravery. He is represented as a lame schoolmaster who invented the elegiac couplet, because its one verse is shorter than the other. His songs were so popular 'that the soldiers sang them around their camp-fires at night, the polemarch rewarding the best singer with an extra piece of meat.

> *stimulating as a marching song by Tyrtaeus*

TZIGANE

A Tzigane is a native of Tzigany, a section of Hungary peopled by gypsies with strongly characteristic customs and music. Just as the Tzigane's temperament is mercurial and passionately emotional, so is his rhapsodic music both melancholy and frenziedly gay in turn, all of which traits are suggested by the name.

> *the barometric nature of a Tzigane*

U

UCALEGON

Ucalegon was a Trojan elder and the friend and counselor of Priam, king of Troy, with whom he sat on the walls of the beleaguered city, watching the progress of the Greek siege. In Vergil's *Aeneid*, ii, 312, his house is mentioned as being adjacent to that of Anchises, father of the epic's hero, Aeneas, and as being burned at the sack of the city. Hence, dictionaries cite the name of Ucalegon as denoting a close or next-door neighbor, or one whose house is burning.

all following the fire-trucks to Ucalegon's house

UGOLINO

Ugolino della Gherardesca (1220-1289) was a Pisan noble and a leader of the Ghibellines, which party he deserted in the hope of usurping supreme power. Defeated in an encounter with Archbishop Ruggiero, he is said to have been imprisoned with his sons in the tower of the Gualandi (since called the Tower of Hunger), where they were left to starve, the keys having been thrown into the Arno. Dante immortalized the name and sufferings of Ugolino in the Inferno, XXXIII, where he is represented as voraciously devouring the head of Ruggiero in hell, both being frozen up together in a hole in a lake of ice.

the hunger pangs of an Ugolino

ULLUR

Ullur, in Scandinavian mythology, was the stepson of Thor, and a warlike deity who presided over single combats, archery, and the chase. Noted for his beauty, he dwelled in Ydaler (the valley of rain) and was accustomed to run so rapidly on snow-shoes or skis that no one was a match for him in skill.

as nimble as Ullur on the ski-jump

ULPIAN, DOMITIUS

Domitius Ulpian (170-228 A.D.) was a celebrated Roman jurist who became chief adviser to the emperor Alexander Severus. The possessor of great legal knowledge, he wrote many treatises and commentaries on Roman law. He perished at the hands of soldiers who forced their way into the palace at night and killed him in the presence of the emperor and his mother.

a jurisconsult as learned as Ulpian

ULRIC, ST.

St. Ulric was a legendary patron much honored by his fisherman wards. He died in 973 on ashes strewn in the shape of a cross upon the floor.

St. Ulric presiding over the haul

ULRICA

Ulrica, in Scott's *Ivanhoe,* is the hideous old sibyl, witch, and prophetess of Torquilstone. The daughter of a Saxon thane, she becomes the victim of Front de Boeuf's father.

a hag as ugly as Ulrica

ULTOR

Ultor, or "Avenger," was a surname of Mars, to whom Augustus built a magnificent temple in his forum in Rome after taking vengeance on the murderers of his great-uncle, Julius Caesar.

prayed to Ultor for satisfaction

ULYSSES

Ulysses, also known as Odysseus, was king of Ithaca, husband of Penelope, and the craftiest of all the Greek leaders. After the Trojan war (1184 B.C.) he suffered incredible adventures during the ten years of wandering that are the subject of Homer's *Odyssey*. They led him to the island of Aeolus, who gave him the winds in a bag; to Circe's island; to the isle of Calypso, who detained him for eight years; to his experience with Polyphemus, the Cyclops. Finally he arrived home, disguised, to find his faithful wife, Penelope, resisting the suitors who were wasting his wealth. After slaying them with the help of Athena and his son, Telemachus, his fantastic adventures are completed.

restless as Ulysses
wise Ulysses, in counsel peer to Jove

UMA

Uma, in Hindu mythology, is a name of the goddess Devi, the consort of Siva. She is famous for her defeat of the armies of Chanda and Munda, two demons, and is represented in art as holding the head of Chanda in one of her four hands and trampling the body of Munda beneath her feet. The heads of the army, strung into a necklace, adorn her body, and a girdle of the same macabre decorations surrounds her waist.

like Uma, has him beneath her feet

UMBRIEL

Umbriel, in Pope's *Rape of the Lock,* is a moody, dusky sprite armed with a bag of sighs and a vial of sorrows supplied by Spleen.

manifold griefs from Umbriel's vial

UNA

Una, the personification of Truth in Spenser's *Faerie Queen,* is there accompanied by St. George, the Red Cross Knight, and is pictured as a "lovely ladie" so pure and beautiful that a lion, ranging the woods for prey and coming upon Una sleeping, is softened by her beauty and becomes her faithful and protecting companion wherever she goes. The allegorical significance is, of course, the power of Truth over brutality. Una marries St. George, who slays the dragon of the story.

a Una who found no lion

UNCAS

Uncas, the son of Chingachgook, and the last of the Mohican Indians, is made the hero of Cooper's novel, *The Last of the Mohicans*. He was noted for his courage and nobility, as well as for his skill in evading danger. He is reported buried in the Moravian Mission cemetery in Bethlehem, Pennsylvania, where many of the Indians are interred in John Eliot's mission.

Uncas now stands by the linefence
of his reservation

UNDINE

Undine, one of the water nymphs created without souls, could acquire a soul only by marrying a mortal. Fouqué's novel pictures her living happily in the fisherman's hut where she has been brought up, but when she marries a mortal and acquires a soul, she acquires all the pains and sorrows of a mortal. When her husband neglects her, the water nymphs come and carry her away.

an unawakened Undine

UPIS

Upis was a surname of Artemis (Diana), as the goddess assisting women in childbirth. It was also the name of a mythical being who reared Artemis and later became one of the nymphs in her train. Later, Upis was simply a goddess who watched over human deeds.

a midwife as perfect as Upis

URANIA

(see *Muse*)
Urania was the Muse of astronomy presiding over all study and investigation of the heavens and the universe. In ancient works she was pictured as carrying a globe of the earth and a pointer. Urania is also another name of Venus (Aphrodite), as representing spiritual rather than sensual love (Pandemos).

her eyes set on the stars like Urania's

URANUS

Uranus, the personification of the heavens in Greek mythology (Coelus, in Roman), was one of the most ancient of the gods and the son and husband of Gaea (Tellus, the earth). Hating his children, he confined them in Tartarus immediately following their birth. In consequence of this, he was castrated by Cronus, at the suggestion of Gaea. The Gigantes and the Melian nymphs sprang from the drops of his blood, as did Aphrodite from the foam gathering around his limbs in the sea. Saturn, the Titans, and the Cyclopes were other children of his.

mutilated like Uranus

URGANDA

Urganda is the name of a potent enchantress and fairy in the romance of *Amadis de Gaul* and in the romances of the Carlovingian cycle and the poems founded on them. She is invested with all the more serious terrors of a Medea.

seeking an Urganda who can read the riddle of his fate

URIAH

Uriah, in *2 Samuel,* xi, is the Hittite captain in the army of Israel who was treacherously exposed in battle by David so that the latter might take his wife, Bath-sheba.

cuckolded like Uriah

URIAN, SIR

Sir Urian, or Herr Urian among the Germans, is a sportive designation of an unknown or unmentionable man who is very little thought of, or who is sure to turn up unexpectedly and inopportunely. In Low German, the name is applied to the Devil.

a nonentity of the Sir Urian type

URIEL

Uriel, in Hebrew meaning "fire of God," is one of the seven archangels mentioned in *2 Esdras* as the good angel. Milton makes him "regent of the sun," and calls him "the sharpest-sighted spirit of all in heaven." He is also an archangel in Longfellow's *Golden Legend.*

as penetrating as Uriel's vision

URIM AND THUMMIM

Urim and Thummim, according to *Exodus,* xxviii, 30, were mystical objects worn in a pouch on the breastplate of the High Priest and employed as a kind of divine oracle and in revelation of the will of God. Though it is not known exactly what they were, they are generally supposed to have been precious stones or small figures employed in sortition or the casting of lots, the one indicating an affirmative, the other a negative answer.

makes his decisions according to the whim of Urim and Thummim

URSULA, ST.

St. Ursula, in Cornish legend and Roman Catholic martyrology, was a princess of the third or fifth century who in the year 238, 283, or 451 A.D. became the patroness and leader of a band of 11,000 virgins on a pilgrimage to Rome. All were slaughtered in protecting their virginity from an army of Huns, whom they encountered at Cologne. The great number of tender martyrs may be due to a misreading of the source's *Ursula et XI M.V.*, in which the "M" may represent either *millia* for "thousands" or simply the word *martyres* preceding the "V" for *virgines*. St. Ursula's festival, in either case, falls on the 21st of October.

innocent as Ursula with her band of virgins

URTH

Urth is one of the three Norse Norns. Originally the only one, she was identified at that time with Death. But when Verthandi and Skuld (*qq.v*) were added, Urth came to represent the past.

rummaging through the archives of Urth

URUGAL

Urugal, or "the great city," was the Hades of the ancient Babylonians.

gone to some ancient Urugal

URVASHI

Urvashi, in Hindu mythology, is "longing" or "desire." She is personified as a woman loved by Pururavas.

covetous of some Urvashi

USAS

Usas is the goddess of the dawn in Hindu mythology, her name being cognate to that of the Greek Eos and Roman Aurora. Celebrated in several hymns of the Rig Veda, she is one of the most graceful creations of Hindu poetry. Borne along on a shining chariot drawn by tawny bulls, she is the daughter of the sky and is beloved by the sun. "Rising resplendent from her bath, showing her charms she comes with light . . . she reveals the paths of men and bestows new life . . . she opens the doors of darkness as the cows their stalls."

Usas tinting the sky with pink gold

UTGARD

Utgard, old Norse for "outer ward" or "inclosure," was a circle of rocks surrounding the vast sea supposed to encompass Midgard, the earth, which was regarded as a flat circular plane or disk. The same as Jotunheim (*q.v.*), it was the abode of the Giants and the region of the dead.

a remote and far-away Utgard

UTGARD-LOKI

Utgard-Loki is the chief and most cunning giant of Utgard, and the personification of physical and moral evil so impervious to attack that the most severe blows of Thor's hammer could not hurt him. Assuming the disguise of Skrymer, he outwits Thor and Loki, taking them with Thialfi to Jotunheim. There fire, disguised as Logi, consumed more voraciously than Loki; thought, disguised as Hugi, ran faster than Thialfi; and old age, disguised as Elli, was stronger than Thor. When Utgard-Loki had revealed all his tricks to Thor, he escaped punishment by vanishing.

as crafty as Utgard-Loki

UTHER

Uther, one of the three chief magicians of ancient Britain, became a legendary king of the island. The son of Constans, he had an adulterous amour with Igerna, the wife of Gorlois, the Duke of Cornwall, and became the father of Arthur, who succeeded him on the throne.

Uther's knack for cuckoldry

UT-NAPISHTIM

Ut-Napishtim was the "Noah" of the Babylonian deluge myth, he and his household being the sole survivors of the great flood. The gods then favor him with immortality, the secret of which his great-grandson, Gilgamesh (*q.v.*), implores him to reveal.

immortalized like Ut-Napishtim

UTOPIAN

Utopian is from More's *Utopia*, an ideal state having a perfect social and political system. Utopian is now used to suggest a state so perfect that it is either non-existent or impossible. The name itself is derived from the Greek for *nowhere*.

waking from our Utopian dream of no foreign entanglements

UTU

Utu, in Babylonian religion, is the sun-god. He has many names, depending on the solar functions of the various seasons of the year. The Sumerian equivalent of Shamash, he is also called Babbar.

Utu blazing in the heavens

UZZIAH

Uzziah, another name of Azariah, was the king of Judah whose reign was marked by many successful wars against Philistines, Arabians, and Ammonites. Acquiring leprosy toward the end of his rule, he was accused of impiety for having usurped the priestly prerogative of burning incense in the Temple (*2 Chronicles,* xxvi, 16-21). His reign was also remembered in later times for a great earthquake that had occurred in it.

smitten, like Uzziah, for his sins

UZZIEL

Uzziel, in Milton's *Paradise Lost,* IV, 782, is the angel next in power and command to Gabriel, who commands him to "coast the south with strictest watch." The name means "Strength of God."

a vigilant Uzziel

a haughty and effeminate man who is led on by the sophistries of a cruel and ambitious mother and the temptations of a malignant genie to commit all manner of crimes, to renounce his faith, and to offer allegiance to Eblis, the Mohammedan Satan, in the hope of seating himself on the throne of the pre-Adamite sultans. His throne proves to be an abode in the abyss of the devil, where he is imprisoned in torment and remorse for eternity.

Vathek-like, blasé and poisoned in youth

VATICANUS

Vaticanus was the Roman religious *numen* or spirit that opened a child's mouth and prompted it to utter its first cry.

a mute never visited by Vaticanus

VAYA

Vaya is the Hindu god of the winds, the second of the evolutionary stages of Parabrahma, the air.

Vaya setting the air in motion

VE

Ve, in Scandinavian mythology, took part in the creation of the world and mankind, along with his brothers Odin and Vili. Slaying the giant Ymir, they made the mountains out of his bones, trees of his hair, the sky of his skull, clouds out of his brain, the seas out of his blood, and Midgard (mid-earth) out of his eyebrows. Then they shaped man (Ask) out of an ash-tree, woman (Embla) out of an elder. To this first couple Ve gave their senses, expressive features, and speech; Vili contributed reason and motion; and Odin presented them with life and soul.

a language never learned from Ve

VEAL, MRS.

Mrs. Veal is the imaginary title-character of Defoe's *True Relation of the Apparition of one Mrs. Veal.* She was supposed to have appeared "the next day after her death, to one Mrs. Bargrave, at Canterbury, on the 8th of Sept., 1705." One of the boldest and most clever of experiments upon human credulity ever made, the pamphlet has long been supposed to owe its origin to the author's desire to help a book-seller rid his shelves of an unsaleable translation of Drelincourt's *On Death.*

looks as though he has just seen Mrs. Veal

VEJOVIS

Vejovis was an obscure Roman deity viewed as the opposite or counterpart of Jove (Jupiter) in the lower world, corresponding to Pluto. Originally an Etruscan divinity, he hurled such fearful lightning bolts that they produced deafness even before they were heard. In his temple between the Capitol and the rock of Tarpeia (*q.v.*) his festival was held on May 21st, and at it sacrifice was offered by the highest priest, the Pontifex Maximus. In art he was represented as a youthful god armed with arrows.

deafened by dread of Vejovis

VELASQUEZ

Diego Rodriguez Velasquez (1599-1660), the famous Spanish painter of portraits and *The Crucifixion,* painted a Spanish admiral so true to life that Felipe IV mistook the picture for the man and reproved it severely for not being with the fleet.

life-like as Velasquez' admiral

VELEDA

Veleda, a member of the ancient German tribe of Bructeri and contemporary with the reign of Vespasian in Rome, was a prophetic virgin who won such great renown for her auguries and predictions that she was revered and worshiped as a divine being.

foretells with the accuracy of Veleda

VENNER, ELSIE

Elsie Venner, the heroine and title character of a novel by Oliver Wendell Holmes (1861), is a girl of abnormal tendencies who owes her peculiarities to a bite her mother received from a rattlesnake. Her name, therefore, connotes any strange psychological phenomenon.

the idiosyncratic Elsie Venner of the town

VENTIDIUS

Ventidius, in Shakespeare's *Timon*, is one of the title-character's false friends.

betrayed by his Ventidius

VENUS

Venus was the Roman goddess of love, beauty, and erotic desire. From her fondness for the myrtle tree she was also known as Murcia, and because brides cut off a lock of their hair and sacrificed it to her on their wedding day, the epithet Calva ("bald") was applied to her. Her worship as Venus Genetrix was promoted by Caesar, who traced his descent from Aeneas, her son. The month of April was considered sacred to her as marking the beginning of spring and the reawakening of the reproductive powers of nature. For her various other attributes see *Aphrodisian, Pandemos, Urania,* and *Verticordia.*

stirred by the impulses of Venus

VENUSBERG

Venusberg is the mountain of fatal delights in the old mythology of Germany. Eckhardt, the Faithful, companion of the knight Tannhaeuser, warned travelers away from it. Translated into English by Carlisle, the legend represents Eckhardt as a good servant who perishes to save his master's children from seduction on the mountain. Tannhaeuser was promised that he should kiss the queen of love (Venus), if he could find the courage to venture upon the Venusberg. Tarrying long among the delicious enchantments of the mountain, he was at last moved to repentance and departed. Wagner described the sensual joys of the place in stirringly bacchanalian music in the Venusberg scene from his opera *Tannhaeuser.*

amorous dalliance on the Venusberg

VERDI, GIUSEPPE

Giuseppe Verdi (1813-1901) was the great Italian composer of perennially popular operas. His works fall into three periods, each marking a steady improvement over its predecessor. From the first period, vulgarly melodious and melodramatic, came *Ernani, Il Trovatore,* and *Rigoletto.* The greater refinement and elegance of his second period began with *Traviata* (*q.v.*) and continued with *Aida* and *A Masked Ball,* and when he was already in extreme old age, in his eighties, he produced his greatest musical masterpieces, *Otello* and *Falstaff,* creations far from the conventionalities of earlier Italian operas. He also composed the sensationally theatrical religious piece, the *Manzoni Requiem.*

an unforgettable Verdian aria

VERE DE VERE, LADY CLARA

Lady Clara Vere de Vere is the title-character of a poem (1842) by Tennyson praising simplicity and goodness, and condemning the supercilious pride of Lady Clara. She is a type of cold, haughty aristocrat, and of "the repose which stamps the caste of Vere de Vere."

the orgulous Lady Vere de Vere of her community

VERGES

Verges is the ingeniously absurd watchman and night-constable, in Shakespeare's *Much Ado about Nothing*

The companion of Dogberry, he is noted for his blundering simple-mindedness.

a watchman as stupid as Verges

VERGILIAN

Vergilian is from Publius Vergilius Maro (70-19 B.C.), the most illustrious and beloved of all Roman poets. He wrote *Eclogues,* pastoral poems of simple and natural beauty, and the *Georgics,* treatises on gardening, beekeeping, and orchardry, written in magnificently rolling hexameter verse. His most famous work is, however, the *Aeneid,* the epic in twelve books concerning the adventures of Aeneas, the Trojan who founded the Latin race and was the hero-son of Venus, from his defense of his native city till his arrival and acceptance in Italy. Vergilian consequently means pastoral, agricultural, epic, and melodiously versified.

with Vergilian diction

VERNE, JULES

Jules Verne (1828-1905) was the imaginative writer of sensational and fantastic pseudo- or semi-scientific romances of adventure, in which many subsequent realities in the way of technological developments and inventions were accurately forecast. Thus, *Five Weeks in a Balloon* told of an extended ascension, *Twenty Thousand Leagues under the Sea* of a submarine submersion, and *Around the World in Twenty-Four Days* of rapid circumvention of the globe by air. *Hector Servadoc* envisaged life on a comet, and *With the English at the North Pole* described elaborate polar expeditions. Verne's novels, like those of Rider Haggard (*q.v.*) and H. G. Wells, achieve a pleasantly plausible verisimilitude.

a Jules Verne piece of fantasy

VERNON, DIANA

Diana, or Di Vernon, is a zealous royalist beauty in Scott's novel *Rob Roy.* A high-born and enthusiastic adherent to a persecuted religion, and a partisan of the exiled king, she receives a masculine education under the superintendence of two learned men, and is predestined to a hateful husband or a cloister.

a high-spirited Di Vernon

VERONICA

Veronica was the compassionate woman of Jerusalem who, as Christ passed her bearing the cross on his way to Golgotha along the Via Dolorosa (*q.v.*), wiped his face clean of blood and sweat with her veil, which miraculously retained the imprint of his countenance. Though her name is probably derived from the Greek Berenice, popular superstition supposed it to derive from the Latin words *vera iconica,* for "true image."

a likeness as faithful as that on Veronica's veil

VERRES, CAIUS

Caius Verres was the extortionate and rapacious Roman propraetorian governor of Sicily from 73 to 71 B.C. Though impeached by Cicero and forced into exile, he retained many of the art treasures he had filched from the residences of wealthy Sicilians. One of his favorite methods of acquiring loot was to order some rich victim to submit to his headquarters a family heirloom to be copied, subsequently returning to the unfortunate prey not the original but the imitation.

loot to charm a Verres

VER SACRUM

A Ver Sacrum ("sacred springtime") was a Roman dedication to the gods, in times of crisis and acute emergency, of the entire produce of the ensuing spring, including children to be born then. Though in early times even the latter were victims of human sacrifice, later they were allowed to grow up to maturity, then expelled from their country. In 217 B.C., during the terrible initial reverses of the second Punic War (see *Trasimene Lake*), all the young of the herds of swine, oxen, sheep, and goats were thus pledged and sacrificed to the gods to avert further disaster.

> the cruel desperation of a Ver Sacrum

VERTHANDI

Verthandi is the Norse Norn who represents the present. She and her sisters, Skuld the future, and Urth the past (*qq.v.*), were giant goddesses who controlled the destiny of gods and men alike. They lived beneath the earth-tree Yggdrasil, which they tended daily with the restorative waters of the well of Urdar. Analogous with the Fates in classical mythology, they too were conceived of as spinning the thread of life, decreeing by inexorable fate the career of each man.

> Verthandi pausing over the thread of life

VERTICORDIA

Verticordia was a Roman epithet of Venus, as the goddess who "turns the human heart." During the general corruption of the year 114 B.C., a temple was built for Verticordia to preserve the integrity of the Vestal Virgins, three of whom had lapsed from their vows of chastity in that year.

> a change-of-heart wrought by Verticordia

VERTUMNUS

Vertumnus (from the Latin *vertere*, to turn or transform) was the god of the seasons and of their variegated products in the vegetable world. He loved Pomona, the goddess of fruit-trees, but, though he tried to gain access to her in a thousand different forms, he was able to effect his desire only in the guise of an old woman. Appearing thus, he told her warning tales of women who had rejected the power of love. When he had moved her to submission, he transformed himself into a beautiful youth and married her. Gardeners offered him the first-fruits of their crops.

> a versatile Vertumnus of a lover
> a mortal Vertumnus busy in his garden

VESPASIAN, FLAVIUS

Titus Flavius Vespasian was emperor of Rome from 69 to 79 A.D., establishing a dynasty that lasted through his two sons, Titus and Domitian, until the year 96. Noted for the simplicity and frugality of his personal life, and the economy and efficiency of his administration, he began the great amphitheater known as the Colosseum, and built the temple of Peace, which Pliny thought to be one of the finest structures in the world. In the latter he placed the golden candlestick taken from the Temple at Jerusalem in the sack of that city by his son Titus.

> simplicity observed from Vespasian

VESTAL

Vestal is from Vesta, goddess of the hearth and, consequently, of the home and of domestic tranquillity. It is also used of the virgins who attended Vesta, hence, virginal, chaste, consecrated. The Greeks called the goddess *Hestia*.

> unquenched, like Vesta's sacred fire

VETURIA AND VOLUMNIA

Veturia and Volumnia were the mother and wife, respectively, of Coriolanus (*q.v.*), legendary Roman autocrat who was impeached and exiled for his haughty bearing in 491 B.C. As he led the Volscian army against his own city to attack it, these women brought his two little children and the noblest matrons of Rome out of the walls to intercede, deprecate, and dissuade him from his traitorous deed. Veturia's reproaches and Volumnia's tears bent him from his purpose, and he retired to the country of the Volscians to die. Veturia and Volumnia are types of fearless patriotism and successful persuasion.

In Shakespeare's *Coriolanus*, the mother is given the name Volumnia, and the wife is known as Virgilia.

no Veturia and Volumnia to save their land

VETURIUS MAMURIUS

Veturius Mamurius, in Roman legend, was the armorer who made eleven *ancilia* (sacred shields), so exactly duplicating the one that fell from heaven in the reign of Numa Pompilius (*q.v.*) that it was impossible to tell the authentic and original one from the copies. Praise of him was the chief subject of the songs of the Salii (*q.v.*).

imitated with the exactitude of Veturius Mamurius

VIA DOLOROSA

The Via Dolorosa, or "road of sorrow," was the street in Jerusalem, from the Mount of Olives to Golgotha, over which Jesus passed on his way to crucifixion. On this road were the house in which the Virgin Mary was born, the church erected on the spot where she fell on seeing her son sink under the burden of the cross, and the house of Veronica (*q.v.*). About a mile in length, the road terminated at the Gate of Judgment.

a life as fraught with sadness as the Via Dolorosa

VICTORIAN

Victorian is from Queen Victoria (1819-1901), ruler of England during more than fifty years, the most settled and prosperous period of domestic progress. It was marked by peace, high social consciousness, and a deep respect for virtue and respectability so thoroughly established that in retrospect it seems prudish, over-conventional, almost absurd, with its formalities and its oppressive "standards."

Victorian stuffed-shirtism

VIDAR

Vidar, the son of Odin and the giantess Grid, in Scandinavian mythology, is the god of wisdom and science whose look is so penetrating that he reads the most secret thoughts of men. He wears very thick shoes, whence he is sometimes called "the god with the thick shoes."

a look as keen as Vidar's

VIGILANTES

The Vigilantes, in California of the early 1850's and in other western districts of a frontier character, were bodies of unofficial police organized among citizens for the purpose of maintaining law and order and of meting out justice.

conceivable need for some Vigilantes' action

VIGILES

The Vigiles were the corps of police and firemen under strict military discipline in ancient Rome. The name, therefore, connotes any official group of constabulary, alert and intent on the preservation of law and order.

as watchful as the Vigiles

VIKINGS

The Vikings were Scandinavian rovers and pirates of the 8th-11th century, strong, adventurous, intrepid conquerors. The name is now loosely used in literature of any group of seafaring men in the extreme northern waters, as it is in Bojer's *The Vikings*.

adventurously sauing the Vikings' main

VILLON, FRANCOIS

François Villon (1431-1485, a French poet who lived a wild bohemian existence, was accused on a serious charge, flogged and condemned to death, but was saved from the sentence by a princess to whom he had addressed poems. His story is romantic, irregular, and has been made the basis of more than one idealized tale.

a Villon-inspired play

VINCENT, ST.

St. Vincent was a Spanish Christian who was tortured and suffered martyrdom at Valencia under Diocletian in 304 A.D. His festival day is on the 22nd of January, and he is regarded as the patron of wine-growers and drunkards, whence the proverb:
If on St. Vincent's day the sky is clear,
More wine than water will crown the year.

a profusion of wines blessed by St. Vincent

VINCENTIO

Vincentio, the Duke of Vienna in Shakespeare's *Measure for Measure*, commits his scepter to Angelo, his untrustworthy deputy, under the pretext of being called to take an urgent and distant journey. He then changes his royal purple for a monk's hood and observes incognito the true condition of his people, and especially the manner and effect of his vice-regent's administration.

the ruse of a Vincentio

VINCI, LEONARDO DA

Leonardo da Vinci (1452-1519), versatile and profound Florentine painter, architect, sculptor, engineer, and scientist, rose from a protégé of Renaissance dukes and a French king to scale the heights of all time as the "complete man" and emblem of intellect and culture. From studies in hydraulics, meteorology, anatomy, mathematics, and engineering he still salvaged enough time to be architect of the Milan cathedral and to paint such masterpieces as the *Mona Lisa*, the *Virgin of the Grotto*, and the fading *Cenacolo*, or "Dast Supper," on the deteriorating refectory wall of the Church of Santa Maria delle Grazie in Milan. The author of philosophical inquiries and a *Treatise on Painting*, he exhibited throughout his entire lifetime a Vergilian desire *rerum cognoscere causas* ("to know the reasons for things").

the complete intellectuality of a Leonardo

VINCY, ROSAMOND

Rosamond Vincy, in George Eliot's *Middlemarch*, is the beautiful, but selfish and narrow wife of Dr. Lydgate, a young physician. Her self-centered indolence prevents his achieving renown.

a drawback like Rosamond Vincy

VIOLA

Viola, the heroine of Shakespeare's *Twelfth Night*, is shipwrecked on the coast of Illyria and, disguised as a male page, enters the services of Duke Orsino until she can gain tidings of her lost twin-brother, Sebastian. Orsino uses her to carry his love-suit to the Countess Olivia, who herself is attracted by the comely youth she takes Viola to be. This excites the jealousy of Orsino, till finally Viola's sex is revealed, the Duke marries her, and her brother Sebastian weds Olivia.

like Viola, she never told her love

VIRAJ

Viraj is the mysterious Hindu primeval being, just at the stage of differentiating itself sexually into male and female.

Viraj had not yet determined its sex

VIRBIUS

Virbius was a primitive Latin divinity of childbirth, worshiped along with Diana in her grove at Aricia on the slopes of the Alban Mount. He was partly identified with Hippolytus (*q.v.*), who was restored to life by Asclepius at Diana's wish.

calling upon Virbius to expedite the delivery

VIRGINIA

Virginia, in the annals of the early Roman republic, was the beautiful and innocent daughter of Lucius Virginius. Betrothed to Lucius Icilius, she tickled the lust of the decemvir Appius Claudius (*q.v.*), who schemed to have one of his clients seize the girl, claiming her as his slave, Claudius then pronouncing legally in favor of his dependent (B.C. 449). Virginius, seeing the girl's fate sealed, asked to be allowed to speak one word to the nurse in his daughter's hearing, in order to ascertain whether she was really his blood child. His request granted, Virginius took both aside, and, plunging a butcher knife into Virginia's breast, cried, "There is no way but this to keep thee free." Brandishing the bloody weapon on high, he rushed to the Roman camp. Both it and the city were incited to rise against Appius Claudius, dragging him to prison where he committed suicide.

the noble death of a Virginia, calculated to preserve honor

VIRTUS

Virtus was the Roman deity who personified manliness and valor. In art she is represented as a stalwart female clad in a short tunic and with right breast uncovered. Her head is helmeted, and she holds a spear in her left hand, a sword in her right, as she stands with her right foot on a captured helmet, sometimes on a shield. Marcellus built a temple in her honor.

Virtus imbuing them with courage

VISHNU

Vishnu is one of the chief deities in Hindu religion, and the second person of the holy Trimurti, or triad. He is regarded as the preserver, while Brahma and Siva, his colleagues, are creator and destroyer respectively. Vishnu accomplishes the objects of his providence by ten successive avatars, or incarnations, in which he appears and acts on earth. Nine of these have already transpired; in the tenth, which is yet to come, he will appear on a white horse, with a flaming sword for the everlasting punishment of the wicked. Buddha and Juggernaut are both regarded as avatars of Vishnu.

preserved by Vishnu

VITALIANS

The Vitalians were a band of pirates operating in the Baltic and the North Seas around the year 1400, marauding, pillaging, and looting wherever they turned their path of destruction.

with Vitalian passion for loot

VITELLIUS, AULUS

Aulus Vitellius (15-69 A.D.) was a good-natured Roman noted for his gluttony, prodigality, laziness, self-indulgence, and licentiousness. An epicure whose chief delight was at the table, on which he spent enormous sums of money, he became the favorite of Tiberius, Caligula, and Nero (*qq.v.*) because of his excesses, and in April of the year 69 he was elevated to the throne on the murder of his predecessor Otho. In December of the same year his brief reign was over, for he was dragged to the Scalae Gemoniae (*q.v.*) and struck with repeated blows until he was dead. "Yet I was once your emperor" were the last and perhaps the most profound words he had ever spoken.

no more worthy of power than Vitellius

VITRUVIUS

Vitruvius Pollio, Roman architect of the days of Caesar and Augustus, was the author of the ten book treatise *De Architectura*, in which he discussed sites and materials for buildings, temples, theaters and private houses as well as water supply, sun-dials and decoration. Illustrated with sketches, it was a handbook for ancient construction engineers and even influenced Renaissance methods of building.

a Vitruvian flair for building

VITUS, ST.

St. Vitus was a Christian child martyr, killed under Diocletian's persecutions in the late third or early fourth century. The disease known as chorea was given its popular name from a belief that he was able to cure it.

twitching as though in the agonies of St. Vitus

VIVIAN

Vivian, in Arthurian legend, is a wily wanton and a sorceress who hates all the knights and tries to seduce "the blameless king." Seducing the magician Merlin instead, she has him, "overtalked and overworn, tell her his secret charm," whereupon she turns the spell against him and imprisons him in an enchanted wood.

a crafty Vivian in her ways with men

VOLPONE

Volpone (Italian for "old fox"), the hero of Ben Jonson's play (1607), is a crafty, hypocritical old Venetian nobleman. He is a type of cunning and shrewd trickster.

a sly and subtle Volpone

VOLSTEAD, ANDREW

Andrew J. Volstead introduced the Volstead Act passed by legislature to enforce prohibition. It became the Eighteenth Amendment, which was later repealed. The Act, passed on October 28, 1919, prohibited the manufacture, transportation, and sale of any beverage containing more than ½ of 1% of alcohol, and was consequently called drastic, comprehensive, and harsh.

dry-in-the-mouth as Andrew Volstead

VOLTAIRE, FRANCOIS

François Voltaire (1694-1778), a brilliant poet and wit, was admitted to the French aristocracy through his grandfather's influence, but his freedom of utterance constantly got him into trouble, especially when he rationalized or ridiculed accepted religious and political truths. *Candide* is his most popular work, *Zadig* perhaps second in favor.

Voltairean brilliance

VOLUND

Völund is the renowned blacksmith and king of the elves in Teutonic legend. Corresponding to the Roman Vulcan and the English Wayland, he is always busy at his forge, executing all manner of smith-work, from the finest golden ornaments to the heaviest suits of armor. Lame from the time when King Nithothr, who had been robbed of his treasures, cut the sinews of his knees and then imprisoned him in a forge on an island, he secured vengeance by killing Nithothr's two sons and raping his daughter. Völund then escaped magically by flying.

jeweled filigree work worthy of Völund

VOLUPIA

Volupia, or Voluptas, was the Roman personification of sensual pleasure. She was worshiped in a temple near the Porta Romanula. Her name is a type of the hedonist and sybarite.

an orgiastic devotee of Volupia

VOPISCUS

Vopiscus was a Roman praenomen, or given name, signifying a twin-child who was born safe, while the other died before delivery. Like many other given names, it ultimately was used as a family appellation.

the Vopiscus of the double birth

VOR

Vor was the Norse goddess of betrothal and marriage. To all who defected from their promises or vows she was harshly vindictive, bringing punishment upon them.

Vor must have shut an eye to their unfaithfulness

VRITRA

Vritra is the Hindu atmospheric demon and spirit which causes droughts. Only when he is killed by Indra does he release rain and rivers.

Vritra scorching the fields

VULCAN

Vulcan was the Roman god of fire (Hephaestus to the Greeks). The son of Jupiter, he was lamed when the king of the gods hurled him from Mount Olympus for having taken Juno's part in a quarrel. He forged Jove's thunderbolts, Achilles' armor, and Hercules' shields in his workshop under Mount Aetna, called the "chimney" of Vulcan's forge. His workmanship was so strong, and yet so exquisite, that he is credited with the arts that distinguish civilization from savagery. The husband of Venus, he caught her in a net with her lover Mars (Ares) and exposed them to view for ridicule in their adultery. *Vulcanize,* of course, has its origin in his name.

like one of Vulcan's quenchless flames
with Vulcan-forged armor

W

WABUN

Wabun, in Longfellow's *Hiawatha*, is the youthful and handsome Indian Apollo who chases Darkness with his arrows over hill and dale, wakes the villager, calls the Thunder, and brings the Morning. He woos and marries Wabun-Annung, a beautiful country maiden, and transplants her to the skies, where she becomes the Morning Star.

> *fleet as Wabun chasing across the dawn*

WADMAN, WIDOW

The Widow Wadman, in Sterne's *Tristram Shandy*, is the comely husband-hunting lady who selects Uncle Toby (*q.v.*) as the target for a partner in her second marital adventure. Pretending that something alien is in her eye, she gets him to look for it, and as he does so, she places her face nearer and nearer his mouth, hoping that he will kiss her and propose.

> *as artful in her pursuit as the Widow Wadman*

WAGNER, CRISTOPH

Cristoph Wagner, borrowed from old German legends as attendant or *famulus*, servant, and companion of Faust in Goethe's *Faust* and Marlowe's *Doctor Faustus*, is a type of the pedant and philister, an outsider devoid of culture and somewhat resembling a modern philistine. He sacrifices himself to books, as Faust does to knowledge. Adoring the letter and the dust of folios, he finds parchment to be the source of his inspiration. He is the sort of person who, in the presence of Niagara, would vex you with questions about arrow-headed inscriptions.

> *as microscopically scholarly as Cristoph Wagner*

WAGNERIAN

Wagnerian is from Richard Wagner (1813-1883), composer of the type of opera called "music drama." In it he demonstrated his theory that opera should consist, not of a series of melodious arias unrelated in dramatic texture (as with the earlier Italian masters of this art-form), but of a combination of *leit-motifs* (leading, or suggesting themes) representing each of the principal characters and events of the story. He thus introduced a new era in that field of dramatic music. His themes are heroic (*Lohengrin, Tannhaeuser*, the *Ring of the Nibelungen* cycle, *Tristan and Isolde, Parsifal*, etc.); the drama is impressive, and the music magnificently fitting.

> *Wagnerian grandeur*

WAGON BOY

Wagon Boy was a popular sobriquet of Thomas Corwin (1794-1865), an American lad destined to become later in life a Representative, Governor of Ohio, Secretary of the Treasury, and minister to Mexico. In his youth, General Harrison and his army were on the northern frontier, almost destitute of provisions, and a demand was made on the patriotism of the people to furnish the necessary subsistence. The elder Corwin loaded a wagon with supplies, which were delivered by his young son, who remained with the army during the rest of the campaign, proving himself "a good whip and an excellent reins-man."

> *needs a little helper like Wagon Boy*

WALDEN POND

Walden Pond was the primitive Eden in which Henry D. Thoreau (*q.v.*) began his two years as a recluse living from the simple bounty of nature. On the edge of a pine-slope by this wooded lake in Concord, Mass., he constructed the hut to which he retired from the world in 1845 in order to record his naturalistic worship of the beauty of nature and the delights of solitude in *Walden, or Life in the Woods.* Feeding himself from a few rows of potatoes and beans which he himself tilled, he made friends with the little creatures of the forest, birds responding to his call, beasts fawning on him, and even fish slipping unafraid between his fingers as he dipped them into the streams. Walden Pond, therefore, is suggestive of any "back-to-Nature" movement and of a life of independence from one's fellow men.

an idyllic atmosphere like that of Walden

WALKER, TOM

Tom Walker is a character used as a warning to usurers in Irving's *Tales of a Traveller,* and his name appears in the proverbial expression, "The Devil and Tom Walker." A poor, miserly man born in Massachusetts in 1727, he is said to have sold himself to the Devil for wealth. Suddenly become very rich, he maintained a fine house in Boston during the panic which prevailed in the time of Governor Belcher. Growing richer and richer, he was foreclosing a mortgage on a poor man one day when a black man on a black horse knocked at the office door. Tom opened the door, went outside and was never seen again. When his office was searched, all his coffers were found empty. During the night his house caught fire and was burned to the ground.

mysterious as Tom Walker

WALKING STEWART

Walking Stewart was the sobriquet of John Stewart (1749-1822), an English traveler and peripatetic who journeyed on foot through India, Persia, Ethi-

opia, the Arabian desert, Europe, and the United States. Thomas De Quincey described him as the "most interesting man whom personally I knew: eloquent in conversation; contemplative in excess; crazy beyond all reach of hellebore (three Anticyrae would not have cured him), yet sublime and divinely benignant in his visionariness; the man who, as a pedestrian traveler, had seen more of the earth's surface and communicated more extensively with the children of the earth, than any man before or since; the writer, also, who published more books (all intelligible by fits and starts) than any Englishman . . . ."

as traveled as Walking Stewart

WALLENSTEIN

Albrecht Wallenstein (1583-1634) was the brilliant Austrian general, statesman, and worker for the unification of Germany during the Thirty Years' War. After campaigning in Hungary and against Venice, he was created Duke and given command of the German forces by the emperor Ferdinand, but after winning more victories over Mansfeld and the king of Denmark, he became the object of the jealousy of the imperial princes. Fallen from favor, he was suspected of being a double-dealer and a traitor for not moving against Sweden on the death of the monarch of that country, and was assassinated by a coalition of officers. Wallenstein is the subject of a great tragic trilogy by Schiller, in which his proud, serious, and imperious character and his unparalleled ability to organize and inspire fighting men are apparent, as well as his bitter struggle against the religious intolerance of the Protestant Reformation.

a patriot as misunderstood as Wallenstein

WALPOLE, HORACE

Horace Walpole (1717-1797) was the eccentric English fourth Earl of Orford who made of his ancestral home on

Strawberry Hill, formerly a villa outside Twickenham, a monstrosity of Gothic architecture that became a visitors' curiosity for all Europe. On the press which he set up here he printed some poems by his friend Thomas Gray, and his own ventures in writing that were to lead to the revival of romance. A novel, *The Castle of Otranto*, and a tragedy, *The Mysterious Mother*, too macabre and grisly ever to be presented on a stage, were his two works that led to a stream of writing called "Gothic" after his idiom, grim fiction of a supernatural and horrible character. Sir Walter Scott extolled to the skies his ability to arouse the emotions of pity and fear, and he did greatly influence the predilection of readers and authors alike for such derivative works as Mary Shelley's *Frankenstein*. His sprightly letters, some 2700 in number, on the other hand, are comparatively neglected, though a monument in English epistolography.

    a murder-story with echoes of Horace Walpole

WALPURGIS

Walpurgis is from St. Walpurga, the English nun (754-779) who converted the Saxons to Christianity. Her festival was on the eve (before) of May-day and supplanted a heathen festival on the same night. Those heathen rites were popularly thought to be the occasion for a great witch festival on the summit of the Brocken, in the Hartz mountains in Germany. The witches arrived on broom-sticks and he-goats and celebrated their evil mass with loud and world-shaking noise. The name is now loosely used of any terribly stormy night, especially one marked by continuous wind and thunder.

    a Walpurgian night

WALSTON, ST.

St. Walston was a Briton who renounced all his wealth and supported himself by manual labor as a husbandman and agriculturist. The patron saint of farmers, he is usually depicted with a scythe in his hand and cattle in the background. He is said to have died while mowing, in 1016.

    presiding like St. Walston over the harvest

WALTHER VON DER VOGELWEIDE

Walther "of Birdmeadow" (1170-1230) was a Middle High German Minnesinger (*q.v.*), wandering minstrel, and lyric bard of noble birth. A courtier of Philip of Swabia, Hermann of Thuringia, Otto IV, and Frederick II, he wrote poems of love, religion, and politics, the latter championing the cause of independence and unity for Germany. All through his life of singing for his lodging and bread, and hoping that some more generous patron would spare him from that "juggler's life," he remained a censorious critic of manners and men, living a strenuous and passionate life to the end. Before his death he had directed that the birds be fed daily at his tomb.

    the minstrelsy of a Walther von der Vogelweide

WALTON, IZAAK

Izaak Walton (1593-1683) is the English author of *The Compleat Angler, or Contemplative Man's Recreation*, specified by Hazlitt as the best pastoral in the English language. Walton's name has become a name for any fisherman who fishes because he likes to fish, and one might well add, likes the place where he likes to fish.

    the Nimrods and the Izaak Waltons of the club

WAMBA

Wamba, in Sir Walter Scott's *Ivanhoe*, is the "son of Witless," and the clown, jester, and zany of Cedric of Rotherwood, in saving whose life he courageously risks his own.

    a buffoon of the Wamba type

WANDERING WILLIE

Wandering Willie, in Scott's *Redgauntlet,* is the itinerant blind fiddler who tells the story of the title-character. His narrative includes the tale of how his piper grandfather, Steenie Steenson, journeyed all the way to hell to get the receipt for his rent from Sir Robert Redgauntlet.

a Wandering Willie with dark glasses and tin cup

WARD, ARTEMUS

Artemus Ward is the pen name of Charles F. Browne (1834-1867), a humorist whose wit is of a distinctly dated type, popular in the early nineteenth century. Ward tells incidents of his own journeyings to and from places his audiences knew, depending for his comedy partly, in his writing, on the natural spelling: "Eye come be4 U 2 ask U'r indulgence 4 my friend & his friends." In speaking he relied on his exaggerated Yankee twang. The whole tone was smart, Barnum-like, cheap, but popular, and welcomed with genuine joy and hearty laughter in a world of inevitable hard work, grim struggle, too strict behaviour, and in a literature heavy with serious reflection.

an Artemus-Ward style

WARDLE, MR.

Mr. Wardle is a stout, genial, and hearty country gentleman and squire in Dickens' *Pickwick Papers.* This elderly man becomes host to the Pickwick Club at Christmas time, constantly prodding his somnolent and fat serving boy, Joe, to keep him awake, for "he goes on errands fast asleep and snores as he waits at table." Yet Mr. Wardle would not "part with him on any account — he's a natural curiosity."

a hospitable Mr. Wardle

WARDOUR STREET

Wardour Street was a London street on which antique shops (many of the antiques spurious) flourished, until it was sometimes called Pseudo Street; hence, spurious, counterfeit, pseudo. The name is now applied to persons who deal in spurious antiques.

a Wardour-Street piece

WARRINGTON, GEORGE

George Warrington, in Thackeray's *Pendennis,* is the friend to the hero and title-character. Cynical, brusque, and melancholy, he is withal clever, generous, and loyal. His family also appears in *The Virginians.*

a pessimistic George Warrington

WARWICK, DIANA

Diana Warwick, the heroine of Meredith's *Diana of the Crossways,* is a beautiful and witty Irish woman. Her character is said to have been modeled on that of Mrs. Caroline Norton, English author who was led by marital troubles to petition the queen against the severity of the divorce laws.

a daughter of Erin, like Diana Warwick

WASHINGTON, GEORGE

George Washington (1732-1799), gentleman born, the Commander-in-chief of the Continental Armies, first president of the United States, counselor, guide, and friend to the American people through the stormy first years of national life, was master of the machinery of government, the organization of parties, and of regulation of commerce and finance. His clear sound judgement, self-control, sense of justice, his personal dignity and fairness, his complete integrity and his wise foresight are all evident in his *Farewell Address,* in which he pointed out many of the advantages and the possible evils of democracy that have become apparent today.

Washingtonian foresight

WATERLOO

Waterloo is the name of the village in central Belgium, south of Brussels, at which Wellington and Blucher crushed the overreaching might of Napoleon. The phrase *to meet one's Waterloo* has ever since that day, June 18, 1815, signified a crushing and final disaster, rout, defeat or fate.

insolently went forth to his Waterloo

WATLING STREET

Watling Street was the name very generally given in England of the Middle Ages to the *via lactea,* or "Milky Way." Found as such in Chaucer's *House of Fame,* it was, however, only an application of the word, not its proper and original meaning, since the real Watling Street was a road extending across South Britain from Dover, through Canterbury, and to London, whence it ran across the island to Chester. An important highway, the portion of it which ran through London still preserves its name. Under the Britons it was simply a forest lane, but the Romans made a great military road of it. This glittering pathway through the sky has been called in other countries also after actual roads on earth, by the Italians being denominated the *Santa Strada di Loretto,* by the Germans as *Euringstrasse.*

spectacular as Watling Street by night

WATSON, DR.

Dr. Watson is the friend and confidant of Sherlock Holmes in Conan Doyle's series of books built on the adventures of that fictitious detective. To him, and through him, Holmes makes clear his methods, his deductions, his processes of analysis; hence, consultant, confidant, intimate.

Watsonian acquiescence

WATTEAU, JEAN

Jean Antoine Watteau, a Frenchman (1684-1721), painted the beauty and grace of shepherds and shepherdesses in gay, light, pastoral scenes with a suggestion of the delicate frolic of the French court and of innocent pleasure. He set his scenes against a background of trees, water, and sky. Strangely enough, Watteau is remembered today chiefly for the fashion of the court costumes he pictured, with "Watteau pleats" from the neck or the shoulder to the hem.

the Watteau lightness of touch

WAVERLEY

Edward Waverley, the hero of Sir Walter Scott's romance of the same name, was a young captain in the English army who was involved in an insurrection in the Highlands at the time of Charles Stuart's invasion of the island. Resigning his commission, he became an adherent of the Young Pretender. Later he received the royal pardon and was married to Rose Bradwardine, who had saved his life. They then settled down in Waverley Honour.

a life as romantic as that of Edward Waverley

WAYLAND THE SMITH

Wayland the Smith was a mythical, supernatural and invisible blacksmith (see *Völund*) in English tradition. Haunting the Vale of White-Horse in Berkshire, he shod horses left by their owners who had never seen Wayland, charging sixpence for his fee and offended, unlike other workmen, if offered more. Three squarish flat stones supporting a fourth are pointed out as his smithy. Sir Walter Scott, somewhat anachronistically, introduced him into *Kenilworth* as a person living in the reign of Elizabeth.

a fee as low as that of Wayland the Smith

WEBSTERIAN

Websterian, from Noah Webster (1758-1843), indicates adherence to the principles of spelling, pronunciation, and meaning that he established in his Dictionary of the English Language, a book that is an authority on those matters wherever the English language is spoken.

Websterian also suggests Daniel Webster (1782-1852), American statesman and orator whose powerful mind and weighty utterance have never been surpassed. "His power of setting forth the truth was magnificent," one historian records. His voice was deep-toned, musical, and resolute, his reasoning unimpeachable. He was considered the greatest and most fearless of American statesmen. Thomas Carlyle called him "a parliamentary Hercules."

Websterian oratory
Websterian accuracy

WEDGEWOOD, JOSIAH

Josiah Wedgewood was famed for a now valuable sort of fine, hard porcelain called Wedgewood after him and marked by a tinted background with a raised figure, distinct as a cameo, usually of classical design and delicate detail.

a Wedgewood taste and a Woolworth purse

WEEPING PHILOSOPHER

"Weeping Philosopher" was a sobriquet given to Heraclitus, a Greek philosopher of Ephesus who flourished about 500 B.C., because of his gloomy and melancholic disposition. He is said to have been perpetually shedding inconsolable tears because of the vices of mankind.

morose as the "Weeping Philosopher"

WEGG, SILAS

Silas Wegg, in Dickens' *Our Mutual Friend,* is a wooden-legged and rascally huckster employed to read "The De-cline-and-Fall-Off-the-Rooshan-Empire' to the ignorant Boffin, the benefactor whom he tries to blackmail. When he read, "His laboring bark became beset by polysyllables, and embarrassed among a perfect archipelago of hard words." This insolent humbug had a "face carved out of very hard material ... when he laughed, certain jerks occurred in it."

a Silas Wegg when he read advanced English

WEIRD SISTERS

The Weird Sisters, in Shakespeare's *Macbeth,* are three prophetesses of destiny. Wholly different from any representation of witches in contemporary writing of that time, they were found by Coleridge to be "shadowy obscure and fearfully anomalous of physical nature, the lawless of human nature — elemental avengers without sex or kin."

as direful as the Weird Sisters

WEISSNICHTWO

Weissnichtwo ("I know not where") is the name given to a purely imaginative and unreal place in Carlyle's *Sartor Resartus.* Probably meant for London, it is spoken of as containing the university in which Professor Teufelsdroeckh (*q.v.*) does his research on "Things in General," and particularly on clothes.

as non-existent as Weissnichtwo

WELLER

Sam Weller, the factotum of Pickwick, is attractive for his shrewdness, his quaint low-life humor, his alertness, his inimitable wit, his easy and arch impudence, coolness in emergency, and, above all, his fidelity to his master. He represents all the best qualities of low life, according to Thackeray.

the colorful Wellerism of English service

WELLER, TONY

Tony Weller, father of Sam, proud of his son and watchful of him, is a great, fat, broad-beamed coachman, mottled by the weather and undisturbed by any emergency.

the cheerful competence of a Tony Weller

WELLINGTONIAN

Wellingtonian is from the "Iron" Duke of Wellington (1769-1852), military leader noted in history for defeating Napoleon at the battle of Waterloo. Wellington was famed for his decisive military sagacity, his honesty in assuming responsibility for his own defeats, his iron will and constitution, his steady, heavy method of attack and consequent victories, and his wisdom as victor. In France he shortened the time of allied occupation and insisted on complete evacuation of the country. Hence, the name means wise, honest, quick, sagacious, truthful.

Wellingtonian solidity
Wellingtonian military instinct

WELLS, H. G.

Herbert George Wells (1866-1946) is a brilliant writer who assumes to diagnose the troubles of the world, suggest remedies, deliver his opinions, and leave his mark on the social, economic, and political thinking of his day. He wrote realistic novels with a light touch, and fantastic stories based on science a little farther advanced than it actually was at the time. Hence, his name suggests a little fantastic at the moment, but extremely popular. His *Outline of History* commanded attention both for its style and for its ambitious scope, and paved the way for other "outlines" quite as ambitious.

Wellsian pipe-dreams

WEMMICK, JOHN

John Wemmick is the confidential law clerk of Mr. Jaggers, in Dickens' *Great Expectations*. A dry bachelor with frayed linen, he is sentimental out of business hours only, as when he tries to embrace Miss Skiffins while the Aged Parent whom he supports is reading. "A dry man with a square wooden face of imperfect, incomplete expression," he must have sustained a good deal of bereavement, "for he wore at least four mourning rings" and was "quite laden with remembrances of departed friends." Wearing the mechanical appearance of a smile, he never really smiled at all. When asked for a loan, Mr. Wemmick opines that "a man should never invest portable property in a friend."

a dismal John Wemmick

WERTHERIAN

Wertherian is from Werther, the hero of Goethe's sentimental romance *The Sorrows of Young Werther*. He is a love-lorn spirit, a morbidly sentimental youth who has become disgusted with life and its disenchantments. The name, therefore, connotes idle, futile repining.

a passionately Wertherian young man

WESLEYAN

Wesleyan is from John Wesley (1703-1791), who, with his brother Charles, founded a club at Oxford, scoffingly called "the methodists" because of the extremely methodical program the members of the group imposed upon themselves. By means of democratic, evangelistic, itinerant preaching quite opposite to the practices of the Established Church of England, and in the face of sometimes perilous situations, Wesley and his followers assembled many adherents to their doctrines, until Methodism now figures among the prominent religious denominations all over the world.

Wesleyan doctrines

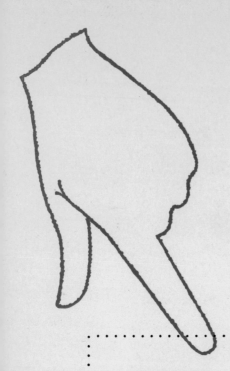

METAPHOR
FINDER

EMMAUS, PENNSYLVANIA

RODALE PRESS, INC.

Introduction

THE ORIGINAL PURPOSE of this volume was to present to the writer
a convenient and useful collection of colorful and pictorial phrases
that would serve to strike sparks from descriptive writing by the substitution of an occasional "picture-phrase" for a plain and simple word
with which it is synonymous. In the pursuit of this purpose, the
writings of thousands of British and American authors from the
"classical" days of our literature on down to modern times were examined for their picturesqueness of content, and the desired phrases
catalogued under file-words, or functional synonyms, suggested by
their literal meaning.

Since the most liberal collection of such "photographic" phrases
came from the department known as "figures of speech" in our high-
school and collegiate study of English composition, it was to be expected that the bulk of the material accumulating would be cast in
the nature of either *simile* or *metaphor*. Reminding ourselves of the
difference, we set before us this cheerful daily reminder to serve as a
touchstone in their detection: "She looks like a dream" (simile);
"She *is* a dream" (metaphor). Proceeding along this happy road, we
resolved that our product should eventually be known as a dictionary
of metaphors, since a metaphor is, after all, simply the kernel of a
simile. To these errant metaphors we would add all similes that
established a beachhead on our desk, and by the simple expedient of
clipping their wings and shearing them of their *like's* and *as'es,* affix
them permanently to some page of our book.

Confident of the superiority of metaphor to its more deliberate
and stilted cousin, simile, we found it to be everything our composition teachers had taught us "way back when." Immediate and intense
in effect, it assumes the likeness between two objects to be so blatantly
obvious as to make them, to all intents and purposes, identical. And
as the excerpted phrases avalanched breath-takingly on our desk, we
found that they had quite another virtue besides that of the color and
vividness for which they were being sought. They enabled their users
to say a great deal more in a great deal less space. As laconic as the

speech of ancient Sparta, they are compact and economical. This is, of course, the reason for which the metaphor, or figurative speech, is the staple diction of poetry and of all imaginative writing. Its effectiveness rests in its sudden surprise, its bold and exciting leaps of fancy from one thing to another. With its concrete and specific visualization of a thing which *is* as a thing which it is *not,* it is the indefatigable companion of all fine descriptive writing, filling in the work left undone by adjectives and adverbs, overworked as these too often are.

The original orientation of this book then changed in favor of making it a dictionary of all types of picturesque speech that could be effectively alphabetized under key-word synonyms. This was due to our ultimate admission that metaphor has played such a heavily historical role in our language as to fill it today with many originally metaphoric coinings that have since lost their meaning as such, in that their erstwhile sense of imagined comparison has quite entirely faded from our memories. Such vestiges of a metaphoric past are now hollowly preserved in words like "backbite," "blueblood," "curfew," "firebrand," and "postmaster." But when, despite this loss of caste, we found such words and phrases to be still of sufficiently "cinematic" effect in current speech, we included them. Thus, though "weed out" will be found under index-word SELECT, it may not actually create a mental picture of a gardener ripping undesirable tares out from among his pet flowers and vegetables in order to keep his patch pure. "Glean" was also kept under this same index-word, whether it always succeeds or sometimes fails in its intent to convey a strong picture of the process of selection that is carried out in a grain field by a second operation after the first harvesters, the reapers, have finished their work. Still another addition to SELECT is, however, of unimpugnable metaphoric rights, "pick from the tree."

Each of these picture-projecting phrases is alphabetized under the word or phrase which best defines or explains it, and should be looked up under that word as it occurs to the user of this book. Thus, if he were to thumb his way to WRITE, the very word which sent him in search of aid, he would find, among other graphic phrases: "weave the threads of a sentence; wear a typewriter to the bone; carve out a path with one's pen; butcher words; open the floodgates of inkland; embark on a page; mesh a lacework of words," etc.

Each alphabetized collection of phrases is further supplemented by a list of cross-references, directing the reader's attention to words synonymous with the one he has consulted, so that he may expand his search for the precise word-picture he wants. No longer need a writer "catch at a straw" if he wishes to express the idea of FUTILITY. By counseling with that word he can, for example: "employ a steam-engine to crack a nut; hurry toward a dead-end; make bricks without straw; cut a whetstone with a razor; beat the wind; extract sunbeams from cucumbers; break a fly on a wheel; milk a he-goat into a sieve; go on a sleeveless errand," etc. But if he does not find what he requires, he refers to other words cross-referenced at the bottom of the group. For example he may look under USELESS, which offers additional colorful phrases from which to choose such as: "sending a sprat to catch a whale; carrying owls to Athens; whistling jigs to a milestone; shoeing the goose; grasping at a shadow," etc.

The figurative value of many of the commoner words and phrases in this collection will depend, it should be warned, on the way in which the individual writer puts them to use. For example, under SHARP are found such entries as "razor-edged" and "tapered to point," which, if used to describe literally a knife-blade or a piece of whittle-wood, are devoid of metaphoric content. But when a harsh, grating voice is called "razor-edged," or an emphatic and menacing one is said to "taper to a point," a true metaphoric image is presented. Similarly, under ORDER is listed "shout injunctions at," which can become a picturesque phrase not if applied to a person (who can actually "shout" if he is so inclined), but to a thing (which actually cannot), as in "The letter shouted its injunctions to him."

Finally, some cautions are in order, and should be remembered by all writers who seek the assistance of word-pictures from these pages. *Avoid mixed metaphors,* that is, the use of two or more figurative expressions that collide in incongruity of meaning, like: "Education is the *Aladdin's lamp* with which *we unlock the door to success.*" Or like the phrase with which the cockney concluded his soap-box oration: "An' that, lidies and gentlemen, is the 'ole kettle o' fish in a nutshell."

Secondly, do not copy phrases slavishly. Refabricate. Readjust. Use them to stimulate your thinking.

Avoid, also, excessive use of picturesque expressions. Though metaphors and the like flash dramatically clear pictures on the screen of a reader's comprehension, in superfluity they are as cloying as (and a lot more artificial than) too many adjectives, however well chosen they may be. The highly stylized and metaphoric writings of men as individualistic in their mode of expression as Lafcadio Hearn, Joseph Conrad, John Steinbeck, and William Faulkner are models of proportion. They are neither excessively simple nor excessively "literary." Roman Horace, prime exponent of the "felicitous phrase," found the philosopher's stone in the *aurea mediocritas* which he himself minted; present-day writers too should take a firm hold on that "golden mean."

EDWARD FLUCK

A

ABANDON (v.)
wash one's hands of; cast or throw to the winds; take French leave; leave in the lurch; leave high and dry; leave in the basket; leave on someone's doorstep; turn one's back upon; throw someone over; throw to the wolves; sell down the river; make someone wear the willow (said of a jilted lover); drop; turn one's face from; ditch; shake the dust off one's feet; cast into the well; throw overboard; let go down the drain; shake off; put on the shelf.
(see *leave, quit, desert, surrender, yield, resign, renounce*)

ABILITY
a turn for; a gift for; a sharp ear for; knowing one's way about; knowing the score; being in form; having things at one's finger-tips; knowing one's stuff.
(see *power, force, efficient, genius, energetic, skillful, facilitate*)

ABSENT
play truant.
(see *neglect, disregard, withdraw*)

ABSENT MINDED
lost in thought; in a brown study; napping; dreaming; wool-gathering; looking a thousand miles away.
(see *inattentive, dream, loss*)

ABSOLUTE
cold (reason); hard (fact); beyond a shadow of doubt; dead (right); hairline (accuracy).
(see *realistic, certainly, unconditionally*)

ABUNDANCE
flocks of; swarms of; a cascade of; a deluge of; a flood of; a tidal wave of; an ever-running fountain of; a torrent of; a gush of; a sea of; a tempest of; a galaxy of; a stream of; a gale of; a treasure trove of; an arsenal of; an avalanche of; a landslide of; mountains of; generous helpings of; a rush of; clouds of; shoals of; a shower of; fistfuls of; kettleful of; a crop of; a snowstorm of; legions of; constant flow of; endless coil of; a big slice of; a carload of; bushels of; rivers of; sheaves of; the high tide of; a thunder of; a rash of; a bucketful of; an eruption of; a ton's weight of; great gulps of; a cornucopia of; a groaning sideboard of; a riot of; a Niagara of; a rain of; an exhaustless fount of; flow with milk and honey; ooze with; wallow in; be pregnant with; overflow with; reek with; brim with.
(see *luxury, wealthy, rich, many, full of, replete*)

ABUSE (v.)
bite; snap at; give a lick with the rough side of the tongue; trample on; hurl burning lava at; blacken; lash out at; heap red-hot coals on; hound from pillar to post.
(see *dishonor, betray, injure, hurt, reproach, slander, disparage, violate*)

ACCEPT
swallow; stomach; face (a fact); take wear; jump at; resign oneself to.
(see *estimate, regard, interpret, agree, approve, embrace, valuable*)

ACCOMPANY
go hand in hand with; have in tow; follow someone's steps; row in the same boat.
(see *follow*)

ACCURATE (to be)
hit the nail on the head; be a sure shot; hit the target; do dead reckoning; cite chapter and verse; act with

clockwork precision; show dictaphone accuracy; speak by the card.

(see *exact, correct, truthful, strict, faithful, careful, severe*)

ACCUSE

give the lie to; fire a charge at; throw in one's face; throw in one's teeth; lay at one's door; trump up a charge; brand with reproach; stigmatize; put in the black book; bring home to; cast the first stone at; keep a rod in pickle for; have a crow to pluck with; tax with; put the finger squarely on; pin the blame on.

(see *blame, reproach, complain, censorship*)

ACHIEVE

score a point; carry something off; bring home the bacon; scale the heights; pull off; knock off; win one's way to.

(see *successful, complete, finish, perfect, gain, win, get*)

ACT (in the theater)

tread the boards; be behind the footlights; wear the buskin; smell of greasepaint; barnstorm.

(see *tragedy, chorus girl*)

ADD

inject; graft on; tack on; pump into; sprinkle on; heap; whip in (something additional) .

(see *join, unite, connection*)

ADJUST

push into line; put in tune to; mend one's fences; trim one's sails; gear to; key to; find one's feet in the world; find one's level; bend to one's own end; mold to; stretch on the bed of Procrustes; temper the wind to the shorn lamb; fit a thing into a pigeonhole.

(see *arrange, reconcile, conform, regulation, harmony, orderly*)

ADVANTAGE (to gain)

get the better of; get the bulge on; get the laugh on one's side; hold the trump card; have (or catch) on the hip; give odds; steal a march on; take opportunity by the forelock; brandish a bargaining weapon; make use of God's gift.

(see *profit, favorable, conquer, defeat, superior, opportunist*)

ADVERTISE

trumpet; beat the drum; hawk; plug; ballyhoo; huckster; make a splash; window-dress.

(see *publish, proclaim, inform, knowledge*)

ADVISE

give a word to the wise; lend an earful; be an admonishing angel.

(see *suggest, inform, warn, consider, cautious*)

AFFECT

touch; melt; pierce; smite; cut deeply into; strike; stamp; color; rock; sink into the heart; play on; turn (someone's head); warp; twist; strike home; punch a hole in; bite into; penetrate; play tunes upon; strike a tender chord.

(see *influence, change, transform, impress, touch, overcome, moved*)

AFRAID

be visited by fear; have one's heart shoot downward with sickening effect; lose one's grip; shrink back; be seized by panic; be frightened out of one's senses; shake (or shiver) in one's shoes; not dare to call one's soul one's own; be scared out of a year's growth; be chilled to the marrow; break out in cold perspiration; hide under the rainspout; have the tail in water; have one's soul faint within one; have one's blood run cold; feel one's flesh creep;

have one's heart in one's mouth; feel the blood freeze.

(see *frightened, fearful, terrify, scare, timid, distrust, anxious*)

AGE (old)

evening's dusk; the crown of years; the quick-gathering sands of time; the sear and yellow leaf; the frosty finger-tips of age; the summit of one's years; the last chapter of a life; the graying period; pursuing the path to the grave; being on one's last legs; the dark dregs of age; the Wintertime of life; having one's vital fires burning low; a century of life resting on one's head; heavy-laden with years; a frail and broken reed.

(see *old, senility, old-fashioned, obsolete*)

AGGRAVATE

add fuel to the flame; fan the flame; push someone's patience; pour oil on the flames; heap coals of fire on someone's head.

(see *annoy, increase, worse, irritate, tease, anger, offend*)

AGGRESSIVE (to be)

beard the lion in his den; take the bull by the horns; go after someone with a meat axe.

(see *attack, hostile, opportunist, ambition*)

AGITATOR

a human whip-lash; a fire-brand; the left flank.

(see *radical, restless, energetic, excite, tumult, arouse, disturbance, dispute*)

AGREE

fit to a T; pay lip service to; chime in with; come to an understanding with; see eye to eye; hit it off with; fall in with; be in tune with; make oneself solid with; be of one mind; go with the stream; swim with the tide; take part with; work side by side; take the same line; stand shoulder to shoulder; walk arm in arm with; express with one voice; be all of a piece; be in key with; be harmonious; be attuned to; abide by; give the green light; bow the head in obedience; play ball with; turn a willing ear to; flow in the same channel with.

(see *conform, harmony, unanimous, uniform, obedient*)

AIM (v.)

steer for; let fly at; level (a weapon) against; set one's sights for; shoot at.

(see *shooting*)

AIMLESS

leading to no end; whistling down the wind; shuffling through life; fiddling away time; rudderless; drifting along the stream of existence.

(see *useless, wasteful, haphazard, futility, unconcerned*)

AIR

the cold wind of the mountains; a breath of wind; a sigh of wind; a pulse of air.

(see *wind, breathe*)

AIRPLANE

cloud chariot; man-created wasp; twentieth-century Pegasus; throbbing cello-drone of planes.

(see *fly*)

ALERT (to be)

be on the watch; keep a sharp lookout; keep one's eye (or one's weather eye) open; know a hawk from a hernshaw; be on tiptoe; stand a-tip-toe; have all one's wits about one; have all one's eyes about one; understand trap; be up to snuff; not suffer the grass to grow under one's feet; have no flies on one; be owl-eyed; have a sharp ear; be on one's toes; be awake in mind; catch fire (under the eye of someone);

have the air of a hunted animal; stand mentally on tiptoe; be clear-headed; prick up one's ears; never miss a trick; sit up and take notice.

(see *watchful, cautious, quickly, ready, observant, prudent, careful*)

ALOOFNESS

the ice-barrier that separates one's private self from his public life; the rigid handle of formality with which to hold off all acquaintances; the steely blankness of a smile; frozen-faced reserve.

(see *formal, unfriendly, distant, remote, privacy, unemotional*)

AMBITION

an eagle born to soar; flaming zeal; the upward climb; castles in the air; the rung just above one's head; the fire of youth; itching fingers; the early bird; shooting at the stars; climbing the ladder.

(see *eager, hope, desire, yearn, energetic, aggressive, fame*)

ANALYZE

dissent; unravel; explore (or plumb) the depths; read between the lines; lay bare the facts; strip to the bones; put the scalpel to; break a thing down; go behind the plain facts; get to the heart of; lay a cold finger on a hot pulse.

(see *interpret, study, expose, understand, examine, investigate, criticize*)

ANGER (n.)

vials of wrath; a glitter in the eye; fire in the eye; heat in the eye; a blaze of fury; a flame of fury; a tearing temper; darts of rage; spleen; ulcer; a fire at the heart; the bursting of a storm-cloud; a storm of anger that clutches by the throat and eyeballs; lava-like eruptions from the crater of the nerves; a hair-trigger temper; a flash of fire; a driving storm of anger;

the lash of a tongue; threads of red cut in the eyeballs; baring the fangs; formidable array of teeth; red spots burning in the cheeks; eyes like bits of steel; blood-red emotions; heated words; smouldering fires.

(see *rage, resent, temper*)

ANGER (v.)

inflame; drive mad; get a rise out of; set on fire; ruffle the temper; draw sparks from; make hackles rise; make blood boil; lash into fury; get someone's shirt; provoke to the boiling point; drive into a black anger; put in a glout.

(see *irritate, annoy, displease, offend*)

ANGRY (to be or become)

feel the barometer rise; scorch with a glance; grind (or gnash) ones' teeth; vent one's spleen; be burning up; blow off steam; flare up; boil with anger; have the blood up; boil over; open (or pour out) the vials of one's wrath; flame up; hit the ceiling (or roof); turn up the whites of one's eyes; lash into madness; fly off the handle; blow up; foam at the mouth; be all in a smoulder; take pepper in the nose; fly into a rage; fly up; get one's Irish up; raise one's back (or dander); snap (or bite) someone's head off; have something get under the skin; have battle in one's eyes; have it in good and heavy for someone; see red; bridle up; snort fire and brimstone; scuttle burning hot words off one's lips; blaze and fulminate with anger; have the blood rocking like a sea in one's veins; lash oneself into a rage; walk off on one's ears; feel a hot flush run through one; spit fire from the eyes; go on the warpath; be in hot blood; be in a stew; be black as thunder; go white with rage; be white-hot; be wrought up; be in the heat of passion; be up in arms; run out of temper; be in a ruffled temper; be on fire; blaze;

snap; set the eyes to kindling; shoot fire; be on fire.

(see *resent, temper, savage, sullen, scowl, glare at*)

ANNOY

rub or stroke the wrong way; peck at; hound; ruffle; play the gadfly; play Old Harry (or Nick) with; sour the temper; set someone by the ears; be a thorn in the side; be an ulcer in the flesh; slam someone's nerves to blazes; throw someone into a fever; put a drop of vinegar in the cup; be gall and wormwood; make bad blood; step on toes; play the deuce against; saddle with; plague; weigh down with; corrode; send away with a flea in the ear; worry someone into the grave; press someone hard; touch to eruption.

(see *irritate, troubled, pain, worry, tease, disturbance*)

ANTICIPATE

look forward to; taste in advance; smack the lips; take time by the throat; take the bull by the horns; steal a march on; beat the gun; scent trouble; smell a rat.

(see *expect, foresee, look for, prospect, wait*)

APOLOGIZE

eat one's words; eat humble pie; eat crow.

(see *retract, regret, repent, remorseful, excuse*)

APPEAR

come to light; dawn; swim into ken; make a bow; sail in; loom; crop up; spring up; mushroom; leap up; turn up; bob up; pop up; knock (of opportunity).

(see *emerge, visible, show, come, occur*)

APPEARANCE

face; cut of one's jib; bib and tucker; outer wrappings; complexion.

(see *show, fashionable*)

APPLAUD

bring down the house; pin an orchid on; thunder approval; make the walls ring; shake the rafters; thump applause.

(see *cheer up, praise, approve*)

APPRECIATIVE (to be)

do justice to; know on which side one's bread is buttered; not look a gift-horse in the mouth.

(see *prize, valuable*)

APPROACH (v.)

bend one's steps toward; pull up alongside of; creep up to; grope toward; drift toward; bear down upon; come up to the threshold; wing one's way toward; shoulder one's way toward; skirmish toward; make a beeline for; flit toward; buzz up to; pick one's way toward; thread one's way toward; march up to; gravitate toward; plummet toward; beat a path toward; trace one's way toward; bounce up to; head for.

(see *come, near*)

APPROVE

put under hand and seal; rubberstamp; pat on the back; smile upon; applaud; clap on the shoulder; give the nod to; give the green light to; "clear"; give a certificate to; bless.

(see *praise, appreciative, valuable, prize*)

ARGUE

bandy words; pick a bone with; fall to conversational blows; thresh out; split hairs; chop logic; pound the table for; do battle on; go at a discussion hammer and tongs; toss the ball of conversation back and forth; struggle verbally with someone.

(see *dispute, discuss, quarrel, scold, squabble, disagree, differ, contend*)

ARGUMENT

knock-down-and-drag-out verbal fisti-cuffs; a verbal pillow-fight; verbal thunderclaps; a battle of words; a duel of brains; a cock-fight; a tongue-lash-ing tournament; a verbal scrimmage; hot words; a skirmish of ideas; verbal guns; a stormy session; a duel of words; a bloodless chasm.

(see *dispute, differ, disagree, contro-versy, discord, strife*)

ARISTOCRACY

the carriage trade; blue blood; gen-tle blood; silk-stocking; crême-de-la crême; high-born; (on a) social pedes-tal; have a white-columned past.

(see *nobleman*)

AROUSE

kindle; light; inflame; stir; galvanize; prod; whet; stab at; bristle up; drum up sentiment; set fire to; rake up; fan; sing to; whip up; fire; spur to.

(see *stimulate, urge, incite, excite, agi-tator*)

AROUSED

up in arms; wound up; inflammable; on fire; having one's blood up; strung up; stirred; dragged up from; heated to the boiling point; wakened to life; catching fire.

(see *excited, stimulate, eager, fervent, passionate, enthusiastic*)

ARRANGE

fix one's flint; hitch; put to rights; put straight; line up; marshal; fix up.

(see *prepare, organize, adjust, plan, provide, ready, orderly, correct*)

ARTIFICIAL

hot-house; veneer; toy; fashion-plat-ed.

(see *false, unreal, sham, pretense, fake*)

ASHAMED (to be)

out of countenance; crest-fallen; with drooping banners; with one's tail be-tween one's legs; hang-dog; shame-faced; hide one's face; cover one's head in shame; hang one's head.

(see *disconcert, repent, shame, em-barrassed, sorrowful, humiliate, blush*)

ASK

besiege with questions; pop a ques-tion; pepper with questions; shoot a question; let fall a question; fire off questions; bombard with questions; make suit.

(see *question, inquisitive, request, solicit, seek, implore, demand*)

ASSISTANT

second; a lesser cog in the wheel; aco-lyte; satellite; tool; partner in crime; doer of the dirty work.

(see *help, subordinate*)

ATTACK (v.)

hack away at; swing hatchet against; tear at; fly at; tackle; strike a blow at; blast; fall afoul of; spring a mine; ride full tilt against; put under fire; fire broadsides; knife; go on the war-path; be on the pounce for; fight the dragon in its lair; fall upon; stab at; bombard; pelt.

(see *aggressive, fight, war, struggle*)

ATTEMPT (v.)

tackle; make passes at; try one's hand at; take in hand; grapple with (a problem); set one's cap at; take a shot at; make overtures to.

(see *try, endeavor, undertake, strive*)

ATTRACT

catch the eye; rivet; magnetize; fix with the eye; polarize; grip; speak to (the imagination); capture; beckon; take the fancy of.

(see *lure, tempt, fascinate*)

AUDIENCE
wall of faces; forest of faces; sea of faces; a vessel for his outpouring.
(see *group, listen, watchful*)

AUTOMOBILE
the king of travel; horseless carriage; bird on wheels; throbbing monster.
(see *locomotive, airplane*)

AUTUMN
fall of the leaf; the painting fingers of October; blue-and-gold autumn days.
(see *springtime, summer*)

AVOID
turn one's back on; set one's face against; duck out of; run away from; keep out of range of; fight shy of; shy away from; steer clear of; detour; blink a fact; hide in the background give a wide birth to.
(see *shun, reject, outcast, eliminate*)

B

BACKGROUND
canvas; frame; pedigree.

(see *source, origin, setting, scene*)

BALANCE (v.)
walk a tightrope; offset; sit in the middle of a seesaw; walk a chalk-line between.

(see *compensate, equal*)

BALD
billiard-ball.

(see *hair*)

BANKRUPT
driven to the wall; "broke"; stony-broke; have one's economic throat cut; be smothered economically.

(see *poor, ruin, poverty-stricken*)

BARGAIN (v.)
sell ones' soul; demand a pound of flesh; strike a bargain.

(see *agree, sell, trade*)

BASIS
ground; taproot; bedrock; core; framework; cornerstone; groundwork; root; pillar; footing; rib; well-spring; nerve-center; kernel; fountainhead; anchor; scaffolding; key-stone.

(see *source, fundamental, bottom, support*)

BATTLEGROUND
theater of war; no-man's-land; vale of destruction.

(see *fight, war, conflict*)

BEAUTIFUL (of a woman)
music to the eyes; nectar from the gods; an eye-opener; a sight for sore eyes; blooming; an exquisite tea-rose; a lyrical vision; a flame of loveliness; the magnolia on the family tree.

(see *woman*)

BEAUTIFY
doll up; grace; put a bloom to; paint the lily; touch up with color; embroider; frost the cake; wake the Sleeping Beauty with a lipstick; set a patch at the corner of Helen of Troy's eyes.

(see *embellish, improve, decorate*)

BEGIN (v.)
raise the curtain; give birth to; hatch; launch; buckle down to; start the ball rolling; embark upon; strike up; set the machinery in motion; open; lead the way; cut the first turf; plant the seed of; break ground; plunge into; burst into; hurl oneself into; break the ice; enter the calendar; make a bow; set in train.

(see *start, originate, undertake*)

BEGINNER
tenderfoot; neophyte; pioneer; in one's novitiate; greenhorn; one in leading strings.

(see *learn, inexperienced, unskillful*)

BEGINNING
springs; cradle; threshold; gate; the first step; the first chapter; the prelude; the rise (or rising) of the curtain; the thin end of the wedge; seed; root; first shadow; dawn; (to start from) scratch; the germ of; the spores; embryo; microcosm; the first link in the chain; infancy; chrysalis; the blueprint stage; in the bud; genesis; opening gun; the first blush; spade-work; birth-throes.

(see *origin, source, start, opening*)

BEHIND
in the wake; at the heels of.

(see *follow*)

BELIEVE

swallow; swallow the bait; gulp down; take the word of; take someone at his word; take to heart; get into one's head; fall for.

(see *gullible, trust, faithful*)

BEST (adj.)

crowning; crack (of a regiment); of the first water; banner (of a year).

(see *superior, excellent, perfect, high-priced, unique*)

BEST (n.)

the flower; the cream; the pick of; the salt (of the earth); the fat (of the land); the pearls of.

(see *perfect*)

BETRAY

sell down the river; play false; blow the gaff; let the cat out of the bag; tell tales out of school; give over to the foe; turn King's or Queen's evidence; stab in the back.

(see *abandon, traitor, treachery, deceive, mislead, lure, violate, false*)

BETTER

greener (pastures); rosier (picture); sunnier (aspect).

(see *superior, preference, advantage*)

BIG

fat; land-office; record-breaking; staggering; Texas-sized; mountainous; thumping.

(see *large, mass*)

BIND

cement; tie to the apron-strings; tie down; chain; shackle; manacle; peg; tether.

(see *join, unite, confine, restrain*)

BIRDS

feathered tribes; musical instruments with wings.

(see *fly*)

BIT (little)

atom; crumb; grain; germ; scrap; fragment; patch; shred; shadow; puff; rav (of hope); smithereen; spark; lick (of work); pebble; whisper; glimmer; dash; mouthful; morsel; splinter; whiff; spoonful; a spice of; a glimmering of; nugget; iota.

(see *tiny, small amount, minimum, scarce, slight, particle, speck*)

BITE (v.)

bury fangs in; mouth.

(see *eat*)

BITTER

acid; vinegar; salty; looking as if butter would not melt in one's mouth.

(see *sharp, unpleasant, harsh, stern, severe, pain*)

BITTERNESS

poisoned feelings; the soured wine (of loneliness); gall; tears hardened to crystal; iron (entered one's soul); wormwood.

(see *intense, regret, despondency, grievance, hate, grieve, malicious, sorrowful, spiteful*)

BLAME (v.)

point an invidious finger at; lay at the door of; throw in someone's teeth; pin the foul deed on; nail to.

(see *accuse, condemn, disapprove, reproach, censorship*)

BLAME (to take)

take the rap; be elected the goat.

(see *victimize, misfortune, misjudge*)

BLAMELESS

with a safe conscience; with the hands clean.

(see *innocent, virtuous*)

BLASPHEMOUS
spiritual poison-gas; a human revolver in oaths.

(see *profanity, ungodly, swear*)

BLIND (to be)
locked in darkness.

(see *conceal, dark, dim, unseen*)

BLOND (hair)
the color of a jar of strained honey seen through sunlight; curls spun out into a cloud of gold; the color of warm ashes.

(see *light (n.), hair*)

BLOW (n.)
shock; a nasty one in the eye; a slap in the face; a dagger in the heart.

(see *misfortune, disaster, hardship, distressed, troubled*)

BLOW (v.)
(of the wind) sing; moan; whip; whisk.

(see *wind, breathe*)

BLUNDER (v.)
stumble in one's speech; make a slip of the tongue; get the wrong sow by the ear; fly in the face of facts; strike a wrong note; muff the ball.

(see *mistake, wrong, clumsy*)

BLUSH (n.)
crimson mantling on the flushed cheek; brightness bursting from one's lids to the cheeks; a wave of scorching red; a fine color running over the cheeks; a sudden rush of rosy color; the angry blood burning in one's face; a flame of scarlet creeping across one's cheeks; apple-cheeked; tell-tale rose; crimson-masked; peony-red flood; a flood of carmine; slow color rising in one's cheeks until it overflows into the whites of one's eyes; wild-rose hue.

(see *shame, ashamed, shy, timid, embarrassed, red*)

BLUSH (v.)
go red all over; burn with embarrassment; flood with color (of the cheeks); flush to the red steaminess of a boiled beet; flame; turn poppy-red.

(see *red, embarrassed*)

BOAST (v.)
throw one's weight about; talk big; toot one's own horn; talk through one's hat; ring one's own bell; cry roast meat; hallo before one is out of the woods; peacock about; become inflated; crow; ride the high horse; blow one's own trumpet; put on the dog; be a windbag.

(see *exaggerate, triumphant, vain, pretentious*)

BOASTING (n.)
much cry and little wool; loud drumming in front and no soldiers behind; windy conceit; purple language.

(see *conceited, pretend*)

BODY
the human temple; the human vessel; the shell; the house of the spirit; the prison cell of the soul.

(see *substance, strong*)

BOLD (to be)
enjoy climbing steep ladders; be a lone wolf; use full rigging.

(see *courageous, dare, brave, self-reliant, confident*)

BOOKS
literary menu; magic carpets to carry one to the other side of the moon; intellectual treasure-troves.

(see *read*)

BORDER (v.)
fringe; skirt; hedge; rim.

(see *touch, edge, surround*)

BORE (v.)
talk a person's head off; talk a person

to death; put a person to sleep; buttonhole.

(see *tedious, uninteresting, dull, monotonous, stupid*)

BORED (to be)
be lost in a fit of yawning; yawn oneself to death; have time hang heavy on one's hands; suffer mental dry-rot; drift over stagnant pools of the mind; be crushed by monotony; find things dry as dust; stagnate; sit back weakly; have things leave one cold.

(see *tired, unconcerned*)

BORN (to be)
join the human cavalcade; be ushered into the world; see the light of day; come into the world; enter the theatre of one's own life; break the shell; have one's soul enter its clay tabernacle.

(see *child, beginning*)

BOTTOM
root; cellar; (of the sea) Davy Jones's locker; foot.

(see *basis*)

BRANCHES (bare)
fleshless arms.

(see *autumn*)

BRAVE (to be)
lion-hearted; unfettered by fear; show a bold front; look danger in the face; march up to the cannon's mouth; play the man; run the gauntlet; screw up one's courage; put a bold face on the matter.

(see *courageous, bold, dare*)

BREAK (v.)
give way; jump contract; cut in; shatter; put out of joint.

(see *sever, disrupt, spoil*)

BREATHE
drink in air.

(see *air*)

BREATHLESS
winded.

(see *excited*)

BRIBE (n.)
hush money; blood money.

(see *reward, graft, extort, price, gift*)

BRIBE (v.)
cross the palm with silver; tickle the palm; grease the palm; bait with a silver hook; make speech silver.

(see *influence*)

BRIEF
in a nutshell; in brochure terms; on the fly; one-glance (explanation); capsule version; vestpocket (size); thumbnail picture.

(see *shorten, concise, short-lived*)

BRIGHT (luminous)
garnished and spangled with light; brazen and unclouded; glowing with fire; burning blue; lit up; gilded; splashed with sunshine; tinged with gold; flaring with white; washing with a sea of light; blinding brilliance; flowering with light; pouring forth golden sunshine; playing a fountain of light; opalesque and full of fire; blooming with radiance; shooting out beams; painted with sunbeams.

(see *light, sunlight, shine, sparkling*)

BRILLIANCE (intellectual)
stroke of genius; lightning mind; luminous talent; a shining example; dazzling understanding; incandescent wit; glittering intellect.

(see *intellectual, intelligent, wise*)

BRUNETTE
mahogany-visaged; raven-haired; caramel-colored; a lick or dash of the tarbrush about one.

(see *hair, dark*)

BRUSH (v.)

give one's hair a brief lick (with the brush).

(see *hair*)

BUILD

timber with oak; translate into bricks and concrete; patch together.

(see *structure*)

BUILDINGS

towering masses of concrete and steel; temples of the religion of business.

(see *house, skyscraper, structure*)

BURDEN (n.)

tax; weight; yoke; iron crown (of suffering); dead weight; millstone around one's neck; albatross (around one's neck); a clanking chain to drag after one; psychological knapsacks too heavy for the shoulders beneath them to bear; the excessive freight of one's offenses.

(see *oppress*)

BURDENED

groaning (of a table); saddled with.

(see *full of, troubled*)

BURN

(of flames) lick; curl; turn something into a flaming cauldron; eat their way; twist restless tongues of fire.

(see *fire*)

BURY

put to bed with a shovel; screw down in his coffin; put someone in his last resting place.

(see *die, death, funeral, grave*)

BUSINESS

irons in the fire; matter in hand; walk of life; (get down to) brass tacks; hive of industry; (talk) shop; many-tentacled octopus.

(see *trade, office, work, industrious*)

BUSINESS (to do)

hold a portfolio; play a part; fill an office.

(see *work, labor, trade, bargain, buy, sell*)

BUSY (to be)

have a hand in; have many irons in the fire; keep on foot; be wide awake; let no grass grow under foot; gather no moss; kick up one's petticoats; bustle with; be in harness; be in the swim; seethe with; buzz with; hum with; whirr and swish; exist in a hive of industry; be up to one's ears in work; have one's hands full; be snowed under; have fish to fry; be closely closeted with; be heaped high with duties; have much on one's hands; be immersed in; have one's hands tied for some time to come; be monopolized by; have no time to kill; be turned into a mere machine.

(see *industrious, work, labor, energetic*)

BUTT (n.)

laughingstock; the whetstone for someone else's wit; food for laughter.

(see *joke, laugh*)

BUY

snap up; gobble up; snatch up.

(see *get, possess, gain, invest*)

C

CALM (adj.)

unruffled: halcyon; sleeping (of the sea); iron (nerves).

(see *tranquil, peace, rest, quiet*)

CALM (to be)

pull oneself together; not turn a hair; keep a cool head; keep one's shirt on; iron the creases from one's temper; keep one's head; pull down one's jacket; gather up one's wits; stand on one's own feet; display a marble calm; not bat an eye; have the meekness of a lamb.

(see *impassive, self-possessed, unexcitable, controlled*)

CALM (v.)

smooth troubled waters; pour oil on troubled waters; set at ease; set someone's mind at rest; pour healing balm on; cast a cooling shadow upon; act as a sedative; smooth the rough edge of; keep on an even keel; cause to sail in calm waters.

(see *soothe, relief, pacify, ease*)

CAMPAIGN (v.)

run for an office; carry the banner; hit the sawdust trail; kiss damp babies; lay hands on babies' brows; woo (a constituency).

(see *politics*)

CANCEL

strike off (a score); consign to the dust-bin; do away with; blot out; rub out; cratch out; wipe out; cross out.

(see *obliterate, destroy, erase*)

CANDLELIGHT

flowers of light; restless tongues of flame.

(see *light, fire, burn*)

CANDY

bait for a sweet tooth.

(see *sweet*)

CAREFUL (to be)

handle with tongs; handle with gloves; pull gently at a weak rope; keep out of harm's way; save one's bacon; take heed at one's peril; sleep with one eye open; tread on delicate ground (or eggs, thin ice); mind one's P's and Q's; draw in one's horns; mind what one is about; look sharp to; toe the line; keep off the grass; not leap in the dark; keep out of troubled waters; keep an ear to the ground; have delicate ears; keep a hawk-eye on; handle on a loose rein; rake over with a fine-tooth comb.

(see *cautious, watchful, discreet, prudent*)

CARELESS (to be)

be off one's guard; be caught off base; play fast and loose; give a lick and a promise; see with half an eye; throw caution to the winds; go off half-cocked; get off on the wrong foot; have one's shoe strings dangling; act in a hit-or-miss fashion; be slap-dash; go once over lightly; be slipshod; have butter fingers; be breezy; act in a helter-skelter manner; be slam-bang; go free-wheeling.

(see *negligent, indifferent, inattentive, unconcerned*)

CATCH (v.)

ensnare; set one's bait for; pinch; collar; bring to book; lay hands on; run down; run to earth; put salt on the tail of; close in upon; cast a net; spin a web around; whip tentacles around; hold in the meshes of one's will.

(see *trap, seize, snatch, snare, possess*)

CAUGHT (to be)

wriggle on a hook; be brought to book; trapped; netted; skewered; fallen into the hands of; caught in a "bag"; hoisted on one's own petard; be roped in.

(see *victimize*)

CAUSE (n.)

root; seed-bed; germ.

(see *basis, source, origin*)

CAUSE (v.)

give birth to; lie at the root of; be at the bottom of; breed; be father to; sow the seeds of; dictate; invite; light the fuse of; spark; awaken (comment, etc.); stir; bring into play; kick up.

(see *originate, produce, create*)

CAUTIOUS (to be)

be on one's guard; feel one's way; pick one's steps; keep on the safe side; keep out of harm's way; steer safely; look before one leaps; wait to see how the cat jumps; wait to see how the wind blows; tread on eggs and break none; pull one's punches; play safe; count the cost; keep one's weather eye open; sit tight; measure one's footsteps; be on the defense.

(see *careful, watchful, prudent, discreet*)

CELEBRATE

hold high festival; kill the fatted calf, roast an ox; paint the town red; mark with a red letter; do things up brown; lark about; put on the cap and bells; blow a tin horn; let off steam.

(see *joyful, rejoice, gay, happy*)

CELEBRITY

lion; noble animal; star.

(see *fame, renown, glorify*)

CENSORSHIP

the Iron Curtain; blue-penciling; veil of secrecy.

(see *criticize, blame, disapprove, condemn, reprimand*)

CENSUS

counting of noses.

(see *citizen*)

CENTER

bosom; heart; kernel; seat (of memory, etc.); belly; melting pot; pivot; kingpin; focal point; mainspring; navel; fulcrum; nucleus; clearing house.

(see *middle*)

CERTAINLY

rain or shine; without a shadow of doubt; beyond a shade of doubt; come what may; even if the worse come to worse.

(see *inevitable*)

CHALLENGE (v.)

throw down the gauntlet; throw down the glove; hold in defiance; look in the eye; call in question; beard; call someone's bluff; force the hand (of Destiny); grasp (Fate) by the horns; fly in the face of; draw the bow against; throw in the teeth of; put on the spot.

(see *defy, dare*)

CHAMPAGNE

the sparkling sin.

(see *drunk*)

CHANCE (n.)

pot luck; cross and pile; a toss up; heads or tails; a fair field; a leap in the dark; a random shot; a pig in a poke; a blind bargain; a flyer; the turn of Fortune's wheel; the whirl of Fortune's giddy wheel; the scales of Fate; the lottery of Fate; the hazard of the die; a turn of the cards; a turn of the table; a stroke of luck; a lucky hit;

innings; the fourth down; the long arm of coincidence; the flower in the crannied wall (*i.e.*, by chance); life's chessboard.

(see *lucky, fortunate, possibility, fate, risk, uncertain*)

CHANCE (to take a)

risk one's neck; run the venture of; tempt fortune; skate on thin ice; leap in the dark; go out on a limb; pitch one's lot; risk the odds; take a shot in the air; cast one's bread on the waters.

(see *risk, dare, gamble*)

CHANGE (n.)

turn of the tide; reshuffling; new departure; ebbing and flowing tides; about-face; turning point; shake-up.

(see *alteration, vicissitudes, varied, turn, transients*)

CHANGE (v.)

take a new turn; turn over a new leaf; play a different tune; sing to another song (or tune); turn the corner; ring the changes; turn (of the tide); wheel about; switch; bend one's course; shift one's ground; turn one's boats; congeal; doctor; reupholster; shuffle the cards; thicken or darken (of emotions); put new wine into old bottles; shift gears; flow (of one season into another); turn one's coat; leap from one thing into another; add a jot or tittle; lift to a different level; change the face of.

(see *transform, varied, replace, turn*)

CHANGEABLE

kaleidoscopic; chameleon-like; fluid; mercurial; barometric; floating; the sport of the winds and the waves.

(see *fickle, undecided, inconsistent, unsettled, unsteady, uncertain, vacillate, unstable*)

CHARACTER

the length of one's foot; true colors;

backbone; complicated twist of moral fibers.

(see *reputation, virtuous*)

CHEAP

catchpenny; trashy; bargain-counter; for a mere song; for an old song; on a shoestring.

(see *common, low-class, inferior, poor*)

CHEAT (v.)

stack the cards; grease the road; fleece; juggle the books; cog the dice; play with marked cards; have one's hand in the till; double-cross; two-time; chisel; give short measure; take in; be a sharper.

(see *trickery, deceive, outwit, mislead, swindle, victimize*)

CHECK-UP

count noses; send to the rightabout; tick off points on one's fingers.

(see *investigate, observant, watchful*)

CHEER (v.)

raise the spirits; warm the soul; warm the cockles of the heart; drive dull care away.

(see *incite, encourage, solace*)

CHEERFUL (to be)

come up smiling; take heart; keep up one's spirits.

(see *happy, joyful, pleasant, pleased, gay*)

CHILD

chick; offshoot, chip off the old block; olive branch; fruit of the womb; be still in swaddling clothes; live under the pellucid sky of babyhood.

(see *born*)

CHILDREN

litter; fragile flowers; pledges of affection; little pitchers; one's own flesh and blood; toddlers; small fry;

nymphs of the perambulator.
(see *son, young, immature*)

CHILL (n.)
the shakes; icy current; pierced to the marrow.
(see *cold, shiver*)

CHOICE (no)
not a pin to choose; Hobson's choice; between the devil and the deep blue sea, the horns of a dilemma.
(see *necessity, inevitable, requisite*)

CHOICE (second)
runner-up; second fiddle; the second string to the bow.
(see *preference, substitute*)

CHOOSE
fix upon; single out; take for better or for worse; make one's "dish"; weigh a choice; espouse; pick.
(see *select, preference*)

CHORUS GIRL
hourglass soubrette.
(see *dance, singing*)

CIRCLE
wreath; halo; radius; girdle.
(see *round, surround*)

CIRCUMSTANCES
the web of life; the wheel of life; (to stand) in such shoes.
(see *vicissitudes, chance*)

CITIZEN
John Doe; Richard Roe; pillar of the community; son.
(see *reside, census, common people*)

CITY
urban agglomeration; monstrously swollen caravanserai; a titanic honeycomb of cells.
(see *skyscraper*)

CIVILIZATION
light; Nature brushed and combed.
(see *refined, educated, enlighten*)

CLASSIC
toga-draped; down the ages.
(see *old, obsolete, model, elegant, refined*)

CLEAN (adj.)
lavender-clean; cauterized (conscience); burstingly immaculate.
(see *innocent, virtuous*)

CLEAR (adj.)
looking-glass (of a river); all daylight (of a mind); written on the wall; untarnished; transparent; speaking for itself; telling its own tale; unblurred; with its meaning lying on the surface; staring one in the face; rearing its head; that which meets the eye; the face-value of a thing; at the first blush.
(see *obvious, evident, conspicuous, visible*)

CLEAR (to make)
blow the cobwebs away; make a clean sweep; get it across to; bring it home to; present a thing nakedly; etch a thing sharply; erase a blot; unravel; focus; express in liquid notes.
(see *show, reveal, explain, solution, represent, self-evident, unencumbered*)

CLIMAX (n.)
the high tide; the crowning stroke; the bright star; the crest of the wave; the point; (come to) a head; crescendo; the last straw; the peak; cap-

stone; the flash point; (at) white heat.
(see *maximum, top*)

CLIMAX (v.)

top off; cap; come to flood-crest; crown.
(see *increase, grow, height*)

CLIQUES

closed rings; solidly knit groups.
(see *group*)

CLOSE (adj.)

under one's nose; at the threshold; on the heels of; within an inch of; within a stone's throw of; a hair's breadth from; hardly wider than an eyelash; neck and neck; within shadow-reach; on the brink of; without elbow room; toe-to-toe; a shave from; on hand; at one's finger's ends; bow to bow; stem to stem; cheek by jowl; in pace with; within arm's length; hugging the land or shore; sharp to.
(see *near, join, immediately, thick, border, intimate, snug, tighten, imminent*)

CLOSE (v.)

fold up; shut up shop; wind up (of affairs); put up the shutters; put the seal to ;wall up; lock.
(see *stop, obstruct, finish, end, complete*)

CLOSELY

by the skin of one's teeth.
(see *difficulty*)

CLOTHES

rig-out; rag; get-up; sartorial embellishment; full panoply; best bib and tucker.
(see *cover, fashionable*)

CLOUDED

veiled; shrouded; frowning.
(see *obscure, darkness, dim, shadows*)

CLOUDS

mackerel sky; mares' tails; thunderheads; white galleons; smoke puffs.
(see *mist*)

CLUE

thread; key; missing link.
(see *solution, guide, hint*)

CLUMSY (to be)

cut a sorry figure; fumble with butter fingers; heavy-handed (or footed); be a bull in a china shop; all thumbs; left-handed; clownish.
(see *blunder, unskillful, inadequate*)

COLD (weather)

raw; icy; glacial; frosty; bone-chilling; marrow-freezing; teeth-chattering; nipping; lacing in a girdle of solid ice.
(see *wind, snow*)

COLLAPSE (v.)

fall on one's face; go to pieces; break down; go up the spout;
(see *fall, sink, ruin, fail, upset*)

COLLECT

glean; reap; send the hat around; tie together in a bundle; sweep up; corral; round up; bundle; collect in a dragnet;
(see *gather*)

COLLECTION

potpourri; mosaic; hodgepodge; montage; bulging file; a circus of; pool; sandpile; a rich pudding from which to pull out plums.
(see *group, mass, store, crowd*)

COME

stray in; float in; drift in; steal in; filter in; creep in; glide in; trickle or dribble in (as news, money, etc.); blow in; sail in; come upon the stage; pour in; stream in; swarm in; rain in (as complaints); flow in; breeze in; shuffle in; toddle in; beat a path to; fall, descend or shut down (as stillness, silence, etc.); swim (as tears into the eyes); crawl out of; burst from; flow from (as words from a pen); pop into (as an idea into a head); dawn upon; bloom within (as words); fly into (the mind); burst into flower.

(see *approach, originate*)

COMMIT (oneself)

stick one's neck out; climb out on a limb; burn one's bridges or boats; cross the Rubicon.

(see *chance, obligated, promise*)

COMMON (adj.)

bread and butter; a dime a dozen; garden-variety; stock.

(see *cheap, ordinary, low-class, uninteresting, usual*)

COMMON PEOPLE

the man in the street; the great unwashed; the swinish multitude; king Mob; rank and file; common herd; tag, rag and bobtail; Tom, Dick and Harry; Brown, Jones and Robinson; chaff; hewers of wood and drawers of water; weary Willie; chawbacon; sheep.

(see *citizen, crowd, people*)

COMMUTER

traffic; whip between; flit between; strap-hanger.

(see *travel, wanderer*)

COMPARE

measure noses; stack alongside; hold a candle to.

(see *balance, similar, resemble, estimate*)

COMPENSATE

make up for; make something good; make casting weight.

(see *replace, restitution, repay, satisfied*)

COMPETITION

marathon race; a run for one's money; dog-eat-dog; competitive web; keeping up with the Joneses; jockeying for advantage; fencing with; running race; tug-of-war; the open door; cut-throat (affair).

(see *rivalry, struggle, oppose, contend, strive*)

COMPLAIN

beef; squawk; moan; bellyache; raise a rumpus; weep on someone's shoulder; howl one's head off; kick; croak; raise a riot; whine; growl; raise a hue and cry; sing the blues; groan over; be a sorehead; chew a bitter cud.

(see *lament, accuse, quarrel, mourn, weep*)

COMPLETE (adj.)

clean (sweep); (the wheel has come) full circle; full-bloom; from alpha to omega; fron Dan to Beersheba; lock, stock and barrel; the whole meat in the coconut.

(see *whole, perfect, thorough, utter, absolute*)

COMPLETE (v.)

give the final touch to; put the finishing touch on; wind up; go the round; make short work of; set the seal on; crown; run its course; run the whole gamut of; bring to a head; go the whole hog; carry through.

(see *finish, end, close, stop*)

COMPLETELY

lock, stock, and barrel; head over heels; to the teeth; to the quick; to the very nerve ends; to the fingertips; up to the neck; from head to foot; down to the ground; to the core; out and out; to the brim; neck and crop; the whole hog; root and branch; at one fell swoop; from both sides of the fence; every inch.

(see *thorough, wholly*)

COMPLICATION

wheels within wheels; the plot thickens; web; labyrinth; tangle; interknotted plaits; jungle; maze; tangled threads; spider-web; thickening fog; hydra; many-sided development.

(see *intricate, confusion, mixture*)

COMPOSE (v.)

take up one's pen; frame (a letter); polish or chisel (phrases, etc.); knock off (a tune); weave (a tale).

(see *invent, originate, write, form, imagine, create*)

COMPROMISE (oneself)

dirty one's boots.

(see *embarrassed, dishonor, disgrace, defame*)

COMPROMISE (v.)

hedge; meet half-way; go half-way; come to terms with; patch up; strike a bargain; accept a half loaf; find a half-way house; give quarter.

(see *bargain, agree, adjust, settle*)

CONCEAL

bury; mask; draw a veil over; cloak; shroud; drown (voices, etc.); screen;

keep in the dark; keep in the shade; put on the mask; hide (one's light) under a bushel; put under a cloud; keep under cover.

(see *cover, hide, secret, disguise*)

CONCEITED (to be)

be wrapped up in oneself; think one's penny silver; mount on one's high horse; have something go to one's head; have a big head; have a swelled head; feel one's oats; not to think small beer of oneself; have one's head turned; sit on a dizzy pinnacle; be puffed up; have a diseased ego; be hoisted by one's own petard.

(see *egotistic, vain, self-sufficient, self-satisfaction*)

CONCENTRATE

focus; bring into focus; buckle down to study; train one's guns on; bend one's thoughts; stick to a point.

(see *think, intense, eager, tense*)

CONCISE

in a nutshell; the long and the short of it; make a long story short; come to the point.

(see *brief, summarize, shorten, reduce, diminish, direct*)

CONDEMN

seal someone's doom; pass sentence upon; point the finger at.

(see *accuse, doom, judge, censorship, disapprove, blame, reprove*)

CONDESCEND

step down from one's pedestal; come down a peg.

(see *self-abasement, self-effacement, yield, submissive*)

CONDUCT (oneself)

shift for oneself; play the game; play one's cards; steer a course; paddle one's canoe; run a race.

(see *self-possessed, self-reliant, self-sufficient*)

CONFESS

get something off one's chest; make a clean breast of; unlock one's heart; disburden or unpack one's heart; pour out one's heart; tear one's heart asunder; uncork or bare one's soul; strip oneself naked; shed one's sins; lay oneself bare; come clean; put or lay one's cards on the table; let one's hair down; break the seal; bring to light; drag in the truth; lift the curtain; lift the veil.

(see *repent, regret, remorseful, rueful, self-condemnation, self-reproach*)

CONFIDENT (to be)

feel the world is one's oyster; lift up one's head; reckon one's chickens before they are hatched; bet one's boots.

(see *self-possessed, self-reliant, dare, bold*)

CONFINE (v.)

pin down; tie up; coop up; house up; cage; fetter and chain; corral; shut up in a bottle; hem in; keep under one's thumb; put a ring fence around.

(see *imprison, limit, restrict*)

CONFLICT (n.)

whirlpool (of emotions); volcano; duel; surf and undertow.

(see *struggle, fight, strife, interfere, oppose*)

CONFORM

fall in with; chime in with; do as the Romans do; move in a groove; tread the beaten path; go with the stream (or tide or current); swim with the stream (or tide or current); follow the fashion; toe the line (or mark); get into line; hold with the hare and hounds; run with the pack; hew to a party line; goose-step; run to pattern; wear a flexible harness; cling to the skirts of; wear Chinese shoes; adhere to the social landscape.

(see *agree, adjust, imitate, copy, conservative, obedient, harmony*)

CONFUSE

throw off the rails; put out of gear; tangle up; trip up; scramble; play the deuce with; throw dust in the eyes; strike dumb; rattle; cloud up; fog up.

(see *perplexed, mystery, disturbance, disconcert, disrupt*)

CONFUSED

tangled; blurred; fuzzy; scrambled; all at sea; in a black haze; lost in the fog; under a cloud; wrapped in a mist; in a ferment; in the dark; (put) to the blush; not knowing one's way around in the dark; not able to make head or tail of; thrown off one's center; out of joint; (with one's head) swimming, going round, whirling, spinning, or reeling; at sixes and sevens; rough and tumble; entangled in coils; lost in a swirl; screwed up; with the house brought about one's ears; with one's threads mixed; topsy-turvey; pell-mell; higgledy-piggledy; helter-skelter; harum-scarum; thrown out of gear; petrified; unable to see the forest for the trees.

(see *puzzled, uncertain, uncontrolled*)

CONFUSION

muddle; labyrinth; maze; jungle; to-do; pucker; a pretty piece of work; tangled skeins; tangle; riot; vortex; whirlpool; wilderness; ferment; maelstrom; boiling cauldron; turbulent river; pretty kettle of fish; hash.

(see *turbulent, dizzy*)

CONGESTION

log-jam; bottleneck.

(see *crowd, excessive, collect*)

CONNECTION

tie; link; stepping stone; bridge; umbilical cord; chain; thread.

(see *unite, join, relationship*)

CONQUER

chain; trample under foot; sweep all before one; put to the worst; take the wall; drive into a corner; take someone's scalp; bestride (the world); take a dilemma by the horns; drag at one's chariot wheels; bring to bay; storm the gates; mop up the earth (floor or ground) with; knock down and drag out; thrash; bring down to one's knees; grind under foot; set one's heel on; send under the yoke; bridle and curb; humble to the dust; take by storm.

(see *defeat, overcome, subdue, victorious, restrain, win*)

CONSCIENCE

the still small voice; inner voice; silent tormentor; struggling with oneself; haunting ghost; the temple of one's soul.

(see *self-punishment, self-analysis, self-condemnation, morality*)

CONSERVATIVE (n.)

a pillar of orthodoxy; the right-wing side of the fence; middle-of-the-road; old-guard.

(see *conform, cautious, prudent, discreet*)

CONSIDER

play or flirt with (an idea, etc.); sift; collect (one's thoughts); take counsel of one's pillow; weigh; explore the possibilities of; count (the cost); cast one's mental shoe across; tackle (problems, etc.); have an eye to; stretch on the tapis (or carpet); toy with.

(see *ponder, meditate, study, examine, think*)

CONSISTENT

hanging together; on one level; of a piece.

(see *conform, harmony, agree*)

CONSPICUOUS (to be)

at the top of the tree; shining (example, etc.); headlined; stand out; spotlighted; high-lighted; be under the nose of.

(see *evident, obvious, self-evident, visible, clear, notice*)

CONSUME

drink up; suck up; swallow up; soak up; eat into; snuff up; take in through all one's pores; gobble up; engulf; breathe in; gnaw away at.

(see *eat, destroy, wasteful, exhausted, squander, use up, dissipate*)

CONTEMPT (to feel or show)

think small beer of; take no account of; set no store by; not care a straw for; snap one's fingers at; turn up one's nose; curl one's lip; turn the cold shoulder to; laugh in one's sleeve; pluck by the beard; toss in a blanket.

(see *disdain, scorn, mock, self-effacement, self-abuse, self-condemnation*)

CONTEND

swim against (the stream); measure swords; enter the lists; come to grips with; tackle; jockey for position; grapple with; throw one's hat in the ring; take up the cudgels.

(see *struggle, strive, endeavor, labor, exertion, fight*)

CONTENTMENT

heart's ease; peace of mind; cup of satisfaction; lotus-eating heaven; vegetable beatitude; purring on the hearth.

(see *satisfactory, self-satisfaction, ease, happy, pleased, peace*)

CONTINUE

carry over; keep up the ball; keep the ball rolling; keep the field; keep the pot boiling; remain smoldering; go right on shooting; plunge on; drag on; hang on.

(see *persevere, endure, steadfast, resolute*)

CONTRIBUTE

put one's hand in one's pocket; kick in; chip in; ante up.

(see *give, help, gift, offer*)

CONTROL (v.)

have (keep) in hand; have (gain) the upper hand; have the whip-hand; hold (keep) a tight hand; have the cards (game) in one's hands; take matters into one's own hands; hold in the hollow of one's hand; get one's clutches on; twist around one's little finger; have in one's fingers; have under one's thumb; have one's finger on; be in the chair; have someone coming and going; run the show; keep an iron heel on the throat of; mould or shape (destiny, etc.); hold the reins; keep a rein on; hold in leading strings (or leash); pull the strings; hold at the sword's point; hold the threads; call the signals; get the bit between one's teeth; have on the hip; have it all one's own way; have the ball at one's feet; be in the saddle; bring to heel; stage-manage; be at the helm; be in the driver's seat; keep under one's boots; sit on the lid; tame and harness; seize by the nape; call the tune

for someone to pipe to; ride herd on; wear the peer's robes; lead by the nose; put a bridle on; have both hands in the puppet show; be at the steering wheel; keep one's foot on the brakes; have others eat out of one's hand; trim and clip with the shears of control; hold the reins; pull the strings; hold in line.

(see *dominate, order, manage, regulations, rule, direct, supervise*)

CONTROVERSIAL

hot potato; explosive; sizzling; flaming; red-hot.

(see *dispute, argue, challenge*)

CONTROVERSY

bone of contention; duel of brains; literary bonfire.

(see *discuss, strife, contend, dispute, argument*)

CONVERSATION

flow of talk; babble; prattle; ball (of conversation); chit-chat; flood-tide of talk; buzz of voices; running fire.

(see *talkative, gossip, speech*)

CONVERTED (be)

hit the trail; follow the sawdust trail; stray back to the sheep; come into the fold.

(see *reform, transform, redeemed, regenerated, correct*)

CONVINCE

bring someone around; drive the nail home; get around someone's objections; open the eyes; break down the wall; bring home to; "sell" someone on; lead by a silken thread; melt another; bring over to one's own camp.

(see *prove, influence*)

COOPERATE

work shoulder to shoulder; do business with; pull together; play ball; play the game with; join hands; sail in the same boat; sail on the same tack; fall in with; rally around; be hand in hand with; lend a hand; give a hand to; help a lame dog over a stile; put heads together; dovetail.

(see *assistant, help, contribute, participate*)

COPY (n.)

a carbon; second edition; a chip off the old block.

(see *similar, facsimile, duplicate*)

COPY (v.)

walk in the shoes of; take a leaf from (someone's book); steal thunder from; catch a likeness.

(see *imitate, conform, forgery, follow*)

CORRECT (v.)

put to rights; put straight; mend (matters).

(see *arrange, improve, reform*)

COURAGEOUS (to be)

lion-hearted; with a heart of oak; keep one's heart up; keep a stiff upper lip; have a strong stomach; face the music; run the gauntlet; go through fire and water; march up to the cannon's mouth; stand to one's guns; hold up one's head; put on a bold face; beard the lion in his den; bell the cat; take the bull by the horns; have starch in one's spine.

(see *bold, brave, dare, steadfast*)

COVER (v.)

sheathe; veneer; cloak; mantle; screen; shroud; coat; wrap; blanket; carpet; roof over; crown; shelter; powder over; drape over; stud (with stars, etc.); bathe (as the sun); creep (with insects); drench (with light); robe; hood; veil; mask; whitewash; plaster.

(see *conceal, hide, disguise*)

COWARDLY (to be)

be pigeon-hearted; be chicken-hearted; be faint-hearted; be milk-livered; be white-livered; be afraid of one's shadow; show the white feather; have cold feet; show a yellow streak; take something lying down; drink Dutch courage (false courage acquired by inebriation).

(see *fearful, timid, afraid, irresolute*)

CRAZY (to be)

half off one's head; out of one's wits; cracked; with one's brains turned; with one's reason unscrewed; lose one's head; tear one's hair; have bats in one's belfry; be off the beam; have one's mind unhinged.

(see *insane*)

CREATE

call into being; give birth to; be the vehicle of the race; hatch; build; whip up; generate; spawn; be pregnant with; be fertile or fruitful; hammer out; forge; pull out of thin air; coin (a phrase); kindle (enthusiasm); spin or weave (a story); awaken (confidence).

(see *originate, produce, invent, form*)

CRISIS

explosion; 11:59 on the clock; the cards down; crossroads; before the clock strikes.

(see *danger, emergency*)

CRITICIZE

take to task; pick to pieces; pick holes in; rake over the coals; heave a harpoon into; lecture; rag; step on some one's toes; damn with faint praise; cast a reflection on; lick with the rough side of the tongue; lash with the tongue; raise one's voice against; maul; stone; rap; blackmail; put under fire; muckrake; give a left-handed compliment; bring a hornet's nest about someone's ears; throw vitriol at; pitch into; cast stones at; tear into fragments; heap coals of fire on someone's head; get a knife into; sharpshoot at; throw bricks at; wither someone; see the mote in another's eye; scorch; give a whipping to; pound; shake one's voice at; snap at; flay the skin off; fly off; blister someone.

(see *insult, scold, judge, examine*)

CROWD (n.)
a sea of faces; a forest of faces; a human wall; a human sea; a phalanx of people; a sandstorm of humanity; a battalion of bodies; waves of countenances; a herd of sheep; a crush of populace.
(see *mass, congestion, people, excessive*)

CRUEL (to be)
out-herod Herod; shut the gates of mercy; give no quarter; be hardhearted; be stony-hearted; be coldblooded.
(see *ruthless, savage, unjust, uncompromising, unfeeling, bitter, severe*)

D

DANCE

dance oneself off one's legs; switch a skirt; trip it on the light fantastic toe; sail across the floor; sweep over the ballroom; shake one's leg (or feet); hoof it.

(see *move, music, grace*)

DANGER (n.)

breakers; maelstrom; brink of disaster; dark silence; death in the pot, the lion's den; pad in the straw; perilous undertow; pitfall; snare; quicksands; shallows; shifting sands; shoals, brewing storm; sword of Damocles; snake in the grass; viper in one's bosom; dynamite; thin layer of ice, edge of the precipice; shooting the rapids; break-neck undertaking.

(see *risk, hardship, injure, crisis, predicament, precarious, misfortune*)

DANGER (to be in)

hang by a thread (or a hair trigger); fall outside the breastworks; be in the jaws of death; be not yet out of the woods; be between Scylla and Charybdis; be in the lion's den; be at the point of a sword; stand on a volcano; sit on a barrel of gunpowder; be too near the falls; have one's life be not worth an hour's purchase; have a halter around one's neck; put the fat in the fire; have the devil to pay; be on a hot griddle; tread on dangerous ground; have the bull by the tail; come out of the frying pan into the fire; sit in the shadow of death.

(see *precarious, insecure, uncertain, unsteady, unstable, ominous, doubtful*)

DARE

take the bull by the horns; beard the lion in his den; bell the cat; present a bold front; face the music, screw one's courage to the sticking point; take courage in one's two hands, march up to the cannon's mouth; walk through fire; go through fire and water; beat down the flames of fear; run the gauntlet.

(see *risk, presumptuous, bold, brave, defy, challenge, courageous*)

DARK (adj.)

frowning; clouded; burnt-umber; mahogany; shorn of its beams; drenched with ink; dirtily dim; sooty; blotted out; leaden; cast in the shade; thrown into deep darkness.

(see *dim, dusk, shadows, blind, cloudy, obscure, mystery*)

DARKNESS

dead of night; wall of darkness; vault of darkness; enormous night; shadow of the brooding forest; witching time; curtain of black velvet; inky blackness; thick blackness; deep-napped velvet; dim cavern; black canyon; owl-light; inky robe of darkness.

(see *despondency, ignorant, dusk, shadows*)

DASH (v.)

bolt; boom; plunge headlong; scuttle; scorch; streak; fly; fly on the wings of the wind; shoot along; bowl along.

(see *rush, hurry, strike, fly*)

DAWN

day is born; day peers forth; sky cracks with light; first blush of the morning; morning smiles; break of day; peep of day; silvery morning light; ripening of light; wind of dawn blows out the stars.

(see *sunrise*)

DAYDREAM (n.)

castle in the air; castle in Spain; wool-gathering; fringes of our minds; riding the clouds; silken cocoon of reverie; rapt in hypnosis; lost in an inward vision.

(see *dream, visionary, absent-minded*)

DEATH

break-up of the system; cold secrecy; day of judgment; fall of the curtain; ebb of life; everlasting night; final trap; greatest of all adventures; king of terrors; life closing in finality; life snuffed out; swan song; Stygian shore; valley of the shadow; void of blackness; coffin shrouds; crossing the bar; molded smile of peace; when night draws the curtain over life; years are soon cut off; silence which presages the worldlessness of eternity; dangling over eternity; locked under the ice of sleep; hands clasped in the handshake of death; departure of the soul; release from the prison of the body; the waves of Acheron; the journey to the Cocytus; the grim reaper; that huge abyss, wide as space and dark as night; that terrible waxen peace; the icy clutch; the blowing out of the candle; the wages of sin; the great desertland.

(see *die, depart, mourn, funeral*)

DEATH (has come)

the breath is out of the body; fateful seventy closed life's book with a snap; one's race is run; Death knocked at the door; one's heart abdicated its duties; life has fled; streams of life circulate not; the grave closed over one; wrapped in the torpor of the grave; the bloom is gone.

(see *grave, lament, extinct*)

DEATH (is near)

one's hour is come; one's doom is sealed; have one foot in the grave; totter on the brink of the grave; hear the rustling of the wings of Azrael; at death's door; nearing one's belated sunset; Death stares one in the face; near one's end; waiting for the angel Gabriel to blow his horn; look death boldly in the face.

(see *sick, pale, frail*)

DEBT (to be in)

drown in red ink; be in the red; borrow of Peter to pay Paul; outrun the constable; be up to one's knees in obligations; dig a financial hole; have a top-heavy credit structure; fly a kite; raise the wind; go on tick; put on the cuff; be head over ears in debt; plunge into debt.

(see *obligated*)

DECEIT

juggling with words; murder in the robes of justice; tongue in the cheek; web of intrigue; borrowed plumes; deceiving mists of pleasure; blind guidance; iron fist in the velvet glove; snake in the grass; mist of fine words.

(see *lie, imposture, trickery, cheat*)

DECEITFUL

two-faced; winding; double-tongued.

(see *vain, rottenness, mislead, evade, false*)

DECEIVE

beat about the bush; blind; blind one's eye; cast dust into one's eyes; cog the dice; clean the outside of the platter; draw a herring across the trail; fool to the top of one's bent; gild the pill; give a color to; give a gloss to; give one the bob; hypnotize; juggle; keep the word of promise to the ear and break it to the hope; kid, lay a trap; lead one a dance; make a cat's-paw of; play a double game; play fast and loose; play at hide-and-seek; play a part; play possum; play (or tip) the traveler; play one tricks; pull (or draw) the wool over one's eyes; put a false coloring upon; put on the mask; put something over on; sail under false colors; say the grapes are sour; slip over on; send on a wild goose chase; steal a march on; swing the lead; take in; take for a ride; tell a tissue of lies; throw a tub to the whale; throw off the scent; varnish right and puzzle wrong; play with one; play the snake; kick up a dust; dangle bait before; feed with false promises; put new wine in old bottles; pull one's leg.

(see *foolish, outwit, false*)

DECEIVER

ass in lion's skin; snake in the grass; viper; wolf in sheep's clothing; stool pigeon; Judas.

(see *hypocrite, sly, pretend*)

DECELERATE

lose ground; slacken one's pace; put the engines astern; clip the wings; rein in; take in sail; put on the drag.

(see *slow, delay, late*)

DECIDE

cross (or pass) the Rubicon; set a question at rest; turn the scale; seal; thrash out; swing; make up one's mind; plunge through a crisis; nail one's color to the mast; cast the die; throw the dice on the table; fight out; swing the balance.

(see *settle, determine, end*)

DECLARE

speak one's mind; air an opinion; voice one's opinion.

(see *say, speak, proclaim, advertise, utter*)

DECLINE (n.)

dimming torch of culture; clearance sale of the warehouse; half way down the descending slope; twilight; nose-dive; decay; greased chute; toboggan; ebbing tide; fall of the leaf; dry-rot; lag; tailspin; downswing; dip; downgrade; drop; sag; softening; comedown; sharp slide.

(see *deteriorate, degenerate, diminish*)

DECLINE (v.)

dip; fall into decay; go down hill; get a wee thought rusty; lose ground; parachute; tumble; fall off; sink; fall down the ladder; wither up; drop back; slip back; be on the skids; crack; ride on a receding wave; stiffen up; die down; drip away.

(see *die, fall, worse, sink, fail, lessen, diminish*)

DECORATE (v.)

jewel; festoon; embroider; put frills on; hang lace on; bejewel; sauce up; play a grace note to a common chord; make flame with purple passages; set in bloom; wake the Sleeping Beauty with a lipstick; set a patch at the corner of Helen of Troy's eyes.

(see *beautify, elaborate, embellish*)

DECREASE (v.)

chop; crumble; cut to the bone; die away; drop off; fall away; fall to a low ebb; fritter away; melt away; lower the ceiling on (debts); pare; plummet; prune; retire into the shade; shrink; wither; shrivel; slide; slip; slump; take a reef in; trim; tumble; wane; whittle down; taper off; slacken; slow up; dip; sag; knock down; wilt;

hack a slice off; crumple; narrow; shave off; dive; nosedive; falter.

(see *lessen, diminish, decline, reduce*)

DEFAME
drag through filth; drag through the mud; make one's name as mud; pick a hole in one's coat; smear; smear one with treacle; pull to pieces; tarnish; shadow one's royal sunlight; drag down; brand; drag in the mire; throw one's name in shadow; put spots on.

(see *slander, malicious, abuse*)

DEFAULT
apply the sponge; draw the purse-strings; fly kites; muzzle the ox that treads the corn; pay over the left shoulder; gets white-washed.

(see *neglect, fail, lack, untrustworthy*)

DEFEAT
batter down opposition; beat the ears off one; break the neck (or back) of; bring one low; crush; cut the ground from under one; flatten at the polls; have on toast; give one a set-down; make a hash of; make a monkey out of one; make the enemy bite the dust; make short work of; not leave a leg to stand on; play rings around one; put to flight; put *hors de combat;* put one's nose out of joint; roll in the dust; scatter to the winds; send to the right about; sink the ship of state; skin; strip one of the last of one's self-esteem; take the wind out of one's sails; take the wall of; trample under foot; unhorse; yank the rug from under; be one too much for someone; shatter the lamp of; batter to a pulp; floor; shellac; kick in the pants; lay into; knock spots out of; dress down someone's jacket; dust someone's jacket; lace to a fare-ye-well.

(see *conquer, subdue, repulse, overcome, thwart*)

DEFEATED (be)
be broken; be slapped down by the heavy hand of Fate; hide one's diminished head (to retire defeated); bite the dust; get the worst of it; be knocked out; be reduced to smoke and ashes.

(see *frustrated, disappointed, ruin, surrender*)

DEFECT
fly in the ointment; hole in one's coat; rift within the lute; wrinkle on one's horn; feet of clay; fly in the amber; spot on the sun; stumbling block; sore spot; lees in the wine; mote in the eye.

(see *lack, deficient, fail*)

DEFECTIVE
rusty; out of kilter.

(see *inadequate*)

DEFEND
bolster up; furnish a handle; glaze; gloss over; varnish; whitewash; help a lame dog over a stile; lend a color; put a good face upon; stick up for; swear by someone; take up the cudgels for; throw one's full support to; pick up.

(see *protect, help, support, encourage*)

DEFENSE
a hedge against; iron-curtain; wooden wall; aegis; Palladium.

(see *protect, secure, refuge, safe*)

DEFENSIVE
back-to-the-wall; at bay; hold-the-line.

(see *fight, resist*)

DEFERENCE
worship of the cloth of aristocracy and even reverence of the fringe; obeis-

ance; bow; curtsy; proscynesis.

(see *respect, obedient, honored, submissive*)

DEFIANTLY

in spite of hell and high water.

(see *resist, bold, dare, courageous*)

DEFICIENT (be)

fall short; not cut a very good figure. be weighed in the balances and found wanting.

(see *inadequate, defective, scarce, unsuccessful*)

DEFINE

nail down; sharpen; chart a course.

(see *limit, explain*)

DEFINITE

clear-cut; sharply etched.

(see *determined, exact, unconditionally, define*)

DEFY

dance the war dance; do under one's very nose; fly in the face of; put on a bold front; lock horns with; snap one's finger at; shake one's fist in someone's face; double the fist; clinch the fist; do in spite of one's teeth; take the law in one's own hands; kick over the traces; face someone down; bite the thumb; wield the sword; sound the clarion of defiance.

(see *resist, oppose, challenge, dare, disregard, scorn*)

DEGENERATE

crumble; have seen one's best days; topple to pieces; decay; go to rack and ruin; go to seed; rot; lose one's touch; fall into decay, lose caste; fall from one's high estate; be a barrel going

downhill; fall into spiritual catalepsy; lie in the dirt.

(see *decline, deteriorate, worse, pervert, inferior*)

DEJECTED

bowed down; a cup too low; crushed by burdens; down in the mouth; down on one's luck; heart-sick; heart-stricken; heavy-hearted; hang down the head; huddled in a pathetic little heap, with dejection stamped on features and form; in a cave of despair; sick at heart; laughing on the wrong side of the face; in a slough of despond; long-faced; broken-hearted; dampened.

(see *sad, depressed, melancholy, unhappy, despondency*)

DEJECTION

broken heart; damp on the spirits; failure of heart; heart sinking; fallen countenance; prostration of soul; skeleton at the feast; weight on the spirits; nausea of the spirit.

(see *depression, melancholy, dreary, sad, distressed*)

DELAY (v.)

beat about the bush; bog down; lead one a dance; drag one's feet; drift aside into an eddy; hang fire; hold up the parade of; stall for time; stave off (hunger).

(see *hinder, pause, retard*)

DELICATE

lavender-pillowed; velvet; gossamer; silk-stockinged; flower-soft; rose-leaf; kid-gloved; such stuff as dreams are made of.

(see *frail, weak, tender, refined, pure*)

DELIGHT (v.)

bring down the house; take one's fancy; tickle one's fancy; warm the cockles of one's heart; titillate the palate.

(see *pleased, rejoice*)

DEMAND (v.)

clamor for; howl for; lay claim to; thump the tub for; squeal; cry for.

(see *ask, question, solicit*)

DEMOCRACY

the many-headed body politic; the soil of freedom; red corpuscles in the blood stream; a ludicrous chicken farm where everybody cackles.

(see *free, politics, citizen*)

DENOUNCE

rail against; scald with boiling invective; turn sentences in serpentine fury at; lash out at; flay; thunder at; call down curses on one's head; blast; breathe fire at; discharge an ammunition-load of black curses at.

(see *disapprove, threaten, censorship*)

DEPART

be on the wing; be on the move; bolt; cut and run; cut one's stick; fly away; give leg-bail; go off the stage; skip the country; march out; hook it; sling one's hook; take off; take ship; take wing; walk one's chalks; wing homeward; wing one's flight; fling one's cap over the windmill; strike one's tents; slip away; weigh anchor; scuttle from; wiggle off; sally forth; glide off; decamp; buzz away.

(see *abandon, leave, disappear, vanish, withdraw*)

DEPEND

count on; fall back upon; hang on the sleeve of; hinge on; lean upon; pin one's hopes to; pin one's faith upon another's sleeve; rest on one's laurels; revolve around someone; stand on one's record; throw oneself on (the chances of the future); hang on the crook of one's little finger; hang on one's door-knob; tie oneself to another's chariot wheels; lean on one's seasoned staff; ride someone's coat-tails; hook on; cling to; lie in the lap of (Destiny lies in the lap of the gods); be in someone's hand; be bound to someone; be led by the nose; be tied to someone's apron strings; be chained to; play the puppet.

(see *trust, hang*)

DEPENDABLE

a tower of strength; built on a solid basis of fact; pillar of support; a rock to lean on.

(see *reliable, trust, strong*)

DEPRESS

blacken (spirits); dam one's enthusiasm; weigh down; eat (homesickness eats); strike cold on one's heart; put a damper on.

(see *sad, discourage, despondency, dejected*)

DEPRESSED (to be)

look blue; lose heart; be down in the mouth; be governed by gloom; one's heart sinks; feel hollow; be in the doldrums; misty depression clings to one's nerves and darkens one's mind; one's spirits are a leaden weight; float in gloom; etch the black pictures deeper and deeper into one's consciousness; feel one's spirit constricted; feel a noose tighten around one's spirit; feel the bottom drop out of; have a feeling of lead at the heart.

(see *self-pity, despondency, sad, melancholy, unhappy*)

DEPRESSION

dark cloud; gray fog; mood to fit a sullen sky; sorrow clad in a somber gown; gloom seated upon one's features; damp; ebb tide; down-wave; shake-out; bog.

(see *sad, dejection, melancholy*)

DEPRIVE

shut out from; shear (shorn of power); take the bread out of someone's mouth; cut off from; rob of; strip of; widow of.

(see *take, loss*)

DEPTHS

black abysses (of pain); black pools; bowels of the earth; dark cellar (of despair); limpid pools (of eyes); private recesses (of one's heart); quagmire (of fear and hate); cavernous shade; tunnels (of the spirit).

(see *bottom, low point*)

DESCRIBE

color (as with adjectives); descend to details or particulars; draw a portrait of; dramatize and embroider; paint; sketch; hold up a mirror to; capture on paper; clothe with verbal drapery; draw a profile of; cross-stitch (as with detail); weave a clear-cut figure into a tapestry.

(see *explain, trace, represent, report*)

DESERT (v.)

cast adrift; ditch; leave in the lurch; leave to shift for oneself; quit one's hold on; throw into neglect; wash one's hands of; leave a sinking ship; jump off the bandwagon; stray from the fold; run out on; turn the back upon; drop all idea of; throw up the cards.

(see *abandon, leave, quit, renounce*)

DESIRE (n.)

appetite; one's own heart's leading; height of one's ambition; hunger; river of lusts; itching palm; thirst after more from the same spring; torment of Tantalus; unquenchable thirst; ache; touch of a magic wand.

(see *eager, impulse, self-indulgent, want, yearn*)

DESIRE (v.)

be on thorns for; cast a sheep's eye at; cry out for; famish for; find it in one's heart to; give one's eyeteeth for; have appetite for; have a mind to; hanker in a hungry adoration for; hunger for; itch for; look sweet upon; pant after; play a good knife and fork; set one's cap for; set one's eyes upon; set one's heart on; thirst for; drool for; be starved for; give one's right hand for; burn for.

(see *want, ask*)

DESPAIR (n.)

abandoned hope; black vapors of remorse; blackness of the night of agony; blackness of spirit; long night of the spirit's exile; black turmoil; black whirlpool; hard-knotted despondency; cloud settled over one's soul; clouds of gloom; darkness for many a heart and hearth; fathomless depths; fixed gulf of hopeless age; heavy stone resting on one's heart; heart of lead in one's breast; hope vanished from one's withered heart; life's dismal swamp; mud of dreariness; sick thud of one's soul; spirit fallen headlong into black waters; wave of creeping despondency; wave of depression; drowning spiritual isolation; zone of delusion.

(see *desperate, despondency, hopeless*)

DESPAIR (v.)

crush one's hope; fall into the slough of despond; grow sick at heart with hope deferred; break hopes into colored dust in one's hands; reap the harvest in the whirlwind of desolation; soul go down into a Gehenna of torture; clutch at straws; sink into deep swamps of self-mistrust; start down on a toboggan to unhappiness; heart consumed and sunk to sudden ashes; swallowed by an abyss, with waters closing over one's head; dwell among lost souls.

(see *sad, melancholy, mourn*)

DESPERATE

driven to bay; catching at straws; eleventh-hour (appeal); at the end of one's rope; with one's back to the wall; driven to the wall; fluttering and beating one's wings, as a bird making desperate war with the hand that clenches it.

(see *hopeless, rash, reckless, frustrated*)

DESPONDENCY

laughing on the wrong side of the mouth; carrying a lump of lead in one's bosom; sinking down in the mildew of abject melancholy; eternal night brooding in one's spirit; a numbing shadow; a sack of darkness inside one; a starless night of darkness in one's spirit; valley of *douleur;* one's bulk a sodden monument to melancholy; one's head upon one's hands; obstructing the sun with clouds of gloom; plunged into the darkness of one's own soul; one's spirit plunged to zero; tears blotting out the stars; crumpling of the soul.

(see *sad, melancholy, dejection, discouraged, depressed, low-point*)

DESTROY

beat down (conventionality); blast (love); blast to dust (beauty); blot out (civilization); blow sky-high (plans); break the chain of (habit); break down (belief); break the neck; burn and scorch the soul from out one's citadel (*i.e.,* kill); freeze the channels of young blood into that ice which no sun can melt (*i.e.,* kill); crumble into dust; crumble to ash (hope); crush; dash (hopes or expectations); devour (ambition); drown; eat; end up in smoke (be destroyed); erase; explode (theory); give a death-blow to; gnaw like a cancer; go by the board; go down to ruin; go to pot (be destroyed); gobble up; knock the bottom out of (hopes); kill the goose that lays the golden eggs; make hash of; make mince-meat of; nip and blight; nip in the bud; pluck up by the roots; pick to pieces; quench; reduce to chaos; reduce to the last extremity; rip to shreds; rub away (sorrow); sap the foundations of; scuttle; shatter; shrivel; (time has a way of) shooting holes through (one's pet illusions); smash; spike (scheme); stamp out (competition); strangle; strike at the root of; swallow up; sweep away; take to pieces; tear up by the roots; throw to the wolves; uproot (existence); wash out; wipe out of existence; wither; stifle (truth); level to the ground; grind the broken atoms; put the torch to; uproot the seeds of; deal a mortal blow; steam-roller; deal destruction.

(see *kill, ruin, wasteful, extinct*)

DESTROYER

a charnel house (of morals and human emotions); cancer eating at the vitals.

(see *undermine*)

DESTRUCTION

death's wings; hand of death; digging one's own grave with one's teeth (self-destruction); go to wrack and ruin (go utterly to destruction); pulling down the pillars; blight; thunderbolt; tumbling to pieces; corrosive acid; bombshell; go by the board.

(see *loss, ruin, extinct*)

DETAILED

day-by-day; chapter-and-verse; microscopic; blow-by-blow; round-by-round; nooks and crannies; hocus-pocus; red tape; fine point; shredded minutiae.

(see *exact, particle*)

DETAIN

buttonhole.

(see *retain, stop, restrain, delay, hold*)

DETECT

put one's finger on a false note; unearth; catch; play the sleuth-hound; scent; nab red-handed.

(see *determine, discover, expose*)

DETERIORATE

be on the down grade; catapult downhill; crumble into dust; fall into decay; fall into the sear and yellow leaf; go farther and fare worse; go from bad to worse; go to pieces; go to grass; go to seed; go to waste; jump out of the frying pan into the fire; lie down with the autumn leaves; rush toward disintegration; see its day; wither; rust; fall to ruin; go to pot; go to the devil; bog down; wear thin.

(see *degenerate, decline, self-abuse, worse*)

DETERIORATION

deadly fungus of decay; dismal swamp; hopeless toboggan (of senility); dry-rot.

(see *senility, worse*)

DETERMINE

shape (a career); mold (a life); peg down; set the pace for; set the pattern for.

(see *influence, settle, decide, adjust, end, verify, define, resolute*)

DETERMINED (to be)

be hell-bent; be purse-lipped; beard the lion in his den; burn one's bridges behind one; go down with colors flying; go blindly and obstinately toward one's object; go through fire and water; have a will of one's own; have it all one's own way; kick down the ladder; make a point of; nail one's colors to the mast; put one's foot down; put one's heart into it; ride in the whirlwind and direct the storm; screw one's courage to the sticking point; set one's back against the wall; set one's face like a flint; set one's heart upon; set one's shoulders to the wheel; set one's lips (mouth or teeth); stand firm; stand one's ground; stick at nothing; steel oneself; take the bit between one's teeth; take the bull by the horns; take the law into one's own hands; take upon oneself; go the whole hog; run the gauntlet; buckle to; not stick at trifles; throw away the scabbard; nurse a fixed idea; have an iron will; set one's feet firmly on the ladder of success; have the tenacity of a crannied flower; stick by one's guns.

(see *resolute, steadfast, strong, bold, persevere*)

DEVELOP

blossom; brew; bud; come to fine flower; crystallize into concrete proposals; fire (imagination); flower; gain ground; grow new industrial limbs; nurture; pan out; ripen; sprout; tune up; unravel; weave; come to a head; come up the ladder; shape up; turn out; broaden out; mushroom; build up; spring up; ferment; hammer out; put one's swaddling clothes behind one; cut one's teeth; embroider; feel growing pains; come on the scene.

(see *grow, mature, expand*)

DEVIATE

alter one's course; fly off at a tangent;

go off the rocker; meander around Robin Hood's barn; travel by-paths and crooked ways.

(see *differ, wanderer, divert, varied, err, digress*)

DEVOTION

chains of affection; wedlock with one's idols; sacrifice of the last drop of one's blood; the gift of a heart; worship of one's rising sun; incense which one burns before someone; unflickering fire; its wings burnt at one's heart, love cannot fly away; being bound up in another; having one's roots attached to another.

(see *love, religion, worship, sanctimonious*)

DIE

be all over with one; be gathered to one's fathers; blink out; come to dust; cross the bar; cross the Stygian ferry; flicker out into the night; cut down before one's time; cut one's cable; be dispatched to meet one's Maker; dodder off life's stage; be dropped back into the immense design of things; drop into the grave; fade; have one's thread cut by the Fates; give up the ghost; go behind the veil; go down to the dust; go the way of all flesh; pass to another sphere; pass to dust; join one's ancestors; find one's last home; go to one's long account; go under; go West; lay down one's life; launch oneself into eternity; melt away; pass on to one's reward; pay the debt to Nature; receive one's sailing orders; receive the kiss of death; return to earth; retire from life; resign one's breath; shuffle off the mortal coil; sing one's swan song; sleep like the stones; go out with the sun; take one's last sleep; taste the bitterness of death; turn up one's toes; pay court to Death; become gray ashes; fall asleep;

knock at Heaven's gate; enter into rest.

(see *death*)

DIFFER

be at sixes and sevens; have a crow to pluck with; pick a quarrel; wear a chip on one's shoulder; pitch oneself in a different key; split away from; be poles (or worlds) apart; be cast in a different mold; sing another tune; be out of tune (or step); stand out from the rest; draw a line; build a barrier.

(see *disagree, deviate, varied, argue, quarrel*)

DIFFERENCE

spiritual chasm; gulf; rift; steep step; a horse of a different color; an apple from another tree; another pair of shoes; a shoe on the other foot; a far cry; a breed apart; a long jump.

(see *deviate, oppose, disagree, quarrel, dispute*)

DIFFICULT

crabbed; heavy; knotty; mind-tearing; back-breaking; sense-rending; pressing; prickly; thorny; tough; ticklish; steep and stony; uphill; stiff; brittle; to be handled with kid gloves.

(see *hard, obscure, intricate, rigid, perplexed*)

DIFFICULTIES

bottlenecks; a bed of thorns; no bed of roses; rugged hills; rough seas; cog in the machinery; fly in the ointment; barriers to scale; stumbling blocks and holes; hurdles; deep waters; log jam; not all beer and skittles; rough sledding; a heavy cross to bear; Gordian knot; hard row to hoe; nut to crack; rub (there's the rub); a hitch; pulling teeth.

(see *troubled, obstacle, obstruct, hinder, emergency*)

DIFFICULTY (in)

aground; at one's wit's end; at the end
of one's tether; caught in the teeth of
the storm; driven into a corner; driven
from pillar to post; driven to the wall;
in a cleft stick; in a fine pickle; in
deep water; in a fix; in hot water; in
a scrape; in the suds; in the wrong
box; hard-pressed; not out of the
woods; out of one's depth; pinched;
put to one's shifts; reduced to straits;
running against the stream; sorely
pressed; surrounded by breakers; surrounded by quicksands; surrounded
by shoals; up a tree; hard-bitten; on
a shaky limb; in a bog; in sore straits;
knee-deep in a thing.

(see *embarrassed, perplexed, danger*)

DIGRESS

alter one's course; fly off at a tangent;
meander around Robin Hood's barn;
travel by-paths and crooked ways;
travel out of the record; detour from
the main road (of one's narrative);
branch out; ramble; beat around the
bush; rhapsodize.

(see *deviate, wanderer, divert, turn*)

DIM (adj.)

cloud-cloaked; full of drowned light;
pale with ineffectual fire; scarfed in
light; thrown through a fog; tarnished, the shadow of a shade.

(see *dark, indistinct, mist, obscure,
shadows, cloudy*)

DIMINISH

begin to flag; bite deeply into; burn
low; chip a little of (diminish slightly); crumble; cut down; die down to
a whisper; ebb (tide of one's philosophy ebbed); fall; go into a tailspin;
melt away; reduce to a trickle; run
thin; slide off; take a nosedive; thin;
trail off; wither; dampen; cool; faint
away; shrink; shrivel up; dry up (as

a flood); taper off.

(see *decrease, lessen, reduce*)

DIRECT (v.)

be at the helm; be behind someone;
be in the chair; be in the driver's seat;
bend (energy) toward; slant (attention) toward; throw (business) toward;
bend one's course; bend one's steps
toward; bend to rules; cast (a look);
center one's fire toward; channel; cut
out work for; handle the ribbons; lay
down the law to; lead one by the nose;
point; pull the strings; pull the stroke
oar; rule the roost; shape one's course;
steer; take hold; take the lead; take
the reins; train to fire; wave (someone to a place); aim something at
someone; keep in the current.

(see *control, order, manage, rule*)

DIRECTOR

captain; charioteer; guiding star;
head; helmsman; man at the wheel;
pilot; power behind the throne; steers-
man; whip; wire-puller.

(see *leader, supervise, advise, guide*)

DISABLE

clip the wings of; draw the teeth;
floor; hamstring; put a spoke in one's
wheel; put out of gear; spike the guns
of; throw a wrench; cripple.

(see *injure, ruin, reduce, diminish,
decrease*)

DISADVANTAGEOUS

stand in one's own light; have a strike
called against one; have the cards
stacked against one.

(see *injure, prejudiced, hurt, unfair*)

DISAGREE

be at loggerheads; be at sixes and
sevens; be out of key (or tune); break-
squares with; break with; play at cross-
purposes; war; take a different road

from; be out of character; fall out; pick a bone; lean the other way; clash with; be out of step with; come to grips with; be at sabre-points with; split away from; divide camps with; rift with; wear a chip on one's shoulder; war with words.

(see *quarrel, differ, dispute, argue*)

DISAPPEAR

blur out; die out; dissolve; evaporate; fade away; fume away; go up in smoke; go off the stage; go out the window; go overboard; go up in the air; leave no trace; leave not a rack behind; decamp; make oneself scarce; melt away; slip away; be swallowed up; be eaten up (as a road under the wheels); be drunk up (as a light by darkness); take wings; vanish into thin air; vanish into the mist; walk one's chalks; seep away; be lost to sight; blot oneself out (in a crowd); go under; slip the leash; dry up; blow away; take to one's heels; drop by the wayside; slip below the horizon; pass out of the picture; cover up one's tracks; shoot away from; run down the drain; vanish up the spout; flicker out.

(see *vanish*)

DISAPPOINTED (be)

be sick at heart; laugh on the other side of the face; live on sour grapes; look blue; pull a long face; one's face falls; one's heart sinks; light goes out of one's eyes; be broken-hearted; be crushed; have one's spirits dashed to the ground; be dampened; have one's hopes withered (or defeated); be given the finger by someone; have the cup dashed from one's lips; be given a knock-down blow; have a dream turn to ashes; feel let down.

(see *frustrated, thwart, discouraged*)

DISAPPOINTMENT

blighted hope; the bubble burst; hard-

ening knots in the strands of time; milk of human kindness turned sour; more grief than gravy; much cry and little wool; poison of disillusion; a slip 'twixt cup and lip; a cup of bitters.

(see *discouraged, disillusion*)

DISAPPROVE (v.)

frown on; look with a cold eye upon; make a long face; turn up one's nose at; set one's face against; weigh in the balance and find wanting; have no relish or taste for; be down upon; have no use for; shrink from; view with dark eyes; show no love for; have no time for; bend the brows; bring a hornet's nest about one's ears; bring over the coals; bring under the ferrule; damn with faint praise; draw up a round robin; give one a lick with the rough side of the tongue; give one a wipe; have a snap at; look with an evil eye; look black upon; make a wry mouth at; pick a hole in one's coat; pick to pieces; pluck a crow with; raise a hue and cry against; read a lecture to; throw a stone in one's garden; view with jaundiced eyes; speak daggers.

(see *rebuff, rebuke, condemn, reject*)

DISASTER

avalanche (that falls upon something); (having drunk of) tragic springs; valley of misfortune; shattering blow; knock-down ruination.

(see *misfortune, ruin*)

DISCARD

cast off (moodiness); cast or throw to the dogs; cast or throw to the winds; fling away (joy); heave or throw overboard; lay by the wall; lay on the shelf; shelve; lay up in a napkin; shed (a mood); throw out of the window; toss into the fire or wastebasket; heave out of the window; shake off (a habit); wash one's hands of a thing;

bury (a hope); toss back into the bin.
(see *reject, abandon, dismiss*)

DISCERN

(before my mind could) give a meaning to (what my eyes told it); know a hawk from a handsaw; read between the lines; see through a millstone; see one's way clear to; read in someone's face; have a sharp eye; be eagle (hawk or Argus)-eyed.
(see *distinguish, perceive, see, discriminate*)

DISCHARGE

cut off one's head; get someone off one's hands; give the axe; give the gate; give one the heave-ho; give one the sack; give one one's walking papers; sack; cause a head or two to roll; lop off personnel; bounce an employee; strike off the payroll, bundle out of service.
(see *dismiss, emit, discard*)

DISCIPLINE

bring someone to heel; put one's head to the chalk-mark; make someone toe the line.
(see *correct, teach, punish, control*)

DISCONCERT

bowl over; put out of countenance; kill one's thinking faculties.
(see *confuse, frustrated, perplexed, disturbance, embarrassed*)

DISCONTINUE

throw over; throw overboard; break off; pull out of; sever the thread; put a hole in the fabric of (a story).
(see *abandon, stop, interrupt, quit*)

DISCORD (n.)

bone of contention; cross questions and crooked answers; division in the camp; a house divided against itself; no love lost between them; rift within the lute; cat-and-dog; two ill-matched horses in harness together.
(see *disagree, contend, dispute, differ*)

DISCORD (v.)

be at drawn daggers; be at loggerheads; fasten a quarrel on; fish in troubled waters; have a bone to pick with; have a crow to pluck with; pick a quarrel; rub up the wrong way; set together by the ears; spar with; stir up dissension; turn the house out the window; widen the breach; rob of tranquility; strike a sour note.
(see *quarrel, disagree, strife, oppose, disrupt*)

DISCOURAGE

break one's spirit; cast a shadow; crush (one's hopes); dash cold water on; dim (hopes); choke off (ambition); chill (hopes); knock down; lay a wet blanket on; dislodge (humor); pale one's ineffectual fire; put a damper on; put an extinguisher on; take the heart out of; strangle (love); take the wind out of one's sails; throw cold water on; clip one's wings; rot the apple of content; blight one's aspirations; dash one's spirits.
(see *despair, obstruct, oppose, disparage, disprove*)

DISCOURAGED (to be)

down in the dumps; down in the mouth; bowed down by hopelessness; sick at heart; look on the dark side (be discouraged); lose heart (become discouraged); set back on one's heels; have leaden heart and feet; walk away from Hope; feel one's castle of imagination fallen about one's feet; feel a sinking of the heart.
(see *disappointed, depressed, dejected*)

DISCOVER

bring to light; unearth; hit upon (an answer); ferret out; spot; stumble over; comb out; dig out; dredge up.

(see *find, invent, reveal, detect, show, expose*)

DISCREET (be)

keep one's eyes on the ground; go along and peddle one's papers; mind one's P's and Q's; pull down the blinds and stuff paper in the keyholes; tend strictly to one's knitting; tend to one's own geranium; tend to one's spaghetti; show tea-party manners.

(see *careful, prudent, cautious, wise*)

DISCRIMINATE

know what is what; know a hawk from a handsaw; separate the sheep from the goats; split hairs; winnow the chaff from the wheat; know the ins and outs of a thing; draw a line; sift the fine flour from the bran; separate the kernel from the chaff; make fish of one and flesh of another.

(see *distinguish, prejudiced, insight, judge, discern*)

DISCUSS

hash over; talk turkey; thrash out; have a word with someone (discuss with someone); air (an opinion); descant; carry something (topic) along with a whirl; swap talk.

(see *argue, agitator, reason, consider*)

DISDAIN

snap one's fingers at; turn up one's nose at; look down upon; see a mutt dog when one is looking for a thoroughbred.

(see *scorn, contempt, superior, arrogant, haughty*)

DISFIGURED

one's mother wouldn't know one from a pot roast; beaten to a mummy.

(see *injure, spoil, ugly*)

DISGRACE (n.)

blight; blot on one's escutcheon; blur; brand; spot; stain; a fall from high estate; a fall afoul of.

(see *dishonor (v.), reproach, scandal, disparage, shame*)

DISGUISE (v.)

put new wine in old bottles; clean the outside of the platter; cloak; gild the pill; clothe; mask; veil; put a false coloring upon; wash a blackamoor white; whitewash; put candy-coating on; employ stage get-up; bury a thing beneath something else; perfume reality; camouflage the truth.

(see *change, hide, conceal, cover, pretend*)

DISGUST (v.)

do something *ad nauseam* (do something so as to produce disgust); leave a bitter taste in one's mouth; make one sick; turn one's stomach; stink in the nostrils (be disgusting).

(see *revulsion, offend*)

DISHONEST (be)

break one's faith; hang out false colors; hit below the belt; live by one's wits; play with marked cards; be slippery; be cut on the bias; bestow the kiss of Judas.

(see *untrustworthy, false, deceitful*)

DISHONOR (v.)

bring low; cast into the shade; drag through the mire or mud; eclipse; heap dirt upon; hold up to shame; put a blot upon; put down in the world; put under a cloud; seal someone's infamy; put in the stocks; put a halter around someone's neck; brand; fling dishonor upon; blackball; put on the black list; drum out; tread under foot; tarnish (someone's good name); cause to lose face; send to Stellenbosche or Coventry.

(see *ostracize, disgrace, disparage, scandal*)

DISILLUSION (v.)

drag one's castle of hope to ruin; destroy an illusion; cause a delicate dream to turn to ashes; prick the bright balloons of one's hopes; cast one's idol off his pedestal; overthrow one's dazzling hopes; cause a mirage to fade; topple one's house of cards; lock against the intrusion of old dreams; poison faith in the sap; reveal the worm at the core of the apple; sweep one away from his anchor; blow one's air castles away; sting one out of his dreams; see the fair feet turn clay; shatter the vase and depetal the flowers; make dreams tinkle into fragments.

(see *ruin, realistic, destroy*)

DISINHERIT

cut off with a shilling; cast out of one's will.

(see *reject, repudiate, slight, renounce, denounce*)

DISMISS (v.)

bow someone out; slam the door on; turn adrift; send packing; send about one's business; cashier; turn out; scatter to the winds; show one the door; bundle one out; get someone off one's hands; settle someone's hash; give the sack; weed out; give the gate.

(see *release, discharge, discard, depart*)

DISPARAGE

dip the pen in gall; give a dog a bad name; make light of; make little of; pick a hole in one's coat; run someone down; pull from a pedestal; put one's pipe out; hit at; speak lightly of.

(see *reproach, defame, criticize, underrate, disdain, scorn*)

DISPLAY (v.)

cut a figure or a dash; make a splash; prick oneself up; parade one's wares; flash one's virtues; frame and glaze; turn on (temperament); grow (a smile); present with fanfare and flourish of trumpet.

(see *flaunt, ostentatious, show, pretentious*)

DISPLEASE (v.)

go against the grain; jar upon the feelings; make one sick; fall sour on one's ears; make one turn in one's grave; cause one to knit his brow.

(see *annoy, offend, disgust, irritate, anger*)

DISPROVE

blast or destroy a legend; explode a theory; uproot a belief; take the wind out of an argument.

(see *false, disapprove*)

DISPUTE (v.)

fasten a quarrel on; be neck-deep in controversy; thrash out; plunge into a battle of ideas; have a bone to pick with; have an ax to grind; jockey over (a contract).

(see *argue, quarrel, squabble, challenge*)

DISREGARD (v.)

brush to one side; fling to the winds; give one the back; jettison; knock reason on the head; lose sight of; set little store by; shut one's eyes to; shrug one's shoulders at; snap one's fingers at; toss overboard; turn a deaf ear to; take the law into one's own hands; let in one ear and out the other.

(see *neglect, contempt, ignore, indifferent*)

DISRUPT

throw a bombshell; throw out of gear; blow to smithereens; throw a wrench into.

(see *destroy*)

DISSIPATE

burn the candle at both ends; sow one's wild oats; foul one's nest; break the pale; go to the dogs; go on a racket; have one's fling; keep bad hours; live fast; wallow in voluptuousness; dally by the fleshpots of Babylon; plunge into dissipation.

(see *wasteful, lavish, squander, excessive*)

DISTINGUISH (v.)

split hairs; cut a feather; have a fine ear; balance on a razor edge; separate the cream.

(see *separate, divide, prejudiced, discriminate, discern*)

DISTRESSED (to be)

be sick at heart; drain the cup of misery to the dregs; fall on evil days; look blue; be harrowed of soul; be weighed down; have one's feelings wounded; be in a black mood; be in deep waters; face a calamitous darkness; be torn of heart; have storm-tossed emotions; be wrung with sorrow; have a keyed-up temperament; be haunted by something; flutter; stew; boil; be ready to burst; be driven to wit's ends.

(see *disaster, misfortune, tribulation, troubled, pain, unhappy*)

DISTRIBUTE

parcel out; spread thin; pigeonhole.

(see *divide, share*)

DISTRUST (n.)

web of doubt; world of iron curtains and dirty windows; shutters down and closed doors; imp of suspicion.

(see *doubt, suspicious*)

DISTURBANCE (cause a)

kick up a devil's delight; kick up a dust; make a scene; raise a storm; rock the boat; blow a thing from its anchorage; rip the stillness; ruffle the calm; shake from quiet; send a thing off its balance; turn house out of window; turn topsy-turvy; churn up a row; raise a storm in a teacup; stir up a hornet's nest; let a simoon loose; put out of gear; put on its beam end; toss in a blanket; raise Cain; be a gadfly; upset the house.

(see *agitator, confuse, upset, excite, incite*)

DIVERT

go off at a tangent; lead (conversation) into other paths; put on a new scent; short-circuit; sidetrack; throw off the scent; shut one's thoughts away; wander away at a tangent; put off to a sidetrack.

(see *disturbance, interfere, digress, deviate*)

DIVIDE

drive a wedge between; split down the middle; cut up; parcel; checker-board.

(see *separate, sever, split, distribute, share*)

DIVORCE (v.)

break one's domestic chains; shed one's mate; strain at the marital leash; quarrel irreparably with one's bread and butter.

(see *separate, unloved, estrange*)

DIVULGE (v.)

tell tales out of school; let the cat out of the bag; let something leak out; breathe something to someone; let roll off the tip of one's tongue; let slip.

(see *reveal, expose, publish*)

DIZZY (be)

brain flies in circles; brain swims; head seems full of the fumes of alcohol; one's senses are blurred; things seem to swim in a sort of blurred mist before the eyes.

(see *confused, careless*)

DOMINATE (v.)

lead by the nose; throw one's shadow over another; throw another into the shade; shine forth in the world; hold in the hollow of one's hand; turn around one's little finger; make a puppet of another; chain by loyalty; get the upper hand; soar to an eminence over another; have the game in one's own hand; put another under a yoke; have under one's thumb; play first fiddle; have the ball at one's feet; carry with a high hand; bring another to his knees; set the fashion; lay down the law; ride in the whirlwind and direct the storm; rule with a rod of iron; ride a high horse; ascend the throne; take the reins in one's own hand; keep in one's grasp; bestride another; wear the breeches; lead the parade; hold the field; rule the roost; swallow opposition; ride roughshod over; browbeat into submission; lord it over another; wrap in an octopus grasp.

(see *rule, control, order*)

DOOM (v.)

spell ruin for; mutter a frightful oracle over; cut the Achilles cord; cast the evil eye at; encircle with prophecy; lay a fateful hand on.

(see *condemn, judge, fate, ruin, predestined*)

DOUBT (n.)

a fog of uncertainty; a mist of agnosticism; if's and's and but's; a shadow of mistrust; a cloud.

(see *hesitate, irresolute, uncertain, vacillate, suspicious, distrust*)

DOUBT (v.)

flutter with misgiving; lift an eyebrow at; view with a suspicious eye; look the gift-horse in the mouth; call into question; shake one's head; float in a sea of doubt; take with a grain of salt; twist one's features into a question mark.

(see *question, hesitate, suspense, uncertain*)

DOUBTFUL

a pig in a poke; a blind bargain; a toss-up.

(see *chance, gamble, obscure, undecided*)

DREAM (n.)

castle in the clouds; happy hunting-grounds of sleep; the films of sleep; winged fancy; phantoms of the subconscious; the nightmare and it's Hydra heads; dim night-fire of the mind.

(see *imaginary, visionary*)

DREAM (v.)

fly kites in sleep; unfurl the wings of the imagination; chase a flower of fancy; sink into reverie; drift in the subconscious; ride on the clouds of sleep; float in the clouds of a night sky; fall prey to silent fancy; wear a faraway look; be held in the meshes of a dream.

(see *imagine, daydream, sleep*)

DREARY

monotonous gray pageantry of clouds; cold wrinkled lips of winter; a day gone two shades darker; bleak stony tints of sky.

(see *dark, monotonous, uninteresting, dull*)

DRINK (v.)

drain the glass; finish in one draught; force down; wash down repast; wet one's whistle; crook the elbow; soak in; suck up; swallow the waters of affliction; take a pick-me-up; drown one's sorrow in the wreathed cup; drown one's wits.

(see *drunk*)

DRIVE (v.)

taxi picks its way; laces its way in and out of a stream of vehicles; threads through traffic; slides importantly up a street; spins along; rocks with speed; purrs to a halt; hums along; snorts pompously up a road; sputters to a standstill; tunes itself up to a song; quakes in protestation.

(see *automobile*)

DROWN

go to Davy Jones's locker; sink to a watery grave; take a lethal draught of brine; sport with the mermaids; go to Amphitrite's bower; take residence in Poseidon's realm; have one's hair festooned with seaweed.

(see *flood, sea, ocean, waves*)

DRUNK (to become)

drown frustration in rum; get a furred tongue; be far gone in one's cups; become tight; be the worse for liquor; be sewed up with booze; carry a tight load; become muddle-headed; be soaked in rye; spin on the merry-go-round of cocktails; hug the bottle; have one's pots on; be put under the table; have three sheets in the wind; take a hair of the dog that bit one; be illuminated by champagne; bow to the bottle; wet one's whistle; become half seas over; be one over the light; become tipsy; become numb with drink; find Dutch courage in the flask; become blurred and fogged with moonshine; keep one's nose in the cup; have a brick in one's hat; bring the smell of whisky with one; have one's malt above one's meal (or wheat); be drugged with wine; be heated with brandy; have the senses reeling; be staggered by fire-water; swallow a tavern token; lace one's coffee or tea (*i.e.,* add brandy or rum to).

(see *drink*)

DULL (adj.)

back-water; pedestrian; cabbage-headed; stagnant; cold porridge; skim milk; plodding; ponderous; blunted; slumbering; dry; cold dish water; dried stockfish; stick of wood; dry rot; doldroms; flat; arid; sagging; unsalted; dead-alive; deadening; beaten track; heavy-gaited; dreary; milk-and-water.

(see *tedious, uninteresting, monotonous, bored, stupid*)

DUSK

a symphony of gray and gold; thickening darkness; the hour of pinkish mist; the flickering spread of twilight's cloak; the quivering approach of shadows and winking stars; a pale blue light through the fog; the descent of Phoebus.

(see *evening, sunset, shadows*)

DUTY (n.)

inward monitor; still small voice within; acting one's part; redeeming one's pledge; one's lot; that which lies at one's door; that which lies on one's shoulders; that with which one is saddled.

(see *obligated, responsibility*)

E

EAGER (to be)

glow with; be feverish over; leap to; be breathless with; kindle to; hunger for; thirst for; feel a gnawing for; feel one's heart run out to; bluster with efforts; be heated with; tear oneself to shreds with trying; die to; clamor for; have one's appetite whetted for; run madly after; burn to; put one's heart into; send one's soul toward; bend one's every effort; strive with might and main to; be hot for; itch to; give one's eyetooth for; jump at.

(see *enthusiastic, fervent, yearn, desire, impatient*)

EARLY

up with the sun; in the bud; raw (dawn); young (evening).

(see *premature, dawn*)

EARN (a livelihood)

scrape together; wring gold from; chalk up; net; bring grist to the mill; grub; get in the harvest; bring in the sheaves; keep the pot boiling; squeeze out subsistence; keep the head above water; keep afloat; keep the wolf from the door; make both ends meet; gain by the sweat of one's brow; make one's bread and butter; win one's daily bread; have a grip upon the wheel of fortune; keep a roof over one's head; earn one's salt; grind one's grist; turn an honest penny.

(see *work, labor, effort, achieve, get*)

EARTH

a mote of dust; a windblown anthill; rich dampness; the bowels of the earth.

(see *world*)

EASE (n.)

Peacock Alley; primrose path; bowl of cherries; bed of roses; the sunny side of the road; royal road; honeymoon.

(see *leisure, contentment, luxury, rich*)

EASE (to put at)

break the ice; take a load off someone's heart; smooth the bed of discomfort; soften a blow; dull the sharp edge of; relax pressure on; grease the grinding wheels; help someone unburden his mind; make someone feel at home; bring a glow of warmth to; put someone in his element; temper the wind to the shorn lamb; cushion an impact; take the sharp edge off.

(see *tranquil, pacify, rest, peace, quiet*)

EASY (adj.)

smooth-or plain-sailing apple pie; mutton handed to one on a skewer; going along at a saunter; child's play; preaching to the converted; walking away with; presented on a silver platter; smooth water; fair wind; making hay of; seeing with half an eye; flowing with the stream; swimming with the tide; having the game in one's own hands; winning at a canter; being at home in; without a hitch; with a wet finger.

(see *facilitate, satisfied, yield, submissive*)

EAT

play a good knife and fork; address oneself to luncheon; tackle dinner; work the jaws; play with meat; crunch celery; dig into a sundae; dive into dinner; attack one's food; peck at salad; wolf up a repast; swill soup; line one's stomach; be deep in dinner;

scoop into one's mouth; shovel down food; tear away at a steak; snap up a meal; line one's paunch.

(see *consume, hungry, food*)

EAVESDROPPER
a twitching squirrel busily gathering acorns; a slumbrous cat slyly pricking up her ears.

(see *inquisitive, meddlesome, elicit, listen*)

ECCENTRIC (to be)
walk on stilts; have a maggot on the brain; be an old or queer fish; be a crackpot; run off the trolley.

(see *strange, unusual, unique*)

ECHO
a full revolution of the mystic wheel of sound; words caught by the wind and flung back for sport; sounding board; overflow of tone from the depths of the woods.

(see *repeat, imitate, sounds, reverberate*)

ECONOMIZE
make both ends meet; tighten one's purse strings; cut corners; cut to the bone; tighten one's belt; stretch one's dollars; pinch pennies; cut one's coat according to one's cloth; provide against a rainy day; save cheese parings and candle ends; keep within compass; keep one's head above water; stay out of the red; think hard about nickels; be penny-wise without being pound-foolish; operate on a thin financial shoestring.

(see *scrimp, save, cheap, miserly*)

EDGE
fringe; brow; outer ripples; shoulder; frame; skirt; rim.

(see *border, confine, limit*)

EDITOR
literary mid-wife to those in labor; blue penciler.

(see *correct, revise, write, publish*)

EDUCATED (become)
be brought up at the feet of Gamaliel; be escorted from the threshold of Wisdom into its temple; have an old head put on young shoulders; become a learned owl; be cradled in learning; be steeped in study; burn the midnight oil; find a fathomless mine of information; go out on a branch of learning; extend the frontiers of knowledge; carry the fringes of the great garment of learning.

(see *study, learn, knowledge, teach*)

EFFETE
rest on one's laurels; be pumped out.

(see *exhausted, worn out, uninspired*)

EFFICIENT (to be)
well-oiled; clockwork; sharpen one's skill; move into high gear; goose-step.

(see *energetic, skilful, vigorous*)

EFFORT (to exhibit)
do one's stint of leg-work; wear out shoe-leather; elaborate a stitch of work; not grudge a stroke of work; scramble for approval; fight one's way to accomplishment; make a drive for approval; earn one's salt; employ a steam engine to crack a nut.

(see *earn, endeavor, attempt, struggle*)

EGOTISTIC (to be)
live in a narrow prison-house of self-centered interest; hug oneself with delight; admire the fine skin of one's vanity; see oneself (only) as large as life; burn incense before oneself; hoist oneself on one's own petard.

(see *conceited, vain, self-centered, self-praise, self-love*)

ELABORATE
window-dressing; embroidered; lacquered; flowery; Pelion-upon-Ossa (adjectives); colorful; groomed; curry-combed; Shakespearian (diction); ultra-précieuse.

(see *intricate, detailed, embellish, beautify*)

ELATED (to be)
be in fine feather; have one's head in the clouds or stars; feel one's soul bubble over with joy; radiate sunshine; set one's eyes to dancing; be flushed with the strong wine of exaltation; be lifted to the stars; be in a delirium of intoxicated feeling; be transported with gladness.

(see *joyful, happy, excited, proud*)

ELEGANT
fine-feathered; gold-lace; silk-stockinged; patent-leather; swallow-tailed; top-hatted; silk-hatted; soup-to-nuts; perfumed; white tie and tails; tea-party; cocktails-at-five; hand-kissing; manicured; lacquered; enameled.

(see *refined, suave, fashionable, grace, beautiful*)

ELICIT
wring (information) from; worm something out of someone; "pump".

(see *eavesdropper, inquisitive, extort*)

ELIMINATE
cut out; wipe out; erase; uproot; push out of; send to the right about; throw out; screen out; rub out; blot out; sweep away; set at nought; plow under; throw overboard; grind to dust; weed out; shut down on; shake out.

(see *remove, reject, destroy, erase*)

ELOQUENT
speak volumes; have a tongue in one's head; roll words off one's tongue; wing one's words; be silver-tongued; have a tongue of silver; flower with speech; unleash glowing words; flow with oratory.

(see *orate, impressive, express, speak*)

EMBARRASSED (to be)
be red-faced with chagrin; feel a bronze blush mount to one's temples; have ears tipped with flame; be cornered; be red to the teeth; feel oneself on the spot; be tongue-tied; get oneself entangled in a clothesline; feel something stick in one's throat; feel a flush creep slowly up one's throat; feel choked with shyness; experience a painful pause.

(see *disconcert, distressed, troubled, ashamed, shame, self-conscious, blush*)

EMBELLISH
wake the Sleeping Beauty with a lipstick; set a patch at the corner of Helen of Troy's eyes; gild the lily.

(see *beautify, elaborate, decorate*)

EMBRACE (v.)
entwine in honeysuckle clutches; lock with; melt in arms; clasp to the breast; enfold; make a wreath of arms; take to the bosom; take into the arms; sweep into the arms.

(see *passionate, kiss, love*)

EMBROIL
have irons in many fires; fish in troubled waters; sow dissension; fall foul of; get into hot water.

(see *involved, troubled, confuse, disturbance*)

EMERGE
spring from the stem; step out of the mists; swim through the mist; spring out of.

(see *escape, come, appear, visible*)

EMERGENCY

a shot in the locker (shot stored away for an emergency); the hour of trial; stand-by; a pinch.

(see *necessity, crisis, difficulty*)

EMIT

belch forth; shovel out; snort; spurt; shoot out.

(see *discharge, dash*)

EMOTIONAL

a sea, full of deep-down currents and smooth on top; an elevator dropping in sheer descent; valley of tears and laughter; hemming and hawing of the heart; volcanic flames; electric storm; tide ebbing and flowing; soul overflow; cross-currents; lump in the throat; waves of humor and sadness; fiery wing of passion; choked with pity; heart full of tears; surging bosom; overcharged heart; quickening of the pulse; heart on the sleeve; hot-blooded; whirl of emotions.

(see *passionate, sentimental, sensitive, pity, romantic, intense*)

EMPHASIZE

punctuate one's remarks; hammer home; harp on; underline; spotlight; take off one's gloves to drive a point home; put a steady focus on; highlight; lay stress upon; bear one's weight down on; sharpen one's voice; put in a flutter of headlines; ride full tilt at; make one's words ring; deliver machine-gun style; punch away at; cannonade with rhythm; seal with a round oath; rub a thing in.

(see *impressive, strenuous, intense, eloquent, force, pressure, violent, convince, fervent*)

EMPTY (adj.)

naked; sterile; stripped to the bone; denuded; hollow; dead; featureless; arid; desert; yawning with space; husked.

(see *useless, exhausted, reduce*)

EMPTY (v.)

clean out; clear decks; sweep off; drain to the dregs; make a clean sweep of; create a vacuum; dry the fountain; spill out; root out.

(see *withdraw, discharge, eliminate, remove*)

ENCLOSED

fenced in; bottled up; swathed in; encased in; wrapped in; have a cocoon spun around; sealed up.

(see *surround, circle, wrapped, envelop*)

ENCOUNTER

brush elbows with; run into; run across; run head against; bump into; speak of an angel and hear his wings; have a brush with; collide with; clash with; fall upon.

(see *meet, encounter, find, join, unite*)

ENCOURAGE

fan into a flame; stir the embers; whip up; feed the fires of; lend wings to; keep the door open to; give the green light to; spur on; nurture; nurse; add fuel to the fire; buoy up; pat on the shoulder; screw up (courage); warm the heart; nerve one's arm; smile upon; feed the longing for; clap on the back; drum up; give new life to; fortify the spirits of.

(see *cheer, stimulate, urge, strengthen, support, inspired*)

END (v.)

give up the ghost; dethrone; wind up; fizzle out; wither; trail off; crown by; burn out; lower the curtain; give a last gasp; drop away; die out; crumble away; be on the homestretch; write finis to; extinguish the flame; draw to an end; give a final turn of the screw to; run out; run dry; bring the wheel to full circle; kill (a hope); bury (a notion); burst (a bubble); fade out; blow the final whistle on; sound the death-knell of; give a death blow to; let the sand run out on; close the book on; number the days of; sing the swan-song; go down the drain; meet the day of Judgment; hear the crack of doom; run the length of one's tether (or rope); strangle; dissolve.

(see *close, complete, stop, finish, discontinue*)

ENDANGERED

be on the verge of a precipice (or a volcano); sit on dynamite; be between the hammer and the anvil; be at the point of a sword; hang by a thread; sit on an open barrel of gunpowder; tremble in the balance; be on slippery ground; be between two fires; nod to one's fall; be between wind and water; sail near the wind; scuffle along the brink of chaos; be on the wrong side of the wall; get into hot water; jump out of the frying pan into the fire; be behind the eight ball; rock on the edge of an abyss; tread a quicksand; be between Scylla and Charybdis; be between the devil and the deep blue sea; be gripped by the throat; have a halter around one's neck.

(see *risk, danger, troubled, tragedy, fearful, suspense, predicament*)

ENDEAR

win all hearts; grow upon someone; build oneself a chalet in someone's heart; plant one's feet in someone's heart; thaw a person up; soften dislike.

(see *love, tender, friendly, kind*)

ENDEAVOR

move heaven and earth; act with might and main; do one's level best; drag a lengthened chain; buckle down to work.

(see *attempt, effort, exertion, struggle, labor, try, strive*)

ENDURE

eat the bitter bread of; stomach something; swallow the medicine of; weather the storm; survive a shakeup; bear with submission; bear the brunt of; weather a difficulty; bear a cross; hold out until; groan and sweat with a martyr's perseverance.

(see *suffer, submissive, patient, persevere, obedient*)

ENERGETIC (be)

be a live wire; be a human steam engine (or dynamo); have inextinguishable vitality; be full of fire and go; be a human tornado; be a wire charged with a high-voltage current; be a grindstone requiring something to grind; have the red blood of ambition; make things hum; act in a high pressure manner; have backbone; be a demon of energy; have drive; forge full-steam ahead; use elbow-grease; have punch; be in full bloom; put one's best leg forward; move mountains; let no flies settle on one; let no grass grow under one's feet.

(see *power, ambition, vigorous, zestful, strengthen, industrious*)

ENGROSSED (be)

be wrapped up in; be up to one's ears in; sink oneself in; be absorbed by; soak oneself in; be engulfed in; be lost to everything else but.

(see *industrious, involved, interested, inspired*)

ENJOY

get a kick out of; wallow in; feel at home in; lap up; drink up; savor with zest; reap the benefits of; chew on with relish; eat the sweet fruits of; warm up to; devour with zest; eat up an experience; feast on; taste with approval; smack one's lips; lick one's chops; bask in the sunshine of; drink deep of; laugh one's way through; sun oneself in; make a cult of; make the welkin ring; suck up the pleasure of; dissolve delight in brandy; find all beer and skittles; live the life of Riley; have one's fling.

(see *pleasure-seeking, delight, happy, dissipate, joyful, laugh*)

ENLIGHTEN

throw light on; turn on full daylight; shed light upon; open the eyes of; cause the scales to fall from the eyes of; cause to see with new eyes; cause to dawn upon.

(see *inform, teach, educated*)

ENTER

glide into; break into; crash the gates; worm oneself into; plunge into; launch into; pour into; steal into; slip under the covers of; drop from the clouds; leap into; dive into; jump into; swing into; flow in; stream in; slither into; sweep into; pop into; swim into; wade into; barge into; set foot in; jump up to one's neck in; filter into; storm into; dip one's hands into; seep into; bounce into; drift into; gravitate into; swarm into.

(see *penetrate, insert, push*)

ENTHUSIASTIC (to be)

go to town; warm up to; take fire at; burn bright after; glow with enthusiasm for; break out in a rash of cheers for; light up; become ignited by; be all on fire; bubble over with; be touched with excitement; burst with; catch the contagion; have one's heart in; wax rhapsodic over; boil with fervor; go hog-wild over; be carried away by; let a thing run away with one.

(see *arouse, eager, passionate, fervent, vehement*)

ENTRUST

throw oneself into the arms of; pour oneself into the keeping of; put oneself in the hands of; set a fox to keep one's geese (entrust one's valuables to sharpers).

(see *believe, rely, trust, depend*)

ENVELOP (v.)

surge over; spread about; settle on; twine around; fold over; ensheathe; leap up around; suffocate; creep over; swallow up; close over; enshroud; bathe in.

(see *enclosed, surround, circle, hide, involved, cover*)

ENVY (v.)

taste sour grapes; bite into the apple of discord; turn green eyes toward; fall victim to the green-eyed devil; cast lustful eyes upon; feel one's nose swell; feel one's mouth water; have a tinge of green in; be green with envy; be consumed by envy; feel heartburn smoldering in one's breast; feel the old dragon is about ready to rear its hoary head; burst with envy; be yellow-eyed; view with a jaundiced eye; have one's nose be put out of joint; have a canker in one's heart; have one's brain twisted by envy.

(see *jealousy, hate, desire, spiteful, malicious*)

EQUAL (v.)

be a match for; add up to; be on a par with; keep pace with; feel like a fighting-cock (be equal to one's task);

catch up with; take rank with; measure up to; hold a candle to; lie on a level with; walk hand-in-hand with; be up to the mark; be neck and neck with; be parallel to; leave not a pin to choose; stand up to; break even with; run abreast; be as broad as long; strike a balance between; be on an equal footing with; peg even with; be stretched on the bed of Procrustes; be six of one to half a dozen of the other.

(see *identical, sameness, exactly, competition*)

ERASE

blot out; apply the sponge; rub a sponge over; smother.

(see *obliterate, cancel, destroy*)

ERR

strike a wrong note; sound off key; get out of step; put the cart before the horse; fumble the ball; land a shot out of the bull's-eye; slip a cog; put a foot into it; put all the fat in the fire; put the saddle on the wrong horse; make a bull; make a slip; bark up the wrong tree; see out of focus; be on the wrong track; fall wide of the mark.

(see *deviate, blunder, mistake, misjudge*)

ESCAPE (v.)

give the slip to; take to one's legs; slip the collar (or leash); slip through someone's fingers; take French leave; make a break for; save one's skin; take to one's heels; slip out of someone's grasp; beat a retreat; turn tail; take flight; show a clean pair of legs; decamp; do a bolt; creep out of; fly away; vanish into thin air; tear loose from; burst one's coils; unchain one's chains; skip; do a disappearing act; give leg-bail; jump clear; escape by the skin of one's teeth; get away by a hair's-breadth.

(see *avoid, shun, evade, flee*)

ESTABLISHED (to get)

get a footing; be squarely based; take root; be launched; find a seat; plant one's flagstaff; be berthed; take up one's abode; plant oneself; get set up.

(see *settle, reside, live, start*)

ESTIMATE (v.)

take one's measure; size up; gauge; weigh; touch for appraisal; juggle with bits of paper; eye up; sum up from head to foot; pigeonhole; put in its proper place; take stock of; study the barometer; use a yardstick.

(see *judge, self-analysis, analyze, discern*)

ESTRANGE

poison a mind against someone; divorce incompatibles; cause a river to flow between; cause a veil to hang between.

(see *separate, sever, divide, disparage*)

EVADE

fence; juggle; beat about the bush; give the go-by to; dodge the question; pass the buck; play at hide-and-seek; shuffle; hedge; mince words.

(see *escape, quibble, subterfuge, maneuver*)

EVANGELIST

pulpit-pounder; Book-thumper; Satan-wrestler; traveling-salesman of religion.

(see *religious, preach, converted*)

EVENING

the day's epitaph; blind man's holiday; cock-shut; curfew; tail o' the day; angelus-time; gray dusk; quick-falling dusk.

(see *night, sunset, dusk*)

EVENT

milestone; inning; landmark; a pig to be shaved (a humorous explanation of the reason for the assembling of people to watch an event of interest); a constellation in someone's sky.

(see *important, occur*)

EVERYBODY

all the world and his wife; all hands on deck; the butcher, the baker, and the candlestick maker; the whole kit.

(see *crowd, mass, congestion*)

EVERYWHERE

at every turn; the four corners of the earth; on the face of the earth; under the sun; toward all points of the compass; to the four winds; the highways and byways; from pillar to post; every hole and corner; right and left; Dan to Beersheba; from every nook and cranny; through thick and thin.

(see *whole, completely, ubiquitous*)

EVIDENT (to be)

need no ghost to tell people; be written on someone's face; break through the clouds; cry aloud; stare one in the face; leave footprints; stand forth naked; lie in one's ears and eyes.

(see *clear, obvious, openly, visible, conspicuous, reveal, display*)

EVIL

devil's broth; the cloven hoof; scourge of the human race; foul play; ills that flesh is heir to; crying sin; devil sitting in men's hearts; gaping jaws of destruction; sink of vice; breath from the infernal regions; machinations of the devil; taint; stain; rottenness; poison; infection; dry-rot; Pandora's box; the powers of darkness; the rulers of darkness.

(see *wicked, villainous, hell, Satan*)

EVIL (to do)

tear down the walls of hell to gain one's ends; sow dragon's teeth; be in the clutch of the devil; do a bad turn; have a dirty soul; sell oneself to the devil; be a bad actor; thirst for destruction; play the viper; strike in serpent fashion.

(see *sinful, offend, malicious, wicked, self-indulgence, scoundrel, err)*

EXACT (to be)

put the saddle on the right horse; hit the nail on the head; pin down to fact; follow the letter of the law; act with pin-point accuracy; have a steel-trap mind; be a stickler for correctness; go step by step; bring down to cases.

(see *strict, accurate, rigid, correct, careful, definite*)

EXACTLY

to a tittle; to an inch; by clock-work; to the letter; word for word; to a hair; ship-shape.

(see *exact, uncompromising, orderly*)

EXAGGERATE

stretch a point; embroider on the truth; make a mountain out of a mole hill; throw the hatchet; strain one's conscience; be high-flown; prettify fact; puff a thing up; make two bites of a cherry; stir up a tempest in a teapot; spin a long yarn; use false coloring; indulge in a flight of fancy; draw a long bow; overlay with ornament; overshoot the mark; walk on stilts; lay it on thick; indulge in mile-high musings; overplay a thing; clothe with the witchery of fiction; swell up reality; heighten the truth; draw verbal hyperboles; play a game of bluff and bluster; tell a tall story; see a glowworm and report a fire; say all one's geese are swans; leaven the loaf of truth; play Baron Munchausen; let off hot air; overheat the dish of facts; knock oneself out with overdoing; be much cry and little wool; raise an anthill to the height of a mountain; gush over; carry to extravagant lengths; make up out of whole cloth; overstep credibility; ride a thing too hard; color too highly.

(see *lie, embellish, elaborate, imagine, ostentatious, glorify, sensationalistic*)

EXAMINE

put someone through his paces; pick someone's brains; sift for truth; thump one about; dig into the corners; prospect for something; plow a thing through; turn over the leaves; comb through a thing; grapple with a thing; set one's eyes to raking (or sweeping) a subject; have one's eyes devour a thing; paw a thing over; turn one's looks upon; dig down into the raw roots; leave no stone unturned; perform an autopsy on; take a mental tour through; finger an object; catechize a person.

(see *inquisitive, observant, investigate, consider, study, test, explore, survey, verify, check-up*)

EXCEL

lead in the dance; hold top place; shine forth from the crowd; win hands-down; win in a canter; outdistance one's rivals; get the best of; beat; cast in the shade; eclipse; win the palm; bear the bell; outstrip; cap; win the prize; stand out from the crowd; be singular; be a world-beater; dance rings around others.

(see *surpass, rivalry, triumphant, outdo, competition*)

EXCELLENT

above par; on a high plane; first-rate; sterling; salt of the earth; of the first water; cracker-jack; brightest jewel in the crown; gem; flower of the flock; cream of the crop; gilt-edged; Simon Pure.

(see *valuable, superior, excel, celebrity, perfect*)

EXCESSIVE (to be)

carry coals to Newcastle; carry owls to Athens; paint the lily; gild refined gold; kill the slain; do a thing till one is blue in the face; overshoot the mark; teach one's grandmother to suck eggs; have too many irons in the fire; run riot; soar sky-high; butter one's bread on both sides; put butter upon bacon; lay it on with a trowel; create a back-wash; burst the seams; out-Herod Herod; go beyond the length of one's tether; overbait the hook; set a patch at the corner of Helen of Troy's eyes; wake the Sleeping Beauty with a lipstick.

(see *superfluous, unrestrained, extravagant, exaggerate, foolish, wasteful, lavish, embellish*)

EXCITE

set on fire; tickle the desire; apply the torch to; stir the blood; take the breath; set stagnant blood in motion; whet the appetite; shake up; set a chord in vibration; warm the blood; kindle desire; fire with desire; whip the senses; call up the blood; make the heart thump; give new life to; work up; set the heart aflame; lash into desire; set the blood dancing; cause hair to stand up; raise a whirlwind; electrify; galvanize; make red corpuscles race; set pulsating; send the heart leaping into the mouth; set blood to roaring in the arteries; raise to a white heat; send blood pressure up; cause burning blood to ebb and flow.

(see *arouse, waken, stimulate, incite, agitator*)

EXCITED (to be)

keyed up; ablaze; feel one's blood leap up; be in a lather; feel one's heart begin to hammer; flail one's arms about; be electrified over; be stirred by; work oneself into a state; blow up; run berserk; feel one's blood racing in the veins; have one's brain in a whirl; feel hot and cold all over; feel burning with emotion; feel aflame with passion; be wrought up to a high pitch; toss on one's pillow; champ the bit; be in a fever of excitement; feel one's pulse quicken; light up with anticipation; boil over; be in a stew; be steamed up; fly off the handle; froth at the mouth; burst out with emotion; feel intoxicated with excitement; get one's heart to racing; feel tingling with emotion; have one's heart set off at a gallop; fly off at a tangent; flame up with passion; feel hot-headed; take fire; feel all wound up and tight inside; be mercurial; be high-strung; bubble over; fly up the gamut; be a tinder box; be volcanic; be explosive; be combustible; lose one's head; be in a ferment.

(see *inspired, aroused, passionate, eloquent, temperamental, turbulent*)

EXCOMMUNICATE

ban with bell, book, and candle.

(see *dismiss, expel, denounce, ostracize*)

EXCUSE (n.)

whipping the devil round the stump; a loophole; a dodge; sheltering oneself under a plea; having a leg to stand on; furnishing a handle; hemming and hawing; cooking up a reason; having a peg to hang on; giving grounds for.

(see *apologize, defense*)

EXECUTIVE

front-office sahib; spark plug; mahout; shogun; titan; big-wig; mogul; topstring man; high-priest; generalissimo.

(see *law, leader, business, official*)

EXERTION

dragging a lengthened chain; sweat of one's brow; wading through; uphill work; leaving no stone unturned; stretching a long arm; tugging at the oar; bending the bow; buckling to; putting one's shoulder to the wheel; burning the midnight oil; fighting one's way; taking the laboring oar; hammering at; playing one's best card; putting one's best leg forward; going at something with hammer and tongs; acting with heart and soul; straining every nerve; moving heaven and earth; going to all lengths; tackling with tooth and nail; bringing the mountain to Mohammed.

(see *work, labor, strive, endeavor*)

EXHAUSTED (to be)

feel oneself a limp rag; wrapped in a pall of lassitude; drained of energy; sucked dry; feel washed out; be on one's last legs; be worn to a thread; be worn to the bone; feel shop-worn; be run to the ground; feel dead on one's feet; be sapped of strength; be played out; peter out; droop; feel run through the wringer; feel one's knees worn away; be burnt out; feel tired from the eyeballs down; feel one's bolt shot; dog-tired; be down and out; be at low ebb; be more dead than alive; feel drained to the dregs; feel drawn through a loophole.

(see *empty, effete, consume, tired*)

EXPAND

grow elbow room; bloom; swell the ranks; spread wings; stretch lower limbs; blow up; practice ripening powers; dilate; throw arms outward; bud out; spade up new ground.

(see *spread, open, develop, increase*)

EXPECT

be on tenterhooks; be on the rack; count chickens before they are hatched; hold one's breath; hang on (an answer); have in view; reckon upon; pin hopes on; get drunk with hope; wait for dead men's shoes; watch the baton of the future; be in the antechamber; hold one's breath for.

(see *anticipate, hope, prospect, suspense*)

EXPEL

brush out; give the gate; smoke out; bundle out neck and crop; cast out of doors; chuck up.

(see *eliminate, remove, transfer, separate*)

EXPENSIVE

have a white elephant on one's hands; heavy pull upon the purse; too dear for one's whistle; paying through the nose; dent the pocketbook; cost a pretty penny; hand-tailored; high-flying; beyond one's pocket; the route to the poorhouse; priced higher than the roof; require a mortgage on the old homestead; plush.

(see *high-priced, extravagant, lavish, wasteful*)

EXPERIENCED (to be)

be an old hand at; have a practiced eye; pass through the mill; know where the shoe pinches; have looked in the glass of life; have a vivid patch in one's life; drain life to the dregs; be beaten by the rough winds of life; have cut one's eye-teeth; be dry behind the ears; be an old bird; taste of a thing; cut a slice of life; be refined in the fire; be hardened in the mold

of time; have traveled a hard road upward; turn many leaves in the book of life; drink deep of life; have many old threads; be hard-boiled; be hard-bitten; have the hand of a master; be a cunning blade; be a shark at; be a gourmet in; have acquired the ease of the man on the flying trapeze; be crack at a thing; graduate to first fiddle.

(see *knowledge, wise, skilful, self-intelligence*)

EXPERIMENT (v.)

fire a random shot; take a leap in the dark; cast one's net; beat the bushes; try one's hand at; send up a pilot balloon; watch how the wind blows; consult the barometer; feel the pulse; see how the land lies; "monkey" with; tinker with; get one's feet wet; put to the acid test; use a rule of thumb; employ a touchstone; use a guinea pig; cut-and-try.

(see *test, explore, examine, investigate, observant, try*)

EXPLAIN

throw (or cast) light upon; shed light on; illuminate; ventilate; dissolve the mists; cast a searchlight into; flood with light; unravel; unveil; unmask; put one's cards on the table; clear the air; paint an allegory; open people's eyes; draw a clear picture of; untangle the knots; hold the key to; find the common denominator; show the keystone to; sweep away the clouds.

(see *interpret, clear, reason, solution, describe*)

EXPLOIT (v.)

milk the cow; ride a thing for all it is worth; put on the make; make capital out of; suck the juice out of; put in a sweatshop.

(see *use, work, advantage, extort*)

EXPLORE

dig one's toes in new soil; stray into strange paths; creep into the unknown; roam through strange fields; poke one's nose into; beat the bush.

(see *investigate, search for, examine, travel, seek*)

EXPOSE (v.)

tear the lid off; throw a harsh light on; fluoroscope the anatomy of; strip naked; let the cat out of the bag; put in a glass house; ventilate a situation; lay bare; put the cards on the table; get to the bottom of; unroll before the mind's eye; show up in its true colors; put on the rack; hold up to view; lay wide open; send crawling out from under their rocks; drag through the streets in rags; let daylight into; open the curtain on; peel the hearts of; air a situation; open a door to; show someone up; tear the mask from; bring to light; rip raiment from the body of.

(see *detect, show, reveal, open, publish, divulge, betray*)

EXPRESS (orally)

speak one's mind; clothe in words; mirror a thought; breathe a suggestion; frame with words; pour out one's feelings; open one's mind; air an opinion; voice one's ideas; drape with words; find expression; wing one's words; distil into words; open one's mouth in a fishy gasp; give accent to a thought; taste one's words; give sorrow words; effervesce with words; do verbal gymnastics; make one's words an effective tool; lash forth into speech; flower into expression; speak volumes; flame with speech; set one's words in a mask.

(see *utter, speak, declare, voice, eloquent*)

EXTEND

flow into the distance; swoop ahead; yawn into the beyond; stretch away; deepen unfathomably; creep upward and out; cover a broad front; ramble afar; retreat into the distance.

(see *spread, expand, envelop, continue, increase*)

EXTINCT

Dead-Sea fruit; stamped out; smothered in the abyss of the past; dead; lost in time.

(see *vanish, destruction, disappear, end*)

EXTORT

wring from; wrench; pump; milk; put the squeeze on; suck the blood of; leech on to; tear out of; worm out; funnel off; drain out; bleed poor.

(see *use, work, advantage, exploit*)

EXTRAVAGANT (to be)

let money run through the fingers; have money burn one's pocket; cut a flash; burn the candle at both ends; run up a bill; fly high; pour forth like water; throw money around, pay dearly for one's whistle; pay through the nose; blow away money; fritter away cash; be pound foolish; knock a hole in one's pocketbook.

(see *excessive, wasteful, lavish, spend*)

EYES

cold blue stones; extinct volcanoes; clouds of blue mist; wells with Truth at the bottom of each; long green-glinting slits; lamps; flashing fires; dancing coquettes; bottomless pools; distant stars; pale veils.

(see *see, sharp, look, observant*)

F

FACE (visage)

sealed books; disks; mask of white stone.

(see *appearance, eyes, jaw, beautiful, ugly, smile, frown, sharp-faced*)

FACILITATE

smooth the ground; pave the way for; open the door to; bridge over; lighten the labor; disencumber.

(see *ease, ability, resourceful, advantage, unencumbered*)

FAIL

crack up; come to naught; wither on the vine; end in smoke; fall between two stools; sputter out; get the wrong sow by the ear; run one's head against a stone wall; crumble away; see one's hopes blighted; go to the wall; go to the dogs; go to pot; bite the dust; miss fire; flash in the pan; upset the apple cart; be thrown off one's balance; be thrown on one's beam ends; be unhorsed; fall through; go up the spout; get stuck; bog down; muff the ball; take a false step; sit in on one's own funeral; miss the mark; go up in smoke; go on the skids; fall flat; make a mess; go under; go by the board; go on the rocks; fall short of expectation; fizzle out; hit the shoals; miss one's footing; come a cropper; expire at birth; lose ground; wash out; go flat; draw blank cheques against destiny; fold up; stub one's toe against; hang fire; head downhill; have the ground cut out from under one; go out of one's depth; sink of one's own weight; have the third strike called against one; make a poor fist of a thing; go to seed; make a spoon or spoil a horn; be broken at the wheel in the attempt; be headed for the auctioneer's block; make the keystone fall out of the arch; deliver still-born; be a frost; make a slip 'twixt cup and lip; be the black sheep of a good flock; come to flotsam and jetsam; fail thumpingly; fall out of the run; become a fragment of flotsam tossed on the tide of failure.

(see *defeated, weak, err, frail, break, decline, sink, misfortune, mistake*)

FAINT (v.)

feel the light in one's brain go out; have the curtain of unconsciousness black out the daylight; sink to the earth; fall in giddiness.

(see *fall, weak, sick, exhausted*)

FAIR (just)

play the game; shoot square; give the hare a sporting chance; abide by the rules; hold the scales even; give the devil his due; put the saddle on the right horse; leave the door open.

(see *judge, frank, honest, unbiased, truthful*)

FAITHFUL

true to one's salt; true to the core; earn a solid reputation; die in harness; stay safe in harness; remain in the fold; fight to the last ditch; stand to one's colors (or guns); cling to one's principles; burn with unflickering flame.

(see *reliable, steadfast, trust, loyal, devotion, conscience, courageous, fervent*)

FAKE

more bark than bite; ass in lion's skin; fair-weather sailor; fish out of water, fresh-water sailor; horse-marine; jackdaw in peacock's feathers; lord of misrule; mare's nest; man of straw.

(see *pretend, cheat, deceitful, untrustworthy, imposture, insincere, forgery, worthless*)

FALL (v.)

take a header; plunge; sag; plummet; slide off; landslide; nose-dive; topple; sink; pitch over; careen down a precipice; flutter in a cloud to the floor.

(see *sink, collapse*)

FALLING (prices)

skidding; crumbling; softening; tumbling down-hill; melting away; deflating; slipping; riding down; cracking; taking a sharp plunge; losing altitude; taking a dip; sagging.

(see *bankrupt, low point, cheap, decline, diminish, lessen*)

FALSE (to be)

ring hollow; part company with facts; fly far from the truth; cry wolf; shed crocodile tears; bestow a Judas kiss; have a cardboard character; counterfeit; draw a red herring across the trail; be rotten at the core; play fast and loose with; wear a garment of false pretenses; make a bridge of one's nose; lie out of whole cloth; doctor the account; fly kites; juggle the truth.

(see *dishonest, mislead, lie, misdirected, imposture, insincere, treachery, deceive, hypocrite, betray, fickle, swindle*)

FAME (to achieve)

make a name for oneself; find one's place in the sun; see one's star rise; set foot upon the ladder of prominence; flow in praise; have one's name on the world's lips; glow in the limelight; secure a niche in the Temple of Fame; flame resplendent in the sky; make a name for oneself; find one's way to the top; be a great gun; become a myth; catapult into fame; bask in the glare of Fame; have a name that shouts through the archives of history; wear a halo; take high rank; be on a high footing; have a face to be saved, not slapped; have a name that is in every household.

(see *popularity, reputation, glorify, honored, renown, self-satisfaction, proud, excel*)

FAREWELL

swan song; valedictory; bon voyage.

(see *depart, leave, end, quit, retire, withdraw*)

FARMER

wrestler with the earth; dresser of the ground; son of the soil; man with a green thumb; man with a hoe; ploughboy; resident of the brown corduroy of plowed fields.

(see *labor, work, food*)

FASCINATE

set on fire; get hold of; sweep someone off his feet; steal someone's heart; carry away; wind around the heart; cast a spell over; intoxicate.

(see *romantic, embrace, endear, emotional, love, sentimental, lure*)

FASHIONABLE (to be)

have the right cut to one's jib; be in the pink of fashion; cut a figure in society; rub shoulders with the elite; keep one's carriage; be a silk-stocking; go with the stream; fall in with the fashion; pass current; be all the rage; roll in the squirrel-cage of fashion; be a fashion-plate; be a clothes-horse; be all the go.

(see *elegant, appearance, beautify, model*)

FAST (adj.)

move on a whirlwind; gather speed;

fly on the wings of the wind; march in double time; get up the speed of a buck being passed; put one's best leg foremost; move with breakneck speed; be eagle-winged· travel on a lightning bolt; make tracks; shake a leg; be light-legged; be light of heel; make short work of; show fiery hoofs; get under full steam; forge ahead full blast; rush hell-bent-for-leather; send out sparks; be electric; be telegraphic; move at space-eating tempo; crowd sail; travel on a whirligig; go by leaps and bounds; go at a gallop; have the speed of a mushroom growing; go like hot cakes.

(see *swift, quickly, reckless, speed*)

FASTIDIOUS

be thin-skinned; be strait-laced; mince the matter; turn up one's nose; see spots on the sun; look a gift horse in the mouth.

(see *delicate, sensitive, strict, exact*)

FAT (adj.)

plump and pulpy; dumpling; mountain of flesh; melon-shaped; padded; a second edition to the chin; lard-faced; spherical; enveloped in suet; clothed in fat; upholstered; beef-trust; pot-bellied; swag-bellied; wrapped in flesh; support a prosperous abdomen.

(see *self-indulgence*)

FATE

clock of fate begins to chime; knees of the High Gods; fate rapping one on the knuckles; fate's tracery in the sands: one's true dark path; dark path of the future; caught in the mesh of fate; the moving finger writing on; the numberer of one's days; written in the book of fate; what falls to one's lot; the punishment of an ironic nature; fate's stacked cards; the mistress of one's destiny; the cast of the die;

the strings that jerk like puppets in unending repetition of the same patterns; the sharpened ax of destiny; what is in the cards; Ides of March; wheel of fortune; the pattern in the threads of destiny; the womb of time; loaded dice of fate; stars of destiny.

(see *doom, predestined, prediction, premeditated, premonition*)

FATHER

the head of the house; the sire of the flock.

(see *patriarch, heredity*)

FAVOR (v.)

do a good turn; smile on someone; bend the knee of fortune to; throw one's weight to; make someone's course run smooth.

(see *indulge, encourage, approve, support, kind*)

FAVORABLE

a red-letter occasion; sailing before the wind; the goose hanging high; the one patch of blue; the sunny side; with bright prospects; hope shining again; one white ball amid the black.

(see *lucky, happy, fortunate, successful*)

FAVORITE

the apple of one's eye; a pet lamb; whiteheaded boy; one on whom the world will never grow cold; the spoiled child of one's heart; the jewel of one's heart; darling of the gods; one's leading lady (or man).

(see *sweetheart, preference*)

FAWN

dance to someone's tune; bow obeisance to; salaam before; kowtow to; bow to the earth before; pin oneself upon; lick (or kiss) boots; hang on the sleeve of; eat honey out of someone's hand; sun oneself in the smiles of; kiss the hem of someone's garment; kiss the feet of; pin oneself upon.

(see *flatter, praise, obedient*)

FEAR (n.)

nightmare; skeleton; hobgoblin; the invisible worm; bogey; that bit of ancient hard black flint.

(see *frightened, afraid, terrify, scare*)

FEARFUL (to be apprehensive)

feel one's blood run cold; be sickly-livered; feel one's heart sink; be under the lash of terror; feel an ominous sensation sitting at one's heart; be gnawed by anxiety; feel a glacial shiver run down one's spine; feel a sinking in the stomach; wear fear on one's sleeve; feel a gnawing in one's breast; get gooseflesh; hear a bell clang upon one's heart; feel one's face disintegrate in shadow; widen one's eyes in distress; feel cold wet sheets wound round one's body; feel a tightness in one's breast; sit in accidental stillness; feel a great pang grip one's heart; feel one's heart in one's throat; feel one's hair curl; have one's spine turn to jelly; feel one's legs turn to water; have one's brain run riot in terror; sweat with terror; have one's heart in one's boots; shy away from; fold one's petals; hide in dread; feel one's courage shattered; feel the clammy paws of; hear one's heart pound against one's ribs; feel one's mouth run dry; feel the sockets of one's eyes go icy cold; feel one's blood turn to ice; feel one's heart fail one; feel one's flesh creep; be in a gale of terror; feel an icy tension; have one's thoughts ripen into dread; stay close to the lamplight; whistle in the dark; drink Dutch courage; be afraid of one's own shadow; hold one's breath; feel the fingers of fear at one's throat;

become infected with dread; petrify with fear; be held in the clutch of fear.

(see *nervous, cowardly, timid*)

FEELING (emotion)

a net-work of sensitive strings, waiting to be played on by every factor in life; pulse of the emotions; hurry of spirits; the distillation of the heart; wave of sensitivity; the withering fires of emotional intensity; an undercurrent of reaction; the faint tide of emotional response; the stab of immense admiration; a spasm of compunction; the heart's strings; a touch of sympathy; hurt to the quick; the contents of the heart; a taste of relief; inner burning; a jolt of emotion.

(see *sensation, emotional, passionate, sympathetic, sentimental, moved*)

FERVENT

feverish; warming; burning; scalding; flaming; carried away with; feeling deeply.

(see *eager, aroused, zestful, enthusiastic, intense, passionate, vehement, violent*)

FEW

a sprinkling of; scraps of; a handful; a dribble; to be counted on one's fingers; enough to be comfortable in a telephone booth; easily numbered; few and far between.

(see *small amount, scarce, speck, bit, particle, scrap*)

FICKLE

mercurial; fair-weather friend; weathercock; barometric; Cynara of the minute; elastic; changing horses; a rock set in quicksand.

(see *unsteady, untrustworthy, unsettled, unstable, undecided, uncertain, changeable, irresolute, irresponsible*)

FIGHT (v.)

live by the sword; turn into a shambles; rain hailstones of knobby fists; cause the fur to fly; grind in the dust; come to points; measure swords; ready to eat up one another; lay on the mailed fist; bite heads off; club right and left; go into scrimmage; scratch eyes out; beat into a soft pulp; rend limb from limb; give a going-over; cut to ribbons; give a lacing; fly at throats; spill blood; thrash within an inch of life; make mincemeat of; hurl lances at; unsheathe the sword; lay about one; come to grips with; be at loggerheads; sharpen the claws; enter a tug of war; lead a cat-and-dog life; pack a vicious punch; take up the gauntlet; turn the buckle of the belt; tangle talons with; don armor; take up the hatchet; battle tooth-and-nail; play the bantam-cock; pound to a jelly; go on the warpath; lock horns with.

(see *conflict, strife, quarrel, struggle, encounter, oppose, discord*)

FILL

saturate; flood; sprinkle heavily with; cause to brim with; glut; make rich with; cause to bristle with; overflow with; drown in; choke with; jam to the eaves; pack to the beams; litter with; load to the gunwales; pepper with; speckle with.

(see *sated, congestion, gluttony, excessive, replete, abundance*)

FIND (v.)

dig up; fish up; put the finger on; unearth; hit on; stumble upon; bump into; lay hands on; ferret out; uncover; pick up the scent.

(see *discover, detect, solution, expose, divulge, reveal*)

FINISH (v.)

put the coping stone on; rest one's case; drive the last nail in; ring down the curtain on; bring to a full cycle; top off; round out and seal; add the final push; make a clean sweep of; wind up; bring to the end of the tether; bring to the end of the course; see a thing through; come to the fag end of; come to the uttermost inch; tie up all loose ends; bring to the home stretch; polish up; chisel off rough edges; put the finishing touch on.

(see *complete, end, stop, close*)

FIRE (n.)

garland of sparks; wreath of flame; licking tongues; shower of light; blazing furnace; cauldron of flame; sizzling crater, licking its lips and cracking its jaws; angry red tongue.

(see *burn*)

FIRM (to be)

keep to one's course; stand one's ground; take a square stand; keep one's footing; keep one's backbone; stand four-square; turn oneself to stone; stick to one's guns; stand on an unassailable rock; keep a tight hand on; have nerves of steel; strike root deeply; stand with flat determination; be iron-willed; stick one's chin out antenna-wise.

(see *steadfast, resolute, determined, strong, self-control, self-reliant, self-sufficient, immovable*)

FIRST

curtain-raiser; maiden (as of a speech or voyage).

(see *beginning, opening, start, origin, source*)

FISH (n.)

fruits of the rod and reel; members of

the finny tribe.

(see *sea, ocean*)

FLATTER

butter someone up; worm oneself into another's graces; curry favor with; turn someone's head; have honey in the mouth; be soft-tongued; hang on the sleeve of; lick someone's boots; offer food to vanity; burn incense before; lay on thick; puff someone up; "soft soap"; "oil"; "blarney"; pay court to.

(see *fawn, praise, favor, applaud*)

FLAUNT

throw in the face of; cast in the teeth of; parade before the eyes of; wave under the nose of; let fly before; present with fanfare and flourish of trumpet.

(see *display, ostentatious, sensationalistic, show-off*)

FLEE

take to one's heels; turn tail; get up the dust; cut and run; decamp.

(see *run, escape, vanish*)

FLIRT (v.)

make mash; drop the handkerchief; hang a rag on every bush; mechanize love-making; play the fish in every pond.

(see *love, woo, sentimental, sensual, sweetheart*)

FLOOD

wall of water; body of water jumping its banks; storm of water sweeping the land.

(see *waves, drown, disaster, river, sea*)

FLOW (v.)

stream; rush; leap in torrents; rain; glide; gush; dance down; ripple and

laugh its way; creep by; purl.

(see *rush, splash, spray, river, waves*)

FLOWER (n.)

ghostly little faces; bride of the woodland (the dogwood); butterfly flight of orchids; candle-flames of crocus.

(see *grow*)

FLUCTUATE

careen up and down; see-saw; ebb and flow; shuttle; dance; wave up and down; swing with the pendulum; hit the peaks and valleys; move on a roller coaster.

(see *varied, changeable, irresolute, inconsistent, unsettled, unsteady, uncertain*)

FLY (v.)

trace patterns over the sky; wing one's way; drift through the clouds; whistle past; winnow one's way; sail on extended pinions.

(see *soar, birds, airplane, height*)

FOLLOW

dog another's footsteps; press hard after; keep in the wash of; tread on another's heels; tread in the steps of; follow in the wake of; be in the trail of; hang on the skirts of; keep at the tail of; walk in the shoes of; bring up the rear; hound after; steer by another; skirmish in pursuit of; set one's bloodhounds after; stay on the scent; follow in full cry.

(see *accompany, proceed*)

FOOD

the staff of life; belly timber; grist for the mill.

(see *sustenance, survive, eat, hungry, consume*)

FOOLISH (to be)

catch the wind with a net; put on the

cap and bells; be feather-headed; cut off one's own nose in the interest of universal ugliness; quarrel with one's bread and butter; have a soft spot in one's head; get oneself tangled in nonsense; act without rime or reason; play the monkey; be a mountain in labor and give birth to a mouse; make an ass of oneself; teach one's grandmother to suck eggs; trust to a broken reed; put a square thing in a round hole; cut a caper; seem half-baked; squeeze the saint and let the sinner slip; throw good money after bad; draw water in a sieve; break a butterfly upon a wheel; live in a fool's paradise.

(see *reckless, weak, vain, ridiculous, senseless, nonsense, stupid*)

FORCE (v.)

press into service; make a demand bid; push to the wall; apply a squeeze hold; put at sword's point; wield an iron hand; use the straight-arm appeal; wrestle into subjection; resort to a strong-arm policy; lay down the law; push another into a thing; bend to one's will; carry by the sword; put teeth to a thing; sledge-hammer one's way; dragoon another into a thing; turn on the screw; steam-roller a person into action; use a pressure-play; catapult another into something; strike hammer blows; stampede a thing through; blast one's way; tear from another with wild horses; resort to the mailed fist; rule with a rod of iron; drive into a corner; cram down the throat; drive sheep; ride herd; force another's hand; browbeat someone; use brass knuckles; shoehorn into power; rope another into something; rig the balance; wedge one's way; railroad another into a thing; make another fit the Procrustean bed; put the bee on; put under the lash; batter into consent; crack down on; pin another down to; wring from another; elbow one's way to.

(see *power, vigorous, violent, strong, stern, energetic, pressure, overcome, ruthless, aggressive*)

FOREIGN

the old-world look; an international flavor; beyond seas; profane soil.

(see *strange, remote, classic*)

FORESEE

direct one's trustful thoughts far down the stream of time; look beyond the mists that fill the present; have an eye to the future; scent from afar; feel in one's bones; peep into the future; see how the land lies; watch how the wind blows; put aside the veil of futurity; keep one's sights on tomorrow; be eagle-eyed.

(see *fate, future, anticipate, prudent, prediction, premonition*)

FORESHORTEN

nip in the bud; prune; mow; reap; crop; snub.

(see *shorten, short-lived, reduce, diminish, lessen*)

FORGERY

manufacture out of wedlock.

(see *fake, false, dishonest, imposture, swindle, treachery, deceive*)

FORGET

lose sight of; rub out; wash out of one's mind; erase; put out of mind; drown the past; consign to oblivion; discharge from the memory; lay aside in folds of soft tissue; swallow in time; burn one's bridges to the rear; slip from the memory; shake out of the memory; have the mind play hide-and-seek with the memory; banish from the mind; spin into oblivion; cut adrift from the past; throw away the baggage of the past; wean away from the past; let memories grow rusty; let sleeping dogs lie; cast out of one's thoughts: blur the memory; drop the recollection; lose touch with; cause to dim and tarnish with the years; bury the hatchet; come in at one ear and go out at the other; send one's mind into the pit of oblivion; drop into the jaws of darkness; give a thing the go-by; let the past bury its dead; throw to the winds; blot out the past; cast behind one's back; rub a sponge over the memory; tear one's thoughts from the past; relegate to the limbo of history; let a thing sink below the horizon of awareness; seal up in the burial cave of oblivion; let memory accumulate dust; let the past die of old age; have melt from the mind; let the past fade; cause to go out of the memory; bury memory in its neglected grave; let the dead past lie in its halo; watch a thing fade into the indifferent past; embalm in the past; let go by the board; empty the mind of the past.

(see *neglect, oblivious, obsolete, disregard, indifferent*)

FORGIVE

lift the load of anguish from another's tormented soul; let bygones be bygones; let the wound heal; clean the slate; bury the hatchet; hold out the hand of pardon; pocket the affront; wash white from crimson sins; grant a reprieve.

(see *reconcile, pacify, apologize, confess, reunion, repent*)

FORM (v.)

place on the anvil; weave; mold; cause to congeal; carve; frame; engrave: make crystallize; lick into shape; whip into shape; manufacture.

(see *shape, pattern, build, create, produce, invent, originate*)

FORMAL

arctic; aldermanic; on stilts; on a pedestal; under the yoke of convention; the tone of a bread-and-butter note; stuffed-shirt.

(see *strict, rigid, stiff, exact*)

FORTUNATE (to be)

bear a charmed life; have opportunity knock for one; have one's bread buttered on both sides; acquire a windfall; have fortune smile on one; be a child of fortune; be pursued by luck; shake the pagoda tree (British-Indian).

(see *successful, favorite, lucky, advantage, happy*)

FRAIL

glass house; house of cards; hothouse flower; a child's balloon, merely bright air inflated and thinly armored.

(see *delicate, weak, unstable, sensitive, tender*)

FRANK (to be)

meet a thing face to face; open a piece of one's mind; call a spade a spade; relate a naked truth; make no bones; speak four-square; wear one's thoughts upon the sleeve; be above-board; drop the mask; unveil one's mind; call to a show-down; prefer the unvarnished; lay the cards on the table; cast tact to the winds; tell an uncorseted tale; speak one's tongue; strip one's words of rhetorical ornament; not mince words; put off one's academic robes.

(see *sincere, direct, straightforward, truthful, honest*)

FREE (to become)

cast off the yoke; slip the collar; be shot of; dissolve one's bondage; overthrow subjection; tear oneself from thraldom; shake off fetters; cut loose from control; give oneself reins; be set at liberty; tear bonds asunder; break the shackles; clear one's path of obstacles; break out of the cage; be foot-loose; slip out of harness; find a passkey out of prison; strike off the chains; burst the bonds of restraint; cut oneself free; be delivered out of the hand of; loosen one's bonds; kick over the traces.

(see *independent, unrestrained, lax, release, unencumbered*)

FRESH

a rose with the dew on; a rain-washed April look; forest-fresh; green; virgin; new-born; raw; new ground broken; the smell of newly turned earth.

(see *new, renew, revive, springtime, sweet, refresh*)

FRIENDLY (to be)

hold out the hand of friendship; keep another in one's books; have the heart in the right place; make up to another; strike in with people; hit it off with another; be a brick; be a good old scout; make others feel at home; blow away formalities; put up horses together; enter into the feelings of another; walk hand in hand with another; talk the same language as another; meet half way; receive with open arms; scrape acquaintance with; be an ice-breaker; extend the right hand of fellowship; have a leaning to; be warm-hearted; come out of one's shell.

(see *kind, pleased*)

FRIGHTENED (to be)

quake before; have one's heart in his mouth; feel one's hair curl; feel one's blood freeze; be in the clutch of fear; have one's breath taken away; feel one's flesh creep; get one's wind up; break into a cold sweat; shiver in one's boots; balance on the plank; feel ice go up and down the back; have one's teeth chatter; have one's spine chilled: lose one's head; become petrified (or paralyzed) with fear; freeze with horror; feel the chill breath of fright; be frightened out of the seven senses; have one's blood curdle.

(see *fearful, terrify, afraid, scare*)

FRONT

face; grandstand seat; front of the stage; façade; vanguard.

(see *background*)

FROWN (v.)

give a glance that smoulders with rebuke; knit the eyebrows; give a dark smile; screw up the eyes; have the brows furrowed; contract the brow; draw down the eyebrows; have a forehead rutted by disapproval; turn on a black look; have a cloud come over the face.

(see *scowl, stern*)

FRUSTRATED

find oneself in the shoals; have one's goose cooked; be blighted by defeat; have intentions hamstrung; eat the air; be mocked by fate; have the soul warped by disappointment; be chained to defeat; dash oneself against an unyielding wall; feel bottled up; be brought to nought.

(see *defeated, disappointed, hinder*)

FULL (of)

crowded to suffocation; pregnant; groaning with excess; filled to the neck (or brim); swarming with; steeped to the lips; brimming over; saturated with; boiling over; honeycombed with; bristling with; crammed to the scuppers; packed to bursting; black with; filled to the core; bulging with;

alive with; choked with.

(see *gluttony, sated, abundance, replete*)

FUNDAMENTAL

bare bones; cornerstone; backbone; hard tacks; bread-and-butter; deep roots.

(see *rudiments, important*)

FUNERAL

passing bell; dead march; muffled drum.

(see *bury, death, mourn, grave*)

FUTILITY

employing a steam-engine to crack a nut; catching at a straw; cutting a whetstone with a razor; locking the stable-door after the horse is stolen; chasing nothing; teaching one's grandmother to suck eggs; running one's head against walls; hurrying toward a dead-end; chasing a wild goose; crying for the moon; going on a sleeveless errand; making bricks without straw; baying the moon; beating the wind; rolling the stone of Sisyphus; carrying water in a sieve; extracting sunbeams from cucumbers; running around in circles; breaking a fly on a wheel; milking a he-goat into a sieve; looking for a blade of corn in the stack of chaff.

(see *impossibility, useless, worthless*)

FUTURE (n.)

horizon; womb of time; time drawing on; on the knees of the gods; a new vista; the shadow on tomorrow's wall; the unborn tomorrow; the shape of things to come; the golden morning of Sometime; the file of the next decade; the blueprint of what is to come.

(see *fate, foresee, premonition, time*)

G

GAIN (n.)

reaping the fruits; black figures; the coin of plenty; grab bag; loaves and fishes; dollars-and-cents profit; feathering the nest; filling one's pockets.

(see *profit, increase, add, advantage, achieve, self-gain, earn, spoils*)

GAMBLE (v.)

spin the wheel; make a book; shuffle the cards; live on one's wits; tempt the gods; buck the tiger; take a blind leap.

(see *money, spend, sporting, swindle, risk*)

GATHER

marshal; herd; garner; scrape up; rake up; knit the skein.

(see *collect, group*)

GAY (to be)

ride on the howdah of happiness; flit with the butterflies; kick up the heels; bathe in charged waters; sow wild oats; bubble over with gaiety; shine with good spirit; be feather-headed; be tickled by aerial champagne.

(see *lively, cheerful, joyful, happy, laugh, pleasure-seeking*)

GENERALLY

in the long run; wholesale; blanket; bird's-eye view.

(see *universal, wholly, maximum*)

GENEROUS (to be)

give away the shirt off one's back; chuck about gold purses; flow over with gifts; be lavish with the sweet oils of life; give a baker's dozen; have a big heart; overflow with the milk of human kindness; do the handsome thing; be large-hearted; throw one's treasures and storehouses open; have a heart of gold; cast one's bread upon the waters; have one's heart in the right place; give with both hands; be free-handed; loose one's purse strings; shower upon; deluge with; rain upon; bless with a drumstick; kill the fatted calf; have a generous soul; be princely.

(see *abundance, give, gift, superfluous, sympathetic, kind*)

GENIUS (to be a)

be a meteor flashing across the sky; be a mental giant; stride on the highroads of mankind's aspirations; be the great white hope; have the spark; be a shining light; have one's creative sap flowing strong; have the green fingers of a born (writer); have one's lark lose itself in the skies; have the divine fire; carry the torch of genius.

(see *intellectual, create, imagine, visionary*)

GET

scrape up; pick up; "bag"; scoop up; bring into one's clutches; capture; snare; rope in; wring from; corral; land (a contract); garner; fish out; harvest; reap; roll up gains; draw from a well; dig out; wrangle; net; nail; pry loose; comb out.

(see *achieve, earn, secure, win*)

GIANT

a mountain of a man; a Triton among minnows; colossus.

(see *large, big*)

GIFT

a plum dropped in one's lap; a windfall; manna from heaven.

(see *favor, indulge, help*)

GIST

the milk in the coconut; the whole thing in a nut shell; heart; core; breath; flower; distillation; kernel; nub; pivot; marrow; meat of the thing; root; where the hen scratches; bedrock; flavor; life-blood; salt; germ; pith; essence.

(see *important, necessity, requisite, summarized, basis*)

GIVE

fork out; shell out; cough up; cross palm with; hand over; put into one's purse; pour on; shed; blow in; dish out; toss; fling; slip over; feed.

(see *entrust, contribute, pay, money*)

GIVE (up)

throw up the sponge; turn one's back upon; turn upon one's heel; dance the back-step; beat a retreat; throw up one's hands; surrender; hang up one's harp; wash the hands of; cry quits; cry quarter.

(see *retreat, retire, retrace, surrender, yield*)

GLANCE (at)

throw a glance; feed the eyes on; bring the eyes to dwell on; exchange a glance; fasten the eyes on; rivet the eyes to; flirt an eye at; catch one's eye; sweep with the eyes; whiskbroom the eyes over; dart a lightning look at; take a bird's-eye view of; run the eyes over.

(see *look at, see, eyes, regard*)

GLARE (at)

look daggers; battle with eyes; set one's eyes to blazing; kill with a look; scorch with a glance; launch a steely glitter from the eyes; flash flames from the eyes; make the forehead gloom with thunder.

(see *frown, angry, scowl, sullen*)

GLORIFY

clothe in shining armor; scrub to so bright a lustre that the baser metal mixed with the gold is not noted; dress up in robes of state; surround with a halo; enroll among the gods; represent in full-bearded dignity; cause to bask in the sunshine of fame; sound the fanfare for; enthrone in golden pomp; genuflect before; extol to the skies.

(see *honored, renown, fame*)

GLUTTONY

have the stomach of an ostrich; eat out of house and home; play a good knife and fork; be a belly-god or slave; be a cormorant; have a hog's capacity; have a greedy-gut; wallow with the swine at the sty; eat one's head off.

(see *hungry, greedy, self-abuse, self-indulgence*)

GOD

the Great Gardener; the Great Artificer; Sun of Righteousness; Light of the World; Prince of Peace; Bread of Life; Lamb of God; Ruler of Wind and Wave; Overseer of the Universe; Author of all things; the Great Architect; the Father; the Bestower of Gifts; Maker, Preserver, and Destroyer.

(see *heaven, religion, religious, worship*)

GOSSIP (n.)

chewing the rag; babel of tongues; tongue or breath of scandal; sewer-system of society; wag of tongues; buzz; tittle-tattle; muckraking; washing dirty linen in public; verbal tearing to pieces; click-clack of tongues; ripples of rumor; head-wagging; chaff bandied across the table; juicy talk; telling tales out of school; rain of scandal; flying of rumor; journey of a whisper; winged rumor; shuffling and re-dealing the lives of others; grapevine; leak-out; noising abroad; over-the-transom reports; vulture of reputations; scandal rolling under tongues; making a curtain of buzzings.

(see *talkative, rumor, scandal, scathe*)

GRACE

poetry of movement; smoothly flowing line.

(see *elegant, refined, dance, smooth*)

GRADUALLY

step-by-step; inch-by-inch; drop-by-drop; foot-by-foot; veil-by-veil; snowballing.

(see *slow, consider, cautious, careful, prudent*)

GRAFT (n.)

overfeeding at the public trough; shaking the political tree; passing out the plums; lining one's pockets.

(see *illegality, gain, violate, spoils, profit, swindle, self-gain*)

GRASS

emerald carpet.

(see *earth, woodland*)

GRATEFUL (to be)

know on which side one's bread is buttered; not look a gift-horse in the mouth; overflow with gratitude; rise on wings of gratitude; thank one's stars; thank heaven; bless one's stars; write a bread-and-butter note.

(see *obligated, reward, appreciative, gift*)

GRAVE (n.)

narrow house; long home; house of death; potter's field; God's acre; field of bones; permanent dwelling-place;

eternal resting place.

(see *bury, shroud, death, funeral*)

GRAY-HAIRED

pepper-and-salt hair; hair threaded with silver; hoar frost of gray at the temples; a head covered with patches of gray astrakhan; grayish smoke stealing over hair.

(see *age, old, white-haired, middle-age, wrinkles*)

GREEDY (to be)

have an itching palm; have a thirst for; gorge the hook; employ wolf-pack methods; be tight-fisted; have a hard fist; be a vulture; drink greedily of; eat one's cake and have it too; be excited by a fever for; be a pig for; be given an inch and take an ell; take the lion's share; want the earth with a gold fence around it; insist on one's pound of flesh; be a catch-all.

(see *selfish, self-gain, get, seize, self-centered*)

GRIEVANCE

have a crow to pluck; have a bone to pick; have a chip on the shoulder; nurse a grievance; have an ax to grind.

(see *bitterness, complain, irritate, aggravate, quarrel*)

GRIEVE

taste the bitters in the ambrosial cup; be gnawed at the heart; feel an aching emptiness; feel absence a permanent pain; dwell in the chilling vapor that is loneliness; have one's heart lacerated; be dissolved in grief; have the heart stabbed; founder in a sea of grief; have a wordless grief overspread the face; be cut to the quick; have weigh upon the heart; tear one's heart in two; move in a fog of grief; lay to heart; break one's heart; have a soul that is sick within one; have one's feelings wounded; have the iron entered into one's soul; have a face that is clouded with grief; nurse a sorrow that deepens into darker colors; eat one's heart out for; be stabbed through and through by grief.

(see *mourn, sorrowful, pain, weep, regret, loss, lonely, worry, solace*)

GROUP (n.)

posse; coagulation; line-up: bundle; knot; pack; brood; circle; stable; family; crop; chain; sprinkling; stream; covey; galaxy; cluster; caravan; flock; herd; clot; nucleus.

(see *mass, crowd, collection, gather*)

GROW

sprout; flower; bud; creep up on the vine; take root; germinate; climb steadily; tower up; loom up; soar; bulk large; put forth leaves; mushroom; run riot; ripen; shoot up suddenly; bloom; reach man's estate; swell; burst the chrysalis.

(see *mature, expand, complete*)

GUIDE (n.)

yardstick; polestar; barometer; touchstone.

(see *advise, influence, rule, standard, estimate, judge*)

GULLIBLE (to be)

fall hook, line, and sinker; be taken in; nibble at the bait; believe the moon is made of green cheese; have something put over on one; set a fox to keep one's geese; play into the hands of; take for gospel; take the shadow for the substance; swallow the bottle without reading the label; be wide-eyed; be blind to flaws; find a mare's nest; get sucked in.

(see *unaware, undiscerning, trust, inexperienced*)

GUN (n.)

shooting iron; engine of destruction; fire-squirter; bullet-belcher.

(see *war, battleground, fight, kill*)

H

HABITUAL
staying on the beaten path; moving in a rut; running in a groove; following the well-trodden track; going round in a mill; having a web wound about one; being wedded to; sticking to one's mind-soil; being addicted to the narcotic of one's ways; being given over to a thing.

(see *common, faithful, ordinary, sameness*)

HAIR
undergrowth; dense shrubbery; flowing locks; crowning glory; mop; mane; thatch; crest; ambrosial cloud; fringe; filigreed gold.

(see *bald, gray-haired, blond, whitehaired, brunette*)

HAND (n.)
hairy paw; talons; pointer; claw; meathook.

(see *touch, hold*)

HANDSHAKE
pump another's hand off; put another's hand through a wringer; extend a paw.

(see *friendly, welcome*)

HANG
depend stalactite-fashion; stab space downward; trail down.

(see *depend*)

HAPHAZARD
hit-or-miss; catch-as-catch-can; hit-and-run.

(see *chance, aimless, unsteady, uncertain*)

HAPPY (to be)
brim over with ecstasy; tread on sunbeams; have a sparkle in one's eye; feel the heart leap with joy; spend rapture prodigally; have a light heart; feel one's spiritual barometer rise another notch; have dancing eyes; give a loose to mirth; breathe gaiety from the air; tread on air; view life through rose-tinted spectacles; have sunshine in one's nature; purr with happiness; feel the cup of joy flowing over; put a smiling face upon; be in a glow; warm the cockles of the heart; carry sunshine; be in high feather; view the bright side of the picture; be on stilts; feel an agreeable flow of spirits; feel cock-a-hoop; be in mellow, loose-shod days; live and let live; be in Elysium; be tickled; pass a golden hour; sit on top of the world; throw off the mantle of severity; drive dull care away; feel one's heart leap into a waltz; walk in an earthly heaven; feel one's heart sing; let the face light up with bliss; live sun-filled hours; catch the contagion of good spirits; be in clover; be in a melting mood; be intoxicated with joy; carry a holiday in one's eye; bathe in bliss; put wings to one's feet; gild the hour; be in a haze of enchantment; be a bird let out of a cage; bloom with joy; see only sunshine and flowers; warm to the occasion; collect memories woven on a fabric of sunshine; walk under arches of rainbows; be a blue-bird; feel emotions of iridescent colors; taste joy; live days winged with delight; feel joy dawn on one; feel the heart at rest; light up with a bonfire of joy; soar skywards; be in a simoon of rapture; put a gavotte to the heartbeat; have a song in one's heart; dance a jig of joy; keep a nest of singing birds in one's heart; live

in an Eden untroubled existence.

(see *joyful, elated, gay, cheerful, contentment, laugh, pleased, rejoice*)

HARD

granite; marble; flinty; indigestible; rough and tough; thorny; stone; hickory-nut; concrete petrifaction, tempered-steel; cast-iron.

(see *firm, immovable, rigid, unfeeling, strengthen, strong, uncompromising*)

HARDSHIP

storms and stress of life; confused waters of life; a dog's life; working fingers to the bone.

(see *suffer, tribulation, troubled, misfortune, distressed, work*)

HARMONY

piping times of peace; safe walls of conformity; chiming in with; striking the same chord; blending with; going well with.

(see *conform, agree, peace, friendly, understand, kind*)

HARSH

metallic; rasping; grating on the ear; speaking through the nose; vocal daggers of corroded brass; blistering; punctuated with an icy rap.

(see *discord, rude, hoarse, stern*)

HASTILY

by fits and starts; hop, skip and jump; head over heels; feverish; headlong; break-neck; darting; flying; scuttling; going off half-cocked; by forced march.

(see *quickly, swift, speed, fast, rash, hurry*)

HATE (v.)

look daggers at; show a sparkle of malice; dart venom from the eyes; shoot a jagged glance; be at drawn daggers; let no love be lost between; poison with ill-will; owe a grudge; crop flints and thorns; have bad blood between; bite one's glove; burn in the eyes with bitterness; have all one's thoughts dyed red; vomit forth one's hatred.

(see *hostile, frown, malicious, evil, rage, bitterness, retaliate, revengeful, unrestrained, grievance*)

HAUGHTY (to be)

hand someone a cold-boiled stare; be on one's high ropes; recoil on one's summit; turn on the ice; strike a frost; be high-handed; puff up; plume oneself; give oneself airs; set one's back up; act the grand seigneur; assume a lofty bearing; be stuck-up; be toplofty; carry with a high hand; ride roughshod; be admirable in small doses; play the part of the upper dog; put one's nose out of joint.

(see *disdain, self-love, vain, conceited, self-centered, proud, snobbish, scorns, contempt*)

HEALTHY (to be)

be sound of wind and limb; be without a scratch; be in full bloom; be in fine feather; keep on one's legs; keep one's lease on life; keep body and soul together; have a clean bill of health; be in the pink of condition; burst with health; be a picture of health.

(see *vigorous, strong*)

HEAR

catch a sound; be all ears; strain the ears; prick up the ears; hang on the lips of; drink in with the ear; get wind of; feed the ears with; soak up a sound; mark someone's words; keep a sharp ear.

(see *sounds, eavesdropper, whisper, listen, gossip*)

HEAVEN

the pearly gates; Islands of the Blessed; eternal home; abode of the blessed; inheritance of the saints in light; the kingdom of God; bowers of bliss; the rainbow land; happy hunting grounds.

(see *God, hell, saintly, virtuous, reward, religion*)

HEIGHT

peak; crest; full blaze; high-water mark; arch; heyday; pedestal; flood tide.

(see *utmost, climax, top, surpass, surmount*)

HELL

bottomless pit; lake of fire and brimstone; fire that is never quenched; frying fire of torture; place of torment; the bad place; the worm that never dies; the bowels of the earth.

(see *wicked, evil, torment, Heaven, Satan*)

HELP (v.)

lend a hand to; stretch out a helping hand; bear a helping hand; give a handle to; give line (or rope) to; fly to the defense of; put weapons into the hands of; do someone a turn; see someone through; set one on his legs; take one in hand; give new life to; rally around; enlist under the banners of; give a lift to; feed the fire of; work hand in hand with; have a finger in the pie; pull an oar; smooth the path of; oil the wheels; step into the breach; hand on the torch; stand at the elbows of; give tools to; help one back to his feet; throw out the lifeline; hold up by the chin; take up the cudgels for; be a staff (or prop) to; help a lame dog over a stile; be leg-man to; hold the candle for; be

someone's other fist; play handmaiden to.

(see *assistant, relief, support, cooperate*)

HELPLESS

have the ground cut away from under one's feet; step off a sudden bank into the deep; have the claws; be up a tree; be driven into a corner; be a broken reed; catch at straws; be out on the end of a limb; be a shuddering chip on the torrent; have hands and feet tied; be hemmed in; have one's back to the wall; flounder in a slough; butter no parsnips; crawl off, a wounded snake, to die alone; have the chance of a violet in the five-o'clock rush; sink between hawk and buzzard.

(see *weak, powerless, predicament, difficulty, defeated, disable*)

HEREDITY

blood instinct; traditions of the blood; running in the blood; blood of the ancestors leaping within the veins; the sap of the soil.

(see *inherit, relationship*)

HESITATE

hang back; hang fire; shrink from; stand on the side lines; get the tail down; balance between; act in fits and starts.

(see *pause, delay, doubt, doubtful, irresolute, uncertain, undecided, unstable*)

HIDE

push into a corner; bury; screen; veil; cloak; mask; go underground; swallow up; flee to cover; blot out; cover one's tracks; lie low; camouflage; shelter behind cover; wrap in a mantle; draw a curtain over; go into ambush; becloud; eclipse; lock away in a strong room; smother; put under a bushel;

leave in the dark; keep up the sleeve. (see *cover, suppress, withdraw, secret, shelter, obscure*)

HIGH-PRICED

pedigree price; steep; fat; runaway; stiff; fancy; lofty; fantastic; mountainous; peak; astronomical; coiled upward; cloud-high; stratospheric; spiraling upward; jumping upward; garbed in fancy prices; priced out of the market.

(see *expensive, rich, extravagant, valuable, money, inflation*)

HINDER

scotch the wheel; tie one's hands; cramp a style; strike a blow to advancement; act as a drag; lock the wheel; cripple an attempt; put to the door; throttle; choke; spike; clip the wings; clog the wheels; toss a wrench into the machinery; tie in a knot; dam up; put on the brake; throw cold water on; hedge in; nip in the bud; turn aside; weigh down; put a kink in; trip the heels of; load with fetters; stop by a vacuum; paralyze; cause to stick in the mud; cloud the path; put a spoke in the wheel; blockade; trap; stymie; throw a wet blanket on; put a lion in the path; cast a pall over; cause the anchor to drag; put a stumbling block in the way; direct to a blind-alley; create a bottleneck; tie a mill-stone around the neck; ensnare in a booby-trap; put grit in the oil; put the Old Man of the Sea on Sindbad's shoulders; snag.

(see *prevent, obstruct, stop, oppose, thwart, restrain*)

HINT (v.)

tip off; put a bee in the bonnet; give a pointer; give a word to the wise; send away with a flea in the ear; reveal the shadow of the truth; sound a distant rumbling; throw a straw in the wind; put something behind what one says; let someone read between the lines; give the ghost (or a glimmer) of an idea; worm an idea into; drop hints of; plant a seemingly stray thought; cast a pale shadow of a suggestion.

(see *suggest, indirect, inform*)

HISTORY

the scrap heap of history; the flowing waters of history; the human record; Clio, the Muse of history; intricate morass of miracles.

(see *record, past*)

HOARSE (to be)

have a hairy voice; wrap one's vocal cords in sandpaper; thicken the voice; croak.

(see *voice, talkative, harsh, discord, express*)

HOLD (v.)

pitch upon; harbor (a feeling); nurse (a package); cradle in the hand; bottle something in the hand; cup something in the hand; rivet (attention); bate (the breath).

(see *seize, possess, retain, confine, stop, receive, restrain, restrict, bind, snatch, imprison, detain*)

HOLIDAY

red letter day.

(see *celebrate, pleasure-seeking, revelry*)

HOME

one's own roof; one's own backyard; one's nest; one's doorstep; familiar stamping grounds; the roost; one's den; one's own vine and fig-tree; the bulwark of one's security; one's private kennel; a fortress against life; the arsenal of democracy; in the bosom of one's family.

(see *house, native, intimate, relationship, isolated, homeless, contentment, homesick*)

HOMELESS
the scattered shards of a broken vessel; uprooted spirits; no place whereon to lay the head; tennis balls of fortune.

(see *poverty-stricken, solitary, disinherit, house, outcast, homesick*)

HOMESICK (to be)
feel one's torn roots ache; feel home pluck at one's heart.

(see *home, homeless, lonely, nostalgic, relationship*)

HONEST (to be)
look another in the face; be open and aboveboard; be true steel and straight blade; lay one's cards on the table; stick to a bargain; clothe in truth; call a spade "a spade"; throw off all disguise; pull no punches; be fair and square; play the game; tell to one's face; have clean hands; have singleness of heart; tell the truth and shame the devil; put the saddle on the right horse; make sincerity ring; be as good as one's word; have no shield before one's eyes; be straight; give the devil his due; not to depart from the channel of truth; balance the scales of justice; sail under one's true colors; keep one's moral fabric whole.

(see *straightforward, fair, truthful, virtuous, frank, sincere*)

HONORED (to be)
get a feather in one's cap; hand one's name down to posterity; find one's place in the sun; win golden opinions; lead the van; have the crowd fall at one's feet; win one's spurs; win a niche in the temple of fame; be haloed with glory; win the laurels; have the mantle of a hero draped around one; be a star; have obeisance paid one; be enthroned in men's hearts; have hats removed in one's presence; be the ornament of one's time.

(see *fame, glory, revere, worship, respect, deference, reputation*)

HOPE (v.)
see the bright side of the dark cloud; catch at a straw; take heart; view on the sunny side; see the silver lining of the cloud; be a Pollyanna; build castles in the air; pin faith upon; reach into the bottom of Pandora's box; get balm from Gilead; keep one's spirits up; lay the flattering unction to one's soul; see a bit of blue sky; be of good heart; put the best face upon; anchor one's trust; never say die; believe in the golden dream; warm the heart with hope; cross the fingers; blow bright bubbles of promise; count one's chickens before they are hatched; hug hope to the breast.

(see *trust, anticipate, optimistic, solace*)

HOPELESS (to be)
see one's hopes dashed; see one's days numbered; watch the last ray of hope sink below the horizon; feel the damp of hopelessness sink into one's soul; be forced to entreat the wind; taste the bitterness of despair; be a gone man; dwell in the cove of despair; be in the Slough of Despond; see black spots on the horizon; see a bird of ill-omen; be at one's last gasp; feel one's heart sink; yield to despair.

(see *despair, despondency, depressed, discouraged*)

HOSTILE (to be)
live in a miasma of hate; be at drawn

daggers; be at open war with; be up in arms against; have a cancer of hostility planted in the heart; be in a freezing depth of silence; shut the hand of friendship into a fist; be at swords' points; hold at arm's length; be at loggerheads; conduct a feud with; harden the heart against; feel goodwill turn sour; turn icy.

(see *war, hate, oppose, discord, strife, conflict*)

HOT WEATHER
a gray blanket of woolly humidity; July coming in leonine range; broiling sun; a red and fiery sky; a sizzling wind; scorching sidewalks; melting asphalt; steaming streets.

(see *summer, sun*)

HOUSE
a man's castle; marble palace; roof; ivory-tower; red-brick immensity; hollyhocks by the front door and rosy faces around the hearth; monster of gray stone; human nest.

(see *home, reside*)

HUMAN
feet of clay; flesh and blood; a piece of clay; fumbling men of good will; rag of flesh; the full palette of human pigments; stream of human life; an unfeathered angel; a rag, a bone and a hank of hair.

(see *man, people, life, common people*)

HUMILIATE (v.)
teach one his distance; push into a corner; put in the background; shear one of his glory; rub down; take down a peg or two; bring low; pale one's ineffectual fire; bring one to his knees; bring to the dust; put one out of countenance; send away with a flea in one's ear; put to the blush; cast into the shade; strike dumb; make one sing small; bring one to his all-fours; take the starch out of; bring down on one's marrow bones; bring down into the dust; soil one's pride; humble in the dust; cause one to fall from his high estate; make one draw in his horns; make down-in-the-mouth; make crest-fallen; make eat humble pie; force to eat dirt; force to eat one's words; make one drink the cup of humiliation to the dregs; force one to put pride in his pocket; make someone black one's boots; bring one down from his perch; make one's pedestal topple; quench one's pride; make one swallow his pride; force to lick one's feet for mercy; grind one down; trample one under foot; reduce one to powder; force one to crawl; leave one beat and bleeding; freeze one stiff; blister one with the fires of scorn; put one's nose out of joint; force one to go to Canossa; force someone to be the carpet under one's feet; scatter one's high spirits; pierce one's ego; take the wind out of one's sails; prick the bladders of; pull about one's ears; stab one's pride; cause the mighty to fall.

(see *shame, disdain, disgrace, injure, contempt, ridicule, dishonor*)

HUMOROUS (to be)
let the quips fall where they may; don the sock (in contrast to the buskin); breed a laugh; show contagious wit; tickle ribs; flash with hoary-headed jest; be a wit-snapper; empty one's kit of smart jests; crack a joke; be salty; wear the cap and bells; be a pickled-herring; be a card; be a merry-andrew; lend a touch of salt to; be a wag; toss off glittering epigrams; have a storehouse of wit in the mind; have inexhaustible resources of wit; flash a sparkling gem of wit.

(see *joke, pleasant, laugh*)

HUNGRY (to be)

be pinched with hunger; have a gnawing stomach; feel the stomach go right down into one's heels; have a horse's appetite; feel as though one could eat a house; dine with Duke Humphrey; feel one's mouth water; be pierced with an arrow of hunger; smack one's lips; lick one's chops; hear the wolf at the door; have a stomach that is a bottomless bucket.

(see *food, stomach, starve*)

HURRY (v.)

whisk around; bustle; sail by with pennants flying; apply the spurs; tear around; go under full steam; make a bee-line; scurry through; bolt; step on it; leap over the hedge before you come at the stile; shake a leg; have flying feet; devour space; shoot along; dart along; gallop; wing one's way; stir one's stumps; set off at a score; outstrip the wind; fly on the wings of the wind; trot on a forced march; mend one's pace; whip along; make a charge at; open up the throttle; pick up speed; march at double-time; step fast and fancy; quickstep; swing into;

(see *speed, hastily, fast, quickly, urge*)

HURT (v.)

cut to the quick; pommel; drench with blood and tears; sting; bite; hit hard; stab; pinch; bruise; scorch; jolt; wound; cut to the bone; burn; pierce the heart; touch on the raw; scald; lacerate; ride roughshod over; hammer nails in another's coffin.

(see *injure, suffer, ruthless*)

HYPOCRITE

wolf in sheep's clothing; stuffed shirt; polished shell enveloping the yolk of piety; lump of affectation; snake in the grass; Pecksniff; double-faced; praying-mantis; poseur; wire-drawn; smooth-faced; one who talks out of both sides of the mouth; one who carries water on both shoulders.

(see *deceiver, imposture, cheat, false, strategy, mislead, trickery, fake*)

I

IDEAL
shining example; angel on earth; lotus-dream; magic dreamland; walking the earth with a star in the pocket; having a Garden of Eden attitude; heaven-scaling spirit.

(see *perfect, visionary, illusory, unreal*)

IDENTICAL
two peas in a pod; in the same shoes; speaking the same language; leave not a pin to choose from; being in the same boat; sister (as of ships, etc.); on all fours (corresponding identically); similarly labeled; branded with the same iron.

(see *sameness, similar*)

IGNORANT (to be)
not know chalk from cheese; be shallow; see through a glass darkly; be unable to make head or tail out of a thing; be beyond one's depths in a matter; be deprived of the lights of knowledge; keep oneself in blinkers; blindly lead the blind; be in perpetual dark; be a zero; have a blind-folded mentality; exist in a naked state of nescience; be a cracked pipkin discovered by its sound; live in a fool's paradise. .

(see *unaware, stupid*)

IGNORE
shut the eyes to; blind oneself to a fact; brush something aside; shrug the shoulders at; turn the back to; turn into scraps of paper; turn a deaf ear to; dismiss from the mind; skip over; make nothing of; close one's ears to; let a thing go by the board; let warning fall in the grass; throw caution to the winds; gloss over; cold-shoulder; leave out in the cold; look wide of; let go hang; turn on the other side and go to sleep; wink at; not give a tumble; give the go-by to.

(see *neglect, disregard, indifferent, avoid*)

ILLEGALITY
making the law a dead letter; taking the law into one's own hands; pursuing a shadowy legal line; indulging gun-running activities; operating on the gray (or black) market; taking forbidden fruit.

(see *legal, unauthorized*)

ILLEGITIMATE BIRTH
born on the wrong side of the blanket; woods colt; sub-rosa progeny; lovechild; left-handed child.

(see *propriety, prostitute, virtuous, err, morality*)

ILLOGICAL
with a lame and impotent conclusion; cobwebs of sophistry; playing fast and loose with reason; proving that black is white; tongue-fencing; reasoning in a circle; straining at gnats while swallowing camels; divorcing oneself from reason.

(see *inconsistent, unstable*)

ILLUSORY
house of cards; moon's face; rope of sand; wrapped in a shining armor of illusion; mists and shadows floating over truth; myth.

(see *visionary, unreal, unstable, false, imaginary*)

IMAGINARY
fairy-infested; divorced from reality; the footlights and gauze of fiction; air-drawn; soap-bubbles; air castles;

flight of fancy; reinless fancy; imaginative stretch; castle-building; mental mirages; play of the brain; gray vision; kaleidoscope of the mind; dreams seen through a mist; phantom of the brain; mythical chimaera; day-dream world; man of straw.

(see *visionary, unreal, illusory, dream*)

IMAGINE

see through the eyelids; star-gaze; stay in the realm of guesswork; frame in phantasy; work at the plastic art of phantasy; gather wool; voyage mentally.

(see *dream, visionary, pretend*)

IMITATE

play ape to; model oneself; walk in another's shoes; take a leaf out of another's book; take another off; follow suit to; keep pace with; echo; strut in the cast-off finery of another; parrot another; take pattern; follow in another's footsteps; go with the stream; mould oneself on another; be a second-hand copy.

(see *follow, resemble, forgery, pattern, echo*)

IMMATURE

wet behind the ears; green within; sophomoric; puerile puppy-doggerel; half-baked; sprung from the shallow soil of youth; unripe.

(see *young, unprepared*)

IMMEDIATELY

in the twinkling of an eye; before the ink is dry; on the nail; the time has come; (stop) cold; (stop) dead in its tracks; fresh from; at the drop of a hat; in a wink; right off the bat; in the first inning; at a clip.

(see *close, near*)

IMMINENT

in the wind; on the cards; hanging over one's head; at hand; brewing; in embryo; on the knees of the gods.

(see *near, approach*)

IMMOVABLE

carved in granite; rooted to the floor; glued to the spot; petrified; held in a vise; frozen to the spot; not stir a peg; riveted to the chair; anchored; sit like an idol; surrounded by a wall of brass.

(see *firm, stabilize, steadfast, unmoved, unchangeable, permanent*)

IMPASSE

dead end; bottleneck; blind alley; cul-de-sac.

(see *finish, end, limit, complete*)

IMPATIENT (to be)

champ the bit; beat the devil's tattoo; drum the table; feel one's supply of patience running low; bite one's fingernails; have time hang heavy on one's hands; gnaw the leash.

(see *restless, eager, irritate, vehement, violent, unrestrained, unsteady*)

IMPLORE

throw oneself at the feet of; cry mercy; fall on one's knees; come down on one's marrow-bones; knock at the door of; cry out to.

(see *solicit, request, ask*)

IMPORTANT

pivotal; all-absorbing; having stature; weighty; trump; landmark in history; world-shaking; root; throwing all else into the shade; playing first fiddle; a Triton among the minnows; red-letter; big-wig; cornerstone; making history; top-notch; marked with a white stone; tossed high on the stream; holding the center of the stage; kingpin; key; life-blood; big game; focal; outweighing all else; biggest toad in the puddle; shining light; top-flight; playing a conspicuous role; looming large; big-league business; top-drawer; top-echelon.

(see *valuable, serious, celebrity, fame, prominent*)

IMPOSSIBILITY

making a silk purse out of a sow's ear; making bricks without straw; skinning a flint; washing a blackamoor white; discovering the elixir of life; finding the philosopher's stone; squaring the circle; getting blood from a turnip; reaching out for and grabbing the moon; being in two places at once; blending fire and water; getting what is out of reach; achieving what is beyond the bounds of reason; digging a well with a needle; climbing a rainbow; having not a ghost of a chance; taking advantage of "a fat chance".

(see *futility, useless, worthless, hopeless*)

IMPOSTURE

man of straw.

(see *cheat, deceiver, strategy, mislead, outwit*)

IMPRESS

stamp on the memory; strike home; make a dent; electrify; make a thing sink in; engrave on the memory; plough a furrow on the memory; drive a point home; print on the mind; hammer into; catch the ear (or eye) of; grind facts upon; bowl someone over; strike a chord; make leap to the eye; get home a hit; burn into the memory; puncture someone's shell; bite deep; mark with an indelible rubber stamp; leave a welt; etch sharply upon the brain; sow seed on fertile soil; blaze an impression on people's consciousness.

(see *pressure, force, strike, affect, influence, emphasize*)

IMPRESSIVE (to be)

cut a figure; make a stir in the world; make a splash; send out wide ripples; galvanize people to attention; stagger description; dazzle society; have a gilt-edged name; flash upon a scene; hold the limelight.

(see *affect, power, subdue, irresistible*)

IMPRISON

clap one in quod; keep under lock and key; lay by the heels; send to reform school for a post-graduate course; invite one to be a guest at Alcatraz; send to the stonepile for several months; file one away in a cell; assign one a number.

(see *prisoner, confine, restrain*)

IMPROVE

pull one out of the mud; lift by the bootstraps; hoist oneself up; patch up; give tone to; raise above the level of the mediocre; dress up; tidy up relationships; give sauce to; polish up; elevate taste; be on the mend; be on the up-grade; take a favorable turn; turn over a new leaf; turn the corner; spruce up; raise one's head; touch up; appeal from Philip drunk to Philip sober; infuse new blood into; sharpen up; ease a situation; lick into perfection; show a fairer face.

(see *progress, correct, ambition, develop*)

IMPUDENT (to be)

act with a high hand; lift up the heel against; show a face of brass; give lip to; have cheek; have gall.

(see *insult, bold, presumptuous, rude, abuse, contempt, disdain*)

IMPULSE (to have an)

feel the tug of temptation; act on the spur of the occasion; say what comes uppermost; obey a magnet; have flash on one's mind; yield to enkindled desire; have half a mind to.

(see *rash, passionate, reckless, uninhibited, unrestrained*)

INADEQUATE

take half-and-half measures; send a baby on an errand; fall short of; walk lame; be a flash in the pan; fire a blank cartridge; be sent to Stellenbosche; give a thimbleful of water to a parched man; be in short supply.

(see *unequal, inferior*)

INATTENTIVE

hear with half an ear; let a thing in one ear and out at the other; close one's eyes to; have a turn-off switch in one's mind; float off on a cloud.

(see *careless, absent-minded, undiscerning, day-dream*)

INCENTIVE (to have an)

warm one's hands at the fire of ambition; have a motor that drives one; be spurred on by the subconscious; have all one's plugs sparking; have a rudder to propel one; have an additional starter in one's mental engine.

(see *stimulate, inspired, impulse, encourage, cause, motive, energetic, incite*)

INCITE

stir the cauldron; sow the seed of discontent; light the torch of warfare; put the spurs to; fire with zeal; stir up the blood; touch the match to the powder keg; whip up to action; feed the flames; heat up men's brains; make swell with indignation; wave a bloody shirt; add the last straw of insult; fan into a blaze; pour oil on troubled flames.

(see *stimulate, arouse, excite, urge, encourage, influence, embroil, sway*)

INCLUDE

embrace; weave into the fabric; bring into the fold; bind up with; tie in; throw in; draw into the whirl; embed in.

(see *hold, embrace, involved, enclosed, seize, snare, lure*)

INCONSISTENT (to be)

be cast in one mould and finished in another; hold with the hare but run with the hounds; wish to eat one's cake and have it too; hang one's opinions from a pendulum; veer with the winds and the tides; blow hot and cold; turn mental somersaults; chop logic.

(see *illogical, unstable, changeable, vacillate, fickle*)

INCREASE (v.)

rise with the tide; mushroom; spurt ahead; break into a gallop; balloon; grow louder and louder; reach a crescendo; multiply; inch upward; scale upward; swell to a flood; fatten up; hoist on its own petard; gain ground; step up; spiral upward; soar into the clouds; skyrocket; rocket; skyride; race upward; snowball; fan to a pitch; lift the sights; mount with the tide; crowd sail; edge upward; stiffen; climb higher; bolster up; snap; shoot up; speed up; boil up; put the heat under; drum up; bounce up; boost; lengthen the span; pump; zoom up; pick up; go on the rise; kindle; run up (a bill); hike; rise sharply; whack up; expand; add fuel to the flame; stretch; sweeten the pot; jack up; jump.

(see *grow, expand, extend, develop, gain, spread*)

INDEPENDENT (to be)

be master in one's own house; have a free hand; be given free rein; paddle one's own canoe; stand on one's own legs; take one's own course; go on free-wheeling; be a lone wolf; break ties with control; shift for oneself; go it alone; choose one's own path; have one's own head; hold one's own; be a free lance; go under one's own steam.

(see *free, self-control, unrestrained, unencumbered, self-reliant*)

INDESCRIBABLE

defy the pen; beggar description; stagger the imagination.

(see *understate, unimaginable, impossibility, unique, unusual, surpass*)

INDIFFERENT (to be)

feel emptiness of mind and heart; have one's emotional motor idling; be unroused by; preserve a stony silence to others; show coolness; be tepid about; wallow in a morass of apathy; be half-hearted; not give two hoots; not care a straw; not give a fig for; snap one's fingers at; think small beer of; not care a cent; be icy about; be blind to; sit loose; put a good face on; watch with half an eye; be lukewarm; have a dead-or-alive air; be a backslider; give a devil-may-care shrug.

(see *unbiased, dull, unconcerned, unenthusiastic, unfeeling, unmoved, unemotional, unsympathetic*)

INDIRECT (to be)

beat about the bush; use veiled words; make an oblique approach; maneuver in a roundabout way; make two bites of a cherry; go around Robin Hood's barn; go off sideways; enter by the back door; come by a side wind.

(see *deviate, wanderer, maneuver, digress*)

INDISTINCT (to be)

be covered with a veil of mist; become blurred; reel before the eyes; trail away; fade before the eyes; be but a shadow; have neither head nor tail made of a thing; hem and haw.

(see *obscure, vague, mist, shadows, dim, uncertain, doubtful*)

INDULGE

give reins to; nurse; nourish; stretch (imagination); traffic in; wet-nurse; live on the fat of; wade into.

(see *favor, yield, spoil, self-indulgence*)

INDUSTRIOUS (to be)

lie to one's work; not suffer the grass to grow under one's feet; bend to one's oars; be a clanging power-hammer; throw oneself into one's work; be a baggage-bearer; go at one's work hammer and tongs; join the spinners and the toilers; peg away at; keep the wheels turning; keep the pot boiling; burn the midnight oil; pound the anvil.

(see *work, labor, achieve, persevere, busy*)

INEFFECTIVE

bear no fruit; be a ham; fall still-born; overshoot the mark; potter around; cure the itch by scratching the skin off; flash in the pan; use blank cartridges; create kinks and gaps; flounder beyond one's depth; have things go over one's head; be a dead-letter; have butter-fingers; fall flat; be stale and bloodless; make a mull of.

(see *inadequate, unskilful, useless, futility, weak, powerless*)

INEVITABLE (to be)

be in the cards; be the writing on the wall; follow as day pursues night;

compel to bow before circumstances.
(see *necessity, irrevocable, irresistible, fate, predestined, doom*)

INEXPERIENCED (to be)

flutter on untried wings; be a fledgling; be green; be in one's salad days; have a green hand; have green in one's eye; be still in swaddling clothes; have tender feet.

(see *uncertain, unprepared, unskilful, vulnerable, young, innocent*)

INFATUATED (to be)

go crazy about; be set off one's head; go mad over; be head over ears in love; turn the head after; be drunk with desire for; be beside oneself over; be absorbed to folly by.

(see *foolish, desire, passionate*)

INFERIOR (to be)

be weighed in the balance and found wanting; be the under dog; have one's nose out of joint; have little wheat in the chaff; be forced to hide one's diminished head; retire into the shade; yield the palm; lay an egg; smell; be dirt in others' eyes; be below the salt; be not fit to hold a candle to; play second fiddle; take a back seat; be beyond one's depth; fall below average; be of a petty breed; be an "also ran"; be low-brow; be counted as scum; not fit to patch with; be found the baser coin.

(see *mediocre, deficient, inadequate, humiliate, secondary, shabby, low-class, insignificant*)

INFLATION (economic)

today's kite-high prices; the tide of increasing costs; the lofty stakes of prices; boosting prices; a consuming spree.

(see *high-priced, money, rising prices*)

INFLUENCE (v.)

lay a spell on; offer food of hope; add to the stature of; sweep by crosscurrents; create currents flowing beneath; strike to the heart; throw weight into the scale; pull the strings; set the fashion; have a hand over; get claws into; strike savagely into; pour banana oil into ears; lure out of; pull wires; lead the dance; turn the scale; fan the flame; cut ice with; infect with fever; curry favor with; be in solid with; foist upon; pack power; lay a brilliant veneer over; put pressure on; gain others' ears; bring to bear; flow through; throw weight about; carry others off their legs; cast rays upon; exert powers of persuasion; brand; pull by the sleeves; sway by; blow a chill (or warmth) upon; mould; shed light upon; cut a wide swath; intoxicate; carry weight; leave seeds behind; needle; be a guiding star; get others' faith pinned in one; rivet faith in; rush to others' hearts; exert a force in the world; poison; warp; drug; have ears and power; tip the beam; touch the nerves; bend to one's will; cast a vote; pull this way and that; tug at the heart; color; be the pulling tide; overshadow; leave an imprint; seize men's minds; drive a wedge into; blow a high wind into; corrode; cast waves on the shore of; top the scale; drug; point out paths; be the tail that wags the dog; manipulate the ropes; put new leaves into the notebook of history; have a finger in the pie; magnetize; have a grip on; tap people's credulity; be the salt of the earth; speak with a mighty voice; be a tower of strength; gain a footing; strike root in; play a leading role in; move mountains; inoculate.

(see *sway, power, strong, dominate, control, leader, direct*)

INFORM

publish far and wide; open people's eyes; post people on; verse others in; tip another off; bring others behind the scenes; wise others up; give the scent to; bring to people's ears; be a stool pigeon; shed light on; whisper in the ear; let tumble from one's lips; keep others abreast of developments; give an inkling of; put into others' heads; display a well furnished mind; turn the searchlight on; give a line on; give intellectual nourishment to; feed others' minds; cast nuggets of information before; let out a leak; be a walking advertisement for.

(see *tell, talkative, advertise, teach, enlighten*)

INHERIT

step into (or stand in) the shoes of another; step into a fortune; have bred in one's bones; have handed down to one; follow the bent of one's ancestors; have characteristics built into one's frame; derive from the living roots of the past; be to the manner born; be born so; have a thing in one's blood.

(see *heredity, native, origin*)

INITIATIVE

do things under one's own steam; have enough spirit to accomplish miracles; have wits that can carry one through; take matters into one's own hands; score off one's own bat; face issues out of one's own head.

(see *energetic, originate, overcome, begin, original*)

INJURE

make short work of; play the very devil with; hit between wind and water; drive a nail in a coffin; play the mischief with; make battle-scarred; stab in the back; perpetrate acts of sabotage; wreak one's malice on; fly in someone's face; poison; bring into trouble; have a sting; hit hard; hurt the hairs of someone's head; draw blood; stick a barbed arrow in someone; break another's neck; make bleed; sear; throw a stone in someone's garden; apply a poisoned dart.

(see *abuse, insult, dishonor, hurt, spoil*)

INNOCENT (to be)

keep one's hand clean; be still turning the first page in the book of life; be blameless as a new-born babe; be a lamb; be a spotless dove; remain unmarked by the clumsy fingers of life; let naivete conquer cunning; stay unhardened; remain above suspicion; carry no sting; hold the white flower of a blameless life; be April innocent; have a madonna face; offer white-robed thoughts upon the altar of one's heart; have a naked soul; be free from stain; keep the heart clean; pass through flames unharmed; grow in a hot-bed of sanctity.

(see *young, clean, simple, blameless, child, virtuous, meek, modest*)

INQUISITIVE (to be)

look behind the scenes; pry into every hole and corner; follow the trail; beat up one's quarters; seek a clue; suck the brains of; feel the pulse; grapple with; thresh out; probe to the bottom; take a nibble at; put out feelers; leave no stones unturned; have a searching look; be all ears; burn with a perpetual curiosity; crane the neck; prick up the ears; itch for information; thirst for news; be devoured by curiosity; stick one's nose into others' business; be a moth; worm out information; go smelling into another's affairs.

(see *investigate, search for, meddlesome, examine, inform, news, explore, spying, eavesdropper*)

INSANE (to be)

have one's mind give way; be off center; have one's brains turned; lose one's faculties; have a loose screw; be off one's head, undergo softening of the brain; have a tile (or slate) loose; have wheels in the head; be fit for the bug-house; have rats in the upper story; have one's mind be beaten to the ground; be possessed with a devil; have a bee in one's bonnet; go to crack; have the brain unhinged; be out of one's head; have bats in the belfry; have a wheel unhinged in the mind; have one's reason snap; have a twisted mentality; have one's reason go under a cloud; have but a mile to midsummer; have a disordered mind; have too many flies in one's nostrils; inhabit the desert realm of insanity; have the mind a blank; be moonstruck; have a perverse kink in the brain.

(see *crazy, confused, obsessed*)

INSECURE (to be)

weave a rope of sand; feel the ground sliding from under one; live in a bubble; feel the thinness of the thread of life; live in a fool's paradise; hang by a fragile thread; be on a sandy basis; feel up in the air.

(see *unstable, uncertain, precarious, weak, danger*)

INSERT

sandwich between; inject; implant; infuse; inoculate; impregnate; pour into; inweave; parenthesize.

(see *fill, penetrate*)

INSIGHT (to have)

see through a sudden loophole; have the truth in its full light appear to one; be struck by an idea; have an extra eye; read someone's soul; see a light of blinding brilliance; grasp with penetrating vision; have an X-ray eye; see through people; see the soul bare; note through the rind; have an inner barometer; have a microscopic eye in one's mind.

(see *discern, understand, perceive, sharp, shrewd*)

INSIGNIFICANT

atom; molecule; microbe; shoestring; teapot tempest; a fig; a straw; fading into the background; born to the day of small things; a splinter; in the backwater; an insect; not worth a hill of beans; a surface ruffle.

(see *unimportant, inferior, contempt trifle, mediocre, minimize*)

INSINCERE (to be)

weep crocodile tears; be a lip-servant of virtue; pay lip-service to; give soft soap to; be syrupy to; be cannily hospitable; turn oily eyes on; play up to; wear a perpetual phony smile; retreat quickly from sincerity; ring hollow; have a double tongue; give double talk to; be two-faced; show bad faith; be empty of sincerity.

(see *false, fake, dishonest, hypocrite, mislead, sham, deceiver, artificial, shallow, subterfuge*)

INSISTENT (to be)

harp on a subject; press for something; drum a point in; hug a belief; make a point of; ram down someone's throat; bear down upon; lay down the law; pin down to a point; pound the table for; assert stoutly; thump the tub for.

(see *persevere, urge, tease, argue, orate, obstinate*)

INSPIRED (to be)

act at white heat; taste the warm wine of life; see in a burst of sunshine; have one's thoughts drawn by the

stars; soar to aquiline heights; be cata-
pulted from the springboard of inspiration; feel the flashing wings of
thought; have a shining fixed star;
warm oneself in the fire of genius;
burn with hard gem-like flame; feel
a deep flame burn within one; brush
the stars; take fire; have the foam of
inspiration on one's lips; drink from
the Castalian spring; receive a high-
voltage charge; get an electric spark;
traffic with the stars; be rapt up into
a lyrical heaven; be breathed into by
the Muses; find wings to expression;
have one's capacities awakened; be
lifted to the clouds; break open the
fountains of song; be lifted in one's
stirrups; feed fire into one's veins;
break into flame; be lifted out of this
world; catch flame; be kindled to
ardor; be moved to genius; have one's
heart opened; have one's spark fanned;
breathe the mountain air of high art;
have one's brain set on fire; be spurred on to; have a wave of inspiration
flood one's soul; have one's soul touched by genius; feel the heart expand in
a poem; be struck by inspiration; feel
one's breast warmed by the divine
afflatus; be melted to fire; have one's
spiritual eyes opened; have one's
thoughts stirred by the mother of Art;
awake to a world of fantastic visions;
feel elevated; be filled with the breath
of Apollo; be quickened by inspiration; live in a single flaming point of
time; dwell on the heights of Parnassus; ride Pegasus through the skies.

(see *stimulate, enthusiastic, eloquent,
elated, genius*)

INSULT (v.)

blacken someone's name; give a smack
in the eye; brand; slight; throw a
stone at; give the unkindest cut of all;
fly in the face of; dart in a sure stab;
slap in the face; drag a name through
the mire; twist one's tail; slam the
door in one's face; hurt one's pride;
thumb the nose to; cut one to the
quick; shoot an arrow into the soul;
sting with scalding laughter; drag by
the beard; cover one with mud; tread
on the toes of; give a gratuitous slap
to; sear to the bone; pin-prick one;
thrust a dagger into the flesh; plant
a sting; ride contemptuously over;
fling taunts in one's face.

(see *offend, abuse, violate, defame,
hurt, taunt*)

INTELLECTUAL (to be)

have a soul above buttons; carry a
heavy load of philosophical discourse;
have a highly polished wit; come from
a race of bookworms; have a high
brow; have the air of a tall encyclopedia; shine in conversation; have the
restless and fiery operations of a working mind; be well stocked with gray
matter; carry a lot of mental luggage;
be wise in one's generation; show a
bundle of intellectual fire; wear one's
hair long; mount the peaks of knowledge.

(see *knowledge, intelligent, mind,
wise*)

INTELLIGENT (to be)

have a head on one's shoulders; have
one's wits sharpened; feast on reason;
have elevated wisdom; have all one's
wits about one; stay on the cool
heights of reasoning; keep a beehive
of ideas; know which way is up; be a
monument to common sense; be up to
snuff in matters; have one's head
screwed on the right way; have more
than half an eye; be up to trap; be
well stocked with intellectual equipment; have the finer threads of apprehension.

(see *intellectual, knowledge, insight,
wise, mind*)

INTENSE (to be)

be keyed high; burn for; be feverish over; make the air thick with; engage in a life-or-death struggle; keep the fists tight; be in hot haste; throb with; have the air of going through fire; feel at the darkness; be sharpened; be hot for; listen religiously.

(see *eager, energetic, vigorous, violent, aroused, passionate, over-ambitious, tense, fervent*)

INTENTION

one's special target; the be-all and the end-all; a bent for; what one has in view; what one has in his mind's eye; what one has on the anvil; what one has an eye to; the bull's-eye; what one keeps at stake; going into a thing with one's eyes open; one's special axe to grind; what one takes into his head to do; one's "would-be."

(see *aim, plan, scope*)

INTERESTED (to be)

be glued to a thing; find a thing juicy, have one's fingers in the pie; find spice under the sugar coating; be feverish over; taste cider in a story; be wrapped up in; be bug-eyed over; be capsized with surprise; be steeped in concern; have one's appetite whetted; have one's imagination fired by; have one's tongue tempted; have the attention caught; keep the ball rolling; add spice to a thing; find one's meat; be keyed to a pitch of animation; be stung by curiosity; have an eager ear for; be bitten with the desire to; find one's hobby and ride it; have a ruling passion for; keep the ball rolling; find a thing palatable; enjoy the flavor of; find a thing good to the last drop; find a thing salty; have one's attention held by; have one's eye caught by; be set by the ears with interest; be gripped by.

(see *concentrate, regard, excite*)

INTERFERE

thrust one's nose in; raise a hand to check the storm; open one's mouth and put one's foot in it; stick one's neck out; put a spoke in the wheel; put one's own oar in; horn in; upset the applecart; have a finger in the pie; introduce the thin end of the wedge; step in; stand in the way of; muscle in; throw a monkey wrench into; throw out of gear; break in; march between; step into the torrent; act the *deus ex machina*; put oneself upon others; sandwich oneself in; butt one's way in; tie up in red tape.

(see *meddlesome, oppose, thwart, conflict*)

INTERPRET

shed new light on; disentangle the meaning; find the key to; read between the lines; unravel the significance; unwrap the riddle; spell a thing out; paint a picture for; dredge up the meaning; unveil a hidden meaning; explain an enigma.

(see *explain, define, describe, solution*)

INTERRELATION

crisscrossing; cross-currents; counterpoint; interweaving; intertwining.

(see *mixture, together*)

INTERRUPT

break the thread; cut off; break in; chime in; puncture; horn in; chase words off another's lips; break a spell; snap at the continuity; cut short.

(see *disturbance, stop, break, hinder, separate, divide*)

INTERVIEW (v.)

closet oneself with; screen applicants.

(see *meeting, conversation, talkative*)

INTIMATE (to be)

be thick as thieves; be hand in glove

with; rub elbows with; be on the inside with; have a heart-to-heart talk with; stand in solid with; be thick with; have a tie knit by nature with; be the other pea in the pod; be behind the scenes; strip to one's shirtsleeves.

(see *friendly, close, near*)

INTRICATE

labyrinth; maze; web; cobweb; finespun; devilishly deep; a long song and dance about; the plot thickens; crisscrossed with by-ways; entanglement; subterranean currents beneath the fair surface of; hydra-headed.

(see *complication, obscure, perplexed, confused*)

INTRODUCE

usher in; launch a person into; lead the horse to water; set loose upon the world; springboard a person into; raise the curtain on; administer baptism to; play the prelude to; open someone's eyes to.

(see *begin, open, start*)

INTROSPECTIVE (to be)

contemplate oneself; take stock of oneself; root around in the soil of one's own character; live within oneself; have one's thoughts sink back into oneself; live in one's own mind; turn one's back on the world; hold a mirror to one's own mind; look deep into oneself; sit lonely amid one's mental worlds; probe into one's shell; go back into one's own world.

(see *self-centered, self-analysis*)

INVENT (v.)

coin a phrase; incubate ideas; hatch a scheme; spin something out of one's own fancies; strike out something new; devise from the fertility of one's mind.

(see *create, imagine, originate*)

INVEST (v.)

put out a penny to fatten; sink one's money in; pour dollars into; dabble in investments.

(see *money, save, safe, entrust, speculate*)

INVESTIGATE

call (or put) on the carpet; get to the root of a matter; take soundings; see how the land lies; take stock of; pry into every cloud; put out feelers; get on the track of; paw over the affairs of; explore another life; canvass a subject; walk carefully through; bolt to the bran; spy out; dig into; wade through records; cast about for; pump for information; crawl underground in quest of; run an analytical eye over; probe into the depths of; dive into an inquiry; loose the bloodhounds on; undertake a house-cleaning; throw a little light on; peep behind the curtain; go forth with the lantern of Diogenes; sift the facts; nose into the state of affairs; pour forth a long tide of inquiry; burn one's fingers over; peer into the face of reality; make blind reaches into; fish out facts; follow a whim of curiosity; turn a situation inside out; put under the microscope; sound out a situation; turn the searchlight on; taste the air of; subject to trial by jury; touch all dubious points; pour over one's notes on; play the Grand Inquisitor; feel the pulse of; sound the depths of.

(see *inquisitive, search for, examine, inform, explore, expose*)

INVOLVED (to be)

have a finger in the pie; be shoulder-deep in problems; get one's hand in;

be entangled with; be dragged into; be entwined around; be caught in the net; stand neck-deep in; be mixed up with; be thrown into; be tied up in; be sunk in; get caught in the red-tape; be in deep waters; be held in an intricate web; get oneself interwoven in; be laced up in.

(see *include, comprise, complication, envelop, intricate, embroil*)

IRONY

rapier-wit; bite; sting; bitter nip; barbed point; shooting folly as it flies; fine-blade; cutting edge of wry humor.

(see *mock, sarcastic, contempt, scorn*)

IRREGULARLY

by fits and starts; by fits and snatches; spotty; ragged; fitful; pell-mell; at sixes and sevens; the cart before the horse; following a snake-like path.

(see *uncertain, undecided, unsteady, unstable, spasmodic, changeable, irresolute, deviate*)

IRRESISTIBLE

with the faithfulness of the needle to the magnet; with the irresistibility of tide for moon and moon for tide.

(see *subdue, conquer, submissive, control*)

IRRESOLUTE (to be)

go off on another tack; draw in one's horns; eat one's words; retrace one's steps; come back to one's first love; turn from leaf to leaf; skip from one side to another; go to the right about; box the compass; shift one's ground; act in a piecemeal way; be spineless; swing from the pendulum; say yea-and-nay; not know one's own mind;

be the sport of the winds and the waves.

(see *changeable, spasmodic, uncertain, inconsistent, vacillate, fickle, hesitate, unsettled, unsteady*)

IRRESPONSIBLE (to be)

be feather-brained; go on a continuous free-wheeling; be a happy-go-lucky gypsy; be a racing spring lamb; play fast and loose with a thing; fiddle while the world smolders; be a babe in a toyland of gadgetry; be trigger-happy; cast off responsibility.

(see *untrustworthy, unrestrained, unsteady, fickle, fluctuate, unsettled*)

IRREVOCABLE (to do the)

cross the Rubicon; burn one's bridges behind one; give the Fates an oath to weave.

(see *unchangeable*)

IRRITATE

sting; get someone's back up; pour fuel on; bite; give the needle to; set one's teeth on edge; rub the wrong way; make one's eyes blaze; stick in the stomach; fan the flame; set the teeth on edge; get someone by the hair; grate on the ear; go far enough to provoke a saint; stink in the nostrils; have the effect of static; be enough to drive one mad; draw blood; light a smoldering glow of exasperation in the eyes; ring in the ear; stir up a tempest in the blood; put out of sorts; badger; get a hair in someone's neck; put out of humor; get one's goat; get on one's nerves; wake an echo in one's nerves; give a burning sore to; make the shoe pinch; be a thorn in the flesh; fray one's temper; spice with ill-humor.

(see *annoy, anger, tease*)

ISOLATED (to be)

live in a glass house; be shut up in an ivory tower; keep out of the swim; be frozen in a block of ice; bury oneself; keep in one's own groove; be shut up in a water-tight compartment; be hermetically sealed; immunize oneself to outside influence; be ice-bound by loneliness; stay in one's shell; shut oneself up into solitude; be locked away from the world.

(see *separate, solitary, segregate, seclusion*)

J

JAW
lantern-jawed; anvil-jawed; galley-prow jaws.

(see *face*)

JEALOUSY
the new toy delivered as an accessory to love.

(see *envy, suspicious, resent, watchful*)

JOIN
couple; yoke; link; tie; marry; mate; wed to; rub shoulders with; be hand in glove with; twin with; take up with; join the ranks; grow upon; tie to apron strings; cement; entwine; chain; bridge the gap between; string together; hook on; knit together; band together; interlace; hump together; stir together; throw one's lot with; fasten on; be a recruit in; meet hand to hand; weld; form the uniting bridge; fuse together; melt into one; solder; cast one's lot with; fall in with; rivet together; glue together; hop aboard; hitch; tack on; pin; go over to; render one; swell the ranks.

(see *add, connection, unite, marry, meet*)

JOKE (v.)
crack a joke; poke fun at; indulge in horseplay; pull one's leg; rag someone; have a lark with; be a wag; have one's tongue in cheek.

(see *humorous, laugh*)

JOYFUL (to be)
hug bliss to the heart; fling up one's cap; click heels; feel a leaping of the heart; bark with joy; see heaven on earth; have one's heart sing songs; have a ring in one's voice; jump with joy; feel life to be one long picnic; be drenched with the sunshine of joy; feel a lightening of the heart; enjoy the flavor of life; feel a thrill of untarnished radiance; be a nightingale of joy; climb to a high rung on the ladder of pleasure; enjoy a rhapsody of wine, women, and song; cut up; have a fling; kindle a convivial fire; have lights dancing in one's eyes.

(see *happy, pleased, rejoice, delight, enjoy*)

JUDGE (v.)
weigh in the balance; weigh each side of a question; preside over a court of appeal; umpire a contest; weigh in the scales of one's judgment; hold the scales; set a question at rest; weigh with a glance; measure a matter; sit upon a decision; bring up for the count; appraise by rule of thumb; weigh the pros and cons; referee a match; sit at the broad green cloth; reflect the great eye of justice; call to stand before the higher court; enroll another in the Doomsday book; bring to book; hold the scales even; administer even-handed justice; give a square deal.

(see *decide, determine, doom, law, condemn, legal, lawyer, official, rebuke*)

K

KEEP (v.)
nurse a hope; nourish a dream; chain something to one; tuck a thing away; embalm the memory of; hug to one's heart; freeze into a static.

(see *retain, detain, hold, possess, protect, preserve, confine, remember*)

KIDNAP
spirit away; pounce on; shanghai.

(see *stealthy, take, hold*)

KILL
put to the sword; bring down to the grave; commit mayhem; put away; stifle a heart; make a blood-stained occasion; make away with; launch into eternity; nail down; blow out brains; worry one into the grave; nip in the bud; dash out brains; dip one's hands in blood; bump off; unclose the shears of the Fates; welter in blood; imbrue hands in blood; wade knee-deep in blood; run amuck; give no quarter; plow under; give one the works; do another in with a knife; rub out; spill blood; put out of the way; tread down; smother; send to one's last account; strike the death knell of; wipe off the earth; sign a death warrant; drive a stake through a heart; tear to pieces; dispatch to one's maker; put out of misery; mow down; snuff out a life; take toll of; embalm; close a mouth forever; blot out; knock on the head; brain; put an end to; ring down the curtain on; dissolve; reduce to dust; make bite the dust; sweep up in a dust pan; immerse in a blood bath; butcher.

(see *death, attack, grave, destroy, rage, battleground, fight, stab*)

KIND (to be)
have one's heart in the right place; be large-hearted; be soft-hearted; not hurt a fly; have a heart of gold; dispense the milk of human kindness; divide one's cloak with another; throw a bone to a dog; receive into one's warmth; have a heaven of kindness in one's heart; have a warm heart.

(see *friendly, love, tender, indulge, sympathetic, mild, pity*)

KISS (v.)
lend the lips; brush lips across; exert a burning pressure of lips; surrender lips; crush the wine-red nectar of lips; give one's lips; drink in perfume from lips; fuse mouths; peck at; give a chaste salute with the mouth; bunch the mouth; screw up the mouth.

(see *love, passionate, feeling, sweetheart, sentimental, endear, emotional*)

KNOCK OUT
floor someone; lay one horizontal; hammer one down; nail one flat; bowl over; give a swing that blows out a fuse; spread on the canvas; administer an anaesthetic.

(see *fall, blow, rage, strike, defeated, fight*)

KNOWLEDGE (to have)
see the light; have one's eyes open; taste knowledge; have in one's head; have at the finger ends; be master of; be no stranger to; become acquainted with; savor knowledge; be high-brow; be grounded in; be blue; know the facts of life; fall into the abyss of philosophy; glory in light; put one's finger on trends; have an island of text; taste the fruits of learning; have food for the mind; take part in the

march of intellect; live in a republic of letters; explore to the boundaries of knowledge; drink to the dregs of wisdom; have everything an open book to one; break through clouds. (see *understand, learn, intelligent, wise, intellectual, discern, educated, study*)

L

LABOR (v.)

shed the sweat of one's brow; be a son of toil; fish in troubled waters; lumber along ruts; put one's hand to the plow; roll one's stone up the mountain; live in a nest of ants; work one's fingers to the bone; keep the pot boiling; be a rivet in a machine; struggle along.

(see *work, worker, strive, industrious, earn*)

LACK (n.)

poverty; bankruptcy; drought; innocence; flight.

(see *poverty-stricken, need, deficient, debt, deprive, scarce*)

LAMENT (v.)

tell a tale of woe; sing a long dirge of sadness; beat one's breast; swim on a sea of tears; carry one's gray hairs with sorrow to the grave; cry into one's beer; rain tears over; stand by the wailing wall.

(see *mourn, grieve, sorrowful, complain, weep*)

LANDSCAPE

Nature's canvas; a backcloth of meadows.

(see *scene*)

LARGE

fat; hefty; lion's share; behemoth; Texas-sized; Brobdingnagian; elephantine; amazonian; monster; king-size; thumping; swollen; whopper; man-size; sprawling; healthy; monolithic; shovelful; torrential; mountainous; heavy; bumper; untold; big-boy; record-breaking; wholesale; mass-production; big-scale; monumental.

(see *abundance, big, vastness, full of, generous, maximum, abundance*)

LASTING

time-defying; inextinguishable; weathering the storm; clinging; standing up well.

(see *endure, permanent, remains, continue, dependable*)

LATE

eleventh hour; autumnal; Indian-summer; late in the day; the dead of night; a day after the fair; an afternoon-farmer.

(see *slow, overstay, delay, detain, behind*)

LAUGH (v.)

shake with mirth; be in stitches; surrender oneself to a roar of laughter; hold one's sides; break into a laugh; be thrown into giggles; fall to pieces with mirth; split one's sides; grow a smile; cackle; guffaw; ripple with amusement; bubble with laughter; double up; spurt out a geyser of laughter; laugh in one's sleeve; fire a barrage of giggles; burst with mirth; chuckle to oneself; pour forth a laugh from urns of mirth; riot with joy; emit a staccato laugh; have a laugh like glass beads falling from a snapped chain.

(see *gay, joyful, enjoy, delight, rejoice, humorous*)

LAVISH (v.)

wield an unsparing hand; pay too dear for one's whistle; be penny wise and pound foolish; feel money burning one's pocket; shower; strew one's path with.

(see *extravagant, wasteful, squander, spree, excessive, spend*)

LAW

legal weapon; rule laid down; legislative ambush; that which throws into court.

(see *lawyer, legal, judge, rule, order, discipline, regulations*)

LAWYER

limb of the law; gentleman of the long robe; silk gown; stuff gown; one who takes silk.

(see *law, judge, condemn, official, doom*)

LAX (to be)

go beyond the length of one's tether; give the reins to; hold a loose rein; give rope enough; have one's swing; snap the string; play fast and loose with.

(see *relax, soft, facilitate, rash, reckless, negligent, self-indulgence, dissipate*)

LAYER (n.)

armor; chrysalis; encrustation: carpet; stratum; bed.

(see *cover*)

LAZY (to be)

let the grass grow under one's feet; fold one's arms (or hands); twirl one's fingers; let things lie on one's hands; rest on the oars; whistle for want of thought; vegetate; keep the hands in one's pockets; keep the hands behind one's back; have time on one's hands; eat one's head off; burn daylight; kill time; be a lotus-eater; loaf around; slumber with the eyes open; be a slow coach; be an afternoon farmer; be a dormouse; gather no honey; be a

drone; not lift a finger; sit on the sidelines; let things take their own course; lie on the shelf; sleep at one's post; go to sleep over; eat the bread of idleness; loll in the lap of inertia; talk against time; relax one's efforts; cool one's heels; slip idle hours through one's fingers; be pillowed in idleness; rust in desuetude; spend time in drydock; stagnate; live days swollen with inertia; lack ginger; be a stranger to spinning; never lift a finger; drone in the sunshine; give a lick and a promise; be imprisoned in inertia.

(see *slacker, slow, unemployed, ease, loaf*)

LEADER

bellwether; brains; chieftain; leading light; sparkplug; spearhead; cock of the walk; shepherd; first fiddler; master spirit of the group; path-blazer; pioneer; way-paver; tune-setter; captain; head; pace-setter; rein-holder; helmsman; pilot; pacemaker; shining light; bigwig; first trumpet; pillar of the earth; big shot; major-domo; kingpin; prince; torch-bearer; sheep-dog; top spot winner; lord of the ascendant.

(see *guide, superior, rule, excel, order, supervise*)

LEARN

drink in learning; get to the bottom of; take pointers from; get into the way of; cut one's eye-teeth; digest intellectually; sharpen the wits; make friends with; coquet with; feel one's way around; soak up; master; pick up; make one's mind a pigeon-holed desk; get the hang of; absorb; be a revolving bookcase; acquire a sixteenth-edition-Britannica range of erudition.

(see *knowledge, understand, wise, intelligent, study, intellectual, discern, educated*)

LEAVE (v.)

shake the dust from one's feet; sail out of; ebb away; fly away; get up and dust; seep out of; melt off; get out from under; cut oneself adrift; tear oneself away; turn on one's heel; turn to the right about; pack up; cut loose from; whip away; whisk oneself off; take wing; get one's feet going; make oneself scarce; walk out on; fold up one's tent and silently steal away; sever oneself from; break away from the fold; pull up stakes; strike camp; turn one's back on; ditch a thing; fly the country; vamoose the ranch; sally forth; bustle out of; bundle out of; show a light pair of heels; quit the field; dump a thing; kick out of; step out of; drift from.

(see *abandon, desert, withdraw, quit, depart, renounce*)

LEGAL

to the signet; in the eye of the law; aboveboard; to the letter of the law.

(see *law, orderly, conform, blameless*)

LEGS

pins; pegs; shanks; broom-handles; piano-legs; props; silk-stocking forms.

(see *walk, hurry, run*)

LEISURE (to be at)

be under easy sail; be at a loose end; have time hanging on one's hands; be master of one's time; live the life of Riley; while away time; enjoy *dolce far niente;* be a vagabond in broadcloth.

(see *ease, rest, tranquil, quiet, peace, time, slow, unemployed, relax*)

LENGTHWISE

fore and aft; from head to heels; from head to foot; from top to toe; from end to end; from the crown of the head to the sole of the foot; stem to stern.

(see *extend, continue, height, depths, scope*)

LESSEN (v.)

take a bite out of; siphon off; take a nick into; use the pruning shears on; shrink; fade; shrivel up; reduce to a handful of dust; dry up; cause to fall away; eat into; melt down; nibble at the edges of; soften; beat down; knock a hole in.

(see *diminish, decrease, reduce, small amount, degenerate, decline*)

LIE (fib)

be a charter member of the Ananias Club; have some elastic in one's truth-telling; tell a cock-and-bull story; not ring true; have a false tongue in one's mouth; be parsimonious with regard to the whole truth; run a bit thin; leak a little; tell a trumped-up story; tell a traveler's tale; tell a tall story; tie oneself in knots; produce a figment of the imagination; weave a tissue of lies; live in grottoes of dishonesty; make a swinish invention; throw lots of dirt and some will stick; burn the tip of the tongue with a lie; bend the truth out of shape; tell a bare-faced lie; make a thing up out of whole cloth; tell a white lie (a venial falsehood); give a Roland for an Oliver; lie oneself black and blue; tell a fish story; say the grapes are sour (give an untrue reason for not taking something); warp the truth.

(see *false, untrustworthy, mislead, cheat*)

LIFE

the turning wheel of the world; the bluepencil on men's plans; the period of one's earthly sojourn; red corpuscles; the great ocean of existence; the unending campaign which death wages with life; the dark avenue of human folly; the pageant of men's lives; the breath of one's nostrils; the battle for existence; this side of the grave; the passing parade; the number of one's days; a sleep and a forgetting; a losing game; the dance of life; a big, complicated machine; the ups and downs; a hurly-burly; from cradle to grave; the human drama; the breath of life; the road we all travel; the elastic span of time to its utmost golden length; the beating pulse; the current of life; the corner of life; life's fitful fever; risking one's neck for existence; what makes one tick; life-blood; sap; marrow; the experiences of men under the sun; the busy hum of men.

(see *live, survive, long-lived, time, born*)

LIGHT (adj.)

gossamer; feathery; kicking or striking the beam (light in weight); airy; shallow.

(see *gay, unsteady, fickle, unsettled, free, grace*)

LIGHT (n.)

dim phosphorescence; cross of pale fire; golden specks; coruscating swirls; the gold eyes of cats; flood of light; a warm pool; constellations of flame; an edge of radiance; blaze of brilliance; a huge conflagration; inundation of light; fingers of light catching the landscape; a bronze robe of light; gold borrowed from the sun; long necklaces of brilliants strung against the sky; shots of flame piercing the clouds;

blinking of a cyclopean reflector-eye.

(see *bright, sun, sunlight, dawn, shine, candlelight*)

LIKE (v.)

take to one's heart; take a shine to; cotton to a thing; eye with favor; feel one's heart warm to; be enamored of; dote on; have a weakness for; be wedded to; be sold on a person; have a mad passion for; have a mania for; eat out of someone's hand; rave about; find meat and drink in; get sweet on; be in tune with; have one's fancy taken by; eat up a thing; keep a corner in the heart for; be smitten with; find the apple of one's eye in; take a liking to; put on one's good side; bear good-will for; adore; be soft on; have a leaning toward; gather to one's bosom.

(see *love, relish, approve, favor, attract, susceptible*)

LIMIT (v.)

draw the line; set a horizon for; curb; put a ceiling over; ground a thing; hedge around; put on a shoestring; establish a breaking point; fix to rock bottom; tether; clamp a top on; put on short allowance; tie a string to; make stop at the water's edge; keep stocks tight.

(see *border, confine, control, restrict, restrain, hinder, hold, prevent, rule*)

LISTEN

lend an ear; prick up ears; have an eager and thirsty ear; hang upon another's lips; be all ears; cup the ears in the hands; turn a willing ear; drink in the ears; perk up the ears; bend one's head to catch a whisper; hang on another's words; lend a critical ear; have a thirsting ear; bend or apply the mind to another's words; bend back one's ears; give ear to; incline an ear; prick the ears forward; put an ear to the ground; cock an ear; sharpen the ears; soak up words; give heed to; focus upon another's words; be riveted to a speaker; be wrapped in another's words.

(see *hear, sharp, speech, speak, alert, sounds, audience, eavesdropper*)

LIVE (v.)

pulse with life; strut and fret one's hour upon a stage; walk the earth; drink deep of the spring of life; feed oneself on life; pursue the tenor of one's way; romp through one's paces; take life by the tail; take root in the earth; wallow in life; toss on life's tempestuous billows; burn with the joy of life; exist in space; nourish oneself on life; meander up life's road; jostle and elbow along the road of life; meet the days that are in store; unravel the skein of one's life; chart one's course in the world; follow one's life span; roost on the earth; soar through life; navigate on the stream of time; swing the course of the ship of life; sail upon the tide of present things; draw the breath of life; have the tide of life licking at one's feet.

(see *life, survive, long-lived, time*)

LIVELY (to be)

be full of the Old Nick; light up; kindle to life; be alive with; sparkle; be caloric; frisk and romp; be racy; keep one's tempo at allegro; kick one's heels.

(see *vigorous, energetic, gay, joyful, nervous, playful, zestful*)

LOAF (v.)

eat the bread of idleness; kill time; fritter away hours; be a carpet knight; fool around; hang around; fiddle away time; poke about; take one's time.

(see *lazy, slow, ease, unemployed, irresponsible*)

LOCATE

come to an anchor; strike root; take up one's quarters; plant oneself; moor oneself; squat; perch; bivouac; take footing; pitch one's tent; mark out one's boundaries.

(see *place, established, settle, reside, situated, stay*)

LOCK (v.)

button up (one's house) tightly; bolt in; padlock.

(see *secure, imprison, safe, protect, self-protection*)

LOCOMOTIVE (railroad)

an iron courser stamping titanic hoofs; a throbbing monster; an iron king; on iron horse pounding out with clamorous hoofs his seventy miles an hour; a galloping iron horse with a swarthy smoke mane whipped back by the wind.

(see *railroad, travel*)

LOCOMOTIVE (sound of)

shriek; screech; wail; stammers; sputter; puff; shuffle; pant.

(see *noisy, shrieks*)

LONELY (to be)

taste the bitterness of separation; feel a gnawing in one's heart; plow a lonely furrow; perish with loneliness; live in barren desolation; nurse a bruised and lonely soul; rummage about in the barren attic of loneliness; drown in a sea of loneliness; weep in one's beard; have in one's heart a void never to be filled; tiptoe through the cold and dreary chambers of one's heart; be a floating iceberg; be sicken-ed by loneliness; carry a sack of darkness inside one; be empty of heart; be insulated with living silence.

(see *solitary, seclusion, dreary, desert, despondency, remote, dejected, aloofness, homesick, outcast, yearn, nostalgic*)

LONG AGO

time out of mind or memory; when the Indians were only knee-high; when the Rock of Gibraltar was only a pebble; since Sitting Bull was a calf.

(see *history, past, obsolete*)

LONG-LIVED (to be)

hold on to the last rung of life; hug the emptying tankard of life; crowd a lot of life in the tiny space left in one's box; outwit the grave; match a donkey's ears; live a coon's age; live to see the walls of one's life crumbling in dilapidation about one.

(see *old, old man, senility, wrinkles, age*)

LOOK AT (v.)

take someone in with the eyes; direct the eyes to; cast an eye at; throw glances at; steal a look at; turn the gaze upon; strain the gaze toward; rest the eyes on; pour out a look; cock an eye at; keep the eyes glued on; rivet the eyes upon; unrobe with a glance; fasten the eyes on; give another the eye; feast one's eyes on; screw up the eyes; bend an eye on; fix a stare at; shoot a glance at; devour with the eyes; apply an eye to.

(see *glance at, glare at, eyes, notice, examine, see, observant*)

LOOK FOR (v.)

beat the bushes for; hunt for a needle in a hay mow (a hopeless search); comb for (news); scramble for; scour around for; cast eyes around; rummage through; stir the ground for; ferret around; wait for dead men's shoes (look for inheritance); run the eye over; fish for; sweep with a glance; hawk about for; set one's gaze straying through; have one's glances wandering around; travel through with one's eyes; set one's eyes sliding this way and that; wear a searching expression; throw swift glances around; dart glances around; scratch around for; go in quest of; root around for strain one's eyes; explore for; crane one's head for; go on the hunt for poke through; breeze through things (other than the one wanted).

(see *search, seek, explore, investigate, find*)

LORE

the ancient and mysterious perfume of the past centuries.

(see *history, past, long ago, record*)

LOSS (to suffer)

have things go to the bad; have the worse end of the staff; take a beating; have slip through the fingers (or from the grasp); have a thing chipped away from one; get sunk; see one's sun set; come off second best; fall very low; take a spill; be left holding the bag; be swamped; get stranded or shipwrecked; be capsized; founder; run aground; be drowned in; get swamped by; be swallowed up by; be flotsam; fall out of; see the fat all in the fire; slip; be forced to drink the hemlock; see nothing but hara-kiri for one; operate in the red; see thrown to the winds; see one's walls toppling about one; lose one's grip on.

(see *fail, deterioration, degenerate, ruin, defeated, decline, frustrated, bankrupt*)

LOUD

enough to wake the Seven Sleepers of Ephesus; bull-roaring; explosive; air-splitting; trumpet-toned; at the top of one's voice; enough to wake the dead; thunder in the ear; head-splitting; enough to make one's windows shake; echo-awakening; enough to drown the beat of drums; heaven-rending; bursting on the ear; enough to make the welkin ring; ringing in the ears; titanic-toned; enough to drown out a band; volcanic.

(see *noisy, vehement, turbulent, shrill shrieks, scream, resound, reverberate*)

LOVE (to be in)

lay seige to someone's heart; enthrone in love; place on a pedestal; worship; have one's heart-strings tied around; devour another with one's eyes; dance attendance upon; take to; be bitten; crouch in the depths of love; spoon; feel a fulness of heart; have one's heart won by another; blend hearts; enter paradise; warm one's heart with a stream of love; shower blind adoration on; be gone on another; lose one's heart to; fall head over heels over; be smitten by love; enjoy a brief rhapsody; be shot through the heart; fall victim to Cupid's bow; set one's cap at; burn with the genial flame of love; be the slave of Venus; yield to Eros; go down at the first shot; find one's flame; be in the toils of Aphrodite; hang on to another's lips; concentrate on the apple of one's eye; blow a kiss to; give more than a side glance to; have eyes for only one person; bill and coo to; be sweet on; cast sheep's eyes at; pop the question to; be love-sick; fall under a glittering enchantment; take to one's bosom; sing serenades to; tie a lover's knot; have love-light shining in one's eyes; give one's soul to another; sit on a star with; crawl into another's vest pocket; give away one's heart; smell the rose of romance; feast one's eyes on; be over head and ears in love; feast one's eyes on; idolize another; look moon-eyed at; be mashed on; be tied to another's chariot; pitch one's heart into another's lap; burn with the fires of passion; have one's heart go out to; find someone to be of one's heart; have one's heartstrings plucked; feel the heart flutter; lay one's heart at another's feet; have the compass in one's heart point to another; wear one's heart on the coat sleeves; feel an awakening of the flesh.

(see *passionate, friendly, tender, kind, devotion, like, sweetheart, romantic, sentimental*)

LOW CLASS

scum of the earth; those who walk in the gutter; on the wrong side of the kerb-stone; seamy folk; shady characters; vermin; slum-denizens; back-alley character.

(see *degenerate, shabby, common, riff-raff, common people, tawdry, sordid*)

LOW POINT

in the cellar; at the bottom of the scale; at rock-bottom; on the floor; in a valley; in an abyss; in the depths; at the nadir; in a hollow.

(see *bottom, basis, depths, fall, hopeless, worthless*)

LOYAL (to be)

be true blue; be true to one's colors; chain one's soul to another; stick by; show dog-true eyes; adhere to one's stripes; have the heart choked by loyalty.

(see *faithful, honest, trust, truthful, steadfast, sincere, duty, obedient*)

LUCKY (to be)

get a break; be born under a lucky

star; have the stars with one; bear a charmed life; have fortune smile on one; have one's star in the ascendant; be born with a silver spoon in one's mouth; be a darling of the gods; be the favored child of fortune; get a windfall; have occasion to thank one's lucky star; bask on the sunny side of the hedge; have one's life all ups; find the cap of Fortunatus; have all water run to one's mill; see fate smile on one's endeavors; be a spoiled child of fortune; have everything smile upon one; have luck serve one kindly; warm oneself in the smiles of fortune; get a shower of red roses out of blank winter skies; tap the jackpot of fortune.

(see *fortunate, favorite, favorable, successful, prosperous, advantage*)

LURE (v.)

lead by the nose; suck another in; give come-on bait; scoop in the public; court Mr. Citizen; sing a Siren song to; attract the eyes of; spread honey for; dangle bright bait before; bait the hook; use window-dressing; give a call to.

(see *attract, tempt, seduce, betray, mislead, deceive, shrewd, gullible*)

LUXURY (to enjoy)

live on the fat of the land; have life a bed of roses; be bred in the lap of luxury; have all milk and honey (or all loaves and fishes); live in clover; loll on feather-bedding; eat nothing but cake and caviar; love the plush of life; suck the honey of the world; roll in money; be a silk-stocking; be nursed in the lap of luxury.

(see *self-indulgence, pleasure-seeking, sensual, enjoy, delight*)

M

MACHINERY

mechanical monstrosities; metal monsters; mechanical marvels; soulless robots.

(see *mechanical, tools*)

MAGAZINE

a literary bulwark; an organ; a slick-paper periodical; a polite monthly; capsule-containing literary chest.

(see *publish, news*)

MAGICIAN (to be a)

practice sleight of hand; wave a magic wand; mumble abracadabra; indulge in legerdemain; rely on mumbo jumbo; dabble in uncanny alchemy; have Aladdin's lamp; be an initiate to witchcraft.

(see *visionary, illusory, imaginary, fake, unreal*)

MAKE

have or put on the stocks; whittle; tailor; rack up; chalk up; hang up (a record); shape; strike (a partnership); boil into (consistency); churn out; erect the framework of; pour out; whip up; weave; brew; hew out; screw into; drive a deal; hammer out; fall into (a mistake); throw out (a suggestion); gear a thing for; whack out; sharpen (a point); set the machinery in motion; roll out (tools).

(see *create, shape, form, produce*)

MALICIOUS (to be)

throw stones at; imbrue one's hands in blood; plant a thorn in the breast; be cold-blooded; be stony-hearted; act hard of heart; pour vinegar on; hunt down; play the devil with; break a butterfly on the wheel; wreak one's malice on.

(see *bitter, evil, injure, victimize, villainous, slander, destroyer, spiteful, abuse*)

MAN (general)

a reed that thinks; frail skiff; a musical instrument given to the other sex; two-legged animal; a good skate; a dry stick; gay dog; grinning ape; male beast; a buck; a plucked rooster; flesh and blood; lord of creation; a thinking creation; a skill-hungry animal; a tough bird; frail parasite of life; one of the herd; a collection of vultures, foxes, and fat pink pigs.

(see *human, people*)

MANAGE

run the show; pull the strings; play the tune; make ends meet; break even; oil and run the machinery; hoe one's own row; crack a crisis; take in one's stride; juggle several things at once.

(see *direct, self-sufficient, guide, rule, control, supervise, maneuver*)

MANEUVER (v.)

thread one's way between; jockey for position; take steps to.

(see *manage, scheme, plan, strategy, plot, trickery, shrewd*)

MANY

a bundle of; a shower of; a flood of; swarms of; a vast net of; a galaxy of; a potpourri of; loads of; a host of; heaps of; coming thick; a blizzard of; a deluge of; tons of; a string of; mountains of; a snowstorm of; a parcel of; a raft of; a torrent of; clouds of; a volley of; a vast pool of; bushels of; a sea of; a stack of; a world of; a downpour of; a plague of; shoals of;

a legion of; an ocean of; a wave of; an avalanche of; a landslide of; herds of; a crowd of; a forest of; a rash of; constellations of; slews of; stockpiles of; drawerfuls of; honeycombed with; a trunkload of: a whole archipelago of; a harvest of; an army of; a cargo of.

(see *abundance, lavish, full of, replete, many, mass, quantity*)

MARK (n.)

stain; rust; stamp; imprint; shadow; trail; seal; scar; fingerprint; brand; tarnish; talisman.

(see *sign, trace, impress*)

MARRIAGE

the odor of orange blossom; the gold bonds of matrimony; the velvet bonds of Hymen; the nuptial knot; the bond of union; Hymen's torch; what is made in heaven; the tie that binds; becoming one bone and one flesh; wedlock; the silken-cord (*i.e.,* of Yue-laou, Chinese old man of the moon, who unites all predestined couples in wedlock with this unbreakable bond).

(see *unite, love, wife, marry, divorce*)

MARRY (v.)

take for husband or wife; lead to the altar; bestow one's hand upon; take the public plunge; retire into the nuptial shade; anchor one's destiny on; share one's lot with; ankle up the aisle; be spliced; rope someone in; take a grab in the matrimonial bran-pie; tie oneself to by law; embark on matrimonial seas; tie the Gordian knot; take for better or for worse; marry into the purple; slip the ring on a finger; put a halter around one's neck.

(see *wife, unite, marriage*)

MASS (n.)

a torrent of; volumes of; a tower of; a cloud of; a swamp of; an avalanche of; a sea of; a squadron of.

(see *abundance, full of, many*)

MATURE (v.)

shed childhood ideas; become mellow; soar out of the parental nest; become full-blown; bud; be weaned from the bottle of babyhood; be abloom; cut the eyeteeth; become dry behind the ears; flower; ripen; awaken to adulthood; grow to stature; come to full flower; become golden-ripe; be heavy with over-ripeness; go up a rung on the ladder of living; come to a head.

(see *grow, complete, prime*)

MAXIMUM

high-water mark; full tilt; running full; hitting the peak.

(see *limit, height, full of, vastness, utmost, unlimited*)

MEANINGFUL (to be)

look one's words; have an edge in one's words; be pregnant with meaning; signal a meaning; pack words with significance; spell out for; charge words with significance; show what is between-the-lines (or in-back-of-the-line).

(see *explain, interpret, emphasize, important, impressive*)

MEANINGLESS

dead letter; sounding brass and tinkling cymbal; a tale told by an idiot, full of sound and fury, signifying nothing; empty vessels; high-sounding phrases gone sour on the tongues of their speaker; lip-babble; a tasteless, thrice-warmed dish; hollow; musty words; Greek; Tower of Babel.

(see *inadequate, ineffective, insignificant, unconvincing, worthless*)

MEANS TO (n.)

avenue; channel; road; pathway; trail; vehicle; transmission belt; weapons; detour; spectacles to view through; cards to play; strings to one's bow; magic formula for; instrument; stepping-stone; broad highway.

(see *resources, resourceful*)

MECHANICAL

going by clockwork; push-button; robot; automaton; machine-minded.

(see *machinery, tools*)

MEDDLESOME (to be)

put an oar in another's boat or business; thrust one's nose in another's affairs; horn or chime in on another; have crust; shoot with another's bow.

(see *interfere, oppose, disturbance, tactless, presumptuous*)

MEDIOCRE

sailing in midstream; run-of-the-mill; worth a piece of carrion; garden variety; lukewarm; tepid; one who will not set the Thames on fire; the quicksands of mediocrity.

(see *ordinary, poor, inferior, temperate, common, conservative*)

MEDITATE

chew the cud upon; take counsel of one's pillow; ruminate; sort one's thoughts; contemplate the soul; put a thing in one's pipe and smoke it; throw the mind back; peer into the clutter of the mind; feed the mind on; chase thoughts about; be deep in thought; turn over in the mind; withdraw behind the iron curtain of contemplation; sit in judgment; sleep upon a thought; spin logic; go into a brown study; be lost in thought; weave a web of thoughts; dine on food for fancy.

(see *ponder, study, think, introspective, self-analysis*)

MEEK (to be)

turn the other cheek; eat out of a hand; be weak-kneed; have a hangdog mien; be sheep.

(see *yield, submissive, mild, sensitive, servile, fawn, timid, pacify, weak, self-effacement*)

MEET

run into; cross someone's horizon; fall in the way of; intersect another's life; cross the path of; bump into; run head-on into; come face to face with; stumble across; rub shoulders with.

(see *encounter, join, unite*)

MEETING (n.)

pow-wow; talkfest; love feast; Council of War.

(see *interview. gather, controversy, discuss*)

MELANCHOLY

funereal; sepulchral; long-faced; sour-faced; moody; darkened by brooding sorrow; sunk in a morose spell; in the blues; low in spirit; downcast; heartsick.

(see *sad, self-pity, sorrowful, dejected, dejection, despondency, discouraged, distressed, dreary, unhappy*)

METHODICAL

follow a pattern; follow a recipe; make a clinical case-study; have one's instruments at hand; plan a line-of-attack; believe that the first stroke is half the battle; use one's brains in a matter; mount the ladder rung-by-rung; take inventory of the ways and means; find a workable approach to a thing; know the right door by which to enter.

(see *exact, orderly, system, schedule*)

MIDDLE (in the)
at the half-way house; in the dead of (night); at the heart of; in the thick of; in mid-stream; at the crossroads.

(see *center, centered*)

MIDDLE-AGE
past the morn of life; in the afternoon of one's time; reach the top of the hill of life! in the soft October of one's time; in the fattening forties; past the middle of the second act of life; in the autumn of one's years; the early falling leaves of life.

(see *mature, age, prime*)

MIDDLE-CLASS
the white-collar workers.

(see *ordinary, temperate, conservative*)

MIDNIGHT
the witching time of night; the strike of twelve; a blind man's holiday; getting on to bull's-noon.

(see *night, dark, darkness, late*)

MIDST (in the)
in the bosom of; in the teeth of; in the very jaws of; up to the neck in; in the face of; at the storm center of; in the circle of.

(see *center, centered, involved, surround, envelop*)

MILD
milk-and-water; tame; low-pitched; lamblike.

(see *meek, submissive, sensitive, yield, tender, calm, suave*)

MIND (n.)
the private chamber of the ego; mental mirror; reasoning faculty; gray matter; upper story; the high plateau of the mind; seat of thought; the trap-door of the subconscious; the racing engine of the brain; mental equipment; the picture-making mechanism; a well-oiled thinking machine; the austere asylum of the soul; a loom weaving a tapestry of one's plan of action; soil fertile in thought-seeds.

(see *intellectual, intelligent, think, self-intelligence, subconscious, psychoanalysis*)

MINIATURE
microcosm; pocket-edition; on a small scale.

(see *diminish, small, small amount, tiny, insignificant, trifle*)

MINIMIZE
soft-pedal; view through the wrong end of a telescope; gloss over; make mole-hills out of mountains.

(see *smooth, disguise, excuse, soothe, calm, lessen, underrate, understate*)

MINIMUM
drop in the ocean or bucket; thimbleful; nutshell; reduced to a skeleton; on a shoestring; squeeze (noun).

(see *small, small amount, tiny, trifle, insignificant, scrap, speck, unimportant*)

MINISTER
a black coat; a shepherd; the pulpit; the cloth; a soul-winner; a pulpit-pounder; a gospel-pusher; a traveler on a theological road.

(see *worship, soul, religion, religious*)

MISCELLANY
a rag-bag, a rope of many strands; a pie you can shove anything into; all baked in one pie; mish-mash; a potpourri; an olio; a hodge-podge; a medley; a gallimaufry; a hash; a ragout; a mulligan stew.

(see *mixture, varied*)

MISDIRECTED (to be)

lay one's foundations on a lie; be thrown off the track; be thrown off the scent; bark up the wrong tree; look for an apple on a weeping willow tree.

(see *mislead, deceive, cheat, trickery, gullible, false*)

MISERLY (to be)

pinch pennies; squeeze a cent; nurse a nickle; skin a flint; live upon nothing; drive a hard bargain; stop one hole in a sieve; close the purse strings; button up one's pockets; be grasping; have an itching palm; grub money; be a pinchfist; be a lickpenny; scrimp; skin a flea for its hide and tallow; be close-fisted; be purse-proud.

(see *stingy, scrimp, close, save*)

MISFIT (n.)

a round peg in a square hole; a big frog in a small puddle; a fish out of water; a stone that Providence heaves into the tranquil pool of humanity.

(see *inadequate, illogical, inconsistent*)

MISFORTUNE (to suffer)

go down in the world; have seen better days; make a slip 'twixt cup and lip; take a tumble; live through stormy days; jump out of the frying pan into the fire; drink the cup of affliction; undergo a crack-up; sail on a sea of trouble; bring a hornet's nest about one's ears; get kicked by destiny; see gloomy spots on the horizon; have one's gray hairs brought down with sorrow to the grave; have one's luck rot; sit under a shadow; have fate turn thumbs down on one; endure smoke and gas; have it not rain but pour on one; be searched out by the bony fingers of hard times; be a tennis ball of fortune.

(see *disaster, distressed, troubled, defeat, ruin, defeated*)

MISJUDGE

put the saddle on the wrong horse; put the cart before the horse; bark up the wrong tree; follow a false scent; put all the fat in the fire; cast pearls before swine; see things in false colors; play one's cards badly; stride over Truth's body; have one's blows go wild; overshoot the mark; give weight to smoke.

(see *mistake, misdirected, mislead, err, underrate*)

MISLEAD

throw dust into someone's eyes; point out a false trail; throw one off the track; lead up a blind alley; throw off one's guard; draw a red herring across the trail; throw off the scent; play with someone's beard; give one the mitten; double-cross one; cheat one with wealth; blind one with delusion; put one's wits to sleep; take someone out of his element; give a false coloring; put a thing in a false light; put out of focus; give a wrong cue.

(see *deceive, deceiver, cheat, trickery, misdirected, treachery, victimize*)

MIST

the faint exhalation of the earth; a stingy rain; a river of mist streaming out of the hills; a crawling vapor; a palpitating haze; a trailing scarf of mist; little wisps of meandering mist.
(see *cloud, clouded, cloudy*)

MISTAKE (to make a)

sound a wrong note; take a false step; make a slip of the tongue; put one's foot in a thing; make a false start; take the wrong sow by the ear; take the shadow for the substance; take a wrong turn; go on a wrong track; pick a lemon; fumbie a thing; reckon without one's host; wake up the wrong passenger; kill the goose that lays the golden egg; aim at a pigeon and kill a crow; jerk at the wrong strings; make a slip 'twixt cup and lip; look in the wrong box; preach to the wise; misread the symptoms.

(see *misjudge, err, blunder, stupid, fail*)

MIXTURE

a tapestry; a carnival; a glutinous amalgam; a mosaic; Noah's ark; a melting pot; a French *pot-au-feu,* with everything in the kettle; a welding together; a magpie's nest; a potpourri; a hash; a patchwork quilt; pottage; hodge-podge; the broth of a Vanity Fair; a scrambling together; pepper-and-salt; a churning; a symphony (of color); polyglot (population).

(see *miscellany, varied*)

MOCK (v.)

poke fun at; heap mockery on; give a horse-laugh to; laugh up one's sleeve; laugh to scorn; smirk in one's sleeve; caricature; burlesque; laugh in a thin soprano with ice in it; rain mockery down on.

(see *scorn, ridicule, taunt, tease, sarcastic, scathe*)

MODEL (n.)

the glass of fashion; a man of wax; a glass in which many things are revealed; a perfect icicle of decorum; salt of the earth; trump; rough diamond.

(see *pattern, fashionable, propriety, copy*)

MODERN

the last word (*le dernier cri);* the last cry; electric age; live (advertising); clothed in modern dress; dolled-up; daisy-fresh; with none of the dust of the ages.

(see *fashionable, new, progress, fresh*)

MODEST (to be)

hide one's light under a bushel; pursue the noiseless tenor of one's ways; make no bones; draw in one's horns; hide one's face; keep oneself in the background; put one's talent in a napkin; think small beer of oneself; take a reef in one's pride; pocket one's pride; live without beat of drum; act without ceremony; be poor in spirit; cut one's coat according to one's cloth; lay aside affectations; not put oneself on a pedestal.

(see *timid, virtuous, self-conscious, self-effacement*)

MONEY

bankroll; dough; admission to the grandstand; fat checkbook; kitty; cash rolling across counters; a jet of coppers; high-stake; a pocket of money; slippery money; a nest egg; the almighty dollar; a mint; pursestrings; filthy lucre; brass; boodle; a heap of coin; tinkling profits; the ring of gold; the root of all evil; the wherewithal (*de quoi);* small change; flush.

(see *wealthy, rich, save, squander, invest, spend*)

MONOTONOUS (to be)

reduce to a grind or formula; singsong; go on and on in the same narrow rut; rotate inside the dull daily groove; be cut-and-dried.

(see *tedious, sameness, dull, uniform, uninteresting, unimaginative, trite*)

MOON (n.)

the Queen of Heaven; a silver boat sailing over the rooftops; the sickle of a new moon swinging in the sky; the pale feather of the crescent moon; a slice of lemon peel in the evening sky; the moon trailing a ribbon of silver mist; a lamp of silver light; the silvery drapery which the moon throws pell-mell over everything; the shimmering, billowing depths of white light; a sickle with a faint cast of gold.

(see *sky, night, light*)

MORALITY

the odor of respectability; the strait-jacket of society; cast-iron conventions; a strait-laced garment; sermon-preaching.

(see *righteous, sanctimonious, honest, self-control, self-respect, virtuous*)

MOTIVE

the why and wherefore; springboard; driving force; crusade; magnet; the pro and con.

(see *incentive, impulse, incite, stimulate, cause, influence, drive, reason, force*)

MOUNTAIN

straight-falling cloak of stone; frowning peak; icy-capped, snowy giant; plunging waves of mountains; bristling spines of mountain ranges.

(see *height, tall, tremendous, woodland, ridge*)

MOURN

wear the willow; lament in sing-song voice; clothe oneself in the trappings of grief; intone a wordless chant of despair; toll the bell; sit in mournful shadows.

(see *grieve, lament, despair, weep, sorrowful, sad, melancholy, unhappy, sob, sigh*)

MOVE (physical)

surge; flow; pulse; trip; flutter; shift gears; dodge; creep; grind on; trudge along; roll; stir the earth; shuffle; bottle up; go on a hard-driving pace; storm about; trace one's script on; race along; weave one's way; wend on a path; steal along; float towards; bowl along; lurch; uproot oneself; fleet on; rove over; stream on; cut a feather; fly along; swim along; stir oneself; crawl along; prod oneself forward; churn through; whirr into full speed; sail along; dance ahead; bounce along; stumble along; take a step; sweep ahead; waltz along; leap ahead; ebb and flow; pulsate; ripple; flit along; edge forward; transplant oneself.

(see *drive, force, progress, rush, run, speed, walk, travel, energetic*)

MOVED (to be)—emotional

feel one's heart melt; have one's frozen surface broken; be cut; be magnetized; have one's heartstrings touched.

(see *sympathetic, distressed, excited, emotional*)

MUSIC

the speech of angels; the international language; the moan of strings; rippling melody; squealing of fifes; a violin fit of fortissimos; the sigh of the instruments; the lilting music of a voice; swelling tones; a spray of notes; brass bands shrieking; a drenching melody; rattling tunes; a sobbing, sawing, and singing tango; the twilight musings of Chopin; singing strings; ear-filling cacophonies.

(see *sounds, piano playing, harmony, singing*)

MYSTERY

unchartered seas; mumbo jumbo; a riddle; wheels within wheels; huggery-muggery; dark hint; a tomb; a closed book; wrapped in mystery; missing link; a fog; puzzledom of life; under a murky cloud; murky; a plot thick enough.

(see *secret, obscure, hide, unknown, plot, perplexed*)

N

NAME (v.)

tie a label to; tag one with a name; brand; dub; christen.

(see *speak, specify, describe, title*)

NARROW-MINDED (to be)

be single-eyed; be hidebound; have slender experience of the facts of life; hold narrow views; have a primitive narrowness of outlook; be short-sighted; have warped opinions; have a narrow soul; hold contracted views; not see beyond one's nose; have a blind side; not see the forest for the trees; have a mote in one's eye; have only one idea; look at only one side of the shield; be one-sided; be purblind; have a hunch-backed view of a subject.

(see *prejudiced, unfair, unjust*)

NATIVE (adj.)

home-grown; home-spun; in one's element; mother (country or tongue); inborn; bred in the bone.

(see *home, original*)

NEAR (to be)

be at someone's heels; be at hand; have at one's elbow; be hot on the trail of; be within earshot of; be on the highroad to; be hard by; knock at the door; be on the threshold; be within a stone's throw; edge close to; have under one's nose; have a thing stare one in the face; press the hard edge of; have in one's grasp; be within hollering distance; tread close on the heels of; be within gunshot of; be near to the edge of; be within a squirrel's leap of; be in the neighborhood of; have a ringside seat to; be within an ace of; get the scent of; hug one's goal; be within the shadow of; be one or two notches short of;

be in the jaws of; brush against; hang on the skirts of.

(see *close*)

NECESSITY

crying want; meat and drink; the staff of life; bread-and-butter; needs must when the devil drives; scornful dogs will eat dirty puddings; no two ways about it.

(see *need, poverty-stricken, inevitable, fate, requisite*)

NECKLACE

a caravan of pearls.

(see *embellish*)

NEED (v.)

thirst for; be hungry for; cry for; be starved for; feel the pangs of hunger for; be pressed for; be hard up for; feel the pinch of.

(see *requisite, fate, poverty-stricken, want*)

NEGLECT (v.)

allow to lie on the shelf; wrap up in a napkin of neglect; lose sight of; shut one's eyes to; turn a deaf ear to; fling to the winds; set aside; put in the shade; leave a loose thread; turn the cold shoulder to; hang a thing by the wall; give the go-by to; leave a hole in the fabric; let go by the board; be deaf to the call of.

(see *disregard, fail, default*)

NEGLIGENT (to be)

skim the surface of; skip over; slip over; slur over; take a cursory view of; let the grass grow under one's feet; be caught napping; take a liberty from; mislay.

(see *inattentive, careless, lax, slacker, unconcerned, indifferent*)

NEPOTISM

providing places at the same trough for one's relatives.

(see *relationship, unfair*)

NERVOUS (to be)

feel one's composure smashed to fragments; have one's nerves frayed at the edges; bite the lips; chew one's nails; have butterflies in one's stomach; feel acid poured on one's raw nerves; be in a shattered state; feel one's ganglia twanging; be on edge; be on pins and needles; have one's teeth set on edge; work one's nerves into tattered rags; feel jittery; feel one's nerves shot to pieces; feel the nerves cry aloud; sprout neuroses.

(see *uncertain, unsettled, unsteady, upset, fearful, timid, insecure, tense*)

NEVER

on the day when icicles freeze in hell; not by a long shot; when the devil is blind; not once in a blue moon; not in a month of Sundays; on the Greek Kalends; not on your tintype; when there are two Sundays in one week; not for all the world.

(see *none, impossibility, no*)

NEW

warm; fresh; embryonic; hot from the brain; bib and jumper stage; new-fangled; undigested; green; in the egg; virginal; raw; glossy; spick and span; dew-fresh; neophytic; up-to-date; damp behind the ears; making its bow; just baptized; undergoing birth pains; a new twist; a new wrinkle; just out of the shell; up-to-the-minute;

latter-day.

(see *fresh, modern, discover, strange, unusual*)

NEWS

delectable morsels of gossip; ripples of social tides and currents; press-feeders; the unfolding of a scroll; what is in the wind; what is the good word?

(see *gossip, inform, report*)

NEW YORK

the cerebrum of the Western World; the land of Big Business.

(see *city, skyscraper*)

NIGHT

the velvety magic of night; black velvet sprinkled with stars; unpainted darkness; the curtains of night; cloak of darkness; the sable mantle of night; the closing in of dark; the heart of darkness; flood of black; the draining of light from the earth; pool of darkness; the end of the pause of twilight; when the full moon rides the sky; glittering fairyland; the death of day; the muting of the tune of the streets; the tottering fabric of day.

(see *evening, dusk, sunset, darkness, shine, moon*)

NO

thumbs down; not by a long shot.

(see *none, never*)

NOBLEMAN

born or cradled in the purple; born with a silver spoon in the mouth; three-tailed bashaw; blue blood of Castile; *pur sang* (pure blood); high descent; *haut monde* (high life); of the ten-thousand; upper-class; of gentle blood; high-born; big-wig; silk-stocking; swell.

(see *aristocracy, rich, superior*)

NOISY (to be)

raise a storm of sound; rattle around; thunder about; roar; haul a racket over cobblestones; make the windows shake; din in the ear; fill or split the air; trumpet loudly; raise bedlam or pandemonium; make the welkin ring; raise a hue and cry; rasp; drum; crash cymbals; go into a crescendo; shatter silence; thunder at the top of one's voice; set off an explosion; beat in great waves of sound; make the air solid with sound; create a madhouse; shoot a cross fire of sounds; gouge the silence; rage against the wind; throb with sound; tumble in a flood of sound; beat a tattoo; raise the roof; make people unable to hear themselves think.

(see *loud, turbulent*)

NONE

not a breath of; without an iota of.

(see *no, never, lack*)

NONENTITY

a mobile flea of a man; a polyp; a dwarf; a cipher; a nobody; a man of straw; a figurehead.

(see *insignificant, futility, unimportant, uninteresting, unnecessary*)

NONSENSE

rubbish; rot; maudlin twaddle; fudge; bunk; monkey business; drivel; balderdash; buncombe; rigmarole; fol-de-rol; piffle; clap-trap; moonshine; stuff and nonsense; guff; bilge; Jabberwocky language; without rhyme or reason; trash; trumpery; flummery.

(see *foolish, unimportant, insignificant, unreal*)

NOSTALGIC (to be)

find the lamplight yellow with remembrance; have one's memories stirred; ponder over the broken threads of the past; feel the nameless sadness that is born of moonlight; suffer a long pain of remembrance; throb to a constant stream of rhythmic memories; have the turbid flood of memories come pouring in; be haunted by a restless ghost desirous of troubling one's heart; swim in an undercurrent of pensive thought; recall "auld lang syne"; sink in sentimentality; measure the past with one's heart; have one's heart drenched in homesick tears; smile with a light choke in the throat; bewail one's lost youth.

(see *homesick, lonely*)

NOTICE (v.)

turn the head after; have a thing dawn on one's horizon; not be blind to a thing; have something strike one; have one's eye caught by.

(see *observant, perceive, see, regard*)

NUDE (to be)

wear one's birthday suit; dress in nature's garb; be in a state of nature; sit around in one's bones; go native.

(see *native, shame*)

O

OBEDIENT (to be)
mind one's P's and Q's; toe the chalk-line; toe the mark; walk the straight and narrow path; answer to the whistle; plod uncomplainingly along the road of duty; bow to another's dictates; bend the knee to; follow the dictates of another; follow rules; follow the lead of; follow to the world's end; be wax before another's wishes; give way to another; be at one's beck and call.

(see *submissive, deference, observant, duty, respect*)

OBLIGATED (to be)
be bound to another; be chained to; owe another a debt of gratitude; be taken by duty; be held by the bond of duty; fetter oneself by obligations.

(see *debt, bind, duty*)

OBLITERATE
blot out; wipe off the map; lay the ghost of the past; sponge away; draw a curtain over; draw the pen through; leave no trace of; stamp out.

(see *erase, cancel, extinct*)

OBLIVIOUS OF (to be)
drink the waters of Lethe; live in lotus-land; make a thing fade from the memory; escape the memory of; wean one's thoughts from; relegate to limbo; have one's thoughts wrapped in mist and fog; sink into the bottomless pit of nothingness; cast memory into a maelstrom of black emptiness; cast behind one's back; put memory under a long eclipse; sink into oblivion; have everything come in at one ear and go out the other; drown memory; empty one's brain of;

be blind to all that goes by; keep one's head in the clouds.

(see *forget, careless, neglect, negligent, unaware, unconcerned*)

OBSCURE (to make)
veil in mist; cover with fog; eclipse; make muddy; stir up the muddy depths; cloud; throw into the shade; put out of focus; make shadowy; throw in the background; becloud; drown out; blot out; blur; make a thing retreat behind; draw a curtain over; cut off from vision; make murky; emit the velvet breath of vagueness; flatten into nonentity; keep behind the scenes; keep in a secret pocket; cut off light from; clog with vapors; make pale; lay a heavy smoke screen.

(see *dark, darkness, clouded, shade, dim, shadows, disguise, hide, conceal, cover*)

OBSERVANT (to be)
have an eagle's eye; be needle-sharp; see how the wind blows; keep a watchful eye on; see with one's own eyes; see how the cat jumps; take stock of; bend one's looks upon; have an eye for; be a mirror that goes in and out with others; keep an eye peeled on; scout around; keep one's eyes wide open.

(see *notice, regard, obedient, watchful*)

OBSESSED (to be)
have an *idée fix;* not be able to get a thing out of one's head; have one's thoughts haunted by; be dogged by; have a notion press thick upon one; have one's imagination taken possession of; meet one's *bête noir* at every

turn; have a perverse kink in the brain.

(see *dominate, psychoanalysis, insistent*)

OBSOLETE

covered by the dust of centuries; moth-eaten; a museum piece; behind the age; of the old school; stagnating in a backwater; out of date; fallen behind the times; moldy; creaking; dilapidated; fossilized; grandfather-method.

(see *old-fashioned, past, neglect, long ago*)

OBSTACLE

millstone round one's neck; a sea of troubles; snag; man-made paralysis; excess baggage; bottle-neck; the pebble in the path; high wall; thorn in the side; the monkey-wrench that stopped the machinery; the stone in the road; tripping-rope; a dead end; a rope upon the wheel of Joy; a ball and chain; lion in the path; iron curtain; a bit of grillwork between; hurdle; barrier; stumbling-block; the main rub.

(see *hinder, obstruct, difficulty, impasse*)

OBSTINATE

dogged; stiff-necked; stony; bulldog; adamantine; die-hard; stiff-backed; hide-bound; deaf to advice; hard-mouthed; impervious to reason; last-ditch; bitter-ender; wedded to opinionation; stiff-kneed; not yielding an inch; hugging a belief; fighting against destiny.

(see *stubborn, uncompromising, immovable, insistent, firm, resolute, unchangeable*)

OBSTRUCT

put a spoke in the wheel; throw a monkey-wrench into the machinery; truss in red tape; hedge in; hold up traffic; barricade; put on the brake; spike guns; clog the wheel; cross the path of; snow under; make heavy; strand on the sandbar of inactivity; tie in a knot; clog pipelines; block the steamroller; clot with dust; snag; build a bloc against; dam up.

(see *obstacle, hinder, impasse, difficulty, close, stop, oppose*)

OBVIOUS (to be)

be transparent; show through; stick out a mile; have written on every line of the face; wear one's heart on the sleeve; stare one in the face.

(see *evident, visible, self-evident, clear*)

OCCUR

dawn on; shoot up in the mind; come into one's head; flash on the mind; pop up; rear its head; spring up to the mind; cross the mind; flit across the view; come uppermost; run in one's head; fasten itself on the mind; occupy the mind; bob up; burst upon the mind; sprout out; break out; strike one.

(see *event, appear*)

OCEAN

the seven seas; a garden of water flowering in foam; the iron seas; the wine-dark sea; steamer-track; herring pond; the vasty deep; watery waste; briny waters; high seas; the moving gray plain; the cool clean lungs of the world; Davy Jones's locker: the big drink; the big pond; sharks' hunting ground; Amphitrite's bower; the court of Neptune; the mad cavalry charge of creaming billows.

(see *sea, waves, tide*)

ODOR

a day perfumed with hidden flowers; a little whisper of cologne; the intoxicating smell of printer's ink; the smell of newly turned earth clinging to one; musty smells flying to the nostrils; the odor of bourbon from a block away; smell hovering over the land; an empty flask still redolent; a room pervaded with the appetizing aroma of sizzling fowl; the offense of a smoking-car atmosphere.

(see *smell of*)

OFFEND

flick on the raw; step on the toes; tread on the corns; cut to the quick; draw blood; stick in the craw; stab; nauseate; hurl insults; wither with a frown; needle with words; grate upon the ear; talk down to; sting; make sore-hearted; step over the boundary; be a snake to be scotched.

(see *displease, annoy, irritate, anger, err*)

OFFER (v.)

lay at one's feet; throw in the path; throw at one's head; be at one's service; open the door to; deluge with; give a nibble to; dangle bait before; feed with; make overtures to; throw a thing open to someone.

(see *show, give*)

OFFICE (business)

a steel chapel where loafing and laughter are raw sin; a pigeon-holed vault; a coop partitioned with frosted glass; the boss's lair; an overflowing cupboard; a stall and harness.

(see *business, work, worker*)

OFFICIAL (n.)

bigwig; big-head; brass hat; high brass; authoritative functionary.

(see *leader, superior, supervise*)

OLD (to be)

withered; antique; bearded; barnacle-encrusted; creaky; moss-grown; running to seed; shop-worn; landlocked within the harbor of the years; ready to be gathered to its ancestors; ripe for the harvester; having one foot in the grave; measured for a coffin; dry-as-dust; gnarled; battered; mellowed; tarnished; weather-beaten; laden with age; rusty; lost in the dust of time; faded; ravaged by time; moth-eaten; burned down to the butt end; time-worn; cobwebbed with antiquity; stricken by years; superannuated; wrinkled; frosted with white whiskers; draped with the cobwebs of old age; on the shady side of life's afternoon; with the snows of many winters nestling in the beard; when the dusk of the evening begins to gather over the watery eye; when one mounts age's silver-rimmed hill; in the peaceful evening of life; drift toward life's late afternoon; fall victim to the autumn haze of senescence; surrounded by the chilling fogs of senescence; within walking distance of death; descend swiftly into the valley; travel toward the sunset; have run its course; have had its day; totter to the grave; outgrow one's usefulness; have spent one's fires; have a dried-apple appearance; have age creep over one; have swapped all of one's hair with the years in exchange for a face full of wrinkles; have most of the gilt worn off; droop on one's stalk; reach the mumbling stage of life; flow with the ebb tide; find one's second childhood; bask in one's twilit hours; belong to the "old guard"; be of the old school; be far advanced in years; be of the oldest rock; be covered with mildew; be in one's dotage; find old age to be an incurable disease (Seneca); be shriveled up by the years; be a dead hearth.

(see *age, gray-haired, white-haired, senility, long-lived*)

OLD-FASHIONED (to be)

be born in the ark; follow the way of the stage-coach and the canal; stay in the ox-cart stage; be wedded to antiquity; cling to tradition; be a pastel-tinted remnant of the old order; be pre-Model T; attend the old school; rummage in the arsenal of antiquity; wear ancient garb; date from the pyramids; cultivate ancestral virtues; come from beyond the tomahawk age; date from the age of gas-lights; belong in an old curiosity shop; be a stick-in-the-mud; drive a horse and buggy.

(see *obsolete, past, untimely, long ago*)

OLD MAN

ghost; relic; old vintage; fossil; buzzard; old dog; old donkey; old volcano; old coot; geezer; graybeard.

(see *old, gray-haired, white-haired, senility, patriarch*)

OMINOUS

shadow on the wall; calm before the storm; handwriting on the wall; gathering clouds; raven; harbinger of evil; heavy-heavy-hanging over.

(see *premonition, threaten, fearful, foresee*)

OPEN (v.)

pick the knot; keep a thing fluid; throw the gates wide; break the land; unlock; peel; yawn; unfold.

(see *spread, expand, reveal, begin, extend, clear*)

OPENING (n.)

mouth; yawn; loophole.

(see *beginning, first*)

OPENLY

above-board; before one's eyes; under one's nose; in the light of; on the stage; in the face of day; face to face; to one's face; baldly.

(see *frank, unhesitatingly, uninhibited, unrestrained, straightforward*)

OPINION (to state one's)

give a piece of one's mind; reveal one's views; speak one's piece; throw in one's own two cents; say one's two-bits worth; show one's point of view; say how one sees a thing with one's own eyes; take one's stand upon a thing; show how a thing looks from where one sits; beat the tom-tom for a thing.

(see *divulge, reveal, orate, declare, preach, speak, say, straightforward*)

OPPORTUNIST (to be an)

take time by the forelock; make hay while the sun shines; come in pudding-time; strike while the iron is hot; play one's best card; know what tune to dance to; jump at an opportunity; butter one's bread on both sides; pull one's chestnuts out of the fire in time; hear opportunity knock at the door; feel the quick finger of chance laid on one; know which door to open; seize the moment of free stage and no favor; scent an opening; find a loophole for one's aim; get the world at one's feet; make a gold mine of a thing; get a second helping from heaven; know when the time is ripe; find new pastures; get the gods to toss a thing into one's lap; know when the hour of destiny is upon one; make one's way to the gate of paradise; use a thing as a stepping-stone.

(see *self-gain, advantage, initiative, profit, useful, resourceful*)

OPPOSE (v.)

fly in the face of; stem the tide; go against the grain; raise one's hand or voice against; set one's face against; be at cross-purposes with; turn upon; be dead against; pull a different way; declare war on; pit or set oneself against; grapple with; cry out against; fight back to the ropes; hurl oneself against; run counter to; kick against the pricks; get the wind in one's teeth; dress in hostile array; feel a quiver of resistance run through one; make a stand against; buck the current; cross bayonets; be at drawn daggers; counterpoint against; hack away at; hurl defiance at; buffet the waves; fall foul of; fly into a headwind; sail in the eye of the wind; be up in arms against; breast the flood; break a lance with; stand front to front; be the shoe that pinches; subject to a cross-pull; raise a storm of hostility; come to grips with; tangle with; war to the knife; wage a running grudge fight; engage in cross fire; start an undercurrent; row against the current; fly to the opposite pole.

(see *resist, thwart, obstruct, prevent, stop, rebuff, repulse*)

OPPRESS (v.)

grind the face of; put on the screw; trample under foot; rule with a rod of iron; lay a heavy hand on; bear down upon; crush under an iron heel; ride roughshod over; rivet the yoke; force down the throat; hit hard at; drive down to the deeps; weigh upon another; be a bird of prey; conduct a reign of terror; force to labor under; tie up in red tape.

(see *overcome, cruel, subdue, severe, hardship, hard, persecuted, unjust*)

OPTIMISTIC (to be)

see through rose-colored glasses; look on the bright side of; see a ray of hope; take the side of the angels; be starry-eyed; buoy up with hopes; keep on the sunny side; see the silver lining; glow with optimism; take heart; offer food for hope; sing the bluebird's song; paint the world in rose.

(see *cheerful, encourage, enthusiastic, happy*)

ORATE (v.)

hold the floor; step on a soapbox; hold forth; make a necklace of well-turned phrases; wield a verbal sledgehammer; sail on a Niagara of monologue; ripple with a liquid rhythm of speech; descant in a silvery voice; have a silver tongue; have a golden tongue; embroider speech with purple passages; have the gift of gab.

(see *opinion, preach, speak, eloquent, say, declare*)

ORDER (v.)

lay down the law; snap fingers at; throw thunderbolts; call the tune; run the show; rule the waves; ram a thing down someone's throat; serve notice to; push around; snap the whip at; shout injunctions at; achieve by a dash or stroke of the pen.

(see *direct, rule, dominate, control, power*)

ORDERLY (adj.)

neat as a pin; ship-shape; according to Cocker; in apple-pie order; in tune with the music of the spheres; licked into shape; pigeon-holed; a hole for every peg; cut and dried; in battle array; marching in procession.

(see *methodical, system, regulations, regimentation*)

ORDINARY (adj.)

run-of-the-mill; rank-and-file; homespun; bread-and-butter; man-on-the-street; rubber-stamp; common clay;

stripped of all romantic disguise; with the novelty worn off.

(see *mediocre, poor, habitual, common*)

ORGANIZE

set up the framework; assemble the machinery; line up; get the wheels turning; whip into order; bind the bundle; turn the flow into an orderly current; shape up; weave together the strands; weld the parts into a strong whole; unsnarl the threads; tie up the ends; blend the ingredients; build into service.

(see *arrange, established, regimentation, system, form, make, shape, adjust, reorganize*)

ORIGIN

fountainhead; seat of; germinal cell; soil out of which a thing springs; root; genesis; gateway.

(see *source, beginning, start, cause*)

ORIGINAL (to be)

strike a new note; break fresh ground; blaze a trail; pioneer a thing; be first-hand; be no mere phonograph.

(see *invent, create, model, pattern, unusual*)

ORIGINATE (v.)

bud from; stem from; flow from; spring from; hail from; float from; drift from; hatch; crop up; shoot up; sprout from; be rooted in; launch; father; mother; sire; be parent to; be the architect of.

(see *create, cause, begin, proceed*)

OSTENTATIOUS (to be)

play to the grandstand; appear with beat of drum; come with flourish of trumpet; be escorted by fanfare; have pontifical pretensions; wear one's best bib and tucker; keep one's colors flying; arrive with an eleven-gun salute; cut a wide swath; cut a figure or a feather; throw oneself about; wear high-collared pomposity; hold the center of the stage; fashion-plate oneself on a sofa.

(see *display, flaunt, pretentious, show off, boast, vain*)

OSTRACIZE

put someone beyond the pale; quench the candle and ring the bell for someone (medieval service of excommunication); send to Coventry; show the door to; shake someone off; keep another off one's grass; put on the blacklist; blackball another from; cause another to lose caste; bundle someone out neck-and-crop; put under the ban.

(see *dishonor, reject, expel, excommunicate*)

OUTCAST (n.)

black sheep; ugly duckling; desert rat; dog; castaway; flotsam and jetsam; driftwood.

(see *ostracize, abandon*)

OUTDO (v.)

leave in the shade; eclipse; outdistance; drown a band; dim another; out-herod Herod.

(see *surpass, superior, excel*)

OUTLET

safety-valve; vent; loophole; letting off steam.

(see *express, unrestrained, self-protection, uninhibited*)

OUTLINE (n.)

skeleton; bare bones; scaffolding; keynote; frame; larger canvas (not including the details).

(see *pattern, plan*)

OUTWIT

beat the devil around the stump; think rings around another; catch a weasel asleep; outgame another; lead another a merry dance; tilt the balance in one's own favor; steal a march upon; out-maneuver.

(see *outdo, overcome, cheat, deceive, swindle, victimize*)

OVAL

pear-shaped; egg-shaped; within a horseshoe belt.

(see *shape, circle*)

OVER-AMBITIOUS

have too many irons in the fire; bruise oneself against one's own ambitions; let ambition run away with oneself; go nap on a thing; try to put a large peg in a small hole.

(see *greedy, unlimited, ambition, excessive*)

OVERCOME (v.)

swing one from his moorings; run away with one; lick; buck; tackle; beat; wear down another's resistance; roll through opposition; strangle; override; cause another to beat a retreat; blot out; paralyze opposition; outride; numb another with want; fight through a thing; smother; crush; make short work of; bowl over; drown out; throw on the last straw; floor; hurdle; carry off a situation; swamp; flood; cause to break down; bridge over a difficulty; choke; spell the end of; close about a thing; beat down; trample under; prostrate; unhorse; sweep away; cause to tumble; snow under; sweep down on; engulf; knock the breath out of; outweigh; burst the bonds of.

(see *defeat, conquer, victorious, subdue, triumphant*)

OVERCOME BY (to be)

be swept over by; be intoxicated with; be deluged or swamped by; suffer more than flesh can bear; be staggered by; be electrified by; be consumed or eaten up by; get lost in; be dissolved by; be hip-deep in; fight a losing battle; be devoured by; be stunned by; have one's cup of woe run over.

(see *defeated, give up, yield, despair, surrender*)

OVERSTAY

sit eggs; the best fish smell when they are three days old; wear out one's welcome.

(see *tedious, unlimited, unnecessary, bore, unpopular, untimely*)

P

PACIFY

throw a sop to; set the mind at rest; pour oil on troubled waters; bury the hatchet; patch up a quarrel.

(see *peace, harmony, calm, soothe, tranquil*)

PAIN (to suffer)

feel a long tongue of living fire; roll in agony; gnash the teeth in pain; be torn with pain; be knotted with cramps; feel the head split; fester with pain; be ground down by grating pain; suffer more than flesh and blood can bear; be corroded by gnawing pain; feel pins and needles inside one; be on the rack; sit on thorns; drain the cup of misery to the dregs; writhe the lips in agony; whirl in a storm of suffering; be stabbed by aches; have a bad time of it; fall on evil days; labor under afflictions; bear a cross; sink between hawk and buzzard; tear away one's bandages in pain; be pierced by a javelin of pain; be burned by a biting little spark of pain.

(see *troubled, sick, distressed, suffer, hurt, torment*)

PAIR

mate; twin; brace; twain.

(see *together*)

PALE (to become)

become a death's-head on a mopstick; look pulled down by pallor; become white about the gills; have the color drained out of one's face; look bleached out; be painted with milky light; have the pallor of a magnolia blossom; have bloodless cheeks; be silvery-skinned; sicken with white.

(see *sick*)

PARASITE

leech; sponge; bloodsucker; toad-eater; hanger-on; pick-thank; satellite; flunky; trencher-friend; tuft-hunter; carpet knight; lap-dog; smell-feast.

(see *servile, fawn, flatter, submissive, sponge*)

PARK (n.)

a little island of soil in the midst of the asphalt.

(see *grass, flower, landscape, woodland*)

PARTICIPATE

have a finger in the pie; have a hand in; come in for a share; act a part in; taste a dish for several; have a voice in.

(see *share, cooperate*)

PARTICLE

piece; parcel; slice; chunk; fragment; thread; strand; corner; warp and woof; drop in the bucket; cog; niche; patch; streak; grain; scrap; atom; corpuscle; molecule; granule; mote; shred; crumb; spark; ion; driblet; iota; tittle; speck; glimmer; electron; scintilla.

(see *small amount*)

PARTY (social)

the feast of reason and the flow of soul (Pope); Tuesdays at home; snug carousal; soirée.

(see *sociable, pleasure-seeking*)

PASS (v.)

stream past; whirl by; shoot past; ripple by; roll away; zip by; swim by; course through; flash by; stagger by;

dart past; drift by; fly past; shoot ahead of; breeze by; sweep by; flit by; slip ahead; float past; sail by; blow over; run out, drag away, wear away (of time); ooze by.

(see *move, proceed, travel, disappear, vanish*)

PASSIONATE (to be)
be at white heat; have a flame in one's gaze; undress with a glance; feel one's nerves tingle and one's body burn; burn with desire; rise to fever heat; flame with desire; be enlaced with the ardor of passion; feel fever burn in one's blood; have a sultry eye; feel fire in one's pulse; have a hammering heart; be devoured by desire; feel set afire; feel rivers of fire course through one's body; be consumed by ardor; feel one's blood quicken; be stung by passion; be ablaze with desire; feel volcanic fires burn within one; be hungry for someone; feel vague stirrings of desire; be breathless with passion.

(see *love, embrace, kiss, desire, sexual, sensual*)

PASSIVE
hanging fire; smoldering; stagnating; dead.

(see *quiet, unresponsive, submissive, patient, endure, unfeeling*)

PAST
over the dam; in the abyss of things gone; gone with the wind; woven in the tapestry of time past; among the dead days of long ago; water under the bridge; with the snows of yesteryear; a row of half-dead seeds, some of which may be revived; on forgotten shores; among the dusty tombstones of dead years.

(see *end, finish, obsolete, yesterday, history, long ago*)

PATIENT (adj.)
armed with patience; knowing that Rome was not built in a day.

(see *submissive, endure, persevere*)

PATRIARCH ,
a battle-scarred stallion who disposed of disputants; an old bull-moose who brooked no interference; a herd-protecting old buck; an old seal with tusks.

(see *old, old man*)

PATRIOTIC (to be)
be married to one's country; burn with an intense nationalistic flame; heed the call to arms; be a flag-waver; follow the flag; seal one's loyalty with blood; go down wrapped in the flag.

(see *citizen, soldiery, war*)

PATTERN (n.)
checkerboard; mosaic; tapestry; warp and woof; tracery.

(see *outline, shape, model, sample*)

PAUSE (v.)
rise from one's loom; bring the eyes to rest; take a breathing spell; arrest oneself; feel the wing of silence sweep down; hold one's breath for a moment; make a cavity in time.

(see *stop, delay, rest, wait, interrupt, hesitate*)

PAY (money)
shell out; come across; pay sauce for all; dig down in one's jeans; pony up for; cough up; ante for; lay one's money on the line; untie the purse strings; foot the bill; fork over; plunk down; pay one's footing; square up; pay on the nail; bring one's wallet out of hiding; wipe off a score; come down with the dust; put one's hand in the pocket; clear oneself of en-

cumbrance; pay the piper; sing for one's supper.

(see *money, spend*)

PEACE (to have)
put up the sword; beat swords into ploughshares; bury the hatchet; hold out the olive branch; lay down arms; smoke the calumet; close the temple of Janus; sheathe the sword; cause the lion to lie down with the lamb; send forth the white-winged dove of peace; progress down the thorny path of peace; see the storm blow over; heal the breach; row in still water; knit bonds of harmony; live in unruffled times; stray in the calm meadows of peace.

(see *pacify, harmony, calm, soothe, tranquil*)

PENALTY (to pay the)
sow the wind and reap the whirlwind; pronounce a curse that comes home to roost; pay the piper; be given a bitter pill to swallow; sing for one's supper; have the devil to pay; pay the price for a thing; be forced to pay a pound of one's flesh.

(see *punish, retribution, remorseful, compensate*)

PENETRATE
filter in; seep into; pierce; thrust tentacles into; trickle through; probe to the roots of; spread creeping fingers into; see through a millstone; see far into a brick wall; have a worm's-eye view; cut one's way through; worm one's way; pour into; thread one's way into; weave through the fabric of; read to the bottom of a soul; shoot through; sweep over; tear the fog away from the secrets behind it; make an incision in; grow into; infect; flow through; percolate through; flicker

into; bore into; swim through; creep in.

(see *enter*)

PEOPLE
jumping jacks; cattle; vermin; web of human existence; automatons; the porcelain-clay of humanity; the human family; lions; stream of humanity; fish in an aquarium (when seen through a window); small fry; big fish; rank-and-file; pieces of human furniture; human ant-heaps; branches on the tree of humanity; melting pot.

(see *human, man, common people*)

PERCEIVE
see through a millstone; pierce the changes wrought by years; see through the dust; have knife-like eyes; turn a mental flashlight on; have a trained eye; train mental antennae on; read between the lines.

(see *see, discern, understand, discover, notice, detect, observant*)

PERFECT (adj.)
twenty-four carat gold; sterling silver; utopian; untarnished; right man in the right place; wearing a halo; apple-pie order.

(see *complete, whole, excellent, ideal*)

PERMANENT
evergreen; rock-principled; cut in marble; deep-rooted; standing dish; for good and all.

(see *endure, lasting, continue, steadfast, unchangeable, immovable*)

PERPLEXED (to be)
knit one's brow over; look blank; be over a barrel; hover in a bit of a fog; be in the dark; have a ticklish card to play; be thrown off balance; find oneself at sea; be out on a limb; be left

hanging in the air; get caught in a web; find oneself in a maze or labyrinth; be forced to choose between the horns of a dilemma.

(see *puzzled, uncertain, undecided, confuse, difficulty, troubled, complication*)

PERSECUTED (to be)

get pushed to the wall; be hounded from pillar to post; be bound to the rack; get kicked around; be trodden under foot; have the bloodhounds loosed on oneself; be confined within a ring-fence; pass through the mill; be compelled to run the gauntlet.

(see *hardship, distressed, worry, oppress*)

PERSEVERE

cling to a belief; leave no stone unturned; stick to one's guns; keep a stiff upper lip; pick the flint; keep one's nose to the grindstone; maintain one's ground; have bulldog tenacity; stick to one's text; stem the current or tide; weather the storm; be in at the death; fight to the last ditch; keep one's head above water; nail one's colors to the mast; go on to the last drop; plod along in determination; stand one's ground; go through fire and water for; grapple with an affair; struggle through flames toward a goal; have a resolve remain hot in one's mouth; never say die; hug a purpose; stick a thing out; press toward an end; pound away at a thing; keep feeding the flame; ride a hobby; have iron tenacity; work around the clock for; harp on the same string; shove a thing through; drive a bargain; hammer away at; have sleepless energy; be chronic about; continue in spite of one's teeth; see a thing through; keep to one's course; move heaven and

earth; stand firm.

(see *lasting, endure, steadfast, firm, continue, uncompromising, resolute*)

PERSPIRE

shake a gallon of sweat; wear beads of perspiration; flow with sweat; have sweat trickling from one; mop one's brow; exude liquid; pour forth salt droplets; let loose a monsoon.

(see *hot weather*)

PERVERT (v.)

warp; prove that black is white and white is black; torture an argument; twist; stand a thing on its head; shipwreck an endeavor.

(see *mislead, change, spoil*)

PESSIMISTIC (to be)

forecast the future in gray; see black spots on the horizon; wear dark-colored glasses; view a thing through a bit of black glass; be a prophet of doom; take a sour view of a thing; be a croaking owl.

(see *despair, depressed, melancholy, hopeless*)

PIANO PLAYING

digital gymnastics; caressing a piano; piano-pounding; skipping along a keyboard; journeying over keys; rattling the ivories; waking the strings; riding an avalanche down the keyboard; dancing among the black keys; fingering the keys; strumming on the strings.

(see *music*)

PIONEER (v.)

act the apostle; carry the flag; blaze the trail; open a new vista; crusade; launch; show the path; pave the road; cut the underbrush.

(see *show, first*)

PITY (v.)

have one's heart torn in two; feel pulls upon the heartstrings; have one's heart touched; make one's heart bleed for; wipe the tears; be a magnet of sympathy; melt; offer food for sympathy; eye with pity; touch the soul; be soft-hearted; wring the heart; feel one's heart squeezed; keep the heart open to sympathy; enter into the feelings of; thaw; pluck at the heart; share another's misery; have one's heart go out to; open the bowels of compassion; salve another's feelings.

(see *sympathetic, feeling*)

PLACE (n.)

perch; stronghold; niche; arena; theater; hole; courtyard; scene; station; post; sphere; seat; fortress; berth; billet.

(see *situated, locate*)

PLAN (v.)

draw a blueprint for; frame an idea; hatch a plot; cut a pattern; map out an idea; manufacture an intention; cut out work for; tailor a measure; hold a council of war; shoot for a goal; cook up an idea; put on the carpet; mark out a course; set one's wits to work; concoct a scheme; set one's sights for a thing; build the castle of one's future; lay out the gardens of one's future; hammer out a plan; chart a course; set a thing afoot; count one's chickens; tinker with a program; revolve a scheme; be the architect of a project; sketch out a plan; plot a possibility.

(see *scheme, arrange, plot, prepare, invent*)

PLAYFUL (to be)

act kittenish; fiddle with; toy with; juggle; loop the loop.

(see *humorous, lively, gay*)

PLEASANT

sun-drenched; sugar-coated; warming; glowing; smiling; sweet; delicious; tasty; taking one's fancy; soul-gladdening; finding favor in one's eyes; heart-warming; mouth-watering; laying unction to one's soul; hitting one's fancy; meeting one's wishes; warming the cockles of one's heart; tickling one's fancy.

(see *delight, enjoy, sparkling*)

PLEASED (to be)

smack the lips; lick the chops; be ready to burst; be tickled; hold one's sides in laughter; emit a peal of laughter; sing a paean of joy; have one's face light up; feel one's blood run riot in the veins; be in clover; luxuriate in; relish; enter into the spirit of; tread on enchanted ground; walk on clouds; have one's eyes dance.

(see *enjoy, relish, joyful, happy*)

PLEASURE-SEEKING

go on a round of pleasures; make a holiday of; have a fling; go on one continuous joy-ride; have a whale of a time; seek the manna in the wilderness; live high days; burn the candle at both ends; play at high jinks.

(see *self-indulgence, revelry, drunk, spree, holiday*)

PLOT (v.)

lay heads together; dig a mine; go into a huddle; do dirty work at the crossroads; spin a web; lay a snare; unloose the foxes of the mind; attempt a frame-up; lie in ambush; hatch a plot; form a combination against; be bent on evil designs; lay a net.

(see *scheme, arrange, plan, strategy, invent*)

POETIC (to be)

jingle a few silver coins in the ragged garment of life; be a wild-winged bird pouring down one's music on others; traffic with the Muse; be intoxicated with the waters of the Castalian spring; be touched by Apollo; ride Pegasus through the skies.

(see *imagine, singing, romantic, visionary*)

POINT (n.)

arrow-tip; notch; finger; tongue (of land).

(see *place, situated, locate*)

POLICEMAN

an arm of the law; copper; bull; flat-foot; watch-dog; peeler; bobby; man-hunter.

(see *law, detect*)

POLITE (to be)

be the very pink of politeness; cultivate the amenities and civilities; shun to break the bounds of courtesy; observe the proprieties; maintain a velvety mien; never lay aside the polished armor of imperturbable courtesy.

(see *elegant, refined, suave*)

POLITICS

turbulent excursions into political fields; political medicine; erupting political volcanoes; party house-cleaning; political heat turned on; political grapevine; shifting of political winds; party machines; cesspool of politics; playing pork-barrel politics; political puppets; an island of plums entirely surrounded by politicians.

(see *citizen, official, campaign*)

PONDER (v.)

range one's thoughts; smoke some pipes on a matter; turn ideas over in one's mind; toy with the possibility of a thing; weigh in the scales; play with a supposition; entertain an idea; juggle a thing in one's head.

(see *meditate, think, consider, study*)

POOR (in quality)

garden-variety; kitchen-pot; sterile; faded; barren, lamedog; anemic; flat; stale; killing; ailing; grease-paint and gauze; narrow; over-worked.

(see *mediocre, ordinary, inferior, inadequate, shabby, deficient*)

POPULARITY (to enjoy)

be on the beam with the public; ride a wave or crest of popularity; enjoy top billing; have a place in the sun; have a path beaten to one's door; score a bull's-eye of success; ring the bell; have one's favor courted; have a niche in the Hall of Fame; be a reigning toast; sweep the country before one; have the pendulum of public opinion swing toward one; be the brightest star in heaven; be quite the vogue.

(see *fame, reputation, favorite, celebrity, prominent*)

POSSESS

get between one's finger and thumb; get into one's hand; have on one's hands; pocket a thing; make stick to one's fingers; hang up one's hat (*i.e.,* take possession); take a grip on; have an air of legal possession.

(see *have, hold, keep, control, seize*)

POSSIBILITY

on the cards; on the dice; run a good chance; the toss of chance; a ray of hope; the spectre of a chance; have a leg to stand on; potential in the germ; ten to one.

(see *chance, risk, fate*)

POSTPONE

wrap up in camphor; table a matter; sleep on a question; lay a thing on the shelf; put something on ice; pigeon-hole a plan; stave a thing off; play a delaying game.

(see *delay, retard*)

POVERTY-STRICKEN

down and out; down at the heels; seedy; stripped; unable to keep the wolf from the door; unable to make both ends meet; reduced to painful poverty; live from hand to mouth; go down in the world; go to the dogs; broke; have seen better days; drained of resources; slender living; shabby; out at the elbows; ill-nourished; re-duced to one's bedroom slippers; frayed at the edges; live in lean; come upon the parish; be on the county; not a shot in the locker; cooped in stinking poverty; grub along; be on one's uppers; out of pocket; dollar-hungry; born with a wooden ladle in one's mouth; embarrassed for money; smell the ground; live in rags; down on one's luck; not have a leg to stand on; threadbare; drag or eke out an existence; stony-broke; without a dime; crippled flat; walk in broken boots; have a beggarly account of empty boxes; be on the downhill side of life; eat the bitter bread of exist-ence; sink into the mire of poverty; be struck in the cash box; feel the pinch of need; live on crusts; gnaw one's finger-nails; be not worth a sou; fall on lean days; belong to the very thin of purse; have slender means; have one's money at low tide; without a bean in the world; fall to the bot-tom of the ladder; have a light or barren purse; have an empty cup-board; be thrown into the bowl with greased sides; live with the tenement rats; poorer than Job's turkey; fall off one's hobby-horse; go over the hills to the poor-house; have the black cloud of poverty hang over one's house; stir around ashes; be luxury-starved; have a kitchen horizon; live on bread and water.

(see *need, necessity, difficulties, hard-ship, shabby*)

POWER (to have)

wield the lightning; hold the trump card; have the whip-hand; keep one's claws sharp; pull out all the stops; make one's talons felt; keep a club in one's hands; keep one's teeth sharp; have the law in one's own hands; wield the sword of judgment; turn with iron hand the great wheels of Fate; grasp the rod of empire; hold the baton; keep the sceptre; have a free hand; make a thing a matter of trousers (masculine preeminence); have the last word; get footing on solid ground; wield a policeman's club; wave the wand of power; pull the leading strings; breathe empire; send Jovian thunder rolling; detonate dynamite; be a lion; have a long arm; be firmly seated in power; whip crea-tion; have indestructible roots; be mighty in Gath; shake the pillars of the temple; be a tower of strength; be host in oneself; be a dynamo in breeches; be a whole row of steam-hammers; be a pillar of society; rain one's influence; have the force of a pile-driver; unleash the hurricane; bring Atlas to his knees; wear the crown; sit firmly on the throne.

(see *force, direct, dominate, influence, strong*)

POWERLESS

have one's hands tied; have not a leg to stand on; be laid on one's back; be a bit of waste paper; suffer paralysis; be a sailing ship before a typhoon; drift rudderless; be water-logged; get laid on the shelf.

(see *weak, helpless, vulnerable*)

PRACTICAL (to be)

follow a rule of thumb; have horse sense; be a monument of common sense; be down-to-earth; have a hard head.

(see *experienced, skilful, ability, un-imaginative, realistic*)

PRAISE (v.)

take off one's hat to; have a good word for; hail with satisfaction; speak well for; put a feather in another's cap; chant the praises of; cheer to the echo; clap on the back; extol to the skies; shed approval upon; pour forth the praises of; sing a hymn to; sing loud hosannas to; rave on about; go into rhapsodies over; give a pat on the back; feed the milk of adulation to; oil another's ego; pour praises at the feet of; give a good account of an-other; give a well-turned compliment to; pay tribute to; give the palm to; cry up another's virtues; adore with hymns; indulge in hero-worship of an-other; give a golden opinion of an-other; whitewash another's defects; do homage to.

(see *approve, applaud, glorify, wor-ship, fame, celebrity, renown*)

PRAY

batter the gates of heaven; slap the carpet; call down a blessing from; tell the beads; take a matter to God; drop to one's knees; sit on one's knees; seek the throne of grace; accost the Supreme Being; approach the Mercy Seat.

(see *implore, request, ask, solicit, re-ligious*)

PREACH (v.)

harp on the fiddle strings of one's be-liefs; spread the gospel; pontificate; preach sulphur and brimstone; trum-pet against; peddle platitudes; hand on the torch; press urgently for; ser-monize over; speak *ex cathedra*.

(see *teach, urge, propagandize*)

PRECARIOUS

walk on eggs; hang by a thread; be on the spot; walk on knives; live from hand to mouth.

(see *risk, danger, chance, uncertain, unsettled, doubtful, insecure*)

PRECEDE

spearhead; take rank of; go in the van; usher in; herald; head; lead the dance; steal a march; lead the way; foreshadow.

(see *leader, introduce, guide, antici-pate*)

PREDESTINED (to be)

have one's life float in the ether of "what must come, will"; have one's name irrevocably written in the book of fate; have one's pattern cut out for him; have one's fate pigeonholed in the desk of Life.

(see *fate, doom, necessity, inevitable, unchangeable*)

PREDICAMENT (to be in a)

have a pretty kettle of fish; be driven from pillar to post; have the devil to pay; be in the fork of a cleft stick; ride the horns of a dilemma; flounder between Scylla and Charybdis; get oneself into a blind alley; be in a fix; be on the spot; be betwixt the devil and the deep blue sea; have to choose between the frying pan and the fire; be in the same boat with an unfor-tunate.

(see *danger, impasse, emergency, in-volved, undecided, problem, puzzled*)

PREDICTION

the handwriting on the wall; the voice of destiny; the shadow of the future; foregleams and foreshadows of things to come; the prophet business; the scent of the future; showing the way the gods are pointing; a message tapped from the future; reading the cards; watching the birds; showing what is in the cards; removing the cast from the mold of fate.

(see *prophesy, foresee, premonition, ominous*)

PREFERENCE

a leaning to one side; one's "dish"; a singling out.

(see *choose, select, choice*)

PREJUDICED (to be)

be firmly rooted in one's opinions; view with jaundiced eyes; make fish of one and flesh (or fowl) of another; pack facts in cotton wool; have one's mind poisoned against; be unable to see the forest for the trees; have one's mind grow up crooked; direct a spray of propaganda against; create a social distance between; view through distorting spectacles; be wedded to one's own opinion; have a set of ready-made opinions; weigh a thing heavily in favor of one and against another; be bound by one's own opinions; be cut on the bias; look through colored glasses; be blinded by opinionation; erect a barrier between; be covered by the thick scales of prejudice.

(see *unfair, disadvantageous*)

PREMATURE (to be)

count one's chickens before they are hatched; cross the bridge before we come to it; leave before the final curtain is rung down; run before one is sent; count or reckon without one's host.

(see *untimely, hastily, unprepared, immature*)

PREMEDITATED

with one's eyes open; in cold blood; with the view of; with the cards stacked; cut-and-dried.

(see *plan, plot*)

PREMONITION (to have a)

feel a thing in one's bones; walk on one's own grave; see a foreshadowing of; receive an omen of; beware of the Ides of March.

(see *foresee, ominous, warn, insight*)

PREPARE

gird or brace up one's loins; arm oneself for; steel oneself against; erect the scaffolding; do the spade work; lay the cornerstone; hold a dress rehearsal; set one's house in order; sound A; clear the decks; get to one's legs; smooth or pave the way for; dig the foundations; do the groundwork; take steps toward; beat up for recruits; make all snug; open the door; whet one's scythe; warm up for; mount the podium; shuffle the cards; serve an apprenticeship; get into harness; get the steam up; buckle on one's armor; prime and load the guns; shoulder arms; put the horses to; have a rod in a pickle; provide against a rainy day; feather one's nest; lie in wait for; keep one's powder dry; have a thing cut and dried; get into gear; close one's ranks; smell of the lamp; be in full feather; get out one's best bib and tucker; put on war paint; mount in the saddle; trim one's sails; put up one's "dukes"; prime one's pumps; have a thing made to one's hand; get armed to the teeth; square off for battle; ripen for; gird oneself for the fray; take sword in hand;

mend one's fences; grease the ways for; make a good lather to require only half a shave; count one's cards; speak softly but carry a big stick; put on boots and spurs; soften up the opposition; sound the note of preparation; sow the seed; dress the ground; lick into shape; set the stage for; cook up preparations; lay a stepping-stone; brief one's troops; plow the scene for; forearm oneself; lay down a plan; clear the air for; have all one's eyes about one; put one's weapons to the whetstone; sharpen one's tools; oil the machinery; have an eye on the future; draw up a course of action; observe the calm before the storm; watch a thing while it is still in the egg.

(see *ready, provide, orderly, arrange*)

PRESERVE (v.)

keep to one's course; die in harness; maintain one's ground; be game to the last; die at one's post; persist through evil report and good report; keep body and soul together; continue through thick and thin; go through fire and water; sink or swim; at any price; in sickness and in health; keep one's head above water; tide over; save one's bacon; ride out the storm; possess nine lives; weather the storm; find a hole to creep out of; bear a charmed life; come through with a whole skin; light upon one's feet; slip through the hands; slip the collar; close shave; hairbreadth escape; without a scratch; stolen away; embalm; freeze up; put on ice; hold things together; keep one's countenance; leave a fly in amber.

(see *keep, protect, defend, rescue, secure, safe*)

PRESSURE (to exert)

high-powered tactics; strain; drain; running a thing fast and hard; burrowing into; turning the screw; put-ting the squeeze on; thumb-screwing; putting a great concrete weight upon; putting the screws on; steamrollering; driving into a corner.

(see *force, urge, insistent, hurry, strict*)

PRESUMPTUOUS (to be)

tempt Providence; fly in the face of Fate; teach one's grandmother to suck eggs; show cheek; have brass; count one's chickens before they are hatched; have the face to.

(see *rash, overambitious, confident, foolish, bold, uninhibited, unrestrained*)

PRETEND

sail under false colors; wear a mask; live in a gingerbread house; be a stuffed doll; live in a strange never-never land; mince the truth; make a parade of; act a part; keep up a bluff; play possum; hide one's head in the sand; be an ostrich; play at a thing; juggle with words; dress the part; play-act; sham Abraham; keep gloves on; window-dress reality; cloak the truth; put on a false face; mask in another's robes; find Dutch courage; whistle in the dark; have a bark worse than one's bite; shadow-box with reality; be all tinsel; keep behind a false facade; put a smiling face upon.

(see *sham, lie, imposture*)

PRETENTIOUS (to be)

blow one's own trumpet; make a splash; cut a figure; make a dash; clean the outside of the platter; assume a hyphenated name; put on airs; clothe one's voice in a silken envelope; be high-flown; wear a stuffed shirt.

(see *boast, exaggerate, conspicuous, show off, self-love, self-praise, ostentatious, conceited*)

PREVENT

cut the bridge; take up a loose thread;

stop up a hole; choke off; chain with impediment; keep the lid on; keep at bay; head off; stave off; shut out; vaccinate against; raise a barrier against; bind in iron chains; stay a hand; save the necessity; stem the tide; block the way; halt progress; knock on wood; fight a rear-guard action; wave a veto arm; outlaw; clip the wings of; dash the cup from one's lips; turn a flaming sword against.

(see *interfere, obstruct, hinder, stop, restrain, thwart, interrupt*)

PRIME (of life)

in one's hey-day; in the spring of one's years; in the bloom of life; in flaming youth; in the June of life.

(see *healthy, maximum, middle-age, mature*)

PRINCIPLE

chief plank in one's platform; keynote; keystone; fountain-head; main-spring; groundwork; substratum.

(see *source, cause, basis, fundamental, virtuous, righteous, honest*)

PRINK (v.)

set a patch at the corner of Helen of Troy's eyes; wake the Sleeping Beauty with a lipstick; gild the lily.

(see *decorate, fastidious, fashionable, ostentatious, beautify, embellish*)

PRINTING

spinning out an edition; emerging from the press; splashing opinions across a page; setting down in black and white; spreading across news pages; blooming front pages; news breaking on page one; a smear of printer's ink.

(see *publish, editor, news, reporter*)

PRISONER

ticket-of-leave man; member of a chain-gang; jail-bird; one under lock and key; one bound seemingly in iron chains.

(see *imprison*)

PRIVACY

locked-door session; behind closed doors; off-stage; cloistered; the world forgetting, by the world forgot (Pope).

(see *secret, conceal, seclusion, solitary, reticent, retire*)

PRIZE

fat plum; quarry; stake; the milk in the coconut; meed; laurel; palm; cup; trophy; medal; bays; chaplet; garland.

(see *reward, gain, advantage*)

PRIZE-FIGHTER

leather slapper; braggart of the squared circle; gladiator; cauliflower ears; haymaker.

(see *fight*)

PROBLEM

a hard nut to crack; a fearful knot; a horny dilemma; pretty kettle of fish; grasping the nettle; question mark; a headache; sick old lady; a hurdle to clear; hard sledding; a bone of contention; a puzzle; a jigsaw; one's funeral; an ill; scaling the next range; a labyrinth; holding a hot potato; a mental foxhole.

(see *puzzled, solution, uncertain*)

PROCEED

wind one's way; jog along; swirl and eddy through; flow; dart on; thread a labyrinth; establish a bridgehead; defy the winds; wag along; follow in the footsteps of; sweep on; flicker along; crawl on; pour into; fire ahead; go

full steam ahead; follow a pattern.
(see *continue, move, progress, conduct*)

PROCLAIM

hang out a banner; blow the trumpet; sound the fanfare; broadcast; blaze abroad; noise abroad; publish; scream in headlines; thunder from the house tops.
(see *declare, publish, advertise*)

PRODUCE (v.)

give birth to; generate; beget; procreate; hatch; bring forth; bring into view; give rise to; manufacture; grind one's grist; roll off the assembly line; pour forth a flood of; push out; breed; turn out; graduate; yield fruit; whip up; call up; grind out; rake up; shovel out; throw out; rattle out; breathe; forge.
(see *create, make, originate*)

PROFANITY

a garbage-scow of talk; the talk of a Billingsgate fishwife; strong language; talk to make the air blue with obscenity; a Chinese-cracker string of profanity; raw-boned language; purple with profanity; a volley of oaths; foul-mouthed language; a flow of bitter curses; smoky words.
(see *swear, blasphemous, ungodly*)

PROFIT (to make)

ride the gravy train; make hay; feather one's nest; make a killing; cut a melon; reap the harvest; drive a roaring trade; pocket profits; bring grist to the mill; turn red ink into black; have an interest pay off heavily; find a gold mine; be in velvet; fish well for oneself; keep the pot boiling; turn an honest penny; reap the fruits of; get for one's pains; find all to be fish that come to one's net; find the years

fat for one; skim the cream off; ripen the fruits of enterprise; ride the wind; find to one's account; have the better end of the staff; fill one's pockets; put dollars in one's till; make a corner of; hit stride; get others' scalps; fatten on an investment; make capital out of.
(see *prosperous, advantage, self-gain, successful, lucky, luxury, fortunate, rich*)

PROGRESS (to make)

jump ahead; push one's fortune; edge into the foreground; gain ground; work one's way up; take a long step; make a plunge ahead; shoot ahead; sweep on; plow one's way on; grind on; march on; elbow one's way ahead; make an upswing; dig in; pass a milestone; go up the ladder; blossom out; make headway; carve one's way; stride forward with seven-league boots; be on the right road to; overflow with aggressiveness; make one's way in the world; march with rapid strides; be on the main highway to; be on the wing; be on the forward march; move up a bracket; ride the foam-crested wave of prosperity; establish a beachhead; keep pace with; teach the young idea how to shoot; roll ahead; creep steadily onward; swim ahead; gain a point; thread one's way on; make things hum; keep up-to-the-minute; open the throttle; run steadily on; throw a bridge over a gap; shake off restraining fetters; crusade ahead; live in a go-ahead world.
(see *grow, improve, increase, proceed*)

PROMINENT (to be)

be in the spotlight; be in the public eye; be of the first water; be at the top of the tree; exalt one's horn; leave one's mark; be exalted to the skies; hand one's name down to posterity; blow the trumpet; be crowned with laurel; have a lustre shed on one; play first fiddle; be a star; be a shining light; sit high on a throne of royal state; be a bigwig.

(see *celebrity, conspicuous, popularity, fame, reputation*)

PROMISE (v.)

lead one to expect; commit oneself; give one's hand upon anything; pay lip service to; get another to pin his hopes on one; make one's head answer for; put under hand and seal; bid fair; swear upon a stack of bibles; be big with fate; hold out a dazzling prospect.

(see *agree, bargain, undertake, swear*)

PRONOUNCE

have one's voice slip along vowels in a creamy way; roll sounds over and under one's tongue.

(see *speak, voice, utter, declare*)

PROPAGANDIZE

warm over the old apple-sauce; hand out manufactured opinions; fire psychic artillery; engage in mental mine-sowing; infect with false ideas; poison the climate of opinion; inject into the intelligence a daily dose of poison.

(see *opinion, mislead*)

PROPHESY

pry into the future; open the curtains of the future; gaze into a crystal; be a weathervane; herald the future; interpret the handwriting on the wall; foreshadow the future; unseal fate; write the future in red letters.

(see *prediction, foresee, premonition, ominous*)

PROPOSAL (marital)

popping the question; offering another one's hand and heart; playing the overture to love.

(see *woo*)

PROPRIETY

the ritual of society; the corset of convention; keeping one's foot (Biblical for decorum).

(see *respect, formal*)

PROSPECT (n.)

the silver lining of the clouds (Milton); irons in the fire; fish to fry; axes to grind; a budding.

(see *hope, expect, anticipate, foresee, trust*)

PROSPEROUS (to be)

drop into a good thing; cut a wide circle; be in clover; be on Easy Street; get on in the world; line one's pockets; fill one's coffers; land on one's feet; have one's day; come up in the world; escape from the prison of poverty; fall into luck; get a windfall; feather one's nest; reap a golden harvest; get into black ink; bask in the sunshine; get fat on living; have the Midas touch; ride the crest of the wave; have a bulging bank account; go from rags to riches; fatten on profits; live in palmy days; puff up with well-being; swim with the tide; sail before the wind; run on all fours; bear a charmed life; have a well-larded bank account; work one's way to the top of the ladder; raise one's head high in finances; be on the pig's back; have fertile coffers; be well-to-do; be made of money; roll in riches; keep one's head above water; light on one's legs; live on the fat of the land; drive a roaring trade; have one's ship come in; live in green pastures; blossom with dollars; have icing on one's cake; sweeten one's lemonade; have fat years; have everything in full sail; have sudden wealth float to one; have one's golden age; rain dollars; own the horn of plenty; have a boom; go on a spree of money-making; have lush times; live in fair weather; be out of the woods; have a dollar deluge fall on one; have a landslide business; live in a springtime of prosperity; blow a financial bubble.

(see *profit, rich, wealthy*)

PROSTITUTE (n.)

daughter of joy; merchant of human flesh; loose woman; street-walker; daughter of shame; member of the sorority of corruption; white-faced Camille of the dawn; lady of sin; lady of the road; pavement nymph; denizen of a sink of vice; fallen woman; kept woman; woman of the half-world; lady of easy virtue; scarlet woman.

(see *sexual, sensual, sinful*)

PROTECT

put on the gloves; shepherd; launch oneself in defense of; screen; shield; take under one's wing; harbor; take in tow; cushion; blanket; ring down a curtain of security; cloister; entrench; convoy; throw up earthworks; act the watch-dog; be a guardian angel; be a messiah; provide an umbrella for; throw sheltering arms around; hold the fort; be a hedge; give cover to; grow a shell around; don armor-plate against; mother; provide with weapons against; be a bulwark against; throw a wall around.

(see *defend, watchful, cover, shelter, preserve, secure, safe*)

PROTEST (v.)

raise one's voice against; unchain a torrent; emit a howl of defiance; burst out against; button up one's pockets; thump a bang of remonstrance; sow a revolutionary seed; kick up the dust; kick up one's heels; cry to heaven; yell bloody murder; move a finger against; let out an angry scream.

(see *disagree, criticize, revolt, rebuff, refuse, reject, renounce, repudiate, resent, resist*)

PROUD (to be)

plume oneself; not put one's talent in a napkin; not think small beer of oneself; not hide one's light under a bushel; hold one's head high; keep one's nose in the air; be puffed up; act with a high hand; put oneself on a pedestal; be on one's high horses; stalk about; look one in the face; set one's back up; give oneself airs; look big; be high-blown; button oneself up in pride; wear robes of dignity; hug oneself in the consciousness of security; walk on tight ropes; have pride swell one's bosom; get chesty; consider oneself set apart; be strait-laced; be bloated with ego; burst with pride; be swollen; be flushed with success; ride a tide of glory; be purse-proud and mighty; be "high-hat."

(see *vain, conceited, self-love, egotistic, haughty*)

PROVE

bring home the truth to; cite chapter and verse; bring to a show-down; establish the burden of evidence; get the goods on; insure against; have one dead to rights; stand the test; make air-tight; pursue an objective; try in the furnace; give the acid-test to.

(see *show, verify, test, examine, try*)

PROVIDE

keep the pot boiling; feather a nest; be left to shift for oneself; settle money on; play the role of groceryman for; bring grist to the mill; be the bread-basket for; be the meal-ticket for; pour out help; throw one's protection around; make a life for.

(see *sustenance, earn, supply, support*)

PRUDENT (to be)

cut one's coat according to one's cloth; lay up against a rainy day; keep one's sights on tomorrow; be a long-eyed prophet.

(see *discreet, careful, cautious, watchful, foresee, wise, economize, save*)

PSYCHOANALYSIS

libido strip-tease; pressing into the libido.

(see *analyze, mind, self-analysis*)

PUBLISH (v.)

bring to light; usher into the light of day; chronicle an event; hammer out a bulletin; generate in the catacombs of a publishing company; blazon news about; shout from the housetops; hawk a journal; introduce in public headlines; exhibit in the journalistic arena; throw into limelight; launch a story with fanfare and fusillade; trumpet the news; beat the tom-toms in announcement of; sound the clarions for notice; make an open book of; show in a looking-glass; exhibit in the face of day; introduce in the great artificial universe of books and newspapers; take behind the scenes.

(see *printing, editor, news, reporter, declare, proclaim, divulge, reveal*)

PUNISH

break on the wheel; lace or dust someone's jacket; put to the rack; beat to a jelly; send one to cool his heels; box the ears; make an example of; give a dog a bad name and hang him; make one pay a toll of tears; rub down with an oaken towel; take it out of one's hide; apply the cane to; baste or tickle one's rib-roast; wring one's neck; make one dance upon nothing; give one his gruel; call to account; roast over a fire; give one his medicine; make one's claws felt; teach a lesson to; pitch into; treat to a cat-o-nine tails; apply the birch-rod; grind beneath the iron heel; eat someone up; make sit on a wooden horse; have a rod in pickle for; get in behind; make face the music; put under the lash; give a whipping to; flog the offense out of.

(see *discipline, correct, revengeful*)

PUPPET

straw-man; tool; pawn; manikin; lay-figure; stooge for the big-shots; cat's-paw.

(see *miniature, assistant*)

PUSH (v.)

straight-arm one's way; shoulder or elbow one's way; clap into; wedge one's way between elbows; forge ahead; butt against; jolt in the back; sweep along.

(see *shove, force, pressure, attack*)

PUT (v.)

clap into; couch in; drop into; sandwich between; pour into; herd into; dot about with; plant; glue to; toss into; shed over; pop into; launch into.

(see *locate, settle*)

PUZZLED (to be)

scratch one's head over; be in the dark; be stumped; cudgel one's brains; be at one's wit's end; be in a blind alley; find oneself in deep water; wander around in a maze; be in the labyrinth without a clew; ride the horns of a dilemma; be up a tree; be out on a limb; have one's wits knocked out; ponder over a knotty point; be between the devil and the deep blue sea; straddle two horses; be all at sea.

(see *confused, problem, uncertain, undecided, unsettled, perplexed, intricate*)

Q

QUANTITY (large)

a rain of; bucketfuls of; a thick-set hedge of; a barricade of; a covey of; cascades of; a deluge of; an enormous dose of; a flood of; a trackless wilderness of; a wagonload of.

(see *abundance, large, mass, full of, replete, many*)

QUARREL (v.)

pluck a crow with; make the fur begin to fly; fall foul of; pick up a row; draw the sword against; raise Cain; break a straw with; set together by the ears; have words with; gnaw a bone of contention; go into a dog-fight; flare up; raise a storm of words; get on someone's neck; spit fire at; lead a cat and dog life; be ready to take on the whole world; act the wild boar; be a fire-eater.

(see *argue, argument, squabble, dispute, disagree, discord, differ, contend*)

QUESTION (v.)

pounce on with questions; fire inquiry at; squeeze information out of; suck the brains of; discharge streams of inquiries; probe into the inner recesses of another's mind; bleed with questions; pump a person; sound one out; call one to catechism.

(see *ask, examine, inquisitive*)

QUIBBLE (v.)

break butterflies on wheels; mince matters; split hairs; chop logic; beat the air.

(see *evade, argue, inconsistent*)

QUICKLY

in a brace of shakes; on the run; rapid fire; at the drop of a hat; in a twinkling; in one gulp; on the dot; in the tick of a clock; in hot haste; in the shake of a lamb's tail; in a couple of shakes; at the speed of a thunderbolt; in a flash; before one can say "Jack Robinson"; with the scratch of a pen; before the ink is dry; at one fell swoop; right off the reel; hair-trigger; headlong; in the nick of time; on the wing; sharply; whirlwind; lightning; quicksilver; while the iron is hot; thumbnail; post-haste.

(see *immediately, swift, fast, hastily, speed, soon, hurry*)

QUIET (to be)

hold one's tongue; listen for a pin to drop; not let a word escape one; be becalmed in a trough of silence; let silence fall; have a sleeping tongue; seal the lips; put a bridle on one's tongue; sit in silken silence; have a hush settle down; command calm to reign; fade into silence; stop the wheels of conversation; exist in an icy hush; listen for a feather to drop; have a drowsy tongue; fling into silence; cover oneself with a blanket of silence; allow no ripples in the pool of silence; muffle one's tongue; be filled with hush; let words dry up on one's tongue; let death-like stillness prevail; have a hush hang heavy; catch dying sounds; be under the influence of aphasia; be struck speechless; let the dust of silence settle; put the tongue to rest; have the cat get one's tongue; draw a veil of silence over things; be a little mouse; strangle conversation; thin away sound; simmer in silence.

(see *silent, tranquil, calm, rest*)

QUIT (v.)

throw the cap up; take a holiday;

shut up shop; get out from under; wash one's hands; abdicate; throw up the cards; vacate one's seat; go off the stage; take flight; take wing; give up the ghost; throw in the sponge; throw in the towel; quit the game.

(see *yield, give up, renounce, resign, stop, surrender*)

R

RADICAL

fire-brand; screwball; left-wing; anarchistic rebel against the crime of power; bright pink; red; left-bank; one who swerves or shrinks from conservatism; one who savors of the pan; rabble-rouser.

(see *unrestrained, revolt, agitator, reform*)

RAGE (v.)

turn an apoplectic hue; burn with volcanic fire; feel the blood boiling in one's veins; burst into a flame; show one's teeth; flame with fury; blaze with rage; blast out rage; be in an eruptive mood; fly into a tantrum; be out in full cry; raise Cain; be in a towering passion; gnash one's teeth; foam at the mouth; boil over; reach the boiling point; flash lightning.

(see *angry, storm*)

RAILROAD

an engraved necklace of steel; kilometers of arterial steel.

(see *locomotive*)

RAIN (v.)

come down in bucketfuls; rain cats and dogs; rain pitchforks; come down in sheets; pour with rain; slash the windowpanes with rain; flog the face with rain; weep soddenly from the heavens; stitch long, silent needles of rain; let down a curtain of rain; open the heavens; spring a leak from the sky; rain, whipped by a stinging wind; open the floodgates of heaven; stain with weeping rain; sprinkle; let loose torrents of rain; feel the winds whip a spray of rain; hear the mad patter of rain; beat a tattoo of rain; cover with a veil of rain; melt leaden clouds into rain; make of the streets ambulating meadows of mushrooms; wrap in a shroud of rain and hail; spit rain; swell rivers with rain.

(see *storm, mist, clouds*)

RARITY

a rare bird; one in a thousand; a black swan; missing link; a flying fish; a freak of Nature; few and far between; a blue diamond; once in a blue moon; a centaur; a Chimera; a cockatrice.

(see *unusual, unique, seldom, scarce*)

RASH (to be)

run away with an idea; rush headlong into; rush head foremost; tempt Providence; lean on a broken reed; catch at straws; fly in the face of Fate; leap in the dark; have caution flee; throw caution to the winds; act in a hare-brained way; indulge in fire-eating; be devil-may-care; tumble heels over head; have a hot-head; go break-neck; count chickens before they are hatched; go neck or nothing; be hot-blooded; be quixotic; be madcap; sail without ballast; go out of one's depth; ride at single anchor; buy a pig in a poke; sail too near the wind; carry too much sail; play with fire; fly too near the candle; run pell-mell into danger; play a desperate game; put all one's eggs in one basket; knock one's head against a wall.

(see *reckless, dare, impulse, hastily*)

REACT

feel one's heart leap at; bat an eyelash; feel waves of excitement rise within one; be hit in the face by; feel a wind in the air.

(see *responsive*)

READ

coast through pages; wade through; devour a scrap of print; plow through; stick one's nose into a page; bury one's head in a book; nuzzle one's way through a paper; digest headlines; wallow in books; spell out a page; leaf through; be an armchair traveler; be a slave to books; canter along through pages; haunt literature; expose oneself to a volume; thumb through pages.

(see *study, interpret, understand, discern, learn, scholar*)

READY (to be)

be ripe for; be poised for; have the boards cleared; rap the down beat for; have work cut out for one; be in harness; be on one's guard; have a thing made to one's hand; have the stage set for; have on tap; have on ice; be on the point of; be in line for.

(see *alert, unhesitatingly, smart, prepare*)

REALISTIC (to be)

face facts; be hard-boiled; be cold-blooded; be earthy; keep one's feet on the ground; set a down-to-earth value on things; keep one's face to the world; hold the mirror up to nature; free oneself from fancy; rip out the stitches of fancy; be all flesh and blood; see things in the flesh; burn with the vital spark of life; break down the barriers of fancy; see things in their true colors; come into the daylight; step out of the clouds of romance; swallow the bitter pill of reality; look things in the face; face the raw truths of life; look in the teeth of the facts; come to grips with the truth; be wide-awake to reality; see the light; take the gilt off the gingerbread.

(see *unimaginative, practical*)

REASON (conclude)

add two and two together; chop logic; come to the point; find the milk in the coconut; come to one's senses; feel that a thing stands to reason; have a belief born of logic; look at an issue with one's head.

(see *think, ponder, meditate*)

REBUFF (v.)

keep at arm's length; shut the door in one's face; give a slap in the face; accord a chilling reply; hit in the face; give a kick in the pants; beat back; be deaf to; close one's hand to; not be at home to; not yield an inch; send away with a flea in the ear; send to the right-about; set one's face against; shake one's head; turn a deaf ear to; turn one's back upon; wash one's hands of; bend the brows; put under a cloud; bring to book; call over the coals; cry down; give a rap on the knuckles; give one a lick with the rough side of the tongue.

(see *disapprove, resist, reject, oppose*)

REBUKE (v.)

call down; throw something up to one; cast in the teeth; flail; raise an eyebrow; fling words in one's face; give a spanking to; scorch with a look; give hell to; rip one with words; wither with a glance; give a trimming to; call the kettle black.

(see *disapprove, scold, criticize, blame, reprimand, reproach, reprove*)

RECEIVE

have fall into one's hand; put into one's pocket; drink up; get one's come-uppings; rake in.

(see *get, accept, take*)

RECESS (n.)

secret chamber; nook and cranny; re-

treat; corner; niche; alcove; hollow.
(see *conceal, hide, seclusion*)

RECKLESS (to be)
throw caution to the winds; fling discretion to the four waves; proceed in an unguarded moment; play fast and loose; sail too near the wind; burn the candle at both ends; trust to a broken reed; rush headlong into; fling the helve after the hatchet; put one's hand into the fire; be blind to caution; skate on thin ice; dance on the edge of a precipice; not care which end goes forward; take a leap in the dark; carry too much sail; rush in where angels fear to tread; twist the lion's tail; live on a devil-may-care diet; have a nothing-to-lose attitude; kick one's life about contemptuously; make a blind bargain; be a fire-eater; live in a fool's paradise; gamble with chance; buy a pig in a poke; catch at straws; count one's chickens before they are hatched; go out of one's depth; knock one's head against a wall; play at a desperate game; play with edged tools; play with fire; ride at single anchor; reckon without one's host; swim in troubled waters; sail without ballast; go down a precipice with open eyes.
(see *foolish, rash, impulse, hastily, dare*)

RECONCILE
bridge the gap; heal the breach; pour oil on the troubled waters; patch things up; bury the hatchet; make up with; smoke the peace-pipe; fly the flag of truce; declare an armistice; accept the olive branch; close the temple of Janus; lay down one's arms; put up the sword; shake hands; beat swords into plowshares; sheathe the sword; give absolution.
(see *forgive, pacify, reunion, unite*)

RECONSIDER
appeal from Philip drunk to Philip sober; view in a new light; think better of a matter; put a thing under one's pillow; sleep on a matter; find a new perspective for.
(see *consider, ponder*)

RECORD (v.)
keep tabs on; mark the zigzags in the fever chart of; chalk up; put on paper; hand down to posterity; trace the record of; inscribe in the book of Fate; enter in the album of.
(see *watchful, observant*)

RECOVER
be on the mend; be on the up-grade; rise from one's ashes; be oneself again; take a new or fresh lease on life; pull through; return to health; rise from the grave; raise one's head again; heal ones' wounds; come to oneself; get one's balance again; struggle out of the fiery pit of pain; find oneself; call to one's aid all one's frail physical strength; lick one's wounds; set foot on the road to recovery; reanimate one's bones; put on the new man.
(see *improve, revive, refresh, regenerated*)

RED
rosy-cheeked; wild-rose; rusty-sheened; blossom-blush; flame-like; carnation-hued; damask-rose; ruby-fired; blood-red; brick-colored; carroty; cherry-colored; claret; wine-dark; peach-colored; lobster-red; turkey-cock red; salmon-colored.
(see *blush, ruddy*)

REDEEMED (to be)
wash away one's sins with one's tears; make one's soul; be pulled out of hell by the root; balance one's books with the past; ransom one's soul; find sal-

vation; buy oneself back from the devil; stand in a white sheet.

(see *repent, rescue, safe, converted, regenerated*)

REDUCE (v.)

slice off pieces; take the gilt off the ginger-bread; trim down; cut into; melt down; whittle down; boil down to; streamline; whack with the axe; cut down; make a hole in; cut in half; drain off; hack away at; snip off; narrow down; dwarf; hammer down; file away at; pare down; drag down; put a brake on; knock down; water down; prune off; blunt the edge of; dilute; deplete; wilt; carve off; strip of; cut corners; lop off; tighten the belt; weed out; nip off; hack down; put through a slimming process; hack a chunk off; cut back; slash away at; wring down; taper; shrink; relax holdings; put a crimp in; thin down; knock down; jew down prices; take a slide; get out from under high-cost inventories.

(see *diminish, lessen, decrease, minimize, shorten*)

REFINED

polished; etherealized; caviar to the general; pleasure-distilling; tasteful.

(see *elegant, polite, suave*)

REFLECTION (of light)

mirroring lake; mirrors catching and holding a sight; willows curling their long green hair in water of polished ebony; floor tiles dancing with every swing of light; stars showering dark water with a spray of golden coins; scintillating jewels kissed by innumerable lights; catching the light of a poet's dream; a fierce glowing breath of light; play of sunbeams; swimming glorified in a sea of light; silver light lapping against somber shapes; an arc of light thrown by a lamp; figures routed out of shadow into light.

(see *light*)

REFORM (v.)

turn over a new leaf; suffer a change of heart; change one's tactics; do spiritual house-cleaning; return to the right path; clean up the slate; make an honest person of oneself; chase the devil out of one; become a knight-errant crusader; mend one's ways.

(see *improve, converted, correct, redeemed*)

REFRESH (oneself, to)

tarry in a flourishing oasis; feel the pulses leap a n e w; renew one's strength; infuse new blood into oneself; inhale the witching influence of the air; bask in medicinal sunshine; find a pool into which one's soul may dip its curse; wash away the dust of a journey in wine; feel a tonic in one's blood; raise one's head from a sparkling beaker.

(see *fresh, renew, drink, recover*)

REFUGE (n.)

anchorage; haven; sea-port; asylum; ark; sanctuary; retreat; stronghold; fastness; keep; hearth; nest; sheet-anchor; bosom; port of safety; covert; breakwater; life-boat; *sanctum sanctorum;* shield.

(see *sanctuary, safe, shelter, secure, protect*)

REFUSE (n.)

scum that rises to the surface of a boiling kettle; the lint of living; dregs; lees; rubbish; garbage; sediment; junk; chaff; sweepings; litter; trash; offscouring; offal; slag; leavings; dross; candle ends; cheese parings; fag end; orts; debris; stubble.

(see *useless, riffraff, scrap, remnant, relic*)

REFUSE (v.)

put one's foot down; take exception; roar in protest; turn a thing down; chuck a thing up; turn thumbs down; close the hand; turn a deaf ear to; set one's face against; not hear of; wash one's hands of; be deaf to; stand aloof; turn one's back upon; set aside; cast behind one; not yield an inch; shake one's head; take no hand in; harden one's heart to; balk at; not be at home to.

(see *reject, repudiate, rebuff, repel, renounce*)

REGAIN

recover lost ground.

(see *restitution, recover*)

REGARD (v.)

set eyes on; cast eyes upon; look sweet upon; fix a blaze of feeling on; keep an eye on.

(see *glance at, look at*)

REGARDLESS OF

come thick or thin; come hell or high water; ride rough-shod to.

(see *uncompromising, disregard, reckless, unconcerned*)

REGENERATED (to be)

win a little human islet from the waters of animalism; be put into the crucible; undergo palingenesis; be resuscitated; act the phoenix.

(see *redeemed, reform, renew, recover, revive*)

REGIMENTATION

machine-like order; clock-work precision.

(see *orderly, uniform*)

REGRET (n.)

a penitential procession of bygone petulances; a heart full of tears; a ghost of remorse.

(see *disappointment, self-condemnation, self-reproach*)

REGRET (v.)

pay in disillusion for one's impulses; feel the stings of conscience; eat one's words; cry over spilt milk; have memories that scorch and burn; realize it is too late to lock the stable-door when the steeds are stolen.

(see *repent, remorseful, sorrowful, lament, grieve, mourn*)

REGULATIONS

red-tape.

(see *regimentation, uniform*)

REINFORCE

fortify; fill up the ranks.

(see *support, strengthen*)

REJECT (v.)

push outside the main stream of; slam the door on; freeze out; pack off to the storehouse; toss overboard; push away with one's hands; cast away; turn one's back on; wave aside; send one about one's business; send one off with a flea in his ear; send packing; keep at arm's length; thumb one's nose at; send to the dust bin; chuck into the ashcan; give the basket (reject an offer of marriage); give the mitten instead of the hand (reject a marriage proposal); cast behind one; turn a cold shoulder upon; relegate to the attic; put on the shelf; turn thumbs down on; send down the drain; close the door to; give the brush-off to; throw overboard; cashier; pluck (reject at examinations in English universities); cast to the dogs; fling to the winds; send adrift; send to Coventry; blackball.

(see *discard, excommunicate, refuse, repudiate, repel, rebuff, disapprove, renounce*)

REJOICE (v.)

throw up one's cap; dance in the streets; kill the fatted calf; feel one's heart leap with joy; bless one's stars; clap one's hands; hold jubilee; rub one's hands; give a loose to mirth; cast away care; frisk; gambol about; be merry as a marriage-bell.

(see *joyful, delight, pleased, elated*)

RELATE (connect)

hitch a thing to something else; tie to; gear to; link to.

(see *join, unite*)

RELATE (tell)

spin a long yarn; fight one's battles over again; reel off a string of; dive backward into one's experiences; carry the budget of gossip; spout a tale; rattle off a tale; unreel a story; draw a picture; pour out an opinion; weave a narrative.

(see *story-teller, tell, report, describe*)

RELATIONSHIP (kin)

fruit that dangles on the family tree; one's own flesh and blood; ties of blood; that which is thicker than water (*i.e.,* blood); family-tie; next of kin.

(see *father*)

RELAX (v.)

shut up shop; experience a vacation-effect; soften; unbend; get away from things; break the ice; make oneself at home; loll about; keep one's temperature down; let off steam; feel the heart melt; rest on one's oars; eat of the sweet fruits of leisure; take one's hair

down; throw off strain; let oneself down gradually; fling away restraint; put away one's frets.

(see *leisure, divert, ease, loaf*)

RELEASE (v.)

undam a flood; unstopper; cut oneself adrift; cut a thing loose; give the reins full swing; unlock; blow the lid off; give rein to; snap the binding link; break the connecting chain.

(see *discharge, dismiss, free*)

RELENT

call off the dogs; relax one's iron grasp; give quarter; open the bowels of compassion.

(see *repent, remorseful, soften*)

RELEVANT (to be)

return to one's muttons; get down to brass tacks; get to the point; get to the milk in the coconut; get down to cases.

(see *involved*)

RELIABLE

be on the beam; be as good as one's word; expound an idea that holds water.

(see *dependable*)

RELIC

a broken shell wave-tossed on shore; a mote of dust from a passing breeze; the shadow of a ship that once sailed the seas; a tattered page from a wind-scattered volume; a grain left over from the gleaning; a broken stem, without root or seed; a footprint on the sands of time; a vestige of the past.

(see *remnant, remains, scrap, remembrance*)

RELIEF (n.)
breath of respite; a break; cushion; poultice; balm in Gilead; crumb of comfort; softening; oasis.

(see *sustenance, refresh, remedy, ease*)

RELIEF (to afford)
send in the water-boy; take a load off one's mind; take the weight off one; take off a load of care; cheer the heart; nurse one; remedy a situation; set the heart at rest; lift a weight off one's mind; wipe the tears from one's eyes; give a breathing spell; unburden one's mind; temper the wind to the shorn lamb; smooth the ruffled brow of care; pour oil on troubled waters; pour balm on; ease one's cares; remove the pinch; let off steam; remove an obstacle from the path; iron out rough spots; wear out the heat of the day in the shade; drop a burden from the shoulders; open the pores of the mind; hear a black cloud gather itself and roll away; throw off care; disarm a tension.

(see *help, support, soothe, ease*)

RELIGION
spiritual territory; sanctified odor; ocean of belief; a lamp unto one's feet; the ladder of spiritual promotion; a ticket for one's soul that leads to God; a rash of ritual; the pressure of the ecclesiastical yoke; a citadel of the spirit.

(see *God, worship, minister*)

RELIGIOUS (to be)
live close to God; be God-fearing; understudy an angel; be a Sunday-schooler; rest in the bosom of the church; walk humbly before God; dwell in holiness; stay on the side of the angels; glow with piety; be a leading sheep; be a pillar of the church; take the veil; mingle with the priests; quaff fine spiritual draughts from the reservoir of religion.

(see *saintly, sanctimonious, preach, pray*)

RELISH (food)
smack the lips; lick the chops; tickle the appetite; do justice to a meal.

(see *savor, tasty, food, hungry*)

RELUCTANTLY
in spite of oneself; in spite of one's teeth; with a heavy heart; against the grain; sore against one's will; with an ill-grace; far be it from oneself.

(see *unwilling, hesitate*)

RELY
pin one's faith upon; hang upon the lips of.

(see *trust, depend*)

REMAINS
swine-husks; mutilated fragments; *disjecta membra;* ruins; corpse; ashes; residue; candle ends; cheese-parings; odds and ends; heel-tap.

(see *remnant, scrap, remembrance, relic, refuse*)

REMARKS (conversational)
happy-go-lucky slings and arrows; shots.

(see *story-teller, conversation*)

REMEDY (n.)
cure-all; labeled jar of panacea.

(see *relief, help*)

REMEMBER
have a scene printed on one's memory; pry into the crevices of one's memory; drag out of one's past; hop mentally back to days gone by; thumb through one's yesterdays; nurse a

memory; bend the mind toward a memory; throw a flash-light on the past; bring out of the rich darkness of one's memory; stir to recollection; cast one's memory back to; bring before the mind's eye; have recorded in the heart; rake up memories; have one's memory brace itself to deal with the past; wallow in the past; feel one's ears still echoing with; summon up in the mind; treasure fragments of the past; smell a scent that haunts the air; treasure up in the memory; have a thing fasten itself on the mind; have one's memory haunted by; have stamped on the mind; reflect on the past; embrace an old dream of; bottle up in the memory; engrave in one's memory; have lights and shadows of reviving memory cross one's face; keep in the thoughts; know by heart; keep the wound green; bear in mind; sink into a reverie; travel down through the avenues of time; note things down on the imperishable tablets of one's subconscious; rummage through the past; burn into one's memory; conjure up a host of phantoms in the memory; be stabbed by a sharp recollection; shear away the years with the scissors of the memory; withdraw the veil from the past; wrestle with the phantoms of the past; see the face of the past hanging over one; keep the memory green with tears; show eyes opaque with memories; court the pain of memories; have float in the mind; hear the music of unforgotten years sound again in the soul; store in the memory; have one's thoughts claimed by the past; hear an echo in one's mind; rub up one's memory; preserve a memory in the treasure-chamber of one's mind; traverse the silent halls of memory; carry with one the picture of; send the mind flying back; drift into the past; hear a note that rouses a thousand memories; have the mind wander to; have an old dream that

dies hard; set the strings of the memory to vibrating; redden the lips of an old wound; have the memory quicken dull aches to stinging torture; hang on to a dream; see a succession of ghosts crowd in upon the memory; have some strand in one's fancy caught by a memory; set adrift in one's mind; have an experience forever marked with a white stone; figure back to the past; see in the dark-shadowed mirror of the past; carry one's thoughts back to; unravel tangled recollections; have a memory touch one's heart with a cold finger; set the mind to stalk with the ghosts of the past; dig out a memory that is swathed in gray chiffon; dredge out of the mind; look back upon; dwell in the mind; have something run in one's head; pull memory by the sleeve; have a memory sink deep and imbed itself in the mind; roll time back; untie some knotted memories; search through a tricky memory; cling to the past; have tossed up on the waves of memory; rip up old sores; clear the memory from stain; have pass across the consciousness; hark back to; leap from ancestor to ancestor through the long centuries; have memory be one's winged host; be at the mercy of a softening wave of reminiscence; be brought up with a nostalgic jolt against a childhood fantasy; be caught by a recollection; have flash on the mind; bring the mind back to; hear the babble of dead years; fan the embers of the past; sit in the gray ashes of memory; break the mirror of recollection into splinters; chew the cud of memory; read the mirror-writing of the mind; not be able to get a thing out of one's head; hear ring through one's mind; carry in the thoughts; have a love for another's shadows; soak up in the mental sponge; have flash on the inner eye; follow memory's tricksy finger; forage in the cupboard of memory; count one's keepsakes in the closet of memory; rekindle the ashen past into colors of flame; repass a recognized mental milestone; study the patches on memory's quilt; search for the dreams of one's childhood; relive tales that come floating back in the trailing mists of memory; watch the pageant of the past speed before one's eyes; be assailed by the ghosts of memory; look at the imperishable pictures impressed on one's mind; drift to a familiar harbor on the tides of memory; recapture the experiences of youth; read what is written in indelible ink on the psyche.

(see *remind, reminisce, retrospect*)

REMEMBRANCE

echo; shadow of the past; cloud of images; dried roses of regret; stirring of the sleeping past of life; subterranean channels of the past; vivid tints and clear tones of the past; the moment on which a soul is pinned; tidal wave of remembrance; the shimmering on the expanding rim of memory; the breaking into light of a dim picture of the past; the vibrating chords of remembrance; memory's picture gallery; wandering back through the pages of the past; swimming of the past before one.

(see *relic*)

REMIND

strike a chord of memory; have a familiar flavor; send trailing across one's consciousness; have a thing run in one's brain; touch a sleeping chord; ring a bell in one's mind; have a ripple of memory stirred by; feel a thing burnt on one's brain in letters of fire.

(see *remember, resemble*)

REMINISCE

fight old battles over again; chew the cud of memory; subside into a dream; blow on old ashes; listen to echoes; have one's mind embedded in deposits of the past; be lost in the mists of the past; take a leisurely stroll down memory lane; throw one's mind back across the years; soar on the wings of memory; page through the family album.

(see *remember, retrospect, introspective*)

REMNANT

ghosts of; embers of; trace of; crumbs on the table; last sparks of; last shade of.

(see *relic, remains, refuse*)

REMOLD

put into the crucible.

(see *shape, transform*)

REMORSEFUL (to be)

bite one's tongue; beat the breast; feel a dart of remorse stab through one; sear one's memory; feel a pang twist one's heart; feel a centipede bite at one's heart; feel a sting of conscience.

(see *regret, repent, self-punishment, self-reproach, sorrowful*)

REMOTE

a snow-clad mountain-peak; far as the star from the moth; a far cry from; a star far-off and inaccessible; in another world.

(see *past, history, old, seclusion, isolated*)

REMOVE

wash from; tear from; peel off; make a clean sweep; unload; shake-out; shed; shear of; efface from; divorce from; burn out; blot from; erase; drain; pluck out; grind out; whack off; clip from; knock out; strip; cut off; break off; wipe out; weed out; sponge out; screen out; lift bodily from; wipe off the floor; unlace from.

(see *transfer, withdraw, suppress, separate, dismiss, expel, move*)

RENEW

fan into fresh flames; pump new blood into; awaken; freshen; reknit the thread of; fire anew; resurrect; spruce up; polish up; raise from hell to heaven; cause to put out a bright green leaf; cause the dry bones to stir; give a face-lifting to; shake the dust from.

(see *redeemed, reform, regenerated, repair, refresh, revive*)

RENOUNCE

wash one's hands of; go back on one's word; bid a long farewell to; turn Turk; backtrack; shake one's head; fling to the winds.

(see *reject, repudiate, disinherit, abandon, resign, surrender, desert*)

RENOWN (to give — to)

put a thing on the map; engrave a name upon the walls of time.

(see *reputation, fame, celebrity*)

REORGANIZE

re-form the ranks of; clean house; pick up the threads of; churn up thoroughly.

(see *organize, remold*)

REPAIR

keep the corners up; patch up; stop a gap; face-lift; plaster up; sew up the seams.

(see *renew, correct*)

REPAY

set one his supper; pay one's shot; give measure for measure.

(see *restitution, return, compensate, reward, retaliate*)

REPEAT

drum in the ear; ring the changes; echo; parrot; traverse beaten ground: go over the same ground; go the same round; do till one is black in the face; retrace one's steps; harp on the same string; din in the ear; backtrack; cut and come again; run mechanically off the tongue; retell a twice-told tale; grind on the same groove.

(see *relate, echo*)

REPEL

hold at bay; keep at arm's length; slam the door in one's face; go against the grain.

(see *oppose, resist, rebuff, reject, refuse, disgust*)

REPENT

turn over a new leaf; put on the new man; take to sackcloth and ashes; set one's house in order; return to the fold; stand in a white sheet; wipe off one's score; eat humble pie; knit the lips in a grimace of regret; salve the conscience; wade through lakes of repentance.

(see *remorseful, sorrowful, regret*)

REPERTORY

bag of tricks.

(see *store, reserve*)

REPLACE

stand in the shoes of; fill the shoes of.

(see *substitute*)

REPLETE

full to the brim; overflowing; packed; trimmed to the eyes.

(see *full of, abundance, sated*)

REPORT (v.)

herald; trumpet; sound the news.

(see *tell, describe, declare, publish, record*)

REPORTER (newspaper)

member of the fourth estate; ink-slinger; newspaper scribe; one of the writing fraternity; knight of the quill; pad and pencil boy; sob sister.

(see *write, publish, story-teller*)

REPRESENT

walk in the shoes of; stand in the stead of; be the mouth-piece for; hold the mirror up to.

(see *act, describe, show*)

REPRESS

drive underground; trample down; damp the flush of; chain up; bottle up; strangle.

(see *suppress, subdue, silent, overcome, control restrain*)

REPRIMAND

call on the carpet; call to task; give a spanking to; tread on another's tail; boil in oil; tell one off; rake over the coals; give one Hail Columbia; give a piece of one's mind to; shoot at sunrise; read one a chapter; teach one a lesson; give a tongue-lashing to; give a black look to; deliver a curtain lecture; give a dressing down; rap on the knuckles; trim down; bark at; put under a cloud; bring a hornet's nest about one's ears; bring to book; bring under the ferule; frown down; give one a lick with the rough side of the tongue; snap at; load with reproaches; make a wry mouth at; pick a hole in one's coat; pluck a crow with; raise one's voice against; shake the head at.

(see *reprove, rebuke, censorship, criticize, reproach, blame*)

REPRISAL

a game at which two can play; a Roland for an Oliver; tit for tat; blow for blow; counterstroke; diamond cut diamond; give and take; measure for measure; the biter bit; paying in the same coin.

(see *retaliate*)

REPROACH (v.)

hold up to shame; crush beneath a weight of odium; cast in one's teeth; put in the pan; lay one out; send away with a flea in one's ear; frame a bitter reproach on one's lips; glare at.

(see *reprove, rebuke, blame, reprimand, defame, condemn, accuse, disparage*)

REPROVE

give a rap on the knuckles; put down a peg; read the riot act; give a piece of one's mind to.

(see *criticize, blame, condemn, reprimand, scold, rebuke*)

REPUDIATE

wash one's hands of.

(see *discard, reject, renounce, divorce*)

REPULSE

send away with a flea in the ear; send to the right about; close the door against; cause to lose ground.

(see *repel, refuse, reject*)

REPULSIVE

slimy; terrible as a plucked hen on a butcher's block.

(see *ugly, disfigured, revulsion*)

REPUTATION (to gain a)

have a name to conjure with; acquire blushing honors; move in a blaze of glory; win the laurels; be the talk of the town, a man of mark, a great card, a lion, a man of rank, a pillar of society, a master spirit, or a star; occupy the center of the stage; be the pink of fashion; be in one's flower; make a figure; be at the top of the ladder; win a fair name; occupy a niche in the temple of fame; acquire lustre; leave one's footprints on the sands of time; shine forth; wear a public halo; move in high mightiness; have a face to save; be given top billing; have a build-up to maintain.

(see *fame, popularity, celebrity*)

REQUEST (v.)

knock at the door; whistle for; cry to; kneel to; beg hard; offer up prayers; stand cap in hand; beg one's bread; send the hat around; come down on one's marrow bones; throw oneself at the feet of; dance attendance on.

(see *ask, solicit, desire*)

REQUISITE

an admission ticket.

(see *necessity*)

RESCUE (v.)

show the door of escape to; snatch from the jaws of death; help a lame dog over a stile; get the wheel out of the rut; launch the lifeboat; pull out of the fire; lend a helping hand; set on one's legs.

(see *safe, secure, release, preserve*)

RESEARCH (to do)

dig beneath the surface; do spade-work.

(see *study, lore, investigate, analyze, examine*)

RESEMBLE

take on the color of something else; take after; have something of another distilled in oneself; be a chip off the old block.

(see *imitate, copy*)

RESENT

explode; be all fire and fury; look black; have hot blood; speak high words; find a crow to pluck; wave the red flag to the bull; flare up; knit the brow; look daggers; boil with indignation; grind one's teeth; vent one's spleen; lose one's temper; bite one's thumb; champ the bit; stand on one's hind legs; kick up a row; fly off the handle; cut up rough; burst with resentment; raise Cain; take a fling at; stir up bile; fan into a flame; add fuel to the flame; be stung; have one's blood stirred; have one's resentment kindled; have stick in one's gizzard; be put out of humor; put one's monkey up; raise one's gorge; put one's back up; get worked up into a passion; feel one's blood boil; feel one's ears tingle; lash into a fury; storm; feel set by the ears; be thrown into a ferment; find something a sore subject; be in a towering passion; have ill blood for; chafe under a stubborn sore; feel one's heart stiffen against; have a militant spark flash in one's eye; feel rankled inside one; feel a protest creep through one's veins; open the vials of resentment; bring a hornet's nest about one's ears; squirm under the halter; feel slapped in the face by; bristle up; have one's dander raised; take in ill part; be up in arms; be in high dudgeon.

(see *angry, revengeful*)

RESERVE (v.)

keep up one's sleeve; keep a large untapped reservoir; stockpile; have a nest egg; have a backlog; keep a cushion against; keep in a hidden corner; save one's bacon; have to fall back upon.

(see *save, store, provide, cautious, retain, resources*)

RESIDE

pitch one's tent; stay where one's lot is cast; infest; haunt; be a barnacle fastened to a place; perch; roost; bunk.

(see *live, house, home*)

RESIGN (v.)

drop the reins; throw in the towel; bow oneself out; throw up one's hands; throw in the sponge.

(see *give up, yield, surrender, discontinue, quit, abandon, withdraw, retire*)

RESIST (v.)

keep at bay; sell one's life dearly; ride out the storm; hold one's ground; fly in the face of; swim against the tide; take the bit between the teeth; offer heavy opposition; hold out tooth and nail against; balk; claw at; flap the wings of a wild eagle in a cage; hold at arm's length; wrestle with; come to grips with; breast the wave; stand up against; make head against; show a bold front; kick against the pricks; lift the hand against; rise up in arms; draw up a round robin; lock out; bar out; turn out; be allergic to; grow bullet-proof against.

(see *oppose, attack, stop, hinder, rebuff, obstruct, thwart, repulse*)

RESOLUTE (to be)

square the jaw; keep the chin up; harden one's lips; keep a strong hand; be on one's mettle; insist on neck or nothing; hold one's ground; be in a thing heart and soul; screw up one's resolve; show backbone; keep an iron will; set a firm tone; pluck up heart of grace; put a bold face upon; present a bold front; act in bull-dog fashion; kick down the ladder; throw away the scabbard; be game to the backbone; have the courage of the British lion.

(see *determined, firm, steadfast, persevere, rigid, unchangeable*)

RESONANT

a plucked violin string; steps magnified by their echo.

(see *sounds, music*)

RESOUND

fling back echoes; ring the rafters; toll in one's ears; ring in the ears; echo a reflection; shimmeringly chime from a rich life to a long echo; make the roof echo; send an organ roll.

(see *echo, reverberate, noisy, sounds*)

RESOURCEFUL (to be)

bubble with ideas.

(see *smart, self-reliant*)

RESOURCES

cards to play; a shot in the locker; stock in the trade; storehouses; two strings to one's bow.

(see *reserve, money, wealthy*)

RESPECT (to show)

bend the knee; fall down before; kneel to; bow to; prostrate oneself before; kiss the hem of one's garment; stand upon ceremony; look up to; take one's hat off to; kiss the rod; sit at the feet of; worship at someone's altar; regard with an eye of favor.

(see *polite, deference, formal*)

RESPITE (to take)

ride at anchor; repose on laurels; rest on oars; hang fire; mark time; put on brakes.

(see *delay, pause, rest, postpone, refresh, stop*)

RESPONSIBILITY (to take)

take the laboring oar; take on one's own shoulders; allow oneself to be saddled with; allow a thing to be fathered upon oneself; have one's shoulders sag under obligations; take on shackles; have laid at one's door; pay the piper; bear the burden; have the responsibility on one's own head.

(see *obligated, reliable*)

RESPONSIVE (to be)

mirror; be a clear pool reflecting every change in a shifting sky.

(see *sensitive, sympathetic, reflection*)

REST (to take)

take a breathing space; take time out; recline on a bed of down; stay one's hand; refresh one's weariness; shut up shop; lie on one's oars.

(see *respite, refresh, sleep*)

RESTITUTION (to make)

pay the piper; face the music.

(see *repay, penalty, compensate*)

RESTLESS (to be)

be in a state of ferment; be on pins and needles; not be able to keep one's seat; be a surging ocean; toss on one's pillow; paw the earth; champ at the bit.

(see *unsteady, unstable, unsettled, transients, changeable, irresolute, vacillate, wanderer, turbulent*)

RESTRAIN

keep a rein on; hold in leash; stem the stream; nip in the bud; hang on to someone's coattails; draw in one's horns; keep the curb on; pen up; cage and chain; bottle up; keep a lid on; smother; shackle; throw cold water on; keep within compass; act as a drag; put the brakes on; fetter; hamper by chains around the ankles; keep at arm's length; hold in check; stem the torrent; draw up; cramp one's effort; stem the tide; pull the check strings; straitjacket; tie by the leg; lay by the heels; harness; hold to a minimum; hobble; keep within bounds; keep under lock and key; tie one's hands; throttle; tighten up on; keep under hatches; fence in; stay one's hand.

(see *confine, hinder, prevent, stop, restrict*)

RESTRICT

put a damper on; tighten the brake on; slap a curb on; pin down to; bind to an agreement; tie down to; chain; "freeze"; shackle; straitjacket; quarantine; squeeze; pinch; coop up; put a cramp on; peg down; bottle up; hedge about; clamp down on; put a ceiling over; shackle; barricade; hem in by iron walls; put a damper on; spin a cocoon around; tighten the reins; crack down on; keep within iron grooves; take a reef in.

(see *confine, limit, restrain*)

RESULT (to have)

bear fruit; yield return; flower in; have outgrowth; produce harvest; have a backwash to the wave; have a final distillation; produce an off-shoot; have upshot; pan out.

(see *produce, originate*)

RESUME (v.)

take up the thread; catch up the echo; weigh anchor.

(see *continue*)

RETAIN

hang tight to; harbor; cling to; store up; keep footing.

(see *keep, hold, reserve, preserve*)

RETALIATE

have one's inning; get even with; have a Roland for an Oliver; cross fire with; pay in coin; trade blow for blow; demand an eye for an eye; settle old scores; be hoist on one's own petard; throw a stone in one's garden; square the account between; turn the tables on; take out of one's hide; serve the same sauce; serve one out; turn the war back into the enemy's country; play at battledore and shuttlecock; play at puss in the corner; return the compliment; play at a game for two; give measure for measure; scratch back; pay off an old debt; play at a nip-and-tuck proposition; cut diamond with diamond; return the bitter bit.

(see *revengeful, repay, reprisal*)

RETARD (v.)

tie the hands of; pin down; create a bottleneck; cripple; "freeze"; gum up.

(see *delay, slow, obstruct, hinder, postpone*)

RETICENT (to be)

keep one's own counsel; stiffen into silence; wrap oneself in reserve; bottle oneself up; go into a shell; build walls around oneself; creep into a corner; hole up.

(see *silent, secret*)

RETIRE

shrink from the whirl of life; vacate one's seat; take a back seat; save one's wind; slip out of harness; hide oneself in the bosom of one's family; recede into a hole; recede into the shade; go to Coventry; keep good hours; go to bed with the fowls; slip into the backwater of life; rest on one's laurels; put oneself on the shelf; bow out of a picture; cloister oneself; take the veil; put one's hands in one's pockets.

(see *withdraw, discharge, retreat, depart, resign*)

RETORT (v.)

throw back a reply; throw a paper pellet; fire at another; barb a reply; fling back an answer.

(see *speak*)

RETRACE

turn upon one's heel; turn tail; beat a retreat; dance the backstep; retrace one's steps; turn one's back upon; go back on oneself.

(see *retreat, return, review, trace*)

RETRACT

eat one's words; eat the leek; draw in one's horns; take back one's words; drive one's words down one's throat.

(see *renounce*)

RETREAT (v.)

back water; lose ground; put about; fall astern; crawfish; turn tail; take the back track; melt away.

(see *withdraw, retire*)

RETRIBUTION (to suffer)

sow the wind and reap the whirlwind; reap the fruit of one's faults; see the high walls of sin rise about one; be paid out; be engulfed in the pit one has digged.

(see *compensate, reward, retaliate, penalty*)

RETROGRESS (v.)

turn back the clock of progress; get further from one's goal instead of nearer to it; suffer stagnation; decay.

(see *decline, deterioriate, degenerate*)

RETROSPECT (v.)

look back over the years; turn back the clock; review the long vista of life.

(see *reminisce, review*)

RETURN (v.)

come home to roost; wing homeward; darken a door-step again; snap back; bounce back; roll back; hark back; sweep back; stream back; float back; drift back.

(see *retrace, retreat*)

REUNION

love feast.

(see *meeting, unite*)

REVEAL

unfold; let the cat out of the bag; show one's hand; let escape one's lips; have printed on one's face; proclaim from the housetops; lift the mask; raise the curtain; draw aside the veil; pour out; unbosom oneself; drag into the open day; tip the wink; bring to the front; bring to light; open another's eyes; betray the pot to the roses; show one's colors; bring out into strong relief; show the light of heaven to; let ooze out; tear the clothes off; cause the scales to drop from the eyes; drop a hint of; let into a secret; spring a leak; unburden oneself of; tip the hand; hold up to the mirror; throw light on; bring to the surface; lay open; direct a searchlight on; put to the acid test; unfurl the flag; uncork; unseal; bare; strip naked; tell tales out of school; "spill"; turn inside out; break news; blow the gaff; wear one's heart on one's sleeve; show one's hand; let slip from one's lips; cause to break through the clouds; tell a piece of one's mind; make a clean breast; make crop out; let the water out; make flash on another's mind; tear the veil from; reveal the secrets of the prison-house; penetrate the fog; breathe information; cause to peep out; paint in its true colors; nail one's colors to the mast; show one's weak point; make time itself bald; stir the dust from the unknown; burst the bubble; be a telescope to; shoot off a star; mirror; reflect the rays of.

(see *divulge, declare, tell, expose*)

REVELRY

cut-up; human cyclone.

(see *dissipate, drunk*)

REVENGEFUL (to be)

harbor vindictive feelings; be out for blood; demand blood for blood; feel vengeance hot at one's heart; feel a lump of fury rise in one's throat; have accounts to settle; have a crow to pluck; feel screaming for blood; pay off old scores; demand an eye for an eye; keep one's wounds green; settle a score; pay one back in coin; get back at; savor the sweet taste of revenge; call the day of reckoning; clean the slate; give no quarter; have vengeance rankle in one's breast; hug revenge and keep it warm; thirst for revenge; take the law into one's own hands.

(see *malicious, spiteful, resent, retaliate*)

REVERBERATE

hurl back an echo; boomerang from a sounding board; saw sound in the ears.

(see *resound, echo, noisy, sounds*)

REVERE

bow down in the house of Rimmon; make a religion of; enshrine on an altar; make a sacred cow of; lift up one's heart to.

(see *worship*)

REVERSE (n.)

the cart before the horse; the boot on the other leg; somersault; boomerang; flip-flop; turn-about; about-face; turn turtle; turn of the tide; turn of the tables.

(see *undo, change, vicissitudes, misfortune, misfit, setback, roundabout*)

REVIEW (v.)

go over old ground; take stock of; see swift films of old scenes pass before one's eyes.

(see *retrace, reminisce, retrospect, survey*)

REVISE (v.)

lick into shape; overhaul; hash up.

(see *change, correct, review, remold*)

REVIVE (v.)

dust off; lever out of a rut; turn a fresh stream upon; chase away the shadows of the grave; galvanize the corpse; put back into business; make rise from its sepulchre; give a new lease on life; stir the embers; fan the ashes into flame; blow the coals; set on its feet again; exhume; resurrect; rake up the fire; put into the crucible; take out of the dustbin; bring back from the brink of death; keep alive; give a shot in the arm to; cause to spring anew.

(see *refresh, arouse, renew, strengthen, regenerated*)

REVOLT (v.)

rise up in arms; set authority at naught; seethe with mutiny; fan public opinion to a flame; rise up against; spring up in revolt; stage a revolution; raise the red flag; chafe under the hand of authority; raise the banner of revolt; murder the state; raise a rebellious eye; fan revolution's embers; plot a violent upheaval of authority; breathe rebellion; stage a ruthless shake-out; sweep a land with the wind of revolt; raise the fist against; savor the bitter taste of authority in one's mouth; change the face of government.

(see *desert, renounce, resist*)

REVOLVE

swirl before; whirr around; eddy around; swim before one's eyes.

(see *turn, dizzy, circle, return*)

REVULSION (to feel)

shudder under one's skin at; twist and shrink in the presence of another; be overwhelmed by a wave of nausea.

(see *sick, disgust, repulsive*)

REWARD (to receive)

have medals pinned all over one; be given the palm; reap the advantage; reap the fruits of; receive a slice of profit; have the plums passed to oneself; see all one's schemes crowned by;

get the prize bag; get something for one's pains; hit the jackpot; collect a bonanza; come to the end of the rainbow; see the silver lining.

(see *advantage, compensate, pay, prize*)

RICH (to be)

worship the Golden Calf; have well-filled money-bags; wallow in gold; be well-heeled; roll in riches; be in full feather; feather one's nest; wade around in money; have money choke one's wallet; be in clover; have a bottomless purse; suffer from coupon thumb; have a gold-lined pocket-book; be born with a gold spoon in one's mouth; have plenty of champagne money; feel flush; overflow with milk and honey; live in gilded regions; make a heap of coin; rake in the thousands; have hefty resources; have shoals of money; own a barrel of money; make money hand-over-fist; rise to the two Rolls-Royce status; be crawling with money; follow the dollar; be made of money; command an army of iron men; be among the carriage clientele; belong to the upper brackets; roll in velvet; live in the silk-stocking district; be filthy with lucre; be in easy circumstances.

(see *prosperous, wealthy*)

RID (v.)

slough off; trade off; shake off; prune away; weed out; shovel away; get off one's hands; brush off; toss to the winds; throw overboard; wash out of; sweep away; shuffle off.

(see *free, release, finish, divorce, disinherit, destroy*)

RIDE (v.)

whip over to; rattle across the miles; grind up distance; shoot past landscape; thread one's way through milestones.

(see *move, travel*)

RIDGE (n.)

saddle of a hill; crest; rib; spine; weal; wrinkle; chine; hogback; watershed; ledge.

(see *top, mountain*)

RIDICULE (v.)

pour scorn on; pooh-pooh; put to the public blush; tweak the nose; laugh off the stage; grind to mincemeat; hoot down; plant a thorn in someone's side; lay open to scorn; point the finger of scorn; make an April fool of; prick another's bubble; make a laughingstock of; toss in a blanket; take by the beard; crush beneath the weight of ridicule; make a hare of; make the butt; couch the lance of levity at; make game of; make an ass of.

(see *mock, taunt, disparage, sneer*)

RIDICULOUS (to be)

make an Irish bull; pass from the sublime to the ridiculous; wear the cap and bells; make a monkey of oneself; act the buffoon; be the mountain in labor that produced a mouse; be an old fish; play the fool.

(see *nonsense, eccentric*)

RIFFRAFF

scum; dregs of society; underling; roughneck; guttersnipe; vermin; outcast of society.

(see *refuse, low class*)

RIGHTEOUS (persons)

salt of the earth; pillar of the church.

(see *virtuous, religious, saintly, honest, fair*)

RIGID

iron-clad; starched; petrified; icy; congealed; frozen; iceberg; tough; rooted to the spot.

(see *stiff, firm, hard, stern, strict*)

RISING (prices)

soaring; kiting up; jumping forward; flying high; mushrooming; spurting upward; zooming ahead; climbing; racing upward; going on a flight through the roof; kicking up; galloping; hitting a new peak; spiraling; snapping upward; shooting up; skyrocketing; soaring out of reach; springing up; hiking up; running up; clambering up; boosted ahead; jacked up; knocked higher than a kite; ballooning; propped up; soaring audaciously into space; hoisted up; securing a place in the skies; astronomical; blooming into the heavens; borne aloft; vaulting; piercing the sky; leaping; moving on the upswing; towering; running the scale; holding a rocket by the tail; scaling; mounting; standing on tiptoe; working their way up; aspiring to the skies; lifting their heads above the rim of the world; flaring up.

(see *inflation, high-priced, expensive*)

RISK (v.)

put the chestnuts into the fire; swap horses in mid-stream; go out on a limb; hang by a thread; buy a pig in a poke; trust to the chapter of accidents; leap in the dark; take a bear by the tooth; put one's head into a lion's mouth; tread on soft ground; play with fire; walk a thin line between; gamble for high stakes; chase the wild goose; fly in the face of fate; play with edged tools; put at stake; play at a desperate game; put into a lottery; gamble life on; stand the hazard of the die (or dice); sleep on a volcano; rush on destruction; play at chuck-farthing; walk on a thin crust over an abyss; lean on a broken reed; run the gauntlet; court chance; wander into the jaws of death; sit on a barrel of gunpowder; live in a glass house; sail too near the wind; take a flyer at; put one's life in another's hands; skate over thin ice; throw the great cast; go it one (or more) better; ride at single anchor; walk on a tight-rope; play at a ticklish chance; put too many eggs in one basket; steer a wobbling course; jump out of the frying pan into the fire; come through a crisis by the skin of one's teeth; take the chance of having to run for it; embark on suicidal missions; proceed into the gathering clouds; loiter on the road to ruin.

(see *dare, danger, endangered, speculate*)

RISQUE

showing a naked shoulder; uncorseted; sheathed in silk stockings; paprikaed.

(see *uninhibited, sensual, sexual, unrestrained*)

RIVALRY (to show)

play at cross-purposes; pit against; pitch against; run against; set against; run counter to; exchange friendly shots; cut each other's throats; spoil one's trade; spar for the best position.

(see *oppose, competition, contend, equal*)

RIVER

a ribbon of silver; a necklace of amethyst collaring the valley; a dun-colored serpent twisting sinuously; a silver serpent slipping over stones; a musical voice talking through its throat of sand.

(see *ocean*)

ROAD
a broad white ribbon; arteries carrying life-blood to great cities.
(see *travel*)

ROMANTIC (to be)
pass through the ivory gates; dream of castles in Spain; move in a moon-soaked phantasy; feel words of flame scorching one's lips; feel the eager flush of young love; don the cloak and sword; see Love wave a white hand from her lattice; have dreamy and faraway eyes.
(see *love, imaginary, sentimental*)

ROOF (v.)
cap a building with black slate; stir the tar-pots.
(see *cover, top*)

ROOM (n.)
the size and bareness of a packing case; a hole; a refuge.
(see *place, space*)

ROTTENNESS
a spreading cancer.
(see *spoil, degenerate, deteriorate, tainted*)

ROUGH (to be)
handle without mittens; take off one's kid gloves; have a character with the bark on; act in a rough-and-tumble fashion; be rugged; thunder orders.
(see *irregularly, unpolished, rude, harsh, sharp*)

ROUNDABOUT (to be)
weave circles; beat about the bush; parade an exception to prove a rule; make two bites of a cherry.
(see *indirect*)

RUDDY (complexioned)
cheeks whereon the paths of the blood-vessels were scrawled in red; a complexion burnt to red leather; cherry-cheeked.
(see *red*)

RUDE (to be)
act in a bear-like manner; lose one's temper; send another away with a flea in his ear; show the door to; be a rough diamond; act iron-handedly; give the cold shoulder to; go wild; be offensive to polite ears; pluck by the beard; be an unlicked cub; be a bruin.
(see *unpolished, rough, unskilful, savage, ignorant, impudent*)

RUDIMENTS
dry bones; embryo; germ; root; seed.
(see *principle, basis*)

RUEFUL
sour.
(see *regret, repent, lament, mourn, sorrowful, grieve*)

RUGGED
sea-bitten; wintry; shaggy; cragged; wrinkled; seamed; bristly; stormy.
(see *rough, hard, severe, rude, harsh, turbulent*)

RUIN (to go to)
crumble into dust; turn to dust; come apart at the seams; go to pigs and whistles; go all to smash; go by the board; go to the dogs; go to pot; play a losing game; split on a rock; march on the road to perdition; wreck oneself on the rock of ruin.
(see *defeated, fall, destruction*)

RUIN (v.)
cast to the dogs; deliver sledge-ham-

mer blows upon; make a hash of; break the life of; reduce to ashes; strip of life; massacre; break the back of; knock for a loop; swallow up; torpedo; strike the vitals of; lay by the heels; make mincemeat of; kill; cripple; deal the death-blow to; foreclose the mortgage on; knock to atoms; blast to smithereens; kill the goose that laid the golden eggs; eat out of house and home; wipe out; smirch; split; take the brick out of the dam that shut back the waters; shipwreck.

(see *destroy, defeat, violate, seduce, disaster, doom, undo, sacrifice*)

RULE (n.)
letter of the law; standing order; standing dish; key-note.

(see *regulations, guide, methodical, orderly, system*)

RULE (v.)
carry with a high hand; reign in unquestioned sovereignty; wear the breeches; play the emperor; be at the top of the upper crust.

(see *control, dominate, judge, manage, direct, advise, decide, determine, order*)

RUMOR (v.)
noise abroad; let leak out; buzz; send on the grapevine; commit to hearsay; pour into the cup of gossip; put in everyone's mouth; send all over town; put a tip in the air.

(see *report, news, gossip*)

RUN (v.)
show the heels; click the heels; scuttle along; romp along; make one's feet one's friends; take to one's heels; show a light pair of heels; swirl through streets; bolt along; fly down the street; whip forward; stir one's stumps; shoot along.

(see *quickly, hastily, hurry, speed*)

RUSH (v.)
scamper away; stampede; move in a whirlwind; fly toward; break down the doors; dive at; create a flurry; tear into; railroad; press hard upon; surge along; move in a torrent; hightail it for.

(see *dash, drive*)

RUSTLING
whispering.
(see *whisper, sounds*)

RUTHLESS
dog-eat-dog; cut-throat.
(see *cruel, savage*)

S

SACRIFICE
toss to the wolves; carry a life to the altar; kill the goose that lays the golden egg; force to pay the price; purchase a thing at the cost of; empty the veins of.

(see *surrender, give up, offer, destroy, destruction, loss*)

SAD (to be)
burst with grief; be heavy-laden; feel a load on the heart; be sore at heart; give a protracted shiver of grief; tread the winepress of woe; tear one's hair; force a smile that hovers on tears; be prostrated with grief; be engulfed in a sea of sorrows; feel a pall hang over one; be steeped to the lips in misery; have weight upon the heart; look heavily on; be within a cloud of sadness; take a thing to heart; feel grief that saps the heart; wear the buskin of tragedy; be bathed in tears; feel one's spirits damped; see everything look black; wear sadness with contrition; have memories that make the heart ache; have the blues; be devoured by longing; have a bruised heart; feel a melancholy monotone beat on one's heart; have a pitiable smile that dies on the lips; weep tears that are salt; wear a cloud on one's brow; be stricken wordless; feel one's heart bleeding; droop the tattered banner of hope; have a heart that cracks with grief; break one's heart; feel gravel-throated; have eyes blistered with sorrow; feel the sun gone out of one's eyes; move in a cloud of depression; have the look of a stricken St. Bernard dog; feel one's heart cry out; hear a tale for tears; live in an inferno of misery; feel an ocean of sadness moan, surge, and break over one; feel one's heart dissolved within one's breast; wring one's soul over; feel a tearing at one's heart; wring tears of sympathy from one's heart; feel a nibbling at one's heart.

(see *sorrowful, melancholy, mourn, despondency, depressed, dejected, unhappy, dreary, grieve, tragedy*)

SAFE (to be)
be in God's hands; be on firm ground; find the coast clear; get out of the woods; run into port; be above water; be under the shield of; be high and dry; rest at anchor; be under the shadow of someone's wing; let the portcullis down; find a tower of strength; make port; be on the side of the angels; weather the storm; save one's skin; set one's heart at rest; keep one's head above water; keep one's withers unwrung; secure a rock of refuge; have hold of the lifeline.

(see *unharmed*)

SAFE (to make)
put under lock and key; take to the hills; have an anchor to windward; take in a reef; double reef the topsails; take up a loose thread; raise the drawbridge; take to the woods; be light on one's legs; place a stepping-stone; take a middle-of-the-road position; lock a secret in one's bosom; lower the sheet anchor; bar the gate; lock the door; throw oneself into the arms of; wait till the storm blows over.

(see *secure, protect, defend, preserve*)

SAGE (n.)
a venerable graybeard.

(see *wise, old man*)

SAIL (v.)

plow through the sea; take ship; put to sea; find one's sea-legs; get under steam; spread sail; spread canvas; make sail; have way on; gather way; carry sail; plow the waves; ply the oar; walk the waters; plow the deep; wing one's way; rock through the sea; plow the main; ride the storm; get under canvas; plow the ocean; get under way; be under sail; hug the shore; hoist blue Peter; take wing; buffet the waves; dance on the waves; tear the brine; buffet the wind; be on the wing; gather barnacles; be an old shellback; follow the sea.

(see *ocean, waves, ship, travel*)

SAINTLY (to be)

be on the side of the angels; be a giant of the spirit; have a diamond soul.

(see *religious, sanctimonious, pray*)

SALESMAN

the selling fraternity; trade emissary abroad; order-taker; scrapper for the public dollar.

(see *sell*)

SALLOW

tallow-faced; pasty-complexioned.

(see *sick, pale*)

SALOON

sink of iniquity; sin den; elbow-bending spot; rum-hole.

(see *drunk*)

SAMENESS

six of one and half a dozen of the other; tarred with the same brush; of a piece; chip off the old block; standing dish; steady diet; running in a groove; standing order; in the mold;

new wine in old bottles.

(see *similar, resemble, monotonous, identical*)

SAMPLE

cross-section; a dip into; a taste of.

(see *pattern, model*)

SANCTIMONIOUS (to be)

exhale an odor of sanctity; carry religion in one's pocket; wear a strait-waistcoat of dogma; wears a halo about one's head; feel one's wings sprouting; bless oneself.

(see *hypocrite, self-love, self-praise, self-satisfaction*)

SANCTUARY

one's private preserve; the secret recesses of one's inner dwelling; one's ivory tower.

(see *refuge, shelter, religion, God*)

SANE (to be)

follow the main highway of normal psychology; hold on to one's reason; keep one's equilibrium; retain one's peace of mind.

(see *intelligent, mind*)

SARCASTIC (to be)

have a withering tongue; edge one's language with brimstone; shoot a verbal broadside; rain a shower of abuse; put a bite in one's words; barb the arrows of one's words; give a sabre-cut; speak cutting words; have an acid quality in one's words; treat to the rough edge of a fishwife's tongue; dip one's words in vinegar; etch a speech in acid; be sharp-tongued; show an irritable mouth; have one's tongue dwell ironically on one's words; have none of the milk of human kindness in one's words; put a tart flavor in one's words; be a master of the pin prick; pillory with words; load beneath an arsenal of insult; scald with one's words; have a fang or two in one's mouth; shoot a red-hot reply.

(see *taunt, ridicule, sharp, mock*)

SATAN

the cloven foot; the angel of the bottomless pit; the unclean beast; hellborn fiend; the author of evil; the Prince of Darkness; the power of the air.

(see *tempt, evil, sinful*)

SATED (to be)

be swollen with wine and food; have one's appetite satisfied; drink one's fill; have a jaded taste.

(see *fill, full of, eat, sufficient, gluttony*)

SATISFACTORY (to be)

deliver the goods; live up to; come up to the scratch; make the best of a bad job.

(see *sufficient, convince*)

SATISFIED (to be)

purr with satisfaction; gratify one's senses; still one's hunger; feel a feather-weight of satisfaction; have a run for one's money; let well enough alone; rest upon one's oars; repose on one's laurels; have the bell rung for one; have one's bill filled; smell into a tumbler with its sides still wet from a rare vintage; have one's desires quieted; have one's cup splashing over the rim; have all one's demands paid in full; take the will for the deed; warm oneself by satisfaction; take the good the gods provide; lay the flattering unction to one's soul.

(see *contentment, pleased*)

SAUNTER (v.)

advance with measured gait.

(see *walk*)

SAVAGE (to be)

act in cold blood; rub off the varnish of civilization; be a tiger; act the wildcat; take more than flesh and blood can stand; live with dog-eat-dog corruptness; satisfy chill-hungry clients; be a beast.

(see *rough, rude, unpolished, cruel, ruthless*)

SAVE (money)

pinch one's pennies; pinch the dollars; beat out shillings; put money by for a rainy day; put a veto on spending; tuck one's money in one's sock; hide one's dollars away in the lining of the mattress; salt one's money away; stretch the nickels; hang onto one's dollars; put a sou on one side; be close-fisted; feather one's nest; build a nest egg; make a stocking for oneself; keep a backlog; realize that money does not grow on bushes; cut one's coat according to one's cloth; save a scrap for one's old age.

(see *economize, scrimp*)

SAVOR (v.)

roll under one's tongue; tickle the appetite; flatter the palate; smack the lips; lick the chaps.

(see *tasty, smell of*)

SAY

snarl; grunt; bray; croak; coo; cast out words; breathe words; snap; chirp; flame out in speech; bring words past one's lips; point out verbally.

(see *speak, declare, tell, utter, pronounce*)

SCANDAL (to spread)

give a two-column sneer; raise a fiery storm of slander; drag a name in the dust; wash soiled linen in public; show the blot on the scutcheon; rattle the skeleton in the closet; unleash the hounds of gossip; put under a cloud; bring under the ferule; give a bad name to; bring a hornet's nest about another's ears.

(see *gossip, defame, slander, disparage*)

SCARCE

at a premium; in the barrel-scraping stage; tight; pinch; scraping the bottom of the food bin; few worms to catch; a capful of (wind, *i. e.*, a stray puff of air inadequate to propel a sailing vessel; a nautical expression).

(see *rarity, unusual, unique, deficient, lack, scattered, bit*)

SCARE (v.)

send shudders up and down; raise gooseflesh; give the creeps; haunt; make hearts skip a beat; give a grip at the throat; raise hair; shake the big stick; freeze blood.

(see *frightened, afraid, terrify, fearful*)

SCATHE

hack to the bone.

(see *hurt, injure, destroy*)

SCATTERED

few and far between; straggling; sown throughout the lands; cast to the winds; dotted throughout the land.

(see *scarce, few, rarity, separately*)

SCAVENGER

bird of prey.

(see *destroy, destroyer*)

SCENE

arena; domestic drama; tapestry; backdrop.

(see *place, background*)

SCEPTRE

rod of empire; sword of state.

(see *power, rule*)

SCHEDULE (v.)

table for discussion; bring a thing off.

(see *arrange, plan*)

SCHEME (v.)

practice backstairs influence; play one's cards right; have cunning grow in one's eyes; have fish to fry; indulge in bald speculation; put a rock into motion; cook up an idea; cast one's nets in the right direction; play a game; worm one's way toward; weave a spider's web; move with the serpent.

(see *plot, plan*)

SCHOLAR

blue stocking (female); an athlete of scholarship; a learned Theban; a high-brow; a big-wig; one brought up at the feet of Gamaliel; a pundit; a thirster for learning; a book in breeches; a walking encyclopedia.

(see *study, intellectual*)

SCOLD (v.)

shoot off a volley of words; give someone a piece of one's mind; snap another's head off; be wasp-tongued; dish it out to another; bark at; have a sharp tongue; give a dressing down to; bite someone's head off; give one Jesse; bawl one out; stab with the tongue; blow sky-high; fry one verbally; give it to; rag another; put one on the pan; give one the length of one's tongue; thunder at; snap another up; backbite.

(see *reprimand, reprove, rebuke, blame, criticize, denounce, condemn*)

SCOPE

elbow-room; leeway.

(see *room, space, span, extend, aim, intention*)

SCORE (v.)

ring the bell; hit the jackpot; reach high C.

(see *successful, record*)

SCORELESS (to be)

make a pair of spectacles.

(see *unsuccessful, defeated*)

SCORN (v.)

toss the head at; view with a scornful eye; look down on; spit upon; look down one's nose at; curl up one's lip; turn up one's nose; snap one's fingers at; laugh up one's sleeve at; think small beer of; send one's eyes through another like a lightning flash; raise up the horn (Biblical); "ritz" another; "Park Avenue" someone; give the cold shoulder to; put to the blush; freeze one with silence; trample under foot.

(see *contempt, disdain, disregard, mock, sneer, snobbish*)

SCOUNDREL

a lower breed of the human animal; dog-in-the-manger; skunk; beast; clay-eating trash.

(see *villainous, swindle, cheat, trickery*)

SCOWL (v.)

give a black look at; have one's face become a thunder cloud.

(see *glare at, disapprove, frown, sullen*)

SCRAP

a bone to throw to a dog.

(see *refuse, remnant, bit*)

SCREAM (v.)

roar in anguish; thin the lips in a scream of anguish.

(see *shriek, shrill, shout, yell*)

SCRIMP

pinch one's pennies; crumble one's money away in small doses.

(see *save, economize, reduce, shorten, limit*)

SEA

the boundless gray waste; the gray sweet mother; the cradled mold of the moon; a magnified wash-hand basin; the cradle of the deep.

(see *ocean*)

SEARCH FOR (v.)

beat the bushes; scour; rummage through; cast about for; have restless eyes; browse through; comb the woods for; cast one's nets for; fish for; prowl through; conduct a tour of investigation for; dig for; ferret out; plough deep; get on the trail of; nose around for.

(see *seek, look for*)

SEASICK (to be)

feed the fishes.

(see *sea, ocean, sick*)

SECLUSION (to put in)

draw a curtain round; send to Coventry; cut off from; put in a corner; keep at arm's length; cut dead; turn one's back on; shut the door to outside; cause to retire from the world; take the veil; bar to outsiders; shut away; hive away; place in closed compartments; nourish with seclusion;

make a stay-at-home of; lay an embargo on.

(see *hide, conceal, separate, withdraw, privacy, secret, isolated, solitary, segregate*)

SECONDARY
backwash; second fiddle; back seat; minor league.

(see *inferior, subordinate*)

SECRET (to keep)
keep a thing under one's hat; not let the cat out of the bag; seal one's lips; be an inscrutable sphinx; keep in a sealed book; keep up one's sleeve; not let the skeleton out of the closet; stay underground; keep behind the curtain; keep on the sly; keep behind closed doors; keep behind one's back; lock in the labyrinth of one's heart; keep a thing dark; know more than meets the eye; keep a thing dry; cloak with silence; keep on the Q. T.; blanket in secrecy; give a hideout to; clothe in a cloak of silence; draw a veil of secrecy over; say mum's the word about; lock in one's secret chamber; draw an iron curtain over; nourish in secrecy; afford a Shangri-La to; keep behind the veil of night; keep one's thoughts lurking in the interlunar cave of one's heart; keep the word in one's ear; not let leak out; look ignorant about; keep backstage; muffle in discreet silence; build a wall of silence around; help the dog to hide his bone; keep behind the scenes; regard as not meant for public ears; syndicate a secret; keep deep within the black privacy of one's consciousness; wear a mask concerning; preserve a security screen; keep in a back room; store in the attic of one's mind; keep one's tongue between one's teeth; keep under the rose (*sub rosa*, the rose being an attribute or symbol of the Egyptian deity Horus and the Greek god of silence, Harpocrates).

(see *silent, reticent, seclusion, hide, conceal*)

SECURE (to make)
anchor a thing; nail down; pin down; keep in the hollow of one's hand; find sanctuary for; rest a thing on firm ground; build on solid foundation; keep water-tight; safe bind, safe find; fit like a glove.

(see *safe, protect*)

SEDUCE
deflower.

(see *mislead, tempt, betray, violate*)

SEE
catch sight of; follow with the eyes; clap the eyes upon; set eyes on; fasten one's gaze upon; have a thing catch one's eye; catch a glance of; command a view of; drink in with one's eyes; cast a look at; bend one's looks upon; get a slant on.

(see *look at, glance at, survey, perceive, notice, observant, discern, regard*)

SEEK
fish for; grope for; court; throw one's net for.

(see *look for, search for*)

SEGREGATE
weed out.

(see *distinguish, separate*)

SEIZE
collar; snatch at; pounce on; buttonhole; clap one's hands on; lay hands on; swoop upon.

(see *snatch, catch, hold, take*)

SELDOM
once in a blue moon; once in a coon's age.
(see *rarity, scarce*)

SELECT
pick from the tree; weed out; glean.
(see *choose, preference*)

SELF-ABASEMENT
sackcloth and ashes.
(see *repent, humiliate, meek*)

SELF-ABUSE
foul one's own nest.
(see *pervert, dishonor, injure*)

SELF-ANALYSIS
hold the mirror up to oneself; experience a regenerating thrust of self-knowledge; look into one's own heart.
(see *introspective, psychoanalysis*)

SELF-CENTERED (to be)
bend in on oneself; spin one's own cosmos; live in a world of one's own; have an unbruised ego; carry inside oneself the boundaries of one's universe.
(see *introspective, self-love, selfish, egotistic*)

SELF-CONDEMNATION
feel the knife of remorse and shame stab one fiercely.
(see *remorseful, condemn*)

SELF-CONSCIOUS (to be)
wriggle on the hook of someone's glance; have a burning face; be chained to the rock of self-consciousness.
(see *embarrassed*)

SELF-CONTROL
master one's feelings; bridle the im-

pulses; pull oneself together; keep one's head; keep the heel of one's spirit on the neck of one's flesh.
(see *self-possessed*)

SELF-DEFENSE
hold one's ground against an enemy; keep one's head and one's back to the wall.
(see *self-protection, defense*)

SELF-EFFACEMENT
shrink into one's shell.
(see *meek*)

SELF-EVIDENT
tell one's own tale; let one's past speak for itself.
(see *clear, evident, obvious*)

SELF-GAIN
play for one's own hand; take care of number one.
(see *selfish*)

SELF-INDULGENCE
indulge one's fancy.
(see *selfish, indulge*)

SELF-INTELLIGENCE
have a head of one's own.
(see *independent, self-analysis*)

SELFISH (to be)
eat one's cake and have it too; be given an inch and take an ell; feather one's nest; begin one's charity at home; be a fortune-hunter; be a dog in the manger; dance to nothing but one's own pipe; hog everything; have an agate core of egocentric desires; have eyes only for oneself; roll one's own logs; wait for dead men's shoes; have a cash register instead of a heart; be close-handed; fight for one's

own hand; consult one's own pleasure; be a time-server.

(see *narrow-minded, egotistic*)

SELF-LOVE

fall in love with one's own reflection.

(see *egotistic, show-off*)

SELF-PITY

lick one's wounds; warm one's hands
at one's sorrows.

(see *pity*)

SELF-POSSESSED

possess one's soul; be master of oneself.

(see *self-reliant, courageous, confident*)

SELF-PRAISE

pat oneself on the back; burn candles
to oneself.

(see *vain, conceited*)

SELF-PROTECTION

bring oneself in out of the rain; save
one's skin.

(see *protect, defense, defensive*)

SELF-PUNISHMENT

lash oneself; cut off one's nose to spite
one's face.

(see *self-abasement, conscience, repent*)

SELF-RELIANT

sail one's own boat; paddle one's own
canoe; stand on one's own feet; not
need a crutch to lean on.

(see *independent, self-sufficient, confident*)

SELF-REPROACH

hold a sense of hot shame to one's

sober memory.

(see *remorseful, blame, repent, shame*)

SELF-RESPECT

feel one's pride as a rational animal
revolt against; feel self-respect flow
through one's veins.

(see *proud*)

SELF-SATISFACTION

warm one's coat-tails at the glow of
one's own virtue; feel one's heart
swell with self-satisfaction; hug oneself; feel one's bosom thrill with
pride.

(see *pleased, smugness*)

SELF-SUFFICIENT

proceed under one's own steam; let
one's proud heart feed on itself; be
one's own bread-winner.

(see *proud, confident, haughty*)

SELL (v.)

bring under the hammer; turn into
money; conduct a Dutch auction;
let flow into the channels of trade;
dump one's stocks; ring up a sale;
unload one's bonds; cause a change
of hands; hawk; get whisked off store
shelves.

(see *business, shopkeeper, salesman*)

SEMBLANCE

shadow.

(see *resemble, similar, appearance*)

SEND

waft; wireless; fire; catapult; pour
into; pack off to; scuttle off to; nudge
out of; drive off to.

(see *emit, drive, give*)

SENILITY

the unproductive vineyard of seventy.

(see *old, old man*)

SENSATION

a wave of; a blur of; vibration; a flavor of; rippling.

(see *feeling, thrilled, excited*)

SENSATIONALISTIC

atomic; bright yellow; screaming; splashing.

(see *startle, impressive, unusual*)

SENSELESS

without rhyme or reason; a tale told by an idiot; take leave of one's senses; forty to the dozen (British for 'senseless chatter'); live in a fool's paradise.

(see *meaningless, foolish, nonsense, silly*)

SENSITIVE (to be)

scale an emotional ladder; have a thin skin; take things too much to heart; "die of a rose in aromatic pain" (Pope); have a hair-trigger sensitivity; feel to the quick; feel the shoe pinch; respond to the inmost core; be allergic to; be touchy; be coated over with sensitiveness; be ticklish; have a jeweled soul; shoot out unrestrainedly in all directions; be alive to.

(see *emotional, responsive, susceptible, moved*)

SENSUAL (to be)

swill voluptuousness; be goatish; smack the lips over; yield to the weakness of the flesh; plunge into dissipation; uncorset desire; sow wild oats; slake one's appetite; burn the candle at both ends; live hard and fast; be nursed in the lap of sensuality; intoxicate oneself from the Circean cup; lie on a bed of roses; wallow in sensuality; show the cloven hoof; carouse on an endless round of pleasure; feel brutish passions; dip one's feet in a moral mire; give a loose to; run riot; be full-fed with pleasure; subject oneself to the exquisite slavery of the flesh; stroke the silk of; drag Venus through mud.

(see *pleasure-seeking, passionate, sexual*)

SENTIMENTAL (to be)

wear one's heart on one's sleeve; be sucked in a molasses lake of sentiment; be sticky; slop about in the ooze of sentimentality; wear a veil of nostalgia; have a soft streak in oneself; be reduced to emotional pulpiness; be syrupy; spread on the sentimental jelly overthick.

(see *emotional, romantic, tender*)

SEPARATE (v.)

punctuate; divorce; part company with; curtain off; drift away from; break the tie between; stray away from; cut adrift; throw out of gear; break apart; draw a line between; weed out; erect a Great Divide between; part ways; wall off; fence off; follow roads that fail to cross; open an abyss between.

(see *divide, divorce, remove, eliminate, segregate*)

SEPARATELY

one by one; piecemeal.

(see *detailed, gradually*)

SEQUENCE

train (of events); march; parade.

(see *follow, series*)

SERIES

a string of; a web of; a train of; a chain of; a tissue of.

(see *sequence, connection, relate*)

SERIOUS (to be)

burning; sobering; not lightly; wearing no smile; critical; cold; taking to heart; keeping a straight face.

(see *sober, important*)

SERVICE (to give)

sell one's sword to; dance attendance on; die in harness.

(see *useful, work*)

SERVILE (to be)

go with the stream; hold with the hare and run with the hounds; hang on the sleeve of; lick the feet of; kiss the boots of; kiss the hem of one's garment; pin oneself upon; be one's lap-dog; be a spaniel; make oneself a door-mat for; wear the badge of servility; serve an apostleship to.

(see *slavery, fawn, submissive*)

SET (adj.)

geared; framed; braced.

(see *ready*)

SETBACK (to cause a)

give a blow in the midriff; put back the clock; give the cheese to.

(see *undo, reverse, undermine*)

SETTING (n.)

backdrop; canvas; stage; fabric.

(see *background, scene*)

SETTLE (v.)

set at rest; pass in one's checks or chips; clinch; pull together; draw up the loose threads; iron out; wipe the slate clean; thresh out; smooth out; have it out with; clear off old scores; quit scores; turn the scales; face up to a question; umpire; referee; liquidate.

(see *adjust, arrange, finish, close, balance, calm, pacify, stabilize*)

SEVER

throw out of gear; loosen ties; cut off from; cut the knot.

(see *divide, divorce, remove, segregate, separate*)

SEVERE (to be)

look daggers; sharpen one's teeth; barb the dart; be hard; rule with a rod of iron; lay a heavy hand on; be black-browed; tighten one's belt; be astringent.

(see *stern, hard, harsh, rigid, sharp, bitter, stiff, methodical, accurate, sarcastic, cruel*)

SEW

stitch wandering gypsy trails.

(see *bind*)

SEXUAL (to be)

sow the seeds of vice; sink into moral turpitude; play fast and loose; head for the gutter; stir the flesh-pots; lick with one's eyes; undress with a glance; feel the fires of desire blaze fiercely in one's heart; yearn for flesh; slop about in the oozy slime of sex.

(see *sensual, passionate*)

SHABBY

moth-eaten; rusty clothed; tumble-down; down-at-the-heels.

(see *worn-out, poor, poverty-stricken*)

SHADE

a hanging-garden of parasols.

(see *shadows, dusk, shelter, cover, darkness*)

SHADOWS

the creeping fingers of night; pools of shadow.

(see *shade, clouded*)

SHALLOW (in character)

be content to scratch the surface of things; think with only the husk of the mind.

(see *superficial, silly, unintelligent, ignorant*)

SHAM

much cry and little wool; shadow.

(see *unreal, imposture, pretend, false, cheat*)

SHAME (to feel)

hide one's diminished head; feel the sting of shame; have coals of fire heaped on one's head; be spiritually tarred and feathered; be stained by; have a scarlet letter branded on one; cry for shame.

(see *ashamed, remorseful, embarrassed*)

SHAME (to put to)

take one down a peg; throw into the shade; put to the blush; tear away from one the veil of respect.

(see *humiliate, disgrace, dishonor, disconcert*)

SHAPE (v.)

lick into shape; whip into shape.

(see *form, create, make, produce*)

SHARE

take pot luck; have a voice in; get one's rake-off; have one's fingers in the pie; get a slice of; take up the ball; get a dose of; get a chunk of.

(see *participate, distribute*)

SHARP (adj.)

razor-edged; stinging; sheet steel; acid; diamond-sharp; stiletto-like; snapping; surgically incisive; whetstone; needle-shaped; conical; pyramidal; spiked; knife-edged; arrowy;

searing; briery; arrow-headed; thistly; studded; tapered to a point; tangy; burning; spiny; thorny; peaked; toothed; dagger-sharp; pungent.

(see *bitter, bite, burn, harsh, severe, sarcastic, hard, rigid, penetrate*)

SHARP (of hearing)

listen with both ears.

(see *listen, hear*)

SHARP (of sight)

basilisk-eyed; eagle-eyed.

(see *watchful, observant, see*)

SHARP-FACED

hatchet-faced.

(see *face*)

SHEEP

a dirty-white sea of sheep.

(see *timid*)

SHELTER (n.)

a refuge from the storm; a shadow from the heat; a port in a storm; a cloud; a cloistered existence; a walled-in life; a smokescreen; a shield.

(see *protect, cover, safe, secure, refuge, sanctuary*)

SHIFTINESS

passing the buck; robbing Peter to pay Paul; backing and filling.

(see *evade, insincere, unstable, unsteady*)

SHINE (of the stars)

kill the darkness with silver light; linger, remotely burning; wink; reach down silvery fingers; throb with golden spangles; brood down radiantly; catch on fire; beacon down; throw down silver arrows; twinkle with incandescence; lie prostrate in the sky; put glittering sequins on the velvet of the sky; powder the darkness with starlight; peep; sprinkle the night with fireflies.

(see *light, moon, bright, evening, night*)

SHINE (of the sun)

make a shimmering path; pour down torrents of light from a blazing sky; fire a salvo of scarlet and gold behind it (sunset); burn lavishly; beat down on; glare on; fling nooses of light around; flame with summer; blaze fiercely; drench the earth with light; touch the treetops, filling their limbs with fire; dance over the grass; pour down in golden blessing; stab with great golden light; resemble a great flare of fire igniting the horizon; lay bright carpets; shoot blinding rays of light; leap into sight like a friendly morning caller; play brilliantly over the earth; dance and gleam with intense joy; sprinkle sunbeams to and fro; strike particles of snow, covering them with cold fire.

(see *sunlight, sunrise, sunset*)

SHIP (n.)

a floating palace; an ocean greyhound.

(see *sail, ocean, sea*)

SHIVER (v.)

feel one's blood run cold.

(see *cold*)

SHOCKED (to be)

be pierced to the marrow; have news explode in one with a colossal reverberation; feel a concussion inflicted on one's brain; receive a stunning blow; suffer a nightmare paralysis; feel one's heart leap to one's mouth; get an eye-opener; be electrified; feel a sharp pang of surprise; get a smack in the eye; receive a jolt; be stag-

gered; feel palsied; receive with the impact of a thunderbolt; feel struck by a bombshell.

(see *stun, surprise*)

SHOOTING

the murmur of the six-shooter; the barking of guns; vomiting iron jaws; a rain of remorseless death; a hail of bullets; fire-spitting revolvers; the speaking of rifles; the silken whish and whistle of bullets; spitting balls of fire; rocketing fire; a shower of sparks.

(see *gun*)

SHOPKEEPER

a licensed thief.

(see *business, sell*)

SHORE (n.)

iron-bound coast; loom of the land.

(see *sea, ocean, waves*)

SHORTCOMING

one's weak side; falling short of.

(see *deficient, err, fail, defect, weak*)

SHORTEN

boil down; put in a capsule; distill; blue pencil (edit); draw in; deflate; dwarf; telescope; clip; squeeze; pinch; drain; short circuit.

(see *diminish, lessen, reduce, confine, hinder, restrain, restrict, foreshorten*)

SHORT-LIVED

mushrooming; spectral; flash in the pan; flying; May-fly.

(see *brief*)

SHOUT (v.)

make a trumpet of one's hands; hoot wildly; thunder forth; pour out orders; hurl a command; lift up one's voice; boom through a loudspeaker; fling out one's voice; crow.

(see *yell, loud*)

SHOVE (v.)

elbow one's way; force one's way; edge one's way.

(see *push, force*)

SHOW (v.)

unveil; lay before one's eyes; hold up the mirror; parade; highlight; have written on one's face; have creep into one's face; tell the story of; flash an expression; write the record across the face of; register; mirror; loom out; unmask; draw the curtain from.

(see *display, reveal, flaunt, divulge, proclaim, explain, prove, direct, inform, teach, interpret*)

SHOWMANSHIP

a flipped coin up and down Broadway; gingerbread.

(see *ostentatious, stage, act*)

SHOW OFF (v.)

play to the gallery; play to the grandstand; sound the fanfare for; flourish trumpets; dangle before the eyes; flash oneself in public; put oneself forward; rear up one's head; ride the high horse; cut a wide swath; flex one's muscles.

(see *exhibit, ostentatious, display, boast, exaggerate, self-love*)

SHREWD (to be)

have a slippery mind; have a hard head; indulge in cold-blooded calculation; know how many beans make five; have a sharp mind; have a mind that is a steel trap; use every trick in the book; be too hard a nut to crack; drive a hard bargain; have a knife-edged mind; play one's cards right;

swim away from a bare hook.

(see *sly, sharp, discern, wise, discriminate, knowledge, skilful*)

SHRIEKS (n.)

a shrill babble of tongues; a savage symphony of wailing.

(see *yell, scream, shrill*)

SHRILL (voice)

women's screeching parrot and peacock voices; a thin, squeaking voice.

(see *shrieks, voice*)

SHROUD (n.)

the garment of death.

(see *bury, death, grave*)

SHUN (v.)

give one the run-around; give one a wide berth; cut someone; give one the go-by.

(see *avoid, evade, escape*)

SHY (to be)

be tongue-tied; cast a sheep's eye; hide in a shell of reserve.

(see *timid, self-effacement, self-conscious, cautious, distrust*)

SICK (to be)

be laid up; keep to one's bed; be laid low with; have a churchyard cough; suffer a general breaking up of the system; have the ills that flesh is heir to; have hereditary poison in one's veins; be doomed to the eternal bondage of an invalid chair; be tied to bed; have food turn the stomach; have one foot in the grave; have food sit badly in one's stomach; go green around the gills; be on one's last legs; feel a wave of nausea; be laid up for repairs; have death show in one's face; take to one's bed; have one's tongue wearing a morning coat; bear the seeds of death in one; feel things go against one's stomach; be a physical wreck; hear one's deadbeat in the distance; be on the sick list; be out of health; be in a bad way; be flax-faced.

(see *pale, sallow, weak, faint*)

SIGH (v.)
be an old glove just about ready to flatten out and deflate; heave a sigh.

(see *grieve, complain, lament, mourn*)

SIGN (n.)
handwriting on the wall.

(see *ominous, mark*)

SIGNAL (v.)
give the cut; tip the wing; give the watchword; flash a telegraph; ring the bell; raise the finger; saw the air; sound the trumpet; beat the drum; show one's colors; light a beacon-fire.

(see *mark, inform*)

SILENT (to be)
seal one's lips; dry up; thrust words, unspoken, into a sheath; keep one's mouth shut; not breathe a word; keep one's tongue between one's teeth; not let a word escape one; put under shelter of one's tongue; have stick in one's throat; hold one's tongue; let go without saying; drown one's words; freeze up; place the finger on one's lips; remain in a startled hush; blanket one's words; plunge into a gulf of silence; put a padlock on one's mouth; stop one's mouth; hold one's peace; bite one's lips; keep under one's hat; be close-lipped; not have a word to say for oneself; hold one's jaw; lose one's tongue; have the cat get one's tongue; be as quiet as a tortoise asleep; guard one's tongue; be close-mouthed; keep one's own counsel; glue the lips; conduct a dumb show; be tight-lipped; let one's words fall unspoken; clam up; lock one's tongue; be a sphinx whose riddle no man can read; be a man of few words.

(see *reticent, quiet, speechless*)

SILENT (to make)
muzzle; talk down; drown out; snuff out; lay the finger on the lips; settle one's hash; stop the mouth; cut one short; spread a wing of silence; put a bridle on one's tongue; beat sound dead; hush up; rear a tower of silence; cause silence to fall; create a conversational Yukon before the ice breaks in the spring; eat in sound; make a hush hang heavily; make quiet settle down; ply the spur of silence; cause conversation to grind to a stop; tie up talk.

(see *stop*)

SILLY (to be)
play the fool to the top of one's bent; take on the cap and bells.

(see *foolish, senseless, nonsense, stupid, shallow*)

SIMILAR
of a piece; cut out of the same cloth; cast in the same mold; in the same kettle; rowing in the same boat; daubed with the same brush; having common ground; both of a hair; twin peas in a pod; birds of a feather; brother to another; chip off the old block; striking a familiar note; rhyming with; one's second self; of like kidney; running in pairs; savoring of; smacking of; taking after; tarred with the same stick; by the same token; *deux gouttes d'eau;* the very image (or picture) of; going on all fours; carbon copy.

(see *resemble, uniform, sameness, semblance*)

SIMPLE

homespun; duck soup; babes in the wood; plain unvarnished; cut and dried; monolithic; to be seen with half an eye; pure and simple; home-cooked; primer-like; straight; black-and-white.

(see *ordinary, easy, sincere, frank, straight-forward, clear*)

SIMPLICITY

resolve into its elements; narrow down.

(see *reduce, shorten, explain, clear*)

SINCERE

hold water; ring of truth; call a spade a spade; to the core; at the bottom of one's heart; stripped of the shining plastic of its surface; above-board; heart and soul; rough diamond; wear one's heart upon one's sleeve; look one in the face; unvarnished; in good faith; over head and ears.

(see *truthful, honest, frank, straight-forward*)

SINECURE

snap of a job.

(see *easy*)

SINFUL (to be)

stray from the right path; wrestle with Satan; take a bite out of the apple; wallow in a sink of debauchery; be of loose character; be of easy virtue; be a loose fish; backslide; put one's soul in pawn; wrap oneself in sin; be weighed in the balance and found wanting; be an ugly, cut-throat customer; be caught red-handed; be a monster; fall into evil ways; belong to the frail sisterhood; become hardened; be stained with spiritual contamination; be sunk in iniquity;

suffer looseness of morals; be one of the children of darkness; be an offending Adam; be the devil incarnate, the scum of the earth; be a dog; be a rake-hell; emulate a mongrel; be a whelp, a hound, a cur, a black sheep, a sad dog, a fallen angel, a hell-hound, a serpent, a reptile, a viper; drag Venus through the mire; make one's nest in vice; go to the bad; worship the flesh and the devil; be of a deep dye; be guilt-edged; be a strayed lamb; sell one's soul to sin; tread the foot awry.

(see *wicked, evil*)

SINGING

a tenor calling to his mate; flinging up a song like a curve of gold; spraying a room with a great fire hose of liquid music; flinging upward the broken beat of a melody; indulging in vocal gymnastics; pouring out an elaborate vocal fretwork; taking up the thread of a song; blissful bellowing; rolling words with a voice; droning of singers.

(see *music, voice*)

SINK (v.)

drop to the bottom; fall down with a thud; go down in a caldron of flame.

(see *fall, collapse, fail, decline, decrease*)

SIT

curl up in a chair; snuggle into; loop oneself over furniture; be festooned over a chair; fling oneself into; perch on; crouch in an easy chair; drop into; sink into.

(see *rest*)

SITUATED

nestling; anchored; huddled.

(see *locate, place*)

SKEPTICAL (to be)
be a doubting Thomas; hold aloof; turn a deaf ear; shut one's ears to; cock horn-rimmed spectacles at; shut one's eyes to.

(see *doubt, question*)

SKILFUL (to be)
have all one's wits about one; play one's cards well; handle a subject well; live by one's wits; carry the torch of genius into; exercise one's discretion; feather the oar; sail near the wind; stoop to conquer; be at home with; make hay while the sun shines; be a good hand at; be up to snuff; not be caught with chaff; be neat-handed; be fine-fingered; be sure-footed; know on which side one's bread is buttered; know what's o'clock; know a thing or two; have cut one's eye-teeth; put the saddle on the right horse; see one's way; see where the wind lies; have one's hand in; cut one's coat according to one's cloth; hit the right nail on the head; play one's best card; have cut one's wisdom teeth; make a hit; have the eye of the master; be a practiced hand; have a turn for; know a hawk from a handsaw; manage a good stroke; have mother wit; be polished at.

(see *resourceful, ability, experienced*)

SKINNY
hatchet-faced; knobs of protruding neckbone; elbows, and shoulder blades; stringy; shriveled to a mummy; bag of bones.

(see *thin*)

SKY
a blue lava field; a blue meadow full of gardenias; a washed-blue bowl; a high roof of mist; light-drenched ceil-ing of cloud; a black velvet strip of sky.

(see *heaven, sun, moon, clouds*)

SKYSCRAPER
a blasphemy in stone; a pile of stick and stone and steel; massive hunks of masonry; a dark herd of buffalo marching against the sky-line.

(see *tall, buildings*)

SLACKER (n.)
an unfaithful shepherd.

(see *careless, negligent, inattentive, unconcerned, loaf*)

SLANDER (v.)
speak behind one's back; sling mud at; fling dirt; cast a slur upon; backbite; bespatter; give tongue; indulge in muck-raking; dip the pen in gall; sling slime at; throw lots of dirt and some will stick; heap foul accusations upon; have the poison of asps under one's lips; throw stones at.

(see *disparage, defame, scandal, reproach*)

SLANG (n.)
words that dislocate the jaw; words that break the teeth; words offensive to ears polite; language out of the gutter.

(see *express, speak, low class*)

SLAVERY
yoke; entangling web; chains; coil; a mere machine; a heavy dosage of black Africa; badge of servitude; the ebony trade.

(see *servile, dominate*)

SLEEP
open the casements of sleep; lie in the arms of Morpheus; feel dead to the world; have one's consciousness

stumble away into the mazy woods of sleep; drift away to Nothing; be visited by the sandman; feel the cool silver depths of sleep close over one; pound one's pillow; feel the dews of sleep fall on one; seal up one's eyes; have one's eyelids weighed down; snatch forty winks; drift into dreamland; consult one's pillow; have sand in one's eyes; turn in; feel the eyes begin to draw straws; be a dormouse; join the Seven Sleepers of Ephesus; vanish from consciousness; have heavy lids; be gathered to the bosom of sleep; be drunk with sleep; have sleep assault one; grope in the mists of sleep; have the eyes fringed with sleep; hug the pillow; sink into a coma; feel the stars pour glittering cups of snow upon one's eyelids; soothe oneself with the priceless balm for a weary soul; find sleep the best doctor; be blind with sleep.

(see *rest, snore*)

SLEET

whips of ice.

(see *snow, rain*)

SLIGHT (adj.)

at low ebb; (win) by a nose, or a head; fragile; mild; only a jump ahead; razor-edge margin; a shade of difference; the ghost of a notion; slim; thin; a hair's breadth; reedy; the shadow of a shade; the foggiest idea of; a suspicion of.

(see *low point, bit, small amount, trifle, unimportant*)

SLOGAN

battle-cry.

(see *motive*)

SLOW (v.)

move with tortoise speed; put on the drag; take in sail; move with a heavy tread; clip the wings; have time hang heavy; apply the brake; move with a snail's pace; let hang fire; proceed at a funeral pace; creep along; slacken one's pace; linger over a step; mince along; worm one's way; limp along; hold one's horses; snore along; ebb; move by degrees; go at a poky pace; trickle along; take a piecemeal approach; crawl along; move snailwise; have the legs of a weary ploughman; have the speed of a funeral march; crawl with the speed of a beetle; lag behind; bog down; slacken one's gait; loiter along; move little by little; confine one's pace to a dribble; take a let-up; proceed at half speed; lag along; drag one's slow length along.

(see *delay, late, behind, gradually, decelerate*)

SLUM

a reeking backwater.

(see *poverty-stricken*)

SLY (to be)

live by one's wits; stoop to conquer; steal a march upon; throw off one's guard; snatch from under one's nose; not be caught with chaff; be too clever by half; be up to snuff; be double-tongued; be foxy; have an axe to grind; be diamond-cut-diamond; play tricks with; come by a sidewind; play a deep game; have cut one's eyeteeth; apply the thin end of the wedge; snatch a verdict; have a cunning right hand; not let the left hand know what the right is doing; be a squirrel.

(see *resourceful, cautious, shrewd, stealthy, secret*)

SMALL

a matchbox; a pin-point; pocket-handkerchief; a bandbox; capsule-size; pocket-size; sparrow-like; embryonic; the size of a telephone booth; toy-size; slender; slim; at vanishing point; at low ebb; pint-sized; vestpocket edition; iota; mote; dot; dwarf-size.

(see *miniature, tiny, trifle*)

SMALL AMOUNT
trickle; driblet; pinch; crumb; drizzle; shred; twinkle; ripple; ghost; rag; thimbleful; spot; just a pin prick; just enough to swear by; flicker; farthing; penny-worth; a shade of; a thread of; sprinkling; an inch of; sketchy; a glimmering of; a snatch of; a note of; a patch of; the shadow of; a suspicion of; spotty; a mere flea-bite; a fraction of; a drop in the ocean (or bucket); a splinter of; a doctor's dose of; a hair of; next to nothing of; the shadow of a shade of; within an inch of; within an ace of; enough to keep a bird alive; a molecule of; a particle of; an atom of; a dab of; a fleck of; a speck of; a grain of.

(see *bit, minimum, insignificant, scarce, slight, particle, speck*)

SMART (to be)
have cut one's wisdom teeth; know all the answers; be nobody's fool; know what it's all about.

(see *intelligent, resourceful, shrewd, sly, skillful*)

SMELL OF (to)
exude a multiplicity of odors competing for attention; assail another's nostrils; assault the sense of smell; hit with smell; radiate an aroma of; reek of scent.

(see *odor, savor*)

SMILE (v.)
pin a smile on one's face; light up a face with a smile; shed pleasant rays from one's face; gash a face with a grin; have a smile play on the lips; have dancing eyes; put a good face upon; have a crescent moon of a smile lie deeply into one's face; express amusement with the eyebrows; wear a smile on one's face; have a nervous smile flit across one's face; shine upon another; laugh in one's beard; screw up the eyes in a smile; wear a twist on one's mouth; have a smile sweep one's face; be prodigal of smiles; repay in dimples; have crystals of light in the eyes; display the warm sunshine of a smile; have one's face wreathed in wavering smiles; do some snappy sparkling with one's eyes and teeth; turn on a smile; have a smile sicken and die on one's face.

(see *laugh*)

SMOKE (v.)
suck one's pipe; fire up a pipe; look naked without a pipe; blow a bundle of smoke; be a chimney of smoke; eat cigarettes; solace oneself with tobacco; seek solace in nicotine.

(see *fire*)

SMOOTH (adj.)
creamy; glassy; velvet; caressing; slick; glib; sleek; silver-toned; with the edges taken off; without an acid edge; on an even keel; silken.

(see *soft*)

SMUGGLE
filter through illegal channels.

(see *stealthily, illegality*)

SMUGNESS
a George Washington yarn.

(see *self-satisfaction, righteous, sanctimonious*)

SNARE (n.)
a sucking whirlpool.

(see *trap, catch*)

SNATCH
snap up; seize upon.

(see *take, seize, catch*)

SNEER (v.)
slap in the face with a sneer; grin as a Cheshire cat; curl the lip.

(see *scorn, mock, ridicule, disdain, contempt*)

SNOBBISH (to be)
dwell in high glacial latitudes; put oneself on a pedestal; be altitudinous; lose the common touch.

(see *haughty, pretentious, self-praise, condescend*)

SNORE (v.)
trumpet in one's sleep; raise a typhoon of snoring.

(see *noisy, sleep, hoarse*)

SNOW (n.)
diamond dust; white star dust; frosting for a wedding cake; copious white fuzz; shining gems in the earth's white velvet cup; etching with white.

(see *cold*)

SNUB (v.)
keep at arm's length; turn the cold shoulder; be down on.

(see *humiliate, rebuke, disdain, contempt*)

SNUG (fit)
fit to a T.

(see *close, tighten*)

SOAPY
a white mud of lather.

(see *clean*)

SOAR
hitchhike on a breeze; kite upward; flame up; describe an arc.

(see *fly, height*)

SOB (v.)
flood oneself with tears; have a knot in one's throat; have every syllable a tear; emit a sigh that heaves all the cavities of one's chest; let sobs sweep through one's frame; chant tearfully; make one's throat a cave of the winds for one's unreleased sobs.

(see *tearful, weep, sigh*)

SOBER (to be)
keep one's countenance; have a frozen expression on one's face; keep an orderly face; curb levity; bridle mirth; be dry; stay on the water wagon.

(see *serious, temperate, sane, calm, quiet*)

SOCIABLE (to be)
come out of one's shell; break the ice; make advances to; beat up one's quarters; go on a round of visits; keep company with; walk hand-in-hand with; eat off the same trencher; club together; go arm-in-arm with; bring into the family circle; give a warm reception to; kill the fatted calf; keep open house; be at home to; pay a visit to; drop in on; live at free quarters; look one up; take pot luck with; crack a bottle with; make oneself at home with; look in on.

(see *friendly*)

SOCIALIZE
seine big names from the social sea; sit enthroned in the Golden Horse-

shoe; travel on the social merry-go-round; be in the social swim; join the social parade; move in top circles; travel with the fashionable herd; live in a blaze of splendor; know the gossip of the leonine world; be of the upper stratum; turn one's salon into a den of "lions"; be sprucely maned and elegantly tailed; hobnob with bluebloods; have residence in the silk-stocking district; collect pedigrees.
(see *fashionable, elegant, party, rich, luxury, pleasure-seeking.*

SOFT
silky; liquid; velvet; melting; buttery; padded; feather-bed; downy; waxen; tan-colored; putty.
(see *smooth, submissive, weak, irresolute, mild, delicate, tender*)

SOFTEN
have time softly press its velvet palm upon; make the first crack in a hard surface; take the edge off; temper the wind to the shorn lamb; use soft fire to make sweet malt; mellow; fur; dissolve.
(see *soothe, soft*)

SOILED
a mass of shop-worn merchandise; an unswept chimney.
(see *spotted, tainted, sordid*)

SOLACE (n.)
crumbs of comfort.
(see *relief, cheer, soothe*)

SOLDIERY
battalion of boots; brass and braid; knights of the knapsack; rank and file; standard bearers; cannon fodder; shavetail; food for powder; horse and foot.
(see *war, fight*)

SOLICIT
crusade for; court; woo the charitable.
(see *ask, request, implore, urge, arouse, excite*)

SOLICITOUS (to be)
sow one's thoughts in.
(see *careful, troubled, eager*)

SOLITARY
lone wolf; the sweets of silence; treading the wine-press alone.
(see *aloofness, lonely, seclusion, isolated*)

SOLUTION (to find the)
piece together a broken chain; unravel the tangle; find the key to; find the missing link; get out of a blind alley; find one's way out of a labyrinth; cut the Gordian knot; thread one's way out of a difficulty; break a mystery; iron out a problem; ferret out a mystery; find the master-key for unlocking; arrive at the truth; get to the bottom of.
(see *explain, clear, interpret, clue*)

SOLVENT (to be)
stay in the black; keep one's head above water.
(see *unencumbered, pay, debt*)

SOMETIMES
once in a blue moon; once in a coon's age.
(see *rarity, scarce, spasmodic*)

SON
the grape from the vine of one's family; a consolation; a chip off the old block; the youngest shoot on the family tree; the family cupbearer.
(see *child, children*)

SOON

before the candles are burned out.

(see *early, quickly*)

SOOTHE

set the mind at ease; smooth the ruffled brow of care; cool down to the soul; pour balm into; pour oil on; change the blood to light; silence with a gentle caress; give an angelic message to; salve; nurse; dull the edge of; remove the sting from; soften.

(see *relief, calm, pacify, ease*)

SOPHISTICATED (to be)

be a man of the world; give oneself airs; get up on the high horse.

(see *experienced, artificial*)

SORCERY (to practice)

look on with the evil eye; wave a wand at; raise ghosts; call up spirits from the vasty deep; cast a spell; rub the ring; raise spirits from the dead; rub the lamp; magnetize; gaze into a crystal; lead a ghost dance; have second sight; draw a magic circle around.

(see *magician, prophesy*)

SORDID

on the seamy side of human nature; bituminous.

(see *soiled, selfish, sinful, stingy*)

SORROWFUL (to be)

feel one's heart bleed; be a dejected little figure of grief; waft a sigh from Indus to the pole; sigh like a furnace; feel the heart drum with sobs; feel edged with a flame of regret; have a sense of heaviness; be a model of sorrow; have the black ox tread on one's foot; have tears stand in one's eyes; open a spring of tears; be bankrupt in heart; have cheeks furrowed with tears; traverse dark pastures; eat one's heart out; have the heart ache with anguish; flog one's conscience; have a heart that drips blood; lacerate the heart; feel a dagger plunged in one's heart; be torn by emotions; have tears in one's voice; cry one's eyes out; burst into tears; put on mourning; wear sackcloth and ashes; wear the willow; give sorrow words; have words stick in the throat; bring one's gray hairs with sorrow to the grave; have haunt the memory; have a broken heart; wail with woe; feel the iron entering into one's soul; have prey on the heart; drink the cup of sorrow to its dregs; carry around a lacerated heart; be touched to the quick; wail by the waters of sorrow; have the bruise of sorrow on one's heart; feel sorrow in the most secret fibers of one's soul.

(see *sad, grieve, dejected, depressed, mourn, distressed, melancholy, dreary, rueful*)

SORT OUT (v.)

winnow.

(see *arrange, distribute, discriminate, select, choose*)

SOUL

a spark of God; the innermost shrine of humanity; the most secret fibers of the body.

(see *spirit, mind*)

SOUNDS (n.)

clatter; ringing of a bell in one's ears; tolling of a knell; singing; whispering; grunting; purring smoothly; snarling; stuttering; laughing; the voice of a pair of agitated clippers; ripple; the song of hurrying waters; clashing; strange music; beating; yawping; lisping; crashing; barking;

a great untiring lullaby, rising and falling like t h e ocean; echoing; rhythmic throbbing; a cry that cleaves the stillness; the soft plunk of rubber heels; grating on the ear; the dream-spun cadence of the surf; creaking; hissing; the delicate whisper of leaves; throbbing beats of drums; sound breaking across darkness; chattering; words falling softly on perfumed air; waves of familiar sound; pealing on the ears; muttering thunder; crow-ing; rumbling; crackling.

(see *voice, noisy, loud, whisper, express, utter, music, singing, resonant, resound, reverberate, echo, rustling*)

SOURCE (n.)
the sea of life; the tree of knowledge; the secret springs of life; the fountain-head of life; the world, a winepress of sensation and happiness; the river of life; the loom of life; the cradle of civilization; the seedbed of popula-tion; the deep roots of trouble; the soil for the seeds of fear; a mine of information; the core of the matter; feeding streams; the beacon of desire; a hotbed of cliches; vials of hate; the key of knowledge; rivulets of power; a harvest of truths; an engine of power; a feeding ground; nuggets of information; the springboard; the perennial fountain of prosperity; the deep wellsprings of the spirit; the thumb of his memory; the backbones of the stories; a reservoir of informa-tion; the fount of desire; a bed of sanctity; a vein of humor; canals for communication; the heart of the question; the seed of epidemics.

(see *origin, cause, beginning*)

SOUTH (n.)
enchanted sunlit lands.
(see *hot weather*)

SPACE (n.)
elbow room; chinks; gap; to the four winds; the face of the earth; the wide world; under the sun; gulf.

(see *extend, expand, spread, room, remote*)

SPAN (n.)
bridge.
(see *extend, scope*)

SPARE (v.)
give (or show) quarter; mince words.
(see *pity, forgive, tolerant, mild*)

SPARKLING
blazing; dancing; glistening; wink-ing; jeweled; like champagne; sun-like.
(see *gay, bright, light*)

SPASMODIC
by fits and snatches.
(see *sometimes, short-lived, irregularly*)

SPATTERED
a drift of poppyseed.
(see *scattered, sprinkle, scarce*)

SPEAK
let fall from the lips; bring to the tip of the tongue; come to the point; throw a word over one's shoulder; spit out words; let speech tumble out; toss out words; cut in with words; flail the air with speech; oil one's words; rap out an order; clip one's words; thunder forth; break silence; twitter; chirp; fling a speech out; have words leave one's mouth; illum-inate with words; let one's voice pop out; pour out speech; bubble up into speech; launch winged words at a mark; gabble; lift up the voice; trip on the tongue; find one's tongue;

voice an opinion; have on one's lips; rave wildly; draw words from one's mouth; wring speech; discharge a final round of words; take the words out of the mouth of; fling out a word; struggle to find voice; take the plunge; clack; cackle; mouth words; frame one's words; launch a statement; be the mouthpiece for; taste one's words; take the stump; wag the tongue; sweep silence aside; spit words through one's teeth; have words burn on one's tongue; ham through one's lines; toss a b o u t phrases; scatter one's words; sow words around.

(see *express, utter, pronounce, say, tell, declare, orate, preach, proclaim, conversation*)

SPECIAL
red-letter; not for everyday; one's long suit.

(see *unusual, rarity, scarce, holiday, unclassified*)

SPECIFY
descend from generalities; enter into detail; descend to particulars; come to the point; put one's fingers on; earmark; brand.

(see *define, detailed*)

SPECK
a superfluous atom; molecule; corpuscle.

(see *bit, small amount, particle*)

SPECTATOR
one with an armchair view.

(see *viewpoint, see, look at*)

SPECULATE
take a flyer; dabble in; play the business.

(see *trade, business, meditate, consider, ponder, gamble, invest*)

SPEECH
cutting drawl; slow, mechanical voice; rolling speech; string of words poured forth; crisp dialogue; riot of words; whirlwind of words; freezing tones; knuckle-rapping intonation; interminable defile of words; a long, fine-spun yarn; burst of eloquence; quiet pearls of words; stump speech; flowering oratory; arrows of words; words tolling alternate dirge notes; fiery oratorical chariot; wordy ammunition; diluted language; white-hot speech; verbal caress; oratorical guns turned loose.

(see *conversation, speak*)

SPEECHLESS (to be)
have one's voice freeze; hold the tongue; have the cat get one's tongue; see a wolf; lose the tongue; choke back words; be smitten into silence; have words die away on the tongue; make a poor mouth; have words stick in one's throat; be tongue-tied.

(see *silent, quiet*)

SPEED (to travel with)
show a clean pair of heels; clip along; go at an eye-blinking pace; tear up a street; move at a dizzy tempo; travel on the wings of the wind; quicken one's pace; open up the throttle; see the telegraph poles flying by; borrow momentum; fly along in seven-league boots; travel at the top of one's speed; step on the accelerator; get under full steam; move under press of sail (or canvas); go by leaps and bounds; apply whip and spur to; fly along.

(see *fast, swift, run, rush, flee, hastily, hurry, quickly, fly*)

SPEND (v.)
lay out one's money; turn money loose; fool away money; throw dollars

away; shoot the works; turn on the tap; pour out money; devour a fortune; lavish one's cash on; scatter money to the winds; open the sluices; open the flood-gates; eat up money; open one's purse-strings; pour water into a sieve (spend without purpose or result); make money flow like water; incur a crushing financial outlay; untie the purse-strings; shell out; see money swallowed up by; watch the flow of coin across counters; melt one's money away; feel money burn a hole in one's pocket.

(see *pay, extravagant, lavish, expensive, squander*)

SPINSTER
a wallflower; a woman left on the shelf.

(see *virtuous, old*)

SPIRIT (n.)
a soul of white fire; the shadow of the body as it walks the world.

(see *soul, mind*)

SPITEFUL (to be)
have a worm in one's tongue; put venom into one's words; be a slave of malice.

(see *malicious, resent, hate, annoy, injure, offend*)

SPLASH (v.)
rise in showers.

(see *swimmer, spray*)

SPLENDID
blazing; dazzling.

(see *bright, conspicuous, excellent, fame, renown, celebrity, best, ideal*)

SPLIT (v.)
cause to fly in pieces; open up a cleavage in.

(see *divide, break, separate*)

SPOIL (v.)
cloud; scar; make worm-eaten; smear a streak across; puncture; cripple; poison; knock into a cocked-hat; impale; prick; tarnish; clip the wings of; reduce to a skeleton; cause to become moth-eaten; take off the hinges; cast a shadow over; put one's foot into; spoil the food in cooking; curdle; shatter; crack; upset the applecart; mess up; make a hash of; send to rack and ruin; throw out of gear; make an eyesore of; butcher; blight; cause to yield dead fruit.

(see *defect, destroy, injure, hurt, disfigured, ruin*)

SPOILS (to get)
shake the plum tree; be in on the rake-off; make hay.

(see *thief, extort*)

SPOKESMAN
mouthpiece.

(see *represent*)

SPONGE (live off another)
have one's fingers in someone else's pocket.

(see *parasite*)

SPONSOR (v.)
be the angel for; back; plug; push.

(see *support*)

SPORTING (to be)
be a good soldier; have one's sense of fair play surge on top.

(see *fair, gamble*)

SPOTTED
checkered; freckled.
(see *spattered, sprinkle, scattered, mark*)

SPRAWL (v.)
make a long arm; drag one's slow length along.
(see *loaf, lazy, ease*)

SPRAY (n.)
a bouquet of liquid.
(see *splash, sprinkle*)

SPREAD (v.)
mushroom; swell; trowel on; scatter in all directions; cause to go the rounds; deploy; sow; throw out roots; shoot out; filter through; fan out.
(see *extend, expand, distribute*)

SPREE (to have a)
go on a bat.
(see *revelry, drunk, indulge, self-indulgence*)

SPRINGTIME
the curve of the year; the coming of earth's green mantle; the peeping out of buds.
(see *young, grow, fresh, prime*)

SPRINKLE (v.)
pepper; season; lard between; stud with; powder; sand; dust; bedew.
(see *spray*)

SPYING
walls have ears; underground activities.
(see *detect, discern, inquisitive, search for, examine, watchful, undermine*)

SQUABBLE (n.)
a teapot tempest; a quick confetti of flung insults.
(see *quarrel, disagree, discord, dispute, contend*)

SQUANDER (v.)
play ducks and drakes with one's possessions; fritter away a legacy; drink one's patrimony down in one brimming cupful.
(see *lavish, extravagant, spend, wasteful, dissipate, use up*)

SQUARE (n.)
a checkerboard block.
(see *shape, form*)

SQUELCH (v.)
put out the flame of; crush.
(see *subdue, suppress, silent*)

SQUINT (v.)
screw up the eyes; swivel the eyes.
(see *look at, indirect*)

STAB (v.)
give an inch of cold iron to.
(see *injure, blow*)

STABILIZE
give anchor to; give sea-legs to; establish on an island of rock; keep a floor under; weather the storm; keep on an even keel.
(see *firm, immovable, unchangeable, secure*)

STAGE (n.)
milestone; step; turn.
(see *point*)

STAMMER (v.)
have one's tongue trip itself; have words stick in one's throat; be unable to put two words together.
(see *hesitate*)

STAND (v.)

plant the foot; bounce to the feet; rock to the feet; be on one's legs; find one's footing; take up position.

(see *stay*)

STANDARD (n.)

golden mean; rule of thumb; yardstick; up to the mark; the established line that must not be crossed; touchstone; a mark to shoot at; cut-and-dried; pace.

(see *model, rule*)

STARE (v.)

fix the eyes upon; cast a hawk's glance at; look full in the face; rivet the eyes upon; have eyes burning like coals; fasten a lingering glance upon; glue the eyes on; feed the eyes on; fix a long piercing look upon; pierce with the eyes; fix with a threatening eye; be marble-eyed; have a basilisk stare.

(see *look at*)

START (v.)

set one's face for; kick off; spark; unfurl the wings; sow the seeds of; jump from a spring-board; embark; take off; get on the first leg of; fire the first shot; set in motion the train of; get a foot in the stirrup; touch off; be in the bud; sprout; flicker into action; kindle the fire of; spring into action; appply the match to; unleash; let loose; bubble in ferment; blaze the trail for; plunge into; bring to birth; erupt; father; clear out for Guam; let it rip; launch; pioneer; whip up; get underway; tackle; turn the wheel; break ground; dig a new foothold; set the ball in motion; take the first step; lay the first stone; hit the trail; set on foot; get the ball rolling; light out for.

(see *begin, invent*)

STARTLE (v.)

explode a bombshell; light a firecracker under; take away one's breath; jolt out of complacency.

(see *surprise, scare, disturbance*)

STARVE

have the bread taken out of one's mouth; dine with Duke Humphrey; make two bites of a cherry; perish with hunger; not have a morsel of food to swallow; be on a meager diet.

(see *hungry*)

STAY (v.)

pitch one's tent; cast anchor; come to roost; cling to; stick in.

(see *continue, endure, wait*)

STEADFAST (to be)

be moored; stick to one's guns; show not a shadow of turning; persevere through thick and thin; dare hellheat or Arctic cold; keep in the straight path of duty; maintain one's course; be anchored to; have a heart that never swerves; have true steel quality; hold a light that adversity cannot quench; sit tight in the saddle; have both feet on the ground; be a rock of resolution; have a stomach defiant of wind and wave; hold one's life on an even keel; have the firmness of a fixed star; not yield an inch.

(see *preserve, resolute, firm, faithful, unchangeable, determined*)

STEALTHY (to be)

pussyfoot around; go as silent as the air; steal a glance; have the air of a hunted animal.

(see *sly, secret, undermine*)

STERN (to be)

shoot a chilling glance; direct a basilisk look at; be parchment-faced; have a forbidding aspect; be grim-visaged; be iron-fisted; have a stony face; have a cast-iron character.

(see *severe, strict, harsh, cruel, bitter, hard*)

STIFF (adj.)

stone-image; ramrod; petrified; rugged; old-maidish; corrugated; stony; rigid; marble.

(see *rigid, immovable, unchangeable, firm, obstinate, stubborn, formal*)

STIMULATE (v.)

fire the soul; galvanize to action; ply the spurs to; awaken the interest of; electrify into activity; kindle the light of; give a shot-in-the-arm to; stir the spirit of; give a stinging challenge to; whet the appetite for; whip up enthusiasm; fan the fire of; warm up the fire; fire the imagination; kindle the pulse of; open avenues of thought; give food for thinking; slip a hot needle into; add fuel to the flame; inflame to action; play on the feelings of; set a melody singing in one's blood; key up for effort; make a bonfire out of dead ashes; set afire; quicken the interest of; set hearts leaping for; add yeast to; spark; sweep on a billow of enthusiasm; give a tonic to; recharge the brain cells; plough up and fertilize; give an infusion of new blood; serve as a whetstone; quicken the pulse; add oil to the fire; put under the whip-lash.

(see *incite, excite, encourage, urge, arouse*)

STINGY (to be)

live cheek by jowl; be tight-fisted; pinch pennies; be fast-handed; be a penny-saver; pile penny upon penny; pinch the purse; keep the purse-strings tight.

(see *miserly*)

STOLID

wooden; stuffed-shirt; strait-laced.

(see *formal, dull, unmoved, stupid, slow, narrow-minded*)

STOMACH (n.)

bread-basket; asbestos-lined catch-all; food-bin.

(see *relish, eat*)

STOP (v.)

stay one's hand; nip in the bud; freeze; knock off with; crack; break; cause to die out; dry up; slither into nothing; paralyze; crumble; halt; ground; arrest motion; fade; hold up; kill; cut adrift; pull up; scrap; stem the tide; sink into rest; check; fall exhausted; bring to a deadlock; put the brakes on; shut off; block; put into cold storage; checkmate; hold in; repose on one's laurels; rest on one's oars; mark time; ride at anchor; plague progress; toss in the towel; blunt; drop anchor; curb; stall; jolt to a halt; throttle; clamp silence on; stick in the mud; pull the check string; smother; pitch one's tent; draw the line; crash into silence; dam the stream of; shut up shop; break a hush; cut out; harness; turn thumbs down on; hit a snag; cause a thing to spend itself; explode opposition; strangle; choke; bring to a dead end; bring to the point of cessation; pull up short; block; cut off; break off; drop the reins; split a hush; stop dead in its tracks; cut short; grind to a flickering halt; shut down on; apply a tourniquet to; bring to a stalemate; cause to pipe down.

(see *end, close, obstruct, impasse, restrain, hinder, suppress, interrupt, prevent, delay, discontinue, pause*)

STORE (v.)

put on ice; lay in the hold; treasure

up; hive.

(see *preserve, keep, reserve, save*)

STORM
blown sheets of rain; millions of waves rearing up and wrestling with each other; a snow volcano; groaning waves of the tortured sea; heavy sea; ground swell; clap of thunder; the sky leaning low; raising the wind; sea lashed into fury; a crack running up the golden bowl of the sky; leaden clouds reaching spectral fingers to smother the sun; a brooding sky; thunder hammering across the sky; storm sucking in the air.

(see *wind, rain, snow*)

STORY-TELLER
a spinner of yarns; a narrator of tall stories.

(see *relate, tell, talkative*)

STRAIGHT
a chalk line; a beeline; a ramrod.

(see *direct*)

STRAIGHTFORWARD (adv.)
right between the eyes; straight to the point; without beating about the bush; straight f r o m the horse's mouth; in a beeline; squarely; man to man; by a straight path.

(see *direct, immediately, quickly*)

STRAIGHTFORWARD (to be)
meet four-square; call a spade a spade; tell without any draped accessories; give a good square look.

(see *truthful, frank, sincere*)

STRANGE
a fish out of water; the devil riding on a fiddlestick; beating the Dutch; a person one doesn't know from Adam;

something far-fetched.

(see *unusual, foreign, new, unclassified, unexpected, unimaginable, unique*)

STRATEGY
pulling strings in the interests of; keeping something up one's sleeve; killing two birds with one stone; recoiling to leap the better; playing one's cards well; having an ace in the hole.

(see *subterfuge, maneuver, trickery, mislead, deceive*)

STRENGTHEN
dig in to resist; prune the deadwood off; stiffen the temper of; sharpen; bolster up; stiffen the sinews of; steel oneself; cement together; lay stone upon stone to build the fortress of; ballast by.

(see *reinforce, stimulate, encourage, support*)

STRENUOUS
back-breaking; dog's life.

(see *energetic, vigorous, eager, resolute, bold, strong, determined*)

STRICT
tight-belted; strait-laced; hard-and-fast rule; within a wall of convention; ruling with an iron hand; whip-cracking; iron-clad; cast-iron; air-tight.

(see *severe, rigid, stern, harsh, uncompromising, accurate, exact, careful, tense*)

STRIFE (to promote)
sow dragons' teeth; blow the coals or the fire; sow dissension.

(see *incite, embroil, estrange, evil, discord, disrupt, disturbance, victimize, agitator*)

STRIKE (v.)

plant a haymaker; knock one's block off; hit one in the eye; belt over; rain blows on; sport with one's flesh; swing at; ruffle against.

(see *blow, knock out, whip, punish*)

STRIVE

sweat away at; breast the current; bend over backwards; push higher and higher; let the wish be father to the thought.

(see *try, endeavor, labor, struggle, attempt, exertion, aim, utmost*)

STRONG (to be)

have fingers that are bands of steel; be broad-beamed and well-buttressed; be made of cast-iron; be a husky; have nerves that are whipcords; be set in one's legs; be strong enough to blow down the walls of Jericho; have a bite; have the constitution of a Nubian lion; be full-blooded; be thick-ribbed; be fresh as a daisy; have rich sap in one's veins; have sinews of steel; be well-knit; be in fine fettle; have tensile strength; have backbone; be as strong as a rock; be as strong as a lion (or a horse); be at the zenith of one's power; have a body of oak; have iron in one's amalgam; be made of metal; be hardened against pain; have veins of iron; be all blood and iron; have a back of steel; have the splendid strength of a raging lion; be a rock of defense; have iron control; win by the weight of one's armor; be a blood-and-thunder strong man; whip one's weight in wild cats; hold in an iron embrace; have a touch of whalebone in one's system; be made of granite; have the hold of a band of iron; be in the pink.

(see *vigorous, tough, power, healthy, firm, vehement, efficient, energetic, intense, bold, violent, sharp, strenuous*)

STRUCTURE

fabric; framework; architecture.

(see *basis, build, building, form, compose*)

STRUGGLE (v.)

wade through deep waters; flounder in the path; scramble to find one's feet; lumber up through; heave painfully upward; wrestle with; lead a rough-and-tumble e x i s t e n c e; beat against; grapple with a problem; have hard sledding; wallow through difficulties; worm one's way upward; groan away at; have a hard time making ends meet; be involved in a tug-of-war; grub along; do battle against; be together by the ears; be hard put to it.

(see *strive, endeavor, hardship, try, exertion, utmost, labor, effort, contend, fight, conflict*)

STUBBORN (to be)

be deaf to advice; kick against the pricks; have bulldog tenacity; be blindly unreasonable; be pig-headed; be a tough nut to crack; be set in one's ways; have mule-like determination; have stubbornness run through one's veins; run rusty; be dogged about; be a stickler for; continue in spite of the pie; steel the heart.

(see *obstinate, persevere, stiff*)

STUDY (v.)

pore over; chew the truth of; come to grips with; bone up on; keep a studious eye on; bury oneself in books; dig deep into; burn the midnight oil; comb books; probe deeply into; store the vacuum of one's mind with; amass information; weigh; turn over the leaves; run the eye over; wade through; watch with an eagle eye; revel in the library; burrow into books; dig through facts; imbibe a strong drink of logic; size up; imprison oneself among books; stretch one's hand back down the centuries; mug up; mount the ladder to thorough knowledge; boil down an idea; feed one's scholarly curiosity; rake the dust piles of knowledge; drink at the springs of the past; have the mind take an impression of; tackle a problem; set forth on an intellectual voyage; sit under a tutor; fathom the depths of; take stock of; hammer away at; do some window-shopping for ideas.

(see *research, investigate, examine, meditate, ponder, think, analyze*)

STUN

rock a person on his heels; petrify; paralyze; root to the pavement; hit between the eyes; freeze into form.

(see *surprise, shocked, confuse, overcome*)

STUPID (to be)

do an intellectual tail-spin; feel one's brains fallen into one's boots; have a soft head; be wrapped in a mental fog; have one's garret unfurnished; be feather-headed; have a bird-brain; not see an inch beyond one's nose; be muddle-headed; be weak-headed; have a bovine brain; be knuckle-headed; play the monkey; knock one's head against the wall; be buried in the quicksands of ignorance; be weak in the upper story; be chuckle-headed; not have a grain of sense; take leave of one's senses; play the goat; be short-sighted; be crackbrained; have a thick skull; have one's few mental buttons all fly off; need every bit of brains one can lay one's hands on; be a donkey; be a blockhead; have the intellect of a cabbage; have one's mind a perfect blank; be sunk to the ears in a mental bog; be lame above the neckband; be slow on the uptake;

have one's brain work on a part-time basis; have only a spoonful of brains; have one's head a complete vacuum; have a mind like a sieve; be empty-headed; be seven kinds of an imbecile; have one's brains full of cobwebs; do some muscle-bound thinking; have a rhinoceros hide; be mule-headed; have a wooden head; have one's skull untenanted; be mentally asleep; have an ivory-head; have one's brains all soup; be a mental virgin; be muddle-witted; be mentally drugged; not be one to invent gunpowder; be an ass; have an impoverished intellect; be all in the dark.

(see *senseless, stolid, foolish, uninteresting, tedious, dull, undiscerning, unimaginative, unintelligent*)

SUAVE

oily; of high polish; silken; velvety; kid-gloved.

(see *smooth, polite, pleasant*)

SUBCONSCIOUS (n.)

the dark continents of one's mind; the dust-bin of the mind; a tossing ocean of thoughts; the back of the mind; the kitchen that prepares our ideas for us.

(see *psychoanalysis, mind*)

SUBDUE

make one sing small; drive to the wall; throw into the shade; get under one's thumb; browbeat; muzzle; take down a peg; mute one's strings; prison; bottle up; trample over; crush; put through the mill.

(see *conquer, overcome, defeat, surmount, break, reduce, restrain, soften, suppress, repress, control*)

SUBJECT (n.)

a peg to hang one's ideas on; literary pole; point; choice of fare; grist to the mental mill; running thread; the core of a book.

(see *point, resources*)

SUBMISSIVE (to be)

give one's head for the washing; lie at the feet of; have another's foot on one's neck; take a thing sitting down; have one's hat in hand; be another's puppet; sacrifice oneself on the altar of; eat out of another's hand; play second fiddle to; lower one's horns; grin and abide; bend to another's yoke; swallow the pill; eat humble pie; pocket the affront; make a virtue of necessity; knuckle under; bend the knee; bend before the storm; eat dirt; bite the dust; swallow the leek; kiss the rod; deliver up one's arms; hand over one's sword; turn the other cheek; withdraw from the field; throw oneself into the arms of; haul down one's flag; bow to the inevitable; surrender to necessity.

(see *obedient, patient, passive, meek, deference, self-abasement*)

SUBORDINATE (to be)

play second fiddle; sit at the feet of; take a back seat; be a satellite.

(see *secondary, inferior, depend, underrate*)

SUBSTANCE

body and weight; flesh and bone; fabric; stuff; wine for the goblet; heart; core; drift; burden; pith; soul; weight.

(see *body, mass, resources, fundamental*)

SUBSTANTIAL

a square meal; something you can get your teeth into; solid.

(see *realistic, strong, firm*)

SUBSTITUTE

step into the shoes of; pinch-hit for; be a stop-gap; take on another's cargo; make a shift for; be employed as a diversionary vehicle.

(see *choice, change, represent*)

SUBTERFUGE

dust thrown in the eyes; a blind; moonshine; glossing over; furnishing a handle; lending a color to; a tub thrown to a whale (from the whaling custom of throwing a tub into the sea when a ship was threatened by a school of whales, whose attention was thus diverted to the substitute object).

(see *evade, excuse, shiftiness, trickery, pretend*)

SUBURB

"fringe" area; periphery.

(see *city, edge*)

SUCCESSFUL (to be)

come out on top; rise to the surface; make a crooked track turn in one's direction; hit the bull's eye; get to first base; come Yorkshire over one; carry one's point; have one's shadow never grow less; get along; come off with flying colors; have one on the hip; have the ball at one's feet; take by storm; have the game in one's own hands; flare up like a rocket; keep one's head above water; climb on the bandwagon; gain the day; carry the field; win one's spurs; make the riffle; bear away the bell; win hands down; see land; hurdle a difficulty; brush aside impediments; collar the corners of the earth; make a killing; cut a swath; pull big; carry to a profitable conclusion; get the wheel out of the rut; cover oneself with glory; bear fruit; win the day; make one's way; waltz to fame; earn a place; climb the ladder; "'click"; get one's wings; plunge through; score a point; develop a roar; pocket the plums; ring a bell; leap the fences; make good; hit a home run; do the trick; ride the crest of; be a shining light; crack the shell of the oyster; get a feather in one's cap; hit with a bang; make a touchdown; make a hit; find a gold mine; wring gold from the world; make a long run; make a field goal; come to fruition; wrap oneself in a blaze of glory; stand on the heights; set the town on fire; accept one's throne and sceptre; scale the heights; be flushed with triumph; go from rags to riches; have a streak of luck; get in the harvest; carry the ball of fortune; have one's cake and eat it too; carry all before one; crack a tidy crust; strike pay dirt; have the world by the tail; be on the top rung; have success heaped in one's lap; mop up; see time well spent; bring home the loot; see one's name lead all the rest; go over with a bang; ride the top wave; bring home the bacon; strive to some purpose; be on velvet; go on swimmingly; hit the right nail on the head; reap golden sheaves; see one's star in the ascendant; have the world at one's feet; hit the jackpot; take a sturdy stance in life; have solid foundations; remain a waterspout; occupy a strategic perch; be on one's footing; have everything come one's way; be in full swing; be crowned with success; make the enemy bite the dust; trample obstacles under foot; carry the flag; run up from a shoestring; strike oil; ride smoothly over; arrive socially; eat the sweet fruits of; be on the road to fame; sail through life; have a walkover; make one's pile; keep one's legs; make a go of; reach up and touch the stars; make one's mark; be mellowed by the sun of prosperity; get there with both feet; march to greatness; hold the trump card; have the whip-hand; have the upper hand; direct a master-stroke; be

at the top of the tree; soar to success; secure a place in the skies; win the honors; keep a good house; have a run of luck; turn up trumps.

(see *fortunate, prosperous, lucky, victorious, win, triumphant*)

SUDDEN
greased lightning; at a stroke; volcanic; whirlwind; spur of the moment; at one fell swoop; in the twinkling of an eye; at one jump; at a gulp; coming around the corner; beginning on the up beat; staccato; lightning-like; in the opening and shutting of an eye; before one can say "Jack Robinson"; swift; flashing; like a shot; with a bang; a bolt; meteoric; with a stab; in a flash; pop; darting out and away.

(see *unexpectedly, immediately, quickly*)

SUFFER
reap a bitter harvest; labor under affliction; take a thing in the raw; be choked by a viper of agony; feel one's pain nerves come alive; walk through fire, bear one's cross; taste hell; be broken on the wheel; groan beneath oppression; have the pig on one's back; stew or fry in one's own juice; bear the burden of; walk in hell; take a thing on the chin; be swept away on a rushing tide of suffering; have a deep scar; sit on pins and needles; make a wry face; be cut to the quick; be torn by suffering; go through the mill; take the bumps; sit on thorns; be a toad under the harrow; pay the piper; know where the shoe pinches; burn one's fingers; lie prostrate in hopeless misery.

(see *penalty, feeling, endure, tolerant, receive, indulge, pain, loss*)

SUFFICIENT
with no sparing hand; to one's heart's

TALL (to be)

threaten the gas globes; draw oneself to a trooper-like stature.

(see *height, big, soar*)

TASTELESS

ashes in the mouth; food without personality; a dish drained of savor.

(see *dull, uninteresting, savor, tasty*)

TASTY

mouth-watering; fitting the palate; tickling the palate.

(see *savor, relish*)

TAUNT (v.)

rag; twit; deliver a caustic remark to; sting with jibes; stab with a jibe.

(see *mock, ridicule, reproach, sneer, butt*)

TAWDRY

ginger-bread.

(see *ostentatious, cheap, low class*)

TEACH

sharpen the wits; take in hand; sow the seeds of; polish the wits; ground in; point a lesson; shed the light of one's learning; school in; launch into a classroom; pump rudiments into another's head; beat into the head; lead to knowledge; guide the footsteps; force down another's throat; be an intellectual wet nurse.

(see *inform, enlighten, train, discipline, interpret, explain, guide, show, advise, direct*)

TEARFUL (to be)

struggle through rain-clouds; weep in dropped pearls; dampen one's handkerchief; have glistening moisture under the lashes; feel a curious moisture at one's eyes; be salt-bitten; launch a flow of misery; be an onion; collapse in a vale of tears.

(see *sob, weep, sorrowful, mourn*)

TEASE

pull another's leg; make game of; twit.

(see *playful, annoy, torment, irritate*)

TEDIOUS

dragging its weary length along; limping along lengthy corridors; cut-and-dried; spun out; harping on the same string; long-winded; microscopically detailed.

(see *monotonous, dull, uninteresting*)

TELL

pour out a story; unwind a story; reel off; break news to; breathe a tale; unravel a story; unfold a tale; breathe a word about; unfurl; picture; take a story into one's hands; pour into another's ears; spin a yarn; retail news; come out with; get a thing off one's chest; put a bee in one's bonnet; let the cat out of the bag; insert in an ear; sob out a tale; spill a tale; spin out; pass from mouth to mouth; proclaim at Charing Cross; bombard with news; feed a tale to; weave a yarn.

(see *relate, report, describe, reveal, divulge, declare, teach, inform, explain, express, utter, speak*)

TEMPER (to have a)

fly into a passion; fly off the handle; go into a black fit; flare up; hold the weapon of one's temper by the blade.

(see *angry, rage*)

TEMPERAMENTAL

caught away in the claws of a mood; volcanic; mercurial; barometric.

(see *changeable, sensitive*)

TEMPERATE (to be)

look not upon the wine when it is red; know when one has had enough; take the pledge; deny oneself; strike an average; hit the happy mean.

(see *sober, self-control, self-possessed*)

TEMPORARY

only from day to day; fleeting; a flash in the pan; in the short run; a sliding scale set up on a quicksand; fair-weather; month-to-month; May-fly; nine days' wonder; writ in water; stop-gap.

(see *brief, short-lived*)

TEMPT

bait with a silver hook; sing the Siren song; have the voice of the tempter; offer forbidden fruit; grease the palm; draw the trail of a red herring; magnetize; throw a sop to; gild the pill; make one's mouth water; extend the bait to; seduce; sling a net over; dangle a carrot before the donkey's nose; cause to wrestle with the devil; get the fish to bite; not make Satan take to his heels; fly in the face of; be an emissary of Satan; drag the insidious coils of a serpent; be the serpent in Paradise.

(see *lure, seduce, fascinate, attract, incite*)

TENDENCY

undercurrent; leaning; s h a d i n g toward; a bump for.

(see *susceptible, trend*)

TENDER

liquid; melting; trickling; compassionately bosomed; softened.

(see *soft, delicate, weak, sensitive, kind, mild*)

TENSE (to be)

have the rigid quiet of a stretched spring; be in an electric atmosphere; be high-strung; have the fibres strung to concert pitch; be stiff; feel the atmosphere drop to zero.

(see *tighten, rigid, stiff, nervous, excited*)

TERRIFY

freeze the blood; make the blood run cold; make one's hairs stand on end; make one tremble; seize the heart; seize with panic; have a blood-and-thunder effect; make the spine tingle; give a nightmare to; have an ungodly effect on; throw into consternation; prostrate with terror; fasten a baleful face on; draw a circle of terror around.

(see *scare, startle*)

TEST (v.)

put to the proof; see how the land lies; feel the pulse of; put to the question; send up a pilot balloon; throw out a feeler; hold a touchstone to; measure with a yardstick; gauge with a barometer; take the temperature of; make a proving ground of; put through the mill; put a straw in the wind; plumb the depth of; put through the fiery f u r n a c e; put through one's paces; haul over the coals.

(see *try, prove, examine, experiment*)

THERE

on the spot.

(see *place, locate*)

THICK

put on with a pastry tube; caked with; in a white glue of.

(see *fat, full of, replete, abundance*)

THIEF

light-fingered gentry; shop-lifter; finger-smith; shark; land-shark.

(see *stealthy, swindle*)

THIN

mere skin and bones; reduced to a skeleton; worn to a shadow; weedy; wasp-waisted; hawk-faced; rail-faced; dressed-up w i s h b o n e; raw-boned; bare-bone; bag of bones; ribby; scarecrow; mosquito-limbed; a sparse umbrella of a person; escaped from the temptation to fatness; herring-gutted; an iron gas-pipe of a figure; the midsection of an hour-glass; a mere thread; finger's breadth; eggshell.

(see *skinny, slight, small, delicate*)

THINK

hunt in one's mind; play a game with one's thoughts; start the mental wheels grinding; dream up; pull ideas out of a hat; do intellectual gymnastics; crack one's brains; have pass in the mind; chew the cud of thought; have flit through the mind; set the wheels within one's brain to endless revolutions; make mental notes; stretch the imagination; collect one's thoughts; have one's mind uncoil and strike off in a certain direction; have run in one's head; set one's brain to work; rack one's brains; have cross the mind; cudgel one's brains; beat one's brains; have float in the mind; bend the brows; have flash across the mind; have come into one's head; sleep upon a thing; toss one's brain about; have thoughts awaken; chew on a fact; chew a thing over; unbend the mind; look about in one's mind; digest a thought; sweat one's brains; clear the brain of cobwebs; ransack one's brains; pass in review before one's mind; have flit across the brain; connect links in the chain of reasoning; feel a clattering mill of thought go round in one's head; search one's mind; turn mental somersaults; be immersed in thought; set the mind to a feverish speed; have one's brain whirl with ideas; set the mind sailing down a channel; set one's wits to work; knit the brows; frame in fantasy; grope for an idea; toy with a plan; adjust one's mental balances; pace about one's mind; crank up one's mind; hook one's mental tentacles into an idea; look before one leaps; bring forth from the back of one's mind; scratch one's head for an idea; give birth to an idea; consult one's intellectual menu; fry in one's mind; put on one's thinking cap; set a thought to percolating in one's brain; cloud one's forehead; weigh an idea; have one's brain buzzing with ideas; set scurrying through the mind; be rich in meditation; be lost in thought; fall into thought; be wrapped in thought; bend one's mental eye; advise with one's pillow; be devoured by thought; be up to one's ears in thought; be knee-deep in ideas; be sunk in thought; go into a brown study; go woolgathering; have one's mind pick up a thought; be struck by an idea; have the shadow of a thought fall across one's mind; rummage in the inner recesses of one's mind; put a long reflective finger on; face an idea; feel fiery swords play about one's mind; walk in the meadows of meditation; be hit by an idea; go on a mental journey; find food for thought; unravel the threads of one's musings; throw one's mind to a thing; sit in spacious mental solitude.

(see *meditate, ponder, reason, consider, judge, determine, imagine, viewpoint*)

THOROUGH

double-dyed; to the core; dyed in the wool; head over heels; every whit;

head and shoulders; head to foot; every inch; giving the whole meat in the coconut; running the gauntlet of; taking one thing with another; many-sided; leaving not a rack behind; going down to the roots; leaving no stone unturned; cleaning up well behind; making a clean sweep of; going from attic to cellar; running the gamut; to the fingertips; with "bell and book."

(see *completely, complete, absolute*)

THREATEN

hang a sword over one's head; give one something to sing for; browbeat; look thunder; have the unnatural calm of a sleeping volcano; rear an ugly head; set under a dark and lowering cloud; show the mailed fist; show one's teeth; speak daggers; stare one in the face; gather the storm clouds; point a big gun at; thunder with approaching d o o m; scorch with a glance; cast a black look; carry a warning of; shake a stick at; overcloud the sky; set trouble brewing; send clouds on the blue; start a shaking avalanche; look daggers at; brandish the big stick; shake a fist at; parade one's fangs; show the face of death; simmer with anger; send a scowling cloud scurrying over; make stare into a pit that yawns at one's feet; maneuver into the position of an ogre; stir up a hornet's nest; darken by a shadow; haunt by a spectre; level a scourge at; take by the throat.

(see *menace, scare, terrify, warn*)

THRILLED (to be)

feel a line of fire run along one's entire being; be electrified; feel one's heart hammer; be lifted to the stars; feel lifted out of a saddle; feel the heart swell with emotion; tingle with emotion; have one's blood pressure played havoc with; be dazzled by.

(see *arouse, excited, moved, sensation, inspired*)

THWART

drive into a corner; put a spoke in one's wheel; spike one's guns; draw the teeth; clip the wings; put out of gear; take the wind out of one's sails; hamstring; swaddle in red tape; throw off the scent; bring to the end of one's rope.

(see *obstruct, frustrated, hinder, oppose, disconcert, defeat, impasse*)

TIDE (n.)

the white waves pacing to and fro; the sound of the great sea's voice; the sea pouring itself out on the beach.

(see *ocean, sea, waves, flow*)

TIGHTEN

clamp down; pinch; squeeze; weave a tangled maze; make fit like a glove.

(see *close, firm, tense*)

TIME

the whirligig of time; seconds that fly on elfin wings; the march of years; the moving fingers of time; the swinging pendulum of time; the washing of the waves of time; the sands of time running out; the fall of the years; the rolling years; the years waxing and waning; the running by of time; time running off into the shadows; the swift waters of time flowing under the bridge; creeping hours; the flight of time; a majestic stream gliding to the ocean of eternity; a handful of years; the maze of time.

(see *lasting, endure, age, long-lived, short-lived, long ago, immediately, soon, past, future, old, old-fashioned, quickly, week, yesterday, night, autumn, springtime, summer, slow, fast, early, late, premature, mature, permanent*)

TIMELY

high time; hot off the griddle.

(see *opportunist, early*)

TIMID (to be)

be unable to say boo to a goose; be lily-livered; act in a mouse-like way; have the heart of little dog Fido; look shyly upon life; have the air of a shy rabbit.

(see *afraid, modest, fearful, nervous, cowardly, shy*)

TINY

a mote; a midge in the sun; pin-point; pin-prick.

(see *miniature, small, bit, particle, speck*)

TIRED (to be)

feel washed out; be worn out; feel half-dead; be done in; have a drawn look; be used up; be footsore; be weather-beaten; feel ready to drop; feel more dead than alive; feel pumped out; be on one's last legs; feel frayed; be fed up; feel faded; look shopworn; feel floored; feel time hanging heavily on one's hands; be dog-tired; drag one's weary length along; feel parched in spirit; have one's slight form crushed by fatigue.

(see *exhausted, worn out*)

TITLE (n.)

a handle to one's name.

(see *name, nobleman*)

TOGETHER

hand-in-hand; in league; coupled; hand-in-glove; in the same boat (or cart); neck-to-neck; in chorus; side by side; cheek by jowl; arm-in-arm.

(see *unite, join*)

TOLERANT (to be)

uproot the tares of prejudice; maintain an unwarped judgment; bask in the sunshine of tolerance; grin and bear a thing; keep the door open to; stand for a thing; stomach an idea; swallow an affront; give the reins to tolerance.

(see *patient, indulge*)

TOOLS

mechanical fingers that drill, whittle, plane and shape.

(see *machinery*)

TOP (n.)

crown; zenith; brow; pinnacle; high-water mark; saddle; ceiling; cap; head; crest; apex; vertex.

(see *height, climax*)

TORMENT (v.)

drive from pillar to post; break on the wheel; hound; harrow upon the soul; wring the heart; make hell upon earth; put on the rack; stone with; worry into the grave; making a living death for; pierce with the sword of agony; crush beneath the feet; rend the bosom; cause to run the gauntlet; finger the wounds; burn at the stake; stick pins into.

(see *pain, tease, irritate, annoy, provoke*)

TOUCH (figurative, v.)

melt the heart; play on the heart-strings; make stones weep.

(see *feeling, moved, affect, sensation, soften, injure*)

TOUCH (literal, v.)

lay hand on; finger; graze; sweep; lay a finger upon; kiss; caress.

(see *hold*)

TOUGH

hard-shell; horny; leathery; rhino-ceros-hide; crusty; bad-egg; thick-skinned; hard - boiled; roughneck; weather-beaten; hard-headed.

(see *hard, stiff, rigid, strong, firm, stubborn*)

TRACE (v.)

run to earth; smell out; track the lion to his den; follow the hoof-marks of.

(see *search for, look for, investigate, find*)

TRADE (v.)

rig the market; drive a bargain; send across the counter; huckster; have the pawnshop in one's blood; horse-trade.

(see *shopkeeper, bargain, business buy, sell*)

TRADITION

the clogging vapors of the past; the eternal pull of the past.

(see *lore, history*)

TRAFFIC

morass of congestion; wildly tossed stream of pedestrians; weaving glitter of the street; thin black stream of beings; pouring stream of vehicles.

(see *people, transients, move, auto-mobile, drive, congestion*)

TRAGEDY

the angel of death stooping to swing his sickle; literary bitumen.

(see *disaster, sad, death*)

TRAIN (v.)

nurse; school; break in; burn in; acclimate.

(see *teach, guide, discipline, show, advise, direct, explain*)

TRAITOR

turncoat; rat; snake in the grass; serpent; the hand that holds the dagger; wolf in sheep's clothing.

(see *betray, treachery, deceiver, revolt, desert, deceitful*)

TRAITS

earmarks.

(see *mark, character*)

TRANQUIL (to be)

shiver into quiet; cool down; find all quiet along the Potomac; see the storm-clouds roll away; abide in the realm of peace; simmer down; move in an unclouded heaven; have cool judgment.

(see *peace, calm, quiet, unmoved*)

TRANSFER (v.)

shift the burden; transplant; switch; drift; cause to change hands; hand down; pitch; dump in another's lap.

(see *send, change, pass*)

TRANSFORM

hoist a thing to a plane it has never touched before; lift out of one groove and set in another; build a nest in a foreign tree; mold the face of.

(see *converted, change*)

TRANSIENTS

bits of seaweed tossed up on a strange shore; birds of passage.

(see *commuter, temporary, short-lived, traffic, travel*)

TRAP (v.)

drive up a tree; weave a tangled web; bait the hook; catch in a quagmire; lure into a mucilaginous web.

(see *snare, catch, strategy*)

TRAVEL (v.)

take to the road; trek; globe-trot; jog-trot; knock around the planet; see life; dash to the ends of the earth; wing one's way; sail along; stir one's stumps; hurl through the stratosphere; make a sortie to; thread the highroads; bowl along; hit the highway; cross-country; kick around; spread the wings in flight; bend one's steps; plough one's way; run through the country's veins; put a girdle around the earth; become footsore; go on a pilgrim's way; be a rolling stone; gather no moss; leap over gulfs of space.

(see *move, transients, traffic, progress, explore, wanderer*) ·

TREACHERY

stab in the back; foul ball; knife up the sleeve; stab in the dark; handing the poisoned chalice.

(see *traitor, betray, deceiver, untrustworthy, undermine, deceit*)

TREMENDOUS

towering; volcanic; astronomical; mountainous.

(see *vastness, unimaginable, unlimited*)

TREND

tide; current; drift; road leading to; flowing tide; climate of opinion; wetting one's finger to the wind; undercurrent.

(see *tendency, turn*)

TRIBULATION (to suffer)

have a much tried heart; be worn out by grief and toil; be tried by fire; be put under the screw; carry a cross; be in the hour of need; be on the rack.

(see *distressed, difficulty, troubled, suffer, grieve, sorrowful, unhappy, pain*)

TRICKERY

a mare's nest; trap; a bit of hanky-panky; double-dealing; playing fast and loose; living by one's wits; playing wary poker; shiftiness; stealing a march; taking for a ride; juggling; legerdemain; playing the fool; tricks-of-the-trade; a new wrinkle; thin end of the wedge; side-blow; pulling the wool over people's eyes; twisting the arm.

(see *deceit, strategy, cheat, imposture, swindle*)

TRIFLE (n.)

a piece of bric-a-brac; no great shakes; a mere flea-bite; the shadow of a shade; small beer; bread crumbs; the ashes of emptiness; a fig's worth; a grain of sand on the beach; a row of pins; a button's worth; the hair on a fly's leg; a straw; a goose egg; a shoestring's worth; something made from scratch; just enough to swear by; little apples.

(see *worthless, nonentity, unimportant, useless, insignificant*)

TRITE

worn thin; threadbare; dulled at the edge; stale; warmed-over; moth-eaten; mildewed; shabby with clichés.

(see *ordinary, common, worn-out, mediocre*)

TRIUMPHANT (to be)

marching off with the flag; playing the trump card; coming off with colors flying; sweeping off the trick.

(see *conquer, win, victorious, glorify, elated, joyful, rejoice, successful*)

TROUBLED (to be)

fish in troubled waters; ride the horns of a dilemma; be gnawed by a cankerworm of care; be in hot water; have one's mind corroded; watch for the pot to boil; go into a fiery furnace; have the devil to pay; have the mind corrupted with a festering mass of doubt; have harrowed eyes; have hell upon earth; carry a peck of troubles; suffer the ills that flesh is heir to; flounder in a sea of troubles; have a thorn in one's side; haul a full cargo of woes; be swept by storms on the sea of life; go through the wringer; have a hornet's nest brought about one's ears; swim against the stream; be in a pickle; buffet the waves; scud under bare pales; grope in the dark; lose one's way; weave a tangled web; walk among eggs; be in a stew; have one's heart bleed; have a dagger planted in one's breast; bog down in a quagmire; see clouds on the horizon; scent brimstone; have a spoke put in one's wheel; come to a standstill; stick in the mud; get tangled up; feel the shoe pinch; taste gall and wormwood; hear heavy news; have disaster swoop upon one; be "on the spot"; be in a jam; be forced to take the bumps; be made old before one's time; be in the soup; smell a wind blowing up; see the swell of new combers; bear a cross; have one's heart eaten out; be tangled in trouble; watch the clouds gather; have a heavy feeling on one's chest; find oneself on the rocks; have a thing prey on one's mind; be painfully shaken; put one's neck into the waiting wringer; come to a stumbling block; feel a thing go against one's grain; be at one's wit's end; grapple with difficulties; have one's ear wounded; feel the dull prick of conscience; grab a tiger by the tail; wipe a feverish brow; breathe heavily; come to grief; shed blood and tears; plunge into an abyss; wake up a sleeping dog; be cursed by; be up to one's ears; feel one's bowels reached; have an eruption descend upon one; have the cup dashed from one's lips;

have tough sledding; stir up a bee's nest; nurse a headache; find a fly in one's ointment; go too far out on a limb; wander into a den of lions; see a bogey; have a pretty kettle of fish; put all the fat in the fire; be worried sick; have a bad time of it; have all hell break loose; pass through the mill; be plagued by; feel out of joint.

(see *tribulation, distressed, difficulty, suffer, discouraged, dejected, depressed, worry, confused, perplexed*)

TRUST (v.)

pin one's faith to; make an investment of faith in; build on; be a lamb that eats out of the hand of.

(see *believe, confident, reliable, dependable, entrust*)

TRUTHFUL (to be)

be true to the letter; show oneself in one's true colors; speak one's mind; be true to life; make a clean breast; come clean; tell the gospel; stand the test; hold water; speak from the bottom of one's heart; put one's cards on the table; tell an unvarnished tale; tell cold facts; have the ring of truth; have the fabric of fact; speak naked words; make Truth the law of one's mouth; not cast a shadow of doubt; be straight as an arrow; be sterling.

(see *frank, sincere, reliable, honest, straightforward*)

TRY

make a dash at; give it a whirl; take a whack at; chin oneself up to a level; have a go at; put one's best foot forward; double oneself into knots; make a stab at; have a shot at; take a fling at; grapple with; tackle; grope for; stretch out a hand to; risk the bogs and the blind-alleys.

(see *attempt, endeavor, aim, strive, seek, effort, utmost, experiment, examine, test, prove*)

TURBULENT (to be)

have live coals of unrest toss on one's soul; have a stormy spirit; be volcanic; be a sputtering pack of firecrackers; put all the fat in the fire; have the surge of a heavy sea; feel a hurricane sweep through one; feel the ground rock under one's feet; be torn in two; spill from a boiling caldron.

(see *disturbance, agitator, restless, violent*)

TURN (v.)

wheel around; face about; whirl back; switch off; port one's helm; spin around; loop the loop.

(see *change, move, revolve, deviate, sway, transfer, reverse, transform*)

TUXEDO

a bobtail jacket for a ringtail monkey.

(see *formal, clothes*)

U

UBIQUITOUS (to be)
be a social eel; be one whom others meet at every turn.

(see *everywhere, travel*)

UGLY (to be)
be an eyesore; have the face of an old war horse; be a nightmare; be sorry-looking.

(see *repulsive, unpleasant*)

ULTIMATELY
in the long run; first or last; as the world goes; as the tree falls; at the eleventh hour.

(see *late, remote*)

UNANIMOUS (to be)
present a solid front; move in a body; speak with one voice; be at one with; be in every mouth; chime in with; go with the stream; join in the chorus; say aye to; nod assent; say ditto to; say amen to; strike in with; vote for; be of one mind.

(see *harmony, agree*)

UNAUTHORIZED
wildcat.

(see *illegality, unjust, uncontrolled, unofficial*)

UNAWARE (to be)
be blinded to defects; be shortsighted; be caught with chaff; be caught flat-footed; be unconscious of it all; live in a fool's paradise.

(see *blind, oblivious of, inattentive, ignorant*)

UNBEARABLE
more than flesh and blood can bear; the last straw.

(see *excessive, pain*)

UNBIASED (to be)
have an open mind; be a man without a sword; maintain a balanced attitude.

(see *fair, indifferent*)

UNCERTAIN (to be)
stand upon a crumbling sand-heap; grope through an intricate labyrinth; be in a blur of doubt; cast one's anchor in the dark; be off one's balance; be all at sea; have cobwebby remembrances; entertain suspicions; tremble in the balance; be adrift; be caught tripping; teeter on the horns of a dilemma; be at one's wit's end; be torn between; have one's faith shaken; sit on the fence; be in the dark; see a question mark; have Fate's iron scale hang in suspense; be skittish about; see a problem dimly before one; blow hot and cold about; be in the touch-and-go phase; be between the devil and the deep blue sea; look at a cloud of conjectures; move in a fog of formless uncertainty; sense something in the air; be swathed and muffled in the fog of Fate; be tossed between; have gusty sailing; sway between; see things plunged in the mists of uncertainty.

(see *undecided, unsettled, doubtful, indistinct, precarious, insecure, changeable, vague*)

UNCHANGEABLE
the Law of the Medes and the Persians; a firm rock; blown-in-the-bottle; in a groove.

(see *irrevocable, permanent, lasting*)

UNCLASSIFIED

neither fish, flesh, nor fowl (or good red herring).

(see *miscellany, varied, vague*)

UNCOMFORTABLE

sit on pins and needles; tread on thorns; have things too hot for one; be a fish out of water.

(see *distressed, restless, unpleasant*)

UNCOMPROMISING

hard-shell; die-hard.

(see *obstinate, stiff, rigid, stubborn, strict*)

UNCONCERNED (to be)

fiddle while Rome burns; not care a straw about; shrug one's shoulders; not care a fig; lose no sleep over; be in a chill of indifference; not care a hoot; mask all interest; not shed tears over.

(see *indifferent, careless, unmoved*)

UNCONDITIONALLY

with no strings attached.

(see *absolute, unlimited, complete*)

UNCONTROLLED (to be)

run riot; get out of hand; run away with; spread like wildfire; be a violent, unreasoning torrent; lose one's head; be inextinguishable.

(see *unrestrained, violent*)

UNCONVINCING (to be)

ring hollow; advance weak-kneed arguments.

(see *weak, inconsistent, illogical*)

UNDECIDED (to be)

hover on the brink; leave a matter up in the air; be lukewarm about; be torn between; hang in the balance; be between stools; starve between two bundles of hay; leave a thing on the knees of the gods; be on the fence; come to a deadlock; wait to see how the cat will jump; blow hot and cold about.

(see *uncertain, unsettled, vague, irresolute, doubtful*)

UNDERMINE

sap the strength of; knock the bottom out of; gnaw at the root of; eat into the fibre of; knock the props from under.

(see *ruin, thwart, undo*)

UNDERRATE

damn with faint praise; set no light by; dwarf to unimportance.

(see *misjudge, ridicule, minimize*)

UNDERSTAND

be alive to the nature of a thing; catch the drift of; see the light; have dawn upon one; glean an idea of; know the ropes; enter into the ideas of; see one's way; make it add up; grasp the fact; catch on; digest a thing; have the know-how; be no stranger to; hit the nail; sow seeds of understanding; etch with insight; read each word in the mosaic; dope a thing out; make head or tail of; let the tide of understanding wash over one; see through; keep things straight; grasp wisdom; grip the words; dissect a problem; plumb the true significance; read the riddle; seize the meaning of; open one's eyes to; follow a thought; see in the mind's eye; get next to; see into the heart of; fathom a thing; tumble to the fact; have insight into; touch bottom; have the scales fall from one's eyes; read the signals of; pierce the veil of; see through brick walls; see the daylight; take in; catch the spirit of; have light

thrown on; have a flair for.
(see *knowledge, perceive, discern, learn, interpret, intelligent*)

UNDERSTATE
soft-pedal; mute; tone down.
(see *minimize, underrate*)

UNDERTAKE
ride one's hobby; launch a project; cook the porridge; take upon oneself; take in hand; take up; have an iron in the fire; take upon one's shoulders; lay one's shoulder to the wheel; lay one's hand to the plough; turn one's hand to; put in hand; set up shop; tackle a job; jump into a job; embark upon; take up the thread of.
(see *attempt, begin, endeavor, effort*)

UNDISCERNING (to be)
fail to see the forest for the trees; have uncut wisdom teeth.
(see *ignorant, stupid, blind, unintelligent*)

UNDO
put back the clock; wash away all trace of.
(see *spoil, remove, obliterate, cancel, open, ruin, destroy*)

UNEMOTIONAL
glacial; frigid; frosty; cold; chilly; cold-blooded; in spiritual cold storage; banking the emotional fires.
(see *indifferent, unfeeling, passive, unresponsive*)

UNEMPLOYED
out of the labor market; thrown out of work; on the wallaby track.
(see *leisure, loaf*)

UNENCUMBERED (to be)
travel light in life; keep one's elbows

free; go with empty hands.
(see *free, independent*)

UNENTHUSIASTIC (to be)
throw cold water on; be lukewarm; be colorless about; speak in a cold voice; lay a wet blanket on; fall flat upon the ear; not have fire struck in one; hang fire.
(see *indifferent, unsympathetic, unmoved, unresponsive*)

UNEQUAL (to make)
make lop-sided; turn the scale; kick the beam; give the advantage; make over-balanced; make top-heavy; make out of line.
(see *prejudiced, favor, unjust*)

UNEXCITABLE (to be)
master one's feelings; stay level-headed; be easy-going; have the patience of Job; submit with good grace; keep one's presence of mind; have command of one's temper; keep one's mind at ease; put a good face on; keep one's countenance.
(see *calm, self-control, self-possessed*)

UNEXPECTED
out of a clear sky; out of the blue; manna in the wilderness; a windfall; a trick of Fortune; something dropped into one's lap; dropped from the clouds; off one's guard; in an unguarded moment; what Fate shakes from its spangled sleeve.
(see *sudden, surprise, shocked*)

UNFAIR (to be)
cheat the umpire; give an inch and take an ell.
(see *prejudiced, unjust, unequal, insincere, hypocrite*)

UNFEELING
hard-boiled; blank-eyed; stony; drain-

ed of emotion; cold-blooded; icy-hearted; narrow-souled; dry - eyed; soul-less; frigid; deaf to; thick-skinned; hard-hearted; blind to; made of iron; stony-hearted; steeled against; glacial; made of ice; flint-eyed; petrified; callous; m a d e of s awdust; marble; coarse in texture; anaesthetized.

(see *unemotional, unsympathetic, indifferent, cruel*)

UNFRIENDLY (to be)
surround with the cold atmosphere of unfriendliness; cast cold eyes at; look icily at; be stony toward; be at swords' points; be sour toward; fix with a frigid stare.

(see *hostile, malicious, oppose*)

UNGODLY (to be)
break away from deity; go to the devil in one's own way; bear a spiritual blight; backslide from deity.

(see *blasphemous, swear, wicked, sinful, profanity*)

UNGRATEFUL (to be)
bite the hand that feeds one; be a monster of ingratitude; look a gift horse in the mouth; be a dog-in-the-manger.

(see *offend*)

UNHAPPY (to be)
bear a scar on one's soul; have one's soul punctured; wear a look of naked misery; have a heart that distils tears of blood; have one's soul chilled; live in black days; have a sunless future; sit with clouded eyes; laugh on the wrong side of the mouth; feel empty-hearted; have one's spirit seared; have a soul steeped in indigo; be tortured by unhappiness; have a bruised heart; quaff the bitter cup; lacerate one's soul; have a bleeding heart; feel

ill-starred; feel drowning in misery; have the corners of one's mouth pulled down in distress; have the wine of life run to vinegar; weep the light out of one's eyes; have a spirit surrounded by a gray atmosphere; have a clouded face; feel the dark shadow of unhappiness; be empty of smiles; groan through one's days; drink the cup of bitterness to its dregs; have a heavy heart; be starved of the sunshine.

(see *unlucky, distressed, dejected, sad, sorrowful*)

UNHARMED
with a whole skin.

(see *safe, survive*)

UNHESITATINGLY
without turning a hair; making no bones about.

(see *immediately, quickly, ready*)

UNIFORM (adj.)
even tenor; dead level; of a piece; across-the-board.

(see *consistent, smooth, monotonous, stabilize, sameness*)

UNIMAGINABLE (to be)
beggar description; stagger the imagination.

(see *impossibility*)

UNIMAGINATIVE
stiff-jointed; near-sighted.

(see *practical*)

UNIMPORTANT
straw; pin; fig; button; pinch of snuff; dust in the balance; feather in the scale; drop in the ocean; old song; child's play; figurehead; storm in a teacup; small beer; nine days' wonder; much ado about nothing; flash in the pan; side issue; flea-bite; snap of the

fingers; fudge; no great shakes; pricked balloon; dead leaf whirling in the street; small fry.

(see *insignificant, trifle, small, slight, mediocre*)

UNINHIBITED (to be)

throw one's pride out of the window; let down one's hair.

(see *uncontrolled, unrestrained, self-indulgence*)

UNINSPIRED (to be)

have the fountains of one's inspiration dry at their source; have a mind with the plodding precision of a mathematical problem.

(see *unimaginative, unmoved, dull*)

UNINTELLIGENT (to be)

plunge at things blindly; make neither head nor tail of; see through a glass darkly; be all at sea; be unendowed with reason; have things be Greek to one; be a blind leader of the blind; be a stupid animal; live in a fool's paradise.

(see *stupid, ignorant, foolish*)

UNINTENTIONALLY (to act)

let things slip.

(see *haphazard*)

UNINTERESTING

dry; tasteless; flat; sleepy; dusty; milk and water; cold turkey; pale; lukewarm; gray gruel.

(see *dull, tedious, monotonous*)

UNIQUE

the only pebble on the beach; in a class by itself.

(see *unusual, rarity*)

UNITE

wed; put in a melting pot; band to-gether; fuse; bridge the gap between; cement together; interweave; join forces; weld; narrow the gap between; bind the bundle; roll into one; seal together; join hands with; knit together; club together; lump into one; link; marry; bind together; piece together; put in the same boat; stand shoulder to shoulder; stand side by side; place hand in hand; hang together; make stick together; make close-knit; join in a body; join in oneness.

(see *join, bind, relate, connection*)

UNIVERSAL

embracing all humanity; in all quarters; epidemic.

(see *everywhere, unlimited, generally, complete, whole, world*)

UNJUST (to be)

take all the meat and give another all the bones; take the lion's share; banquet on unrighteousness; have customs more honored in the breach than in the observance.

(see *unfair, unequal, insincere, favor*)

UNKNOWN

a pig in a poke; a dark horse; a big question mark; wrapped in a mystery; a new ship on a strange new sea; wrapped in the darkness of the unknown; a sealed book; uncharted.

(see *mystery, dark, obscure, unseen*)

UNLIMITED

unbridled; knowing no bounds; abysmal.

(see *universal, unrestrained, absolute*)

UNLOVED (to be)

suffer from the gnawing hunger of an underfed heart; be a kitten relegated to the back yard because no longer loved.

(see *lonely, spinster*)

UNLUCKY (to be)

spill the salt; lead a star-crossed life; see a bird of bad omen; feel an ill wind that blows no good; have hell upon earth; find life to be a plot against one; suffer the frowns of fortune; wear the badge of slavery; be born under an evil star; be under a cloud; be down on one's luck; go down in the world; be a tennis ball of fortune; be on one's last legs; be born with a wooden ladle in one's mouth; be defeated at every turn by chance; have Fate's hand against one; have one's prospects clouded; have one's star on the wane; have the winds of chance be cruel to one; go on the road to ruin; live the life of a Jonah.

(see *unsuccessful, disaster, unhappy*)

UNMOVED (to be)

maintain a dead silence; keep undazzled eyes; be left cold; have hard eyes; have pleas fail to pierce one.

(see *unfeeling, unsympathetic, firm, steadfast, calm, self-possessed*)

UNNECESSARY (person)

too many cooks; fifth wheel; *persona non grata;* figurehead.
(see *useless, superfluous*)

UNOFFICIAL

off the record; back-stair; grapevine.
(see *unauthorized, rumor*)

UNPLEASANT

bitter; citrine; soul-searing; snaggy; rocky; creeping and black; sour; crabbed; too hot to hold; mouse-gray; bitter pill; thorny; nightmare; scarred; vinegary; stick in one's gizzard; stink in the nostrils; sore; chilling; stormy; wormwood; unpalatable; throw a shadow.

(see *displease, repulsive, offend*)

UNPOLISHED

unlicked cub; diamond in the rough.
(see *rugged, rough, rude*)

UNPOPULAR (to be)

be in the doghouse; lose caste; be beyond the pale; fall into the shade; be a cast-off old shoe; be booted out of favor.

(see *unloved, unpleasant*)

UNPREPARED (to be)

be caught napping; be off one's guard; be caught with one's hair down; be caught with one's back turned.

(see *misfit, sudden*)

UNREAL (to be)

step out of the pages of fiction; be bathed in a colorless fluid of unreality; be made of cardboard; be a phantom; be up in the clouds; come from a shadow - world; exist in a vacuum; be airy; be built of air.

(see *imaginary, visionary, illusory, dream*)

UNRESPONSIVE (to be)

strike no chord; be stiff to; be frigid to; let a thing fall dead.

(see *unsympathetic, unfeeling, stiff, rigid, silent*)

UNRESTRAINED (to be)

let oneself go; shake off the checkrein; break one's bonds; loosen the iron shackles of convention; give free rein to; kick over the traces; do one's sweet will; be unbridled; hold a loose rein; take enough rope; shoot the works; know no curb; be without anchor and without port; know no bounds; have one's swing.

(see *uninhibited, uncontrolled, lax*)

UNSEEN

under an eclipse; behind the scenes; under the table; behind the curtain; blotted out.

(see *unknown, illusory, evade*)

UNSETTLED (to be)

have loose ends dangling; hang in doubt; be unhinged; be untamed; be unseated.

(see *doubtful, uncertain, restless, vacillate, unsteady, fickle, unstable, changeable, undecided, troubled*)

UNSKILFUL (to be)

not see an inch beyond one's nose; overshoot the mark; put one's foot in it; be heavy-handed; get rusty; catch a Tartar; lose one's head; cut one's throat; get the dirty end of the stick; put the saddle on the wrong horse; put a square peg into a round hole; put new wine into old bottles; cut a whetstone with a razor; hold a farthing candle to the sun; fight with a shadow; grasp at a shadow; catch at straws; lean on a broken reed; reckon without one's host; miss one's way; lose one's way; go farther and fare worse; go on a sleeveless errand; go on a fool's errand; pursue a wild-goose chase; stand in one's own light; have a screw loose; send a sprat out to catch a whale; make two bites of a cherry; put oneself out of court; strain at a gnat and swallow a camel; put the cart before the horse; lock the stable door when the horse is stolen; not know on which side one's bread is buttered; quarrel with one's own bread and butter; throw a stone in one's own garden; kill the goose that lays the golden egg; pay dear for one's whistle; burn one's fingers; knock one's head against a stone wall; fall into a trap; bring the house about one's ears; have too many eggs in one basket; have too many irons in the fire; take the shadow for the substance; be in the wrong box; aim at a pigeon and kill a crow; take the wrong sow by the ear; have too many cooks to make the soup; have all the seams showing; have a hand that has forgot its cunning; not know enough to get out of the rain.

(see *clumsy, rough, rude, inexperienced*)

UNSTABLE

rise and fall of the barometer; flash in the pan; such stuff as dreams are made on; baseless fabric of a vision; castles in Spain; fool's paradise; tottering air-castle; man of straw; moonshine; weak-kneed strength; thin air.

(see *unsteady, insecure, precarious, changeable, fickle, weak, vacillate, irresolute*)

UNSTEADY (to be)

play fast and loose; be time-serving; wait to see how the wind blows; wait to see how the cat jumps; be on one's last legs; live on a roller-coaster; blow hot and cold; hold with the hare but run with the hounds; move on shaky ground; travel a slippery path.

(see *unsettled, fluctuate, unstable*)

UNSUCCESSFUL (to be)

draw a blank; be a rocket going up and a stick coming down; lay an egg; roll no dice; do an act that dies right on the stage; not amount to a hill of beans; not amount to a pinch of salt; cut a poor figure; be a penny-soul never come to twopence; make a flash in the pan; come a day after the fair.

(see *fail, ineffective, futility, unlucky*)

UNSYMPATHETIC (to be)

have one's soul untouched; harden the heart; dismiss consolation; have no spark of sympathy; shut the heart against; be ice-cold; have one's withers unwrung; be stony-hearted; be marble-hearted; give a frosty reception to; have ice water run in one's veins; have a heart that has an edge of slivered ice.

(see *unemotional, unfeeling, unresponsive*)

UNTEMPTED (to be)

wear Joseph's coat; swim away from a bare hook.

(see *innocent, virtuous*)

UNTIMELY

after death the doctor; after meat the mustard; in an unfashionable moment.

(see *immature, premature*)

UNTRUSTWORTHY (to be)

play fast and loose; have a fishy eye; be a loose fish; be a broken reed; be a weathercock; play the hypocrite; bear false witness; show Punic faith; give a Judas-kiss; indulge in sharp practices; be shuffling; break one's faith; go over to the enemy; be double-tongued; be two-faced; catch on to a rope of sand.

(see *false, deceitful, treachery, dishonest*)

UNUSUAL

rare bird; out of the common run; earth-shaking; electrifying; set the Thames on fire; above the salt (from custom of seating guests and persons of distinction between the head of the table and the salt cellar, which was placed in the middle of the table to be reached by both those "above the salt" and those "below the salt," the latter being ordinary members of the household).

(see *unique, rarity, strange*)

UNWILLING (to be)

not find it in one's heart to; not have the stomach to; have a bone in the arm; be not in the vein; stick at; recoil from; shrink from; have a thing go against the grain.

(see *disagree, oppose, reluctantly*)

UPSET (to be)

get off balance; have the mind unhinged; put the mind in a turmoil; be thrown off the rails; have quivering nerves; be worked up to a pitch; have scattered faculties; have a firecracker set off in one's face; have the tides of one's soul alternate from ebb to flow; be frazzled; have one's nose put out of joint; be thrown off one's center; be at war with oneself; be set by the ears; have one's reason unstrung; tear one's hair; have one's disposition ruffled; have the crystal calm of one's heart shiver; have one's brain turned; be out of gear; see things topsy-turvy; see things upside down; have one's calm heel over; be curdled; be all shot to pieces.

(see *disconcert, shocked, embarrassed, troubled, excited, startle*)

UPSTART (n.)

pig in clover; round peg in a square hole; mushroom; one with the cosmopolitan polish of a floor-walker.

(see *snobbish, pretentious*)

URGE (v.)

press one hard; hound; prick; spur; goad; clap spurs to; prod; push; pinprick.

(see *encourage, incite, stimulate, push*)

USE (v.)

lay one's hand on; subject to wear and tear; exercise; employ; make a shift with; bring something into play;

have the run of; make free with; make a handle of; dog-ear.

(see *consume, advantage, profit, improve, work, exploit, train, manage*)

USEFUL

grist for the mill; general utility nag; effective tool; step in the right direction.

(see *practical, service, help, efficient, valuable*)

USELESS

seed sown upon rock; dead wood; sown sand; work of Penelope; water poured into a sieve; a bucket dipped into an empty well; preaching to the winds; holding a farthing candle to the sun; wild-goose chase; white elephant; dead branch; dead-sea fruit; grasping at a shadow; sending a sprat to catch a whale; sleeveless errand; casting pearls before swine; washing a blackamoor white; spiked guns; clipped wings; put out of gear; fit for the dusthole; fit for the wastepaper basket; beating the air; lashing the waves; fishing in the air; milking the ram; baying at the moon; whistling jigs to a milestone; kicking

against the pricks; labor of Sisyphus; broken meat; off-scourings; struggling with destiny; carrying coals to Newcastle; bring owls to Athens; shoeing the goose; rope of sand; sad rubbish; dead donkey; not worth a penny; dear at any price; laid on the shelf; not worth a straw; stale, flat, and unprofitable; sterile; gone by the board; gone a-begging.

(see *valueless, worthless, futility, ineffective*)

USE UP (v.)

eat up; swallow up; feed on; drink thirstily from; drain off; gobble down; soak up; consume; dip deeply into the well of; eat deeply into.

(see *consume*)

UTMOST (to do)

leave no stone unturned; squeeze the moment dry; play to the hilt.

(see *exertion, effort, endeavor*)

UTTER (v.)

give forth; crow; pour forth; fling out words; breathe a syllable.

(see *pronounce, speak, express, tell, reveal, divulge*)

V

VACILLATE
blow hot and cold; skip from one side to another; play fast and loose; see-saw; swing about from side to side; be a reed shaken by the wind; swim with the tide; swing with the pendulum; practice petticoat diplomacy; move with the shifting sands of impulse; be a feather for each wind that blows; have a flabby will; box the compass; be a weathercock; run with the hare and hunt with the hound.

(see *fluctuate, sway, unsteady, unsettled, hesitate*)

VAGUE
fuzzy; softly focused; cloudy; misty; nebulous; phantom; dim; cotton-wool; swaddled in fog; wrapped in a haze; twilit; shrouded in mystery; airy; dusky; loosely worded; floating in the mind.

(see *indistinct, uncertain, dim, doubtful, obscure, unsettled, lax, unauthorized*)

VAIN (to be)
have too high an opinion of oneself; be a coxcomb; blow one's own horn; flatter oneself; be a preening peacock; put oneself forward; not think small beer of oneself; blind oneself as to one's own merit; pique oneself; wallow in self-admiration; put a halo on oneself; give oneself airs.

(see *conceited, egotistic, self-love, proud, ostentatious, self-sufficient, self-satisfaction, self-praise*)

VALUABLE
of the first water; worth its weight in gold; gold-plated; sterling; blue chips; jewel; gem; worth a king's ransom; worth the price of admission; a bird in the hand.

(see *useful, service, expensive*)

VALUELESS
not worth the candle; not worth the powder and shot; not worth a hill of beans; not worth a row of pins.

(see *useless, worthless, cheap*)

VANISH
evaporate; melt away; leave not a trace behind; shrivel up into a burned cobweb; fizzle out; melt into the distance; pass out of the picture; fade into nothingness; slip out of sight; trail off into fumes.

(see *disappear, die, pass, unseen*)

VARIED
many-sided; assorted, checkered; spotted; kaleidoscopic; rainbow-hued; crazy-quilt; layered; patchwork.

(see *miscellany, mixture, changeable*)

VASTNESS
ocean; sea, cosmos; universe; abyss; wilderness.

(see *tremendous, extend, big, giant*)

VEHEMENT
white-hot; burning; fiery; red-hot.

(see *violent, passionate, eager, fervent, enthusiastic, strong*)

VERIFY
quote chapter and verse; set one's hand and seal to; prove one's point; sign and seal; cause to hold water.

(see *prove, truthful*)

VETERAN
old hand; old war-horse; dried her-

ring; seasoned; grayheaded; old soldier; old campaigner; graybeard; old stager; practiced hand.   ,

(see *experienced*)

VIBRATION

upward-surging tide of sound; air shivering with sound; pulsating beat of sound; twanging tones.

(see *sway, sounds, reverberate, resonant, resound*)

VICISSITUDES

ups and downs; tossing ocean of fortune; run of assorted luck; ebb and flow of life; bitter-sweet of life; tennis ball of Fortune.

(see *change, changeable, varied, circumstances*)

VICTIMIZE

make a cat's-paw of; bleed; milk; make a handle of; lure into the toils; catch flies with honey; quarry; make another a fool for his pains; stalk for prey; make another the whetstone for one's aims; offer the fruit of deception; bait the hook.

(see *cheat, trickery, deceive, swindle*)

VICTORIOUS (to be)

bear away the bell; chain victory to one's car; win the day; capture the palm; be a winning giant; score a touchdown; win by a landslide; beat hollow; carry all before one; carry by storm; carry the day; come off with colors flying; be crowned with success; drive to the wall; gain the upper hand; gain the ascendancy; have one on the hip; have the ball at one's feet; have the game in one's hands; hit the mark; make short work of; make the enemy bite the dust; gain possession of the field;

trample under foot; play the trump; checkmate.

(see *triumphant, win, conquer, successful*)

VIEWPOINT (to take)

see through the eyes of; open the window on; take a bird's-eye view of; bring into focus; fix the eye on; study the horizon of; see in perspective.

(see *survey, regard, examine, see, consider*)

VIGOROUS

all sinew; strapping; high-powered; rich in life-sap; full of the lust for action; blooming; delivering the punch; tooth-and-nail; high pressure; striking hard; double-shotted; all steam up; made of iron; blood and iron; in full swing; thick-ribbed; electric current; live wire.

(see *strong, power, energetic, strenuous, vehement, healthy, lively, bold*)

VILLAINOUS (to be)

have the poison of asps under one's lips; have a cloven foot; be of a deep dye; be a hound of hell; doublecross; be a black sheep; be a colossus of crime; be a veritable dragon; be a limb of Satan; be a snake in the grass; be a beast of prey; be a wolf; be a demon in human shape; put Attila to shame; be blackened by sin; be a serpent; conceal a viper in one's bosom; hug one's villainies.

(see *wicked, sinful*)

VIOLATE

chip little bits off the law; run athwart the barriers of the law; trample all laws under foot; drive a coach and six through the law; break the Sabbath.

(see *illegality, seduce, injure, hurt*)

VIOLENT (to be)

make the fur (or feathers) fly; make

the lid blow off; unsheathe the sword; lash into fury; attack with tooth and nail; raise a storm; unleash hell; ride roughshod over; out-Herod Herod; pour fuel on the flames; impale on the point of a bayonet; descend at one fell swoop; show the mailed fist; go at with hammer and tongs; be incendiary; smell of gun powder; make a riot.

(see *vehement, turbulent, insane, rage, rough, strong, sharp, severe, intense*)

VIRTUOUS (to be)

be a knight in shining armor; follow the straight and narrow path; have a soul that is a palace of truth; be steel true and blade straight; have starched morals; be a pillar of virtue; have virtues that cause the angels to rejoice; have a spotless character; lead a stainless life.

(see *honest, righteous, blameless, excellent, morality, modest, innocent*)

VISIBLE (to become)

break through the clouds; show its face; come upon the stage; heave in sight; meet the eye; burst upon the view; make its appearance.

(see *appear, appearance, evident, obvious, conspicuous, clear, distinguish*)

VISIONARY (to be)

have dreams with intricate designs; glow with imagination; be an opium-eater; build castles in the air; dream the dream of Alnaschar; be moonstruck; play truant from a wearisome universe; have a boiling imagination; dwell in cloudland; coin in the imagination; inhale the fumes of fancy; bask in the happy valley; see in the mind's eye; see with mental vision; see a bright picture paint itself on darkness.

(see *imaginary, romantic, unreal, ideal, illusory, daydream*)

VISIT (v.)

drop in; leave one's calling card; pay one's respects; beat up one's quarters (look up one's relatives); besiege a host (or hostess).

(see *examine, survey, stay, socialize*)

VOICE

a sharp knife that cuts; thin tinkling accents; broken-wing lameness of voice; timbre of a singing wire; splitting of silk; fog-horn; liquid music; penetrating whinny; thunder; cracked bell; creamy tenor.

(see *speak, utter, speech, sounds, pronounce*)

VULNERABLE (to be)

have Achilles' heel; lay oneself open; have a weak spot; be ripe to be cut and hurt; live in a glass house; be open to attack.

(see *susceptible, weak, helpless*)

W

WAIT (v.)

cool the heels; sit on the doorsteps; sweat out; sit tight; chin oneself on the mantle; whittle a pencil; have time hang heavy on one's hands; watch how the wind blows; sit on the lid while the pot boils; drool around; keep one's shirt on; hold one's horses; let the world go by; bide one's time.

(see *stay, delay, watchful, expect*)

WAKEN

lift an eyelash; rouse oneself from slumber; come to life; return to life; bounce into wakefulness; be jarred into consciousness.

(see *arouse, excite*)

WALK (v.)

go on shank's mare; stamp up to; hobble; breeze up to; sweep along; roll about; worm one's way; thread the way; leg it; glide; weave one's way; fly; float; speak from the soles of one's shoes; take the air; streak to; stumble on; steer oneself around; tramp along; coast round to; trip along; flit by; jog along; mince with a marionette gait; waddle about; dart along; beat a path; wade through; potter along; dance along; take steps clogged with leaden weights; frisk onto; shuffle along; ride in the marrow-bone coach; travel on shoeleather express; ooze along; clump toward; rap the sidewalk; stalk abroad; scuff along; walk among eggs; foot it; gallop along; pity the grass one's feet press; have one's legs; waddle past; stump on; meander; gad about; map one's way; prowl about; knock around; go by Walker's 'bus.

(see *saunter, depart, move*)

WANDERER

rolling stone; tumbleweed; street Arab; beachcomber; flotsam and jetsam; nomad; bedouin; gypsy.

(see *deviate, digress, travel, roundabout*)

WANT (v.)

itch to; ache for; fish for; thirst for; hunger for; be greedy for; be filled with desire for; strain for.

(see *desire, need, lack, requisite, deficient, shortcoming, fail*)

WAR (to make)   ,

go on the warpath; appeal to arms; feed the voracious belly of the war machine; unsheathe the sword; do mischief with the sword; draw a jagged scar across the face of human history; flood the earth with blood; give over to fire and sword; infect with military fever; burst the thunderclap of war; swamp with an ocean of blood; beat the waves of barbarism against the dykes of civilization; write edicts in blood; draw maps in blood; travel an all-red route; roar for blood; rise up in arms; take up the cudgels; sow with tented fields; dig up the hatchet; bathe the world in blood; re-carve the world by sword; open the mouth of hell; paint the map pink; sound the trumpet call; set the world ablaze; unleash the hounds of war; light the torch of war; raise one's banner; send round the fiery cross; hoist the black flag; throw away the scabbard; take the field; spot the pages of history with mud and blood; keep record in blood; sing a song of the sword; flesh one's sword; measure swords with; draw the trigger; break lances with; shoulder muskets;

smell gunpowder; put under fire; imbrue hands in blood; go over the top; cut one's way through; wield the scourge of the human race; cause Armageddon to break out; bristle with arms; open the cannon's mouth; make human life cheap; stoke the furnaces of war.

(see *battleground, fight, soldiery, hostile, shooting, strife*)

WARN

put on one's guard; sound the ram's horn of danger; send away with a flea in one's ear; read the Riot Act; give a word to the wise; speak the language of danger; show the handwriting on the wall; send a cloud no bigger than a man's hand; give the signs of the times; catch another's eye; wave a threat at; flash the caution signal; sound a note of caution; throw in a warning hint; hoist storm signals.

(see *inform, threaten*)

WARNING

bird of ill omen; gathering clouds; Mother Carey's chickens; clouds on the horizon; handwriting on the wall; yellow flag; ghost in the mirror; storm signals; fog signal; straw in the wind; threatening cloud; nod of Fate; gathering clouds; impulses of disaster; death-watch; preventive medicine.

(see *ominous, sign*)

WASTEFUL (to be)

whistle away money; make ducks and drakes of one's money; fritter away time; fool away money; burn the candle at both ends; cut blocks with a razor; break a butterfly on a wheel; cast one's pearls before swine; throw the handle after the blade; have money to burn; pour water into a sieve; waste one's sweetness on the desert air; cast one's bread upon the

waters; employ a steam hammer to crack a nut; fiddle away resources; tilt at windmills; be penny-wise and pound-foolish; pad the payroll; bay the moon; flog the dead horse; kill time; throw away money; fling away time; whistle jigs to a milestone; sink money.

(see *lavish, extravagant, squander, dissipate*)

WATCHFUL (to be)

keep an eye out; keep under glass; camp on one's trail; fasten a look upon; look about one; keep track of; glue an eye to; watch and ward; be on the look-out; keep a sharp eye on; keep in sight; sleep with one eye open; be on one's guard; keep tabs on; shepherd; keep a wary eye on the horizon; be on the alert; be Argus-eyed; let nothing lull one to sleep; follow with one's eyes; keep an eye cocked on; rivet the eyes on; keep one's eyes peeled for; sit up and take notice; have an eye to the main chance; keep a sharp lookout; have an eagle's eye for; guard the gates of; have the gift of wakefulness; be on the *qui vive;* be a watchdog.

(see *observant, search for, look for, careful, cautious, prudent*)

WAVES (ocean)

laughing waters; wall of ship-engulfing water; mad cavalry charge of creaming billows; thundering spray; white sea-horses; soft song of the sea; purple sea breaking in a tangled fringe of silver; cringling splash of gossiping waves; high lacy ruffs among rocks; tossing manes of foam; whitecaps showing their flashing teeth.

(see *tide, ocean, sea*)

WEAK

tremble in the wind; have chilled

blood; be spineless; become crippled; feel life streaming through one's open pores; lie haggard; live in a house built on sand; be a broken reed; be jelly-spined; feel about to draw one's last breath; be boneless; be sick; have a senile gaze; be putty in another's hands; be on one's last legs; live in a house of cards; be at low ebb; feel shattered; be thin-spirited; have one foot in the grave; be namby-pamby; feel one's head swim; hang by a thread; feel one's legs turn to water; be a physical wreck; be shaky; wobble about loose at the edges; feel light-headed; feel bowel-less; tread the path of least resistance; feel one's strength ebb; be anemic; have brittle resolution; crawl on the ground; weave a rope of sand; feel one's courage oozing out; fray out; have one's hold shaken; go down on quaking knees; have the wind taken out of one's sails; be diluted; be milk-and-water; be sapped by paralysis; have one's guns spiked; sag; take water; allow oneself to slip out of one's own hands; fall into frailty; feel strength dissolve; melt before opposition; fall away; go to the wall; not have the upper hand; feel a drain on one's strength; have weakened foundations; be gnawed at the roots; be watered down; die out in soul; have the consistency of a marshmallow; be a tenderfoot; have liquid legs; be soft-boiled.

(see *sick, exhausted, worn out, frail, delicate, vulnerable, soft, vacillate, unstable, unsteady, undecided, unsettled, irresolute, senseless, stupid, foolish, ineffective, helpless, slight*)

WEALTHY (to be)

be born with a gold spoon in the mouth; be a child of the dollar; find the purse of Fortunatus; make one's pile; fill one's pockets; live on the fat of the land; own the mint; have one's ship come home; control a torrent of riches; be on the highroad of prosperity; be a man of money; have money to burn; marry a big dowry; be well-heeled; have easy circumstances; clean up; worship Mammon; worship the golden calf; have a well-lined purse; be yellow-gilded; have a mine of wealth; have a heavy purse; roll in money; wallow in riches; be made of money; live in the lap of luxury; live on Easy Street; have command of wealth; overflow with riches; wax fat; coin golden coins; wear silk stockings.

(see *prosperous, rich*)

WEEK

six days looped up by the rosette of Sunday.

(see *time*)

WEEP

be filled to overflowing; have tears struggle to one's eyes; be wrenched by sobs; have a voice damp with tears; have tears stand on the cheeks; drop large, pear-shaped tears; set free prisoned sobs; let loose an April shower of tears; cry one's eyes out; dash tears from one's eyes; spill a torrent of tears; weep one's heart out; be dissolved (or bathed) in tears; have tears raining down the face; be bedewed with tears; open the floodgates; have one's eyes swimming; bleed tears; melt in tears; be a knot of sobs; weep till a leaden pressure sinks in one's chest; have diamond-dripping eyes.

(see *sob, tearful*)

WELCOME (to make)

open the door to; take into the fold; roll out the red carpet; toss a word of welcome; sound a flourish of trumpets; hold open house; give the glad-hand to; hail with open arms; salute; keep the latch-string hanging out; stretch out hands to.

(see *embrace, receive, handshake*)

WHIP (v.)

thrash within an inch of life; cure by repeated applications of a birch rod; give a dressing to; lace one's jacket; have a persuader; razor-strop one's hide; take to the woodshed.

(see *strike, punish, hurt*)

WHISPER (v.)

rend the silence with the tear of silk; speak between the teeth; speak with bated breath; speak in one's ear; drop the voice; buzz; sibilate a murmured stream of talk; breathe between motionless lips; rustle words; stir silence with a gurgling whisper.

(see *breathe, sigh, hint, sounds, voice*)

WHITE-HAIRED

winter roosting in Alpine hair; snow of the hair.

(see *old, age*)

WHOLE

lion's share; Benjamin's mess.

(see *complete, perfect, firm, strong, healthy*)

WHOLLY

to the top of one's bent; down to the ground; head to heels; beginning to end; from first to last; end to end; head to foot; top to toe; fore and aft; up to the brim; up to the ears; root and branch; out and out; all out; neck and heel; head and shoulders; neck and crop; through thick and thin; for good and all; over head and ears; heart and soul; part and parcel; every inch; length and breadth; lock, stock, and barrel; the sweep of; unpruned.

(see *completely, clean, absolute*)

WICKED (to be)

have the devil's own light in one's eyes; weave a web of villainy; be spawn of hell; have dark and disreputable ties; embrace the devil; have a mind that is a perfect sink.

(see *sinful, ungodly, profanity, worthless, villainous, evil, unjust*)

WIFE

helpmeet; helpmate; better half; bedfellow; reflexive minor deity beaming worshipfully upon her husband; consort; second self; *alter ego;* gray mare; wife of one's bosom.

(see *marry, woman*)

WILDERNESS

virgin country; howling wilderness; wild-and-woolly land.

(see *rough, rude, savage, isolated*)

WILLING (to be)

welcome with open arms; do a labor of love; do a thing with all one's heart; undertake with heart and soul; gorge the hook; nibble at the bait; swallow hook, line, and sinker; make no bones of; make a virtue of necessity; be clay in another's hands.

(see *eager, ready, desire*)

WIN (v.)

bear away the bell; win the palm; take the prize; capture the trophy; reap a conquest; nose out competition; steal the honors; walk away with the honors; get away with; play one's trump card; walk over the course; mop up opposition.

(see *conquer, triumphant, victorious, surpass, successful*)

WIND (n.)

surging tide in the tree-tops; the breath of heaven; capful of wind; howling, restless nomad; sea-wind with cold spray in its teeth.

(see *air, blow, breathe*)

WISE (to be)

know what's what; play one's cards well; be in advance of one's age; have the wisdom of a serpent; be possessed of the philosopher's stone; see the world in a grain of sand; be a young Solomon; be an unfeathered owl.

(see *prudent, reason, intelligent, intellectual, scholar, sly*)

WITHDRAW

slip cable; haul up anchor; take French leave; retire into a shell; retire into oneself; wean oneself of a habit; tear oneself away from.

(see *leave, depart, retire, retreat*)

WOMAN

the distaff side; weaker vessel; pretty trinket; idol of men; little cat; arch-spider; wren; she-wolf; Siren.

(see *wife, spinster, beautiful*)

WONDER (v.)

have eyes that are homes of mystery; scratch one's head; open one's mouth; send one's wits a-woolgathering.

(see *ponder, meditate, speculate, question*)

WOO

aspire to the hand of; cultivate the affections of; dance attention on; get on bended knee before; pay court to; offer the moon and stars to.

(see *love*)

WOODLAND

deer-dappled vistas of woodland; wall of trees; labyrinth of branching foliage.

(see *park, mountain*)

WORK (v.)

turn an honest penny; wrestle with; make one's tucker; pour one's talents into; wear one's pencils down; stay in harness; dig in; pound away at; hammer at; plow through; be in gear; earn by the sweat of one's brow; break one's back over; sing for one's supper; bring grist to the mill; keep one's shoulder to the collar; keep one's face to the grindstone; be on one's taps; take the laboring oar; work one's fingers to the bone; be a bread-winner; punch a time clock; peg away at; lay one's shoulder to the wheel; grind away at; root, hog, or die; grapple with; have work on one's hands; keep the pot boiling; churn out one's work; slave over; get in one's licks; buckle down to; plug away at; fiddle with; cultivate one's garden; get the cobwebs out of one's hair; stick to one's last; raise more hogs and less hell; turn one's hand to; be ready to hit the ball; plunge into the caldron of work; grind away body and soul for; get the bit between one's teeth; burn the midnight oil; do a hand's turn; bend the bow; earn one's salt; hole up with; be ready to pitch for; scratch for a living; be in one's shirt sleeves.

(see *labor, industrious, strive, endeavor, aim, attempt, exertion, produce, cause*)

WORKER

wheel - horse; anchor - man; factory robot; h a n d; slavey; dinner-pail crowd; busy bee; breadwinner; human machine.

(see *earn*)

WORLD

every quarter of the compass; the hollow of nature's hand; man's oyster; horizon; arena.

(see *earth, life, people, man*)

WORN-OUT

fit for the dust-hole; dropping to pieces; dog-eared; thumbed over; frayed; coming apart at the seams; moth-eaten; the worse for wear.

(see *worthless, useless, exhausted, shabby*)

WORRY (v.)

sit on thorns; have prey on one's mind; be on pins and needles; be on edge; have a heart torn with anxiety; feel a pang at the heart; be in a gray anxiety; have a headache over; have one's nerves frayed by; have one's rest disturbed by; stir uneasily at; pinch one's face in anxiety; have weigh heavy on one; knit the forehead; have a weight on one's mind; tie oneself in knots over; get gray hairs over; draggle one's wings with sordid cares; see the skeleton at the feast; take a thing to heart; have anxious thoughts roll over one's mind; be in a stew; have a thorn in one's heart; have one's eyes clouded by worry; be in a fever over; have one's spirits overcast by clouds of anxiety; have beat against one's brain; be burdened with cares; be fluttered by; be the cat killed by worry; carry a corroding secret; have some bad half-hours; furrow one's brow; fret one's gizzard; be at one's wits' end; be on one's beam-ends; stew in one's own juice; have a long face.

(see *troubled, perplexed, solicitous, fearful*)

WORSE

out of God's blessing into the warm sun; from lambent flame into passionate fire; out of the frying pan into the fire; blacker; bleaker.

(see *deteriorate, degenerate, sick*)

WORSHIP (v.)

set upon Olympian heights; fall on one's face before; set on a pedestal; apotheosize; bow down before; prostrate oneself to; bend the knee; humble oneself before; pay homage to; lift up the heart to; send one's soul up in a prayer.

(see *revere, pray, love*)

WORTHLESS

not worth the candle; of small consequence; a plugged nickel; a straw; gone to the dogs; not worth a snap; scum of the earth; dregs; not worth a rush; not worth the powder to shoot at; not worth one's salt; fallen to zero; a thoroughly bad egg; not amount to a row of stringbeans; hogwash; a discarded bit of humanity; rubbish; flotsam and jetsam; full of chill emptiness; a rope of sand.

(see *useless, valueless, futility, ineffective, refuse, riffraff, superficial, trifle*)

WRAPPED

enveloped; packaged in a jacket; blanketful.

(see *cover, enclosed*)

WRINKLES

spiderwebs of wrinkles; seamed visage; lacework of lines; fingers of age; furrowed and grooved countenance; crumpled skin; hieroglyphics of life's old age; crows' feet; the fingerprints of time; brackets of time; corrugated skin; network of wrinkles; barnacle-encrusted; intersections of wrinkles at the corners of the eyes; lines of cordage in the face.

(see *old, age*)

WRITE

smudge paper; set the pen racing; put down in black and white; set pouring from a pen; bring a pen to life; dash off with a pencil; weave the threads of a sentence; pound out a letter; dictate one's brain children; knock out a column; wear a typewriter to the bone; slash with a corrosive pen; carve out a path with one's pen; touch on with a pen; toss words around a page; be lured into print; embark on a page; butcher words; sling the ink; dip one's pen in vitriol; have veins that flow with printer's ink; make pen drippings; mesh a lacework of words; open the flood-gates of inkland; entrust to pen-strokes.

(see *compose, record*)

WRONG (to be)

go off the beam; follow the wrong scent; land wide of the mark; bark up the wrong tree; talk through one's hat; put a false construction upon; not play the game; fall into an error; live in a fool's paradise; reap where one has not sown; give an inch and take an ell; rob Peter to pay Paul; do one's cost.

(see *err, mistake, unjust, unfair, false, bad, wicked, evil, sinful*)

Y

YEARN
die for want of; eat one's heart out; have a hungry heart; ache with desire; feel one's soul clamor for; feel one's mouth begin to water.
(see *desire, want*)

YELL (v.)
bark; blow a cyclonic blast; roar; bellow.
(see *shout, scream, shrieks, loud*)

YESTERDAY
the long unholy road called the past; the hidden corners of the past; chapters of the dear dead past; the scrap-heap of the past.
(see *past, time*)

YIELD
accept the apple; feel a foretaste of submission; wither before; eat humble pie; resign oneself to; answer the helm; knuckle under; bend before the storm; knock under; give ground to; give grass; retire into the shade; yield the palm; thaw; cave in.
(see *give up, surrender, submissive, obedient, relent*)

YOUNG (to be)
be in the morning of life; bud with youth; have the closed buds of immaturity; be fresh from the cradle; be in the bloom of youth; be in embryo; have a green heart; be new-born and clean; have the tide of life run high; be unripe; be in the spring-time of life; be a fledgling; be in the flower; be a young sapling; have a smile that is a festival of youth; be in the flush of life; be in the age of ignorance; have puppy teeth; live one's salad days; be in the seed-time of life; be in the flower of one's days; live the golden season of life; be a young eagle; be the bright shoot of the house; bloom with youth; be in the plastic season of life; be of the rising generation; be an unlicked cub; have the fires of youth kindle in one; start to climb the hill of the years.
(see *immature, inexperienced, innocent, child, children, prime*)

Z

ZESTFUL (to be)
be spiced; be full of the fire of life; have a healthy appetite for life; fall head over heels for.

(see *relish, enjoy, thrilled, tasty, savor*)

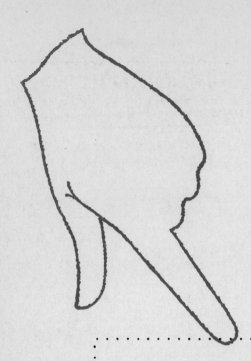

SOPHISTICATED

SYNONYMS

EMMAUS, PENNSYLVANIA

RODALE PRESS, INC.

SOPHISTICATED
SYNONYMS

EMMAUS, PENNSYLVANIA

RODALE PRESS

Introduction

Sophisticated Synonyms is a humorous and smart synonym book, a thesaurus of sparkling phrases, slang, and sonorous-sounding expressions. It is a record of living and lively speech garnered from the pages of current and recent books and magazines, from the burlesque proscenium, from the lips of the man on the street. It is an action photograph of a lusty language caught on the jump. It is the King's English in action.

This book has been compiled to serve a definite end: to aid the worker in words by injecting electricity into his style—be he writing a novel, preaching a sermon, or inscribing an affectionate letter to his mother-in-law. It is for conversationalists, senators, doctors, tax collectors, lawyers, and other hold-up men.

Somebody or other said that humorists are born and not manufactured. Well, according to that we can't guarantee that this book will turn anybody into a Jack Benny in seven easy lessons. However, Don Marquis once said, "I do not think anyone can be taught anything about humor, but I do think that certain persons may be taught the mechanism of producing humorous copy."

The purpose of Sophisticated Synonyms is to serve as an aid in producing humorous copy. It should be the bible of the individual desirous of a striking style. It should be read not once, but again and again. The weakness of most of us as wielders of the pen is our tendency to slip into the commonplace and the monotonous. When properly employed, this collection is an antidote for the deadly style.

The text is arranged alphabetically. Referring to the word which best expresses the thought he has in mind, the reader finds certain words and phrases bearing upon that thought. Immediately, and graphically, he discovers how others have expressed the same or approximately the same thought in words that dart direct to the funny-bone.

The public speaker will find enormous profit in perusing this book diligently—for the public speaker must have his witticisms. He will find here the spur to spicy and uproarious originality, for *Sophis-*

[1127]

ticated Synonyms is primarily a thought stimulator. Gag-men, comedians, radio script writers, and those lesser lights, the amateur jokester and the Romeo seeking to slay his Juliet with the bubbling tongue of wit—all of them have known the moment when they'd have given their good right arm for a book built as *Sophisticated Synonyms* is built. Newspaper columnists too.

Dip into *Sophisticated Synonyms* from time to time—read a page here and there in your leisure moments, and at your writing desk whenever inspiration lags—and acquaint yourself with the humorous ways and means by which contemporaries secure their effects. The words and phrases will lie fallow in your brain, and when the right moment comes you will discover that these same words and phrases will burst forth new-gilded and entirely your own by virtue of your own personality and talent.

J. I. RODALE

A

ABANDON
Leave in the lurch; leave him hanging on a limb; dump him in the alley; tie a can to him; give him the air; throw him to the wolves; be sold down the river; ditch the whole business; give him the heave-O; abandon on the doorstep of the Republican Party; let everything go hang; be left suspended from a chandelier.
(See *leave alone, resign.*)

ABILITY
She has something of the *je ne sais quoi;* one whom the Good Lord made on purpose for such business; this lad is tops; one of those lads Horatio Alger wrote about; he had a mean ball and two strikes on the world; a Johnny-on-the-spot; to know how to jockey the hurdles; ability doth hit the mark where presumption over-shooteth and diffidence falleth short (prov.); fried pigeon doesn't fly into your mouth (prov.); to have something on the ball.
(See *talent, genius, strength, experienced.*)

ABOLISH
Consigned to the dust-bin; make it null and void; you might just as well abolish the Indian Ocean.
(See *end, extinct.*)

ABSENT-MINDED
His mind resembles a pawnbroker's window; he'd be an absent-minded professor, if he was a professor.
(See *dreamer, memory-poor.*)

ABSURD
Reductio ad absurdum.
(See *silly, nonsense, stupid, ridiculous.*)

ACCENT (Foreign)
A closely woven English accent.
(See *talk, speech, French.*)

ACCIDENT
Contretemps; a cataclysm; he was sewn together by the nearest taxidermist; skid on one ear; bark my shins on; sustain painful abrasions; the resulting contusion on my brow; to step on the business end of a rake; he was set down for a ten-yard loss; emulate the daring young man on the flying trapeze; the sly banana skin snares the unwary foot; at the hospital he was in a plaster cast with pulleys attached all over him.
(See *mistake, chance, lucky, smash-up.*)

ACCOUNTANT
Error hound.
(See *bookkeeper, cost, money.*)

ACHIEVEMENT
An achievement worthy of ranking with the invention of the safety pin.
(See *work, do.*)

ACQUAINTED WITH
On terms of social intimacy with.
(See *friendship, society.*)

ACROBAT
Turn flip-flops; the daring young man on the flying trapeze; poetry in motion.
(See *theatre, shows, dancing.*)

ACTION
Fireworks; to do a Douglas Fairbanks; the lets-go school; to be on the *qui*

vive; a spirit of *joi er de vivre;* possessed of a great deal of bounce; to keep the whirligig going; he was out and about and up and doing; get-up-and-go; to lash about; with all guns in action; grab the bull by the horns; with gusto; full tilt; raring to go.
(See *energy, do, strength.*)

ACTING

To emote; do their stuff; played his part with passion and with whiskers; barnstorming; ad lib; the pash stuff; the purple art of sock and buskin; he stopped shows; he burns 'em alive; he took the big city like Grant took Richmond; he stole the show; he acted his ears off; worst bit of dramatic hooey; laryngeal creakings; he goes a little hammy near the end; he played the king as though someone had led the ace; the act smelled; the show laid an egg.
(See *theatre, shows.*)

ACTIVE

As active as a mouse in a cheese factory; as active as a dog in a butcher shop; no flies on him; there is life in the old dog yet.
(See *excited, anxious, busy.*)

ACTOR

Thespian; gallery God; dramaturgic magnifico; dime-a-dozen hams; spotlight-loving hams; so-so actors; practically born in a wardrobe trunk; his name will be in lights within the year; his head got baked by the spotlight (conceited); he was not the Shirley Temple of his era (when he was a boy); he expected to run the Barrymores completely off the stage.
(See *movies.*)

ACTOR (Vaudeville)

The small fry of vaudeville; a bunch of rank vaudeville throw-aways; ten-twenty-thirty vaudevillians.
(See *vaudeville.*)

ACTRESS

Sarah Bernhardt had nothing on her; in her war paint; actorines; ladies of the theatre; a lady of some renown in the dramatic industry; tossing her torso all over the stage; she has a warble and a wiggle; she had a higher voltage than Garbo; she is no great shakes as an actress.
(See *movies.*)

ADAM'S APPLE

His Adam's apple slipped a cog; swallowed his Adam's apple; his Adam's apple was just bob-bob-bobbing along.
(See *body.*)

ADMIRATION

Evoke screams of admiration; having endeared his work to the cognoscenti; the hoarse bravos of an admiring throng.
(See *praise, cheers, applause.*)

ADVANTAGE

Eat the sweet fruits of; better be the head of an ass than the tail of a horse (prov.).
(See *good, better, opportunity.*)

ADVERTISING

Blurbs; the pulsing life blood of business; doing business without advertising is like winking at a girl in the dark.
(See *description, publicity, want-ads.*)

ADVICE

Pontifical advice; advice is like kissing, it costs nothing and is pleasant to do; to give advice by the bucket but take it by the grain; if you do not hear reason she will rap you on the knuckles; pregnant advice; over-weening advice.

(See *warn, cautious, careful.*)

AEROPLANE

Cloud chariots; a sweet flying crate; went for a buggy ride; doesn't expect to fly until an aeroplane lays an egg.

(See *aviator.*)

AFFECTING (Disgust)

It gets me down; it lays me flat; put the damper on the opening; makes me break down and weep; cramps my style; gets in my hair; gets under my hide; wouldn't that melt you down; gets my gander; gets my nannie; af-fected him to a point where the doc-tors had to be called in.

(See *disgust, anger.*)

AFFECTION

The apple of his eye.

(See *love, like, passion.*)

AFFECTS

It makes him fold his petals and droop like a dying lily.

(See *hurt, sentimental, sad.*)

AFRICA

Slapping off tsetse flies; where there ain't no Ten Commandments; the Veldt of Africa.

(See *negroes, jungle.*)

AGAIN

A return engagement.

(See *encore, time, returned.*)

AGAINST IT

Heresy; dead against it; an icono-clast; thunder forth denunciations; frosty to my suggestion.

(See *critic, disagree, opposition.*)

AGE

She must be shoving on toward forty; here I am admitting to twenty-eight; I am, for life insurance purposes, in my thirty-first year; her years on this earth have been eighteen; sixteen years of old age; he is on the wrong side of forty; at the age of almost nothing; man's allotted span is three score and ten; attained to the sober age of sixteen; she was at the boy-crazy age.

(See *old, birthday, young.*)

AGE (Era)

This decadent age; this age of chro-mium steel; in these tantivy days; in this age of encyclopedias on easy terms; in this steam-boiler age.

(See *time.*)

AGREE

You said a mouthful; you took the words right out of my mouth; I am wholly at one with our critic; to talk turkey; agree like a bell and its clap-per.

(See *yes, contract.*)

AIM

He shoots at a pigeon and kills a crow.

(See *shooting, gun.*)

AIR

To get a gulp of fresh air.

(See *wind.*)

AIRS

Poseur; was a bundle of annoying self-assurance; he plays God so convinc-ingly; every ass loves to hear himself bray.

(See *show-off, brag.*)

ALBUM

A family album containing faded tin-types showing "Aunt–".

(See *photograph, cameraman.*)

ALERT
Alert as a chamois.
(See *smart, ready, prompt.*)

ALL
In toto; which runs the whole gamut of.
(See *complete, lot.*)

ALLEGATION
Prepared to meet the allegation and defy the alligator.
(See *lawyer, courts, excuse.*)

ALL OVER
From pillar to post.
(See *everywhere.*)

ALL RIGHT
Okydoke.
(See *fine, O. K.*)

ALL THE TIME
The livelong time.
(See *often, always, long.*)

ALONE
I am alone, save for the sea and the clouds; to leave him to his own devices; a dog in the kitchen desires no company; just me and my memories.
(See *lonesome, forgotten.*)

ALTHOUGH
Albeit.
(See *if.*)

ALWAYS
As a steady diet; rain or shine; from time immemorial; forevermore; and you can talk to me from then on; forever and a day; the livelong time.
(See *long, all the time.*)

AMATEUR
Tyro; novice; a rank, amateur; greenhorn; duffer; sophomoric; that's freshman stuff; neophyte; verdant; kindergartner.
(See *begin, inexperience.*)

AMAZED
Staring in pop-eyed wonder; I was struck right between the ears.
(See *surprised, shock.*)

AMBITION
He was ambitious with fatal results; bitten on the ankle by ambition; bitten by the bug of ambition; the fires of ambition burning in his breast.
(See *famous, importance.*)

AMBULANCE
The meat wagon.
(See *sick, hospital, accident.*)

AMERICAN
A nation of salesmen; as American as buckwheat cakes; as American as pie-in-the-face two-reelers; bed-rock Americanism; steak-fed Americans; America, the land of chickens and pots; as American as a college yell; liberty-loving Americans.
(See *patriotism, Uncle Sam, U. S. A. South.*)

AMUSE
He slays me.
(See *entertainment, fun.*)

ANALYZE
To see what makes corporation executives tick; to sift the wheat from the chaff; he had his number.
(See *think.*)

ANCESTRY

Fungus on his family tree; you'd imagine he owned a whole forest by the way he talks about his family tree; the blood of the Vikings flowed in her veins; to carry the torch for the Dubbs; from fine old Southern stock, slightly watered; George Washington came very near sleeping under their roof.

(See *family, relatives.*)

ANGELS

Pink cherubs twanging their harps; demountable wings.

(See *heaven, religious.*)

ANGER

Going into great yelps; he raised six kinds of a row; vented his spleen; made him hopping mad; flew into a passion; in a huff; flung into a violent pet; high dudgeon; vials of wrath; magnificent jet of French pique; all het up; churned him up; fly off the handle; up in arms; conniptions; get into a lather; he took on at her something terrible; gets his dander up; gets his Irish up; threw him into a small rage; fit to be tied; like a red rag to a bull; in a great wax; to take umbrage; mad clear through; his blood pressure reached the danger point; choler; bile; flabbergasted; fumed; as mad as a March hare; that was the straw that tickled the camel's shoulder blades; stung to the quick and piqued to the marrow; made his blood pressure go up alarmingly; red, rolling ball of fury; working off his spleen; weeping, wailing and gnashing of their aristocratic molars; a bit huffy; a little gall spoils a great deal of honey; angered to the point of apoplexy.

(See *temper.*)

ANGER (Action)

I felt like immersing her in boiling glue; I could bite my monogram on her what-have-you; felt like luring her out on the landing and tipping her over the banisters; I could have wrung his neck; I felt like patting him on the head with some blunt instrument; I could slit his throat; I could have thrown him to the lions; I could tear off the wall paper; so angry I could spit; felt like biting the fuselage in twain; I could have flung her round my head and played handball with her against the wall.

(See *fight, swearing.*)

ANGER (Facial contortions)

Got green around the gills; bared his fangs; due to burst a blood vessel; frothing at the mouth; frothing at the gills; eyes gave off glittering sparks of rage; face crimson as a sausage; flame practically curling from his nostrils; fire flashed from her eyes; his brow black like thunder in the summer sky; go mauve around the gills; face clotted with anger; the veins in his neck standing out like livid welts; ground his teeth with insane rage.

(See *frown.*)

ANGER (Heat)

His blood was boiling; sizzling inside; seething inside; to blaze with righteous indignation; Emerson said, "We boil at different degrees"; came to a slow, intense boil; smouldering with indignation; flamed up like a kerosene torch; steaming; erupts; burned him up; burned him to a cinder.

(See *hot, heat.*)

ANGER (Looks)

Looked at him in a way that froze his blood; a look of condensed venom; looked daggers at him; directed a lethal glare after; glared at him like a dose of small pox; looks mad enough to lick his weight in wildcats; anger oozed out of him.

(See *frown.*)

ANGER (Physical Action)

Threw his derby on the floor and jumped on it; he threw seventeen fits; hit the ceiling with anger; tearing his hair out by the handful; he pulled the telephone out by the roots; annihilated ash trays; reared up on his hind legs; he lit into him thumbs down and hell bent; pyrotechnics; threw his wig at him.

(See *battle, fight.*)

ANGER (Sounds)

Emits bellow of rage; sputtered; snorted; spluttered; snarled; yelling bloody murder.

(See *scold, storms.*)

ANTICIPATE

Taking time by the throat.

(See *expect, prepare.*)

ANXIOUS

He was in a ferment to; to be waiting on pins and needles; I would give my eye tooth to; a rarin' to go.

(See *careful, desire.*)

ANYHOW

And I might as well be hanged for a sheep as a lamb.

(See *regardless.*)

ANYONE

Any fishwife can; almost anybody above the rank of a half-wit can.

(See *everyone.*)

ANYTHING

He would give, he does not know what, if.

(See *everything.*)

ANYWHERE

Anywhere, in sunshine or shadow, in rain or sleet or snow; from hither and yon.

(See *everywhere.*)

APARTMENT

An apartment with all the modern gadgets; the apartment fitted him as well as the cell of a honeycomb fits the bee; he returned to his pot-closet and bath; apartment so small the dog had to wag his tail up and down; this bird cage.

(See *home, house.*)

APOLOGY

To eat those words.

(See *excuse, explain.*)

APPEARANCES

Not all is gold that is gold-plated; all are not hunters that blow the horn (prov.); a straight stick is crooked in the water (prov.).

(See *deceive.*)

APPEARED

He bobbed up again in Oshkosh; blossomed out.

(See *come.*)

APPETITE

Appetite depressants; gastric possibilities.

(See *hunger.*)

APPLAUSE

Bravo bravissimo; the applause shook the rafters; beat appreciative palms together; and there was applause (clap,clap,clap); there was a spat-spat of applauding hands; they pounded their palms together till the chandeliers rocked; mistaking vigorous mosquito-slapping for a burst of applause; brought down the house. They charged us for repairs; he mistook the noise in the rear of the house for applause and inflicted a second verse; what good are two hands if they can't slap 'em together once in a while.

(See *approve, praise, audience.*)

APPLE

Too many apples a day may fetch the undertaker.

(See *food.*)

APPROACH

Buttonhole someone; he approached like Sir Henry Irving riding to the Crusades.

(See *come, nearby.*)

APPROVE

Smiled upon the alliance.

(See *yes, praise.*)

APRIL 1ST

When the milk of human kindness is at its lowest ebb.

(See *fool.*)

ARCHITECTURE

It looked as though it had been designed by an accomplished pastry cook; it looked like an architect's bad dream; it was patterned after an Italian abattoir of the sixteenth century; early Michigan architecture; Steamboat Gothic.

(See *house, style, gasoline station.*)

ARGUING

You can't reason with a bulldog with a bone; a tiff; ruction; a run-in; imbroglio; tongue-lashing tournament; tempest in a teacup; I gave him tit for tat; knock the spots out of an argument; the warmth of the argument heated the room; he opened the throttle another notch; out-argue; quibble

with me; bandy bitter words; cudgels; kissed and made up; at loggerheads; argue ourselves to a standstill; like cat and dog spitting at each other; he stepped clean into the middle of my pet theory; sinking their teeth into each other's flesh; we heard snarls of dissension; the Smith-Wilson contretemps.

(See *debate, discuss, conversation, fight.*)

ARISE

awakened at the crack of noon; awoke with a song on his lips and a heart as light as a feather; roll out of bed the third time he's called; awoke from a sweet dream of peace; they don't believe this early-bird-and-the-worm stuff; to be yanked from bed; gets up so early that even the roosters complain.

(See *sleep.*)

ARISTOCRACY

What he really has in his veins is about 98 per cent alcohol; azure-blooded persons; only those whose blood runs blue; there may have been some little flaw, some fleck in his pure blood; being asked to dine en famille at Buckingham Palace; of the flower of British aristocracy.

(See *nobility, royalty.*)

ARMS

Her alabaster arms.

(See *hands.*)

ARRESTED

Pinched; to beat the rap; run afoul of the law; in the toils of the law; to have the law on him; to be scooped in by the constabulary.

(See *policeman, criminals, caught.*)

ARROGANCE

To hurl insults into the teeth of; sassed him.

(See *insult, ego.*)

ART

He oozed art; as artistic as a cigar-store Indian; got too dog-goned arty.

(See *trades, business.*)

ARTIST

Nom-de-brush; he was hung in the Metropolitan; I'd rather be a painter of hydrants and lamp posts; lives among the ateliers of Paris.

(See *painting, music, dancing.*)

ASHAMED

A hang-dog expression; hang their heads in civic disgrace; his tail between his legs; fie, for shame; how the gods must laugh; shame still clung to him like an u n p a i d mortgage; ashamed, like Elisha before the entreaties of Elisha's disciples.

(See *confused, scandal, humiliation.*)

ASS

Every ass thinks himself worthy to stand with the king's horses (prov.).

(See *stupid.*)

ASSISTANT

Stooge; did you ever notice that all assistants look just alike; yes-yessed him all over the place; these yes-indeed, Mr. Bushkill, young men; he was one of the lesser cogs in the great wheel.

(See *help, partner.*)

ASTRONOMY

He could call all the planets by their first names.

(See *moon, scientist.*)

ATTACK

Nip an attack in the bud.

(See *fight.*)

ATTIC

Contained the wrecks of his broken dreams.

(See *house, room.*)

AUDIENCE

Grease paint lovers; theatre was packed to the beams; a sell-out; Mr. Jones didn't wait for the last cough; he brought out the finest feathered first-night audience; the customers laughed themselves into the aisles; audience went into a state approximating dementia; the a u d i e n c e practically swooned with joy; audience gave him the bird.

(See *theatre, shows, applause.*)

AUNT

A few assorted aunts were present; oh, my sainted aunt.

(See *relatives, uncle.*)

AUSTRALIA

Australia, the kangaroo-infested continent.

(See *British, distance, foreigner.*)

AUTHORITY

The country's leading authority on Steamboat Gothic.

(See *experienced.*)

AUTOMOBILE

These modern baubles; the old buzz-box; boat; buss-wagon; teakettle; gasoline buggy; this old crock; a sardine tin; lawn mower; it carries five large passengers and twelve small monthly payments; a block long Rolls pulls up; Rolls Rerce.

(See *traffic, travel.*)

AUTO (Action)

Came pelting down Monterey Road; flivver over the continent; slid the car towards the park; we were bowling down Eighth Avenue; came zooming down Main Street; twiddled some levers; scoot through the landscape; was aiming his Dodge at Philadelphia; the rear of the Ford rose up; the car went ka-lumping down the street.

(See *smashup.*)

AUTO (Dashboard)

A dashboard equipped with everything but an electric stove; much gadgeted roadster; the dashboard resembled the conning tower of a submarine.

(See *speed.*)

AUTO (Driver)

A windshield viper.

(See *park.*)

AUTO (Old)

Use it to scare crows with; car rattled like a bad set of false teeth; it had about sixty-nine rattles evenly distributed; a dilapidated car playing hookey from the junk heap; but she (auto) was kind to children; that museum piece of his; an auto of ancient and honorable lineage; in a series of ear-shattering crashes, rattles and bangs, they staggered away; went into another convulsive paroxysm; was shaking like a wet dog; his relic; my venerable roadster; that load of junk; get a horse.

(See *old.*)

AUTUMN

Nature's annual funeral; the kind of day which is soft and warm in the middle but crisp about the edges; when the leaves bid the trees goodbye.

(See *seasons, winter.*)

AVIATOR

The pilots bumped him from cloud to cloud; the airman who flew into a passion.

(See *aeroplane.*)

AVOID

Eschew; shun; avoiding it as a burned cat avoids a shovelful of live coals; gave me the run-around; give him a wide-berth; to give him the go-by.

(See *disagree, escape, stay away from.*)

AWAY

Away, like a ghost at break of day; away, like mists that flee from summer sea.

(See *go, disappeared.*)

AWED

I felt like a sardine; I have met only three famous persons in my life and each time a bell inside of me went "dung! dung! dung!"

(See *embarrassed, impression.*)

AWKWARD

Young hobble-de-hoys; a contretemps; awkward as a pig in a parlor; awkward as a cow on ice; awkward as a blind dog in a meat shop.

(See *clumsy.*)

B

BABY
A pretty pig makes an ugly sow; you were a bundle of pink and white; at the age of almost nothing.
(See *children, birth.*)

BABY-TALK
"Is oo nice oogy-oogums. Es oo is."
(See *speech, talking.*)

BACHELOR
Benedict; steer clear of matrimony; footloose and fancy free.
(See *man-about-town.*)

BAD
(See *terrible.*)

BAD (Action)
They are so wicked they belabor their parents with hockey sticks; robbers who steal Gideon Bibles from hotel rooms; he had Machiavelli beaten hollow; low cunning; he battens on; he winds his slimy coils around; when he gives you decadence he makes it stink; phenagling; plays fast and loose; a bad cat deserves a bad rat (prov.); he is every other inch a gentleman; he strikes women, frightens babies and steps on flowers; he must have a long spoon that sups with the devil (prov.); he is worse than the wolf that ate grandma.
(See *sin, sex, kill, steal.*)

BAD (Person)
Churlish lout; the black sheep of a somewhat greyish family; a no good guy; a high-ridden gentleman; rapscallion; scalawag; a double-crossing louse; filthy scoundrel; these hounds of hell; these minions of evil; rotters; a snake in the grass; a viper in my bosom.
(See *criminals, gangsters, villain, gunman.*)

BAD (Thing)
The act smelled; went haywire; it went screwy; such tripe; lousy; the best that could be said for it is that it smelled; the vicissitudes; his reputation stood at zero; beastly putrid; bad medicine; deadly; normal quota of bitchiness; rubbish; piffle; garbage; truck; trash; refuse; bilge; slush; rotten; unconscionable; I wouldn't wish it on a dog; it's the nasty way he says it; pretty goshawful; a dud film; shoddy; over the meal that resulted I draw a veil; a punk picture; it looked like a black mark against; bad as the itch.
(See *poor quality, unpopular.*)

BALD
Pyorrhea of the scalp; very little foliage on his egg; when he was sixteen and had some thatch on his dome; bald-headed on his father's side; thinking the hair off his head; he needed a wig to keep his brains warm; bald as an egg; bald as the palm of your hand; bald as a Greek monk; bald as is the winter tree; bald as a coot; bald as a cannon ball; as bald as a boiled egg with the shell off.
(See *hair.*)

BANJO
The way he handles that banjo he must be a bear at necking.
(See *music.*)

BANK
We were orphans at that bank; bilked its depositors; a counting house.
(See *money.*)

BANKRUPTCY
To drag him by his suspenders out of bankruptcy.
(See "broke.")

BARBER
What the barber needs is new blood.
(See haircut, hairdresser.)

BARE
As bare as Egypt when the locusts got through with it; bare as a schoolboy's diary; bare as a bird's tail; bare as a pig in a sty; bare, like a carcass picked by crows; bare as a beggar; bare as shame.
(See empty, nude.)

BARGAIN
To bargain with the fates; to smell a bargain; haggle; a thing you don't want is dear at any price; to wangle.
(See contract, agree.)

BARTENDER
With his gates-ajar collar; those mix-masters behind the bar.
(See whiskey, beer, drinking.)

BASEBALL
He occasionally stole second with the bases full; to swoon them in the stands; the Braves stayed in the League only because of the rule that there must be eight teams in there.
(See games.)

BASEBALL (Batting, good)
The guy who had stood the big-league pitchers on their ears; he was slapping Jones all around the lot; a sizzling daisy-cutter; he slams one; he leads the league in everything but beauty treatments; he gobbled those balls up nicely; he blasted two home runs; slapping the ball around to the tune of a .440 batting average; the boys could dust them off at the plate; he busted fences down with line drives; he maced the missile at a .420 clip; he stung that onion for a .440 percentage; he could parse a ball batted to him; to convert a curve ball into three bases without using logarithm tables; kid, go up there and slap one; the ball went whizzing in the general direction of Spokane, Washington.
(See hit.)

BASEBALL (Batting, bad)
He batted like a girl; he couldn't hit the ball with a paddle; which couldn't qualify him for anything but the grapefruit league.
(See failure.)

BASEBALL (Fielding)
He did everything in the field but make the ball jump up and sing Yankee Doodle; he and the ball stuck together like ham and eggs; he couldn't stop a bunt in an alley; as fancy a job of second-basing; scooping; he surely can field that apple; sometimes he'd throw to the guy sitting in Row 3 instead of second base.
(See far, distance.)

BASEBALL (Big fields)
The center field fence is a good three-day bus ride from the plate; an outfield that should have been covered by greyhounds; it is so big, that men play out there for weeks sometimes without seeing their teammates.
(See big, large.)

BASEBALL (Pitching)
Pitching with the old noodle; curving that ball around the batter's neck; you couldn't touch him with a flagpole; his arm was so much rubber; he blew the ball past the batters; the

loud plunk of the ball in the catcher's mitt.
(See *throw.*)

BASEBALL (Rookie)
Onion-green rookie; I'm going to ship him to Poughkeepsie as soon as I can get a good excursion rate; came from some clambake league; down in the grapefruit league; polished the bench all through the World Series.
(See *amateur.*)

BASEBALL (Scores, big)
It had been a grand Roman holiday; a baseball game with a football score.
(See *umpire.*)

BASHFUL
He was so bashful his voice blushed when he used it; mealy-mouthed; coy; many a flower is born to blush unseen; bashful as an egg at Easter.
(See *timid, modesty.*)

BASSO
Basso cooing in a fatuous falsetto; a basso profundo hitting on all six.
(see *singing, opera.*)

BATH
Lolling back in the tub; wallowing in a nice hot bath; firm bosom yielding its voluptuous contours to the caress of a soapy sponge.
(See *washing oneself.*)

BATHING BEACH
Bathing beach exposure; I don't dive into the sea, I belong to the school that goes in inch by inch; all the difference between a bathing beach and nudist camp you can put in your eye; if they ever went in over the waist they were rated as channel swimmers;

the beach looks like an Earl Carroll finale; promenade into the deep.
(See *ocean, swimming.*)

BATHING SUIT
The tent-like atrocities of the Gay Nineties; a bathing suit that came within four sizes of being large enough to contain his corpulent anatomy; they fit her shape like a non-skid tire fits thirty-six pounds of air; a moth's haven.
(See *clothes.*)

BATTLE
Bullets came zinging at you; he collided with a cannon ball; he is not one to sneeze when he smells gunpowder.
(See *fight, war.*)

BATTLESHIPS
Those big battle wagons.
(See *navy.*)

BEAR
He was a bear with the lady bears.
(See *embrace, rough.*)

BEAR (To)
Some women can stomach it.
(See *suffer.*)

BEARD
He had enough beard to thatch a hut; trellis whiskers; chin whiskers; foliage; in a dimity beard; spit through his whiskers; two yards of spinach; messianic beard; sporting the snappiest Van Dyke beard; gazing at his bearded visage; the hirsute mattress; a positively frightful array of whiskers; sideburns; his fingers caressed his beard; goatee; an apostolic beard; a false beard; a thicket of whiskers that was a perpetual temptation to owls

requiring a nesting site; behind this zareba; penetrate the undergrowth; he reveled in them; the youngsters would frolic in and out of his beard; a spade beard; mangy beard; faces were shrouded in a dense shrubbery; a brace of ludicrous side-whiskers; muttonchop whiskers; his beard is cut like the spire of a steeple; a beard like an artichoke; beard like foam swept off the broad blown sea; his Moscowitchy whiskers; grew a beard to prevent his face from getting chapped while playing hockey; facial decoration; a patriarch with a three-foot beard.

(See *hair, shave, barber.*)

BEAT (Win)

Simply played him off the stage; to get the whey beaten out of me; knocks the socks off all others; I can slap you down at golf; howl them down; beat him to a fare-ye-well; standing the other golfers on their heads; took the wind out of his sails; beat the ears off you; make a monkey out of them; he played rings around him; to outsmart.

(See *win, defeat.*)

BEAUTIFUL

She was music to my eyes; she was like the bees buzzing, the water lapping, the trees swishing in the breeze; she strove to improve on the Lord's handiwork; the most beautiful blonde I have ever seen outside a bad dream; a raving beauty; these slavering beauties; she was a pip; very tasty-looking young doll; pulchritudinous; the chicest of the chic; a well-kept female face is more agreeable to contemplate than an old-fashioned gasmeter or a spotted Peruvian goat-lizard; the cream of the country's beauties; she doesn't shape up badly on the hoof; that gorgeous bundle; these beauteous dames; modern Venus; she was tall, and slim and lovely as the morning; she had the figure of an angel on a church ceiling; she was absolutely the "goods"; downright pretty; a fawn-eyed, timid-looking young thing; she had the face and she had the chassis; she was a rip-snorter for looks; a looker all right; regular fruit-stand type; peaches and cherries; she was an eye-opener; an eyeful; her eyes were like the bluebirds in the spring and her hair like finches' feathers a-wing; she had what it takes; she has élan and is distingué, dainty, darkly orchidaceous; Heaven's gift to the white race; that lovely feminine helplessness which you often read about and so seldom encounter; lace-lidded sirens; she has the oo la la; dewey-eyed young creatures; she was like thistledown dancing along through sunny places; beautiful flowers are soon picked; she was so sweet, he almost cried; when he saw her he licked his lips several times; every man is licking his chops over the sight of her; beauty may have fair leaves yet bitter fruit (prov.); beautiful as is the rose in June; beautiful as the seraph's dream; every woman would rather be beautiful than good; she looked like the girl on the barber's calendar; beauty, like an almanac, lasts a year; a true houri of Fairyland; she was nectar from the Gods.

(See *good-looking, body.*)

BEAUTY PARLOR

Cosmetician; cosmetologist; beautician; cosmetic counsellor.

(See *cosmetics, hairdresser.*)

BECOMES

Waxes tearful.

(See *changes, begin, is.*)

BED

a bed that sags in the middle; it was his second best bed; the bed needed tuning up; a place to flop at; Mark Twain said, "Don't go to bed because so many people die there"; safely tucked away in bed.

(See *sleep, rest.*)

BEE
A dead bee maketh no honey.

(See *flowers.*)

BEER
He considered beer a drink for children; a scuttle of brew; schooner of pilsener; malt; while the beer ebbs and flows; a tankard of bitter; mellowed by two steins of beer; a man well primed on beer; black velvet; let's slop up a couple of scuttles of beer; what couldn't I do to a glass of beer; the low detonating-power of the beer.

(See *drinkers.*)

BEFORE
Ere this.

(See *first.*)

BEG (Cajole)
Talked to her like a Dutch uncle; I pleaded with him, the tears in my eyes; to sponge off us.

(See *pray, request.*)

BEGGAR
Give a beggar a bed, and he'll repay you with a louse.

(See *poor, poverty.*)

BEGIN
Turned on the steam; started off with a bang; blaze the trail; carry on; from the word go; the mills of the gods have begun to grind; still in the bib and jumper stage; gave birth to an idea; start from scratch; he had the first inning; in the blueprint stage; it was in its Stone Age.

(See *opening, go.*)

BEHAVE
How to comport themselves; so long as he was a good boy.

(See *etiquette.*)

BEHIND
Always behind like a donkey's tail.

(See *later.*)

BELCH
Belch as loud as a musket; belching like a torn balloon.

(See *indigestion.*)

BELIEVE
It is a little too stiff to take; keep up a pretense of believing; they ate it up; half kidded himself into the belief; the quaint theory is generally cherished; the populace consumed it with gusto; swallowed the bait like an innocent codfish; to swallow the stuff; they swallowed the egg.

(See *trusted.*)

BELIEVING TYPE
He believes that a horsehair put into a bottle of water will turn into a snake; he believes in Santa Claus and the good fairies.

(See *truth.*)

BELL
The bonging of Big Ben; bells ring out their gladsome chime.

(See *music.*)

BELL-HOP
The buttons.

(See *servants, hotel.*)

BEND
Bend like a field of corn in a hurricane.
(See *curves, bow.*)

BENEFIT
It's an ill-wind that does no blowing.
(See *advantage, good.*)

BEST
Its palmiest day; he was tops in taps; ace; the Napoleon of all gamblers; the greatest show this side of oblivion; all-American; this one cops the prize; creme de la creme.
(See *good.*)

BET
Bet a dollar to a cookie; bet your bottom dollar; a dollar says; ten'll get you thirty; bet your last dollar; the "wise" money was on; it's dollars to doughnuts; put up the family china and chintz on their team; put a half dollar on Broadway Bill's nose; I'll bet your boots; two new topcoats against your grandfather's old clay pipe; bet your best hat; to bet on how many times two is four; he had them in the bag.
(See *poker, dice, card games, race track.*)

BETTER
He can sell rings around any two salesmen.
(See *beat, win.*)

BEWARE
Beware when the hawk coos like a dove.
(See *cautious, careful.*)

BIG
The lion's share; a tidy sum; the mind reels; a whale of an income; big as

bull beef; big as a church debt; this behemoth; big as a whale; Texas-sized.
(See *large.*)

BIG-SHOT
High muckety-muck; pooh-bah; big gun; the grand moguls; factotum; titans of big business; big-wigs; higher-ups; a somebody; sit in the seats of the mighty; the head man; overlords; the octopuses of; mahouts; front office sahibs; generalissimo; the Napoleon of; these apostles; high priests; his nibs; king-pins; oracles; these subway and surface car tycoons; shoguns; all-highest; these Lords of creation.
(See *importance, officers, executive.*)

BILL (Congress)
Bill flipped through Congress; to grind out bills.
(See *law.*)

BILL-PAYING
Dead beats.
(See *credit, honest.*)

BILLS
The best way to keep down bills is to use a paper-weight.
(See *cost, expensive.*)

BIRDS
The birds in the trees wake up and go tweet-tweet.
(See *chickens, crow.*)

BIRTH
Had begotten five children; had a visit from the stork; had a visit from the connubial bird.
(See *children, born.*)

BIRTHDAY
Natal day.
(See *celebrating, age.*)

BITE

Pardon me, sir, but is that your mouth that has my ear in it?
(See *chew, eating.*)

BITTER

Bitter as gall.
(See *sour.*)

BLACK

Black as the hinges of hell; black as despair; black as the womb of darkness; black as ink; black as Egypt's night; black as a crow; black as the king of Ashantee; black as black; black as a stack of black cats; black as snow in Pittsburgh.
(See *darkness, night.*)

BLAME

Animadversions; taking the rap; pin the foul deed on; there must be a goat; blaming him for everything from the Mexican War to the boll weevil; blame is the lazy man's wages; I might as well be hanged for a sheep as a lamb.
(See *criticism, fault.*)

BLANKETS

Covered with so many blankets, they had to put in a book mark to know where I was.
(See *bed.*)

BLESS

A benison upon you!
(See *thank you, happy.*)

BLIND

In the land of the blind the one-eyed is king (prov.).
(See *eyes, darkness.*)

BLIZZARD

The weather broke into a Hatteras blizzard; a juicy blizzard.
(See *snow.*)

BLONDE

A blonde of the platinum persuasion; a lusty efflorescent blonde; a blonde extrovert; a b r i g h t, gin-guzzling blonde; gilt-headed blonde; squiring a chemical blonde; blonde with a platinum voice.
(See *hair.*)

BLOW

A nasty jar; a bit of a jolt; a haymaking left.
(See *hit, fight, prize-fighter.*)

BLUSH

Blushing like an underdone beefsteak; blushed like a red bull-calf; like a young virgin on her wedding night; like a red cochineal; resembled a sudden prairie fire; looked like an explosion at a beet-root factory; she blushed to the locket line; blushed to my boots; going red all over; face as crimson as a sausage; blush through my tunic; blushing coyly; he looked like and explosion at a paint works.
(See *ashamed, embarrassed.*)

BOAT

Wave choppers; gondola; galleon; in this swankiest of gilded chariots of the Atlantic; one of those water gliders; the Queen Mary, "a hunk of ship"; was sloshing up and down the North Sea; the ship was nuzzled into her berth; an officious little tug; boats tossed about like paper cups.
(See *liners.*)

BOAT (Actions on)

Betting on the sex of seagulls; he shipped aboard a collier; sailed the ocean blue; peering behind every wave; tossing their baggage aboard

the —— for the happy romp to Bermuda; to hitch aboard one of those water gliders; life on the ocean wave; out there on the bounding waves; steer the boat so fast the fish couldn't get out of the way.
(See *sailors, seasickness.*)

BODY (Male)
Carcass; his chassis; torso; corpus delicti; he hasn't any more figure than an airport hangar; he has the kind of torso that sculptures dream about.
(See *muscles, strength.*)

BODY (Woman, beautiful)
The figure of a Juno; his eyes swept over her body; her sinuous body; tossing her torso about.
(See *fat, thin, thighs, bosom, hips, nose, eyes, face, feet, mouth.*)

BOLD
To lick their jowls and become bolder.
(See *daredevil, courage, brave.*)

BOMB THROWING
Hurled a large pineapple.
(See *war, fight.*)

BOND
Bonds must be clipped regularly, like asparagus.
(See *capitalist, stockmarket, brokers.*)

BOOKKEEPER
Behind a stack of dog-eared ledgers.
(See *accountant.*)

BOOK-REVIEWERS
He ate novelists for breakfast.
(See *writing.*)

BOOKS
Sometimes things get so desperate you have to read a book or something; opus; to curl up with a book; tome; the binding is read but not the books; the book-of-the-moment club; a documentary tome about Boston; he reads more book reviews than books; the book was a sell.
(See *reading, literature.*)

BOOKS (Appearance)
This book may be slipped into the vest pocket, or, still better, into the garbage can; the edges of the pages are so dirty that they feel like the underside of a mushroom; bound in leather that looks like Morocco but smells more like Constantinople; the edges are so deckle that they look as if they had been chewed by a puppy; with pages so thin that turning them is like peeling an onion.
(See *large, little.*)

BOOKS (Bad)
Reads like a very dull dish of Hollywood mush; it isn't the book of our dreams.
(See *melodrama.*)

BOOKS (Big)
An excellent example of the wet wash laundry (12c a pound) school of literature; picked it up, that is with the help of a block-and-tackle; could be used as a trouser press; they're hard on your hands.
(See *pages.*)

BOOKS (Titles)
Elsie's First Mistake; Through Turkestan on a Tandem Bicycle; The Report of the Commission of Inquiry into the Recent Outbreak of Spotted Mumps in the Gasfitting Industry; A Handbook of Chinese Music; One Thousand Ways of Hashing Veal; Prophecies for 1887; Whither and Why; The Life of a Tadpole; How

to get the most from your Loud-Speaker; Through Turkestan in Tartan Trousers; Seventy Years a Verger; The By-Laws of Battersea Park.
(See *college subjects.*)

BOOKS (Types)
These penny dreadfuls; shilling shockers.
(See *serial stories.*)

BORE
He never intrudes himself on people after they have intimated with a shotgun that they are weary of him; die of ennui; Dr. Dryasdust; bored to tears; she would pounce upon me as soon as I entered; wasn't exactly holding him spellbound; gave me a pain in the neck that reached all the way down to the small of my back; a filthy bore; to bore them to the very verge of delirium; he bores me close to the sneering point; abysmal boredom; bore them to the verge of hysteria; had a thin time of it.
(See *uninteresting, unpopular.*)

BORN
He first saw the light of day; when he was born the signs were all wrong; he was born on the wrong side of the railroad tracks; where he joined the human cavalcade; he was born at a cost of $18.00.
(See *birth.*)

BORROW
To sponge; bums all her cigarettes; cadging groceries from his friends; a thrush paid for is better than a turkey owing for (prov.); I promise to pay everything in one month positively, and, who knows, perhaps I shall; the probability is that the loaned article will never again sojourn beneath his roof; he that goes a-borrowing goes a-sorrowing; a borrowed cat catches no mice.
(See *credit, take.*)

BOSOM
To emphasize amply the luscious contours of her bosom; luscious bosom; the gorgeous swells of her ripe bosom; her pliant bosom; inviting curves of her bosom.
(See *body, brassiere.*)

BOSS
The king pin; to have a tete-a-tete with the boss; he was a law and czar unto himself; monarch of all he surveyed; his liege lord; he's the whole works; he's the big cheese; the boss of the ranch; his nibs.
(See *executive, big-shot.*)

BOSTON
The Bean City; Faneuil Hall, the cradle of liberty; where the Cabots speak only to the Lowells and the Lowells speak only to God; like giving a Boston debutante a codfish; when a Boston male fell for a Bostonienne he indicated his love by reading Ralph Waldo Emerson aloud to her.
(See *city, culture.*)

BOTHER
Plague; pester; she wished no truck with Miss; to badger people; do not pox him; a passion for getting into the hair of anyone; upset my equilibrium.
(See *bore, pest, unpopular.*)

BOTTLE (Liquor)
A be-diapered bottle.
(See *liquor, whiskey, champagne.*)

BOW
His little dancing-master bow.
(See *bend, respect, etiquette.*)

BOX OFFICE
There was a rustle of notes and a tinkle of coins in the treasurer's office; that made a big difference at the turnstiles; laid 50c on the line for his show; the show laid an egg in the box-office.
(See *tickets, theatre.*)

BOY (Names for)
Guttersnipe; a young buckaroo; most offensive-looking young toad; whippersnapper; he was just passing his nonage; squirt; squabs; these young cavaliers; a dashing young blade; the young man from the wrong side of Chicago; a rootin' tootin' young galoot; blade; this young goat; the pup; the young ruffians; young bucks.
(See *names.*)

BOY (Description)
A tall, horsefaced boy; a pimply boy; only last winter that he started shaving his chin; a tall, gangling youth.
(See *body, face.*)

BOY (Growing up)
To reach man's estate; he was going to be a man among men; was getting hair on his chest; not far removed from his first shave; youngsters coming up from knee pants; out of his swaddling clothes; before they are fairly out of their diapers; growing pains.
(See *young, children.*)

BRAG
Braggart; cackling; his skin is too large for his body; chesty; strutting; every ass loves to hear himself bray; he had better put his horns in his pocket than blow them.
(See *talker, exaggerated.*)

BRAIN
The fungus growth which you refer to as your brains; through your adamantine skull; sweat their brains; she's got a bean; his cerebellum; to wear your brain to the bone; if brains were books you could pack a library; the brains of a Minerva; a good head will get itself hats; such cerebration; brain titivation; brains of an Einstein; think tank; an encyclopedic brain; clear the brain of cobwebs.
(See *think, mind.*)

BRAKES
He yanked his emergency brake; sklitch.
(See *stop, automobile.*)

BRASSIERE
A hammock for midgets; a 6 ply, double duty brassiere.
(See *bosom, clothes.*)

BRAVE
Intrepid; he that scratches a bear must have iron nails (prov.); he was a bold man that first ate an oyster (prov.).
(See *bold, courage.*)

BREAKFAST
His breakfast is an affair of a hand groping out from behind a paper; a "farmer's breakfast"; and passed it off as breakfast; after breakfast the time is put in to good advantage looking forward to the time when dinner will be ready; *petit dejeuner.*
(See *meal, food.*)

BREATH
You can chin yourself on his aroma;

oh, if someone would only invent odorless whiskey.
(See *odor*.)

BRIBE
A bribe will enter without knocking (prov.).
(See *reward, graft*.)

BRIDEGROOM
To serve in the capacity of bridegroom; get some altar practice; a "'catch"; bought a copy of "What Every Young Bridegroom Ought to Know."
(See *wedding*.)

BRING
Fetch; coolied the coats safely home.
(See *leader, guide, get, give*.)

BRINGING UP
A woman's bringing up can be estimated by her method of eating asparagus; a good cow may have an ill calf (prov.); in a fiddler's house all are dancers (prov.).
(See *education, teach*.)

BRITISH
The roaring of the British lion.
(See *Australia, conservative, England*.)

BRITTLE
Snaps like an icicle.
(See *weak*.)

BROADWAY
The main stem; to be shagging around Broadway; neon lights are transforming Broadway into the Great Pink Way; the jeweled lane of light that was Broadway; he looked like one of good breeding glossed over with a thin veneer of Broadway; Broadway, the rue of rues, gleaming white like the cicatrix of an ancient and honorable wound; heartbreak boulevard; hard Times Square; mazda lane.
(See *city, New York*.)

BROKE
He was so broke that a pickpocket going through his pockets would get nothing but practice; financially crippled; demolished; wind up without a dime; stony broke; considerable monetary prostration; reduced to his bedroom slippers; wouldn't stake her to a thin dime; I'm on the county; broke as a China plate; a man without money is like a bow without an arrow (prov.); a moneyless man goes fast through the market (prov.); his exchequer was at a low ebb; a terrific hole in the sock.
(See *poverty, poor*.)

BROKERS
The roaring of the angry brokers; the old oaken bucketshop.
(See *bond, stockmarket*.)

BROOKLYN
And there was sadness in Flatbush, Canarsie, and all along the Gowanus Canal; Brooklyn, where they say if you can't have turkey take chicken.
(See *New York*.)

BROTHER
(See *relatives*.)

BULLY
He bullyrags a lot of relatives; a beetle-browed bully; bulldoze.
(See *scare*.)

BUNK
Bunkum; blarney; hooey; what kind of a song and dance is this; the good old bunk; what are you giving us; the apotheosis of hooey; tripe; ah, foosh;

rubbish; whangdoodle; is sheer three-ply tosh; it's a lot of eyewash; bugs; it's hokum, and inferior hokum at that; unmitigated twaddle; such pish posh; slice her where you like, she's still baloney; feeding us taffy; to hell with it; aw, buttermilk; fiddlesticks; the old apple-sauce will be only warmed over; dryrot.

(See *nonsense, lie.*)

BURGLARS

She moated the possibility of them all being murdered in their beds; he looked like the kind of person who would enter even his own home by means of a window, out of force of habit; a gentleman who was in the habit of going to other people's houses at odd hours and abstracting therefrom valuable articles for which he gave the family no pecuniary equivalent; a real genius at entering enclosed premises; collects a nice lot of loose trinkets; hang a thief when he is young, and he'll not steal when he is old (prov.); stole everything but accumulated tax bills; all are not thieves that dogs bark at.

(See *steal, gangster, safe-cracker.*)

BURGLAR'S TOOLS

A dainty set of up-to-date burgling irons; blunderbuss.

(See *gun.*)

BURLESQUE

Strip-tease; the flesh-pots; to see ten tons of assorted sex-appeal wearing old lamp shades, come charging up the runway; burlesque, the slum of show business; a peep show; between the flesh-pots and rouge-pots back stage; it had a sawdust flavor; the garter snatching of burlesque; you can't distinguish it from a stag smoker of the Sewer Digger's Union; burlesque rowdy-dowdy; the cooch dance; snatching gals off the runway.

(See *dancing, undress, underthing, shows.*)

BUSINESS

He controls the output of trouser-buttons for the whole country; racket; a slave to the advertising business; in the banking dodge; to go into the counting-house; plebeian uncle who was in trade.

(See *trades, work, prices.*)

BUSINESS (Bad)

The thermometer of its affairs stood way below zero; ups and downs, his fat months and his lean; don't worry about the business, as there isn't any business to worry about; things were a little wobbly.

(See *depression.*)

BUSINESS (Good)

A land-office business; when the going was good; boomed us off our feet; got a tremendous shot in the arm; a feeling of upswish; things are on the mend.

(See *prosperity.*)

BUSINESS (Lack of capital)

Shoestring operator.

(See *poor.*)

BUSINESS MAN

Has his finger deep in every pie; I'm somebody on this boulevard; he was talking into three telephones at once; those entrepreneurs of industry; seeking surcease from their crushing labors.

(See *capitalist, worker.*)

BUSINESS MAN (Inexperienced)

He would not have recognized a merger if one had jumped out of a bush and snarled at him.

(See *inefficiency*.)

BUSY

As busy as a one-armed goalkeeper; as busy as a cat in a butcher shop; steeped to the eyebrow; tied up; busy as pipers; up to his neck; was so busy that he never read the Sunday papers before Monday or Tuesday; up to their eyes in plans for; I am so busy I do not know whether I am afoot or ahorseback; busy as a one-armed obstetrician delivering quintuplets.

(See *active, work*.)

BUSYBODY

He has a tremendous capacity for bleeding when others are wounded; refrain from inserting my oar in the wheel; ambassador without portfolio.

(See *inquisitive, curiosity*.)

BUT

"But" me no "buts."

(See *on the contrary*.)

BUTLER

His dickey was always falling off; a gentleman's gentleman; he was the gentleman who said "The carriage awaits without."

(See *servants*.)

BUTTONHOLES

Buttonholes large enough to drop horsechestnuts through.

(See *clothes*.)

BUY

I mortgaged my little home and bought it; splurged himself to seats in the third row; and he threw in two out-fielders; lay a certified check on the line; dug down into his pants for the money; plunked down his money; bought sight unseen; cat in a bag; wished to be accommodated with a shirt.

(See *prices, pay, cost*.)

C

CABBAGE
No man devoted to orchids can care for cabbages.
(See *food*.)

CABLE
The cables sizzled with messages.
(See *telephone, letter*.)

CALIFORNIA
Californiacs; California, the sun-parlor of the nation; the sunkist region.
(See *Wild West*.)

CALM (To be)
He took it without batting an eye; he has the placidity of a barnacle; placidly chewing his cud; the bromidic effect of her personality; bovine, that describes her; her damnable calm; a nation that has complacently chewed its gum; she didn't bat the traditional eyelash; alas, this deceptive calm was but the lull before the storm; sangfroid; to act as a kind of sedative.
(See *quiet, peace*.)

CAMEL
A camel with a hump that sagged like an empty sack; a tame old dromedary; a horse with a wart on his back.
(See *elephant*.)

CAMERA MAN
To fall into the evil clutches of the camera man.
(See *photographer, movies*.)

CAMPAIGN
Comic opera campaign.
(See *plan*.)

CAMPING
To light a fire you rub two boy scouts together.
(See *vacation*.)

CANADA
A few years ago it was just a place where our absconding cashiers went.
(See *British*.)

CANDIDATE (Weak)
There is not a stick of G. O. P. presidential timber which is not worm-eaten and affected with dry-rot; he couldn't be elected to a street conductor's job in Boston; if they made him official dog catcher he would be doing very well indeed; he was running for bogey man (ugly candidate); he would much rather run for office than hold it.
(See *politics, vote*.)

CANDY
Bon-bons; yum-yum; an Oogly-Googly bar.
(See *sweet, pie*.)

CANDY SHOP
Yum-yum shop.
(See *food*.)

CANE
He is in walking partnership with a cane; there are not enough canes being used on the avenues these days to kindle a fire.
(See *walk*.)

CANNIBALS
A boiling cauldron with red-pepper and other counter-irritants; they

danced the Highland fling around this royal barbecue; epicurean chieftain; to include Mr. Witherspoon in the ingredients of an appetizing stew.

(See *eating*.)

CAPITALIST

A reeking capitalist; bloated capitalist; unregenerate capitalists.

(See *stockmarket, bond*.)

CAPERS

Hoydenish capers.

(See *fun, trick, playful*.)

CARD GAMES (Crooked)

Who gets rheumatism in his hands so bad he can no longer shuffle the cards; dealers that slid them off the bottom of the pack; cards are the devil's prayer-book; when you play with him there are 52 reasons why you can't win.

(See *bet, deceive, poker*.)

CARDS (Picture postal)

When this you see remember me.

(See *photograph, letter*.)

CARE (Not to care)

Snap her fingers in his face; makes no bones about it; nobody cares a cuss; such wild abandon; I'm fainting with excitement (feigned); making that gesture of thumb to nose; he didn't give a whistle in a whirlwind; not to care a hoot; only when the spirit moves him; there may be a panic on the Bourse, Holland may go off gold; it makes no never mind; they aren't shedding tears about it; I don't care a fig; I don't care a hoot, in fact, I don't care two hoots; with a flirt of her skirts; she didn't care a dump; he doesn't give a rip; I do not care tuppence; I don't care if you're the Archbishop of Canterbury, or the vicar's

great aunt or uncle; I have nothing to lose; after us the deluge; rolls off him like fleas leaving a deloused dog; ordinarily we can take our panacea or leave it alone; lose no sleep over.

(See *disregard, contempt*.)

CAREER

To carve out a name for herself; he had quite a niche in the Temple of Fame; should he become an actor or remain true to the wholesale knit goods game; be not a baker if your head be of butter (prov.).

(See *work, living*.)

CAREFUL (Care)

Really gives a hoot; a whoop; the type that squeezes the toothpaste from the bottom; as careful as a nudist crossing a barbed wire fence; gives a whoop in Hades; cagy; never pick a cherry blossom unless you are sure that it doesn't have a wasp hidden in it; like an elephant, he tests every bridge before putting his weight on it; sleeps with one eye open; the kind of nice young man who never forgets his rubbers; nice boys who do deep-breathing exercises every morning and see the dentist at least twice a year; a fox is not taken twice in the same snare (prov.); a scalded cat dreads cold water; a short cut is often a wrong cut; he that hath a head of wax must not walk in the sun; always keep behind a gun and in front of a mule.

(See *anxious, cautious*.)

CARELESS

To get off on the wrong foot; willy-nilly; might just as well keep dynamite in the house; a hotchpotch; wiping his sticky fingers on the bedclothes; a spirit of laissez faire; playing fast and loose; haphazard; higgledy-piggledy; by rule of the thumb; firing his gun at whim; slap-dash methods; hit-or-miss method; helter-skelter shifts of allegiance; go off half-cocked; didn't rate one-two-three with her; catch-as-catch can; his mind resembled a pawnbroker's shop window; ragtag; let his wardrobe slide; throwing caution to the winds.

(See *disregard, regardless*.)

CARPENTER

"Well done, Chippendale"; things that looked like the remains of a hen-house that had been struck by lightning (bits of wood); he worked by rule of thumb; a wood butcher.

(See *architecture, house*.)

CARRIAGE

I am afraid the bottom will fall out from under me; the clippity-clop of the hansom; Mrs. Belmont's coach and four with its caracoling horses.

(See *horses*.)

CARRY

Loaded down like a pack mule; carrying a load that would kill a mule.

(See *take*.)

CARVING (Meat)

When I start to carve, it is advisable to remove the women and children to a place of safety, and guests should get under the table; I never knew until then that a duck was built like a watch; that his works were inclosed in a burglar proof case; use dynamite; as delicate an art as ivory carving; you draw the carving knife lovingly across the bosom of the turkey; he was the family carver; to manage it without losing a thumb; disfigured a duck; dismember a turkey.

(See *knife*.)

CATS

The catnip conservatory (fence); the cat poured itself through the fence; the cat strength of the establishment had been reduced by one; she came charging out at forty miles an hour; the cat yowled; miauw; the cats, between whom and man there are unremitting hatred and cruel, eternal war; tabbies; did you ever see a cat walking with wet feet; a mouser; puss; catch-as-cats-can; he had lived many more than the proverbial nine lives attributed to cats; play puss-in-the-corner; a purring cat left its motor running; a cat having a fit is a beautiful sight; the cat's whiskers; never throw stones at a cat who is sitting on a greenhouse; nocturnal music; feline; cacophonous cat-noises; a large cat named Dr. Mary Walker; a veteran tomcat.

(See *dog*.)

CAUGHT

Brought to book; nailed her; caught him red-handed; fell into the clutches of the law; I have you dead to rights; to get hooked; to have his number.

(See *arrested*.)

CAUTIOUS

Once bitten, twice shy; what makes me a little leery; wait to see how the wind blows; yield nothing and keep our powder dry; to be on the side with the angels; he cast no bread upon the water unless he was sure it would return a three-tiered layer cake; I know which side of the fence is buttered.

(See *beware, careful*.)

CAVE-MAN

To go back to primeval ooze.

(See *rough*.)

CELEBRATING

There was a great hooray; the huzzas for the home-coming heroes; "bust

loose"; huroo; he did things up brown.
(See *party, cocktails.*)

CELLAR
Full of busted rocking chairs, potato crates, furnaces, ash sifters and barrels full of empty tomato cans; it smelled fearfully of cat and hot oil and dust.
(See *house.*)

CEMETERY
In the marble orchard.
(See *death, funeral.*)

CEREMONY
A slap-up church ceremony.
(See *wedding.*)

CERTAIN
Surefire stuff; beyond the cavil of a doubt; was by all odds the; on the other hand is certitude that.
(See *confidence.*)

CERTAINLY
Beyond the peradventure of a doubt.
(See *sure.*)

CHAIN STORES
Five and dime.
(See *prices cheap.*)

CHAINS
Go clinkety-clank.
(See *jail, jewelry.*)

CHAIR
A Morris chair collapsed with all on board; tottering to a chair; he was festooned over a chair; he looped himself over furniture; he waved her to a chair; an old museum piece; snuggling into a chair; one leg dangling across the side.
(See *sit.*)

CHAMPAGNE
The bubbles tickled her nose; he said it tasted exactly like licking a dusty window pane.
(See *drinking parties.*)

CHANCE
He had the same chance as a baby fly with a Maine spider; to get another crack at; as much of a chance as a snowball in Hades; palpitating for a chance; you'll wind up behind the eight ball; as much chance as a toupee in a windstorm.
(See *luck, accident, opportunity.*)

CHANGE
There is going to be a clean sweep, and you are going to be the broom; the idea should be reupholstered; iconoclasts; come out of his cocoon; why not try a new tune on your concertina; fumigated and disinfected; you can't improve the weather by tampering with the mercury in a barometer; to be simonized; the old apple-sauce will be only warmed over; the same rye bread delivered by the same baker every day; you've got to have sponge cake once in a while.
(See *different, exchange.*)

CHANGE (No change)
As is; maintain the status quo; a myrtle among thorns is a myrtle still (prov.); an old dog cannot alter his ways of barking; unchangeable as concrete; as unchangeable as the multiplication table.
(See *same.*)

CHAPERONE
Or latter-day duennas.
(See *protection, careful.*)

CHAPPED HANDS
Caused by writing long letters with inadequately-heated fountain pens.
(See *hands, cold.*)

CHARACTER

Character was revealed by handwriting, fingernails and the way one wore down one's rubber heels.
(See *disposition, personality*.)

CHARGE OF
(See *chief*.)

CHARITY

Handouts.
(See *kind, generous*.)

CHARM

Charm turned on as if with a grease gun; an air of *je ne sais quoi*; embodiment of all the attractions of Cleopatra, Ninon de Lenclos and Peggy Joyce; she had the nuance of chic.
(See *beautiful, love*.)

CHASE

Shoo them; executed a flying tackle which brought him down; all went pelting after the screaming young porker; let a young reporter loose on him.
(See *follow*.)

CHEERS

Three cheers for . . . . make it two; do I hear one; two cheers and a hay nonny nonny; hooray.
(See *applause, hurrah*.)

CHEMISTRY

The study of the erratic behavior of oxygen atoms on the binge.
(See *scientist, education*.)

CHESS

Rigor mortis sets in; each player is provided with eight pawns, two castles, two knights, two bishops, one king, one queen, one alarm clock, one camp bed, and one small cooking stove; his pieces consisted of seven pawns, two peppermint drops, three vest buttons, two knights, one bishop, an eye-cup, one king and a kidney bean; a chess master is a cross between a logarithm table and an adding machine; chess addict.
(See *games*.)

CHEST

Has a chest like the front of a granite quarry; the many ringlets on his chest.
(See *body, bosom*.)

CHEW

Scrunching; gnawing; masticating her gum.
(See *bite, eating*.)

CHEWING GUM

The chew in his mouth suddenly felt as big as a magnolia ham; champing away like a cow in a meadow; tireless'v grinding the inevitable piece of gum; to start chewing her gum where she had left off.
(See *candy*.)

CHICAGO

Windy City; we're going to open a restaurant in Chicago that will put that town on the map; the back rooms of the Loop.
(See *city*.)

CHICKENS

He liked that part of the chicken that went under the fence last; fowl play; they were all excited, clucking and crowing, and talking to each other.
(See *food, farm*.)

CHIEF

Factotum; major domo.
(See *leader, bigshot*.)

CHILDISHNESS

Maybe you ought to pass me my bib; no childish hickory-dickory-dock for me.

(See *foolishness, silly*.)

CHILDREN

Every child is just a quivering little mass of individuality; commit infanticide; before they are fairly out of their diapers; by the ripe age of nine; these gallumphing youngsters; the neighborhood brattery; the egg is trying to teach the chicken; incorrigible hoydens; as the twig is bent the cradle will fall; whether he would grow up to be a president or a shortstop; grow up to be a steam roller.

(See *young, boy, girl*.)

CHILDREN (Names for)

A small shaver; offspring; his chicks; little toddler; young prodigies; unimaginative little stoics; how's the wife and colleens; a litter of offsprings; progeny; junior; he left no issue.

(See *youth*.)

CHILDREN (Pet names)

Mother's lambie; my little cabbage.

(See *twins, names, pet*.)

CHIN (Receding)

A chin that was a bugle call for a retreat; slack-chinned.

(See *face, mouth, jaw*.)

CHINA (Porcelain)

She handled china like Japan.

(See *vase*.)

CHINAMAN

Rat-eater; lowly heathen; China, rickshas and temple bells; I wish I could speak Chinese, it looks like a good language to swear in; no tickee, no launlee; heathen Chinee; he looked chop suey; our knowledge of Chinese is so limited, we can't even handle a menu in a chop-suey parlor; a Chinaman's chance; not for all the tea in China.

(See *foreigner*.)

CHOOSE

Put the saddle on the right horse.

(See *want, take, right*.)

CHORUS GIRL

Doing their stuff; ladies of the ensemble; chorine; an hour-glass soubrette; bothered with stage door Johns or the manager's pals; she had the oo-la-la; man in the front row was enjoying forty winks.

(See *shows, night clubs, dancing*.)

CHRISTENING

Christened by a man who stuttered.

(See *names*.)

CHRISTMAS

Yuletide season; under the Christmas truce; succumb to the strange madness prevalent at Christmas; annual epidemic of Yuletide generosity; a merry Christmas and a fancy New Year; theme song "Then Yule Remember Me."

(See *Santa Claus*.)

CHRISTMAS GIFTS

Scout knives; air rifles; kill-me-quick cigars.

(See *thing, things*.)

CHUMMY

Got quite matey; hail-fellow-well-met fraternizing; very pally; as inseparable as a pair of pants; as chummy as two peanuts in a pod; got very clubby.

(See *pal, friendly*.)

CHURCH

I wonder what church he stays away from; in the amen corner.

(See *religious*.)

CIGAR-BUTT

Cigar-butts over one inch long should be turned into the lost and found dept.

(See *smoking*.)

CIGARETTE

Smoked down to the point where it was a menace to his mustache; he could smoke a cigarette under a shower bath.

(See *smoking*.)

CIGARS

His fourth matutinal cigar; a cigar that we call imported is about as appropriately named as the hired-girl we call domestic; he suggests a volcano in violent eruption; a cigar as black as the inside of a horse; he was clinging to a tobacco rope about two feet long; eats cigars; smoking a brand-new cigar; a cigar tucked in the corner of his mouth; a cigar that you can smoke in the house or out.

(See *smoking*.)

CIGARS (Bad)

Cigars mostly filled with pieces of Colorado maduro overalls; each cigar has a spinal column to it and this outer debris is wrapped around it; he must have forgotten to take the cellophane off; he was smoking a cigar that must have been in the Smith family for generations; a five-cent cigar that doesn't side-rip like Gertie's stocking; those kill-me-quick cigars of Christmas; and the druggist asked me as a favor not to light it in the store; smells like you're cremating a toadstool; a Roman candle; after luncheon, over a couple of cigar bands.

(See *odor*.)

CIGARS (Action)

Rolling his fat cigar round his mouth; doing gymnastics with his cigar; he contemplated the debris of his cigar; he was savaging the end of a cigar; lit a large black cigar, as General U. S. Grant used to do when he went into battle; sucking a cigar; he removed the wreck of the cigar from his mouth; in his mouth was an unlighted cigar which he revolved methodically with his teeth and tongue; a limp cheroot drooping beneath his moustache; he would make a cigar virtually talk; he undressed the cigar; he goes to work on a cigar with the same technique that Paderewski handles a piano; handle a cigar like a bachelor holding a baby.

(See *chew*.)

CIGARS (Adjectives)

Morose-looking cigar; vile; disheveled; rat-tailed; aromatic; wicked; black; indefensible; villainous-looking.

(See *smoking, give up*.)

CIGARS (Names)

A sheaf of cheroots; stogie; weed; puffing at his old stinkaroo; he knows all the ropes; El Ropo's Havana cigar; Bouquet de Gluefactoro cigar; common Mexican stinkaro.

CIRCUMSTANCE

He felt around his neck the tightening noose of circumstance.

(See *fate, destiny*.)

CITIZEN

Citizenry; woo the constituency; rabble.

(See *vote, politics, taxpayer*.)

CITY

Ah, city of golden dreams come true; I love every cobblestone in this city; the big burg.

(See *New York, Brooklyn, Chicago, Hollywood, London, Paris, Philadelphia, Reno, Washington.*)

CIVILIZATION

Civilization, they say, consists of good plumbing.

(See *education, culture.*)

CLEAN

Well-scrubbed look; rejuvenating the cuspidors; looking scrubbed; he had just been sapolioed; her house looked like an operating room; a highly prophylactic appearance; spic and span; he kept the whole place like a fifteen dollar hotel room; as clean as a hound's tooth; had been scrubbed and ironed within an inch of its life.

(See *bath, washing oneself.*)

CLEANING (House)

Scrubbed clean of its whorls of grime (bldg.); her regular setting-up exercises in the kitchen; the spring-cleaning festivals; a house which never knows the cares of a feather duster; and when the turmoil has finally subsided, and every chair, teaspoon, photograph, antimacassar, piano-stool and candelabrum is back in its appointed place; to hear the plaintive murmur of the vacuum cleaner.

(See *houses.*)

CLERK

Clerks fluttered about.

(See *salesman, sell.*)

CLEVER

That's slick.

(See *smart, experienced.*)

CLIMB

To do a Douglas Fairbanks.

(See *mountain climbing.*)

CLIQUE

A Philistine (one not in the clique); are very "clique-y"; I and my mob.

(See *club, society, friends.*)

CLOCK

It refused to run unless it was slanted so that the II was where the XII ought to be; it developed a nasty attack of hiccups.

(See *time.*)

CLOSE

Ran nip and tuck all the way; neck and neck; stick around Blair like a poultice; and she came within an ace of; on the five yard line.

(See *nearby, next to, inseparable.*)

CLOSED

Bottled up the territory.

(See *stop, finish, end.*)

CLOTHES (Men, flashy)

Dressed up like a horse; slick-looking feller; "Where's the banjo that went with it?"; his patent-leather elegance; resplendent in his checked vest, pearl derby and spats; barbered to a gloss; what the well-dressed man will dare; he resembled the lilies of the field in variegated hues; he wore a suit of beer-bottle green; his plaid cap looked like a relief map of the Land of Oz; his rig-out; bunch of forget-me-nots in his lapel; they looked like what was left of a minstrel show; dressed up like Astor's pet horse; he was a sight to behold; he reminds me of a hillbilly, fresh from the ready-to-wear department of Montgomery-Ward, bound for the county fair; he was got up like the colonel of the Horse Marines; silly sartorial fol-de-rols; to go on a sartorial binge; that tailor that designed them must have had a hangover.

(See *suit, trousers, shirt, collar, vest.*)

CLOTHES (Good dressers)

A young gentleman in silk hat, striped trousers, boutonniere and monocle; a Don Juan; I regarded him merely as a haberdasher's manikin; stuffed shirt; his sartorial snobberies; a collection of exclusive metropolitan labels; Beau Brummel; dandies; a stickler for fashion; a fop foppishly dressed; clothes horse; lapel posy; silly sartorial conceits; *le dernier cri;* decked himself in metropolitan splendor; the human "clothes horse"; nattily upholstered; bravely caparisoned; sartorial splendor; I could tell by the cut of his jib; people who have more than one suit of clothes; nicely turned out; his clothes fit him as the skin of a potato; dapper; well-turned-out lads; dressed to kill; togging up; man is judged by the umbrella he carries; he had the front all right.

(See *necktie, spats, effeminate.*)

CLOTHES (Men—Names for)

Trappings; togs; he had some nifty-looking rags; his duds; his sartorial effects; every stitch of clothes that he wore; habiliments; glad rags; raiments; rig-out; store clothes; ensemble.

(See *suit, pants, trousers, suspenders, spats.*)

CLOTHES (Men—dressing)

Sliding into his togs; he went forth in full panoply; donning fancy duds; leaped into his clothes; wriggled into his overcoat.

(See *shoe shine.*)

CLOTHES (Men—old-fashioned)

Peg-top trousers; clothes which were the sine qua nons of the elegant eighties and the mauve decade.

(See *underwear, coat.*)

CLOTHES (Evening)

Plug-hatted, frock-coated gentlemen; stuffed shirts; a coat with long tails; embellished themselves with boiled shirts; a cutaway; all done up in soup and fish; getting himself trussed in a boiled shirt; he was in white tie and tails; evening clothes, a costume in which the ordinary man looks like something dragged in by an undiscriminating cat; he practically lives in evening clothes; tricked out in frock coat; French silk socks as thin as tissue paper.

CLOTHES (Men—careless)

His moccasins were down at the heels; coffee sack; dressed like a wagon-driver for the Salvation Army; he was a pretty sloppy dresser; it looked like an empty gunny sack; he zigged where he should have zagged, and bagged where he should have bulged; his white suit looked as if it had been fricasseed; one of the ten worst-dressed men in N. Y.; a hand-me down suit about four times too big for him; his new clothes felt like a Chinese torture jacket.

(See *shoes, hats.*)

CLOTHES (Women)

Her clothes have the week-before-last look; I will deck you in; she looked so expensive; stodgy; an instinct for the wearing of clothes which made a couturier's dream; a first class dress dummy; the most extravagant sartorial embellishments; beruffled in oodles and oodles of pale greenish net; and all the folderols; dressed up like Mrs. Astor's plush horse; "poured" into her evening gowns; a plushed up Mrs. Astorbilt; one of the ten worst-dressed women in N. Y.; she did not look soignée; she was a sartorial sight for the eyes; stopped on the steps for a minute and gave the mink coat a chance to kill 'em.

(See *dress, stocking, fur coat, hats.*)

CLOTHES (Women—Old-fashioned)

As dead as bustles; passementerie; the old-time girl was a veritable hedgehog of pins; and huge coiffures suggesting the presence of rats; in the days when a bombazine skirt was glamorous; used to scream when a male saw her with her sleeves rolled up.

(See *old-fashioned.*)

CLOTHES (Women-scanty)

Whose garment you could have sent to any part of the world with a one-cent stamp; abbreviated costume; one of the ten least-dressed women in; brevity is the soul of lingerie.

(See *under thing, brassiere.*)

CLOWNS

Merry Andrews; a wit of the Lambs; his clownish posturing; dons cap and bells and busts out again; playing the role of mountebank; bar-room clowning; a Pagliacci.

(See *funny, humor, fool.*)

CLUB

To go and grouse at his club; the serried rows of members, embedded to their ears in commodious arm-chairs.

(See *clique, fraternity, sorority.*)

CLUBS (Names of)

The Ancient Order of Beer-Buyers.
(See *lodge.*)

CLUMSY

He is all thumbs; he had two left feet.
(See *awkward, heavy.*)

COAL

Black diamonds.
(See *meat.*)

COAT

She slid out of her mink coat; peeled off his coat; his coat fit him like the raincoat on an army truck.

(See *clothes, fur coat.*)

COCKTAILS

She dallied over martinis and high-balls; downed by two side-cars; a mickey fin; cocktailing everywhere; a lady who drinks only creme de menthe when she wears a red or a green dress; the average hostess is still committed to the belief that a liberal dash of grenadine syrup improves any drink; the pale terra-cotta cocktails.

CO-EDS

The Petticoats' Dean.
(See *college, girl.*)

COFFEE

A demi-tasse, bah! Bring me a bowl of coffee; they give you an eye dropper full of black coffee; the coffee was almost as discouraged as we were; gulping his Sanka; with his chin in his cup of Java; finishing his second slug of coffee; enough coffee to float a navy; toying with his coffee; asked if he wanted a demi-tasse, he said, "Yes, and a small cup of coffee, too"; coffee thick enough to hold a spoon upright; he was drinking a cup of well-advertised coffee; O. Henry described a certain restaurant coffee as "black as night, sweet as sugar, hot as hell"; drank that cupful of synthetic coffe to its bitter dregs; stirring his coffee with my stogie.

(See *tea.*)

COINCIDENCE

The long arm of coincidence; more

than just something washed in from the sea.
(See *accident, chance.*)

COLD (Cold-blooded)

The girl was like a chunk of ice cream with spikes all over it; the atmosphere dropped to zero; he had iced arteries; the thawed perceptibly; colder than a blonde's heart; colder than a traffic cop's heart; felt the blood turn to ice in her veins; hints of glaciers in her.
(See *hard-boiled, disregard.*)

COLD

He pulled the zodiac over himself to keep warm; as cold as an iceman's pants; chilblains; hardy snowbirds; it was so cold I thought some bankers were around; colder than a blonde's heart; it was so cold I saw a statue of Lincoln put his hands in his pockets; so cold it froze the fire in our fire-place; cold as a hot-water bag in the morning; cold as an enthusiastic New England audience; cold as the rocks on Torneo's hoary brow; cold as a skeleton; cold as a fish; cold as a dead man's nose; the mercury dropped to the nose-nipping point; this weather puts hair in your mittens; it's a coat colder this morning; frost-bitten ears; the thermometer was sitting on its bottom; freeze the buttons off the coat of a state trooper; the heating was poor but the ventilation was perfect (meaning the house was not well insulated against the cold); as cold as an airedale's nose in January; icicles were hanging on the chandelier.
(See *winter, snow, shaking.*)

COLD (Sickness)

The sniffles; entertaining la grippe; a full influenza cold with a temperature and curious buzzing noises in the ears; a plain cold with loud hacking cough; he hauls off and catches a cold;

how I caught my cold I have no idea, it's just a knack I have.
(See *sick.*)

COLLAPSED

Collapsed like a farm-relief plan; fallen by the wayside; folded up; deflated; went galley west; had been given the hook; it was a body blow to; although it was hanging on the ropes anyway; several shows will fold their wings before March 1; went to pieces; collapsed with all on board.
(See *end, failure.*)

COLLAR (Men)

Smoke-stack collar; gates-ajar collar; a collar with an edge on it like that of a buzz saw; the wearing of a starched collar for a man with a short neck is a minor surgical operation; turn-down collar, turned down by every laundry in town; his collar must've been mad at his neck; choker collar; he sported a celluloid collar a horse could jump through.
(See *shirt, necktie.*)

COLLECTOR

Collector was using their door mat as a sleeping porch.
(See *bills, bill-paying.*)

COLLEGE

Prexy; he had a whole alphabet of degrees; came in with a tall blue-eyed stranger, just like one of those Yale boys, only bright-looking; four years in college do very little damage to a really bright young fellow; he escaped from Amherst back in 1904; he looks salt-water college; chief ornament of our campus; a college with stadium attached; I flunked out of three colleges; an institution of higher learning; a university had dipped him very casually into education; booted out of Harvard.

(See *education, intellectual.*)

COLLEGE CHEERING
He yelled for Oxford till he was a bad case of sandpaper-throat.

(See *cheers.*)

COLLEGE SUBJECTS
The theory of diminishing returns; the orations of Cicero; the binomial theorem; the dramas of Ibsen; Archimedes's principle about bodies immerged in fluid.

(See *intellectual.*)

COLOGNE
Dabbed a bit of cologne under his arm pits.

(See *perfume.*)

COLOR
Whistler said mauve was pink trying to be purple; as black as the hinges of hell; as pink as the break of day; in the putty-colored twilight; puce-colored underwear; blue like the Mediterranean; a suit of beer-bottle green; lilies of the field in variegated hues; looked like an explosion at a paint factory; colors that defy a rainbow on a drunk.

(see *painting.*)

COLOR (Names of)
Fire-patrol red; such heavenly colors; like bittersweet and rusticana; mauve; pistachio; beige; midnight blue.

(See *blush.*)

COLOSSAL
It's colossal in a small way.

(See *big, large.*)

COLUMNIST
Many of the tid-bits that appear in his column.

(See *newspaper, writer, reporter.*)

COME
Come busting out; idea popped into his head; coax the water up this side; actors blow in now and then; Lafayette, I am here; along breezes Katie; these gentlemen swarmed in like flies to honey; she toddled in; trot round to my place; slipped into town; barged into the room; his goings and comings; shuffled in; come out, come out, wherever you are!

(See *appeared, go.*)

COMEBACK
He's back in the chips again.

(See *success, prosperity.*)

COMEDIAN
A knock-down comic; the cap and bells; if a comedian is lucky enough to make up a joke, it lasts him all season; he rocked a Hollywood audience.

(See *humorist, clowns.*)

COMFORT
In our shirt-sleeves; a crumb of comfort.

(See *satisfactory, support.*)

COMPANY
A going concern, but we don't know which way it is going.

(See *business.*)

COMPARISON
What is hash to some people is steak to others.

(See *different, change.*)

COMPLAIN
Something to snark at; yipping; slams; squawks; split the heavens with my

outcries; what's the use of yelping; such a hue and cry; raising a rumpus; railed at everything; he was always grousing about something; howling his head off about; belly-aching; crab about; beefing; putting up quite a beef.
(See *criticism, grouchy.*)

COMPLETE
From soup to nuts; all encompassing scope; shooting the works; run the whole gamut of; from pillar to post.
(See *all, perfect, thorough.*)

COMPLEXION (Female)
Was the color of rare old linen; a stain of color came to tint the girl's complexion; a complexion like Grade-A milk; a peaches and cream complexion.
(See *skin, cosmetics.*)

COMPLICATED
And down will come the madhouse; if complications had not fermented; it was rapidly becoming a sort of matrimonial Fourth Dimension.
(See *confused, mixed up.*)

COMPLIMENT
To receive the wreath of verbal posies.
(See *praise, flattery.*)

CONCENTRATE
Trained his guns.
(See *strength.*)

CONCERTS
Don't hum sea chanteys during a concert of chamber music.
(See *music.*)

CONDUCTOR (Music)
The conductor has mounted his soapbox with a waggle of his little stick; conductor who controls all these warring elements with a little cudgel; he prevents the First Fiddle from throwing bread-pellets, etc., at the third trombone; wields the baton; foreman of the orchestra; headman; he let loose the pandemonium.
(See *orchestra.*)

CONFERENCE
In a seance; love-feast; filled the room full of conference and smoke; a council of war.
(See *meeting, talking.*)

CONFESS
Breaks down and confesses; come clean.
(See *tell, truth.*)

CONFIDE
He was a sort of mother-confessor.
(See *trusted, secret.*)

CONFIDENCE
He had an air of *je ne sais quoi;* an air of savoir faire; his aplomb; to be cocky; sight unseen.
(See *certain, believing type.*)

CONFUSED
He couldn't tell t'other from which; I found myself adrift in a cockle-shell between Scylla and Charybdis; a smoke screen.
(See *complicated, mixed up.*)

CONGRESS
A collection of 435 dumbbells; what was once known as the world's greatest deliberative body; the popular congressional game of fool-the-voters; legislation by blocks, alliances and log-rolling; it's one-third honest, one-third fool and one-third knave; you are more impressed by the spittoons than by the congressmen; law mong-

ers; bloodthirsty and savage bucca-
neers; he plays to the Star Spangled
gallery; he was elected to congress
where he was lost in the shuffle; buy a
big black hat and go to congress.
(See *law, government.*)

CONSCIENCE

It was yanked out along with his tonsils; his conscience was three sizes too
large, yet it pinched him.
(See *morals.*)

CONSCIENTIOUS

God-fearing.
(See *honest, careful.*)

CONSERVATIVE

They are an old British tradition;
Tories; hidebound Britons; hard-
shells; an affront to every bit of sound
four-and-a-half per cent advice which
has ever been given to young men;
a die-hard; I had rather ride on an ass
that carries me than a horse that
throws me (prov.).
(See *politics, cautious.*)

CONSPICUOUS

Stand out like a walrus at a goldfish
ball; sticking up like the proverbial
sore thumb; they stand out like pins
on a 1929 Hoover vacuum cleaner
sales manager's map.
(See *noticeable, prominent.*)

CONSTITUTION

People can't eat the Constitution; the
eighteenth commandment; is the constitution a set of laws or a punching
bag?
(See *government, law.*)

CONSULTATION

Council of war.
(See *conference, advice.*)

CONTEMPT

Like laughing at God; if I stomp on
the delicate sensibilities; that gesture
of thumb to nose; I wouldn't wipe my
hoofs on the likes of you.
(See *disdain, disregard.*)

CONTENTED

He was contented in the sense that
cows are contented.
(See *happy, satisfactory.*)

CONTEST

Too many contests and not enough
prizes.
(See *battle, debate, fight.*)

CONTRACT (Legal)

We whereased and thereuponed; long
documents full of whereases.
(See *agree, bargain.*)

CONTRIBUTE

To blow in.
(See *co-operate, part of.*)

CONTROL

To keep an iron heel upon the throat
of.
(See *orders, manage.*)

CONVENIENCE

At your beck and call.
(See *comfort, easy.*)

CONVERSATION

Short-circuted the conversation; he
had been relying on the topic to carry
him nicely through at least a couple
of courses (meal); to be au courant in
matters of small talk; he could say
nothing well; tête-a-tête; this constant
buzz-buzz-buzz; put her oar in the conversation; she shifted conversational
gears; telling obvious but pleasant lies
to one another; never open your

mouth unless you have something to say; a valetudinarian; pleasant chit-chat; his conversation wasn't really of the sort that makes you grab both arms of your chair while you're listening to it; idle persiflage; prattle; babble; subjects which men simply do not consider talkworthy; ball of conversation; their smart alec talk; she held up her end of the conversation until it was practically perpendicular; it keeps splashing through her conversation; conversational rigor mortis setting in; the weather lasted about a minute.
(See *talking, debate, speech.*)

CONVERSATION (Subjects)
The influence of medieval archaeology on modern football tactics; the influence of medieval cookery on modern baseball tactics; the best method of boiling imported tripe; bimettalism; is the Red Sea a vivid scarlet or merely a mild pink; the latest axe murder; the Ukrainian budget; the price of fish; the decline and fall of the Roman Empire; the tendency of cuckoos to lay eggs in postmen's hats.
(See *discussion.*)

COOK (Good)
She was born in a kitchen.
(See *kitchen.*)

COOKING
Bouillabaise; its fourth basting (turkey) to fill the kitchen with the odors of paradise; he was skillful at basting a stuffed capon.
(See *food, eating.*)

COOKING (Poor)
Wasn't able to cook anything more complicated than hot water; which eventually solidified into something resembling macadam; couldn't ever

persuade a sardine to lie down on a canape with touching grace; God sends meat, the devil sends cooks (prov.).
(See *indigestion.*)

CO-OPERATE
Work hand in glove; gang up among themselves; blow not against the hurricane; co-operate like a bell and its clapper; to play ball.
(See *contribute, help.*)

CO-OPERATE (Not to)
Working at cross purposes.
(See *opposition, object.*)

COPY
To crib; a carbon copy; he lifted that from; took their cues from Broadway; these tuppenny imitators; steal some thunder; aping; copy-cats.
(See *imitate, same.*)

COQUETTING
They turned to mush for Grace when she did those things with her eyes; her hello smile; the flirt of her skirt.
(See *flirt.*)

CORDIAL
Who oozed cordiality.
(See *friendly.*)

CORNET
Hiccup a little on the cornet.
(See *instruments.*)

CORRECT
I like plausibility, logicality; it adds up right; the figures jibed.
(See *right.*)

COSMETICS
Cosmetic allure; sweet-smelling unguents; plied herself with; freshen-

uppers; drew out her compact and quite calmly renewed her beauty; her lipstick was skewy; lip-rouge laid on in provocative twirls; their rouge pots; her hair and complexion came out of a couple of bottles; with the aid of cosmetics and unguents and false eyebrows and what not; and subject their winsome faces to a searching scrutiny about 873 times between breakfast and curfew; whose healthy color comes in any shade desired and not from setting-up exercises in the kitchen; her lips could stop an express train; after a session with her hairdresser; who will delay her own funeral ceremony if she suspects the slightest shine upon her well-shaped nose; perfumed dust (powder); varnished with make-up; to kalsomine her cheeks; giving her a primary coat of sizing; to demonstrate novel hideosities in which lacquer, gold leaf, shellac, and (for all I know) deck paint are used; made up to the whites of her eyes; a gory trail of Mephistophelean makeup; she had a vast arsenal of makeup supplies.

(See *beauty parlor.*)

COST

I nicked him for seven dollars; the pearls would fetch close to; "What's the damage?"; it set me back three dollars; we'd be swindling if we asked more than $3,000; nicked his purse for something like; it cost either $7,000 or $11,000, according to who is telling the story.

(See *buy, pay, prices.*)

COSTUMES

They were got up like the Colonel of the 'Orse marines.

(See *dress, masquerade.*)

COUCH

A Chesterfield.

(See *bed, chair, sit, divan.*)

COUGH

I began to cough; it seemed the top of my head came off and flew up to the ceiling.

(See *cold.*)

COUNTRY

If you've seen one tree you've seen 'em all; lying on the grass and having potato bugs crawling up and down your spine; a place with a sheep in the clover and the cows in the corn; the larks fluting in heaven's blue vault.

(See *hunting, fishing, farm.*)

COURAGE

Look a whole regiment of experts in the eye and tell them to go chase themselves; he didn't care a blamed cent; "It is a bold mouse that nestles in the cat's ear"; he had the guts; a stiff upper lip; his spine stiffened; he was very brash; which emboldens me to; it takes a big hunk of nerve; nobody can speak out at meetin' like; at last he screwed up his courage; his Irish; sheer, cast-iron courage; the courage of a saxophone player; intestinal fortitude.

(See *bold, brave, hero.*)

COURTEOUS

A Galahad.

(See *etiquette.*)

COURT-PLASTER

Stuck to him with great tenacity of purpose.

COURTS (General)

Being flayed by the district attorney; miscarriage of justice; making a mockery of the law.

(See *judge, law, jury.*)

COW

Acting as nurse-maid to a milk cow;

the cows are to be made into meat balls; a sward swallower; the cows were cropping daintily at the lush grass; gentle brown-eyed creatures.

(See *milk*.)

COWARD

Fence straddler; to take it lying down; fraidy cat; rushing for the iodine bottle for the slightest scratch; lily-livered; he won't tackle anything unless he's got an ace in the hole and at least a king showing; pusillanimous; chicken-breasted; chicken-hearted; turn tail and run like a hunted stag; are you man or mouse?; if he had said "Boo!" she'd have run for dear life; he didn't have guts; he had all the aplomb of a frightened rabbit.

(See *fear, timid*.)

CRAZY

He goes screwy; has bees in his bonnet; he was dropped on the head by his nurse when a boy; he used to put beans up his nose; he's gone potty; a crackpot; go gaga; cutting out paper dolls; walking on your heels; drive him slightly batty; has gone absolutely scrammy; I am hopelessly cuckoo; his mind completely unbuttoned; essence of dementia; goofy; unscrew his reason; he was potted; he is cracked; twisted; off; as daffy as a coot; it's going to run me nuts; crack-brained; he has delusions of grandeur; entirely off his nut; daffydil; he is a little screwy, or if he is not screwy he will do very well as a pinch-hitter until a screwy guy comes to bat; go berserk; a crazy loon; going plum bughouse; plum locoed ones; as fascinating as the inside of a looney-bin; go gaga and start chewing the carpet; bats in his belfry; made noises like a bird called the cuckoo when; he was chipped china; loco in the coco; went into a state approximating dementia; bat-

ty; somewhat balmy in the bean; had chipped a little more china off the crack pot; sensible people snickered and tapped their foreheads; his lunacies; wrong in the head; a state of jibbering idiocy; your metaphors are slightly mixed; we ought to get out immediately with the butterfly nets; and finally take refuge, gibbering slightly, at his club; softening of the dome.

(See *insane asylum*.)

CREDIT

Cash-and-carry, with very little to carry away.

(See *borrow, bill-paying*.)

CREEPY

Gives us the woolies.

(See *fear*.)

CRIMINALS

Brought to book; good pickings; working in cahoots; a refined entrepeneur of crime; a jolly crew of bank robbers; thieves, hijackers and murderers; as pretty a bunch of cut-throats; an accessory to the crime; he ought to be in six state penitentiaries; post-graduates at Sing Sing.

(See *gangster, gunman, steal, murder*.)

CRITIC

Digging nightly into the rubbish can of the theatre; Mr. Nathan dozed through 38 plays; criticians; the critics doubled themselves into knots; the limburger school of criticism; judges plays by his liver; never uses one adjective where two will suffice; a subway circuit critic; writes in neutral.

(See *book-reviewers, writer*.)

CRITICISM

Criticism mixed with tabasco; hand his show the roast; to heave the old harpoon into; he withers under criticism and folds his petals; panned him; animadversions; while we leave off our critical cap and gown; canned the picture; he panned the pants off; more sinned against than sinning; critical brickbats; put you on the pan.

(See *blame, complain.*)

CROOK

Sharper; he is so crooked that tailors break their necks in measuring him for a suit; he cries wine and sells vinegar (prov.); crooked as a dog's hind leg.

(See *steal, dishonest.*)

CROPS

The consumptive lettuce.

(See *farm, food.*)

CROSS-EYED

She wasn't exactly cross-eyed, but one of her eyes just ignored the other; those go-funny eyes; her eyes did not seem to know the value of team work.

(See *eyes.*)

CROSS YOUR HEART

Honest Injun; honor bright.

(See *swearing oaths.*)

CROW

Sky-thief.

(See *birds.*)

CROWDS

My feet stepped on, my ribs poked and my eye glasses knocked off; gathered together like sheep in a storm; crowds began to thicken; you couldn't get into the French Casino with a shoehorn the other night; is still jammed to the sweatband; practically sitting in each other's laps.

(See *people, city, crowds.*)

CRUELTY

As cruel as a taxi meter; *Schrecklichkeit*.

(See *torture.*)

CRY

Nose was red from sniveling all day; weep to slow music; he was shedding crocodile tears; sniffling softly; winked back scalding tears of rage; a real weepy letter; wept softly in his soufflé; lachrymatory glands are so sensitive; all of which makes me call for my crying towel; he then burst into a torrent of tears; cry into their beer at the mere mention of; Aunt Ella was weeping softly and all seemed right with the world; but the onion fell out of her handkerchief; crying his eyes out; cry softly into someone else's beard; cried till he got all dough-eyed and dithery; prolonged crocodile sobs of woe; black tears ran down her cheeks from the ruins of her eyelashes; from her eyes there rolled a large one-and-half carat tear; tears didn't affect him; his heart was waterproof; tears began to flow like lovely crystal beads over Joyce's cheeks; felt a tear fall on his manly bosom; he cried all over Mr. Jetty's purple vest; to drop a tear.

(See *sad.*)

CRYBABY

He is able to bleed when others are wounded.

(See *melancholy.*)

CULTURE

She began to have culture pains; soaked his system full of culture; read fifteen minutes a day; the sophisticates; went highbrow on us.

(See *civilization, education.*)

CURIOSITY

Stung by the gadfly of curiosity; too

nosy; pique my curiosity; poking his beezer into other people's business; put her oar in everybody's business; his bump of curiosity had enlarged considerably; he was the type who would toss a raw egg into an electric fan, to see what would happen; she was a buttinsky.

(See *busybody, inquisitive.*)

CURLS

Catch-me-if-you-can curls.

(See *hair.*)

CURVES

The diaphanous black lace accentuated every line of her delectably proportioned curves; the voluptuous curves of her body; revealing round, alabaster-like curves; she was curvy in wonderful places; she had hairpin curves.

(See *hips, bosom.*)

CUSPIDOR

Yawning brass cuspidor; spittoon out of focus.

(See *tobacco chewing.*)

CUSTARD

It was an old Spanish custard.

(See *food.*)

CUSTOMS (Duty)

The customs Johnnies.

(See *tax.*)

CUTE

She's a cute little trick; cute as a bug's ear.

(See *beautiful.*)

CYCLONE

If your ears are large and stand out, be sure the wind doesn't get behind them; caught on one of the most destructive cyclones that ever visited a republican form of government.

(See *wind.*)

CYNIC

Scoffer at truth; hoary-headed unbeliever; his Harvard sneer; curl the upper lip at woman; professional sneerer; how the gods must laugh.

(See *skepticism, pessimist.*)

D

DAMAGE
Mayhem.
(See *hurt, mischief.*)

DANCERS (Men)
Hoofers; the boy with the electric
feet; dime-a-dozen hoofers; those ball-
bearing ankles.
(See *shows.*)

DANCERS (Women)
Hip-weavers.
(See *burlesque.*)

DANCING
Pirouetting; across the floor they sailed, a coquettish yacht convoyed by a
stately cruiser; he could tear a tango
to pieces; postage stamp dance floor;
she had to be "sat out" with; his long-
suffering partner; hoofing; swing her
elegantly in a waltz; to gyrate; these
nimble-toed dancers; his love for
Terpsichore; the Lindy hop is a barbaric throwback to the dervishes of
the jungle; a dance with kisses in the
clinches; let's do a brace of rhumbas;
the dance floor was big enough for an
honest dogfight but no more; would
you care to tread a stately measure
with me?; shake a leg; you've got to
be a stevedore to dance with that
woman; it's like hauling a bale of hay
around; a hop around with Mrs.; I
don't think Mrs. Murgle's done much
of the light fantastic since the minuet
went out; treading a hobnailed measure with; the elephant squad; hip-
tossing tangos; bending low and fer-
vently over a semi-recumbent partner
is one of the more erotic moments of
the tango; this terpsichorean academy;
he was doing a little of what passes
for dancing; they twisted, turned,
dipped, tangoed, continentaled and
glode; he shook a neat leg; where
they pay real money to be showed
around the floor; good dancers have
mostly better heels than heads (prov.);
watching them heaving a thigh; everyone who dances is not happy (prov.).
(See *night clubs.*)

DANCING (Classical)
A troupe of hop, step and jump specialists who had sprained their ankles
hurdling buttercups; a cross between
pogo-stick hopping and ballet dancing; she was like thistledown; from
the first step to the last leap; hopping
about in cheesecloth to the Meditation from Thais and the Death of the
Swan; tossing her torso all over the
stage; she was in the contortions of
an exotic polka; put his right forefinger on his head and his left hand
on his hip and made what he thought
were oriental dance turns; acrobatic
dancers turning flip-flops; ability he
displays in tossing her ladyship
through the air and catching her in
the catch-as-catch-can fashion; adagio
dance; she can dance like the flames:
"Whoops, Pavlova"; performing a sort
of pas de deux.
(See *artist.*)

DANDRUFF
Dusting the snow off my coat.
(See *hair.*)

DANGER
Flirting with hazards that would make
an insurance actuary swoon; deadly:
the jaws of death; with only a rope
ladder and the grace of God between

us and eternity; they were gone goslings; the business end of a snake; he came to grief between the Scylla of "sour" and the Charybdis of "sweet." (See *trouble, narrow escape.*)

DARE

Anyone who dasts pass up.
(See *courage.*)

DAREDEVIL

His attitude, which is that of a daredevil about to go over the Niagara Falls in a barrel.
(See *bold, reckless.*)

DARKNESS

Plunged into stygian darkness.
(See *black, night.*)

DARTING

Darting through Congress like pains in a rheumatic leg.
(See *run, hurry.*)

DATE

You must have been out with the Social Register last night; she stood him up; I've a date for beer and pretzels with the duchess; and never the twain shall meet; I spent a buck and a half of my relief money; he is playing host to Gladys tonight.
(See *entertained, rendezvous.*)

DAUGHTER

If my daughter does that I'll turn her out in the snow.
(See *relatives.*)

DAWN

But the dawn's early light this morning saw; wee hours yesterday morning at sunup; the dawn borne on the wings of a soft breeze which is helping to usher in a new day; milkman's mat-inee hour; I'd lie awake until the sparrows began to twitter and the first milkman started yodelling; the hour when night throws off its shadowy cloak to become another day; the dawn of a new day peeping coyly over the gasworks.
(See *morning.*)

DAY

The live-long day; day breaks but does not fall; night falls but does not break; the days fly past like telegraph poles on a railway journey.
(See *light, time.*)

DAYDREAMS

Wool-gathering.
(See *dreamer.*)

DAYS (Old)

The palmy days; those free-and-easy days; in those naive days; the mauve decade; as of yore; in those days of the Coolidge era; when whiskey was only fifteen cents a gallon; hang-the-expense era (Coolidge); in those days when Grandpa was a boy. The Fabulous 50's; in the days when monarchs were absolute as well as dissolute; when dollars fell off every tree; when Harry Lauder was making his first farewell performance; when swashbuckling was in its prime; in the days when men wore the tight pants of the family; in those good old days when knights were bold; giddy nineties.
(See *past, long time ago.*)

DEAD (Extinct)

Would soon take their place on the scrap heap of history with smallpox and the buggy whip; as dead as the Queen of Sheba's camel; as obsolete as the great auk; vanished like the diplodoccus; died out long ago, like the chin whiskers and the spotted dinosaur; as dead as bustles and peg-top trousers; as dead as last Tuesday; these cafes that open so bravely and die aborning; commit hari-kari; fox hunting is dying of pernicious anaemia; is on the toboggan; doomed to follow the bison; to drive the ultimate nail in capitalism's coffin; a greased chute.

(See *extinct.*)

DEADLOCK
An impasse.
(See *disagree.*)

DEALINGS
To have any truck with.
(See *business, friendly.*)

DEATH
Dispatched to meet his maker; life was snuffed out; to assist at her obsequies; passed on to his reward; long since gathered to his fathers; he was careless enough to lose his life; who entered into Eternal Rest; and he wasn't playing possum neither; to liquidate persons who; to croak; when I shove off; stiffs; put in his last resting place; breathed her last; joined the angelic choir in the Elysian Fields; when the time comes for the angel Gabriel to toot that cute little trumpet; doing your exit with your boots on; his demise; he is extremely dead; have gone to another sphere; died of old age; gave up the ghost; an ignominious end; the jaws of death; his heart just naturally hauls off and quits; gone where the woodbine twineth; as dead as a hammer; shuffling off this mortal coil; a box with silver-plated handles on the outside; he went to bed feeling well and the next morning woke up dead; pushing up the daisies; went to the happy hunting grounds; gone off to Valhalla; the slender cord of life so often snaps; a piece of churchyard fits everybody (prov.); he died young of curdling; and then, oblivion; he was found dead with a long word in his mouth; rapped at death's door; when the summons came; and soon you'll be shaking St. Peter's hand; may the earth rest lightly on his bones; dead men bite not (prov.); toothy defiance of death.

(See *end, cemetery, funeral.*)

DEBATE
The rough and tumble of debate.
(See *contest, arguing.*)

DEBUTANTE
It was supposed to be her coming-out, but she did not come, she had to be pushed; Grade A "debbies"; debutantitis; that annual Mayfair malady is just like the measles; the budding juniors simply must go through it once; Mary is so young she is not yet "out" officially; gay, giddy debutante season; the high-priestess of smart debutante functions; one of the upper register belles; sub-debutantes; she "debuted" in the green room; to bring out daughter with a bang that would shake even the calm of a Herald Tribune society editor; support her in the same manner to which her parents had spoiled her; debutante slouch, he stoops over when she stands up; she is just too, too Junior League; this year's crop of debutantes.

(See *girl, society.*)

DECEIVE
Hornswoggle, shortchanged; thimble rigged; chicanery; to pull the wool over his eyes; play both ends against the middle; flimflamming.

(See *lie, fool someone.*)

DECLINE
The greased chute.
(See *failure, downward.*)

DEEP

In the bowels of.

(See *inside, far.*)

DEFEAT

They steam-rollered Jim; also ran; sink the ship of state; flattened at the polls.

(See *win, downfall.*)

DELIRIUM TREMENS

The jimjams; imagine being chased by a pale blue armadillo on a tricycle; the D. T.'s.

(See *drunk.*)

DEMAND

He wanted his full sixteen ounces of flesh.

(See *insist, want.*)

DEMOCRAT

Where the followers of Jefferson and Jackson pursue the peculiar practices of their sect; red-white-and-blue democrat.

(See *politics.*)

DENTIST

Was turning the pages of a three-year-old copy of the Tatler; the man behind the forceps; was straining at the forceps; the extraction of his bicuspid; a fang-wrencher.

(See *teeth.*)

DEPENDABLE

Someone, as you might say, who can button their own pants; gold-plated predictions.

(See *loyal, trusted.*)

DEPENDENT

Had all his relatives on his back.

(See *hangers-on; relatives.*)

DEPRESSION

Before the blight.

(See *business, decline.*)

DESCRIPTION

His general tout ensemble; a slight, bespectacled gentleman; a fly-looking man; looked like somebody invented by Ring Lardner; a little bald-headed man with pop-eyes; he was a wisp of a man who looked as if he had been left out in the rain; he looked like a porcupine; a scurvy fellow; half man and half devil; a hatchet-faced man; a man with a moustache, a last year's derby and a little dust on his shoulders; a bean-headed bartender; he was one of those little egg-shaped men who bulge in all the wrong places; mouse-faced bachelor; he was a tall young man with considerable brilliantine; that gives the whole meat in the coconut; described her to her last toenail; a blow-by-blow description of her appearance; had the innocent mien of a cherub; a cross between a Wagnerian soprano and the rear end of a bus; woman with a cast-iron marcel; rouged, finger-waved and what-notted; warm as the breast that rose and fell under the shimmering gown; she is inclined to be a bit of a clinger; struck a Mae West pose; the thunder storm with lightning flashes known as Lupe Velez.

(See *story, talking.*)

DESERVE

He rates it.

(See *merit, worth.*)

DESIRE

Hankering; hell-bent for comic effects; passion for; can still animate the human breast; when the spirit moves him; I wanted, oh, how I wanted; this hue and cry after.

(See *want, love, wish.*)

DESIRE (Not to desire)

He had no stomach at all for discussing; fighting shy of; who had salesmanship thrust upon her; steer clear of.

(See *avoid, disdain.*)

DESK

A desk of rococo splendor.

(See *office, writer.*)

DESPERATE

Pushed to the wall; a toughish time of late.

(See *hopeless.*)

DESTINY

Destiny gave him a kick; but always the star of their destiny burned brightly.

(See *fate.*)

DETECTIVE

Goes around looking stern and solemn, talking out of the corner of his mouth, wearing his hat indoors like all detectives do; tailing; snooper; he made Sherlock Holmes look like a country constable; disguise; a set of false whiskers; he can see around corners without twisting his head; playing hide and seek with his agents; like a mail order detective; go in for some fancy snooping; like a stage detective; story book sleuth; gum shoes; their slinking steps and shifty glances; flatfoot; a dick; gum-shoe men; polishing his detective shield; detectives who, contrary to all rules, take off their hats in the house, don't smoke cigars and are plenty smarter than the amateur dick; he looked more like an old-clothes man than a plainclothes one.

(See *policeman, secret service, spy.*)

DETECTIVE STORIES

It is guaranteed to raise your blood

pressure alarmingly; the servants find their master's body in bed and his head in the ash tray; a villain who exudes cyanided from every pore.

(See *criminals.*)

DETERMINATION

And wild horses couldn't stop me; he was hell-bent on my salvation; bivouacking on his doorstep; is one of t h o s e never-say-die persons; with leech-like tenacity; all creation and fifty locomotives couldn't change his attitude.

(See *resolution, stubborn.*)

DEVIL

Fight the devil with the devil's own weapons; he believed in a devil with horns, hoof and a tail.

(See *sin, temptation.*)

DIAMOND

Sparkler; regarding diamonds, suppose you write to Tiffany, Cartier or Peggy Joyce; a walnut-sized diamond; better a diamond with a flaw than a pebble without.

(See *jewelry, ring.*)

DICE

To bet their poke on the spots of the dice; snake eyes (2); African golf; with the right dice.

(See *bet, games.*)

DICTATE

To call the tune.

(See *orders.*)

DICTATION (Steno.)

Daily bout of dictation.

(See *stenographer.*)

DIET (Reducing)

For dessert you lick a postage stamp; Lent lasts forever when you're on a diet; shedding embonpoint; melt your hips; fearing she might begin to bulge in the wrong places; to take three or four feet off his waistline and make it possible for him to buy ready-made pants; and after I had introduced a lamb chop to a piece of pineapple.

(See *eating, food, vegetarian.*)

DIFFERENCE

As well be hanged for a sheep as a lamb (prov.).
(See *distinguish.*)

DIFFERENT

That's a horse from a different stable; that's a different horse race; this apple pie is all by itself; have suggested that I try a new tune on my concertina; the American species is a good three whoops and a holler removed from the European variety; sing another tune; what is hash for some people is steak to others; that's a different pair of shoes; as different as a pea is from a cabbage; the shoe was on the wrong foot.

(See *change, comparison.*)

DIFFICULT

The job takes a bit of doing; all was not beer and skittles; as difficult as doing a ballet dance in a telephone-booth; it was easier for a camel to go through the eye of a needle; as difficult as rolling off a log; as easy as getting a shirt out of a tree in a cyclone; the ups and downs; is no bed of roses; it is very much like eating spaghetti for the first time; this'll be a bit of a teaser; it isn't all beer and duck pins; that would ensnarl the brain of an Einstein; as difficult as to nail a custard pie to the wall; a very tough cross for him to bear; is a dashed difficult thing to be; you know what a chore it is.

(See *impossible, useless.*)

DIGNITY

Dipped deep into his reservoir of dignity; Arctic dignity; aldermanic dignity.
(See *cold, glory, famous.*)

DIMPLE

Turn it inside out and it's a pimple.
(See *smile, face.*)

DINNER

We are having dinner en famille.
(See *meal, food, eating.*)

DIRTY

A pig used to dirt turns his nose up at rice boiled in milk (Jap. prov.); on his boiled shirt he has left enough thumb prints on the bosom to keep Scotland Yard busy for two weeks; the flotsam and jetsam.

(See *bath, clean.*)

DISADVANTAGE

The proverbial Ethiopian in the woodpile.
(See *drawback.*)

DISAGREE

Like a dose of castor oil, for instance; they were as far apart as the poles; at sixes and sevens; I find myself something considerably more than a mere nonconformist; you and I are simply not talking the same language.

(See *arguing, different.*)

DISAPPEARED

Dried up; pushed right off the map; fade into the limbo; their manager had melted like a cloud; vanish into thin air; it had scooted toward all points of the compass; do the vanishing act; until they melt away like the Cheshire cat; he disappears as quickly and completely as a magician's trick egg; but his anger soon vanished like a morning mist; disappears like water down a rathole.

(See *away, lost.*)

DISAPPOINTMENT

Gnashing their teeth in disappointment; took it on the chin; he got it where the chicken got the axe; falling from the empyrean; her life is more ashes than attar; disappointment like the little boy who crawled under a tent to see a circus and discovered it was a revival meeting.

(See *hopeless, unlucky, disillusion.*)

DISCHARGE

Sack; give the gate; give him the heave-o; can; gets the axe; summary dismissal; he is planning to sell us down the river; I am going to ship you back home as soon as I can get a good excursion rate; she would be on the streets in no time; he's due for the skids; getting the knife.

(See *fire, rid of.*)

DISCIPLINE

A little hair-brush discipline.

(See *punish.*)

DISCONTINUE

Drop me like a hot potato; cast off like an old shoe; he quit cold; a bust-up; and down came the madhouse.

(See *stop, end.*)

DISCOURAGE

Put the damper on.

(See *don't.*)

DISCOVERED

So that's your little game; word has just filtered into the; the jig was up; I have you dead to rights; the cat came out of the bag.

(See *find, learn.*)

DISCUSS

To thrash it out.

(See *talking.*)

DISCUSSION (Subjects for)

Influence of medieval folk-dancing on modern therapeutics; fiscal situation of Siam; tomato culture; influence of early Renaissance architecture on the National League prospects; the correct method of frying a sausage.

(See *conversation.*)

DISDAIN

Snap your fingers in disdain.

(See *contempt, disregard.*)

DISEASES (Names of)

Beriberi; sciatica; alopecia; dandruff; rigor mortis; a bad attack of the bends; flat feet; fits; see spots before his eyes; housemaid's knee; palsy; spotted mumps; heebie-jeebies; chilblains; tennis-elbow; chicken pox; galloping schizophrenia; acidosis; hardening of the arteries; the blind staggers; cirrhosis of the liver; stamp collector's tongue; adenoids; allergy; glanders; spavin; rinderpest; turmeric fever; hammer toe; housemaid's knuckles; phagocytosis; leukocytes; ingrowing toenails.

(See *sick.*)

DISGUST

Fill me with revulsion—which is a pretty unpleasant thing to be filled with at my age; I'm just about crammed to the gizzard with all this; I'm sick of the whole dashed business; by now the crowd was pretty well fed up on the Constitution; and I, for one, felt in need of a glass of beer.

(See *nauseated, anger.*)

DISHES

The maid handled china like Japan.

(See *meal, food, eating.*)

DISHONESTY

Fenagling; he was a fraud; didn't come clean; it stinks to high heaven; chiseling; skullduggery; this here to-day and gone tomorrow business; double-crossing him; unprincipled scoundrel; his honesty was not his strongest point; crooked; I may be a little bent, but not crooked; crooked as a dog's hind leg; to cover up various financial peccadilloes.

(See *lie, deceive.*)

DISH-WASHING

Pot-walloper; the best way to wash dishes is to have somebody else do it; he manicured the dishes cheerfully.

(See *cleaning.*)

DISILLUSION

Time has a way of shooting holes through your pet illusions; she awaits him in her fool's paradise; pricked the bright balloons of his hopes.

(See *deceive, disappointment.*)

DISPOSITION

A consistently even-tempered man, he stays mad all the time.

(See *character, temperament.*)

DISREGARD

Riding roughshod over prejudice; he paid no more attention to me than if I were a piece of good advice.

(See *care, contempt, disdain.*)

DISSATISFACTION

Diehard; malcontent; bitten with dis-content.

(See *unhappy.*)

DISSIPATE

Let off steam; to play the hot spots; they have night work; a Bachanalian orgy.

(See *man-about-town.*)

DISTANCE

To be there by proxy; from the rock-bound coast of Maine to the sun-kiss-ed shores of the Pacific; anywhere from an igloo at the North Pole to the deck of a Venezuelan haddock-boat; shrieks could be heard for at least three miles as the crow flies.

(See *far.*)

DISTINGUISH

Distinguish between fried haddock and a secondhand opera hat.

(See *difference, separate.*)

DISTRICT

Bailiwick; in the smug and cultivated purlieus of Hollywood.

(See *neighborhood.*)

DISTURBER

Monkey wrench.

(See *spoil, damage, trouble-maker.*)

DIVAN

Leading me to an overstuffed Grand Rapids.

(See *couch, sit.*)

DIVORCE

Come on and eat something, you can't get divorced on an empty stomach; I am withdrawing from marriage; the "Reno route"; domestic smashup; a marriage which crashed on the di-vorce rocks; hitting the marital shoals; the knot would be severed via the di-vorce courts; and seems to be satisfied with one divorce; hit the well-trodden trail to Reno; a marriage headed for the last round-up.

(See *marriage, trouble.*)

DIZZY

I am too groggy; as I reeled toward the elevator.

(See *nauseated, careless.*)

DO

Bringing the message to Garcia; dabble in; doing their stuff; I'll bat it right out for you; had some irons in the fire; I did it for King and Country; he dashes them off; would do the trick; and hers not to reason why; carry on; I go through all the rigmarole; to hold the torch for; he did things up brown; was engineered by; I'm going to town on this idea; everyone must kill his own bull (Spanish); she liked to take the bit between the teeth; all meat's to be eaten, all maids to be wed; every herring must hang by his own tail (prov.).

(See *achievement, work.*)

DO (Not to)

I wouldn't do it for all the tea in China.

(See *refuse, no.*)

DOCTOR (Name of)

His name was Dr. Streptococci; Doctor Sawbones; medico; high priests of health; chirugeon; herb-expert.

DOCTOR

He then took my temperature and fifteen dollars; specialist; any time he ventured below the thorax he was out of bounds and liable to be penalized; he is with us when we come into the world and with us when we go out of it, oftentimes lending a helping hand on both occasions; he had two ailments that endeared him to doctors, he was incurable and he paid cash; he is a doctor of medicine in those hours when he can tear himself away from golf; who did some plain and fancy carving on his lithe chassis; the medical fraternity; a good surgeon must have an eagle's eye, a lion's heart and a lady's hand; he had his finger on my pulse or in my pocket all the time; herb-expert whose products have been known and feared for 30 years.

(See *osteopath, hospital, operation.*)

DOG

Do not tie a tin can to the tail of a mad dog on Friday the 13th; escorting her dog on a tour of the lampposts in Gramercy Park; took a nip at; the poodle never made any faux pas on the rugs; burst into barker; a one-man daschund; always run after a dog and he will never bite you; the puppy wagged ecstatically everything behind its ears; a yellow dog in an advanced stage of mange; a living dog is better than a dead lion (prov.); a dog will not cry if you beat him with a bone; a dog in the kitchen desires no company; a dog never laughs at a man chasing his hat in a high wind; exchange sniffs; every dog is a lion at home (prov.); family kioodles; a cross between a muff and a chrysanthemum (Pekinese).

(See *cats.*)

DOG (Highclass kennels)

Tossing a dead horse into the kennels once a week: the modern kennel is equipped with diet kitchens, ultra violet lamps, hot and cold showers and sanitary drinking fountains.

(See *veterinary.*)

DON'T

Lay-off; verboten; don't light a match over a gasoline tank even if it is a safety match.

(See *discourage, void.*)

DOOR

He poured himself through the doorway; the door popped open.

(See *entrance.*)

DOORMAN

The doormen who were once Russian generals; beside a pillar loitered a concierge in the full-dress uniforms and gold-laced kepi of a Prussian field marshal; a fellow in much uniform; the gold-braid boys; with a drum major's high fur hat.

(See *janitor.*)

DOUBT

"Of that there could be no manner of doubt, no possible, probable shadow of doubt, no possible doubt whatever. In other words, there couldn't be any doubt"; to pooh-pooh; "Sensible, my eye"; non-plussed; there were doubts in their breasts; oh,yeah?; charged with ifs, ands and buts; he sniffed the possibility of; tut, tut.

(See *suspicious, suspense, skepticism, problem.*)

DOWAGER

She sailed into the room.

(See *widow, old woman, society.*)

DOWNFALL

As Anthony had his Cleopatra.
(See *defeat.*)

DOWNWARD

Growing downward like the cow's tail.
(See *decline.*)

DRAWBACK

Fly in the ointment; pig in a poke; a fly in the amber; fly in the molasses; there is an insect in the ointment.

(See *disadvantage.*)

DREAMER (Day time)

Pipe dream; blowing bubbles, pretty bubbles in the air; whose feet are in the subway, while his head is sniffing in the clouds; soar into the stratosphere; he plays big; he is a painter of ideas, whose canvas is the illimitable heavens.

(See *daydreams.*)

DREAMS

Weaving pleasant dreams; a sweet dream of peace.

(See *sleep, imagination.*)

DRESS (Cheap)

My black frock with the green polka dots; her dress had an air about it that showed she wore it while she cooked pancakes and fried the doughnuts; Mrs. Jones in blue bombazine, and Mrs. Murphy in what looked like a brown nightgown; she wore a two-buck dress that must have been made in a nut hatch.

(See *clothes.*)

DRESS (Highclass)

Her frock was what flowery ink-slingers would term a "sartorial poem"; that's a swell piece of broccoli she's wearing.

(See *fashions.*)

DRINK

He swilled huge quantities of orange juice; he wrapped himself around a cooling drink.

(See *water, drought.*)

DRINKERS (Heavy)

Hefty drinkers; drink the river front dry; he can inhale more brandy bouquets; it seemed he could drink a whole ocean; whiskey-guzzling louts; he was anything but a teetotaler; toss off a dozen hefty glasses of rye; he uses a funnel; boozers; gin-hoister.

(See *intoxicated, drunk.*)

DRINKING (Names for)

Have a shot with me; a nightcap; a snifter; a couple of ponies of brandy; have a snort with me.

(See *cocktail, whiskey.*)

DRINKING (To)

Sit down over a few seidels; guzzling; crack a bottle of the best; take a nip now and then; step in at various places and chew a clove or two; drown

his sorrows in the flowing bowl; they quaffed; went down his esophagus; sitting around and hoisting friendly steins; "fortify" themselves against assignments; his long drooping moustache curled lovingly over a stein; we drank up the rest of the dinner; a quart of beer under his belt; the. liquor brings you back alive; let us lubricate ourselves; he poured himself a mighty hooker; downed another slug of; he grabs a couple of bottles, bites the heads off, and hands one to me, "Suck away on that"; it's the most delicious concoction you ever wrapped your tongue around; drink a bottle of lunch; treated me to a firkin of old ale; imbibed; imbibed not wisely but too well; some tall drinking; began to get consolation out of the neck of a bottle; bathed his tonsils in a generous libation of thirty-year old bourbon; he was doing some serious drinking; these simply tear me to pieces; Old John Barleycorn; he was always on hand with a highball when Bill's nose needed a treatment; to drink yourself into an alcoholic stupor; absorbing strong drinks by the bucketful; take nips out of his flask.
(See *beer, liquor*.)

DRINKING (Morning after)

A taste in my mouth like a bird-and-animal store; the higher I get in the evening, the lower I feel in the morning; a dark brown taste in the mouth; your head is so large that you can't possibly get it out through your bedroom door; with a knot in his head as big as a pineapple; Jeeves, another ice pack, and some more of that bromo seltzer; a hangover; my head was going "Whango! Whango! Whango!"; we all finish up in the ice house; has the morning jitters from sloe gin; he had fuzzy-tongue.
(See *headache, morning*.)

DRINKING PARTIES

They were having an uncorking good time; he was sitting about four tables and six drinks ahead of us; the swishing of the soda water and the whoosh of opened gingerale bottles; jested over their cups; when there aren't enough glasses to go round, drink out of soap dishes, flower vases, etc.; throw out the lifeline; his growing fondness for the life jocund.
(See *party*.)

DROUGHT

It was so dry he tried to spit after sunup and pretty near choked to death on his own tongue; it was so dry that folks had to prime their mules to get 'em to sweat; the dust-encrusted inhabitants of — where it's so dry that one's morning tub consists of a rub-down with sandpaper; it was so dry the people couldn't lick their stamps, they just pinned them on.
(See *weather*.)

DROWNING

She precipitated the professor, head over teakettle, as the girls say, into the brook; there appeared to be quite a lot of ocean intervening between his exploring feet and solid sand; so without a moment's hesitation, never even removing his wrist watch, he rushed into the sea; like throwing a toothpick to a drowning man.
(See *swimming*.)

DRUG-ADDICT

The hop-head with his doe-startled glance.
(See *nervousness*.)

DRUGGIST

A pillroller.
(See *medicine*.)

DRUM

Tom-tom.
(See *music, noise*.)

DRUNK

Three sheets in the wind; become fluent drunkards; had a jag on; potted; puts you under the table; he went native; zigzagged; he hiccoughed; well lathered; on a big bender; stewed; too convivial; a swell binge; then I drink until I fall down in a stupor and hit my head on the radiator; a quartette of three-sheeted play boys; get jagged; soused; they get blotto; when he had his pots on; tipsy; pretty well oiled; gutter drunkard; a rum-soaked blighter; plastered; in his cups; on a continual drinking merry-go-round; toss a few drinks into him and he begins to spill; he loved the bottle; gin-crazed; the pie-eyed piper; even in their most plastered moments; he had imbibed very copiously; he got wide open; stiff as a ramrod; he was in his cups; getting lit up; hopped to the eyelids; cockeyed; drunk as a coot; from slight inebriation to alcoholic petrification; sloshed to the ears; soused to the gills; everyone getting simply stinko; on a tipple; put you under the table; gentlemen in their cups; some pickled gent; spiffed; besottedness; pie-eyed; to get beautifully lit; as drunk as a lord; rye-soaked males; let's get high together.

(See *whiskey, beer.*)

DRUNKARD

Stupid sot; whisky-addled sot; when did he start sucking the bottle.

(See *intoxicated.*)

DRUNK'S ACTIONS

Eating lobster salad out of his high hat; lying on the hall mat imitating Cerberus (so he announced from the floor) guarding the gates of hell; was at the point where he started taking off his shoes; and whenever he gets tight he burns down the cottage; teetered uncertainly; could play any musical instrument after three drinks of beer; wake me early, mother, for I'm to be Queen of the May; a quavering song, richly alcoholic, was wafted to them; he hiccuped after me; singing "The Bottle Hymn of the Republic."

(See *dizzy.*)

DULL

Like warming up cold porridge; it didn't exactly thrill me to pieces; the doldrums; possessed of the *joie de vie* and sparkle of a weary dish of oatmeal; a putrid time.

(See *stupid, bore.*)

DUMB

Too bad you're not beautiful, then you'd be beautiful and dumb; empty vessels make the most noise; stripling dunces of the purest ray; he has a thick skull; he is singularly obtuse; crack-brained; broken sacks will hold no corn (prov.); ignoramus; boob; in the land of the blind the one-eyed is king; he thinks kittens come from pussy-willows; he thinks corn syrup is good for corns; mule-headed; he generally leads a singleton after bidding six spades vulnerable; he is seven kinds of an imbecile.

(See *illiterate, fool.*)

DUMB (Thing)

It's like winking at a girl in the dark; he will burn his house to warm his hands.

(See *stupid.*)

DUN AND BRADSTREET

Bradstreet and Doom.

(See *credit, business.*)

DYNAMITE

An entangling alliance with a stick of dynamite.

(See *end.*)

E

EARNINGS

Making money by the bucketful; rake in the thousands.
(See *salary, profits.*)

EARRINGS

Earrings like chandeliers; two things resembling incipient chandeliers hanging from her alabaster ears.
(See *jewelry.*)

EARS

The set of his ears; double-breasted ears; his ears hung hopefully onto the side of his head; broccoli ears; ears that looked like a drum-major's plume; jug-handled ears; bats-wing ears; his flappers; ears like the delicate petals of some lovely flower unfolding to the caress of the zephyrs; whose ears were so large and outstanding that he seemed almost incidental to them; he has that Clark Gable look in his ears; ears like ventilators; ears of the jug-handled pattern; satchel-eared.
(See *listen, body.*)

EARTH

In the bowels of the earth; God's green earth.
(See *world, ground.*)

EARTHQUAKE

Seismic disturbances.
(See *shaking.*)

EASTER

He ate so many eggs he won't be able to ever look a hen in the face.
(See *Christmas.*)

EASY

A pushover; it was all beer and skit- tles; soft snap; a picnic; a sinecure; a bed of roses; a pipe; pip; to be insultingly simple; to be pie for him; with the utmost impunity; with his hands tied behind him; a set-up; clear sledding; open and shut; you can see that with one eye peeled; it didn't lay any of them low with brain-fag; handed it to them on a skewer; it's a cinch; they are his mutton; he's an ill cook that cannot lick his own fingers; it doesn't take an auditor to prove; as easy as falling off a cliff; he could do it without working up a sweat; a lead-pipe cinch; a thin meadow is soon mowed (prov.).
(See *simple, possible.*)

EASY (Similes)

As easy as getting a shirt out of a tree in a cyclone; as easy as milking; as easy as convincing a child there's a Santa Claus; as easy as it is for a politician to make a speech on the Fourth of July; easy as an old shoe; as easy as going down the river; as easy as lying.
(See *natural.*)

EATING

Nuzzling his bouillon; to take coffee together; load her festive holiday boards; lapping up; start your jaws going; stuffed himself with; let's put on the feed-bag; nibble at a joint; she sat over a saddle of lamb; let's rip a herring in half; gulp; sat around the festive board; munched on a caviar sandwich; snatching a bit of salad; toying with the dessert; partaking of their Bismarck herring; gastronomy; break bread with me; let's talk it over over a few hot groceries; gobble up; we debauched; they sat them down to

dine; stuff themselves sick; wrecking a large and well-filled sandwich; tucking away a; a rush of hamburgers to the abdomen; he snatched a hot dog on the run; toying with coffee; mopping up hot cakes; up to the eyebrows in griddle cakes and maple syrup; take your oats with me; mangle a pastrami sandwich; grab a bite; filled him to the brim with costly groceries; he wolfed those beans up; he eats like a couple of horses; to be ankle-deep in gherkins and sausages; a bellyful's a bellyful, whether it's meat or drink (prov.); hurl it down the gullet; he laid into the buckwheat cakes; so we snag a head of cabbage; he stuffed himself; performed valorously with knife and fork; was deep in his breakfast; pecked away at a lettuce salad; he makes camel noises when eating wheat cakes.
(See *food, meal.*)

EATING (Big eater)
Stow away double orders; five square meals a day; had done himself well in that restaurant; orgy; heavy fodder; to gather his forces together for an assault upon the groaning board; the orgies of food which he inflicted on his digestive apparatus; his appetite was the joy of all the restaurants; he swilled huge quantities of cider; to eat toe to toe with the best of them; gorged himself; gourmet; glutton; the Jones ice chest is in for another beating from Joe; he ate like a horse; ingrowing gluttony; he loves bacon well that licks the swine-sty door; he loves mutton well that eats the wool; gastronomical orgies; ate it until it came out through the eyes; outeat everybody in Ohio; he eats bananas with their skins on; eat themselves into an early grave; his culinary prowess.
(See *fat.*)

EATING (Girls)
Dames thank you for bringing them flowers, but they love you when you feed them steaks; did you ever see her eat when nobody was looking?
(See *date.*)

ECONOMY
False economy; saving at the spigot and wasting at the bunghole.
(See *saving, miser, thrift.*)

EDITOR
Loud editorial snort; it was spoken of in editorial sanctums; leather-chaired editing; who graced the editorial swivel; omniscient editor.
(See *writer, publishing.*)

EDITORIALS
To take some of the sting out of the tail in our editorials; pen drippings; he cuts slashes and rips, snorts and paws the air and slings mud; launches anathemas against all institutions.
(See *writing, newspaper.*)

EDUCATION
Read fifteen minutes a day; soak his system full of a college education in seven easy lessons; he had been briefly exposed to education at; exposure to knowledge; he's so highly educated that he can spell words of four syllables, do compound division in his head; his early education gained in the Little Red Schoolhouse; a university had dipped him very casually into education; I want you to be able to go anywhere and spell the hardest word; he knew how to get the square root of a barrel of pork; to extend the frontiers of knowledge; he could read Walter Winchell in the original; he's so educated he talks Latin in his sleep; he learned his three R's.
(See *college, knowledge.*)

EFFECT
With all flags set and the band playing.
(See *showoff, fancy.*)

EFFECTIVE
Competition with teeth in it; it was grist to his mill.
(See *energy, active.*)

EFFEMINATE
Who's the pretty boy?; he looks like a cousin of the Prince of Wales; a flaxen moustache, and a handkerchief was concealed in his cuff; sissy; he smokes cigarettes in a holder nearly a foot long; he wears a watch on one wrist and a slave bracelet on the other; he was kicked by a butterfly when a child; a namby-pamby; embroidered suspenders; "Oh, deary me"; who wore puce-underwear; pluck a petal off that pansy; "Whoops, dearie;" wears a corset and long silk stockings.
(See *feminine.*)

EFFICIENCY
Such hideous efficiency.
(See *ability, energy.*)

EGGS
These eggs were in their second childhood; they were like Chinese antiques; can be used for omelettes, thrown at bum actors, or can be hatched.
(See *food.*)

EGO
Hoisted by his own petard; he hugged himself with delight; thinking himself one of nature's rare gifts; he shook hands with himself; egomaniac; his enameled ego began to chip; such magnificent self-esteem; delusion of grandeur; amour-propre (self esteem); he that is full of himself is empty (prov.).
(See *vanity, selfish.*)

ELEMENTARY
A sophomoric version.
(See *begin, easy, simple.*)

ELEPHANT
Pachyderm; if the front part is the trunk, his tail must be a valise; an elephant came trapezing along; sure an elephant never forgets, what has he to remember?; bring those elephants and tell them to bring their trunks along.
(See *camel, heavy, large.*)

ELOCUTION
Clamp your glottis firmly against the tonsils; take care of your consonants and your vowels will take care of themselves.
(See *speech, talking.*)

EMBARRASSED
A sort of contretemps; his adam's apple slipped a cog; he sputtered like a string of fire crackers; the atmosphere dropped to zero; went all zigzag in their speech; I'd have been grateful for a typhoon instead; how the gods must laugh.
(See *awed, confused, ashamed.*)

EMBRACE
Melted into my arms; felt the warm undulations of her thigh against him, the subtle fragrance of her in his nostrils; her heart was thudding against his.
(See *kiss, love.*)

EMOTIONS
His bosom was surging with emotions; emotions have run dry; the emotion in his bosom twittered like a swarm of humming birds.
(See *love, sentimental.*)

EMPTY (Similes)
As empty as a traffic cop's head; empty as a bird's nest in December; empty as a politician's address to the people; empty as a church on a weekday;

empty as a cobbler's curse; empty as wind.
(See *useless, unsatisfactory.*)

ENCORE

He mistook the noise in the audience for applause and inflicted a second verse.
(See *applause, again.*)

END

Sounds the death-knell of; dropped me like a hot potato; surcease; the game blew up; a show-down; the book season toils out; gone where the woodbine twineth; he was all washed up; he was content to call it quits; when the final whistle blows; to a no-good end; she was beached, but she refused to be a beach-comber; unhorse the Old Guard leadership; then it all conked out; that was the straw that tickled the camel's shoulder blades; and they scrapped happily ever after; your swan song; all over but the shouting; the windup; the payoff; sank with all on board; then came the deluge; he had his Gethsemane; the business folded up; to drive the last nail in the coffin; it's curtains; it has gone aglimmering.
(See *complete, stop.*)

ENEMY

A positive genius for making enemies; we get along pretty well together, especially when one of us is not around; arch-enemy; dog eat dog; anything dreadful happening to either would be regarded with genuine calm by the other; stopped wearing each other's neckties; could never hit it off; outflank his enemy; when they met the thermometer dropped to zero.
(See *opposition, fight.*)

ENERGY

Sheer animal spirits; possessed of infinitely more bounce; git-up-and-go; I've got plenty of salve but no place to smear it.
(See *active, strength, pep.*)

ENGAGED

All signed on the dotted line; you're m o r t g a g e d property; engagement wringer.
(See *proposal, marriage.*)

ENGINEER

He is so good he can open a can of sardines, if given plenty of time.
(See *smart, experienced.*)

ENGINE TROUBLE

Engine set up a series of ominous knocks and thumps; step on the starter and say a prayer.
(See *accident.*)

ENGLAND

The shores of Albion; ultra-conservative Britishers; hidebound Britons; the far-flung British Empire; God save us all; Britannia rules the waves; perfidious Albion; to inject himself into English swelldom; Merrie England; these lime-juicers; a limey; it is not statesmanship, nor mutual affection, nor even tarred string, that holds the Empire together.
(See *British.*)

ENGLAND (Cockney)

"H"—less cockney; dropping his aitches with care.
(See *accents.*)

ENGLAND (Money)

Thruppence ha' penny.
(See *money.*)

ENGLAND (Towns)

Upper-Tooting-on-Hants.
(See *town.*)

ENGLISHMAN (Expressions)

I say, old thing; old dear; so deuced hard; frightful looking; who is this person; by Jove! quite so; silly ass; the old bean; bit of rot, eh what?; bally beggar; all that sort of thing; quite top-hole cheerio; become so muzzy; deuce take it, sir; he said, "What ho"; buzzed off; a dashed fascinating chap; rummy; cheerio; pip-pip, dear Old Boy sort of stuff; carry on; fancy; my lad; his dashed memory is quite all right; old chap; the blighter; a tram; his daily bahth; ra-ther; jitters, old bean; I'll be down in a jiff; toodle-oo and pip-pip; bally well.

(See *language.*)

ENGLISHMEN

He followed her everywhere, bleating; a drawing-room Englishman; in his Picadilly accent.

(See *conservative.*)

ENJOYMENT

High-jinks; to read back numbers of the National Geographic; I have wallowed in his plays; hope your ribs will be tickled by it; tickled his risibilities.

(See *happy, contented.*)

ENOUGH

Say uncle.
(See *satisfactory.*)

ENTERTAINED (To be)

To be wined and dined.
(See *date.*)

ENTERTAINMENT

He can oscillate his ears; seeking surcease from their crushing labors.
(See *shows, happy, party.*)

ENTHUSIASM

Gusto; he carried on with a bright zip; zest; rhapsodizing over the view; the way he bubbles; the fires of his enthusiasm; we can't let our enthusiasms bounce us around; sprightly zest; then he goes into a nose dive about her ears; his sophomoric enthusiasm; pump up enthusiasm; ardent as the lips of love; to be in a lather; the boiling point.

(See *passion, impatience.*)

ENTRANCE

To pass within the magic portal.
(See *door.*)

ENVY

He got green around the gills with envy.
(See *jealousy.*)

EPITHETS

Hurl vituperative epithets.
(See *swearing, names.*)

ERRATIC

He gets up steam in the engine, but he can't stop at the platform.
(See *excited, out of place.*)

ESCAPE

Gave them the slip.
(See *run away.*)

ESKIMO

You look so tired, why not lie down for a few months.
(See *stronger.*)

ETC.

And all points West; or what you will; and so on at five dollars a paragraph for a chapter or two; and heaven knows what-all; et cetera; and no end of; and all that sort of thing; and where not; and what not; et al; or what have you; wigs, noses, paint and the usual impedimenta of an actor; etc. ad nauseum; animal, vegetable or mineral.

(See *all, complete.*)

ETIQUETTE

His right ankle was black and blue from June kicking it under the table: she was so excited she used all the wrong forks; he evidently believed that fingers were made before forks; they don't know which fork goes with salad and which with pie; that'd give Emily Post a headache for a week; commit social solecisms; he must have been brought up by a stable boy; his panama hat almost leaped into his hand; sticklers for etiquette; as courteous as a dog in a kitchen.

(See *courteous.*)

EVANGELISTS

A prophet not without honorarium in his own country; his audiences came and listened and went away to sin some more; made plenty of thumping the Book and wrestling Satan; screamed for gore; promised his disciples heaven and harps; by rolling with groans of contrition in the sawdust; his pious billingsgate; scream his recipe for salvation; many would come forward and wrestle triumphantly with Satan in the sawdust; the old pulpit pounder.

(See *religious, minister.*)

EVASIVE

As evasive as a borrowed umbrella.

(See *deceive, fool someone.*)

EVERYONE

One and all; the whole kit; the butcher, the baker and the candlestick maker; boys and girls; all and sundry; as everyone over the age of eleven is aware; by everybody from the Vicar's great-aunt down; all the world and his wife; everyone, from man to mollusk.

(See *all, people, crowds.*)

EVERYTHING

The works; shebang; reject the whole caboose; that gives the whole meat in the coconut; runs the gamut from; the whole dashed business; everything under the sun.

(See *complete.*)

EVERYWHERE

Wherever the eye may rove; right and left; exists up and down this country; a battery of waffle irons that stretched from here to yonder; in every far-flung outpost of civilization; hither and yon; all over the lot; toward all points of the compass; we must carry our message into the highways and byways.

(See *all over.*)

EXACT

Exact to a tittle, to an inch, to a nicety, to a hair; that hits the nail smack on the conk; bring it down to cases.

(See *strict, correct.*)

EXACTLY

He filled the bill to a "T"; hit it on the nose.

(See *right.*)

EXAGGERATED

A pretty well varnished account.

(See *brag, overdue.*)

EXCHANGE

I would gladly have exchanged him for a good second baseman and a brace of suspenders.

(See *change, trade.*)

EXCITED

In a dither; all agog; to go berserk; keep your shirt tails properly tucked in; wrought up to a high twitter; hopping about; all a-twitter; the house was just a frothing maelstrom: all het up; are even more smoked up with the thought; all steamed up; excitement ran high; all heated up; played tag with her blood pressure; a flutter of excitement; be still, my heart; I'm all jellied with excitement; great to-do; keep your shirt on; his glands were misfiring; his reflexes were popping; hang on to your suspenders.

(See *enthusiasm*.)

EXCLUSIVE

Had it sewed up exclusively; of which he was the sole proprietor; he was so exclusive he talked only to himself.

(See *lonesome, alone, snob*.)

EXCUSE

A dodge; a thousand pardons; alibi; stalling him that; hemmed and hawed; his raison d'etre; without a by-your-leave; a pre-fabricated excuse; the old song and dance; if a woman with red hair wants to see me, I went to Italy to visit Mussolini; long-winded stories; what's my out.

(See *evasive, apology, pretend*.)

EXECUTION

And the next morning his head was thumping about in the wastepaper basket; the chief executioners ran him through the royal sausage grinder.

(See *kill, hanging*.)

EXECUTIVE

Sit at a roll top desk, eating cigars, pushing buttons; Jones gave the commands; Smith executed it the next year.

(See *big-shot, boss*.)

EXERCISE

Hang by their eye teeth on a hook in the closet while they count fifty; the only real exercise he ever got was lifting an occasional glass of beer.

(See *work, playing, muscles*.)

EXIST

Worry along.

(See *living*.)

EXPAND

Expanded or contracted at will like an opera hat.

(See *opening, increase, spread*.)

EXPECT

So wait for things to float in over the doorsill.

(See *wait, anticipate*.)

EXPENSES

Her board and keep.

(See *cost*.)

EXPENSIVE

It must cost a packet to keep up; pay too much for your whistle; it was a holdup; $8.75 for defense, but not a cent for silk pajamas; fancy prices; it cost like sixty.

(See *prices, pay*.)

EXPERIENCED

A perfect wizard at; knew the ins and outs, the ups and downs; he became a whiz; he'd been through the mill; he is quite a hand at; sweet are the uses of adversity; a fox is not taken twice in the same snare (prov.); their first bumps on that well-known Road of Hard Knocks; an old ox makes a straight furrow; experience, purchased at the highest market price; experience keeps a dear school, but fools will learn in no other (prov.).

(See *authority, smart*.)

EXPLAIN

Give us the low-down; let me go into my dance; and thereby hangs a tale; to expound the intricacies of; for the benefit of my Chinese readers I will explain; that gives the whole meat in the coconut; in other words, it's that which nothing else is whicher, if you get what I mean.

(See *reason, why.*)

EXTEMPORANEOUS

Ad lib.

(See *unprepared.*)

EXTINCT

As extinct as the dodo bird.

(See *dead.*)

EXTRA

To boot.

(See *etc.*)

EXTRAVAGANT

He treats money as though it were rice and he was at a wedding; you'll drive me to the poorhouse; with a month's pay burning holes in his pocket.

(See *spendthrift, lots of.*)

EYEBROWS

Dense thickets of eyebrows; was so bushy you could walk barefoot through it; his eyebrows interfered with his knee action.

(See *hair.*)

EYEBROWS (Female)

Their eyebrows pruned until they resemble small pieces of string; her string-like eyebrows.

EYE GLASSES

On his nose was perched a pair of nose glasses; big horn cheaters; gold-rimmed cheaters; bifocals.

(See *see.*)

EYELASHES (Women)

Are those lashes honest-to-God, or are they spares; lace-lidded sirens.

(See *hair.*)

EYES (Adjectives)

Her cold, blancmange eyes; googly; twinkling little black shoebutton eyes; pansy-soft; I'm-comin'-right-over-there-and-get-you eyes; come-hither eyes; owl-eyed; her lovely gentian eyes; star-struck eyes.

(See *face, beautiful.*)

EYES (Names for)

Optic; bum glims; orbs; peepers; lamps.

EYES (Black)

Looks like the autograph of an army mule; his eyes were in mourning; a shiner; and put a blue forget-me-not under his eye; who hung that shanty on your eye?; your eyes, they shine like the pants of a blue serge suit.

(See *hit, black.*)

EYES (Description)

Eyes like those of a dead codfish; dull eyes, rather like a llama; eyes like craters on the moon; her eyes are about the same color and temperature as the Gulf of Mexico; a cod-like bulginess to the eyes; black eyes, like a heifer calf; her eyes like twin stars sinking into an azure sea; eyes like two teaspoonfuls of the Mediterranean; little green pig-eyes.

EYES (Glass)

Sported a crockery glim; it kept staring two points over the port bow.

(See *blind.*)

EYES (Good eyesight)
He could see a needle in a haystack;
his eyesight is so good he can distinguish mild from bitter without the
aid of binoculars.

(See *see, look.*)

EYES (Poor eyesight)
He wore two pairs of spectacles and
used a magnifying glass besides; a
myopic dowager; he's so near-sighted
he couldn't find a bass drum in a telephone booth; without his spectacles
he couldn't tell a comma from a cockroach.

(See *eyeglasses.*)

EYES (Sore)
My eyes looked like the day after a
fire at a jam factory; his eyes resembled holly wreaths.

(See *cry.*)

EYES (Misc.)
The eyes are the windows of the soul.

F

FACE
Mug; pan; map; puss; beezer; smush; kisser; esophagus; phiz; facade; dial.
(See *eyes, nose, mouth.*)

FACE (Beautiful)
Her petal-like face.
(See *beautiful.*)

FACE (Blank)
A poker face; dead pan face; a vacuous expression; his face gave no evidence of what was frying in his mind.
(See *stupid.*)

FACE (Cold)
One of those cold, inscrutable faces you read about in books.
(See *cold.*)

FACE (Description)
It was more of a landscape than a face; placid expression of a well-fed cow.
(See *dimple, frown.*)

FACTORY
Treadmill.
(See *machinery.*)

FAILURE
Wallflowers in the dance of life; what a washout you turned out to be; he was just another firecracker that didn't go off; musically he is a total loss; to play second fiddle; a has-been; stay-at-home; a bust; wallowing in the slough of despond; how the gods must laugh; as Anthony had his Cleopatra; a dismal flop; was something less than a wow; went phooey; venture blew a fuse; he was a fluke as a policeman; a fiasco; how hath the mighty fallen;
to wind up behind the eight ball; a washout; went on the rocks; fizzle; gone to the bow-wows; a flop; the show demised; my vacation went flooey; his business went phut; went up in smoke; but he didn't get to first base; handed him an Easter egg that time; a dud.
(See *decline, mistake.*)

FAIR
All's fair that comes to the net.
(See *allright, O.K.*)

FAKE
Hokum; bogus; phoney; hornswoggles his way to Washington; a crass fake.
(See *deceive, lie.*)

FALL
Fell off the cliff and turned to jelly on the rocks below; did a Brodie; he went down ker-wallop; and suddenly find yourself impersonating the Face on the Barroom Floor; slipped from his grasp like an oiled eel; and cause her to bite the dust.
(See *decline, downward.*)

FALSE TEETH
Store nippers.
(See *teeth.*)

FAMILY
Family-ish; his tribe; lolling in the bosom of your family; God-fearing family.
(See *relatives.*)

FAMILY (Reunions)
Pulling chairs from under maiden aunts at family reunions.
(See *meeting.*)

FAMILY (Secrets)
The family skeleton.
(See *secret.*)

FAMOUS
In the money; a blue chip; he got an offer to pose for a hay fever cure; his name was sprinkled all over the page Ones and; he had become a myth; famed in song and story for; a theory which will go clattering down the halls of time; the males that matter; top flight men; watch for my name in lights, kid, I'm going places; limelight-minded; there is no Horatio Alger fairy tale angle to the rise of—.
(See *glory, reputation.*)

FANCY
Doodads; with a lot of gingerbread on it; "Go to town"; parlor brand of insincerity.
(See *overdo, complicated.*)

FAR
I'll go so far it will take a ten dollar postage stamp to reach me; so far that it takes three months for a letter to reach him if nobody shoots the mailman; away to hell-and-gone out there among; a good biscuit's toss from.
(See *distance, away.*)

FARM
His farm was about as large as a door mat; his rutabaga conservatory; the cowery (barn).
(See *country.*)

FARM (City man on a)
He couldn't tell a ploughshare from a Buff Alderney; I'd sooner eat mutton than watch it grow; if you've seen one tree you've seen 'em all; becoming familiar with the flora and fauna of rural life in America.
(See *hired man.*)

FARMER
Selling them lightning rods; tiller of the soil; nursemaid to the land; to milk and haul slop for the pigs; sturdy agriculturists.
(See *crops, garden, hick.*)

FASHIONS (Women)
Schiaparelli; Paton and Hattie Carnegie; coats are practically de rigueur; all the go; depending upon the current decrees from the Rue de la Paix; in the ateliers of the Continental fashion centers.
(See *clothes.*)

FAST
Alongside of it a woman with St. Vitus would be a comparatively fixed and stationary object; like all get out; he went through them (pages) as if he were a streamlined train; in a wink; like a shot; like a bat out of what-is-this; it's his way of beating to the punch; in the twinkling of an optic; to keep one jump ahead of; I shan't be two ticks; drive like billy heck; she'll go like steam-o; in a jiffy; the sixteenth part of a second; posthaste; pronto; hair-trigger speed; in the batting of an eyelid; he burned the wind to his office; like a flash; faster than a fireman can slide down the pole when the alarm goes off; with the speed of a greased eel; like a house afire; a hasty man never wanteth woe; bald heads are soon shaven; in practically no time at all; before you can say Metro-Goldwyn-Mayer.
(See *quickly, speed.*)

FAT
Boasted considerable girth; wee bit of embonpoint; his figure became a perfect scandal; looked like a blowfish before the seams give way; pudding-bellied; a few years of that diet would reduce his perimeter; the roly-poly

Mr.——; has taken on a bit of excess poundage; he carries his pudgy little form with a waddle; as fat as a beer-barrel; too fat to fit between the handles of a wheelbarrow; a door had to be open pretty wide for him to go through; circular physique; a man with a pouched stomach; a man with a front porch; look at my front bumper; he weighed 220 pounds, mostly stomach.

(See *heavy, big*.)

FAT (Females)
She was built in terraces; she was so bulbous; her proportions were anything but meagre; the rotund Mrs. ——; those ladies who get their penny's worth out of a weight machine; these stout women, eight to the ton; a plumpness that was extremely cuddlesome; a lady who might well have posed as model for the Rock of Gibraltar itself; a cross between a Wagnerian soprano and the rear end of a bus; she's so fat she has to use inner tubes for garters; the large chesty lady; while not what you would call fat, she is definitely overemphasized.

(See *large*.)

FAT (Adjectives)
Paunchy, pudgy; a tubby man; globular; the over-stomached Mr. ——; amplitudinous.

FAT (Chins)
The cantilever construction of his chins; already a second edition of his chin had been published; had more than his quota of chins; well-reefed chin.

(See *chin*.)

FAT (Weight)
Weighs two hundred on the hoof; weighs 250 lbs. before dinner.

(See *weight, heavy*.)

FAT PEOPLE (Actions)
Waddled to the door.

(See *eating, big eater*.)

FATE
To succumb to the first jabs of fate; the frivolous caperings of fate; a pawn of fate; a trick that fate played; fate made a tracery in the sands, a map of destiny; a gadget of fate; a football of fate; and here comes stealthily the finger of fate fumbling; I stand on the Rubicon rattling the dice; had been dealt one final, finishing blow by the spiteful fist of fate; fate rapped him on the knuckles; fate decreed.

(See *destiny, necessary*.)

FATHER
Pater; the governor; the paterfamilias.

(See *family, mother, children*.)

FAULT
You make your bed and you must lie in it.

(See *weak, failure, wrong, mistake*.)

FAVORITE
Darling of the Gods; a pet of; is your dish; lies nearest my heart; one of my pet enthusiasms; to be the chosen people; fish to one and fowl to; the apple of his eye.

(See *like, sweetheart*.)

FAWN
To go lollygagging around you all the time; bootlicker; the way he would suck up to the old man; it was "Yes, Mr. Sullivan" and "of course, Mr. Sullivan"; he cringed into his office; it amounts to fetishism; to oil up to; salaamed and worshiped; to traipse after him; he crawled; I had him pawing at my trouser-legs; he knows what tune to dance to; he groveled abject-

ly; kowtowing; curry favor with; worm himself into his good graces; to bow obeisance to; knew in which direction to tip his plate of turtle soup; he would be glad to drink his bathwater; adhesive as a postage stamp; and wish to prostrate themselves before him.

(See *flattery.*)

FEAR

He got green around the gills; he retired into his cyclone-cellar; he was a flutterbudget; he was afraid to step on a rug without a permit; mealymouthed; send cold shivers racing up and down my spine; rubbed his rabbit's foot; got me buffaloed; finicky; he cringed into his office; he was the bogey man; petrified with fear; afraid of a mouse; put the fear of God back into; with trepidation; a bit gun shy of street crowds; he shies from; hobgoblins; turned his spine to jelly; churned his soul into a froth of dread; it made my hair curl; threw him into a very spasm of terror; swallowed his Adam's apple; gooseflesh; a sinking feeling in the pit of his stomach; he suffered a constriction of the epiglottis; his blood turned to cold jellied consomme; trembled like an aspen; fear clutched at his heart with icy hands; bring out the cold sweat; will give you the vertigo; coming out all goose-pimples; he blanched and beat his breast; cause the dew of anguish to bead his brow; sleep with one eye open; his spine turned to rubber; who see hobgoblins sitting atop every; they were scared and scurried like rabbits to cover; in fear of being eaten up by the Wall Street ogre.

(See *coward, timid, frightened.*)

FEARLESS

Not caring a snap of his fingers.

(See *courage, brave.*)

FEAST

The Lucullan feast.

(See *dinner, meal.*)

FEEL BAD

Give you a bad moment or two; he had a bad attack of the bends; you look as if you've been chewing barnacles; and when they were over I could have doubled for any brand of Swiss cheese; I get a woozy feeling in the stomach; feel as if the white corpuscles and the red corpuscles have been getting up teams and playing hockey in our veins; I'm so low I could walk under a dachshund; a seal-brown taste in my mouth.

(See *sick, sad.*)

FEEL GOOD

The words warmed his ears; warmed the cockles of his heart; running on all cylinders; that'll make the corpuscles riot madly through your veins; feeling his oats; feel chipper; I feel full of caper; warms my old bones; feel I want to yell and skip and push houses over; warmed his liver; I feel so good, I feel like kicking over a street car; with a light heart and a gay snatch of song; I feel chirpy; to be in the pink of condition; in fine fettle; as fit as a fiddle; and my hair is getting thicker on top; my health is absolutely tophole; as sound as a Stradivarius fiddle.

(See *healthy, happy.*)

FEET

We need our feet for hurrying to the office, kicking cats, evading creditors; free-wheeling feet.

(See *body.*)

FEET (Action)

Unscrambled his long legs.

(See *walk, run.*)

FEET (Bandy)

Legs that said "O" to you; he couldn't stop a pig in an alley; was it really Shakespeare who said "What ho! What manner of man is this, who carries his feet like a parenthesis."

FEET (Description)

His arches having fallen in 1861, along with Fort Sumter; his elegantly spatted feet; Leon Errol's gutta percha leg.

(See *shoes.*)

FEET (Large)

His feet would come in handy for stamping out forest fires; his feet are like gunboats; his large, flat, Bronx feet.

(See *large.*)

FEET (Names for)

Skinny stems; hoofs; his dogs; pins; his shafts; pedal extremities; pedals; his puppies; shanks.

FEET (Tired)

My feet felt as if somebody was massaging them with a red-hot poker.

(See *tired.*)

FEET (Women)

Swell pair of gams; lavish display of feet; so dear to the hearts of the ship-news photographers; whose legs were not too bad, and who knew it; spindle shanks; chiffon-clad legs.

FEET (Large)

Her feet which nature had made all too ample; small feet are undeniably appealing to the eye, but big ones are better to stand on; she looked all feet; some girls have big feet, others wear white shoes.

(See *large.*)

FEMININE

Feminine to the last lash.

(See *woman, effeminate.*)

FEUD

He follows in his father's feud-steps.

(See *fight.*)

FEW

Shy on undershirts; I know a brace of poetesses; a scant handful; few and far between; can be counted on the toes of one foot; he didn't have a corporal's guard; could have held the meeting in a telephone booth.

(See *numerous as, scarce.*)

FIGHT (Names for)

Fisticuffs; a tiff; a friendly argument; a row; run-in; rumpus; brawling; a knock-down-and-drag-out argument; a street brawl; massacre; love-feast; free-for-all scuffle.

(See *battle, war.*)

FIGHT (Women)

A public hair-pulling.

(See *temper.*)

FIGHT

He got rambunctious; it wasn't exactly a maypole dance; dealt out plenty of punishment; was doing him a maximum of bodily harm; stood off the gang; wade into; manhandle him; ready to sell his life dearly; riding roughshod; to fight to the last ditch; he ran amuck; to outfight; for a time he was all over Barney like a swarm of bees; with no respect at all for each other's physiognomy; thought the roof had fallen on him; snarled at each other; wipe the floor with him; there was something pretty potent about the way he pushed his mallets; made an attempt to exterminate him; cuffing him around; she grabbed him by the ears, although his lapels were just as handy; kick the gizzards out of him; kick the slats off of; the massacre began in earnest; his Irish; sounded like a free-for-all in a madhouse; ground him in the dust; ready to eat up another; kicked him from Dan to Beersheba.

(See *anger.*)

FIGHT (Beginning a)

The war horse scenting battle smoke; he pulled his suspenders far out and then let them smite him in; girded himself for the fray; put up his dukes; he made earnest attempts to incite Mr. —— to riot; they stood back expecting to catch me on the rebound; the glad light of battle leaped into his eyes; he spit on his hands; all set to mash his brains out; sharpening his claws; got into more fights than Popeye the Sailor.

(See *arguing.*)

FIGHT (Free-for-all)

Turned the place into a shambles; the place was turned into a second battle of Antietam; a brickbat hits him under the right ear, and he begins wobbling about very loose at the hinges; commit mayhem; causing the fur to fly.

(See *hit, blow, beat.*)

FIGHT (Loser)

My chassis looks like I'd been run over by a flock of wild elephants; he pulverized him; and his lips looked as though someone had injected air into them; that took the streamline out of my spine.

(See *defeat.*)

FIGHT (Punches)

Smote him in the midriff; punched him right where it did the most good;

let go a straight left to Porkey's beezer; a two-ton rabbit punch; swing back the other way with a swift coup de grace; fought tooth and nail; a right hook to the belly that made his dull eyes pop; solar plexus; and began to take wildcat Evans apart; hit him with everything but the kitchen stove; he hauled off and belted Ambrose over the noggin; a chuck under the chin that came pretty close to busting his jaw; he swung from the ankle; knock him for a graduated series of intercollegiate hurdles; he let go a beautiful right which landed on my nose and uncorked the ketchup bottle; a punch in the umbilicus; lashing out with his hind feet; deal its wearer a nasty buffet in the face.

(See *prizefighter, wrestler.*)

FIGHT (Result)

Polished him off like a brass doorknob; knocked him for a loop; he filed him away for future reference; engaged in fisticuffs and had his beard torn off; knuckles broken in a friendly argument; gave him the works; got the whey beaten out of him; knocked the stuffings out of him; gave him such a thwacking, cuffing; his eyes were in mourning; his face appeared as if it had been through the city sewer system; he folded up like an accordian; knocked Kid Kaplan bowlegged; a shellacking; cut him into ribbons; took a lacing; he got the most thoroughly scientific going-over that any man has ever gotten; beat the hell out of him; jolly good pasting; beat him into a very soft pulp; he was tearing him limb from limb; and when he got through ironing him out, he looked like something a road roller had passed over and then backed up and passed over again; he looked as if he'd been chewing barnacles; broken noses, chipped chins, sloughed jaws and cracked ribs; licked the liv-

ing by-heck out of him; to lay him out like a rug; took the wind out of his sails; smacked him for a row of sleeping powders.
(See *win, defeat*.)

FIGHT (Talk)

I'll break his back for him; I'll thrash him within an inch or an inch-and-a-half of his life; I'll spit in your eye; I'll make mince-meat out of you; I will fight to the last drop of blood in your body; I am ready to fracture your spine; say uncle; I will break your clavicle; I will tear you limb from limb; I'll knock his ears off; I will annihilate; I will put salt on his tail; I'm going to cool you off; I'll beat your ears down; I'd like to scratch your eyes out; I'll lay him like linoleum; I'll grind you down to a pinch of salt; I'll punch you in the snout; get out before I pare off your ears and paste them over your eyes; are you sucking around for a smack in the puss?; I'll beat the daylights out of you; I will guarantee to yank one of his arms off and beat his brains out with it.
(See *arguing, talk back to*.)

FIGURE (Woman)

Bulges in all the wrong places; her figure filled out so it had bumps here and there where a doll is entitled to have bumps; the flowing curves of her lithe youthful figure; the ripe luscious contours of her gorgeous figure; her pink and white, piquant figure; her quivering torso; the voluptuous form, tantalizingly protected by no more than the gossamer wisp of her chemise.
(See *body, fat, thin, bosom*.)

FIGURING THINGS OUT

Wetting stub pencils with the tips of fevered tongues; pit his wits against.
(See *think, explain*.)

FINALLY

At long last; en passant; as a clincher; to make a long story shrink.
(See *late*.)

FIND

Dig up a friend; stir up some food.
(See *discovered, invention*.)

FINE

Bully for you, old boy; a real sweetheart of a story; Jim-dandy.
(See *all right, O. K.*)

FINGERNAILS

His nails looked as if they'd been in mourning for months.
(See *manicurists*.)

FINGERS (Men)

He had fingers that could throttle a horse.
(See *hands*.)

FINGERS (Women)

Her highly polished digits.
(See *cosmetics*.)

FINISH

Just in time to dead-heat with the final spoonful; romance has kicked up her heels; put you off me for life; cast off like an old shoe; peter out; the year will fold its icy limbs and die; shot his bolt; topped off with; all washed up; squelched it; that friendship was all overboard; to be hooted out of public life; his exit; ran dry; on the shelf; my plan is all shot to pieces; doomed for the garbage heap; all washed up; he winds up.
(See *end, complete*.)

FIRE (Discharge)

Give him the air.
(See *discharge*.)

FIRST
Maiden speech; the first crack out of the box; this is the first time I did it again today; his debut.
(See *begin, inexperience*.)

FISH
Our finny friends; denizens of the deep; ichthyologist; members of the finny tribe.
(See *whale, ocean, shark*.)

FISHERMAN
Some ingenious disciple of Izaak Walton.
(See *seasickness*.)

FISHING
Sitting and dangling a disgruntled worm in an unresponsive stream.
(See *country, hunting*.)

FIT (To take a fit)
Having conniptions; throw a spasm.
(See *anger*.)

FLAT
Flatter than eel's hips.
(See *low, thin*.)

FLATTERY
Feed him all the well-known compliments; spreading it on as thick as marmalade.
(See *compliment, fawn, praise*.)

FLIRT
She coquetted over a little spangled fan; mash notes; ogle the boys; that sheik stuff; her "come hither" method; to chuck passing dairymaids under the chin; as a chin-chucker I have few superiors; her eyes and his were giving each other promissory notes for the future; made goo-goo eyes at.
(See *coquetting, petting*)

FLOWERS
Her favorite aspidistra; other local flora; old-maid's whiskers; he presented her with bales of orchids; a cornflower winking in his lapel; bombarded her with long-stemmed roses; where did you get the spinach?; flaura and fauna; stinkweeds.
(See *garden*.)

FLUCTUATE
Its value shifted acrobatically; fluctuated like a monkey on a stick.
(See *change, uncertain*.)

FLUTES
The flutes keep up an intermittent whimpering, very pitiable to hear.
(See *music, orchestra*.)

FOG
Londoners are proud of their fog; you see it and feel it and smell it and taste it; washed-out-green fog; pea-soup fog; got tangled up in one of these fogs; thick blanket of fog; a fog cannot be dispelled with a fan; blackout.
(See *rain*.)

FOLLOW
I tailed him; I camped on his tail; dog his footsteps; pounding up behind him; adhesive as a postage stamp.
(See *chase*.)

FOOD
An insult to his digestive apparatus; at Paris the food was either uneatable or unpronounceable; just served a box lunch; rustling his own grub; gastronomic idiosyncracies; food with a lot of goo on it; fodder; the eats; a gastronomic crime; gastronomic splendor; chow; this article is a gastronomical institution; robust provender; something that will stick to the ribs all morning; boy, I kin hardly wait till

I get them hot wittels stowed below the hatches; when there are tidbits to be had; provender; provisions; fodder; the alleged eatables; they give you such muck to eat; there was no food in the larder; the groceries in the pantry; the proof of the pudding was on the table; nectar from the gods.

(See *eating, meals.*)

FOOD (List)

Goulash; Rehbraten, borscht, Rindeburst mit Sauerkraut und Kartoffel Salad; bouillabaise; pheasant's eyelids; caviar; pate de foie gras; crumpets; a brace of ducks; egg plant a l'opera; all-day sucker; after partaking of fresh-breast-of-fresh-squab-guinea-h e n-served-on-a-canape-of-puree-of-goose - liver-washed-down-with-Musigny-de-Vogue.

(See *vegetarian.*)

FOOD (Bad)

Strangely there is no good food in Hollywood; it is severely tasteless; you feel as if the cattle had grazed on straw in abattoir days; the taste and flavor of venison is still not unlike that of old boiled slippers.

(See *indigestion.*)

FOOD (Fancy)

In a world where people exist who really like anchovies wrapped around olives, canteloupe stuffed with ice cream.

(See *feast, French dishes.*)

FOOL (A) (Names for)

A jackanapes; jackass; a sucker; he was the monkey wrench of the organization; lunatic; chump; little cuss; a rummy; a poor goof; to carry the torch for; I was a mug to back that horse; he was a laughingstock; a lunk; lummox; gump; fathead; a complete ass; milksop; an oaf; a cluck.

(See *stupid.*)

FOOL (A) (Proverbs)

A fool may ask more questions in an hour than a wise man can answer in seven years; a fool demands much, but he's a greater fool that gives it; a fool knows more in his house than a wise man in another's; fools set stools for wise men to stumble at; a fool may throw a stone into a well which a hundred wise men cannot pull out; but alas! a myrtle among thorns is a myrtle still; as the fool thinks, so the bell clinks.

(See *useless.*)

FOOL (Someone)

Inveigle; give him the runaround; wangled a diamond out of him; you can't hand me this jug of molasses; hokum; foist; bamboozle; guilty of chicanery; spoofing the world; shim shamming; left in the lurch; hamstring; jolly; josh; double-dealing; for which I was always a sucker; he filled him up with taffy; what are you giving us? he is up to something machiavellian; ran out of them; hijacked him; buggy ride; greased the road for his foot to slip; leave Europe in the lurch; he was plucked to his pinfeathers; to "shake down"; flimflamming; phenagling; and came out on the wrong end of the bargain; fobbed off on; bilked the depositors; laugh on the wrong side of his mouth; string him along; pull the wool over their eyes.

(See *deceive, lie.*)

FOOL AROUND

His waggery; gallivanting round; most refreshing fol-de-rol; mummery; fiddle around with; monkey with flubdubbery; dilly-dallying; m o n k e y-shines; joshes; a spoofer; shilly-shallying; to fiddle-faddle.

(See *wasting time.*)

FOOLISHNESS

Fol-de-rols; a sap; such tosh; a lot of

god-damn foolishness; jibberish; ho-kum; rigmarole.

(See *childishness, silly*.)

FOOTBALL

He had risked all the breakable por-tions of his large frame playing foot-ball; the game ends in a draw or a hospital; the football guide was his Bible; a football player with a bad heart is like a limousine without a carburetor; raised a nice bunch of cal-louses sitting on the bench; Jones carried that apple down the field; kicking a lopsided pigskin around; who couldn't agree with me that their sons were a little less than All-Ameri-can quarterbacks or ends; twenty-two young men were indulging in a form of physical encounter; wearers of the cleats; the mysterious jargon of the gridiron; triple threat fullback; he came to the conclusion that football in the United States is a cross between Rugby football and the World War; combining most of their less pleasing features.

(See *games*.)

FOOTBALL (Errors)

We'll put handles on that ball for you (fumble); butter fingers; he knew more football and played less than any.

(See *wrong*.)

FOOTBALL (Good playing)

He could do everything with a foot-ball up to and including making it play The Stars and Stripes Forever; was born with a football in his arms; they played heads-up football.

(See *win*.)

FORBIDDEN

Forbidden fruit is sweetest.

(See *no, refuse*.)

FORCED

Dragooned into voting for it; hijack me; was hustled and jostled and shouldered and trod upon; forced down the throat of; log-rolling; what's sauce for the goose is sauce for the croquettes; muscle in; mooch our way in; foist something on.

(See *unfair, strength*.)

FOREIGNER

That hairdresser; he comes from 'way across the seas; a frowsy foreigner; answering to a name like a burst siphon; these hunyaks; squarehead.

(See *Chinaman, French, Spain, Irish, Germany, Hawaii, Japs, British, Italy, Russia, Eskimo, Turkey, Switzerland*.

FOREIGN EXCHANGE

The value of the ruble shifts acrobat-ically.

(See *stock market*.)

FOREIGN LANGUAGE

There wasn't enough French to go around; a French irregular verb would be torn to tatters in a Wagner opera; Scandinavian jabber.

(See *accent*.)

FORGET IT

Skip it; file it away for future refer-ence; drop it; pour it down the drain; bury the hatchet.

(See *care—not to, never mind*.)

FORGOTTEN

Lost in the dust of time.

(See *past, neglected*.)

FORTUNE TELLER

Pries into the future at cut rates; reads the past, present and future at so much per read.

(See *prophet, future*.)

SOPHISTIC[...]

a couple of merry Andrews; he has[...] an ill-natured bone in his body; do[...] listen to this if you have a cracked li[...] he's a hot sketch; he's quite a spoof[...] lay 'em in the aisles; excruciating[...] funny; was a howl.

(See *ridiculous, humor.*)

FUNERAL
Obsequies.

(See *death, cemetery.*)

FUR COAT
A fur coat that made you look like[...] polar bear with the dropsy; a fam[...] ished fur coat; she has enough fu[...] coats for a tribe of Eskimos; out [...] the cocoon of furs; women don't wea[...] furs, they fairly drip them.

(See *clothes.*)

FURNITURE
All the furniture was Louis Some[...] thing; a family two years ahead of it[...]

FORWARD
As forward as a set of buck teeth.

(See *fresh, bold.*)

FOUL PLAY
Dirty work at the cross-roads; double-crossing louse; does her dirt.

(See *unfair.*)

FOUR
The Four Horsemen of the Apocalypse.

(See *mathematics.*)

FOURTH OF JULY
The Declaration of Independence has been read; fireworks on the village green.

(See *celebrating.*)

FRANK
Call a cad a cad; stories larded with old-fashioned, nothing-up-my-sleeve-gentlemen sincerity; man to man; laid all the cards on the table; to speak out at meetin'; she called her shots; call a spade a spade; show-down; he made no bones about it.

(See *truth.*)

FRATERNITY
His frat pin was over some other girl's seventh rib.

(See *club, college.*)

FREEDOM
Where tyrant foot hath never trod nor bigot forged a chain.

(See *Fourth of July.*)

FRENCH
You can't be French unless you were brought up on snails; that frog-eater; Gallic vivacity; the French they are a funny race; la belle France; speak French like a couple of natives; I say "my French" because it is a peculiar patois shared by no one else; French conversation is not a sedentary occupation, it calls into play all the muscles of the face, to say nothing of the arms, shoulders and spine; Frenchmen have a habit of wearing spats with evening dress; those frogs.

(See *foreigner.*)

FRENCH (Talk)
Oui, oui, yes; it ees asking too moch; tell heem; you say soch verry sweet theeng; he sends you of the caresses; sacre tonnerre; le bon Dieu; mon ami; sacre bleu.

(See *foreign language.*)

FRENCH DISHES
Caneton a la Palisse; poulet de bonne femme; Crepe Suzette.

(See *food—fancy.*)

FRESH (Nervy)
A sassy letter.

(See *forward, bold.*)

FRESHMAN
Verdant freshman.

(See *college.*)

FRIEND
Who will go anywhere there's free drinks; hobnob with; doesn't care which of the Goulds are bowing to each other; cronies; have always been quite persona grata; the dove of peace now chirps over; it was nice to feel that one's friends rallied round one; save me from my friends, I can take care of my enemies; a friend to everybody is a friend to nobody (prov.); a man may see his friend need, but he will not see him bleed (prov.); a friend's frown is better than a fool's smile (prov.); compatriots; friends are like fiddlestrings, they must

not be screwed too tight (prov
(See *company, pal.*)

FRIENDLY
Trying to be folksey; hit it off
hobnob with cabinet officers;
slapping; everything is hotsy-tot
tween them; with whom he beca
thick as raspberry jam.
(See *cordial, kind.*)

FRIENDSHIP
Camaraderie; my palliest pal; w
along pretty well together, espe
when one of us is not around; n
the whole world kin; he would ra
have him than an oil well; with
testations of undying friendship;
for all and all for one.
(See *affection, love.*)

FRIGHTENED
Could feel goose flesh sprouting
all over me; strike terror into
breast; frightening the wits out
him; frightened out of a mon
growth; malediction sent the outf
ers scurrying toward the fence.
(See *fear, scare.*)

FROWN
A Ciceronian frown ennobled
brow; a friend's frown is better th
a fool's smile; glowered.
(See *discourage.*)

FULL OF
Chock full of; his singing is jamm
with all three qualities; the subje
simply bristles with fallacies; sh
through with sports writers; for hir
it is loaded to the gunwales with sen
mental association.
(See *lots.*)

FUN (To have)
Rollicking high-jinks; shenanigans

G

GAMES (Childrens')
Duck-on-rock; cops and robbers; shin-
ny on your own side; pepper, salt and
mustard; a jolly game of hop-scotch
with the kiddies; pum-pum; pullaway
in the parlor; a game of going to Jerusalem; eeney meeney miney mo.

(See *playing, hide.*)

GAMES (Grown-up)
A rousing game of Post Office or Spin
the Bottle; Scavenger Party (treasure
hunt); tiddleywinks; to play Copen-
hagen; to play upsy daisy; puss-in-the-
corner.

(See *chess, football, baseball, hockey,
golf, tennis.*)

GANGSTERS
A mob; mobsters; he's a craftsman
with the knife; his criminal cohorts.

(See *gunman, criminals.*)

GARBAGE
To air-condition the garbage can.
(See *food, germs.*)

GARDEN
Pottering in the garden; flitting bee-
like from flower to flower; and the
aspidistra badly needs decarbonizing;
in the geranium bed; flung himself at
the soil; trying to kill bugs by giving
them nasty looks.

(See *farm, flowers.*)

GARLIC
Soft attar of garlic.
(See *odor—bad, onion.*)

GASOLINE
Petrol.
(See *automobile.*)

GASOLINE STATION
A gas station build along the lines of
the Taj Mahal; a sprawly, large, California filling station, made of ginger-
bread and red jam, with towers, min-
arets and a moat; a gasolinery.

(See *architecture.*)

GAY
To go gay and gigglish.
(See *laugh, lively, happy.*)

GENEROUS
Open-handed; good old Morton, he'd
split his last infinitive with you.
(See *charity, kind.*)

GENIUS
Fresh-water genius; he lets his hair
grow and tells people he's a genius.
(See *intellectual, artist.*)

GENUINE
He's the real McCoy.
(See *real, frank, honest.*)

GERMANS
With their goose-step efficiency; uttering little soothing, clucking sounds in
German; and get to thinking about
the buxom little fraulein who served
Munchner to you in the Spatenbrau
hall in Munich; German war lords
dressed like Zulu chiefs; their soldiers
goosestepped; they eat blood and iron;
lisping in German is rather serious;
a voice thick with Teutonic gutterals;
the Berliner; Teutonic thoroughness;
the Krauts; in genuine sauerkraut
fashion; he was born in Germany;
God save the mark.

(See *foreigner.*)

GERMS

In those days germs had not been invented yet; whiskers are such fine winter quarters for germs; the influenza germ is rearing its ugly head in our midst; you cannot bar the entry of germs by means of a microbe net; you do not realize you are capable of conveying 5,000,000,000 germs, even in the off season; bacilli; germs are, like the poor, always with us; from far and near could be heard the patter of grippe germs as they marched by the sextillion onto the nation's tonsils.
(See *disease, unhealthful.*)

GET

Grab off a bit of; get his clutches on; to wheedle; to collar; rustle; wangle
(See *earnings, influence, have.*)

GET EVEN

Squared t h e account between us; laugh from the other corner of his mouth; work off his spleen; to take his measure; two can play at this game as well as one; settle his score; I am laying for him; pay you back in your own coin; wipe off some old scores; an eye for an eye; when I hit you in the back remind me to have a knife in my hands.
(See *revenge.*)

GHOSTLY

Eerie; the heebie-jeebies; a shivery tete-a-tete; makes a Nick Carter tale seem milder than McGuffey's Fourth Reader.
(See *death.*)

GIGOLO

Papier mache gigolos; daffydill.
(See *man-about-town.*)

GIRL (Anxious to get married)

She's had a boy complex with a decided weakness for dashing off to a minister's; to rope him in; set her cap for him; some floosie had got her hooks into Tim; loved by the man she hated, hated by the man she loved; she was far too emotionally man-conscious.
(See *marriage, husband, wife.*)

GIRL (Names)

A dish like you, girly; a wight; damozels; this airy baggage; damsel; blight young thing; this pancake; pagan wench; a frail; this little tramp; a winsome lass; deadlier species; Jane; the little duck; doll; moll; this little honey; gal; skirt; floosie; colleen; dame; mademoiselle; senorita; his lady fair; biscuit; nice little filly; wren; the gel; a fetching midge; a cute little piece; that little red-headed mutt; one of nature's loveliest manifestations; a twist; creature; baby; donkey; oh, you little goose; that veal cutlet.
(See *sweetheart.*)

GIRL (Girl-crazy)

He was doll-dizzy; a Lothario; a sucker for dames; a lady-killer; and always he is on the grab for young dolls; petticoat fever; a woman can get him ga ga; dame dizzy.
(See *lady-killer.*)

GIRL (Gold-digger)

She pulled the people's legs; "gimmies"; the kind of a girl who likes to eat her cake and have yours too; a heart-working girl; first in war, first in peace and first in the pockets of her countrymen; she can do more tricks with a man than a monkey with a cocoanut; better an old man's darling than a young man's slave.
(See *expensive.*)

GIRL (Hot stuff)

Looking as though she'd hiss if a drop

of water touched her; and was she a torrid baby; knowing her was like shaking hands with the devil; frivolous minx.
(See *sex*.)

GIRL (Popular)

An appendix girl, the kind that gets taken out; but when the men step out with a girl they want something snappy for street wear.
(See *beautiful*.)

GIRL (Simple)

The kind of a girl whose contact with men consisted of brief talks with the laundry man, the bread man and the collector from the dairy; an appearance bespeaking a clandestine rendezvous with the kitchen stove; to go domestic; little girls are made of sugar and spice and everything nice; she thought Rex Beach was a summer resort.
(See *plain, old maid*.)

GIVE

Fork over; blow in; dig up; sling; feeding him; he loaded them down with; dish it out; slip it over.
(See *generous*.)

GIVE UP

Rest my case right here; throw in the towel; he blew up; is going to crack.
(See *submit*.)

GLAD TO SEE YOU

Clasped me to her rugged bosom.
(See *welcome, embrace*.)

GLORY

You can't eat glory.
(See *mighty, famous*.)

GLOVES

Gauntlets.
(See *clothes*.)

GO

I'll just pop over; scat; be gone; go, and never darken these doors again; you needn't think you can come around darkening our doors just whenever the mood takes you; toddled off; lights out the front door; scuttled like a crab from the room; barged into the room; tottered out of the room; go dashing over to her house; Mr. Monroe crept whitely through the streets; buzzed off; let's mooch along; shuttled over to; mushed on; let's shove off; glided off; flitting lightly from dance to club; repaired to his room; ambled off; jumped into the taxi and made off; scuttled back to the kitchen; betook himself to a night club; shuffled out; we're going places; she wiggles off; hies herself to; leg it to the movies; we're lamming; they pushed-off together; rolled like a bowling ball on its way to a ten-strike; he chanced into a small London playhouse; he sashayed to the party; he beat it right over to; made a bee-line for; he shoved off; hit it off to the shore; he reeled to the elevator; check me out; goes galumphing off into the night; get into your car and high-tail it out of here; and oozed about the island perfectly happy; so David pikes off; gravitate to N. Y.; get to blazes out of here; he is bowing out; he swept from the place.
(See *travel, progress, run, hurry, speed*.)

GOAT

He has a fragrance of which he is the sole proprietor; eating his midday meal of boot heels and barrel staves; those under-privileged goats; a goat under the influence of mumps; sits around all day and eats old blotters and telegraph envelopes (in an office.).
(See *odor*.)

GOD

The great Ruler of the universe; the

inscrutable workings of Providence; the General Manager of the universe; Most Sublime Overseer of the Universe; the Great Architect; the dear Ruler of Wind and Wave.

(See *religious*.)

GOLF

At that kind of a golf club a good many members will be compelled to take up golf sooner or later in order to kill time; her father's stroke-by-stroke defense of his afternoon's playing; you and your tribe who live on divots and stymies; her papa is a ball-knocker; he dressed a swell game of golf; who packed a nasty wallop with his mid-iron; the course over which, now and then, he whacked a golf ball; watched the species at their gambols on divers golf-courses; a man who has just sliced his seventh at the short fourteenth into a casual hazard is in no mood to; he does it for the sake of his liver; a complicated method of taking a walk; golf is all very well in small doses; golfo-maniac; he was a confirmed hole-claimer; the course is rather washboardy; floundered about in the rough; I walk from the first tee to a sand trap where I generally remain for the rest of the day; it looks as if I will have to blast; flirts with par; knock off eighteen holes of golf.

(See *games*.)

GOOD

Tip-top; rattling good book; bang-up reading; these people were the salt of the earth; things were rosy; nifty; the ne plus ultra of good legs; a scrumptious holiday; Garland's rave review; everything was perfectly hacha; it was a honey; no slouch of a joke; grade A; was a pip; she is a natural; he became a whiz; this apple pie is all by itself; the pattest first-night performance; he was a right guy; this is nectar from the gods; that was a grandpa, all right; a

lulu; he was a whale on geology; the berries; he was tops; top-notcher; a "number one" dinner; a fetching letter; a good cat deserves a good rat; an all-star idea; a crackerjack; his drive was a darb; a world-beater; Cleo was absolutely the elephant's earrings; is something to behold; he could write rings around Shakespeare; it's good for us, just like cod-liver oil; was a howl; a ducky prospect; top-flight men; a triple-threat fullback; a picture with some guts to it; it was the nuts.

(See *best, fine, advantage, virtue*.)

GOOD-BYE

Step on it, big boy, and see if you can't smother yourself in your own dust; if I never see you again before your funeral, it will be too soon; if I never see you again it will be twice too soon; adieu; ta-ta; bid him a hearty Goodspeed; Auf Wiedersehn; well, have yourselves a time; toodle-oo; happy landing; with a by-your-leave; so long; pack your flimsies, we're pushing off.

(See *go, leave*.)

GOOD-LOOKING (Male)

These flannel-trousered young Apollos; he thinks he is a handsome dog; their magnificent male pulchritude; baby-faced; Adonis; he looked too good to be true—and was; he didn't scare any hosses in his young days; this guy's a Gable; sleek young blade with the Leyendecker profile; a fair face may hide a foul heart (prov.); the ladies would accept him in overalls and gum boots; collar-model youths.

(See *beautiful, man*.)

GOOD-NATURED

He hasn't a mean hair on his chest; oozed cordiality.

(See *kind, generous*.)

GOOD TIME

Let's go out and play with the slot machines; a hot time; stepped out; frolicking around with.

(See *party, happy*.)

GOSSIP

She's a regular teakettle and occasionally boiling over; panning her; scandal-mongering; chattering like a cageful of agitated monkeys at the zoo; chit-chat; the village pump (gossip); the L o n d o n tabbies; loosen the tongues of the garrulous gossips; a gossipy tidbit; swap scandal with Mrs. ———; gutter gossip; choice morsel of gossip; old-wives' tales; tongues waggel; a honey tongue, a heart of gall (prov.); to get it hot from the griddle (backyard gossip); anything you tell a woman goes in one ear and over the back fence; half the world delights in slander and the other half in believing it; they settled down to exchange the latest dirt.

(See *tattle-tale, busybody, rumor*.)

GOUT

He had the gout and felt as if he was walking on his eyeballs.

(See *sick*.)

GOVERNMENT

Even the toot of a railroad train is now regulated by law.

(See *congress, politics, law*.)

GRADUALLY

Feather by feather the goose is plucked (prov.).

(See *slow*.)

GRAFT

Overfeeding at the public trough; passing out the plums; shaking the political tree; spoilsmen; the politician's feed box; grabbers; handouts; pickings; it has the odor of graft; a blot on our national escutcheon; largesse smeared around like marmalade; grease the palm.

(See *bribe*.)

GRAMMAR

In due course I was exploring the mazes of the subjunctive; my first excursion along the thorny paths of syntax; let him do the worrying about the irregular verbs; he must have learned grammar by mail in 10 easy lessons; he had a solid gold infinitive splitter on his desk; Dr. Thraddle got caught on a dangling participle, it took us the better part of a day to extricate him.

(See *language*.)

GRAPEFRUIT

She finally learned that grapefruit is cut latitudinally.

(See *food*.)

GRATITUDE

Bows himself out with mumbled and acrobatic gratitude; gratitude, a lively sense of favors to come.

(See *thank you*.)

GRAVE (To turn over in his)

Would cause him to indulge in acrobatic stunts in his last resting place; he must have been turning over so fast that he looked like a squirrel in a revolving cage; I can hear a snort from the grave of; your father would absolutely rotate in his grave; the shade of P. T. could not rest easily in his noisy Valhalla.

(See *cemetery, surprised*.)

GRAVY

And enough gravy to give the dumplings a decent burial in a savory sea.

(See *food*.)

GREAT

Grandiose; and the idea was a wham; everything is hotsy-totsy between them; the all-American half-wit.

(See *good, wonderful.*)

GREED

Greed gnaws the vitals.

(See *envy, jealousy.*)

GREEK

Stromberry pie.

(See *foreigner.*)

GREENWICH VILLAGE

Greenwich Village tea rooms such as the Green Gazelle, the Orange Ostrich and the Purple Plesio-saurus.

(See *New York, artist.*)

GREETING

He gave me good-day; to buttonhole someone; he didn't burst into a how-I've-missed-you line; "meet 'cha"; bon jour monseer; "what's doing?"; how's tricks?; hello, Harry, you old turtle, haven't they hung you yet?; so he gives me a large hello, so I hello him right back; is that you Mr.——, I didn't know you since you washed your face; to perform the perfunctory gesture of hat-lifting; "greetings and salutations."

(See *glad to see you, welcome.*)

GRIEF

A corroding grief.

(See *sorry, sad.*)

GRIN

Grin-deep.

(See *smile, laugh.*)

GROUCHY

Cantankerous; grumpy; a terrible old crab; on liverish days; a consistently even-tempered man, he stays mad all the time; a hard-boiled old crosspatch.

(See *unhappy, pessimist.*)

GROUND

Terra firma.

(See *earth, world.*)

GUESS (Reckon)

I trow not.

(See *think.*)

GUESS

To call the turn.

(See *figuring things out.*)

GUIDE

A Moses to guide them.

(See *chief, leader.*)

GUN (Names for)

Fowling piece; gat; a BB gun; six-shooter; our trusty old flintlock; this double-barreled popgun; engines of destruction; shooting iron; a Tommy gun; cowboy outfit.

GUN (Sound of)

The roaring of the six-shooter; the guns barked; the gun goes rooty-toot; tat-a-tat-tat.

(See *noise.*)

GUN (Receiving end)

Look down the barrel of a gun; swallow a dose of lead; bullets come zinging at you.

(See *victim.*)

GUN (Business end)

Packed a big gun; to punctuate somebody; I'll mow you off the spot; he sprayed him with a machine gun; emptying his; quicker'n greased lightning on the draw; who knew the

poetry and beauty of his gun.
(See *villain*.)

GUN (Misc.)

Didn't know a shotgun from an air-rifle; a miniature pop-gun; it's my old pal, put-put-put; well, then put-put-put it away.
(See *shooting*.)

GUNMAN

Got himself a habeas corpus; to rub out the rat; his moll; pay-off man; their cohorts; two-bit gangsters; gent whose chief claim to distinction lies in the excessive number of nicks in his gun butt; looks like mugs in the police line-up; he's Louis' fixer, his go-between, his messenger boy; yegg.
(See *gangster, criminals*.)

GUNMEN (Names)

Big Nig; head mobster; as tough a gangster as ever packed a rod; Up-state Red; Crowbars Connolly; Swifty Moran; One-eye Zigo; Jimmy the Bopp.
(See *names*.)

GUSH

They gurgled on.
(See *talking, gossip*.)

GUTTER

A boy's best friend is his gutter.
(See *street*.)

GUY

Daffydill.
(See *man*.)

H

HABIT
To be weaned away from; dull ritual; like taking opium; he that lives with wolves will learn to howl (prov.).
(See *used to.*)

HABITS (List of)
Throwing cigarette butts out of windows; biting fingernails; custom of hurling his trousers on a chair any old way when retiring; paying the check when it isn't my turn.
(See *action.*)

HAIR (Male)
Pompadour; his raven locks; his thatch; patent-leather hair; his white mane; he looked as if he had just come from Oberammergau; his hair in a lion tamer's roach; a gollywog mop of bushy hair, his bushy hair, spanked and brushed to lie straight back; his ambrosial locks.
(See *head, haircut, beard, moustache.*)

HAIR (Female)
Coiffure; her blonde mop; torturing ladies' hair into new and horrifying arrangements; her hair as soft as scented night on breezes newly borne; her crowning glory fluttering in the breeze.
(See *beauty parlor.*)

HAIR (Redheads)
When a redheaded person meets another redheaded person, it is almost certain that an explosion will take place immediately.
(See *blonde.*)

HAIRCUT (Man)
Badger haircut; collegiate haircut; shampooed and all but drowned in bay rum; army haircut; got his hair landscaped.
(See *barber, shave.*)

HAIRDRESSER
Cast iron marcel; to toy with her locks.
(See *beauty parlor.*)

HANDKERCHIEF
Hanky.
(See *clothes.*)

HANDS (Names for)
Paw; his lunch hooks; mitts; dukes; claws.
(See *fingers, fingernails.*)

HANDS
Hands were maded for gesticulating, fisticuffs and hailing of taxicabs; hands like the ears of little white rabbits; took her little leg-o-mutton fist in mine; her fat hand corseted with rings; her hands which suggested all too clearly that she had spent her girlhood milking cows.
(See *body.*)

HANDS (Big)
Hands like toasting forks; hands that looked like they had first baseman's mitts on them; his hand was as big as a watermelon; how did he wind his watch; sported a pair of dukes bigger than a pot roast.
(See *body.*)

HANDWRITING
Take your mittens off when you write that scrawl; chirography; the whole-

[1211]

arm movement; his Alpine scrawl; mincing flourish; it has an exasperating sameness of letters that drives printers to despair; most of it must be read through a microscope.
(See *signature*.)

HANGERS ON
Almoners; ward-heelers; henchmen; minions; liegemen; satellites.
(See *dependent, ward-heelers*.)

HANGING (Death)
Your worthless body will swing from Execution Dock at the next assizes; it will be his first appearance on the gallows, his debut; a "necktie" party.
(See *execution*.)

HAPPENING
A happenstance; goings on; come to pass; it was pulled off; something went flooey in the; the plot thickens; things began to pop.
(See *circumstance, result*.)

HAPPY
There was dancing in the streets; I was so happy I gave three short barks of joy; his cup of joy was about ready to slop over; tickled pink; she purred proudly; unalloyed bliss; a great deal of oh-ing and ah-ing; a chink of heaven; seized her in a bear hug; wept with joy; if he had owned two tons of firecrackers he would have set them all off at once; were thrown into a frenzy of delight; they emitted a war-whoop of delight; pleased as Punch; with a light heart and a gay snatch of song; a hey-nonny-nonny and a hi-de-ho; a man of gladness seldom falls into madness (prov.); humming a gay snatch of song; as happy as a mouse in a cheese factory; to tread on air; embraced me with whoops of joy; she didn't know whether she was eating ice cream or cement; do a jig for joy.
(See *bless, contented, feel good*.)

HARD-BOILED
Hard-bitten; couldn't penetrate his rhinocerous hide.
(See *cold, rough*.)

HARE
A hare is a sort of a rabbit's uncle.
(See *rabbit*.)

HARMLESS
As harmless as a bag of marshmallows.
(See *O. K., good*.)

HASH
"Sweep the floor"; you can serve your patrons on hash and call it 'ris de veau noisette.'
(See *feed, mixed up*.)

HASTE
Make haste slowly.
(See *hurry, speed*.)

HAT-CHECK
The guests were robbed of their hats and coats; hat snatcher; hat-check pirate.
(See *night clubs*.)

HATE
Shun; he had no stomach at all for discussing; I never liked it in the first place, now I like it twice as much; you're leprosy to me right now; he snatched it from me as if I was poison; he's going to be sorry that my grandfather was ever born; who loves Hitler slightly less than he does a rattlesnake; he is poison to chisellers; I haven't got anything against——— except that I don't like him; implanted a cancer of hatred in his heart; ready to eat up one another; hate each other

like poison; about as pleased as Socrates was when they handed him the hemlock; she will have no part of them; she did not relish it; no more affinity for each other than a robin for a goldfish; turns up its nose at; I will have no part of him whatever; hadn't been able to see me with a telescope.

(See *disgust, enemy, horror.*)

HATS (Women—old-fashioned)
On her head rocked a gay "90" model with a regular farm yard sprouting all over it; a venerable confection.

(See *old-fashioned.*)

HATS (Women)
Queen Mary's hats; her tiny hat nuzzled one ear fetchingly; she doffed her toque; it had a sassy look; the daffiest hats; pertly toqued; in summer they wear postage stamps for hats; hat that hung on the back of her head through the most sheer magic; some of them (hats) are like damp cabbage leaves; seems to be held in place by willpower or suction; the top crushed in like a muffin; it looks as if it had made a forced landing; moored on her skull by long steel skewers.

(See *clothes.*)

HATS (High hat)
Bunged-up old stovepipe hat.

(See *high class.*)

HATS (Description)
Hat that gave the impression of having been dropped from a great height; doff my topper; clap on his bowler; with the ridiculous hat perched up high; wore his hat a trifle more slappity-bang.

(See *fashions.*)

HATS (Names)
Ten-gallon hat; yarmarka; lid; old bowler (derby); kady; top-piece; topper; chapeau; fedora; headgear, sombrero; bonnet.

HAVE
Eat the sweet fruits of.

(See *get, own.*)

HAWAII
I'm Wicki and she's Wacki.

(See *foreigner.*)

HAZING
To "fan the frosh."

(See *college.*)

HEAD
Conk; bean; cranium; noodle; egg; dome; onion; his noggin; scratching his poll; sconce; dial; top-piece; he thinks the only thing the head is for is to keep their ears apart.

(See *hair, mouth, nose, lips, ears, eyes, eyebrows.*)

HEADACHE
Non-stop headache; if the bells in my head would stop ringing; my head feels like a bucket of rivets; my head feels like a Russian samovar; I've got a head full of hornets.

(See *sick.*)

HEADLINES
With all this Page One news breaking; for five days this subject has been to the entire United States a smear of printer's ink; extra editions of the newspapers would scream at us; the papers spread the thing on page one; and bitten by first-page hounds.

(See *newspaper, news.*)

HEALTHY
As healthy as a battleship; disgustingly healthy.
See *feel good*.)

HEART (Names)
His ticker; a bum ticker.
(See *body*.)

HEART
Had a pawnbroker's heart; give her your heart to tear; my heart thumped at my ribs; his heart played a soft obligato; his heart turned a somersault; his heart was making twenty-seven knots; build a fire under his heart; her heart gave a little flutter; heart went plop-plop; suddenly his heart, which had been tumbling like a ball on a fountain; wear and tear on his heart; his heart stuttered.
(See *emotions, sentimental*.)

HEART BREAKER
Plucking heart strings; he fancies himself as a ladies' gentleman; a number one sheik; who caused so many feminine hearts of all vintages to flutter; gay Lothario; gigolo; young cavaliers; a matrimonial "catch" of the season; modern Casanova; Don Juan; can cause such a heaving of feminine bosoms; and ladies have been known to simulate the panther when coming within range of him; these virtuosi of love; I gobble up lovely girls.
(See *love*.)

HEAT
When the weather gets hot you can realize the wisdom of the Chinese who wear their shirt tails outside their trousers; it was so hot the lead in our pencils began to melt; it was so hot that eggs fried in four minutes on Pennsylvania Avenue's tar; it was so hot it was melting the enamel off the kitchen sink; one of those days when the heat story is on the front page; it was so hot folks were pulling boiled catfish out of the ponds; it was so hot the cows were giving evaporated milk; hot as hell; stick a fork in me, I think I'm done; the mercury was shooting up.
(See *hot, sunburn*.)

HEAVEN
The pearly gates.
(See *God, religious*.)

HEAVY
The parcels were as heavy as though filled with scrap iron and telephone books.
(See *clumsy, awkward, weight, fat*.)

HEDGE
Pussyfoot about.
(See *evasive, avoid*.)

HELL
Going to hell in carload lots, collect.
(See *religious, devil, punish*.)

HELP
To aid and abet; he expects me to rally round; he doesn't butter my parsnips; a dog in the kitchen desires no company (prov.); to stooge for him; throw him a parachute.
(See *co-operate, support, remedy*.)

HELPER
Flunky.
(See *assistant*.)

HENPECK
He was afraid to step on a rug without getting a permit; she had him buffaloed; henpecked; she didn't 'arf put me through the 'oop; a fall guy.
(See *wife, scold*.)

HEREDITY
In a fiddler's house all are dancers.
(See *inherit*.)

HERO

The nation apotheosized him; acclaim for the conquering hero; an Algeresque hero; the satellites about him.

(See *courage, man, brave, ideal man.*)

HICK

He looked as if he had just climbed out of a hay mow; he looked to her like a bushel of oats; these fresh-water geniuses; he looks like he just climbed out of a tree; yokelism; a plow boy; a country jake; hinterland hot-sports; a crossroads philosopher; in his store clothes; hadn't removed the oats from his whiskers; Mr. Dubuque; gullible peasants from Oneonta and Painted Post; bucolic environment; come from the forest primeval; the hickiest of hicks; shoots the works in the barber shop; he hung around the cracker barrel; he had straw in his hair.

(See *farmer.*)

HICK TOWN

The Michigan Dunes; Hinterland; Hickory Corners; Tank Town; The Tall Grass; a Flag-stop; Jerkwater Town; One-horse Town; The Tall Celery; Whistle S t o p s; Tall-corn Country.

(See *town.*)

HIDE

She had cached it away; he hid out in the Jersey dunes; to hide under the rainspout.

(See *disappeared, lost.*)

HIGH

It reached the high-water mark; up above the world so high.

(See *tall.*)

HIGH CLASS

Bang-up; parlor brand of insincerity; 18-karat newspaperman; snooty;classy; up stage; top-flight gangster; a high-hat reception; in the Rococo manner; a silk-hat way of.

(See *society.*)

HIPS (Female)

The soft hips swaying rhythmically; the delectable roundness of her hips; the curved lushness of her hips; a deliciously intoxicating quiver to her hips.

(See *curves, body.*)

HIRED MAN

We had a hired man to take care of the cows and to brush the dew off the grass.

(See *farmer.*)

HISTORY

The very Uncivil War.

(See *past.*)

HIT

Pops him over the conk; socks; delivered a haymaker; hit him with everything but the bell; it sounded like a hog getting hit on the head with an axe; the lights went out; took a nose dive; kissed the canvas; being pasted around by; bounced his fist against his silky skin; commit mayhem; socking him; gave him a good smack across the vestibule; took the hatchet and gave him a larrup of it across the neck; he boffs him over the skull; clout him; whanged Jake on the nose; felt as if a pile driver had hit him in the diaphragm; belabor him about the head with.

(See *blow, fight.*)

HIT (To make a)

It rang the bell; clicked; it was a literary bull's-eye; she panicked him.

(See *success.*)

HOBBY

Take up fretwork; to collect Byzantine pewter; mediaeval hat-stands of Icelandic sword sticks; collecting tail feathers of rhinoceri; study of filling-station architecture; collection of bent china; assistant sub-hobby to keep from going stale on his hobby; counting the cracks in the cement sidewalks as I walk along; many retired business men, otherwise quite sane, go in for collecting things; there is hardly anything which is not being collected somewhere at this moment by a retired business man; to collect other people's umbrellas; dabbles in; passion for raising petunias.

(See *amateur, postage stamp collecting.*)

HOCKEY

The game either ends in a draw or in a hospital; there's one nice thing about being a hockey player, you meet all the best nurses; those razor-blades on his feet; goal-keeper, the poor goat, padded out like an old Michelin tire advertisement.

(See *games.*)

HOLE

A broken sack will hold no corn (prov.); a hole the size of the Hudson tunnel; this hole is a dimple compared with the grand canyon.

(See *empty, opening.*)

HOLLYWOOD

Where you can get anything from a cup of coffee to a mountain by paying a down payment of a few cents; Hollywood is only an artery of Broadway; the City of Impossible Distances; cinema capital.

(See *movies, actress.*)

HOME (Names for)

Diggings; bailiwick; stamping ground; habitat; menage; anchorage; the old homestead; hut; flea bag; snug little billet; the parental rooftree; roost; domicile; harem; seraglio; paternal domicile; nest; shanty; dugout; kennel; sty; wigwam; coop; igloo; love nest; fold; this little Eden.

(See *house, apartment.*)

HOME

A place to go when all the other joints are closed; she went home to her vacuum sweeper; a man's house is his castle; Home Sweet Home; in the bosom of his family.

(See *living.*)

HONEST

On the level; on the up and up; Diogenes and his lantern.

(See *conscientious, genuine.*)

HONORS

Gallops off with the honors; stewing in the glories of; to carry the torch for the Allisons.

(See *win, prize, reward.*)

HOPE

There's always tomorrow; she nugged every bit of it to her breast; he that lives in hope danceth without music.

(See *anticipate, expect, confidence.*)

HOPELESS

Abandon hope all ye who enter here; incurable as as amputated thumb; as hopeless as the cow that falls in love with a Bull Durham advertisement.

(See *desperate, melancholy.*)

HORROR

Hold up their aristocratic digits in holy horror; clicked her tongue twice at such doings.

(See *fear, frightened.*)

HORSEBACK RIDING

Repeating the process daily until one's money, time, or trouser-seat gives out; what you do when you have a horse is you get some boots and sit on top of the horse, and the horse goes, over hill, over dale; to ride a horse, one of the most unstable creatures known; he didn't know one end of the horse from the other; the outside of a horse is good for the inside of a man.

(See *travel*.)

HORSES

Horses, horses, it's a w o n d e r he wouldn't cry "wolf" once in a while; mustang; its tail looked as if the moths had been in it; he grew up to fit a horse's back; a sorry-looking piece of horse flesh; he jabs the Mexican spurs into the foamy flank of his noble cayuse; plug; nag; stallion; that horse is spavined, blind and got the staggers, also has the heaves; a good general utility nag; horse, caracoling with much vigor; he is a nice tame old dromedary; the clippity clop of the horses on the cobbles; and tells dobbin to giddap, and dobbin is giddaping very nicely; I set spurs to my steed; my mount; my rangy beast; swishing their tails at us in pleasant greeting; he swung off his bay gelding; a melancholy and ribby horse; a horse between his knees; clumpety-clumpety; horseflesh; a thousand pounds of horseflesh; that bag of bones; what is the power you have over horses, I guess it must be a horsepower; a good horse never lacks a saddle; decrepit nag.

(See *race-track*.)

HOSPITAL

He was horizontal in the hospital; he was due to escape from the hospital; he is in a pesthouse suffering from smallpox; hauled off to the hospital;
"vagrants, peddlers and fathers not admitted"; bed-pan alley.

(See *operation, doctor, diseases*.)

HOT

It was so hot the woodwork was breaking out in large blisters.

(See *heat*.)

HOT DOGS

I'm going to see a man about a bunch of hot dogs.

(See *food*.)

HOTEL (High Class)

Stowed ourselves away at the Riverside Hotel; ensconced at the Park Lane hostelry, where they will soak you fifty cents for a cup of coffee; you could get a very good second-hand automobile for the price of a modern dinner there; the rooms fitted its tenants as the cell of a honeycomb fits a bee; felt quite comfortable, right down to its monogrammed guest soap.

(See *living, apartment*.)

HOTEL (Lower type)

The fly hotel; a run down hotel; the biltmore—built more like a stable; gentlemen-only lodging houses; a flea bag.

(See *saloon*.)

HOUSE

House is his castle; a glorified barn; a modest thing of about thirty-four rooms.

(See *home*.)

HOUSE (Things around the house)

Receipted grocery bills; a busted flashlight.

(See *furniture, things*.)

HOUSES (Work around)

To air-condition the garbage can.

(See *work*.)

HOUSES (Dirty)

The house would have fallen down if the spider webs and cockroaches had been removed.

(See *clean*.)

HUMAN NATURE

Human nature continues to do business even during a cataclysm.

(See *character, disposition*.)

HUMILIATION

I felt like a sardine in that big house; you get taken down a peg; her nose scraped her shoes; then there would be nothing left but to crawl into a hole and pull the hole in after him; to take some of the starch out of his dress shirt; a comedown socially; how the gods must laugh; oh, the ignominy of it all; how hath the mighty fallen.

(See *ashamed*.)

HUMOR

Let the quips fall where they may; I had meant to fling off several bright, spontaneous quips; witticism; he uses a sledgehammer with which to make his humorous touches; up in the tall brackets of humor; we had to diddle him.

(See *fun, amuse*.)

HUMORIST

He was top fool; gagmen, the wet-nurses of wit; he occasionally gets a good cry out of my humorous articles.

(See *clowns, joker*.)

HUNCH

A copper-riveted hunch.

(See *idea, notion*.)

HUNGER

I'm so hungry I could eat an old straw hat, if it had enough mayonnaise slopped over it; I was so hungry that I could have eaten a stalled ox; had the expression of a pup hearing his dish rattled in the kitchen; hungry maw; they were so hungry they could have dined on unicorn stew and breakfasted off dodo eggs; one time I was so hungry I thought the three balls in front of Uncle Moses' store were apples; to stay the pangs of hunger; hungry dogs will eat dirty puddings.

(See *appetite*.)

HUNTING

A crackling gallop across good country with a jolly fine kill at the end of it, what, what?; hark forrad, yoicks, tallyho, I mean to say, and all that sort of thing; riding to hounds; fifty people running wild over the countryside; rides to the hounds with the best of them; a sport where red-faced lads in pink coats rush madly around yelling "Tally Ho"; as he approaches the kill; hunt by yourself in the privacy of your own home for such small game as keys, collar-studs, and last month's gas bill; "We're going ahead to see the kill. Yoicks! Yoicks! As one who enjoys a good yoick as much as the next fellow"; the landed gentry from the neighboring estate joined; "Oh, a-hunting we will go, a-hunting we will go—Tantivy, tantivy, tantivy. A-hunting we will go"; fetch down a pheasant with a bean shooter at 50 paces.

(See *country, fishing*.)

HURRAH

Banzai; huzzas; there was great hooray about; 32 cheers for; hurroo; yipee.

(See *cheers, applause*.)

HURRY

To hump himself with the spinach;

she shot him up to his room; to dress like a streak; hustle out; dash into; step on the gas; hop to it; there was a grand scramble; harum-scarum; shake a leg; I'm practically on my doorstep; leaped into his clothes; make it snappy; to make a long story shrink; get a wiggle on; are you in a sweat; he used to eat his breakfast at night to save time in the morning.
(See *darting, haste, speed*.)

HURT (Spiritually)

Cut me like a knife; his spirit was dented; he got it where the chicken got the axe; how the gods must laugh.
(See *damage, sad*.)

HUSBAND

He's away grouse-shooting in the highlands; spouse; was just a piece of handy furniture in his own home; it is a well-known fact that husbands chew holes in socks and pull off a button a day; he had "wife trouble"; her future life-helpmate; her liege-lord; breadwinner; men are all different, but husbands are all alike; he became her slave for life; friend husband; the pilot of my ship of life; her man.
(See *marriage, henpeck*.)

HYPOCRITE

Pharisees.
(See *deceive, lie*.)

I

ICE-SKATING
Those razor blades on his feet.
(See *winter*.)

IDEA
Take it apart to see what makes it tick; an idea struck him right between the fifth and sixth drink; an idea was percolating around in the old bean; idea hit me like a ton of bricks; was a beehive of ideas; to plug the idea; his brainchild; his mind gave birth to an idea; he is too full of ideas, they break out in a rash; he sells me a goofy idea; idea burst into flower; smitten with the idea; pet idea; hunch; notion; thought; wrinkle; that gives the whole meat in the cocoanut; brainstormed the idea; sophomoric idea.
(See *hunch, imagination; opinion, think*.)

IDEA (Poor)
Ideas of the sort propounded are not likely to cling to the mind and cause convulsions.
(See *nonsense*.)

IDEAL (Man)
A composite of Lord Byron, Achilles, Jack Dempsey, Sir Gallahad, John D. Rockefeller, and Mussolini.

IDENTIFICATION
For all we know he is the Marx Brothers; all cats are grey in the dark.
(See *recognize*.)

IDLER
He that does nothing finds helpers (prov.); they toil not, neither do they spin.
(See *wasting time*.)

IF
I warn you just in case; perchance; if——, then I'm the Swedish Ambassador's aunt; if there's any fun in that, I am the eldest unmarried daughter of a retired Swiss Admiral; if ——, then I'm a full-blooded weasel; if ——, then I'm the rear end of a horse; if if's and and's were pots and pans.
(See *although*.)

ILLITERATE
She can't read, she saves old magazines and makes paper hats out of them; he never saw the inside of a schoolhouse.
(See *stupid, dumb*.)

IMAGINATION
Stretch his imagination to the snapping point.
(See *daydreams, dreamer*.)

IMITATE
To double for.
(See *copy*.)

IMMEDIATELY
Right off the reel; at one fell swoop; wanted him to answer on the button; right off the bat.
(See *next to, quickly,*)

IMMORAL
They are not immoral, they are unmoral; she'll be my girl with all the trimmings.
(See *sin, vice, sex*.)

IMPATIENCE
Kept him on the tenterhooks of ex-

pectations; gills working up and down with impatience; feet began to twitch with impatience; keep your shirt on; such a difficult witness that he would have had the recording angel coughing behind his hand; she did a fandango of impatience.

(See *enthusiasm, haste.*)

IMPORTANCE
Wherever he sat was the head of the table; he dominated the scene; something to write home about; it is not to be sneezed at; the very life-blood; the old sachem.

(See *great, big-shot, valuable.*)

IMPOSSIBLE
He looks around for a new rabbit to take out of a hat; you can't buy caviar in the five and ten; after that the deluge; to ask a cobblestone to waltz; like reaching up into the sky in an effort to pull down the comets by their tails; you cannot rebuild the tracks while the trains are running; you can't tear up confetti; one might just as well try to improve the weather by tampering with the mercury in a barometer; a dead bee maketh no honey (prov.); a fog cannot be dispelled with a fan; they said the Panama Canal was impossible; you can't play tennis without a racket; a pint can't hold a quart; a mouse must not think to cast a shadow like an elephant; a man cannot whistle and drink at the same time; a man cannot spin and reel at the same time.

(See *difficult, hopeless.*)

IMPOSSIBLE (Similes)
As impossible as drawing an all-spade hand at bridge; as finding a bottle of Scotch at a W. C. T. U. meeting; as pushing the waters of Niagara back to their source with a broom; as impossible as vamping a pile of discarded oyster shells; like trying to persuade an African elephant to enter a smallish dog-kennel; impossible, like eating fried eggs without a napkin.

(See *absurd.*)

IMPRESSION (To make an)
Punctures his shell; wooing them; make himself solid with her father; it gave him "face"; show-window stuff; you must approach him on his good ear; dazzling them; doing my very best to look like a vice-chairman at least; the gal gits me here; are ace-high with her; put his best foot forward; when the statement has sunk well in.

(See *show-off, effective.*)

IMPRESSION (Poor)
He didn't rate one-two-three with her.
(See *failure.*)

INACTIVE
A stage (the theatre) that has seemed to be edging toward the morgue; comes out of his cocoon.

(See *quiet, idler, lazy.*)

INCOME TAX
A certain amount of income taxery is necessary.
(See *tax, customs.*)

INCREASE
His losses swelled; the ignorance of parent-hood increases as the cube of the root and the square of the distance.

(See *expand, raise.*)

INCURABLE
As incurable as an amputated thumb.
(See *hopeless.*)

INDEPENDENT
The testiest of stars.
(See *freedom.*)

INDEX
An old thesaurus with a very cross index.
(See *point.*)

INDIANS
Present day Indians will not go on the warpath without their valises; John Smith amused a hostile band of Indians by showing them his compass and new suspenders; his moccasins were down at the heels; Sitting Bull; Kicking Bird; lo, the poor Indian—squaw, papooses, tepees; Aborigines; Rain-in-the-face; our red brothers.
(See *American, foreigner.*)

INDIGESTION
Blushing after meals.
(See *cooking, belch.*)

INDIGNATION
Sophomoric indignation.
(See *anger, temper.*)

INDISCREET
Discretion flung to the four winds.
(See *fool, reckless.*)

INDULGE
Wallow; dabbles in fortune telling.
(See *spoil.*)

INEFFICIENCY
The world is like a board with holes in it, and the square men get into the round holes; clear the brain (or system) of cobwebs; your quantity is much better than your quality; like tossing a drowning man a toothpick.
(See *weak.*)

INEVITABLE
As inevitable as snake eyes to a crap shooter; as Anthony had his Cleopatra; as inevitable as the crop of kittens at our house.
(See *necessary.*)

INEXPERIENCE
Green; greenhorn; a tenderfoot; he must have learned it from a mail-order house.
(See *amateur, begin.*)

INFERIORITY COMPLEX
Sub-cellar complex.
(See *psychology.*)

INFLUENCE
A man in the know; some special drag; he was in solid.
(See *reputation.*)

INFORMED
In the know.
(See *knowledge.*)

INGRATITUDE
Has been biting the hand that feeds him, or, at least, he's been snapping at it a little.
(See *selfish.*)

INHERIT (Character)
A throwback to some former golfless generation; a good cow may have an ill calf (prov.) .
(See *heredity.*)

INQUISITIVE
All these will be an open book to the Paul Prys of science.
(See *busybody.*)

INSANE ASYLUM
Completed his junior year at the state asylum for the insane; Nut Foundry; cuckoo house; the laughing academy.
(See *crazy.*)

INSEPARABLE
Inseparable as a pair of pants.
(See *close, together.*)

INSIDE
Boring from within; once inside the portals; in the very bowels of.
(See *entrance.*)

INSIDE STUFF
Give me the low-down.
(See *secret.*)

INSIST
I'll trouble you to.
(See *demand.*)

INSTALLMENTS
So passionately addicted to payments.
(See *pay, part of.*)

INSTRUMENTS (Brass)
A complicated brass affair which is worn round the body and resembles an amateur's attempt at simple plumbing; instruments of which one end is inserted in the mouth and blown violently into, so that the required noise has no option but to escape hurriedly at the other, seaward, extremity; the perpetual blowing and fingering involved was liable to produce corns on the lungs, knots in the larynx, dents in the diaphragm, and a tendency to bubble harshly when annoyed; those big brass instruments contribute nothing but loud grumphing noises whenever they feel so disposed.
(See *cornet, trombone, saxophone.*)

INSULT
A man threw me about forty feet, I asked him if he meant anything personal about that; slur; the words cut like the lash of a knout; cut him to the quick.
(See *hurt, ridicule.*)

INTELLECTUAL
Low-grade parlor bunk; he knew all about Ming pottery and Blue Delft China; Haute Monde; infrallectuals (lower than); the literati of our day; ultra-sophisticated booksy people; savants; cognoscenti; literati.
(See *genius, philosophy.*)

INTENTIONS
Hell is paved with good intentions.
(See *plan.*)

INTERESTED
I sit in wide-eyed adenoidal vacuity when she talks; listened to him with his mouth open; everything outside of baseball was just ping-pong to him; he was so steamed up over this stranger; everyone hung on his words; society was on its ear; he dabbles in fortune-telling.
(See *curiosity.*)

INTERESTING
Little tidbits; hot stuff; more interesting than a barrel of monkeys.
(See *entertainment.*)

INTERFERE
Muscled in; treading on the tail of; poach on one another's preserves; she seldom sticks in her oar; to horn in; upset that Washington applecart.
(See *opposition.*)

INTERIOR DECORATION
Whether a maroon or an eggplant rug would look best with yellow walls.
(See *artistic, furniture.*)

INTERRUPTION
Interregnum.
(See *interfere, discontinue.*)

INTERVIEW
Pray be seated; the air became so thick with interviewing.
(See *interview, conference.*)

INTOXICATED
Up to his eyebrows in liquor; feeling his drinks; sloshed to the ears; they were boiled.
(See *drunk.*)

INTRIGUE
Back-room intrigue.
(See *plot, scheme.*)

INTRODUCTION
Send-in; the guy who gave me an "in" with her.
(See *acquainted with.*)

INTRUDE
Muscled in.
(See *interfere.*)

INVENTION
The inventor of the water cress; gadget; invent new uses for old typewriter ribbons, or how to make Pullman-car windows open easily; dingus; doodads.
(See *find, discovered.*)

INVESTIGATION
Something in need of formaldehyde.
(See *search.*)

INVESTMENT
Buying an interest in a Siberian soap-mine.
(See *stock market.*)

INVITATION
Have their cognomens festooned on the invitation cards; to wangle an invitation; come on, smell our kitchen sink; come and take a dish of tea with us some time; an invite; she crashed in; women cut their throats and drown themselves in bathtubs when they're not invited.
(See *request, party.*)

IRISH
A harp; a mick; paddy; God takes care of boys and Irishmen (prov.).
(See *foreigner.*)

IS
It smacks of an elopement; is what I am practically nothing else but.
(See *becomes.*)

ISSUE
Spew forth memoranda.
(See *produce.*)

IS THAT SO?
Pish tush; tut tut; thasso?; that's definite, is it?; top that.
(See *yes, real.*)

ITALY
At Naples, entirely surrounded by mandolins, fruit and lovely ladies; sunshine and spaghetti; wops; bilious blend of green and yellow; dago; Italy, where they sing all day and go to the opera at night; "Mamma Mia"; Italians have a low boiling point, they steam readily but cool off quickly.
(See *foreigner.*)

J

JACK-OF-ALL-TRADES
A jackass of all trades.
(See *talent, hired man.*)

JAIL
Had completed his sophomore year at the state prison; taken to the jug; the cooler; calaboose; in the pokey; hoosegow; hauled off to the nearest lockup; lug her away to the ——; cooling his heels in the clink; a few months in gaol; managed to get sprung before the jurors got home; they gave him five years in the shade.
(See *prison.*)

JANITOR
The yanitor.
(See *doorman.*)

JAPS
The Nipponese; the land of the Shoguns; Japan is a little boiler with too big a fire underneath, some day there is bound to be an explosion; these slant-eyed folk; the Japs have something up their kimono sleeves.
(See *foreigner.*)

JAW
Anvil-jawed; galley-prow jaws; lantern-jawed.
(See *face, chin.*)

JAZZ
Jazz spurted into the room.
(See *dancing, music.*)

JEALOUSY
Those who would pull me from my pedestal; he went green, absolutely green; tear his hair out; the green-eyed monster.
(See *envy.*)

JEW
Semite; this little Yid Kid.
(See *religious.*)

JEWELRY
Ransacked her jewel caskets; bejewelled lady; cheap jewelry which is nothing much but slum; was given vigorously to jewelry, which they wore at random; festooned with jewels.
(See *diamond, earrings, ring, pearls.*)

JOB
I was riding the see-saw of theatrical ad soliciting; I had a job, something to eat and the price of clean laundry; every man should be given a chance to select the job he intends to make a failure of; daily grind; one of the lesser cogs in the great wheel; a job filling ink wells in a bank; a lousy salary and the privilege of working twelve or fourteen hours a day; a job wangled for him.
(See *work, professionals.*)

JOKE
Wheezes that would set them all cackling; it didn't raise a titter; a gag; petrified circus jokes; no slouch of a joke; got off a pretty good joke; Phoenician joke; prehistoric joke; japes; whimsies; jokes already told by Bunker Hill and Burdock; toss out gay jests; how the gods must laugh; a few hearty quips; coarse jibes; risqué jokes; double-entendre; the farmer's-daughter joke; pale magenta anecdotes.
(See *humor, fun.*)

JOKE (Practical)
Putting an eel in Slimey's pants; slip

a hot stove-lid into his chair; placed a number of sharp fish bones in her bed; fools set stools for wise men to stumble at; pulling chairs from under maiden aunts at family reunions; to slip a live watersnake or a mud turtle into somebody's bed, or a dead fish (if he knew the party had high blood-pressure); the butt of rude and unkind pranks; insert dead cats beneath his drawing room floor; he tried to ring himself at his office, but he was always out or else the line was engaged; put itching powder in the wife's corsets; astounded the socialites present at the swanky affair by dropping eggs into their pockets and then smashing them by affectionate hugs.

(See *amuse*.)

JOKER
Prankster; funster.

(See *humorist, clowns*.)

JUDGE
A tête-a-tête with a judge; had been an ornament to the judiciary for thirty years; and before the rustling of his gown had died away; justice was enthroned.

(See *courts, lawyer*.)

JUMP
Out hops; jumped like a gazelle; to do a Douglas Fairbanks; jumping like grease out of a frying pan.

(See *leaps*.)

JUNGLE
Far off in the brake a cougar scream-ed.

(See *Nature*.)

JUNK
Cast-off gods waiting to be consigned to their Valhalla.

(See *useless*.)

JURY
Twelve good men and true.

(See *courts*.)

K

KEEPER
A governess of some trained fleas.
(See *chaperone*.)

KICK
Booted him out of the Casino.
(See *thrown out*.)

KIDNAP
Shanghai them; m a d e away with Lotta; the snatch.
(See *forced*.)

KILL
Rub out; blow his brains out; she "did in" her husband with a pitchfork; liquidate him; plowed the old man under; killed him dead; I want to drill him full of holes; gave him the business; someone cooled off Mr.——; outs with the old thing, and gives it to him as follows; bang, bang; he was done to death; finally succumbing to a baptism of lead; plugged him in the bridgework; the deceased gentleman had deliberately placed his head in the way of bullets from Daisie's gun, just to embarrass her; killed him deader than boiled haddock; I shoot you so dead you stink before you touch the ground; he brings him back as stiff as a herring; you'll go on that lead diet; you'll be buzzards' food; if you do, your girl friend will start eating bullets; as tough an hombre as ever bisected a gunman; they employed a little shotgun arithmetic and put a minus-sign before him.
(See *execution, murder*.)

KIND (Gentle)
The angel of mercy; with freedom towards all and malice towards none; he hasn't an ill-natured bone in his body; one of nature's noblemen; filled his heart with the milk of human kindness; a dog will not cry if you beat him with a bone (prov.); noblesse oblige; Mark Twain once said his mother was so kind she would warm the water when she drowned kittens.
(See *charity, friendly*.)

KISS
Kisses taste better at close range; a chaste salute; they went through the travesty of a kiss; it was like kissing an old cab horse; he kissed a girl once and they had to pry him loose with a crow-bar; his kiss against her hungry mouth seemed to be setting her afire; he found her heart-shaped lips; no more would his lips be liquid fire on hers; pressing his kisses upon her yielding flesh; ooze me a slobber; crushing the wine-red nectar from her ripe, moist lips; he fused his mouth to hers; pressed his own quivering lips down on their damp, sweeter-than-honey succulence; his clinging mouth sent rivers of fire through all her body; his lips began swift journeys over the lovely curves of her lips.
(See *embrace, love*.)

KITCHEN
The scullery.
(See *cook, food*.)

KNIFE
Boiled potatoes and Julius Caesar both wound up on the end of a knife; a poniard; to manage it without losing a thumb; dirk; a broadax; running his thumb playfully over the

edge of his meat ax; dagger; wield a mean stiletto; scimitar.

(See *carving*.)

KNIGHTHOOD

His winter armor and his summer armor.

(See *courteous*.)

KNIT

Purled her way through to the bitter end; knitting away; she drops a mean stitch.

(See *sweater*.)

KNOTS

Seaman's knots.

(See *complicated*.)

KNOW (Not to)

I wouldn't know the Sherman Act if it passed me on the street, unless it wore a white carnation.

(See *dumb, stupid*.)

KNOWLEDGE

The facts of life; to thirst for knowledge.

(See *education, understand*.)

L

LADY-KILLER
All meat's to be eaten, all maid's to be kissed; making a play for the ladies.

(See *girl-crazy, man.*)

LANDLORD
"Stood him off" from month to month.

(See *own.*)

LANDLUBBERS
In terror of their lives while riding in a rowboat on the six-inch waters of Central Park's lake; landlubbing hearties; his nautical experience is limited to ferry rides; he doesn't know the difference between a sextant and a hydrant.

(See *seasickness.*)

LANGUAGE
Lingo; housemaid's jargon; argot; raw-boned language; in language that sounded like a rasp of the thesaurus; the prose is neatly washed, ironed and starched; his overheated, imaginative style; your metaphors are slightly mixed; mutilating the English.

(See *grammar, speech, slang.*)

LARGE
Brobdingnagian; a whacking great Alsatian; the behemoths of city traffic; Leviathan; as large as Gog and Magog; elephantine; elephant-sized volume; Texas-sized hot dog.

(See *big, tall, fat.*)

LATE (Appointments)
She'd be late for her own funeral; I've never known either of 'em to be more than ten seconds late for a free meal; laggards.

(See *finally.*)

LATE (In the evening)
It's getting to be all hours.

(See *late.*)

LATE HOURS
No one ever went to bed; I've always been home well ahead of the milk.

(See *party, celebrating.*)

LATER
Anon.

(See *behind.*)

LAUGH
She laughed her L y n n Fontanne laugh; a big abdominal laugh; he was laughing fit to split his face; makes me snicker; titter; chortle; cachinnate; hawhaw; he laughed my head off; he laughed his pants off; he was in stitches; a titter ran through; he laughed in his beer; laughed like a paper bag bursting; rolled in the aisle; sniggered audibly; laughed his heartless laugh; broke out into a glad ripple of childish laughter; laughing a low, gurgling laugh; fall to pieces with mirth; burst into wild hilarity; he was an easy and extemporaneous laughter; an honest mid-section laugh; wound up with a corrosive laugh; almost had hysterics; who broke into treble titters; she laughed (Hanh! Hanh! Hanh!); a man with a bull-roar laugh; "Ho, ho, ho," laughs Tim; laughed all over the place; laugh till his belly hurt; and there she sat, stuffing her handkerchief into her mouth and nearly going pop; I ain't had such a laugh since old man Jim—my dead husband—fell offin a beer truck; apoplectic with laughter; sending them

into gales of silent laughter; horse-laugh.
(See *smile, grin.*)

LAUGH AT
The merry ha-ha; why, they'd laugh me right out of the knit-goods game.
(See *fun.*)

LAUGHTER
Vitamin L (laughter); the young lady, after bursting sixteen sequins off her evening gown trying not to laugh; her laugh was like raindrops on moss; "went into gales of laughter, har, har, har"; rib-busting laughter; a laugh that makes dogs drop their bones; salvos of laughter; he wrung a laugh from them; he that laughs on Friday will weep on Sunday (prov.); laughter that will make you split your doubtlet and briskin; body-heaving laughter.
(See *gay, wit.*)

LAUNDRY
Pulls off a button a day; a button-ripper-off machine.
(See *clean.*)

LAW
To do a little dental work that will put "teeth" in this law; making a mockery of the law.
(See *bill, congress, government.*)

LAWNMOWER
Argue with a 12-inch lawnmower.
(See *hired man.*)

LAWYER
He whereased and thereuponed; as he brief-cases through life; swung out his shingle; always glad to meet a lawyer with his hands in his own pockets; always count your fingers after shaking hands with an attorney; making a mockery of the law.
(See *courts, judge.*)

LAWYER (Names for)
Mouthpiece; a "lips"; a counselor; an attorney and counselor-at-law; solicitor-in-chancery, and proctor-in-admiralty; legal lights; these legal johnnies; barrister.
(See *Supreme Court.*)

LAZY
Throw off that air of ennui and languor; dolce far niente; he was sitting on his hands; sits all day and plays catch-thumbs; the old glad light was not in her eye; lazing; he dawdled for an hour; drool around; rigor mortis about to set in; a stranger to toil and spinning; get the cobwebs out of your hair; what are you daddlin' around here for?; he spit in his palm and did nothing; to mooch around; fried pigeon doesn't fly into your mouth; human vitality at its lowest ebb; just the right degree of loungitude and lassitude; he called him Theory because he so seldom works; a lazy horse must have a sharp spur; he was in a coma all the time; his dog used to lean against the wall to bark.
(See *idler, wasting time.*)

LEADER
A Moses who had led his people into the Promised Land.
(See *chief.*)

LEAP
Leap like a jumping bean.
(See *jump.*)

LEARN
Soak up; take pointers from; instructive to the mind and fertilizing to the beard; still in the embryonic or what-do-I-do-next stage.
(See *knowledge.*)

LEAVE

Pulling up stakes; making tracks for home; sent her packing off to; to fold up your tent like an Arab and silently steal away; took French leave of her; so he picked up and left.

(See *good-bye.*)

LECTURER

Professional ear-benders.

(See *speech.*)

LEFT

Two lefts do not make a right; distinguished right from left, port from starboard; he doesn't know left from right or wrong.

LEFT-HANDERS

Southpaw; should one-arm lunches be lefthanded?

(See *baseball.*)

LEGAL

Get me a habeas corpus.

(See *Supreme Court.*)

LEGS

(See *feet.*)

LEISURE

Eaten of the sweet fruits of leisure.

(See *idler, wasting time.*)

LET'S

How's for taking.

(See *will.*)

LETTER (Ending)

Yours till the anti-saloon league recommends whiskey for the flu.

(See *writer.*)

LETTER

A written and grammatical request; writing bales of soggy letters; Aunt Mad's semiannual letter; love and lilies from; it was letter perfect; billet-doux; valentine; missive; epistle; took some paper from her escritoire and; I hate to write to you in this tone of voice; he apologized for the long letter, saying he didn't have time to write a brief letter.

(See *telephone, cable.*)

LETTERS (Alphabet)

Y is a V with a tail on it.

(See *knowledge, learn.*)

LETTERS (Business)

In reply to your letter of the Umpth Inst.

(See *business.*)

LICKED

He ran off with his tail at half mast; you're sunk.

(See *defeat, downfall.*)

LICKINGS

A good, durable birch rod; cured by repeated applications of a large, flat hand; licking for pulling chairs from under maiden aunts at family reunions; I'll razor-strop your hide; the heir-conditioning apparatus consisted of a woodshed and a couple of shingles; he had a persuader.

(See *punish, whip.*)

LIE

An 18-karat fibber; your story begins to leak a little; it is a little too stiff to take; whopper; the story was running a bit thin; parsimonious with regard to the facts; play hide-and-seek with the truth; bluff; spoofing; joshing; jollying; stalling; lying canards; boloney; figment of the imagination; he puts some elastic into his truth-telling; to blacken your immortal soul with lies; pusillanimous, lop-eared, blue-nosed liar; he begins tying himself in knots; it has as much truth to it as Jack and the Beanstalk; his specialty was telling lies; Ananias Club; the lie burned the tip of her tongue; a story that would at once extinguish Diogenes' lantern and cause Baron Munchausen to swoon; bent the truth out of shape; the only thing that saves you from being a barefaced liar is your mustache; one should never tell more than the other fellow will believe; there are three kinds of lies—lies, damnable lies and statistics; some men are liars, others have active imaginations; which makes us both out to be Johnny-Come-Latelys.

(See *bunk, deceive.*)

LIFE

And I murmured "Ah, I too have lived"; the outlook for mankind was far from bright; life got you; the ups and downs; to suit every layer of our seven-layer cake of life; the dance of life; youth is a blunder, manhood a struggle, old age a regret; it has done me good to be somewhat parched by the heat and drenched by the rain of life (Longfellow); in the hurly-burly of modern life.

(See *living.*)

LIFE OF THE PARTY

The wag of the party; he stole the show.

(See *lively, humorist.*)

LIGHT

It gave out about as much glare as two sick lightning bugs.

(See *moon.*)

LIKE

To be passionately fond of; to have a yen for; about whom he is plumb daffy; was very much hipped on the lovely Miss Barlow; take a fancy to; is your dish; it's my meat; we ate it up; they had us eating out of their hands; he clicked; she raved on about the canvas; N. Y. is nuts about college wrestlers; a phobia; a mad passion for guns; his life began and ended with baseball; she was cracked about him; so hell-bent for comic effects; dotes on; he is coo-coo about; greater love for the piano hath no man; doesn't love him for himself alone; for which a man would leave home; so enamored of America; are right up my boulevard; something about her made his heart turn a somesault; go for him; goes right off his Ka-Zip about her; I never did fancy it; he is a sucker for authors; I'm a fool for a horse; eat out of her hand; took a shine to Efra; I tumbled for you; will go CurRazy about wrestling; "I care not who makes the nation's laws, if I may"; was sold on him completely; wedded to his auto; was all hopped up about bridge; you're my cookie; is all choked up about some jane; fighting was their meat and drink; he had a crush on this feeding place; he would get up in the middle of the night to play ball; to catch her fancy; I love them to pieces; you're a miniature train fancier; pie fancier; I always went for Dan; it was grist to his mill; form a deep attachment for her soup tureen.

(See *praise, admiration.*)

LIKE (As, similar)

The like of which no one had ever seen; gave her a $10 bill, zip like that.

(See *same, type.*)

LIMITED

A man must plough with such oxen as he hath (prov.); a muzzled cat is no good mouser.

(See *few, scarce.*)

LINERS (Ocean)

Trans-Atlantic gondolas; a few face liftings in the waterfront beauty parlors (repairs); the big houseboat; there is a cocktail shaker for every porthole; a romp across the Atlantic; the swanky section of the ship; strode up the gangplank to the strains of Rule Britannia; for riding the tubs back and forth between here and Europe; and when they hauled in the gangplank; when we reached our mooring.
(See *boat, ocean.*)

LION

Did you ever hear the midnight twitter of the mountain lion?; the old Bert Williams maxim to the effect that there's a difference between the lions now and the lions den; he might take it into his head to chew off my arm.
(See *jungle.*)

LIPS (Male)
His liver-thick lips.
(See *mouth.*)

LIPS (Female)

Slavering lips; with lips like red slashes; her lips were sweet, like dew-dropped rose that waking greets the morn; bright-red, bee-stung lips; red-lipped; crimsoned lips.
(See *kiss.*)

LIQUOR

He was filled with liquor to his eyebrows; he pawned his wife's false teeth to buy liquor; the venerable vintage had lapsed into its second childhood; to run the gamut of beer to whiskey.
(See *whiskey, cocktails.*)

LISP

Lisping in German is rather serious.
(See *stutter, talk.*)

LISTEN (Give an ear to)

Bend an ear; lend me your ear; listen to me with his mouth open; bend back your ears; soak up; get a load of this; but list, list, O list, as Shakespeare says; psst, psst, psst; fall to, old dear; get an earful; he gave ear; she put both ears to the ground at the same time; unfold your ears; has listened too well but not too wisely; listening as if their lives were on his words depending; harken to the words of.
(See *ears.*)

LITERARY
Literary buzz-fuzz.
(See *writer.*)

LITERARY LEADERS
Leader of the beaumonde; the leading light.
(See *intellectual, culture.*)

LITERATURE

Confirmation lists in the Sunday *Times,* the movements of naval vessels, police department orders in the *Herald-Tribune,* arrival of a buyer in Women's Wear; a judge of literature in the raw.
(See *writing.*)

LITTLE

Not one tittle; trivia; not one whit; there were only enough for a sick corporal's squad; you couldn't swing a cat in it; the tiniest suspicion of; teentsy-weentsy smidgin; wee bitsy; a measly hundred dollars; just a mite whimsical; postage stamp size; if there's anything left it won't take over two cents postage; lived there a spell; lean pickings; a leetle bit; would not fill the back of a punctured postage stamp; in 1898, when the industry was just a gleam in somebody's eye; a drop in the bucket; I haven't a smitch of intellect; a splash of travel might help; a slight modicum of bitterness; one infinitesimal fraction of an iota; he had only a spoonful of brains; teeny-weeny; payment in thin driblets; and she not knowing beans about; that sum was chicken feed, a bagatelle, mere pocket change; a two-by-twice sandwich stand; can hold a meeting in a telephone booth; a drop in the bucket; there wasn't a corporal's guard; he would never amount to a hill of beans; doesn't amount to a pinch of salt; all the difference between you can put in your eye; with no more social standing than a fireplug; a little gall spoils a great deal of honey (prov.) ; there wasn't enough French to go round; a little leak will sink a great ship; just a thimbleful; what she knows about it can be put in her vanity case.

(See *small, few.*)

LIVELY

As lively as a barrel of monkeys; as lively as a barrel of fleas.

(See *active, gay.*)

LIVER

Liver in a bad state of repair; you look kind of liverish; a disorganized liver.

(See *body.*)

LIVING (Residence)

Where she is bivouacking; infests a large house; she clutters my doorstep; Macungie, where he wanted to sink his roots.

(See *home.*)

LIVING (a)

On which they depend for beer and skittles; to earn his caviar; a person has a job, something to eat, and the price of clean laundry; all he wants is a chance to make a buck; to sponge off his relatives; they are taking the caviar right out of our mouths.

(See *career, exist.*)

LOBBYIST

Double-jointed lobbyist..

(See *politics.*)

LOBSTER

She began to explore her first lobster.

(See *food.*)

LOCK

A bad padlock invites a picklock.

(See *steal.*)

LODGE

He is a big Rotary man from Wheeling; he was posted for non-payment of dues.

(See *club.*)

LONDON

Was a little late for the first official fog of the season; looks like a gentleman coal-miner after a bath; jolly old London; Lunnon.

(See *England, British.*)

LONESOME

He was as lonesome as a rubber oyster in an oyster stew.

(See *alone.*)

LONG

An egg's age; a coon's age; will keep us unwedded until you are a grey-haired old lady with one tooth; hasn't been here in "yahrs and yahrs"; haven't seen you for donkey's years; a whale of a long time; an aeon passed; had not been disturbed since the sinking of the Maine; to me the next day was ten thousand hours long; a knock-down-and-drag-out argument;

and in less time than it takes to get through on the telephone to some places—that is, by next Saturday; he had known Julia since her milk teeth; a Yankee he'll remain for many a July Fourth; for going on ten years; to the end of time; to make a long story shrink; days without end; back at the time when Paul Revere was still an active memory; a good while a-soaking; he has been acting even since George Arliss was in short trousers; until the bad place freezes over; as she looked when she was a girl, 50 pounds ago.

LONGEVITY
Outwitting the grave.
(See *old man*.)

LONG ISLAND
Longuyland.
(See *New York*.)

LONGSHOREMAN
Dock walloper.
(See *liners*.)

LONG TIME AGO
That was a long time ago, as the political clock ticks; many a ball's been knocked over the fence since then; when the Indians were only about knee high; when the Rock of Gibraltar was only a pebble; since time out of mind; since Sitting Bull was a calf.
(See *past, days old*.)

LOOK
He gave her a look you could have poured on a waffle; goggling at her; took a peek; to gawk at; he shot a look at; have a looksee; takes a gander at; ogles; keeping his eyes glued to the horse's tail; that meets the naked eye; we spotted Jim; gave him the "once over"; poured out a look; a look that would have burned a hole in any other man; I gave him such an old-fashioned look; he draped his eyelids; if you care for records, wrap these up; give her a tumble; gawping at; he used to cock an eye at the heavens; she gave him the double O; get a hunk of that; gape at; give this guy a load of your fiddle; he gave her a sepulchral look; had a look as if he was sucking a lemon; keep your eyes skinned.
(See *see*.)

LOOK AWAY
Tear his eyes from.
(See *avoid*.)

LOOKING FOR
A man walking around with a comb, "I am combing the city for that;" he peeped out; having scanned the terrain narrowly; looked in every direction of the compass; dig up; and the search for one often makes Jason's quest for the Golden Fleece look like a trip to the corner grocery for a pound of coffee.
(See *search*.)

LOSE
Forced to drink the hemlock; it was hari kari for him; given the gate.
(See *defeat*.)

LOST
It is with the snows of yester-year; gone where the woodbine twineth; it looks as if they are gone goslings.
(See *disappeared, away*.)

LOT (End to end)
If they were laid end to end they would reach to where things laid end to end usually reach to; if all the Charleston experts in this city alone

were placed end to end, a good place would be the Delaware river; which laid end to end would be unbearable; if all the students who slept in class were placed end to end they would be much more comfortable; if all the copy that was thrown into the waste can were laid end to end it would reach Shanghai, which would be of very little avail, since they don't read much English there, and are probably lucky at that.

(See *all, complete.*)

LOT (More than)

She had more automobiles than the King of England.

(See *extra.*)

LOTS (Similes)

As plentiful as blackberries; plentiful as bacteria in bad butter.

(See *much.*)

LOTS

No end of; fit to kill; a fistful of francs; bushel of; a carload of; gobs and gobs of; quite a mess of; umpty-ump thousand tons; scads of; flock of your friends; bales of; oodles; he's won tons of blue ribbons; the stories about him were legion; to have shoals of motor cars; quite a raft of; dinners galore; a plague of French restaurants; is being played right and left; a good helping of comedy; the whole caboodle of Pilgrims; a wheen of times; a slew of; reams of description; she could make pots and pots of money; go about distributing gifts in a perfect frenzy; to be a drug on the market; a string of yachts; a barrel of money; he hired show girls in hordes; whole platoons of pigs; battalions of lambs; crawling with; my tooth hurts like the dickens; please the natives no end; a covey of blighters; a battery of waffle irons; shovelfuls of; we

had a right smart bit of snow; in a muckle of trouble; more celebrities than you could shake Alexander Woollcott at; were eaten up with causes; got plenty oiled; he made a slather of silent pictures; heaps.

(See *full of.*)

LOTS OF

Losing money hand over teakettle; just crawling with servants; it's been aching like tarnation; like nobody's business; snowed under with a blizzard of ads; puffed profits; there is an unceasing Niagara of publications; by a vast segment of its citizenry; honeycombed with instances; so many gross of jokes; vibrating like all get out; bushels of letters; an orgy or series of orgies in stamp collecting; amid a snowstorm of press clippings; copiously; it takes a bit of finding; gallons of temperament; a spot of shoveling; he not only knows football but he feels it and eats it; shoveling coal hell bent for leather; the high road to wealth beyond the dreams of whats-a-name; it pleased her no amount; cost a slather to make.

(See *enough, many.*)

LOVE

To go sparking; let's just loaf along and smell the spring night; try to shove me out into the moondrenched rhododendrons with that precious brother of his; in the putty-colored twilight; he laid siege to her heart; managed to persuade Miss Dixie that he was the cream in her coffee; had succumbed to his blandishments; under the gibbous moon; besieging the stronghold of a woman's heart; you and him tripping through the rhubarb; the lovers chasing each other through the California shrubbery; he paid ardent court to; lovey-dovey attitude; he is better than a raw hand at making love; "I've got a frightful

problem on my mind"; "Tell me about her"; fell head over teakettle; it was over Niagara with the pair of them; is all choked up over some jane; moon-struck boy; amorous as a pair of love-birds; bill and coo; profane and sacred love; silly mooning; it's love-love-love; affairs du coeur; love began to burgeon; platonic turned out to be plutonic; she was cracked about him; making plaintive, moon-calf noises; love-spasm; he's ga ga over; he had it bad; he fell head over appetite; the gal gits me here; the smitten male; luscious amours; along the bumpy road of love; giving him all of me; the pash stuff; I love him so much that it's oozing out of my ears.
(See *affection, passion, sex.*)

LOVE (Comparison)
She loves me better than anything else in the world, barring the dog; I love her more than Solomon loved all his wives put together.
(See *wife—a lot of husbands.*)

LOVE (Villain)
A wolf of a man who yearns for her tender flesh.
(See *man-about-town, villain.*)

LOVE (Talk)
"Let us fly, my dove"; those itsy-bitsy ankles of hers; don't worry, lamb; don't sweet-talk me; "Get out of the room, you big yap," she said, "before I go all soft on you, like meringue"; light of my days; you know, cherub; you're my cookie; you're my moment supreme; you great big man of muscle; listen, honey chile.
(See *talking, proposal.*)

LOVE (Symptoms)
Moon too much; for years he had been simmering; the same old tingling, almost electric something, was leaping between them now; I can see the old love light shining so brightly in their eyes; waiting in the garden all trembly-like; got kittenish; romancing about; such sticky love.
(See *desire, sigh.*)

LOVE (Promises)
He was ready to tackle dragons on her behalf.
(See *promises.*)

LOVE (One-sided)
An unrequited yen; he's giving her his soul to do as she likes with and she's just feeding it to the cat; or else she's sitting on a star and he's at the bottom of a well with no ladder handy; love was unrequited; "I wouldn't marry you if the old maid's home yawned at me"; "I wouldn't marry you with a last year's dog license."
(See *old maid.*)

LOVE LETTERS
Billet d'amour; petting by mail.
(See *letter.*)

LOVING CUP
He won enough loving-cups to open a German beerkeller.
(See *prize, honors.*)

LOW
Nadir; at low ebb; America today is in the cellar of the league of faith; he was so low he would have to go to hell in a balloon; I feel so low I could crawl under a caterpillar, carrrying an umbrella; they are so low that if they stand on their heads they would still be unable to reach the level of a snake's belly.
(See *mean, dirty.*)

LOYALTY
I wouldn't be doing right by my little Chester unless.
(See *dependable*.)

LUCK
Darling of the gods; take pot luck; an especially favored child of fortune; it was the kind of luck you get from walking under ladders and lighting three on a match; he was one of those fellows who couldn't poke an umbrella in the ground without getting covered with oil; a windfall; thank my lucky stars; sitting pretty.
(See *chance*.)

LUCKY (Unlucky)
It is unlucky to find a green snake in your bath; it's bad luck, of course, to fall down a hole in the road at midnight.
(See *unfortunate, unhappy*.)

LUNCH
Let's have a spot of lunch.
(See *meal*.)

LURE
Siren songs.
(See *charm*.)

M

MACHINE
Gadget; dingus; doodads.
(See *things*.)

MACHINERY
Mechanical monstrosities.
(See *factory*.)

MACHINERY (Mechanical ability)
I can't even change the ribbon on a typewriter; thinks it an invention of the devil; I couldn't even run a hot dog stand.
(See *engineer*.)

MAGAZINE
An organ; the polite monthlies; and other literary bulwarks of the republic; Satevepost; the long-faced monthlies; slick monthlies.
(See *publishing, news*.)

MAGAZINE ARTICLES
Basket-weaving in the Sudan.
(See *discussion*.)

MAGIC
Abracadabra; legerdemain; mumbo-jumbo; Aladdin's lamp; a piece of celestial hocus-pocus; wave a wand.
(See *mystery*.)

MAGICIANS
Because a man does card tricks he cannot be considered a magician.
(See *trick*.)

MAIDS
It seems all German maids have an aunt in Brooklyn; the last maid handled china like Japan.
(See *servants*.)

MAIL-ORDER COURSE
He that is taught only by himself has a fool for a master—Ben Johnson.
(See *college subjects*.)

MAN (Abstract)
As Shakespeare (?) said, All men are alike, the only point of difference from one to the other is their neckties; a sort of moral and social cockroach; reached man's estate; man starts on a milk diet and finishes on one; it takes more to make a man than a smooth head of hair and a swell pair of dancing legs; that swollen-headed insect, man; Madame De Sevigne said, "The more I see of men, the more I like dogs"; a set of vocal chords wrapped up in a suit of clothes; we male beasts are made of tough meat; man is the only animal that can be skinned more than once.
(See *people*.)

MAN (Names for)
Homo sapiens; a sprout like that dictating to me; chap; a lout; a pretty frightful young slab of damnation; bird; gazabo; bozo; a young sprig; not one of these blisters; some human carbuncle; loon; waited upon by these glossy snips; these customs johnnies; zany; every able-bodied man-jack; duffer; blighter; stinker; such a pish-tush as; the trousered sex; man, that despised yet oddly necessary insect; gay blade; this walrus; this yegg; the brute; a strange Lochinvar came out of the West; the man-in-the-street; a punk named Anderson; the seventh son of a seventh man; a good looking goof; bimbo; this old goat; that big stiff; galoots; mug; gazooney; that fallen arch.
(See *youth, boy, girl, old*.)

MAN (Bad to women)

A seducer; conceited; contemptible; curly-headed parlor snake; he is every other inch a gentleman.
(See *bachelor*.)

MAN (Popular with women)

"Where are all my women? I want women rushing at me"; he is the deb's delight; Jimmy dusted women off the doorsill regularly; had the esoteric magic that makes all the feminine hearts flutter; these Don Juans, Casanovas, Rasputins, and Valentinos; women swooned at his touch or approach.
(See *lady-killer*.)

MAN (Unpopular with women)

You haven't got enough on the ball to play in my league; women have never shown a disposition to make passes at me.
(See *love—villain*.)

MAN (Woman crazy)

Blonde crazy; a fool for a pretty face; he's a sucker for a trim ankle; he loved life, liberty and the pursuit of women.
(See *girl-crazy*.)

MAN (Famous)

A Casanova (Love); Don Juan, Valentinos, Rasputins; a Machiavelli (Crafty); a Lucifer (Proud); a Beau Brummel (Clothes); a Galahad (Courteous); a Lothario (Love); a Macauley (Good memory); a Minerva (Brains); a Croesus (R i c h); an Einstein (Brains); Atilla the Hun (Barbarian); John Dillinger (Crook); Peter Pan (Dreamer); Baron Munchausen (Liar); Ananias (Liar); Diogenes (Honest).
(See *hero*.)

MAN-ABOUT-TOWN

A consistent diner-out; a bon vivant.
(See *dissipate, gigolo, rounder*.)

MANAGE

He'd held the whip over them, making them jump.
(See *control, orders*.)

MANAGEMENT

Under the slight-of-hand management of.
(See *executive, boss*.)

MANDOLIN

To plunk a mandolin.
(See *music*.'

MANICURISTS

Ladies of the nippers; like getting a manicure with a meat-ax; hands required a weekly overhauling.
(See *fingernails, beauty parlor*.)

MANUSCRIPT

Came home to roost; that piece of junk; to receive envelopes bulging with emolument from; what do you think of an author who sends in an MS of 10,000 words and a return envelope about 2 x 4 inches?; filed them away in the waste basket; manuscript was so bad they had to rewrite it before even throwing it in the waste basket; sweet-scented manuscript; such is his genius he doesn't know what a rejection slip looks like.
(See *writing*.)

MANY

With copious gestures.
(See *numerous, crowds*.)

MARGIN (Wall St.)

Hush money.
(See *profits*.)

MARRIAGE

Publish the banns; her sturdy ankles have not as yet swung to the tempo of a wedding march; he needed a friendly shove toward the altar; we are now man and wife in the sight of; tied the Gordian knot; a life-time guarantee; took to holy matrimony like a duck to water; embark on the matrimonial seas; take unto himself a wife; wedding bells may peal out; marital bark; alliance; are galloping along in happy double-harness; the nuptials; a little band of gold; they had "I willed"; ankled up the aisle last week; folks got tied; to share his humble cot; was sealed to his bride; merger; they crashed the altar; they were welded; I'll get Fred Linder to help hold me up; before we plighted our troth; their amalgamation; committing matrimony; joined by the velvet bonds of hymen; a man may woo where he will, but he will wed where he is destined (prov.); she murmured, "I do"; I thought sure he was going to ask me if I'd mind a Justice of the Peace; he put his property in her name; support her in the same manner to which her parents had spoiled her; b e i n g matrimonially united; shoot the works; get spliced; all meat's to be eaten, all maids to be wed; we are going to have a Justice of the Peace, although why they call it "of the Peace" when it comes to performing the marriage ceremony is a mystery; marriage is an ideal or an ordeal; offering her the prison house of marriage; proffering the ball-and-chain; soldered in the bonds of matrimony.
(See *wedding, bridegroom.*)

MARRIAGE TROUBLE

Mr. and Mrs. Jones were straining at their marital ties; those who marry where they do not love, will be likely to love where they do not marry.
(See *divorce.*)

MARRY AGAIN

Second fling at matrimony; she was married a few times before that, but never for more than a minute.
(See *wife—a lot of husbands.*)

MASQUERADE

Heavily upholstered costumes.
(See *costumes.*)

MATHEMATICS

A rush of figures to the head; perform arithmetical acrobatics; to do sums; the square of the hypotenuse of a right triangle is equal to the sum of the squares of the other two sides.
(See *exact, college subjects.*)

MATHEMATICS (Count)

You could have counted it on the fingers of six hands, an odd thumb and that stub of pencil in my waistcoat pocket; count noses.
(See *numerous.*)

MATHEMATICS (Divide)

Divvy.
(See *take.*)

MATHEMATICS (Figures)

Dig up figures; it was put on at a cost of either $7,000 or $11,00, according to who is telling the story.
(See *bookkeeper, accountant.*)

MATHEMATICS (Numbers)

About Umpteen and a half miles from anywhere; her steenth novel.
(See *three, two, four, nine.*)

MAY

Merry month of May.
(See *seasons.*)

ME

Watch the old Maestro go to work.
(See *ego.*)

MEAL

His meal consisted of coffee and a slap in the face from the waitress; (bringing someone for dinner) told her to boil and extra potato; when her luncheon arrived she addressed herself to it; a dainty collation; the meal was a masterpiece, a Rembrandt or a Raphael of the cookstove; even Harold was subdued by the time we got to the fromages assortis; they smeared everything with cheese dressing.

(See *food, breakfast, dinner, feast, lunch.*)

MEAL (Big)

One of those Diamond Jim Brady meals.

(See *feast.*)

MEAN

A stinker; he is such a guy as will give you a glass of milk for a nice cow; you can't eat your cake and have it; Mr. Harris is a little less than the best-loved man in town; he was in the mood to jostle old ladies off the pavement and snap at his elderly aunts; he that keeps malice harbors a viper in his breast; the only sincere word in his vocabulary is "good-bye."

(See *low, miser, selfish.*)

MEDALS

Three bushels of medals; for all the medals that rattled on his chest; he was round-shouldered from hanging them on his shallow chest.

(See *prize, honors, reward.*)

MEDICAL EXAMINATION

He thumped me all over with a tack hammer and found no loose boards; he wrapped an inner tube around my arm and took my blood pressure; a sort of living autopsy on me; pleased with my blood-pressure, charmed with my valves, and tickled to death with my reflexes.

(See *doctor, body, unhealthy.*)

MEDICINE

It tasted like drippings from an automobile; it tasted like a bird and animal store; it should be taken on rising with a grain of salt.

(See *druggist, sick, diseases.*)

MEDIUM QUALITY

Was so-so; run-of-mine; Grade B; Class B stuff; also ran.

(See *ordinary.*)

MEETING

Council of War; they could have held it in Macy's basement for all I cared.

(See *conference, interview.*)

MELANCHOLY

As funny as a shroud; a fit of cold blue golly-wobbles; neither of 'em is the life of the party, unless it is a funeral party; a friend that frowns is better than a smiling enemy.

(See *sad, hopeless.*)

MELODRAMA

Well-lubricated melodrama; heart-throbs planted in my bosom with a shoehorn; the tearjerker of his guild, he flushes sobby little threnodies out of the; rip-snorting melodrama; poisonings, seductions, murders, table-poundings, rapidly changed blond and grey wings and make-up boxes; where the hero went forth in answer to the call of duty; recoups the family fortune; cast for the villain of the piece; an Algeresque hero; tear-jerker; UncleTom's bungalow; Tank-town performance of Uncle Tom's Cabin— the dogs were poorly supported by the

cast; this heart-yanker; the plot thickens.
(See *theatre, shows, Wild West.*)

MELODRAMA (Language)
Unhand me, villain; saved her daughter from the clutches of a wastrel.
(See *speech.*)

MELODRAMA (Names of)
Nugget Nell; Lost in London.
(See *shows.*)

MELTED
Melted like an ice cream cone dropped on a hot pavement.
(See *heat.*)

MEMORY
Again there comes to me the scent of pansy and mignonette as I go back in memory; I have scars on my memory; that come trooping up in my memory; filthy old memory; if your memory needs jogging; through the corridors of memory; a man of great memory, without learning, hath a rock and a spindle and no staff to spin.
(See *remember.*)

MEMORY (Good)
Copy-book mind; the memory of Macaulay; compared to me an elephant is a mouse when it comes to remembering; the memory of a radio comedian.
(See *long.*)

MEMORY (Poor)
Has a mind like a sieve; I haven't got any more memory than a billy goat.
(See *forgotten.*)

MERIT
Hot stuff.
(See *deserve.*)

METHOD
A drop of honey catches more flies than a hogshead of vinegar; Tinkers to Evers to Chance; name your poison; a silver key can open an iron lock; all bread is not baked in one oven.
(See *plan, rules.*)

MIDDLE
He stepped clean into the middle of.
(See *medium, quality.*)

MIDDLE-AGE
By people below the forty line; he is beginning to feel the years, when he has to sneak in a masseur now and then to help him along; past their first youth; to keep youthful ebullience within the bounds of decorum; in the afternoon of his life; still in the heyday of life; is no longer in the first flush of youth; you're beginning to look a bit shop-worn.
(See *age.*)

MILD
A milk and water report.
(See *kind, tender.*)

MILK
Canned cow.
(See *cow.*)

MILLIONAIRE
Whose vast fortune, if converted into $1 bills and placed end to end, would reach from Philadelphia to Oshkosh; how much her income would weigh if she changed it into nickels; who has a big chest in his bed-room full of brand-new million-dollar bills; plutocrats; dirty with dough; slippery millions; millionaires, both multi and plain.
(See *rich, capitalist.*)

MIND

A mind that threshes about; her mind lashed about frantically for a point of contact; No! the mind is a fiction, no one's ever seen a mind; he has a marvelous mind; he lives in his mind; it was a pleasure to inspect her elegantly appointed mind; the mind reels; what was frying in his mind; her mind is like a timetable, subject to change without notice; his erstwhile exuberance seemed to have curdled; sent all his good resolution galley west.
(See *brain*.)

MIND YOUR OWN BUSINESS

Tend strictly to their knitting; it is none of your put-in; go along and peddle your papers; nonya business; mind your P's and Q's; tend to your own geraniums; tend to your spaghetti.
(See *busybody, inquisitive*.)

MINISTER

Found out just in time that a clerical collar wouldn't fit him; the old pulpit pounder.
(See *evangelists, sermon*.)

MISCHIEF

Skulduggery; high-jinks; shenanigans; di-does; at her pranks; she mocked 'em, and shocked 'em; thanks to some too-prankish person; play such a scurvy trick; just like small boys can never refrain from poking a stick into a wasp's nest.
(See *damage, trouble-maker*.)

MISER

You old scrooge; penny-pincher; a nickel-nursing Frenchman; tightwad; a cheese-paring skinflint; he pinched it (coin) till the eagle screamed; niggling; so stingy he wouldn't give you the right time if he had nine clocks in his house; who knows where yellow lady-slippers grow but will not tell even his intimate friends; he's left-handed and keeps all his change in his right-hand pocket; extreme parsimony; he's so tight if you ask him to sing "Old Hundred" he would sing the "Ninety and Nine" and save one percent; tight-fisted; to squeeze a nickel till the buffalo snorted.
(See *saving, mean, tight*.)

MISSIONARY

The Society for the Promotion of Trousers among the Heathen.
(See *evangelists*.)

MISTAKE

Mistook him for her first husband; a typographical error; miscue; bungle; pulled a boner; botch everything up; how come you foozled it?; a bloomer; mistakes cannot be rectified after 24 hours; next time it will be so terrible you'll wish it were a typographical error, so you can erase it; you batted into a double play; froth is not beer; do not put the saddle on the wrong horse; blow not against the hurricane; idiot who was stealing a typewriter (he thought it was a cash register).
(See *fault, wrong*.)

MIXED UP

A fudged-up currency; a sorry mess; a jangle of conflicting thoughts; topsy-turvy; all tangled up; smoke-screen; he was so dazed he was using his shaving cream to clean his teeth; hindside foremost; making a pretty pickle of things ashore; helter-skelter of confusion; harum-scarum; general pandemonium reigned; hurly burly.
(See *complicated, confused*.)

MODERN

As modern as tomorrow.
(See *new*.)

MODESTY
As devoid of vanity as an octogenarian wart-hog; he still wears the same size hat; to hide our virtues under a bushel; a little bird is content with a little nest (prov.); never blew his own trumpet.
(See *proper, plain.*)

MONEY
Dollars lurking behind those brass buttons; piling in; the smell of money; he held the family purse-strings; writing sonnets doesn't butter parsnips; he had three goals in life (money, jack and dough); dragging a sack of specie; money is like manure, of very little use except it be spread—Francis Bacon; the almighty dollar; a slush fund; tainted money—"taint yours and taint mine"; if you would know the value of money try to borrow some.
(See *economy, capitalist.*)

MONEY (Names for)
Doubloons; smackers; kale; mazuma; coin of the realm; sugar; potatoes; kopecks; cucumbers; dough; plenty of wampum; silk; jack; making plenty of scratch; pelt; bullion; he spent his last frog skin; the wherewithal; hay; coconuts; lucre; pesos; sheckels; ducats; four rocks a day; spondoolix; government literature (bills); marks; pfennigs; groschen; Chinese yens; iron men; money bags; payable in OKlahoma wooden nickels; pelf; boodle.
(See *salary, prices.*)

MONEY (Paper)
This one was a fiver, aged and tired-looking, but still game.
(See *bills.*)

MONEY (Little)
A plugged nickle; the money left wasn't enough to buy a gnat a pair of sandals; started on a shoe string but soon had to use that to keep the scenery together; wouldn't cost her a thin dime; cake and coffee money; and so far we haven't saved enough to buy a knitted waistcoat for a smallish gnat; chicken feed; I couldn't get beans for 'em; but that's flap-jacks to what I get; small change; we couldn't turn in our shares for a bowl of chili; I couldn't use it for a down payment on a bull dog; a shoestring.
(See *poor.*)

MONEY (Lots)
A nest egg; has more currency than you could shovel with two shovels in two weeks; a barrel of money; piles of cash; he pulled out a water-logged wad of bills; it costs him more than the annual check-room ransom of a Broadway playboy's topper; rake in my thousands; slippery millions; bank roll; a ton of money; a nice piece of change; to have made a packet of money.
(See *rich.*)

MONKEY
Where does one garage a monkey?
(See *fool around.*)

MONOTONOUS
It evoked something less than enthusiasm; monotonous as mutton.
(See *dull, bore.*)

MOON
Under the spell of a full harvest moon; a nickle-plated moon; a movie-set moon; walked there in the moonlight, doubtless, to catch the murmur of the trees in leafy whisper; a romantic and inexpensive place to look moon-eyed at your little lady.
(See *night, light.*)

MORALS

The Watch and Ward Society; her morals were starched throughout; to soar into the stratosphere of purity; morality isn't the light, it is only the polish on the candlestick; souls in Pawn.
(See *honest, virtue.*)

MORNING

On such matutinal excursions; in the gray morning while the early worm is getting his just deserts; your bath awaits.
(See *dawn, day.*)

MORNING (After drinking)

I feel like a tin can on a stormy sea; mouth feels like a bird and animal store.
(See *drinking.*)

MORTGAGE

To foreclose as soon as we have a nice snow-storm to turn folks out into; slap on a mortgage.
(See *borrow.*)

MOTHER

Mater; muzzy.
(See *father, children.*)

MOTHER-IN-LAW

Maxim-silencer for mother-in-law.
(See *relatives.*)

MOTHS

Moths get at the curtains, reducing them to the semblance of fishing-nets; moth sang a song, "My little grey hole in your vest."
(See *hole.*)

MOUNTAIN CLIMBING

Leaping blithely from crag to crag.
(See *climb.*)

MOURNING (In)

Woman clad in the trappings of grief.
(See *funeral, death.*)

MOUSE

The mouse that has but one hole is quickly taken (prov.).
(See *search.*)

MOUSTACHE (Action)

Twirls his flourishing moustache; his little moustache stiffened like a pointer's tail when he scents a bird; don't stand there bristling your moustache at me like that; "Mon dieu!" he exclaimed, twisting the needle-point ends of his waxed moustache; his waxed moustache bristled like thorns on a rose bush.
(See *hair, lips, face.*)

MOUSTACHE (Adjectives)

Dispirited moustache; drooping moustache; cream-separator moustache; handlebar moustache; gauze moustache; movie villain moustache; airplane moustache; walrus moustache.
(See *beard.*)

MOUSTACHE (Description)

He wore a small black moustache in the only way that a small black moustache should be worn; a black, narrow moustache decorated his short upper lip; a moustache like a badly-broken comb; a footling little moustache; one of the finest handle-bar moustaches in the history of barberdom; a tallow-colored moustache with ends like rope ends.

MOUTH

A taste in my mouth like a bird-and-animal store; keep your trap closed; don't open your yap; as big as Joe E. Brown's mouth; satchel mouth.
(See *lips, face, teeth, tongue.*)

MOUTH (Women)

She had a permanent pout which men found fetching but which the girls said was due to adenoids; a mouth that made everyone think of kisses.

(See *beautiful*.)

MOVIE PRODUCERS

The movie moguls.

(See *camera man, press agent*.)

MOVIES (The)

Moom picksures; the cinema; the flickers; the flicks; I've ever seen on celluloid; to sit through a newsreel we'd already seen four times; flesh-pots of Hollywood; flickerdom; film-land; in the fabulous land of filmdom.

(See *shows*.)

MOVIES (Acting)

His celluloid heroics; rave notices; Hollywoodishness; she makes most of the other movie queens look like spear toters; finding an actor in Hollywood is like finding a needle in a haystack.

(See *acting*.)

MOVIES (Actors)

To borrow stars like a woman would borrow a half pound of butter; Cinemadonna; you can see one and see them all; his mailman is threatened with a nervous breakdown; a pretty prominent nib in celluloid circles; these lilies who blossom in the Hollywood fields of celluloid; the knights and ladies of the films; that screen siren who has always sent you into swoons.

(See *actor, actress*.)

MOVIES (Bad)

A dud film; I've felt jollier in a dentist's chair than I have watching that film; it's the usual dull dish of Holly-wood mush; it's one of those colossal movies with everything in it but a clambake; the kind of movies you reluctantly go to see in Broken Foot, Utah, while waiting for a train; a hunk of tripe.

(See *melodrama*.)

MOVIES (Directors)

They had a man named ——— who ought to be directing traffic; these megaphone maniacs; he is Jovian thunder rolling out of a megaphone; to urge his minions.

(See *theatrical company*.)

MOVIES (Extras)

Spear toters.

(See *crowds*.)

MOVIES (Fan mail)

His fan mail kept an extra clerk stepping; almost gave the postman a nervous breakdown.

(See *raves, letter*.)

MUCH

He would never amount to a hill of beans; that will jolly well force them to; a goodish bit.

(See *lots*.)

MUD

Get so thoroughly entangled in the gumbo of West Texas.

(See *rain*.)

MURDER

Homicide; denticide; commit infanticide; to liquidate persons.

(See *kill*.)

MUSCLES

His muscles stood out like the fenders on a truck; the muscles under his skin looked like a snake that had just swallowed a rabbit.

(See *body, strength, exercise*.)

MUSIC

The resultant noise, or music as it is sometimes called; music is an assortment of twanging, thudding, plunking, and tweedling sounds roughly sorted out and arranged in chronological order; a piece consists merely of notes—some sharp, some flat, and some simply awful—with here and there a quaver or a crochet to hold the thing together and impart a touch of variety; good music—the kind that is performed in long chunks by large orchestras for the benefit of pallid-looking audiences with green shirts and longish hair; musical slush; you can hear the cries of the injured and the moans of the dying; he likes hum-my music; to him, music is just a more or less organized noise.

(See *orchestra, singing.*)

MUSIC (Ignorance of)

I have a cauliflower ear for music; can't tell a fugue from an oratorio.

(See *stupid.*)

MUST

Theirs not to reason why; theirs not to make reply.

(See *necessary.*)

MYSTERY

Had not yet cracked the murder; huggery-muggery; mumbo-jumbo; wheels within wheels.

(See *unknown, secret.*)

N

NAILS
He had enough nails to build a courthouse.
(See *carpenter*.)

NAMES
We will call him Ethelbert because I always wanted to call somebody Ethelbert; his name is John Viper, of the Windshield Vipers; Grace always called her grandmother Uncle Moe—ask me why?; one of my friends whose name is Legion; a boy whom we call ———— because that was his name; called him Theory, because he so seldom works; yclept; he was dubbed; monicker; the family cognomen; their front names; his tag; reading from left to right, we were myself and; the name sounded like a cook-stove falling downstairs; Mrs. Folliot-ffoliot (pronounced Finkle); answered to the name of; sobriquet; his handle; he must have been christened by a man who stuttered; a myrtle among thorns is a myrtle still (prov.).
(See *epithet*.)

NAMES (Comic)
Lila Butt; Mlle. Sprouts from Brussels; Etta Herring; General Stiffneck.
(See *fun*.)

NAMES (Second)
Gog and Magog; Clementine Unthank; Widgerley; Sam Toogood; George E. Porgey; Simcox; Pootles; Aunt Dido; Currier and Ives; Cafoozalum and Dudderley; Doolittle; Donner Wetter; Xthenttisvitch; Mr. Eczema; Dingle Foot; Mrs. Milfret; Chitterling; Pyrzztchwll; Chudwell; Oddleigh; Schnittzlchaumberg; Buxtable; Ponderby; Dillweather; Mrs. Penwyper; Suggs; Higginbotham; Abeddy; Twifflenfinks; Dinwiddy; Hey, Diddle-Diddle; Miss Cadenza; Isaac Finklebottom; Captain Bilge; Mrs. Tinwhistle; Mr. Throttlebottom; Mr. Bumble; Mr. Fussbudget; Mr. Bunderby; Mr. Flathead; Mr. Twirp; Mr. Screwball; Mr. Ticklebritches; Mr. Blowhard; Mr. Barnsmeller; Mr. Pennifeather; Bloodbersby.
(See *men, famous*.)

NAMES (Effeminate)
It was dangerous to live in that neighborhood with a name like Clarence.
(See *effeminate*.)

NAMES (First names, male)
Eustace; Adelbert; Clementine; Murgatroyd; Cholomondeley; Willoughby; Osric; Arbuthnot; Nicodemus; Pegitty.
(See *boy*.)

NAMES (First names, female)
Guinevere; Arabella; Abigail; Heloise; Monica; Hephzibah; Clarissa; Anaemia; Ermintrude; Natacha.
(See *girl*.)

NAMES (Funny)
You old cow; old irresistible; you old Dachshund; you old scourge of God; the old billy-goat; the old sausage; old pipsqueaks; you lump.
(See *humor*.)

NAMES (Trick)
There were 4 Footes but not 2 pairs.
(See *pun*.)

NAMES (Of companies)
Attar-of-Rose Hide and Tallow works; Mr. Tittlejot (third from the left in

the legal firm of Tittlejot, Tittlejot, Tittlejot and Tittlejot and Iota; the Non Compos Mentis Beef Co., Ltd.

NAMES (Pet)

Her wudgi gudgi; her pidgie widgie; ducky; chickie; lambie; turtle dove; honey-cake; my little pet lamb; sugar; itty-bitty; funnyface.
(See *sweetheart, favorite.*)

NAMES (Pet)

pipsqueaks; you lump.
(See *favorite.*)

NARROW ESCAPE

Close shave.
(See *danger, trouble.*)

NATURAL

It is natural to a greyhound to have a long tail; he felt he could let down his hair to speak; to regain her amour propre.
(See *easy, possible.*)

NATURE

The deafening shriek of the cuckoo; the floura and fauna of rural life in America.
(See *jungle, human nature.*)

NAUSEATED

Sits badly on a tender stomach.
(See *disgust, sick, seasickness.*)

NAUTICAL TERMS

Ay, ay, sir; sea-dogs; I was luffing or jibbing or something (sail boat); "No harm meant, matey"; "An old seadog wot's been battered by wind and wave, blow me down"; "Belay there!"; "Blast you for an interfering swab"; "Shiver my timbers"; the spring wire jammed on the winch drum; give her a couple of turns to starboard; knew a scupper from a dog watch; go down the fo'c'stle ladder; threw a hawser to what he thought was a stanchion; stood poised upon the galleon's bulwark; the poop; ranged the Seven Seas with their jibbooms flying gaily from the Mizzen-forepeak and the first mate flying gaily from his creditors.
(See *sailors.*)

NAVY

Why should the admirals rattle their epaulets at the expense of the army; join the navy and see the girls.
(See *boat, battleships.*)

NEARBY

A hop-skip from Fifth Avenue; hard by the railway tracks; so nearby you can spit on it; nearer to him than a tight vest; brought within hailing distance; it isn't any further than you could throw a Yale full-back; hits your neck of the woods; on the five yard line.
(See *close, next to.*)

NEATNESS

Natty; a place for everything and everything in its place.
(See *clean.*)

NECESSARY

Do the Gods decree; if we did not have Christmas we should have to invent it; Mrs. Vanderbilt is to N. Y. society what starch is to blanc mange pudding.
(See *inevitable, must.*)

NECESSITY

Necessity is invention's father's wife.
(See *destiny, fate.*)

NECKING

Passionate posturing.
(See *petting, embrace.*)

NECKTIE

One of the Venetian awning ties; the oldest Ascot, or puff tie, is being revived; he sports one; his gleaming collar drawn taut by a striped cravat and fastened just this side of the garrote stage by a gold pin; tie was held in place by the kind of collar pin that always seemed to strangle him; a tie like a fire in a pin-wheel store; kept diddling with his necktie; sported a red, black and grey tie which he insisted, in all seriousness, symbolized moonlight on the Adriatic; red four-in-hand; nifty tie; if his neckties do not clash too violently with his socks; eye-filling necktie; a roaring red necktie.
(See *clothes.*)

NEGLECTED

What am I, the forgotten man?
(See *forgotten.*)

NEGROES

A high yaller; cornfield darkie with a month's pay burning holes in his pocket; that ebony fiend; the poor cough drop; he's the white sheep of his family; Senegambians; a Senegambian in the woodpile.
(See *Africa, people.*)

NEIGHBORHOOD

He approached the familiar purlieus of the coffee pot.
(See *district.*)

NEIGHBORS

Everyone has neighbors, except lighthouse-keepers.
(See *friendly.*)

NERVE

Had more sap than a sugar maple; he had the chromium-plated impudence; I was brash enough; supreme gall; you have to have an iron chin to write a column; he had the brass to say.
(See *bold, forward.*)

NERVES

The nerves which usually danced a jig at the back of his neck; his overwrought ganglia; feels like a palsied derelict from the home for old wreck; hair-trigger nervousness.
(See *body, emotions.*)

NERVOUS BREAKDOWN

She kept ahead of a nervous breakdown by traveling too fast for it to catch up with her; as soon as he could spare the time, George intended to have a nervous breakdown.
(See *sick.*)

NERVOUSNESS

He locked himself in the bathroom and bit his nails; being nervous and fretful as a canary's mother; I was so nervous I could yell; works his nerves into tattered discharge; his jiggles and jousts; tore a lace handkerchief to shreds; cause strong men to break down and weep; fluttery nervousness; megrims; I twitter, I jitter; five more minutes of being polite would reduce her to a jittering pulp; gives me the Iks; as jittery as a tree full of elephants; it makes me want to chew gum and cry; his nerves are all shot to pieces; to a point where they will scream if a woman looks at them; gives us the fidgets; the willies; what's eating you; as nervous as a mouse in a revolving door; twiddled his fingers irritably; pour acid on the raw nerves of; she had the fidgets, like a hen on a hot griddle; her nerves were high tension wires radiating in all directions; chewing the nails; got out of bed on the wrong side that morning; stop jittering; tugged at his moustache; he became pitter-pattery; a soul in torment; what's biting you; his nerves were crying out loud; every time a nerve rang a bell; keep your pants on; he all but burst into tears; I'm going upstairs to have some hysterics; biting his underlip; fuss and fripper; is doing my nervous system no good; go to bed and have cold compresses applied; fretfully gnawing his moustache; her fellow players are in a state of nervous exhaustion and galloping ennui; "stop acting like a butterfly and light some place"; the jitters.

(See *shaking, fear.*)

NEUROTIC

Hypochondriac; rushing for the iodine bottle for the slightest scratch; his favorite literature is the medical dictionary; spends most of his life counting the vitamins in his porridge; the neurotic, the erotic and the tommy-rotic.

(See *psychology, inferiority complex.*)

NEUTRAL

There are two sides to everything except a short piece of string.

(See *unbiased, fair.*)

NEVER

They never, just never will; and I never will, till there's two Sundays in one week; and never the twain shall meet; well practically never; never in all my born days.

(See *no.*)

NEVER MIND
"Skip it."
(See *forget it.*)

NEW

The project was still in the egg; was in the bib and jumper stage; newfangled ideas; made its bow; virginal; why not try a new tune on your con-certina; the birth pains of the New Deal; baptism of fire.

(See *modern.*)

NEWLYWEDS
First-nighters.

(See *marriage.*)

NEWS

Spill the news; what "copy" they are; dished up in lurid phrases; provide the society "ink-slingers" with no end of "copy"; nothing less catastrophic than the elopement of the Queen of England; material must be dug up to keep the whirligig going; he knocks boldly who brings good news (prov.).

(See *rumor, gossip.*)

NEWSPAPER

A newspaper so respectable that even bishops do not hesitate to light their fires with it; when the paper goes to bed; it comes out on Fridays if there's nothing to stop it; while searching the morning paper for the Kiddies' Korner.

(See *publishing, editor, reporter.*)

NEWSPAPER (Names)

One of the morning rags; Gazette; Sheet; the public prints; newssheet.

(See *Sunday papers, tabloids.*)

NEW YEAR

Gathered to welcome a cherubic little fellow and bespatter him with champagne; "go gay" on New Year's eve; ridiculous to start the new year with a headache; resolutions go in one year and go out the other; it looks as if 1952 is here to stay.

(See *welcome, day, resolution.*)

NEW YORK

Gotham; Pa Knickerbocker's skyline; the lobster belt; grabbing at the brass rings of the Manhattan merry-go-round; New York, an eastern seaport town 'near Bridgeport; adventuring into the dangerous purlieus of the Sodom of New York, of the Gomorrah of Boston; New York—a winner-take-all-town; down below the Macy and Gimbel line; Seventh Avenue—home of the "kluck and soot" business; Manhattan Isle, where visitors get the impression that all motorists are morons studying to be maniacs; some day this is going to be a great city; Hemingway called New Yorkers "angleworms in bottles"; many go to N. Y. too early and stay too long; a stenographer's tears on Tenth Ave. mean more to me than all the lions in Africa.

(See *Broadway, Long Island, Brooklyn*.)

NEXT TO
Toeing the road.
(See *close*.)

NICE
The old world charm of mine; he is a likeable little shad; positively ripping of you; that would be too, too ducky; pretty doggone white of me; nectar of the gods; but the dinner! Ah-h-h! many Ah's; honeyed matter; he's the salt of the earth; sober and honest citizens who seldom kick dumb animals and hardly ever push their unmarried aunts over cliffs for the sake of insurance money; a regular paragon of all the virtues.
(See *fine, good*.)

NIGHT
Dress up o' nights; at eventide; curfew; the night wind stirred in the vines.
(See *darkness, late*.)

NIGHT CLUBS
Gallivanting around in night clubs; the cover charge made the James Bros. look like pikers; you'll land in your neighbor's soup if you move an inch; practically sitting in each other's laps; made the rounds of the night clubs; repaired to the night club; they catered to the best dress-suit and red fingernail trade; clip joints; swank night spots; postage stamp dance floors; a night dive; if you hunger for a little trampling, jostling, plunging a n d rib-slugging; hotcha joints; wassail palaces; push-the-button-and-ask-for Tony places; he played the hot spots; crude and sweaty little holes; gentleman who comes in with the idea of amusing himself by tossing the tables into the mezzanine; his shabby caravansary; a dingy side-street hey-hey hut; a honky-tonk; his place had the oo-la-la!; a late spot; one of the midtown night asylums; pay real money to be shoved around the floor.

(See *dancing, party*.)

NIGHTGOWN
Nightie, nightgear.
(See *clothes, pajamas*.)

NIGHT LIFE
Back home they used to sit up and listen to the owls; she lives not far from the dazzle that once knew her so well; saw as little daylight as a mule in the mine; night-lifers; helling around.

(See *entertainment, theatre*.)

NINE
The nine muses.
(See *mathematics*.)

NO
Not by a jugful; *jamais de la vie;* no go; no dice; no can do; not a lick; nary a lick; nil; wondering in just what words he was going to say "No!";

to hell with it; not by the hair on your chinny chin chin; it was no soap; thumbs down; null and void; turned a deaf ear; forget it; pretend you didn't hear anything; no thank you; absolutely, utterly and irrevocably No; not by a brimming jugful; 'raus mit it; not a scrap of evidence; not a shred of evidence; thumbed his nose at it; not on your tintype; said he would go to hell first; he stood pat; no, a 1000 times no; I wouldn't do it for all the tea in China; always say no and you will never be married (prov.); he could say "No!" like a person driving a rivet; that was out; perish the thought; to blithering blazes with it; all he did was stick his head in the ground like an ostrich. (See *never*.)

NO?

Nicht wahr?; *n'est-ce pas?*; eh, Mrs. Murgatroyd, you lump?; it had to be thought of by somebody originally, had it not?

(See *is that so, yes*.)

NOBILITY

Duchess who was seeking a little sideplay after duchess hours; noblesse oblige; Burke's Peerage; a scion of England's royal family; her ladyship; a poor old broken-down duke; can a Grand Duke do first-class duking in socks like those; Grand Dukes, and even people with regular jobs, are; today, Russian dukes are about as useful as dandruff; bogus Marquis; Lord Stick-in-the-mud; the Duke and Duchess of Blah; their castle in Umpshire; were unable to breathe unless surrounded by courtiers in knee breeches, and flunkies in powdered wigs, and gold and silver dishes; the Gaekwar of Glunk; Lord Leftover; and asked out to tea by peeresses in their own right; a nod from a lord is a breakfast for a fool (prov.). (See *nobility*.)

NO GOOD

The best that can be said about it is that it's lousy, so you can't imagine the worst; the shoddy of Broadway. (See *useless*.)

NOISE

Sounded like the crack of doom; a crash that made the welkin ring; his hat fell down on the church floor and sounded like a twenty-one gun salute; he bully-rags (to abuse loudly); rambunctious; no noise is good noise; pendemonium; bedlam; hullooing; a madhouse; howl them down; noisy as a cookstove falling downstairs; noisy as burial-howlers in full cry; noisy as a living skeleton having a fit on a hardwood floor; noisy as women bathing in a river; as noisy as a hen with one chicken; general pandemonium reigned; a great hue and cry arose; the truck goes smack-dab into the wall with a loud kuh-boom; he could beat a drum so loud it rattled the teeth of Eskimos in Greenland; with a plunk; noise like the crack of doom; a sort of swooshing noise; it made enough noise to wake the Seven Sleepers, whoever they were; hubbub; noisy as a milkmen's convention; like walking through a bog with squeaky shoes; hullabaloo; a big dredger was working out in the river, making a noise like a big dredger; the loud plunk of the ball in the catcher's mitt; noise sounded like a gang war on a cat farm; confused uproar resembling the last words of a moribund duck; whoop-te-do; he made a noise like a blotter when a dope comes into the office.

(See *gun, sound of, music*.)

NOISES (Examples)

The mating-cry of the boll weevil. (See *cry*.)

NONE

Run shy of cars; never did a stroke of work; she can't swim a lick; disturbed me not at all; she hasn't got a brain in her head; none worthy the name.

(See *not, anything, nothing.*)

NONSENSE

Twaddle; drivel; spittle; buncombe; balderdash; fingle-fangle; flapdoodle; rigmarole; fol-de-rol; purely personal piffle; claptrap.

(See *bunk.*)

NOSE

The olfactory orifices; Etruscan noses; a lobster-claw nose; he had a Roman nose which ran the entire length of the Suez Canal; and one of those funny noses that are made in Poland; a long, long nose, which grew pinker and pinker toward its point; ruby nose; the Dantesque line of his nose; a nose of a most retroussé variety; a breezer; shnozzle; one of those noses you could stop a train with, if there wasn't a signal handy; it looks like a printer's error; snout; snoot; sneezer; Cyrano (big); beak.

(See *face, odor.*)

NOSE (Adjectives)

Rubicund; lavender-tinted; buttonlike; broad and flowery; bulbous; tip-tilted, clumsy; saucy; beaked; hawklike; pendulous; obtuse; broad-nostriled; pug; lumpy; formidable; grubby little; knobular; fleshy; cherry.

(See *noticeable.*)

NOSE (Rose)

The complexion of whose nose convinced me that he knew whereof he spoke; the soft bloom on his nose; noses glowed like stop signals on a traffic light.

(See *blush.*)

NOSE (Picking)

Can you do it up to your second knuckle?; why don't you use a buttonhook, it looks better; an old Chinese proverb says, the best way to pick your nose is with your elbow; I'm going to hang a bell on your nose.

(See *sneeze.*)

NOT

Nary a one; women cut their throats and drown themselves in bathtubs when they're not invited; didn't rate one-two-three with her.

(See *none.*)

NOTE IT

Paste it in your hat.

(See *remind.*)

NOTHING

From scratch; not a sausage; the ashes of emptiness; I've never had so much as a sausage from.

(See *none.*)

NOTICEABLE

Stood out like a sunbonnet in the rain; stand out like a walrus at a goldfish ball.

(See *conspicuous.*)

NUDE

Cavorting about in the altogether; until I could have passed almost anywhere for September Morn's father; he appeared in next door to his birthday suit; coming out all goose-pimples; gooseflesh sprouted all over him; let's go native.

(See *bare.*)

NUDE (Female)

About all she had on was some talcum powder; she was dressed in her dignity and some beads; an advanced stage of nudity; to go Eve; to go native; nekkid female loveliness; her pink and white, piquant figure; her deshabille; as lovely and unabashed as Eve in her pristine glory; *au naturel;* nothin' on but long silk stockin's an' little what-you-call-'ems; a glorious pink and white statue from her tiny twinkling feet to the top of her dark-haired head; à la nude.

(See *body*.)

NUMEROUS

And before long, elephants will be as numerous on Broadway as autumn leaves in Vallombrosa, wherever that may be.

(See *scarce, few*.)

NURSE

I'm a registered nurse, but if people get sick they keep the symptoms to themselves; a white-robed female.

(See *sick, hospital*.)

NUTSHELL

And there is the root and center and gist of the matter.

(See *short time*.)

O

OATH
Eggs and oaths are easily broken.
(See *cross-your-heart*.)

OATHS
Du lieber Gott; Donnerwetter.
(See *swearing*.)

OBJECT
Cry to high heaven; objurgated mightily; I rise to squawk.
(See *protest*.)

OBSERVANT
Those of us who keep both our ears to the ground.
(See *careful*.)

OCEAN
In the briny; he shot back into the sea so fast he practically started a tidal wave; sea looked as flat as an ironing board; Kid Neptune; it wasn't any mill pond; the rip-snorting Atlantic; and cast it into the maw of the sea; American shipping rides proudly on Britannia's waves; the cabbage-green sea; to sail the Seven Seas (or eight, if we include the Caspian); on the bosom of the Atlantic.
(See *waves, sailors, boat*.)

ODOR (Bad)
An odor of which he was the sole proprietor; he-man odor; the nose is quicker than the eye; hold their noses; I had won by a nose—held tightly between the thumb and forefinger; what did he do, step on a skunk?; it didn't smell like Quelques Fleurs; lusty stench; which makes Chicago smell like your favorite zoo; sweet-smelling as an Iowa pig sty; malodorous; to perfume with piety whatever muck exists; go out and let the wind blow the stink out of you; could smell it a block away; you could chin yourself on the bourbon aroma; put a stench in the nation's nostrils which can never be blown away; a smell like burning tennis shoes; aromatic.
(See *breath, garlic, onion*.)

OFFICE (Big)
Outside the gilded portals of big business he sat in a half-acre private office; he guarded the outer portals of his office (office boy); the Holy of Holies on the twelfth floor; overpoweringly handsome office resembling the refectory of a monastery with a throne room decorative scheme; it was hard to tell at a glance whether the boss was sitting behind a desk or behind a pool table.
(See *business, work*.)

OFFICE (Little)
A small glass-enclosed cubbyhole; yon fusty cubicle.
(See *little*.)

OFFICERS (Army)
Beribboned and bemedaled; bespangled with medals; retired with the rank of a captain and the reputation of being the best poker player in the Indian service; the gold-braid boys; he has gold braid from his cuff to his neck; medal-hung majors.
(See *war*.)

OFTEN
Ofttimes.
(See *lots of, many*.)

O. K.

Everything is lollypops now.

(See *all right*.)

OLD (Idea)

Covered with mildew; mouldy; proved to be a rehash of the kind of play all Frenchmen stopped going to soon after the Franco-Prussian War; the ghost of the old flying wedge came out of its cupboard; old vintage; superannuated; the relic of an earlier and more barbaric day.

(See *days—old*.)

OLD (Man)

You old fossil; an old dog; the old boy; codger; was in the dotage; the old blighter; gnarled and withered like a sour apple in vinegar; the old buzzard; old-fogy; the darling old dote; I had a mind to ask this old disease if; the old gaffer; old Methuselah; mildewed; geezer; the old coot; doddering; he cackled; his step has lost its old elasticity, and so have his suspenders (or, but not his suspenders); the old bird; it made him old before his time; an old tomato; patriarch; bald-headed old sinners; an oldster; an old stinker; the old weasel; old and crotchety; graybeards; he had the bends; white-haired cavaliers giving Methuselah a run for his money; a little shriveled-up old guy; a little old pappy guy with chin whiskers; when I begin to dodder; he is up so far in the 70's he's brushing the octaves; old Sourpuss; his joints are creaky; the old curmudgeon; outwit the grave; like most old men, creak a little in the morning; the old waster; octogenarian; old pieface; older than Noah's Ark; older than Job's boils; he's so old, he gets winded playing chess; superannuated; he was 75 years old and had seven of his own teeth left; a hard-boiled old cross-patch; lived to be an octopus; vintage; many a tune can be

played on an old fiddle; septuagenarian; an antediluvian; his eyes were beginning to dim; he was on the wrong side of 70; many a tune left in an old violin; its age creeping up; the best time for a man to sow his wild oats is between the age of 85 and 90; he is old and given to stroking his long white whiskers; an old man is twice a child; an old goat is never the more reverend for his beard; an old dog can not alter his way of barking; an old ox makes a straight furrow; an old fox needs not be taught tricks; some men are born old, and some never grow so; the evening of a well-spent life; he was a good old wagon, but he broke down; fogyism; when the dusk of the evening begins to gather over the watery eye; his opinions were not ossified; a lot of old crocks; old? he knew the Big Dipper when it was nothing but a drinking cup; the snows of many winters; nestled in his beard.

(See *age, man*.)

OLD (Thing)

A suit which hadn't been new for some time; gathering dust through the years.

(See *past*.)

OLD (Woman)

A little nosegay of an old lady; an old gal; to talk like an old rip; she doesn't neck, drink, swear, smoke, go to parties, stay out late or diet; elderly siren; a bobbed-haired old beldame of sixty-odd dressed like Janet Gaynor.

(See *dowager, age, woman*.)

OLD-FASHIONED

Don't be mediaeval; none of these latter-day prejudices; these old-style females; little politenesses which were all the go in Queen Victoria's time; about the time Halley's Comet was flaming across the sky; diehard; malcontents; cling to old favorites; vintage of; a parlor which must have been furnished when Victoria was a girl; called them the Camphor Ball Set; go the way of the stagecoach and the canal; a throwback to the old-fashioned days; the great dames of another day; like a breath of lavendar and old lace; in the old days when a mug was something to drink from and when a raspberry was a fruit; in the old days when John was good looking, Helen was pretty, and even the cabs were handsome; when pompadours were in fashion; gone where the woodbine twineth; a bit old-timey; the last hold-out of the old American guard in Paris; peg-top pants days; since Ward McAllister put over the cotillion; Gay Nineties, of whiskers streaming amain, of pup dogs, hansom cabs and rubber plants; a place of faded plush, dusty gilt cupids, and laundry-soap-color walls; it was old before the pyramids; the "ox-cart stage"; old days when trousers were strapped under the boots; a thing of the past, like muttonchop whiskers; the good old days when a corset was not a collector's item; the old-fashioned pants pocket will be in a glass jar in the Smithsonian Institution in no time; the era when women thought it was coy to flirt from behind a fan, and wear lace pantalettes down to their ankles; elegant eighties.

(See *behind, ancestry.*)

OLD MAID
Shanghai herself a man; on the shelf; I am 30 and have yet to be taken on the davenport and given a chance to struggle.

(See *spinster, girl, simple.*)

OLYMPICS
The spoon and egg event.

(See *games.*)

ONCE IN A WHILE
Ever and anon.

(See *scarce, seldom, rare.*)

ONION
Know my bermudas; onions as large as saucers; I can fry an onion as well as anybody, it's only that my lachrymatory glands are so sensitive; I like a dash of onion in everything; I don't practice breath control.

(See *garlic.*)

ON THE CONTRARY
Au contraire.

(See *but.*)

OPENING
Throws everything wide open.

(See *expand, hole.*)

OPERA
Some of the Social Registerites who sit enthroned in the "Golden horseshoe"; "golden horseshoeite"; in the days of Sembrich and Pol Plancon, attendance at Grand Opera was limited to property owners possessing one or more diamond tiaras; light opera—we have light or dark; red-blooded operagoers; an opera without a few murders and some suicides is a failure right off.

(See *theatre.*)

OPERA SINGERS
She shattered the notion that an opera star must be a cross between a Wagnerian soprano and the rear end of a bus; operatic diva.

(See *soprano, tenors, basso, singing.*)

OPERATION
Pruning or remodeling at the hands of a physician; carved him; the surgeons had to do a good deal of guessing as they worked on the jig-saw

puzzle of her face; we'll have to blast or amputate; they gave him a bullet to bite while the operation was going on; had his appendix clipped.

(See *doctor, hospital.*)

OPINION

An opinion that would smoke the hide off an alligator.

(See *idea, notion.*)

OPPORTUNITY

Dumped in his lap; mislaid the opportunity; seize the opportunity by the forelock; the gods tossed it in his lap; fortune knocks but fools do not answer; he that will not when he may, when he will he shall have nay.

(See *chance, luck.*)

OPPOSITE

Every white hath its black, and every sweet its sour; eats are eats and drinks are drinks and never the twain shall meet.

(See *on the contrary.*)

OPPOSITION

Scattered those who tried to bar his path as a tornado scatters paper dolls; Horatius at the Bridge.

(See *co-operate, not to, enemy.*)

OPTIMISTIC

Pipe-dream; that ray of sunshine; synthetic sunshine; he is a Peter Pan; scattering a few sunbeams; to view life through rose-tinted spectacles.

(See *happy, wonderful.*)

ORATOR

Tear-brewing spellbinders; he weeps rhetorical tears and musses his hair in passionate attacks; bristles with such philippics as; everyone hung on his words; stealing the bombast and bonhommie of; he slings his arms;

his oratorical style; eyes and head rolling, twisty forelock askew, arms larruping the atmosphere; rabble-rousing tendencies.

(See *talker, speech.*)

ORCHESTRA (Musicians)

The orchestra fiddling away for dear life; the stale rhythms of the orchestra; in the middle of a wandering obligato; there was a sounding of cymbals, a tweedle of flutes, and uproar of trumpets, a booming of 'cellos, and other ingredients; each and every instrument went its own wailful way; the net result of these various activities sounds like a gang-war in a busy boiler-works; brass bands shrieking.

(See *conductor, music.*)

ORCHESTRA (Jazz)

Moan of a jazz band; toe-tickling lyrics; torrid music by——and his Toot Sweeters.

(See *dancing.*)

ORDERS (Giving)

Laying down the law to.

(See *control, dictate.*)

ORDINARY

The usual syrupy doings of; he's acting ornery; he was just a cabbage; run-of-the mill liar; a self-respecting diaper pin.

(See *medium, quality*)

ORIGINALITY

Undetected plagiarism; every herring must hang by its own tail.

(See *new, modern.*)

OSTEOPATH

To take the streamline out of my spine; save the pieces; he employed a half-nelson; the aviation test, jump on his back, pull his ears out of gear and tie his neck into a lover's knot.

(See *doctor.*)

OUTCAST
Pariah.

(See *thrown out.*)

OUT OF PLACE
Looking as though she belonged there about as much as a canary belongs at a crows' convention.

(See *stranger.*)

OVERDO
The formula on which he depends is wearing so thin.

(See *exaggerated.*)

OWN
Has a small piece of the joint; it's yours to have and to hold until death do us part; they regard the land as their own, just as the mosquitoes claim New Jersey; possession is nine points of the law; he owned everything in town except a couple of corner groceries.

(See *have, get.*)

OYSTERS
Bivalves; an oyster's hungry maw; he was a bold man that first ate an oyster.

(See *food.*)

P

PAGES
Measuring 800 pages from stem to stern.
(See *books*.)

PAINTING
That awful smear of misfit paints; who put pain in painting?
(See *art*.)

PAIR
Tweedledum and Tweedledee.
(See *two, names*.)

PAJAMAS
Slumberwear; red curduroy ice-cooled house pajamas.
(See *nightgown, sleep*.)

PAL
Palsy-walsy days; a crooked stick will have a crooked shadow (prov.).
(See *chummy, friend*.)

PALE
Pallid as a Botticelli cherub.
(See *blonde, sick*.)

PANTS
Insert himself into a pair of middle-aged pantaloons.
(See *trousers, suit*.)

PARENTS
Too many parents are not on spanking terms with their children; in a fiddler's house all are dancers (prov.).
(See *mother, father*.)

PARIS
To drive in the Bois or have tea on the Champs Elysées; France exports Bohemians, champagne, and; the Rue de la Paix; to loaf expensively.
(See *city, French*.)

PARK (A car)
He could park a car on a dime and have nine cents left over.
(See *automobile*.)

PARTICULAR
One must, I mean to say, draw the line somewhere; a great stickler for.
(See *strict, correct*.)

PARTICULAR (Not)
Any stick is good enough to beat a dog with; any port in a storm; make no bones about.
(See *neutral, careless*.)

PARTIES
There isn't much difference between the major parties; the donkey brays and the elephant has a trunk, but they both get hay from the same manger.
(See *politics*.)

PARTNER
My sidekick; partner in crime.
(See *pal, assistant*.)

PART OF
She had been "in" and "of" the summer colony for a long time.
(See *contribute, some, piece*.)

PARTY
A debauch; table-hopping; a blowout; the dizzy whirl; partying; where a cute blond in pink tights would

come out of a huge pit at midnight; passing trays of cakes to each other with lovely rhythm; a shindig; when the party finally broke up, along with the furniture; sashayed to the party; the radio had been reduced to scrap, someone had burned the curtains and we were ankle-deep in gherkins and sausages; soirées; a house party at his mansion, and people keep running in and out of bedrooms for two days and two nights.

(See *celebrating, cocktails.*)

PARTY (Dull)

We're just pouring out the lifeline; whose house parties are in danger of going flat; it was a tepid affair.

(See *dull, bore.*)

PARTY (Gate crashing)

Do we walk into the dance backwards to give the impression that we're coming out, or what?

(See *invitation.*)

PARTY (Society)

A caviar round-up; the table decorations were miniature lakes filled with camellias and a bank effect of violets and certified checks (mine); made the court of Versailles look like a meeting of Quakers; kid glove affairs.

(See *society tea.*)

PASSION

The flesh-pots; or is it the asthma that made him breathe that way?; the thermometer went up; raised his blood pressure alarmingly; the Clyde Beatty in my system came to the fore; she did something that made your toes wiggle; she was bringing out the Casanova within him in six easy lessons; his heart hammered dizzily, swelling his veins with surge after surge of hot, eager blood; she struggled a little to no avail, increasing the fire and surge of her pulses; setting her afire; and the way her breasts pushed out against the single layer that covered them was enough to bring on a fever; they rode on blazing gusts of passion, like birds before a wind; rivers of fire ran through his veins; every time I look at you, I feel as if I were going to melt and run right down into my shoes.

(See *sex, love.*)

PAST (The)

It's water under the bridge; to burn her bridges to the rear; all that was rain down the spout; as you go rolling down the corridors of time; but that is all down the hatch.

(See *days-old.*)

PAST

A past as black as the ace of spades; a past as black as the hinges of hell.

(See *reputation.*)

PATIENCE

Keep your shirt on; but there is a point at which patience ceases to be a virtue.

(See *wait, virtue, quiet.*)

PATRIOTISM

Flag-waving; dollar patriots; you can't sing the Star-Spangled Banner on an empty stomach.

(See *citizen, hero.*)

PATROL WAGON

The Black Maria.
(See *policeman, arrested.*)

PAWNBROKER

The tabernacle of the gilded spheres; the old "shent per shent."
(See *borrow, "broke."*)

PAY

You pays your money and you takes your choice; to unbelt; that doesn't get me any pork chops; to fork over; shell out; footed the bill; dig down in his jeans; pawning everything except his underwear; ransack the nursery money-box; to pony up for; to ante for; cough up; to kick back; to lay 50c on the line.

(See *buy, prices.*)

PEACE

Ice picks were hammered into knitting needles; the dove of peace now chirps over; waving a drooping olive branch.

(See *quiet, calm.*)

PEARLS

Rope of pearls; strands and strands of priceless pearls; satan's teardrops; do you like pearls? here's an oyster.

(See *jewelry.*)

PEDDLER

Costermonger calling attention to his Brussels sprouts.

(See *sell, clerk.*)

PEOPLE

Smaller fry; stooge.

(See *human nature.*)

PEOPLE (Common)

Plebeians; riffraf; pagans; hoi polloi; barbarians; the shanty element; the elite of toity-toid street; the "masses"; the dregs; a lot of pots; I feel like a worm; don't be steerage.

(See *crowds, vulgar.*)

PEP

To shoot some tabasco into; alert as a mongoose; he was full of pep as a yeast ad.

(See *energy, active.*)

PERFECT

Aces; Jones can do no wrong; a crack outfit; top-notcher; letter perfect; it was a home-run; nonpareil.

(See *thorough, great.*)

PERFUME (General)

Perfume made his head spin; turn the dressing table and bathroom into a romance; the old-fashioned cologne and perfume scents that suggest crinolines and the minuet; she wanted some perfume that would make her smell dangerous; romance and allure in the caress of this bewitching *odeur.*

(See *cologne.*)

PERFUME (Names)

A Night in a Swamp; Nightingale's Breath; Who socked McGinness?; a new perfume—Attar Boy; Woods at Night; *De Toi Je Chante;* Moment Supreme; Ginsberg's Herring; Coty's Sheep.

(See *fashions.*)

PERMISSION

Without asking a by-your-leave.
(See *invitation, let's.*)

PERSON (In person)

In propria persona; seen in the flesh.
(See *everyone, anyone.*)

PERSONALITY

That old world charm of mine; he could wiggle his ears; she turned on a thousand volts; turning the white heat of his personality on; he had "Umpah"; he lacks the swish and swash; he had yumph.

(See *character, temperamental.*)

PESSIMIST

One of those people who are always standing at the grave before the doctor has even begun shaking his head; a crape-hanger; Gloomy Gus; he has liver complaint and looks at the world darkly; tear jerkers; an old stick-in-the-mud; a killjoy; Calamity Jane;

those birds of doom who flutter around; viewed life with a highly jaundiced eye; a this-is-the-end expression on his face; a crank and a killjoy; a defeatist; a markedly jaundiced outlook on life in general; professional sneerer; black lookout; these prophets of gloom; in viewing with alarm and pointing with premonition; as soon as a man is born he begins to die.
(See *cynic, worse.*)

PEST
One of those women who go through life demanding to see the manager; our little pestilence; you may be all the world to the Boy Scouts, but you're only a headache to me; a pain in the neck; obstreperous; some fuss-budget on the committee; with that precious brother of hers; boil on the neck of the Administration; have to chloroform him to get him out of the kitchen.
(See *bother, bore.*)

PETTING
Make passes at her; chucking the girls under the chin; he was on the five yard line; squeeze her right out through the top of her gown like toothpaste out of a tube; catch-as-catch-can; an arms conference; we had to sweep him off the front porch with the cigarette ashes; he gets mushy; went into a clinch; in a séance; some girls may like wrestling for their dinner; he's all the time pawing you; look out for that guy with the flying-trapeze act; fellows who steer a car with their knees; I don't want to be forced to kick your teeth out; pinch-hitter; what are you, an interior decorator?; he's a laplander, he keeps one lap ahead of me; the blood in her veins was liquid fire; a quiet little spoon; somehow or other, they found themselves side-by-side on the couch; his hands wandered all over the lot; she nibbled at the lobe of his ear; he spends several bucks on a girl and wants a receipt.
(See *necking, embrace.*)

PHILADELPHIA
The Quaker City; the City of Brotherly Love; Philly.
(See *city.*)

PHILOSOPHER
Home-spun philosopher.
(See *wise, intellectual.*)

PHILOSOPHY
Long-haired philosophy; the Q. E. D. air of a philosopher handing out.
(See *college subjects.*)

PHOTOGRAPH
Snoopshot.
(See *cards.*)

PHOTOGRAPHER
While the photographer is going through his preliminary focus-pocus; he had one of those cameras that remind you of the time when you used to watch for the dicky bird.
(See *camera man.*)

PIANO
A regular Paderewski; then the lunatic falls all over the piano keys; piano-pounding; spent many hours at the pianoforte; thumping of the ivories; tinkling of the piano keys; will tickle the ivories; keyboard virtuoso; caress piano; whang the keyboard; can you play that ice-box?; he slapped the piano around until it hollered for help; digital gymnastics; belabor the piano; ivory masseur.
(See *music.*)

PIANO (Electrical)

Large quantities of galloping melody.
(See *machinery.*)

PICKPOCKET

Light-fingered gentry; finger-smith.
(See *burglars.*)

PICNIC

A middle-class bourgeois picnic; a bunch of Elks at a clam bake; strawberry festival.
(See *meal, parties.*)

PIE

A piece of store pie; the skush of a custard pie; apple pie à la apple pie; two sectors of pie; a slab of pie; a wedge of warm apple pie; and from innocent slabs of pastry the little green gooseberry raises its treacherous head; cherry pie must be eaten with a blue print.
(See *food, candy.*)

PIECE

A big hunk of.
(See *part of.*)

PIG

The screaming young porker; stood the piglet on its little legs and surreptitiously pinched one of his tender hams; piggy porkers; a pretty pig makes an ugly old sow (prov.); a pig used to dirt turns up its nose at rice (prov.).
(See *farm.*)

PIMP

Merchants of human flesh.
(See *prostitutes.*)

PIN

A pinhead with the Lord's Prayer written on it; it is no exaggeration to say that without pins civilization would crumble, people would come undone in all directions.
(See *clothes.*)

PING-PONG

Belaboring the little celluloid pellet; a family game; table tennis is something sightly more masculine than tiddly-winks; pingle pongle.
(See *tennis, games.*)

PIPE (Smoking)

A pipe is as much a part of the seasoned smoker's face; to curl up with a pipe; it's one of those very old gnarled pipes that bubble a good deal and give visitors the idea that there's something wrong with the drains; he did look sort of naked without his pipe; suck my pipe; fired up his pipe.
(See *smoking.*)

PIRATES

Captain Kidd; Long John Silver.
(See *sailors, steal.*)

PLAIN

As commonplace as pie.
(See *simple, ordinary.*)

PLAN

Upset the applecart; the project was still in the egg.
(See *campaign, plot.*)

PLATFORM (Political)

It mentions about everything except a good hair-restorer; I have made my platform and I must lie in it; my platform stands for the following splinters.
(See *politician's language.*)

PLAY

In that stirring opus.
(See *theatre, shows.*)

PLAYFUL
Crotchety.
(See *capers, humor, tease.*)

PLAYING
Gallivanting 'round; to fiddle with; of play-boyish propensities; toy with; letting off steam; dabble in; play-as-you-go system.
(See *games, card games.*)

PLEASED
As pleased as a child with a Christmas toy.
(See *contented, amuse.*)

PLOT
Dirty work at the cross-roads; hatch a conspiracy.
(See *intrigue, scheme.*)

PLOT (Movies)
All of the action takes place on the back of a postcard; the lovers chasing each other through California shrubbery; movie in which the heroine had a tough time defending her honor, but won by a Hollywood nose; happy ending we can suggest is for the management to give the audience their money back; the play takes place on the inside of a clothes closet.
(See *story, movies.*)

POET
A fellow long of hair and short of cash; when he puts his lyre away forever.
(See *writer.*)

POETRY
Commit a volume of verse; write a sonnet on an empty stomach; an epic in eighty-eight cantos; a poem one hundred thousand lines long, with scattered sections yet to be heard from; poetry is the jingling of a few silver coins in the ragged garment of life.
(See *literature, writing.*)

POINT (Come to)
Get down to brass tacks; the hub of the matter; let us return to our muttons; let's get to the milk in the coconut; let's get down to cases.
(See *exact.*)

POISON
Poison, an unpleasant thing to have in one's belly; put "barn arsenic" in the blancmange; put Paris green in the pipe; drink the hemlock; serve powdered glass in his breakfast food; tempted to feed her arsenic.
(See *druggist, unhealthful.*)

POKER
A few rounds of Seven-card Pete; with the deuces and one-eyed jacks running wild.
(See *card games, bet.*)

POLICEMAN (Name for)
The local gendarmerie; American OGPU; John Law; flat-foot; copper; a member of the local constabulary; guardian of the law; worthy minion of the law; bull.
(See *detective, patrol wagon.*)

POLITICIAN
Political high-priest; knows what tune to dance to; promises a brand-new millennius every afternoon; always glad to meet a politician with his hands in his own pocket; bush-beating politicians; experienced politician that ever talked an audience to sleep; sentiments of the Republic; he knows what's going to happen and who's going to do it, the Wednesday before; these old Wheel Horses; these party

apostles;   red-white-and-blue   politician.
(See *patriotism, ward-heeler, candidate, vote.*)

POLITICIAN'S LANGUAGE

The bulwark; under our starry banner; the old apple-sauce will be warmed over; from the rockbound coast of Maine to the sunkissed shores of California; the heel of the tyrant; of the people, by the people, for the people; on God's green earth; "I tremble to think."
(See *platform, vote—speeches.*)

POLITICS (Speech)

Take the stump; a real rabble-rouser; turning his oratorical guns loose; bursting with mob-igniting spirit; white-hot oratory; he flails his arms about his head violently; scalding his opponents with boiling hyperbole; his speeches smelled of gunpowder; delegations of citizens, brought to a boil by fiery oratory; political windbaggery.
(See *politician's language.*)

POLITICS

An island of plums entirely surrounded by politicians; with its speeches, hand-shakings and chicken-liver orgies; back-alley deals; funds wherewith party machinery is kept greased.
(See *parties.*)

POOL ROOM

Drop into a poolroom and help along the chalk industry; billiard balls are made from ivory, and work out at about forty to the elephant; an undulating, rectangular table; to bet their poke on the slot a scurrying pill will drop into; an errant cue-ball ricochets against the cuspidor; instruct them in the erstwhile gentle art of making one ball hit two other balls.
(See *games, ping-pong.*)

POOR (Quality)

Goofy; botched work; when I say it is lousy I'm praising it; are rather a scratch lot; shoddy goods; his golf was consistently wretched; aren't any particular shakes as actors; he must have learned his swimming from a mail-order house; also-ran; to see any old sissy pictures; a few moth-eaten specimens.
(See *useless, no good.*)

POOR (Poverty)

Down-at-heel peddler; as poor as a beggar man; as poor as Job; several steps ahead of the sheriff.
(See *poverty.*)

POPULARITY

On the band wagon; which were all the go; the apple of his eye; is getting a big play; quite the vogue; to be all the rage; has become one of Hollywood's fair-haired boys; he is a type on which the gods dote; the sidewalk cafe is to whoop this spring; was beating a path to her door for ten years; set the seal on his popularity; to be given the keys to the city.
(See *favorite, famous.*)

POPULATION

It couldn't claim three hundred people, even on election day.
(See *crowds, numerous.*)

POSSIBLE

A silver key can open an iron lock.
(See *easy, natural.*)

POSTAGE STAMP COLLECTING

The payment of enormous sums for little old fragments of unclean paper; the gum on its back has lost its pristine flavor.
(See *hobby, stamp collecting.*)

POSTURE

Posture that would be the despair of physical culture instructors; looked as if she had the bends.

(See *body, standing.*)

POTATOES

A mound of mashed potatoes; spuds; looked like a hunk busted off a tombstone; potatoes, be they fried, boiled, or hanging on the vine; tubers.

(See *food.*)

POVERTY

The poor man accumulated more and more poverty; like some shanty person; fell on lean days; living on crusts; down-at-the-heel; finances were approaching the vanishing point; cottonstocking waifs; not so well heeled with money; poverty rears its ugly head on all sides; felt the pinch of want; he kept the family in hock all the time; he didn't know there was any coin larger than a dime; for the very thin of purse; he was so poor he didn't own the buttons on his vest; impoverished; who had fallen on evil days; the seamier side of life.

(See *poor, beggar.*)

PRACTICAL

Apple blossom is beautiful, but dumplings are better (Japanese prov.).

(See *worth while, use.*)

PRAISE

With loud hosannahs; ring a bell in the carillon of praise; she raved on about the canvas; slipped him sugarcoated words of praise; a pat on the back; to sing hymns of praise; they oh'd and ah'd; go around chanting the praises of; laying the butter on; 64 cheers for; a paean of praise; the syrupy eulogies poured upon it; it's a little late to clap hands for Mr. Jones; mutual admiration society.

(See *admiration, bless.*)

PRAY

He salaamed three times; he called upon powers seldom invoked; he prayed like a jackrabbit eating cabbage.

(See *religious.*)

PREGNANT

She has two children, going on three.

(See *children, birth.*)

PREPARE

To cook up; the stage is being set; a beard well lathered is half shaved (prov.); fried pigeon doesn't fly into your mouth.

(See *ready, plan.*)

PRESCRIBING

Like prescribing Scott's Emulsion for a broken leg; to get some arnica for his chilblain.

(See *doctor, advice.*)

PRESENT

Better an egg today than a hen tomorrow.

(See *nearby, immediately.*)

PRESS-AGENT

Their blurbs; overhullabalooed; ballyhoo; I get the situation you're trumpeting; ballyhoo the pants off it; then the ballyhoo broke loose; over-theatricalized; beating the tom-toms; the clarions of the press-agents; is the town papered?; buried at once under a landslide of superlatives; a lot of extravagant hoop-la about him; with fanfare and fusillade the picture was launched; his grinning map had been three-sheeted all over Columbus for the last two weeks; transformed a flop into a smash hit by the Barnumian

trick of hokum ballyhoo; silk-hatted species of theatrical trumpeting; who disdains adjectives less than three leagues long.
(See *publicity*.)

PRETEND

Play possum; with a wink.
(See *imagination, lie, real*.)

PRETZELS

Some pretzels put a contortionist to shame; a soda cracker with the cramps.
(See *food*.)

PREVENT

Has me stymied.
(See *stop, interruption*.)

PRICES (Reasonable)

Without taking the shirt off your back or putting an extra mortgage on your house.
(See *cost*.)

PRICES (Cheap)

Murdered prices; had become suddenly two a penny; it was literally thrown at him; dime-a-dozen; subway money; two-bit gangsters.
(See *low*.)

PRICES (High)

The price rose to remarkable altitude; a stiffish price; isn't it a bit too steep?; cost him a pretty penny; boosts the price to stratospheric heights; astronomical; requires mortgaging the old homestead; the prices were higher than the roof.
(See *expensive*.)

PRISON

Took a post-graduate course at Ossining; expiate his crime at; so it's the Big Rock for you; several months on the stone pile; and filed him away in a cell; to be put where your meals come through a hole; did a stretch; turn him over to the mercies of the Federal authorities; in durance vile; the royal suite; he is now in one of the better hoosegows; are guests of the United States Government in Atlanta.
(See *jail*.)

PRISON (Escape)

To spring them.
(See *escape, run away*.)

PRIVACY

About as much privacy as a goldfish; in the sanctity of his own chamber; as private as a love letter in the tabloids.
(See *alone, exclusive*.)

PRIZE

Plum.
(See *honors, win*.)

PRIZEFIGHT

Orgy; fracas; massacre; tussle; the squared circle; tangles with Joe Louis; I had a date to step fifteen frames; the whiskerweight championship.
(See *fight*.)

PRIZEFIGHT (Knockout)

Count faster or he'll die of old age; knocked him colder than an ice cube; he could hear the birds singing and the referee counting.
(See *hit, blow*.)

PRIZEFIGHTER

Glaring at him as if he was so much red meat; to knuckle those ears of his until they flower like a truck garden; he belted over everything he could persuade to stand up in front of him; and never looked even approximately the same afterwards; he could keep

his feet south of his neck; packed a nasty wallop; a dumb but willing war horse; he could sock; murder in his hard hairy fists; the Simms orgy; back in the days when Knighthood was in Cauliflower; he was in the big league; he could dish it out; he took him apart somewhat like a medical examiner performing an autopsy.
(See *wrestler.*)

PRIZEFIGHTER (Second-rater)
A ham-and-egger; spent his days inspecting canvases; a pork-and-beans fighter; he had broccoli ears.
(See *fight—loser.*)

PRIZEFIGHTER (Talk)
Spread him on the canvas; mother won't know him from a pot roast; will lay him horizontal.
(See *fight—talk.*)

PRIZEFIGHTER (Audience)
"When do they go into their dance?"; kill the Mick; yelling homicidal encouragement; what is this, the Follies?
(See *audience.*)

PRIZEFIGHTER (Blows)
A right uppercut to the button; every blow is a minor concussion of the brain; plant a haymaker; given him an anaesthetic; a swing that almost blew out his fuse; a right that was sheer poetry in motion.
(See *fight—punches.*)

PRIZEFIGHTER (Fighting)
And was counted out examining the weave of the canvas; knocked him for a row of garbage cans; he took the dive; for years picking resin out of his konk.
(See *beat.*)

PRIZEFIGHTER (Foul)
He hit him on the ankle.
(See *unfair, foul play.*)

PRIZEFIGHTER (Loser)
His nose looked like a flattened sweet potato; battered gladiator; punch-drunk; his head was securely screwed on; looking like the burned remains of an air crash; to take a bad lacing; he sat down in a corner and asked for a little weak tea with lemon; blocking with his chin; he was knocked down so often he had a cauliflower back; he swallowed his bridge work; I never got so sick and tired of looking at a guy in my life; his ears looked like watersoaked biscuits.
(See *fight—loser.*)

PRIZEFIGHTER (Name for, general)
Pug; bruiser; scrapper, a broken-down old plug; gladiator; the knights of the knobby ears; palookas; leather slappers; braggart of the squared circle.
(See *free-for-all.*)

PRIZEFIGHTERS (Names for)
Rough House Brown; Haymaker Hogan; the New Rochelle Bruiser; One Poke McGregor.
(See *names.*)

PROBABLE
As improbable as a salary increase.
(See *possible, impossible.*)

PROBLEM
You couldn't get rid of it like they do Chinese girl babies; eating like a canker into the soul of England; and this brings us bang up against the problem.
(See *questions*)

PRODUCE
Dig up.
(See *effective, work.*)

PROFANITY

Uncorked some brocaded profanity; blank such a blankety blank blank; he said something that sounded like the squeak of an old-fashioned bedstead; he said something derogatory about; not fit to print; swore violently in several languages; cursed softly; I wish I could speak Chinese, it looks like a good language to swear in; spit out swear words; bellowed a volley of what-the-hells; a purple epithet; and was told to go to a warm spot; she castigated me; overworking their supply of oaths; raw-boned language; to indulge in recriminations; shouted vitriolic invective; cellophane-wrapped curse; milk-and-water maledictions; four-motored curses; in language that would make a Billingsgate fishwife blush; his diatribes; launches anathemas; the epithet is father to the epitaph; made the air blue with curses; a few unmuffled oaths; a Chinese cracker string of profanity.
(See *swearing.*)

PROFESSIONALS

It should be reserved for professionals, like tight-rope walking.
(See *experienced.*)

PROFESSOR

Professor with his knapsack full of theories; he adorns our faculty; some pale and prissy professor; he'd split his last infinitive with you.
(See *teach, intellectual.*)

PROFILE

That stern and rockbound profile.
(See *face.*)

PROFITS

A slice of the profits.
(See *margin, earnings.*)

PROGRESS

Upon the foam-crested wave of pros-

perity; we move up a bracket; the impressive forward march during the past century; is going great guns.
(See *increase.*)

PROMINENT

Persons who have been nodded at by Dukes.
(See *famous, conspicuous.*)

PROMISES

Big noises; he is poor indeed that can promise nothing (prov.).
(See *words, engaged, contract.*)

PROMPT

A stitch in time saves nine.
(See *ready, quickly.*)

PROPER

In the Rococo manner; it is considered de rigueur; things were back in their appointed places.
(See *correct, right, thing to do.*)

PROPHECY

She put both ears to the ground at the same time.
(See *future.*)

PROPHET

A Jeremiah; water-front prophets.
(See *fortune teller.*)

PROPOSAL

The occasion he selected for pressing the button.
(See *engaged.*)

PROSPERITY

Upon the foam-crested wave of prosperity.
(See *business.*)

PROSTITUTES (Etc.)

That old procuress; fallen woman;

habitués of sinks of vice; Kansas City Kitty; some floosie; damaged by the fleshpots; a white-faced Camille of the dawn; she wasn't exactly a paragon of virtue; the ladies of the hey-hey haciendas; one of the ladies of the road; ladies of sin; pavement nymph; courtesan of the boulevards; amateur magdalene; ladies of the parlor.

(See *sex*.)

PROSTITUTES (House of)

Spots with the Oo-la-la; den of iniquity; he played the hot spots; bordelo; brothel; bawdy joints; merchants of flesh; one of Philadelphia's flossiest bordellos; sink of vice; hey-hey hacienda.

(See *pimp*.)

PROTECTION

Looks around for the nearest storm cellar; under the aegis of Mrs. Treadwell.

(See *chaperone, keeper*.)

PROTEST

The welkin was ringing with popular protests.

(See *object, rebuke*.)

PROUD

He got chesty; take another reef in your pride; proud as Lucifer; pride so great he had tripped on it; you'd think he had just been given the Congressional medal; proud as a peacock; fairly bursting with pride; he nearly busted wide open when he saw her; swelling out his chest like a fan-tailed pigeon.

(See *vanity, ego*.)

PSYCHOLOGY

Pressing deeper into their libidos.

(See *mind, brain*.)

PUBLIC

Mr. and Mrs. John Q. Public; the pee-pul's acclaim; a plain John Citizen; the great bat-headed public.

(See *people*.)

PUBLICITY

In the presence of the newsreel cameraman; blistering *rays* of the publicity spotlight;

(See *press-agent*.)

PUBLISHING

Retired to the catacombs of a publishing company.

(See *editor, books*.)

PUN

He was quite a punnist, therefore he had to be a punster.

(See *joke*.)

PUNISH

To crack down on; they were surprised that I wasn't stricken by a bolt from the skies; boiled in oil; shot at sunrise; papa spank; he would tread on his tail; a bad cat deserves a bad rat; men have been shot and left dying in dark alleys for less reason.

(See *discipline, lickings*.)

PUSH

Straight-arm my way through the crowd.

(See *hurry, crowds*.)

PUT

He planted (slang); coaxing the edge of a rug under a piano.

(See *bring*.)

Q

QUESTIONS

Asking him questions which had no answers; he asks me answers and tells me questions; is he fast?, gwan, ask me, is he fast?; after someone has asked a lot of questions say "What is this anyway, a schoolhouse?"; the question fell on the floor unanswered; a fool may ask more questions in an hour than a wise man can answer in nine years.

(See *problem*.)

QUESTIONS (Celebrated)

Who killed cock robin?; who put the overalls in Mrs. Murphy's chowder?; who put the itching powder in Mrs. Carter's corsets?

(See *doubt, debate*.)

QUICKLY

I won't be two shakes doing it.

(See *fast, immediately, speed*.)

QUIET

As quiet as the morgue; mousey; it was so quiet you could hear a person changing his mind in the next room; let's have more quiet and less Rigoletto; a closed mouth catcheth no flies (prov.); pipe down; it was so quiet you could hear a watch tick in the next street; tip-toes about shushing everybody; in self-effacing tip-toe; in the pianissimo manner; so quiet you could have heard a cough drop (drug store); as silent as Harpo Marx; maxim silencer; all quiet on the Potomac; became especially tip-toey; shushed him; as quiet as a Trappist monastery; silent as the tomb; congealed silence; as quiet as a frost-be-numbed cicada; sh—you'll wake my foot up—it's asleep.

(See *calm, peace*.)

R

RABBIT
The rabbit softly cooing to his mate.
(See *hare.*)

RACE TRACK
At the race track he couldn't shuffle the horses; he was hitting the ponies; "horsey" set; "horsey" c i r c l e s; I haven't picked any wrong ones yet, well, hardly any wrong ones; where the bangtails run; where they bet their pokes on the gallop of a horse; bet on that sneezer of his.
(See *horseback riding.*)

RACE TRACK (Fast horses)
By the time the rest finished, I'll bet he was on his way to supper; the only way he can lose the race is to have somebody shoot him at the quarter pole.
(See *horses, fast.*)

RACE TRACK (Names)
A plug by the name of Miracle; Timbuctoo; Breezing Along; Meat Ball.
(See *names.*)

RACE TRACK (Poor horses)
Finished among the "also rans"; I can outrun this horse myself; if you were to place a bet on any one of them it would have broken his back; I picked one that looked as if he might last a couple of laps if he took care of himself; and by the time he ran one furlong he looked as if he had cannon balls on his feet; and if I'd known then what I know now, I wouldn't have put the tail of an old shirt on him; he can run far enough, but it takes him too long; that goat; your

horse can stay four miles, but he takes a hell of a long time to do it.
(See *slow, lose.*)

RACE TRACK (Tips)
Tips so hot they must have scorched the feedbox whence they came; a hot horse is a horse that is all readied up to win a race.
(See *bet.*)

RACKET
A sweet racket; by working this dodge.
(See *unfair, trick.*)

RADIATOR CAP
Fur-trimmed radiator cap.
(See *automobile.*)

RADIO
To belabor the air; "Marconi's Folly"; to hear things you cannot see.
(See *invention.*)

RADIO ANNOUNCER
Engaged a new man to do the coughing into the microphone.
(See *actor, advertising.*)

RAILROADS
An antiquated streak of rust; choo-choo company.
(See *travel, trains.*)

RAIN
The sky sprang a leak; the heavens opened and a flood of rain swashed down; I suppose it's raining on Mars and Jupiter and; honest-to-goodness rainstorm; it was raining outside! drip! drip! drip; the rain came down in bucketfuls; it rained like hellen

gone; splish-splashing rain; rained cats and dogs; a-knock-em-down rain; water squished inside his boots; rain pelted down with unremitting vindictiveness; Florida people say "That's not rain, that's just heavy dew."

(See *fog, storms.*)

RAISE (Salary)

A tilt; raised beyond recognition.

(See *salary.*)

RAISE (Children)

Raised her children with a good hickory.

(See *family.*)

RAISED

Ascends like the hoof of a camel; gesture that somehow ballooned our self-respect.

(See *increase, excited.*)

RAKE

To step on the business end of a rake.

(See *farm.*)

RARE

As rare as a Pekingese with a haircut; as rare as an antelope egg; rare as a dodo; as rare as snow in midsummer; rare as a mind that is chaste; rare as a fat man in a clothing advertisement; rare as humility in a grizzly bear; as rare as a clam in restaurant chowder; they are few and far between.

(See *scarce, once in a while.*)

RAVES

Then he goes into a nose-dive about her glims.

(See *exaggerated, praised.*)

READING

Cling to it till the fire went out; spelling out a newspaper; I have wallowed in these books; pouring breathlessly over; bent his beetle-browed gaze upon its pages; a confirmed reader-in-bedder; he had corns on the thumbs from book-holding; this is not the pabulum I would select for a Sunday morning in bed; plowing through; read what he has begot; I couldn't hear myself read; seeking success from his crushing labors in; they read more book reviews than they do books; expose themselves to the National Geographic.

(See *books, writing.*)

READY

The zero hour was at hand; ready at any time, like the undertaker.

(See *prepare, prompt.*)

REAL

The real McCoy; an 18-karat newspaperman; competition with teeth in it; he is the real goods; honest-to-goodness; a dyed-in-the-wool fan; all-wool; Grade-A.

(See *genuine, truth.*)

REAR-END

The buttocks; his fat imperial rump; his rumble seat; posterior; her what-have-you; a pat on her pistol pocket; a pat on her southern aspect; she was big, especially where she sat down.

(See *body, hips.*)

REASON

I owe it all to Bilge Reducing Gum; the whys and wherefores; no one knows the exact why.

(See *explain.*)

REBUKE

A bawling out that would smoke the hide off an alligator; soak them; give him Hail Columbia; would like to roast him over a fire; give them a piece of her mind; telling her off about it; a good rousting around; a sulphuric tirade; the greatest shellacking; raked him over the coals; using his tongue on her like a sergeant-major; to catch hell from; he gave her the length of his tongue; her trenchant tirades filled the air; he railed against; he tiraded against the verdict; tongue-lashing; to put you on the pan; lambasting.

(See *protest.*)

RECIPE
Look your egg firmly in the eye.
(See *cooking.*)

RECKLESS
Rush in where angels fear to tread; playing fast and loose; she doesn't care two cents; with reckless abandon; twist the British lion's tail; played bean-bag with the opposition; harum-scarum.

(See *daredevil, indiscreet.*)

RECOGNIZE
Never gives him a tumble.
(See *identification.*)

RECORD (Good)
Record as clean as a hound's tooth.
(See *reputation.*)

RECORD (Bad)
It is a blot on our escutcheon.
(See *dishonesty, failure.*)

RECORDS
My gory dossier.
(See *bookkeeper.*)

RECORDS (Break)
Crack all records.
(See *succes, win.*)

REFERENCES (For a job)
I can refer you to the World Almanac and Motley's Rise of the Dutch Republic; her references were falling apart in the creases.
(See *job, approve.*)

REFORM
That sent him to the carpet-slippers-and-pipe stage; Moses leading them out of the cesspools.
(See *change.*)

REFUSE
Turn thumbs down; hardened his heart; and who shall say me nay?
(See *"No."*)

REGARDLESS
Come weal, come woe.
(See *anyhow.*)

REGULAR
Cut and dried; as regular as being a democrat in Texas or a Presbyterian in Scotland; a steady diet; according to Hoyle.
(See *correct, ordinary.*)

REGULARLY
On and off.
(See *thorough.*)

REJOICING
There was dancing in the streets.
(See *thanksgiving.*)

RELATE
He reeled off his story; unwinds her life story.
(See *tell.*)

RELATIVES
A pack of hyenas; blood and kin; kinfolk; kith and kin; but my aunts were

thrust upon me; a miscellaneous collection of aunts, cousins, etc.; kinsman.
(See *aunt, brother, daughter, uncle, mother-in-law, son.*)

RELATIVES (On payroll)
Glued wives and daughters to the federal payroll.
(See *selfish, protection.*)

RELIEVED
He eased himself into a chair; "wheww-w-w!; relieved like a reprieve from the governor.
(See *feel good.*)

RELIGIOUS
Underneath the white robe of religion; in the amen corner in church.
(See *church, pray.*)

RELIGIOUS (Not)
His taste did not run to church-basement suppers.
(See *profanity.*)

REMARKS
A few cracks.
(See *repartee, speech.*)

REMEDY
Different sores must have different salves; desperate diseases have desperate remedies (prov.).
(See *medicine.*)

REMEMBER
What makes the story stick; paste that in your hat; go clattering down the halls of time; the corridors of your memory; it's right at the tip of my tongue, but I can't bite it off.
(See *memory.*)

REMIND
May I dust your memory back to the time.
(See *note it.*)

RENDEZVOUS
Happened upon his trysts.
(See *date.*)

RENO
Out in the graveyard of shattered romances; the famous Nevada melting pot; Cupid's Graveyard.
(See *city.*)

REPAIR
Patch up; bandage it up.
(See *good.*)

REPARTEE
The continuous explosion of firecrackery repartee; badinage; banter; persiflage; a *jeu d'esprit;* bon-mot; fluffy banter; verbal give and take; giving and taking outrageous repartee; he is quite a one on the happy retort; repartee, like vinegar, should be used with discretion; his devastating sallies.
(See *wise crack, conversation.*)

REPORTER
Newshawk; a young man of the press; the ink-slingers; newspaper scribe; hell hounds of the press; sob sisters; members of the fourth estate; typewriter jockeys; one of the better jotter-downers; ink-throwers; the writing fraternity; knights of the quill; pad and pencil boys; a press representative (he's never just a plain reporter); gazetteering; "semicolon boys"; news-hound; these potential Brisbanes; our local Margaret Higgins; a real, honest-to-goodness reporter.
(See *newspaper, news.*)

REPUBLICANS
And in their house "Democrat" is a bad word to the children; their Republican orthodoxy; an off-color Republican.
(See *politician.*)

REPUTATION

His lustre would have been more enduring.

(See *famous, influence*.)

REQUEST

At the behest.

(See *invitation*.)

RESIGN

Handed in his dinner pail.

(See *fire, discharge, stop*.)

RESOLUTION

So bang goes your good resolution; go ahead and resolute; resolution proved as brittle as.

(See *determination*.)

RESPECT

He takes his hat off to the law; doffs his topper to; takes off his chapeau to.

(See *bow, admiration*.)

RESPONSIBILITY

Stoop-shouldered with the new responsibility; pass the buck; these old shoulders sagging under obligations.

(See *trusted*.)

REST

To relax and rest on my nud caps; lolling; surcease from emotion.

(See *quiet, sleep*.)

RESTAURANT

They serve coffee for nothing, but charge 10c for the cream; she was so excited she used all the wrong forks; this restaurant served the best sixty cent dinner for a dollar you ever ate; she ordered as one to the menu born; the gleaming napery; with neat cubicles to which the hungry one may retire; "what do you call the meat balls today, John?"; a pie foundry; a beanery; dirty-spoon restaurant; a flip café;

going there for a snack; restyrong; smart people in New York lunch and have their pieds á terre at the; eating joint; grubbery; hash foundry; a penny beanery; ham and eggery; a high-class pie-and-coffee joint.

(See *eating, food*.)

RESTAURANT (High class)

One of the crack feeding spots; in some rococo restaurant; where you can pick up a fair meal for about $20.

(See *night club*.)

RESTAURANT (Head waiter)

With the air of a Caesar leading a triumphal march into Rome; by the exercise of that black magic known only to head waiters; without the use of a shoe-horn he had squeezed us cozily into our seats; he waved me to a small table.

(See *hotel—high class, waiter*.)

RESTAURANT (Waitress)

Got a job dealing 'em off the arm; slinging hash in a restaurant.

(See *servants*.)

RESULT

The upshot of it was; he that lies with dogs rises with fleas (prov.); he that sows thistles shall reap prickles (prov.).

(See *happening, end*.)

RETURNED

He was refunded to the bosom of his family.

(See *come, visiting*.)

REVENGE

I'll get your hide; at the first opportunity he was going to put powdered glass in her breakfast food.

(See *get even*.)

REVOLUTION

The tail wagged the dog.

(See *change, upset*.)

REWARD

Passing out the plums; munificences; to pin medals all over him; the way an animal trainer throws a seal a fish; I'd take good care of a guy who.

(See *bribery, honors, prize, win.*)

RICH

He was so rich he wore tailor-made underwear; the high-priced carriage clientele; cater to the upper-bracketed few; a good liver; he looked as if his pocket was well lined; he's in clover; rolling in velvet; he suffered agonies from coupon thumb; as rich as Croesus; wealth is a disease, but it never becomes an epidemic; he's filthy rich; a few hundred dollars mean as much to him as paper matches mean to a cigar store; catered to the best dress-suit and red fingernail trade; the white-tie and champagne trade; he got rich by buying tables for $8.50 and selling them reduced from $50 to $27.50; Mr. Moneybags; upper bracketeers; as rich as mud; who made a fortune during the war selling condemned meat to the army; he owns everything in town except a couple of gasoline stations; has money dripping out of all of his pockets.

(See *big-shot, money—lots.*)

RICH (To become)

Came into the money; rise to the two-Rolls-Royce status; wrought a fortune out of iron.

(See *saving, stock market.*)

RICH (Young men)

Playboys; bloods; too much swelling around; an international dilettante.

(See *man-about-town.*)

RIDE

Whip over to.

(See *horseback riding.*)

RIDICULE

A razzing; how the gods must laugh; held his nose in polite aversion; why, they'd laugh him right out of the knit-goods game; it's a yell, isn't it?; my story was widely pooh-poohed.

(See *fun, sarcasm.*)

RIDICULOUS

Like throwing a toothpick to a drowning man; like the lady who tried to keep out the Atlantic with a mop; reductio ad absurdum.

(See *funny, joke.*)

RID OF

Thinking of liquidating persons who; getting it out of our hair; figuring to ditch me; smoked her out; made short shift of; whom we wish he would trade Sir Malcolm Campbell and an outfielder.

(See *fire, discharge.*)

RIGHT

As right as rain; dead right; "I'm never wrong, I may not always be right, but I'm never wrong"; I do not err; as authentic as the Indian on the buffalo nickel; I wouldn't be doing right by my little Chester unless; I haven't picked a wrong one yet, well hardly any wrong ones; an aura of authenticity; just as there is a wrong and a right way of cooking smelts, of climbing Matterhorns; you have called at the right address.

(See *correct, proper.*)

RING (Jewelry)

A fat hand corseted with rings.

(See *jewelry.*)

RIVER

The lap-lap of the water.

(See *waves, ocean.*)

ROLE

A role that he could sink his teeth into.

(See *play, plot—movies, villain, hero.*)

ROMANCE
Pretty-pretty romance.
(See *love*.)

ROMANTIC
You go in for romance with both feet.
(See *passion, sentimental*.)

ROOM (Noun)
You couldn't swing a cat in it; it resembled a Ligget drugstore; repaired to his room; a room large enough for a giraffe to swing his mother in.
(See *house, apartment*.)

ROUGH
The untutored savage; a diamond in the rough; riding roughshod over; roughhouse; rough-hewn; a rowdydow; tough as nails; gentleness was not one of his characteristics.
(See *cave-man, hard-boiled*.)

ROUNDER
A philanderer; playboys; leads a life of the deepest infamy; a bon vivant; helling around.
(See *man-about town*.)

ROYALTY
Dark purple blood in their veins; the peerage as compared to the seepage.
(See *nobility, aristocracy*.)

RUIN
Going to rack and ruin; went to the bow-wows; put the kibosh; go to pot; roon; killed the goose that laid the gilded bricks; to foreclose the mortgage on his health.
(See *spoil, damage, wreck*.)

RULES
Catch-as-catch-can.
(See *method, orders*.)

RUMOR
Scotched these rumors; rumors riding every wind; rumor that had just arrived by the grapevine route; Dame Rumor; a rumor had rippled through the store; this rumor is completely destitute of foundation; rumors flew thick and fast.
(See *gossip, scandal, news*.)

RUN
Scoots; hotfoots it; run like all get out; lammed for the exits; ran lickety-split; came charging out at forty miles an hour; ran for the bus like a stag with the hounds at its heels; sailed into the yard; lit out for; pell mell; higgledy-piggledy; with his knees hitting his eyebrows; came tearing out of the joint; rush off clippity-cloppety; take to their heels; flitting; came running into the room in high gear; turns on such a burst of speed that he almost runs right out of his collar; dashed to the; trotted up to; lope; sprinted out of there in nothing flat; I gave my dogs the gas; scampered through the various rooms; ah looked at mah feet an' said, 'do yo' duty'; ran like the south wind; he ran like tarnation; "lit out" at top speed; take to the woods; to go racing like a young Lochinvar; and leg it to; scurried; ran like sheep before the wolf.
(See *darting, feet, hurry, speed*.)

RUN AWAY
And went away from that spot; let's fly, my dove; taking it on the Dan O'Leary away from there; to take it on the lam.
(See *escape*.)

RUSSIA
Kossacks; Moujik; the steppes; Khamschatka; the caviar punishers; Russia, the bear that wants to walk like a man; Russian men wear their shirts hanging outside their pants; Vasili Ivanovitch.
(See *foreigner*.)

S

SACRIFICE
One must take the bitter with the sweet.
(See *lose, yield, unselfish.*)

SAD
He was the opposite of mirth; as sad as a lightning bug in a milk bottle; he had laugh trouble; acting as if she were playing the title role at a funeral; woebegone; affected to the point of tears; alas and alack; life turns to aloes; nostalgic moments; as much gay abandon as a W. C. T. U. convention; felt herself go funny inside; voice freighted with woe; looking about as happy as a wet hen on a fox farm; a countenance from which all hope had fled; as sad as a woodpecker in a petrified forest; sad as a subpoena; sad as raindrops on a grave; woe is me; he looked like a man who has signed up to go over Niagara in a barrel; he rolled his eyes in the manner of a dying frog; was wrestling with her chagrin; looking like that traditional victim of the wrath of God; time out for a good old-fashioned mope; is in the dumps; Rembrandtesque gloom; who assured me with some wringing of the hands; in the depths of a dolor; with the demeanor that Mary Queen of Scots might have adapted en route to the scaffold; a painful, oh-the-pity-of-it business; a God-help-us-all distress signal in his eyes; a sorrow is an itching place which is made worse by scratching; unhappy as a hill-billy without a sponsor; get out your handkerchief and proceed to weep, Brother; his life is more ashes than attar; a picture of woe unutterable; into every life a little rain must fall.
(See *cry, feel bad.*)

SAFE-CRACKER
To cuddle a safe-door; croon to it; cracking a bank.
(See *burglars.*)

SAID
Said he in a basso profundo; said he in his kind Massachusetts voice; said he in a voice that sounded oddly like Alexander Woollcott's; said he in a voice that sounded like pebbles dropping on a tin roof; said Mr. ———in a tut-tutting voice; said he with a whale in each eye; "tush tush," he tush-tushed; he said it as if he was prepared to take it back at half price.
(See *talking, voice.*)

SAILORS
A pack of women-chasing scamps; sea dog; gobs; tars; God loves United States sailors; sailed the seven seas; jolly tars (English); the men who "go down to the sea in ships"; he stank of sea water; in maritime circles; a gnarled old sea-dog; a bit of an old sea-dog.
(See *nautical terms, pirates.*)

SALAD
There was everything in that salad except a few Republicans; a good salad is the prologue to a bad supper (prov.).
(See *food.*)

SALARY
He was making coffee and doughnut money; dragging down $20 a week; a salary rumored to be mighty close to two figures; stipend; I knock out thirty smackers a week.
(See *earnings, raise, wages.*)

SALES
And lie in wait for customers.
(See *sell.*)

SALESMAN
He would have difficulty selling a famished dog a bone.
(See *clerk, peddler.*)

SALESMAN (Good)
He can sell rings around any two salesmen; he was ready to go out selling lighthouses.
(See *business, busy.*)

SALOON
Liquor foundry; the new suds parlor; blind pig; filling station; bar-flies; a corn dispensary; pubs of Boston; the sawdust palaces of Eighth Avenue; giggle-water emporium; it had a sawdust flavor; gin mill; grogshop; barroom clowning.
(See *drinking, drunk.*)

SAME
A carbon copy of Red Grange; like peas in a pod; if you've seen one tree, you've seen 'em all; a mare's shoe and a horse's shoe are both alike (prov.).
(See *change—no change, copy.*)

SANTA CLAUS
Kris Kringle; crepe whiskers; the old gent.
(See *Christmas gifts.*)

SARCASM
In that case we shall go off in a corner and weep bitterly for democracy; I ought to burst into tears; his Harvard sneers; a professional sneerer; "tush, tush," be tush-tushed; how the gods must laugh.
(See *ridicule, fun.*)

SATISFACTORY
Hope everything is lollypops; Eddie will fill the bill; everything is hunky-dory; it will ring the bell.
(See *comfort, contented.*)

SAVING
Had more than twelve grand tucked away in the old sock; to hide away in the lining of the mattress.
(See *economy, miser, tight.*)

SAXOPHONE
Can tote a pretty fair sax; a saxophone player with asthma; a patent static eliminator for saxophones.
(See *instruments, brass.*)

SAY
Like father used to say; "Son," used father to say; utter a sentiment; spit it out.
(See *speech, talk.*)

SAYINGS
To peddle platitudes; has become a shiboleth.
(See *remarks, speech.*)

SCALES
Scales so delicately adjusted that you can weigh your signature on a piece of paper.
(See *weight, heavy.*)

SCANDAL
Rattled a few skeletons in the Gould closet; a public laundering of the soiled family linen; dragged his name in the dust; to sully the reputation of; his campaign of vilification against me; a lie has not legs, but a scandal has wings (prov.).
(See *gossip, rumor.*)

SCARCE

As scarce as orchids in an Arizona desert; shy on undershirts; no fifty dollar jobs are hanging around on bushes.

(See *few, numerous as.*)

SCARE

The goblin'll get you if you don't watch out; scare him into his cyclone-cellar; he was scared out of a year's growth; regarded him like the pox; chilled him to the marrow; his eyes popped; break out in cold perspiration; to make his spine crinkle.

(See *frightened.*)

SCARF

Adjusted his tippet.

(See *clothes, ascot.*)

SCHEME (To)

Sharp-shooting; chiseling; log-rolling; sitting up nights devising new and subtle ways of; hatch a scheme; dirty work at the cross-roads; to spike his scheme.

(See *intrigue, plot.*)

SCHOOL (Elementary)

McGuffey's reader.

(See *college.*)

SCIENTIST

The Paul Prys of Science.

(See *chemistry.*)

SCOLD

Tongue-lashing.

(See *rebuke.*)

SEARCH

They frisked him; snoop around Washington.

(See *investigation, looking for.*)

SEASICKNESS

Felt like last Wednesday's blanc-mange; he was beginning to look queer and unwholesome; all greenish round the gills; get his feet on terra cotta; mal-de-mer (French, for "You can't take it with you"); my own case was a victory of mind over matter; grouchier than a seasick traveler rolling down to Rio on a slow boat; trying to hold on to his breakfast; the boat commenced rolling like a porpoise; Jack was no sailor; he made a judicious dash for the rail; regarded sea-sickness as a social error.

(See *ocean, nauseated.*)

SEASONS

Change to their light or heavy underwear, depending on the season.

(See *spring, winter, autumn.*)

SECRET

None of this mumbo-jumbo and lodge secrecy; hugger-muggery; sub rosa; unbeknownst; nurtured the secret longing; a dark secret; to whisper secret tidings brought by little birdies from the north; the grapevine system; tend to your own geraniums; and it shan't go further than these four walls; honor bright; utsnay to you umpchays; pull down the blinds and stuff paper in the keyholes.

(See *mystery, hide.*)

SECRETARY

Privut secrity; he has a secretarial sort of face.

(See *typewriter, shorthand.*)

SECRET SERVICE

American cheka; ogpu.

(See *spy, detective.*)

SEE
He spotted her; descried.
(See *look*.)

SELDOM
Once in a blue moon.
(See *rare, scarce, one in a while*.)

SELFISH
You're a dog in the manger; the man who lives for himself alone will be sole mourner at his own funeral; he thinks charity begins at him; he will dance to nothing but his own pipe; he loved his friends well, but himself better.
(See *ego, mean*.)

SELL
Peddle to.
(See *salesman, clerk*.)

SEND
He relays this one.
(See *throw, give*.)

SENTIMENTAL
Sprinkling fragrant lavender between each little lost hope; vivacious slobber; smear on the sentimental jelly overthick.
(See *emotions, love*.)

SENTIMENTALIST
A mushy fuddy-duddy.
(See *romantic*.)

SEPARATE
Wheat from the chaff.
(See *distinguish*.)

SERIAL STORIES
Blood and thunder serials.
(See *writing, books*.)

SERIOUS
As serious as a tree full of owls.
(See *sober, importance*.)

SERMON
When he turned on the hell fire; his squirming congregation.
(See *minister*.)

SERVANTS
The first cook, the second cook, door-opener, superintendent of collar-buttons; the imported hair-fixer; the footman has eloped with the parlor-maid; and quite an entourage; below-stairs gentry.
(See *butler, maids, waitress, valet*.)

SEX (Desires)
His eyes glassy with pent-up anticipation; had whipped up Lee's desires to fever pitch; the fires of desire blazed fiercely in Lee's heart; he yearned for her tender flesh; his eager little eyes licked over her, undressing her mentally; his look, a look that peeled off her pink taffeta uniform; 'Gay night in Paris'; 'What the Butler Said'; flesh-pots; gad, this stuff is dynamite; playing fast and loose; sow the seeds of vice and wickedness; living in sin; he is the Boccaccio of the white-way Decameron; moral turpitude; you are heading for the gutter; sex is here to stay.
(See *passion, love*.)

SEX (Perversion)
He was obsessed with every known sexual perversion and some perversions never heard of before.
(See *criminals, vice*.)

SHAKE HANDS
He must mitt about 1,000 hands; pumped his hand up and down; gave him the lodge grip; thrust her small

paw out; to glad hand the patrons; so I unscrewed my hand from his; he shook hands with me up to the elbow; always count your fingers when shaking hands with a lawyer; let me press your cuticle.

(See *welcome, glad to see you.*)

SHAKING (Shivering)

Shaking all over like a reaping-machine with palsy; like a blancmange with palsy; like a shirt in a hurricane; like jelly; his flesh quivered; shivering like a Model-T Ford fender.

(See *nervousness.*)

SHARK

And then a thing like an old wet rubber boot top hove up out of the water; did you ever hear of a woman-eating shark.

(See *ocean, fish.*)

SHAVE

To shave with a blowtorch; he needed a shave so bad he could strike a match on his chin; a beard well lathered is half shaved; he had to take an anaesthetic every time he shaved; he used Dutch cleanser.

(See *beard, barber.*)

SHE

She it was, who.
(See *girl, woman.*)

SHIP

(See *liners.*)

SHIRT

I puts on a clean shirt and finds the buttonhole at the back big enough to put your head through; and this time the laundry left a little more shirt on the cuffs; he busts out in something in shirts.

(See *clothes, collar.*)

SHOCK

That would make your grandmother throw her apron over her head and shriek.

(See *amazed, surprised.*)

SHOES

His moccasins; shod; noise like walking through a bog with squeaky shoes; canal boats; destroyers; his shoes were full of feet.

(See *feet, clothes.*)

SHOE SHINE

Shoes shined up so that we can see our faces in them.

(See *clean.*)

SHOOTING

Felt the bite of bullets; let him have both barrels.

(See *gun.*)

SHOPPING

She loved to walk down Fifth Avenue and breathe on the jewelers windows; snarling through the shops.

(See *buy, spend.*)

SHORE

By the shores of Gitchie Goomie.
(See *ocean, river.*)

SHORTHAND

The art of "pothooks."
(See *secretary.*)

SHORT PEOPLE

Knee-high to a grasshopper; runt; you little snipe; runty; he isn't any bigger than an air-mail stamp; to stand on a penny to look over a nickle; he was no taller than a shortish piece of string; a little man may cast a great shadow (prov.); he's so small he can walk under the dachshund.

(See *little.*)

SHORT TIME
Her story is the briefest of the brief; she hadn't been in the house long enough to powder her nose, when; have had short shrift; held brief sway; 2 by 4 visit.
(See *small, temporarily*.)

SHORT WOMEN
What a fetching midge she appeared; little bitsy women.
(See *girl, woman*.)

SHOW-OFF (A)
Such a pish-tush.
(See *impression*.)

SHOWS
A few second-rate plays by third-rate hacks; "Way Down East"; the first of the big b'gosh shows; he was going to make Shakespeare look sick; like a Chinese drama, it lasts all day and there is no plot; the show demised in three brief days; the play, in short, was so much grease-paint; he put everything in it but the kitchen stove; polished drawing room dramas; this heart-yanker.
(See *theatre*.)

SHOWS (Bad)
A turkey; laid an egg in the box office; the play smells in nine different keys; the soggiest flop of the season; it smelled to high heaven; the whole play went phut; dramatic bellyache; the customers stayed away by the thousands; should have given away the tickets to the show itself and charged the customers for the intermissions; a story that must have been written by some shortstop in a nut hatch; a Broadway debacle; this play registered zero; it was hooted out of the theatre; wasn't even brought within hailing distance of Broadway; the play

was packed off promptly to the storehouse; this show was so bad that even the ushers failed to show up on the third night; it was one of those plays in which all of the actors, unfortunately, enunciated very clearly.
(See *melodrama, burlesque*.)

SHOWS (Good)
Lay 'em in the aisles; was standing 'em in the aisles; scheduled to slay the public; capsized everyone; wowed the public; set the town by the ears; packing them in; bowled them over; a rip-roaring success; lays 'em in rows; a sell-out; took London by storm; knock 'em for a row of gilded ash cans; smash hit; a home-run; a first-rate show, if only a second-rate play; the bacchanalian orgy.
(See *success*.)

SHOWS (Names, musicals)
The Tantrums of 1935; leg-and-lyric extravaganzas.
(See *opera, vaudeville*.)

SHOWS (Sad)
If you don't pretty nearly cry, I hate you.
(See *sad*.)

SHREW
A sandpaper tongue.
(See *scold, woman-sharp*.)

SHRUGGED
C'est la guerre.
(See *disregard*.)

SHUT UP
"Cut the lyrics."
(See *quiet*.)

SIBERIA
The tundras of Siberia.
(See *Russia*.)

SICK

There is seldom anything wrong with her that a certified check will not cure; got green around the gills; he was sick in bed with two nurses; highly expensive ailments; you look kind of liverish; just crumbling to pieces; had a spot of malaise; discovered what a whited sepulchre he was; was laid up for repairs; splendid array of symptoms; smitten with five spectacular ailments; went to bed and had cold compresses applied; but something happened to the physician for a few days so that he could not attend to me, and I recovered; she had been given up by both Mayos; he got the willies.

(See *diseases, feel bad, headache, nauseated, operation.*)

SIDE SHOWS

Side-show barking; tent spieling.

(See *theatre, shows.*)

SIGH

Hove a sigh that rattled the windows; he heaved a sigh that seemed to start somewhere down in his high-top boots.

(See *sad, sentimental.*)

SIGHT

They were a yell.

(See *ugly.*)

SIGNATURE

Sign on the dotted line; give me your autograph; your John Hancock.

(See *handwriting.*)

SILLY

Reductio ad absurdum; absurd as giving bread-pills for a broken leg; as silly as winking at a girl in the dark; absurd as to ask if the flowers love the dew.

(See *foolishness, nonsense.*)

SIMPLE

Simple as milking.

(See *easy, plain.*)

SIN

Sold his soul to the devil; the Seven Deadly Sins; living in sin; everything was wide open; bound in the chains of Satan; playing fast and loose; habitué of sinks of vice; seed of Satan; in league with the devil; contact with the fleshpots; primrose dalliance upon the Great White Ways of sin; Sodom and Gemorrah; sin—the invention of the devil; following the straight and narrow is all right, but it's more exciting to follow the one with curves; living in a lover's paradise.

(See *devil, temptation.*)

SINGING

She was having her voice done over; to lapse into song; she can warble; sending his lyric winging upon the otherwise inoffensive morning air; Miss Cadenza; he tears apart "Il Trovatore"; humming a gay snatch of song; vocal gargling; lifting a childish treble; I can't sing a straight line; songs that you can't sink your teeth in.

(See *voice, music, opera.*)

SIT

Pray be seated; rest your fetlock; sat there like a bump on a log; drape yo'self in an ole easy chair; park the frame; rest your bones.

(See *chair.*)

SKEPTICISM

And there would be a bit of tut-tut-tutting; bushwa; it is the bunk; poppycock; too, too kind; then, I'm the Swedish Ambassador's aunt; a doubting Thomas; pooh-pooh the idea.

(See *cynic, doubt.*)

SKIN (Male)
Skin like a rhinocerous.
(See *face*.)

SKIN (Female)
Her skin was white like tinted summer clouds.
(See *complexion*.)

SKIRT
With a flirt of her skirts.
(See *dress, clothes*.)

SKUNK
Saturated with essence of skunk; admired and respected by all.
(See *odor*.)

SLANG
And if the word "okay" had never been invented she would have been practically speechless.
(See *language, grammar*.)

SLEEP (Names for)
Beauty-sleep; cat-nap; snooze; siesta; shut-eye; forty winks.
(See *rest*.)

SLEEP (Go to)
Wafted in the land of dreams; tuck myself to sleep; grab off a bit of shut-eye; I'll be off to slumberland soon; climb into my pajamas and slide deftly beneath the eiderdown; hit the hay; popped right off to sleep; it is nappy nappy time; wrapped in slumber; in the arms of Morpheus; goes beddy-bye-lo; crawl in the hay; I think I'll consult my pillow; to woo slumber.
(See *bed*.)

SLEEP (Not)
To swap anything she might have left for a good night's sleep; sheep are made to be eaten, not counted.
(See *daydreams*.)

SLEEP (Action)
He is in the hay pounding his ear; she slept in her corsets to keep warm.
(See *snore*.)

SLEEP (Misc.)
A place to flop at; lay asleep like green waves on the sea.
(See *dreams*.)

SLEEPER (Heavy)
Wouldn't wake for an air raid; his ability to fall asleep amounts to a genius.
(See *tired*.)

SLOW
We were off like a streak of greased molasses; the mills of the gods grind slowly; a laggard; as the returns trickled in; it was knockdown and dragout; Saturday came like a snail scaling a cliff; make haste slowly.
(See *gradually, lazy, inactive*.)

SMALL (Amount)
The mere trickle of passers-by; don't blame you a nickle's worth; capsule biography; demi-tasse size.
(See *little, short time*.)

SMART (Persons)
These cognoscente; bulgeheads; such luminaries.
(See *intellectual*.)

SMART
Such perspicacity; it takes a seventh son of a seventh son; gad, the man is an Einstein; she is the bright shining light of; am I a brain trust?; she had her head screwed on the right way; this particular pundit; as smart as a treeful of owls; the so-called "wise ones"; and terribly, terribly wise; intelligence enthroned on the seat of authority; possess the seven brands of

wisdom; just a smart guy from Brooklyn who knows all the answers; he is nobody's fool; can give him "cards and spades"; outsmart; a good head will get itself hats (prov.); damn clever, these Japanese; he knows how many beans make five; and he didn't learn it by mail in ten easy lessons; such cerebration.

(See *clever, experienced.*)

SMASHUP

The truck goes smack-dab into the wall with a loud kuh-boom; found that the stern of a coal truck was stouter than the bow of a Dodge; exactly how it happened is a secret between my wife and a pole belonging to the local electric light company; there is a scientific law that two autos cannot occupy one space at one time.

(See *accident.*)

SMILE

He beamed and burbled; he smiled up his sleeve; a push-button grin; simper; the one who wins is the one who grins; grinning like a Cheshire cat; a castor-oil smile that looks as if it is painted on; toothsome grin; wearing a perpetual phony smile; ear-spanning grin; his good-natured smile had been practically tattooed on his face; turned on his million-candle-power smile; smiled like a tooth paste ad; never judge a woman's smile by her teeth, both may be artificial; an adenoidal smile.

(See *grin, laugh.*)

SMOKING

He smoked like a chimney; he eats cigars; flicking cigarette ashes into the potato chips; for a dash of nicotine; I'm going out for a fag; dragging on a butt.

(See *pipe, cigarette, cigars.*)

SMOKING (Cure, give up)

To cure yourself of the smoking habit get someone to put something secretly into your tea; I hereby resolve to give up smoking, and if there's a slump in the tobacco trade you'll know who's to blame.

(See *temperance.*)

SNAKE

An "old sarpint"; the business end of a snake.

(See *poison.*)

SNEEZE

An atchoo.

(See *cold.*)

SNOB

High hatitude; a stately, nose-uppy duchess; nose elegantly in the air; he is able to strut, even when sitting down; snooty; they sniff at; his sartorial snobberies; lifting a snooty nose; giving you the "once-over" via the lorgnette route; an upper register "fawncy"; her hoity-toity attitude; snobbism; the rather offish Mrs.——; she is too upper register; very upstage; carry their "honor" like a chip on their shoulders; we get high-hatted all over the dump; considered themselves rather a race apart; ritz some one; to give anyone a tumble; the way she Park Avenued everybody; come out from under your high hat; anyone would think she was a duchess on a slumming party; and plainly regarded us as not quite the right people; hauteur and noblesse oblige; delusions of grandeur; these six-penny snobs; the holier-than-thou complex; with nose up in the air as if we smelled bad.

(See *exclusive, vanity, proud.*)

SNOOPING
Deploying around; willing to turn snooper.
(See *inquisitive*.)

SNORE
Snored in the night like the blast of a fog horn; and snores begin to issue from beneath their moustaches; soft-p a l a t e calisthenics; two - hundred pound snore; was emitting snores like the soughing of the wind in a grave-yard cypress; nostril opera; like the droning of a steam shovel; night con-cert.
(See *sleeper—heavy*.)

SNOW
It was snowing a copious white fuzz.
(See *blizzard*.)

SOBER
As sober as a judge.
(See *serious*.)

SOCIALISM
Parlor Pinks; most of them were 'ists of one sort or another; with the *New Masses* protruding from their hip pockets; they stand for caviar for e v e r y o n e; Pharisees; hair-trigger, crack-brained radicalism; wild-eyed radicals; his Marxist strain has be-come too brilliantly ruby; carmine streak; the old and new shades of pink; the brotherhood of man; near-communists; pent-house communists; back-alley red; bright reds and pale pinks; agents of the Third Interna-tionale; the red menace; those frizzle-haired, wild-eyed clucks.
(See *politics*.)

SOCIETY
Punctuality is again coming into fashion; road leading to the social Nirvana; slapped fresh gilt on the gilded set; your old man is Park Ave-nue; lousy with class; the best dress-suit and red fingernail trade; you're in the big time now; it is not consid-ered soigné on Fifth Avenue; it is not the proper caper; she'll bust you one with her tiara; she has been through the social mill; giddy young fool on the social trapeze; the social racket; with their diamond dog-collars; sas-siety; high-handshake (Park Ave.).
(See *high-class, aristocracy*.)

SOCIETY (Individuals)
Mingle only with the socially anoint-ed ones; he is New York's most inde-fatigable social gadabout; blueblood; Mayfairites; the creme-de-la-creme of society; the scion of the Morgans; the lorgnetted Southamptoners; socially sacrosanct Morgan clan; such social luminaries; the plutocracy.
(See *snob*.)

SOCIETY (Ladies)
Is one of the "great ladies" of Phila-delphia swelldom; the foremost of metropolitan society's grand dames; the de luxe ringmaster of internation-al society; top-lofty ladies; pillars of our smart set; high priestess; the doughty dowagers.
(See *dowager, debutante*.)

SOCIETY (Names for)
The four hundred; the Mayfair mer-ry-go-round; sassiety; the Park Ave-nue social sector; the upper social strata; the gilded set; the upper crust; in the higher brackets of society; silk-stocking district; carriage trade.

SOCIETY (Social register.)
Burke's Peerage; pedigree; the Social Registered Thomas Whelans; they have a nice Social Register rating; she is too upper register; who knows

the Social Register backwards and forwards; Social Registerites; both social
and cash registers.
(See *exclusive, high-class.*)

SOFT DRINKS
Luscious ambrosia.
(See *drinking.*)

SOME
A spell of; a batch of mail; a splash
of travel.
(See *part of.*)

SOMETHING
She was dragging, look what.
(See *anything, everything.*)

SON
His sun rises and sets with his son;
offspring; in a fiddler's house all are
dancers; looks like a splinter off the
old block; my own flesh and blood.
(See *family, boy.*)

SONG
Chantys; the merry roundelay; litany.
(See *singing, music.*)

SONG-WRITER
Fashioner of ditties; Tin Pan Alley.
(See *opera.*)

SOPRANO
The coloratura soprano, at whose
cackling even the taxi-drivers halt;
her singing voice was a trifle strident
in the upper register.
(See *opera singers.*)

SORORITY
A henhouse where the coeds live.
(See *club, college.*)

SORRY
In that case we shall go off in a corner and weep bitterly for democracy;

my heart bleeds for you; oh, the ignominy of it; I'm all broken up about
it; made clucking noises with their
tongues against their teeth.
(See *grief, sad, sympathy.*)

SOUP
Who put the overalls in Mrs. Murphy's chowder; guzzle; nothing could
be heard but the gentle murmur of
the soup.
(See *food.*)

SOUR
As sour as a spinster with the screws.
(See *bitter.*)

SOUTH (The)
The Mason-Dixon line separates those
who say "you all" from those who
say "hadn't ought"; a conservative of
the Ole Massa School; the furbelowed
South of long ago; said he, in soft
South Carolina accents; draggy talk;
damyankees.
(See *American.*)

SPAGHETTI
Shoveling it in and humming Italian
arias; like water-soaked shoestrings.
(See *food.*)

SPAIN
Castanets and passionate glances; a
ten-gallon comb on a Spanish senorita; caballeros; they say she knows
only two words of Spanish—manana,
meaning tomorrow, and pajama,
meaning tonight.
(See *foreigner.*)

SPATS
Heliotrope spats.
(See *clothes.*)

SPECULATE (Stocks)

He will end up by sleeping in the subway; he will wind up behind the eight ball; the market runs up and down like a monkey on a stick.
(See *bond, brokers, stock market.*)

SPEECH

Delivering this oratory to the umbrella stand; laryngeal creakings; vocal garglings; spread-eagle oratory; soap-box orations; philippics; his speed was "oppressed by metaphor, dislocated by parentheses, and debilitated by amplification"; oiled his cords and got ready for his spiel; flailed the air with his old vigor; spellbinding them with a masterly flow of genitives, past participles, conjunctions, neuter nouns, and; "And now ladies and gentlepeople"; spellbinders.
(See *talking, elocution.*)

SPEED

Annihilate space; you have to open a car up pretty wide; his accelerator foot hit the floor boards; drive like Billy Heck; drive like all get out; we were going lickity-split.
(See *fast, quickly, speed.*)

SPELLING

2 P's, one on top of the other.
(See *language, grammar.*)

SPEND

To shoot the works; he spent a buck and a half (his relief money); with a month's pay burning holes in his pocket; dish out the spondoolix; he spends as if it were stage money; blow in his money.
(See *buy, shopping.*)

SPENDTHRIFT

Fritter away a week's salary; his money was melting; like pouring money into a rat hole; he spent it like a cowboy on a spree; spent $500 as casually as if it were something growing around the back porch; spending hand over teakettle; if he continues he'll soon be down to his last $50,000,000; he tossed a nice bundle of currency into circulation; he believed that a shroud had no pockets; beside him Solomon was a miser.
(See *extravagant.*)

SPINSTER

Congeal into a spinster.
(See *old maid.*)

SPOIL

To coddle; pamper; mess up his plans.
(See *disturber, indulge.*)

SPREAD

Spread like athlete's foot at an athletic meet; spreads the pink eye.
(See *expand.*)

SPREE

On a bender; on a binge; go on the loose; and began knocking about the public houses; go on the razzle-dazzle; on a tipple; primed for his semi-annual spree; going the pace; make the rounds; frolicking around with; helling around; went on a rampage.
(See *drinking, rounder.*)

SPRING

When the sap flowed and the birds mated; tra-la-la, and all that sort of stuff; spring, when the sap runs in the baseball bats; to come forth from hibernation; spring has definitely arrived (subject to change without notice); no doubt spring will come at the same time as usual this year, not having heard any plans to the contrary.
(See *seasons.*)

SPY

A spy system that makes Mata Hari look like a near-sighted Albino; spies and agents provocateurs; they were not allowed to send letters showing the fortifications or revealing the seating capacity of our large movie palaces.

(See *secret service*.)

SQUEAL

Holler copper; our gals put the finger on them; the tip-off.

(See *yell, tattle-tale*.)

STAGE FRIGHT

He looked like the man who had strolled on by mistake and regretted the whole incident.

(See *acting*.)

STAIRS

Clumped up the stairs; to nip downstairs; he toddled up the stairs; scuffed up the stairs.

(See *house*.)

STAMP COLLECTING

Stamp collector's tongue; fuzzy-tongue.

(See *postage stamp collecting*.)

STANDING

Broke their arches standing at bars.

(See *posture*.)

STAND UP

Bounced to his feet; rocked to his feet.

(See *arise*.)

STATISTICS

Bandy statistics with the ease of the man on the flying trapeze; plague of statistics; statistics culled by loving hands; there are three kinds of lies— lies, damnable lies, and statistics.

(See *accountant*.)

STATUE OF LIBERTY

The old maid of Bedloe's Island.

(See *American*.)

STAY

Tarry in our midst.

(See *living, wait*.)

STAY AWAY FROM

Playing hookey from.

(See *avoid*.)

STEAK

One of the aristocrats of the cow kingdom; baked potatoes and steak are old college chums; wheeled the steak into the operating room; steak-lovers; even an alligator couldn't have eaten that steak without a struggle; he beamed at a large steak.

(See *food*.)

STEAL

To cop a phrase; frisked him; swipe; he went through them as if he were a streamline train; went through him like an electric shock; burgled; jimmied; filched nickles from; to steal the family jewels; sneak-thieving.

(See *burglars, crook*.)

STENOGRAPHER

She was more of a blonde than a typist, but she would spell a word right every once in a while; banging a typewriter.

(See *dictation, typewriter*.)

STEP-INS

Burlap step-ins with non-skid tread.

(See *clothes, underthings*.)

STICKY

The fly-paper stuck to her feet with great tenacity of purpose; stuck to him like a mortgage.

(See *hangers on*.)

STOCK COMPANY
They'd have played *Ben Hur* with six people and a mule.

(See *theatrical company.*)

STOCKING
She darned them so often that they began to look like exquisite pieces of tapestry.

(See *clothes.*)

STOCK MARKET
Stock market played jumping jack; stocks and blondes; these stocks were cats and dogs; blue ribbon stocks turned purple.

(See *bond, brokers, speculate.*)

STOMACH
His interior felt like the Battle of Gettysburg after the second days' fighting; midriff; solar plexus; innards; his epigastrium; his vitals.

(See *body, hunger.*)

STOP
Nip in the bud; hold everything; hang fire; pipe down; squelched it; lay off that nonsense.

(See *brakes, discontinue.*)

STORMS
Trees were blown down which were never blown down before; sure was blowing big guns; I couldn't put a dog out on a night like this.

(See *cyclone, blizzard, rain.*)

STORY
Swap stories; regaled us with many stories; exchanging hot ones; spin you a sea yarn; opus; and thereby hangs a tale; saga; concocted a story; retailed a story; two-fisted he-man yarns; pale magenta anecdote; this story be-gins at seventy miles an hour, but quickly gathers speed.

(See *talking, writing, serial stories.*)

STRANGER
A strange Lochinvar came out of the vest; I don't know you from a bowl of beans.

(See *foreigner.*)

STREET
The main stem; the main drag.

(See *city.*)

STRENGTH
His blood and thunder style; a perfect dreadnought of a woman, looking for whom she might sink; able to bite rifle barrels in two; a real panther-man; he had some Clyde Beatty in his system; full of panther sweat; he was constructed of concrete and cast iron; the assassin; his rough-hewn manner; he'd fight anybody at the drop of a hat; a hell-cat; hellion; you could hit him all day in the stomach and only bruise your knuckles; ruffian; built like two gorillas; he looked like a mixture of Londos, Carnera and Zbyszko rolled into one; he had fingers that could throttle a horse; it was like trying to knock over the Bank of England; he looked like a toss-up between Frankenstein and something that lived in a swamp; he had that icicle glance that sends the tiger slinking back to the jungle; he had that something in his eye which fetches waiters.

(See *energy, muscles.*)

STRICT
Her morals were starched throughout; strait-laced; was run in Prussian style.

(See *exact.*)

STRONG
(See *strength.*)

STUBBORN

Cussedness; pig-headed; m u l i s h; balky; plant his little heels in the gravel and refuse to budge; set in her ways; puts his fingers in his ears and will not hear.

(See *determination*.)

STUCK

Stymied.

(See *sticky, failure*.)

STUPID (Mild)

Slow on the uptake; gentle benign boobery; his few mental buttons all fly off; he is the kind of man who pulls doors marked "push"; obtuse child; skip-stop mind; wooden-headed; mentally soggy; lame above the neckband; doltish, addlepates; he isn't anything to 'phone home about; has he got a good head?; it ought to be good, he hasn't used it much; a state that was practically non compos mentis; he didn't know the difference between single tax and left hook; he looks as if he doesn't know what time it is; if she only had the brains God gives geese; his thinking is muscle-bound; you chuckle-head; his brain was full of cobwebs; his addled intellect; a nod is as good as a wink to him; about as temperamental as a dish of oatmeal; sunk to the ears in a bog; mental dyspepsia; he does not know who wrote the autobiography of Cellini, or when the war of 1812 was fought; his brain works on a part-time basis; he gave no outward symptoms of being ready to help Lloyd George solve problems of statecraft; not exactly a master mind; he wasn't exactly the seventh son of a seventh son; a mouse must not think to cast a shadow like an elephant (prov.).

(See *dumb, nonsense*.)

STUPID (Zero)

A mosquito is way ahead of him mentally; he knew that Monday always comes after a Tuesday; he knew how many beans make ten; imitate zero; he knew which way was up; he didn't have a grain of sense; apartments to let upstairs; his skull has no tenant; he is one of life's imponderables; didn't have enough sense to pound sand in a rat hole; the brains of a mosquito; he'll never be worth hell-room as a; with weak heads and delayed reflexes; present but not voting; he knows so little and knows it so fluently; his adamantine skull; halitosis of the intellect; hasn't got a single brain in his head; horse-car minds; their heads, such as they are, are complete vacuums; has a mind like a sieve; he had only a spoonful of brains; he was just barely able to tell when water came to a boil; pure bone between the ears; he's so dumb he couldn't find a bass drum in a telephone booth; has that air of cast-iron nitwittedness; he was muscle-bound from the neck up; the All-American half-wit; having been dropped on his head when young.

(See *illiterate*.)

STUPID (Proverbs)

A cracked bell can never sound well; a broken sack will hold no corn; among the blind the one-eyed is king.

(See *foolishness*.)

STUPID (Names for)

Dumb cluck; a hundred per-cent chump; dope; dullard; sap; greenhorn; dumbbell; cabbage head; prize dope; teak-head; dolthead; ninny; nitwit; half-wit; addle-pate; ignoramus; fat-headed cluck; a bunch of dim-witted coons.

(See *fool*.)

STUTTER

He stuttered like a string of fire-crackers; he sputtered; his tonsils get tied in a knot.

(See *lisp.*)

STYLE

Had a style which was dégagé; a masterly flow of genitives, past participles, conjunctions, neuter nouns, and other Latin parts of speech; this sentence can be set to music and sung at ships' concerts.

(See *language, writing.*)

SUBMIT

To take it lying down; I bend the knee; I made him come to heel.

(See *give up.*)

SUBSTITUTE

To be there by proxy; pinch-hitting.

(See *change, exchange.*)

SUBWAY

The public be jammed; I wish I had been given a little time to select a lady whose lap I could prefer to sit down in; Chambers of Horror and Black Hole of Calcutta; strap-hanging in the subway.

(See *trains.*)

SUCCESS

A wow of the first carat; he was knocking them over like a boy playing war with tin soldiers; to panic 'em; wallow in success; on top of the world; made the grade; on top of the pile; struck pay dirt; Horatio Alger type; they are in the clover; took London by storm; winning his spurs; she rode the Hollywood top wave; to click like a carload of dynamite; had the world by the tail; victory was heaped into his lap; "Local Boy Makes Good"; his name led all the rest; the title is a sell; he was on the top rung; they mopped up; in the bright lexicon of success; sitting as pretty as an ermine coat on a blonde's shoulders; he that would have what he hath not should do what he doth not.

(See *hit, prosperity.*)

SUDDENLY

With one fell swoop; it happened whamo.

(See *quickly, surprised.*)

SUFFER

To take the bumps.

(See *feel bad.*)

SUICIDE

Throw herself with a hysterical shriek from the belfry; commit hari-kari; he'll throw himself off Pier 14; he turned to jelly on the rocks below; but I do not have the price of a rope; he was going down to the cellar to end it all; to muss up the carpet with his brains; his head ached and he did not feel like shooting into it.

(See *kill.*)

SUIT (Man's, cheap)

It looked like a set of slip covers; an atrocity; jig-saw puzzle you call a suit; a mail-order suit; use it to scare crows with; you - can - be - nifty - for - $13.50; a suit which hadn't been new for some time; last time he was caught in the rain with this suit on, the vest disappeared.

(See *clothes.*)

SUNBURN

His nose peeling like wallpaper in a damp room; like lamb chops, to be broiled first on one side and then on the other; never expected to see the day when the girls would get sunburned in the places they do now.

(See *heat.*)

SUNDAY PAPERS

Ten pounds of Sunday papers.

(See *newspaper*.)

SUPERSTITIONS

Bugbears; for the bride to be run over on the left side of the road by a black truck on Friday the 13th is considered to be definitely unlucky; her knuckles were skinned from knocking on wood.

(See *believe, worship, fear*.)

SUPPORT

Help feather the nest; to keep us in sables.

(See *living, help*.)

SUPREME COURT

Legislature makes laws, executive bodies carry them out, and the supreme court throws them out.

(See *law, judge*.)

SURE

Beyond the peradventure of a doubt; it's in the bag; gold-plated predictions; dead sure; as sure as a gun; it's on the griddle; I have it on the ice.

(See *certain*.)

SURPRISED (To be)

Surprising as a wooden wedding in Hollywood; this will destroy you; he started as if bitten by a snake; shocked and reshocked; a source of wonder and amazement even to ourselves; his eyes popped; bombshell was hurled into the situation; your eyes are popping out of your head with astonishment; his eyes bulged with amazement, like two huge globules of tapioca; a great deal of oh-ing and ah-ing; I nearly swallowed my gum; his jaw fell to the pavement; like a bolt from the blue; a dark horse; "Emmagine!"; "GK!" said Mrs. ——; you could have

knocked me down with a crowbar; gave a gasp like a stranded cod; he almost jumped completely out of his white-canvas spats; he looked at it with the same amazement that he might regard a seven-legged chorus girl with; this will knock you for a row of aluminum ash-cans.

(See *amazed, shock, suddenly*.)

SUSPENDERS

Capt. John Smith once amused a hostile band of Indians by showing them his compass and new suspenders; galluses; sock-suspenders.

(See *clothes*.)

SUSPENSE

Tongue hung out of his mouth; the zero hour had arrived.

(See *doubt, fluctuate*.)

SUSPICIOUS

I smelled it in the beginning; I smelled a rat; there was something odoriferous in Denmark; there was a nigger in the vestibule somewhere.

(See *doubt, jealousy*.)

SWEAR

He swore a wicked swear; opprobrious epithets; he allowed himself the luxury of a very bad word; master of invective.

(See *profanity*.)

SWEAR (Promise)

To swear upon a stack of bibles; cross my heart; honor bright.

(See *cross your heart*.)

SWEAR (Trump that)

Laugh that off; tie that; put that in your old clay pipe; put that in your sock.

(See *beat*.)

SWEARING

Horsefeathers; horse-chestnuts; nuts; that's a lot of noise; bushwa; sez you; phooey; hells bells; aw, spinach; it is all too, too quaint; baloney; apple-sauce and tripe; rubbish; rats; piffle; the heck with it; "tut, tut"; oh, scissors; I wish he would sit on a rock and get a black eye; they should stick his head in water three times and pull it out twice; few miles, your grandmother; blooie; bosh; utsnay; a fig for you; gadzooks and gollywogs; oh, rats; fumadiddles; pfui; stuff; run along and peddle your papers; pishy-posh; pish tush; you go 'long; oh stuff; you Turks can go climb a Halvah tree; go whistle; golly; it's a mercy; tsk! tsk!; aw, shoot; for gosh sakes; my good suffering gosh; good golly; good crimminy cripes; gadzooks; zowie; dad-burn-it; horrors; holy saints; Holy Crow; mercy; my stars; perish me; great guns; oh, Judas Priest; by jumpin' Jupiter; for crimp's sakes; crimminy; mein gott im himmel; gosh all fish-hooks; well, I swan!

(See *oath.*)

SWEARING (Darn)

Blamed manners; who in the name of George Washington; a blasted idiot; a blooming fool; a dog-gone fool; he was so gee-dee sure of himself; what in the name of the incandescent hinges on the trapdoors of Hades does he; what the heck; a danged varmint; the bloody flavor; in your confounded society; your precious cousin; this blinking fool; where the *enfer* is my; how in what-Sherman-said-war-was did you; drat the question of talent.

(See *anger.*)

SWEARING (Exclamations)

Bully for you; strike up the band; heh! heh!; hot ziggity dam!

(See *pleased.*)

SWEARING (Name calling)

Dead beats; you big lug; you lousey punks; you're a beastly old slut; clods; philistines; fatheads; nit-wit; you're an awful pill; you hussy; cad; bounder; lout; why, you dirty offspring of a not too scrupulous parent; you beast, you; you old porous plaster; you old weasel; wind-bag; listen, egg; old frozen puss; beetlepuss; monkey-face; and this bit of refuse imagines; a slug; a low gasterpod; moocher; talk to that piece of pork; that churl; the shoemakers have a word for it (heel); low-lifer; insect; you dumb, shabby-ankled, good-for-not-a-thing, bum; that female snake in human form; dirty blackguard; cheap-skate; proved himself seven different kinds of unscrupulous heel; low down scallywag; you poor she-fool; you stubborn mule; a soulless plug-ugly; sniveler; Chinese stinkpot; clam; blatherskite; bloated toad; sniveling hypocrite; the graceless old widget; taking digs at him; you're a no-good so-and-so.

(See *names.*)

SWEARING (Names, mild)

That old scallop; you old baggage; go ahead, stinkweed.

(See *epithets.*)

SWEARING (Oaths)

By the sacred ashes of my ancestors; by the beard of the Prophet; by gad; not by the hair of your chinny-chin-chin; odsblud; a pox on it; a pox take him; gad; by heaven; shut my beard; shiver me timbers; burn my shorties; strike me pink; I'll be jiggered; I'm blowed; I'll be a son-of-a-gun; I'll be blithered; as I live and breathe; begob; may Allah lengthen thy days; Allah be praised; by the Lord Harry; bless my soul; God save the King; dummed if the dang thing didn't turn white; but to save my neck; by gow;

by gum; they'd be so-and-so-ed if they would; a plague on thee; well, for crying out loud; rot me if; for the love of Aunt Het; for the luvva Pete; dog my cats; bless my mildewed soul; by the two-headed gods of ancient Erin; why rip me; I'll be diddledy—daddledy—durned; may the recording angel write down.

(See *cross-your-heart.*)

SWEARING (Telling them where to go)

You go jump in the river; go fly a kite; go chase yourself; go chase your Aunt Minnie; go to blazes; go home and take yourself a pill; rats; pooh; go sit on your hat; put that in your old clay pipe; go bite yourself; please take two running jumps and go to "H——"; go lay an egg; go down to the ocean and pull a wave over your head.

(See *disgust.*)

SWEAT

Sweat running from your garters to your sock tops and tickling like sand fleas; perspiration bedews their pinkish brows; he perspires fluently; the beads of perspiration roll from his manly brow in great globules; he sweated like a suspect in a murder case under police examination.

(See *heat.*)

SWEAT (Women)

My dear child, only animals sweat, men perspire, but young ladies merely glow.

(See *hot.*)

SWEATER

It hugged her body.

(See *clothes.*)

SWEET

As sweet as a secretary's "hello"—when her boss is in; it isn't fair to sugar to be as sweet as you; she said, in those honeyed accents; with unholy sweetness.

(See *candy, taste.*)

SWEETHEART

He's my deep breath; my all-that-matters; a new flame; the lady of his choice; his "One and only"; his inamorata; the girl of his dreams; you are my moment supreme; my sweety pie.

(See *pet, girl, favorite, love.*)

SWIMMING (Good)

Swimming as though he was old man ocean himself; he cut through the waves like a porpoise.

(See *bathing beach.*)

SWIMMING (Bad)

He must have learned his swimming from a mail order house.

(See *bathing suit.*)

SWINDLE

Leave in the lurch; hoodwink; working in cahoots; their professional gaucheries; bilked the depositors; they had been sold down the river.

(See *crook, steal, dishonesty.*)

SWITZERLAND

To pick edelweiss in the Alpine twilight; chortle their tooralays.

(See *foreigner.*)

SYMPATHY

Her womanly sympathy had been turned off at the main; his bleeding heart; made little clucking noises to indicate their sympathy; this miserable sob-stuff; I made sympathetic noises to indicate that.

(See *sorry, kind.*)

T

TABLOIDS
Does his lurid lulus for the tabloids.
(See *newspaper*.)

TAKE
Snakes out a copy of.
(See *get, have*.)

TAKE AWAY FROM SOMEONE
Frisked him; plucked two million of its men; pried loose; wooed many a writer from us; bunco you out of your last cent; separate the victim from a roll of bills; waltzed off with his dough; to tap the till; he is clipping these poor people; Mussolinied it out of him; to be simonized.
(See *swindle*).

TALENT
He oozed talent; his metier is the theatre; he had what it takes; these wunderkinder.
(See *ability, genius*.)

TALK (Back to)
Sassed; I'll have no more lip out of you.
(See *rebuke*.)

TALK (Diction)
Take the blackboard erasers out of their mouths.
(See *lisp*.)

TALK (Sparingly)
A closed mouth catcheth no flies; he hemmed and hawed; without saying as much as boo; kept his trap closed; didn't open his yap; he didn't talk much because his bridgework always came loose; as unloquacious as a Trap-pist monk that stuttered; he makes the sphinx look like a tattle-tale; it is better to remain silent at the risk of being thought a fool than to talk and remove all doubt of it; got a stiff tongue from sitting in a draft.
(See *quiet*.)

TALKER (a big)
The old windbag; piping off his puss; trying to tune him out; he opens his mouth to crack wise; shooting off too much; talks a blue streak, shoots off his mouth; babbling; hurts my eardrum; excessive verbosity; windjammer; developed corns on his tongue; has a tongue a mile long, and every inch of it as lively as a flea; he is very gabby; he is warming my ears with his talk; his jaws work on ball-bearing hinges; words pour forth like oil; a fool's tongue is long enough to cut his own throat; a woman's hair is long—her tongue is longer; an earbender.
(See *brag, exaggerated*.)

TALKING
Jabbering, grousing; line of twitter; line of spiel; beefing about his; spouting to harangue them; gabble; dishing out the latest scandal; chatterbox; the art of blather; repetitious patter; racy pitter-patter; chin awhile; talked like a turkey gobbler; gift of gab; chattering like a cageful of monkeys; chewing the fat; mumbles in his beard; gassing; gaseous palaver; holding forth; they were in a huddle; lip; full of sound and fury; babble; prattle; expanding the mouth from time to time and letting parts of speech emerge; gabble like a lot of women; yield to his blandishments; yawping;

[1301]

tongues wagged; chin music; ventilating the same opinions; mouthings.
(See *conversation*.)

TALKING (Foolishly)

Talk through the roof of his hat; he babbled along; a mouthful of clotted nonsense; you utters plenty words but they don't say nothin'; if you talk too much you'll get a blister on your tongue; an ox is taken by the horns, and a man by his tongue; his tonsils got tied up in a knot; he blab-blabs; to jibber away.
(See *speech, repartee, bunk*.)

TALL

Sixteen hands high; he measures a full fathom from keel to masthead; men the size of first-basemen; how is it in the stratosphere up there?; a human Alp; a tall drink of water; she was one of those tall, rangy, Queen Elizabeth sort of women.
(See *high*.)

TASTE

A taste in my mouth like a bird-and-animal store; bitter as Penthea's curse.
(See *sweet, bitter, sour*.)

TATTLE-TALE

She "blowed" on him; let the cat out of the bag; she spilled it.
(See *gossip, squeal*.)

TATTOO

He had battleships, snakes and naked dames tattooed all over him.
(See *body*.)

TAX

He pays taxes on $50,000 so he must be worth at least $100,000.
(See *customs, income tax*.)

TAXICABS

Roaming gyps; a couple of hacks; his meter curvetted; poured into a taxi (drunk).
(See *automobile*.)

TAXPAYER

Holding the taxpayer upside down.
(See *citizen*.)

TEA

Oolong; to balance saucers on their knees; sipping tea; I wouldn't do it for all the tea in China; a dish of tea.
(See *party*.)

TEACH

Hammer into their thick heads.
(See *education, college*.)

TEACHER

Schoolmarm.
(See *professor*.)

TEASE

Played tag with her blood pressure; tantalizing.
(See *playful, fun*.)

TEETH

His tusks; molars; he has two of the finest teeth I've ever seen in any face; herring-destroyers; bicuspid.
(See *dentist, mouth*.)

TEETH (False)

Choppers; I'm just after paying the dentist two hundred smackers for a new set of dishes; the time he cracked his upper plate on a walnut cooky; a new set of uppers; store teeth.
(See *false teeth*.)

TELEPHONE

He hung up so hard he bent the hook;

he gave me a buzz; roused by a phone jingle; afflicted with telephonitis; instrument of torture; he dropped the phone into the cradle; the telephone, Mr. Bell's invention; croon to his girlfriends on the.

(See *cable*.)

TELEPHONE BOOK

Telephone books may be thrown at cats.

(See *books—big*.)

TELL

Word has just filtered into; retailed the days activities; spill the beans; come clean; tingling the ears of.

(See *confess, relate*.)

TEMPER

Exploded; a filthy temper; a thunderstorm with lightning flashes.

(See *anger*.)

TEMPERAMENT

Throw an occasional tantrum; mercurial didoes; as temperamental as a prima donna; gallons of temperament.

(See *personality, disposition*.)

TEMPERANCE

Going on the wagon; sniff the pink lemonade suspiciously; who experience a uniform size of head from year to year; taking the corn cure; a dyed-in-the-wool teetotaler; whose lips have never touch liquor; want the nation to go off the cocktail standard; eschew the flowing bowl; he never touched ardent spirits.

(See *sober*.)

TEMPORARILY

For the nonce; as permanent as a movie star marriage; a flash in the pan.

(See *short time*.)

TEMPTATION

To forswear the fleshpots of the Great White Way; get thee behind me, Satan; open not the door when the devil knocks; the next time he heard the dulcet call of Broadway; an open door may tempt a saint (prov.).

(See *devil, sin*.)

TENDER

As tender as a sunburned neck; tender as a scrambled egg.

(See *mild*.)

TENNIS

He had been using my rackets for snowshoes.

(See *games, Ping-pong*.)

TENORS

Tenors lose as many as 25 or 30 lbs. during the singing of a single Wagnerian opera; there is a reason why all tenors have empty heads, they must have lots of empty space for resonance chambers; half man and half tenor; he is practically the only tenor who can reach high B-flat without standing on a step-ladder; that guy can sure bust a lung; bath-room tenor; but you cannot shoot them, they are still protected by law; at his high C's, women swooned; listening to a tenor calling his mate; during a violent fit of fortissimos; slopoozing sounds.

(See *opera singers*.)

TERRIBLE

His accent simply vile; putrid; with that precious brother of his; he thinks the professors are a gripe; it's enough to make a man strike a minister; the copiousness of the English language was perhaps never more apparent than in the following character description by a lady, of her own husband: "He is," she says, "an abhorred, barbarous, capricious, detestable, envious, fastidious, hard-hearted, illiberal, ill-natured, jealous, keen, loathsome, malevolent, nauseous, obstinate, passionate, quarrelsome, raging, saucy, tantalizing, uncomfortable, vexatious, abominable, bitter, captious, execrable, fierce, grating, gross, hasty, malicious, nefarious, obstreperous, peevish, restless, savage, tart, unpleasant, violent, waspish, worrying, acrimonious, blustering, careless, discontented, fretful, growling, hateful, inattentive, malignant, noisy, odious, perverse, rigid, severe, teasing, unsuitable, angry, boisterous, choleric, disgusting, gruff, hectoring, incorrigible, mischievous, negligent, offensive, pettish, roaring, sharp, sluggish, snapping, snarling, sneaking, sour, testy, tiresome, tormenting, touchy, arrogant, austere, awkward, boorish, brawling, brutal, bullying, churlish, clamorous, crabbed, cross, currish, dismal, dull, dry, drowsy, grumbling, horrid, huffish, insolent, intractable, irascible, ireful, morose, murmuring, overbearing, petulant, plaguy, rough, rude, rugged, spiteful, splenetic, stern, stubborn, stupid, sulky, sullen, surly, suspicious, treacherous, troublesome, turbulent, tyrannical, virulent, wrangling, yelping, dog-in-a-manger."

(See *bad*.)

TEST
Put me through the wringer.
(See *try*.)

THAN
Than aught else.
(See *etc*.)

THANKSGIVING
Who started this thing called Thanksgiving?; she wished the Indians had done away with the Pilgrims.
(See *rejoicing*.)

THANK YOU
I'll dance at your wedding; thanks a million, Sir; a thousand thanks to you; thank you very much; much obliged please.
(See *gratitude*.)

THEATRE
A wayside shrine to the Muse (a country theatre); the outhouses of Thespis; to go fourth-rowing to the theatre; amusement factory; show business; the nuances of the dramatic art; the dramatic industry; nickelodeon.
(See *shoes, acting, movies*.)

THEATRICAL COMPANY (Poor)
A down-at-heel company.
(See *stock company*.)

THEORY
Stepped clean into the middle of his theory.
(See *idea, opinion*.)

THERE
Thither; yonder.
(See *anywhere, everywhere*.)

THICK
A three-ply-bus-shelter.
(See *large, fat, big*.)

THIGHS (Female)
The delectable roundness of her hips verging into the sheer white flesh of her thighs; her svelte, rounded thighs; the entrancing revealment of tapering thighs, undulating flanks; the lushness of her thighs and hips.
(See *body, figure*.)

THIN
His attenuated frame; built like a croquet wicket; he wouldn't have weighed one hundred and ten with the Sunday papers under his arm;

built like a slat; a skinny will-o-the-wisp; elongated people; cadaverous; a bony lady.

(See *figure, weight*.)

THING

Gadget; dingus; doodad; doohickey; whatchamacallit; thingamajig; gimmick; trinket; devil's contraption; the whole shebang; knick-knacks; jigger; gewgaw; bric-a-brac; instrument of torture; thingumabob; these whatsits; animal, vegetable or mineral; gimcrack; flotsam and jetsam; chef's-d'oeuvre; objets d'art; it was a pleasant little ringledingle; the eighth wonder of the world; monstrosity; dingbat; these minutiae; folderols; flora and fauna.

(See *anything, everything*.)

THING (To do)

It is not the proper caper; the wheeze really is to have gone.

(See *proper, necessary*.)

THINGS (List of)

An earthenware pipkin; bottle of digestive tablets; a curious metal gadget which is either a patent tin-can-opener or a thing for lighting fires; a stuffed seamew; a pre-war overcoat; a gross of assorted buttons; antimacassar; spare socks, hard-boiled eggs.

(See *house, furniture*.)

THINK

Methinks; to go into a huddle; an orgy of cogitation; she does a good deal of her thinking in quotation marks or italics; he could think it out to four decimal points; think the hair off his head; he stood there, pulling his forelock; it was then that the bright (well, fairly bright) thought came to me; whose minds were bent all out of shape with much thinking; and nearly worked herself into a sanitarium thinking it up; and he furrowed his brow in deep reflection; some reptile thought stirring in the dark jungle of his mind; puts on a thinking cap; he cudgelled his brain; was frying in his mind; if you don't care to risk concussion by turning it over in your mind; I was thinking, yes, thinking, dear reader; to clear the brains of cobwebs; brainstormed the idea; needed every bit of skull he could lay hands on; let me go into committee on this mater; chew it over.

(See *understand, mind*.)

THINK (Not)

Mental dyspepsia; in the depths of a mental bog.

(See *understand—not to*.)

THOROUGH

Let's go the whole hog; with all the trimmings; he took London as Grant took Richmond; well lathered is half shaved; got him coming and going; goes in for romance with both feet; from A to izzard; milked the subject dry; described her to her last toenail; from stem to stern; runs the gamut; from Alpha to Omega; scratch the bottom of every barrel; to the Nth degree; she is feminine to the last lash; from pillar to post.

(See *all, perfect*.)

THREATEN

He bullyrags.

(See *warn*.)

THREE

A trinity; this triumvirate; trio; triplets; triplicate; trilogy; thrice; treble; trisect; triple; threefold; sisters three; the three graces; like Gaul, it is divided into three parts.

(See *mathematics*.)

THRIFT

A penny saved is a penny saved; many a nickle makes a muckle; money doesn't grow on bushes; "pinch-penny" attitude; a shroud has no pockets; take care of your pennies and the tax collector will take care of your dollars; as the old saying is, two checks in the bank are better than one.

(See *saving, economy*.)

THRILL

Thrilled to my toes; made her heart hammer; played havoc with his blood pressure; thrilled to pieces.

(See *feel good*.)

THROAT

He had a case of sandpaper-throat; frog in his throat; his voice sounded like a concertina that has been left out in the rain.

(See *mouth, voice*.)

THROW

Slapped down the steak.
(See *send*.)

THROWN OUT

Given the gate; he was forward-passed into 46th Street; boot him out of the Casino.

(See *outcast*.)

TICKETS

Splurged himself to tickets in the third row orchestra; two pasteboards; when I pay six dollars for a seat I expect Joe Penner taking tickets at the door and Garbo showing me to my seat.

(See *box office, theatre*.)

TIGHT (Money)

He could go out for an evening with a dime and have nine cents left over; he was the world's greatest exponent of the one-way pocket; scrimping; tighter than a tick; he could make one highball last a week; close fistedness; with him it's "easy come—go slow."

(See *saving, miser*.)

TIME

She had bushels of time; came a day; down through the dim vista of coming years; ofttimes; time gets a few licks; eons later; ever and anon he would; a few weeks frittered by; it's high time; time has a way of shooting holes through your pet illusions; fortnight; Father Time is hurrying us along; came the week-end, followed as usual by Monday, Tuesday, and Wednesday; the vicissitudes of time; you'd be surprised how fast five years can lope over the hills; time certainly bounces along; frittering away time.

(See *day, future, past, age, night*.)

TIME (By the clock)

My watch says 11 so it must be 10:30; it was three bells; the hour being hard by the stroke of midnight.

(See *clock*.)

TIME (Length of)

For sixteen years, come Micklemas.
(See *long*.)

TIMID

He wouldn't say "boo" to a goose; a quiet mind-your-own-business fellow.

(See *fear, coward*.)

TIP

Munificences; gratuities; handouts; trinkgeld; pourboire.

(See *generous*.)

TIRED

So weary he had no more to go in him than an unwound clock; the old glad light was not in her eye; looked like a white sepulchre; plumb worn out; who is all tuckered out; worn to a frazzle; I was ready to be carried out on a shutter; feeling like an exploded firecracker on July fifth; worn to a whisper; I looked like a dishrag; oh, was I tired?; worn down to a nub.

(See *weak*.)

TOBACCO CHEWING

Masticator of the weed; he wasn't a handsome chewer; he shifted his quid; people as far back as the third row in the balcony were splashed; a misdirected shot broke a window; he could hit a size 6 spittoon at 25 feet in a room with the shades pulled down.

(See *cuspidor*.)

TOGETHER

Hand-in-glove.

(See *inseparable, two*.)

TOILET

Primping.

(See *clothes, cosmetics*.)

TONGUE

Lapper.

(See *mouth*.)

TOOTHPICKS

Like throwing a toothpick to a drowning man.

(See *meals, teeth*.)

TORTURE

Put him on the rack and applied hot irons to the soles of his feet.

(See *cruelty*.)

TOUGH

Tough as a twenty-cent steak.

(See *rough, hard-boiled*.)

TOURIST

Tourists, the "shock troops" of travel.

(See *traveler*.)

TOWN

The town fathers; it was one of those towns where you would naturally stay just long enough to have a suit pressed.

(See *hick town*.)

TOY

Trinket.

(See *playing*.)

TRADE

Will trade him for a good third baseman; will trade him for a set of "Monopoly"; will trade him for a good inner tube.

(See *exchange*.)

TRADES (Work)

Knot-hole picker-outer in a lumber yard; a job of soldering sausage casings in a hot dog foundry; he puts the lacy trimmings on postage stamps; friller of paper panties for lamb chops; domino-dotter; bank-vault inspector; whistle tuners; cistern diggers; chocolate-eclair stuffer; buttonhole counter.

(See *work*.)

TRAFFIC

It requires a lawyer to explain the traffic code; traffic you couldn't shoot a bullet through; waiting in traffic for the cop's nose to turn green.

(See *crowds, automobile*.)

TRAFFIC OFFICER

Had a tete-a-tete with a traffic officer; (seeing motorcycle cop coming from distance) "We got company."

(See *policeman*.)

TRAINS

So he climbed aboard a rattler; on an early milk-train; used up five yards of railroad tickets; vibration that forces elderly passengers to hold in their upper plates with both hands; tuck myself into a Pullman berth; the rhythmic clackings of the wheels; we clackety-clacked along; a dinky local tooted into the station; riding the rods.

(See *railroads*.)

TRAINS (Old-fashioned.)

The red plush seats that Rutherford B. Hayes used to admire as a boy.

(See *old-fashioned*.)

TRAMP

A tatterdemalion; a mooching bum.

(See *unemployed, traveler*.)

TRANSFER

Shunted to.

(See *change, travel*.)

TRAVEL

The wanderlust; a long trek; gadding about the world; feet began to twitch with impatience; chasing around the Orient; China, here I come; have gone gypsy on us; hitting the trail for the West; globe girdling; the heavy hegira southward; to honor Gotham with his presence; shove your nightie in a sponge bag and go; packed up their evening gowns and their rouge pots and; add a new country to your "collection"; so he packed up his Ipana; and so the Gulliver days of Mr. Van Dyke are drawing to a close; in his peregrinations abroad; wondered what the Sahara looks like and what Tibetans have for tea; he lived in a suitcase; shook the dust of Phila. off his heels; slumming expedition; all I have to show is a lot of Pullman stubs; getting ready for another dash up the gangplank.

(See *vacation, go*.)

TRAVEL (Not to)

We stay-at-homes.

(See *contented, lazy*.)

TRAVELER

Modern Marco Polo; a rolling stone; a gad-about; who no doubt spent 15 minutes in Abyssinia; it's the Halliburton in me.

(See *tourist*.)

TRIANGLE

(Woman.) It was more than a triangle, it was a quadrilateral.

(See *three*.)

TRICK

He learned it while visiting a cousin in Philadelphia; to wiggle his ears; he can do more tricks than a monkey with a coconut.

(See *capers, magic*.)

TRICKY

Wiles; his knavish tricks; he was a sharper.

(See *deceive, fool someone*.)

TROMBONE

It requires an ability to twiddle both hands simultaneously; there is no more charming spectacle than a trombonist in full cry.

(See *instruments*.)

TROUBLE

To be in the soup; found himself on the rocks; in dutch; was on the "spot"; it made him old before his time; to take the bumps; we shall eat nothing but trouble; in a jam; stirred up a hornet's nest; a positive genius for getting into trouble; what a dance that bird led me; disaster swooped upon them; landed in a kettle of hot water; we were tossed from the horns of one dilemma to another; wallowing helplessly in the Slough of Despond; a pretty kettle of fish; a tempest in a teapot; hell's been poppin' loose; on the horns of a dilemma; a sorrow is an itching place which is made worse by scratching; olive oil on troubled waters; you'll wind up behind the eight-ball; was in low water financially.

(See *danger, narrow escape*.)

TROUBLE MAKER
Stormy petrel; the monkey wrench.
(See *mischief, upset*.)

TROUSERS
Any trousers that could be negotiated over those feet (big) ; hand-me-downs; reach me-downs; trousers wide enough to be put on over your head; worn thinner than a joke when Ed Wynn gets hold of it; his wrinkled trousers looked like a concertina; the tailor that designed them must have had a hangover; his trousers had a crease that you could have sharpened a pencil on; grab him by the seat of his inexpressibleness; pantaloons; ledger-ruled trousers.

(See *pants, suit*.)

TRUCK
The truck was coming lickity-split.
(See *automobile*.)

TRUCK DRIVER
Jockey of a beer truck.
(See *work*.)

TRUSTED (Not)
It is not to be trusted any farther than a pugnosed man can sneeze; she couldn't trust her brainy husband any further than a clam could gallop on a dusty road; would you send cabbage leaves by a rabbit?; I wouldn't trust him any further than I could carry soup on a pitchfork.

(See *unconvincing, responsibility*.)

TRUTH
Honest Injun; now come clean; the truth; I am telling the gospel; speak the truth, and shame the devil; the straight-out; the God's truth; the beautiful, unvarnished truth; children and drunken folk speak the truth; truth crushed to earth shall rise again.

(See *confess, frank, real*.)

TRY
Coaxing the edge of a rug under a piano; trying tooth and nail; to chin himself up to their level; get another crack at; put her best foot forward; having a go at one of; have a whirl at; give it a whirl; take a whack at it; try that over on your Wurlitzer; tearing himself to shreds trying; to double themselves into knots.

(See *test*.)

TRY (Not to)
Never lifted a finger to; one cannot, after all, construct an omelette without cracking at least one egg.

(See *give-up, lazy*.)

TUMBLE
Tumbled smack-dab.
(See *fall*.)

TURKEY
The land of the viscous coffee; Sultan Ibrahim's castle; Hassan; salaam aleikum; Abdul Hamid; Caliph of Islam; in this land where they wore bedslippers curled up at the toes; may Allah lengthen thy days.

(See *foreigner*.)

TWINS

One pair of twins and an ordinary child, born by itself; Tweedledum and Tweedledee.
(See *children*.)

TWO

The twain; Siamese Twins; twins; dual game at which two can play; kill two birds with one stone; two strings to his bow; twofold; duplicate; double; coming to grief between the Scylla of "infer" and the Charybdis of "imply"; runner-up; a double-header.
(See *mathematics*.)

TYPE

Their ilk; or any others of her guild.
(See *same, like*.)

TYPEWRITER

Pounding a typewriter; the tapping sounded like a woodpecker; the clackety-clack, clack of the typewriters; a tipper-tapper; it was hot from his ypewriter; and I'm supposed to skip to my typewriter, tra, la, and tap out airy nothings—frothy stuff; his typewriter ribbon was generally in shreds before he had finished the simplest yarn; pecking away at typewriters; a typewriter of museum vintage; and the old typewriter is in its red flannels for the night; typewriter carriage rang bells and went back with a bang for new loads of words; it's been a long time since I put key to ribbon.
(See *secretary*.)

U

UGLY

As homely as a mud fence; a face like the old oaken bucket; that some cat dragged in out of the rain; he would never win any beauty contest; listen, Frankenstein; a toad among orchids; he's no prize package; he was no sight for sore eyes; he does not exactly resemble an Apollo; as ugly as a warthog; faces only suitable for scaring crows; little children run screaming to their mothers; if he hadn't been left out in the rain so much; a face that doesn't even arouse mother-love; looks rather like an Assyrian goat; his face was not a mural painting; sloppy puss; he once got out of bed, looked into a mirror and jumped back in, he stayed there for 3 days; he was no bargain; a pie-face; he isn't exactly an oil painting; pickle puss; a trout-faced man; skunkpuss; he looked like a lobster a la stewpan; puss-face; he didn't look like the answer to any maiden's prayer; strangers who do business with him demand their money in advance; a face that curdles milk.

(See *sight*.)

UGLY WOMEN

She had not been overlooked by the pruning-hook of time; ugly-duckling; was she a mess; these simple-faced Sallies; unpretty; hatchet-faced woman; but she makes the most extraordinary pickled cabbage; she's simply a pop-face; technically, she was not a beauty; mutt; a thick-ankled hausfrau; if she was cast as Lady Godiva, the horse would steal the scene; she looked like rain on the eaves.

(See *woman, girl*.)

UMPIRE

Expressing a desire to cut the umpire's throat from ear to ear; he had to change his address.

(See *baseball*.)

UNBIASED

Let the chips fall where they may; we're on the fence.

(See *neutral, fair*.)

UNCERTAIN

Shilly-shallying; wishy-washy; namby-pamby; an old softie; dilly-dallying; left us high and dry; stand pat.

(See *fluctuate*.)

UNCLE

My carbuncle; my uncle, not the one who is living, the one who is married· maiden uncle.

(See *relatives, aunt*.)

UNCLE SAM

The old gent.

(See *American*.)

UNCONVINCING

As convincing as a government denial.

(See *weak*.)

UNDEPENDABLE

Leave in the lurch.

(See *uncertain, trusted—not*.)

UNDERDOG

Every dog is a lion at home.

(See *unimportant, weakling*.)

UNDERSTAND

Wise up to themselves; not hep to; we are jerry to the idea; let this trickle

through your dome: gives me a chink of light on; are right up my boulevard; and you'll have a stranglehold on one of the best ways; a sudden rush of common sense to the head; could understand it with one hand tied behind his back; the cat came out of my bag; tear blinders from my eyes; you're over 21; to have the low down; he had his number.
(See *think, knowledge.*)

UNDERSTAND (Not to)
Is more than I can fathom; I cannot make head or tail of; something utterly beyond our ken; I could not adumbrate this situation.
(See *think—not.*)

UNDER THING (Women)
Demi-tasse shorts; clothed only in the most nonsensical of lingerie; clad only in the brevity of a chemise which caressed her charms as intimately as a lover.
(See *brassiere, step-ins.*)

UNDERWEAR (Man)
I am a confirmed two-piece underwear man.
(See *clothes.*)

UNDESIRABLE
The game is not worth the candle.
(See *unwelcome.*)

UNDRESS
Peeled off her clothes.
(See *clothes, burlesque.*)

UNEMPLOYED
Out of work for two years running.
(See *tramp.*)

UNFAIR
Socking below the belt; it wasn't cricket.
(See *foul play.*)

UNFORTUNATE
Hapless.
(See *poor, sad, hopeless.*)

UNFRIENDLY
Have never been as close together as Brown's cows; not worth having much truck with.
(See *enemy.*)

UNHAPPY
I have never been able to gloat with satisfaction; I was so happy I made faces at cows; her life is more ashes than attar.
(See *dissatisfaction.*)

UNHEALTHFUL
Is a menace to my glands and arteries.
(See *sick, germs.*)

UNIMPORTANT
He's a very small patch on the seat of government; we did not rate; nothing over which to hold the newspaper presses for extras; bush league stuff; this piddling little syndicate; a nonentity; two-penny, half-penny; a small sore wants not a great plaster (prov.).
(See *underdog, small.*)

UNINTERESTING
It is cold turkey; as interesting as a back-garden in December.
(See *bore.*)

UNKNOWN
As unknown as an Auk in the Third National Bank; unwept, unhonored and unsung.
(See *mystery.*)

UNLUCKY
(See *lucky.*)

UNNATURAL

Acting as natural as a man waiting for the birth of his first child.
(See *embarrassed.*)

UNNECESSARY

As unnecessary as a hitching-post; as unnecessary as paper pants on lamb chops; a mole wants no lantern (prov.); you don't have to use a silver key to open an iron lock (prov.); crows are never the whiter for washing themselves (prov.); burn not your house to fright away the mice (prov.).
(See *useless, extra.*)

UNPOPULAR

As popular as spinal meningitis; stinko; hooted out of public office; could stage their mass meeting in a telephone booth; you'll lose caste; persona non grata; public stays away by the thousands.
(See *unwelcome, disgust.*)

UNPREPARED

Catch me with my hair down; the mouse that hath but one hole is quickly taken (prov.).
(See *extemporaneous.*)

UNSATISFACTORY

It was no dice.
(See *no good.*)

UNSELFISH

Didn't seem to have a selfish bone in her body.
(See *sacrifice, generous.*)

UNWELCOME

As welcome as blueberry pie to a white linen suit; given the gate; I feel like an immigrant down here; unwelcome as water in your shoe; unwelcome to a woman as a looking-glass after the smallpox.
(See *undesirable, unpopular.*)

UP MY ALLEY

Grist to my story mill; right up my boulevard.
(See *understand.*)

UPSET

Upset the applecart; to create internecine disorder.
(See *trouble maker.*)

U. S. A.

These Utopian States of America.
(See *California, American.*)

USE

Use a mashie; it has gained considerable currency.
(See *action, work, do.*)

USED TO

In time you get used to it, but you never really care for it; to orientate myself; accept it as they accept rain, hunger and the Fourth of July.
(See *habit.*)

USELESS

As futile as trying to convince a communist; a crow is never whiter for washing herself often (prov.) ; a blind man will not thank you for a looking-glass (prov.) ; as useless as rubbing salve on a cancer; all they are good for (things) is to scare away burglars; you're about as useful as lumbago; as useful as dandruff; a dead bee maketh no honey (prov.); as useless as a pocket in a shroud; as useless as an amputated thumb; as useless as water in a sieve; like a windmill without wind; as useless as a one-armed paperhanger; as useless as boiling stones in butter.
(See *no good.*)

USHERS

Uniformed flunky; a gaudy major general with his bandbox staff.
(See *theatre.*)

V

VACATION
Is "rusticating" in Maine; his sabbatical year.
(See *camping, travel.*)

VAGUE
Beat around the bush; to sound mealy-mouthed.
(See *mystery.*)

VALET
His man Friday, Saturday and Sunday.
(See *servant.*)

VALUABLE
Would give his right eye for it.
(See *importance.*)

VALUELESS
Not worth the powder.
(See *useless.*)

VAMP
Turn on a thousand volts.
(See *flirt, coquetting.*)

VANITY
Pricked by vanity; his God-given gifts; swollen craniums; most of his forty words are "I," and the rest are "me"; turkey-gobbler strut; tilt his hat over one eye and swagger up and down the promenade; chestiness; had his hats made in a tent factory; looking as smug as a cat licking cream off its whiskers.
(See *ego, proud, snob.*)

VASE
The not-quite-ming vase.
(See *china.*)

VAUDEVILLE
Vaudevillians.
(See *shows.*)

VEGETARIAN
He wouldn't eat anything he couldn't pat; rabbit food; he won't even count sheep to fall asleep, let alone eat them; confirmed spinach-addict; vegetarianism fills a person with wind and self-righteousness.
(See *food, diet.*)

VENTILATION
Windows hermetically sealed.
(See *windows.*)

VERY
So all-fired efficient; with precious little to carry away; too, too kind; being, oh, so attentive; right bright; wilder than all get out; it gets really cold, I mean positively; she wanted, oh how she wanted; she will be no end grateful; helluva good ball player; guilty as hell; he's an out-and-out pest; has been far and away, and above and below, and to one side, the worst offender; very well indeed; she was worried all to pieces; copiously; jolly well; downright scholarly.
(See *lots.*)

VERY MUCH
Fit to kill; head and shoulders above; utterly; a teensy-weensy bit too much.
(See *lots of.*)

VERY WELL
He can play golf to beat the mischief; like nobody's business; it is all too, too quaint.
(See *good, O.K.*)

VEST

Waistcoat; a strange Lochinvar came out of the vest; a gay fellow known for his fancy weskits; checkered vest; vest from Vest Va.

(See *clothes, suit.*)

VETERINARY

Goat doctor.

(See *dog, cats.*)

VICE

Flesh-pots; vice-bitten towns; you are heading for the gutter; just because vice is beginning to bore you is no sign you are getting virtuous, you may only be getting old.

(See *immoral, sex, sin.*)

VICTIM

The quarry.

(See *suffer, torture, sacrifice.*)

VILLAIN

Windshield viper; fiends of the same ilk or elk; an oily villain; ogre; the dastardly deed; foiled; our hero arrives in the nick of time; "unhand my"; their dastardly clutches; I'm looking for a god hissing part; the arch-villain.

(See *role, plot, role.*)

VIOLINIST

A regular Paganini on the violin; his fiddle waving; a fiddle-scratcher.

(See *music, orchestra.*)

VIRTUE

Having a spasm of virtue; God-fearing; from now on I am as the driven snow; a regular paragon of all the virtues; defended her virtue with the vinegar cruet.

(See *morals, worth, merit.*)

VISITING

Sojourn beneath our roof; popped in one afternoon; come in and take off your spats; at whose house I spent a week one night; some people can stay longer in an hour than others can in a week; I don't like him to stay so long that I have to adopt him; stopped to pass the time of day; repaying a calling obligation that was contracted by his grandparents fifty years ago; a guest and a fish both stink after three days; I like to have visitors around to limber up our upholstery.

(See *travel, stay.*)

VOCABULARY

A steady diet of alphabet soup will not improve your vocabulary; his vocabulary burgeoned fast; his copious, tumbling vocabulary.

(See *language, words.*)

VOICE

He dropped his voice to half a gale; so bashful that his voice even blushed; sotto-voce; his voice sounded as if he ate spinach with sand in it; in a rich dark red voice; cursed softly in his childish treble; she had a dulcet voice; basso profundo; a piping falsetto; her voice was like a cat's purr; a voice that sounds as if it comes out of a cellar; a voice like a concertina that has been left out in the rain; roostery voice; they hear him for miles on a clear day; wail not unlike that of the banshee; a blonde with a platinum voice; a voice as tender as a three-minute egg; a tut-tutting voice; he's got a good voice, if you don't like music; chromium-plated voice; the sounds coming through his bridgework.

(See *said, opera singers.*)

VOTE

Vote-snaring; laying hands on baby's brows; on the first Tuesday after the first Monday in November the voters; plebiscite; he has a lot of votes in his capacious paw; woo the constituency; kiss damp babies.

(See *candidate, politics*.)

VOTE (Straw vote)

The straw gave out on the last vote and corn shucks had to be used.

(See *test, type*.)

VOTE (Speeches)

If I get elected there will be a subway on every corner; promising voters everything from 3-piece suits to South Sea Island cruises; a vote for me means more butter on buttered toast.

(See *politician's language*.)

VULGAR

Plebeian.

(See *low, people—common*.)

Y

YAWN
"Ho hum," he said, turning a yawn into a yap just in time; nearly made me yawn the top of my head off; a Grand Canyon yawn; a windy yawn.

(See *tired, sleep.*)

YELL
Bark at; answered with a yell which practically tore my tonsils from their moorings; he published a loud yell; a yell rent the air; Freddy let out a heart-stricken yip; let loose a forty-acre bellow; "they can't do that to me," he yammered; emit bellows of rage; yowl; to cry wolf; hollering; he let out a bellow that blew the flags clean off the poles; bellowing fit to scare the ferries out of their slips; stop that caterwauling; let out an Indian war whoop; I'm a bad case of sandpaper-throat from yelling; the yell almost rent his suspender button; maniacal gurgle; a series of wild and blood-curdling yells; groans, gurglings, yelps, shrieks, roars, bellows; yell like an auctioneer.

(See *squeal.*)

YES
Honest, Injun; a yes indeed man; a yes-indeed-Mr.-Johnson man; yes-yessing him all over the place; bully for you, old boy; I'll go you once; yerse; yep; okey-dokey; ay; no sooner said than done; check; you said it; that's the one thing I ain't gwine do nothin' else but; you took the words right out of my mouth; waggled her head in the affirmative.

(See *is-that-so.*)

YIELD
She might unbend.

(See *give up, submit.*)

YOU
Hey, you, with the double-breasted ears.

(See *anyone.*)

YOUNG
When he was knee-high to a grasshopper; he was no longer a larva; in his salad days.

(See *boy, children, girl.*)

YOURS
Yours till the Siamese Twins sleep in twin beds.

(See *own.*)

YOUTH
In the early springtime of our existence; youth not far from his bib and jumper days.

(See *age.*)